The Church of England Year Book

1999

115th Edition

CHURCH HOUSE PUBLISHING

CHURCH OF ENGLAND YEARBOOK

The Official Year Book of the General Synod of the Church of England

115th edition 1999

Editor: Jo Linzey

Published 1999 by
Church House Publishing
Church House
Great Smith Street
London SW1P 3NZ

© *The Archbishops' Council 1999*

All rights reserved. No part of this publication may be reproduced in any form or by any means, electronic or mechanical, including photocopying, recording, or any information storage and retrieval system, without written permission which should be sought from the Copyright Manager, The Archbishops' Council, Church House, Great Smith Street, London SW1P 3NZ

Cover design by Julian Smith

Typeset by RefineCatch Limited
Printed and bound by Biddles Ltd,
Guildford and King's Lynn

ISBN 0 7151 8103 3
ISSN 0069 3987

Contents

INDEX TO ADVERTISEMENTS *iv*
REVIEW OF THE YEAR *xxiii*
CALENDAR FOR 1999 *xxxvi*

THE GENERAL SYNOD 3 • THE ARCHBISHOPS' COUNCIL 15 • THE CHURCH COMMISSIONERS 43 • THE CHURCH OF ENGLAND PENSIONS BOARD 46 • OTHER BOARDS, COUNCILS, COMMISSIONS, ETC. 48 • THE CONVOCATIONS OF CANTERBURY AND YORK 51 • THE ECCLESIASTICAL COURTS 52

CENTRAL STRUCTURES — 1

THE DIOCESES 55

DIOCESES — 2

GENERAL INFORMATION 157 • SELECTED CHURCH STATISTICS 181 • ROYAL PECULIARS, THE CHAPELS ROYAL, ETC. 193 • RELIGIOUS COMMUNITIES 199

GENERAL — 3

ORGANISATIONS 209

ORGANISATIONS — 4

THE ANGLICAN COMMUNION 271 • THE LAMBETH CONFERENCE 272 • THE ANGLICAN CONSULTATIVE COUNCIL 275 • CHURCHES AND PROVINCES OF THE ANGLICAN COMMUNION 277 • UNITED CHURCHES IN FULL COMMUNION 326 • THE HOLY CATHOLIC CHURCH IN CHINA 332 • OTHER CHURCHES IN COMMUNION 335 • MAPS OF THE ANGLICAN COMMUNION 337 • THE PORVOO COMMUNION 353

ANGLICAN AND PORVOO COMMUNIONS — 5

ECUMENICAL 363

ECUMENICAL — 6

WHO'S WHO 385

WHO'S WHO — 7

LATE INFORMATION 480 • INDEX 481

INDEX — *i*

INDEX TO ADVERTISEMENTS

CHURCH FURNISHINGS AND BUILDINGS
Avon Silversmiths xii
The Building Conservation Directory 504
James Chase & Son (Furnishings) Ltd xiv
The Necropolis Company xxi
Pruden & Smith Silversmiths vii
Watts & Co Ltd xii
Whitechapel Bellfoundry .... *inside back cover*
Wippell's 510

RESOURCES
Autosave v
Dunphy Ecclesiastical Heating xiii
ICC Duplication xxi
RG Jones xvi

RELIGIOUS SOCIEITIES AND CHARITABLE INSTITUTIONS
Additional Curates Society viii
Bromley & Sheppard's Colleges x
The Central Church Fund 505
The Church Lads' and Church Girls' Brigade 510
The Church of England Pensions Board 508
The College of St Barnabas xiii
Corporation of the Sons of the Clergy 509
Corrymeela 510
The English Clergy Association xix
The Friends of the Clergy Corporation viii
The Lesbian and Gay Christian Movement x
London City Mission xv
The Missions to Seamen 503

The Mothers' Union 504
The Prayer Book Society xi
Siloam Christian Ministries 504
Siloam TransAid vii
St Luke's Hospital for the Clergy xvii
St Paul's Cathedral 512
Trinity Care 506

PUBLISHERS AND PUBLICATIONS
The Sign and *Home Words* 507
The Church of England Newspaper xviii
Church Times xxii
Guildford Diocese Productions 507
The Tablet xx

FINANCE AND FUNDRAISING
Community Counselling Services vi
Debt Solutions vii
Ecclesiastical Insurance .... *inside front cover*
Lockie Envelopes xiii
Russell Plaice & Partners ix

CONFERENCE CENTRES, SCHOOLS AND TRAVEL
Inter-Church Travel 511
King Edward's School xv
Rydal Hall xxi

The inclusion of an advertisement is for purposes of information and is not to be taken as implying acceptance of the objects of the advertiser by the publisher.

AUTOSAVE - THE BEST WAY TO BUY YOUR NEXT CAR

Unique suppliers to schools, churches, charities and now church members

NEW OR USED, AT SPECIAL DISCOUNTS

In the last 15 years Autosave has continued to develop its special scheme **achieving the best possible prices** for our wide range of clients including churches, schools and numerous leading charities. These special prices are now **available to church members as well.**

LATEST RANGE OF MINI-BUSES

Autosave's commercial minibus department is able to offer an extensive range of new and second hand vehicles.

Every need catered for, from small economical models to prestige marques and people carriers

FREE — USED CAR LOCATION SCHEME

FREE of CHARGE Autosave will scan the car market for a vehicle to your specification. We have access to huge stocks of 1990 onwards registered vehicles including very high quality ex-demonstration cars.

WE PROMISE THE BEST SERVICE

- Inspections up to AA/RAC standard
- Up to 36 months warranty with the RAC
- Competitive insurance cover
- Your old car in part-exchange
- Free delivery nationwide - to your door
- Competitive finance and leasing rates

HAVING DIFFICULTY SELLING YOUR OLD CAR?

autosave will give you a telephone valuation and if it is acceptable we will collect your car free of charge from anywhere in the UK

AUTOSAVE ✞

Ivy House, The Dale,
Sheffield S8 0PS   Fax: 0114 255 4949

RaC Aftercare Warranty

Tel: 0114 255 4040

Call today for your FREE Motor Information Pack

Name ....
Address ....
....
....
.... Tel: ....

Freepost - no stamp needed
Autosave, FREEPOST, Ivy House, The Dale, Sheffield S8 0PG

Symbols of Success

CCS CELEBRATES 50 YEARS

Community Counselling Service Ltd

Fund Raising/Public Relations

CCS has designed special planning and feasibility studies, development audits and capital campaigns for leading institutions worldwide including

University of Manchester Institute of Science & Technology (UMIST)

Christ Church Cathedral, Dublin

Royal Free Hospital School of Medicine, London

St. Anne's Cathedral, Belfast

Wolverhampton Grammar School

Royal College of Surgeons of Edinburgh

Royal College of Surgeons in Ireland

University of Nottingham Trent

University of Salford

De Montfort University, Leicester

Diocese of Leeds

27/29 Cursitor Street
London EC4A 1LT
Tel: 0171.731.3439
Fax: 0171.731.1051
E-mail: ccslondon@email.msn.com

London • Dublin • New York •
Chicago • Toronto • San Francisco

Royal College of Surgeons of Edinburgh

Christ Church Cathedral

Royal Free Hospital School of Medicine

UMIST

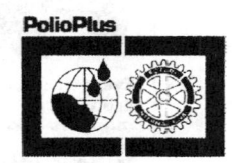

WOLVERHAMPTON GRAMMAR SCHOOL

PolioPlus

The Nottingham Trent University

SUMMIT

SILVERWARE IN THE BEST TRADITION

Third generation silversmiths producing individually designed, hand-made contemporary silverware for clients that include Ampleforth Abbey & Durham Cathedral. Chalice commissions a speciality. Figurative work by Dunstan Pruden.

Turner Dumbrell Workshops, North End, Ditchling, East Sussex BN6 8TD.
Telephone 01273 846338
Fax: 01273 846684
Tuesday to Saturday 10am to 6pm
Registered with the Council for the care of Churches

PRUDEN & SMITH
silversmiths

Siloam – TransAid

Fax us on:
01926 431193

SILOAM TransAid
A Moving Ministry for Churches & Missions

VANS & TRUCKS UP TO 38 TONS TO EASTERN EUROPE

Could we move your aid to your relief project in Eastern Europe?
Let us quote you today.
'Phone 01926 335037

Siloam uses medical, educational, social and other relief as a vehicle for the life-changing gospel of the Lord Jesus Christ.
SILOAM CHRISTIAN MINISTRIES
FREEPOST, 5, Clarendon Place, Leamington Spa, Warwickshire CV32 5BR
Registered under the Charities Act 1960 No. 327396.
Registerd in the United Kingdom No. 2104165

Debt advice from Christian professionals, free of charge
(with no obligation)

- debt and insolvency advisers specialising in personal finances & small businesses - serving the whole of England and Wales
- friendly, personal, confidential
- details of **all** options presented (incl costs), - arrangements (less formal & "IVA"), bankruptcy, Co Ct Admin Order (or the option to "do nothing")
- we will not "hurry" the client - we always have time
- if further assistance is requested with an arrangement then costs are usually paid by the creditors
- debt & insolvency advice training for professionals, advice centres and voluntary gps

Write for further information, or telephone to speak to Mike Reeves or Julie Taylor without obligation Mike Reeves is a licenced insolvency practitioner.

**Debt Solutions,
Havering Grange Centre,
Havering Road, Romford, Essex
RM1 4HR
Tel 01708 750093 / Fax 736292**

Justice & mercy
to satisfy
creditors & debtors

If only we could get away..

"If only we could get away – just for a few days!" How often we hear clergy say that. Living 'over the shop' is one of the main causes of clergy stress and breakdown. Just getting out of the house is a break. A proper holiday – which is what hard-pressed clergy really need – is beyond the reach of many of them.

The Friends of the Clergy Corporation gives holiday grants to clergy and their families in time of need. It also provides grants for general welfare, for school clothing, at times of retirement, resettlement, and bereavement, and during the trauma of marriage breakdown.

Grants of money cannot in themselves solve all the problems, but they can remove some of the causes of stress. And occupational stress affects the clergy probably more than anyone else in the community.

Please help us to continue this work – with a donation or covenant – and by remembering the Corporation in your Will.

And if you, or someone you know, needs our help, do get in touch with the Secretary.

THE FRIENDS OF THE CLERGY CORPORATION
27 Medway Street, Westminster, London SW1P 2BD. Telephone 0171-222 2288. *Registered Charity 264724.*

Additional Curates Society

gives grants for assistant priests
in poor and populous parishes
and fosters vocations to the priesthood.
Every penny donated to A.C.S.
is used to provide parishes with priests

Donations and enquiries to:
The General Secretary
The Reverend Stephen Leach
ADDITIONAL CURATES SOCIETY
Gordon Browning House, 8 Spitfire Road, Birmingham B24 9PB
Tel: 0121 382 5533   Fax: 0121 382 6999

Registered Charity No. 209448   Founded 1837
Patron: Her Most Excellent Majesty The Queen

Where in the World do you go for good Financial Advice?

We specialise in the Clergy Sector and understand the financial needs of Clergy men & women. We have established ourselves as the largest Independent Financial Advisers for the Clergy in England.

Travelling the length & breadth of the country, we meet with thousands of members of the clergy to discuss their financial affairs including tax efficiency, investments, mortgages, pensions & life assurance.

As we are Independent, we can offer our clients products from a wide range of top performing insurance companies and investment houses, including ethical investments.

If you would like a free consultation with one of our advisers, please telephone:- **01476 560662**

Russell Plaice & Partners *- for financial peace of mind*
70a Castlegate, Grantham, Lincs NG31 6SH

Regulated by the Personal Investment Authority ★ Mortgages are not regulated by the Personal Investment Authority

BROMLEY AND SHEPPARD'S COLLEGES

Registered Charity 210337

London Road, Bromley, Kent BR1 1PE
Tel (0181) 460 4712

The Colleges, set in 4 acres in the centre of Bromley, offer secure and comfortable accommodation to retired clergy of the Church of England, the Church in Wales, the Church of Ireland and the Scottish Episcopal Church, their spouses, widows, widowers, divorced and separated spouses and unmarried daughters of former residents of Bromley College.

For information contact;
The Chaplain, Chaplain's House, Bromley College

LESBIAN✜GAY CHRISTIANS

. . .*and our friends*
supporting *clergy*
resourcing *debate*
challenging *discrimination*

Membership open to all, irrespective of sexual orientation

LGCM, Oxford House, Derbyshire Street, London E2 6HG

Email lgcm@churchnet.ucsm.ac.uk

Telephone/Fax: 0171 739 1249

Counselling HELPLINE Wed & Sun 7-10pm

Telephone: 0171 739 8134

The Lesbian and Gay Christian Movement is a registered charity No. 1048842
LGCM is a non-profit Company Limited by guarantee registered in England & Wales No. 3092197

THE PRAYER BOOK SOCIETY

Registered Charity 1001783

SAINT JAMES GARLICKHYTHE
GARLICK HILL, LONDON EC4

President: The Rt Hon Lord Charteris of Amisfield, G.C.B., G.C.V.O., P.C.

Ecclesiastical Patron:
The Rt Revd and Rt Hon Richard Chartres, Lord Bishop of London

Lay Patron: The Rt Hon The Lord Sudeley, F.S.A.

Vice Presidents:
The Rt Hon Lord Glenamara, C.H., P.C.
The Rt Hon Viscount Cranborne, P.C.
The Rt Hon Frank Field, M.P., Andrew Hunter, Esq, M.P.
The Rt Hon Baroness James of Holland Park, O.B.E.
The Rt Hon Lord Morris of Castle Morris, The Revd Dr Roger Beckwith, Roger Evans, Esq

Chairman: C. A. Anthony Kilmister, Esq

Deputy-Chairman: Dr Roger Homan

Vice Chairmen: Professor the Revd Raymond Chapman and Neil Inkley, Esq

Hon Secretary: Mrs Elaine Bishop   Hon Treasurer: John Service, Esq

The Book of Common Prayer
contains some of the most majestic and beautiful prose in the English language. Over the centuries it has been the repository of doctrine from which Anglican beliefs could be learned. A devotional power-house, the Book of Common Prayer is a deeply valued means of communication with our Maker.

The Prayer Book Society
★ seeks to defend and uphold that doctrine and to promote the worship enshrined in the Book of Common Prayer
★ does NOT propagate Prayer Book fundamentalism but believes a modest amount of flexibility in usage is both sensible and to be desired

The Prayer Book Society aims
★ to encourage the use of the Book of Common Prayer for the training of Ordinands and Confirmands
★ to spread knowledge of the Book of Common Prayer and the doctrine contained therein
★ to encourage use of the Book of Common Prayer for public worship.

ARE YOU A REGULAR READER OF THE SOCIETY'S TWO MAGAZINES?
ISSUES OF *"FAITH AND HERITAGE"* ALTERNATE WITH *"FAITH AND WORSHIP"*

Please support
THE PRAYER BOOK SOCIETY
write now to:
**PBS OFFICE, ST JAMES GARLICKHYTHE
GARLICK HILL, LONDON EC4V 2AF**

AVON SILVERSMITHS

CHURCH SILVER

AND GIFTWARE FOR ORDINATIONS, ANNIVERSARIES AND BAPTISMS

FREE COLOUR BROCHURE
TEL: 01279 508084   OR WRITE TO : AVON SILVERSMITHS LTD.,
10 AVENUE ROAD, BISHOP'S STORTFORD, HERTS., CM23 5NU

REPAIRS, Replicas, Custom Design, Valuations

DIRECT LINE: 0121 604 2121   OR WRITE TO WORKS:
AVON SILVERSMITHS LTD., 39 AUGUSTA ST., HOCKLEY, B'HAM B18 6JA

Messrs. WATTS & Co. Ltd.

ECCLESIASTICAL FURNISHERS
&
CLERICAL OUTFITTERS

ESTABLISHED FOR OVER 100 YEARS AND
FAMOUS FOR FINE VESTMENTS AND
QUALITY FURNISHINGS

7 TUFTON STREET, LONDON, SW1P 3QE
TELEPHONE: 0171 222-7169/1978   FACSIMILE: 0171 233-1130

THE COLLEGE OF ST BARNABAS
Retirement Accommodation for the Clergy
Licensed Church Workers, Readers and their Wives and Widows

offering two-roomed flats, full catering, Chapels with daily services, nursing care, Library and other residential comforts

(Next to Dormans Railway Station)

Enquiries to: **The Warden, College of St Barnabas, Lingfield, Surrey RH7 6NJ**
Telephone: (01342) 870366

THE TRUTH ABOUT CHURCH HEATING

Dunphy Ecclesiastical Heating can give you the whole truth about church heating. We do not manufacture, so we can design and install all types of systems and advise you with complete impartiality. Our service is professional and personal and comes completely free of charge.

DUNPHY

FREE ADVICE   FREE SURVEY   FREE QUOTATION
CALL US NOW FREE ON 0800 614 100
OR FREEPOST OL 5557 ROCHDALE

THE NATIONS LEADERS IN CHURCH HEATING

We can help to improve the level of your Fund raising

Lockie Envelopes

manufacture envelopes specifically for fund raising, together with a full range of stationery designed to simplify the job of accounting & recording

01942 726146
Fax: 01942 271220

38 HIGH STREET, GOLBORNE,
Nr. WARRINGTON, WA3 3BG

It's comforting to know who you can rely on

The 4000 Chair

The Abbey Lectern

The Kelso Stacking Chair

*O*ur customers have the peace of mind in knowing that we are renowned for our commitment to only using the best raw materials and the highest standards of production in our furniture. Quality of service and product has been our priority since James Chase & Son was established in 1931.

ASK FOR OUR BROCHURE NOW
0345 125488
Calls charged at local rate

We have over thirty years experience as Church Furnishings specialists, so you will be in good hands. Our chairs are in over 5,000 places of worship throughout the UK, so you will be in good company too. If you do need someone to rely on, call us and we will be delighted to discuss your requirements.

OUR RANGE INCLUDES

CHAIRS • TABLES • PULPITS • ALTARS • KNEELERS
SILVERWARE • VESTMENTS

JAMES CHASE
& SON (FURNISHINGS) LTD

191 Thornton Rd, Bradford BD1 2JT. Telephone: 01274 738282 Fax: 01274 737836

CAPITAL MINISTRIES

London City Mission workers are engaged in ministry throughout London, including:

- Street evangelism
- Youth outreach
- Christian Centres
- Hospital visiting
- Door-to-door visiting
- Caring for the homeless
- Attachments to churches
- Industrial chaplaincies

SERVING CHRIST IN THE CAPITAL

LONDON CITY MISSION

175 Tower Bridge Road, SE1 2AH. Tel. 0171 407 7585   E-mail: lcm.uk@btinternet.com   Registered Charity No. 247186

Founded 1553

KING EDWARD'S SCHOOL, WITLEY

An independent day and boarding school for boys and girls from age eleven upwards

founded in 1553 this royal, ancient and religious foundation offers

— first class academic tuition —
— excellent facilities for study and recreation —
— modern houses for both day and boarding pupils —
— new sports complex —
— set in a hundred acres of grounds —
— generous bursaries for families with boarding need —

If you have a talented son or daughter who would benefit from the above, please contact:
**The Headmaster's Secretary, King Edward's School, Witley, Godalming, Surrey GU8 5SG
(Tel 01428 682572)** to arrange a tour of the school and to meet the Headmaster

King Edward's School, Witley, exists to provide a structured approach to education with fine facilities and high academic standards

Registered charity No. 311997

In a church just one of the senses is crucial

One of the commonest problems with church buildings is poor sound quality – the way sound echoes off hard surfaces, pillars and lofted ceilings can cause all sorts of listening difficulties, particularly for the more elderly in a congregation.

Every church has its own unique sound properties... but there is one company who has a reputation for overcoming these difficulties by supplying tailor-made, easy to use sound reinforcement systems at prices within reach of even the smallest place of worship.

RGJONES
SOUND ENGINEERING

RG Jones Sound Engineering 16 Endeavour Way Wimbledon London SW19 8UH
call us on 0181 971 3100... we think you'll be pleasantly surprised

Support the Hospital that cares for our clergy!

Free treatment
St Luke's is the clergy's own hospital, founded just over 100 years ago, and today one of the most up-to-date acute hospitals in London.

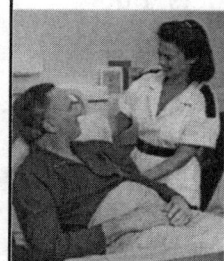

St Luke's extends free treatment to Church of England ordained Ministers, both active and retired, their spouses and dependent children; Ordinands; Monks and Nuns of the Anglican Communion; Officers of the Church Army; Overseas Missionaries, and Priests from Anglican Churches abroad.

Stewardship
St Luke's is a wonderful example of Christian Stewardship in action, for the Hospital is supported largely by private individuals, mostly church members, and treatment is provided by some 150 leading consultants, who give their services without fee.

In addition, St Luke's provides for the laity through its Healthcare Scheme, by which lay church members can receive treatment at greatly reduced costs. The Hospital also runs Couples Counselling services and courses on Stress Management.

Can you help?
There couldn't be a better way of saying, 'Thank you' to those who spend their lives caring for others. Please join our family of supporters by helping us with a donation or a legacy. And if you would like to know more, please telephone, or write to me at the address below.

Paul Thomas
The Revd. Paul Thomas, General
Secretary and Hospital Administrator

St Luke's
HOSPITAL FOR THE CLERGY
Caring for those who care for others

14 Fitzroy Square, London W1P 6AH.
Tel. 0171-388 4954. Fax. 0171-383 4812. Reg Charity 209236

Why the original is still the best

Every week we bring the latest news to all our readers, but there's so much more to *The Church of England Newspaper*.

For clergy, we have news of clergy appointments, retirements, deaths and comprehensive news of General Synod as well as features about the life of the Church around the country.

For lay people, we have a wide range of features that connect the Christian faith to everyday life. And our unique theology page keeps everyone — beginner and expert — up to date with the latest developments.

Ask your newsagent or church agent, or call 0171 878 1510 for a free sample copy to find out what you have been missing for the last 170 years

The CHURCH OF ENGLAND Newspaper

The Original Church Newspaper
Going strong since 1828

THE ENGLISH
CLERGY ASSOCIATION

Patron: The Worshipful Chancellor June Rodgers
Chancellor of the Diocese of Gloucester.
President: Professor Sir Anthony Milnes Coates, Bt., B.Sc., M.D., F.R.C.P.
Parliamentary Vice-President: Sir Patrick Cormack, , F.S.A., M.P.

Vice-Presidents: Sir William Dugdale, Bt., C.B.E., M.C., J.P., D.L.;
The Rt. Hon. Sir Robin Dunn, M.C., P.C.;
The Very Revd. Derek Hole, Provost of Leicester;
The Very Revd. Dr. Peter Moore, O.B.E., M.A., D.Phil., F.S.A.;
The Most Hon. The Marquess of Salisbury;
Dr. D. M. Tyrrell, B.D., M.A., Ph.D., A.C.I.S., A.C.A.;
The Venerable Tom Walker, M.A.;
The Rt. Hon. The Lady Willoughby de Eresby.

The ASSOCIATION supports the integrity of traditional parish and cathedral ministry alongside modern developments, particularly asserting in broad terms the value of the *patronage system and the parson's freehold within* the enduring worth of the Ministry of the Church of England as by Law Established.

PARSON & PARISH, free to Members of the Association, is presently published twice a year: Membership is £10 p.a., £5 to the retired and to ordinands.

HOLIDAY GRANTS of a discretionary kind are made to Church of England clergy upon written application by the form in use to the Hon. Almoner.

LEGACIES & DONATIONS are especially welcome at a time of modest interest-rates. P.C.C.s can become Corporate Members.

**Chairman: The Revd. J. W. Masding, M.A., LL.M.
E.C.A. Office: The Old School, Norton Hawkfield
Near Pensford, Bristol BS18 4HB**
Telephone: (+44) Chew Magna (01275) 83 0017

Deputy Chairman: David Hands, Esq., Q.C.
Vice-Chairman: The Revd. Jonathan Redvers Harris, LL.B., LL.M. (Canon Law)
Treasurer: J. M. Hanks, Esq., LL.M., A.C.A.
Honorary Almoner: The Revd. J. D. Thompstone, M.A.
Editor of *Parson & Parish*: The Revd. M. G. Smith, M.A., B.D. (Oxon.)
Clerk to the Trustees & Hon. Secretary to the Council: J. H. Wearing, Esq., LL.B.

Benefit Fund Registered Charity No.: 258559.
Bankers: Coutts & Co., St. Martin's Office, Strand, London; Bank of Scotland, Birmingham.

Isn't It Time *You* Turned to The Tablet?

For articles of quality by writers drawn from differing faiths, The Tablet, the international Catholic weekly, has no parallel.

Read in over 120 countries, by people who want to know not only what's happening within the Christian Church worldwide, but why, and what people are thinking.

Topical and important issues are discussed and analysed by a network of specialists world-wide, from genetic engineering to the global economic crisis, from the future of the Methodists to the government's housing policy.

All this combined with comprehensive and intelligent book reviews, and columns covering the UK arts scene.

Special Introductory Subscriptions only £25.50 for 6 months
Call 0181 748 8484   Fax 0181 563 7644
The Tablet, CEYearbook Offer, FREEPOST, London W6 OBR
http://www.thetablet.co.uk/

THE NECROPOLIS COMPANY

We specialise in programmes of burial ground reclamation and crypt clearance occasioned by the need for all types of development. The service, whether major or minor, covers both exhumation and reinterment/cremation. All work is conducted by our own experienced staff.

Originally formed by Private Act of Parliament in 1852, the company carries out exhumation and related processes strictly in accordance with the various laws and regulations that govern these matters. As part of its total service the company also offers professional advice on all related aspects of this subject.

Where single or small multiple exhumations are required we normally instruct local funeral directors in these matters. As part of a major group with over 500 branches nationwide we can justly claim to be the premier company in The United Kingdom in this particular context.

For further information please contact:
David Jenkins, BA, General Manager, Bryson House, Horace Road, Kington-Upon-Thames, Surrey KT1 2SL.
Tel: 0181 546 7476   Fax: 0181 974 8895

(A trading subsidiary of Associated Funeral Directors Ltd)

DUPLICATION

BLANK & DUPLICATED AUDIO CASSETTES

CD, CD-ROM & CD-R DUPLICATION

BLANK & DUPLICATED VIDEO CASSETTES

DUPLICATION

ICC Duplication, Hawthorn Road
Ind. Est. Eastbourne, BN23 6QA
Tel 01323 647990 Fax 01323 643095
E-mail: duplication@icc.org.uk

Rydal Hall

in the heart of the Lake District

Conferences Retreats Holidays
(For groups, Families and individuals)

Reproduced under licence for Rydal Hall by kind permission of the artist Karl Stedman   © Karl Stedman

This elegant Georgian Mansion providing full-board accommodation for up to 56 guests together with a 36 bunk self-catering Youth Centre are open throughout the year. A campsite for youth organisations is open from Easter to the end of September (350 persons).

A converted barn provides comfortable seating for 200. Kitchen available.

A 30-acre estate provides opportunites for walking, swimming, painting, ornithology, games, gardening, meditation and prayer.

Members of the resident Community are available to contribute to your programme. Guests are also welcome to join the daily worship of the Community.

Carlisle Diocesan Retreat and Conference Centre, Rydal Hall, Ambleside, Cumbria LA22 9LX.
Tel: 01539 432050   Fax: 01539 434887   E-mail: rydalhall@aol.co.uk

FOR PEOPLE WHO TAKE THE CHURCH SERIOUSLY

CHURCH TIMES

The most widely read Anglican newspaper

Available weekly from your newsagent or by post from our subscription department

Find out why tens of thousands of churchgoers take the Church Times each week

Simply send your name and address to:
Church Times, FREEPOST LON 6705, London N1 0BR
or phone 01502 711171 for your complimentary copy

REVIEW OF THE YEAR 1998
A Personal View by Hugh Wilcox

'I am proud to say,' said the distinguished parish priest as we robed for a diocesan service, 'that I have never seen, still less bought, a copy of the *Year Book* and my ministry has not been impaired thereby one whit.' My friend was teasing me, playing up the role of the remote rural incumbent unimpressed by a Synod activist. But his words are a corrective to those of us who can be so caught up by activities in the triangle of Church House, Millbank and Lambeth that we can fall prey to the temptation to overvalue the Synodical and the national and undervalue the quiet, daily, local, offering of prayer and praise and service, which is the constant and most important work of Christ's body, the Church. As those whose names and activities fill the columns of this volume scurry about the corridors of ever illusive power, it is all too easy to lose sight of whose power it is that is being exercised and on behalf of whom we speak.

The Archbishops' Council takes up its duties from 1 January 1999. Coming as it does close to the new millennium, this provides a vital watershed, a new point of departure, a chance for the restating of old perspectives and the adoption of new ones. It is an opportunity for self-examination. It will not be easy for the new Council to address, still less to remedy, the problems of discontinuity and disconnection between the national, the diocesan, the deanery and the parish.

Just as difficult is the image and role of the Church in contemporary society and culture. How far is the Church in danger of being seduced, as some allege it is, by the spirit of the age, the constant demand for novelty, the compulsions bred and fed by commercial forces whose fortunes depend on over-stimulated appetites? Those who hold the reigns of power in the media and communications are the masters and manipulators of these commercial forces – small wonder that the Church, amongst our other historic English institutions, is under constant attack. For the Church, if it is to be true to the Gospel, has to stand against many of the underlying principles of contemporary culture and its concomitants – 'please yourself morality' and 'design your own deity'. It is not in the interest of those who promote this consumer culture to draw attention to the numerous signs of growth and vitality in our Church. But growth and health there is, and the one institution, the Christian Church, which has survived not one millennium but two can look ahead to the next with confidence.

LITURGICAL REVISION
1998 was dominated synodically by the immense weight of liturgical revision. How strange it is – save that it is an example of disconnection between church at large and parish – that it seems to come as a shock to some church members that *The Alternative Service Book 1980* coming to the end of its authorization as it does in the year 2000, should need to be replaced service by service. The synodical process of liturgical revision is indeed cumbersome. Those of the 'for heaven's sake get on with it' school of ecclesiastical management need to remember that there is always suspicion in the wider Church about change being forced at pace on unsuspecting congregations. If there are still congregations who know nothing of the possible changes in store it is because so few Church members bother to read a Church newspaper and because ministers have failed in their duty to preach and teach about the work which is in progress, about the extensive consultations with parishes in every diocese and the process which permits anyone, member of Synod or not, access to texts, drafts, revisions, and the revision process itself. The Liturgical Commission has done much to publicize its work in progress and with the work of *Praxis*, Grove publications and other supporting literature there can be little excuse for liturgical revision to be a surprise.

Those members of Synod who find the process of revision tedious beyond endurance may well ask if this is the best way to do this kind of business. But our worship is so central to our very being as the Church that the working out of its formalization must be a priority. The bringing about of as great a consensus as is possible makes necessary consultation and much revision and above all skilful listening and redrafting. No one can level at the

Liturgical Commission or the several revision committees the charge that they have not done their best to hear and engage with a proliferation of conflicting demands and proposals, and at the same time to maintain the momentum. The work of Church House Publishing is also to be commended, especially in the positive meeting of the demand for material on disk. It is good that this work is being done from within Church House and that the Church itself is taking responsibility for the production and promotion of its new liturgy.

HEALING AND WHOLENESS

Among the liturgical work of the Synod was consideration of services for ministry to the sick. These we recommitted for revision and it was proposed that a working party be set up to consider the state of the healing ministry of the Church. The development of this ministry is itself a sign of growth and one which demonstrates again the important work which is done quietly at parish level, offering comfort and support to all who need it, regardless of allegiance or commitment. Those in need, whether suffering illness themselves, or through the illness of loved ones, turn of course to the medical services, but they turn also in grief and stress and pain to those who can offer comfort and compassion. This 'suffering with' is one of the gifts of Christ which he offers through the rediscovered ministry of healing. Its continuing growth throughout the Church is to be encouraged. At the same time we need guidance to help us cope with a growing range of alternative solutions being offered. The proposed working party is therefore timely.

CROWN APPOINTMENTS

The decision to set up a review of the working of the Crown Appointments Commission provides an opportunity to examine afresh this most thorny of problems. In an age which seems to think there is truth in the adage *Vox populi vox Dei*, despite all the evidence to the contrary, the case against open elections on the political model is not easy to sustain. The New Testament model is of the post-Resurrection apostles choosing two candidates and leaving the choice to the Holy Spirit in the drawing of lots. Those reviewing our current arrangements will need to consider how far they can be said to reflect that pattern, if indeed it is felt that they should. They will need to wrestle too with the current system which discusses potential candidates for high office without their knowledge and without personal interview. The members of the Commission have to rely on the assessments of others. Are there selection methods in current use in other disciplines which would be appropriate for the Church? The review group will need also to take account of the criticism recently voiced by several commentators, including Lord Habgood, that current practice ensures that the Commission cannot have a role in strategic planning; since each Commission is concerned only with one diocese it cannot be easy for long term strategy to be seen as part of the agenda, except perhaps in the minds of the Archbishops and their advisors.

Underlying this discussion is the wider question of establishment, one which has implications not only for other churches, but also for other faiths. While establishment is seen by some as a relic of a bygone age, others, including many leaders of other faith communities, see it as a recognition of the place of religious faith in national life and would see its abolition as a threat to all faith. This discussion does not, at its widest, concern only the Church of England, for the Church of Scotland is 'established' in a way that recognizes its unique role as the national church, and the Roman Catholic Church is possessed of a far greater 'church and state' establishment than any other church in its diplomatic representation throughout the world. It can be argued that this and other kinds of 'establishment' is a responsibility through which the concerns and interests of not just one but all the Christian Churches, and indeed of other faiths, can be pursued in the corridors of power. The question has to be asked – is this so?

MEASURING ATTENDANCE

One focus of controversy was the complex question of church membership and attendance. It may come as a surprise to those commentators who love to derive from church statistics tales of our imminent demise, that in the parishes ministers and lay leaders alike have much better things to do than continually agonize about numbers. Indeed, our assurance about our task of being the Church depends more on the promise of Jesus Christ that 'where two or three are gathered together in my name there am I' than on a 'successful' turn-out in secular terms. There are falling electoral rolls in some parishes – especially since there has been a shift in perception from the wish to maintain as large an electoral roll as possible, to the desire to make the electoral roll an accurate reflection of actual attendance and stewardship commitment. In some parishes it is observable that while numbers have remained steady, perhaps may have increased, it is not the same people who are attending each week, but a larger number of folk who are attending with a pattern of regularity which may be two- or three-weekly. The faithful in the pew, those hesitating on the fringe and those who can be regarded as friendly observers, need to be reassured that it is the sincerity of our witness, the warmth of our welcome, the compassion of our listening and the offering of word and sacrament which authenticate our discipleship, not our scores on some kind of ecclesiastical league table. While we should never miss a chance to welcome new members, we should not allow ourselves to be talked down by those who apparently do not understand the Old Testament concept of the faithful remnant or the faithful few of Christian history. The more we can discover ways of accurately analysing the new patterns of church attendance which are emerging, the more effectively we can address our mission.

MILLENNIUM

In July the General Synod was given a presentation about the Millennium and the presenters given a positive hearing. Many share the concern, certainly heard in the parishes, about the apparent Christlessness of what, after all, only has meaning as the celebration of two thousand years of Our Lord and support the churches' effort to put Christ at the heart of the millennium event. The Churches' Millennium unit has done its best to voice these concerns and its work has been a good example of how churches can work together successfully in building an effective inter-church staff team able to deliver a combined approach to Government and others on millennium policy. Sadly, it already seems clear that the millennium will be celebrated in a Christ-centred way only in those places where churches and the local community have forged imaginative links and where initiatives have not been stifled by waiting for endorsement from anywhere else, or by an understandable lack of enthusiasm for what seems to be yet another imposition from the top.

Good ideas and good practice need to be shared and the millennium mailings are helping in that process. Greatly to be commended is the Cheshire initiative, begun by an incumbent who asked for a simple millennium notice board. Now these have spread through the area and have begun to appear elsewhere, stating simply, outside churches of all denominations, 'The Millennium is Christ's 2000th Birthday, Worship Him Here – now'. Simple, to the point, good communication, well presented. The proposals for national observance on Friday 31st December 1999 need as sharp a focus if the party mood is to embrace the deeper considerations summed up in the Millennium Resolution. We should be encouraged by the research which suggests that most people will be looking for something special on that night to differentiate it from all others. The proposed candle lighting, silence and reading of the resolution may provide that difference, though the candle in every home idea could prove expensive for churches expected to provide them.

ARCHBISHOPS' COUNCIL
Also in July the Synod added the finishing touches to the legislation necessary for the Archbishops' Council to begin its work in January 1999. The Council faces real problems, not the least of which is the burden of expectations, some impossible to realize, others impossible to reconcile with each other. Those who are called on to become the Council and to serve it as its officers will need to beware of the temptations to arrogance which come with power. The doctrine of trust, used, or some might think overused, in debates in Synod about the Turnbull process, is not to be used as a weapon to silence questions about accountability which should be at the forefront of the Council's thinking and of its subsidiaries. Nor can trust be regarded as an excuse for avoiding proper consultation, or for elitist management of the many by the few. Chief among the challenges will be that of deciding on priorities. Given a quantifiable budget, staff and staff time, what

should the Church's central bodies be doing, and what should they lay aside? Will the Council be able to develop the new kind of working in which all the components, Boards, Councils and so on can take decisions and establish priorities corporately? Closely allied to these areas of difficulty is that of bringing together matters of policy and finance. This will be seen at its most critical in decisions concerning stipends.

STIPENDS

The Church has two pressures: on the one hand, the needs of the stipendiary clergy, needs which are recognized by one or two dioceses which choose to ignore central pay guidelines, and the problems of parishes in raising the level of contributions, from which stipends are paid – problems recognized by dioceses which feel they can only pay at the average level. Will the stipendiary clergy feel that their interests are being represented at every level of the new structure, even though it might seem from the vicarage study to be more Byzantine than that which it replaces? Will the new Council initiate a new in-depth look at stipends? Those few dioceses and individuals who have actually consulted clergy and their families have a complex set of circumstances. Underlying it all is the unpalatable fact that the stipendiary ministry of the Church is being subsidized in practice by working spouses, and to a small extent by those who have private means or expectations. Those ministers who have none of those advantages and are entirely reliant on the stipend find it very difficult to cope, especially if they have ageing relatives or dependent children – and dependency can go on well beyond the teenage years. Living in a large house is itself an expensive business especially if the house was badly built and inadequately maintained. Comparisons are frequently made between stipends and the salaries of 'comparable professions', but these miss the most salient difference. Service and experience and responsibility have financial recognition in other professions, but a parish priest with thirty years service and perhaps with a considerable responsibility in diocesan affairs will receive this year exactly the same as the youngest new incumbent fresh to the job after a couple of curacies. Few of the clergy solely dependent on the stipend have any savings at all, and it is no wonder that they and their families look ahead with apprehension to retirement, despite the admirable improvements both to pensions and to housing now available.

Why are such facts not more widely known? Because the clergy are not given to complain, they are trapped by perceptions of vocation which seem to imply, contrary to the scriptural view that the labourer is worthy of his hire, that we must not be seen to ask for more, and because the current systems of consultation have been thought by some to be inadequate. If we are to hear soon proposals about clergy conditions of service and clergy discipline, these will need to be set within the context of factual analysis of the present financial situation facing our stipendiary ministers.

All this is of especial importance at a time when the numbers of those offering themselves for ministry of various kinds is increasing. Much depends on how the Church is perceived to view its ministers, how it affirms them, and their families, not only in words, but in the practicalities of housing, stipend and pension, and in sympathetic understanding of the stresses and dangers sometimes, which stipendiary ministry imposes on those who answer God's call to serve his Church. The Council will be expecting much of its clergy in the shared task of leading the people of God in mission in the new millennium; those ministers, and those men and women we hope will follow their example, will equally be expecting much of the new Council and hoping that it will give a lead on these important issues.

WORKING TOGETHER
Centralization as a concept can set alarm bells ringing, especially to those of us who rejoice in the history of a Church peopled by eccentrics, by independent thinkers and by a variety of liturgical and doctrinal nuances. We might fear a prescriptive and monochrome church, in which the spiritual dimension is marginalized. Some change in management style will be welcomed by those who point to the fact that the Church of England, far from being a unity, is a loose federation of forty-four fiercely independent dioceses. Any kind of working together has to be negotiated and will demand a network of checks and balances.

Ecumenical working together also has its challenges, despite the achievements of Porvoo and Meissen. The continued refusal of the Vatican to recognize Anglican orders, reinforced by the recent restatement refusing permission for Roman Catholics to receive communion at Anglican altars, reinforces the importance of the ARCIC process and the need for more, not less, work in the pursuit of unity. Yet it is understandable that church people at parish level, faced with the challenge to go out on a cold winters evening to a 'unity' event may well wonder what the point is, and whether the time, effort and money spent on such dialogue could not be better expended elsewhere, if there are no clear signs of any potential progress. Anglicans for their part cannot be complacent. There are some who are profoundly worried at the decision to proceed with renewed talks with the Methodist Church. This is not necessarily because they do not wish them to go forward, but because of the fear that when, and if, such talks result in a proposal for rapprochement, whether on the Porvoo, Meissen or other lines, the Church of England will once more fail to agree to proceed. Far better, say some, not to talk at all than to run the risk of failure. Understandable as this attitude is, it allows little room for the guidance of the Holy Spirit or for the capacity of the Church at large to have a vision for the future. Nor does it recognize the immense progress made in church relationships and in theological agreement, the fruit of years of work by those who serve the Church in the pursuit of church unity.

INTER-FAITH DIALOGUE
Difficult issues confront us also in inter-faith dialogue. At a time when the human rights of our Muslim brothers and sisters in England – human rights which Christians should be prepared to defend – are threatened both by racism and by a demonization of Islam in the media, our own co-religionists in Islamic states are under attack. How do we grapple with the historic Muslim belief that there can be no freedom to leave Islam, and the use of the Blasphemy Law against Pakistani Christians? Human rights are under threat for many communities in many parts of the world, and we need to work with Muslims to eliminate the conditions which give rise to their abuse – whether that is the victimization

of Muslim women who choose to wear the veil, the ethnic cleansing of Muslims by Bosnian Serbs or the desperate terrorism of Islamic radicals who attribute all their ills to the influence of the West and so of Christianity.

LAMBETH CONFERENCE

What, if anything, did this year's conference mean to the parishes of the Church of England, or to those of the worldwide Anglican Communion? The sheer number of words makes it difficult to assay the task of assessing their weight in terms of spiritual leadership, of theological insight and of an Anglican vision for the future. It is easy to criticize the gathering as expensive, though in fact it yielded a surplus. But it was the experience of meeting others from across the spectrum of backgrounds, cultures and experiences which was reported most enthusiastically. To be in a milieu where the office and role of a Bishop of the Church of God is affirmed must be of profound support to those who at home endure at least marginalization and in some cases persecution. But can these undoubted benefits justify the huge expense of time and money and effort? The Anglican Consultative Council itself has to face challenges about its role, its financing and its authority. Just as the parishes in England need to be encouraged to see that diocesan and national structures are taking them seriously and make a difference to their problems and the success of the ministry, so in the same way national churches need to be sure that the worldwide structures of our Communion are vehicles of gospel and community, accessible but not manipulated by particular interest groups.

A thorough-going review needs to be carried out – perhaps by independent assessors – to look at the questions of size, organization, management and communication raised by the conference. Having said that, just as parishes in England need to guard themselves and be guarded from the dangers of sliding into independency and congregationalism, distancing themselves from deanery and diocese and province, so there is a danger of dioceses and provinces wanting to take refuge from confrontation of the real issues which membership of this worldwide communion poses, in a mere lip-service to our common calling in Christ as

Anglicans. Much will depend on how the Lambeth experience is assessed, communicated and criticized, and whether lessons are learnt and acted upon.

PEOPLE

The rapidly changing ecclesiastical scene this year has been paralleled by changes in leadership. As we move to a new era of financial and national organization, Alan McLintock, one of its most assiduous, hardworking and kindly advocates, retires after remarkable service to the national Church. What a sign it is of the vibrant and thriving life of the Church of England that at a time of 'fat-cattery' in industry, lay men and women of the highest calibre are prepared to serve the Church for no reward at all.

From the Church's senior staff we lose through retirement two remarkable people whose influence has been very considerable. Dr Mary Tanner, theologian, ecumenist, diplomat, reconciler, administrator, has worked tirelessly for the Church of England at the heart of the pursuit of unity. Her academic gifts, her commitment to mission, her intellectual rigour, always delivered with humour and sensitivity, have been placed at the service of the worldwide church through her work at the World Council of Churches and in so many theological encounters. She will be greatly missed. Influential in a way less obvious, but as important, was Patrick Locke who has retired this year after four decades of service to the Church Commissioners; his last few years as Secretary, bearing the brunt of the 'post-debacle' trauma there. His massive calm, rigorous attention to detail and accuracy, his personal encouragement of the staff and of new Commissioners, and his commitment to what he saw as the Commissioners' chief purpose – the support of the clergy – made a vital contribution to the Commissioners' reclamation of its losses, the establishment of new assets controls, and their positive participation in the movement towards integration into one central administration.

James Jones was appointed to be Bishop of Liverpool and Thomas Butler to be Bishop of Southwark. Alec Knight became Dean of Lincoln early in the year and it was to be hoped that an end to a damaging saga of Trollopian proportions, together with implementation of the new legislation on cathedrals, would usher in new perspectives in the work and mission of these most compelling of our sacred places. The current controversy at Westminster Abbey casts a shadow, we may hope temporarily, over these hopes.

The deaths of Alistair Haggart and Lesslie Newbiggin ended the witness of two men who in differing ways were icons of a committed ecumenism and a dedication to mission. It was good that Archbishop Trevor Huddleston lived long enough to see the defeat of the apartheid regime in South Africa. His personal witness and teaching on the implications of the Gospel for contemporary issues was of profound influence, rooted as it was in Anglican catholicity and spirituality.

The deaths of Michael Vasey and Brian Masters deprived the Church of priests at opposite and indeed opposing ends of the theological spectrum, but united in pastoral zeal, integrity and personal courage and kindness. Michael Vasey will be sorely missed in Synod and in the Church at large both for his trenchant interventions in the debate on homosexuality, an evangelical challenging assumptions about Bible teaching, and for his work on liturgical renewal marked as one obituary put it 'by strong theological comment and a precise sense of detail'. Brian Masters, who was Bishop of Edmonton for fourteen years, gave leadership and encouragement to those who, while opposed to the decision to ordain women to the priesthood, intended and intend to remain members of the Church of England. Anthony Dyson served the Church as theological college principal and as Professor of Social and Pastoral Theology and was an influential figure in the development of theological training, pastoral theology and medical ethics, a 'model', one commentator wrote, 'of how theologians should work on the issues of their time with those of other disciplines and without any theological hauteur.'

BEING THE CHURCH

It is to be hoped that 1999 will be a year in which the world at large will be enabled to hear the true and exciting story of today's Church of England as its parish clergy and its faithful laymen and women see it day by day. It is a Church of growth; the contribution of Church schools increasingly recognized; new parishes being formed; new churches being built; new church extensions in every diocese of the land, ensuring better facilities for service and for worship; churches being reordered; new organs and bells being installed – and all of this supported by churchgoers and local communities working together, recognizing and welcoming the work of the Church at the heart of local life. It is a church in which increasingly the rich human resources of leadership, ordained and lay, male and female, full and part-time, are being harnessed in the service of God; in which faith is constantly renewed and strengthened, in which the enquirer becomes the committed, in which all are valued and welcomed.

There is of course another strand to the story, the strand told so often as though it is the only truth, of parishes which are struggling, of low morale among worshippers and ministers, of doubt, of doctrinal disagreement, of marital infidelities and worse. Such events are gleefully told as though the Church claims to be the company of the perfect. But that has never been our boast – only that we are the company of the sinful who hope through God's love and help to become the company of the redeemed. That is not news – nor is the third strand of church activity, the unspectacular, quiet work of parishes and people and clergy, who get on with their work of worship and witness and service, loyal to their faith and to the Church, and to our special calling to minister to the whole community. Especially we need to affirm that quiet work of ministry, the significance of the presence of church buildings, mute but powerful witnesses to every community, of the love, grace and healing power of God, and the work of men and women, paid and unpaid, ordained and lay, who are the Church, the Body of Christ in each place.

Canon Hugh Wilcox is Vicar of St Mary's, Ware, has been a member of General Synod since 1989 and is Prolocutor of the Lower House of the Convocation of Canterbury. From 1 January 1999 he will be a member of the Archbishops' Council

The views expressed in this review are personal ones and should not be construed as expressing the policy of the Church of England.

CALENDAR 1999–2000

According to the Calendar, Lectionary and Collects authorized pursuant to Canon B 2 of the Canons of the Church of England for use from 30 November 1997 until further resolution of the General Synod of the Church of England.

Key

BOLD UPPER CASE – Principal Feasts and other Principal Holy Days
Bold Roman – Sundays and Festivals
Roman – Lesser Festivals
Small Italic – Commemorations
Italic – Other Observances

JANUARY
1 **The Naming and Circumcision of Jesus**
2 **Basil the Great and Gregory of Nazianzus, Bishops, Teachers of the Faith, 379 and 389**
   Seraphim, Monk of Sarov, Spiritual Guide, 1833
   Vedanayagam Samuel Azariah, Bishop in South India, Evangelist, 1945
3 **The Second Sunday of Christmas**
   (*or* **The EPIPHANY** *if transferred from 6 January*)
6 **THE EPIPHANY**
10 **The Baptism of Christ** – The First Sunday of Epiphany
11 *Mary Slessor, Missionary in West Africa, 1915*
12 Aelred of Hexham, Abbot of Rievaulx, 1167
   Benedict Biscop, Abbot of Wearmouth, Scholar, 689
13 Hilary, Bishop of Poitiers, Teacher of the Faith, 367
   Kentigern (Mungo), Missionary Bishop in Strathclyde and Cumbria, 603
   George Fox, Founder of the Society of Friends (the Quakers), 1691
17 **The Second Sunday of Epiphany**
18 *Week of Prayer for Christian Unity until 25th*
19 Wulfstan, Bishop of Worcester, 1095
20 *Richard Rolle of Hampole, Spiritual Writer, 1349*
21 Agnes, Child-Martyr at Rome, 304
22 *Vincent of Saragossa, Deacon, first Martyr of Spain, 304*
24 **The Third Sunday of Epiphany**
25 **The Conversion of Paul**
26 Timothy and Titus, Companions of Paul
28 Thomas Aquinas, Priest, Philosopher, Teacher of the Faith, 1274
30 Charles I, King, Martyr, 1649
31 **The Fourth Sunday of Epiphany**
   (*or* **THE PRESENTATION OF CHRIST IN THE TEMPLE** *if transferred from 2 February*)

FEBRUARY
1 *Brigid, Abbess of Kildare, c.525*
2 **THE PRESENTATION OF CHRIST IN THE TEMPLE – CANDLEMAS**
3 Anskar, Archbishop of Hamburg, Missionary in Denmark and Sweden, 865
4 *Gilbert of Sempringham, Founder of the Gilbertine Order, 1189*
6 *The Martyrs of Japan, 1597*
   Queen's Accession
7 **The Second Sunday before Lent**
10 *Scholastica, sister of Benedict, Abbess of Plombariola, c.543*
14 **The Sunday next before Lent**
15 Sigfrid, Bishop, Apostle of Sweden, 1045
   Thomas Bray, Priest, Founder of the SPCK and the SPG, 1730
17 **Ash Wednesday**
21 **The First Sunday of Lent**
23 Polycarp, Bishop of Smyrna, Martyr, c.155
27 George Herbert, Priest, Poet, 1633
28 **The Second Sunday of Lent**

MARCH
1 David, Bishop of Menevia, Patron of Wales, c.601
2 Chad, Bishop of Lichfield, Missionary, 672

7 **The Third Sunday of Lent**
8 Edward King, Bishop of Lincoln, 1910
   Felix, Bishop, Apostle to the East Angles, 647
   Geoffrey Studdert Kennedy, Priest, Poet, 1929
14 **The Fourth Sunday of Lent**
   Mothering Sunday
17 Patrick, Bishop, Missionary, Patron of Ireland, c.460
18 *Cyril, Bishop of Jerusalem, Teacher of the Faith, 386*
19 **Joseph of Nazareth**
20 Cuthbert, Bishop of Lindisfarne, Missionary, 687
21 **The Fifth Sunday of Lent**
24 *Walter Hilton of Thurgarton, Augustinian Canon, Mystic, 1396*
   Oscar Romero, Archbishop of San Salvador, Martyr, 1980
25 **THE ANNUNCIATION OF OUR LORD TO THE BLESSED VIRGIN MARY**
26 *Harriet Monsell, Founder of the Community of St John the Baptist, Clewer, 1883*
28 **Palm Sunday**
29 Monday in Holy Week
30 Tuesday in Holy Week
31 Wednesday in Holy Week

APRIL
1 **MAUNDY THURSDAY**
2 **GOOD FRIDAY**
3 Easter Eve
4 **EASTER DAY**
5 Monday in Easter Week
6 Tuesday in Easter Week
7 Wednesday in Easter Week
8 Thursday in Easter Week
9 Friday in Easter Week
10 Saturday in Easter Week
11 **The Second Sunday of Easter**
16 *Isabella Gilmore, Deaconess, 1923*
18 **The Third Sunday of Easter**
19 Alphege, Archbishop of Canterbury, Martyr, 1012
21 Anselm, Abbot of Le Bec, Archbishop of Canterbury, Teacher of the Faith, 1109
23 **George, Martyr, Patron of England, c.304**
24 *Mellitus, Bishop of London, first Bishop at St Paul's, 624*
25 **The Fourth Sunday of Easter**
26 **Mark the Evangelist** (*transferred from 25 April*)
27 *Christina Rossetti, Poet, 1894*
28 *Peter Chanel, Missionary in the South Pacific, Martyr, 1841*
29 Catherine of Siena, Teacher of the Faith, 1380
30 *Pandita Mary Ramabai, Translator of the Scriptures, 1922*

MAY
1 **St Philip and St James, Apostles**
2 **The Fifth Sunday of Easter**
4 English Saints and Martyrs of the Reformation Era
8 Julian of Norwich, Spiritual Writer, c.1417
9 **The Sixth Sunday of Easter**
10 *Rogation Day*

xxxvi   Calendar

11 *Rogation Day*
12 *Rogation Day*
13 **ASCENSION DAY**
14 **Matthias the Apostle**
16 **The Seventh Sunday of Easter** – *Sunday after Ascension Day*
19 Dunstan, Archbishop of Canterbury, Restorer of Monastic Life, 988
20 Alcuin of York, Deacon, Abbot of Tours, 804
21 *Helena, Protector of the Holy Places, 330*
23 **PENTECOST**
24 John and Charles Wesley, Evangelists, Hymn Writers, 1791 and 1788
25 The Venerable Bede, Monk at Jarrow, Scholar, Historian, 735
   Aldhelm, Bishop of Sherborne, 709
26 Augustine, first Archbishop of Canterbury, 605
   John Calvin, Reformer, 1564
   Philip Neri, Founder of the Oratorians, Spiritual Guide, 1595
28 *Lanfranc, Prior of Le Bec, Archbishop of Canterbury, Scholar, 1089*
30 **TRINITY SUNDAY**
31 **The Visit of the Blessed Virgin Mary to Elizabeth**

JUNE
1 Justin, Martyr at Rome, c.165
3 **The Day of Thanksgiving for the Initiation of Holy Communion (Corpus Christi)**
   The Martyrs of Uganda, 1886 and 1978
5 Boniface (Wynfrith) of Crediton, Bishop, Apostle of Germany, Martyr, 754
6 **The First Sunday After Trinity**
8 Thomas Ken, Bishop of Bath and Wells, Non-Juror, Hymn Writer, 1711
9 Columba, Abbot of Iona, Missionary, 597
   Ephrem of Syria, Deacon, Hymn Writer, Teacher of the Faith, 373
11 **Barnabas the Apostle**
13 **The Second Sunday After Trinity**
14 *Richard Baxter, Puritan Divine, 1691*
15 *Evelyn Underhill, Spiritual Writer, 1941*
16 Richard, Bishop of Chichester, 1253
   Joseph Butler, Bishop of Durham, Philosopher, 1752
17 *Samuel and Henrietta Barnett, Social Reformers, 1913 and 1936*
18 *Bernard Mizeki, Apostle of the MaShona, Martyr, 1896*
19 *Sundar Singh of India, Sadhu (Holy Man), Evangelist, Teacher of the Faith, 1929*
20 **The Third Sunday After Trinity**
22 Alban, first Martyr of Britain, c.250
23 Etheldreda, Abbess of Ely, c.678
24 **The Birth of John the Baptist**
27 **The Fourth Sunday After Trinity**
28 Irenæus, Bishop of Lyons, Teacher of the Faith, c.200
29 **Peter and Paul, Apostles** *or* **Peter the Apostle**

JULY
1 *John and Henry Venn, Priests, Evangelical Divines, 1813 and 1873*
3 **Thomas the Apostle**
4 **The Fifth Sunday After Trinity**
6 *Thomas More, Scholar, and John Fisher, Bishop of Rochester, Reformation Martyrs, 1535*
11 **The Sixth Sunday After Trinity**
14 John Keble, Priest, Tractarian, Poet, 1866
15 Swithun, Bishop of Winchester, c.862
   Bonaventure, Friar, Bishop, Teacher of the Faith, 1274
16 *Osmund, Bishop of Salisbury, 1099*
18 **The Seventh Sunday After Trinity**
19 Gregory, Bishop of Nyssa, and his sister Macrina, Deaconess, Teachers of the Faith, 394 and 379
20 *Margaret of Antioch, Martyr, 4th Century*
   Bartolomé de las Casas, Apostle to the Indies, 1566

22 **Mary Magdalene**
23 *Bridget of Sweden, Abbess of Vadstena, 1373*
25 **James the Apostle – The Eighth Sunday After Trinity**
26 Anne and Joachim, Parents of the Blessed Virgin Mary
27 *Brooke Foss Westcott, Bishop of Durham, Teacher of the Faith, 1901*
29 Mary, Martha and Lazarus, Companions of our Lord
30 William Wilberforce, Social Reformer, 1833
31 *Ignatius of Loyola, Founder of the Society of Jesus, 1556*

AUGUST
1 **The Ninth Sunday After Trinity**
4 *Jean-Baptist Vianney, Curé d'Ars, Spiritual Guide*
5 Oswald, King of Northumbria, Martyr, 642
6 **The Transfiguration of Our Lord**
7 *John Mason Neale, Priest, Hymn Writer, 1866*
8 **The Tenth Sunday After Trinity**
9 Mary Sumner, Founder of the Mothers' Union, 1921
10 Laurence, Deacon at Rome, Martyr, 258
11 Clare of Assisi, Founder of the Minoresses (Poor Clares), 1253
   John Henry Newman, Priest, Tractarian, 1890
13 Jeremy Taylor, Bishop of Down and Connor, Teacher of the Faith, 1667
   Florence Nightingale, Nurse, Social Reformer, 1910
   Octavia Hill, Social Reformer, 1912
14 *Maximilian Kolbe, Friar, Martyr, 1941*
15 **The Blessed Virgin Mary – The Eleventh Sunday After Trinity**
16 **The Blessed Virgin Mary** (*if transferred from 15 August*)
20 Bernard, Abbot of Clairvaux, Teacher of the Faith, 1153
   William and Catherine Booth, Founders of the Salvation Army, 1912 and 1890
22 **The Twelfth Sunday After Trinity**
24 **Bartholomew the Apostle**
27 Monica, mother of Augustine of Hippo, 387
28 Augustine, Bishop of Hippo, Teacher of the Faith, 430
29 **The Thirteenth Sunday After Trinity**
30 John Bunyan, Spiritual Writer, 1688
31 Aidan, Bishop of Lindisfarne, Missionary, 651

SEPTEMBER
1 *Giles of Provence, Hermit, c.710*
2 *The Martyrs of Papua New Guinea, 1901 and 1942*
3 Gregory the Great, Bishop of Rome, Teacher of the Faith, 604
4 *Birinus, Bishop of Dorchester (Oxon), Apostle of Wessex, 650*
5 **The Fourteenth Sunday After Trinity**
6 Allen Gardiner, Missionary, Founder of the South American Mission Society, 1851
8 The Birth of Blessed Virgin Mary
9 *Charles Fuge Lowder, Priest, 1880*
12 **The Fifteenth Sunday After Trinity**
13 John Chrysostom, Bishop of Constantinople, Teacher of the Faith, 407
14 **Holy Cross Day**
15 Cyprian, Bishop of Carthage, Martyr, 258
16 Ninian, Bishop of Galloway, Apostle of the Picts, c.432
   Edward Bouverie Pusey, Priest, Tractarian, 1882
17 Hildegard, Abbess of Bingen, Visionary, 1179
19 **The Sixteenth Sunday After Trinity**
20 John Coleridge Patteson, First Bishop of Melanesia, and his Companions, Martyrs, 1871
21 **Matthew, Apostle and Evangelist**
25 Lancelot Andrewes, Bishop of Winchester, Spiritual Writer, 1626
   Sergei of Radonezh, Russian Monastic Reformer, Teacher of the Faith, 1392
26 **The Seventeenth Sunday After Trinity**

Calendar xxxvii

27 Vincent de Paul, Founder of the Congregation of the Mission (Lazarists), 1660
29 **Michael and All Angels**
30 *Jerome, Translator of the Scriptures, Teacher of the Faith, 420*

OCTOBER
1 *Remigius, Bishop of Rheims, Apostle of the Franks, 533*
  Anthony Ashley Cooper, Earl of Shaftesbury, Social Reformer, 1885
3 **The Eighteenth Sunday After Trinity**
  (**or Dedication Festival**)
4 Francis of Assisi, Friar, Deacon, Founder of the Friars Minor, 1226
6 William Tyndale, Translator of the Scriptures, Reformation Martyr, 1536
9 *Denys, Bishop of Paris, and his Companions, Martyrs, c.250*
  Robert Grosseteste, Bishop of Lincoln, Philosopher, Scientist, 1253
10 **The Nineteenth Sunday After Trinity**
11 *Ethelburga, Abbess of Barking, 675*
   James the Deacon, companion of Paulinus, 7th century
12 Wilfrid of Ripon, Bishop, Missionary, 709
   Elizabeth Fry, Prison Reformer, 1845
   Edith Cavell, Nurse, 1915
13 Edward the Confessor, King of England, 1066
15 Teresa of Avila, Teacher of the Faith, 1582
16 Nicholas Ridley, Bishop of London, and Hugh Latimer, Bishop of Worcester, Reformation Martyrs, 1555
17 **The Twentieth Sunday After Trinity**
18 **Luke the Evangelist**
19 Henry Martyn, Translator of the Scriptures, Missionary, 1812
24 **The Last Sunday After Trinity** – *Bible Sunday*
25 *Crispin and Crispinian, Martyrs at Rome, c.287*
26 Alfred the Great, King of the West Saxons, Scholar, 899
   Cedd, Abbot of Lastingham, Bishop of the East Saxons, 664
28 **Simon and Jude, Apostles**
29 James Hannington, Bishop of East Equatorial Africa, Martyr in Uganda, 1885
31 **The Fourth Sunday before Advent** – *All Saints' Sunday*
   (**or ALL SAINTS' DAY** *if transferred from 1 November*)

NOVEMBER
1 **ALL SAINTS' DAY**
2 Commemoration of the Faithful Departed (All Souls' Day)
3 Richard Hooker, Priest, Anglican Apologist, Teacher of the Faith, 1600
  Martin of Porres, Friar, 1639
6 *Leonard, Hermit, 6th century*
  William Temple, Archbishop of Canterbury, Teacher of the Faith, 1944
7 **The Third Sunday Before Advent**
8 **The Saints and Martyrs of England**
9 *Margery Kempe, Mystic, c.1440*
10 Leo the Great, Bishop of Rome, Teacher of the Faith, 461
11 Martin, Bishop of Tours, c.397
13 Charles Simeon, Priest, Evangelical Divine, 1836
14 *Samuel Seabury, First Anglican Bishop of North America, 1796*
14 **The Second Sunday Before Advent** – *Remembrance Sunday*
16 Margaret, Queen of Scotland, Philanthropist, Reformer of the Church, 1093
   Edmund Rich of Abingdon, Archbishop of Canterbury, 1240
17 Hugh, Bishop of Lincoln, 1200
18 Elizabeth of Hungary, Princess of Thuringia, Philanthropist, 1231
19 Hilda, Abbess of Whitby, 680
   Mechtild, Béguine of Magdeburg, Mystic, 1280
20 Edmund of the East Angles, King, Martyr, 870
   Priscilla Lydia Sellon, a Restorer of the Religious Life in the Church of England, 1876
21 **Christ the King** – *The Sunday Next Before Advent*

22 *Cecilia, Martyr at Rome, c.230*
23 Clement, Bishop of Rome, Martyr, c.100
25 *Catherine of Alexandria, Martyr, 4th century*
   Isaac Watts, Hymn Writer, 1748
28 **The First Sunday of Advent**
29 Day of Intercession and Thanksgiving for the Missionary Work of the Church
30 **Andrew the Apostle**

DECEMBER
1 *Charles de Foucauld, Hermit in the Sahara, 1916*
3 *Francis Xavier, Missionary, Apostle of the Indies, 1552*
4 *John of Damascus, Monk, Teacher of the Faith, c.749*
  Nicholas Ferrar, Deacon, Founder of the Little Gidding Community, 1637
5 **The Second Sunday of Advent**
6 Nicholas, Bishop of Myra, c.326
7 Ambrose, Bishop of Milan, Teacher of the Faith, 397
8 Conception of the Blessed Virgin Mary
12 **The Third Sunday of Advent**
13 Lucy, Martyr at Syracuse, 304
   Samuel Johnson, Moralist, 1784
14 John of the Cross, Poet, Teacher of the Faith, 1591
17 *O Sapientia*
   Eglantine Jebb, Social Reformer, Founder of 'Save the Children', 1928
19 **The Fourth Sunday of Advent**
24 Christmas Eve
25 **CHRISTMAS DAY**
26 **Stephen, Deacon, First Martyr** – **The First Sunday of Christmas**
27 **John, Apostle and Evangelist**
28 **The Holy Innocents**
29 Thomas Becket, Archbishop of Canterbury, Martyr, 1170
   or Stephen, Deacon First Martyr (*if transferred from 26 December*)
31 *John Wyclif, Reformer, 1384*

JANUARY
1 **The Naming and Circumcision of Jesus**
2 **The Second Sunday of Christmas**
  (**or THE EPIPHANY** *if transferred from 6 January*)
6 **THE EPIPHANY**
9 **The Baptism of Christ** – *The First Sunday of Epiphany*
10 *William Laud, Archbishop of Canterbury, 1645*
11 *Mary Slessor, Missionary in West Africa, 1915*
12 Aelred of Hexham, Abbot of Rievaulx, 1167
   Benedict Biscop, Abbot of Wearmouth, Scholar, 689
13 Hilary, Bishop of Poitiers, Teacher of the Faith, 367
   Kentigern (Mungo), Missionary Bishop in Strathclyde and Cumbria, 603
   George Fox, Founder of the Society of Friends (the Quakers), 1691
16 **The Second Sunday of Epiphany**
17 Antony of Egypt, Hermit, Abbot, 356
   Charles Gore, Bishop, Founder of the Community of the Resurrection, 1932
18 *Week of Prayer for Christian Unity until 25th*
19 Wulfstan, Bishop of Worcester, 1095
20 *Richard Rolle of Hampole, Spiritual Writer, 1349*
21 Agnes, Child-Martyr at Rome, 304
22 *Vincent of Saragossa, Deacon, first Martyr of Spain, 304*
23 **The Third Sunday of Epiphany**
24 Francis de Sales, Bishop of Geneva, Teacher of the Faith, 1622
25 **The Conversion of Paul**
26 Timothy and Titus, Companions of Paul
28 Thomas Aquinas, Priest, Philosopher, Teacher of the Faith, 1274
30 **The Fourth Sunday of Epiphany** (**or THE PRESENTATION OF CHRIST IN THE TEMPLE** *if transferred from 2 February*)
31 *John Bosco, Priest, Founder of the Salesian Teaching Order, 1888*

Other dates

17 January	Anglican Communion Sunday
31 January	Education Sunday
14 February	Unemployment Sunday
7 March	Tear Fund Sunday
12 May	Christian Aid Week until 18th
30 May	Day of Prayer for Vocations to Religious Life
9 July	General Synod meets in York until 13th
11 July	Sea Sunday
12 September	Racial Justice Sunday
4 October	World Day for Animals
17 October	Hospital Sunday
17 October	One World Week until 25th
24 October	United Nations Day
14 November	General Synod meets this week
21 November	Prisoners Sunday
1 December	World AIDS Day
8 December	Human Rights Day

CENTRAL STRUCTURES OF THE CHURCH OF ENGLAND

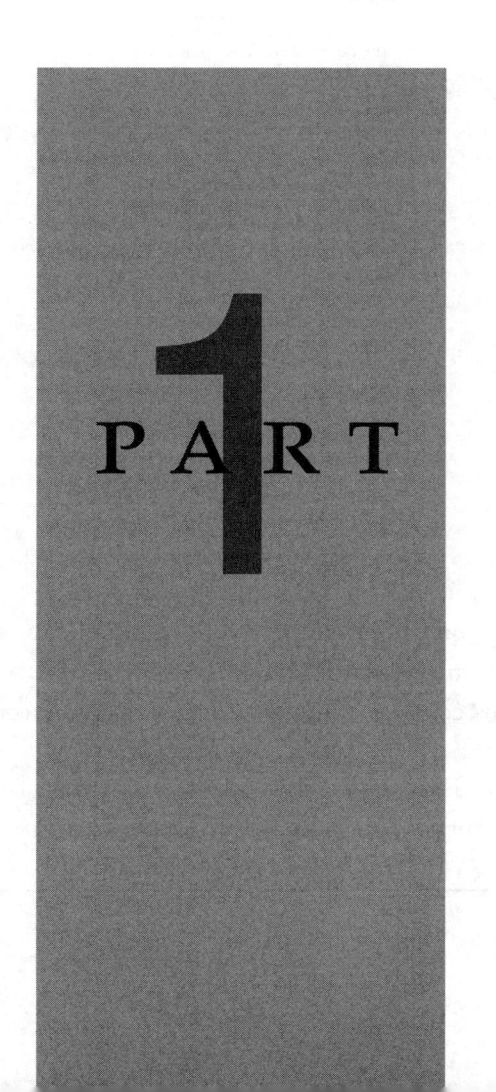

PART 1

PART 1 CONTENTS

All details are fully accurate at the time of going to press.

THE GENERAL SYNOD OF THE CHURCH OF ENGLAND 3
Dates of Sessions 3
Composition of the General Synod 3
House of Bishops 5
House of Clergy 5
House of Laity 5
Principal Committees 5
General Synod Support 6
Legislation Passed 1993–98 7
Constitution 8
General Synod Business 1998 10

THE ARCHBISHOPS' COUNCIL 15
CHURCH AND WORLD 16
The Council for the Christian Unity 16
The Board of Education 18
The Board of Mission 21
The Board of Social Responsibility 23
The Hospital Chaplaincies Council 24
HERITAGE 25
The Council for the Care of Churches 26
The Cathedrals Fabric Commission for England 27
FINANCE 27
General Synod Budget 29
Finance Committee 30
CBF Church of England Funds 31
MINISTRY 32
The Central Readers' Council 35
CENTRAL SERVICES 36
Church House Publishing 37
Church House Bookshop 37
Statistics 37
Records Centre 38
COMMUNICATIONS 38
Enquiry Centre 38
Diocesan Communications Officers Panel 39
LEGAL ADVICE AND SUPPORT STAFF 39
HUMAN RESOURCES 39
Advisory Committees and Permanent Commissions 39
The Cathedral Statutes Commission 39
The Crown Appointments Commission 40
The Dioceses Commission 40
The Doctrine Commission 41
The Legal Advisory Commission 41
The Legal Aid Commission 42
The Liturgical Commission 42

THE CHURCH COMMISSIONERS FOR ENGLAND 43

THE CHURCH OF ENGLAND PENSIONS BOARD 46

OTHER BOARDS, COUNCILS, COMMISSIONS, ETC. OF THE CHURCH OF ENGLAND 48
The Advisory Board for Redundant Churches 48
The Churches Conservation Trust 48
The Corporation of the Church House 48
The National Society (Church of England) for Promoting Religious Education 49

THE CONVOCATIONS OF CANTERBURY AND YORK 51

THE ECCLESIASTICAL COURTS 52

THE GENERAL SYNOD OF THE CHURCH OF ENGLAND

Office

Church House, Great Smith St, London SW1P 3NZ
Tel: 0171–898 1000   *Fax:* 0171–898 1369
e-mail: synod@synod.clara.net

Dates of Sessions

The following periods have been set aside for Groups of Sessions of the General Synod in 1999:

Friday 9 July – Tuesday 13 July (at York)
Week beginning 14 November

2000:   Monday 28 February – Wednesday 1 March if necessary
Friday 7 July – Tuesday 11 July (at York)
Week beginning 12 November

Composition of the General Synod

	Canterbury	York	Either	Totals
House of Bishops				
Diocesan Bishops	30	14		44
Suffragan Bishops	6	3		9
	36	17		53
House of Clergy				
Deans or Provosts	10	5		15
Archdeacons	29	14		43
Service Chaplains and Chaplain-General of Prisons			4	4
Elected Proctors and the Dean of Guernsey or Jersey	126	58		184
University Proctors	4	2		6
Religious Communities	1	1		2
Co-opted places (none filled at present)	3	2		5
	177	82		259

	Canterbury	York	Either	Totals
House of Laity				
Elected Laity*	168	79		247
Religious Communities	2	1		3
Co-opted places (none filled at present)			5	5
Ex officio (First and Second Church Estates Commissioners)			2	2
	170	80	7	257
Either House of Clergy or House of Laity				
Ex officio (Dean of the Arches, the 2 Vicars General, the Third Church Estates Commissioner, the Chairman of the Pensions Board and Members of the Archbishops' Council)			11	11
	383	179	18	580

Seven representatives of other churches have been appointed to the Synod under its Standing Orders with speaking but not voting rights.
* The representatives of laity of the Provinces of Canterbury and York are elected by lay members of Deanery Synods.

OFFICERS OF THE GENERAL SYNOD
Presidents
The Archbishop of Canterbury
The Archbishop of York

Prolocutor of the Lower House of the Convocation of Canterbury
Canon Hugh Wilcox

Prolocutor of the Lower House of the Convocation of York
Canon John Stanley

General Synod

Chairman of the House of Laity Dr Christina Baxter

Vice-Chairman of the House of Laity Dr Philip Giddings

Secretary General Mr Philip Mawer

Clerk to the Synod Mr David Williams

Legal Adviser and *Joint Registrar of the Provinces of Canterbury and York (Registrar of the General Synod)*
Mr Brian Hanson

Financial Secretary Mr Shaun Farrell

Assistant Legal Adviser Miss Ingrid Slaughter

Standing Counsel Mr John Pakenham-Walsh

OFFICERS OF THE CONVOCATIONS
Synodical Secretary of the Convocation of Canterbury
Canon Michael Hodge, The Rectory, Rectory Drive, Bidborough, Tunbridge Wells, Kent TN3 0UL
Tel and Fax: (01892) 528081
e-mail: michaelh@braxton.ndirect.co.uk

Synodal Secretary of the Convocation of York
Ven David Jenkins, Woodcroft, Levens, Kendal, Cumbria LA8 8NQ
Tel: (015395) 61281
Fax: (015395) 61217

NON-DIOCESAN MEMBERS
The following are non-diocesan members of General Synod.

Suffragan Bishops in Convocation
CANTERBURY
The Bishop of Barking
The Bishop of Dudley
The Bishop of Grimsby
The Bishop of Maidstone
The Bishop of St Germans
The Bishop of Woolwich

YORK
The Bishop of Penrith
(Two vacancies)

Deans or Provosts in Convocation
CANTERBURY
The Provost of Birmingham
The Provost of Southwark
The Dean of Ely
The Dean of Hereford
The Dean of Norwich
The Dean of Rochester
The Dean of St Albans
The Dean of St Paul's
The Dean of Wells
The Dean of Westminster

YORK
The Provost of Bradford
The Provost of Newcastle
The Dean of Durham
The Dean of Manchester
The Dean of York

Service Representatives in Convocation
Chaplain of the Fleet and Archdeacon to the Royal Navy
Ven Simon Golding

Deputy Chaplain-General and Archdeacon to the Army
Ven John Holliman

Chaplain-in-Chief, Royal Air Force
Ven Peter Bishop

Chaplain-General of Prisons and Archdeacon
Ven David Fleming

University Representatives in Convocation
CANTERBURY
Oxford
Canon Trevor Williams

Cambridge
Canon John Polkinghorne

London
Revd Dr Richard Burridge

Other Universities (Southern)
Revd Gavin Ashenden

YORK
Durham and Newcastle
Vacancy

Other Universities (Northern)
Canon Prof Anthony Thiselton

Representatives of Religious Communities in Convocation
CANTERBURY
Revd Sister Teresa Joan White CSA

YORK
Fr Aidan Mayoss CR

Lay Representatives of Religious Communities
CANTERBURY
Sister Hilary CSMV
Brother Tristam SSF

YORK
Sister Margaret Shirley OHP

Ex Officio Members of the House of Laity
Dean of the Arches Rt Worshipful Sir John Owen

Vicar-General of the Province of Canterbury
Chancellor Sheila Cameron

Vicar-General of the Province of York
His Honour Judge Thomas Coningsby

First Church Estates Commissioner Sir Michael Colman

Second Church Estates Commissioner Mr Stuart Bell MP

Third Church Estates Commissioner Mrs Margaret Laird

Chairman of the Church of England Pensions Board
Mr Allan Bridgewater

Appointed Members of the Archbishops' Council

Stephen Bampfylde
Michael Chamberlain
David Lammy

Jayne Ozanne
Peter Toyne

House of Bishops

Chairman The Archbishop of Canterbury

Vice-Chairman The Archbishop of York

Secretary Mr Jonathan Neil-Smith   *Tel:* 0171–898 1373

Theological Consultant Dr Gareth Jones   *Tel:* 0171–898 1488

The Standing Committee of the House of Bishops consists of those members of the house who are members of the Archbishops' Council, the Business Committee, and the Appointments Committee and such other members of the House as the Standing Committee shall from time to time determine.

BISHOPS' INSPECTIONS OF THEOLOGICAL COLLEGES AND COURSES
Chairman of the House of Bishops Committee on Inspections
The Bishop of Birmingham

Chairman of the Inspections Working Party
The Dean of St Albans

Secretary to the Inspectorate Miss Jane Melrose
                                    Tel: 0171–898 1379

House of Clergy

Joint Chairmen The Prolocutors of the Convocations

Secretary Mr David Hebblethwaite   *Tel:* 0171–898 1364

The Standing Committee of the House of Clergy consists of the Prolocutors of the Convocations, the two persons elected by the House to serve on the Archbishops' Council, six persons elected by and from the Lower House of the Convocation of Canterbury and four persons elected by and from the Convocation of York.

House of Laity

Chairman Dr Christina Baxter

Vice-Chairman Dr Philip Giddings

Secretary Mr Malcolm Taylor   *Tel:* 0171–898 1375

The Standing Committee of the House of Laity consists of the Chairman and Vice-Chairman, the members of the Business and Appointments Committees elected by the House and the members of the Archbishops' Council elected by the House.

Principal Committees

THE BUSINESS COMMITTEE
Appointed Members 3
Elected Members 7
Secretary   Mr David Williams (*Clerk to the Synod*)
                                    Tel: 0171–898 1559

Assistant Secretary   Mr Malcolm Taylor
                                    Tel: 0171–898 1375
The Committee is responsible for organising the business of the Synod, enabling it to fulfil its role as a legislative and deliberative body.

General Synod   5

THE LEGISLATIVE COMMITTEE
Ex officio Members
The Archbishop of Canterbury
The Archbishop of York
The Prolocutors of the Convocations
The Chairman and Vice-Chairman of the House of Laity
The Dean of the Arches
(Rt Worshipful Sir John Owen)
The Second Church Estates Commissioner
(Mr Stuart Bell MP)

Elected Members
Mr Ian Garden
Prof David McClean
Revd Stephen Trott
Rt Revd Michael Turnbull (*Bishop of Durham*)
Mr David Wright
Revd Jonathan Young

Appointed Members (Three vacancies)

Secretary Mr Robert Wellen   *Tel:* 0171–898 1371

THE STANDING ORDERS COMMITTEE
Chairman Vacancy

Ex officio Members
The Prolocutor of Canterbury
The Prolocutor of York
The Chairman of the House of Laity
The Vice-Chairman of the House of Laity

Appointed Members
Mr David Ashton
Mr James Cheeseman
Rt Revd Rupert Hoare (*Bishop of Dudley*)
Mrs Joanna Ingram
Revd John Rees
Mr Trevor Stevenson

Secretary Mr Malcolm Taylor   *Tel:* 0171–898 1375

THE APPOINTMENTS COMMITTEE OF THE CHURCH OF ENGLAND
Appointed Members 5

Elected Members 7

Secretary Mr Christopher Ball   *Tel:* 0171–898 1362

The Committee, a joint committee of the General Synod and the Archbishops' Council, is responsible for making appointments and/or recommendations on appointments to synodical and other bodies as the Synod or the Archbishops' Council requires.

General Synod Support

Under the overall direction of the Secretary General, staff of the Archbishops' Council provide the secretariat for the General Synod, its three Houses, and its Business and Legislative Committees. Members of staff of the Council serve as secretaries of a number of the Synod's permanent Committees and Commissions, and also as secretaries of *ad hoc* committees as circumstances require. The Clerk to the Synod acts as Secretary to the Business Committee, and provides advice and assistance as necessary to synodical bodies and members.

Secretary General Mr Philip Mawer   *Tel:* 0171–898 1360

Clerk to the Synod Mr David Williams   *Tel:* 0171–898 1559

Legal Adviser (*and Joint Provincial Registrar*)
Mr Brian Hanson   *Tel:* 0171–898 1366

Assistant Legal Adviser
Miss Ingrid Slaughter   *Tel:* 0171–898 1368
(*Secretary* Legal Advisory Commission; Legal Aid Commission)

Standing Counsel Mr John Pakenham-Walsh

Administrative Staff
Mr David Hebblethwaite   *Tel:* 0171–898 1364
(*Secretary* House of Clergy; Standing Committee of the House of Clergy; Dioceses Commission; Liturgical Commission)

Mr Jonathan Neil-Smith   *Tel:* 0171–898 1373
(*Secretary* House of Bishops; Standing Committee of the House of Bishops)

Mr Malcolm Taylor   *Tel:* 0171–898 1375
(*Assistant Secretary* Business Committee; *Secretary* House of Laity; Standing Committee of the House of Laity; Standing Orders Committee; Elections Review Group)

Mr Christopher Ball   *Tel:* 0171–898 1362
(*Assistant Secretary* Archbishops' Council)

Mr Robert Wellen   *Tel:* 0171–898 1371
(*Secretary* Legislative Committee; Fees Advisory Commission; Cathedral Statutes Commission; Appeals Tribunals under the Ordination of Women (Financial Provisions) Measure 1993. Assistant to Mr Hanson)

Miss Jane Melrose   *Tel:* 0171–898 1379
(*Assistant Secretary* House of Bishops; *Secretary* House of Bishops Inspectorate of Theological Colleges and Courses)

Mr Andrew Roberts   *Tel:* 0171–898 1386
Private Secretary to the Secretary General
(*Secretary* Ecumenical Decade: Churches in Solidarity with Women Working Party)

Mrs Angela Cann *Tel:* 0171–898 1377
(*Registry*)

Mrs Susan Score *Tel:* 0171–898 1376
(*Secretary* Anglican Voluntary Societies Forum; *Assistant to Mr Hebblethwaite*)

Mr Francis Bassett *Tel:* 0171–898 1363
(*Assistant to Mr Christopher Ball*)

Miss Judith Egar *Tel:* 0171–898 1389
(*Solicitor seconded part time to the Legal Division from the Church Commissioners*)

Mr David Pite *Tel:* 0171–898 1374
(*Assistant to Mr Taylor and Miss Slaughter*)

Legislation passed 1993–98 together with dates of commencement

The date in brackets is the date when the legislation came into operation. Items of legislation no longer in force are omitted.

MEASURES
Incumbents (Vacation of Benefices) (Amendment) Measure 1993 (1 September 1994)
Priests (Ordination of Women) Measure 1993 (1 February 1994)
Ordination of Women (Financial Provisions) Measure 1993 (5 November 1993)
Pastoral (Amendment) Measure 1994 (1 April 1994)
Care of Cathedrals (Supplementary Provisions) Measure 1994 (1 October 1994)
Church of England (Legal Aid) Measure 1994 (1 September 1994)
Team and Group Ministries Measure 1995 (Section 2, 28 June 1995, Section 13, 12 February 1996, remainder 1 May 1996)
Church of England (Miscellaneous Provisions) Measure 1995 (1 September 1995 – except Section 6)
Pensions Measure 1997 (1 January 1998)
National Institutions Measure 1998 (1 January 1999)

STATUTORY INSTRUMENTS
Church of England (Legal Aid) Rules 1993 SI 1993 No 1840 (1 September 1993)
Diocesan Chancellorship Regulations 1993 SI 1993 No 1841 (1 October 1993)
Payments to Redundant Churches Fund Order 1993 SI 1993 No 2846 (31 March 1994)
Ordination of Women (Financial Provisions) (Appeals) Rules SI 1993 No 2847 (1 February 1994)
Incumbents (Vacation of Benefices) Rules 1994 SI 1994 No 703 (1 September 1994)
Church Representation Rules (Amendment) Resolution 1994 SI 1995 No 2034 (1 October 1995)
Church of England (Legal Aid) Rules 1995 SI 1995 No 2034 (1 October 1995)
Church Representation Rules (Amendment) Resolution 1995 SI 1995 No 3243 (1 January 1996 – part; 1 May 1996 – further part; 1 May 1997 – remainder)
Payments to the Churches Conservation Trust Order 1996 SI 1996 No 3086 (1 April 1997)
Church Accounting Regulations 1997 (1 August 1997)
Church of England Pensions Regulations 1997 SI 1997 No 1929 (1 January 1998)
Church Representation Rules (Amendment) Resolution 1998 SI 1998 No 319 (1 March 1998)
Ecclesiastical Judges and Legal Officers (Fees) Order 1998 SI No 1711 (1 January 1999)
Legal Officers (Annual Fees) Order 1998 SI 1998 No 1712 (1 January 1999)
Faculty Jurisdiction (Appeals) Rules 1998 SI 1998 No 1713 (1 August 1998)
Parochial Fees Order 1998 SI 1998 No 1714 (1 January 1999)
National Institutions of the Church of England (Transfer of Functions) Order 1998 SI 1998 No 1715 (1 January 1999)

Copies of the above legislation may be obtained from the Stationery Office or Church House Bookshop.
The continuous and consolidated text of the Church Representation Rules is published by Church House Publishing (£4.95).

Summary of Measures and Statutory Instruments
A photocopied list of General Synod Measures which received the Royal Assent from 1920 and Statutory Instruments to date which are still in operation, is available from the Legal Adviser, General Synod Office, Church House, Great Smith St, London SW1P 3NZ. Any request should be accompanied by a stamped self-addressed envelope (at least 10" by 7") please.

Notes
Measures and most Rules made pursuant to Measures are sold by HMSO; they are also obtainable from the Church House Bookshop, London SW1P 3BN. Anyone wishing to obtain a Measure which is out of print should write to HMSO, PO Box 276, London SW8 5DT asking for a photocopy, or copies, which will be supplied via the British Library Lending Division at the current rate of £5.50 per publication to be copied. All requests should quote as a reference the number and year of the Measure.
General Synod publications may be obtained from Church House Bookshop. These publications include the *Report of Proceedings* (price on application).

General Synod

Constitution

1 The General Synod shall consist of the Convocations of Canterbury and York joined together in a House of Bishops and a House of Clergy and having added to them a House of Laity.

2 The House of Bishops and the House of Clergy shall accordingly comprise the Upper and the Lower Houses respectively of the said Convocations, and the House of Laity shall be elected and otherwise constituted in accordance with the Church Representation Rules.

3 (1) The General Synod shall meet in sessions at least twice a year, and at such times and places as it may provide, or, in the absence of such provision, as the Joint Presidents of the Synod may direct.

(2) The General Synod shall, on the dissolution of the Convocations, itself be automatically dissolved, and shall come into being on the calling together of the new Convocations.

(3) Business pending at the dissolution of the General Synod shall not abate, but may be resumed by the new Synod at the stage reached before the dissolution, and any Boards, Commissions, Committees or other bodies of the Synod may, so far as may be appropriate and subject to any Standing Orders or any directions of the Synod or of the Archbishops of Canterbury and York, continue their proceedings during the period of the dissolution, and all things may be done by the Archbishops or any such bodies or any officers of the General Synod as may be necessary or expedient for conducting the affairs of the Synod during the period of dissolution and for making arrangements for the resumption of business by the new Synod.

(4) A member of the General Synod may continue to act during the period of the dissolution as a member of any such Board, Commission, Committee or body:

Provided that, if a member of the Synod who is an elected Proctor of the clergy or an elected member of the House of Laity does not stand for re-election or is not re-elected, this paragraph shall cease to apply to him with effect from the date on which the election of his successor is announced by the presiding officer.

4 (1) The Archbishops of Canterbury and York shall be joint Presidents of the General Synod, and they shall determine the occasions on which it is desirable that one of the Presidents shall be the chairman of a meeting of the General Synod, and shall arrange between them which of them is to take the chair on any such occasion:

Provided that one of the Presidents shall be the Chairman when any motion is taken for the final approval of a provision to which Article 7 of this Constitution applies and in such other cases as may be provided in Standing Orders.

(2) The Presidents shall, after consultation with the Appointments Committee of the Church of England, appoint from among the members of the Synod a panel of no fewer than three or more than eight chairmen, who shall be chosen for their experience and ability as chairmen of meetings and may be members of any House; and it shall be the duty of one of the chairmen on the panel, in accordance with arrangements approved by the Presidents and subject to any special directions of the Presidents, to take the chair at meetings of the General Synod at which neither of the Presidents takes the chair.

[(3) Under the Synodical Government Measure the Provincial Registrars are Joint Registrars of the General Synod but since 1980 the responsibility has been exercised by the Legal Adviser to the General Synod whom each Archbishop appointed as his Joint Registrar for this purpose.]

5 (1) A motion for the final approval of any Measure or Canon shall not be deemed to be carried unless, on a division by Houses, it receives the assent of the majority of the members of each House present and voting:

Provided that by permission of the chairman and with the leave of the General Synod given in accordance with Standing Orders this requirement may be dispensed with.

(2) All other motions of the General Synod shall, subject as hereinafter provided, be determined by a majority of the members of the Synod present and voting, and the vote may be taken by a show of hands or a division:

Provided that, except in the case of a motion relating solely to the course of business or procedure, any 25 members present may demand a division by Houses and in that case the motion shall not be deemed to be carried unless, on such a division, it receives the assent of the majority of the members of each House present and voting.

(3) This Article shall be subject to any provision of this Constitution or of any Measure with respect to special majorities of the Synod or of each House thereof, and where a special majority of each House is required the vote shall be taken on a division by Houses, and where a special majority of the whole Synod is required, the motion shall, for the purposes of this Article, be one relating solely to procedure.

(4) Where a vote is to be taken on a division by Houses, it may be taken by an actual division or in such other manner as Standing Orders may provide.

6 The functions of the General Synod shall be as follows:
   (*a*) to consider matters concerning the Church of England and to make provision in respect thereof –

(i) by Measure intended to be given, in the manner prescribed by the Church of England Assembly (Powers) Act 1919, the force and effect of an Act of Parliament, or

(ii) by Canon made, promulged and executed in accordance with the like provisions and subject to the like restrictions and having the like legislative force as Canons heretofore made, promulged and executed by the Convocations of Canterbury and York, or

(iii) by such order, regulation or other subordinate instrument as may be authorised by Measure or Canon, or

(iv) by such Act of Synod, regulation or other instrument or proceeding as may be appropriate in cases where provision by or under a Measure or Canon is not required;

(b) to consider and express their opinion on any other matters of religious or public interest.

7 (1) A provision touching doctrinal formulae or the services or ceremonies of the Church of England or the administration of the Sacraments or sacred rites thereof shall, before it is finally approved by the General Synod, be referred to the House of Bishops, and shall be submitted for such final approval in terms proposed by the House of Bishops and not otherwise.

(2) A provision touching any of the matters aforesaid shall, if the Convocations or either of them or the House of Laity so require, be referred, in the terms proposed by the House of Bishops for final approval by the General Synod, to the two Convocations sitting separately for their provinces and to the House of Laity; and no provision so referred shall be submitted for final approval by the General Synod unless it has been approved, in the terms so proposed, by each House of the two Convocations sitting as aforesaid and by the House of Laity.

(3) The question whether such a reference is required by a Convocation shall be decided by the President and Prolocutor of the Houses of that Convocation, and the Prolocutor shall consult the Standing Committee of the Lower House of Canterbury or, as the case may be, the Assessors of the Lower House of York, and the decision of the President and Prolocutor shall be conclusive:

Provided that if, before such a decision is taken, either House of a Convocation resolves that the provision concerned shall be so referred or both Houses resolve that it shall not be so referred, the resolution or resolutions shall be a conclusive decision that the reference is or is not required by that Convocation.

(4) The question whether such a reference is required by the House of Laity shall be decided by the Prolocutor and Pro-Prolocutor of that House who shall consult the Standing Committee of that House, and the decision of the Prolocutor and the Pro-Prolocutor shall be conclusive:

Provided that if, before such a decision is taken, the House of Laity resolves that the reference is or is not required, the resolution shall be a conclusive decision of that question.

(5) Standing Orders of the General Synod shall provide for ensuring that a provision which fails to secure approval on a reference under this Article by each of the four Houses of the Convocations or by the House of Laity of the General Synod is not proposed again in the same or a similar form until a new General Synod comes into being, except that, in the case of objection by one House of one Convocation only, provision may be made for a second reference to the Convocations and, in the case of a second objection by one House only, for reference to the Houses of Bishops and Clergy of the General Synod for approval by a two-thirds majority of the members of each House present and voting, in lieu of such approval by the four Houses aforesaid.

(6) If any question arises whether the requirements of this Article or Standing Orders made thereunder apply to any provision, or whether those requirements have been complied with, it shall be conclusively determined by the Presidents and Prolocutors of the Houses of the Convocations and the Prolocutor and Pro-Prolocutor of the House of Laity of the General Synod.

8 (1) A Measure or Canon providing for permanent changes in the Services of Baptism or Holy Communion or in the Ordinal, or a scheme for a constitutional union or a permanent and substantial change of relationship between the Church of England and another Christian body, being a body a substantial number of whose members reside in Great Britain, shall not be finally approved by the General Synod unless, at a stage determined by the Archbishops, the Measure or Canon or scheme, or the substance of the proposals embodied therein, has been approved by a majority of the dioceses at meetings of their Diocesan Synods, or, in the case of the Diocese in Europe, of the bishop's council and Standing Committee of that diocese.

(1A) If the Archbishops consider that this Article should apply to a scheme which affects the Church of England and another Christian body but does not fall within paragraph (1) of this Article, they may direct that this Article shall apply to that scheme, and where such a direction is given this Article shall apply accordingly.

(1B) The General Synod may by resolution provide that final approval of any such scheme as aforesaid, being a scheme specified in the resolution, shall require the assent of such special majorities of the members present and voting as may be specified in the resolution, and the resolution may specify a special majority of each House or of the whole Synod or of both, and in the latter case the majorities may be different.

(1C) A motion for the final approval of a Measure providing for permanent changes in any such Service or in the Ordinal shall not be deemed to be carried unless it receives the assent of a majority in each House of the General Synod of not less than two-thirds of those present and voting.

(2) Any question whether this Article applies to any Measure or Canon or scheme, or whether its requirements have been complied with, shall be conclusively determined by the Archbishops, the Prolocutors of the Lower Houses of the Convocations and the Prolocutor and Pro-Prolocutor of the House of Laity of the General Synod.

9 (1) Standing Orders of the General Synod may provide for separate sittings of any of the three Houses or joint sittings of any two Houses and as to who is to take the chair at any such separate or joint sitting.

(2) The House of Laity shall elect a Chairman and Vice-Chairman of that House who shall also discharge the functions assigned by this Constitution and the Standing Orders and by or under any Measure or Canon to the Prolocutor and Pro-Prolocutor of that House.

10 (1) The General Synod shall appoint a Legislative Committee from members of all three Houses, to whom shall be referred all Measures passed by the General Synod which it is desired should be given, in accordance with the procedure prescribed by the Church of England Assembly (Powers) Act 1919, the force of an Act of Parliament; and it shall be the duty of the Legislative Committee to take such steps with respect to any such Measure as may be so prescribed.

(2) The General Synod may appoint or provide by their Standing Orders for the appointment of such Committees, Commissions and bodies (in addition to the Committees mentioned in Section 10 of the National Institutions Measure 1998), which may include persons who are not members of the Synod, and such officers as they think fit.

(3) Each House may appoint or provide by their Standing Orders for the appointment of such Committees of their members as they think fit.

11 (1) The General Synod may make, amend and revoke Standing Orders providing for any of the matters for which such provision is required or authorised by this Constitution to be made, and consistently with this Constitution, for the meetings, business and procedure of the General Synod.

(1A) Provision may be made by Standing Order that the exercise of any power of the General Synod to suspend the Standing Orders or any of them shall require the assent of such a majority of the members of the whole Synod present and voting as may be specified in the Standing Order.

(2) Each House may make, amend and revoke Standing Orders for the matter referred to in Article 10 (3) hereof and consistently with this Constitution and with any Standing Orders of the General Synod, for the separate sittings, business and procedure of that House.

(3) Subject to this Constitution and to any Standing Orders, the business and procedure at any meeting of the General Synod or any House or Houses thereof shall be regulated by the chairman of the meeting.

12 (1) References to final approval shall, in relation to a Canon or Act of Synod, be construed as referring to the final approval by the General Synod of the contents of the Canon or Act, and not to the formal promulgation thereof:

Provided that the proviso to Article 4 (1) shall apply both to the final approval and to the formal promulgation of a Canon or Act of Synod.

(2) Any question concerning the interpretation of this Constitution, other than questions for the determination of which express provision is otherwise made, shall be referred to and determined by the Archbishops of Canterbury and York.

(3) No proceedings of the General Synod or any House or Houses thereof, or any Board, Commission, Committee or body thereof, shall be invalidated by any vacancy in the membership of the body concerned or by any defect in the qualification, election or appointment of any member thereof.

13 Any functions exercisable under this Constitution by the Archbishops of Canterbury and York, whether described as such or as Presidents of the General Synod, may, during the absence abroad or incapacity through illness of one Archbishop or a vacancy in one of the Sees, be exercised by the other Archbishop alone.

General Synod Business

FEBRUARY 1998
Monday 9 – Wednesday 11 February

LEGISLATIVE BUSINESS
The Synod
Considered on final drafting the draft Cathedrals Measure (GS 1219B) and gave Final Approval to the draft Measure. The voting at final approval was as follows: Bishops *Ayes* 34, *Noes* 0; Clergy *Ayes* 174, *Noes* 0; Laity *Ayes* 183, *Noes* 3.

Generally approved draft Amending Canon No 22 (GS 1278).

Approved the draft Church Representation Rules (Amendment) Resolution 1998 (GS 1279). The voting was as follows: Bishops *Ayes* 30, *Noes* 1; Clergy *Ayes* 147, *Noes* 12; Laity *Ayes* 167, *Noes* 11. The rules came into force on 1 March 1998.

Considered on final drafting the draft National Institutions Measure (GS 1228C) and draft Amending Canon No 21 (GS 1228B), and gave Final Approval to the draft Measure. The voting at final approval of the Measure was as follows: Bishops *Ayes* 36, *Noes* 0; Clergy *Ayes* 181, *Noes* 11; Laity *Ayes* 175, *Noes* 27.

Approved the related Amending Canon No 21 and the Petition for Her Majesty's Assent to promulge it, and carried the motion:
> That the Standing Committee be instructed to put in hand the implementation of the new structure on the lines set out in Progress Report No 5 (GS 1277).

LITURGICAL BUSINESS
The Synod
Generally approved the Liturgical Business entitled *Extended Communion* (GS 1230). The voting was as follows: Bishops *Ayes* 24, *Noes* 9; Clergy *Ayes* 128, *Noes* 57; Laity *Ayes* 106, *Noes* 89.

Resumed consideration of the motions for recommittal of Liturgical Business entitled *The Eucharist: The Order for the Administration of the Lord's Supper or Holy Communion* (GS 1211A).

Generally approved the Liturgical Business entitled *The Lord's Prayer* (GS 1269).

Generally approved the Liturgical Business entitled *A Service of the Word; Affirmations of Faith; Prayer for Various Occasions; Canticles at Morning and Evening Prayer* (GS 1280).

OTHER BUSINESS
The Synod
Debated a Diocesan Synod motion on VAT and Church Repairs (GS Misc 576) and carried the motion:
> That this Synod view with great concern the continued imposition of VAT at the standard rate on church repair work and request Her Majesty's Government to levy VAT on all church building work at 5 per cent.

The voting was: *Ayes* 423; *Noes* 2.

Suspended its Standing Orders in order to facilitate a presentation by the Board of Education on the Government's education legislation.

JULY 1998
Friday 3 – Tuesday 7 July

LEGISLATIVE BUSINESS
The Synod
Received a report of the Revision Committee on the draft Care of Places of Worship Measure (GS 1269A) and considered the Measure clause by clause.

Approved the National Institutions of the Church of England (Transfer of Functions) Order 1998 (GS 1309) and the Central Stipends Authority (Amendment) Regulation 1998 (GS 1310).

Carried the following motions in respect to the National Institutions Measure 1998:
> That this Synod determine (pursuant to the power in Schedule 1, paragraph 4(2)) that the persons to be elected to the Archbishops' Council in accordance with the provisions of Schedule 1, paragraph 1(1)(d)(e) and (f) shall serve for three years until 31 December 2001 but request the persons so elected to consider resigning from office with effect from 31 December 2000 in order to allow fresh elections to the Council by the newly elected Synod; and

> That Mr Philip Mawer, Secretary General of the General Synod, be appointed Secretary General of the Archbishops' Council with effect from 1 January 1999 in accordance with Schedule 1, paragraph 16.

Generally approved the Church Representation Rules (Amendment) Resolution (GS 1307) and the Clergy Representation (Amendment) Rules (GS 1308).

Approved the Women Priests (Channel Islands) Order 1998 (GS 1311), the Parochial Fees Order 1998 (GS 1304), the Legal Officers (Annual Fees) Order 1998 (GS 1306) and the Bradford Deaneries Scheme (GS 1314), but did not approve the Southwark Deaneries Scheme (GS 1315). The voting was as follows: *Ayes* 101; *Noes* 142.

Gave deemed approval, under Standing Order 69, to the Faculty Jurisdiction (Appeals) Rules 1998 (GS 1312) and the Ecclesiastical Judges and Legal Officers (Fees) Order 1998 (GS 1305).

LITURGICAL BUSINESS
The Synod
Generally approved that the Liturgical Business entitled *Series 1 Solemnization of Matrimony* (GS 1297) and *Series 1 Burial Services* (GS 1297) be authorised for use until 31 December 2005. The Liturgical Business then automatically stood referred to the House of Bishops.

General Synod

Generally approved the Liturgical Business entitled *Eucharistic Prayers* (GS 1299).

Took note of a report by the Revision Committee on the Liturgical Business entitled: *A Service of the Word, Affirmations of Faith, Prayers for Various Occasions, Canticles at Morning and Evening Prayer* (GS 1280A). The Liturgical Business then automatically stood referred to the House of Bishops.

Took note of a report by the Revision Committee on the Liturgical Business entitled: *Initiation Services – Wholeness and Healing* (GS 1152D). The Liturgical Business then automatically stood referred to the Revision Committee for further consideration.

Took note of a report by the Revision Committee on the Liturgical Business entitled *The Lord's Prayer* (GS 1271A) and approved a motion for the recommittal of the Lord's Prayer for further revision of the lines, in the ELLC text:
'save us from the time of trial
and deliver us from evil.'

Considered the remaining recommittal motions in respect of the Liturgical Business entitled *The Eucharist: The Order for the Administration of the Lord's Supper or Holy Communion* (GS 1211A).

FINANCIAL BUSINESS
The Synod
Took note of the annual report of the Central Board of Finance for 1997 (GS 1295), authorised expenditure by the Central Board of Finance in 1999 and approved the apportionment by the Archbishops' Council between the dioceses of the sum to be provided in 1999 to meet that expenditure.

OTHER BUSINESS
The Synod
Took note of a report by the Board for Social Responsibility entitled *The Misuse of Drugs* (GS 1300) and carried the motion (as amended):
That this Synod, noting the great increase in the amount of drug misuse in our society:
(a) deplore the destructive effects of drugs on individuals and communities;
(b) welcome Her Majesty's Government's intention of improving the co-ordination of efforts to tackle drug misuse;
(c) recognise that such efforts must include serious measures to address the issue of education as well as the symptoms of drug dependence;
(d) commend the efforts of those, including Churches and Christian organisations, giving practical help to those individuals and communities whose lives have been blighted by drugs; and
(e) welcome the introduction of the new drugs court at Wakefield, and call for its further extension into the judicial system after its review and evaluation.

Suspended its Standing Orders in order to facilitate a presentation on a report by the Ecumenical Decade Working Party entitled *The Ecumenical Decade of Churches in Solidarity with Women* (GS 1301), and carried the motion:
That this Synod approve the recommendations in paragraph 12 of GS 1301.

Took note of the Annual Reports for 1997 by the Board for Mission (GS 1283) and the Church Commissioners.

Suspended its Standing Orders in order to facilitate a presentation by the Archbishops' Millennium Advisory Group.

Took note of a report by the Central Board of Finance and the Partnership for World Mission entitled *The Mission Agencies Clergy Pension* (GS 1302) and carried the motion:
That this Synod approve the recommendations in the final paragraph of GS 1302.

Considered the Thirty Sixth Report of the Standing Orders Committee (GS 1296) and proceeded to carry a number of motions amending its Standing Orders.

Debated a Private Members' Motion on Tobacco Promotion, and carried the motion (as amended):
That this Synod, deploring the continued advertising of cigarettes in Britain and the aggressive marketing of tobacco together with the imposition of a tobacco monoculture in the Third World despite overwhelming evidence that smoking kills, welcome the European Union Directive banning tobacco advertising, sponsorship and promotion, and call on the Government
(a) to implement the directive by 31 December 1999;
(b) to ban all point of sale advertising; and
(c) to prohibit the use of tobacco brand names on non-tobacco products.
The voting was as follows: *Ayes* 375; *Noes* 5.

Debated a Private Members' Motion on the Election of Bishops, and carried the motion (as amended):
That this Synod, recognising that it is over twelve years since the procedures of the Crown Appointments Commission were last considered, request the Standing Committee to institute a review of the constitution and methods of operation of the Commission, the review to include consideration of the operation of the Vacancy in See Committees Regulation 1993 and of the

issues covered in the motion tabled by Canon Timothy Yates (Derby) debated at this Group of Session.

Debated a Diocesan Synod Motion on a special day dedicated to the Peace of the World, and carried the motion (as amended):
> That this Synod ask the Archbishops of Canterbury and York to encourage all parishes within the Church of England to pray regularly and urgently for the peace of the world and on occasions, when suitable, to dedicate a special Sunday such as the first Sunday of the calendar year [to such prayer].

NOVEMBER 1998 GROUP OF SESSIONS

LEGISLATIVE BUSINESS
The Synod
Promulged and executed *Amending Canon No 21* (GS 1229B).

Considered on the Revision Stage draft Amending Canon No 22 (GS 1278A) and committed it to the Steering Committee for final drafting.

Considered on the Final Drafting the draft Care of Places of Worship Measure (GS 1269B), and gave final approval to the draft Measure. The voting at final approval was as follows: Bishops *Ayes* 37, *Noes* 0; Clergy *Ayes* 150, *Noes* 0; Laity *Ayes* 171, *Noes* 1.

Considered on the Revision Stage the Church Representation Rules (Amendment) Resolution (GS 1307A) and the Clergy Representation (Amendment) Resolution (GS 1308A) and committed the Instruments to the Steering Committee for final drafting.

Gave deemed approval to the Church of England (Miscellaneous Provisions) Measure (GS 1320) and to draft Amending Canon No 23 (GS 1323).

Approved the Single Transferable Vote (Amendment) Resolutions 1998

Approved the forwarding of a petition to Her Majesty in Council for a change of name to the See of Ripon and Leeds (GS 1313) in accordance with Section 6(2) of the Church of England (Legal Aid and Miscellaneous Provisions) Measure 1998.

LITURGICAL BUSINESS
The Synod
Gave Final Approval to the Liturgical Business entitled *A Service of the Word, Authorized Affirmations of Faith, Prayers for Various Occasions, Canticles, Schedules of Permitted Variations to the Book of Common Prayer, Orders for Morning and Evening Prayer* where these occur in *Common Worship* (GS 1280B). The voting at Final Approval was as follows: Bishops *Ayes* 22, *Noes* 0; Clergy *Ayes* 116, *Noes* 0; Laity *Ayes* 139, *Noes* 0.

Gave Final Approval to the extended authorization for *Series I: Solemnization of Matrimony* (GS 1297A) to 31 December 2005. The voting at Final Approval was as follows: Bishops *Ayes* 18, *Noes* 0; Clergy *Ayes* 110, *Noes* 0; Laity *Ayes* 119, *Noes* 0.

Gave Final Approval to the extended authorization for *Series I: Burial Services* (GS 1297B) to 31 December 2005. The voting at Final Approval was as follows: Bishops *Ayes* 15, *Noes* 1; Clergy *Ayes* 121, *Noes* 8; Laity *Ayes* 127, *Noes* 34.

Took note of the second report by the Revision Committee on the Liturgical Business entitled *The Lord's Prayer* (GS 1271B). The Liturgical Business then automatically stood referred to the House of Bishops.

Took note of the second report by the Revision Committee in respect of the Liturgical Business entitled *The Eucharist: The Order for the Administration of the Lord's Supper or Holy Communion* (GS 1211B). The Liturgical Business (as amended) then automatically stood referred to the House of Bishops.

Took note of a report by the Revision Committee on the Liturgical Business entitled *Sunday Worship with Holy Communion in the Absence of a Priest* (GS 1230A) and recommitted it to the Revision Committee for further consideration.

Generally approved the Liturgical Business entitled *Extended Authorization for the Ordinal in The Alternative Service Book 1980* (GS 1319).

FINANCIAL BUSINESS
The Synod
Approved a supplementary vote for training for ministry and previewed the expenditure by the Central Board of Finance for 2000 (GS 1325).

OTHER BUSINESS
The Synod
Approved, in accordance with Schedule 1 (1) of the National Institutions Measure 1998, the appointment of members to the Archbishops' Council for the period 1 January 1999 to 31 December 2001 and asked the Archbishops' Council to review, early in 1999, the way in which the appointment process had worked.

Heard an address by the Secretary of State for International Development

Took note of a report by the Board of Education entitled *Church of England Schools in the New Millennium* (GS 1321) and carried the motion (as amended) that 'believing that Church Schools stand at the centre of the Church's mission in the nation:

(a) strongly urge:
 (i) Diocesan Synods, in the light of the School Standards and Framework Act, to review the resources available to Diocesan Board of Education to enable them to be involved in all aspects of statutory education;
 (ii) each PCC to discuss how it can serve all schools in the parish;
 (iii) each PCC to commit itself to the greatest possible support for the Church Schools in its area;
(b) welcome the opportunities for Church schools to move to the voluntary aided category and encourage dioceses to support governors in so doing where appropriate; and
(c) invite the Archbishops' Council to review the achievements of Church schools and to make proposals for the future development of Church schools and Church colleges of further and higher education.'

Took note of a report of a Working Party on Local Non-Stipendiary Ministry entitled *Stranger in the Wings* (GS 1316 and GS Misc 532). The voting was as follows: Bishops *Ayes* 34, *Noes* 1; Clergy *Ayes* 128, *Noes* 37; Laity *Ayes* 134, *Noes* 56.

Debated a Diocesan Synod Motion on the Diaconate, and carried the motion (as amended): That this Synod,

(a) mindful of the changing patterns of ministry within the Church of England since the diaconate was last considered; and
(b) conscious of new insight about diaconal ministry arising from discussions both ecumenical and within the Anglican Communion,

request the House of Bishops to set up a working party to consider the concept of a renewed diaconate and to report to Synod.

Debated a Diocesan Synod Motion on Funerals: Business and Vocation, and carried the motion (as amended)

That this Synod 'looking for the resurrection of the dead and the life of the world to come', and recognising the rich history of the Christian pastoral ministry to the dying, and the practice of preparing for a good death,

(a) regret the cultural trends and commercial pressures brought to bear by some funeral directors which tend to discourage funerals in parish churches and to conceal or deny the pastoral and spiritual truths of death and dying;
(b) welcome Parliamentary and Government initiatives to investigate the UK funeral industry;
(c) encourage people when they are having to confront either their own death or burial of others to turn for assistance and support to ministers of religion, such as their local parish priest, or organisations that can offer effective pastoral support to the bereaved;
(d) call on the Archbishops' Council:
 (i) to liase with dioceses to ensure that appropriate training is given to clergy and readers in the conduct of funerals, particularly training in dealing with suicides and sudden and unexpected deaths;
 (ii) to investigate the possibilities of a review in the law covering the re-use of old graves, the re-opening of closed churchyards and appropriate memorialisation; and
 (iii) to examine the possibility of the Church of England participating in the Funerals Ombudsman Scheme;

such review to be made in conjunction with the Churches' Group on Funeral Services at Cemeteries and Crematoria and the Legal Advisory Commission and the results to be reported to the Synod.

Debated a Private Members Motion on Lifelong Celibacy, and carried the motion:

That this Synod commend as something to celebrate the witness of those who fulfil the Christian calling in lifelong celibacy, and honour their vocation.

Debated a Private Members Motion on the Circulation of Synod Papers, and carried the motion (as amended):

That this Synod is of the opinion that, in view of the large quantity of business to be considered at each Group of Sessions, the Business Committee should be encouraged to ensure that, as far as possible, Synod members have a minimum of 21 days to read any Report, proposed legislation or liturgical business before it is considered in Synod.

Heard a presentation on the Lambeth Conference 1998.

THE ARCHBISHOPS' COUNCIL
(and Central Board of Finance of the Church of England)

Central Board of Finance of the Church of England
Company registration no.: 136413
Charity registration no.: 248711
Tel: 0171–898 1000
Fax: 0171–898 1369

Joint Presidents
The Archbishop of Canterbury
The Archbishop of York

Ex officio Members
The Prolocutor of the Lower House of the Convocation of Canterbury
The Prolocutor of the Lower House of the Convocation of York
The Chairman of the House of Laity
The Vice-Chairman of the House of Laity
A Church Estates Commissioner

Elected by the House of Bishops
Rt Revd Michael Turnbull (*Bishop of Durham*)
Rt Revd John Gladwin (*Bishop of Guildford*)
Elected by the House of Clergy
Very Revd Michael Perham (*Provost of Derby*)
Ven Pete Broadbent (*Archdeacon of Northolt*)
Elected by the House of Laity
Mr Brian McHenry
Mrs Christina Rees

Appointed by the Archbishops with the approval of the General Synod
Stephen Bampfylde
Michael Chamberlain
David Lammy
Jayne Ozanne
Peter Toyne
Elizabeth Paver

(The membership of the Archbishops' Council is coterminous with that of the Central Board of Finance of the Church of England)

STAFF
Secretary General Mr Philip Mawer   *Tel:* 0171–898 1360

Deputy Secretary General and Director of Policy Mr Richard Hopgood   *Tel:* 0171–898 1787

Director of Central Services Mr David Williams
Tel: 0171–898 1559

Director of Communications Revd Dr William Beaver
Tel: 0171–898 1462

Financial Secretary and Company Secretary Mr Shaun Farrell   *Tel:* 0171–898 1795

Director of Human Resources Mrs Susan Morgan
Tel: 0171–898 1565

Legal Adviser Mr Brian Hanson   *Tel:* 0171–898 1366

Director of Ministry Ven Gordon Kuhrt
Tel: 0171–898 1390

INTRODUCTION
A key outcome of the reform of the central church structures proposed by the Archbishops' Commission on the Organisation of the Church of England in its report *Working As One Body* is the creation of the Archbishops' Council. The Council will be established on 1 January 1999 following the enactment of the National Institutions Measure 1998, which received Royal Assent in June 1998. The Council will, for the first time, bring together at a national level executive policy and resource decision-making in a single body.

The Council's purpose as set down in the Measure is:
'To co-ordinate, promote, aid and further the work and mission of the Church of England.'

It aims to help the Church to develop a clearer sense of direction, of the opportunities presented to it and of its needs and priorities so that it can fulfil its mission in the world, drawing on the guidance of the House of Bishops, and offering the result for the approval of the General Synod. It aims to ensure that policies and strategies are developed to meet those needs and priorities and to make use of the opportunities accordingly, and to oversee the direction of staff and other resources at the national level in support of the policies agreed by the Synod and the House.

It is responsible for: ministry related functions formerly carried out by the Advisory Board of Ministry and by the

Church Commissioners as Central Stipends Authority (Central Stipends Authority (Amendment) Regulation 1998); financial functions formerly undertaken by the Central Board of Finance and the Church Commissioners; oversight of the range of work carried out by the Boards and Councils, which are accountable to the Synod through the Council; developing pensions policy within the overall remuneration policy for clergy; and developing and executing an integrated communications strategy.

The supporting structure of the Council comprises a number of divisions with responsibility for specific areas of work (see diagram overleaf).

CHURCH AND WORLD

The Church and World grouping brings together a number of Boards and Councils concerned in one way or another with the external face of the Church of England. The Boards relate within it to each other and to the Archbishops' Council, and through the Archbishops' Council, to the Synod.

This grouping together of the Boards provides a new opportunity for developing a strategic overview (for consideration by the Council); helping the Council to assess priorities within a coherent framework; tackling cross-Board issues and working; developing the ecumenical dimension in the working of the Boards; considering resource allocation among the Boards; and addressing work priority questions. The main focus of work in this area will continue to be carried out by the individual Boards, with the Board Chairman continuing to be the Church's principal spokesman in each of the areas covered.

Lambeth Palace, the Anglican Voluntary Societies Forum and the Partnership for World Mission are also represented in this arrangement.

The Council for the Care of Churches (*see* page 26) and the Hospital Chaplaincies Council (*see* page 24) will have a relationship to this grouping in recognition of the public policy aspects of their work.

The Council for Christian Unity

Chairman Rt Revd Ian Cundy (*Bishop of Peterborough*)

Secretary Prebendary Paul Avis PH D   *Tel:* 0171–898 1470

Deputy Secretary Dr Colin Podmore   *Tel:* 0171–898 1479

Secretary for Local Unity Revd Flora Winfield
Tel: 0171–898 1474

Administrative Secretary (*temporary*) Mr Michael Patrick
Tel: 0171–898 1472

Theological Secretary Dr Gareth Jones   *Tel:* 0171–898 1488

Office Church House, Great Smith St, London SW1P 3NZ
Tel: 0171–898 1470
Fax: 0171–898 1483
e-mail: ccu@chho.u-net.com

The Council was established as an advisory committee of the General Synod on 1 April 1991 to continue and develop the ecumenical work formerly undertaken by the Board for Mission and Unity. That Board, set up on 1 January 1972, had inherited the responsibilities of the Missionary and Ecumenical Council of the Church Assembly (MECCA) and the Church of England Council on Foreign Relations (CFR).

FUNCTIONS OF THE COUNCIL
(*Extract from the Constitution*)

(a) To stimulate and encourage theological reflection in consultation with the Doctrine Commission and the Faith and Order Advisory Group and to advise the Archbishops' Council and through it the General Synod on unity issues and proposals in the light of the Christian understanding of God's purposes for the world.

(b) To foster ecumenical work in the Church nationally and in the dioceses.

(c) In conjunction with the Archbishops' Council to promote unity and ecumenical concerns in the work of all Boards and Councils.

(d) In ecumenical concerns on the Archbishops' Council behalf to be the principal link between the General Synod and

  (i) The Anglican Consultative Council;
  (ii) individual provinces and dioceses of the Anglican Communion and the United Churches incorporating former Anglican dioceses.

(e) On behalf of the Archbishops' Council to be the principal channel of communication between the General Synod and

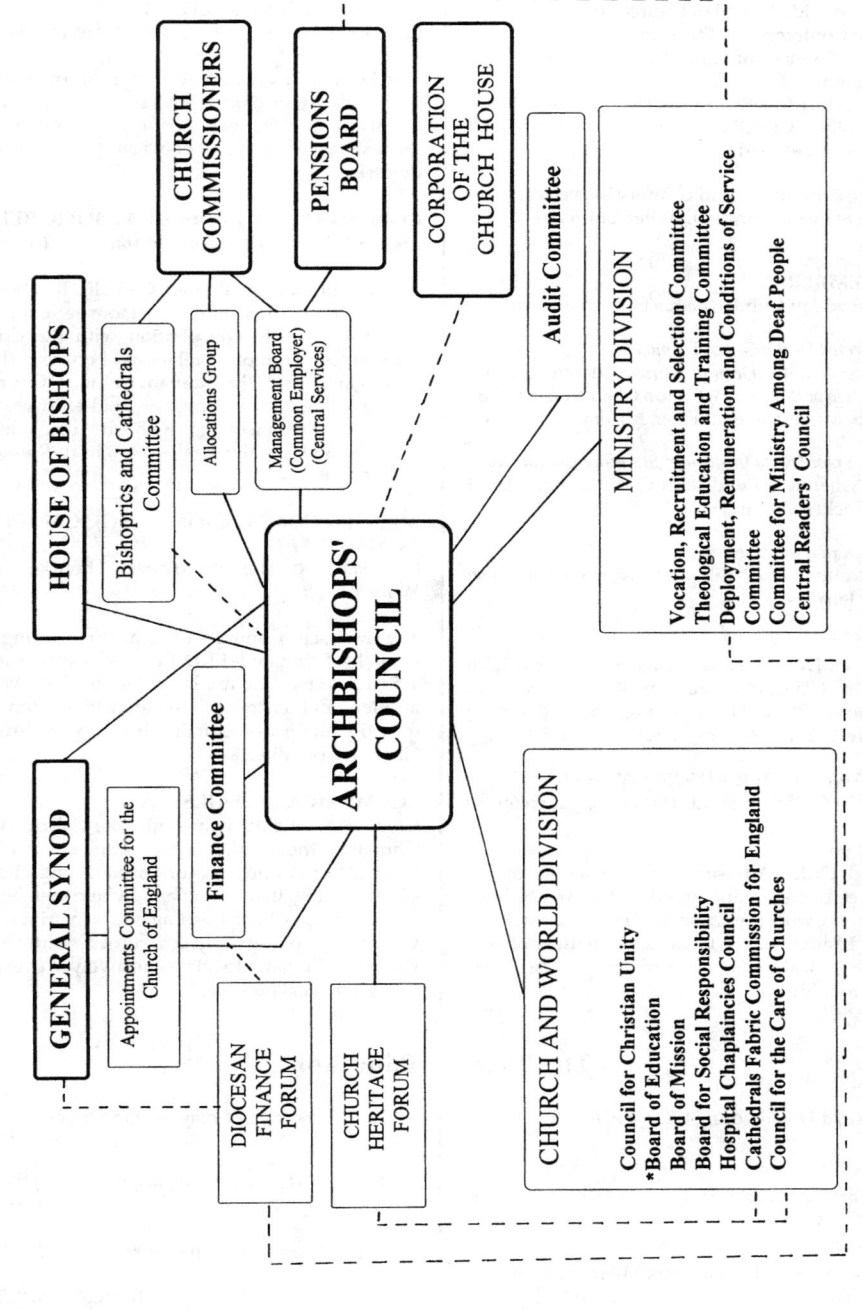

ARCHBISHOPS' COUNCIL : STRUCTURE

GENERAL SYNOD
- Appointments Committee for the Church of England
- Finance Committee

HOUSE OF BISHOPS
- Bishoprics and Cathedrals Committee

CHURCH COMMISSIONERS
- Allocations Group
- Management Board (Common Employer) (Central Services)

PENSIONS BOARD

CORPORATION OF THE CHURCH HOUSE

ARCHBISHOPS' COUNCIL

- DIOCESAN FINANCE FORUM
- CHURCH HERITAGE FORUM
- Audit Committee

CHURCH AND WORLD DIVISION
- Council for Christian Unity
- *Board of Education
- Board of Mission
- Board for Social Responsibility
- Hospital Chaplaincies Council
- Cathedrals Fabric Commission for England
- Council for the Care of Churches

MINISTRY DIVISION
- Vocation, Recruitment and Selection Committee
- Theological Education and Training Committee
- Deployment, Remuneration and Conditions of Service Committee
- Committee for Ministry Among Deaf People
- Central Readers' Council

* The National Society (Church of England) for Promoting Religious Education will continue to work closely with the Board of Education and will maintain a close association with the Archbishops' Council through its integrated publishing programme with Church House Publishing.

CENTRAL STRUCTURES

Archbishops' Council

(i) The World Council of Churches;
(ii) The Conference of European Churches;
(iii) The Council of Churches for Britain and Ireland;
(iv) Churches Together in England;
(iv) all other Christian Churches in the British Isles and abroad.

(f) To service committees and commissions engaged in ecumenical discussions with other Churches.

COUNCIL MEMBERS
Chairman Rt Revd Ian Cundy (*Bishop of Peterborough*)

Six members elected by the General Synod
Very Revd John Arnold (*Dean of Durham*), Rt Revd Colin Buchanan (*Bishop of Woolwich*), Canon Chad Coussmaker, Dr Carole Cull, Mrs Elizabeth Fisher, Mr Frank Knaggs

Four members appointed by the former Standing Committee
Revd Gavin Ashenden, Revd John Cook, Canon David Lickess, Mrs Rachel Moriarty

Four members chosen for expertise
Revd Mark Bratton, Revd Bill Croft, Mrs Terry Garley, Revd Richard Jenkins

Consultants
Rt Revd Michael Doe (*Bishop of Swindon*), Rt Revd John Hind (*Bishop of Gibraltar in Europe*), Rt Revd Bill Ind (*Bishop of Truro*), Rt Revd Barry Rogerson (*Bishop of Bristol*), Canon Richard Marsh (*Lambeth Palace*)

THE FAITH AND ORDER ADVISORY GROUP
Chairman Rt Revd John Hind (*Bishop of Gibraltar in Europe*)

The Faith and Order Advisory Group consists of not more than fifteen persons appointed by the Archbishops after consultation with the Council. The Group advises the House of Bishops or the Council on matters of ecumenical or theological concern referred to it by the House of Bishops or the Council.

LOCAL UNITY COMMITTEE
Chairman Rt Revd Michael Doe (*Bishop of Swindon*)

The Local Unity Committee is concerned to stimulate responsibility in diocese and parish for the unity of the Church. It is a channel of communication and promotes the exchange of ideas between the Council and the dioceses.

COMMITTEE ON ROMAN CATHOLIC RELATIONS
Chairman Rt Revd William Ind (*Bishop of Truro*)

The Committee on Roman Catholic Relations consists of not more than fifteen persons appointed by the Archbishops after consultation with the Council. The Committee promotes relations between the Church of England and the Roman Catholic Church in this country. Regular meetings are held each year, of which two are joint meetings with the equivalent Roman Catholic body in the English Anglican-Roman Catholic Committee.

MEISSEN COMMISSION – ANGLICAN COMMITTEE
Chairman Rt Revd Michael Bourke (*Bishop of Wolverhampton*)

The Meissen Commission (the Sponsoring Body for Church of England–EKD Relations) was established in 1991 to oversee the implementation of the Meissen Declaration and encourage relationships with the Evangelical Church in Germany. It comprises Anglican and German Committees.

ECUMENICAL AFFAIRS
Contact is maintained with the World Council of Churches, the Conference of European Churches, the Council of Churches for Britain and Ireland, and Churches Together in England, where members and staff represent the Church of England at various levels. The Council is particularly concerned with helping the Church of England to relate effectively at every level with the ecumenical bodies.

The Board of Education

Chairman Rt Revd David Young (*Bishop of Ripon*)

General Secretary Canon John Hall Tel: 0171–898 1500

Adult Learning and Lay Training Mrs Hilary Ineson (*also Deputy Secretary*) Tel: 0171–898 1511

Adult and Lifelong Learning Mr Ian Stubbs Tel: 0171–898 1510

Higher Education and Chaplaincy Revd Paul Brice Tel: 0171–898 1513

Children's Work Mrs Diana Murrie Tel: 0171–898 1504

Further Education Mrs Anthea Turner Tel: 0171–898 1517

Education and Administration Finance Officer Ms Daphne Griffith *Tel:* 0171–898 1515

Schools (Curriculum) Mr Alan Brown *Tel:* 0171–898 1494

Schools (Governance and Management) Mr David Lankshear *Tel:* 0171–898 1490

Youth Work Mr Peter Ball, Ms Maxine Green
Tel: 0171–898 1506
Tel: 0171–898 1507

Office Church House, Great Smith St, London SW1P 3NZ
Tel: 0171–898 1500
Fax: 0171–898 1493
e-mail: (insert first name.second name)@boeangel.demon.co.uk

BOARD MEMBERS
Rt Revd David Young (*Bishop of Ripon, Chairman*), Mrs Katy Blake, Mr Peter Bruinvels, Mr A. J. Collier, Mrs Margaret Dean, Prof E. A. V. Ebsworth, Mr Nigel Greenwood, Prof Walter James, Mr Geoff Locke, Mr Peter Middlemiss, Mrs Heather Morgan, Mrs Elizabeth Paver, Prof Arthur Pollard, Ven Robert Reiss (*Archdeacon of Surrey*), Rt Revd Stephen Venner (*Bishop of Middleton*), Ven Paul Wheatley (*Archdeacon of Sherborne*), Mr Peter Williams (*Church in Wales*), (*one vacancy*). Observers: Prof John Dickinson (*Principal, King Alfred's College, Winchester*), Revd John Bailey (*Lincoln DDE*).

The Board's constitution (as laid down by General Synod) sets out three functions: to advise the General Synod through the Archbishops' Council on all matters relating to education; to advise the dioceses similarly; to take action in the field of education (in the name of the Church of England and the General Synod) on such occasion as is required. The work of the Board is divided into three areas, each under the general oversight of a committee responsible to the Board.

COMMITTEES OF THE BOARD
Schools
The work of the Board in connection with schools is carried out in close association with the National Society (Church of England) for Promoting Religious Education (*see* page 49). The two bodies have the same Chairman, General Secretary, Schools Officers, and other members of the staff of the Society and its RE centres are also available to assist the Board in its work.

The Schools Committee reflects and serves the Church's general involvement in the whole statutory system of schooling, with a particular interest in Church schools. It also maintains a link with independent schools of Church of England foundation. It seeks to be concerned with developments affecting the whole curriculum, within which it has a special interest in religious education and school worship in both county and Church schools.

Through its officers, the Committee communicates with the Department for Education and Employment and other national agencies on questions relating to schools, and maintains close links both with professional and educational bodies including the education departments of other churches (particularly through the Churches' Joint Education Policy Committee).

It is responsible to the Board for administering a Loan Scheme for aiding capital works at Church schools.

Further and Higher Education
The current concerns of this Committee are:

1 The development of the Church's presence and witness in Further and Higher Education in the light of careful study of the shifts of emphasis and direction occurring within the national education system (involving mutual consultation with the DfEE and with the FE/HE institutions, attendance at conferences, and the making of time for joint reflection).

2 The making of a particular contribution within the Church's general activity in Further and Higher Education by:
  – working for the extension of church contacts in, and impact on, the field of Further Education;
  – stimulating and developing the Church's practical concern in student affairs;
  – helping the Church to build up its ministry in Higher Education by means of the advisory, liaison, and representative services to chaplaincy work in HE already established;
  – maintaining and strengthening links with Church Colleges of HE in the light of *An Excellent Enterprise* (GS 1134)

Voluntary and Continuing Education
The Committee is concerned with the involvement of the Church in voluntary education. Its task is to explore, identify and communicate how those of differing age and circumstance can grow into fullness of life in Christ.

The Committee is responsible:
  – for servicing the diocesan agencies concerned with voluntary and continuing education including parish development;
  – for co-operating with the committees and staffs of other churches and educational bodies. The purpose of such ecumenical endeavour is to work on behalf of both those within the membership of the Church and those outside it.

The Committee considers and advises on work with children, young people and adults.

Adult Learning and Lay Training

The department exists to encourage adult Christian formation. For a minority this will mean training for a specific ministry in the Church but for most it involves working out the implications of Christian faith in daily life in the world.

The department has the following key functions:
- servicing diocesan and other networks of people working in adult learning and lay training in the Church;
- co-operating with other churches and Christian training agencies;
- collecting and disseminating information about resources in a diverse and expanding field through *Newsboard* and other means;
- providing a National Training Programme in adult education and training;
- developing the church presence and witness in secular adult education;
- encouraging an ongoing critique of current practice through evaluation and research;
- being a 'centre of excellence' in the theory and practice of experiential learning and lifelong learning.

Youth Work

The department works to promote the educational, spiritual and social development of young people between the ages of 11 and 25. This work is for those outside the Church as well as those active within.

The National Youth Officers advise on appropriate training and resourcing of both voluntary and paid youth workers, and provide a Continuing Professional Development Scheme for Diocesan Youth Officers. Action is being taken to enable the better participation of young people in church life with continuing development of a Young Adult Network which includes an Observer Group at General Synod's July meeting. The National Youth Office is managing initiatives to develop youth work in rural areas and among minority ethnic young people.

The National Youth Officers consult regularly with the Diocesan Youth Officers Network in responding to local, regional and national needs.

The Church's youth work also involves collaboration and partnership with a number of Anglican voluntary societies as well as with a variety of other Christian and secular agencies, including the Department for Education and Employment, the National Youth Agency, the National Council for Voluntary Youth Services, Churches Together in England, and Council of Churches in Britain and Ireland. Receipt of a grant from the DfEE under their scheme for National Voluntary Youth organisations has enabled youth work initiatives to be taken at local, diocesan and national level.

Youth A Part (GS 1203), a major report for General Synod on the churches' work with young people, has been, and continues to be, a great stimulus to discussion and action in youth work at every level. This year the book *Accompanying* was published as a resource for parishes. There is ongoing collaborative work with Lambeth Palace and the Archbishop's Adviser in Youth Ministry. This work has focused particularly upon the appointment, training and recognition of youth workers in the Church and plans for a major archiepiscopal event – *The Time of Our Lives* – for young people in 1999.

Childrens Work

1 The National Children's Officer is concerned primarily with the advocacy of the role and value of children in the Church, particularly:
- the Church as a worshipping community,
- the Church as a place of learning for all.

2 The National Officer works primarily with the network of diocesan Children's Advisers, organising the National Conference, implementing induction and in-service training where appropriate, in order to provide laity and clergy at all levels with the necessary resources and training to nurture the faith of children and their families.

3 The Officer instigates and implements reflection and discussion on issues within the Church. Much of this is done in consultation with ecumenical partners and national bodies. Current major issues at present are:
(1) the challenge to the Church of reaching children and their families who have no church contact;
(2) Christian initiation and Communion before Confirmation;
(3) child protection.

4 The Officer works collaboratively with:
Church House Publishing
The National Society
Other Boards and Councils
Lambeth Palace
Other agencies including the Children's Society
The Consultative Group on Ministry among Children (an ecumenical network of CCBI)

For **Chaplains in Higher Education** *see* page 161.
For **Church Colleges of Higher Education** *see* page 165.

The Board of Mission

Chairman Rt Revd Tom Butler (*Bishop of Southwark*)

General Secretary Canon Philip King   Tel: 0171–898 1468

Administrative Secretary Mr Alan Tuddenham
Tel: 0171–898 1467

Partnership Secretary Mr John Clark*

Mission Theology Secretary Dr Anne Richards
Tel: 0171–898 1444

National Officer for Evangelism Vacancy

Mission and Evangelism Secretary Miss Janice Price
Tel: 0171–898 1476

Inter-Faith Relations Adviser Vacancy
Tel: 0171–898 1477

Church of England National Rural Officer Revd Jeremy Martineau*

Archbishops' Officer for the Millennium Revd Stephen Lynas   Tel: 0171–898 1436

Millennium Executive Revd Anne Hibbert
Tel: 0171–898 1437

Office Church House, Great Smith St, London SW1P 3NZ
Tel: 0171–898 1469
Fax: 0171–898 1431
e-mail: (insertfirstname.secondname)@mission.u-net.com
(except where marked *)

BOARD MEMBERS

Eight members elected by General Synod
Rt Revd Richard Garrard (*Bishop of Penrith*), Canon Christopher Hall, Prebendary Robert Horsfield, Mrs Christine McMullen, Dr Peter May, Canon John Moore, Very Revd John Richardson (*Provost of Bradford*), Mr Ian Smith

Three members of the General Synod appointed by the Appointments Committee, having regard to representation of persons representing the Church of England on national and international bodies concerned with mission
Mrs Pat Harris, Mr Nigel Holmes, Rt Revd Michael Nazir-Ali (*Bishop of Rochester*)

Five representatives of mission agencies appointed by the Appointments Committee on the nomination of the Partnership for World Mission
Revd Roger Bowen, Mr Paul Chandler, Rt Revd David Evans, Miss Diana Witts, Rt Revd Manawar Rumalshah

Five persons appointed by the Appointments Committee on the nomination of the Board, chosen for their knowledge of home mission concerns or inter-faith relations, or for other relevant expertise
Revd Dr Brian Castle, Canon Michael Ipgrave, Revd Pradip Sudra, Revd Alison White, Canon Mavis Wilson

Functions of the Board
(*Extract from the Constitution*)
(a) To promote and encourage action, theological reflection and study in the area of mission.
(b) To stimulate and encourage theological reflection, in consultation with the Doctrine Commission, on issues and proposals concerning mission, evangelism, renewal and inter-faith relations in contemporary society, and to advise the General Synod and the dioceses.
(c) To be a channel of communication between the dioceses and the General Synod on the matters referred to in paragraph (b) of this clause.
(d) In conjunction with the Archbishops' Council to promote mission concerns in the work of all Boards.
(e) To bring together the General Synod and the voluntary mission agencies.
(f) In all matters related to the mission of the Church, to be a channel of communication between the General Synod, the Anglican Consultative Council, individual provinces and dioceses of the Anglican Communion, United Churches incorporating former Anglican dioceses, and other Churches.

PARTNERSHIP FOR WORLD MISSION COMMITTEE (PWM)
Partnership for World Mission (PWM) was set up in 1978 as a partnership between the General Synod and the World Mission Agencies of the Church of England. In April 1991 it changed from being an organisation independent of General Synod (but with synodical representation) to a constituent committee of the Board of Mission.

The Committee draws its members from the Board, including General Synod members, from those concerned with World Mission issues, and from the eleven main World Mission Agencies of the Church of England, which are: Church Army, Church's Ministry among Jewish People, Church Mission Society, Crosslinks, Intercontinental Church Society, Mid-Africa Ministry (CMS), the Missions to Seamen, Mothers' Union, South American Mission Society, the Society for Promoting Christian Knowledge, United Society for the Propagation of the Gospel. There are also 25 Associate Members.

Its main tasks are concerned with the Church of England's role in the Partnership in Mission process in the Anglican Communion; with Diocesan Companion Links; and with co-ordinating the policies and selected tasks of the Church of England's World Mission Agencies. It has an advisory role in enabling English dioceses and General Synod to see their way more clearly towards their participation in world mission as members of the Anglican Communion and ecumenically.

Chairman Rt Revd Patrick Harris (*Bishop of Southwell*)

Secretary Mr John Clark

Office Partnership House, 157 Waterloo Rd, London SE1 8XA Tel: 0171–928 8681
Fax: 0171–633 0185

INTER-FAITH CONSULTATIVE GROUP (IFCG)
The Inter-Faith Consultative Group advises the Board on Christian relations with Buddhists, Hindus, Jews, Muslims, Sikhs and other faith communities. It has published material on interfaith dialogue and such topics as multifaith worship, mixed faith marriage and the use of church buildings by other faith communities. It provides a forum for information exchange and co-ordination between Church of England agencies concerned with these and related issues, and acts as a link between the Board and the ecumenical Churches' Commission for Inter-Faith Relations (CCIFR), of which Canon Christopher Lamb is also Secretary.

Chairman Rt Revd John Austin (*Bishop of Aston*)

Secretary Vacancy

MISSION, EVANGELISM AND RENEWAL IN ENGLAND COMMITTEE
The main tasks of the Mission, Evangelism and Renewal in England Committee are to review and evaluate what is happening in evangelism and renewal and to stimulate action accordingly. The Committee also seeks to work with the dioceses to identify and promote good practice in mission, evangelism and renewal. Working with ecumenical partners, the voluntary societies, Partnership for World Mission and within the Anglican Communion forms a vital part of the work of this Committee.

Chairman Rt Revd Nigel McCulloch (*Bishop of Wakefield*)

Secretary Miss Janice Price Tel: 0171–898 1476

MISSION THEOLOGICAL ADVISORY GROUP
The Mission Theological Advisory Group is concerned with the theology of mission and deals with theological issues referred to it by the Board and the Churches' Commission on Mission of the Council of Churches for Britain and Ireland.

Chairman Rt Revd Michael Nazir-Ali (*Bishop of Rochester*)

Secretary Dr Anne Richards

RURAL AFFAIRS COMMITTEE
The Rural Affairs Committee is concerned to reflect to the church structures and policy-makers the special needs and opportunities of rural churches, and to support the work of the National Rural Officer in his practical initiatives in developing rural mission and ministry.

Chairman Rt Revd Paul Barber (*Bishop of Brixworth*)

Secretary Revd Jeremy Martineau

Office The Arthur Rank Centre, National Agricultural Centre, Stoneleigh Park, Warwickshire CV8 2LZ
Tel: (01203) 696969
Fax: (01203) 696460
e-mail: j.martineau@midnet.com

ARCHBISHOPS' MILLENNIUM ADVISORY GROUP (AMAG)
The Archbishops' Millennium Advisory Group works to further plans for the year 2000 within the Church of England. It acts in close co-operation with the Church Together in England Millennium Group to:

1 encourage Government and other official bodies to recognise that the Millennium is a Christian anniversary, and to reflect that as part of their programme;

2 encourage the churches nationally and at local level to mark the year with suitable events and activities.

The Group also liaises with the churches of other parts of the United Kingdom. A quarterly newsletter, *Millennium News*, is published by the Millennium Officer.

Chairman Rt Revd Gavin Reid (*Bishop of Maidstone*)

Secretary Revd Stephen Lynas Tel: 0171–898 1436

The Board for Social Responsibility

Chairman Rt Revd Richard Harries (*Bishop of Oxford*)

Secretary Mr David Skidmore   Tel: 0171–898 1521

Assistant Secretary (Science, Technology, Medicine and Environmental Issues) Mrs Claire Foster
    Tel: 0171–898 1523

Assistant Secretary (Social, Economic and Industrial Affairs) Ruth Badger   Tel: 0171–898 1529

Assistant Secretary (International and Development Affairs) Mr Charles Reed   Tel: 0171–898 1533

Assistant Secretary (Home Affairs) Revd Dr Peter Sedgwick   Tel: 0171–898 1531

Assistant Secretary (Community and Urban Affairs) Revd Andrew Davey   Tel: 0171–898 1446

Overseas Settlement Secretary Miss Patricia J. Hallett   Tel: 0171–898 1535

Office Church House, Great Smith St, London SW1P 3NZ
    Tel: 0171–898 1521
    Fax: 0171–898 1536

BOARD MEMBERS

Six members of the General Synod elected by the General Synod Mrs Elaine Appelbee, Prof Raman Bedi, Canon Paul Brett, Mr Philip Gore, Dr Sheila Grieve, Very Revd George Nairn-Briggs (*Provost of Wakefield*)

Nine members appointed by the former Standing Committee Prof Michael Banner, Rt Revd Robert Hardy (*Bishop of Lincoln*), Mr Dominick Harrod, Rt Revd Richard Lewis (*Bishop of St Edmundsbury and Ipswich*), Canon John Polkinghorne, Mrs Hilary Russell, Rt Revd Humphrey Taylor (*Bishop of Selby*), Revd Dr Mary Seller, Dr Alan Suggate

Up to three members co-opted by the Board Mrs Julia Flack, Rt Revd Roger Sainsbury (*Bishop of Barking*)

The Board was set up by resolution of the Church Assembly on 1 January 1958. It became an Advisory Committee of the General Synod in 1971. Its constitution requires it to 'promote and co-ordinate the thought and action of the Church in matters affecting the life of all in society'.

The Board acts on behalf of the Synod and the Church in its work on a wide range of social issues affecting both domestic and international affairs. Some of this work appears in the Board's publications and reports to Synod. But most of the work is done by staff with the help of *ad hoc* working parties, advisory groups, or standing committees, and through the Board's quarterly journal, *Crucible* (*see* p. 24).

STANDING COMMITTEES OF THE BOARD
HOME AFFAIRS COMMITTEE

Chairman Rt Revd Robert Hardy (*Bishop of Lincoln*)

Secretary Revd Dr Peter Sedgwick

The Committee has a representative membership of ten. Its terms of reference are:

1 to promote Christian theological reflection and appropriate action on criminal justice, substance abuse and mental health;
2 to monitor relevant changes in the light of Christian ethical principles;
3 to liaise with diocesan and ecumenical partners and appropriate statutory, professional and voluntary agencies;
4 to advise the Board on ways in which issues might be drawn to the attention of the wider Church.

INTERNATIONAL AND DEVELOPMENT AFFAIRS COMMITTEE

Chairman Rt Revd Humphrey Taylor (*Bishop of Selby*)

Secretary Mr Charles Reed   Tel: 0171–898 1533

The Committee has a representative membership of ten. Its terms of reference are:

1 to promote Christian theological reflection and action on international affairs and world development;
2 to monitor in particular those areas of the world in which the influence of the British Government is or has been significant, or from which requests for action have been received from member churches of the Anglican Communion or ecumenical partners;
3 to liaise with diocesan and ecumenical partners and appropriate statutory, professional and voluntary agencies;
4 to advise the Board on ways in which issues might be drawn to the attention of the wider Church;
5 to continue the commendation work of Overseas Settlement.

OVERSEAS SETTLEMENT

Secretary Miss Patricia J. Hallett   Tel: 0171–898 1535

The Secretary of the Overseas Settlement work reports to the International and Development Affairs Committee.

Archbishops' Council

She advises and assists members of the Church of England who may be going overseas, either temporarily or permanently. The work provides for people to be met and welcomed on arrival overseas, to make contact in their new parish and be given any guidance needed during the early period of settlement. Contact is maintained with the Foreign and Commonwealth Office and, as appropriate, with other departments representing various governments in London.

COMMUNITY AND URBAN AFFAIRS COMMITTEE
Co-Chairmen Rt Revd Roger Sainsbury (*Bishop of Barking*) and Prof Raman Bedi

Secretary Revd Andrew Davey   *Tel:* 0171–898 1446

The Committee has a representative membership of up to 13 members. Its terms of reference are:

1 to maintain the Church of England's capacity to speak with authority about racism, poverty, social exclusion and social disintegration in society;

2 to promote Christian theological reflection and appropriate action on questions of poverty, racism, social exclusion and social disintegration in society;

3 to monitor developments on those issues and encourage responses to them from Church and Government;

4 to liaise with diocesan and ecumenical partners and appropriate statutory, professional and voluntary agencies;

5 to advise the Board on ways in which issues might be drawn to the attention of the wider Church.

SCIENCE, MEDICINE AND TECHNOLOGY COMMITTEE
Chairman Canon John Polkinghorne

Secretary Vacancy

The Committee is made up of ten members. Its terms of reference are:

1 to promote Christian theological and ethical reflection on the exercise of human power over the natural world;

2 to monitor developments in science, medicine and technology in the light of Christian ethical principles;

3 to advise the Board on ways in which issues might be drawn to the attention of the wider Church.

SOCIAL, ECONOMIC AND INDUSTRIAL AFFAIRS COMMITTEE
Chairman Rt Revd Richard Lewis (*Bishop of St Edmundsbury and Ipswich*)

Secretary Ruth Badger   *Tel:* 0171–898 1529

The Committee has a representative membership of ten. Its terms of reference are:

1 to promote Christian theological reflection and appropriate action on contemporary social, economic and industrial issues;

2 to monitor relevant social and economic trends in the light of Christian ethical principles;

3 to liaise with diocesan and ecumenical partners and appropriate statutory, professional and voluntary agencies;

4 to advise the Board on ways in which the issues might be drawn to the attention of the wider Church.

PUBLICATIONS
The Board is responsible for the quarterly journal *Crucible* (*Editor* Revd Dr Peter Sedgwick). *Crucible* provides Christian comment on contemporary social, economic and political issues. Details about subscription to *Crucible* are available from the Board's office.

The Board also publishes from time to time reports, papers and pamphlets which give perspectives on matters of public concern and the current thinking of the Board on major social questions. These are available from Church House Bookshop.

The Hospital Chaplaincies Council

Chairman Rt Revd Christopher Herbert (*Bishop of St Albans*)

Secretary Revd Robert Clarke   *Tel:* 0171–898 1892

Hospital/Health Care Chaplaincy Training and Development Officer Revd Malcolm Masterman   *Tel:* 0171–898 1893

Administrator Mrs Liz Paffey   *Tel:* 0171–898 1894

Business Manager (*Training*) Miss Elspeth Dawson
    Tel: 0171–898 1895

Office Fielden House, Little College St, London SW1P 3SH   *Tel:* 0171–898 1890; 0171–222 5090
    Fax: 0171–898 1891

MEMBERS
Five members appointed by the former Standing Committee who shall have knowledge of the Health Service, the medical and nursing professions

Dr John Beal, Canon Eddie Burns, Miss Jacquie Flindall, Mrs Alison Ruoff, Ven Frank White

Three members appointed by the former Standing Committee on the nomination of the College of Health Care Chaplains from its Church of England membership
Revd Sandy Borthwick, Canon David Equeall, Revd Michael Stevens

Up to two co-opted members
Mr Tim Battle

Two Observers from the Church in Wales, appointed by the Archbishop of Wales
Revd Berw Hughes, Revd Martyn Davies

Functions of the Council

1 To consider questions of policy and practice relating to spiritual ministrations to patients and staff in medical establishments and community care programmes referred to it by the General Synod.

2 To provide information and advice to the dioceses in their negotiations with Health Authorities and Trusts on the appointment of Hospital Chaplains and on other National Health Service (NHS) matters; to visit and support dioceses involved in such negotiations; and to provide similar services to Hospital Chaplains in their relations with NHS management.

3 To respond promptly to enquiries from Chief Executives and Trusts regarding chaplaincy issues and the best practice for employment of Anglican clergy in the NHS.

4 To monitor and authorise, on behalf of the Church of England, the standards and content of training provided for Hospital Chaplaincy in co-operation with other churches and chaplaincy organisations.

5 To work jointly with the Advisory Board of Ministry in providing the personnel and expertise input from qualified chaplains in preparing theological students for their ministry to the sick in hospital and in the community.

6 To monitor matters affecting spiritual ministrations in all medical establishments and community care programmes, reporting to the General Synod as and when required.

7 To act as a liaison between the Department of Health and the Church of England on all questions relating to spiritual ministrations in medical establishments and community care programmes.

8 To contribute, in co-operation with the Board for Social Responsibility, to the ongoing theological reflections on contemporary medical, ethical and social issues.

9 To exchange information and advice in matters relating to Hospital Chaplaincy with other Christian churches in the British Isles and abroad.

THE CHURCHES' COMMITTEE FOR HOSPITAL CHAPLAINCY

In relation to the Department of Health, the Council works co-operatively with the Free Churches and the Roman Catholic Church in the Churches' Committee for Hospital Chaplaincy (formerly the Joint Committee for Hospital Chaplaincy).

The members of the Churches' Committee for Hospital Chaplaincy are full and equal partners of the Chaplaincy (Health Care) Education and Development Group and, together with the College of Health Care Chaplains, take an equal share in the monitoring of chaplaincy training for the NHS.

TRAINING

One function of the Hospital Chaplaincies Council is to use its contacts in order to encourage, facilitate, co-ordinate where necessary, and generally support all such opportunities for learning about the hospital ministry. To further this role it has with effect from 1 January 1996 jointly funded with the College of Health Care Chaplains the post of Hospital/Health Care Chaplaincy Training and Development Officer.

HERITAGE

This area of the Council's responsibilities relates to the Church's concern with buildings and related matters. The development of closer working relationships between all the church heritage bodies while recognising their separate (often statutory) responsibilities is a high priority.

Archbishops' Council

The Council for the Care of Churches

Chairman Very Revd Raymond Furnell (*Dean of York*)

Vice-Chairmen Mr Tony Redman
Very Revd Graeme Knowles (*Dean of Carlisle*)

Secretary Dr Thomas Cocke   *Tel:* 0171–898 1882

Deputy Secretary Mr Jonathan Goodchild
                                     Tel: 0171–898 1883

Librarian Miss Janet Seeley   *Tel:* 0171–898 1884

Conservation Officer Mr Andrew Argyrakis
                                     Tel: 0171–898 1885

Conservation Assistant Mr Steven Sleight
                                     Tel: 0171–898 1886

Office Fielden House, 13 Little College St, London SW1P 3SH   *Tel:* 0171–898 1880; 0171–222 3793
                                     Fax: 0171–898 1881

MEMBERS

Revd Michael Ainsworth, Revd Peter Cavanagh, Revd Dr Allan Doig, Revd Dr Timothy Ellis, Dr Jennifer Freeman, Ven John Gathercole (*Archdeacon of Dudley*), Mrs Philippa Glanville, Mr William Hawkes, Mr Thomas Hornsby, Miss Jane Kennedy, Mrs Judith Leigh, Ven Trevor Lloyd (*Archdeacon of Barnstaple*), Mr Huon Mallalieu, Mr John McArdell, Mr Jeremy Musson, Mr Nicholas Rank, Mr Tony Redman, Mr William Sanders, Mrs Mary Saunders, Mr Tim Tatton-Brown, Miss Fay Wilson-Rudd

The Council was formed in 1921 to co-ordinate the work of the Diocesan Advisory Committees for the Care of Churches, which advise diocesan chancellors on faculty applications. The Council originally consisted of representatives of all the Committees, but in 1958 it was reconstituted as a Council appointed by the Church Assembly. In 1972, it became a permanent Commission of the General Synod.

The Council advises the General Synod on all matters relating to the use, care and planning or design of places of worship, their curtilages and contents; acts on the Synod's behalf in contacts with Government departments and other bodies and in negotiations with professional bodies over church inspection and repair; and assists in the review or revision of legislation relating to church buildings and their contents.

The Council provides Diocesan Pastoral Committees with detailed reports about the architectural and historic qualities of churches likely to be declared redundant. It also submits specialist advice to diocesan chancellors and Diocesan Advisory Committees on proposals which are the subject of faculty applications, e.g. the construction of church extensions, re-ordering schemes, the sale of church furnishings, partial demolition of churches, etc.

The Council maintains contact with Diocesan Advisory Committees through regular circulation of newsletters, by an annual meeting of members and by personal visits. The membership of DACs is varied: they include both clergy and lay, some with professional expertise in architecture, art history and archaeology and others of no specialist knowledge but of sound judgement and experience, or representing the views of English Heritage, the local planning authority and the amenity societies. Every diocese has specialist advisers on organs, bells, clocks, archaeology and so on.

The Council administers funds (generously provided by charitable bodies) for the conservation of furnishings and works of art in churches, and collaborates closely with English Heritage, the National Heritage Memorial Fund (and its Heritage Lottery Fund) and other grant-making bodies. Advice is available from the Council on specific conservation problems.

The Council is not only concerned with the care and conservation of ancient buildings and objects, but also with the development of places of worship and the encouragement of good new furnishings and works of art. Advice is available and parishes are encouraged to consult the Council's register of artists and craftsmen and to examine photographs of their work.

PUBLICATIONS

The basic title in the Council's programme of publications is *How to Look After Your Church*; other booklets in the series (regularly revised) include *A Guide to Church Inspection and Repair*, *Church Floors and Floor Coverings*, *Heating Your Church*, *Church Organs*, *Redecorating Your Church*, *The Repair and Maintenance of Glass in Churches*, *Sound Amplification in Churches*, and *The Churchyards Handbook*. There is also a 20-minute video called *Looking After Your Church*.

The Council publishes a standard form of *Church Log Book* and a *Church Property Register*, to assist parishes in record-keeping. In addition it has produced technical leaflets and codes of practice, dealing with subjects such as lightning protection, the care of clocks and historic bells and bellframes. The Council publishes three light-hearted guides to the care and presentation of churches, with cartoons by Graham Jeffery: *The Churchwarden's Year: A Calendar of Church Maintenance*, *Handle with Prayer: A Church Cleaner's Notebook* and *Safe and Sound? A Guide to Church Security*. *The Protection of Our English Churches* traces the history and development of the Council from its foundation in 1921. The Council's annual journal *Churchscape* includes articles on everyday care of churches and on their history and design, as well as reviews of books and events of current interest.

A complete list of titles and prices is available on request from the Council.

The Cathedrals Fabric Commission for England

Chairman Dr Averil Cameron

Vice-Chairman Vacancy

Secretary Dr Richard Gem   Tel: 0171–898 1887

Cathedrals Officer Miss Linda Monckton
                               Tel: 0171–898 1888

Office Fielden House, 13 Little College St, London SW1P 3SH   Tel: 0171–898 1880; 0171–222 3793
                                  Fax: 0171–898 1881

MEMBERS
Mr Robert Aagaard, Mr Michael Archer, Mrs Corinne Bennett, Mr John Burton, Ven George Cassidy (*Archdeacon of London*), Mr Philip Cooper, Dr Philip Dixon, Canon Richard Giles, Revd Richard Hanford, Professor Jacques Heyman, Mr Julian Litten, Mr John Maine, Canon Paul Mellor, Mr John Norman, Mrs Diane Nutting, Very Revd Michael Perham (*Provost of Derby*), Mrs Sarah Quail, Mr Michael Reardon, Very Revd Michael Sadgrove (*Provost of Sheffield*), Rt Revd David Stancliffe (*Bishop of Salisbury*), Mr Martin Stancliffe, Very Revd Robert Willis (*Dean of Hereford*)

In 1949, at the request of Deans and Chapters, the Cathedrals Advisory Committee was set up to give help and advice on plans and problems affecting the fabric, furnishings, fittings and precincts of cathedrals.

In 1981, the Committee was reconstituted as a permanent Commission of the General Synod, under the title of The Cathedrals Advisory Commission for England.

In 1991, the Commission was further reconstituted as a statutory body under the Care of Cathedrals Measure and renamed The Cathedrals Fabric Commission. In addition to advisory functions in relation to the architecture, archaeology, art and history of cathedrals and their precincts, the Commission has regulatory powers. Before implementing proposals affecting the cathedral, its contents or its surroundings, the Dean and Chapter require the approval of the Commission in specific cases, or of a local Fabric Advisory Committee appointed jointly by the Commission and by the Dean and Chapter.

CHURCH HERITAGE FORUM

Chairman The Rt Revd Richard Chartres (*Bishop of London*)

Vice-Chairman The Baroness Wilcox of Plymouth

Secretary Vacancy

The Church Heritage Forum, which was established at the beginning of 1997, brings together representatives of national and local church interests in matters relating to the Church's built heritage. It enables the Church to take a more proactive role in anticipating developments in the built heritage field; ensuring that heritage concerns are fed into the Archbishops' Council; providing a mechanism for members to reach a view on matters of common concern; providing a point of focus for contact both within the Church and with outside bodies; promoting a wider public awareness of the Church's work in the built heritage area; and enabling the exchange of information and facilitating mutual support.

Membership comprises representatives from the following: Advisory Board for Redundant Churches, Archbishops' Council, Association of English Cathedrals, Church Commissioners' Redundant Churches Committee, Cathedrals Fabric Commission for England, Churches Conservation Trust, Council for the Care of Churches, and an archdeacon.

FINANCE

The Archbishops' Council's responsibilities, as the financial executive of the General Synod and financial advisory body of the Church of England, are discharged through its Finance Committee. This committee is the focus for the work formerly undertaken by (a) the Central Board of Finance as the financial executive of the General Synod and in relation to Christian Stewardship; and (b) the Church Commissioners, concerning financial provision for the clergy, including the allocation of available monies to support the needier dioceses. The Central Board of Finance will continue in existence as a Trustee body, with the same membership as the Archbishops' Council, with ultimate responsibility for the CBF Church of England Investment, Fixed Interest Securities and Deposit Funds, and for the Central Church Fund and a number of other smaller trusts, although in practice this responsibility will be carried out through the Finance Committee.

The Council's Finance Committee is responsible for the management of the financial business of the Synod and the Archbishops' Council. This includes the raising and administration of money voted by the Synod for the

Archbishops' Council and for other purposes, the apportionment of those costs between dioceses, the presentation of annual reports and accounts, and the presentation of the annual budget. It is responsible for the provision of accounting management information and financial control.

As the financial advisory body of the Church of England the Committee is charged with responsibility for advice and co-ordination on financial matters over the Church as a whole and will periodically produce, in conjunction with the other central church bodies, reports on the Church's general financial position.

Existing consultative arrangements with dioceses have been enhanced by the creation of the Diocesan Finance Forum, a non-statutory body. It provides a formal mechanism for the views of Diocesan Boards of Finance to be obtained on clergy remuneration, conditions of service, and other financial matters (including on the budget for national church responsibilities before it is presented to Synod).

DIOCESAN FINANCE FORUM
Chairman Mr Michael Chamberlain

Members Three members from each diocese chosen by the Bishop's Council of each diocese.

The scope of the Forum includes consultation on: remuneration policy and conditions of service; pensions policy; the national church budget and apportionments; and allocations to dioceses for the support of ministry in poorer areas.

THE GENERAL SYNOD FUND
The revenues of the General Synod, except for a small income from legacies, donations and other sources, are furnished by the dioceses in accordance with a system of apportionment approved annually by the Synod. The Finance Committee is responsible for the preparation of an annual budget, which is produced a year in advance, and a preview of expenditure for subsequent years. As part of this process the Committee takes account of diocesan views through the Diocesan Finance Forum. The budget is agreed with the Archbishops' Council and submitted to the Synod at the summer group of sessions for approval.

ARCHBISHOPS' COUNCIL BUDGET
The budget traditionally covers three main areas: *training for ministry, national church responsibilities* – this latter element covers the cost of the Church's national work through the Archbishops' Council, and a variety of *grants and provisions* which enable the Church of England to play its part in the wider world through the Anglican Consultative Council and ecumenical bodies both in this country and abroad. The General Synod has just agreed to a further item of expenditure known as Inter-diocesan support – Mission Agencies clergy pension contributions. This will allow the dioceses to reimburse the Church Commissioners, through the General Synod budget, for the cost of meeting the pension contributions of clergy employed by specified Mission Agencies.

Two main themes run through the 1999 budget: the continued, and very welcome, increase in the numbers coming forward for ordination training, and the advent of the Archbishops' Council, which brings with it a restructuring of the central church organisations.

Numbers coming forward for training have increased by 23 over the 1998 levels estimated (twelve in colleges and eleven on courses), with a further estimated increase of 20 in the 1999/2000 academic year. The good news does bring a financial cost, however, and training expenditure is budgeted to increase 7.2 per cent above 1998 levels to £7,346,000, of which the dioceses will be asked to meet £6,720,000.

The 1999 budget reflects the first stage of the new administrative structure of the Archbishops' Council, with the transfer of the Stipends and Allocations policy work from the Church Commissioners, and with this transfer comes the responsibility for the distribution – this will feature in future budgets – of the annual stipends allocations to the dioceses from money provided by the Church Commissioners. The transfer of this function will add £281,000 to the General Synod budget, but at the same time this represents a saving of a corresponding sum to the Church Commissioners which they will make available for allocation to the dioceses. (The Archbishops' Council will apportion this additional sum to the dioceses using the present apportionment formula, so neutralising the effect of this transferred cost.) The second stage of the restructuring process will wait upon the consolidation of the Council's staff in the refurbished area of Church House formerly occupied by various Government departments. The areas of work affected include the clergy payments and *Crockford* functions and the common services for all the central church bodies. Apart from some transitional costs associated with the relocation of staff, the impact of which will be spread over several years, total administrative expenditure under the Council is not expected to be any greater than under the existing arrangements.

Core expenditure in *National Church Responsibilities* is budgeted to increase by 3.7 per cent, in line with inflation. However, following consideration by the Policy Committee and Budget Committee, additional expenditure of £105,000 was approved, principally to support the work of the Ministry Division in dealing with the increase in the numbers of ordinands coming forward for training, and for the Council for the Care of Churches to deal with an increase in statutory work. Overall this represents expenditure of £8,222,600, a 5.1 per cent increase

General Synod Budget

	1999 £	1999 £
TRAINING FOR MINISTRY		
Ordination training grants		7,114,800
Other expenditure		231,200
		7,346,000
Financed by:		
Apportionment on the dioceses		6,720,000
Transfer from Reserves (pension liability)		100,000
Transfer from Reserves		396,000
Income from other sources		130,000
		7,346,000
NATIONAL CHURCH RESPONSIBILITIES		
Central Secretariat		836,000
Legal		272,300
Communications		345,600
Personnel		155,700
Ministry Division		
ABM	1,037,100	
CSA work	132,800	
		1,169,900
Church and World:		
Board of Education	599,700	
Board of Mission	442,800	
Board for Social Responsibility	411,700	
Council for Christian Unity	309,800	
Hospital Chaplaincies Council	112,900	
		1,876,900
Finance Division		
Finance	519,800	
Allocations	148,200	
		668,000
Heritage (CCC/CFC)		513,000
Common Services		1,512,600
Turnbull implementation		135,000
Contingency		50,000
		7,535,000
GRANTS AND PROVISIONS		
Anglican Communion Activities		319,700
English ecumenical bodies		138,600
British ecumenical bodies		228,600
Conference of European Churches and other work in Europe		82,200
World Council of Churches		120,900
Other grants and provisions		78,600
		968,600
Financed by:		
Apportionment on dioceses		7,922,300
Grant from Central Church Fund		173,300
Income from other sources		55,000
Savings brought forward / Transfers from Reserves		353,000
		8,503,600
ALLOCATION FROM ARCHBISHOPS' COUNCIL TO NEUTRALISE TRANSFERRED WORK		(281,000)
Net cost		8,222,600
INTER-DIOCESAN SUPPORT / MISSION AGENCIES CLERGY PENSIONS CONTRIBUTIONS		86,000
Financed by:		
Apportionment		86,000

NB: The Office Services cost of £989,200 which includes office rent and service charges, has been apportioned between the divisions of the Archbishops' Council.

Archbishops' Council

To keep the overall amount sought from the dioceses at manageable levels substantial calls have had to be made on the reserves. Accordingly, the net cost to the dioceses of the main elements of the budget has been limited to £14,361,300, a 7.9 per cent increase over 1998. However, the extra cost of meeting the pension contributions of the clergy employed by the Mission Agencies has added a further £86,000 to the budget, resulting in a net increase to the dioceses of 8.6 per cent.

Finance Committee

Chairman Mr Michael Chamberlain

Secretary Mr Shaun Farrell *Tel:* 0171–898 1795

Members Appointed [4]
 Elected [8]

Ex Officio: First Church Estates Commissioner, Chairman of the Pensions Board

Terms of reference

(a) to advise the Archbishops' Council and the dioceses on all financial aspects of the Council's work, including its investment and trustee responsibilities, and on the overall financial needs and resources of the Church;
(b) to make recommendations to the Archbishops' Council as to its annual budget and on mechanisms for monitoring and controlling the expenditure of the Council;
(c) to consult with dioceses on financial matters, and to make recommendations thereon as appropriate to the Archbishops' Council and the dioceses;
(d) to assess and seek to rationalise and simplify the systems for cash flow within the Church;
(e) to provide a central forum for the development and promotion of Christian stewardship and fundraising;
(f) to provide and co-ordinate research and guidance on financial, accounting and related matters;
(g) to provide a channel for communicating on financial matters with Her Majesty's Government, financial regulators and other appropriate enforcement bodies, both directly and through the Churches' Main Committee;
(h) to work in collaboration with ecumenical partners on matters within the Committee's terms of reference;
(i) to carry out such other work as may be entrusted to it by the Archbishops' Council.

OFFICERS
Financial Secretary Mr Shaun Farrell *Tel:* 0171–898 1795

Budgeting Officer/Head of Planning Mr Jeremy Elloy
 Tel: 0171–898 1562

National Stewardship Officer Mr Robin Stevens
 Tel: 0171–898 1540

Senior Accountant Mr Terrence Dawson
 Tel: 0171–898 1568

Head of Internal Audit Mrs Mary Ball *Tel:* 0171–898 1658

CHRISTIAN STEWARDSHIP
Through its Christian Stewardship Committee, the Archbishops' Council plays an active part in affirming the principles of Christian Stewardship in the discovery and use of human and financial resources available to the Church. Initiatives are promoted, support given and ideas exchanged between the members in dioceses of the Christian Stewardship network. In particular, conferences, training courses and publications are used to supplement the personal contact between the Stewardship Officer and diocesan staff.

Stewardship advisers encourage church members to respond to God's love and generosity and resource the mission and ministry of the Church by giving their time, their skills and their money – the latter regularly, tax-effectively and in proportion to their income. The challenge to Church members is to aim at a level of giving to and through the Church of not less than 5 per cent of net income and to review their giving annually. The average level of giving is currently about half this level and the Church's challenge would cover its current financial responsibilities with enough to spare for mission and growth.

Various national publications are available through the Church House Bookshop:

– a legacy strategy for the whole Church, *Your Legacy Will Help*, which raises awareness of the additional need for giving by legacies;
– pads of user-friendly *Deed of Covenant* forms;
– a booklet *Tax-Efficient Giving* for officers of PCCs with guidance on the best ways to give and then obtain tax relief;
– a leaflet *Tax Recovery* which explains how individuals can make their giving tax-efficient;
– *All Things Come from You*, a leaflet that explains the Christian response of the giving of money to resource the mission and ministry of the Church.

As part of the corporate stewardship of the Church's financial resources, a booklet has been published in response to the regulations for accounting, reporting and scrutiny contained in Part VI of the Charities Act 1993. *The Charities Act 1993 and the PCC* complements the *Church Accounting Regulations 1997* and relates the requirements to the particular circumstances of PCCs.

CCLA INVESTMENT MANAGEMENT LIMITED
Investment Manager The Viscount Churchill

Deputy Investment Manager Mr T. H. Lavis

Registered Office St Alphage House, 2 Fore St, London EC2Y 5AQ
Tel: 0171–588 1815
Fax: 0171–588 6291
Telex: 8954509

CCLA Investment Management Limited (CCLA) provides investment services and staff to the Central Board of Finance for its management of the CBF Church of England Funds. CCLA is owned 60 per cent by the CBF Investment Fund, 25 per cent by The COIF Charities Investment Fund and 15 per cent by the Local Authorities Mutual Investment Trust. CCLA, regulated by IMRO, is authorised to give investment advice to churches, charities and local authorities.

The CBF Church of England Funds are Collective Investment Schemes established and regulated by the Church Funds Investment Measure 1958. They are exempt from liability to tax on income and capital gains. Their dividends or interest are paid gross, after recovery of all reclaimable tax.

In the management of the CBF Church of England Funds, the Central Board is an exempted person under the Financial Services Act 1986 and deposits taken by the Board are exempted transactions under the Banking Act 1987.

The three CBF Church of England Funds aim to meet most of the investment needs of a church trust.

Investment Fund
The main CBF Fund for capital that can be invested for the long-term. It has a widely spread portfolio mainly of UK and overseas equities and aims at steady income and capital growth. There are weekly share dealing dates (normally Tuesdays).

Fixed Interest Securities Fund
This Fund invests only in fixed income stocks and is intended to supplement where necessary the initial lower income yield on the Investment Fund. Fixed income investments offer no protection from inflation so this Fund is recommended only for a small proportion of long-term capital. There are weekly share dealing dates (normally Tuesdays).

Deposit Fund
This money Fund is for cash balances which should be available at short notice and with minimal risk of capital loss. Accounts in the Fund obtain a good rate of interest close to money market rates even on small sums. There are daily deposit and withdrawal facilities. The Fund is rated Aaa by Moody's Investors Services.

There are over 50,000 accounts open in the three funds. Contributors include Diocesan Boards of Finance and Diocesan Trusts, Cathedral Chapters, Diocesan Boards of Education, Theological Colleges and Church Colleges of Education, Church Schools and Educational Endowments, Church Societies and the Church Commissioners as well as many Parochial Church Councils.

CBF Church of England Funds

31 May 1997	Investment Fund	Fixed Interest Securities Fund	Deposit Fund
Value of Fund	£813 million	£131 million	£512 million
Net Asset Value per Share	1070.95p	168.80p	–
Income Yield %	3.24	7.58	7.10

A brochure and the latest Reports and Accounts of the CBF Church of England Funds are available from CBF Church of England Funds at the address above.

THE CENTRAL CHURCH FUND
This Fund was established in 1915 and is administered by the Central Board of Finance separately from money raised on the authority of the General Synod. All money received by the Central Board for its general purposes is placed in this Fund, and also money earmarked or appropriated for special purposes, as shown in the accounts.

Grants amounting to £587,169 (1996 £588,483) were paid during the year to 31 December 1997.

The Central Board of Finance welcomes legacies, subscriptions and donations (including covenanted subscriptions) to the Central Church Fund which can be used either for the general purposes of the Church of England at the discretion of the Central Board, or for any special purposes connected therewith specified by the donor.

The Fund helps parishes and dioceses with imaginative and innovative projects of all kinds, especially those that meet the need of local communities. It assists with the cost of training for the ministry, and it makes an annual grant to the General Synod from its unappropriated funds. It is also used to meet unexpected and urgent needs which cannot be budgeted for.

During 1997 the Fund received legacies and donations totalling £61,943.

Further information and application forms are available from:
Mr Terrence Dawson
Secretary to the Central Church Fund
Church House
Great Smith St
London SW1P 3NZ
Tel: 0171–898 1568
Fax: 0171–898 1558

MINISTRY

The provision of a properly trained and supported ministry is critical to the Church's mission. The Council brings together policy on the selection, training, deployment and remuneration of the Church of England's ministry – responsibilities that were formerly scattered at national level between different bodies – thus enabling decisions on ministry policy and strategy to be taken in the round.

The Council's responsibilities in this area are handled by four committees each charged with a specific area of work: Vocation, Recruitment and Selection; Theological Education and Training; Deployment, Remuneration and Conditions of Service; and Ministry Among Deaf People. While the Central Readers' Council continues to fulfil its role in enhancing the contribution of Readers to the overall ministry of the Church, its work is fully integrated into the work of these committees.

The Archbishops' Council's functions as the Central Stipends Authority are discharged under the auspices of the Deployment, Remuneration and Conditions of Service Committee.

STAFF
Ministry Director Ven Gordon Kuhrt   Tel: 0171–898 1390

Vocation, Recruitment and Selection Committee Revd Roy Screech *(Secretary)*   Tel: 0171–898 1402

Theological Education and Training Committee Revd Dr David Way *(Secretary)*   Tel: 0171–898 1404

Deployment, Remuneration and Conditions of Service Committee Margaret Jeffery *(Secretary)*
Tel: 0171–898 1411

Committee for Ministry Among Deaf People Canon James Clarke *(Secretary)*   Tel: 0171–898 1429

AUDIT COMMITTEE
Chairman   Vacancy

Secretary   Mr Shaun Farrell   Tel: 0171–898 1795

Members   Appointed [3]
            Elected   [2]

This Committee ensures an independent oversight of the Council's finances. Its duties are to oversee the discharge of the Archbishops' Council's responsibilities relating to financial statements, internal control systems and internal and external audit, and to report to the Archbishops' Council thereon with recommendations as appropriate.

SELECTION SECRETARIES
Revd Roy Screech (*Senior Selection Secretary*)
Tel: 0171–898 1402
Revd Ferial Etherington (*LNSM Co-ordinator*)
Tel: 0171–898 1395
Revd Margaret Jackson (*Secretary, Continuing Ministerial Education Panel*)   Tel: 0171–898 1408
Revd Marilyn Parry (*Secretary, Pre-Theological Education Panel*)   Tel: 0171–898 1401
Mrs Margaret Sentamu   Tel: 0171–898 1406
Revd Mark Sowerby (*Secretary, Vocations Advisory Panel*)
Tel: 0171–898 1399
Revd Dr David Way (*Secretary, Educational Validation Panel* and *Further Degrees Panel*)   Tel: 0171–898 1404

Finance and Administrative Secretary Mr David Morris (*Secretary to Bishops' Committee for Ministry and Finance Panel*)   Tel: 0171–898 1392

Grants Secretary Dr Mark Hodge   Tel: 0171–898 1396

Assistant Administrative Secretary Miss Sarah Evans
Tel: 0171–898 1394

Honorary Secretary of the Readers' Council Mr Geoff Mihell
Tel: 0171–898 1415

Honorary National Moderator for Reader Training and Honorary Acting National Moderator for the Archbishops' Diploma for Readers Mr John Field   Tel: 0171–898 1414

VOCATION, RECRUITMENT AND SELECTION COMMITTEE
Chairman   Vacancy

Members   Appointed 10
            Elected   4

Terms of Reference

(a)   to advise the Archbishops' Council and the House of Bishops on a strategy for the development of vocation to ministry;

(b) to encourage those in education and careers work throughout the Church in the provision of sustained programmes of vocational development and recruitment for the accredited ministry, both lay and ordained;
(c) to advise the House of Bishops on policy for the selection of candidates for the accredited ministry, ordained and lay;
(d) to oversee and advise the work of staff in the arrangement of and participation in selection conferences;
(e) to oversee the training of bishops' selectors;
(f) to report regularly through the Ministry Co-ordinating Group to the Archbishops' Council on the work of the Committee;
(g) to work in collaboration with Diocesan Directors of Ordinands and others as appropriate on policy and practice related to the selection and care of candidates for ministry;
(h) to work in collaboration with ecumenical partners on matters within the Committee's terms of reference.

THEOLOGICAL EDUCATION AND TRAINING COMMITTEE
Chairman Vacancy

Members Appointed 10
Elected 4

Terms of Reference

(a) to advise the House of Bishops and the Archbishops' Council on a strategy for theological education and training;
(b) to scrutinise and validate programmes for those training under Bishops' Regulations and to keep under review all forms of training for authorised ministry, ordained and lay, including Reader training;
(c) to advise the House of Bishops and the Archbishops' Council on policy concerning theological colleges and courses;
(d) to advise the Archbishops' Council and the House of Bishops on the financial aspects of theological education and training;
(e) to work in collaboration with ecumenical partners on matters within the Committee's terms of reference;
(f) to report regularly through the Ministry Co-ordinating Group to the Archbishops' Council on the work of the Committee.

DEPLOYMENT, REMUNERATION AND CONDITIONS OF SERVICE COMMITTEE
Chairman Vacancy

Members Appointed 9
Elected 7

Terms of Reference

(a) to advise the House of Bishops and the Archbishops' Council on a strategy for ministry, with particular reference to the deployment, remuneration and conditions of service of those in authorised ministry, working in collaboration with dioceses, the Church Commissioners and the Church of England Pensions Board and with ecumenical partners;
(b) to produce, in partnership with dioceses, a framework of national policy for stipends and other related matters, and to advise dioceses as appropriate on such matters;
(c) to produce, in partnership with dioceses, a framework of national policy for the deployment of all ministerial resources, ordained and lay, available to the Church;
(d) to monitor and advise in consultation with interested parties on sector and chaplaincy ministries within the total ministry of the Church;
(e) to work in collaboration with the dioceses and, as far as possible, with ecumenical partners in the provision and development of continuing ministerial education for and review of accredited ministers, ordained and lay;
(f) to report regularly through the Ministry Co-ordinating Group to the Archbishops' Council on the work of the Committee.

COMMITTEE FOR MINISTRY AMONG DEAF PEOPLE
Chairman Vacancy

Appointed Members 11

Terms of Reference

(a) to monitor and advise on the progress of sector and chaplaincy ministries within the total ministry of the Church, in consultation with those responsible for specific areas;
(b) to encourage and strengthen the participation of deaf people in the life and witness of the Church, to represent the views of deaf people to the Church and of the Church to deaf people, and to support the work of the chaplains;

Archbishops' Council

(c) to report regularly through the Ministry Co-ordinating Group to the Archbishops' Council on the work of the Committee.

BISHOPS' REGULATIONS FOR TRAINING
SELECTION

1 Candidates should be commended in the first place by someone who has pastoral responsibility for them to the Diocesan Director of Ordinands or Diocesan Lay Ministry Adviser. Before being accepted for training, they are required:

(1) to have the necessary educational qualifications or show that they have the potential to benefit from a formal course of training;

(2) to satisfy medical requirements;

(3) to be sponsored by their bishop for attendance at a Bishops' Selection Conference according to the following categories:
Ordained Local Ministry;
Ordained Ministry (Permanent Non-Stipendiary Ministry);
Ordained Ministry (Stipendiary Ministry and Non-Stipendiary Ministry);
Accredited Lay Ministry (Permanent Non-Stipendiary Ministry);
Accredited Lay Ministry (Stipendiary Ministry and Non-Stipendiary Ministry).

2 Where it is envisaged that a candidate will exercise a non-stipendiary ministry from the time of ordination such a candidate should normally be at least 30 and well established in a secular occupation before entering training.

EDUCATIONAL QUALIFICATIONS

Candidates are required to have the following qualifications:

1 *Under 25.* Five passes in academic subjects in GCSE, Grade C or above, one of which must be English Language and two at 'A' level: or equivalent qualifications. The only exceptions to this rule are for candidates who are recommended to complete a formal programme of pre-theological education, approved by the Vocation, Recruitment and Selection Committee, to prepare them for training. Bishops' Selectors will need to be assured that candidates are capable of participating in such a course satisfactorily.

2 *Aged 25 and over.* The academic standard is not laid down in terms of GCSE or in any other absolute form, but individuals are considered and assessed in accordance with their existing qualifications and the type of training which they should do, if accepted as candidates. All who are not graduates will be seen by the bishop's examining chaplain, or other person appointed by the bishop. He may ask them to do a course of reading or to take certain examinations before attending a Bishops' Selection Conference.

TRAINING

1 *Pre-theological training.* Candidates may be required to undertake a formal programme of part-time pre-theological education of up to two years, approved by the Vocation, Recruitment and Selection Committee, to the satisfaction of the Assessors. On completion of such a programme, candidates undertake theological training in compliance with the regulations set out below.

2 *Theological training.* Candidates should always consult their bishop or Diocesan Director of Ordinands or Diocesan Lay Ministry Adviser before applying to a theological college or course for admission. A recommendation to train for ordination from the Bishops' Selectors does not carry with it the right of acceptance by any particular theological college or course.

A candidate wishing to undertake a course of training varying from the Regulations approved by the Bishops (including study for a higher degree) should inform the DDO or DLMA in order that the advice of the Vocation, Recruitment and Selection Committee may be sought.

(1) *Candidates under 30*
(a) *Graduates in theology* (where at least half of the degree consists of theology) spend two years on a full-time course at a theological college and have to fulfil the Bishops' requirements by satisfactorily completing a course of education approved on behalf of the House of Bishops by the Theological Education and Training Committee.
(b) *Graduates in subjects other than theology* are required to spend three years on a full-time course at a theological college and have to fulfil the Bishops' requirements by satisfactorily completing a course of education approved on behalf of the House of Bishops by the Theological Education and Training Committee. Only those candidates with an upper second or first class degree may read for a degree in theology or post-graduate diploma in theology, unless the degree course is specially designed as a training course for the professional ministry, is approved by the Theological Education and Training Committee, and involves no additional expense or lengthening of the normal course of training.

Certain special courses and professional qualifications may be regarded as conferring graduate status.
(c) *Non-graduates* are required to spend three years on a full-time course at a theological college and to fulfil the Bishops' requirements by satisfactorily completing a course of education approved on behalf of the House of Bishops by the Theological Education and Training Committee.

(2) *Candidates aged 30 and over*
(a) Candidates over 30 sponsored for the *ordained ministry* (*stipendiary and non-stipendiary ministry*) are required to undertake either two years' full-time training at a theological college, or three years' part-time training on a theological course. In some instances the recommendations for training will indicate a preferred form. Candidates are required to fulfil the Bishops' requirements by satisfactorily completing a course of education approved on behalf of the House of Bishops by the Theological Education and Training Committee.
(b) Candidates for *ordained ministry* (*permanent non-stipendiary ministry*) are required to undertake three years' part-time training on a theological course and to fulfil the Bishops' requirements by satisfactorily completing a course of education approved on behalf of the House of Bishops by the Theological Education and Training Committee.

(3) *Candidates aged 50 and over*
Candidates for *ordained ministry* (*permanent non-stipendiary ministry*) usually undertake three years' part-time training on a theological course. The exact nature of the training is decided by the sponsoring bishop.

NOTES
1 In the above regulations the age refers to the candidate's age at the start of training where the regulation concerns training; and to the candidate's age at time of sponsorship where the regulation concerns category of sponsorship.

2 The above regulations, in terms of age, sponsorship and training, also apply to Accredited Lay Ministry.

3 Exceptions to the above regulations will be considered by the Vocation, Recruitment and Selection Committee.

GRANTS
Candidates who have been recommended for training are eligible for financial help from Church Funds, but should always obtain as much assistance as possible from other sources before applying for such grants. Local Education Authorities almost invariably make awards to candidates who will be undertaking a first degree course during training, but discretionary awards are also available and awards for the support of dependants. Details about grants can be obtained from the Grants Secretary, Ministry Division, Church House, Great Smith St, London SW1P 3NZ.

For **Theological Colleges, Regional Courses** see also pages 179–180

The Central Readers' Council

Patron HRH The Duke of Edinburgh

Presidents The Archbishops of Canterbury and York

Chair Rt Revd Christopher Mayfield (*Bishop of Manchester*)

Vice-Chair Mrs Sarah James

Hon Secretary Mr Geoff Mihell   Tel: 0171–898 1415

Deputy Hon Secretary Miss Pat Nappin Tel: 0171–898 1417

Editor of The Reader Mr Ian Farrimond
                                     Tel: 0171–898 1415/1416

Hon National Moderator for Reader Training (*ABM*) Mr John Field   Tel: 0171–898 1414

Administrative Officer Mrs Sandra Fleming
                                     Tel: 0171–898 1416

Office Church House, Great Smith St, London SW1P 3NZ
                                     Tel: 0171–898 1000
                                     Fax: 0171–898 1419

The Central Readers' Council (CRC) works to enhance the contribution of Readers to the overall ministry of the Church, particularly to encourage the most effective integration with other forms of ministry, ordained and lay. It works in co-operation with the Theological Education and Training Committee, which moderates and co-ordinates the training of Reader candidates and the Archbishops' Diploma for Readers. CRC arranges national conferences for Readers, provides a forum for the exchange of ideas between dioceses on Reader matters and publishes a quarterly magazine, *The Reader*. The annual Summer Course at Selwyn College, Cambridge began in 1881 and is probably the longest established Summer School held in any university. CRC has ecumenical links through the annual Joint Readers' and Preachers' Conference at St Andrew's Hall, Selly Oak, Birmingham.

CRC is a registered charity which derives its income mostly from capitation grants made by diocesan Readers' boards. It has its origins in the revival of Reader ministry in the Church of England in 1866 and particularly in the Central Readers' Board, which was granted a constitution by the Archbishops in 1921. CRC today is the immediate successor to the Central Readers' Conference, under a new constitution adopted in 1994.

Archbishops' Council

CRC has three representatives, including the Warden and Secretary of Readers, from each diocese, and one representative from each of the Armed Forces. Any Reader elected or appointed to the Ministry committees is *ex officio* a member of CRC. A non-voting observer is invited from the Deaf Readers' and Pastoral Assistants Association, the Church of Ireland, the Scottish Episcopal Church and each of the dioceses of the Church in Wales. The annual general meeting is held in March/April each year.

CRC Executive Committee is elected for a five-year term co-terminous with General Synod. In addition to the Chair and Vice-Chair, the present Committee consists of: Mr Ron Black, Revd Christopher Blissard-Barnes, Revd Paul Conder, Mrs Gloria Helson, Dr Kathleen Higgs, Dr Cliff Jones, Miss Catherine Martineau, Mrs Gillian Newton, Mrs Wendy Plant, Canon Alex Whitehead and Mr Raymond Williams.

CENTRAL SERVICES

One of the objectives of the *Working As One Body* reforms was to secure common service arrangements across the central Church bodies in key areas such as legal advice, communications, personnel, and office services. An important step towards this has been achieved through the establishment of a common services division to ensure the development of best practice and the more efficient use of resources.

Among the units located within the division are those responsible for: providing services of appropriate quality to the Archbishops' Council, the other central bodies and, where appropriate, to the wider Church, ensuring their cost-effectiveness; assisting in the collation, analysis, publication and storage of information relating to the Church; providing advice, facilities and goods necessary to enable the day-to-day running of the Council and the other bodies; and providing strategic direction and focus for IT provisions throughout the central bodies.

The Director of Central Services also acts as Clerk to the Synod (*see* page 4)

The Corporation of the Church House, as landlord, is primarily responsible for the building and utilities at Church House, while the Council's Office Services Unit will be responsible for the building and utilities at Millbank and Fielden House. A close degree of liaison operates between the Council and the Corporation.

INFORMATION TECHNOLOGY AND OFFICE SERVICES
Head of Information Technology and Office Services Mr John Ferguson

The Information Technology and Office Services department provides common services for the central Church bodies, including IT systems development, computer support, mapping, reprographics, telephone and central buying facilities.

CENTRAL SECRETARIAT
The Secretariat of the Archbishops' Council provides administrative support to the Council and its committees; the House of Bishops; and the Church of England's Appointments Committee.

COMMITTEE FOR MINORITY ETHNIC ANGLICAN CONCERNS
Chairman The Rt Revd John Sentamu (*Bishop of Stepney*)
Secretary Mrs Glynne Gordon-Carter

The principal tasks of the Committee are to monitor and make recommendations about issues which arise or which ought to arise in the context of the work of the Archbishops' Council, its committees, and Boards and Councils and of the General Synod itself, as far as they have policy implications for minority ethnic groups within the Church and the wider community; and to assist the dioceses in developing strategies for combating racial bias within the Church, encouraging them to make the problem of racism a priority concern in their programmes.

THE INNER CITIES RELIGIOUS COUNCIL
Secretary Revd David Randolph-Horn, Floor 4/K10, Eland House, Bressenden Place, London SW1E 5DU
Tel: 0171–890 3704
Fax: 0171–890 3709

The Council comprises participants from the Christian, Hindu, Jewish, Muslim and Sikh communities. It sponsors a programme of regional conferences and is engaged in development work. It is a forum for Government to meet with the faith communities. The Secretariat is a source of advice to faith communities and Government with a particular emphasis on urban regeneration.

LITURGICAL SUPPORT AND PUBLISHING
The Archbishops' Council also provides administrative support for the Liturgical Commission (*see* page 42), the administration of liturgical business in the House of Bishops and Synod, and the Liturgical Publishing Group.

Church House Publishing

Publishing Manager Mr Alan Mitchell Tel: 0171–898 1450

Liturgy and Reference Editor Ms Rachel Boulding
Tel: 0171–898 1485

Commissioning Editor Mr Hamish Bruce
Tel: 0171–898 1453

Editorial and Copyright Manager Miss Sarah Roberts
Tel: 0171–898 1578

Production Manager Mrs Katharine Allenby
Tel: 0171–898 1452

Sales and Marketing Manager Mr Matthew Tickle
Tel: 0171–898 1454

Office Church House, Great Smith St, London SW1P 3NZ
Tel: 0171–898 1451; 0171–898 1000
Fax: 0171–898 1449
e-mail: info@chp.u-net.com
Web: http://www.chpublishing.co.uk

Church of England Year Book Editor Mrs Jo Linzey
Tel: (01865) 201565
e-mail: jolinzey@aol.com

The Department is jointly funded by the Archbishops' Council and the National Society for Promoting Religious Education. The imprint Church House Publishing is used for titles available through the book trade published on behalf of the Synod and its Boards and Councils. Educational material for churches and schools is co-published with the National Society.

The Department publishes *Crockford's Clerical Directory* and *The Church of England Year Book*. Around 40 new titles are published for the trade in an average year including reports commissioned by General Synod, liturgical material and books on church care and conservation.

Many low-priced, short-lived or highly specialised titles are issued by Boards and Councils under their own name and the Department is involved to a varying degree in producing and promoting them. These, together with most Synod papers, are available only from Church House Bookshop (*see below*).

The Church House Publishing catalogue, supplied on request, contains details of all publications currently available.

Church House Bookshop

31 Great Smith Street, London SW1P 3BN

Retail Co-ordinator Mr Mark Clifford Tel: 0171–898 1300

Bookshop (direct line) Tel: 0171–340 0280
Mail Order Tel: 0171–340 0276/0277/0271
Fax: 0171–340 0278
e-mail: info@chb.u-net.com
Web: http://www.chbookshop.co.uk

The Bookshop, refurbished in 1994, stocks an exceptionally wide range of Christian literature as well as providing the principal retail outlet for material issued by Church House. Recorded music on cassette and compact disc, greetings cards, parochial forms and registers and other items are also carried. All the above items can be obtained to special order if not stocked, and the Mail Order department – posting to anywhere in the world – will accept orders by post, fax, telephone or e-mail, which can either be paid for in advance or charged to most major credit cards. Details of book signings and special events are advertised in the church press – please write for further details. Shop hours: 9.00 am to 5.00 pm Monday, Tuesday, Wednesday, Friday; 9.30 am to 6.00 pm Thursday.

Statistics Unit

Head of Statistics Unit Mr Raymond Tongue
Tel: 0171–898 1542

The Central Board of Finance has been responsible for the collection and tabulation of parochial membership and finance statistics since 1920, and in 1955 it established a separate statistics division. While the gathering of parochial statistics remains at the heart of its work, the Statistics Unit has broadened the range of statistics it maintains and diversified so that it is now providing a service to a number of Boards and Councils. The Unit's role as a central resource has developed with the advent of the Archbishops' Council where it forms part of the Central Services Division.

The Unit is responsible for the collection, collation and

analysis of parochial finance and membership statistics. In recent years the Unit has been able to reduce the time taken to complete the processing of these statistics, so that it is now able to devote more of its resources to researching underlying trends and evaluating the merits of the statistics collected. Working closely with the Board of Mission, the Unit has embarked on a major review of the membership statistics that are collected annually with the aim of providing a range of statistics which will be a tool for mission. The publication in 1998 of *The Church of England Today*, which presented in pamphlet form basic facts about the Church of England and which was distributed to all parishes, represented a first step in improving the way in which statistical information is communicated within church circles.

The Unit maintains a churches database which it is currently enlarging to include details of church location and facilities. This database is to be linked with one being developed by the Council for the Care of Churches to hold information relating to church archaeology and history. Part of the information presently held on the Unit's database concerns urban deprivation, and the Unit is responsible for the maintenance of the Oxlip Index which is used for the identification of Urban Priority Areas. The Unit maintains strong links with the Ministry Division in the preparation and production of *Statistics of Licensed Ministers*, and with the Church Commissioners in the development of the *Crockford* database.

The Unit maintains links with other denominations on statistical matters and has been involved with discussions on the development of an ecumenical database and participation in the organisation of the next church census.

Records Centre

Director Mr Christopher Pickford *Tel:* 0171–898 1864

Address Church of England Record Centre, 15 Galleywall Rd, South Bermondsey, London SE16 3PB
Tel: 0171–898 1860
Fax: 0171–898 1861
e-mail: chris-pickford@chucomm.org.uk

The Centre, which is a combined venture of the Church Commissioners, the General Synod and the National Society, houses the non-current records of the Church Commissioners, the General Synod and the National Society, together with those of some ecumenical bodies. The Centre serves as an advisory point for queries concerning the archives of the Church of England. Enquirers welcome by appointment, Monday to Friday, 10.00 am to 5.00 pm. A small reference library is maintained.

COMMUNICATIONS

Communications are at the very heart of the operation of the Council. Through the development and implementation of an overarching communications and promotional strategy it will support the Church in its mission to communicate the gospel to the nation and beyond.

Director of Communications Revd Dr William Beaver
Tel: 0171–898 1462
Fax: 0171–898 1461

Communications Manager Mr Andrew Male
Tel: 0171–898 1621

Communications Officer Church Commissioner Mr Arun Kataria
Tel: 0171–898 1622

Head of Media Relations Mr Steve Jenkins
Tel: 0171–898 1457

Head of Signal Logistics Revd Jonathan Jennings
Tel: 0171–898 1456

Head of Media Training Revd Martin Short
Tel: 0171–898 1458

Head of Internal Communications Mr Alexander Nicoll
Tel: 0171–898 1623

Enquiry Centre

Enquiries Officer Mr Stephen Empson
Tel: 0171–898 1445
Fax: 0171–898 1461

The enquiry centre was established to deal with questions referred to it by post, by telephone or in person by members of the public on a wide variety of matters relating to church affairs. There is a constant flow of enquiries which come not only from the United Kingdom, but also from overseas. The centre also handles a large number of calls concerning clergy movements and biographical information.

Diocesan Communications Officers Panel

Chairman Rt Revd Graham James (*Bishop of St Germans*)

Secretary Miss Andrina Barnden   Tel: 0171–898 1463

Members
Canon Brian Chave, Mr Jeremy Dowling, Revd John Carter, Revd Richard Thomas, Canon Simon Pettitt, Revd David Marshall

HUMAN RESOURCES

A key objective of the reform of the national church bodies was the creation of a unified staff capability to serve the Church at national level under a joint Management Board and with a single personnel department. The Human Resources Division links personnel policies to the employer's overall strategies; provides a comprehensive personnel service to the central church organisations and to other church bodies that request it; and aims to encourage best practice in all areas.

STAFF
Director of Human Resources Mrs Susan Morgan
   Tel: 0171–898 1565

HR Project Manager Mr Fiske Warren   Tel: 0171–898 1748

Organisational Development and Training Miss Liz Lowe
   Tel: 0171–898 1751

Recruitment and Deployment Ms Francesca Eridani
   Tel: 0171–898 1585

Policy Development Vacancy

Employee Resourcing Miss Mary Carroll
   Tel: 0171–898 1747

Advisory Committees and Permanent Commissions

The Synod's subordinate bodies, other than the Business Committee and the Legislative Committee, fall into two main groups – Advisory Committees and Permanent Commissions – usually made up of a majority of Synod members. Each of the Advisory Committees has responsibility to the Synod through the Archbishops' Council for a major area of synodical business. The Permanent Commissions are concerned with specialised areas of the Synod's business.

ADVISORY COMMITTEES
See main entries on pages 16–24.
The Board of Education (*Chairman* The Bishop of Ripon; *Secretary* Canon John Hall)
The Board of Mission (*Chairman* The Bishop of Southwark; *Secretary* Canon Philip King)
The Council for Christian Unity (*Chairman* The Bishop of Peterborough; *Secretary* Prebendary Paul Avis)
The Board for Social Responsibility (*Chairman* The Bishop of Oxford; *Secretary* Mr David Skidmore)

PERMANENT COMMISSIONS
See main entries on pages 24–26.
The Hospital Chaplaincies Council (*Chairman* The Bishop of St Albans; *Secretary* Revd Robert Clarke)
The Cathedrals Fabric Commission (*Chairman* Dr Averil Cameron; *Secretary* Dr Richard Gem)
The Council for the Care of Churches (*Chairman* The Dean of York; *Secretary* Dr Thomas Cocke)

The Cathedral Statutes Commission

Chairman Prof David McClean

Secretary Mr Robert Wellen

Office Church House, Great Smith St, London SW1P 3NZ
   Tel: 0171–898 1371

MEMBERS
Very Revd Peter Berry (*Provost of Birmingham*), Ven John Duncan (*Archdeacon of Birmingham*), Very Revd Michael Higgins (*Dean of Ely*), Dr Kathryn Morfey, Rt Revd John Saxbee (*Bishop and Archdeacon of Ludlow*)

The Cathedral Statutes Commission, on the application of the consenting body of any Cathedral Church in England (with the single exception of Christ Church, Oxford), has the duty of preparing a scheme under the provisions of the Cathedrals Measure 1976 for revising, or for renewing, the constitution and statutes of that church. The Cathedrals Measure, which received Final Approval from the Synod in February 1998 and was before Parliament at the date of going to press, would supersede the procedure.

The Crown Appointments Commission

Office Fielden House, 13 Little College St, London SW1P 3SH   *Tel:* 0171-898 1875; 0171-233 0393 (Direct line) or 0171-222 7010 Ext 4033
e-mail: ajsadler@asa.clara.net

MEMBERS
Ex officio
The Archbishop of Canterbury
The Archbishop of York

Elected members
Three members of the House of Clergy
Ven Judith Rose
Canon John Stanley
Revd Hugh Broad

Three members of the House of Laity
The Viscountess Brentford
Mr Ian Garden
Mr Brian McHenry

Four members of the Vacancy-in-See Committee of the diocese whose bishopric is to become, or has become, vacant

Ex officio non-voting members
Mr Tony Sadler (*The Archbishops' Appointments Secretary*) Secretary to the Commission

Mr John Holroyd (*The Prime Minister's Appointments Secretary*)

The Commission was established by the General Synod in February 1977. Its function is to consider vacancies in diocesan bishoprics in the Provinces of Canterbury and York, and candidates for appointments to them. At each meeting the Chair is taken by the Archbishop in whose Province the vacancy has arisen. The Commission agrees upon two names for nomination to the Prime Minister by the appropriate Archbishop or, in the case of the Archbishopric of Canterbury or York, by the chairman appointed by the Prime Minister. The names submitted may be given in an order of preference decided upon by the Commission. In accordance with the terms of the Prime Minister's statement to the House of Commons on 8 June 1976, the Prime Minister selects one of the names or may ask for others to submit to HM the Queen for approval.

The Dioceses Commission

Chairman Mr Bryan Sandford

Secretary Mr David Hebblethwaite

Office Church House, Great Smith St, London SW1P 3NZ   *Tel:* 0171-898 1364

MEMBERS
Mrs Janet Atkinson, Ven George Cassidy (*Archdeacon of London*), Chancellor Christopher Clark, Rt Revd Ian Harland (*Bishop of Carlisle*), Dr John Holden, Mr David Kemp, Mr Peter Robottom, Mrs Marion Simpson, Very Revd Colin Slee (*Provost of Southwark*), Rt Revd Martin Wharton (*Bishop of Newcastle*)

The Dioceses Commission was set up in 1978 under Section 1(1) of the Dioceses Measure. That Measure makes provision for such matters as the reorganisation of diocesan boundaries, the creation of Area Bishops and Area Synods, the creation and revival of Suffragan Sees, the delegation of episcopal functions to a Suffragan Bishop by a Diocesan Bishop. The Commission works only within the framework of the Measure, and has two roles. In the first place the Commission is required to consider proposals prepared under the Measure, to report upon them and to make its report available to the diocesan synod of the diocese concerned and to the General Synod. Secondly, it has an advisory role, which is set out in Section 2 of the Measure as follows:

(1) It shall be the duty of the Commission, on the instructions of the General Synod, the Archbishops' Council, or the House of Bishops of the General Synod, to advise on matters affecting the diocesan structure of the Provinces of Canterbury and York or on the action which might be taken under this Measure to improve the episcopal oversight of any diocese therein or the administration of its affairs.

(2) Where it appears to the Commission that there is any such matter as is mentioned in subsection (1) above on which it might usefully advise, it may bring that matter to the attention of the General Synod or the Archbishops' Council with a view to receiving instructions under that subsection.

(3) The Commission shall be available to be consulted by any diocesan synod or the bishop of any diocese on any action which might be taken under this Measure in relation to the diocese.

The Doctrine Commission

Chairman Rt Revd Stephen Sykes (*Bishop of Ely*)

Secretary Dr Gareth Jones

Office Church House, Great Smith St, London SW1P 3NZ
Tel: 0171–898 1488

MEMBERS
Revd Prof Michael Banner, Prof Richard Bauckham, Dr Christina Baxter, Revd Jeremy Begbie, Dr Grace Davie, Prof David Ford, Prof Ann Loades, Rt Revd Geoffrey Rowell, Rt Revd Mark Santer (*Bishop of Birmingham*), Rt Revd Peter Selby (*Bishop of Worcester*), Rt Revd Kenneth Stevenson (*Bishop of Portsmouth*), Canon Prof Anthony Thiselton, Revd Prof John Webster, Dr Linda Woodhead

The functions of the Doctrine Commission are to consider and advise the House of Bishops of the General Synod upon doctrinal questions referred to it by the House of Bishops as well as to make suggestions to that House as to what in its judgement are doctrinal issues of concern to the Church of England.

The Legal Advisory Commission

Chairman Prof David McClean

Secretary Miss Ingrid Slaughter

Office Church House, Great Smith St, London SW1P 3NZ
Tel: 0171–898 1368
Fax: 0171–898 1369

MEMBERS
Mr Roger Arden, Mr Peter Beesley, Chancellor Timothy Briden, Ven Michael Brotherton (*Archdeacon of Chichester*), Chancellor Rupert Bursell, The Worshipful Sheila Cameron (*Vicar-General of Canterbury*), Mr David Cheetham, Chancellor Christopher Clark, His Honour Judge Thomas Coningsby (*Vicar-General of York*), Chancellor Quentin Edwards, Chancellor Michael Goodman, Mr Brian Hanson, Rt Revd Christopher Hill (*Bishop of Stafford*), Mr Nigel Johnson, Mr Lionel Lennox, Professor David McClean, Mrs Heather Morgan, The Rt Hon Lord Justice Mummery, Mr John Pakenham-Walsh, Dr Frank Robson, Revd Stephen Trott, Mr Edward (Ted) Wills

The Legal Advisory Commission gives advice on legal matters referred to it by the General Synod, its Boards and Councils, and also by the Church Commissioners and by diocesan clerical authorities and diocesan lay officials, on matters of general interest to the Church. The Commission will not advise in any contentious matter unless the facts of the dispute are agreed and referred for an opinion by both sides and the subject matter is not, and will not shortly become, the subject matter of legal proceedings.

The opinions of the Commission and its predecessor, the Legal Board, on matters of general interest are published by Church House Publishing in a loose-leaf form under the title *Legal Opinions Concerning the Church of England*. A first supplement was published in 1997 and it is intended that a further supplement will be issued in the near future.

The Legal Aid Commission

Chairman Mr Richard Bowman

Secretary Miss Ingrid Slaughter

Office Church House, Great Smith St, London SW1P 3NZ
Tel: 0171–898 1368
Fax: 0171–898 1369

MEMBERS
Canon Robert Baker, Mr Barry Barnes, Ven Michael Bowering (*Archdeacon of Lindisfarne*), Preb John Brownsell, Revd Helen Chantry, Mr Mark Hill, Rt Revd Edward Holland (*Bishop of Colchester*), Mrs Shirley Jackson, Revd Clive Mansell, Mr John Underwood

The Legal Aid Commission operates under the Church of England (Legal Aid) Measure 1994, and administers the Legal Aid Fund which was originally set up under the Ecclesiastical Jurisdiction Measure 1963 and is continued by the 1994 Measure.

Legal aid under the 1994 Measure may be granted, subject to various conditions, for certain types of proceedings before Ecclesiastical Courts and tribunals; details of eligibility for legal aid and the Commission's procedures, together with an application form for legal aid, are obtainable from the Secretary, on request.

Archbishops' Council

The Liturgical Commission

Chairman Rt Revd David Stancliffe (*Bishop of Salisbury*)

Secretary Mr David Hebblethwaite

Office Church House, Great Smith St, London SW1P 3NZ
Tel: 0171–898 1364

MEMBERS
Revd Andrew Burnham, Revd Dr Christopher Cocksworth, Dr Carole Cull, Canon Jeremy Haselock, Revd Susan Hope, The Baroness James of Holland Park, Rt Revd James Jones (*Bishop of Liverpool*), Mrs Anna de Lange, Canon Stephen Oliver, Very Revd Michael Perham, Canon Jane Sinclair, Mr Timothy Slater, Revd Angela Tilby, Brother Tristam SSF, (one vacancy)

Co-opted members
Revd Jeremy Fletcher, Ven Trevor Lloyd (*Archdeacon of Barnstaple*)

Consultants Rt Revd Kenneth Stevenson, Canon John Sweet DD, Prof Bryan Spinks, Revd Dr Paul Bradshaw

In response to resolutions by the Convocations in October 1954, the Archbishops of Canterbury and York appointed a standing Liturgical Commission 'to consider questions of a liturgical character submitted to them from time to time by the Archbishops of Canterbury and York and to report thereon to the Archbishops'. In 1971 the Commission became a permanent Commission of the General Synod. Its functions are:

1 To prepare forms of service at the request of the House of Bishops for submission to that House in the first instance.

2 To advise on the experimental use of forms of service and the development of liturgy.

3 To exchange information and advice on liturgical matters with other Churches both in the Anglican Communion and elsewhere.

4 To promote the development and understanding of liturgy and its use in the Church.

OTHER COMMITTEES
The Elections Review Group (*Chairman* The Archdeacon of Northolt; *Secretary* Mr Malcolm Taylor)
Ecumenical Decade: Churches in Solidarity with Women Working Party (*Chairman* Mrs Shirley-Ann Williams; *Secretary* Mr Andrew Roberts)

THE CHURCH COMMISSIONERS FOR ENGLAND

Office 1 Millbank, London SW1P 3JZ   *Tel:* 0171–898 1000
                                        Fax: 0171–898 1002
           e-mail: chcomms@dial.pipex.com

Chairman The Archbishop of Canterbury

MEMBERS
The Commissioners are: The Archbishops of Canterbury and York; 3 Church Estates Commissioners; 4 bishops elected by the House of Bishops of the General Synod; 2 deans or provosts elected by all the deans and provosts; 3 clergy elected by the House of Clergy of the General Synod; 4 lay persons elected by the House of Laity of the General Synod; 3 persons nominated by The Queen; 3 persons nominated by the Archbishops of Canterbury and of York acting jointly; 3 persons nominated by the Archbishops acting jointly after consultation with others including the Lord Mayors of the cities of London and York and the Vice-Chancellors of Oxford and Cambridge; the First Lord of the Treasury; the Lord President of the Council; the Secretary of State for the Home Department; the Lord Chancellor; the Secretary of State for the Department for Culture, Media and Sport; and the Speaker of the House of Commons.

BOARD OF GOVERNORS
All Commissioners are Board Members except for Officers of State.

Membership of the Committees below was not available at time of going to press.

ASSETS COMMITTEE
First Church Estates Commissioner (*Chairman*)
(Vacancies)

AUDIT COMMITTEE
(Vacancies)

BISHOPRICS AND CATHEDRALS COMMITTEE
Third Church Estates Commissioner (*Chairman*)
(Vacancies)

PASTORAL COMMITTEE
Third Church Estates Commissioner (*Chairman*)
(Vacancies)

REDUNDANT CHURCHES COMMITTEE
Third Church Estates Commissioner (*Chairman*)
(Vacancies)

OFFICERS
Secretary Mr Howell Harris Hughes   *Tel:* 0171–898 1785

Deputy Secretary (*Finance and Investment*) Mr Christopher Daws   *Tel:* 0171–898 1786

Property Accountant Mrs Marian Adams
                                          Tel: 0171–898 1677
(Management and financial accounting for the Commissioners' property holdings)

Accountant Mr Gerald Baines   *Tel:* 0171–898 1680
(Head of Cash and Accounts Divisions; Financial reporting and control)

Chief Surveyor Mr Andrew Brown   *Tel:* 0171–898 1634
(Head of Commercial Property Department, Agricultural, Residential and Mineral portfolios)

Pastoral and Redundant Churches Secretary Mr Martin Elengorn (Pastoral reorganisation, redundant churches, clergy housing and glebe)   *Tel:* 0171–898 1741

Stock Exchange Investments Manager Mr Antony Hardy (Commissioners' Stock Exchange portfolio; Secretary to the Ethical Investment Working Group and ethical policy monitoring)   *Tel:* 0171–898 1122

Management Accountant Mr Brian Hardy
(Financial analysis and forecasting)   *Tel:* 0171–898 1667

Archivist Mr Christopher Pickford   *Tel:* 0171–898 1864
(Head of Records Centre)

Bishoprics Officer Mr Edward Peacock
(Financial and administrative support for bishops)
                                          Tel: 0171–898 1062

Chief Architect Mr John Taylor
(Head of Architects Department)   *Tel:* 0171–898 1026

LEGAL DEPARTMENT
Official Solicitor Mr Nigel Johnson   *Tel:* 0171–898 1712

Deputy Official Solicitor Miss Susan Jones
                                          Tel: 0171–898 1704

Solicitors Mr Timothy Crow, Miss Judith Egar, Mr Michael Fahy, Mrs Alison Usher, Mrs Ruma Verma, Vacancy

CONSTITUTION

The Church Commissioners were formed on 1 April 1948, when Queen Anne's Bounty (1704) and the Ecclesiastical Commissioners (1836) were united.

The full body of Commissioners meets once a year to consider the Report and Accounts and the allocation of available money. The management of the Commissioners' affairs is shared between the Board of Governors, the Assets Committee and the Audit Committee (which are statutory), the Pastoral Committee, and the Redundant Churches Committee appointed by the Board under statute, the latter including two members who are not Commissioners.

The Church Commissioners' main tasks are to manage their assets, to distribute monies from assets in accordance with the duties laid upon them by Acts of Parliament and Measures of the General Synod and former Church Assembly, and to discharge other administrative duties entrusted to them.

MANAGEMENT OF ASSETS

The Commissioners' income in the year ended 31 December 1997 was:

	£ million
Investments	80.0
Property	43.2
Mortgages and loans	9.2
Other interest receivable	11.3
Income before interest payable	143.7
Interest payable	(3.3)
Asset Management costs	(5.1)
Total income	£135.3

The Commissioners draw no income from the State.

EXPENDITURE IN 1997

The Commissioners' income was distributed in two main ways:

(a) Payment of clergy stipends. The Commissioners' investment income provides around 15 per cent of the stipends of the clergy.
(b) Payment of clergy pensions and pensions to their widows. The Church of England Pensions Board authorises pensions, but the majority of the money is provided and paid by the Church Commissioners. New arrangements to share the cost of pensions with the dioceses in the future came into being on 1 January 1998, with the Commissioners being responsible for service prior to 1 January 1998 and dioceses and parishes for pensions earned after that date. The Commissioners also provided finance for the Clergy Retirement Housing Scheme through the Pensions Board.

The Commissioners used their total income for the year ended 31 December 1997 as follows:

	£ million
Parochial Ministry Support	(19.5)
Clergy and widows' pensions	(82.1)
Bishops and cathedral clergy stipends	(5.3)
Bishops' housing	(2.6)
Episcopal administration and payments to cathedrals	(10.6)
Financial provision for resigning clergy	(2.4)
Church buildings	(0.8)
Administration of central Church functions and Commissioners own administration	(5.6)
Other Church bodies' working costs	(2.6)
Total expenditure	(131.5)
Surplus of income against expenditure for year	3.8

CENTRAL STIPENDS AUTHORITY

This function and its powers were transferred to the Archbishops' Council on 1 January 1999.

ADMINISTRATIVE DUTIES

The Commissioners are responsible for dealing with schemes for pastoral reorganisation proposed by diocesan authorities under the Pastoral Measure 1983. The union of benefices and parishes, the holding of one or more benefices in plurality, the formation of new benefices and parishes, the alteration of ecclesiastical boundaries and the formation of team and group ministries are some of the matters dealt with.

The Commissioners' administrative duties also include considering all proposals for the provision and sale of parsonage houses, cathedral clergy houses and certain transactions affecting diocesan glebe.

REDUNDANT CHURCHES

The Pastoral Measure 1983 provides the procedure for declaring a church pastorally redundant and then settling its future. A Diocesan Pastoral Committee may, after consultation with all the 'interested parties', and with the bishop's approval, ask the Church Commissioners to prepare a draft pastoral scheme for declaring redundant a church which is not required for parochial worship.

If, following the consideration of any representations, a scheme comes into operation, without providing for the future of the church, the redundant building will temporarily vest in the Diocesan Board of Finance for care and maintenance. The Diocesan Redundant Churches Uses Committee then has the duty of making every endeavour to find a suitable alternative use for it and of reporting to the Commissioners. The Commissioners are advised as to the historic and archaeological interest and architectural quality of redundant churches by an independent body, the Advisory Board for Redundant Churches. In the light of the Uses Committee's report and the advice of the Advisory Board, the Commissioners must prepare and publish, normally within a period of three years, a draft redundancy scheme providing for the building in one of four ways: appropriation to another suitable use; retention by the Diocesan Board of Finance; preservation by the Churches Conservation Trust; or demolition. Having carefully considered any representations, the Commissioners decide whether to make any such scheme.

The Churches Conservation Trust, an independent body whose function is the care and maintenance of redundant churches of historic and archaeological interest or architectural quality vested in it by redundancy schemes, is largely financed by Church and State. In 1997, seven churches (six in 1996) of particular merit for which no suitable alternative use could be found were passed to the Churches Conservation Trust, bringing the total number in its care to 315. The Trust requires adequate money to meet the cost of initial repairs and subsequent maintenance to buildings vested in it. For the triennium 1997–2000 the Department of National Heritage has agreed to contribute up to a maximum of £7.2 million representing 70 per cent of the total budgeted expenditure of the Fund. The Church's 30 per cent maximum contribution of £3.2 million will be made available partly from the net proceeds of sales of redundant churches and sites and partly from the Commissioners' own resources.

RECORDS CENTRE
Director Mr Christopher Pickford
Tel: 0171–898 1864
Fax: 0171–898 1861
e-mail: chris-pickford@chucomm.org.uk

For further details *see* page 38.

FURTHER INFORMATION
Further information is available in the Commissioners' Annual Report and Accounts which, together with other information leaflets, is available free of charge from the Communications Department at 1 Millbank, London SW1P 3JZ. Requests for speakers to give talks about the Commissioners' work are welcomed.

Church Commissioners

THE CHURCH OF ENGLAND PENSIONS BOARD

Chairman Mr Allan Bridgewater

Vice-Chairman Ven Ian Russell (*Archdeacon of Coventry*)

Deputy Vice-Chairman Mr David Wright

Secretary Mr Roger Radford Tel: 0171–898 1807

Chief Accountant Mr Stephen Eagleton
  Tel: 0171–898 1818

Pensions Manager Miss Yvonne de la Praudiere
  Tel: 0171–898 1810

Housing Manager Mr Ian Gibbins Tel: 0171–898 1824

AUDIT COMMITTEE
Chairman Mr Keith Dodgson

HON MEDICAL ADVISER
Dr Trevor Hudson

Office 7 Little College St, London SW1P 3SF
  Tel: 0171–898 1800
  Fax: 0171–898 1801

MEMBERS
The constitution of the Board was reviewed by the General Synod in the light of both the Pensions Act 1995 and the changes made with effect from 1 January 1998 to the financial arrangements for providing pensions for those in the stipendiary ministry. It now consists of 20 members.

Appointed Chairman by the General Synod
Mr Allan Bridgewater

Nominated by the Archbishops of Canterbury and York
Mr Nigel Sherlock, one vacancy

Elected by the House of Bishops
Rt Revd John Yates

Elected by the House of Clergy
Ven Christopher Hawthorn (*Archdeacon of Cleveland*), Ven Ian Russell (*Archdeacon of Coventry*), Canon David Williams, (Vacancy)

Elected by members of the Church Workers Pension Fund
Revd Karen Curnock, Mr Colin Peters

Elected by members of the Church Administrators Pension Fund
Mr Robin Stevens

Elected by the House of Laity
Mr Keith Dodgson, Mr Tim Hind, Mr Geoffrey Hine, Mr Trevor Stevenson, Mr William Taylor, Mr David Wright

Elected by the employers participating in the Church Workers Pensions Fund and Church Administrators Pension Fund
Mr Paul Chandler, Mr Philip Couse

Nominated by the Church Commissioners
Mr Derek Fellows

RESPONSIBILITIES
The Pensions Board was constituted by the Church Assembly in 1926 to serve as the pensions authority for the Church of England, and was made the administrator of a comprehensive pension scheme for the clergy. Subsequently the Board has been given wider responsibilities and powers for securing the welfare of all who retire from the stipendiary ministry, and of their widows and widowers, through the provision of pensions and retirement accommodation.

Operating as a trustee both of pension funds and of charitable funds for many different classes of beneficiary, the Board is directly accountable to the General Synod. While the Church has drawn together under the Board its central responsibilities for retirement welfare, the Board will continue to work in close co-operation with the Church Commissioners and, in the future, with the Archbishops' Council. There is also a partnership between the Board and dioceses in financial commitments towards discretionary grants and housing, and at the level of personal pastoral service through Widows Officers, Archdeacons and Retirement Officers.

PENSIONS
The Board is administrator of the pension arrangements for clergy, deaconesses and licensed lay-workers, and for their widows and widowers, keeping records of pensionable service and corresponding about pensions matters both with pensioners and with those not yet retired. It is corporate trustee of the Church of England Funded Pensions Scheme, to which contributions are currently being paid at the rate of some £32.5 million a year to provide for pensions and associated benefits arising from service after the end of 1997. The Church Commissioners

continue to meet the cost of benefits arising from service prior to 1 January 1998.

The Clergy (Widows and Dependants) Pensions Fund was closed to new entrants after widows' pensions were introduced under the main scheme. It has assets of £24 million and provides an additional benefit to widows and other dependants of those who made contributions to it. As a result of favourable investment performance, the benefits were increased by 45 per cent following the latest triennial actuarial valuation.

The Board is also corporate Trustee of the Church Workers Pension Fund, under which some 170 Church organisations make pension provision for their lay employees, and the Church Administrators Pension Fund. It is responsible for all the activities of these funds including the administration and keeping of records, payment of benefits, collection of contributions and investment of monies currently held in the funds; these now total over £140 million.

RETIREMENT HOUSING SCHEMES

The current retirement housing arrangements were presented to the General Synod by the Board and the Commissioners in July 1982 and were brought into operation by the Board in January 1983. The mortgage scheme is based on loans linked to the value of the properties and an initial low rate of interest. The Board owned approximately 400 rental properties, which it had acquired over time by outright gift or had purchased or built out of gifts in trust for that purpose. To these were added another 400 properties in which the entire equity interest had been charged to the Church Commissioners as security for loan finance. The Commissioners undertook to lend to the Board the funds necessary to finance all future mortgage loans and rental property purchases, subject of course to satisfactory terms as to interest and repayment of capital. The Board does however continue to add further properties acquired by gift. At 31 December 1997 the Board had nearly 1,600 properties for rent and just under 1,700 outstanding mortgage loans.

RESIDENTIAL AND NURSING HOMES

There are eight residential homes and one nursing home which are owned and managed by the Board. Five of these were purpose-designed, including the latest which was completed during 1997, and another was refurbished and extended a few years ago. The nursing home has also recently been modernised and extended. The Board has identified a suitable site on which to build a replacement for another of the older homes, and consideration is also being given to modernising the remaining one. The Board's charitable resources provide the capital for purchasing or building the homes and for their subsequent maintenance.

Each home is run by a professional staff, supported by a local committee. The wardens report to the Board's Housing Manager. Residents and patients are charged fees which, with available State support, are affordable. As the fee income is insufficient to cover the operating costs, the shortfall is met from the Board's charitable resources.

In addition, support may be given with fees payable by the Board's pensioners in privately run homes, if an individual cannot meet the full cost even with the maximum possible assistance available from the State.

THE BOARD AS A CHARITY

The care of the more elderly of its pensioners is an activity of the Board which attracts considerable regular support, voluntarily from within the Church at parochial and diocesan level, and from churchgoers and other people of goodwill everywhere. Money and other property given or bequeathed to the Board has averaged over £1.5 million per annum in recent years. The Pensions Board is registered as a charity. The charitable funds currently have a value of some £79 million.

PUBLICATIONS AVAILABLE FROM THE BOARD

Your Pension Questions Answered
Information about the Pension Scheme for clergy, deaconesses and licensed lay-workers.

The Church of England Voluntary Contributions Scheme
Explains the retirement benefits available to clergy, deaconesses and licensed lay-workers in return for voluntary pension contributions.

Retirement Housing
Explains the assistance which the Board is able to make (with financial support from the Church Commissioners) to clergy, their wives and widowers and also to deaconesses and licensed lay-workers for their retirement housing.

The Church Workers Pension Fund
An explanation of the retirement benefits available to church workers whose employers participate in the Fund.

The Church of England Pensions Board – Our Work is Caring . . .
Describes the discretionary assistance made available to its beneficiaries through the Board's charitable funds and explains how contributions may be made to support that work.

Pensions Board

OTHER BOARDS, COUNCILS, COMMISSIONS, ETC. OF THE CHURCH OF ENGLAND

The Advisory Board for Redundant Churches

Mr Michael Gillingham (*Chairman*), Dr John Blair, Chancellor Peter Boydell, Prof Joe Mordaunt Crook, Mr Ian Curry, Prof Roberta Gilchrist, Rt Revd David Lunn, Revd Dr Nicholas Thistlethwaite, Mr Nicholas Thompson

Secretary Dr Jeffrey West, Fielden House, Little College St, London SW1P 3SH   *Tel:* 0171–898 1872; 0171–222 9603

The Churches Conservation Trust

(formerly the Redundant Churches Fund)

Mr Walter Hayes (*Chairman*), Ms Liz Forgan, Rt Revd John Gaisford (*Bishop of Beverley*), Mr Alan Rome, Mr Peter Rumble, Very Revd Henry Stapleton

Director Miss Catherine Cullis, 89 Fleet St, London EC4Y 1DH
Tel: 0171–936 2285
Fax: 0171–936 2284

Chief Caseworker Miss Sarah Robinson

The Trust was set up in 1969 to preserve churches no longer needed for worship but which are of historic, architectural or archaeological importance. Many are in areas of urban or rural depopulation with no financial resources of their own. They may still be used for occasional services, or for concerts, exhibitions or other events considered by the Trust to be suitable.

The Corporation of the Church House

President The Archbishop of Canterbury

Chairman Mr Oswald Clark

Treasurer The Hon Nicholas Assheton

Secretary Mr Colin Menzies   *Tel:* 0171–898 1310

Office Church House, Great Smith St, London SW1P 3NZ
Tel: 0171–898 1320
Fax: 0171–898 1321

The original Church House was built in the early 1890s as the Church's memorial of Queen Victoria's Jubilee, to be the administrative headquarters of the Church of England and was replaced by the present building to a design by Sir Herbert Baker. The foundation stone was laid in 1937 by Queen Mary and on 10 June 1940 King George VI, accompanied by the Queen, formally opened the new House and attended the first Session of the Church Assembly in the great circular hall. The building was almost immediately requisitioned by the Government and for the rest of the war became the alternative meeting place of both Houses of Parliament; the Lords sat in the Convocation Hall and the Commons in the Hoare Memorial Hall. Oak panels in these halls commemorate this use.

By October 1946 some administrative offices of the Church Assembly returned to Church House and the Church Assembly was able to return for its Autumn Session in 1950. The building is now the headquarters of the new Archbishops' Council as well as being the meeting place for the General Synod each spring and autumn.

Following an extensive refurbishment of the principal rooms, Church House has since become an important national centre for conferences and meetings.

The business of the Corporation is vested in its Council of 30 members: 10 *ex officio*, 9 elected, 6 nominated by the General Synod and 5 co-opted by the Council.

The National Society (Church of England) for Promoting Religious Education

Patron HM The Queen

President The Archbishop of Canterbury

Chairman of the Council The Bishop of Ripon

General Secretary Canon John Hall   *Tel:* 0171–898 1500

Treasurer Mr David Lambert

Deputy Secretaries Mr Alan Brown, Mr David Lankshear
     Tel: 0171–898 1494; 0171–898 1490

Finance and Administrative Officer Mr David Grimes
     Tel: 0171–898 1492

Publishing Manager Mr Alan Mitchell   *Tel:* 0171–898 1450

Commissioning Editor Mr Hamish Bruce
     Tel: 0171–898 1453

Membership Officer Miss Katie Lowe   *Tel:* 0171–898 1497

Office Church House, Great Smith St, London SW1P 3NZ
     Tel: 0171–898 1000
     Fax: 0171–898 1520
     e-mail: (first name.surname)@natsoc.org.uk
     web: http://www.natsoc.org.uk

Archivist Ms Sarah Duffield   *Tel:* 0171–898 1863
     Fax: 0171–898 1861

The Society's archives are held at the Church of England Record Centre (*Director* Mr Christopher Pickford) – for further details *see* page 38.

London RE Centre

Director Mrs Alison Seaman

Address 36 Causton St, London SW1P 4AU
     Tel: 0171–932 1190/1191
     Fax: 0171–932 1199
     e-mail: nsrec@dial.pipex.com
     web: http://dspace.dial.pipex.com/nsrec/

York RE Centre

Head of Religious Studies Mrs Eileen Bellett
Centre Tutor Mrs Carrie Mercier

Address The College, Lord Mayor's Walk, York YO3 7EX
     Tel: (01904) 616858
     Fax: (01904) 612512
     e-mail: c.mercier@ucrusj.ac.uk

The National Society exists 'for the promotion, encouragement and support of religious education in accordance with the principles of the Church of England'. It works in close association with the Board of Education (and the Division for Education of the Church in Wales), but values its status as a voluntary body which enables it to take initiatives in developing new work. The Society has a particular concern for the support of Christian goals and values in education as a whole.

Founded in 1811, the Society was chiefly responsible for setting up, in co-operation with local clergy and others, the nationwide network of Church schools in England and Wales; it was also, through the Church colleges, a pioneer in teacher education. A concern for Church schools is still at the heart of the Society's work; it provides a legal and advisory service for dioceses and schools as well as a range of publications for the guidance of teachers and governors. It trains and accredits inspectors for Church Schools under Section 23 of the School Inspection Act 1996. In co-operation with the Board of Education the Society expresses its views on educational matters to the Department for Education and Employment, the LEAs and other bodies.

While supporting the Church's partnership with the State in statutory education, the National Society has a broader range: those responsible for RE and worship in any school, lecturers and students in colleges, and clergy and lay people in diocesan and parish education can all benefit from the resources of the Society's RE Centres, courses, conferences, archives and publications. The Society has recently established a Special Educational Needs Fellowship which is open to individuals, schools or institutions of Higher Eduction. The intended areas fall within religious education, Christian education, spiritual, moral, social and cultural development, school worship or Church schools.

The London RE Centre is in London Diocesan House in Pimlico. It houses thousands of books and journals currently available for religious education and a comprehensive collection of videos, audio cassettes, slides, posters and artefacts. It is open from Monday to Friday, 9.30 am to 4.30 pm (and at other times by arrangement), when staff are always pleased to assist visitors besides answering telephone and written enquiries. The Centre provides facilities for workshops and runs a variety of courses in

Other Boards, Councils, Commissions, etc.   **49**

RE, worship and pastoral and social education. It also works closely with the London Diocesan Board for Schools.

The York RE Centre is an integral part of the University College of Ripon and York St John. The National Society supports its work financially and through representation on the Centre's Advisory Board. The Centre offers a similarly wide range of resources and a full programme of training opportunities. It is open on weekdays, except for a short period in August, from 9.00 am to 8.00 pm on Mondays, and 9.00 am to 5.00 pm Tuesday to Friday in term-time; and 9.00 am to 5.00 pm Monday to Friday during college vacations. Visitors are always welcome but are advised to telephone beforehand if travelling from a distance.

Recent National Society initiatives with Church colleges include the Church Colleges Certificate in Religious Education and the Church Colleges Certificate in Church School Studies and a Masters degree programme in Church School Education. The Society's own series of training courses for inspectors of Church schools continues to be a valued service.

The National Society has created a Fellowship in Special Educational Needs. Each Fellow will be appointed for one year with the results of their work being published. The fellowship covers the areas of religious education, Christian education, Church schools, spiritual, moral, social and cultural development.

After nearly two centuries of close association with Church schools and colleges the National Society has built up an impressive collection of documents and books in its archives and library. These include about 15,000 files of correspondence with the various National Schools in England and Wales and many published works, including the Society's own. Access is available to *bona fide* researchers by appointment at the Church of England Record Centre.

In support of Christian education in schools, colleges, parishes and the home the National Society produces a range of books and other publications, including the magazine *Together with Children*. Its publishing programme is now integrated with Church House Publishing (*see* page 37), where staff salaries are part funded by the Society. A catalogue giving full details is available from the Society at the address above. Applications for membership from individuals, schools and other bodies wishing to support the Society's work and share its resources are welcomed; a form is included in the catalogue.

THE CONVOCATIONS OF CANTERBURY AND YORK

CONSTITUTION
Each of the Convocations consists of two Houses, an Upper House and a Lower House. The Upper House consists of all the diocesan bishops in the Province and certain elected suffragan bishops, and the Archbishop presides. The Lower House comprises *ex officio* and elected members of the clergy. These are known as Proctors in Convocation. The University and Service representatives are given on page 4.

MEMBERS OF CONVOCATIONS

	Canterbury	York
Upper House		
Diocesan Bishops	30	14
Suffragan Bishops	6	3
	36	17
Lower House		
Deans or Provosts	10	5
Dean of Jersey or Guernsey	1	
Archdeacons	29	14
Service Chaplains	3	
Chaplain-General of Prisons	1	
Elected Proctors	125	58
University Proctors	4	2
Religious	1	1
Co-opted Clergy	0	1
	174	81

OFFICERS
Convocation of Canterbury
President The Archbishop of Canterbury

Prolocutor of the Lower House Canon Hugh Wilcox

Pro-Prolocutors
(Three vacancies)

Standing Committee of the Upper House
The Bishop of London
The Bishop of Winchester
(One vacancy)

Standing Committee of the Lower House
The Prolocutor
The Pro-Prolocutors
(Eight vacancies)

Registrar Mr Brian Hanson

Synodical Secretary, Actuary, and Editor of the Chronicle of Convocation
Canon Michael Hodge, Rectory, Rectory Drive, Bidborough, Tunbridge Wells, Kent TN3 0UL
Tel: (01892) 528081
Fax: (01892) 528081
e-mail: michaelh@braxton.ndirect.co.uk

Ostiarius Mr Clive McCleester, Head Virger of Winchester Cathedral

Convocation of York
President The Archbishop of York

Prolocutor of the Lower House Canon John Stanley

Deputy Prolocutors of the Lower House
(Two vacancies)

Assessors of the Upper House
The Bishop of Ripon
The Bishop of Southwell

Assessors of the Lower House
The Prolocutor
The Deputy Prolocutors
(Seven vacancies)

Registrar Mr Lionel Lennox
Registrar (Provincial Elections) Mr Brian Hanson

Synodal Secretary and Treasurer and Editor of the Journal of Convocation
Ven David Jenkins, Woodcroft, Levens, Kendal, Cumbria LA8 8NQ
Tel: (015395) 61281
Fax: (015395) 61217

Apparitor P. Gibson

ACTS AND PROCEEDINGS
For the Acts and Proceedings of the Convocations, readers are referred to *The Chronicle of the Convocation of Canterbury* and to the *York Journal of Convocation* available from Church House Bookshop. Back numbers are available from Wm. Dawson & Sons Ltd, Cannon House, Folkestone, Kent.

THE ECCLESIASTICAL COURTS

The Ecclesiastical Courts consist of (1) the Diocesan or Consistory Courts, (2) the Provincial Courts, and for both Provinces (3) the Court of Ecclesiastical Causes Reserved and, when required, (4) a Commission of Review. In certain faculty cases an appeal lies from the Provincial Courts to the Judicial Committee of the Privy Council. The jurisdiction of the Archdeacons' Courts is now confined to the visitations of Archdeacons. The Ecclesiastical Courts are in the main now regulated by the Ecclesiastical Jurisdiction Measure 1963. The Court of Faculties is the Court of the Archbishop of Canterbury through which the legatine powers transferred to the Archbishop of Canterbury by the Ecclesiastical Licenses Act 1533 are exercised.

The personnel of the Diocesan Courts is given in the diocesan lists. The personnel of the Court of Faculties and of the Provincial and some of the other Courts is as follows:

THE COURT OF ARCHES
Dean of the Arches The Rt Worshipful Sir John Owen

Registrar Dr Frank Robson
16 Beaumont St, Oxford OX1 2LZ

THE COURT OF THE VICAR-GENERAL OF THE PROVINCE OF CANTERBURY
Vicar-General The Worshipful Sheila Cameron

Joint Registrars
Dr Frank Robson (*as above*)
Mr Brian Hanson
Church House, Great Smith St, London SW1P 3NZ

THE CHANCERY COURT OF YORK
Auditor The Rt Worshipful Sir John Owen

Registrar Mr Lionel Lennox
The Registry, Stamford House, Piccadilly, York YO1 1PP

THE COURT OF THE VICAR-GENERAL OF THE PROVINCE OF YORK
Vicar-General His Honour Judge Thomas Coningsby

Registrar Mr Lionel Lennox (*as above*)

THE COURT OF ECCLESIASTICAL CAUSES RESERVED
Judges
The Rt Hon Ralph Gibson
Rt Revd Eric Kemp (*Bishop of Chichester*)
The Rt Hon Lord Justice Lloyd
Rt Revd Ronald Gordon (*formerly Bishop of Portsmouth*)
Rt Revd Alexander Graham (*formerly Bishop of Newcastle*)

Registrar Dr Frank Robson (*as above*)

THE COURT OF FACULTIES
Master of the Faculties The Rt Worshipful Sir John Owen

Registrar Mr Peter Beesley
1 The Sanctuary, Westminster SW1P 3JT

APPEAL PANEL CONSTITUTED UNDER THE PASTORAL MEASURE 1983 SCHEDULE 4
Chairman The Dean of the Arches

Deputy Chairmen
The Vicar-General of Canterbury
The Vicar-General of York

In addition to the Chairman, a tribunal comprises four clergymen and two laymen drawn from the following panels:

Convocation of Canterbury, Lower House
Canon Ray Adams (Worcester)
Canon Bob Baker (Norwich)
Revd Dr Anne Barton (Winchester)
The Archdeacon of Bedford (Ven Malcolm Lesiter)
The Archdeacon of Buckingham (Ven David Goldie)
Canon Christine Farrington (Ely)
Canon Jeremy Haselock (Chichester)
Revd Stephen Holdaway (Lincoln)
Preb Sam Philpott (Exeter)
Revd Eve Pitts (Birmingham)
Preb Terry Thake (Lichfield)
Revd Jonathan Young (Ely)

Convocation of York, Lower House
The Archdeacon of Auckland (Ven Granville Gibson)
Canon Edward Burns (Blackburn)
Revd Helen Chantry (Chester)
Canon Frank Dexter (Newcastle)
Revd Peter Hill (Southwell)
The Archdeacon of Sheffield (Ven Stephen Lowe)
Canon John Stanley (Liverpool)
The Provost of Wakefield (Very Revd George Nairn-Briggs)
Canon Max Wigley (Bradford)
The Dean of York (Very Revd Raymond Furnell)
(One vacancy)

House of Laity of the General Synod
Mr Anthony Archer (St Albans)
Mr Roger Atkinson (Lincoln)

Mr Stewart Darlow (Chester)
Mr Keith Davidson (Peterborough)
Mr Ian Garden (Blackburn)
Dr Sheila Grieve (Chester)
Dr John Holden (Southwell)
Mr James Humphrey (Salisbury)
Dr Kathryn Morfey (Winchester)
Miss Pat Nappin (Chelmsford)
Miss Diana Parker (Blackburn)
Mr David Wright (Oxford)

Secretary Vacancy, General Synod Office, Church House, Great Smith St, London SW1P 3NZ   *Tel:* 0171–340 0214

APPEAL PANEL CONSTITUTED UNDER THE ORDINATION OF WOMEN (FINANCIAL PROVISIONS) MEASURE 1993
Revd Hugh Broad (Gloucester)
Canon Rex Chapman (Carlisle)
Mr Ian Garden (Blackburn)
Mrs Shirley Jackson (St Albans)
Canon David Lickess (York)
The Archdeacon of London (Ven George Cassidy)
Dr Kathryn Morfey (Winchester)
Miss Diane Parker (Blackburn)
Mrs Elizabeth Paver (Sheffield)
The Archdeacon of Plymouth (Ven Robin Ellis)
Mr Mike Tyrell (Coventry)
Revd Colin Williams (Blackburn)

Secretary Vacancy, General Synod Office, Church House, Great Smith St, London SW1P 3NZ

THE DIOCESES

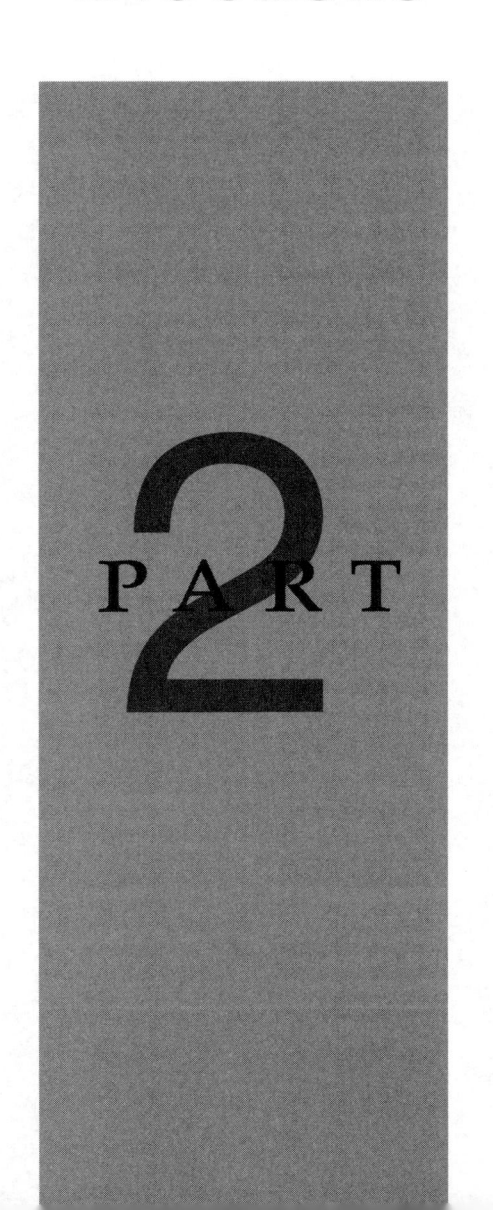

PART 2

Provinces of Canterbury and York

The dioceses in the respective Provinces of Canterbury and York are as below:

The Province of Canterbury Bath and Wells, Birmingham, Bristol, Canterbury, Chelmsford, Chichester, Coventry, Derby, Ely, Europe, Exeter, Gloucester, Guildford, Hereford, Leicester, Lichfield, Lincoln, London, Norwich, Oxford, Peterborough, Portsmouth, Rochester, St Albans, St Edmundsbury and Ipswich, Salisbury, Southwark, Truro, Winchester, Worcester.

The Province of York Blackburn, Bradford, Carlisle, Chester, Durham, Liverpool, Manchester, Newcastle, Ripon, Sheffield, Sodor and Man, Southwell, Wakefield, York.

The entry for each diocese is preceded by a territorial description and a few vital statistics:

Population Derived from the final mid-year estimates of normally resident population for 1996 published by the Office for National Statistics. Calculations are based on diocesan proportions of Ward and Civil Parish populations as at the 1991 Census.

Area in square miles, as calculated from material supplied by the Office of National Statistics and the Church Commissioners.

Stipendiary clergy Full-time clergy, men and women, working within the diocesan framework as at 31 December 1997 and counted under the current deployment formula.

Benefices Figures as at June 1996, compiled from information provided by the Church Commissioners. The figure does not include cathedrals or conventional districts.

Parishes / Churches as listed at June 1996 (with later additions) in the Parish Register maintained by the Statistics Unit of the Central Board of Finance.

In most cases, the Diocesan Secretary is also the Secretary of the Diocesan Synod.

PROVINCIAL LAY OFFICERS

Canterbury
Dean of the Court of Arches Rt Worshipful Sir John Owen, Bickerstaff House, Idlicote, Shipston-on-Stour, Warws CV36 5DT

Vicar-General The Worshipful Sheila Cameron, 2 Harcourt Buildings, Temple, London EC4   *Tel*: 0171–353 8415

Joint Registrars Dr Frank Robson, 16 Beaumont St, Oxford OX1 2LZ   *Tel*: (01865) 241974

Mr Brian Hanson, Church House, Great Smith St, London SW1P 3NZ   *Tel*: 0171–222 9011

York
Official Principal and Auditor of Chancery Court (*York*) Rt Worshipful Sir John Owen, Bickerstaff House, Idlicote, Shipston-on-Stour, Warws CV36 5DT

Vicar-General of the Province and Official Principal of the Consistory Court His Honour Judge Thomas Coningsby, 3 Dr Johnson's Buildings, Temple, London EC4Y 7BA
Tel: 0171–353 4854

Registrar of Province Mr Lionel Lennox, The Registry, Stamford House, Piccadilly, York YO1 1PP
Tel: (01904) 623487
Fax: (01904) 611458
e-mail: denison.till@dial.pipex.com

Registrar (*Provincial Elections*) Mr Brian Hanson, Church House, Great Smith St, London SW1P 3NZ
Tel: 0171–222 9011

Archbishop of Canterbury's Personal Staff

Lambeth Palace, London SE1 7JU
Tel: 0171–928 8282   *Fax*: 0171–261 9836
Web: http//www.archbishopofcanterbury.org
BISHOP AT LAMBETH (Head of Staff)
Rt Revd Richard Llewellin

Secretary for Public Affairs
Mr Jeremy Harris   *Tel*: 0171–898 1272

Public Affairs Officer
Mr Louis Henderson   *Tel*: 0171–898 1290

Secretary for Ecumenical Affairs
Canon Richard Marsh PH D   *Tel*: 0171–898 1232

Assistant Secretary for Ecumenical and Anglican Communion Affairs
Revd Dr Herman Browne   *Tel*: 0171–898 1203

Secretary for Anglican Communion Affairs
Canon Andrew Deuchar   *Tel*: 0171–898 1216

Archbishop's Domestic Chaplain (Lambeth Palace)
Canon Colin Fletcher   *Tel*: 0171–898 1253

Archbishop's Canterbury Chaplain (and Diocesan Missioner)
Revd Stewart Jones   *Tel*: 0171–928 8282

Secretary for Broadcasting, Press and Communications
Ms Lesley Perry   *Tel*: 0171–898 1206

Archbishop's Private Secretary
Mrs Mary Eaton   *Tel*: 0171–898 1225

Administrative Secretary
Miss Julia Hudson   *Tel*: 0171–898 1244

Archbishop's Lay Assistant
Mr Andrew Nunn   *Tel*: 0171–898 1228

Research Officer
Mrs Claire Shirley   *Tel*: 0171–898 1234

Steward
Mr John Dean   *Tel*: 0171–898 1233

Bursar
Vacancy

Archbishop of York's Personal Staff

Bishopthorpe Palace, Bishopthorpe, York YO23 2GE
Tel: (01904) 707021   *Fax*: (01904) 709204
e-mail: office@bishopthorpe.u-net.com

Chaplain to the Archbishop
Revd Michael Kavanagh

Archbishop's Private Secretary
Mrs Mary Murray

Archbishop's Special Adviser
Ven Alan Dean

DIOCESE OF BATH AND WELLS

Founded in 909. Somerset; North West Somerset; Bath; North East Somerset; a few parishes in Dorset.

Population 835,000 Area 1,614 sq m
Stipendiary Clergy 251 Benefices 212
Parishes 481 Churches 571

BISHOP (77th)
Rt Revd James Lawton Thompson, The Palace, Wells, Som BA5 2PD [1991]
Tel: (01749) 672341
Fax: (01749) 679355
e-mail: bishop@bathwells.anglican.org
[James Bath and Wells]

Chaplain/Pastoral Assistant Preb Martin Wright (same address)

SUFFRAGAN BISHOP
TAUNTON Rt Revd Andrew Radford, Bishop's Lodge, Monkton Heights, West Monkton, Taunton TA2 8LU [1998]
Tel: (01823) 413526
Fax: (01823) 412805

HONORARY ASSISTANT BISHOPS
Rt Revd John Waller, 102 Harnham Rd, Salisbury SP2 8JW   Tel: (01722) 329739
Rt Revd Alexander Hamilton, 3 Ash Tree Rd, Burnham on Sea, Som TA8 2LB
Tel: (01278) 783823
Rt Revd Roger Wilson, Kingsett, Roper's Lane, Wrington, Bristol BS18 7NH
Tel: (01934) 862464
Rt Revd John Neale, 26 Prospect, Corsham, Wilts SN13 9AF
Tel: (01249) 712557
Rt Revd Richard Third, 25 Church Close, Martock, Yeovil, Som TA12 6DA
Tel: (01935) 825519
Rt Revd William Persson, Ryalls Cottage, Burton St, Marnhull, Sturminster Newton DT10 1PS   Tel: (01258) 820452
Rt Revd Colin James, 5 Hermitage Rd, Landsdown, Bath BA1 5SN
Tel: (01225) 312720
Rt Revd Peter Coleman, Boxenwood Cottage, Westwood, Weir Bagborough, Bishop's Lydeard TA4 3HQ
Tel: (01984) 618607

CATHEDRAL CHURCH OF ST ANDREW IN WELLS
Dean of Wells Very Revd Richard Lewis, The Dean's Lodging, 25 The Liberty, Wells, Som BA5 2SZ [1990]
Tel: (01749) 670278
e-mail: deanwels@welscathedra.u-net.com
Canons Residentiary
Precentor Canon Paul Lucas, 4 The Liberty, Wells, Som BA5 2SU [1988]
Tel: (01749) 673188
Archdeacon Ven Richard (Dick) Acworth, Old Rectory, The Crescent, Croscombe, Wells, Som BA5 3QN [1993]
Tel: (01749) 342242
Treasurer Canon Geoffrey Walker, 6 The Liberty, Wells, Som BA5 2SU [1994]
Tel: (01749) 672224
Chancellor Canon Melvyn Matthews, 8 The Liberty, Wells, Som BA5 2SU [1997]
Tel: (01749) 678763
Registrar Mr Tim Berry, Diocesan Registry, 14 Market Place, Wells, Som BA5 2RE
Tel: (01749) 674747
Administrator and Chapter Clerk Mr John Roberts, Chain Gate, Cathedral Green, Wells, Som BA5 2UE
Tel: (01749) 674483
Fax: (01749) 677360
Cathedral Organist Mr Malcolm Archer (same address)

ARCHDEACONS
WELLS Ven Richard (Dick) Acworth, Old Rectory, The Crescent, Croscombe, Wells, Som BA5 3QN [1993]
Tel: (01749) 342242
Fax: (01749) 330060
BATH Ven Robert (Bob) Evans, 56 Grange Rd, Saltford, Bristol BS31 3AG [1995]
Tel: (01225) 873609
Fax: (01225) 874110
e-mail: 113145.1175@compuserve.com
TAUNTON Ven John Reed, 4 Westerkirk Gate, Staplegrove, Taunton, Som TA2 6BQ [1999]   Tel: (01823) 323838
Fax: (01823) 325420

CONVOCATION (MEMBERS OF THE HOUSE OF CLERGY OF THE GENERAL SYNOD)
Dignitaries in Convocation
The Dean of Wells
The Archdeacon of Wells
Proctors for Clergy:
Preb Richard Askew
Revd Michael Norman
Preb Rodney Schofield
Preb Penny West

MEMBERS OF THE HOUSE OF LAITY OF THE GENERAL SYNOD
Mrs Ann Clarke
Mr Lewis Currie
Mr Michael Gillingham
Mr Timothy Hind
Mr Peter LeRoy
Mrs Diana Taylor
Mr Jim White
Miss Fay Wilson-Rudd

DIOCESAN OFFICERS
Dioc Secretary Mr Nicholas Denison, Dioc Office, The Old Deanery, Wells, Som BA5 2UG   Tel: (01749) 670777
Fax: (01749) 674240
Chancellor of Diocese The Worshipful Timothy Briden, 1 Temple Gardens, Temple, London EC4Y 9BB
Registrar of Diocese and Bishop's Legal Secretary Mr Tim Berry, Diocesan Registry, 14 Market Place, Wells, Som BA5 2RE
Tel: (01749) 674747
Fax: (01749) 676585

DIOCESAN ORGANISATIONS
Diocesan Office The Old Deanery, Wells, Som BA5 2UG   Tel: (01749) 670777
Fax: (01749) 674240
e-mail: general@bathwells.anglican.org

ADMINISTRATION
Dioc Synod (Chairman, House of Clergy) Preb Penny West, Vicarage, 35 Kewstoke Rd, Weston Super Mare BS22 9YE   Tel: (01934) 416162; *(Chairman, House of Laity)* Mr Lewis Currie, Chapel Cottage, Gills Lane, Rooksbridge, Som BS26 2TU Tel and Fax: (01934) 750676; *(Secretary)* Mr Nicholas Denison, Dioc Office
Board of Finance (Chairman) Mr Alan King, 97 St Ladoc Rd, Keynsham, Bristol BS18 2EN; *(Secretary)* Mr Nicholas Denison (as above)
Finance and General Purposes Committee Mr Nicholas Denison (as above)
Houses and Glebe Committee Miss Susan George, Dioc Office
Board of Patronage Mr Philip Nokes, Dioc Office

Pastoral Committee Mr Philip Nokes (*as above*)
Redundant Churches Uses Committee Mr Philip Nokes (*as above*)
Designated Officer Mr Philip Nokes (*as above*)
Deputy Dioc Secretary Mr Philip Nokes (*as above*)
Accountant Mr Jonathan Cox
Asst Secretary (*Property*) Miss Susan George (*as above*)

CHURCHES

Advisory Committee for the Care of Churches (*Chairman*) Mr Hugh Playfair, Blackford House, Blackford, Yeovil BA22 7EE; *Tel:* (01963) 440611; (*Secretary*) Mr Tim Berry, Dioc Registry, 14 Market Place, Wells BA5 2RE   *Tel:* (01749) 674747
Association of Change Ringers Preb Christopher Marshall, Tap Cottage, High St, Milverton, Taunton TA4 1LL
Tel: (01823) 400419
Choral Association Mr D. B. Chandler, 69 Grenville Court, Waverley Wharf, Bridgwater, Som TA6 3TY   *Tel:* (01278) 427574

EDUCATION

Board of Education Diocesan Education Office, The Old Deanery, Wells BA5 2UG
Tel: (01749) 670777
Dioc Director of Education Mr Mark Evans
Advisers in Religious Education Mr Phil Metcalfe and Mr Mike Brownbill (*same address*)
Youth Officers Miss Yvonne Criddle, Mr Frank Nealis and Revd David Williamson, Dioc Office

COUNCIL FOR MINISTRY

Chairman The Bishop of Taunton
Director of Training Preb Russell Bowman-Eadie, Dioc Office
Lay Training Adviser Revd Graham Dodds, Dioc Office
Director of Ordinands Preb Rodney Schofield, Rectory, West Monkton, Taunton, Som TA2 8QT   *Tel:* (01823) 412226
Dean of Women's Ministry Vacancy
Vocations Adviser Revd Vaughan Roberts, Rectory, Lower St, Chewton Mendip, Bath BA3 4PD   *Tel:* (01761) 241644
Warden of Readers Very Revd Richard Lewis, The Dean's Lodgings, 25 The Liberty, Wells, Som BA5 2SZ
Tel: (01749) 670278

COUNCIL FOR MISSION

Chairman The Archdeacon of Taunton
Dioc Missioner Canon Geoffrey Walker, 6 The Liberty, Wells, Som BA5 3QN
Tel: (01749) 672224

Ecumenical Officer Revd Robert Shorter c/o Dioc Office
Dioc Adviser for the Ministry of Health and Healing Revd David Howell, 60 Andrew Allan Rd, Rockwell Green, Wellington, Som TA21 9DY   *Tel:* (01823) 664529
Bishop's Renewal Adviser Revd Christian Merivale, Quarry Welham, Castle Cary, Som BA7 7NE   *Tel:* (01963) 350191
World Mission Adviser and Exec Secretary Zambia Link Mrs Jenny Humphries, Dioc Office

COUNCIL FOR SOCIAL RESPONSIBILITY

Chairman The Archdeacon of Wells
Social Responsibility Officer Ms Helen Stanton, Dioc Office
Chaplain to the Deaf Sister Susan Bloomfield, St Nicholas Cottage, Newtown Lane, West Pennard BA6 8NW
Tel: (01458) 834171
Fax: (01458) 835136

STEWARDSHIP

Resources Adviser Miss Fay Wilson-Rudd, Dioc Office

LITURGICAL GROUP

Chairman Revd Julian Smith, St Andrew's Vicarage, 118 Kingston Rd, Taunton TA2 7SR   *Tel:* (01823) 332544

PRESS AND PUBLICATIONS

Communications Officer Revd John Andrews, Rectory, Fosse Rd, Oakhill, Bath   *Tel:* (01749) 841341
Fax: (01749) 841098
Editor of 'The Grapevine' (*Dioc Newspaper*) Mrs Celia Andrews (*same address*)
Editor of Directory and Database Manager Mrs Julienne Jones, Dioc Office

WIDOWS' OFFICER

Preb Patrick Blake, 47 Lower St, Merriott, Som TA16 5NN   *Tel:* (01460) 78932

RETREAT HOUSE

Abbey House, Glastonbury (*Warden* David Hill)   *Tel:* (01458) 831112

DIOCESAN RECORD OFFICE

Somerset County Record Office, Obridge Rd, Taunton, Som TA2 7PU (*County and Diocesan Archivist* Mr Adam Green)
Tel: (01823) 278805

DIOCESAN RESOURCE CENTRE

Old Deanery, Wells BA5 2UG
Tel: (01749) 670777
Warden Mrs Joanne Chillington

RURAL DEANS

ARCHDEACONRY OF WELLS

Axbridge Revd Victor Daley, Vicarage, Cheddar BS27 3RF   *Tel:* (01934) 742535
Bruton Revd John Thorogood, Vicarage, Church Lane, Evercreech BA4 6HV
Tel: (01749) 830222
Fax: (01749) 830870
Cary Revd John Thorogood (*as above*)
Frome Revd John Pescod, Vicarage, Vicarage St, Frome BA11 1PU
Tel: (01373) 462325
Glastonbury Revd Gillian Weymont, Vicarage, Othery, Bridgwater TA7 0QG
Tel: (01823) 698073
Ivelchester Preb Trevor Farmiloe, Vicarage, 10 Water St, Martock TA12 6JN
Tel: (01935) 826113
Merston Preb Mark Ellis, St Michael's Vicarage, Yeovil BA21 4LH
Tel: (01935) 75752
Shepton Mallet Revd Bindon Plowman, Vicarage, Vicarage Lane, Wookey, Wells BA5 1JT   *Tel:* (01749) 677244

ARCHDEACONRY OF BATH

Bath Revd David Perryman, St Luke's Vicarage, Hatfield Rd, Bath BA2 2BD
Tel: (01225) 311904
Chew Magna Revd Richard Hall, Rectory, 12 Beech Rd, Saltford, Bristol BS18 3BE
Tel: (01225) 872275
Locking Revd Geoffrey Hobden, 18 Montpelier, Weston-super-Mare BS23 2RH   *Tel:* (01934) 624376
Midsomer Norton Revd James Balliston Thicke, Westfield Vicarage, Midsomer Norton BA3 4BJ   *Tel:* (01761) 412105
Portishead Revd Alastair Wheeler, Vicarage, Christchurch Close, Nailsea, Bristol BS19 2DL   *Tel:* (01275) 853187

ARCHDEACONRY OF TAUNTON

Bridgwater Preb Roger Packer, Vicarage, 7 Durleigh Rd, Bridgwater TA6 7HU
Tel: (01278) 422437
Crewkerne and Ilminster Revd Philip Lambert, Rectory, Curry Rivel, Langport TA10 0HQ   *Tel:* (01458) 251375
Exmoor Revd Barry Priory, Rectory, Parsons St, Polock,, Minehead TA24 8QL
Tel: (01643) 863172
Quantock Revd Andrew Stevens, Rectory, Kilve, Bridgwater TA5 1DZ
Tel: (01278) 741501
Taunton Revd Nigel Venning, Rectory, Rectory Drive, Staplegrove, Taunton TA2 6AP   *Tel:* (01823) 272787
Tone Revd Kevin Tingay, Rectory, Bradford on Tone, Taunton TA4 1HG
Tel: (01823) 461423

DIOCESE OF BIRMINGHAM

Founded in 1905. Birmingham; Sandwell, except for areas in the north (LICHFIELD) and in the west (WORCESTER); Solihull, except for areas in the east (COVENTRY) and in the west (WORCESTER); a few parishes in Staffordshire and in the County of Hereford and Worcester.

Population 1,438,000   Area 292 sq m
Stipendiary Clergy 205   Benefices 156
Parishes 165   Churches 191

BISHOP (7th)
Rt Revd Mark Santer, Bishop's Croft, Harborne, Birmingham, B17 0BG [1987]
Tel: 0121–427 1163
Fax: 0121–426 1322
[Mark Birmingham]

Domestic Chaplain Revd James Langstaff, East Wing, Bishop's Croft, Old Church Rd, Birmingham B17 0BG
Tel: 0121–427 2295 (Home)

SUFFRAGAN BISHOP
ASTON Rt Revd John Austin, Strensham House, 8 Strensham Hill, Moseley, Birmingham B13 8AG [1992]
Tel: 0121–449 0675 (Home)
0121–428 2228 or 0121–427 5141 (Office)
Fax: 0121–428 1114

HONORARY ASSISTANT BISHOPS
Rt Revd Anthony Charles Dumper, 117 Berberry Close, Bournville, Birmingham B30 1TB [1993]
Tel: 0121–458 3011 (Home)
Rt Revd Michael Humphrey Dickens Whinney, 3 Moor Green Lane, Moseley, Birmingham B13 8NE [1989]
Tel: 0121–249 2856
Rt Revd David Evans, 12 Fox Hill, Birmingham B29 4AG [1998]
Tel: 0121–472 2616
Fax: 0121–472 7977
e-mail: SAMSGB@compuserve.com
Rt Revd Peter Hall, 27 Jacey Rd, Edgbaston, Birmingham B16 0LL [1998]
Tel: 0121–455 9240

CATHEDRAL CHURCH OF ST PHILIP
Provost Very Revd Peter Austin Berry, The Provost's House, 16 Pebble Mill Rd, Edgbaston, Birmingham B5 7SA [1986]
Tel: 0121–472 0709
Cathedral Office Birmingham Cathedral, Colmore Row, Birmingham B3 2QB
Tel: 0121–236 4333/6323
Fax: 0121–212 0868

Canons Residentiary
Ven John Barton, 26 George Rd, Edgbaston, Birmingham B15 1PJ [1990]
Tel: 0121–454 5525 (Home)
0121–427 5141 (Office)
Fax: 0121–455 6085
Canon Gary O'Neill, 119 Selly Park Rd, Selly Oak, Birmingham B29 7HY [1997]
Tel: 0121–472 0146
Canon David Lee PH D, Dioc Office, 175 Harborne Park Rd, Harborne, Birmingham B17 0BH [1996]
Tel: 0121–427 5141
Fax: 0121–428 1114
Chaplain Revd Val Cory, Cathedral Office
Lay Administrator and Chapter Clerk Dr Andrew Page, Cathedral Office
Cathedral Organist Mr Marcus Huxley, Cathedral Office

ARCHDEACONS
ASTON Ven John Barton, 26 George Rd, Edgbaston, Birmingham B15 1PJ [1990]
Tel: 0121–454 5525 (Home)
0121–427 5141 (Office)
Fax: 0121–455 6085
BIRMINGHAM Ven John Duncan, 122 Westfield Rd, Edgbaston, Birmingham B15 3JQ [1985]
Tel: 0121–454 3402
Fax: 0121–455 6178

CONVOCATION (MEMBERS OF THE HOUSE OF CLERGY OF THE GENERAL SYNOD)
Dignitaries in Convocation
The Provost of Birmingham
The Archdeacon of Birmingham
Proctors for Clergy
Revd Eve Pitts
Revd George Kovoor
Revd Hayward Osborne

MEMBERS OF THE HOUSE OF LAITY OF THE GENERAL SYNOD
Dr Raman Bedi
Mrs Elizabeth Fisher
Mrs Bridget Langstaff

DIOCESAN OFFICERS
Dioc Secretary Mr Jim Drennan, 175 Harborne Park Rd, Harborne, Birmingham B17 0BH
Tel: 0121–427 5141
Fax: 0121–428 1114
Chancellor of Diocese His Honour Judge Francis Aglionby, 30 The Croft, Houghton, Carlisle, Cumbria CA3 0LP
Registrar of Diocese and Bishop's Legal Secretary Mr Hugh Carslake, Martineau Johnson, St Philip's House, St Philip's Place, Birmingham B3 2PP
Tel: 0121–200 3300
Fax: 0121–200 3330
Dioc Surveyor Mr Alan Broadway, Dioc Office

DIOCESAN ORGANISATIONS
Diocesan Office 175 Harborne Park Rd, Harborne, Birmingham B17 0BH
Tel: 0121–427 5141
Fax: 0121–428 1114

ADMINISTRATION
Dioc Synod (Chairman, House of Clergy) Revd John Hughes, 99 Wentworth Rd, Harborne, Birmingham B17 9ST Tel: 0121–427 4601; *(Chairman, House of Laity)* Dr Terry Slater, 5 Windermere Rd, Moseley, Birmingham B13 8HS; *(Secretary)* Mr Jim Drennan, Dioc Office
Board of Finance (Chairman) Mr Philip Couse, 23 Frederick Rd, Edgbaston, Birmingham B15 1JN Tel: 0121–455 9930
Fax: 0121–455 7254
(Secretary) Mr Jim Drennan *(as above)*
Deputy Secretary (Finance) Mr Paul Wilson, Dioc Office
Parsonages Committee Mr Jim Drennan *(as above)*
Dioc Trustees (Secretary) Mr Paul Wilson *(as above)*
Pastoral Committee Mr Jim Drennan *(as above)*
Designated Officer Mr Hugh Carslake, Martineau Johnson, St Philip's House, St Philip's Place, Birmingham B3 2PP
Tel: 0121–200 3300
Fax: 0121–625 3330

CHURCHES
Advisory Committee for the Care of Churches (Chairman) Mr William Wood, c/o Dioc Office; *(Secretary)* Mr Tim Clayton, Dioc Office

EDUCATION
Dioc Director of Education Dr Stephen Partridge, Dioc Office

MINISTRY
Director of Ordinands and Women's Ministry Canon Marlene Parsons, Dioc Office
Director of Post-Ordination Training The Bishop of Aston *(as above)*

Board for Ministries
Director for Ministries Revd Dr Brian Russell, Dioc Office
Bishop's Adviser for Lay Adult Education and Training Dr Pam de Wit, Dioc Office
Bishop's Adviser for Black Ministry Dr Mukti Barton, Dioc Office
Bishop's Adviser for Children's Work Revd Ruth Yeoman, Dioc Office
Bishop's Adviser for Youth Work Mr Steve Summers, Dioc Office
Bishop's Adviser for Liturgy Revd Brian Hall, Handsworth Rectory, 288 Hamstead Rd, Handsworth Wood B20 2RB
Tel: 0121–554 3407
Dioc Music Adviser Mr Mick Perrier, Dioc Office
Readers' Board (*Secretary*) Dr Kathleen Higgs, 21 Butter Walk, West Heath, Birmingham B38 8JQ   *Tel:* (0121–459 4774

LITURGICAL
see Board for Ministries

BOARD FOR MISSION
Chairman The Bishop of Aston (*as above*)
Director for Mission Canon David Lee PH D, Dioc Office
Bishop's Ecumenical Adviser Canon Richard Bollard, Vicarage, High St, Coleshill B46 3BP   *Tel:* (01675) 462188
Bishop's Adviser for Stewardship Canon Jim Pendorf, 120 Stanhope St, Highgate, Birmingham B12 0XB   *Tel:* (0973) 265037

PRESS AND PUBLICATIONS
Communications Officer Ms Sue Primmer, Dioc Office   *Tel:* 0121–507 0247 (Home)
Editor of Dioc Leaflet Ms Sue Primmer (*as above*)
Editor of Dioc Directory Ms Sue Primmer (*as above*)

INDUSTRIAL RELATIONS
Industrial Chaplain Miss Melanie King, Dioc Office

CIGB Co-ordinator Revd Trevor Lockwood (Methodist), Dioc Office

DIOCESAN RECORD OFFICES
Birmingham Reference Library, Birmingham B3 3HQ, Archives Dept Central Library, *Tel:* 0121–235 4219 (*For parish records in the City of Birmingham*); Warwick County Record Office, Priory Park, Cape Rd, Warwick CV34 4JS, *County Archivist* Mr M. W. Farr, *Tel:* (01926) 410410, Ext 2508 (*For parish records in the Metropolitan Borough of Solihull, together with those still in the county of Warwick*); Sandwell Community History and Archives Service, Smethwick Community Library, High St, Smethwick, Warley, W Midlands B66 1AB *Tel:* 0121–558 2561 (*For parish records in the Metropolitan Borough of Sandwell*)

BOARD FOR SOCIAL RESPONSIBILITY
Community Projects Officer Canon David Collyer, Dioc Office
Bishop's Adviser for Health and Social Care Revd Jim Woodward, The Master's House, Temple Balsall, Solihull B91 0BH
Tel: (01564) 730249

CHRISTIAN STEWARDSHIP
see Board for Mission

ACTION IN THE CITY PROJECTS
Chairman The Archdeacon of Aston (*as above*)
Secretary Canon David Collyer (*as above*)

RURAL DEANS
ARCHDEACONRY OF ASTON
Aston Revd David Newsome, All Saints Vicarage, Broomfield Rd, Erdington, Birmingham B23 7QA   *Tel:* 0121–373 0730
Bordesley Revd Simon Holloway, Christ Church Vicarage, 34 Grantham Rd, Birmingham B11 1LU   *Tel:* 0121–772 6558

Coleshill Canon Christopher Boyle, Rectory, Rectory Lane, Castle Bromwich, Birmingham B36 9DH
Tel: 0121–747 2281
Polesworth Revd Derek Carrivick, Rectory, Dexter Lane, Hurley, Atherstone CV9 2JQ
Tel: (01827) 874252
Solihull Revd Adrian Leahy, St Mary's House, Hob's Meadow, Solihull B92 8PN
Tel: 0121–743 4955
Sutton Coldfield Revd Roger Hindley, 61 Mere Green Rd, Sutton Coldfield B75 5BW
Tel: 0121–308 0074
Yardley Revd Richard Postill, Vicarage, 34 Dudley Park Rd, Acocks Green, Birmingham B27 6QR   *Tel:* 0121–706 9764

ARCHDEACONRY OF BIRMINGHAM
Birmingham City Centre Canon Jim Pendorf, St Alban's Vicarage, 120 Stanhope St, Highgate, Birmingham B12 0XB
Tel: 0121–440 4605
Edgbaston Revd John Barnett, Rectory, 773 Hagley Rd West, Quinton, Birmingham B32 1AJ   *Tel:* 0121–422 2031
Handsworth Canon Rob Morris, St James Vicarage, Austin Rd, Handsworth, Birmingham B21 8NU
Tel: 0121–554 4151
King's Norton Revd Christopher Jackson, St David's Vicarage, 49 Shenley Green, Birmingham B29 4HH
Tel: 0121–475 4874
Moseley Revd Hayward Osborne, Vicarage, 18 Oxford Rd, Moseley, Birmingham B13 9EH   *Tel:* 0121–449 1459/2243
Shirley Revd Michael Caddy, Vicarage, 2 Bishopton Close, Shirley, Solihull B90 4AH   *Tel:* 0121–744 3123
Warley Revd Martin Gorick, Vicarage, Church Rd, Smethwick, Warley B67 6EE
Tel: 0121–558 1763

DIOCESE OF BLACKBURN

Founded in 1926. Lancashire, except for areas in the east (BRADFORD) and in the south (LIVERPOOL, MANCHESTER); a few parishes in Wigan.

Population 1,282,000   Area 878 sq m
Stipendiary Clergy 249   Benefices 222
Parishes 247   Churches 284

BISHOP (7th)
Rt Revd Alan David Chesters, Bishop's House, Ribchester Rd, Clayton-le-Dale, Blackburn, Lancs BB1 9EF [1989]
Tel: (01254) 248234
Fax: (01254) 246668
e-mail: bishop.blackburn@ukonline.co.uk
[Alan Blackburn]

Domestic Chaplain Revd Stephen Ferns, Bishop's House

SUFFRAGAN BISHOPS
LANCASTER Rt Revd (Geoffrey) Stephen Pedley, Shireshead Vicarage, Forton, Preston PR3 0AE [1998]   Tel: (01524) 799900
Fax: (01524) 799901
BURNLEY Rt Revd Martyn William Jarrett, Dean House, 449 Padiham Rd, Burnley, Lancs BB12 6TE [1994]
Tel: (01282) 423564
Fax: (01282) 835496

CATHEDRAL CHURCH OF ST MARY THE VIRGIN
Provost Very Revd David Frayne, Provost's House, Preston New Rd, Blackburn, Lancs BB2 6PS [1992]   Tel: (01254) 52502
e-mail: cathedral@blackburnce.u-net.com
Cathedral Office Cathedral Close, Blackburn BB1 5AA   Tel: (01254) 51491
Fax: (01254) 689666
e-mail: cathedral@blackburnce.u-net.com
Canons Residentiary
Sacrist Canon Andrew Hindley, 22 Billinge Ave, Blackburn, Lancs BB2 6SD [1996]   Tel: (01254) 261152
Chancellor Canon David Galilee, 25 Ryburn Ave, Blackburn BB2 7AU [1995]
Tel: (01254) 671540
Canon Peter Ballard, Wheatfield, Dallas Rd, Lancaster [1998]
e-mail: peter.j.ballard@btinternet.com
Chapter Clerk Mr Thomas Hoyle, Dioc Registry, Cathedral Close, Blackburn, Lancs BB1 5AB   Tel: (01254) 51491
e-mail: registry@blackburnce.u-net.com

Director of Music Mr Richard Tanner, 8 West Park Rd, Blackburn BB2 6DG
Tel: (01254) 56752
e-mail: rtanner117@aol.com

ARCHDEACONS
BLACKBURN Ven Dr John Marsh, 19 Clarence Park, Blackburn BB2 7FA [1996]
Tel: (01254) 262571
Fax: (01254) 263394
e-mail: vendocjon@aol.com
LANCASTER Ven Robert Ladds, Vicarage, Hall Lane, St Michael's on Wyre, Preston PR3 0TQ [1997]   Tel: (01995) 679242
Fax: (01995) 679747
e-mail: venerabilis@ukonline.co.uk

CONVOCATION (MEMBERS OF THE HOUSE OF CLERGY OF THE GENERAL SYNOD)
The Archdeacon of Blackburn
Proctors for Clergy:
Canon Eddie Burns
Revd Brian Pithers
Canon Paul Warren
Revd Colin Williams
(One Vacancy)

MEMBERS OF THE HOUSE OF LAITY OF THE GENERAL SYNOD
Mrs Margaret Baxter
Mr Gerald Burrows
Mr James Garbett
Mr Ian Garden
Mr John Hudson
Mrs Roberta Ladds
Mr John Leigh
Miss Diana Parker
Mr George Phythian

DIOCESAN OFFICERS
Dioc Secretary Revd Michael Wedgeworth, Church House, Cathedral Close, Blackburn, Lancs BB1 5AA
Tel: (01254) 54421
Fax: (01254) 699963
e-mail: diosec@blackburnce.u-net.com
Chancellor of Diocese His Honour Judge John Bullimore, 137 Edge Lane, Thornhill, Dewsbury, W Yorks WF12 0NB
Tel: (01924) 463911
Registrar of Diocese and Bishop's Legal Secretary Mr Thomas Hoyle, Diocesan Registry, Cathedral Close, Blackburn, Lancs BB1 5AB   Tel: (01254) 54421
Fax: (01254) 699963
e-mail: registry@blackburnce.u-net.com

DIOCESAN ORGANISATIONS
Diocesan Office Church House, Cathedral Close, Blackburn, Lancs BB1 5AA
Tel: (01254) 54421
Fax: (01254) 699963
e-mail: diosec@blackburnce.u-net.com

ADMINISTRATION
Dioc Synod (Chairman, House of Clergy) Canon Edward Burns, Christ Church Vicarage, 19 Vicarage Close, Fulwood, Preston PR2 4EG Tel: (01772) 719210; *(Chairman, House of Laity)* Mr Derrick Walkden, 2 Butterlands, Preston PR1 5TJ Tel: (01772) 792224; *(Secretary)* Revd Michael Wedgeworth, Church House
Board of Finance (Chairman) Mr R. M. Edwards, West Bradford Rd, Waddington, Clitheroe BB7 3JD   Tel: (01200) 426625
(Secretary) Revd Michael Wedgeworth *(as above)*
Property Unit (Chairman) Canon J. Duxbury; *(Secretary)* Revd Michael Wedgeworth *(as above)*
Pastoral Committee Revd Michael Wedgeworth *(as above)*
Designated Officer Mr Thomas Hoyle, Dioc Registry, Cathedral Close, Blackburn, Lancs BB1 5AB   Tel: (01254) 54421/52821

CHURCHES
Advisory Committee for the Care of Churches
(Chairman) Vacancy
(Secretary) Vacancy

EDUCATION
Education Council (Dioc Director) Revd Peter Ballard, Church House
e-mail: educn@blackburnce.u-net.com
Principal Adviser Lisa Fenton, Church House
Youth Committee Revd Brian McConkey, Church House
e-mail: youth@blackburnce.u-net.com
Children's Work Adviser Mrs Mary Binks, Church House
e-mail: children@blackburnce.u-net.com

MINISTRY
Director of Ordinands Revd Geoffrey Connor, Vicarage, Church Lane, Whitechapel, Preston PR3 2EP   Tel: (01995) 40282
Director of Training Canon Cyril Ashton,

Charis, 1 Piccadilly Grove, Scotforth, Lancaster LA1 4PP
    Tel and *Fax:* (01524) 841495
Post-Ordination Training Revd John Priestley, Vicarage, Keighley Rd, Colne BB8 7HF   *Tel:* (01282) 863511
Mothers' Union Mrs P. Rothwell, 7 Aldon Grove, Longton, Preston PR4 5PJ
       Tel: (01772) 614045
Readers' Board Mr William McKend, 7 Wolverton Ave, Blackpool FY2 9NT
      Tel: (01253) 51054
Warden of Pastoral Auxiliaries Revd James Burns, St Mary's Rectory, 17 Church Rd, Rutford, Ormskirk L40 1TA
      Tel: (01704) 821261
Resources Officer Mr Dick Clague, Church House
 e-mail: ministry@blackburnce.u-net.com

LITURGICAL
Chairman Canon Paul Warren, Rectory, 13 Rectory Lane, Standish, Wigan WN6 0XA
      Tel: (01257) 421396
Secretary Revd Iain Rennie, Vicarage, Hornby, Lancaster LA2 8JY
      Tel: (01524) 221238

MISSIONARY AND ECUMENICAL
Board for Mission and Unity Rt Revd Donald Nestor, Rectory, South Rd, Bretherton, Preston PR5 7AH *Tel:* (01772) 600206
      Fax: (01772) 600622
  e-mail: sjb@bafs.demon.co.uk
Director for Mission and Evangelism Revd Simon Bessant, 1 Swallow Fields, Pleckgate, Blackburn BB1 8NR
    Tel and *Fax:* (01524) 580176
  e-mail: s.d.bessant@dial.pipex.com
Ecumenical Officer Vacancy

PRESS AND PUBLICATIONS
Dioc Communications Officer Mr Martyn Halsall, 42 Knowsley Rd, Ainsworth, Bolton BL2 5PU *Tel* and *Fax:* (01204) 384996
 e-mail: martyn.halsall@ukonline.co.uk
Dioc Directory Mrs Cate Hart, Church House

DIOCESAN RECORDS
Diocesan Registry, Cathedral Close, Blackburn, Lancs BB1 5AB
      Tel: (01254) 54421;
Lancashire Record Office, Bow Lane, Preston PR1 8ND, *County Archivist* Mr Bruce Jackson   *Tel:* (01772) 254868

SOCIAL RESPONSIBILITY
Social Responsibility Officer Revd Paul Battersby, St Mary's House, Cathedral Close, Blackburn BB1 5AA *Tel:* (01254) 54421
Principal Diocesan Adoption Agency Mr Brian Williams, St Mary's House
      Tel: (01254) 57759
Chaplain with the Deaf Revd Stephen Locke
Interfaith Adviser Vacancy

RURAL DEANS
ARCHDEACONRY OF BLACKBURN
Accrington Revd Michael Ratcliffe, St Paul's Vicarage, 71 Union Rd, Oswaldtwistle, Accrington BB5 3DD
      Tel: (01254) 231038
Blackburn with Darwen Revd Kevin Arkell, Rectory, St Peter's Close, Darwen, Lancs BB3 2EA   *Tel:* (01254) 702411
Burnley Revd Brian Swallow, St Stephen's Vicarage, 154 Todmorden Rd, Burnley BB11 3ER   *Tel:* (01282) 424733

Chorley Revd David Morgan, St Paul's Vicarage, Railway Rd, Adlington, Chorley PR6 9QZ   *Tel:* (01257) 480253
Leyland Revd Arthur Ranson, St Ambrose Vicarage, 61 Moss Lane, Leyland PR5 2SH
      Tel: (01772) 462204
Pendle Revd Edward Saville, Brierfield Vicarage, 22 Reedley Rd, Reedley, Burnley BB10 2LU *Tel:* (01282) 613235
 e-mail: 100553.1707@compuserve.com
Whalley Revd Paul Smith, Vicarage, Somerset Rd, Rishton, Blackburn BB1 4BP
      Tel: (01254) 886191

ARCHDEACONRY OF LANCASTER
Blackpool Revd Michael Wood, St Mary's Vicarage, 59 Stony Hill Ave, Blackpool FY4 1PR   *Tel:* (01253) 342713
Garstang Revd Edward Angus, St Oswald's Vicarage, Lancaster Rd, Knott End on Sea, Poulton Le Fylde FY6 0DU
      Tel: (01253) 810297
Kirkham Canon Godfrey Hirst, Vicarage, Church Rd, Lytham St Annes FY8 5PX
   Tel and *Fax:* (01253) 736168
Lancaster Revd Gary Ingram, Rectory, Church Walk, Morecambe LA4 5PR
  Tel and *Fax:* (01524) 410941 (Home)
     Tel: (01524) 833267 (Office)
Poulton Revd David Reeves, Vicarage, Rough Lee Rd, Thornton-Cleveleys, Blackpool FY5 1DP *Tel:* (01253) 852153
Preston Revd John Powell, Vicarage, 240 Tulketh Rd, Ashton-on-Ribble, Preston PR2 1ES   *Tel:* (01772) 726848
Tunstall Revd Gary Bowness, Vicarage, Arkholme, Carnforth, Lancs LA6 1AX
      Tel: (01524) 221359

DIOCESE OF BRADFORD

Founded in 1919. Bradford; the western quarter of North Yorkshire; areas of east Lancashire, south-east Cumbria and Leeds.

Population 656,000   Area 920 sq m
Stipendiary Clergy 122   Benefices 112
Parishes 131   Churches 166

BISHOP (8th)
Rt Revd David James Smith, Bishopscroft, Ashwell Rd, Bradford, W Yorks BD9 4AU [1992]   *Tel:* (01274) 545414
Fax: (01274) 544831
e-mail: bishbrad@nildram.co.uk
[David Bradford]

Personal Executive Assistant Canon David Bruno (same address)

HONORARY ASSISTANT BISHOP
Rt Revd Peter St George Vaughan, 1 Dawson Lane, Tong Village, Bradford, W Yorks BD4 0ST   *Tel and Fax:* 0113–285 3924

CATHEDRAL CHURCH OF ST PETER
Provost Very Revd John Stephen Richardson, Provost's House, 1 Cathedral Close, Bradford, W Yorks BD1 4EG [1990]
Tel: (01274) 777722
Fax: (01274) 777730
Canons Residentiary
Canon Christopher Lewis, 2 Cathedral Close, Bradford, W Yorks BD1 4EG [1993]
Tel: (01274) 727806
Fax: (01274) 777736
Canon Geoffrey Smith, 3 Cathedral Close, Bradford BD1 4EG   *Tel:* (01274) 777729
Cathedral Adviser in Development and Education Mrs Caroline Moore, Bradford Cathedral, 1 Stott Hill, Bradford BD1 4EH
Tel: (01274) 777724
Fax: (01274) 777730
Cathedral Administrator Mrs Sheila Holmes (same address)   *Tel:* (01274) 777723
Cathedral Organist Mr Alan Horsey, 1 Stott Hill, Bradford BD1 4EH
Tel: (01274) 777725
Fax: (01274) 777730

ARCHDEACONS
CRAVEN Ven Malcolm Grundy, Vicarage, Gisburn, Clitheroe, Lancs BB7 4HR [1994]
Tel: (01200) 445214
Fax: (01200) 445816
e-mail: adcraven@gisburn.u-net.com

BRADFORD Ven David Shreeve, Rowan House, 11 The Rowans, Baildon, W Yorks BD17 5DB [1984]   *Tel:* (01274) 583735
Fax: (01274) 586184

CONVOCATION (MEMBERS OF THE HOUSE OF CLERGY OF THE GENERAL SYNOD)
Dignitaries in Convocation
The Provost of Bradford
The Archdeacon of Craven
Proctors for Clergy
Revd Paul Ayers
Canon Alan Fell
Canon Max Wigley

MEMBERS OF THE HOUSE OF LAITY OF THE GENERAL SYNOD
Mrs Elaine Appelbee
Ms Sallie Bassham
Mr Tony Hesselwood

DIOCESAN OFFICERS
Dioc Secretary Mr Malcolm Halliday, Cathedral Hall, Stott Hill, Bradford, W Yorks BD1 4ET   *Tel:* (01274) 725958
Fax: (01274) 726343
Chancellor of Diocese His Honour David Savill, Priory Cottage, Abbey Rd, Knaresborough, N Yorks HG5 8HX
Tel: (01423) 862309
Registrar of Diocese and Bishop's Legal Secretary Mr Jeremy Mackrell, Diocesan Registry, 6/14 Devonshire St, Keighley, W Yorks BD21 2AY   *Tel:* (01535) 667731
Fax: (01535) 609748
Dioc Surveyors Mr Barry Rawson, The Gatehouse, Skipton Castle, Skipton, N Yorks BD23 1AL *Tel:* (01756) 794881; Mr Michael Greaves, Dacre, Son & Hartley, 24 Devonshire St, Keighley BD21 2BD
Tel: (01535) 605646
Fax: (01535) 610056
Dioc Insurance Adviser Mr John Watts, Hainsworth Watts, Greengates Lodge, 830A Harrogate Rd, Bradford BD10 0RA
Tel: (01274) 619002
Fax: (01274) 619084

DIOCESAN ORGANISATIONS
Diocesan Office Cathedral Hall, Stott Hill, Bradford, W Yorks BD1 4ET
Tel: (01274) 725958
Fax: (01274) 726343

ADMINISTRATION
Dioc Synod (Chairman, House of Clergy) Canon Max Wigley, St John's Vicarage, Barcroft Rd, Yeadon, Leeds LS19 7XZ *Tel:* 0113–250 2274; (*Chairman, House of Laity*) Mr Chris Wright, 15 Walker Close, Glusburn, Keighley BD20 8PW *Tel:* (01535) 634526; (*Secretary*) Mr Malcolm Halliday, Dioc Office
Board of Finance (Chairman) Mr Tony Hesselwood, 38 Bromley Rd, Shipley, Bradford BD18 4DT   *Tel:* (01274) 586613
(*Secretary*) Mr Malcolm Halliday (as above)
Property Committee (Secretary) Mr Malcolm Halliday (as above)
Pastoral Committee Mr Malcolm Halliday (as above)
Ecumenical Officer Canon Bruce Grainger, Vicarage, Oxenhope, Keighley BD22 9SA
Tel: (01535) 42529
Designated Officer Mr Jeremy Mackrell, Diocesan Registry, 6/14 Devonshire St, Keighley, W Yorks BD21 2AY
Tel: (01535) 667731
Fax: (01535) 609748
Resources Centres Administrator Mrs Debbie Child, Dioc Office   *Tel:* (01274) 737870
Fax: (01274) 726343

CHURCHES
Diocesan Advisory Committee (Chairman) Mr Leonard Darley, 16 Aireville Crescent, Bradford BD9 4EU   *Tel:* (01274) 598879
(*Secretary*) Mr Alex McLelland, Dioc Office

CHURCH IN SOCIETY
Bishop's Officer Mrs Elaine Appelbee, 168 Highfield Lane, Keighley, W Yorks BD21 3HH   *Tel:* (01535) 671377
Fax: (01535) 690709
Chaplain to Students Vacancy, Anglican Chaplaincy, 2 Ashgrove, Bradford BD7 1BN   *Tel:* (01274) 727034
Interfaith Adviser Dr Philip Lewis, 9 Garden Lane, Heaton, Bradford BD9 5QJ
Tel: (01274) 543891
Rural Affairs Revd Leslie Foster, The Lune Vicarage, 5 Highfield Rd, Sedbergh, Cumbria LA10 5DH   *Tel:* (015396) 20670
Social Responsibility see Bishop's Officer
Urban Adviser see Bishop's Officer

EDUCATION
Director of Education Vacancy, c/o Dioc Office

MINISTRY AND TRAINING

Bishop's Officer Canon Christopher Lewis, 2 Cathedral Close, Bradford, W Yorks BD1 4EG *Tel:* (01274) 727806 *Fax:* (01274) 722898
Director of In-Service Training see Bishop's Officer
Director of Post-Ordination Training see Bishop's Officer
Directors of Ordinands Revd Richard Hoyal, 14 Queen's Rd, Ilkley LS29 9QJ *Tel* and *Fax:* (01943) 607015
Associate Director of Ordinands Revd Dr Susan Penfold, Rectory, 47 Kirkgate, Shipley BD18 3EH *Tel* and *Fax:* (01274) 583652
Adult Education Officer Dr Stephen Carr, Flat 3, Clergy House, 1 Barkerend Rd, Bradford, W Yorks BD3 9AF *Tel:* (01274) 734723
Registrar for Readers Mr Jeremy Mackrell, Dioc Registry
Warden of Readers Revd Dr Paul Moore, Vicarage, Kildwick, Keighley BD20 9BB *Tel:* (01535) 633307
Retired Clergy and Widows Officer Revd Kenneth Killock, 15 Warwick Rd, Bradford BD4 7RA *Tel:* (01274) 394462

WORLD CHURCH LINKS

Chairman The Archdeacon of Craven (*as above*)
Officer Revd Pauline Ballaman, 12 Laburnum Grove, Cross Roads, Keighley BD22 9EP *Tel:* (01535) 646205

PARISH MISSION AND DEVELOPMENT

Bishop's Officer Vacancy
Children's Work Adviser Revd Elizabeth Thomas, Vicarage, Denholme, W Yorks BD13 4EN *Tel* and *Fax:* (01274) 832813
Adviser in Evangelism Revd Robin Gamble, 6 Glenhurst Rd, Shipley BD18 4DZ *Tel:* (01274) 586414

Healing Revd David Swales, 18 Sunhurst Drive, Oakworth, Keighley BD22 7RG *Tel:* (01535) 647335
Liturgy Canon Geoffrey Smith, 3 Cathedral Close, Bradford BD1 4EG *Tel:* (01274) 777729
Millennium Adviser Vacancy
Mission Audit see Bishop's Officer
Stewardship see Bishop's Officer
Tourism Adviser Vacancy
Youth Adviser Revd Viv Ashworth, Vicarage, Ingleton, Carnforth, Lancs LA6 3HG *Tel:* (015242) 41440

PRESS AND PUBLICATIONS

Communications and Press Officer Ms Alison Bogle, 2 Springfield Terrace, Guiseley, Leeds LS20 9AW *Tel:* (01943) 870367 0468 110175 (Mobile)
Dioc News Ms Alison Bogle (*as above*)
Newsround Mr David Markham, 29 Ashley Rd, Bingley, W Yorks BD16 1DZ *Tel:* (01274) 567180

DIOCESAN RECORD OFFICES

West Yorkshire Archives Service, 15 Canal Rd, Bradford BD1 4AT, *Archivist* Mr Ian Mason, *Tel:* (01274) 731931 (*For parishes in Bradford Metropolitan District*); Archives Dept, Central Library, Northgate House, Halifax HX1 5LA, *Archivist* Mr A. Bettridge, *Tel:* (01422) 357257 (*For parishes in Calderdale Metropolitan District*); Record Office, County Offices, Kendal LA9 4RQ, *County Archivist* Miss S. J. MacPherson, County Record Office, The Castle, Carlisle CA3 8UR, *Tel:* (01228) 23455 (*For parishes in Cumbria County*); County Record Office, Bow Lane, Preston PR1 2RE, *County Archivist* Mr B. Jackson, *Tel:* (01772) 254868 (*For parishes in Lancashire County*); Archives Dept, Leeds District Archives, Chapeltown Rd, Sheepscar, Leeds LS7 3AP, *Archivist* Mr W. J. Connor, *Tel:* 0113–262 8339 (*For parishes in Leeds Metropolitan District*); County Record Office, County Hall, Northallerton DL7 8SG, *County Archivist* Mr M. Y. Ashcroft, *Tel:* (01609) 3123, *Ext* 455 (*For parishes in North Yorkshire County*)

RURAL DEANS

ARCHDEACONRY OF BRADFORD

Airedale Canon Ralph Crowe, Vicarage, St Chad's Rd, Toller Lane, Bradford BD8 9DE *Tel:* (01274) 543957
Bowling and Horton Revd Steve Allen, Vicarage, 30 Bartle Close, Bradford BD7 4QH *Tel:* (01274) 521456
Calverley Revd Simon Bailey, Vicarage, Galloway Lane, Pudsey, Leeds LS28 8JR *Tel:* (01274) 662735
Otley Revd Peter Sutcliffe, Vicarage, Cornmill Lane, Burley-in-Wharfedale, Ilkley LS29 7DR *Tel:* (01943) 863216

ARCHDEACONRY OF CRAVEN

Bowland Canon David Rhodes, Vicarage, Giggleswick, Settle BD24 0AP *Tel:* (01729) 822425
Ewecross Canon John Bearpark, St Margaret's Vicarage, 27 Station Rd, High Bentham, Lancs LA2 7LH *Tel:* (0152 42) 61321
Skipton Revd John Ward, The Beeches, Bolton Abbey, Skipton BD23 6EX *Tel:* (01756) 710326 (Home) (01756) 710238 (Office)
South Craven Revd Peter Endall, St Barnabas Vicarage, Spring Ave, Thwaites Brow, Keighley BD21 4TA *Tel:* (01535) 602830

DIOCESE OF BRISTOL

Founded in 1542. Bristol; the southern two thirds of South Gloucestershire; the northern quarter of Wiltshire, except for two parishes (GLOUCESTER); a few parishes in Gloucestershire.

Population 867,000   Area 474 sq m
Stipendiary Clergy 154   Benefices 119
Parishes 167   Churches 205

BISHOP (54th)
Rt Revd Barry Rogerson, Bishop's House, Clifton Hill, Bristol BS8 1BW [1985]
Tel: 0117–973 0222
Fax: 0117–923 9670
e-mail: 106430.1040@compuserve.com
[Barry Bristol]

SUFFRAGAN BISHOP
SWINDON Rt Revd Michael Doe, Mark House, Field Rise, Swindon SN1 4HP [1994]   *Tel and Fax:* (01793) 538654
e-mail: 106064.431@compuserve.com

CATHEDRAL CHURCH OF THE HOLY AND UNDIVIDED TRINITY
Dean Very Revd Robert Grimley, The Deanery, 20 Charlotte St, Bristol BS1 5PZ [1997]   *Tel:* 0117–926 2443
Cathedral Office Bristol Cathedral, Abbey Gatehouse, College Green, Bristol BS1 5TJ
Tel: 0117–926 4879
Fax: 0117–925 3678
Canons Residentiary
Precentor Canon John Simpson, 55 Salisbury Rd, Redland, Bristol BS6 7AS [1989]
Tel: 0117–942 1452
Treasurer Canon Peter Johnson, 41 Salisbury Rd, Redland, Bristol BS6 7AR [1991]
Tel: 0117–944 4464
Theologian Canon Douglas Holt, 9 Leigh Rd, Clifton, Bristol BS8 2DA [1998]
Tel: 0117–973 7427
Administrator Mrs Joy Coupe, Cathedral Office
Cathedral Organist Mr Mark Lee, Cathedral Office   *Tel:* 0117–926 4879

ARCHDEACONS
BRISTOL Vacancy, 10 Great Brockeridge, Westbury-on-Trym, Bristol BS9 3TY
Tel and Fax: 0117–962 2438
SWINDON Ven Alan Hawker, 2 Louviers Way, Swindon, Wilts SN1 4DU [1998]
Tel: (01793) 644556
Fax: (01793) 495352

CONVOCATION (MEMBERS OF THE HOUSE OF CLERGY OF THE GENERAL SYNOD)
The Archdeacon of Swindon
Proctors for Clergy
Canon David Gillett
Canon George Mitchell
Revd John Risdon

MEMBERS OF THE HOUSE OF LAITY OF THE GENERAL SYNOD
Mrs Katy Blake
Mr David Bone
Ms Jill Dickinson
Dr Matthew Hunt

DIOCESAN OFFICERS
Dioc Secretary Mrs Lesley Farrall, Diocesan Church House, 23 Great George St, Bristol BS1 5QZ   *Tel:* 0117–921 4411
Fax: 0117–925 0460
Chancellor of Diocese Chanc Sir David Calcutt, 35 Essex St, Temple, London WC2R 3AR   *Tel:* 0171–353 6381
Registrar of Diocese and Bishop's Legal Secretary Mr Tim Berry, Harris and Harris, 14 Market Place, Wells BA5 2RE
Tel: (01749) 674747
Fax: (01749) 676585

DIOCESAN ORGANISATIONS
Diocesan Office Diocesan Church House, 23 Great George St, Bristol BS1 5QZ
Tel: 0117- 921 4411
Fax: 0117–925 0460

ADMINISTRATION
Assistant Dioc Secretary Mrs Sally Moody, Dioc Church House
Dioc Synod (*Chairman, House of Clergy*) Canon George Mitchell, Vicarage, Church Ave, Warmley, Bristol BS30 5JJ *Tel:* 0117–967 3965; (*Chairman, House of Laity*) Mrs Margaret Williams, Springfield, Stoppers Hill, Brinkworth, Chippenham, Wilts SN15 5AW   *Tel:* (01666) 510444
Board of Finance (*Chairman*) Mr Neil Porter c/o Dioc Church House; (*Secretary*) Mrs Lesley Farrall, Dioc Church House
Finance Manager Mr Graham Ash, Dioc Church House
Pastoral Committee (*Secretary*) Mrs Lesley Farrall (*as above*)
Dioc Electoral Registration Officer Mrs Lesley Farrall (*as above*)
Designated Officer Mr Tim Berry, Harris and Harris, 14 Market Place, Wells BA5 2RE   *Tel:* (01749) 674747
Fax: (01749) 676585

CHURCHES
Advisory Committee for the Care of Churches (*Chairman*) Canon Peter Johnson, 41 Salisbury Rd, Redland, Bristol BS6 7AS
Tel: 0117–944 4464
(*Secretary*) Mrs Celia Gibbons, c/o Dioc Church House

EDUCATION
Board of Education (*Director and Schools Adviser*) Miss Caroline Barker Bennett, All Saints RE Centre, 1 All Saints Court, Bristol BS1 1JN   *Tel:* 0117–927 7454

BOARD OF READERS
Board of Readers (*Secretary*) Mr Gordon Jobbins, 8 Kyneton Way, Kington St Michael, Chippenham, Wilts SN14 6RF
Tel: (01249) 750733

LITURGICAL
Chairman Revd Paul Roberts, 13 Henleaze Ave, Henleaze, Bristol BS9 4EU
Tel: 0117–962 3535

PARISH RESOURCES TEAM
Director of Parish Resources Canon Douglas Holt, Dioc Church House
Children and Youth Officer Revd Mark Pilgrim, Dioc Church House
Parish Development Adviser (*Bristol Archdeaconry*) Revd Stuart Taylor, Dioc Church House
Parish Development Adviser (*Swindon Archdeaconry*) Mr Alun Brookfield, 16 Fairholm Way, Swindon SN2 6JZ
Tel: (01793) 825658
Fax: (01793) 821554
Dioc Director of Ordinands Revd Paul Denyer, Vicarage, Kington Langley, Chippenham, Wilts SN15 5NJ
Tel: (01249) 750231
Fax: (01249) 750784
Ecumenical Officers (*Bristol Archdeaconry*) Canon Susan Shipp, Vicarage, 85 Bath Rd, Longwell Green, Bristol BS15 6DF
Tel: 0117–983 3373
(*Swindon Archdeaconry*) Revd Brian Fessey, Vicarage, 4 Church St, Purton, Swindon, Wilts SN5 9DS   *Tel:* (01793) 770210
Uganda Link Officer Canon Tony Fensome,

Vicarage, Lords Mead, Chippenham, Wilts SN14 0LJ
Tel and Fax: (01249) 654835
Personal Review of Ministry Revd David James, St Ambrose Vicarage, Stretford Ave, Bristol BS5 7AN   *Tel:* 0117–951 7299
Adviser in Pastoral Care for Clergy and their Families Revd Judith Thompson, St Barnabas Vicarage, Daventry Rd, Knowle, Bristol BS4 1DQ   *Tel:* 0117–966 4139

PRESS, PUBLICITY AND PUBLICATIONS
Communications Officer Revd Tim Daplyn, Vicarage, Church Rd, Abbots Leigh, Bristol BS8 3QU   *Tel:* (01275) 373996
Fax: (01275) 375826
e-mail: dco@easynet.co.uk
Press Officers (*Bristol Archdeaconry*) Revd Tim Daplyn (*as above*)
(*Swindon Archdeaconry*) Revd Stephen Oram, 3 Ockwells, Cricklade, Swindon SN6 6ED   *Tel:* (01793) 750300
Editor of 'Three Crowns' Mr John Hudson, Dioc Church House
Editor of Dioc Directory Mrs Sally Moody, Dioc Church House

DIOCESAN RECORD OFFICES
Bristol Record Office, 'B' Bond, Smeaton Rd, Bristol BS1 6XN, *County Archivist* Mr J. S. Williams, *Tel:* 0117–922 5692 (*For parish records in the Archdeaconry of Bristol*); Wiltshire Record Office, County Hall, Trowbridge, Wilts, *County Archivist* Mr M. G. Rathbone, *Tel:* (01225) 713134 (*For parish records in the Archdeaconry of Swindon*)

DIOCESAN RESOURCE CENTRE
All Saints Centre, 1 All Saints Court, Bristol BS1 1JN   *Tel:* 0117–927 7454
Fax: 0117–925 0404
Administrator Mrs Joanna Bailey

THE CHURCHES' COUNCIL FOR INDUSTRY AND SOCIAL RESPONSIBILITY
Director Canon Tim McClure, St Nicholas House, Lawford's Gate, Bristol BS5 0RE
Tel: 0117–955 7430
Fax: 0117–941 3252
e-mail: isrbristol@gn.apc.org
Administrator Miss Gillian Hiles, St Nicholas House
Industrial Chaplains Revd Heather Pencavel, Revd Gordon Wilson, Revd Michael Massey (*Bristol*); Revd Christine Gilbert (*Swindon*)
Social Responsibility Officer (*Wiltshire*) Mrs Kathleen Ben Rabha
Church and Society Officer Mr David Maggs
Inter-Religious Affairs Adviser Revd Colin Chapman
Church Urban Fund Projects Officer Revd John Harrison
World Development Adviser Revd Gordon Holmes

RURAL DEANS
ARCHDEACONRY OF BRISTOL
Bedminster Revd Peter Huzzey, St Peter's Vicarage, 61 Fernsteed Rd, Bishopsworth, Bristol BS13 8HG   *Tel:* 0117–964 2734
Bitton Revd Stephen Cook, Vicarage, Church Rd, Hanham, Bristol BS15 3AF
Tel: 0117–967 3580
Brislington Canon Keith Newton, Holy Nativity Vicarage, 41 Lilymead Ave, Knowle, Bristol BS4 2BY
Tel: 0117–977 4260
City Revd David Self, St Paul's Rectory, 131 Ashley Rd, St Paul's, Bristol BS6 5NU
Tel: 0117–955 0150
Clifton Revd Frank Smith, St Peter's Vicarage, The Drive, Henleaze, Bristol BS9 4LD
Tel: 0117–962 0636
Horfield Canon David Holloway, St Gregory's Vicarage, Filton Rd, Horfield, Bristol BS7 0PD   *Tel:* 0117–969 2839
Stapleton Revd David Sutch, Rectory, Canterbury Close, Yate, Bristol BS37 5TU
Tel: (01454) 311483
Westbury and Severnside Revd David Harrex, Vicarage, The Glebe, Pilning, Bristol BS35 4LE   *Tel:* (01454) 633409

ARCHDEACONRY OF SWINDON
Chippenham Canon Tony Fensome, St Peter's Vicarage, Lord's Mead, Chippenham, Wilts SN14 0LL
Tel: (01249) 654835
Cricklade Revd Raymond Adams, Vicarage, 54 Furlong Close, Haydon Wick, Swindon, Wilts SN2 3QP
Tel: (01793) 726378
Highworth Canon Brian Duckett, Vicarage, St Paul's Drive, Covingham, Swindon, Wilts SN3 5BY   *Tel:* (01793) 525130
Malmesbury Revd Richard East, Lea Rectory, Malmesbury, Wilts SN16 9BG
Tel: (01666) 823861
Wroughton Revd Michael Johnson, Vicarage, Church Hill, Wroughton, Swindon, Wilts SN4 9JS   *Tel:* (01793) 812301

DIOCESE OF CANTERBURY

Founded in 597. Kent east of the Medway, excluding the Medway Towns (ROCHESTER).

Population 819,000 Area 970 sq m
Stipendiary Clergy 174 Benefices 154
Parishes 267 Churches 330

ARCHBISHOP (103rd)
Most Revd and Rt Hon George Leonard Carey PH D, *Primate of all England and Metropolitan*, Lambeth Palace, London SE1 7JU [Tel: 0171–928 8282] and Old Palace, Canterbury, Kent CT1 2EE [1991]
Fax: 0171–261 9836
[George Cantuar:]

Dioc Chaplain Revd Stewart Jones, The Old Palace, Canterbury, Kent CT1 2EE (*Archbishop's Canterbury Chaplain and Dioc Missioner*)

Matters relating to the Diocese of Canterbury should in the first instance be referred to the **Bishop of Dover** (*see below*)
For the **Archbishop of Canterbury's Personal Staff** see page 58

SUFFRAGAN BISHOPS
DOVER Vacancy, Upway, 52 St Martin's Hill, Canterbury, Kent CT1 1PR
Office 9 The Precincts, Canterbury CT1 2EE *Tel:* (01227) 459382
Fax: (01227) 784945
Hon Chaplain Canon Ronald Diss
MAIDSTONE Rt Revd Gavin Hunter Reid, Bishop's House, Pett Lane, Charing, Ashford, Kent TN27 0DL [1992]
Tel: (01233) 712950
Fax: (01233) 713543
Chaplain Revd Roger Martin
Tel and Fax: (01227) 738177

PROVINCIAL EPISCOPAL VISITORS
EBBSFLEET Rt Revd Michael Houghton, 8 Goldney Ave, Clifton, Bristol BS8 4RA [1998] *Tel:* 0117–973 1752
Fax: 0117–973 1762
RICHBOROUGH Rt Revd Edwin Barnes, 14 Hall Place Gardens, St Albans, Herts AL1 3SP *Tel:* (01727) 857764
Fax: (01727) 763025

HONORARY ASSISTANT BISHOP
Rt Revd Richard David Say, 23 Chequers Park, Wye, Ashford, Kent TN25 5BB
Tel: (01233) 812720

CATHEDRAL AND METROPOLITICAL CHURCH OF CHRIST
Dean Very Revd John Simpson DD, The Deanery, The Precincts, Canterbury, Kent CT1 2EP [1986]
Tel: (01227) 765983 (Home)
(01227) 762862 (Office)
Cathedral Office Cathedral House, 11 The Precincts, Canterbury CT1 2EH
Tel: (01227) 762862
Fax: (01227) 762897
Canons Residentiary
Canon Peter Brett, 22 The Precincts, Canterbury, Kent CT1 2EP [1983]
Tel: (01227) 459757
Canon Roger Symon, 19 The Precincts, Canterbury, Kent CT1 2EP [1994]
Tel: (01227) 459918
Canon Treasurer Canon Michael Chandler PH D, 15 The Precincts, Canterbury, Kent CT1 2EL [1995] *Tel:* (01227) 463056
Ven John Pritchard, 29 The Precincts, Canterbury, Kent CT1 2EP [1996]
Tel: (01227) 463036
Fax: (01227) 785209
Precentor and Sacrist Revd Kevin Goss, Cathedral Office [1998]
Cathedral Organist Mr David Flood, 6 The Precincts, Canterbury CT1 2EE
Tel: (01227) 765219

ARCHDEACONS
CANTERBURY Ven John Pritchard, 29 The Precincts, Canterbury, Kent CT1 2EP [1996] *Tel:* (01227) 463036
Fax: (01227) 785209
MAIDSTONE Ven Patrick Evans, Archdeacon's House, Charing, Ashford, Kent TN27 0LU [1989] *Tel:* (01233) 712294
Fax: (01233) 713651

CONVOCATION (MEMBERS OF THE HOUSE OF CLERGY OF THE GENERAL SYNOD)
Dignitaries in Convocation
The Bishop of Maidstone
The Archdeacon of Maidstone

Proctors for Clergy
Revd Robert Hannaford
Revd Bill Hopkinson
Canon Geoffrey Sidaway

MEMBERS OF THE HOUSE OF LAITY OF THE GENERAL SYNOD
Dr David Bowen
Mr Brian Field
Mrs Caroline Spencer

DIOCESAN OFFICERS
Dioc Secretary Mr David Kemp, Diocesan House, Lady Wootton's Green, Canterbury, Kent CT1 1NQ *Tel:* (01227) 459401
Fax: (01227) 787073
e-mail: d.kemp@diocant.clara.co.uk
Commissary General His Honour Judge Richard Walker, 34 & 36 Castle St, Dover, Kent CT16 1PN *Tel:* (01304) 240250
Fax: (01304) 240040
Dioc Registrar and Legal Adviser to the Diocese Mr Richard Sturt (*same address*)

DIOCESAN ORGANISATIONS
Diocesan Office Diocesan House, Lady Wootton's Green, Canterbury, Kent CT1 1NQ *Tel:* (01227) 459401
Fax: (01227) 450964
e-mail: reception@diocant.clara.co.uk

ADMINISTRATION
Dioc Synod (*Chairman, House of Clergy*) Canon Brian Chalmers, Vicarage, Pett Lane, Charing, Ashford, Kent TN27 0DL *Tel:* (01233) 712598; (*Chairman, House of Laity*) Mr Raymond Harris; (*Secretary*) Mr David Kemp, Dioc House
Board of Finance (*Chairman*) Mr Richard Finlinson, Forge Hill House, Pluckley, Ashford, Kent TN27 0SL
Tel: (01233) 840318
(*Secretary*) Mr David Kemp (*as above*)
Designated Officer Mrs Gillian Marsh, Dioc House
Dioc Accountant Miss Rosemary Collins, Dioc House
Director of Property Services Mr Philip Bell, Dioc House

CHURCHES
Advisory Committee for the Care of Churches Mr Ross Anderson, Cullings Hill, Elham, Canterbury CT4 6TE *Tel:* (01303) 840638
(*Secretary*) Mr Ian Dodd, Dioc House

EDUCATION
Education Committee (*Director*) Mr Rupert Bristow, Dioc House
Education Field Officer Miss Judy Bainbridge, Dioc House
Schools Executive Officer Mrs Pat Gibson, Dioc House

MINISTRY
Director of Ministry and Training Revd Bill Hopkinson, Dioc House

Canterbury

Director of Ordinands Vacancy
Local Ministry Adviser Revd Barbara Way, Dioc House
Youth Officer Mr David Brown, Dioc House
Children's Ministry Adviser Mr Ted Hurst, Dioc House
Association of Readers (*Warden*) Revd Christopher Morgan-Jones, Vicarage, Priory Rd, Maidstone ME15 6NL *Tel:* (01622) 756002; (*Hon Secretary*) Dr James Gibson, 27 Pine Grove, Maidstone, Kent ME14 2AJ   *Tel:* (01622) 673050
Clerical Retirement Officers Canon Ferdie Phillips, 6 South Close, The Precincts, Canterbury CT1 2EJ   *Tel:* (01227) 450891
Revd Alan Frostick, 18 Hawthorn Close, St Mary's Bay, Romney Marsh TN29 0SZ
Tel: (01303) 875158

LITURGICAL
Chairman Revd Fredrik Arvidsson, Rectory, Upper St, Kingsdown, Deal CT14 8BJ
Tel: (01304) 373951
Secretary Miss Mary Ambrose, Zawadi, 15 The Street, Kingston, Canterbury CT4 6JB

MISSION AND ECUMENICAL
Board of Mission (*Chairman*) The Bishop of Maidstone (*as above*)
Dioc Missioner Revd Stewart Jones, The Old Palace, Canterbury CT1 2EE

PRESS AND PUBLICATIONS
Communications Officer Revd Don Witts, Dioc House   *Tel and Fax:* (01227) 763373
0411 410079 (Mobile)
e-mail: don.witts@ukonline.co.uk
Editor of Dioc Directory Miss Tiffany Martin, Dioc House

DIOCESAN RECORD OFFICES
Cathedral Archives and Library, The Precincts, Canterbury CT1 2EH, *Archivist* Dr Michael Stansfield, *Tel:* (01227) 463510 (*For parish records in the Archdeaconry of Canterbury*); Kent Archives Office, County Hall, Maidstone, Kent ME14 1XQ, *Head of Heritage Services* Mr Nigel Yates, *Tel:* (01622) 754321 (*For parish records in the Archdeaconry of Maidstone*)

SOCIAL RESPONSIBILITY
Canterbury and Rochester Joint Council for Social Responsibility/ Senior Adviser Canon David Grimwood, 60 Marsham St, Maidstone, Kent ME14 1EW
Tel: (01622) 755014
Fax: (01622) 693531
Advisers Revd Pearl Anderson, Mr Adrian Speller (*same address*)
Association for the Deaf Revd Tony Old, Dioc House

STEWARDSHIP
Adviser Mr David Noakes, Dioc House

RURAL DEANS
ARCHDEACONRY OF CANTERBURY
East Bridge Revd David Barnes, Vicarage, Queens Rd, Ash, Canterbury, Kent CT3 2BG   *Tel:* (01304) 812296
West Bridge Revd Clive Barlow, Rectory, The Green, Chartham, Canterbury, Kent CT4 7JW   *Tel:* (01227) 738256
Canterbury Canon Peter Mackenzie, Rectory, 13 Ersham Rd, Canterbury CT1 3AR
Tel: (01227) 462686

Reculver Revd Dick Cotton, Christ Church Vicarage, 38 Beltinge Rd, Herne Bay, Kent CT6 6BU   *Tel:* (01227) 366640
Dover Revd Peter Bowers, Vicarage, 23 Lewisham Rd, River, Dover, Kent CT17 0QG   *Tel:* (01304) 822037
Elham Canon Reg Humphriss, Rectory, Saltwood, Hythe, Kent CT21 4QA
Tel: (01303) 266932
Ospringe Revd William Mowll, Vicarage, 101 The Street, Boughton-under-Blean, Faversham, Kent ME13 9BG
Tel: (01227) 751410
Sandwich Revd Bruce Hawkins, Vicarage, St Mary's Rd, Deal, Kent CT14 7NQ
Tel: (01304) 374645
Thanet Revd Mark Hayton, Rectory, Nelson Place, Broadstairs, Kent CT10 1HQ
Tel: (01843) 862921

ARCHDEACONRY OF MAIDSTONE
East Charing Canon Brian Chalmers, Vicarage, Pett Lane, Charing, Kent TN27 0PL
Tel: (01233) 712598
West Charing Revd Brian Barnes, Rectory, Frittenden Lane, Staplehurst, Kent TN12 0DH   *Tel:* (01580) 891258
North Lympne Revd John Tipping, Rectory, Bower Rd, Mersham, Ashford, Kent TN25 6NN   *Tel:* (01233) 502138
South Lympne Revd Lindsay Hammond, Vicarage, Appledore, Kent TN26 2DB
Tel: (01233) 758250
Sittingbourne Revd Gilbert Spencer, Vicarage, Vicarage Rd, Minster-in-Sheppey ME12 2HE   *Tel:* (01795) 873185
Sutton Canon Geoffrey Sidaway, Vicarage, Church Lane, Bearsted, Maidstone, Kent ME14 4EF   *Tel:* (01622) 737135

DIOCESE OF CARLISLE

Founded in 1133. Cumbria, except for small areas in the east (NEWCASTLE, BRADFORD).

Population 485,000 Area 2,477 sq m
Stipendiary Clergy 165 Benefices 174
Parishes 271 Churches 350

BISHOP (65th)
Rt Revd Ian Harland, Rose Castle, Dalston, Carlisle, Cumbria CA5 7BZ [1989]
Tel: (0169 74) 76274
Fax: (0169 74) 76550
[Ian Carliol:]

Bishop's Chaplain Revd Keith Wood

SUFFRAGAN BISHOP
PENRITH Rt Revd Richard Garrard, Holm Croft, Castle Rd, Kendal, Cumbria LA9 7AU [1994]
Tel: (01539) 727836
Fax: (01539) 734380

HONORARY ASSISTANT BISHOPS
Rt Revd Ian Macdonald Griggs, Rookings, Patterdale, Penrith, Cumbria CA11 0NP [1994]
Tel: (0176 84) 82064
Rt Revd George Lanyon Hacker, Keld House, Milburn, Penrith, Cumbria CA10 1TW [1994]
Tel: (0176 83) 61506
Rt Revd John Richard Satterthwaite, 25 Spencer House, St Paul's Square, Carlisle CA1 1DG [1994]
Tel: (01228) 594055
Rt Revd Andrew Alexander Kenny Graham, Fell End, Butterwick, Penrith, Cumbria CA10 1QQ [1997]
Tel: (01931) 713147

CATHEDRAL CHURCH OF THE HOLY AND UNDIVIDED TRINITY
Dean Very Revd Graeme Knowles, The Deanery, Carlisle, Cumbria CA3 8TZ [1998]
Tel: (01228) 523335
Cathedral Office 7 The Abbey, Carlisle, Cumbria CA3 8TZ
Tel and Fax: (01228) 548151
Fax after office hours: (01228) 548164
Canons Residentiary
Canon Rex Chapman, 1 The Abbey, Carlisle, Cumbria CA3 8TZ [1978]
Tel: (01228) 597614
Ven David Turnbull, 2 The Abbey, Carlisle, Cumbria CA3 8TZ [1993]
Tel: (01228) 523026
Canon David Weston PH D, 3 The Abbey, Carlisle, Cumbria CA3 8TZ [1994]
Tel: (01228) 521834

Canon Colin Hill PH D, 4 The Abbey, Carlisle CA3 8TZ [1996] *Tel:* (01228) 590778
Bursar and Chapter Clerk Mr Ellis Amos, Cathedral Office
Administrative Officer Mrs Carolyne Baines, Cathedral Office
Cathedral Organist Mr Jeremy Suter, 6 The Abbey, Carlisle, Cumbria CA3 8TZ
Tel: (01228) 526646

ARCHDEACONS
CARLISLE Ven David Turnbull, 2 The Abbey, Carlisle CA3 8TZ [1993]
Tel: (01228) 23026
Fax: (01228) 594899
WEST CUMBERLAND Ven Alan Davis, 50 Stainburn Rd, Workington, Cumbria CA14 1SN [1996] *Tel:* (01900) 66190
Fax: (01900) 873021
WESTMORLAND AND FURNESS Ven David Jenkins, Woodcroft, Levens, Kendal, Cumbria LA8 8NQ [1995]
Tel: (0153 95) 61281
Fax: (0153 95) 61217

CONVOCATION (MEMBERS OF THE HOUSE OF CLERGY OF THE GENERAL SYNOD)
Dignitaries in Convocation
The Bishop of Penrith
The Archdeacon of Carlisle
Proctors for Clergy
Canon Rex Chapman
Canon Myrtle Langley
Revd Angus MacLeay

MEMBERS OF THE HOUSE OF LAITY OF THE GENERAL SYNOD
Mrs Dorothy Chatterley
Dr Arnold Currall
Mr Nigel Holmes
Mrs Elizabeth Metcalfe
Mr David Mills

DIOCESAN OFFICERS
Dioc Secretary Canon Colin Hill, Church House, West Walls, Carlisle, Cumbria CA3 8UE *Tel:* (01228) 522573
Fax: (01228) 815400

Chancellor of Diocese His Hon Judge Francis Aglionby, The Croft, Houghton, Carlisle, Cumbria CA3 0LD
Registrar of Diocese and Bishop's Legal Secretary Mrs Susan Holmes, Woodside, Great Corby, Carlisle, Cumbria CA4 8LL
Tel: (01228) 560617
Fax: (01228) 562372
e-mail: susan@gt-corby.demon.co.uk

DIOCESAN ORGANISATIONS
Diocesan Office Church House, West Walls, Carlisle, Cumbria CA3 8UE
Tel: (01228) 522573
Fax: (01228) 815400

ADMINISTRATION
Dioc Synod (*Chairman, House of Clergy*) Canon Rex Chapman, 1 The Abbey, Carlisle CA3 8TZ *Tel:* (01228) 597614; (*Chairman, House of Laity*) Mr Nigel Holmes, Woodside, Great Corby, Carlisle CA4 8LL *Tel:* (01228) 560617; (*Secretary*) Canon Colin Hill, Dioc Office
Board of Finance (*Chairman*) Mr Hugh Ellison, 21 Arthur St, Penrith, Cumbria CA11 7TU *Tel:* (01768) 862069; (*Secretary*) Canon Colin Hill (*as above*)
Parsonages Committees (*North, South and West*): Mr Richard Green-Armytage, Dioc Office
Pastoral Committee Canon Campbell Matthews, Dioc Office
Designated Officer Mrs Susan Holmes, Woodside, Great Corby, Carlisle CA4 8LL
Tel: (01228) 560617
Fax: (01228) 562372

CHURCHES
Advisory Committee for the Care of Churches (*Chairman*) Mr Peter Browning, Park Fell, Skelwith, Ambleside, Cumbria LA22 9NP
Tel: (0153 94) 33978
(*Secretary*) Canon Colin Hill, Dioc Office
(*Administrative Secretary*) Mr Richard Green-Armytage (*as above*)

EDUCATION
Board of Education, Church Centre, West Walls, Carlisle CA3 8UE
Tel: (01228) 538086
Fax: (01228) 815409
Director of Education Canon Rex Chapman, Church Centre
Adviser for RE (*North*) Revd Bert Thomas, Church Centre
Adviser for RE (*South*) Revd Philip Barber, Vicarage, Beetham Milnthorpe, Cumbria LA7 7AS *Tel:* (0153 95) 62216
Diocesan Youth Officers (*North*) Vacancy (*South*) Vacancy
Resources Centre Revd Bert Thomas, Church Centre

BOARD FOR MINISTRY AND TRAINING
Principal Carlisle and Blackburn Dioc Training Institute and Adviser for Ministry and

Carlisle 71

Training Revd Tim Herbert, Vicarage, Cotehill, Carlisle CA4 0DY
Tel: (01228) 560323
Adviser for Clergy Training Revd Bob Dew, Vicarage, Skelsmergh, Kendal, Cumbria LA9 6PU
Tel: (01539) 724498
Fax: (01539) 734655
Director of Ordinands Revd Nick Ash, Vicarage, Dalston, Carlisle CA5 7JF
Tel: (01228) 710215
Director of Ordinands Revd Carol Farrer, 18 Skirsgill Close, Penrith, Cumbria CA11 8QF
Tel: (01768) 899540

BOARD FOR SOCIAL RESPONSIBILITY
Officer for Social Responsibility Canon John Higgins, Dioc Office
Council for Agriculture and Rural Life (*Acting Team Leader*) Mr Andrew Humphries, Colonsay House, Itonfield, Southwaite, Carlisle CA4 0NR *Tel:* (01697) 473405
Industrial Mission Revd Ian Davies, St John's Vicarage, James Watt Terrace, Barrow in Furness, Cumbria LA14 2TS
Tel: (01229) 821101
Fax: (01229) 871505

ECUMENICAL AFFAIRS
Dioc Revd Keith Wood, Rose Castle, Dalston, Carlisle CA5 7BZ
Tel: (0169 74) 76274
Fax: (0169 74) 76550
Churches Together in Cumbria (*Secretary*) Revd Andrew Dodd, Dioc Office

PARISH MISSION AND DEVELOPMENT
Team Leader Responsible for Lay Training Revd Peter Wilson, Dioc Office

Council for Stewardship (*Secretary and Dioc Officer*) Vacancy
Council for Evangelism (*Secretary and Dioc Officer*) Vacancy
Partnership in World Mission Mrs Lynne Tembey, 2 High St, Whitehaven, Cumbria CA28 7PZ
Tel: (01946) 64738
Fax: (01946) 599931

WORSHIP ADVISER
Ven David Turnbull, 2 The Abbey, Carlisle, CA3 8TZ *Tel:* (01228) 523026
Fax: (01228) 594399

PRESS AND PUBLICATIONS
Communications Officer Revd Richard Pratt, Dioc Office
Tel: (01228) 521982 (Home)
Editor of Dioc News Ven Lawrie Peat, 17 Railway Terrace, Lindal in Furness, Cumbria LA12 0LC *Tel:* (01229) 468069
Dioc Directory Canon Colin Hill, Dioc Office

DIOCESAN RECORD OFFICES
The Cumbria Record Office, The Castle, Carlisle CA3 8UR *Tel:* (01228) 607282
Cumbria Record Office, County Offices, Kendal *Tel:* (01539) 773540
Cumbria Record Office, 140 Duke St, Barrow *Tel:* (01229) 894363
(*County Archivist* Mr J. Grisenthwaite)
Tel: (01228) 607282

RURAL DEANS
ARCHDEACONRY OF CARLISLE
Appleby Canon Colin Levey, Vicarage, Orton, Penrith, Cumbria CA10 3RQ
Tel: (0153 96) 24532

Brampton Canon Christopher Morris, Vicarage, Lanercost, Brampton, Carlisle CA8 2HQ *Tel:* (0169 77) 2478
Carlisle Canon Geoffrey Ravalde, Vicarage, Longthwaite Rd, Wigton, Cumbria CA7 9JR *Tel:* (0169 73) 42337
Penrith Canon Richard Frank, Rectory, Greystoke, Penrith, Cumbria CA11 CTJ
Tel: (0176 84) 83293

ARCHDEACONRY OF WESTMORLAND AND FURNESS
Furness Canon Peter Mann, Rectory, 98 Roose Rd, Barrow in Furness, Cumbria LA13 9RL *Tel:* (01229) 821641
Kendal Canon George Howe, Holy Trinity Vicarage, 2 Lynngarth Drive, Kendal, Cumbria LA9 2JA *Tel:* (01539) 712541
Windermere Canon Derek Jackson, St Mary's Vicarage, Ambleside Rd, Windermere, Cumbria LA23 1BA
Tel: (01539) 443032

ARCHDEACONRY OF WEST CUMBERLAND
Calder Canon James Baker, Vicarage, Oakbank, Whitehaven, Cumbria CA28 6HY
Tel: (01946) 692630
Derwent Revd Brian Smith, St John's Vicarage, Ambleside Rd, Keswick, Cumbria CA12 4DD
Tel: (01768) 772130
Solway Ven Alan Davis, 50 Stainburn Rd, Workington, Cumbria CA14 1SN
Tel: (01900) 66190
Fax: (01900) 873021

DIOCESE OF CHELMSFORD

Founded in 1914. Essex, except for a few parishes in the north (ELY, ST EDMUNDSBURY AND IPSWICH); five East London boroughs north of the Thames; three parishes in south Cambridgeshire.

Population 2,651,000   Area 1,531 sq m
Stipendiary Clergy 424   Benefices 359
Parishes 489   Churches 609

BISHOP (8th)
Rt Revd John Freeman Perry, Bishopscourt, Margaretting, Ingatestone, Essex CM4 0HD [1996]   Tel: (01277) 352001
Fax: (01277) 355374
[John Chelmsford]

Bishop's Senior Assistant Canon Richard More, Willowdene, Maldon Rd, Margaretting, Ingatestone CM4 9JW
Tel: (01277) 352472

AREA BISHOPS
BARKING Rt Revd Roger Frederick Sainsbury, Barking Lodge, 110 Capel Rd, Forest Gate, London E7 0JS [1991]
Tel: 0181–478 2456
Office Suite 1B, Cranbrook House, 61 Cranbrook Rd, Ilford IG1 4PG
Tel: 0181–514 6044
Fax: 0181–514 6349
e-mail: bishoproger@chelmsford.anglican.org
BRADWELL Rt Revd Laurence Alexander Green D MIN, Bishop's House, Orsett Rd, Horndon-on-the Hill, Stanford-le-Hope, Essex SS17 8NS [1993]
Tel: (01375) 673806
Fax: (01375) 674222
e-mail: lauriegr@globalnet.co.uk
COLCHESTER Rt Revd Edward Holland, 1 Fitzwalter Rd, Lexden, Colchester, Essex CO3 3SS [1994]   Tel: (01206) 576648
Fax: (01206) 763868

HONORARY ASSISTANT BISHOP
Rt Revd James Johnson, St Helena, 249 Woodgrange Drive, Southend on Sea, Essex SS1 2SQ   Tel: (01702) 613429

CATHEDRAL CHURCH OF ST MARY THE VIRGIN, ST PETER AND ST CEDD
Provost Very Revd Peter Judd, The Provost's House, 3 Harlings Grove, Chelmsford, Essex CM1 1YQ [1997]
Tel: (01245) 354318 (Home)
(01245) 294492 (Office)
e-mail: provost@chelmsford.anglican.org

Cathedral Office 53 New St, Chelmsford CM1 1TY   Tel: (01245) 294480
Fax: (01245) 294499
Canons Residentiary
Vice-Provost Canon Timothy Thompson, 115 Rainsford Rd, Chelmsford, Essex CM1 2PF [1988]   Tel: (01245) 267773 (Home)
(01245) 294493 (Office)
Canon Theologian Canon Andrew Knowles, 2 Harlings Grove, Chelmsford CM1 1YQ [1998]   Tel: (01245) 355041 (Home)
(01245) 294484 (Office)
Canon Precentor Canon David Knight, The Precentor's House, 1B Rainsford Ave, Chelmsford CM1 2PJ [1991]
Tel: (01245) 257306 (Home)
(01245) 294482 (Office)
e-mail: precentor@chelmsford.anglican.org
Chaplain Revd Katy Hacker Hughes, 7 Rainsford Ave, Chelmsford CM1 2PJ
Tel: (01245) 350362 (Home)
(01245) 294483 (Office)
Hon Associate Chaplain Revd Ivor Moody, 4 Bishopscourt Gardens, Springfield, Chelmsford CM2 6AZ
Tel: (01245) 261700 (Home)
(01245) 493131 (Office)
Chapter Clerk and Administrator Mr Terry Mobbs, Cathedral Office
Tel: (01245) 294488
Master of Music Dr Graham Elliott, 1 Harlings Grove, Chelmsford CM1 1YQ
Tel: (01245) 262006 (Home)
(01245) 294485 (Office)
e-mail: music@chelmsford.anglican.org
Assistant Master of Music Mr Neil Weston, Cathedral Office   Tel: (01245) 294486

ARCHDEACONS
COLCHESTER Ven Martin Wallace, Archdeacon's House, 63 Powers Hall End, Witham, Essex CM8 1NH [1997]
Tel: (01376) 513130
Fax: (01376) 500789
e-mail: a.colchester@chelmsford.anglican.org
HARLOW Ven Peter Taylor, Glebe House, Church Lane, Sheering, Essex CM22 7NR [1996]   Tel: (01279) 734524
Fax: (01279) 734426
e-mail: a.harlow@chelmsford.anglican.org
SOUTHEND Ven David Jennings, 136 Broomfield Rd, Chelmsford CM1 1RN [1992]   Tel: (01245) 258257
Fax: (01245) 250845
e-mail:
a.southend@chelmsford.anglican.org
WEST HAM Ven Michael Fox, 86 Aldersbrook Rd, Manor Park, London E12 5DH [1996]   Tel: 0181–989 8557
Fax: 0181–530 1311

CONVOCATION (MEMBERS OF THE HOUSE OF CLERGY OF THE GENERAL SYNOD
Dignitaries in Convocation
The Bishop of Barking
The Archdeacon of Southend
Proctors for Clergy
Canon Paul Brett
Revd Julie Eaton
Revd Anthony Higton
Canon John Howden
Canon David Lowman
Revd Peter Walker

MEMBERS OF THE HOUSE OF LAITY OF THE GENERAL SYNOD
Dr Susan Atkin
Mrs Joy Halstead
Mr Julian Litten
Mr Harry Marsh
Mr Vijay Menon
Mr David Morgan
Miss Pat Nappin
Dr James Rawes
Mr William Walker

DIOCESAN OFFICERS
Dioc Secretary Mr David Phillips, Diocesan Office, Guy Harlings, 53 New St, Chelmsford, Essex CM1 1AT   Tel: (01245) 294400
e-mail: mail@chelmsford.anglican.org
Chancellor of Diocese Chanc Sheila Cameron, Diocesan Registry, 53A New St, Chelmsford, Essex CM1 1NG
Tel: (01245) 259470
Registrar of Diocese and Bishop's Legal Secretary Mr Brian Hood, Diocesan Registry, 53A New St, Chelmsford, Essex CM1 1NG
Tel: (01245) 259470
Legal Advisers to the Board of Finance Winckworth Sherwood, 53A New St, Chelmsford CM1 1NG
Tel: (01245) 262212

DIOCESAN ORGANISATIONS
Diocesan Office Guy Harlings, 53 New St, Chelmsford, Essex CM1 1AT
Tel: (01245) 294400
Fax: (01245) 294477
e-mail: mail@chelmsford.anglican.org

ADMINISTRATION

Dioc Synod (*Chairman, House of Clergy*) Revd Tim Potter, Vicarage, Broomfields, Hatfield Heath, Bishops Stortford CM22 7DH Tel: (01279) 730288; (*Chairman, House of Laity*) Mr Gordon Simmonds, 'Cartref', 2A Castle Drive, Rayleigh, Essex SS6 7HT; (*Secretary*) Mr David Phillips, Dioc Office
Board of Finance (*Chairman*) Mr Philip Hawkes, Greenfields, Dunmow Rd, Felstead, Essex CM6 3LF
Tel: (01371) 856480
Fax: (01371) 856872
(*Secretary*) Mr David Phillips (*as above*)
Asst Dioc Secretary Mr Peter Hobbs, Dioc Office
Dioc Accountant Mr Mac Mackay, Dioc Office
Director of Property Services Mr Alan McCarthy, Dioc Office
Designated Officer Mr Brian Hood, Dioc Registry, 53A New St, Chelmsford CM1 1NG Tel: (01245) 259470
Dioc Pastoral Committee (*Chairman*) Mr Mark Cole, 4 Achnacone Drive, Braiswick, Colchester CO4 4RL (*as above*); (*Secretary*) Mr David Brown, Dioc Office

CHURCHES

Advisory Committee for the Care of Churches (*Chairman*) Revd Andrew McIntosh, St Mary's Rectory, Park Drive, Maldon, Essex CM9 7JG Tel: (01621) 857191; (*Asst Secretary*) Mr Peter Hobbs (*as above*)
Redundant Churches Committee (*Secretary*) Mr David Brown, Dioc Office
Ringers Association Mr Michael Bishop, 56 Edinburgh Gardens, Braintree, Essex CM7 6LH Tel: (01376) 325281

DIOCESAN RESOURCE TEAM

Resource Team Leader Ven Peter Taylor, Dioc Office
Director of Education Canon Peter Hartley, Dioc Office
School and RE Advisers Chris Firth, Mark Plater, Dioc Office
Ministry Development Officer Canon Robin Greenwood, Dioc Office
Dioc Director of Ordinands Canon David Lowman, 25 Roxwell Rd, Chelmsford CM1 2LY Tel: (01245) 264187
Children's Officer Mrs Margaret Withers, Dioc Office
Lay Training Officer Revd Chris Burdon, Dioc Office
Lay Development Officer Revd Veronica Hydon, Dioc Office
Interfaith Adviser Mrs Ann Davison, Dioc Office

Youth Officer Mrs Lynn Money, Dioc Office
Asst Adviser for CME Revd Julia Mourant, Dioc Office
Barking Area CME Officer Mr Peter Harding, 26 Station Rd, Walthamstow, London E17 8AA Tel: 0181–521 2026
Mission Officer Revd Roger Matthews, Dioc Office
Social Responsibility Officer Mrs Alison Davies, Dioc Office
Stewardship Adviser Mr Brian Pepper, Dioc Office

PRESS AND COMMUNICATIONS

Communications Manager Mrs Jenny Robinson, Dioc Office
Tel: (01245) 294400 (Office)
(01376) 516727 (Home)
(0385) 545223 (Mobile)
Fax: (01245) 280633
Press Officer Revd Philip Banks
Tel: (01277) 352456 (Office)
(01206) 822431 (Home)
Fax: (01206) 822155

OTHER COMMITTEES

Committee for Clergy Aid and Officer for Widows and Dependants of Clergymen Vacancy
Readers' Committee Mr John Woods, Low Roofs, Parsons Hill, Lexden, Colchester, Essex CO3 4DT Tel: (01206) 573735
Liturgical Committee (*Chairman*) The Provost
Secretary Canon David Knight, The Precentor's House, Rainsford Ave, Chelmsford CM1 2PJ Tel: (01245) 257306

DIOCESAN RECORDS OFFICE

The County Archivist, County Hall, Chelmsford, Essex CM1 1LX (*County Archivist* Mr Ken Hall)
Tel: (01245) 267222, Ext. 2100

DIOCESAN HOUSE OF RETREAT

Pleshey, Chelmsford, Essex CM3 1HA (*Warden* Canon John Howden)
Tel: (01245) 237251

RURAL DEANS
ARCHDEACONRY OF WEST HAM

Barking and Dagenham Revd John Fletcher, Vicarage, 10 St Chad's Rd, Chadwell Heath, Romford, Essex RM6 6JB
Tel: 0181–590 2054
Fax: 0181–503 8982
Havering Revd Hugh Dibbens, 222 High St, Hornchurch, Essex RM12 6QP
Tel: (01708) 441571

Newham Revd Ann Easter, St Luke's House, Stratford St, London E14 8LT
Tel: 0171–538 9316
Redbridge Canon Michael Cole, All Saints Vicarage, 4 Inmans Row, Woodford Green, Essex IG8 0NH
Tel: 0181–504 0266
Waltham Forest Canon David Ainge, St Mary's Vicarage, 4 Vicarage Rd, London E10 5EA Tel: 0181–539 7882

ARCHDEACONRY OF HARLOW

Epping Forest Revd David Driscoll, Vicarage, 2 Piercing Hill, Theydon Bois, Essex CM16 7JN Tel: (01992) 814725
Harlow Revd Martin Webster, Vicarage, Betts Lane, Nazeing, Waltham Abbey, Essex EN9 2DB Tel: (01992) 893167
Ongar Revd Charles Masheder, Lavers Rectory, Magdalen Laver, Ongar, Essex CM5 0ES Tel: (01279) 426774

ARCHDEACONRY OF SOUTHEND

Brentwood Canon Robert White, St Thomas Vicarage, 91 Queens Rd, Brentwood, Essex CM14 4EY
Tel: (01277) 225700 (Home)
Tel and Fax: (01277) 201094 (Office)
Basildon Canon Peter Ashton, Rectory, 40 Laindon Rd, Billericay, Essex CM12 9LD
Tel: (01277) 622837
Chelmsford North Vacancy
Chelmsford South Revd David Atkins, Rectory, Castledon Rd, Downham, Billericay, Essex CM11 1LD Tel: (01268) 710370
Hadleigh Revd Peter Sandberg, Rectory, Church Rd, Thundersley, Benfleet, Essex SS7 3HG Tel: (01268) 792235
Maldon and Dengie Canon Peter Mason, All Saints Vicarage, Church Walk, Maldon CM9 4PY Tel: (01621) 854179
Rochford Revd David Williams, Rectory, 36 Millview Meadows, Rochford, Essex SS4 1EF Tel: (01702) 530621
Southend Canon Michael Ballard, Rectory, 8 Pilgrim's Close, Southend-on-Sea, Essex SS2 4XF Tel: (01702) 466423
Thurrock Revd Robert Springett, Vicarage, 121 Foyle Drive, South Ockendon, Essex RM15 5HF Tel: (01708) 853246

ARCHDEACONRY OF COLCHESTER

Braintree Revd John Shead, Vicarage, Finchingfield, Braintree, Essex CM7 4JR
Tel: (01371) 810309
Colchester Revd Anthony Rose, Rectory, 21 Cambridge Rd, Colchester CO3 3NS
Tel: (01206) 560175
Dedham and Tey Revd Gerard Moate, Vicarage, High St, Dedham, Colchester, Essex CO7 6DE Tel: (01206) 322136

Dunmow Revd Tim Pigrem, Rectory, Stortford Rd, Leaden Roding, Dunmow, Essex CM6 1QZ *Tel:* (01279) 876387
Harwich Revd Stephen Hardie, Rectory, 51 Highfield Ave, Dovercourt, Harwich, Essex CO12 4DR *Tel:* (01255) 502033
Hinckford Revd John Suddards, Rectory, Church Rd, Great Yeldham, Halstead, Essex CO9 4PT *Tel:* (01787) 237358

Newport and Stansted Revd Christopher Bishop, 24 Mallows Green Rd, Manuden, Bishop's Stortford, Herts CM22 1DG *Tel:* (01279) 812228
Saffron Walden Revd Jeremy Saville, Ashdon Rectory, Saffron Walden, Essex CB10 2HP *Tel:* (01799) 584897

St Osyth Revd Norman Issberner, Vicarage, 7 St Alban's Rd, Clacton-on-Sea, Essex CO15 6BA *Tel:* (01255) 424760
Witham Revd Michael Hatchett, Vicarage, 1 Hall Road, Great Totham, Maldon CM9 8NN *Tel:* (01621) 893150

Chelmsford

DIOCESE OF CHESTER

Founded in 1541. Cheshire south of the Mersey; Wirral; Trafford, except for an area in the north (MANCHESTER) and in the east (DERBY); the eastern half of Tameside; a few parishes in north Derbyshire; a few parishes in Manchester; a few parishes in Flintshire.

Population 1,572,000   Area 1,017 sq m
Stipendiary Clergy 292   Benefices 240
Parishes 282   Churches 369

BISHOP (40th)
Rt Revd Peter Robert Forster PH D, Bishop's House, Abbey Square, Chester CH1 2JD [1996]   Tel: (01244) 350864
Fax: (01244) 314187
[Peter Cestr:]

Bishop's Chaplain Revd Brian Perkes (*same address*)   Tel: (01829) 751265 (Home)

SUFFRAGAN BISHOPS
BIRKENHEAD Rt Revd Michael Laurence Langrish, Bishop's Lodge, 67 Bidston Rd, Oxton, Birkenhead, Merseyside L43 6TR [1993]   Tel: 0151–652 2741
Fax: 0151–651 2330
e-mail: bpbirkenhead@clara.net
STOCKPORT Rt Revd Geoffrey Martin Turner, Bishop's Lodge, Back Lane, Dunham Town, Altrincham, Cheshire WA14 4SG [1994]   Tel: 0161–928 5611
Fax: 0161–929 0692

HONORARY ASSISTANT BISHOPS
Rt Revd Alan Leslie Winstanley, Vicarage, Ferry Rd, Eastham, Wirral, Merseyside L62 0AJ   Tel: 0151–327 2182
Rt Revd Lord David Stuart Sheppard of Liverpool, Ambledown, 11 Melloncroft Drive, West Kirby, Wirral L48 2JA

CATHEDRAL CHURCH OF CHRIST AND THE BLESSED VIRGIN MARY
Dean Very Revd Stephen Stewart Smalley PH D, The Deanery, 7 Abbey St, Chester CH1 2JF [1987]   Tel: (01244) 351380
e-mail: dean@chestercathedral.org.uk
Cathedral Office 12 Abbey Square, Chester CH1 2HU   Tel: (01244) 324756
Fax: (01244) 341110
e-mail: office@chestercathedral.org.uk
Vice-Dean Canon Michael Rees, 5 Abbey Green, Chester CH1 2JH [1990]
Tel: (01244) 347500
e-mail: rees@chestercathedral.org.uk
Canons Residentiary
Canon Owen Conway, 9 Abbey St, Chester CH1 2JF [1991]   Tel: (01244) 316144
e-mail: conway@chestercathedral.org.uk
Canon Trevor Dennis, 13 Abbey St, Chester CH1 2JF [1993]   Tel: (01244) 314408
e-mail: dennis@chestercathedral.org.uk
Canon James Newcome, 5 Abbey St, Chester CH1 2JF [1994]
Tel: (01244) 315532
e-mail: newcome@chestercathedral.org.uk
Chapter Clerk Mr Randal Hibbert, 20 White Friars, Chester CH1 1XS
Tel: (01244) 321066
Cathedral Administrator Mr David Burrows, Cathedral Office
e-mail: burrows@chestercathedral.org.uk
Director of Music Mr David Poulter, Cathedral Office   Tel: (01244) 351024
e-mail: music@chestercathedral.org.uk
Cathedral Surveyor Mr Ronald Sims, 8–11 College St, York YO1 2JF
Tel: (01904) 655682

ARCHDEACONS
CHESTER Ven Christopher Hewetson, 8 Queens Park Rd, Queens Park, Chester CH4 7AD [1994]   Tel: (01244) 675417
Fax: (01244) 681959
MACCLESFIELD Ven Richard Gillings, Vicarage, Robin's Lane, Bramhall, Stockport SK7 2PE [1994]   Tel: 0161–439 2254
Fax: 0161–439 0817

CONVOCATION (MEMBERS OF THE HOUSE OF CLERGY OF THE GENERAL SYNOD)
The Archdeacon of Macclesfield
Proctors for Clergy
Revd Helen Chantry
Revd Stephen Foster
Revd John Staley
Revd John Sutton
Revd David Walker
Canon Michael Walters

MEMBERS OF THE HOUSE OF LAITY OF THE GENERAL SYNOD
Mrs Kate Allan
Prof Tony Berry
Dr David Blackmore
Mrs Isobel Burnley
Mrs Rosalind Campbell
Mr Stewart Darlow
Dr Sheila Grieve
Mr Colin Richardson
Mr Arthur Tomlinson
Mr Paul Williams

DIOCESAN OFFICERS
Dioc Secretary Mr Stephen Marriott, Diocesan House, Raymond St, Chester CH1 4PN   Tel: (01244) 379222
Fax: (01244) 383835
Chancellor of Diocese Chanc David Turner, 14 Gray's Inn Square, Gray's Inn, London
Registrar of Diocese and Bishop's Legal Secretary Mr Alan McAllester, Friars, White Friars, Chester CH1 1XS
Tel: (01244) 321066
Fax: (01244) 312582

DIOCESAN ORGANISATIONS
Diocesan Office: Diocesan House, Raymond St, Chester CH1 4PN
Tel: (01244) 379222
Fax: (01244) 383835

ADMINISTRATION
Dioc Synod (Vice-President, House of Clergy) Canon Michael Walters, Rectory, Chapel St, Congleton, Cheshire CW12 4AB Tel: (01260) 273212; (*Vice-President, House of Laity*) Dr David Blackmore, Coniston, Newton Lane, Newton, Chester CH2 2HJ Tel: (01244) 323494; (*Secretary*) Mr Stephen Marriott, Dioc House
Board of Finance (Chairman) Mr Stewart Darlow, 6 Harboro Grove, Sale, Cheshire M33 5BA Tel: 0161–973 4697; (*Secretary*) Mr Stephen Marriott (*as above*)
Director of Finance and Administration Mrs Helen Wappett, Dioc House
Houses Committee Mrs Helen Wappett, Dioc House
Dioc Surveyor Mr Michael Cram, Dioc House
Pastoral Committee Mr Stephen Marriott (*as above*)
Designated Officer Mr Stephen Marriott (*as above*)

CHURCHES
Advisory Committee for the Care of Churches (*Chairman*) Mr Derek Lawson, 1 The Serpentine, Curzon Park, Chester CH4 8AF Tel: (01244) 678216 (*Executive Secretary*) Mr Simon Sayer, Dioc House
Redundant Churches Uses Committee Mr Stephen Marriott (*as above*)

EDUCATION
Director of Education Mr Jeff Turnbull, Dioc House
Children Mrs Alison Harris, Dioc House
Youth Revd Peter Chantry, Revd Helen Chantry, Dioc House

R.E. Adviser Ms Gaynor Pollard, Dioc House

MINISTRY AND TRAINING
Director of Ministry Canon James Newcome, Bishop's House, Abbey Square, Chester, CH1 2JD   *Tel:* (01244) 319169
Training Officer Revd Amiel Osmaston, Dioc House
Vocations Officers Revd Stephen Foster, Vicarage, 99 Chatham St, Edgeley, Stockport, Cheshire SK3 9EG
   Tel: 0161–480 5515
Revd Anne Samuels, Vicarage, Castle Rd, Halton, Runcorn, Cheshire WA7 2BE
   Tel: (01928) 563636
Officer for NSMs Revd Dr Roger Yates, 3 Racehorse Park, Wilmslow, Cheshire SK9 5LU   *Tel:* (01625) 520246
Advisers for Women in Ministry Revd Dr Judy Hunt, Rectory, Inveresk Rd, Tilston, Malpas, Cheshire SY14 7ED
   Tel: (01829) 250628
Revd Jane Brooke, 45 Brookfield Ave, Poynton, Stockport, Cheshire SK12 1JE
   Tel: (01625) 872822
Clergy Widows and Retirement Officers (Chester Archdeaconry) Canon Harold Aldridge, Vicarage, Vicarage Lane, Burton, S Wirral L64 5TJ   *Tel:* 0151–336 4070
(Macclesfield Archdeaconry) Canon Peter Hunt, Rectory, Brereton, Sandbach, Cheshire CW11 9RY   *Tel:* (01477) 533263
Society of Readers Mr A. Buckley, 55 Dalmorton Rd, Wallasey, Merseyside L45 1LG   *Tel:* 0151–639 2407

LITURGICAL
Chairman Ven Richard Gillings
Secretary Mr Stephen Marriott (*as above*)

MISSIONARY AND ECUMENICAL
Dioc Missioner Canon Michael Rees, 5 Abbey Green, Chester CH1 2JH
   Tel: (01244) 347500
Partners in World Mission Rt Revd Alan Winstanley, Vicarage, Ferry Rd, Eastham, Wirral, Merseyside L62 0AJ
   Tel and *Fax:* 0151–327 2182

County Ecumenical Officer and Cheshire Church Leaders Consultation Canon Michael Rees (*as above*)
Dioc Ecumenical Officer Vacancy
Sen Industrial Missioner Revd John Staley, 261 Oxford Rd, Macclesfield, Cheshire SK11 8JY   *Tel:* (01625) 423851

PRESS AND PUBLICATIONS
Dioc Communications Officer Revd David Marshall, Dioc House
Editor of Dioc News Revd David Marshall (*as above*)
Editor of Dioc Year Book Mr Stephen Marriott (*as above*)

DIOCESAN RECORDS OFFICE
Cheshire Records Office, Duke St, Chester CH1 2DN (*County Archivist* Mr J. Pepler)
   Tel: (01244) 603391

SOCIAL RESPONSIBILITY
Director of Social Responsibility Revd Bob Powley, Dioc House
Urban Officers Revd David Walker, Rectory, 29 Park Rd West, Birkenhead, Merseyside L43 1UR   *Tel:* 0151–652 1309
Revd Paul Robinson, St Paul's Vicarage, Huddersfield Rd, Stalybridge, Cheshire SK15 2PT   *Tel:* 0161–338 2514

STEWARDSHIP
Director of Parish Development (Acting) Revd Paul Reynolds, Dioc House

RURAL DEANS
ARCHDEACONRY OF CHESTER
Birkenhead Revd Bob Toan, Vicarage, St Peter's Rd, Rock Ferry, Birkenhead, Merseyside L42 1PY
   Tel: 0151–645 1622/643 1042
Chester Canon Christopher Samuels, Rectory, Handbridge, Chester CH4 7HL
   Tel: (01244) 671202
Frodsham Revd David Felix, Vicarage, 37 Lime Grove, Runcorn, Cheshire WA7 5JZ
   Tel: (01928) 574411
Great Budworth Revd Tom Owen, St James Vicarage, Manx Rd, Warrington, Cheshire WA4 6AJ   *Tel:* (01925) 631893
Malpas Revd Tony Boyd, Vicarage, Farndon, Chester CH3 6QD
   Tel: (01829) 270270
Middlewich Revd Dr Paul Gardner, Vicarage, The Green, Hartford, Northwich, Cheshire CW8 1QA
   Tel: (01606) 775577/783063
Wallasey Canon Richard Orton, St Hilary's Rectory, Church Hill, Wallasey, Merseyside L45 3NH   *Tel:* 0151–638 4771
Wirral North Revd Paddy Benson, Vicarage, Barnston, Wirral, Merseyside L61 1BW   *Tel:* 0151–648 2404
Wirral South Canon Harold Aldridge, Vicarage, Vicarage Lane, Burton, South Wirral L64 5TJ   *Tel:* 0151–336 4070

ARCHDEACONRY OF MACCLESFIELD
Bowden Canon Brian McConnell, Vicarage, Townfield Rd, Altrincham, Cheshire WA14 4DS   *Tel:* 0161–928 1279
Chadkirk Revd Mike Lowe, Vicarage, 155 Church Lane, Marple, Stockport, Cheshire SK6 7LD   *Tel:* 0161–449 0950/427 2378
Cheadle Revd Peter Isherwood, Vicarage, 36 Sagars Rd, Handforth, Wilmslow, Cheshire SK9 3EE
   Tel: (01625) 250559/532145
Congleton Revd Nigel Elbourne, Odd Rode Rectory, Scholar Green, Stoke-on-Trent, Staffs ST7 3QN
   Tel: (01270) 882195
Knutsford Canon Brian Young, Vicarage, Church Lane, Alderley Edge, Cheshire SK9 7UZ   *Tel:* (01625) 583249
Macclesfield Canon David Ashworth, Vicarage, Prestbury, Macclesfield, Cheshire SK10 4DG   *Tel:* (01625) 829288/827625
Mottram Revd Dr John Darch, Vicarage, 85 Edna St, Hyde, Cheshire SK14 1DR
   Tel: 0161–367 8787
Nantwich Revd Bill White, Rectory, 44 Church Lane, Wistaston, Crewe CW2 8HA
   Tel: (01270) 665742 (Home)
   (01270) 567119 (Office)
Stockport Canon John Roff, St George's Vicarage, 28 Buxton Rd, Stockport, Cheshire SK2 6NU   *Tel:* 0161–480 2453

DIOCESE OF CHICHESTER

Founded in 1070, formerly called Selsey (AD 681). West Sussex, except for one parish in the north (GUILDFORD); EAST SUSSEX, except for one parish in the north (ROCHESTER); one parish in Kent.

Population 1,471,000   Area 1,459 sq m
Stipendiary Clergy 347   Benefices 294
Parishes 387   Churches 513

BISHOP (102nd)
Rt Revd Eric Waldram Kemp DD, The Palace, Chichester, W Sussex PO19 1PY [1974]
Tel: (01243) 782161
Fax: (01243) 531332
[Eric Cicestr:]

Domestic Chaplain Revd Ian Chandler, The Palace (*as above*)

AREA BISHOPS
HORSHAM Rt Revd Lindsay Goodall Urwin OGS, Bishop's House, 21 Guildford Rd, Horsham, W Sussex RH12 1LU [1993]
Tel: (01403) 211139
Fax: (01403) 217349
e-mail: bishhorsham@clara.net
LEWES Rt Revd Wallace Benn, Bishop's Lodge, 16A Prideaux Rd, Eastbourne BN21 2NB [1997]
Tel: (01323) 648462
Fax: (01323) 641514
e-mail: wallace@lewes.clara.net

HONORARY ASSISTANT BISHOPS
Rt Revd Mark Green, 27 Selwyn House, Selwyn Rd, Eastbourne, E Sussex BN21 2LF [1982]
Tel: (01323) 642707
Rt Revd Edward George Knapp-Fisher, 2 Vicars Close, Chichester, W Sussex PO19 1PT [1987]
Tel: (01243) 789219
Rt Revd Morris Henry St John Maddocks, 3 The Chantry, Canon Lane, Chichester PO19 1PZ [1987]
Tel: (01243) 788888
Rt Revd Simon Wilton Phipps, Sarsens, Shipley, W Sussex RH13 8PX
Tel: (01403) 741354
Rt Revd Christopher Charles Luxmoore, 42 Willowbed Drive, Chichester, W Sussex PO19 2JB [1991]
Tel: (01243) 784680
Rt Revd Michael Eric Marshall, 97A Cadogan Lane, London SW1X 9DU [1992]
Tel: 0171–235 3383
Rt Revd John William Hind, Bishop's Lodge, Church Rd, Worth, Crawley, W Sussex RH10 7RT [1993]
Tel: (01293) 883051
Rt Revd Michael Richard John Manktelow, 2 The Chantry, Canon Lane, Chichester, W Sussex PO19 1PX [1994]
Tel: (01243) 631096

Rt Revd David Peter Wilcox, 4 The Court, Hoo Gardens, Willingdon, Eastbourne, E Sussex BN20 9AX [1995]
Rt Revd Michael Edgar Adie, Greenslade, Froxfield, Petersfield, Hants GU23 1EB [1996]
Tel: (01730) 827266

CATHEDRAL CHURCH OF THE HOLY TRINITY
Dean Very Revd John Treadgold, The Deanery, Chichester, W Sussex PO19 1PX [1989]
Tel: (01243) 787337/782595 (Office)
(01243) 783286 (Home)
Fax: (01243) 536190
Cathedral Office The Royal Chantry, Cathedral Cloisters, Chichester, W Sussex PO19 1PX Tel: (01243) 782595
Fax: (01243) 536190
Precentor Canon Roger Greenacre, 4 Vicars' Close, Chichester, W Sussex PO19 1PT [1975]
Tel: (01243) 784244
Fax: (01243) 536190
Chancellor Canon Peter Atkinson, The Residentiary, Canon Lane, Chichester, W Sussex PO19 1PX [1997]
Tel: (01243) 782961
Fax: (01243) 536190
Treasurer Canon Frank Hawkins, 12 St Martin's Square, Chichester, W Sussex PO19 1NR [1980]
Tel: (01243) 783509
Fax: (01243) 536190
Other members of the Administrative Chapter
Ven Michael Brotherton, 4 Canon Lane, Chichester, W Sussex PO19 1PX [1991]
Tel: (01243) 779134
Fax: (01243) 536452
Rt Revd Michael Manktelow, 2 The Chantry, Canon Lane, Chichester, W Sussex PO19 1PX [1997]
Tel: (01243) 531096
Fax: (01243) 536190
Priest-Vicar Revd David Nason, 1 St Richard's Walk, Chichester, W Sussex PO19 1QA
Tel: (01243) 775615
Fax: (01243) 536190
Chapter Clerk Mr Clifford Hodgetts, 5 East Pallant, Chichester, W Sussex PO19 1TS
Tel: (01243) 786111
Fax: (01243) 775640

Communar Capt Michael Shallow, Cathedral Office
Cathedral Organist Mr Alan Thurlow, 2 St Richard's Walk, Chichester, W Sussex PO19 1QA
Tel: (01243) 784790
Fax: (01243) 536190

ARCHDEACONS
CHICHESTER Ven Michael Brotherton, 4 Canon Lane, Chichester, W Sussex PO19 1PX [1991]
Tel: (01243) 779134
Fax: (01243) 536452
HORSHAM Ven William Filby, The Archdeaconry, Itchingfield, Horsham, W Sussex RH13 7NX [1983]
Tel: (01403) 790315
Fax: (01403) 791153
LEWES AND HASTINGS Ven Nicholas Reade, 27 The Avenue, Lewes, E Sussex BN7 1QT [1997]
Tel: (01273) 479530
Fax: (01273) 476529

CONVOCATION (MEMBERS OF THE HOUSE OF CLERGY OF THE GENERAL SYNOD)
The Archdeacon of Chichester
Proctors for Clergy
Revd Roger Combes
Canon Jeremy Haselock
Revd Clay Knowles
Ven Nicholas Reade
Revd Doris Staniford
(One Vacancy)

MEMBERS OF THE HOUSE OF LAITY OF THE GENERAL SYNOD
Viscountess Brentford
Mrs Daphne Brotherton
Mrs Margaret Brown
Mrs Jill Loveless
Mrs Rachel Moriarty
Mrs Mary Nagel
Mr John Pope
Mr Peter Robottom
Mr Trevor Stevenson
(Two Vacancies)

DIOCESAN OFFICERS
Dioc Secretary Mr Jonathan Prichard, Diocesan Church House, 211 New Church Rd, Hove, E Sussex BN3 4ED
Tel: (01273) 421021
Fax: (01273) 421041
e-mail: diosec@diochi.org.uk
Chancellor of Diocese The Worshipful Quentin Edwards, 13 South Grove, Highgate, London N6 6BJ   Tel: 0181–340 4861
Registrar of Diocese and Bishop's Legal Secretary Mr Clifford Hodgetts, 5 East Pallant, Chichester, W Sussex PO19 1TS
Tel: (01243) 786111
Fax: (01243) 775640

DIOCESAN ORGANISATIONS
Diocesan Office Diocesan Church House, 211 New Church Rd, Hove, E Sussex BN3 4ED Tel: (01273) 421021 Fax: (01273) 421041 e-mail: admin@diochi.org.uk

ADMINISTRATION
Dioc Synod (Chairman, House of Clergy) Ven Nicholas Reade, 27 The Avenue, Lewes, E Sussex BN7 1QT Tel: (01273) 479530; *(Chairman, House of Laity)* Viscountess Brentford, Cousley Place, Wadhurst, E Sussex TN5 6HF Tel: (01892) 783737; *(Secretary)* Mr Jonathan Prichard, Dioc Church House
Dioc Fund and Board of Finance (Incorporated) (Secretary) Mr Jonathan Prichard *(as above)*
Finance Committee Mr Jonathan Prichard *(as above)*
Stipends Committee (Secretary) Mr Jonathan Prichard *(as above)*
Parsonages Committee (Surveyor and Property Manager) Mr David Brown, Dioc Church House
Pastoral Committee (Secretary) Mr Andrew Robinson, Dioc Church House
Designated Officer Mr Clifford Hodgetts, 5 East Pallant, Chichester, PO19 1TS Tel: (01243) 786111 Fax: (01243) 775640

CHURCHES
Advisory Committee for the Care of Churches (Chairman) The Dean of Chichester *(as above)*; *(Secretary)* Mr Andrew Robinson *(as above)* e-mail: buildings@diochi.org.uk

COUNCIL FOR PASTORAL CARE
Secretary Mrs R. Sewell, Folly Cottage, Duke's Rd, Fontwell, Arundel, W Sussex BN18 0SP Tel: (01243) 542116

EDUCATION AND TRAINING
Schools
Adviser (Director of Education) Revd John Joyce, Dioc Church House e-mail: schools@diochi.org.uk
Schools Administration Mrs Elizabeth Yates, Dioc Church House
Schools Support Mrs Chris Fitton, Dioc Church House
Children and Young People
Children's Work Adviser Miss Rachel Bennett
Youth Officers Capt Bob Carrington, Revd Stephen Gallagher, Dioc Church House
Education and Training of Adults
Adviser Revd Dr John Mantle, Dioc Church House
Readers Board (Secretary) Mrs J. Derbyshire, 9 Wheatsheaf Gardens, Lewes BN7 2UQ Tel: (01273) 483835

MINISTRY
Bishop's Adviser on Ministry, Lay Ministry and Director of Ordinands Canon Frank Hawkins, 12 St Martin's Square, Chichester, W Sussex PO19 1NR Tel: (01243) 783509
Asst DDO (Women's Ministry) Revd Doris Staniford, 1 Church House Close, Downsway, Southwick, Brighton BN42 7WQ Tel: (01273) 594084
Continuing Education of the Clergy and Full-time Lay Workers Revd Stephen Tucker, St Wulfran's Rectory, 43 Ainsworth Ave, Ovingdean, Brighton BN2 7BG Tel: (01273) 303633
Post-Ordination Training Revd Stephen Tucker *(as above)*
Training for the Non-Stipendiary Ministry Vocations Consultants
Revd Roger Caswell, St Mary's Vicarage, 34 Fitzalan Rd, Littlehampton BN17 5ET Tel: (01903) 724410
Revd Kathleen Lefroy, 12 Rodmill Drive, Eastbourne, E Sussex BN21 2SG Tel: (01323) 640294
Revd Trevor Buxton, 24 Stanford Ave, Brighton BN1 6EA Tel: (01273) 561755
Revd Graham Piper, 1 Sandy Vale, Haywards Heath, W Sussex RH16 4JH Tel: (01444) 450173
Revd Keith Wood, Rectory, St Thomas St, Winchelsea, E Sussex TN36 4EB Tel: (01797) 226254

MISSION AND RENEWAL
Adviser Canon John Ford, 27 Gatesmead, Haywards Heath, W Sussex RH16 1SN Tel: (01444) 414658
Evangelist Revd Mark Payne, 12 Walsingham Rd, Hove BN3 4FF Tel: (01273) 326193
Resources Officer Mr Mark Forster, Dioc Church House
Overseas Council (Secretary) Canon David Pain, Vicarage, Billingshurst, W Sussex RH14 9PY Tel: (01403) 782332

ECUMENICAL
European Ecumenical Committee (Chairman) Canon Roger Greenacre, 4 Vicars Close, Chichester, W Sussex PO19 1PT Tel: (01243) 784244
Senior Ecumenical Officer Revd Terry Stratford, Stapleﬁeld Vicarage, 14 Ledgers Meadow, Cuckfield, W Sussex RH17 5EW Tel: (01444) 456588
Archdeaconry Ecumenical Officers (Chichester) Revd Terry Stratford *(as above)*
(Horsham) Revd Geoffrey Driver, Vicarage, Cowfold, Horsham RH13 8AH Tel: (01403) 864296
(Lewes and Hastings) Revd Simon Crittall, St Richard's Vicarage, Hailsham Rd, Heathfield TN21 8AF Tel: (01435) 862744

LITURGICAL
Liturgy Consultant Revd Ian Forrester, Dioc Church House
Music Consultants Revd Ian Forrester *(as above)*

SOCIAL RESPONSIBILITY
Adviser Canon Michael Butler, Dioc Church House
Association for Family Social Work (Secretary) Mr Neil Morgan, Dioc Church House

PRESS AND PUBLICATIONS
Communications Officer Canon Will Pratt, Dioc Church House Tel: (01273) 748756 (Home) e-mail: media@diochi.org.uk
Editor of Dioc Directory Canon Will Pratt *(as above)*
Editor of 'The Chichester Leaflet' and 'The Chichester Magazine' Canon Will Pratt *(as above)*

DIOCESAN RECORDS OFFICES
East Sussex Mr R. Davey, *(County Archivist)*, The Maltings, Castle Precincts, Lewes, E Sussex BN7 1YT Tel: (01273) 482356
West Sussex Mr R. Childs *(County Archivist)*, County Records Office, County Hall, Chichester, W Sussex PO19 1RN Tel: (01243) 533911

RURAL DEANS
ARCHDEACONRY OF CHICHESTER
Arundel and Bognor Revd Robert Harris, Felpham Rectory, 24 Limmer Lane, Bognor Regis PO22 7ET Tel: (01243) 842522
Brighton Canon Douglas McKittrick, St Peter's Vicarage, 10 West Drive, Brighton BN2 2GD Tel: (01273) 682960
Chichester Revd Victor Cassam, Rectory, St Peter's Crescent, Selsey, Chichester PO20 0NA Tel: (01243) 602363
Hove Canon John Caldicott, Vicarage, Wilbury Ave, Hove, E Sussex BN3 3BP Tel: (01273) 733331
Worthing Revd Roger Russell, 63 Manor Rd, Lancing, W Sussex BN15 0EY Tel: (01903) 753212

ARCHDEACONRY OF HORSHAM
Cuckfield Vacancy
East Grinstead Revd Gordon Bond, Vicarage, Windmill Lane, East Grinstead RH19 2DS Tel: (01342) 323439
Horsham Canon David Pain, Vicarage, East St, Billingshurst RH14 9PY Tel: (01403) 782332
Hurst Revd Richard Clarke, Rectory, Keymer, Hassocks, W Sussex BN6 8RB Tel: (01273) 843570
Midhurst Vacancy
Petworth Revd David Pollard, Rectory, Petworth, W Sussex GU28 0DB Tel: (01798) 342505

Storrington Revd Gerald Evans, Lindens, Kithurst Park, Storrington RH20 4JH
Tel: (01903) 742206
Westbourne Revd Tom Inman, Vicarage, Bosham, Chichester, W Sussex PO18 8HX
Tel: (01243) 573228

ARCHDEACONRY OF LEWES AND HASTINGS

Battle and Bexhill Revd John Cotton, Rectory, Old Town, Bexhill-on-Sea, E Sussex TN40 2HE *Tel:* (01424) 211115

Dallington Revd Roger Porthouse, St Mary's Vicarage, Vicarage Rd, Hailsham BN27 1BL
Tel: (01323) 842381
Eastbourne Canon Gordon Rideout, All Saints Vicarage, Grange Rd, Eastbourne, BN21 4HE
Tel: (01323) 410033
Hastings Revd Roger Combes, Rectory, St Matthews Rd, St Leonards on Sea TN38 0TN
Tel: (01424) 423790

Lewes and Seaford Revd Hugh Atherstone, Vicarage, 46 Sutton Rd, Seaford BN25 1SH
Tel: (01323) 893508
Rotherfield Revd Andrew Cornes, Vicarage, Chapel Green, Crowborough, E Sussex TN6 1ED *Tel:* (01892) 667384
Rye Revd Martin Sheppard, Rectory, Gun Garden, Rye, E Sussex TN31 7HH
Tel: (01797) 222430
Uckfield Revd Geoffrey Daintree, Vicarage, Framfield, Uckfield, E Sussex TN22 5NH
Tel: (01825) 890365

DIOCESE OF COVENTRY

Re-founded in 1918. Coventry; Warwickshire, except for small areas in the north (BIRMINGHAM) and south-west (GLOUCESTER) and one parish in the south (OXFORD); an area of Solihull.

Population 763,000   Area 686 sq m
Stipendiary Clergy 149   Benefices 138
Parishes 195   Churches 240

BISHOP (8th)
Rt Revd Colin James Bennetts, Bishop's House, 23 Davenport Rd, Coventry CV5 6PW [1998]   Tel: (01203) 672244
   Fax: (01203) 713271
   e-mail: bishcov@clara.net
[Colin Coventry]

SUFFRAGAN BISHOP
WARWICK Rt Revd Anthony Martin Priddis, Warwick House, 139 Kenilworth Rd, Coventry CV4 7AP [1996]
   Tel: (01203) 416200
   Fax: (01203) 415354
   e-mail: bishwarwick@clara.net

CATHEDRAL CHURCH OF ST MICHAEL
Provost Very Revd John Fitzmaurice Petty, Pelham Lee House, 7 Priory Row, Coventry CV1 5ES [1987]   Tel: (01203) 227597
   Fax: (01203) 631448
e-mail: prov@coventrycathedral.org.uk
   Web: www.coventrycathedral.org.uk
Canons Residentiary
Vice-Provost and Canon Pastor Canon Vivienne Faull, , 35 Morningside, Coventry, W Midlands CV5 6PD [1994]
   Tel: (01203) 675446
Precentor Canon Christopher Burch, 35 Asthill Grove, Coventry CV3 6HN [1995]
   Tel: (01203) 505426
International Adviser Canon Andrew White, 7 Priory Row, Coventry CV1 5ES [1998]   Tel: (01203) 227595
Canons Theologian
Canon David Mead (*Lay Canon Theologian*), 7 Priory Row, Coventry CV1 5ES [1996]   Tel: (01203) 227597
Canon Christopher Lamb PH D, 5 Waterloo St, Coventry CV1 5JS [1992]
   Tel: (01203) 257523
Canon Christina Baxter PH D (*Lay Canon Theologian*), St John's College, Bramcote, Nottingham NG9 3DS   Tel: 0115–925 1114
Very Revd Tom Wright D PHIL, The Deanery, The Close, Lichfield WS13 7LD [1992]
   Tel: (01543) 256120

Bursar Canon David Mead, 7 Priory Row, Coventry CV1 5ES   Tel: (01203) 227597
e-mail:
   information@coventrycathedral.org
Chapter Clerk Mr John Coles, 23 Bayley Lane, Coventry CV1 5RJ
   Tel: (01203) 553311
Director of Music Mr Rupert Jeffcoat
   Tel: (01203) 227597

ARCHDEACONS
COVENTRY Ven Ian Russell, 9 Armorial Rd, Coventry CV3 6GH [1989]
   Tel: (01203) 417750 (Home)
   (01203) 674328 (Office)
WARWICK Ven Michael Paget-Wilkes, 10 Northumberland Rd, Leamington Spa, Warks CV32 6HA [1990]
   Tel: (01926) 313337 (Home)
   (01203) 674328 (Office)

CONVOCATION (MEMBERS OF THE HOUSE OF CLERGY OF THE GENERAL SYNOD)
The Archdeacon of Coventry
Proctors for Clergy
Canon Mark Bryant
Canon John Moore
Revd Peter Watkins

MEMBERS OF THE HOUSE OF LAITY OF THE GENERAL SYNOD
Mr David Jones
Mrs Margaret Sedgwick
Mr Michael Tyrrell

DIOCESAN OFFICERS
Dioc Secretary Mrs Isobel Chapman, Church House, Palmerston Rd, Coventry CV5 6FJ   Tel: (01203) 674328
   Fax: (01203) 691760
e-mail: Isobel.Chapman@btinternet.com
Chancellor of Diocese Chanc W. M. Gage, The Royal Courts of Justice, Strand, London WC2 2LL

Registrar of Diocese and Bishop's Legal Secretary Mr David Dumbleton, Rotherham & Co, 8 The Quadrant, Coventry CV1 2EL
   Tel: (01203) 227331

DIOCESAN ORGANISATIONS
Diocesan Office Church House, Palmerston Rd, Coventry CV5 6FJ
   Tel: (01203) 674328
   Fax: (01203) 691760

ADMINISTRATION
Dioc Synod (*Chairman, House of Clergy*) Ven Ian Russsell, Dioc Office; (*Chairman, House of Laity*) Mr Julian Hall, 'Larkfield', Ashlawn Rd, Rugby CV22 5QE Tel: (01788) 543588; (*Secretary*) Mr Douglas Little, Church House
Board of Finance (*Chairman*) Mr J. R. Boswell, Peacock Farm, Hollywell, Shrewley CV35 7BJ Tel: (01926) 842365; (*Secretary*) Mrs Isobel Chapman, Church House
Parsonages Committee Mrs Isobel Chapman (*as above*)
Trustees Mr David Dumbleton, Rotherham & Co, 8 The Quadrant, Coventry CV1 2EL
   Tel: (01203) 227331
Pastoral Committee Mrs Isobel Chapman (*as above*)
Designated Officer Mrs Isobel Chapman (*as above*)

CHURCHES
Advisory Committee for the Care of Churches Revd Kenneth Phillips, Vicarage, Priors Marston, Rugby, Warks CV23 8RT
   Tel: (01327) 260053

EDUCATION
Schools Canon John Eardley, Bubbenhall Rectory, Coventry CV8 3BD
   Tel: (01203) 302345
   and (01203) 674328

MINISTRY
Dioc Director of Ordinands and Head of Department Revd Stuart Beake, Vicarage, Church Lane, Shottery, Stratford-upon-Avon CV37 9HQ   Tel: (01789) 293381
Dioc Adviser for Women's Ministry Revd Frances Tyler, Vicarage, 4 Farber Rd, Walsgrave, Coventry CV2 2BG
   Tel: (01203) 615152
Vocations Team Leader Revd Malcolm Tyler, Vicarage, 4 Farber Rd, Walsgrave, Coventry CV2 2BG   Tel: (01203) 615151
CME Adviser Revd David Tilley, 6 Church Rd, Baginton, Coventry CV8 3AR
   Tel: (01203) 302508

Lay Training Adviser Revd Tony Bradley, Vicarage, 24 Mallory Rd, Bishop's Tackbrook, Leamington Spa CV33 9QX
Tel: (01926) 426922
Readers (Hon Registrar and Secretary) Mr L. W. T. Sharp, 9 Evenlode Close, Stratford-upon-Avon CV37 7EL *Tel:* (01789) 293019
Ministry Amongst Deaf People Revd Richard Livingston, Wolverton Rectory, Stratford-upon-Avon CV37 0HF
Tel: (01789) 731278

PRESS AND PUBLICATIONS

Dioc Communications Officer Revd Lawrence Mortimer, Wootton Warren Vicarage, Solihull B95 6BD
Tel: (01564) 792659
Editor of Dioc Directory and 'Diamond' Revd Lawrence Mortimer (*as above*)

DIOCESAN RECORDS OFFICE

Warwickshire County Record Office, Priory Park, Cape Rd, Warwick CV34 4JS, *County Archivist* Miss M. Ory
Tel: (01926) 410410, Ext 2508

ECUMENICAL AND SOCIAL RESPONSIBILITY

Officer Revd Liz Cowley, Cathedral Offices, 7 Priory Row, Coventry CV1 5ES
Tel: (01203) 227597

STEWARDSHIP

Dioc Adviser Revd Michael Peatman, St James Vicarage, 171 Abbey Rd, Coventry CV3 4PG *Tel:* (01203) 301617

RURAL DEANS
ARCHDEACONRY OF COVENTRY

Coventry North Revd Barry Keeton, St John's Rectory, 9 Davenport Rd, Coventry CV5 6QA *Tel:* (01203) 673203
Coventry South Revd Charles Knowles, St Mary Magdalen's Vicarage, Craven St, Coventry CV5 8DT *Tel:* (01203) 675838
Coventry East Revd David Howard, 68 Brandon Rd, Coventry CV3 2 JF
Tel: (01203) 636334
Kenilworth Revd George Baisley, Rectory, Meriden Rd, Berkswell, Coventry CV7 7BE *Tel:* (01676) 533605

Nuneaton Revd John Philpott, Chilvers Coton Vicarage, Nuneaton CV11 4NJ
Tel: (01203) 383010
Rugby Revd Peter Watkins, Wolston Vicarage, Coventry CV8 3HD
Tel: (01203) 542722

ARCHDEACONRY OF WARWICK

Alcester Revd John Ganjavi, Rectory, Beaudesert Lane, Henley-in-Arden, Solihull, W Midlands B95 5JY
Tel: (01564) 792570
Fosse Revd Stuart Beake, Vicarage, Church Lane, Shottery, Stratford-upon-Avon CV37 9HQ *Tel:* (01789) 293381
Shipston Revd Gordon Benfield, Ivy Cottage, Butlers Marston, Warwick CV35 0NG *Tel:* (01926) 640758
Southam Revd Roy Brown, Rectory, 2 Church Lane, Harbury, Leamington Spa CV33 9HA *Tel:* (01926) 612377
Warwick and Leamington Revd Bill Merrington, St Paul's Vicarage, 15 Lillington Rd, Leamington Spa CV32 5YS
Tel: (01926) 427149

DIOCESE OF DERBY

Founded in 1927. Derbyshire, except for a small area in the north (CHESTER); a small area of Stockport; a few parishes in Staffordshire.

Population 981,000   Area 997 sq m
Stipendiary Clergy 200   Benefices 178
Parishes 248   Churches 331

BISHOP (6th)
Rt Revd Jonathan Sansbury Bailey, Derby Church House, Full St, Derby DE1 3DR [1995]
Home The Bishop's House, 6 King St, Duffield, Derby DE56 4EU
Tel: (01332) 346744 (Office)
(01332) 840132 (Home)
Fax: (01332) 295810 (Office)
(01332) 842743 (Home)
e-mail: bishopderby@clara.net
[Jonathan Derby]

SUFFRAGAN BISHOP
REPTON Vacancy, Repton House, Lea, Matlock DE4 5JP   Tel: (01629) 534644
Fax: (01629) 534003

HONORARY ASSISTANT BISHOPS
Rt Revd Kenneth John Fraser Skelton, 65 Crescent Rd, Sheffield S7 1HN [1984]
Tel: 0114-255 1260
Rt Revd Robert Beak, Ashcroft Cottage, Butts Rd, Ashover, Chesterfield S45 0AX
Tel: (01246) 590048

CATHEDRAL CHURCH OF ALL SAINTS
Provost Very Revd Michael Perham, The Provost's House, 9 Highfield Rd, Derby DE22 1GX [1998]
Tel: (01332) 341201 Ext 25 (Office)
Tel and Fax: (01332) 342971 (Home)
Cathedral Office St Michael's House, Queen St, Derby DE1 3DT   Tel: (01332) 341201
Fax: (01332) 203991
e-mail: Derby.cathedral@btinternet.com
Canons Residentiary
Sub-Provost Canon Geoffrey Marshall, 24 Kedleston Rd, Derby DE22 1GU [1993]
Tel: (01332) 343144 (Home)
(01332) 341201 Ext 23 (Office)
Ven Ian Gatford, Derby Church House, Full St, Derby DE1 3DR [1984]
Tel: (01332) 382233 (Office)

Canon Theologian Canon Tony Chesterman, 13 Newbridge Rd, Ambergate, Belper DE56 2GR [1989]
Tel: (01773) 852236 (Home)
(01332) 382233 (Office)
Canon Pastor Canon David Truby, 22 Kedleston Rd, Derby DE22 1GU [1998]
Tel: (01332) 341201 Ext 28 (Office)
NSM Canon Sheana Barby, 2 Margaret St, Derby DE1 3FE   Tel: (01332) 383301
Chapter Clerk Mr Michael Mallender, 35 St Mary's Gate, Derby DE1 3JU
Tel: (01332) 372311
Administrator Mr William Hall, Cathedral Office   Tel: (01332) 341201 Ext 21
Master of Music and Organist Mr Peter Gould, 3 Cathedral View, Littleover, Derby DE22 3HR
Tel: (01332) 366692 (Home)
(01332) 345848 (Office)
Assistant Organist Dr Tom Corfield, 109 Palmerston St, Derby DE23 6PF
Tel: (01332) 762251 (Home)
(01332) 345848 (Office)

ARCHDEACONS
CHESTERFIELD Ven David Garnett, The Old Parsonage, Taddington, Buxton SK17 9TW [1996]   Tel: (01298) 85607
Fax: (01298) 85583
DERBY Ven Ian Gatford, Derby Church House, Full St, Derby DE1 3DR [1993]
Tel: (01332) 382233
Fax: (01332) 292969 (Office)
72 Pastures Hill, Littleover, Derby DE23 7BB   Tel: (01332) 512700 (Home)
Fax: (01332) 523332 (Home)

CONVOCATION (MEMBERS OF THE HOUSE OF CLERGY OF THE GENERAL SYNOD)
The Archdeacon of Derby
Proctors for Clergy
Revd Cedric Blakey
Canon Geoffrey Marshall
Canon Timothy Yates

MEMBERS OF THE HOUSE OF LAITY OF THE GENERAL SYNOD
Mrs Joanna Ingram
Mrs Christine McMullen
Mrs Jennifer Radford
Mr David Wilkinson

DIOCESAN OFFICERS
Dioc Secretary Mr Bob Carey, Derby Church House, Full St, Derby DE1 3DR
Tel: (01332) 382233
Fax: (01332) 292969
Chancellor of Diocese His Honour Judge John Bullimore, 137 Edge Lane, Thornhill, Dewsbury, W Yorks WF12 0HB
Tel: (01924) 463911
Registrar of Diocese and Bishop's Legal Secretary Mr James Battie, Derby Church House

DIOCESAN ORGANISATIONS
Diocesan Office Derby Church House, Full St, Derby DE1 3DR   Tel: (01332) 382233
Fax: (01332) 292969

ADMINISTRATION
Dioc Synod (Chairman, House of Clergy) Canon Tony Chesterman, 13 Newbridge Rd, Ambergate, Belper DE56 2GR; Tel: (01773) 852236; *(Chairman, House of Laity)* Mrs Christine McMullen 114 Brown Edge Rd, Buxton SK17 7AB Tel: (01298) 73997 Fax: (01298) 72448; *(Secretary)* Mr Bob Carey, Derby Church House
Board of Finance (Chairman) Canon Martin Hulbert, Vicarage, 6 Pursglove Drive, Tideswell, Buxton SK17 8PA
Tel: (01298) 871317
Fax: (01298) 872621
(Secretary) Mr Bob Carey *(as above)*
Parsonages Board Mr Jim Blackwell, Derby Church House
Dioc Surveyors (Derby Archdeaconry) Mr Ben Roper, Smith & Roper, Buxton Rd, Bakewell DE45 1BZ
Tel: (0162 981) 2722
Pastoral Committee Mr Jim Blackwell *(as above)*
Designated Officer Mr James Battie, Derby Church House

CHURCHES
Advisory Committee for the Care of Churches (Chairman) Canon Raymond Ross; *(Secretary)* Ms Belinda Bramhall, Derby Church House

EDUCATION
Dioc Education Office Derby Church House, Full St, Derby DE1 3DR
Tel: (01332) 382233
Fax: (01332) 291988

Derby   83

Director Mr David Edwards
Schools Adviser Mr Andrew Burns
Children's Adviser Canon Sheana Barby
Laity Adviser Revd Michael Alexander
Youth Adviser Vacancy
Warden, Champion House Revd Adrian Murray-Leslie, Champion House, Edale, Hope Valley S33 7ZA
Tel and *Fax:* (01433) 670254

MINISTRY
Secretary and Director of Ordinands Canon Geoffrey Marshall, 24 Kedleston Rd, Derby DE22 1GU
Tel: (01332) 343144 (Home)
(01332) 341201 (Office)
Bishop's Adviser on CME Canon Tony Chesterman, Derby Church House
Bishop's Officer for NSMs Canon Tony Chesterman (*as above*)
Director of Ordinands Canon Sheana Barby, 2 Margaret St, Derby DE1 3FE
Tel: (01332) 383301
Readers' Board Mr Norman Stanley, 24 Ella Bank Rd, Marlpool, Heanor DE75 7HF
Tel: (01773) 714821

MISSIONARY AND ECUMENICAL
Council for Mission and Unity (*Chairman*) The Bishop of Repton
Ecumenical Officers Canon Richard Orchard, Vicarage, Curbar, Hope Valley S32 3YF
Tel: (01433) 630387
Revd John Henson, St Mary's Vicarage, Ilkeston DE7 5JA
Tel: 0115–932 4725
World Development Officer Revd David Murdoch, St George's Vicarage, Church Lane, New Mills, High Peak SK22 4NP
Tel: (01663) 743225
Dioc Missioner Revd John Morison, St Paul's Vicarage, 149 Church Rd, Quarndon, Derby DE22 5JA
Tel: (01332) 559333

Interfaith Adviser Revd Basil Scott, 11 Harrington St, Derby DE23 8PG
Tel: (01332) 772360

PRESS AND COMMUNICATIONS
Office Derby Church House, Derby DE1 3DR
Tel: (01332) 382233
Fax: (01332) 292969
Communications Officer Mr Bryan Harris, Derby Church House
Tel: (01332) 553394 (Home)
Editor of Dioc News Mr Bryan Harris (*as above*)

DIOCESAN RECORDS OFFICE
Derbyshire Record Office, County Offices, Matlock DE4 3AG (*County Archivist* Dr Margaret O'Sullivan) Tel: (01629) 580000, Ext 7347

SOCIAL RESPONSIBILITY
Dioc Adviser for Social Responsibility Dr Rosemary Power, Derby Church House
Assistant for Social Responsibility Revd Maggie McLean, Derby Church House
Industrial Mission in Derbyshire (*Local Ecumenical Project*) *Chairman* Revd Keith Orford, 27 Lums Hill Rise, Matlock DE4 3FX
Tel: (01629) 55349

PARISH DEVELOPMENT
Parish Development Adviser Revd Barrie Gauge, Derby Church House

RURAL DEANS
ARCHDEACONRY OF DERBY
Ashbourne Revd Christopher Harrison, Vicarage, Parwich, Ashbourne, Derby DE6 1QD
Tel: (01335) 390226
Derby North Revd Gerry Reilly, St Philip's Vicarage, Taddington Rd, Chaddesden, Derby DE21 4JU
Tel: (01332) 673428
Derby South Canon Donald Macdonald, St Osmund's Vicarage, London Rd, Derby DE24 8UW
Tel: (01332) 571329

Duffield Revd David Perkins, Christ Church Vic, Bridge St, Belper DE56 1BA
Tel: (01773) 824974
Heanor Revd Peter Swales, Vicarage, Horsley, Derby DE21 5BR
Tel: (01332) 880284
Ilkeston Revd Ian Gooding, Rectory, Stanton-by-Dale, Ilkeston DE7 4QA
Tel: 0115–932 4584
Longford Revd Stewart Rayner, St Helen's Rectory, Rectory Court, Etwall, Derby DE65 6LP
Tel: (01283) 732349
Melbourne Revd Robert Harris, St Mary's Vicarage, 1 St Mary's Close, Boulton Lane, Alvaston, Derby DE24 0GF
Tel: (01332) 571296
Repton Revd Joseph Lister, Netherseal Rectory, Swadlincote DE12 8DF
Tel: (01283) 761179

ARCHDEACONRY OF CHESTERFIELD
Alfreton Revd David Ashton, Vicarage, Broadway, Swanwick, Alfreton DE55 1DQ
Tel: (01773) 602684
Bakewell and Eyam Revd Edmund Urquhart, Bakewell Vicarage, Bakewell DE45 1FD
Tel: (01629) 812256
Bolsover and Staveley Revd John Easton, Vicarage, Bolsover, Chesterfield S44 6BG
Tel: (01246) 824888
Buxton Canon Martin Hulbert, Vicarage, 6 Pursglove Drive, Tideswell, Buxton SK17 8PA
Tel: (01298) 871317
Chesterfield Revd Tom Johnson, Rectory, Narrowleys Lane, Ashover, Chesterfield S45 0AU
Tel: (01246) 590246
Glossop Revd David Rowley, Vicarage, 7 Station Rd, Birch Vale, Stockport SK12 5BP
Tel: (01663) 743350
Wirksworth Revd Dr Ian Mitchell, All Saints' Vicarage, Smedley St, Matlock DE4 3JG
Tel: (01629) 582235

DIOCESE OF DURHAM

Founded in 635. Durham, except for an area in the south-west (RIPON), and two parishes in the north (NEWCASTLE); Gateshead; South Tyneside; Sunderland; Hartlepool; Stockton-on-Tees, north of the Tees.

Population 1,486,000   Area 987 sq m
Stipendiary Clergy 241   Benefices 227
Parishes 252   Churches 300

BISHOP (70th)
Rt Revd Anthony Michael Arnold Turnbull, Auckland Castle, Bishop Auckland, Co Durham DL14 7NR [1994]
Tel: (01388) 602576
Fax: (01388) 605264
e-mail: bishdur@btinternet.com
[Michael Dunelm:]

Bishop's Senior Chaplain Revd Stephen Conway (*same address*)

SUFFRAGAN BISHOP
JARROW Rt Revd Alan Smithson, The Old Vicarage, Hallgarth, Pittington, Durham DH6 1AB [1990]   Tel: 0191–372 0025
Fax: 0191–372 2326

CATHEDRAL CHURCH OF CHRIST AND BLESSED MARY THE VIRGIN
Dean Very Revd John Robert Arnold, The Deanery, Durham DH1 3EQ [1989]
Tel: 0191–384 7500
Fax: 0191–386 4267
Canons Residentiary
Canon Prof David Brown, 14 The College, Durham DH1 3EQ [1990]   Tel: 0191–386 4657
Ven Trevor Willmott, 15 The College, Durham DH1 3EQ [1997]
Tel: 0191–384 7534
Canon Martin Kitchen PH D, 3 The College, Durham DH1 3EQ [1997]
Tel: 0191–384 2415
Canon David Whittington, 6A The College, Durham DH1 3EQ [1998]
Tel: 0191–384 5489
Canon Nigel Stock, 7 The College, Durham DH1 3EQ [1998] Tel: 0191–386 1891
Precentor Revd Michael Hampel, 16A The College, Durham DH1 3EQ
Tel: 0191–384 2481
Chapter Clerk Mr Paul Whittaker, Chapter Office, The College, Durham DH1 3EH
Tel: 0191–386 4266
Cathedral Organist Mr James Lancelot, 6 The College, Durham DH1 3EQ
Tel: 0191–386 4766

ARCHDEACONS
DURHAM Ven Trevor Willmott, 15 The College, Durham DH1 3EQ [1997]
Tel: 0191–384 7534
AUCKLAND Ven Granville Gibson, Elmside, 2 Etherley Lane, Bishop Auckland DL14 7QR [1993]   Tel: (01388) 451635
Fax: (01388) 607502
e-mail: vengg@gibven.demon.co.uk
SUNDERLAND Ven Frank White, Greenriggs, Dipe Lane, East Boldon NE36 0PH [1997]   Tel: 0191–536 2300
Fax: 0191–519 3369
e-mail: F2awhite@aol.com

CONVOCATION (MEMBERS OF THE HOUSE OF CLERGY OF THE GENERAL SYNOD)
Dignitaries in Convocation
The Dean of Durham
The Archdeacon of Auckland
Proctors in Convocation
Revd Graeme Buttery
Revd Stephen Conway
Revd Penny Martin
Revd Dr Philip Thomas
Ven Frank White

MEMBERS OF THE HOUSE OF LAITY OF THE GENERAL SYNOD
Mrs Janet Atkinson
Dr James Harrison
Mr Paul Jefferson
Mrs Irene Oakley
Ms Anne Williams
Mrs Ioné Rippeth

DIOCESAN OFFICERS
Dioc Secretary Mr Jonathan Cryer, Dioc Office, Auckland Castle, Market Place, Bishop Auckland, Co Durham DL14 7QJ
Tel: (01388) 604515
Fax: (01388) 603695
Chancellor of Diocese The Worshipful the Revd Rupert Bursell, Diocesan Registry, 3 The Gate House, Auckland Castle, Bishop Auckland DL14 7NP   Tel: (01388) 450576
Fax: (01388) 604999
Deputy Chancellor His Honour Judge Thomas Coningsby, (*same address*)
Registrar of Diocese and Bishop's Legal Secretary Mr A. N. Fairclough, (*same address*)
Deputy Registrar Ms H. Monckton-Milnes, Dioc Registry
Dioc Surveyor Mr D. L. Renton, Dioc Office

DIOCESAN ORGANISATIONS
Diocesan Office Auckland Castle, Market Place, Bishop Auckland, Co Durham DL14 7QJ   Tel: (01388) 604515
Fax: (01388) 603695

ADMINISTRATION
Dioc Synod (*Chairman, House of Clergy*) Canon Eric Stephenson, St George's Vicarage, 2 Ashleigh Villas, East Boldon, Tyne and Wear NE36 0LA Tel: 0191–536 3699; (*Chairman, House of Laity*) Mr Geoffrey Taylor, 14 Academy Gardens, Gainford, Darlington, Co Durham DL2 3EN Tel: (01325) 730379; (*Secretary*) Mr Jonathan Cryer, Dioc Office
Board of Finance (*Chairman*) Ven Granville Gibson, Elmside, 2 Etherley Lane, Bishop Auckland DL14 7QR Tel: (01388) 451635; (*Secretary*) Mr Jonathan Cryer (*as above*)
Glebe Advisory Committee (*Chairman*) Ven Granville Gibson (*as above*); (*Secretary*) Mr Jonathan Cryer (*as above*)
Parsonages Committee (*Chairman*) Revd Jon Bell, St Cuthbert's Vicarage, 1 Aykley Court, Durham DH1 4NW Tel: 0191–386 4526; (*Secretary*) Mr G. W. Heslop, Dioc Office
Pastoral Committee (*Chairman*) Ven Granville Gibson (*as above*); (*Secretary*) Mr G. W. Heslop (*as above*)
Church Buildings Committee (*Chairman*) Ven Granville Gibson (*as above*); (*Secretary*) Mr Jonathan Cryer (*as above*)
Redundant Churches Uses Committee (*Chairman*) Ven Granville Gibson (*as above*); (*Secretary*) Mr Jonathan Cryer (*as above*)
Designated Officer Mr A. N. Fairclough, Dioc Registry (*as above*)
Tel: (01388) 450576

CHURCHES
Advisory Committee for the Care of Churches (*Chairman*) Mr Geoffrey Thrush, 9 Brierville, Durham DH1 4QE Tel: 0191–386 1958; (*Secretary*) Mr I. A. Richardson, Dioc Office   Tel: (01388) 450577

EDUCATION
Director of Education Canon David Whittington, Carter House, Pelaw Leazes Lane, Durham DH1 1TB
Tel: 0191–384 3692
Assistants (*RE Adviser*) Revd Valerie Shedden (*same address*)

(*Children's Adviser*) Revd Paul Allinson (*same address*)
(*Youth Officer*) Vacancy (*same address*)
(*Adult Education Officer*) Revd Colin Patterson (*same address*)

MINISTRY
Board for Ministries and Training (*Chairman*) The Bishop of Durham (*as above*); (*Secretary*) Canon Adrian Dorber, Rectory, Brancepeth, Durham DH7 8EH
Tel: 0191–378 0503
Bishop's Adviser for Continuing Ministerial Education Revd Dr Nick Chamberlain, Rectory, Burnmoor, Houghton-le-Spring DH4 6EX Tel: 0191–385 2695
Director of Post-Ordination Training Revd Dr Nick Chamberlain (*as above*)
Director of Ordinands Revd Alison White, Greenriggs, Dipe Lane, East Boldon NE36 0PH Tel: 0191–536 2300
Fax: 0191–519 3369
e-mail: F2awhite@aol.com
Woman Adviser in Ministry Canon Penny Jones, Rectory, Stanhope, Bishop Auckland DL13 2UE Tel: (01388) 528308
Pensions Officers Mr W. Hurworth, 34 Castlereagh, Wynard Park, Wynard, Billingham TS22 5QF Tel: (01740) 644274
Revd Peter Welby, 21 York Villas, Tudhoe, Spennymoor, Co Durham DL16 6LP
Tel: (01388) 818418
Readers' Board (*Warden*) Canon Alex Whitehead, St Peter's Vicarage, 77 Yarm Rd, Stockton-on-Tees TS18 3PJ
Tel: (01642) 676625
(*Registrar*) Mr Philip Smithson, 2 Sea View Gardens, Roker, Sunderland SR6 9PN
Tel: 0191–548 6827

LITURGICAL
Chairman Canon Eric Stephenson (*as above*)
Secretary Mrs K. Venning, 10 South Bailey, Durham DH1 3EE Tel: 0191–386 9950

MISSION AND UNITY
Co-Chairmen Mr A. J. Piper, 11 Briardene, Durham DH1 4UQ Tel: 0191–384 4040; Ven Trevor Willmott (*as above*)
Secretary Vacancy

ECUMENICAL
Ecumenical Officer Revd Sam Randall, Vicarage, Holmside Lane, Burnhope, Durham DH7 0DP Tel: (01207) 529274

PRESS AND PUBLICATIONS
Press and Communications Officer Revd Stephen Conway, Auckland Castle, Bishop Auckland DL14 7NR
Tel: (01388) 602576
Fax: (01388) 605264
Editor of Dioc Yearbook Mr Jonathan Cryer (*as above*)
Editor of Dioc News Revd Paul Judson, Vicarage, St Mark's Terrace, Millfield, Sunderland SR4 7BN Tel and Fax: 0191–514 7872
Chaplain for Information Technology Revd Stoker Wilson, 76 Merrybent Village, Darlington DL2 2LE Tel: (01325) 374510

DIOCESAN RECORDS OFFICE
Durham County Record Office, County Hall, Durham DH1 5UL (*County Archivist* Miss J. Gill) Tel: 0191–386 4411, Ext 474

SOCIAL RESPONSIBILITY
Chairman Revd Geoff Miller, 26 Upsall Drive, Darlington DL3 8RB
Tel: (01325) 358911
Secretary Revd Paul Judson (*as above*)
Social Responsibility Officer Canon Brian Hails, 5 Hepscott Terrace, South Shields, Tyne and Wear NE33 4TH
Tel: 0191–456 3490
Family Welfare Council (*Chairman*) Canon Maurice Simmons, 11 Roecliffe Grove, Stockton-on-Tees TS19 8JU Tel: (01642) 618880; (*Director*) Mrs Sue Rayner, Agriculture House, Stonebridge, Durham DH1 3RY Tel: 0191–386 3719
Northumbrian Industrial Mission (*Chairman*) Mr J. G. Smith, The Durdans, Fellside Rd, Whickham, Newcastle-upon-Tyne NE16 4LA Tel: 0191–488 1631; (*Secretary*) Mrs C. Paul, East Thorn Farm, Kirkley, Ponteland, Newcastle-upon-Tyne NE20 0AG Tel: (01661) 25950
Teeside Industrial Mission (*Chairman*) Mr J. Wills, 14 Kirk St, Stillington, Stockton-on-Tees TS21 1JR Tel: (01740) 630473; (*Secretary*) Mr K. Brookfield, 38 St Leonard's Rd, Guisborough TS14 8BV
Tel: (01287) 632404
Arts and Recreation Chaplaincy: (*Chairman*) Mr K. Bates, 96 Junction Rd, Norton, Stockton-on-Tees TS20 1PT Tel: (01642) 553794; (*Secretary*) Revd Robert Cooper, Rectory, Sadberge, Darlington, Co Durham DL2 1RP Tel: (01325) 333771

STEWARDSHIP
Stewardship Development Officer Mr J. E. Roberts, Dioc Office Tel: (01388) 604823
Fax: (01388) 603695

AREA DEANS
ARCHDEACONRY OF SUNDERLAND
Chester-le-Street Revd Kevin Dunne, 37 Brancepeth Rd, Oxclose, Washington NE38 0LA Tel: 0191–416 2561
Gateshead (Acting) Canon Ray Knell, 40 St Andrew's Drive, Low Fell, Gateshead NE9 6JU Tel: 0191–442 1069
Gateshead West Canon Hazel Ditchburn, Rectory, Shibdon Rd, Blaydon on Tyne NE21 5AE Tel and Fax: 0191–414 2750
Houghton-le-Spring Revd Michael Beck, Rectory, Houghton Rd, Hetton-le-Hole, Houghton-le-Spring DH5 9PH
Tel: 0191–517 2488
Jarrow Canon Eric Stephenson, St George's Vicarage, 2 Ashleigh Villas, East Boldon, Tyne and Wear NE36 0LA
Tel: 0191–536 3699
Wearmouth Canon Richard Davison, 7 St Bede's Park, Sunderland SR2 7DZ
Tel: 0191–565 8077

ARCHDEACONRY OF DURHAM
Durham Revd Jon Bell, Vicarage, St Cuthbert's Vicarage, 1 Aykley Court, Durham DH1 4NW Tel: 0191–386 4526
Easington Revd Neville Vine, Rectory, 5 Tudor Grange, Easington, Peterlee SR8 3DF Tel: 0191–527 0287
Hartlepool Revd David Couling, Greatham Hall, Greatham, Hartlepool TS25 2HS
Tel: (01429) 871148
Lanchester Revd Peter Waterhouse, Lanchester Vicarage, 1 Lee Hill Court, Lanchester, Co Durham DH7 0QE
Tel: (01207) 521170
Sedgefield Revd Peter Baldwin, Vicarage, Trimdon Grange, Trimdon Station TS29 6LX Tel: (01429) 880872

ARCHDEACONRY OF AUCKLAND
Auckland Canon Stuart Bain, St Paul's Vicarage, Horswell Gardens, Spennymoor, Co Durham DH16 7AA
Tel: (01388) 814522
Barnard Castle Canon Timothy Ollier, Gainford Vicarage, Gainford, Darlington DL2 3DS Tel: (01325) 730261
Darlington Revd Dr Philip Thomas, Vicarage, Heighington, Darlington, Co Durham DL5 6PP Tel: (01325) 312134
Stanhope Revd Andrew Featherstone, Rectory, Hartside Close, Crook, Co Durham DL15 9NH Tel: (01388) 764024
Stockton Canon Richard Smith, St Cuthbert's Vicarage, Church Rd, Billingham TS23 1BW Tel: (01642) 553236

DIOCESE OF ELY

Founded in 1109. Cambridgeshire, except for an area in the north-west (PETERBOROUGH) and three parishes in the south (CHELMSFORD); the western quarter of Norfolk; a few parishes in Essex; one parish in Bedfordshire.

Population 625,000   Area 1,507 sq m
Stipendiary Clergy 161   Benefices 248
Parishes 310   Churches 341

BISHOP (67th)
Rt Revd Stephen Whitefield Sykes, The Bishop's House, Ely, Cambs CB7 4DW [1990]
Tel: (01353) 662749
Fax: (01353) 669477
e-mail: bishop@ely.anglican.org
[Stephen Ely]

SUFFRAGAN BISHOP
HUNTINGDON Rt Revd John Robert Flack, 14 Lynn Rd, Ely, Cambs CB6 1DA [1997]
Tel: (01353) 662137
Fax: (01353) 669357
e-mail: suffragan@ely.anglican.org

CATHEDRAL CHURCH OF THE HOLY AND UNDIVIDED TRINITY
Dean Very Revd Michael Higgins, The Deanery, The College, Ely, Cambs CB7 4DN [1991]
Tel: (01353) 667735
Fax: (01353) 665658
Canons Residentiary
Vice-Dean Canon Dennis Green, The Black Hostelry, Ely, Cambs CB7 4DL [1980]
Tel: (01353) 662612
Canon John Inge, Powchers Hall, The College, Ely, Cambs CB7 4DL
Tel: (01353) 663662
Precentor and Sacrist Revd Peter Moger, The Precentor's House, The College, Ely, Cambs CB7 4JU [1995]
Tel: (01353) 662526
Cathedral Chaplain Revd Janet McFarlane, The Porta, The College, Ely, Cambs
Tel: (01353) 666781
Chapter Clerk Mrs Constance Heald, Chapter House, The College, Ely, Cambs CB7 4DN
Tel: (01353) 667735
Organist Mr Paul Trepte, The Old Sacristy, The College, Ely, Cambs CB7 4DS

ARCHDEACONS
ELY Ven Jeffrey Watson, 1a Summerfield, Cambridge CB3 9HE [1993]
Tel: (01223) 515725
Fax: (01223) 571322
e-mail: archdeacon.ely@ely.anglican.org

HUNTINGDON Ven John Stuart Beer, Rectory, Hemingford Abbots, Huntingdon, Cambs PE18 9AN [1997]
Tel: (01480) 469856
Fax: (01480) 496073
e-mail:
archdeacon.huntingdon@ely.anglican.org
WISBECH Ven James (Jim) Rone, Archdeacon's House, 24 Cromwell Rd, Ely, Cambs CB6 1AS [1995]
Tel: (01353) 662909
Fax: (01353) 662056
e-mail:
archdeacon.wisbech@ely.anglican.org

CONVOCATION (MEMBERS OF THE HOUSE OF CLERGY OF THE GENERAL SYNOD)
Dignitaries in Convocation
The Dean of Ely
The Archdeacon of Wisbech
Proctors for Clergy
Canon Christine Farrington
Canon Fred Kilner
Revd Jonathan Young

MEMBERS OF THE HOUSE OF LAITY OF THE GENERAL SYNOD
Mrs Penny Granger
Mr William Sanders
Mr Stephen Tooke
Mrs Ruth Whitworth

DIOCESAN OFFICERS
Dioc Secretary Dr Matthew Lavis, Bishop Woodford House, Barton Rd, Ely, Cambs CB7 4DX
Tel: (01353) 663579
(01353) 652702 (Direct Line)
Fax: (01353) 652700
Chancellor of Diocese The Hon Mr Justice William Gage, The Royal Courts of Justice, The Strand, London WC2 2LL
Registrar of Diocese Mr Bill Godfrey, 18 The Broadway, St Ives, Huntingdon PE17 4BS
Tel: (01480) 464600
Joint Registrar (Legal Secretary) Mr Peter Beesley, 1 The Sanctuary, London SW1P 3JT
Tel: 0171–222 5381

Deputy Registrar Mr B. Halls, 18 The Broadway, St Ives, Huntingdon PE17 4BS
Tel: (01480) 464600

DIOCESAN ORGANISATIONS
Diocesan Office Bishop Woodford House, Barton Rd, Ely, Cambs CB7 4DX
Tel: (01353) 652701
Fax: (01353) 652700
e-mail: d.secretary@office.ely.anglican.org

ADMINISTRATION
Dioc Synod (Chairman, House of Clergy) Canon Michael Wadsworth D PHIL, Vicarage, 12 Church St, Great Shelford CB2 5EL
Tel: (01223) 843274; *(Chairman, House of Laity)* Mr Stephen Tooke, Rectory, Church Rd, Christchurch, Wisbech PE14 9PQ Tel: (01354) 638379; *(Secretary)* Dr Matthew Lavis, Dioc Office
Finance Committee (Chairman) Mr Hugh Duberly; *(Secretary)* Dr Matthew Lavis *(as above)*
Dioc Accountant Vacancy, Dioc Office
Dioc Surveyor Mr Tony Wilding, Dioc Office
Asst Secretary (Pastoral) Vacancy, Dioc Office
Board of Patronage (Secretary) Mr William Sanders, Dioc Office
Designated Officer Dr Matthew Lavis *(as above)*

CHURCHES
Advisory Committee for the Care of Churches (Secretary) Vacancy
Council of Church Music (Secretary) Mr B. E. Eaden, 64 Green End Rd, Cambridge CB4 1RY
Tel: (01223) 424363

EDUCATION
Dioc Board of Education (Secretary) Revd Tim Elbourne, Dioc Office
Director of Education Revd Tim Elbourne *(as above)*
Children's Council (RE Adviser) Mrs Gill Ambrose, Dioc Office
Dioc Youth Council (Youth Officer) Revd Anthony Chandler, Dioc Office
Adult Education Council (Adult Education and Training Officer) Revd David Cockerell, Dioc Office
RE Adviser (Schools) Dr Shirley Hall, Dioc Office

MINISTRY
Co-Director of Ordinands and Warden of Post-Ordination Training Ven John Beer, Rectory, Hemingford Abbots, Huntingdon, Cambs PE18 9AN
Tel: (01480) 469856
Fax: (01480) 496073

Director of Women's Ministry and Co-Director of Ordinands Canon Christine Farrington, St Mark's Vicarage, Barton Rd, Cambridge CB3 9JZ   Tel: (01233) 363339
Continuing Ministerial Education Revd Dr John Parr, Vicarage, Church St, Harston, Cambridge CB2 5NP   Tel: (01223) 872496
Readers' Board (*Hon Sec*) Mrs Julia Jones, 39 Westlands, Comberton, Cambs CB3 7EH
Tel: (01223) 262251
Warden The Bishop of Huntingdon

LITURGICAL
Secretary Revd Jonathan Young, Ascension Rectory, 95 Richmond Rd, Cambridge CB4 3PS   Tel: (01223) 61919

MISSIONARY AND ECUMENICAL
Council of Mission and Unity (*Secretary*) Mr William Sanders, Dioc Office
Ecumenical Officer Canon Frank Fisher, Stapleford Vicarage, Stapleford, Cambridge CB2 5BG   Tel: (01223) 842150

PRESS AND PUBLICATIONS
Press and Communications Officer Revd Dr Tom Ambrose, Witchford Vicarage, Witchford, Ely CB6 2HQ
Tel: (01353) 669420
Fax: (01353) 669609
Editor, 'Ely Ensign' Mr S. Levitt, 15 The Elms, Milton, Cambridge
Editor of Dioc Directory Dr Matthew Lavis, Dioc Office

DIOCESAN RECORD OFFICES
Dioc Archivist P. M. Meadows, c/o University Library
Cambridge Record Office, Shire Hall, Castle Hill, Cambridge CB3 0AP, *Archivist* Mrs Elizabeth Stazicker   Tel: (01223) 317281 (*For parishes in the Archdeaconry of Ely*); Cambridgeshire Record Office, Grammar School Walk, Huntingdon PE18 6LF   Tel: (01480) 52181 (*For parishes in the Archdeaconry of Huntingdon*); Cambridge Record Office, Shire Hall, Cambridge (*see above*) (*For parishes in the Deaneries of Ely and March*); Norfolk Record Office, Central Library, Norwich NR2 1NJ, *City and County Archivist* Miss J. M. Kennedy Tel:

(01603) 22233 (*For parishes in the Deaneries of Feltwell and Fincham*); Wisbech and Fenland Museum, Museum Square, Wisbech PE13 1ES Tel: (01945) 3817 (*For parishes in the Deaneries of Wisbech and Lynn Marshland*)

DIOCESAN RESOURCE CENTRE
Contact Mrs Sally White and Mrs Annette Norman, Dioc Resource Centre, Dioc Office

SOCIAL RESPONSIBILITY
Board for Social Responsibility (*Chairman*) Canon Hugh Searle, Vicarage, Barton, Cambridge CB3 7BG   Tel: (01223) 262218 (*Secretary*) Dr Hilary Lavis, Dioc Office
Tel: (01353) 652720
Committee for Family and Social Welfare (*Chairman*) Revd Allan Viller, Vicarage, 30 Church Lane, Littleport, Cambs CB6 3TB
Tel: (01353) 860207
Cambridgeshire Deaf Association (*Ely Dioc Association for the Deaf*) (*Chairman*) Dr G. Cumming, 8 Romsey Terrace, Cambridge
Mothers' Union (*President*) Mrs Della Fletcher, 12 Redhill Close, Great Shelford, Cambridge CB2 5JP   Tel: (01223) 841783

STEWARDSHIP
Stewardship Adviser Mr Rodger Sansom, Dioc Office

RURAL DEANS
ARCHDEACONRY OF ELY
Bourn Revd Jeremy Pemberton, Rectory, 2 Short St, Bourn, Cambridge CB3 7SG
Tel: (01924) 719728
Cambridge Canon Michael Diamond, St Andrew the Less Vicarage, Parsonage St, Cambridge CB5 8DN   Tel: (01223) 353794
Fordham Revd Mark Haworth, Vicarage, Green Head Rd, Swaffham Prior, Cambridge CB5 0JT   Tel: (01638) 741409
Linton Canon Bill Girard, Rectory, 19 West Wratting Rd, Balsham, Cambridge CB1 6DX   Tel: (01223) 894010
North Stowe Revd Hugh McCurdy, Vicarage, Church St, Histon, Cambridge CB4 4EP   Tel: (01223) 232255
e-mail: hugh.mccurdy@dial.pipex.com

Quy Revd Brian Kerley, Rectory, Apthorpe Street, Fulbourn, Cambridge CB1 5EY   Tel: (01223) 880337
Shelford Canon Frank Fisher, Vicarage, Mingle Lane, Stapleford, Cambridge CB2 5BG   Tel: (01223) 842150
Shingay Revd Shamus Williams, Vicarage, Church St, Guilden Morden, Royston, Herts SG8 0JP   Tel: (01763) 853067

ARCHDEACONRY OF HUNTINGDON
Huntingdon Revd Walter King, Rectory, 1 The Walks East, Huntingdon PE13 6AP
Tel: (01480) 412674
Leightonstone Canon John Hindley, Tilbrook Rectory, Church Lane, Tilbrook, Huntingdon PE18 0JS   Tel: (01480) 860147
St Ives Revd Stephen Leeke, Rectory, 15 Church Rd, Warboys, Huntingdon PE17 2RJ   Tel: (01487) 822237
St Neots Canon Bruce Curry, Vicarage, Everton, Sandy, Beds SG19 3JY
Tel: (01767) 691827
Yaxley Canon Michael Soulsby, Holy Trinity Rectory, The Village. Orton Longueville, Peterborough, Cambs PE2 7DN   Tel: (01733) 371071

ARCHDEACONRY OF WISBECH
Ely Revd Allan Viller, Vicarage, 30 Church Lane, Littleport, Ely, Cambs CB6 1PS
Tel: (01353) 860207
e-mail: allan@agfv.demon.co.uk
Feltwell Revd David Kightley, Rectory, 7 Oak St, Feltwell, Thetford, Norfolk IP26 4DD   Tel: (01842) 828104
Fincham Revd David Kightley (*as above*)
Lynn Marshland Revd Tony Treen, Rectory, Walpole St Peter, Wisbech, Cambs PE14 7NX   Tel: (01945) 780252
March Revd Peter Baxandall, St Wendreda's Rectory, 21 Wimblington Rd, March, Cambs PE15 9QW
Tel: (01354) 53377
Wisbech Revd Robert Bull, St Augustine's Vicarage, Lynn Rd, Wisbech, Cambs PE13 3DL   Tel: (01945) 583724

DIOCESE IN EUROPE

Founded 1980 by union of the Diocese of Gibraltar (founded 1842) and the (FULHAM) Jurisdiction of North and Central Europe. Area, Europe, except Great Britain and Ireland; Morocco; Turkey; the Asian countries of the former Soviet Union.

Clergy 128   Congregations 259

BISHOP OF GIBRALTAR IN EUROPE (2nd)
Rt Revd John William Hind, Bishop's Lodge, Church Rd, Worth, Crawley, W Sussex RH10 7RT [1993]
Tel: (01293) 883051
Fax: (01293) 884479
e-mail: 101741.3160@compuserve.com
Bishop's *Chaplain* Vacancy (*same address*)
Bishop's *Secretary* Mrs Lisa Elbourne

SUFFRAGAN BISHOP
IN EUROPE Rt Revd Henry Scriven, 14 Tufton St, London SW1P 3QZ [1995]
Tel: 0171–976 8001
Fax: 0171–976 8002
e-mail: henry@dioeurope.clara.net

HONORARY ASSISTANT BISHOPS
Rt Revd Daniel de Pina Cabral, Rua Henrique Lopes de Mendonca, 253–4 Dto Hab 42, 4100 Oporto, Portugal [1976]
Tel: 00–351–2–617–77–72
Rt Revd Eric Devenport, 32 Bishopsgate, Norwich NR1 4AA *Tel:* (01603) 664121
Rt Revd Carlos López-Lozano, c/o Iere, Calle de Beneficencia 18, 28004 Madrid, Spain [1995]   *Tel:* 00–34–1–445–25–60
Fax: 00–34–1–594–42–72
Rt Revd Michael Manktelow, 2 The Chantry, Canon Lane, Chichester, W Sussex PO19 1PZ [1994]   *Tel:* (01243) 531096
Rt Revd Alan Rogers, 20 River Way, Twickenham TW2 5JP [1996]
Tel: 0181–894 2031
Rt Revd Jeffery Rowthorn, American Cathedral, 23 Ave George V, 75008 Paris, France [1994]
Tel: 00–33–1–47–20–17–92 (Cathedral)
00–33–1–47–20–02–23 (Direct)
Fax: 00–33–1–47–23–95–30 (Cathedral)
00–33–1–40–27–03–53 (Direct)
Rt Revd Arturo Sanchez, Calle de Beneficencia 18, 28004 Madrid, Spain [1995]
Tel: 00–34–1–445–25–60

Rt Revd Fernando Soares, Rue Elias Garcia 107–1 Dto, 4400 Vila Nova de Gaia, Portugal [1995] *Tel:* 00–351–2–304646
Rt Revd John Taylor, 22 Conduit Head Rd, Cambridge CB3 0EY
Rt Revd Ambrose Weekes, All Saints' Vicarage, 7 Margaret St, London W1N 8JQ [1988]   *Tel:* 0171–580 6467

CATHEDRAL CHURCH OF THE HOLY TRINITY, GIBRALTAR
Dean Very Revd Gordon Reid, The Deanery, Bomb House Lane, Gibraltar [1998]
Tel: 00–350–78377 (Home)
00–350–75745 (Office)
Fax: 00–350–78463

PRO-CATHEDRAL OF ST PAUL, VALLETTA, MALTA
Chancellor Canon Alan Woods, Chancellor's Lodge, St Paul's Anglican Pro-Cathedral, Independence Square, Valletta VLT12, Malta [1996]
Tel and *Fax:* 00–356–22–57–14

PRO-CATHEDRAL OF THE HOLY TRINITY, BRUSSELS, BELGIUM
Chancellor Canon Nigel Walker, Pro-Cathedral of the Holy Trinity, 29 rue Capitaine Crespel, 1050 Brussels [1993]
Tel: 00–32–2–511–71–83 (Office)
Fax: 00–32–2–511–10–28

ARCHDEACONS
THE EASTERN ARCHDEACONRY Ven Jeremy Peake, Thugutstrasse 2/12, 1020 Vienna 2, Austria [1995]
Tel and *Fax:* 00–43–1–7–20–79–73 (Home)
00–43–1–66–39–20–92–64 (Office)
NORTH WEST EUROPE Ven Geoffrey Allen, Ijsselsingel 86, 6991 ZT Rheden, Netherlands [1993]   *Tel:* 00–31–26–4953800
Fax: 00–31–26–4954922
e-mail: 106362.1337@compuserve.com
FRANCE Ven Martin Draper, 7 rue Auguste-Vacquerie, 75116 Paris, France [1994]   *Tel:* 00–33–1–47–20–22–51
Fax: 00–33–1–49–52–03–23

GIBRALTAR Ven Kenneth Robinson, Rua da Ginjeira Lote 5, Alcoitao, 2765 Estoril, Portugal [1994]
Tel and *Fax:* 00–351–1–4692303
ITALY AND MALTA Ven William Edebohls, c/o All Saints' Church, Via Solferino 17, 20121 Milan, Italy [1998]
Tel and *Fax:* 00–39–02–655–2258
SCANDINAVIA AND GERMANY Ven David Ratcliff, Styrmansgatan 1, S-114 54 Stockholm, Sweden [1996]
Tel: 00–46–8–663–8248
Fax: 00–46–8–663–8911
e-mail: anglican.church@telia.com
SWITZERLAND Ven Peter Hawker, Promenadengasse 9, 8001 Zurich, Switzerland [1986]
Tel and *Fax:* 00–41–1–252–60–24 (Office)
Tel: 00–41–1–261–22–41 (Home)
e-mail: zurich@anglican.ch (Office)

CONVOCATION (MEMBERS OF THE HOUSE OF CLERGY OF THE GENERAL SYNOD)
Canon Chad Coussmaker
Revd Howell Sasser

MEMBERS OF THE HOUSE OF LAITY OF THE GENERAL SYNOD
Mrs Marion Jägers
Mrs Diana Webster

DIOCESAN OFFICERS
Dioc Secretary Mr Adrian Mumford, Dioc Office
Assistant Dioc Secretary Mrs Jeanne French, Dioc Office
Chancellor of Diocese Sir David Calcutt, c/o The Chambers of Alan Rawley QC, 35 Essex St, Temple, London WC2R 3AR
Tel: 0171–353 6381
Registrar of Diocese and Bishop's Legal Secretary Mr John Underwood, Vestry House, Laurence Pountney Hill, London EC4R 0EH   *Tel:* 0171–626 9236
Fax: 0171–623 6870

DIOCESAN ORGANISATIONS
Diocesan Office 14 Tufton St, Westminster, London SW1P 3QZ   *Tel:* 0171–976 8001
Fax: 0171–976 8002
e-mail: dioeurope@clara.net
Web: http://www.europe.anglican.org

ADMINISTRATION
Dioc Synod (Clerical Vice-President) Ven Ken Robinson, Rua da Ginjeira Lote 5, Alcoitao, 2765 Estoril, Portugal *Tel* and *Fax:* 00–351–1–4692303; *(Lay Vice-President)* Mrs Maryon Jägers, Hoefbladhof 61, Post Bus 37, 3990 DA Houten, The Netherlands   *Tel:* 00–31–30–637–17–80
Fax: 00–31–30–635–10–34
(Secretary) Mr Adrian Mumford, Dioc Office

Board of Finance (*Chairman*) Mr Bernard Day, c/o Dioc Office
(*Secretary*) Mr Adrian Mumford, Dioc Office

CHURCHES
Faculty Committee (*Secretary*) Mr Adrian Mumford (*as above*)

MINISTRY AND TRAINING
Director of Ordinands and Warden of Readers The Suffragan Bishop, Dioc Office
Director of Training Revd Ambrose Mason, Dioc Office

LITURGY
Enquiries to the Bishop's Chaplain

MEDITERRANEAN MISSIONS TO SEAMEN
Administrator Mr Adrian Mumford (*as above*)

PRESS AND PUBLICATIONS
Press and Communications Officer Revd Rob Marshall, Dioc Office   *Tel:* 0181–450 1455
Fax: 0181–450 1454
(0385) 767594 (Mobile)
e-mail: claire@rpm33rpm.u-net.com

Editor of the European Anglican Revd Rob Marshall (*as above*)

DIOCESAN RECORDS OFFICE
The Guildhall Library, Aldermanbury, London EC2P 2EJ   *Tel:* 0171–606 3030

ARCHBISHOP'S APOKRISARIOI AND REPRESENTATIVES
To the Holy See Canon Bruce Ruddock, Centro Anglicano, Palazzo Dorio, Via del Corso 303, 00186 Rome, Italy
Tel: 00–39–6–678–0302
To the Oecumenical Patriarch Canon Ian Sherwood, British Consulate General, Tepebasi, Istanbul, c/o The Foreign and Commonwealth Office, King Charles St, London SW1A 2AH (For correspondence)
Tel: 00–90–212–251–56–16
To the Patriarch of Moscow and all Russia Canon Chad Coussmaker, British Embassy Moscow, c/o The Foreign and Commonwealth Office, King Charles St, London SW1A 2AH (For correspondence)
Tel: 00–7–095–245–3837
To the Catholicos-Patriarch of All Georgia Revd Phillip Storr Venter (part resident in the Caucusus), Bearsden, Tredegar Place, 109 Bow Rd, London E3 2AN
Tel and *Fax:* 0181–981 6195
e-mail: ArchiesDen@compuserve.com
To the Supreme Patriarch of All Armenians Revd Phillip Storr Venter (*as above*)
To the Patriarch of Romania Revd Steve Hughes, British Embassy Bucharest, c/o The Foreign and Commonwealth Office, King Charles St, London SW1A 2AH (For correspondence)   *Tel:* 00–40–1–615–1392
To the Patriarch of Bulgaria Revd Steve Hughes (*as above*)
To the Patriarch of Serbia Revd Steve Hughes (*as above*)
To the Archbishop of Greece Vacancy
To the European Institutions Revd James Barnett, 16 rue Riehl, F-67100 Strasbourg-Neuhof, France   *Tel:* 00–33–88–40–36–15
Fax: 00–33–3–88–39–07–58
e-mail: 101547.3346@compuserve.com

DEANERIES
The Archdeaconry of Scandinavia and Germany has Deanery Synods rather than a single Archdeaconry Synod. The names and addresses of the officers are available from the Diocesan Office.

DIOCESE OF EXETER

Tranferred to Exeter in 1050, formerly at Crediton in 909. Devon, except for one parish in the south-east (SALISBURY) and one parish in the west (TRURO).

Population 1,058,000   Area 2,575 sq m
Stipendiary Clergy 268   Benefices 229
Parishes 504   Churches 613

BISHOP (69th)
Rt Revd (Geoffrey) Hewlett Thompson, The Palace, Exeter EX1 1HY [1985]
Tel: (01392) 272362
Fax: (01392) 430923
[Hewlett Exon:]

SUFFRAGAN BISHOPS
CREDITON Rt Revd Richard Stephen Hawkins, 10 The Close, Exeter EX1 1EZ [1996]
Tel: (01392) 273509
Fax: (01392) 431266
PLYMOUTH Rt Revd John Garton, 31 Riverside Walk, Tamerton Foliot, Plymouth PL5 4AQ [1996]
Tel: (01752) 769836
Fax: (01752) 769818

HONORARY ASSISTANT BISHOPS
Rt Revd Richard Fox Cartwright, 5 Old Vicarage Close, Ide, Exeter EX2 9RT [1988]
Tel: (01392) 211270
Rt Revd Ivor Colin Docker, Braemar, Bradley Rd, Bovey Tracey, Newton Abbot TQ13 9EU [1991]
Tel: (01626) 832468

CATHEDRAL CHURCH OF ST PETER
Dean Very Revd Keith Brynmor Jones, The Deanery, Exeter EX1 1HT [1996]
Tel: (01392) 252891 (Office)
(01392) 272697 (Home)
Cathedral Office 1 The Cloisters, Exeter EX1 1HS
Tel: (01392) 255573
Fax: (01392) 498769
e-mail: admin@exeter-cathedral.org.uk
Web: http://www.exeter-cathedral.org.uk
Canons Residentiary
Treasurer Vacancy
Precentor Canon Kenneth Parry, 6 The Close, Exeter EX1 1EZ [1991]
Tel: (01392) 272498
Chancellor Canon David Ison, 12 The Close, Exeter EX1 1EZ [1995]
Tel: (01392) 275745
Priest Vicar Revd Gregory Daxter, 6A The Close, Exeter EX1 1EZ Tel: (01392) 2258892
Chapter Clerk Col Michael Woodcock, Cathedral Office

Visitors' Officer Mrs Juliet Dymoke-Marr, Cathedral Office   Tel: (01392) 214219
Education Officer Mr David Risdon, Cathedral Office   Tel: (01392) 434243
Cathedral Organist Mr Lucian Nethsingha, 11 The Close, Exeter EX1 1EZ
Tel: (01392) 277521
Asst Organist Mr Paul Morgan, 40 Countess Wear Rd, Exeter EX2 6LR
Tel: (01392) 877623

ARCHDEACONS
EXETER Ven Tony Tremlett, St Matthew's House, Spicer Rd, Exeter EX1 1TA [1994]
Tel: (01392) 425432
Fax: (01392) 425783
TOTNES Ven Richard Gilpin, Blue Hills, Bradley Rd, Bovey Tracey, Newton Abbot TQ13 9EU [1996]   Tel: (01626) 832064
Fax: (01626) 834947
BARNSTAPLE Ven Trevor Lloyd, Stage Cross, Whitemoor Hill, Bishops Tawton, Barnstaple EX32 0BE [1989]
Tel: (01271) 375475
Fax: (01271) 377934
PLYMOUTH Ven Robin Ellis, 33 Leat Walk, Roborough, Plymouth PL6 7AT [1982]
Tel: (01752) 793397
Fax: (01752) 774618

CONVOCATION (MEMBERS OF THE HOUSE OF CLERGY OF THE GENERAL SYNOD)
The Archdeacon of Plymouth
Proctors for Clergy
Ven Richard Gilpin
Revd Hilary Ison
Canon Peter Larkin
Ven Trevor Lloyd
Preb Samuel Philpott

MEMBERS OF THE HOUSE OF LAITY OF THE GENERAL SYNOD
Mr Roger Adcock
Mrs Margaret Behenna
Mrs Sheila Fletcher
Mrs Anne Ellis
Mrs Heather Morgan
Mrs Shirley-Ann Williams

DIOCESAN OFFICERS
Dioc Secretary Mr Mark Beedell, Diocesan House, Palace Gate, Exeter EX1 1HX
Tel: (01392) 272686
Fax: (01392) 499594
Chancellor of Diocese Chanc Sir David Calcutt, Lamb Buildings, Temple, London EC4Y 7AS   Tel: 0171–405 1124
Registrar of Diocese and Bishop's Legal Secretary Mr R. K. Wheeler, 18 Cathedral Yard, Exeter EX1 1HE
Tel: (01392) 421171
Fax: (01392) 215579
Dioc Surveyors Vickery Holman, 22 Lockyer St, Plymouth PL1 2QY Tel: (01752) 266291; Vickery Holman, 16 Southernhay West, Exeter EX1 1PJ   Tel: (01392) 72043
Barnstaple Smith & Dunn, Alliance House, Cross St, Barnstaple EX31 1BA
Tel: (01271) 327878

DIOCESAN ORGANISATIONS
Diocesan Office Diocesan House, Palace Gate, Exeter, Devon EX1 1HX
Tel: (01392) 272686
Fax: (01392) 499594

ADMINISTRATION
Dioc Synod (*Chairman, House of Clergy*) Vacancy; (*Secretary, House of Clergy*) Revd Philip Darby, Vicarage, Paternoster Lane, Ipplepen, Newton Abbot TQ12 5RY Tel: (01803) 812215; (*Chairman, House of Laity*) Mrs Shirley-Ann Williams, Miller's Farm, Talaton, Exeter EX5 2RE; (*Secretary, House of Laity*) Mr Charles Hodgson, Heale Moor Farm, Parracombe, Barnstaple EX31 4QE
Synod Secretary Mr Mark Beedell, Dioc House
Board of Finance (*Chairman*) Mr John Hutchinson, Heath Barton, Whitestone, Exeter EX4 2HJ Tel: (01647) 61401; (*Secretary*) Mr Mark Beedell (*as above*)
Parsonages Committee (*Secretary*) Mr Bob Greig, Dioc House
Pastoral Committee (*Secretary*) Miss Pru Williams, Dioc House
Board of Patronage (*Chairman*) Mrs Shirley-Ann Williams (*as above*)
Trusts Mr Mark Beedell (*as above*)
Designated Officer Mr Mark Beedell (*as above*)

CHURCHES
Dioc Advisory Committee (*Chairman*) Preb Christopher Pidsley, Vicarage, Chudleigh, Newton Abbot TQ13 0JF
Tel: (01626) 863241
(*Secretary*) Miss Janet Croysdale, Dioc House
Redundant Churches Uses Committee (*Secretary*) Miss Pru Williams (*as above*)

EDUCATION

Director of Education Revd Christopher Davidson, Christian Education and Resources Centre, St Mary Arches Church, St Mary Arches St, Exeter EX4 3BA Tel: (01392) 432149 Fax: (01392) 436085
Asst Education Officers Mr Tony Giddings and Mrs Jennifer Pestridge (*same address*)

MINISTRY AND PARISH TRAINING

Director of Ordinands and Adviser for Team Ministries Preb Terry Nottage, 2 West Ave, Pennsylvania, Exeter EX4 4SD Tel: (01392) 214867 Fax: (01392) 251229
Officer for Non-Stipendiary Ministry Canon David Ison, Dioc House Tel and Fax: (01392) 499710
Officer for Continuing Ministerial Education Canon David Ison (*as above*)
Board of Readers (*Secretary*) Mr Ronald Edinborough, 3 Manor Rd, Paignton TQ3 2HT Tel: (01803) 550493
Dioc Adult Training Adviser Revd Viv Armstrong-MacDonnell, 1A The Cloisters, Exeter EX1 1JS Tel: (01392) 498110
Family Life and Marriage Education Co-ordinator Mrs Sheila Fletcher, 11 Troarn Way, Chudliegh, Newton Abbot TQ13 0PP Tel: (01626) 853998
Children's Adviser Vacancy
Youth Adviser Capt Tony Williams, Rectory, Ideford, Newton Abbot TQ13 0BA Tel: (01626) 852828
Widows and Dependants (*Ottery and Honiton Deaneries*) Preb John Mapson, c/o Dioc House Tel: (01392) 272686 (Office)
(01297) 35023 (Home)
(*Other Deaneries*) Revd Gilbert Cowdry, 17 Hillcrest Park, Pennsylvania, Exeter EX4 4SH Tel: (01392) 252662
Chaplain to the Deaf Revd Gill Behenna, Glenn House, 96 Old Tiverton Rd, Exeter EX4 6L Tel: (01392) 278875

ECUMENICAL

Ecumenical Advisers Revd Derek Newport, Rectory, Widecombe-in-the-Moor, Newton Abbot TQ13 7TF Tel and Fax: (01364) 621334
Revd Keith Gale, Vicarage, Lower Town, Halberton, Tiverton EX16 7AU Tel: (01884) 821149

PRESS, PUBLICITY AND PUBLICATIONS

Press and Media Liaison Officer Vacancy – enquiries to the Bishop's Office

Editor of Dioc News Preb John Mapson, Dioc House Tel: (01395) 35023 (Home)
Editor of Dioc Directory Miss Janet Croysdale, Dioc House

DIOCESAN RECORD OFFICES

Devon Record Office, Castle St, Exeter EX4 3PU (*County Archivist* Mr John Draisey) Tel: (01392) 384253

SOCIAL RESPONSIBILITY

Board for Christian Care (*Administrator*) Mr Ronald Harbour, Glenn House, 96 Old Tiverton Rd, Exeter EX4 6LD Tel: (01392) 278875

STEWARDSHIP

Stewardship Adviser Mr Terry Anning, Stewardship Office, 1B The Cloisters, Exeter EX1 1JS Tel: (01392) 272354
Assistant Adviser Mr John Grummett (*same address*)

RURAL DEANS

ARCHDEACONRY OF EXETER

Aylesbeare Revd John Clapham, Rectory, Lympstone, Exmouth EX8 5HP Tel: (01395) 273343
Cadbury Revd John Hall, Rectory, Bow, Crediton EX17 6HS Tel: (01363) 82566
Christianity Revd Mark Bate, Rectory, Alphington, Exeter EX2 8XJ Tel: (01392) 437662
Cullompton Revd Brian Petty, Rectory, Blackdown View, Sampford Peverell, Tiverton EX16 7BE Tel: (01884) 821879
Honiton Revd Nigel Freathy, Vicarage, Mare Lane, Beer, Seaton EX12 3NB Tel: (01297) 20996
Kenn Revd Victor Standing, Rectory, 12 Church Lane, Whitestone, Exeter EX4 2JT Tel: (01392) 811406
Ottery Revd Rik Peckham, St Francis Vicarage, Woolbrook, Sidmouth, EX10 *9XH* Tel: (01395) 514522
Tiverton Revd Michael Partridge, St Paul's Vicarage, Baker's Hill, Tiverton EX16 5NE Tel: (01884) 255705

ARCHDEACONRY OF TOTNES

Holsworthy Revd Leslie Brookhouse, Rectory, Pyworthy, Holsworthy EX22 6SU Tel: (01409) 254769

Moreton Revd David Stanton, St John's Vicarage, Newton Rd, Bovey Tracey, Newton Abbot TQ13 9BD Tel: (01626) 833451
Newton Abbot and Ipplepen Revd Philip Darby, Vicarage, Paternoster Lane, Ipplepen, Newton Abbot TQ12 5RY Tel: (01803) 812215
Okehampton Revd Barry Wood, Vicarage, South Tawton, Okehampton EX20 2LQ Tel: (01837) 840337
Torbay Revd Tony Macey, Vicarage, 22 Monterey Close, Livermead, Torquay TQ9 7HN Tel: (01803) 732384
Totnes Revd Richard King, Rectory, Priory View, Cornworthy, Totnes TQ9 7HN Tel: (01803) 732384
Woodleigh Revd Ronald White, Vicarage, Stoke Fleming, Dartmouth TQ6 0QB Tel: (01803) 770361

ARCHDEACONRY OF BARNSTAPLE

Barnstaple Revd Michael Pearson, Rectory, Sowden Lane, Barnstaple EX32 8BU Tel: (01271) 373837
Hartland Revd Gordon Hansford, Rectory, Weare Giffard, Bideford EX39 4QP Tel: (01237) 472017
Shirwell Revd Keith Wyer, Rectory, Rectory Rd, Combe Martin, Ilfracombe EX34 0NS Tel: (01271) 883203
South Molton Revd Stephen Girling, Vicarage, Chittlehampton, Umberleigh EX37 9QL Tel: (01769) 540654
Torrington Revd John Carvosso, Rectory, Tawstock, Barnstaple EX31 3HZ Tel: (01271) 374963

ARCHDEACONRY OF PLYMOUTH

Ivybridge Revd Tim Deacon, Rectory, Court Rd, Newton Ferrers, Plymouth PL8 1DL Tel: (01752) 872530
Devonport Preb Samuel Philpott, St Peter's Vicarage, 23 Wyndham Square, Plymouth PL1 5EG Tel: (01752) 222007
Moorside Preb John Richards, St Mary's Vicarage, 58 Plymbridge Rd, Plympton, Plymouth PL7 4QG Tel: (01752) 336157
Sutton Revd Stephen Dinsmore, St Jude's Vicarage, Knighton Rd, Plymouth PL4 3BU Tel: (01752) 661232
Tavistock Revd John Rawlings, Vicarage, 5A Plymouth Rd, Tavistock PL19 8AU Tel: (01822) 612162

DIOCESE OF GLOUCESTER

Founded in 1541. Gloucestershire except for a few parishes in the north (WORCESTER), a few parishes in the south (BRISTOL) and one parish in the east (OXFORD); the northern third of South Gloucestershire; two parishes in Wiltshire; a small area in south-west Warwickshire; a few parishes in the southern part of Hereford and Worcester.

Population 593,000   Area 1,140 sq m
Stipendiary Clergy 168   Benefices 161
Parishes 325   Churches 403

BISHOP (39th)
Rt Revd David Edward Bentley, Bishopscourt, Pitt St, Gloucester GL1 2BQ [1993]
Tel: (01452) 524598
Fax: (01452) 310025
e-mail: bshpglos@star.co.uk
[David Gloucestr]

Personal Assistant/Chaplain Canon Roger Grey

SUFFRAGAN BISHOP
TEWKESBURY Rt Revd John Stewart Went, Green Acre, 166 Hempsted Lane, Gloucester GL2 5LG [1995]   Tel: (01452) 521824
Fax: (01452) 505554
e-mail: bshptewk@star.co.uk

HONORARY ASSISTANT BISHOPS
Rt Revd Charles Derek Bond, Ambleside, 14 Worcester Rd, Evesham, Worcs WR11 4JU [1992]   Tel: (01386) 446156
Rt Revd Cyril William Johnston Bowles, Rose Lodge, Tewkesbury Rd, Stow-on-the-Wold, Cheltenham GL54 1EN [1987]
Tel: (01451) 831965
Rt Revd John Gibbs, Farthingloe, Southfield, Minchinhampton, Stroud GL6 9DY [1985]   Tel: (01453) 886211
Rt Revd William Somers Llewellyn, Glebe House, Leighterton, Tetbury GL8 8UW [1973]   Tel: (01666) 890236
Rt Revd Michael Ashley Mann, The Cottage, Lower End Farm, Eastington, Northleach, Cheltenham GL54 3PN [1989]
Tel: (01451) 860767
Rt Revd John Neale, 26 Prospect, Corsham, Wilts SN13 9AF [1994]
Tel: (01249) 712557

CATHEDRAL CHURCH OF ST PETER AND THE HOLY AND INDIVISIBLE TRINITY
Dean Very Revd Nicholas Bury, The Deanery, Miller's Green, Gloucester GL1 2BP [1997]   Tel: (01452) 524167

Canons Residentiary
Canon Norman Chatfield, 6 College Green, Gloucester GL1 2LX [1992]
Tel: (01452) 521954
Precentor Canon Neil Heavisides, 7 College Green, Gloucester GL1 2LX [1993]
Tel: (01452) 523987
Diocesan Residentiary Canons
Canon Roger Grey, 4A Miller's Green, Gloucester GL1 2BN [1982]
Tel: (01452) 525242
Canon Christopher Morgan, 9 College Green, Gloucester GL1 2LX [1996]
Tel: (01452) 507002
Cathedral Chaplain and Visitors' Officer Revd Judith Hubbard-Jones, 10 College Green, Gloucester GL1 2LX [1997]
Tel: (01452) 300655
Chapter Steward Mr Anthony Higgs, 17 College Green, Gloucester GL1 2LR
Tel: (01452) 528095
Fax: (01452) 300469
Cathedral Organist Mr David Briggs, 7 Millers Green, Gloucester GL1 2BN
Tel: (01452) 524764

ARCHDEACONS
GLOUCESTER Ven Christopher Wagstaff, Glebe House, Church Lane, Maisemore, Gloucester GL2 8EY [1982]
Tel: (01452) 528500
Fax: (01452) 381528
CHELTENHAM Ven Hedley Ringrose, The Sanderlings, Thorncliffe Drive, Cheltenham GL51 6PY [1998]
Tel: (01242) 522923
Fax: (01242) 235925

CONVOCATION (MEMBERS OF THE HOUSE OF CLERGY OF THE GENERAL SYNOD)
The Archdeacon of Cheltenham
Proctors for Clergy
Revd Hugh Broad
Canon Michael Page
Canon David Williams

MEMBERS OF THE HOUSE OF LAITY OF THE GENERAL SYNOD
Mr Nigel Chetwood
Mrs Pat Harris
Mrs Sarah James
Mr Timothy Royle
Mrs Elizabeth Ward

DIOCESAN OFFICERS
Dioc Secretary Mr Michael Williams, Church House, College Green, Gloucester GL1 2LY   Tel: (01452) 410022
Fax: (01452) 308324
Chancellor of Diocese Chanc June Rodgers, 2 Harcourt Buildings, The Temple, London EC4Y 9DB
Registrar of Diocese and Bishop's Legal Secretary Mr Chris Peak, Dioc Registry, 34 Brunswick Rd, Gloucester GL1 1JJ
Tel: (01452) 520224

DIOCESAN ORGANISATIONS
Diocesan Office Church House, College Green, Gloucester GL1 2LY
Tel: (01452) 410022
Fax: (01452) 308324
e-mail: glosdioc@star.co.uk

ADMINISTRATION
Dioc Synod (*Vice-President, House of Clergy*) Canon Michael Page, Vicarage, Langley Rd, Winchcombe, Cheltenham GL54 5QP Tel: (01242) 602368; (*Vice-President, House of Laity*) Mr John Young, Silver Birches, Wavereane, Oakridge, Stroud, Glos GL6 7PJ Tel: (01452) 770537; (*Secretary*) Mr Michael Williams, Church House
Board of Finance (*Chairman*) Mr Fraser Hart, Glebe Farm, Hatherop, Cirencester, Glos GL7 3NA Tel: (01285) 750200; (*Secretary*) Mr Michael Williams (*as above*)
Financial Secretary Mr Colin Albert, Church House
Houses Committee (*Secretary*) Mrs Juliet Watkins, Church House
Pastoral Committee (*Secretary*) Mr Michael Williams (*as above*)
Board of Patronage (*Secretary*) Mr Jonathan MacKechnie-Jarvis, Church House
Designated Officer Mr Michael Williams (*as above*)
Trust (*Secretary*) Mr Jonathan MacKechnie-Jarvis (*as above*)
Redundant Churches Uses Committee (*Secretary*) Mr Jonathan MacKechnie-Jarvis (*as above*)
Glebe Committee (*Secretary*) Mrs Juliet Watkins (*as above*)

CHURCHES
Advisory Committee for the Care of Churches (*Chairman*) Miss Mary Bliss, The Old Bakehouse, Beech Pike, Elkstone, Cheltenham GL53 9PL Tel: (01285) 821232;

(*Secretary*) Mr Jonathan MacKechnie-Jarvis (*as above*)

EDUCATION
Education Committee (*Director*) Mrs Sue Devine, 4 College Green, Gloucester GL1 2LB
Religious Education Adviser Canon George Humphrey (*same address*)
Schools Officer Mr Rob Stephens (*same address*)

MINISTRY
Dioc Officer for Ministry Canon Christopher Morgan, 9 College Green, Gloucester GL1 2LX Tel: (01452) 507002
Director of Ordinands Revd Dr Michael Parsons, Rectory, Hempsted, Gloucester GL2 6LW Tel: (01452) 524550
Associate Director of Ordinands Revd David Bowers, Vicarage, The Green, Apperley, Gloucester GL19 4DQ Tel: (01452) 780880
Vocations Adviser Revd Pat Lyes-Wilsdon, Rectory, Cromhall, Wotton-under-Edge GL12 8AN Tel: (01454) 294767
Adviser for Women's Ministry Canon Eleanor Powell, Rectory, Edge, Gloucester GL6 6PF Tel: (01452) 812319
NSM Officer Canon Michael Tucker, Rectory, Amberley, Stroud, Glos GL5 5JG
 Tel: (01453) 878515
Chaplain for Deaf and Hard of Hearing People Revd Stephen Morris, 2 High View, Hempsted, Gloucester GL2 5LN
 Tel: (01452) 416178
Readers' Board Mr W. H. Irving, 80 Melmore Gardens, Siddington, Cirencester GL7 1NS Tel: (01285) 650012
West of England Ministerial Training Course (*Principal*) Revd Dr Richard Clutterbuck, 7c College Green, Gloucester GL1 2LX
 Tel and *Fax*: (01452) 300494
Full-time Local Ministry and LNSM Officer Mrs Caroline Pascoe, 4 College Green, Gloucester GL1 2LB
Part-time Local Ministry Officers Canon Andrew Bowden, Rectory, Coates, Cirencester, Glos GL7 6NR
 Tel: (01285) 770235
Revd Geoffrey Neale, Vicarage, Blockley, Moreton-in-Marsh GL56 9ES
 Tel: (01386) 700283
Revd Hugh Allen, Vicarage, Leonard Stanley, Stonehouse, Glos GL10 3NP
 Tel: (01453) 823161
Mrs Kathy Lawrence, Vicarage, St Anne's Way, St Briavels, Lydney, Glos GL15 6UE
 Tel: (01594) 530345

LITURGICAL
Chairman Canon Neil Heavisides, 7 College Green, Gloucester GL1 2LX
 Tel: (01452) 523987

PARISH DEVELOPMENT
Dioc Officer for Parish Resources Revd Guy Bridgewater, 4 College Green, Gloucester GL1 2LB
Stewardship Adviser Mrs Elizabeth Ward (*same address*)
Dioc Children's Officer Vacancy
Dioc Youth Officer Mr Justin Groves (*same address*)
Ecumenical Adviser Revd Graham Martin, Vicarage, Bibury, Cirencester GL7 5NT
 Tel: (01285) 740387
County Ecumenical Officer Revd Dr David Calvert, 151 Tuffley Ave, Gloucester GL1 5NP Tel: (01452) 301347

PRESS AND PUBLICATIONS
Communications Officer Revd Geoff Crago, Church House
 Tel and *Fax*: (01452) 750575 (Home)
  0802 367033 (Mobile)
  0839 467601 (Pager)
Editor of Dioc Directory Revd Geoff Crago, Church House (*as above*)

DIOCESAN RECORDS OFFICE
Gloucestershire Records Office, Clarence Row, Gloucester GL1 3DW (*Dioc Archivist:* Mr David Smith*)* Tel: (01452) 425295

DIOCESAN RESOURCE CENTRE
Warden Mrs Gill Calvert, 9 College Green, Gloucester GL1 2LX Tel: (01452) 385217

SOCIAL RESPONSIBILITY
Dioc Officer for Social Responsibility Canon Adrian Slade, 38 Sydenham Villas Rd, Cheltenham GL52 6DZ
 Tel: (01242) 253162
 e-mail: glossr@star.co.uk
Community Relations Revd Grantley Finlayson, 36 Howard St, Gloucester GL1 4US Tel: (01452) 423986
Rural Adviser Revd David Green, Rectory, Cowley, Cheltenham GL53 9NJ
 Tel: (01242) 870232
Evangelist Working with Older People Capt Colin Rudge, 10 Billingham Close, Gloucester GL4 7SS Tel: (01452) 423988
Homeless Project Officer Sister Fiona Fisher, 35 St Mary's Square, Gloucester GL1 2QT
 Tel: (01452) 310810

RURAL DEANS
ARCHDEACONRY OF CHELTENHAM
Campden Revd Roy Wyatt, Rectory, Church Lane, Welford-on-Avon, Stratford-upon-Avon CV37 8EL
 Tel: (01789) 750808
Cheltenham Revd Ted Crofton, Christ Church Vicarage, Malvern Rd, Cheltenham GL50 2NU Tel: (01242) 515983
Cirencester Revd Henry Morris, Rectory, Preston, Cirencester GL7 5PR
 Tel: (01285) 654187
Fairford Revd Tony Ross, Vicarage, Coln St Aldwyns, Cirencester GL7 5AG
 Tel: (01285) 750013
Northleach Revd David Hutchin, Vicarage, Cheap St, Chedworth, Cheltenham GL54 4AE Tel: (01285) 720392
Stow Revd Fred Rothery, Rectory, Stow-on-the-Wold, Cheltenham, Glos GL54 1AA Tel: (01451) 830607
Tetbury Canon David Strong, Vicarage, Nailsworth, Stroud, Glos GL6 0PJ
 Tel: (01453) 832181
Winchcombe Canon Michael Page, Vicarage, Langley Rd, Winchcombe, Cheltenham, Glos GL54 5QP Tel: (01242) 602368

ARCHDEACONRY OF GLOUCESTER
Bisley Canon Barry Coker, Vicarage, Church St, Stroud, Glos GL5 1JL
 Tel: (01453) 764555
Dursley Revd Simon Richards, Vicarage, Church Lane, Berkeley GL13 9BH
 Tel: (01453) 210294
Forest North Revd Dr Terence Williams, Rectory, Redmarley D'Abitot, Gloucester GL19 3HS Tel: (01531) 650630
Forest South Revd Andrew James, Vicarage, Oakland Rd, Harrow Hill, Drybrook GL17 9JX Tel: (01594) 542232
Gloucester City Canon Michael Butler, Vicarage, 1 The Conifers, Upton St, Gloucester GL1 4LP Tel: (01452) 422349
Gloucester North Revd John O'Brien, Rectory, Twigworth, Gloucester GL2 9PQ
 Tel: (01452) 731483
Hawkesbury Revd Pat Lyes-Wilscon, Rectory, Cromhall, Wotton-under-Edge, Glos GL12 8AN Tel: (01454) 294767
Stonehouse Revd Graham Minors, Vicarage, 58 Cashes Green Rd, Cainscross, Stroud, Glos GL5 4RA
 Tel: (01453) 755148
Tewkesbury Revd Peter Sibley, Holy Trinity Vicarage, 49 Barton St, Tewkesbury GL20 5PU Tel: (01684) 293233

DIOCESE OF GUILDFORD

Founded in 1927. The western two-thirds of Surrey south of the Thames, except for a small area in the north-east (SOUTHWARK); areas of north-east Hampshire; a few parishes in Greater London; one parish in West Sussex.

Population 933,000   Area 538 sq m
Stipendiary Clergy 207   Benefices 150
Parishes 162   Churches 215

BISHOP (8th)
Rt Revd John Warren Gladwin, Willow Grange, Woking Rd, Guildford, Surrey GU4 7QS [1994]   Tel: (01483) 590500
Fax: (01483) 590501
e-mail: bishopjohn@cofeguildford.org.uk
[John Guildford]

Bishop's Chaplain Vacancy (*same address*)

SUFFRAGAN BISHOP
DORKING Rt Revd Ian James Brackley, Dayspring, 13 Pilgrims Way, Guildford, Surrey GU4 8AD [1996]
Tel: (01483) 570829
Fax: (01483) 567268
e-mail: bishop.ian@cofeguildford.org.uk

CATHEDRAL CHURCH OF THE HOLY SPIRIT
Dean Very Revd Alexander Wedderspoon, The Deanery, 1 Cathedral Close, Guildford, Surrey GU2 5TL [1987]
Tel: (01483) 560328
Cathedral Office Guildford Cathedral, Stag Hill, Guildford GU2 5UP
Tel: (01483) 565287
Fax: (01483) 303350
Sub-Dean and Canon Pastor Canon Maureen Palmer PH D, 2 Cathedral Close, Guildford, Surrey GU2 5TL [1996]
Tel: (01483) 560329
Canons Residentiary Canon John Schofield, 4 Cathedral Close, Guildford, Surrey GU2 5TL [1995]   Tel: (01483) 571826 (Office)
Precentor Vacancy
Cathedral Administrator Commander Bill Evershed, Cathedral Office
Treasurer Mr Miles Roberts, Cathedral Office
Chapter Clerk Mr John Brown, Triggs Turner Barton, 128 High St, Guildford, Surrey GU1 3HH   Tel: (01483) 565771
Cathedral Organist Mr Andrew Millington, 5 Cathedral Close, Guildford, Surrey GU2 5TL   Tel: (01483) 531693

ARCHDEACONS
SURREY Ven Robert Reiss, Archdeacon's House, New Rd, Wormley, Godalming, Surrey GU8 5SU [1996]
Tel: (01428) 682563
Fax: (01428) 682993
e-mail: bob.reiss@cofeguildford.org.uk
DORKING Ven Mark Wilson, Littlecroft, Heathside Rd, Woking, Surrey GU22 7EZ [1996]   Tel: (01483) 772713
Fax: (01483) 757353
e-mail: mark.wilson@cofeguildford.org.uk

CONVOCATION (MEMBERS OF THE HOUSE OF CLERGY OF THE GENERAL SYNOD)
The Archdeacon of Surrey
Proctors for Clergy
Revd Richard Hanford
Revd Malcolm King
Revd Alistair Magowan
Ven Mark Wilson

MEMBERS OF THE HOUSE OF LAITY OF THE GENERAL SYNOD
Mr Peter Bruinvels
Mr William Bryant
Mr David Lambert
Mr Robert Leach
Mrs Ann Warren

DIOCESAN OFFICERS
Dioc Secretary Mrs Kristina Ingate, Diocesan House, Quarry St, Guildford, Surrey GU1 3XG   Tel: (01483) 571826
Fax: (01483) 567896
e-mail: kristina.ingate@cofeguildford.org.uk
Chancellor of Diocese His Honour Judge Michael Goodman, Parkside, Dulwich Common, London SE21 7EU
Registrar of Diocese and Bishop's Legal Secretary Mr Peter Beesley, 1 The Sanctuary, London SW1P 3JT   Tel: 0171–222 5381
Fax: 0171–222 7502
Deputy Registrar Mr Nicholas Richens

DIOCESAN ORGANISATIONS
Diocesan Office Diocesan House, Quarry St, Guildford, Surrey GU1 3XG
Tel: (01483) 571826
Fax: (01483) 567896

ADMINISTRATION
Dioc Synod (*Vice-President, House of Clergy*) Revd Malcolm King, Vicarage, Westcott Rd, Dorking, Surrey RH4 3DP Tel: (01306) 882875; (*Vice-President, House of Laity*) Mr Alan Foster, Pennwood, Chiddingfold Rd, Dunsfold, Godalming, Surrey GU8 4PB Tel: (01483) 200960; (*Secretary*) Mrs Kristina Ingate, Dioc House; (*Asst Secretary*), Mr Michael Bishop, Dioc House
e-mail: mike.bishop@cofeguildford.org.uk
Board of Finance (*Chairman*) Mr Michael Young, Dioc House; (*Secretary*) Mrs Kristina Ingate (*as above*)
Accountant Mr Peter Smith, Dioc House
e-mail: peter.smith@cofeguildford.org.uk
Asst Secretaries Mr Michael Bishop, Mr John White, Mr Peter Smith, Dioc House
Parsonages and Propery Committee Mr John White (*as above*)
e-mail: john.white@cofeguildford.org.uk
Pastoral Committee Mr Michael Bishop (*as above*)
Designated Officer Mr Peter Beesley, 1 The Sanctuary, London SW1P 3JT
Tel: 0171–222 5381
Fax: 0171–222 7502

CHURCHES
Advisory Committee for the Care of Churches (*Chairman*) Mr Hamish Donaldson, Edgecombe, Hill Rd, Haslemere, Surrey GU27 2JN; (*Secretary*) Mr Michael Bishop (*as above*)

EDUCATION
Education Centre The Cathedral, Stag Hill, Guildford, Surrey GU2 5UP
Tel: (01483) 450423
Fax: (01483) 450424
Director of Education and Secretary Dioc Board of Education Canon Tony Chanter
e-mail: tony.chanter@cofeguildford.org.uk
Children's Education Officer Mrs Margaret Dean
Assistant Children's Education Officer Mrs Alison Hendy
Youth Education Officer Revd Karina Green
Adviser in Continuing Adult Education and Development Revd Andrew Knowles
Further Education Adviser Mrs Kathleen Kimber
Schools' Personnel and Development Officer Mr David Ager
Schools' Administration Officer Mrs Dorothy Dellow
Resource Officer Mr Roy Davey
Centre Administrator Mrs Diane Hart

MINISTRY
Director of Ministerial Training and Secretary, Council for Ministry Canon John Schofield, Dioc House
 e-mail: john.schofield@cofeguildford.org.uk
Director of Ordinands Revd John Partington, 13 Heath Drive, Brookwood, Surrey GU24 0HG Tel: (01483) 799284
Director of Post-Ordination Training Canon John Schofield (as above)
Clerical Registry (Registrar) Mr Michael Waide, 6 Leybourne Ave, Byfleet, Woking, Surrey KT14 7HB Tel: (01932) 400487
Readers' Board (Secretary) Dr Bryan Wheeler, 40 Simons Walk, Englefield Green, Egham TW20 9SQ
 Tel: (01784) 432835

LITURGICAL
Secretary Sheila Sandison, 13 Pilgrim's Way, Guildford, Surrey GU4 8AD
 Tel: (01483) 570829

MISSIONARY AND ECUMENICAL
Council for Mission and Unity (Chairman) Ven Mark Wilson, Littlecroft, Heathside Rd, Woking, Surrey GU22 7EZ
 Tel: (01483) 772713
Director for Parish Development and Mission Canon Mavis Wilson, Littlecroft, Heathside Rd, Woking, Surrey GU22 7EZ
 Tel: (01483) 720057
 e-mail: mavis.wilson@cofeguildford.org.uk
Dioc Ecumenical Officer Revd Humphrey Southern, Rectory, 25 Upper Hale Rd, Farnham, Surrey GU9 0NX
 Tel: (01252) 716469

PRESS AND PUBLICATIONS
Press and Communications Officer Mrs Sally Hastings, Willow Grange, Woking Rd, Guildford, Surrey GU4 7QS
 Tel: (01483) 598400 (Office)
 (01252) 629205 (Home)
 e-mail: sally.hastings@cofeguildford.org.uk
Director, Guildford Diocese Productions Canon Geoffrey Curtis, Vicarage, Clammer Hill, Grayswood, Haslemere, Surrey GU27 2DZ Tel: (01428) 644208
Editor of Dioc Newspaper Mrs Sally Hastings (as above)
Editor of Dioc Directory Mrs Sally Hastings (as above)

DIOCESAN RECORD OFFICE
130 Goldsworth Rd, Woking, Surrey GU2 1ND (Archivists: Dr D. B. Robinson and Miss Mary Mackey) Tel: (01483) 594594

SOCIAL RESPONSIBILITY
Council for Social Responsibility (Chairman): Revd Gary Meirion-Jones, Rectory, Spinning Walk, Shere, Guildford GU5 9HN
 Tel: (01483) 202394
Director and Secretary: Miss Bassi Mirzania, Dioc House
 e-mail: bassi.marzania@cofeguildford.org.uk

STEWARDSHIP
Dioc Adviser Mr Syd Giles, Dioc House

RURAL DEANS
ARCHDEACONRY OF SURREY
Aldershot Revd David Holt, Vicarage, Branksome Wood Rd, Fleet, Hants GU13 8JU Tel: (01252) 616361

Cranleigh Revd Nigel Nicholson, Rectory, High St, Cranleigh, Surrey GU6 8AF
 Tel: (01483) 273620
Farnham Revd Julian Hubbard, Vicarage, 2 Middle Ave, Farnham, Surrey GU9 8JL
 Tel: (01252) 715505
Godalming Revd John Ashe, Vicarage, Westbrook Rd, Godalming, Surrey GU7 1ET Tel: (01483) 414135
Guildford Revd Jeremy Collingwood, Vicarage, 25 Waterden Rd, Guildford, Surrey GU1 2AX Tel: (01483) 568886
Surrey Heath Revd Neil Turton, Rectory, Parsonage Way, Frimley, Camberley, Surrey GU16 5AG Tel: (01276) 23309

ARCHDEACONRY OF DORKING
Dorking Revd Andrew Cullis, St Paul's Vicarage, 7 South Terrace, Dorking, Surrey RH4 2AB Tel: (01306) 881998
Emly Revd Julian Henderson, Vicarage, Church Rd, Claygate, Esher, Surrey KT10 0JP Tel: (01372) 463603
Epsom Revd David Smethurst, Vicarage, 35 Burgh Heath Rd, Epsom, Surrey KT17 4LP Tel: (01372) 743336
Leatherhead Revd Bryan Paradise, Rectory, Ockham Rd South, East Horsley, Leatherhead, Surrey KT24 6RL
 Tel: (01483) 282359
Runnymede Revd Alistair Magowan, Vicarage, Vicarage Rd, Egham, Surrey TW20 9JN Tel: (01784) 432066
Woking Revd Malcolm Herbert, Christ Church Vicarage, 10 Russetts Close, Woking, Surrey GU21 4BH
 Tel: (01483) 727496

DIOCESE OF HEREFORD

Founded *c* 676. The western half of the County of Hereford and Worcester, except for a few parishes in the south (GLOUCESTER); the southern half of Shropshire; a few parishes in Powys and Monmouthshire.

Population 281,000　　Area 1,660 sq m
Stipendiary Clergy 117　　Benefices 128
Parishes 353　　Churches 421

BISHOP (103rd)
Rt Revd John Oliver, The Bishop's House, The Palace, Hereford HR4 9BN [1990]
Tel: (01432) 271355
Fax: (01432) 343047
[John Hereford]

SUFFRAGAN BISHOP
LUDLOW Rt Revd John Saxbee, The Bishop's House, Corvedale Rd, Craven Arms, Shropshire SY7 9BT [1994]
Tel: (01588) 673571
Fax: (01588) 673585

CATHEDRAL CHURCH OF THE BLESSED VIRGIN MARY AND ST ETHELBERT
Dean Very Revd Robert Willis, The Deanery, The Cloisters, Hereford HR1 2NG [1992]　　*Tel:* (01432) 359880
Cathedral Office 5 College Cloisters, Hereford HR1 2NG　　*Tel:* (01432) 359880
Canons Residentiary
Precentor Canon Paul Iles, The Canon's House, The Close, Hereford HR1 2NG [1983]　　*Tel:* (01432) 266193
Chancellor Canon John Tiller, The Canon's House, 3 St John St, Hereford HR1 2NB [1984]　　*Tel:* (01432) 265659
Treasurer Canon James Butterworth, Cathedral Office [1994]
Ven Michael Hooper, The Archdeacon's House, The Close, Hereford HR1 2NG [1997]　　*Tel:* (01432) 272873
Non-Residentiary Canon Canon Brian Chave, Cathedral Office [1997]
Succentor Revd Geoffrey Howell, 3 Castle St, Hereford HR1 2NL [1997]
Tel: (01432) 273708
Cathedral Administrator and Chapter Clerk Lt Col Andrew Eames, Cathedral Office
Cathedral Organist Dr Roy Massey, 1 College Cloisters, Hereford HR1 2NG
Tel: (01432) 272011
Asst Organist Mr Peter Pyke, 14 College Cloisters, Hereford HR1 2NG
Tel: (01432) 264520

ARCHDEACONS
HEREFORD Ven Michael Hooper, The Archdeacon's House, The Close, Hereford HR1 2NG [1991]　　*Tel:* (01432) 272873
LUDLOW Rt Revd John Saxbee, The Bishop's House, Corvedale Rd, Craven Arms, Shropshire SY7 9BT [1992]
Tel: (01588) 673571

CONVOCATION (MEMBERS OF THE HOUSE OF CLERGY OF THE GENERAL SYNOD)
Dignitaries in Convocation
The Dean of Hereford
The Archdeacon of Hereford
Proctors for Clergy
Revd Kay Garlick
Preb Robert Horsfield
Preb John Reese

MEMBERS OF THE HOUSE OF LAITY OF THE GENERAL SYNOD
Mr Keith Bladon
Mrs Margaret Cosh
Mrs Mary-Lou Toop

DIOCESAN OFFICERS
Dioc Secretary Miss Sylvia Green, The Palace, Hereford HR4 9BL
Tel: (01432) 353863
Fax: (01432) 352952
Chancellor of Diocese Chanc Jonathan Henty, Office of the Social Security and Child Support Commissioners, Harp House, 83 Farringdon St, London EC4A 4DH　　*Tel:* 0171–353 5145
Registrars of Diocese and Bishop's Legal Secretaries Mr Tom Jordan, Dioc Registry, 44 Bridge St, Hereford HR4 9DN *Tel:* (01432) 352992; Mr Peter Beesley, 1 The Sanctuary, Westminster, London SW1P 3JT
Tel: 0171–222 5381
Dioc Surveyors Hook Mason Partnership, 11 Castle St, Hereford HR1 3NL
Tel: (01432) 352299

DIOCESAN ORGANISATIONS
Dioc Office The Palace, Hereford HR4 9BL
Tel: (01432) 353863
Fax: (01432) 352952
Bishop's Office The Palace, Hereford HR4 9BN　　*Tel:* (01432) 271355
Fax: (01432) 343047

ADMINISTRATION
Dioc Synod (*Chairman, House of Clergy*) Revd John Reese, Vicarage, 107 Church Road, Tupsley, Hereford HR1 1RT *Tel:* (01432) 274490; (*Chairman, House of Laity*) Mr Keith Bladon, 11 Salisbury Ave, Tupsley, Hereford HR1 1QG *Tel:* (01432) 272402; (*Secretary*) Miss Sylvia Green, Dioc Office
Board of Finance (*Chairman*) Mr Richard Mercer, 'Tana Leas', Clee St Margaret, Craven Arms, Shropshire SY7 9DZ *Tel:* (01584) 823272; (*Secretary*) Miss Sylvia Green (*as above*)
Benefice Buildings Committee Mr Graham Horne, Dioc Office
Glebe Committee Mr Graham Horne (*as above*)
Board of Patronage Miss Sylvia Green (*as above*)
Designated Officer Mr Peter Beesley, 1 The Sanctuary, Westminster, London SW1P 3JT　　*Tel:* 0171–222 5381
Pastoral Committee Miss Sylvia Green (*as above*)
Trusts Miss Sylvia Green (*as above*)

CHURCHES
Advisory Committee for the Care of Churches (*Chairman*) Mr Christopher Dalton, Upper Court, Ullingswick, Hereford HR1 3JG *Tel:* (01432) 820295; (*Secretary*) Mr Graham Horne (*as above*)

EDUCATION
Director of Education Mr Tristram Jenkins, Dioc Office　　*Tel:* (01432) 357864
Fax: (01432) 352952
Schools Adviser (*Curriculum*) Mr Jonathan Rendall, Dioc Office
Dioc Youth Officer Mr Richard Betterton, The Cottage, Bishop Mascall Centre, Lower Galdeford, Ludlow, Shropshire SY8 2RU　　*Tel:* (01584) 872334
Children's Adviser Revd Peter Privett, 165 Bargates, Leominster, Herefordshire HR6 8QT　　*Tel:* (01568) 613176 (Home)
(01584) 872334 (Office)
Church Schools Officer Revd Michael Smith, Dioc Office

DIOCESAN CENTRE
Director Revd Graham Earney, Bishop Mascall Centre, Lower Galdeford, Ludlow, Shropshire SY8 2RU
Tel: (01584) 873882

MINISTRY AND TRAINING
Director of Ordinands Preb Robert North, St Nicholas Rectory, 76 Breinton Rd, Hereford HR4 0JY   *Tel:* (01432) 273810
Dioc Director of Training Canon John Tiller, The Canon's House, 3 St John St, Hereford HR1 2NB   *Tel:* (01432) 265659
Local Ministry Officer Preb Gill Sumner, Rectory, Wistanstow, Craven Arms, Shropshire SY7 8DG   *Tel:* (01588) 672067
Readers' Association (Warden) Rt Revd John Saxbee, Bishop's House, Corvedale Rd, Craven Arms, Shropshire SY7 9BT
   Tel: (01588) 673585
Widows and Dependants (Hereford Archdeaconry Clerical Charities) Preb Ralph Garnett, 5 Hampton Manor, Hereford HR1 1TG   *Tel:* (01432) 274985
(Ludlow Archdeaconry) Preb Robert Sharp, 62 Biddulph Way, Ledbury, Herefordshire HR8 2HN   *Tel:* (01531) 631972

LITURGICAL
Chairman Canon Paul Iles, The Canon's House, The Close, Hereford HR1 2NG
   Tel: (01432) 266193

MISSIONARY AND ECUMENICAL
Dioc Ecumenical Officer Revd Jan Fox, Vicarage, Orleton, Ludlow, Shropshire SY8 4HW   *Tel:* (01568) 780863
Ecumenical Committee (Chairman) The Bishop of Ludlow; *(Secretary)* Revd Jan Fox *(as above)*
Council for World Partnership and Development (Chairman) Mrs Margaret Wickstead, Laurel Cottage, Orleton Common, Ludlow, Shropshire SY8 4JG
   Tel: (01584) 831246;
(Secretary) Revd C. Fletcher, Rectory, Bredenbury, Bromyard, Herefordshire HR7 4TF   *Tel:* (01885) 482236
Dioc Co-ordinator for Evangelism Revd Graham Sykes, Vicarage, Breinton, Hereford HR4 7PG   *Tel:* (01432) 273447
Evangelism Committee (Chairman) The Archdeacon of Hereford; *(Secretary)* Revd Clive Williams, St Mary's Vicarage, Church St, Highley, Bridgnorth, Shropshire WV16 6NA   *Tel:* (01746) 861612

AGRICULTURE
Chaplain Revd Nick Read, Vicarage, Lydbury North, Shropshire SY7 8AU
   Tel: (01588) 680609

PRESS, PUBLICITY AND PUBLICATIONS
Dioc Communications Officer Canon Brian Chave, The Gateway Office, The Palace, Hereford HR4 9BL   *Tel:* (01432) 271355
   0589 186316 (Mobile)
   Fax: (01432) 343047
Editor of Dioc Year Book Miss Sylvia Green *(as above)*
Dioc Newspaper Canon Brian Chave *(as above)*

DIOCESAN RECORDS OFFICE
Hereford Records Office, The Old Barracks, Harold St, Hereford HR1 2QX
   Tel: (01432) 265441

SOCIAL RESPONSIBILITY
Social Responsibility Officer Miss J. Boys
Council for Social Responsibility (Chairman) Vacancy

STEWARDSHIP
Christian Giving Adviser Revd John Fearn, Crozen Cottage, Felton, Hereford HR1 3PW   *Tel:* (01432) 820161

RURAL DEANS
ARCHDEACONRY OF HEREFORD
Abbeydore Revd Paul Barnes, Rectory, Cusop, Hay-on-Wye, Hereford HR3 5RF
   Tel: (01497) 820634
Bromyard Preb Walter Gould, Vicarage, 28 Church Lane, Bromyard, Herefordshire HR7 4DZ   *Tel:* (01885) 482438
Hereford City Preb John Reese, Vicarage, Tupsley, Hereford HR1 1RT
   Tel: (01432) 274490
Hereford Rural Preb Jeanne Summers, 99 Walkers Green, Marden, Hereford HR1 3EA   *Tel:* (01432) 880497
Kington and Weobley Revd Stephen Hollinghurst, Rectory, Pembridge, Hereford HR6 9EB   *Tel:* (01544) 388998
Ledbury Revd Dr Colin Beevers, Rectory, Worcester Rd, Ledbury, Herefordshire HR8 1PL   *Tel:* (01531) 632571
Leominster Revd P. Swain, Rectory, Church Street, Leominster, Hereford HR6 8NH   *Tel:* (01568) 612124
Ross and Archenfield Revd Alan Jevons, Rectory, Much Birch, Hereford HR2 8HT
   Tel: (01981) 540558

ARCHDEACONRY OF LUDLOW
Bridgnorth Revd Clive Williams, St Mary's Vicarage, Church St, Highley, Bridgnorth, Shropshire WV16 6NA
   Tel: (01746) 861612
Clun Forest Revd Richard Shaw, Vicarage, Clun, Craven Arms, Shropshire SY7 8JG
   Tel: (01588) 640809
Condover Revd Allan Toop, Vicarage, Clun Rd, Craven Arms, Shropshire SY7 9QW
   Tel: (01588) 672797
Ludlow Revd Duncan Dormor, Vicarage, Church St, Tenbury Wells, Worcs WR15 8BP   *Tel:* (01584) 810702
Pontesbury Preb Paul Towner, Rectory, Great Hanwood, Shrewsbury SY5 8LJ
   Tel: (01743) 860074
Telford Severn Gorge Revd Dennis Smith, Holy Trinity Vicarage, Holyhead Rd, Oakengates, Telford, Shropshire TF2 6BN
   Tel: (01543) 262420

DIOCESE OF LEICESTER

Restored in 1926. Leicestershire, except the former county of Rutland (PETERBOROUGH); one in Northamptonshire.

Population 891,000   Area 835 sq m
Stipendiary Clergy 170   Benefices 137
Parishes 245   Churches 326

BISHOP (6th)
Vacancy, Bishop's Lodge, 10 Springfield Rd, Leicester LE2 3BD   *Tel:* 0116–270 8985
Fax: 0116–270 3288
e-mail: bpsec@leicester.anglican.org

ASSISTANT BISHOP
Rt Revd William Down, St Mary's Vicarage, 56 Vicarage Lane, Humberstone, Leicester LE5 1EE [1995]
Tel: 0116–276 7281
Fax: 0116–276 4504

CATHEDRAL CHURCH OF ST MARTIN
Provost Very Revd Derek Norman Hole, Provost's House, 1 St Martin's East, Leicester LE1 5FX [1992]
Tel: 0116–262 5294
Fax: 0116–262 5295
Cathedral Office 1 St Martin's East, Leicester LE1 5FX   *Tel:* 0116–262 5294
Canons Residentiary
Chancellor Canon Michael Banks, 3 Morland Ave, Leicester LE2 2PF [1987]
Tel: 0116–210 9893
Fax: 0116–210 9894
Treasurer Canon Michael Wilson, 7 St Martin's East, Leicester LE1 5FX [1988]
Tel: 0116–253 0580
Non-Residentiary Canon
Precentor Canon John Craig, 154 Barclay St, Leicester LE3 0JB [1991]
Tel: 0116–255 7327
Canons Theologian
Canon Brian Hebblethwaite, Queens' College, Cambridge; Canon Anthony Thiselton, Dept of Theology, University of Nottingham, University Park, Nottingham NG7 2RD
Chapter Clerk Mr Graham Moore, Messrs Wartnabys, Solicitors, 44 High St, Market Harborough, Leics LE16 7AH
Tel: (01858) 463322
Cathedral Administrator Mr D. H. C. Moore, Cathedral Office

Master of Music Mr Jonathan Gregory, 27 Heron Close, Great Glen, Leicester LE8 0DZ   *Tel:* 0116–259 3891
Asst Master of Music Mr David Cowen, Flat 2, Mapleton Court, 4 University Rd, Leicester LE1 7RB   *Tel:* 0116–255 4437

ARCHDEACONS
LEICESTER Ven Mike Edson, 13 Stoneygate Ave, Leicester LE2 3HE [1994]
Tel: 0116–270 4441
Fax: 0116–270 1091
e-mail: medson@leicester.anglican.org
LOUGHBOROUGH Ven Ian Stanes, The Archdeaconry, 21 Church Rd, Glenfield, Leicester LE3 8DP [1992]
Tel: 0116–231 1632
Fax: 0116–232 1593
e-mail: stanes@leicester.anglican.org

CONVOCATION (MEMBERS OF THE HOUSE OF CLERGY OF THE GENERAL SYNOD)
The Archdeacon of Loughborough
Proctors for Clergy
Revd Nick Baines
Canon Robert Freeman
Canon Jim Wellington

MEMBERS OF THE HOUSE OF LAITY OF THE GENERAL SYNOD
Mr John Higginbotham
Dr Hugh James
Mrs Mary Weston

DIOCESAN OFFICERS
Dioc Secretary Mr Andrew Howard, Church House, 3/5 St Martin's East, Leicester LE1 5FX   *Tel:* 0116–262 7445
Fax: 0116–253 2889
Chancellor of Diocese The Worshipful Nigel Seed, 3 Paper Buildings, Temple, London EC4Y 7ED   *Tel:* 0171–583 8055
Registrars of Diocese and Bishop's Legal Secretaries Mr Richard Bloor, Harvey Ingram Owston, 20 New Walk, Leicester LE1 6TX   *Tel:* 0116–254 5454
Fax: 0116–255 4559

Mr Paul Morris, Winckworth Sherwood, Registry Chambers, The Old Deanery, Deans Court, London EC4V 5AA
Tel: 0171–593 5110
Fax: 0171–248 3221
Dioc Surveyors Martin Jones & Associates, The Reading Room, 33 Main St, Medbourne, Market Harborough, Leics LE16 8DT   *Tel:* (01858) 565567
Fax: (01858) 565433

DIOCESAN ORGANISATIONS
Diocesan Office Church House, 3/5 St Martin's East, Leicester LE1 5FX
Tel: 0116–262 7445
Fax: 0116–253 2889
e-mail: chouse@leicester.anglican.org

ADMINISTRATION
Dioc Synod (*Secretary*) Mr Andrew Howard, Dioc Office
Dioc Synod (*Chairman, House of Clergy*) Canon Jim Wellington, St Cuthbert's Vicarage, Church Rd, Great Glen, Leicester LE8 0FE   *Tel:* 0116–259 2238; (*Chairman, House of Laity*) Mr William Moss, The Coach House, Mill Lane, Kegworth, Derby DE74 2EJ   *Tel:* (01509) 672481
Board of Finance (*Chairman*) Mr Michael Chamberlain, Peat House, 1 Waterloo Way, Leicester LE1 6LP *Tel:* 0116–256 6000; (*Secretary*) Mr Andrew Howard (*as above*)
Deputy Dioc Secretary Mr Harvey Taylor, Dioc Office
Finance and General Purposes Committee Mr Andrew Howard (*as above*)
Property Committee Mrs Maureen Higgins, Dioc Office
Pastoral Committee Mr Harvey Taylor (*as above*)
Board of Patronage Mr Terence Cocks, 24 Beresford Drive, Leicester LE2 3LA
Tel: 0116–270 3424
Widows Officer Ven Hughie Jones, Four Trees, 68 Main St, Thorpe Satchville, Melton Mowbray, Leics LE14 2DQ
Tel: (01664) 840262
Parish Funding Director Mr Brian Tanner, 100 Burnmill Rd, Market Harborough LE16 7JG   *Tel:* (01858) 432371
Designated Officer Mr Andrew Howard (*as above*)

CHURCHES
Advisory Committee for the Care of Churches (*Chairman*) Dr A. McWhirr, 37 Dovedale Rd, Stoneygate, Leicester LE2 2DN *Tel:* 0116–270 3031; (*Secretary*) Mr Harvey Taylor (*as above*)
Redundant Churches Uses Committee Mrs Maureen Higgins, Dioc Office

EDUCATION
Chairman Mr D. Gwynne Jones, 19 Stanton Rd, Sapcote, Leics LE9 6FQ

Board of Education (Director) Revd Peter Taylor, Dioc Office Tel: 0116–253 7676
Youth Officer Mr Colin Udall, Dioc Office
Religious Education Adviser Ms Hardev Grewal, Dioc Office
Children's Adviser Revd Gillian Dallow, Dioc Office

MINISTRY

Advisory Board of Ministry (Chairman) Ven Ian Stanes, The Archdeaconry, 21 Church Rd, Glenfield, Leicester LE3 8DP
 Tel: 0116–231 1632
Director of Lay Training Canon Anne Horton, Rectory, 157 Main St, Swithland, Loughborough LE12 8QT
 Tel and Fax: (01509) 891163
Director of Ordinands and Lay Ministry Adviser Revd Peter Burrows, Rectory, Broughton Astley, Leicester LE9 6PF
 Tel: (01455) 282261
Officer for NSM Revd Geoffrey Mitchell, 36 Brick Kiln Lane, Shepshed, Loughborough LE12 9EL Tel: (01509) 502280
Association of Readers Revd Malcolm Lambert, Rectory, 19 Main St, South Croxton, Leicester LE7 3RJ Tel: (01664) 840245

LITURGICAL

Chairman Revd Stephen Cherry, Rectory, Steeple Row, Loughborough LE11 1UX
 Tel: (01509) 212780
Secretary Revd Richard Curtis

MISSION AND SOCIAL RESPONSIBILITY

Board of Mission and Social Responsibility (Adviser) Revd Martin Wilson, 278 East Park Rd, Leicester LE5 5AY
 Tel: 0116–273 3893
 e-mail: ldbmsr@foobar.co.uk

ECUMENICAL

Ecumenical Officer Revd Barbara Stanton, 25 Atterton Lane, Witherley, Atherstone, Warks CV9 3LP Tel: (01827) 717875

PRESS AND PUBLICATIONS

Press Relations Officer Mrs Sue Kyriakou, Church House Tel: (01543) 473052
Editor of Dioc Directory Mr Andrew Howard (as above)
Editor of 'News and Views' Revd Jeff Hopewell, Vicarage, 5 The Stockwell, Wymeswold, Loughborough LE12 6UF
 Tel: (01509) 891163
 e-mail: jhopewell@leicester.anglican.org

DIOCESAN RECORDS OFFICE

Leicestershire Records Office, Long Street, Wigston, Leicester LE18 2AH
 Tel: 0116–257 1080
 Fax: 0116–257 1120

EVANGELISM

Dioc Evangelist Ven Mike Edson, 13 Stoneygate Ave, Leicester LE2 3HE
 Tel: 0116–270 4441

RURAL DEANS
ARCHDEACONRY OF LEICESTER

Christianity North (Leicester) Canon John Leonard, St Theodore's House, 4 Sandfield Close, Off Nicklaus Rd, Rushey Mead, Leicester LE4 7RE
 Tel: 0116–266 9956
Christianity South (Leicester) Revd Chris Oxley, Vicarage, 10 Parkside Close, Beaumont Leys, Leicester LE4 1EP
 Tel: 0116–235 2667

Framland Revd Charles Jenkin, Rectory, 67 Dalby Rd, Melton Mowbray LE13 0BQ Tel: (01664) 480923
Gartree I Revd Ian Gemmell, Rectory, Great Bowden, Market Harborough LE16 7ET Tel: (01858) 462032
Gartree II Revd Brian Glover, Vicarage, 12 Saddington Rd, Fleckney, Leicester LE8 0AW Tel: 0116–240 2215
Goscote Revd Nick Baines, Rothley Vicarage, 128 Hallfields Lane, Rothley, Leicester LE7 7NG Tel: 0116–230 2241

ARCHDEACONRY OF LOUGHBOROUGH

Akeley East Revd Stephen Cherry, Rectory, Steeple Row, Loughborough, Leics LE11 1UX Tel: (01509) 212780
Akeley South Revd Kerry Emmett, Rectory, 9 Orchard Close, Ravenstone, Coalville, Leicester LE67 2JW Tel: (01530) 839802
Akeley West Canon Charles Dobbin, Rectory, Prior Park, Ashby-de-la-Zouch, Leicester LE6 5BH Tel: (01530) 412180
Guthlaxton I Revd Peter Burrows, Rectory, Broughton Astley, Leics LE9 6PF
 Tel: (01455) 282261
Guthlaxton II Revd Philip Clements, Rectory, Kilworth Rd, Swinford, Lutterworth, Leics LE17 6BQ Tel: (01788) 860221
Sparkenhoe West Canon Brian Davis, St Mary's Vicarage, Hinckley, Leics LE10 1EQ Tel: (01455) 234241
Sparkenhoe East Canon Geoffrey Willett, Rectory, The Nook, Markfield, Leicester LE6 0WE Tel: (01530) 242844

DIOCESE OF LICHFIELD

Founded in 664, formerly Mercia (AD 656). Staffordshire, except for a few parishes in the south-east (BIRMINGHAM, DERBY); a few parishes in the south-west (WORCESTER); the northern half of Shropshire; Wolverhampton; Walsall; the northern half of Dudley; an area of Sandwell.

Population 1,983,000   Area 1,744 sq m
Stipendiary Clergy 374   Benefices 309
Parishes 427   Churches 577

BISHOP (97th)
Rt Revd Keith Norman Sutton, Bishop's House, 22 The Close, Lichfield, Staffs WS13 7LG [1984]   Tel: (01543) 306000
Fax: (01543) 306009
[Keith Lichfield]

Bishop's Assistant Capt David Brown (*same address*)
Bishop's Press Officer Revd Robert Ellis, St Mary's House, The Close, Lichfield, Staffs WS13 7LD   Tel: (01543) 306030
Fax: (01543) 306039

AREA BISHOPS
SHREWSBURY Rt Revd David Hallatt, 68 London Rd, Shrewsbury SY2 6PG [1994]   Tel: (01743) 235867
Fax: (01743) 243296
STAFFORD Rt Revd Christopher Hill, Ash Garth, Broughton Crescent, Barlaston, Stoke-on-Trent, Staffs ST12 9DD [1996]
Tel: (01782) 373308
Fax: (01782) 373705
WOLVERHAMPTON Rt Revd Michael Bourke, 61 Richmond Rd, Merridale, Wolverhampton WV3 9JH [1993]
Tel: (01902) 824503
Fax: (01902) 824504

CATHEDRAL CHURCH OF THE BLESSED VIRGIN MARY AND ST CHAD
Dean Very Revd Tom Wright D PHIL, The Deanery, Lichfield, Staffs WS13 7LD [1994]   Tel: (01543) 306250
Fax: (01543) 306255
e-mail: tom.wright1@virgin.net
Chapter Office 19A The Close, Lichfield, Staffs WS13 7LD   Tel: (01543) 306100
Fax: (01543) 306109
e-mail: lich.cath@virgin.net
Canons Residentiary
Treasurer Ven George Frost, 24 The Close, Lichfield, Staffs WS13 7LD [1998]
Tel: (01543) 306145
Fax: (01543) 306147

Chancellor Canon Anthony Barnard, 13 The Close, Lichfield, Staffs WS13 7LD [1977]   Tel: (01543) 306241 (Home)
(01543) 306240 (Visitors Study Centre)
Precentor Canon Charles Taylor, 23 The Close, Lichfield, Staffs WS13 7LD
Tel: (01543) 306140
Chief Executive Officer Mr David Wallington, Chapter Office
Bursar: Mr Clive Tomlinson, Chapter Office
Master of the Choristers Mr Andrew Lumsden, 11 The Close, Lichfield WS13 7LD   Tel: (01543) 306200
Assistant Organist Mr Robert Sharpe, 10 The Close, Lichfield, Staffs WS13 7LD   Tel: (01543) 306201
Visits Officer Mrs Angela Bayles, Visitors' Study Centre, The Close, Lichfield, Staffs WS13 7LD   Tel: (01543) 306240

ARCHDEACONS
LICHFIELD Ven George Frost, 24 The Close, Lichfield, Staffs WS13 7LD [1998]
Tel: (01543) 306145
Fax: (01543) 306147
STOKE-UPON-TRENT Ven Alan Smith, 39 The Brackens, Clayton, Newcastle-under-Lyme, Staffs ST5 4JL [1997]
Tel: (01782) 663066
Fax: (01782) 711165
SALOP Ven John Hall, Tong Vicarage, Shifnal, Shropshire TF11 8PW [1998]
Tel: (01902) 372622
Fax: (01902) 374021
WALSALL Ven Tony Sadler, 10 Paradise Lane, Pelsall, Walsall WS3 4NH [1997]   Tel: (01922) 445353
Fax: (01922) 445354

CONVOCATION (MEMBERS OF THE HOUSE OF CLERGY OF THE GENERAL SYNOD)
The Archdeacon of Lichfield
Proctors for Clergy
Revd David Butterfield
Revd Sally Chapman

Revd Robert Ellis
Revd Graham Fowell
Preb Horace Harper
Preb Terry Thake

MEMBERS OF THE HOUSE OF LAITY OF THE GENERAL SYNOD
Miss Sue Booth
Mr John Clark
Sir Patrick Cormack
Mr Ian Gaweda
Mrs Wendy Kinson
Mr Geoff Locke
Mr Keith Masters
Mrs Joanna Monckton
Mr Marcel Noël

DIOCESAN OFFICERS
Dioc Secretary Mr David Taylor, St Mary's House, The Close, Lichfield, Staffs WS13 7LD   Tel: (01543) 306030
Fax: (01543) 306039
e-mail: (open)@ lichfield.anglican.org
Assistant Secretaries Mr Ian Gaweda (*Finance*) and Mr Barry Toothill (*Housing*) (*same address*)
Chancellor of Diocese Judge John Shand, St Mary's House
Registrar of Diocese and Bishop's Legal Secretary Mr John Thorneycroft, Messrs Manby & Steward, 1 St Leonard's Close, Bridgnorth, Shropshire WV16 4EL
Tel: (01746) 761436
Fax: (01746) 766764
Deputy Registrar Mr Niall Blackie, Messrs Manby & Steward, Blount House, Hall Court, Hall Park Way, Telford, Shropshire TF3 4N   Tel: (01952) 291525
Fax: (01952) 291921
Dioc Surveyors Wood, Goldstraw and Yorath, Churchill House, Regent Rd, Hanley, Stoke-on-Trent, Staffs ST1 3RH   Tel: (01782) 208000

DIOCESAN ORGANISATIONS
Diocesan Office See individual addresses below

ADMINISTRATION
Dioc Synod (*Chairman, House of Clergy*) Preb Terry Thake, Vicarage, Little Haywood, Stafford ST18 0TS Tel: (01889) 881262; (*Chairman, House of Laity*) Mr Geoff Locke, Narnia II, 88 Ravenscliffe Rd, Kidsgrove, Stoke on Trent ST7 4HX Tel: (01782) 785544; (*Secretary*) Mr David Taylor, St Mary's House, The Close, Lichfield, Staffs WS13 7LD
Tel: (01543) 306030
Fax: (01543) 306039
Dioc Board of Finance (*Chairman*) Mr Glynne Morris; (*Secretary*) Mr David Taylor (*as above*)

Lichfield   101

Benefice Buildings and Glebe Committee (*Secretary*) Mr Barry Toothill, St Mary's House
Pastoral Committee Revd John Porter, Rectory, 9 Vicarage Rd, Wednesfield, Wolverhampton WV11 1SB *Tel:* (01902) 731462
Fax: (01902) 725560
Trust (*Secretary*) Mr David Taylor (*as above*)
Designated Officer Mr John Thorneycroft, St Mary's House

CHURCHES
Advisory Committee for the Care of Churches (*Chairman*) Mr Richard Raven, Wheatlea House, 82 Upper Rd, Meole Brace, Shrewsbury, Shropshire SY3 9JP
Tel: (01743) 362896;
(*Secretary*) Mrs Katie Brown, St Mary's House

EDUCATION
Director of Education Revd Peter Lister, St Mary's House
Assistant Director Mr Alan Butterworth, St Mary's House
Youth and Children's Adviser (*Lichfield*) *and Team Leader* Vacancy, St Mary's House
Youth and Children's Adviser (*Salop*) Dr Leonie Wheeler, Primrose Cottage, Weston Lullingfields, Shrewsbury SY4 2AA *Tel:* (01939) 261571
Youth and Children's Adviser (*Stoke*) Mr Mark Hatcher, Wetley Abbey Cottage, Wetley Rocks, Stoke-on-Trent, Staffs ST9 0AS *Tel and Fax:* (01782) 551145
Warden – Dioc Youth Centre Mr Arthur Hack, Dovedale House, Ilam, Ashbourne, Derbys DE6 2AZ *Tel:* (01335) 350365
Fax: (01335) 350441
Warden – Shepherds Building (*self-catering youth centre*) Vacancy, St Mary's House
Schools Advisers Mrs June Cook, 3 St Agatha's Close, Charlton Manor, Wellington, Telford TF1 3QP
Tel and Fax: (01952) 242589
Mrs Joan Furlong, Station House, Station Rd, Haughton, Stafford ST18 9HF
Tel and Fax: (01785) 780604

MINISTRY
Postal address and telephone Backcester Lane, Lichfield WS13 1JJ
Tel: (01543) 411550
Fax: (01543) 411552
Board of Ministry Team Leader and Director of Local Ministry Preb David Sceats, Backcester Lane
e-mail: dds@uniblick,compu-link.co.uk
Director of Ordinands Revd Mark Geldard (*same address*)
Director of Ministry Development Revd John Wesson (*same address*)
LNSM Course Leader Revd Eileen Turner (*same address*)

Adviser to Women in Ministry Revd Pippa Thorneycroft, Vicarage, 11 Brookhouse Lane, Featherstone, Wolverhampton WV10 7AW *Tel:* (01902) 727579
Dioc Vocations Adviser Preb Ann Hadley, Rectory, Myddle, Shrewsbury SY4 3RX *Tel:* (01939) 290811
Warden of Readers Revd Ian Cardinal, Vicarage, Wigginton, Tamworth B79 9DN *Tel:* (01827) 64537
Local Vocations Advisory Service Revd Mark Geldard (*as above*)
Readers' Association Mr Barry Toothill, St Mary's House
Local Ministry Scheme Preb David Sceats (*as above*)

LITURGICAL
Secretary Canon Charles Taylor, 23 The Close, Lichfield, Staffs WS13 7LD
Tel: (01543) 263337

MISSION AND UNITY
Dioc Missioner Revd Mark Ireland, 14 Gorway Gardens, Walsall WS1 3BJ
Tel: (01922) 626010
Fax: (01922) 625924
World Mission Officer Revd Dr Michael Sheard, 68 Sneyd Lane, Essington, Wolverhampton WV11 3DX
Tel: (01922) 445844
Fax: (01922) 445845
e-mail: michael.sheard@netmatters.co.uk
Ecumenical Officer Vacancy, 66 Heritage Court, Lichfield, Staffs WS14 9ST
Tel and Fax: (01543) 417179

PRESS, PUBLICATIONS AND NEWSLETTER
Communications Officer Revd Robert Ellis, St Mary's House
Press Officer on Duty *Tel:* (01543) 306030
(01283) 820732 (Home)
Editor of Dioc Newsletter 'Link' Revd Robert Ellis (*as above*)
Editor – Dioc Newspaper 'Spotlight' Mrs Pauline Shelton, 23 Kingsway West, Newcastle-under-Lyme, Staffs ST5 3PT *Tel and Fax:* (01782) 662229

DIOCESAN RECORD OFFICES
Staffordshire Record Office, Eastgate St, Stafford ST16 2LZ *Tel:* (01785) 278379, *County Archivist:* Mr D. V. Fowkes (*For parishes in the Archdeaconries of Lichfield and Stoke-upon-Trent*); Lichfield Record Office, The Library, The Friary, Lichfield WS13 6QG, *Tel:* (01543) 256787, *Archivist in Charge* Mr M. Dorrington (*For parishes within the city of Lichfield*); Shrewsbury Records and Research Centre, Castle Gates, Shrewsbury SY1 2AQ, *Tel:* (01743) 255350 *Head of Records and Research* Miss

R. Bagley (*For parishes in the Archdeaconry of Salop*)

CARIS (Care, Action, Responsibility, and Justice in Society)
Social Responsibility Officer Revd Ruth Stables, Shallowford House, Norton Bridge, Stone ST15 0NZ
Tel: (01785) 761763
Fax: (01785) 761764
Local Development Officer Mr Malcolm Carroll (*same address*)
Association for Family Care Vanessa Geffen, 8 Coven Mill Close, Coven WV9 5HX
Tel and Fax: (01902) 791100
Black Country Urban Industrial Mission (*Team Leader*) Revd Olwen Smith
Office St Peter's House, Exchange St, Wolverhampton WV1 1TS
Tel: (01902) 710407
Home Vicarage, 66 Albert Rd, Wolverhampton WV6 0AF *Tel:* (01902) 712935
Dioc Council with Deaf People (*Senior Chaplain and Secretary*) Revd Philip Maddock, Rectory, 56 Uttoxeter Rd, Hill Ridware, Rugeley WS13 3QU *Tel:* (01543) 402023
(*Dioc Chaplain*) Revd John Cowburn, Vicarage, Upper Belgrave Rd, Normacot, Stoke-on-Trent ST3 4QJ
Tel: (01782) 325832
Dioc Adviser in Pastoral Care and Counselling Revd Jeffery Leonardi, New Rectory, Bellamour Way, Colton, Rugeley WS14 3JW *Tel:* (01889) 570897
Black Anglican Concerns Minister Vacancy

PARISH FUNDING UNIT
Team Members Mr Neil Bradley, Mr Bill Proctor, Mr Ian Law, St Mary's House

RURAL DEANS
ARCHDEACONRY OF LICHFIELD
Lichfield Revd Ned Townshend, St Chad's Rectory, The Windings, Lichfield WS13 7EX *Tel:* (01543) 262254
Penkridge Revd Trevor Green, Vicarage, Sandy Lane, Brewood, Stafford ST19 9ET *Tel:* (01902) 850368
Rugeley Preb Terry Thake, Vicarage, Little Haywood, Stafford ST18 0TS
Tel: (01889) 881262
Tamworth Revd Barry Roche, 29 Melmerby, Wilnecote, Tamworth, Staffs B77 4LP *Tel:* (01827) 331163

ARCHDEACONRY OF STOKE-ON-TRENT
Alstonfield Revd Jack Nicoll, Longnor Vicarage, Buxton SK17 0PA
Tel: (01298) 83316
Cheadle Preb Neil Jefferyes, Vicarage, 8 Vicarage Crescent, Caverswall, Stoke-on-Trent ST11 9EW *Tel:* (01782) 393309

Eccleshall Revd Michael Pope, Vicarage, Gnosall, Stafford ST20 0ER
 Tel: (01785) 822213
Leek Revd David Wilmot, Vicarage, Baddeley Green Lane, Stoke-on-Trent ST2 7EY
 Tel: (01782) 534062
Newcastle-under-Lyme Revd Gerald Gardiner, St Andrew's Vicarage, 50 Kingsway West, Westlands, Newcastle ST5 3PU
 Tel: (01782) 619594
Stafford Revd Geoffrey Smith, Rectory, Haughton, Stafford ST18 9HU
 Tel: (01785) 780181
Stoke (North) Revd Brian Williams, Sneyd Vicarage, Hamil Rd, Burslem, Stoke-on-Trent ST6 1AP *Tel:* (01782) 825841
Stoke-on-Trent Revd Godfrey Stone, Rectory, 151 Werrington Rd, Bucknall, Stoke-on-Trent ST2 9AR *Tel:* (01782) 214455
Trentham Revd Godfrey Simpson, Vicarage, Barlaston, Stoke-on-Trent, Staffs ST12 9AB *Tel:* (0178 139) 2452
Tutbury Revd Phillip Jefferies, Horninglow Vicarage, Rolleston Rd, Burton-on-Trent DE13 0JZ *Tel:* (01283) 568613
Uttoxeter Vacancy

ARCHDEACONRY OF SALOP

Edgmond Revd David Butterfield, Vicarage, 25 Church Rd, Lilleshall, Newport, Shropshire TF10 9HE
 Tel: (01952) 604281
Ellesmere (Acting) Revd Maurice Gray, The Pynt, Rhosgadfa, Gobowen, Oswestry SY10 7BN *Tel:* (01691) 661110
Hodnet Revd James Graham, Rectory, Hodnet, Market Drayton TF9 3NQ
 Tel: (01630) 685491
Oswestry Revd David Crowhurst, St Oswald's Vicarage, Penylan Lane, Oswestry, Shropshire SY11 2AN
 Tel: (01691) 653467
Shifnal Revd Roger Balkwill, Vicarage, High St, Albrighton, Wolverhampton WV7 3EQ *Tel:* (01902) 372701
Shrewsbury Revd Kevin Roberts, Vicarage, Vicarage Rd, Meole Brace, Shrewsbury SY3 9EZ *Tel:* (01743) 231744
Telford Revd Dennis Smith, Holy Trinity Vicarage, Holyhead Rd, Oakengates, Telford, Shropshire TF2 6BN
 Tel: (01952) 612926

Wem and Whitchurch Preb Neil MacGregor, Rectory, Ellesmere Rd, Wem, Shropshire SY4 5TU *Tel:* (01939) 232550
Wrockwardine Revd Christopher Cooke, Rectory, Wrockwardine, Wellington, Telford, Shropshire TF6 5DD
 Tel: (01952) 240969

ARCHDEACONRY OF WALSALL

Trysull Revd Michael Hunter, 100 Bellencroft Gardens, Merry Hill, Wolverhampton WV3 8DU *Tel:* (01902) 763603
Walsall Revd David Lingwood, Rushall Vicarage, 10 Tetley Ave, Walsall WS4 2HE
 Tel: (01922) 624677
Wednesbury Preb Ian Cook, Rectory, Hollies Drive, Wednesbury WS10 9EQ
 Tel: 0121–556 0645
West Bromwich Revd Martin Rutter, St James' Vicarage, 151A Hill Top, West Bromwich, B70 0SB *Tel:* 0121–556 0805
Wolverhampton Vacancy

Lichfield

DIOCESE OF LINCOLN

Founded in 1072, formerly Dorchester (AD 886), formerly Leicester (AD 680), originally Lindine (AD 678). Lincolnshire; North East Lincolnshire; North Lincolnshire, except for an area in the west (SHEFFIELD).

Population 927,000   Area 2,673 sq m
Stipendiary Clergy 229   Benefices 258
Parishes 533   Churches 648

BISHOP (70th)
Rt Revd Robert Maynard Hardy, Bishop's House, Eastgate, Lincoln LN2 1QQ [1987]   Tel: (01522) 534701   Fax: (01522) 511095
[Robert Lincoln]

Personal Assistant Canon Raymond Rodger (*same address*)

SUFFRAGAN BISHOPS
GRANTHAM Rt Revd Alastair Llewellyn John Redfern, 243 Barrowby Rd, Grantham NG31 8NP [1997]   Tel: (01476) 564722   Fax: (01476) 592468
GRIMSBY Rt Revd David Tustin, Bishop's House, Church Lane, Irby-on-Humber, Grimsby DN37 7JR [1979]   Tel: (01472) 371715   Fax: (01472) 371716

HONORARY ASSISTANT BISHOPS
Rt Revd Donald Snelgrove, Kingston House, 8 Park View, Barton-on-Humber DN18 6AX [1994]   Tel: (01652) 634484
Rt Revd John Brown, 130 Oxford Rd, Cleethorpes [1995]   Tel: (01472) 698840

CATHEDRAL CHURCH OF THE BLESSED VIRGIN MARY
Dean Very Revd Alec Knight, The Deanery, 12 Eastgate, Lincoln LN2 1QG [1998]   Tel: (01522) 523608
Canons Residentiary
Sub-dean Canon Rex Davis, The Subdeanery, 18 Minster Yard, Lincoln LN2 1PX [1977]   Tel: (01522) 521932
Precentor Canon Andrew Stokes, The Precentory, 16 Minster Yard, Lincoln LN2 1PX [1992]   Tel: (01522) 523644
Chancellor Canon Vernon White, The Chancery, 11 Minster Yard, Lincoln LN2 1PJ [1993]   Tel: (01522) 525610
Chapter Clerk Mr Russell Pond, Chapter Office, The Cathedral, Lincoln LN2 1PZ   Tel: (01522) 530320

Cathedral Organist Mr Colin Walsh, Graveley Place, 12 Minster Yard, Lincoln LN2 1PJ
Asst Organist Mr Jeffrey Makinson, 2A Vicars' Court, Lincoln LN2 1PT   Tel: (01522) 526469

ARCHDEACONS
LINCOLN Ven Arthur Hawes, Archdeacon's House, Northfield Rd, Quarrington, Sleaford NG34 8RT [1995]   Tel: (01529) 304348   Fax: (01529) 304354
STOW Ven Roderick Wells, Hackthorn Vicarage, Lincoln LN2 3PF [1989]   Tel: (01673) 860382   Fax: (01673) 863423
LINDSEY (*as Stow*)

CONVOCATION (MEMBERS OF THE HOUSE OF CLERGY OF THE GENERAL SYNOD)
Dignitaries in Convocation
The Bishop of Grimsby
The Archdeacon of Stow
Proctors for Clergy
Revd Andrew Hawes
Revd Stephen Holdaway
Revd Christopher Lilley
Revd Peter Mullins

MEMBERS OF THE HOUSE OF LAITY OF THE GENERAL SYNOD
Mr Roger Atkinson
Mrs Joy Epton
Mrs Nicolete Fisher
Mrs Sonia Marshall
Mrs Carol Ticehurst

DIOCESAN OFFICERS
Dioc Secretary Mr Philip Hamlyn Williams, Church House, Lincoln LN2 1PU   Tel: (01522) 529241   Fax: (01522) 512717
e-mail: lincolndio@clara.net.co.uk
Chancellor of Diocese Mr Peter Collier, 12 St Helens Rd, Dringhouses, York YO24 1HP

Registrar of Diocese and Bishop's Legal Secretary Mr Derek Wellman, 28 West Parade, Lincoln LN1 1JT   Tel: (01522) 536161   Fax: (01522) 513007
Deputy Registrar Mr Michael Rhodes (*same address*)

DIOCESAN ORGANISATIONS
Diocesan Office Church House, Lincoln LN2 1PU   Tel: (01522) 529241   Fax: (01522) 512717
e-mail: lincolndio@clara.net.co.uk

ADMINISTRATION
Dioc Synod (*Chairman, House of Clergy*) Canon Brian Osborne, Holy Trinity Vicarage, 64 Spilsby Rd, Boston PE21 9NS Tel: (01205) 363657; (*Secretary*) Mr Philip Hamlyn Williams, Dioc Office; (*Chairman, House of Laity*) Mrs Sally Smithson, Pendling, Tattershall Rd, Woodhall Spa, Lincoln LN10 6TW   Tel: (01526) 352332
Board of Finance (*Chairman*) Mr Ian Davey, 53 Cromwell Rd, Cleethorpes Tel: (01472) 693133 (*Secretary*) Mr Philip Hamlyn Williams (*as above*)
Budget, Finance and Co-ordinating Committee Mr Philip Hamlyn Williams (*as above*)
Stipends and Clergy Conditions of Service Committee Mr Richard Wilkinson, Dioc Office
Trusts Committee Mr Philip Hamlyn Williams (*as above*)
Assets (and Glebe) Committee Mr Philip Hamlyn Williams (*as above*)
Clergy Housing and Board Property Committee Mr Philip Hamlyn Williams (*as above*)
Pastoral Committee Mr Richard Wilkinson (*as above*)
Board of Patronage Mr Richard Wilkinson (*as above*)
Designated Officer Mr Derek Wellman, 28 West Parade, Lincoln LN1 1JT   Tel: (01522) 536161
Dioc Electoral Registration Officer Mr Gavin Dix-White, Dioc Office

CHURCHES
Advisory Committee for the Care of Churches (*Chairman*) Canon Raymond Rodger, Bishop's House, Eastgate, Lincoln LN2 1QQ   Tel: (01522) 534701   Fax: (01522) 511095
(*Secretary*) Miss Jane Logan, Dioc Office
Church Buildings Revd Neil Brunning, 11 Drover's Court, Lea Rd, Gainsborough DN21 1AN   Tel: (01427) 732033
Church Extension Committee Mr Richard Wilkinson (*as above*)
Redundant Churches Uses Committee (*Secretary*) Miss Jane Logan (*as above*)

EDUCATION

Director of Education Revd John Bailey, Dioc Education Centre, Church House, Lincoln LN2 1PU   Tel: (01522) 569600
Schools Administrator Mr Maurice Milner (*same address*)
Dioc RE Adviser Mrs Paulette Bissell (*same address*)

MISSION AND TRAINING

Director of Forum Canon Alan Nugent, Dioc Office   Tel: (01522) 528886
Clergy Training Adviser and Co-ordinator Revd P. Mullins, 1 St Giles Ave, Lincoln LN2 4PE   Tel: (01522) 528199
Director of Ordinands Revd Angela Pavey, St Luke's Vicarage, Jasmin Rd, Birchwood, Lincoln LN6 0YR
    Tel: (01522) 683507
Ordinands' Grants Mr Philip Hamlyn Williams (*as above*)
Mission and Training Development Forum (*Secretary*) Mr Hugh Tilney-Bassett, MTDF, Dioc Office   Tel: (01522) 528886
Stewardship Campaign Director Mrs Jane Chard, Dioc Office
Resources Consultant Mr Keith Bourne, Dioc Office
Adult Education Adviser Dr Joan Butterfield, Vicarage, Church Lane, Chapel St Leonards, Skegness PE24 5UJ
    Tel: (01754) 872646
Children's Work Adviser Vacancy
Youth Work Adviser Capt Dave Rose, MTDF, Dioc Office   Tel: (01522) 528886
Local Ministry Officer Revd Kathryn Windslow, Dioc Office   Tel: (01522) 528886
Warden of Readers Revd Leslie Acklam, 165c Carholme Rd, Lincoln LN1 1RU   Tel: (01522) 531477
Director of Readers Revd Rosslyn Miller, 120A Station Rd, Waddington, Lincoln LN5 9QS   Tel: (01522) 720819
Readers (*Secretary*) Mr M.J. Pemberton, 23 Viceroy Drive, Pinchbeck, Spalding PE11 2LG   Tel: (01775) 760437
Clergy Widows Officers Canon and Mrs Ifor George-Jones, 42 Kelstern Rd, Doddington Park, Lincoln LN6 3NJ
    Tel: (01522) 691896
Clergy Retirement Officer Canon Edward Barlow, 8 Pynder Close, Hillcroft, Washingborough, Lincoln LN2 1EX
    Tel: (01522) 793762

LITURGICAL

Secretary Miss R. J. Logan, Dioc Office

ECUMENICAL

Ecumenical Development Officer Revd John Cole, Pelham House, Little Lane, Wrawby, Brigg DN20 8RW   Tel: (01652) 657484
Ecumenical Officer (*Local*) Vacancy, (*same address*)
Church in Society Officer Miss Janet Ratcliffe, Dioc Office   Tel: (01522) 528886
    (01522) 793800 (Home)
    Fax: (01522) 512717
Rural Officer Mr Terry Miller, 120A Station Rd, Waddington, Lincoln LN5 9QS
    Tel: (01522) 720819
Chaplain to Deaf Revd John Clark, 3 Hawthorn Rd, Cherry Willingham, Lincoln LN3 4JU   Tel: (01522) 751759
Industrial Chaplains Revd Adrian Thomas (Baptist), 4 Old Brumby St, Scunthorpe; Revd Doreen Brown, 23 Montaigne Crescent, Glebe Park, Lincoln LN2 4QN Tel: (01522) 526399; Revd Geraldine Kirk, 364 Laceby Rd, Grimsby DN34 5LU Tel: (01472) 873435; Revd Andrew Vaughan, 4 Grange Close, Canwick, Lincoln LN4 2RH   Tel: (01522) 528266

PRESS, PUBLICITY AND PUBLICATIONS

Press and Media Relations Officer Canon Raymond Rodger, Bishop's House (*as above*)
Editor of Dioc Directory Mr Philip Hamlyn Williams (*as above*)
Editor of Dioc Leaflet Mr Philip Hamlyn Williams (*as above*)

DIOCESAN RECORDS OFFICE

Lincolnshire Archives Office, St Rumbold St, Lincoln LN2 5AB (*Archivist* Dr G. A. Knight)   Tel: (01522) 526204

RURAL DEANS

ARCHDEACONRY OF STOW

Isle of Axholme Canon Derek Brown, Rectory, Belton Rd, Epworth, Doncaster DN9 1JL   Tel: (01427) 872471
Corringham Revd Geoffrey Richardson, Rectory, Normanby Rd, Stow, Lincoln LN1 2DF   Tel: (01427) 788251
Lawres Revd Ivan Howitt, Rectory, Owmby, Lincoln LN2 3HL
    Tel: (01637) 878275
Manlake Revd Alan Hayday, St Hugh's Rectory, Ashby Rd, Scunthorpe DN16 2AG   Tel: (01724) 843064
West Wold Revd Michael Cartwright, Vicarage, Market Rasen, Lincoln LN8 3HL   Tel: (01673) 843424

Yarborough Revd Stephen Phillips, Vicarage, Great Limber, Grimsby DN37 8JN   Tel: (01469) 60641

ARCHDEACONRY OF LINDSEY

Bolingbroke Revd Adrian Sullivan, Rectory, West Keal, Spilsby PE23 4BJ
    Tel: (01790) 753534
Calcewaith and Candleshoe Revd Peter Coates, Rectory, Vicarage Lane, Wainfleet St Mary, Skegness PE24 4JJ
    Tel: (01754) 880401
Grimsby and Cleethorpes Revd John Ellis, 120 Queen Mary Ave, Cleethorpes DN35 7SZ   Tel: (01472) 696521
Haverstoe Canon Peter Hall, Vicarage, 344 Pelham Rd, Immingham, Grimsby DN40 1PU   Tel: (01469) 72560
Horncastle Revd Christopher Elliott, Deanery House, 2 Millstone Close, Langton Drive, Horncastle LN9 5SU
Louthesk Revd Stephen Holdaway, Rectory, 49 Westgate, Louth LN11 9YE
    Tel: (01507) 610247

ARCHDEACONRY OF LINCOLN

Aveland, Ness with Stamford Canon John Warwick, Vicarage, Bourne PE10 9LX   Tel: (01778) 422412
Beltisloe Revd Andrew Hawes, Vicarage, Church Lane, Edenham, Bourne PE10 0LS   Tel: (01778) 591272
Christianity Revd Tony Kerswill, Bracebridge Vicarage, 60 Chiltern Rd, Lincoln LN5 8SE   Tel: (01522) 532636
Elloe (*East*) Canon Peter Hill, Vicarage, Holbeach, Spalding PE12 7DT
    Tel: (01406) 22185
Elloe (*West*) Revd Timothy Thompson, Vicarage, 11 Station Rd, Surfleet, Spalding PE11 4DA   Tel: (01775) 680906
Graffoe Revd Richard Billinghurst, St Lawrence Rectory, Vicarage Drive, Skellingthorpe, Lincoln LN6 5UY
    Tel: (01522) 682520
Grantham Revd Richard Eyre, Saxonwell Vicarage, Church St, Long Bennington, Newark, NG23 5ES   Tel: (01400) 282545
Holland (*East*) Revd Chris Dalliston, Vicarage, Wormgate, Boston PE21 6NP
    Tel: (01205) 362864
Holland (*West*) Revd Margaret Barsley, Vicarage, Church Lane, Swineshead, Boston PE20 3JA   Tel: (01205) 820271
Lafford Revd Hall Speers, Rectory, West St, Folkingham, Sleaford NG34 0SN
    Tel: (01529) 497391
Loveden Revd James Hawkins, Rectory, 117 Ermine St, Ancaster, Grantham NG32 3QL   Tel: (01400) 230398

DIOCESE OF LIVERPOOL

Founded in 1880. Liverpool; Sefton; Knowsley; St Helens; Wigan, except for areas in the north (BLACKBURN) and in the east (MANCHESTER); areas of southern Lancashire and northern Cheshire.

Population 1,573,000   Area 389 sq m
Stipendiary Clergy 255   Benefices 203
Parishes 206   Churches 254

BISHOP (7th)
Rt Revd James Stuart Jones, Bishop's Lodge, Woolton Park, Woolton, Liverpool L25 6DT [1998]   Tel: 0151–421 0831

[James Liverpool]

Personal Chaplain Revd Clive Gardner, 48 Babbacombe Rd, Childwall, Liverpool L16 9JW   Tel: 0151–421 0831 (Office)
0151–722 9543 (Home)
Fax: 0151–428 3055

SUFFRAGAN BISHOP
WARRINGTON Rt Revd John Richard Packer, 34 Central Ave, Eccleston Park, Prescot, Merseyside L34 2QP [1996]
Tel: 0151–426 1897 (Home)
0151–708 9480 (Office)

HONORARY ASSISTANT BISHOP
Rt Revd James William Roxburgh, 53 Preston Rd, Southport PR9 9EE [1991]
Tel: (01704) 542927

CATHEDRAL CHURCH OF CHRIST
Dean Very Revd (Rhys) Derrick Chamberlain Walters, The Cathedral, St James' Mount, Liverpool L1 7AZ [1983]
Tel: 0151–709 6271
Canons Residentiary
Chancellor Canon David Hutton, The Cathedral [1983]
Treasurer Canon Noel Vincent, The Cathedral [1995]
Precentor Canon Mark Boyling, The Cathedral [1993]
Bursar Mr Raymond Maher, The Cathedral
Chapter Clerk Mr Roger Arden, Church House, 1 Hanover St, Liverpool L1 3DW   Tel: 0151–709 2222
Cathedral Organist Professor Ian Tracey, The Cathedral

ARCHDEACONS
LIVERPOOL Ven Bob Metcalf, 38 Menlove Ave, Liverpool L18 2EF [1994]
Tel: 0151–724 3956
Fax: 0151–729 0587

WARRINGTON Ven David Woodhouse, 22 Rob Lane, Newton le Willows WA12 0DR [1981]   Tel: (01925) 229247
Fax: (01925) 220423

CONVOCATION (MEMBERS OF THE HOUSE OF CLERGY OF THE GENERAL SYNOD)
The Archdeacon of Warrington
Proctors for Clergy
Canon Neville Black
Revd Peter Bradley
Revd Eric Bramhall
Canon Paul Nener
Canon John Stanley

MEMBERS OF THE HOUSE OF LAITY OF THE GENERAL SYNOD
Mr Keith Cawdron
Mr Allan Jones
Mrs Lesley Michell
Dr Peter Owen
Mr Roy Pybus
Mr Christopher Pye
Mrs Margaret Swinson

DIOCESAN OFFICERS
Dioc Secretary Mr Keith Cawdron, Church House, 1 Hanover St, Liverpool L1 3DW
Tel: 0151–709 9722
Fax: 0151–709 2885
Chancellor of Diocese His Honour Judge Richard Hamilton, c/o Diocesan Registry, Church House
Registrar of Diocese and Bishop's Legal Secretary Mr Roger Arden, Church House
Tel: 0151–709 2222

DIOCESAN ORGANISATIONS
Diocesan Office Church House, 1 Hanover St, Liverpool L1 3DW
Tel: 0151–709 9722
Fax: 0151–709 2885

ADMINISTRATION
Dioc Synod (Chairman, House of Clergy) Revd Eric Bramhall, All Saints' Vicarage, Childwall Abbey Rd, Liverpool L16 9JU   Tel: 0151–737 2169; (*Chairman, House of Laity*) Mr Christopher Pye, 140 Hinckley Rd, Blackbrook, St Helens WA11 9JY   Tel: (01744) 36206; (*Secretary*) Mr Keith Cawdron, Church House
Board of Finance (*Chairman*) Mr Barry Moult, Cranbrook, Higher Lane, Dalton, Wigan WN8 7RP Tel: (01257) 462841; (*Secretary*) Mr Keith Cawdron (*as above*)
Pastoral Committee (*Chairman*) The Bishop of Warrington; (*Secretary*) Mrs Margaret Sadler, Church House; (*Bishop's Planning Adviser*) Revd Bob Lewis, Church House
Parsonages Committee (*Chairman*) Ven Bob Metcalf, Church House; (*Secretary*) Mrs Jackie Duck, Church House; (*Surveyor*) Hardcastle & Hogarth, Church House
Stipends Officer Mrs Pauline Walsh, Church House
Designated Officer Mr Roger Arden, Church House

CHURCHES
Advisory Committee for the Care of Churches (*Chairman*) Canon Malcolm Forrest, The Hall, Wigan, Lancs WN1 1HN
Tel: (01942) 44459
Secretary Revd Noel Michell, Church House

BOARD OF EDUCATION
Chairman The Bishop of Warrington, Church House
Director of Education Canon David Woodhouse, Church House
Youth Officer Mr Richard Turner, Church House
Children's Officer Mrs Jane Leadbetter, 11 Ryegate Rd, Grassendale, Liverpool L19 9AL   Tel: 0151–427 0413
Schools Officer Mr Graham Massey, Church House

BOARD OF MINISTRY
Chairman The Archdeacon of Warrington (*as above*)
Secretary Miss Beryl Smart, 41 Culcheth Hall Drive, Culcheth, Warrington WA3 4PT   Tel: (01925) 762655
Director of Ordinands Revd Myles Davies, St Ann's Vicarage, Derwent Square, Liverpool L13 6QT   Tel: 0151–228 5252
Director of Diaconal Ministries Revd Lesley Bentley, St Philip's Vicarage, 89 Westbrook Crescent, Westbrook, Warrington WA5 5TC   Tel: (01925) 54400
Director of Continuing Ministerial Education Revd Peter Bradley, Rectory, 1A College Rd, Upholland, Skelmersdale WN8 0PY
Tel and Fax: (01695) 622936
Readers' Association (*Warden*) Revd Paul Conder, St Michael's Vicarage, 41 Downhills Rd, Liverpool L23 8SJ
Tel: 0151–924 3424

LITURGICAL
Chairman Revd Myles Davies (*as above*)

BOARD OF MISSION AND UNITY
Chairman Mrs Linda Jones, St Matthew's Vicarage, 418 Stanley Rd, Bootle, Liverpool L20 5AE *Tel:* 0151–922 3316
Secretary Revd Julian Hartley, St Paul's Vicarage, Warrington Rd, Goose Green, Wigan WN3 6QB *Tel:* (01942) 42984
Director of Christian Development for Mission Mr Christopher Peck, Church House
Evangelism Adviser Mr Phil Pawley, 40 Sherdley Rd, Peasley Cross, St Helens WA9 5AB *Tel:* (01744) 737291

PRESS AND PUBLICATIONS
Press Officer c/o Church House
Editor of 'Livewire' Mrs Anne Todd, c/o Church House
Communications Officer c/o Church House

DIOCESAN RECORDS OFFICE
For further information apply to Registrar, Church House, 1 Hanover St, Liverpool L1 3DW *Tel:* 051–709 9722 *or* The Lancashire Record Office, Bow Lane, Preston PR1 8ND (*Archivist* Mr K. Hall)
Tel: (01772) 254868

BOARD FOR SOCIAL RESPONSIBILITY
Chairman Revd Frank Kendall, Cromwell Villa, 260 Prescot Rd, St Helens WA10 3HR
Executive Officer for Social Responsibility Mr Ultan Russell, Church House
Tel: 0151–709 5586
Senior Industrial Chaplain Canon Randell Moll (*same address*)

UPA Link Officer Revd Nicholas Anderson, St Francis's Vicarage, 42 Sherborne Rd, Kitt Green, Wigan WN5 0JA
Tel: (01942) 213227

MERSEYSIDE AND REGION CHURCHES ECUMENICAL ASSEMBLY
Ecumenical Officer Revd Martyn Newman, Friends Meeting House, 65 Paradise St, Liverpool L1 3BP *Tel:* 0151–709 0125

RESOURCES
Resources Officers: Mrs Kath Rogers, Mr Graeme Pollard, Church House
UPA Projects Adviser Mrs Marion Boon, Church House

AREA DEANS
ARCHDEACONRY OF LIVERPOOL
Bootle Revd Chris Jones, St Matthew's Vicarage, 418 Stanley Rd, Bootle, Liverpool L20 5AE *Tel:* 0151–922 3316
Huyton Canon John Stanley, Vicarage, Huyton, Merseyside L36 7SA
Tel: 0151–489 1449
Liverpool North Revd David Lewis, Vicarage, 48 John Lennon Drive, Liverpool L6 9HT *Tel:* 0151–260 3262
Liverpool South – Childwall Canon John Roberts, 67 Church Rd, Woolton, Liverpool L25 6DA *Tel:* 0151–428 1853
Sefton Canon Frances Briscoe, St Stephen's Vicarage, St Stephen's Rd, Hightown, Merseyside L38 0BL *Tel:* 0151–929 2469
Toxteth and Wavertree Revd David Kirkwood, 40 Devonshire Rd, Liverpool L8 3TZ *Tel:* 0151–727 1248
Walton Canon Anthony Hawley, Rectory, Mill Lane, Kirkby, Liverpool L32 2AX
Tel: 0151–547 2155
West Derby Canon Roger Wikeley, Rectory, West Derby, Liverpool L12 5EA
Tel: 0151–256 6600

ARCHDEACONRY OF WARRINGTON
North Meols Revd John Burgess, St Philip's Vicarage, Scarisbrick New Rd, Southport PR8 6QF *Tel:* (01704) 532886
Ormskirk Canon Michael Smout, Rectory, 10 Church Lane, Aughton L39 6SB
Tel: (01695) 423204
St Helens Revd Chris Byworth, 51A Rainford Rd, St Helens WA10 6BZ
Tel: (01744) 22067
Warrington Vacancy
Widnes Canon Brian Robinson, St Mary's Vicarage, St Mary's Rd, Widnes WA8 0DN *Tel:* 0151–424 4233
Wigan East Canon Malcolm Forrest, The Hall, Wigan WN1 1HN
Tel: (01942) 44459
Wigan West Revd Ron Crankshaw, St Anne's Vicarage, 154 Beech Hill Ave, Wigan WN6 7TA *Tel:* (01942) 41930
Winwick Revd Bob Britton, Vicarage, 1 Barford Drive, St Mary's Park, Lowton WA3 1DD *Tel:* (01942) 607705

DIOCESE OF LONDON

Founded in 314. The City of London; Greater London north of the Thames, except five East London boroughs (CHELMSFORD) and an area in the north (ST ALBANS); Surrey north of the Thames; a small area of southern Hertfordshire.

Population 3,400,000 Area 277 sq m
Stipendiary Clergy 551 Benefices 408
Parishes 396 Churches 465

BISHOP (132nd)
Rt Revd and Rt Hon Richard John Carew Chartres, The Old Deanery, Dean's Court, London EC4V 5AA [1995]
Tel: 0171–248 6233
Fax: 0171–248 9721
e-mail: bishop.london@dlondon.org.uk
[Richard Londin:]

Personal Jurisdiction Cities of London and Westminster *(Archdeaconries of London and Charing Cross)*

Matters relating to the other Areas should be referred to the appropriate Area Bishop

Chaplain Revd Mark Oakley
Personal Assistant Mrs Joanna Simms

AREA BISHOPS
STEPNEY Rt Revd John Sentamu PH D, 63 Coborn Rd, Bow, London E3 2DB [1996]
Tel: 0181–981 2323
Fax: 0181–981 8015
e-mail: bishop.stepney@dlondon.org.uk
KENSINGTON Rt Revd Michael Colclough, 19 Campden Hill Square, London W8 7JY [1996]
Tel: 0171–727 9818
Fax: 0171–229 3651
e-mail: bishop.kensington@dlondon.org.uk
EDMONTON Vacancy, 1 Regents Park Terrace, London NW1 7EE
Tel: 0171–267 4455
Fax: 0171–267 4404
e-mail: bishop.edmonton@dlondon.org.uk
WILLESDEN Rt Revd Graham Dow, 173 Willesden Lane, London NW6 7YN [1992]
Tel: 0181–451 0189
Fax: 0181–451 4606
e-mail: bishop.willesden@dlondon.org.uk

SUFFRAGAN BISHOP
FULHAM Rt Revd John Broadhurst, 26 Canonbury Park South, London N1 2FN [1996] Tel and Fax: 0171–354 2334
e-mail: bpfulham@compuserve.com
Assists the Diocesan in all matters not delegated to the Areas

HONORARY ASSISTANT BISHOPS
Rt Revd Maurice Wood, 41 Fir Tree Walk, Enfield, Middx EN1 3TZ [1985]
Tel: 0181–363 4491
Rt Revd Michael Marshall, 97A Cadogan Lane, London SW1X 9DU [1984]
Rt Revd Roderic Coote, Friday Woods, Stoke Rd, Cobham, Surrey KT11 3AS
Tel: (01932) 867306
Rt Revd Donald Arden, 6 Frobisher Close, Pinner HA5 1NN Tel: 0181–866 6009
Rt Revd Michael Baughen, 99 Brunswick Quay, London SE16 1PX
Tel: 0171–237 0167

CATHEDRAL CHURCH OF ST PAUL
Dean Very Revd John Moses PH D, 9 Amen Court, London EC4M 7BU [1996]
Tel: 0171–236 2827
Fax: 0171–332 0298
Canons Residentiary
Ven George Cassidy, 2 Amen Court, EC4M 7BU [1987] Tel: 0171–248 3312
Canon John Halliburton, 1 Amen Court, EC4M 7BU [1989] Tel: 0171–248 1817
Canon Michael Saward, 6 Amen Court, EC4M 7BU [1991] Tel: 0171–248 8572
Canon Stephen Oliver, 3 Amen Court, EC4M 7BU [1996] Tel: 0171–236 4532
The College of Minor Canons
Sacrist and Warden of Minor Canons Revd John Paul, 7A Amen Court, EC4M 7BU [1996] Tel: 0171–248 6151
Chaplain Revd Lucy Winkett, 7B Amen Court, EC4M 7BU [1997]
Tel: 0171–236 3871
Succentor Revd Gordon Giles, 8A Amen Court, EC4M 7BU [1998]
Tel: 0171–248 6115
Headmaster of the Choir School Mr Stephen Sides, St Paul's Cathedral Choir School, New Change, London EC4
Tel: 0171–248 5156
Registrar Brigadier Robert Acworth, Chapter House, St Paul's Churchyard, EC4M 8AD Tel: 0171–236 4128
Warden of St Paul's and Dean's Verger Mr Michael Page, 4A Amen Court, EC4M 7BU Tel: 0171–236 7656

Chapter Clerk Mr David Faull, Chapter House, St Paul's Churchyard, EC4M 8AD Tel: 0171–236 4128
Surveyor Mr Martin Stancliffe (*same address*)
Cathedral Organist Mr John Scott, 4 Amen Court, EC4M 7BU Tel: 0171–248 6868
Sub Organist Mr Huw Williams, 3B Amen Court, EC4M 7BU Tel: 0171–236 4257
Assistant Sub Organist Mr Richard Moorhouse, East Flat, The Chapter House, St Paul's Churchyard, EC4M 8AD
Tel: 0171–248 3314

ARCHDEACONS
LONDON Ven George Cassidy, 2 Amen Court, EC4M 7BU [1987]
Tel: 0171–248 3312
Fax: 0171–489 8579
e-mail: archdeacon.london@dlondon.org.uk
CHARING CROSS Ven William Jacob, The Old Deanery, Dean's Court, London EC4V 5AA [1996] Tel: 0171–248 6233
Fax: 0171–248 9721
e-mail:
archdeacon.charingcross@dlondon.org.uk
HACKNEY Ven Clive Young, St Andrew's Vicarage, 5 St Andrew's St, EC4A 3AB [1992] Tel: 071–353 3544
Fax: 0171–583 2750
e-mail:
archdeacon.hackney@dlondon.org.uk
MIDDLESEX Ven Malcolm Colmer, 59 Sutton Lane South, London W4 3JR [1996]
Tel: 0181–994 8148 (Office)
Fax: 0181–995 5374
e-mail:
archdeacon.middlesex@dlondon.org.uk
HAMPSTEAD Ven Peter Wheatley, 27 Thurlow Rd, London NW3 5PP [1995]
Tel: 0171–435 5890
Fax: 0171–435 6049
e-mail:
archdeacon.hampstead@dlondon.org.uk
NORTHOLT Ven Pete Broadbent, 247 Kenton Rd, Kenton, Harrow, Middlesex HA3 0HQ [1995] Tel: 0181–907 5941
Fax: 0181–909 2368
e-mail: pete@arch.northolt.demon.co.uk

CONVOCATION (MEMBERS OF THE HOUSE OF CLERGY OF THE GENERAL SYNOD)
The Archdeacon of London
Proctors for Clergy
Revd Philippa Boardman
Preb Kenneth Bowler
Ven Pete Broadbent
Preb John Brownsell
Revd John Cook
Revd David Houlding
Revd Malcolm Johnson
Revd Ulla Monberg
Revd David Stone
Revd Ronald Swan

MEMBERS OF THE HOUSE OF LAITY OF THE GENERAL SYNOD
Mrs Molly Dow
Sir Timothy Hoare
Mrs Mary Johnston
Ms Josile Munro
Mrs Alison Ruoff
Mr Christopher Smith
Mrs Elaine Storkey
Mr Frank Williams

DIOCESAN OFFICERS
Dioc Secretary Mr Chris Smith, London Diocesan House, 36 Causton St, London SW1P 4AU Tel: 0171–932 1100
Fax: 0171–932 1113
e-mail: Chris.Smith@dlondon.org.uk
Chancellor of Diocese Chanc Sheila Cameron, The Old Deanery, Dean's Court, London EC4V 5AA Tel: 0171–593 5110
Fax: 0171–248 3221
Registrar of Diocese and Bishop's Legal Secretary Mr Paul Morris (*same address*)
Official of the Archdeaconry of Hackney Mr David Smith, 3 Pump Court, Temple, London EC4
Official of the Archdeaconry of Hampstead Chanc Sheila Cameron, 2 Harcourt Bldgs, Temple, London EC4
Official of the Archdeaconry of Northolt Mr Paul Morris (*as above*)

DIOCESAN ORGANISATIONS
CHAIRMEN
London Dioc Fund (*Dioc Board of Finance*) The Bishop of London
Deputy Chairman and Treasurer Sir Timothy Hoare
Finance Committee Sir Timothy Hoare
Dioc Synod (*House of Clergy*) Revd John Slater; (*House of Laity*) Sir Timothy Hoare
Dioc Board for Schools Ven Pete Broadbent
CARIS (*Dioc Board for Social Responsibility*) Ven Peter Wheatley

ADMINISTRATION
Diocesan Office London Diocesan House, 36 Causton St, London SW1P 4AU
Tel: 0171–932 1100
Fax: 0171–932 1112
Financial Controller Mr Richard Walker
Office Manager and Personnel Officer Mr John Sansom
Finance and Trusts Mrs Karen Smith
Pastoral and Redundant Churches Mr Roger Clayton Pearce
Parsonages and Glebe Revd Roger Hills
Information and Technology Mr Martin How
Dioc Advisory Committee (*Chair*) Vacancy; (*Secretary*) Mr Brian Cuthbertson
Synodical Mr Roy Martin
Designated Officer Mr Paul Morris, (*as above*)

EDUCATION
Senior Chaplain for Higher Education Revd Stephen Williams, University Chaplaincy Office, 48B Gordon Square, London WC1H 0PD Tel: 0171–387 0670
Director, Board for Schools Mr Tom Peryer, London Dioc House

MINISTRY
Ordained Ministry
Dioc Director Revd Dr Christopher Cunliffe, London Dioc House

London
Director of Ordinands (*Men*) Revd John Cowling, St Olave's Rectory, 8 Hart St, Mark Lane, London EC3R 7NB
Tel: 0171–488 4318
Director of Ordinands (*Women*) Revd Ulla Monberg, 11 Ormonde Mansions, 106 Southampton Row, London WC1B 4BP Tel: 0171–242 7533
CME Officer Revd John Slater, St John's House, St Johns Wood, London NW8 7NE Tel: 0171–722 4378
Dean of Women's Ministry Revd Ulla Monberg (*as above*)

Stepney
Director of Ordinands Revd Kevin Scully, 6 Arbour Square, London E1 0SH
Tel: 0171–791 0330
Director of Post-Ordination Training Revd David Paton, St Vedast's Rectory, 4 Foster Lane, London EC2V 6HH
Tel: 0171–606 1863
Dean of Women's Ministry Revd Philippa Boardman, Old Ford Vicarage, St Stephen's Rd, London E3 5JL
Tel: 0181–980 9020
CME Officer Revd Rachel Montgomery, St James the Less Vicarage, St James Ave, London E2 9JD Tel: 0181–980 1612

Kensington
Director of Ordinands (*Men*) Preb John Brownsell, All Saint's Vicarage, Powis Gardens, London W11 1JG
Tel: 0171–727 5919
Director of Ordinands (*Women*) Vacancy
Director of Post-Ordination Training Revd Michael Fuller, 25 Campden Hill Square, London W8 7JY Tel: 0171–727 9486
CME Officer Revd Neil Evans, All Hallows Vicarage, 138 Chertsey Rd, Twickenham, Middx TW1 1EW Tel: 0181–892 1322
Dean of Women's Ministry Revd Ulla Monberg (*as above*)

Willesden
Directors of Ordinands Revd Ann Coleman, 2 Bridle Rd, Pinner, Middx HA5 2SJ
Tel: 0181–866 1263
Revd Trevor Mapstone, 39 Rusland Park Rd, Harrow, Middx HA1 1UN
Tel: 0181–427 2616
Director of Post-Ordination Training Revd William Taylor, St Peter's Vicarage, Mount Park Rd, London W5 2RU
Tel: 0181–997 1620
CME Officer Revd David Neno, 54 Roe Green, Kingsbury, London NW9 0PJ Tel: 0181–204 7531
Dean of Women's Ministry Revd Jacqui Fox, 14 Cumberland Park, Acton, London W3 6SX Tel: 0181–992 8876

Edmonton
Director of Ordinands Revd Dr Perry Butler, 7 Little Russell St, London WC1A 2HR Tel: 0171–405 3044
Director of Post-Ordination Training Revd Paul Taylor, 184 Chase Side, London N14 7EG Tel: 0181–886 7523
Assistant Director Revd Nicholas Wheeler, 191 St Pancras Way, London NW1 9NH
CME Officer Revd Richard Knowling, St John's Vicarage, 1 Bourne Hill, London N13 4DA Tel: 0181–886 1348
Women's Ministry Revd Ulla Monberg (*as above*)
Secretary of Board of Women Candidates for Ordination Revd Ulla Monberg (*as above*)

MISSION AND UNITY
Bishop's Adviser in Evangelism Preb David Saville, London Dioc House

LITURGICAL
Chairman Ven Malcolm Colmer (*as above*)
Secretary Dr Alan Everett, 97 Lavender Grove, London E8 3LR
Tel: 0171–249 2627

PRESS AND COMMUNICATIONS
Director of Communications Preb Eric Shegog, London Dioc House
Tel: 0171–932 1240
0831 120596 (Mobile)
Fax: 0171–233 8670
Editor of Diocese Book Preb Eric Shegog (*as above*)

DIOCESAN RECORD OFFICES
Diocesan Record Offices are situated at the following addresses: London Metropolitan Archives, 40 Northampton Rd, London EC1R 0HB *Head Archivist* Dr Deborah Jenkins, Tel: 0171–332 3824; Guildhall Library, Aldermanbury, London EC2P 2EJ, *Archivist* Mr S. G. H. Freeth, Tel: 0171–606 3030, Ext. 1862/3; Westminster Archives Dept, 10 St Ann's St, London SW1P 2XR, *Archivist* Mr Jerome Farrell Tel: 0171–798 2180

SOCIAL RESPONSIBILITY
CARIS (*Director*) Revd Chris Brice, London Dioc House *Tel:* 0171–932 1121

AREA DEANS
ARCHDEACONRY OF LONDON
City Preb John Oates, St Bride's Rectory, Fleet St, London EC4Y 8AU
Tel: 0171–353 1301

ARCHDEACONRY OF CHARING CROSS
Westminster (Paddington) Revd William Wilson, 6 Gloucester Terrace, London W2 3DD *Tel:* 0171–723 8119
Westminster (St Margaret) Revd William Scott, 30 Bourne St, London SW1W 8JJ
Tel: 0171–730 2423
Westminster (St Marylebone) Revd John Slater, St John's House, St John's Wood, London NW8 7NE *Tel:* 0171–586 3864

ARCHDEACONRY OF HACKNEY
Hackney Revd Malcom Macnaughton, St John's Vicarage, Crondall St, London N1 6PT *Tel:* 0171–739 9823
Islington Revd Stephen Cox, 3 Highcroft Rd, London N19 3AQ
Tel: 0171–272 9084
Tower Hamlets Revd Christopher Chessun, Stepney Rectory, Rectory Square, London E1 3NQ *Tel:* 0171–791 3545

ARCHDEACONRY OF MIDDLESEX
Hammersmith Revd Jonathan Clark, 153 Blythe Rd, London W14 0HL
Tel: 0171–602 1043
Hampton Revd David Vanstone, 40 The Avenue, Hampton, Middx TW12 3RS
Tel: 0181–979 2102
Hounslow Revd David Wilson, St Mary's Vicarage, Osterley Rd, Isleworth, Middx TW7 4PW *Tel:* 0181–560 3555
Kensington Revd Harold Stringer, 25 Ladbroke Rd, London W11 3PD
Tel: 0171–727 3439
Chelsea Revd David Stone, 20 Collingham Rd, London SW5 0LX
Tel: 0171–373 1693
Spelthorne Revd Christopher Swift, Rectory, Church Square, Shepperton TW17 9JY *Tel:* (01932) 220511

ARCHDEACONRY OF HAMPSTEAD
Central Barnet Revd Raymond Taylor, Vicarage, Woodland Rd, London N11 1PN *Tel:* 0181–361 1946
West Barnet Revd Dr Peter Baker, Vicarage, 3 St Alban's Close, North End Rd, London NW11 7RA *Tel:* 0181–455 4525
North Camden (Hampstead) Revd Charles Mason, 13 Kingscroft Rd, London NW2 3QE *Tel:* 0181–452 1913

South Camden (Holborn and St Pancras) Revd Guy Pope, Vicarage, 85 Dartmouth Park Rd, London NW5 1SL
Tel: 0171–267 5941
Enfield Revd Richard Knowling, 1 Bourne Hill, Palmers Green, London N13 4DA
Tel: 0181–886 1348
East Haringey Preb Roy Pearson, The Priory, Church Lane, London N17 7RA
Tel: 0181–808 2470
West Haringey Revd Geoffrey Seabrook, Rectory, 140 Cranley Gardens, London N10 3AH *Tel:* 0181–883 6846

ARCHDEACONRY OF NORTHOLT
Brent Revd John Root, Vicarage, 34 Stanley Ave, Alperton, Middx HA0 4JB *Tel:* 0181–902 1729
Ealing Revd Dr William Taylor, St Peter's Vicarage, Mount Park Rd, London W5 2RV *Tel:* 0181–997 1620
Harrow Revd Paul Reece, Whitchurch Rectory, St Lawrence Close, Edgeware, Middx HA8 6RB *Tel:* 0181–952 0019
e-mail: 101323.2644@compuserve.com
Hillingdon Revd Philip Robinson, St Giles's Rectory, 38 Swakeleys Rd, Ickenham, Middx UB10 8BE
Tel and Fax: (01895) 622970
e-mail: stgilesickenham@compuserve.com

DIOCESE OF MANCHESTER

Founded in 1847. Manchester, except for a few parishes in the south (CHESTER); Salford; Bolton; Bury; Rochdale; Oldham; the western half of Tameside; an area of Wigan; an area of Trafford; an area of Stockport; an area of southern Lancashire.

Population 1,964,000   Area 415 sq m
Stipendiary Clergy 324   Benefices 283
Parishes 310   Churches 363

BISHOP (10th)
Rt Revd Christopher John Mayfield, Bishopscourt, Bury New Rd, Manchester M7 0LE [1993]   Tel: 0161–792 2096 (Office)
Fax: 0161–792 6826
[Christopher Manchester]

Chaplain Revd Paul Richardson, St Gabriel's Vicarage, 8 Bishop's Rd, Prestwich, Manchester M25 0HT
Tel: 0161–792 2096 (Office)
0161–773 8839 (Home)

SUFFRAGAN BISHOPS
BOLTON Rt Revd David Bonser, 4 Sandfield Drive, Lostock, Bolton BL6 4DU [1991]   Tel: (01204) 843400
Fax: (01204) 849652
MIDDLETON Rt Revd Stephen Squires Venner, The Hollies, Manchester Rd, Rochdale, Lancs OL11 3QY [1994]
Tel: (01706) 358550
Fax: (01706) 354851
e-mail: Stephen.Venner@btinternet.com
HULME Vacancy, 197 Old Hall Lane, Fallowfield, Manchester M14 6HJ
Tel: 0161–224 6643

CATHEDRAL AND COLLEGIATE CHURCH OF ST MARY, ST DENYS AND ST GEORGE
Dean Very Revd Kenneth Riley, 1 Booth Clibborn Court, Park Lane, Manchester M7 4PJ [1993]
Cathedral Office The Cathedral, Manchester M3 1SX   Tel: 0161–833 2220
Fax: 0161–839 6226
Canons Residentiary
Canon John Atherton, 3 Booth Clibborn Court, Park Lane, Manchester M7 4PJ [1984]
Canon Albert Radcliffe, 46 Shrewsbury Road, Prestwich, Manchester, M25 8GO [1991]   Tel: 0161–798 0459
Precentor Canon Paul Denby, 2 Booth Clibborn Court, Park Lane, Manchester M7 4PJ [1995]

Chapter Clerk Mr W. A. Brock, Messrs Cobbett Leak Almond, Ship Canal House, King St, Manchester M2 4WB
Tel: 0161–833 3333
Cathedral Organist and Master of the Choristers Mr Christopher Stokes, c/o Cathedral Office
Sub Organist Mr Matthew Owens (same address)
Organ Scholar Mr Jeremy Holland-Smith (same address)

ARCHDEACONS
MANCHESTER Ven Alan Wolstencroft, c/o The Cathedral, Manchester M3 1SX [1998]
Tel: 0161–833 22200 (Cathedral)
0161–839 0093 (Office)
ROCHDALE Ven Dr Mark Dalby, 21 Belmont Way, Rochdale, Lancs OL12 6HR [1991]   Tel and Fax: (01706) 648640
BOLTON Ven Lorys Davies, 45 Rudgwick Drive, Brandlesholme, Bury, Lancs BL8 1YA [1992]   Tel and Fax: 0161–761 6117

CONVOCATION (MEMBERS OF THE HOUSE OF CLERGY OF THE GENERAL SYNOD)
Dignitaries in Convocation
The Bishop of Hulme
The Dean of Manchester
The Archdeacon of Bolton
Proctors for Clergy
Revd Michael Ainsworth
Canon Rosemary Anderson
Canon Wendy Bracegirdle
Revd Charles Razzall
Revd Charles Read
(One Vacancy)

MEMBERS OF THE HOUSE OF LAITY OF THE GENERAL SYNOD
Mrs Jessie Axtell
Dr Peter Capon
Mr Alan Cooper
Mrs Louise Da-Cocodia
Mr Philip Gore
Mr Geoffrey Tattershall
Mr Michael Winterbottom
(One Vacancy)

DIOCESAN OFFICERS
Dioc Secretary Mrs Jackie Park, Diocesan Church House, 90 Deansgate, Manchester M3 2GH   Tel: 0161–833 9521
Fax: 0161–833 2751
Chancellor of Diocese Mr J. L. O. Holden, Willow Bank, 49 Brooklands Rd, Towneley, Burnley BB11 3PR
Registrar of Diocese and Bishop's Legal Secretary Mr Michael Darlington, Dioc Registry, Dioc Church House
Tel: 0161–834 7545
Dioc Surveyor for Parsonage Houses Mr John Prichard, The Lloyd Evans Partnership, 5 The Parsonage, Manchester M3 2HS
Tel: 0161–834 6251

DIOCESAN ORGANISATIONS
Diocesan Office Diocesan Church House, 90 Deansgate, Manchester M3 2GH
Tel: 0161–833 9521
Fax: 0161–833 2751

ADMINISTRATION
Dioc Synod (Chairman, House of Clergy) Canon Anthony Durrans, Rectory, 233 Barton Rd, Stretford, Manchester M32 9RB Tel: 0161–865 1350; (Chairman, House of Laity) Mr Geoffrey Tattersall, 2 The Woodlands, Lostock, Bolton BL6 4JD
Board of Finance (Chairman) Mr Alan Cooper,11 Ravensdale Gdns, Eccles, Manchester M30 9JD Tel: 0161–789 1514; (General Secretary) Mrs Jackie Park, Dioc Office; (Deputy Secretary) Dr Ray Hughes, Dioc Office; (Financial Secretary) Vacancy, Dioc Office; (Legal Secretary) Mr Michael Darlington, Dioc Registry, Dioc Church House   Tel: 0161–834 7545
Property Committee (Property Secretary) Mr Geoff Hutchinson, Dioc Office
Pastoral Committee Mrs Jackie Park (as above); (Planning Consultant) Mr D. W. Buckler, 36 Newbury Rd, St Annes-on-Sea, Lancs FY8 1DG
Designated Officer Mr Michael Darlington, Dioc Registry, Dioc Church House
Tel: 0161–834 7545

CHURCHES
Advisory Committee for the Care of Churches (Chairman) Mr Adrian Golland, Peel House, 29 Higher Dunscar, Egerton, Bolton BL7 9TE; (Secretary) Vacancy

EDUCATION
Director of Education Vacancy, Dioc Church House   Tel: 0161–834 1022
Schools' Officer Mr David Thomas (same address)
Accountant Mr Robert Morgan (same address)

Religious Education Adviser Mrs Jan Ainsworth (*same address*)
Children's Work Adviser Miss I. Booth-Clibborn (*same address*)
Youth Work Adviser Revd S. Howard (*same address*)
Adviser for Further and Higher Education Revd Dr J. I. Bentley (*same address*)

MINISTRY
Board of Ministry (*Chairman*) The Bishop of Bolton
Secretary Mrs J. Read, St Jame's Rectory, Great Cheetham St East, Higher Broughton, Salford M7 0UH
Tel: 0161–792 1208
Director of Continuing Ministerial Education Vacancy, Dioc Office
Tel: 0161–832 5785
Director of Laity Development Ms Margaret Halsey, Dioc Office Tel: 0161–832 5785
LNSM Governing Body (*Chairman*) Ven Dr Mark Dalby, 21 Belmont Way, Rochdale, Lancs OL12 6HR
Tel and Fax: (01706) 648640
(*Director*) Canon Wendy Bracegirdle, Dioc Office Tel: 0161–832 5785
Dioc Director of Ordinands and LNSM Officer Revd Jonathan MacGillivray
Readers' and Lay Assistants' Committee (*Chairman*) The Bishop of Bolton; (*Secretary*) Mr G. Howard, 87 Bury & Bolton Rd, Redcliffe, Manchester M26 0JY
Tel: 0161–797 5548

WORSHIP COMMITTEE
Chairman Revd Simon Tatton-Brown, Rectory, Market St, Westhoughton, Bolton BL5 3AZ Tel: (01942) 813280
Secretary Mrs Sue Usher, St John's Vicarage, 156 Gordon St, Leigh, Lancs WN7 1RT

BOARD FOR CHURCH AND SOCIETY
Chairman Vacancy
Dioc Executive Officer Revd Stephen Little, Dioc Office Tel: 0161–832 5253
Fax: 0161–832 2869
Admin Secretary Mrs J. Beresford (*same address*)
Ecumenical Officer Revd Ian Blay, St Andrew's Rectory, Merton Drive, Droylesden, Manchester M35 6BH
Tel: 0161–370 3242

Advisers on Evangelism Revd Ian Johnson, St Anne's Rectory, St Anne's Drive, Denton, Manchester M34 3EB
Tel: 0161–336 2374
Capt A. Dyer, 9 Macefin Ave, Chorlton-cum-Hardy, Manchester M21 7QQ
Tel: 0161–445 4063
Revd Mike Saunders, St Andrew's Vicarage, 11 Abbey Grove, Eccles, Manchester M30 9QN Tel: 0161–707 1742
Senior Industrial Chaplain Revd Philip Atherton, 192 Windsor Rd, Oldham, Lancs OL8 1RG Tel: 0161–652 2684

PRESS AND PUBLICATIONS
Dioc Press and Communications Officer Mr D. Johnson Tel: 0161–833 9521 (Office)
(01204) 699301 (Home)
(0836) 224444 (Mobile)
Fax: (01204) 667924
e-mail: 100772.1557@compuserve.com
Editor of Dioc Year Book c/o Dioc Office
Editor of Dioc Magazine Ms Jan Heeney
Tel: (01942) 671481

DIOCESAN RECORDS OFFICE
For further information apply to The Central Library, St Peter's Square, Manchester M2 5PD (*Archivist* Miss D. Rayson)
Tel: 0161–234 1980

STEWARDSHIP
Chairman The Archdeacon of Bolton
Christian Giving Officer Mr Ken Wiggans, Dioc Office Tel: 0161–833 9521

AREA DEANS
ARCHDEACONRY OF MANCHESTER
Ardwick Revd William Nelson, St Clement's Rectory, Ashton Old Rd, Manchester M11 1HJ Tel: 0161–370 1538
Eccles Revd Norman Jones, Rectory, 12B Westminster Rd, Eccles, Manchester M30 9EB Tel: 0161–281 5739
Heaton Revd Marcus Maxwell, St John's Rectory, 15 Priestnall Rd, Stockport, Cheshire SK4 3HR Tel: 0161–432 2165
Hulme Revd Richard Gilpin, Rectory, 6 Edge Lane, Chorlton-cum-Hardy, Manchester M21 9JF Tel: 0161–881 3063
North Manchester Revd Dr Christopher Ford, St John's Rectory, Railton Terrace, Moston, Manchester M9 1WE
Tel: 0161–205 4967

Salford Revd Dr John Applegate, St John's Rectory, 237 Great Clowes St, Higher Broughton, Salford M7 2DZ
Tel: 0161–792 9161
Stretford Revd Philip Rawlings, St Bride's Rectory, 29 Shrewsbury St, Old Trafford, Manchester M16 9AP Tel: 0161–226 6064
Withington Revd Norman Dawson, Withington Rectory, 491 Wilmslow Rd, Withington, Manchester M20 9AW
Tel: 0161–445 3781

ARCHDEACONRY OF BOLTON
Bolton Revd Roger Oldfield, St Peter's Vicarage, Harpers Lane, Bolton BL1 6HT Tel: (01204) 849412
Bury Revd Ian Rogerson, St Andrew's Vicarage, Henwick Hall Ave, Broadhey Park, Ramsbottom BL0 9YH
Tel: (01706) 826482
Deane Revd William Brew, Lostock Vicarage, 9 Lowside Ave, Lostock, Bolton BL1 5XQ Tel: (01204) 848631
Farnworth Revd Brian Hartley, New Bury Rectory, 130A Highfield Rd, Farnworth, Bolton BL4 0AJ Tel: (01204) 572334
Leigh Revd Peter Leakey, Pennington Vicarage, Schofield St, Leigh WN7 4HT
Tel: (01942) 673619
Radcliffe and Prestwich Revd Charles Ellis, St Thomas' Vicarage, Heber St, Radcliffe, Manchester M26 2TG Tel: 0161–723 2123
Rossendale Vacancy
Walmsley Revd David Brierley, Walmsley Vicarage, Egerton, Bolton BL7 9RZ
Tel: (01204) 304283

ARCHDEACONRY OF ROCHDALE
Ashton-under-Lyne Revd Ronald Cassidy, Rectory, 131 Town Lane, Denton, Manchester M34 2DJ Tel: 0161–320 4895
Heywood and Middleton Revd Ian McVeety, St Martin's Vicarage, Vicarage Rd North, Castleton, Rochdale, Lancs OL11 2TE
Tel: (01706) 32353
Oldham Revd Charles Razzall, Holy Trinity Vicarage, 46 Godson St, Oldham OL1 2DB Tel: 0161–627 1640
Rochdale Revd Ian Thompson, St Mary's Vicarage, The Sett, Badger Lane, Rochdale OL16 4RQ Tel: (01706) 49886
Saddleworth Vacancy
Tandle Revd David Sharples, St Anne's Vicarage, St Anne's Ave, Royton, Oldham OL2 5AD Tel: 0161–624 2249

DIOCESE OF NEWCASTLE

Founded in 1882. Northumberland; Newcastle upon Tyne; North Tyneside; a small area of eastern Cumbria; two parishes in northern County Durham.

Population 786,000 Area 2,110 sq m
Stipendiary Clergy 159 Benefices 132
Parishes 174 Churches 245

BISHOP (11th)
Rt Revd (John) Martin Wharton, Bishop's House, 29 Moor Rd South, Gosforth, Newcastle upon Tyne NE3 1PA [1998] Tel: 0191–285 2220 [Martin Newcastle]

ASSISTANT BISHOP
Rt Revd Paul Richardson, Close House, St George's Close, Jesmond, Newcastle upon Tyne NE2 2TF Tel: 0191–281 2556

CATHEDRAL CHURCH OF ST NICHOLAS
Provost Very Revd Nicholas Guy Coulton, 26 Mitchell Ave, Jesmond, Newcastle upon Tyne NE2 3LA [1990]
Tel: 0191–281 6554
Cathedral Office The Cathedral, St Nicholas Churchyard, Newcastle upon Tyne NE1 1PF Tel: 0191–232 1939
Fax: 0191–230 0735
Canons Residentiary
Canon Robert Langley, 16 Towers Ave, Jesmond, Newcastle upon Tyne NE2 3QE [1985] Tel: 0191–281 0714
Canon Peter Strange, 55 Queens Terrace, Jesmond, Newcastle upon Tyne NE2 2PL [1986] Tel: 0191–281 0181
Ven Peter Elliott, 80 Moorside North, Fenham, Newcastle upon Tyne NE4 9DU [1993] Tel and Fax: 0191–273 8245
Chapter Clerk Mr Derek Govier, Cathedral Office
Master of Music Mr Timothy Hone, Cathedral Office
Cathedral Secretary Mrs Lesley Wright, Cathedral Office

ARCHDEACONS
LINDISFARNE Ven Michael Bowering, 12 Rectory Park, Morpeth, Northumberland NE61 2SZ [1987] Tel: (01670) 513207
NORTHUMBERLAND Ven Peter Elliott, 80 Moorside North, Fenham, Newcastle upon Tyne NE4 9DU [1993]
Tel and Fax: 0191–273 8245

CONVOCATION (MEMBERS OF THE HOUSE OF CLERGY OF THE GENERAL SYNOD)
Dignitaries in Convocation
The Provost of Newcastle
The Archdeacon of Lindisfarne
Proctors for Clergy
Revd Norman Banks
Canon Richard Bryant
Canon Frank Dexter

MEMBERS OF THE HOUSE OF LAITY OF THE GENERAL SYNOD
Dr John Bull
Mr Colin Keating
Mr Frank Knaggs
Mrs Hazel Simmons

DIOCESAN OFFICERS
Dioc Secretary Mr Philip Davies, Church House, Grainger Park Rd, Newcastle upon Tyne NE4 8SX Tel: 0191–273 0120
Fax: 0191–256 5900
Chancellor of Diocese The Worshipful David McClean, 6 Burnt Stones Close, Sheffield S10 5TS Tel: 0114-230 5794
Registrar of Diocese and Bishop's Legal Secretary Mrs Jane Lowdon, 7 Osborne Terrace, Newcastle upon Tyne NE2 1PQ
Tel: 0191–281 5811
Fax: 0191–231 3608

DIOCESAN ORGANISATIONS
Diocesan Office Church House, Grainger Park Rd, Newcastle upon Tyne NE4 8SX Tel: 0191–273 0120
Fax: 0191–256 5900
e-mail:
church_house@newcastle.anglican.org

ADMINISTRATION
Dioc Synod (*Chairman, House of Clergy*) Canon Frank Dexter, St George's Vicarage, St George's Close, Jesmond, Newcastle upon Tyne NE2 2TF Tel: 0191–281 1628; (*Chairman, House of Laity*) Dr John Bull, 11 Glebe Mews, Bedlington, Northumberland NE22 6LJ Tel: 0191–222 7924 (Work); (*Secretary*) Mr Philip Davies, Church House
Finance Board (*Chairman*) Mr John Squires, Benfield Motors, Asama Court, Newcastle upon Tyne NE4 7YD Tel: 0191–226 1700; (*Secretary*) Mr Philip Davies (*as above*)
Accountant Mr John Hall, Church House
Parsonages Board Mr Eddie Fogg, Church House
Dioc Society (*Trusts*) Mr Philip Davies (*as above*)
Pastoral Committee Mr Nigel Foxon, Church House
Board of Patronage Mr Philip Davies (*as above*)
Designated Officer Mrs Jane Lowdon, 7 Osborne Terrace, Newcastle upon Tyne NE2 1NH Tel: 0191–281 5811
Fax: 0191–281 3608

CHURCHES
Advisory Committee for the Care of Churches (*Chairman*) His Honour John Johnson, Kirk Fenwick, Cambo, Morpeth NE61 4BN Tel: (01670) 774243; (*Secretary*) Mr Nigel Foxon (*as above*)
Redundant Churches Uses Committee Mr Philip Davies (*as above*)

EDUCATION
Director of Education Mrs Margaret Nicholson, Church House
Schools Administrative Officer Mrs Valerie Foxon, Church House

MINISTRY AND TRAINING
Director of Ministry and Training Canon Robert Langley, Church Institute, Denewood, Clayton Rd, Jesmond, Newcastle upon Tyne NE2 1TL Tel: 0191–281 9930
Fax: 0191–231 1452
Director of Ordinands c/o Bishop's House (*as above*)
Board for Ministry and Training (*Secretary*) Mrs Audrey Truman, Church Institute (*as above*)
Post-Ordination Training Canon Robert Langley (*as above*)
Adult Adviser Revd Dr Peter Bryars, Church Institute (*as above*)
Youth Adviser Mr Neal Terry, Church Institute (*as above*)
Children's Adviser Mrs Judith Sadler, Church Institute (*as above*)
Principal of Local Ministry Scheme and Reader Training Course Canon Richard Bryant, Church Institute (*as above*)
Association of Readers Mr Ron Black, 44 Bowsden Terrace, South Gosforth, Newcastle upon Tyne NE3 1RX
Tel: 0191–284 6718
Retreat House Mr Peter Dodgson (*Warden*), Shepherds Dene, Riding Mill, Northumberland NE44 6AF Tel: (01434) 682212

Sons of Clergy Society Mrs Gwenda Gofton, 4 Crossfell, Ponteland NE20 9EA
 Tel: (01661) 820344
Diocesan Widows Officer Mrs Sybil Taylor, 1 Osborne Terrace, North Sunderland, Seahouses, Northumberland NE68 7UH
 Tel: (01665) 720723

LITURGICAL

Chairman Canon Graham Revett, Rectory, Whalton, Morpeth, Northumberland NE61 3UX *Tel:* (01670) 775360

MISSION, SOCIAL RESPONSIBILITY AND ECUMENISM

Dioc Missioner Canon Robert Langley, 16 Towers Ave, Jesmond, Newcastle upon Tyne NE2 3QE *Tel:* 0191–281 0714
Social Responsibility Adviser Mr Barry Stewart, Church House
Board for Mission and Social Responsibility (Secretary) Mr Nigel Foxon, Church House
Ecumenical Officer Canon Clive Price, St Oswald's Vicarage, Wall, Hexham, Northumberland NE46 4DU
 Tel: (01434) 681354

PRESS, PUBLICITY AND PUBLICATIONS

Dioc Communications Officer Mr Vincent Arthey, Church House
Editor of 'The New Link' Mrs Christine Henshall, Church House

Editor of Dioc Directory Mr Philip Davies (*as above*)

DIOCESAN RECORDS OFFICE

For further information apply to The Northumberland County Record Office, Melton Park, North Gosforth, Newcastle upon Tyne NE3 5QX *Tel:* 0191–236 2680

DIOCESAN RESOURCE CENTRE

Contact Karenza Passmore, Church Institute, Denewood, Clayton Rd, Jesmond, Newcastle upon Tyne NE2 1TL
 Tel: 0191–281 9930
 Fax: 0191–231 1452

STEWARDSHIP

Dioc Funding Adviser Mrs Jane Highnam, Church House

RURAL DEANS
ARCHDEACONRY OF NORTHUMBERLAND

Bedlington Revd Richard Pringle, St Bede's Vicarage, Newcastle Rd, Newsham, Blyth, Northumberland NE24 4AS
 Tel: (01670) 352391
Bellingham Revd Reg Harper, Rectory, Bellingham, Northumberland NE48 2JS *Tel:* (01434) 220019
Corbridge Canon Malcolm Fenwick, Vicarage, Riding Mill, Northumberland NE44 6AS *Tel:* (01434) 682811

Hexham Revd Vincent Ashwin, Vicarage, Station Yard, Haydon Bridge, Northumberland NE47 6LL *Tel:* (01434) 684307
Newcastle Central Revd Kit Widdows, 9 Chester Crescent, Newcastle upon Tyne NE2 1DH *Tel:* 0191–232 9789
Newcastle East Revd Michael Webb, St Gabriel's Vicarage, 9 Holderness Rd, Heaton, Newcastle upon Tyne NE6 5RH
 Tel: 0191–276 3957
Newcastle West Revd John Clasper, St James & St Basil Vicarage, Wingrove Rd North, Newcastle upon Tyne NE4 9EJ
 Tel: 0191–274 5078
Tynemouth Revd James Robertson, St Peter's Vicarage, 6 Elmwood Rd, Whitley Bay NE25 8FX *Tel:* 0191-252 1991

ARCHDEACONRY OF LINDISFARNE

Alnwick Revd Brian Cowen, Lesbury Vicarage, Alnwick, Northumberland NE66 3AU *Tel:* (01665) 830281
Bamburgh and Glendale Revd Adrian Hughes, Vicarage, North Bank, Belford, Northumberland NE70 7LT
 Tel: (01668) 213545
Morpeth Revd Richard Ferguson, Vicarage, Kirkwhelpington, Northumberland NE29 2RT *Tel:* (01830) 540260
Norham Revd Jim Shewan, St John's Vicarage, 129 Main St, Spittal, Berwick-upon-Tweed, Northumberland TD15 1RP
 Tel: (01289) 307342

DIOCESE OF NORWICH

Founded in 1094, formerly Thetford (AD 1070), originally Dunwich (AD 630) and Elmham (AD 673). Norfolk, except for the western quarter (ELY); an area of north-east Suffolk.

Population 797,000 Area 1,804 sq m
Stipendiary Clergy 200   Benefices 213
Parishes 580   Churches 642

BISHOP (70th)
Rt Revd Peter John Nott, Bishop's House, Norwich, Norfolk NR3 1SB [1985]
Tel: (01603) 629001
Fax: (01603) 761613
[Peter Norvic:]

Bishop's Chaplain Revd Tom Heffer (*same address*) *Tel:* (01603) 614172
Bishop's Secretary Mrs Brenda Goodson (*same address*)

SUFFRAGAN BISHOPS
THETFORD Rt Revd Hugo de Waal, Rectory Meadow, Bramerton, Norwich NR14 7DW [1992] *Tel:* (01508) 538251
Fax: (01508) 538371
Bishop's Secretary Mrs Maggi Sprange (*same address*)
LYNN Vacancy, The Old Vicarage, Castle Acre, King's Lynn, Norfolk PE32 2AA
Tel: (01760) 755553
Fax: (01760) 755085
Bishop's Secretary Mrs Sheila Fergusan (*same address*)

CATHEDRAL CHURCH OF THE HOLY AND UNDIVIDED TRINITY
Dean Very Revd Stephen Platten, The Deanery, The Close, Norwich, Norfolk NR1 4EG [1995] *Tel:* (01603) 218308
Fax: (01603) 766032
e-mail: dean@cathedral.org.uk
Cathedral Office 12 The Close, Norwich, Norfolk NR1 4DH *Tel:* (01603) 218308
Fax: (01603) 766032

Canons Residentiary
Vice-Dean, Treasurer and Custos Canon Richard Hanmer, 52 The Close, Norwich, Norfolk NR1 4EG [1994]
Tel: (01603) 665210 (Home)
(01603) 764383 (Office)
Precentor Canon Jeremy Haselock, 27 The Close, Norwich, Norfolk NR1 4DZ [1998] *Tel:* (01603) 219484 (Home)
(01603) 218306 (Office)

Librarian Ven Clifford Offer, 26 The Close, Norwich, Norfolk NR1 4DZ [1994]
Tel: (01603) 630525
High Steward The Rt Hon The Earl Ferrers, Ditchingham Hall, Bungay, Suffolk NR35 2LE *Tel:* (01508) 482250
Chapter Clerk Mr Colin Pordham, 12 The Close, Norwich, Norfolk NR1 4DH
Tel: (01603) 764383
Fax: (01603) 766032
Steward Mr Timothy Cawkwell (*same address*) *Tel:* (01603) 764386
Fax: (01603) 766032
Cathedral Organist Mr David Dunnett (*same address*) *Tel:* (01603) 218313
Fax: (01603) 766032
Asst Organist Mrs Katherine Dienes-Williams (*same address*)
Tel: (01603) 218313
Fax: (01603) 766032

ARCHDEACONS
NORWICH Ven Clifford Offer, 26 The Close, Norwich, Norfolk NR1 4DZ [1994]
Tel: (01603) 630525
Fax: (01603) 661104
LYNN Ven Anthony Foottit, Ivy House, Whitwell St, Reepham, Norwich NR10 4RA [1987] *Tel* and *Fax:* (01603) 870340
NORFOLK Ven Michael Handley, 40 Heigham Rd, Norwich, Norfolk NR2 3AU [1993] *Tel:* (01603) 611808
Fax: (01603) 618954

CONVOCATION (MEMBERS OF THE HOUSE OF CLERGY OF THE GENERAL SYNOD)
Dignitaries in Convocation:
The Dean of Norwich
The Archdeacon of Lynn
Proctors for Clergy
Canon Robert Baker
Very Revd Michael Perham
Revd Martin Smith

MEMBERS OF THE HOUSE OF LAITY OF THE GENERAL SYNOD
Mr Tom Gilbert
Mrs Faith Hanson
Mrs Sue Johns
Major Patrick King
Mrs Sue Page

DIOCESAN OFFICERS
Dioc Secretary Mr David Adeney, Diocesan House, 109 Dereham Rd, Easton, Norwich, Norfolk NR9 5ES
Tel: (01603) 880853
Fax: (01603) 881083
Chancellor of Diocese Vacancy
Registrar of Diocese and Bishop's Legal Secretary Mr John Herring, Mills and Reeve, 3–7 Redwell St, Norwich NR2 4TJ
Tel: (01603) 660155
Fax: (01603) 633027

DIOCESAN ORGANISATIONS
Diocesan Office Diocesan House, 109 Dereham Rd, Easton, Norwich, Norfolk NR9 5ES *Tel:* (01603) 880853
Fax: (01603) 881083

ADMINISTRATION
Dioc Synod (*Lay Chairman*) Mr David Pearson, 16/17 North Drive, Great Yarmouth NR30 4EW *Tel:* (01493) 842623; (*Clergy Chairman*) Revd John Simpson, Vicarage, Corton, Lowestoft NR32 5HT *Tel:* (01502) 731272; (*Secretary*): Mr David Adeney, Dioc House; (*Assistant Secretary*) Mr Jonathan Davis, Dioc House
Board of Finance (*Chairman*) Mr David Gurney, Bawdeswell Hall, Bawdeswell, Dereham NR20 4SA *Tel:* (01362) 688308; (*Secretary*) Mr David Adeney (*as above*)
Property Committee (*Chairman*) Mr George Kendall, York Cottage, Blakeney, Holt, Norfolk NR25 7NU; (*Secretary*) Mr Ray Levett, Dioc House
Surveyor Mr Eddie Mann, Dioc House
Designated Officer Mr David Adeney (*as above*)
Dioc Electoral Registration Officer Mr Jonathan Davis (*as above*)

PASTORAL
Pastoral Committee (*Chairman*) Ven Michael Handley (*as above*); (*Secretary*) Mr David Adeney (*as above*); *Assistant Secretary*) Mr Jonathan Davis (*as above*)
Redundant Churches Uses Committee (*Chairman*) Mr Tony Gent, The Paddocks, Little Barney, Fakenham NR21 0NL *Tel:* (01328) 838803; (*Secretary*) Mr Jonathan Davis (*as above*)
Board of Patronage (*Chairman*) Mr Neville Houseago, 159 Drayton High Rd, Drayton, Norwich NR8 6BN *Tel:* (01603) 427042; (*Secretary*) Canon P. H. Atkins, Rectory, West Runton, Cromer NR27 9QT *Tel:* (01263) 837279

Advisory Committee for the Care of Churches (*Chairman*) Mr Donald Ray, 2 Lindford Drive, Eaton, Norwich NR4 6LT Tel: (01603) 57271; (*Secretary*) Mrs Lizzie Halfacre, Dioc House
Ringers' Association Mr G. R. Drew, Munsal, 6 Hall Moor Rd, Hingham NR9 4LB Tel: (01953) 850853
Bishop's Furnishings Officer Mr P. King, 10 Bridewell St, Little Walsingham NR22 6BJ Tel: (01328) 820709

EDUCATION

Board of Education (*Acting Chairman*) Revd Brian Cole, Rectory, Great Dunham, King's Lynn PE32 2LQ
 Tel: (01328) 701466
Director of Education Miss Cynthia Wake, Dioc House Tel: (01603) 881352
Schools Administrative Officer Mr Gerald Ward, Dioc House Tel: (01603) 881352
Youth Officer Mr John Reaney, Dioc House Tel: (01603) 881352
Children's Officer Miss Stella Noons, Dioc House Tel: (01603) 881352
Horstead Centre (*Warden*) Mrs Valerie Khambatta, Horstead, Norwich NR12 7EP Tel: (01603) 737215
 Fax: (01603) 737494
 e-mail: Horstead.Centre@Zoo.co.uk

MISSION AND MINISTRY

Advisory Board for Mission and Ministry (*Chairman*) The Bishop of Thetford (*as above*); (*Secretary*) Revd Richard Impey, Dioc House Tel: (01603) 880722
Director of Parish Development and Training Revd Richard Impey (*as above*)
Dioc Director of Ordinands Vacancy
Asst Director of Ordinands Canon Pamela Fawcett, 47A High St, Mundesley, Norwich NR11 8JL Tel: (01263) 721752
Principal LNSM Scheme Canon John Goodchild, Emmaus House, 65 The Close, Norwich NR1 4DH Tel: (01603) 611196
Asst Director for Lay and Reader Training Revd Clive Blackman
Continuing Ministerial Training Officer Revd C. Way, Dioc House
Dioc Officer for NSMs Revd Roger MacPhee
Readers' Committee (*Chairman*) Ven Clifford Offer (*as above*); (*Secretary*) Mr Neville Houseago (*as above*)
Bishop's Officer for Retired Clergy and Widows Canon John Wilson, 4 Rectory Lane, Chedgrave, Norwich NR14 6NE Tel: (01508) 520259
Clergy Pre-Retirement Adviser Ven George Marchant, 28 Greenways, Eaton, Norwich NR4 6PE Tel: (01603) 58295
Officer for Evangelism Revd Christopher Collison, Rectory, Church Rd, Newton Flotman, Norwich NR15 1QB
 Tel: (01508) 470762
 Fax: (01508) 470487

Evangelism Committee (*Chairman*) Canon Peter Taylor, Rectory, Necton, Swaffham PE37 8HT Tel: (01760) 722021; (*Secretary*) Mrs Mary Brookes, Dioc House
World Mission Committee (*Chairman*) Revd Cathy Milford, Vicarage, Barnham Broom, Norwich NR9 4DB
 Tel: (01603) 759204;
(*Secretary*) Mrs P. Dutton, Pevers Farm, Martin's Lane, Kirkstead Green, Brook NR15 1ED Tel: (01508) 550638
Ecumenical Committee (*Chairman*) Mrs Sheila Ashford, Holly Lodge, Strumpshaw, Norwich NR13 4NS Tel: (01603) 712324; (*Ecumenical Officer*) Revd Robin Hewetson, Rectory, Marsham, Norwich NR10 5PP Tel: (01263) 733249
 Fax: (01263) 733799
Committee for Christian Stewardship (*Chairman*) Revd Philip Harrison, Rectory, Drayton, Norwich NR8 6EF
 Tel: (01603) 868749
Secretary and Adviser Mr Christopher Hedges, Dioc House

LITURGICAL

Chairman Canon Jeremy Haselock, 27 The Close, Norwich NR21 4DZ
 Tel: (01603) 291484
Secretary Revd Kenneth Reeve, Rectory, Goodwins Rd, King's Lynn PE30 5QX Tel: (01553) 771799

PRESS, PUBLICITY AND PUBLICATIONS

Communications Unit (*Chairman*) Revd Michael Paddison, Rectory, Station Rd, Reepham, Norwich NR10 4RA
 Tel: (01603) 870220
Communications Officer Mr Trevor Reid, Dioc House Tel: (01603) 880853 (Office)
 0421 057764 (Mobile)
 Fax: (01603) 881083
Editor of Dioc Directory Mr Trevor Reid (*as above*)

DIOCESAN RECORDS OFFICE

Norfolk Record Office, Gildengate House, Anglia Square, Upper Green Lane, Norwich NR3 1AX (*County Archivist* Dr John Alban) Tel: (01603) 761349
 Fax: (01603) 761885

SOCIAL RESPONSIBILITY

Board for Social Responsibility (*Chairman*) Mr William Armstrong, 122 Norwich Rd, Wymondham NR18 0SZ
 Tel: (01953) 605910
(*Secretary*) Mr Tom Gilbert, Dioc House
 Tel: (01603) 881385
Social Responsibility Officer Mr Tom Gilbert (*as above*)
Industry Committee (*Secretary*) Canon Hereward Cooke, 31 Bracondale, Norwich NR1 2AT Tel: (01603) 624827

Holiday Chaplaincy Committee (*Chairman/Senior Holiday Chaplain*) Vacancy
Dioc Missioner (*Rural Affairs*) Vacancy, Dioc House
Chaplain to the Deaf Revd Gordon Howells, Rectory, Stone Hill, Rackheath, Norwich NR13 6NG Tel: (01603) 720097

RURAL DEANS
ARCHDEACONRY OF NORWICH

Norwich East Canon Hereward Cooke, 31 Bracondale, Norwich NR1 2AT
 Tel: (01603) 624827
Norwich North Canon Michael Stagg, Vicarage, 2 Wroxham Rd, Sprowston, Norwich NR7 8TZ Tel: (01603) 426492
Norwich South Revd Peter Rutherford, 126 Colman Rd, Norwich NR4 7AA
 Tel: (01603) 457629

ARCHDEACONRY OF NORFOLK

Blofield Revd Vivien Elphick, Rectory, Barn Close, Lingwood, Norwich NR13 4TS Tel: (01603) 713880
Depwade Revd Selwyn Swift, Rectory, Carleton Rode, Norwich NR16 1RN
 Tel: (01953) 789218
Great Yarmouth Revd Anthony Ward, Vicarage, Duke Rd, Gorleston, Great Yarmouth NR31 6LL Tel: (01493) 663477
Humbleyard Revd Di Lammas, Rectory, Hethersett, Norwich NR9 3AR
 Tel: (01603) 810273
Loddon Revd Christopher Poulard, Rectory, Rectory Rd, Haddiscoe, Norwich NR14 6PG Tel: (01502) 677774
Lothingland Revd Martin Gray, St Margaret's Rectory, 147 Hollingworth Rd, Lowestoft NR32 4BW
 Tel: (01502) 573046
Redenhall Revd Des Whale, Rectory, Winfarthing, Diss IP22 2EA
 Tel: (01379) 642543
Saint Benet at Waxham and Tunstead Canon Martin Smith, Vicarage, 28A Yarmouth Rd, North Walsham NR28 9RJ
 Tel: (01692) 406380
Thetford and Rockland Revd John Aves, Rectory, Surrogate St, Attleborough NR17 2AW Tel: (01953) 453185

ARCHDEACONRY OF LYNN

Breckland Revd Hedley Richardson, Rectory, Caston, Attleborough NR17 1DE
 Tel: (01953) 483222
Brisley and Elmham Revd Brian Cole, Rectory, Great Dunham, King's Lynn PE32 2LQ Tel: (01328) 701466
Burnham and Walsingham Revd Alan Bell, Rectory, Fakenham NR21 9BZ
 Tel: (01328) 862268
Dereham in Mitford Canon Dennis Rider, Vicarage, 1 Vicarage Meadows, Dereham NR19 1TW Tel: (01362) 693143

Heacham and Rising Canon George Hall, Rectory, Sandringham, King's Lynn PE35 6EH *Tel:* (01485) 540587
Holt Revd Peter Barnes-Clay, Rectory, Weybourne, Holt NR25 7SY *Tel:* (01263) 588268

Ingworth Revd Patrick Foreman, Rectory, Westgate Green, Hevingham, Norwich NR10 5NH *Tel:* (01603) 754643
Lynn Revd Stuart Nairn, Vicarage, Narborough, King's Lynn PE32 1TE *Tel:* (01760) 338552

Repps Canon David Hayden, Vicarage, Cromer NR27 0BE *Tel:* (01263) 512000
Sparham Revd Paul Illingworth, Rectory, Weston Longville, Norwich NR9 5JU *Tel:* (01603) 880163

DIOCESE OF OXFORD

Founded in 1542. Oxfordshire; Berkshire; Buckinghamshire; one parish in each of Bedfordshire, Gloucestershire, Hampshire, Hertfordshire and Warwickshire.

Population 2,076,000   Area 2,221 sq m
Stipendiary Clergy 447   Benefices 334
Parishes 631   Churches 816

BISHOP (41st)
Rt Revd Richard Douglas Harries, Diocesan Church House, North Hinksey, Oxford OX2 0NB
Tel: (01865) 208200 (Office)
Fax: (01865) 790470
e-mail: bishopoxon@oxford.anglican.org
[Richard Oxon:]

Bishop's Domestic Chaplain Revd Dr Edmund Newell (*same address*)

AREA BISHOPS
READING Rt Revd Dominic Walker, Bishop's House, Tidmarsh Lane, Tidmarsh, Reading RG8 8HA [1997]
Tel: 0118–984 1216
Fax: 0118–984 1218
e-mail:
bishopreading@oxford.anglican.org
BUCKINGHAM Rt Revd Michael Hill, Magnolia Cottage, 28 Church St, Gt Missenden, Bucks HP16 0AZ [1998]
Tel: (01494) 862173
Fax: (01494) 890508
e-mail: bishopbucks@oxford.anglican.org
DORCHESTER Rt Revd Anthony John Russell, Holmby House, Sibford Ferris, Banbury, Oxon OX15 5RG [1988]
Tel: (01295) 780583
Fax: (01295) 788686
e-mail:
bishopdorchester@oxford.anglican.org

HONORARY ASSISTANT BISHOPS
Rt Revd Keith Arnold, 9 Dingleder ry, Olney, Bucks MK46 5ES [1997]
Tel: (01234) 713044
Rt Revd Leonard Ashton, 60 Lowndes Ave, Chesham, Bucks HP5 2HJ [1984]
Tel: (01494) 782952
Rt Revd John Bone, 4 Grove Rd, Henley on Thames, Oxon RG9 1DH [1997]
Tel: (01491) 413482
Rt Revd Paul Burrough, 6 Mill Green Close, Bampton, Oxon OX18 2HE [1995]

Rt Revd Albert Kenneth Cragg, 3 Goring Lodge, White House Rd, Oxford OX1 4QE [1982]
Tel: (01865) 249895
Rt Revd Ronald Gordon, 16 East St Helen St, Abingdon, Oxon OX4 5EA [1991]
Tel: (01235) 529956
Rt Revd Stephen Verney, Charity School House, Church Rd, Blewbury, Didcot, Oxon OX11 9PY
Tel: (01235) 850004
Rt Revd Michael Houghton, 8 Goldney Ave, Clifton, Bristol BS8 4RA [1998]
Tel: 0117-973 1752
Fax: 0117-973 1762

CATHEDRAL CHURCH OF CHRIST
Dean Very Revd John Drury, The Deanery, Christ Church, Oxford OX1 1DP [1991]
Tel: (01865) 276162
Fax: (01865) 276238
Dean's Secretary Mrs Jan Bolongaro (*same address*)
Tel: (01865) 276161
Canons Residentiary
Canon Prof Oliver O'Donovan, Christ Church, Oxford OX1 1DP [1982]
Tel: (01865) 276219
Ven John Morrison, Archdeacon's Lodging, Christ Church, Oxford OX1 1DP [1998]
Tel: (01865) 204440
Canon Martin Peirce, 70 Yarnells Hill, Oxford OX2 9BG [1987]
Tel: (01865) 721330
Very Revd Robert Jeffery (*Sub-Dean*), Christ Church, Oxford OX1 1DP [1996]
Tel: (01865) 276278
Canon Prof Keith Ward, Christ Church, Oxford OX1 1DP [1991]
Tel: (01865) 276246
Canon Prof John Webster, Priory House, Christ Church, Oxford OX1 1DP [1997]
Tel: (01865) 276247
Lay Canon Prof H. M. R. E. Mayr-Harting, Christ Church Oxford OX1 1DP [1997]
Tel: (01865) 286334
Precentor Revd Justin Lewis-Anthony, Christ Church, Oxford OX1 1DP
Tel: (01865) 276214
Cathedral Registrar Mr David Burnside, Christ Church, Oxford OX1 1DP
Tel: (01865) 276155

Cathedral Secretary Miss Sally-Ann Ford, Christ Church, Oxford OX1 1DP
Tel: (01865) 276155
Fax: (01865) 276277
Cathedral Organist Mr Stephen Darlington, Christ Church, Oxford OX1 1DP
Tel: (01865) 276195

ARCHDEACONS
OXFORD Ven John Morrison, Archdeacon's Lodging, Christ Church, Oxford OX1 1DP [1998]
Tel: (01865) 204440
Fax: (01865) 204465
e-mail: archoxf@oxford.anglican.org
BERKSHIRE Ven Norman Russell, Foxglove House, Love Lane, Donnington, Newbury RG13 2JG [1998]
Tel: (01635) 552820
e-mail: archber@oxford.anglican.org
BUCKINGHAM Ven David Goldie, 60 Wendover Rd, Aylesbury, Bucks HP21 9LW [1998]
Tel: (01296) 423269
e-mail: archbuc@oxford.anglican.org

CONVOCATION (MEMBERS OF THE HOUSE OF CLERGY OF THE GENERAL SYNOD)
The Archdeacon of Oxford
Proctors for Clergy
Revd Valerie Bonham
Canon Simon Brown
Revd Andrew Burnham
Ven David Goldie
Revd Christopher Hall
Revd Robert Key
Revd John Rees
Revd Philip Tovey

MEMBERS OF THE HOUSE OF LAITY OF THE GENERAL SYNOD
Mr John Bowen
Dr Carole Cull
Dr Philip Giddings
Mrs Viviane Hall
Mrs Penny Keens
Mr Terry Landsbert
Mr Gavin Oldham
Ms Beverley Ruddock
Dr Anna Thomas-Betts
Mr David Wright

DIOCESAN OFFICERS
Dioc Secretary Mrs Rosemary Pearce, Diocesan Church House, North Hinksey, Oxford OX2 0NB   *Tel:* (01865) 208200
Fax: (01865) 790470
e-mail: diosec@oxford.anglican.org
Chancellor of Diocese Chanc P. T. S. Boydell, Diocesan Registry, 16 Beaumont St, Oxford OX1 2LZ   *Tel:* (01865) 241974
e-mail: oxford@winckworths.co.uk
Joint Registrars of Diocese and Bishop's Legal Secretary Dr Frank Robson and Revd John Rees (*same address*)
Registrars of the Archdeaconries Dr Frank Robson and Revd John Rees (*as above*)

DIOCESAN ORGANISATIONS
Diocesan Office Diocesan Church House, North Hinksey, Oxford OX2 0NB
Tel: (01865) 208200
Fax: (01865) 790470

ADMINISTRATION
Dioc Synod (Vice-President, House of Clergy) Canon Simon Brown, The Precincts, Burnham, Slough SL1 7HU Tel: (01628) 604173; *(Vice-President, House of Laity)* Dr Philip Giddings, 5 Clifton Park Rd, Caversham, Reading, Berks RG4 7PD Tel: 0118–931 8207; *(Secretary)* Mrs Rosemary Pearce, Dioc Church House
Board of Finance (Chairman) Mr John Yaxley, Old Housing, Church St, Fifield, Milton-under-Wychwood, Chipping Norton OX7 6HF *Tel and Fax:* (01993) 831385; *(Secretary)* Mrs Rosemary Pearce *(as above)*
Principal Buildings Officer and Dioc Surveyor Mr Roger Harwood, Dioc Church House
Dioc Trustees (Oxford) Ltd Mrs Rosemary Pearce *(as above)*
Pastoral Committee (Secretary) Mrs Mary Saunders, Dioc Church House
e-mail: dac@oxford.anglican.org
Designated Officer Dr Frank Robson *(as above)*

CHURCHES
Advisory Committee for the Care of Churches (Chairman) Sir Timothy Raison, Dioc Church House; *(Secretary)* Mrs Mary Saunders *(as above)*
Redundant Churches Uses Committee (Secretary) Mrs Mary Saunders *(as above)*

STEWARDSHIP, TRAINING, EDUCATION AND MINISTRY
Secretary Canon Keith Lamdin, Dioc Church House
e-mail: training@oxford.anglican.org
Dioc Director of Ordinands and Post-Ordination Training Canon Martin Peirce, 70 Yarnell's Hill, Oxford OX2 9BG
Tel: (01865) 721330
e-mail: ordinands@oxford.anglican.org
Dept of Training and Parish Resources Canon Keith Lamdin *(as above)*
Readers' Association (Warden) Revd Bob Rhodes, Dioc Church House
Dioc Youth Adviser Mr Andrew Gear, Dioc Church House
e-mail: youthofficer@oxford.anglican.org
Dioc Children's Adviser Mrs Jenny Hyson, Dioc Church House
e-mail: childofficer@oxford.anglican.org
Dioc Stewardship Adviser Mr David Haylett
e-mail: steward@oxford.anglican.org

EDUCATION
Director of Education (Schools) Canon Tony Williamson, Dioc Church House
e-mail: schools@oxford.anglican.org

MISSIONARY AND ECUMENICAL
Dioc Advisory Group for Mission Canon David Meara, Buckingham Rectory, 39 Fisher's Field, Buckingham MK18 1SF
Tel: (01280) 813178
Bishop's Officer for Evangelism Revd Colin Horseman, Rectory, 6 Standlake Rd, Ducklington, Witney OX8 7XG
Tel: (01993) 776625
e-mail: evang@oxford.anglican.org
Partnership in World Mission (Secretary) Revd Michael Sams, 13 Hound Close, Abingdon, Oxon OX14 2LU
Tel: (01235) 529084

COMMUNICATIONS
Dioc Communications Officer Revd Richard Thomas, Dioc Church House
Tel: (01865) 553360 (Home)
01893 703279 (Pager)
e-mail: communications@oxford.anglican.org
Editor of Dioc Newspaper 'The Door' Mrs Christine Zwart, Dioc Church House
e-mail: door@oxford.anglican.org

DIOCESAN RECORD OFFICES
County Archivist, Oxfordshire County Record Office, County Hall, Oxford OX1 1ND Tel: (01865) 815203 *(For records of the diocese, and parish records in the Archdeaconry of Oxford)*; Berkshire Record Office, Shire Hall, Shinfield Park, Reading RG2 9XD Tel: 0118-901 5132 *(For parish records in the Archdeaconry of Berkshire)*; Buckinghamshire Record Office, County Hall, Aylesbury, Bucks HP20 1UA Tel: (01296) 395000, Ext. 588 *(For parish records in the Archdeaconry of Buckingham)*

SOCIAL RESPONSIBILITY
Board of Social Responsibility: (Secretary) Mrs Jo Saunders, Dioc Church House
e-mail: socresp@oxford.anglican.org
PACT – (Parents and Children Together) – Council for Social Work Mrs Yvette Gayford, 48 Bath Rd, Reading, Berks RG1 6PQ
Tel: 0118–958 1861
Council for the Deaf (Chairman) Canon David Manship, Dioc Church House

BOROUGH DEAN
MILTON KEYNES
Vacancy

RURAL DEANS
ARCHDEACONRY OF OXFORD
Aston and Cuddesdon Canon John Crowe, Dorchester Rectory, Dorchester, Wallingford, Oxon OX9 8HZ   Tel: (01865) 340007
Bicester and Islip Revd Guy Chapman, Vicarage, Ambrosden, Bicester, Oxon OX6 0UJ   Tel: (01869) 247813
Chipping Norton Revd Graham Canning, 'Moredays', 36 The Slade, Charlbury, Chipping Norton, Oxon OX7 3SY
Tel: (01608) 810421
Cowley Revd Tony Price, Vicarage, Elsfield Rd, Marston, Oxford OX3 0PR
Tel: (01865) 247034
Deddington Canon Timothy Wimbush, Rectory, Sibford Gower, Banbury, Oxon OX15 5RW   Tel: (0129 578) 555
Henley Revd Phillip Nixon, Vicarage, Manor Rd, Goring, Reading RG8 9DR
Tel: (01491) 872196
Oxford Revd Anthony Gann, Rectory, Lonsdale Rd, Oxford OX2 7ES
Tel: (01865) 556079
Witney Revd Cameron Butland, Rectory, Station Lane, Witney, Oxon OX8 6BH
Tel: (01993) 775003
Woodstock Revd Geoff van der Weegen, Rectory, Stonesfield, Oxon OX8 8PR
Tel: (01993) 891664

ARCHDEACONRY OF BERKSHIRE
Abingdon Revd Leighton Thomas, Vicarage, 3 Tullis Close, Sutton Courtenay, Abingdon, Oxon OX14 4BD
Tel: (01235) 848297
Bracknell Revd Sebastian Jones, Vicarage, Vicarage Rd, South Ascot, Berks SL5 9DX
Tel: (01344) 22388
Bradfield Revd Roger Howell, Rectory, 1 Westridge Ave, Purley, Reading, Berks RG8 8DE   Tel: (01734) 417727
Maidenhead Revd David Rossdale, Vicarage, Church Gate, Cookham, Berks SL6 9SP   Tel: (01628) 523969
Newbury Revd David Cook, Rectory, 64 Northcroft Lane, Newbury, Berks RG14 1BN   Tel: (01635) 40326
Reading Canon Brian Shenton, 39 Downshire Square, Reading, Berks RG1 6NH
Tel: 0118–957 1057
Sonning Revd Dr Alan Wilson, Rectory, 155 High St, Sandhurst, Camberley GU17 8HR   Tel: (01252) 872168
e-mail: atwilson@machine.co.uk
Vale of White Horse Revd Andrew Bailey, Vicarage, Coach Lane, Faringdon, Oxon SN7 8AB   Tel: (01367) 240106
Wallingford Revd John Morley, Rectory, 22 Castle St, Wallingford, Oxon OX10 8DW
Tel: (01491) 837280
Wantage Revd Alan Wadge, Ridgeway Rectory, Letcombe Regis, Wantage, Oxon OX12 9LD   Tel: (01235) 763805

ARCHDEACONRY OF BUCKINGHAM
Amersham Revd Roger Salisbury, Rectory, Church St, Chesham, Bucks HP15 1HY
Tel: (01494) 783629
Aylesbury Revd Tim Higgins, Rectory, Parsons Fee, Aylesbury HP20 2QZ Tel: (01296) 24276
Buckingham Revd David Meara, Rectory, 39 Fishers Field, Buckingham MK18 1SF
Tel: (01280) 813178
Burnham Canon Simon Brown, Rectory, The Precincts, Burnham, Slough SL1 7HU
Tel: (01628) 604173

Claydon Canon Judy Rees, 15 Weston Rd, Great Horwood, Bucks MK17 0QR Tel: (01296) 713603
Milton Keynes Revd Ian Pusey, Rectory, 75 Church Green Rd, Bletchley, Milton Keynes MK3 6BY Tel: (01908) 373357

Mursley Revd Norman Cotton, Stewkley Vicarage, Stewkley, Leighton Buzzard, Beds LU7 0HH Tel: (01525) 240287
Newport Revd Maurice Stanton-Saringer, Rectory, 21 School Lane, Sherington, Newport Pagnell MK16 9NF Tel: (01908) 610521

Wendover Revd Alan Bennett, Rectory, Aston Clinton, Aylesbury, Bucks HP22 5JD Tel: (01296) 631626
Wycombe Revd Christopher Bull, Vicarage, 9 Chapel Rd, Flackwell Heath, High Wycombe HP10 9AA Tel: (01628) 522795

DIOCESE OF PETERBOROUGH

Founded in 1541. Northamptonshire, except for one parish in the west (LEICESTER); Rutland; an area of north-west Cambridgeshire, including Peterborough; one parish in Lincolnshire.

Population 756,000   Area 1,149 sq m
Stipendiary Clergy 161   Benefices 166
Parishes 357   Churches 380

BISHOP (37th)
Rt Revd Ian Patrick Martyn Cundy, Bishop's Lodgings, The Palace, Peterborough, Cambs PE1 1YA [1996]
Tel: (01733) 562492
Fax: (01733) 890077
[Ian Petriburg:]

Bishop's Chaplain Canon Richard Cattle

SUFFRAGAN BISHOP
BRIXWORTH Rt Revd Paul Everard Barber, 4 The Avenue, Dallington, Northampton NN5 7AN [1989]   Tel: (01604) 759423
Fax: (01604) 750925

CATHEDRAL CHURCH OF ST PETER, ST PAUL AND ST ANDREW
Dean Very Revd Michael Bunker, The Deanery, Peterborough, Cambs PE1 1XS [1992]   Tel: (01733) 562780
Fax: (01733) 897874

Canons Residentiary
Canon Thomas Christie, Prebendal House, Minster Precincts, Peterborough, Cambs PE1 1XX [1980]   Tel: (01733) 569441
Canon Jack Higham, Canonry House, Minster Precincts, Peterborough PE1 1XX [1983]   Tel: (01733) 562125
Canon Philip Spence, 7 Minster Precincts, Peterborough PE1 1XX [1997]
Tel: (01733) 564899
Precentor Revd Bill Croft, 18 Minster Precincts, Peterborough PE1 1XX [1998]
Tel: (01733) 343389
Chapter Clerk Mr Bernard Kane, Chapter Office, Minster Precincts, Peterborough, Cambs PE1 1XS   Tel: (01733) 343342
Fax: (01733) 552465
Cathedral Organist Mr Christopher Gower, The Norman Hall, Minster Precincts, Peterborough, Cambs PE1 1XX
Tel: (01733) 565165

ARCHDEACONS
NORTHAMPTON Ven Michael Chapman, 11 The Drive, Northampton NN1 4RZ [1991]
Tel: (01604) 714015
Fax: (01604) 792016

OAKHAM Ven Bernard Fernyhough, Rectory, 5 Nook Lane, Empingham, Oakham, Leics LE15 8PT [1977]   Tel: (01780) 460345

CONVOCATION (MEMBERS OF THE HOUSE OF CLERGY OF THE GENERAL SYNOD)
The Archdeacon of Northampton
Proctors for Clergy
Revd David Bird
Canon Thomas Christie
Revd Stephen Trott

MEMBERS OF THE HOUSE OF LAITY OF THE GENERAL SYNOD
Mrs Beatrice Brandon
Mr Keith Davidson
Mrs Sheila Saunders
Mr Malcolm Tyler

DIOCESAN OFFICERS
Dioc Secretary Canon Richard Cattle, Diocesan Office, The Palace, Peterborough, Cambs PE1 1YB   Tel: (01733) 564448
Fax: (01733) 555271
Chancellor of Diocese His Honour Judge Thomas Coningsby, Leyfields, Elmore Rd, Chipstead, Surrey CR3 3PG
Deputy Chancellor Mr George Pulman, c/o The Diocesan Registrar, 4 Holywell Way, Longthorpe, Peterborough PE3 6SS
Registrar of Diocese and Bishop's Legal Secretary Mr Raymond Hemingray, 4 Holywell Way, Longthorpe, Peterborough, Cambs PE3 6SS   Tel: (01733) 262523

DIOCESAN ORGANISATIONS
Diocesan Office The Palace, Peterborough, Cambs PE1 1YB   Tel: (01733) 564448
Fax: (01733) 555271

ADMINISTRATION
Dioc Synod (*Vice-President, Clergy*) Canon Thomas Christie, Prebendal House, Minster Precincts, Peterborough PE1 1XX Tel: (01733) 569441; (*Vice-President, Laity*) Mrs Beatrice Brandon, Clopton Manor, Clopton, Kettering NN14 3DZ Tel: (01832) 720346; (*Secretary*) Canon Richard Cattle, Dioc Office

Board of Finance (*Chairman*) Mr Scott Durward, The Old House, Medbourne, Market Harborough, Leics LE16 8DX Tel: (01858) 565207; (*Secretary*) Canon Richard Cattle (*as above*)
Financial Controller Mrs Sue McMeekin, Dioc Office
Houses Committee (*Chairman*) Mr Alastair Stirling, 14 Redmiles Lane, Kelton, Stamford PE9 3RG Tel: (017880) 720320; (*Secretary*) Mrs Hilary Newton, Dioc Office
Pastoral Committee Mrs Hilary Newton (*as above*)
Board of Patronage Canon Richard Cattle (*as above*)
Designated Officer Mr Raymond Hemingray, 4 Holywell Way, Longthorpe, Peterborough, Cambs PE3 6SS
Tel: (01733) 262523
Trust Committee Mrs Hilary Newton (*as above*)

CHURCHES
Advisory Committee for the Care of Churches (*Chairman*) Mr Stephen Billings, The Church Offices, St Michael's Church, Perry St, Northampton NN1 4HL
Tel: (01604) 603833
(*Secretary*) Mrs Diana Evans (*same address*)
Redundant Churches Uses Committee (*Chairman*) Mr Adrian Christmas, 1 Minster Precincts, Peterborough; (*Secretary*) Mrs Hilary Newton, Dioc Office

EDUCATION
Board of Education (*Schools*) (*Director of Education* (*Schools*) *and Secretary*) Revd John Smith, Dioc Office
Schools Officer Revd Philip Davies, Rectory, 3 Hall Yard, King's Cliffe, Peterborough PE8 6XQ   Tel: (01780) 470314

MINISTRY
Director of Ordinands Revd Bill Croft, 18 Minster Precincts, Peterborough PE1 1XX
Tel: (01733) 343389
Director of Post Ordination Training Revd Ronald Hawkes, Vicarage, 12 New St, Oundle, Peterborough PE8 4EA
Tel: (01832) 273595
Continuing Ministerial Education Revd Stephen Evans, Rectory, 32 West St, Ecton, Northampton NN6 0QF
Tel: (01604) 416322
Warden of Readers Canon John Westwood, St Andrew's Vicarage, Berrymoor Rd, Wellingborough NN8 2AU
Tel: (01933) 222692
Warden of Pastoral Assistants Revd Paul Paynton, Vicarage, 19 Station Rd, Irchester, Northants NN9 7EH
Tel: (01933) 312674

Warden of Parish Evangelists Canon Timothy Partridge, Rectory, Church Lane, Bugbrooke, Northampton NN7 3PB
Tel: (01604) 830373
Lay Training Officer Miss Sheila Addison, Peterborough House, 90 Harlestone Rd, Northampton NN5 7AG
Tel: (01604) 751907
Fax: (01604) 580301
Local Ministry Officer Revd Paul Dunthorne, Rectory, 6 Ridlington Rd, Preston, Oakham LE15 9NN
Tel: (01572) 737287

MISSION
Children's Officer Mrs Pamela Jones, Peterborough House, 90 Harlestone Rd, Northampton NN5 7AG *Tel:* (01604) 751907
Fax: (01604) 580301
Parish Development Director Mr Tony Armitage, Dioc Office
Youth Officer Capt P. Niemiec, Peterborough House (*as above*)
Urban Priority Areas Link Officer and Church Urban Fund Canon David Staples, Vicarage, 4 West End, West Haddon, Northampton NN6 7AY
Tel: (01788) 510207
Ecumenical Officer Revd Robert Giles, Rectory, Gate Lane, Broughton, Kettering NN14 1ND *Tel:* (01536) 791373
Hospital Chaplaincy Adviser Revd Leslie Turner, 4 Stratton Close, Langlands, Northampton NN3 3HQ
Tel: (01604) 635512 (Home)
(01604) 634700 (Office)
Industrial Chaplain Canon Mostyn Davies, 16 Swanspool, Peterborough PE3 7LS
Tel: (01733) 262034

LITURGICAL
Officer Revd Stephen Evans (*as above*)

PRESS, PUBLICITY AND PUBLICATIONS
Media Officer Revd Paul Needle, 106 Wharf Rd, Higham Ferrers, Northants NN10 8BH *Tel:* (01933) 312800
0802 731751 (Mobile)

DIOCESAN RECORD OFFICES
Wootton Park, Northampton NN4 9BQ *County Archivist* Miss R. Watson *Tel:* (01604) 762129 (*For all parishes in Northants and the former Soke of Peterborough*); Leicestershire Record Office, Long St, Wigston Magna, Leicester LE18 2AH, *County Archivist* Miss K. M. Thompson, *Tel:* 0116–257 1080 (*For all parishes in Rutland*)

SPIRITUALITY
Ecton House (Retreat House) Warden Vacancy, Ecton House, Church Way, Ecton, Northampton NN6 0QE
Tel: (01604) 406442
SpirDir Canon Peter Garlick, 120 Worcester Close, Northampton NN3 9ED
Tel: (01604) 416511

RURAL DEANS
ARCHDEACONRY OF NORTHAMPTON
Brackley Revd John Roberts, Pimlico House, Pimlico, Brackley, Northants NN13 5TN *Tel:* (01280) 850378
Brixworth Canon Brian Lee, Vicarage, 2 Church Rd, Spratton, Northampton NN6 8HR *Tel:* (01604) 847212
Daventry Canon David Evans, Rectory, Church Lane, Nether Heyford, Northampton NN7 3LQ *Tel:* (01327) 340487
Northampton Revd Kevin Ashby, Rectory, Church Walk, Great Billing, Northampton NN3 9ED *Tel:* (01604) 784870
Towcester Canon Michael Baker, Vicarage, Towcester NN12 6AB *Tel:* (01327) 350459
Wellingborough Revd David Witchell, St Barnabas Vicarage, St Barnabas St, Wellingborough, Northants NN8 3HB
Tel: (01933) 226337
Wootton Revd Richard Ormston, Rectory, Collingtree, Northampton NN4 0NF
Tel: (01604) 761895

ARCHDEACONRY OF OAKHAM
Barnack Revd Roger Watson, Rectory, Wittering, Peterborough PE8 6AQ
Tel: (01780) 782428
Corby Canon Ronald Howe, Vicarage, Brigstock, Kettering, Northants NN14 3EX *Tel:* (01536) 373371
Higham Canon William Kentigern-Fox, Vicarage High St, Raunds NN9 6HS
Tel: (01933) 461509
Kettering Revd John Simmons, Rectory, Preston Court, Burton Latimer, Kettering, Northants NN15 5LR *Tel:* (01536) 722959
Oundle Revd Dr Judith Rose, Rectory, Aldwincle, Kettering NN14 3EP
Tel: (01832) 720613
Peterborough Canon Haydn Smart, Vicarage, 315 Thorpe Rd, Peterborough PE3 6LU *Tel:* (01733) 263016
Rutland Revd Michael Rogers, Rectory, Cottesmore, Oakham, Rutland LE15 7DJ
Tel: (01572) 812202

DIOCESE OF PORTSMOUTH

Founded in 1927. The south-eastern third of Hampshire; the Isle of White.

Population 710,000 Area 408 sq m
Stipendiary Clergy 116 Benefices 124
Parishes 138 Churches 168

BISHOP (8th)
Rt Revd Kenneth Stevenson PH D, Bishopsgrove, 26 Osborn Rd, Fareham, Hants PO16 7DQ [1995] *Tel:* (01329) 280247 *Fax:* (01329) 231538
[Kenneth Portsmouth]

Bishop's Chaplain Revd Andrew Tremlett, 11 Burnham Wood, Fareham, Hants PO16 7UD *Tel:* (01329) 221326 (Home) (01329) 280247 (Office) *Fax:* (01329) 231538
Secretaries Mrs Jean Maslin, Ms Julia Anderson

HONORARY ASSISTANT BISHOPS
Rt Revd Michael Adie, Greenslade, Froxfield, Petersfield, Hants GU32 1EB
Tel: (01730) 827266
Rt Revd Ernest Edwin Curtis, 5 Elizabeth Gardens, Havenstreet, Ryde, Isle of Wight PO33 4DU *Tel:* (01983) 883049
Rt Revd Henry David Halsey, Bramblecross, Gully Rd, Seaview, Isle of Wight PO34 5BY *Tel:* (01983) 613583
Rt Revd Edward James Keymer Roberts, The House on the Marsh, Quay Lane, Brading, Isle of Wight PO36 0BD
Tel: (01983) 407434

CATHEDRAL CHURCH OF ST THOMAS OF CANTERBURY
Provost Very Revd Michael Yorke, Provost's House, 13 Pembroke Rd, Old Portsmouth, Hants PO1 2NS [1994]
Tel: (01705) 824400 (Home)
(01705) 823300 (Office)
Fax: (01705) 295480
Cathedral Office Cathedral Office, St Thomas's St, Old Portsmouth, Hants PO1 2HH *Tel:* (01705) 823300
Fax: (01705) 295480
Canons Residentiary
Canon David Isaac, 1 Pembroke Close, Portsmouth, Hants PO1 2NX [1990]
Tel: (01705) 818107
Fax: (01705) 295081
Canon Jane Hedges, 51 High St, Portsmouth, Hants PO1 2LU [1993]
Tel: (01705) 731282

Precentor Canon Gavin Kirk, 61 St Thomas's St, Old Portsmouth, Hants PO1 2EZ [1998] *Tel:* (01705) 824621
Fax: (01705) 821356
Canon Ian Jagger, 50 Penny St, Old Portsmouth, Hants PO1 2NL [1998]
Tel: (01705) 730792
Cathedral Administrator, Chapter Clerk and Clerk to Cathedral Council Mr Brian Jones, Cathedral Office
Cathedral Organist Mr David Price, 8 Lombard St, Old Portsmouth, Hants PO1 2HX
Tel: (01705) 430811
Fax: (01705) 295480

ARCHDEACONS
PORTSMOUTH Ven Christopher Lowson, 5 Brading Ave, Southsea, Hants PO4 1QJ [1999]
ISLE OF WIGHT Ven Mervyn Banting, 5 The Boltons, Wootton Bridge, Ryde, Isle of Wight PO33 4PB [1996]
Tel and Fax: (01983) 884432

CONVOCATION (MEMBERS OF THE HOUSE OF CLERGY OF THE GENERAL SYNOD)
The Archdeacon of the Isle of Wight
Proctors for Clergy
Canon John Byrne
Canon David Isaac
Canon Robert White

MEMBERS OF THE HOUSE OF LAITY OF THE GENERAL SYNOD
Mr Christopher Hedges
Mr Peter Lowater
Mrs Anahid Thomas

DIOCESAN OFFICERS
Dioc Secretary Mr Michael Jordan, Cathedral House, St Thomas's St, Portsmouth, Hants PO1 2HA *Tel:* (01705) 825731
Fax: (01705) 752967
Chancellor of Diocese His Honour Judge Francis Aglionby, The Croft, Houghton, Carlisle, Cumbria CA3 0LD

Registrar of Diocese and Bishop's Legal Secretary Miss Hilary Tyler, Messrs Bruttons, 288 West St, Fareham, Hants PO16 0AJ
Tel: (01329) 236171
Fax: (01329) 289915
Parsonage and Property Committee Surveyors *(Portsmouth)* Mr Roger Boyce, Roger Boyce Associates, Purbrook House, Purbrook Gardens, London Rd, Purbrook, Hants PO7 5JY *Tel:* (01705) 266620; *(Isle of Wight)* Mr Robert Biggs, A. G. Biggs Partnership, 66 Carisbrooke Rd, Newport, Isle of Wight PO30 1BW *Tel:* (01983) 522190

DIOCESAN ORGANISATIONS
Diocesan Office Cathedral House, St Thomas's St, Portsmouth, Hants PO1 2HA
Tel: (01705) 825731
Fax: (01705) 752967

ADMINISTRATION
Dioc Synod *(Chairman House of Clergy)* Vacancy; *(Chairman, House of Laity)* Dr Hugh Mason, 32 Chelsea Rd, Southsea PO5 1NJ *Tel:* (01705) 816794; *(Secretary)* Mr Michael Jordan, Dioc Office
Board of Finance *(Chairman)* Mr Peter Lowater, Lower Gubbles, Hook Lane, Warsash, Southampton SO31 9HH *Tel:* (01489) 572156 *Fax:* (01489) 572252; *(Secretary)* Mr Michael Jordan *(as above)*
Parsonages and Property Committee *(Secretary)* Mr Rodney Baker, Dioc Office
Dioc Board of Ministry, Pastoral Committee (Secretary) Mrs Lindie Sawtell, Dioc Office
Patronage Board Miss Hilary Tyler, Messrs Bruttons, 288 West St, Fareham, Hants PO16 0AJ *Tel:* (01329) 236171
Fax: (01329) 289915
Designated Officer Miss Hilary Tyler *(as above)*

CHURCHES
Advisory Committee for the Care of Churches (Chairman) Mrs Sarah Quail; *(Secretary)* Mrs Lindie Sawtell, Dioc Office
Redundant Churches Uses Committee (Secretary) Mr Rodney Baker *(as above)*

EDUCATION
Director of Education Canon David Isaac, Cathedral House, St Thomas's St, Portsmouth, Hants PO1 2HA
Tel: (01705) 822053
Fax: (01705) 295081
Board of Education (Secretary) Canon David Isaac *(as above)*
Youth and Children's Work Adviser and Bishop's Representative for Child Protection Vacancy
Further Education Officer Revd David Gibbons, 6 Carlton Way, Gosport, Hants PO12 1LN *Tel:* (01705) 503921

MINISTRY
Dioc Director of Ordinands Revd Richard Brand, Vicarage, Church Lane, Hambledon, Waterlooville PO7 4RT
Tel and *Fax:* (01705) 632717
Bishop's Chaplain for Continuing Ministerial Education Canon Terry Louden, Vicarage, East Meon, Petersfield, Hants GU32 1NH
Tel: (01730) 823221
Chaplain for Women's Ministry Canon Jane Hedges, Cathedral Office
Dioc Director of NSM Revd Dr Trevor Reader, Rectory, Blendworth, Horndean, Waterlooville PO8 1AB
Tel: (01705) 592174
Fax: (01705) 597023
Warden of Readers Revd Peter Sutton, Vicarage, Victoria Square, Lee-on-the-Solent, Hants PO13 9NF *Tel:* (01705) 550269
Clerical Registry (*Winchester and Portsmouth*) Revd Dr Ronald Pugh, Church House, 9 The Close, Winchester, Hants SO23 9LS *Tel:* (01962) 844644
Widows Officers (*Mainland*) The Archdeacon of Portsmouth; (*Isle of Wight*) The Archdeacon of the Isle of Wight

BISHOP'S ADVISORY GROUP ON WORSHIP
Chairman Canon Gavin Kirk, 61 St Thomas's St, Old Portsmouth, Hants PO1 2EZ
Tel: (01705) 824621
Fax: (01705) 821356
Secretary Vacancy

MISSIONARY AND ECUMENICAL
Dioc Ecumenical Officer Revd Peter Pimentel, St Paul's Vicarage, Staplers Rd, Barton, Newport, Isle of Wight PO30 2HZ
Tel: (01983) 522075

Canon Missioner Revd Ian Jagger, 50 Penny St, Old Portsmouth, Hants PO1 2NL
Tel: (01705) 730792
Council for Mission and Unity (*Chairman*) The Provost of Portsmouth; (*Secretary*) Vacancy

COMMUNICATIONS
Dioc Communications Officer: Vacancy
Dioc Directory All Communications to Dioc Office

DIOCESAN RECORD OFFICES
Portsmouth City Records Office, 3 Museum Rd, Portsmouth PO1 2LE *Archivist* Mrs S. Quail *Tel:* (01705) 827261 (*For Gosport, Fareham, Havant and Portsmouth Deaneries*); Hampshire Record Office, 20 Southgate St, Winchester SO23 9EF; *County Archivist* Miss R. C. Dunhill *Tel:* (01962) 846154 (*For Bishop's Waltham and Petersfield Deaneries*); Isle of Wight County Record Office, 26 Hillside, Newport, Isle of Wight PO30 2EB *Archivist* Mr R. Smout *Tel:* (01983) 823821 (*For the Isle of Wight Deaneries*)

SOCIAL RESPONSIBILITY
Social Responsibility Adviser Canon David Tonkinson, All Saints Church, Commercial Rd, Portsmouth, Hants PO1 4BT
Tel: (01705) 821137
Fax: (01705) 838116

SPIRITUALITY
Warden Revd Dr Philip Newell, St John's House, 102 Copnor Rd, Portsmouth, Hants PO3 5AL *Tel:* (01705) 666535

STEWARDSHIP
Parish Resources Adviser Mr Gordon Uphill, Dioc Office
Part-time Christian Stewardship Adviser (*Isle of Wight*) Dr John Wibberley, Alsace, 48 High Park Rd, Ryde, Isle of Wight PO33 1BX *Tel:* (01983) 564287
Fax: (01983) 566770

RURAL DEANS
ARCHDEACONRY OF PORTSMOUTH
Bishop's Waltham Revd Ian Coomber, All Saints' Rectory, Brook Lane, Botley, Southampton SO30 2ER
Tel: (01489) 781534
Fareham Vacancy
Gosport Revd Peter Wadsworth, Vicarage, 21 Elson Rd, Gosport, Hants PO12 4BL
Tel: (01705) 582824
Havant Canon Robert White, Vicarage, Riders Lane, Leigh Park, Havant, Hants PO9 4QT *Tel:* (01705) 475276
Fax: (01705) 481228
Petersfield Vacancy
Portsmouth Revd John Pinder, Rectory, 27 Farlington Ave, Cosham, Portsmouth PO6 1DF *Tel* and *Fax:* (01705) 375145

ARCHDEACONRY OF THE ISLE OF WIGHT
East Wight Revd Andrew Menniss, Vicarage, Bembridge, Isle of Wight PO35 5NA
Tel: (01983) 872175
Fax: (01983) 875255
West Wight Revd Jon Russell, Shorwell Vicarage, 5 Northcourt Close, Shorwell, Isle of Wight PO30 3LD
Tel and *Fax:* (01983) 741044

DIOCESE OF RIPON

Re-constituted in 1836. The central third of North Yorkshire; Leeds, except for a few parishes in the south-east (SOUTHWELL); an area of south-western County Durham.

Population 780,000   Area 1,359 sq m
Stipendiary Clergy 162   Benefices 125
Parishes 157   Churches 266

BISHOP (11th)
Rt Revd David Nigel de Lorentz Young, Bishop Mount, Ripon, N Yorks HG4 5DP [1977]   *Tel:* (01765) 602045
Fax: (01765) 600758
[David Ripon]

Domestic Chaplain Revd Michael Hepper, Bishop Mount (*as above*)

SUFFRAGAN BISHOP
KNARESBOROUGH Rt Revd Frank Valentine Weston, 16 Shaftesbury Ave, Roundhay, Leeds LS8 1DT   *Tel:* 0113–266 4800
Fax: 0113–266 5649
e-mail: Knaresborough@btinternet.com

HONORARY ASSISTANT BISHOPS
Rt Revd Ralph Emmerson, 15 High St Agnesgate, Ripon, N Yorks HG4 1QR
Tel: (01765) 601626
Rt Revd David Jenkins, Ashbourne, Cotherstone, Barnard Castle, DL12 9PR
Tel: (01833) 650804
Rt Revd John Gaisford, 3 North Lane, Roundhay, Leeds LS8 2QJ
Tel: 0113–273 2003
Fax: 0113–273 3002
e-mail: 101740,2725@compuserve.com

CATHEDRAL CHURCH OF ST PETER AND ST WILFRID
Dean Very Revd John Methuen, The Minster House, Ripon, N Yorks HG4 1PE [1995]   *Tel:* (01765) 603615
e-mail: postmaster@riponcathedral.org.uk
Cathedral Office High St Agnesgate, Ripon HG4 1QT   Tel and *Fax:* (01765) 603462
Canons Residentiary
Canon James Bell, 12 Clotherholme Rd, Ripon HG4 2DA [1997]
Tel and *Fax:* (01765) 604835
Canon Michael Glanville-Smith, St Wilfrid's House, Minster Close, Ripon HG4 1QR [1990]   *Tel:* (01765) 600211
Canon Keith Punshon, St Peter's House, Minster Close, Ripon HG4 1QR [1996]
Tel: (01765) 604108
Chapter Clerk Mr Robert Lambie, Cathedral Office

Cathedral Organist Mr Kerry Beaumont, c/o The Cathedral, Ripon, N Yorks HG4 1QT   *Tel:* (01765) 600237

ARCHDEACONS
LEEDS Ven John Oliver, 2 Halcyon Hill, Leeds LS7 3PU [1992]
Tel and *Fax:* 0113–269 0594
RICHMOND Ven Kenneth Good, 62 Palace Rd, Ripon, N Yorks HG4 1HA [1993]
Tel and *Fax:* (01765) 604742

CONVOCATION (MEMBERS OF THE HOUSE OF CLERGY OF THE GENERAL SYNOD)
The Archdeacon of Leeds
Proctors for Clergy
Revd Penny Driver
Revd Clive Mansell
Revd David Rhodes

MEMBERS OF THE HOUSE OF LAITY OF THE GENERAL SYNOD
Mr Robert Aagaard
Dr John Beal
Mrs Katherine Carr
Mr Nigel Greenwood
Mrs Dorothy Stewart

DIOCESAN OFFICERS
Dioc Secretary Mr Philip Arundel, Diocesan Office, St Mary's St, Leeds LS9 7DP
Tel: 0113–248 7487
Fax: 0113–249 1129
Chancellor of Diocese The Worshipful Simon Grenfell, St John's House, Sharow Lane, Ripon, N Yorks HG4 5BN
Registrar of Diocese and Bishop's Legal Secretary Mr John Balmforth, Ripon Diocesan Registry, Cathedral Chambers, 4 Kirkgate, Ripon HG4 1PA   *Tel:* (01765) 600755
Fax: (01765) 690523
Deputy Registrar Mr Christopher Tunnard (*same address*)
Dioc Surveyor Mr Michael Lindley, Dioc Office

DIOCESAN ORGANISATIONS
Diocesan Office Ripon Diocesan Office, St Mary's St, Leeds LS9 7DP
Tel: 0113–248 7487
Fax: 0113–249 1129

ADMINISTRATION
Dioc Synod (*Chairman, House of Clergy*) Revd Richard Cooper, Rectory, Church Wynd, Richmond DL10 7AQ *Tel:* (01748) 823398; (*Chairman, House of Laity*) Dr Alan Stanley, The Limes, 35 Potterton Lane, Barwick in Elmet, Leeds LS15 4DU *Tel:* 0113–281 2769; (*Secretary*) Mr Philip Arundel, Dioc Office
Board of Finance (*Chairman*) Dr Raymond Head, Walden Cottage, New Row, Birstwith, Harrogate HG3 2NH *Tel:* (01423) 770450; (*Secretary*) Mr Philip Arundel (*as above*); (*Asst Secretary*) Mr Peter Mojsa, Dioc Office; (*Accountant*) Ms Ruth Debney, Dioc Office
Parsonages Board Mr Philip Arundel (*as above*); (*Parsonages Officer*) Mr Michael Lindley, Dioc Office
Pastoral Committee Mr Philip Arundel (*as above*)
Board of Patronage Mr Philip Arundel (*as above*)
Designated Officer Mr Philip Arundel (*as above*)
Dioc Electoral Registration Officer Mr Philip Arundel (*as above*)
Widows and Dependants (*Widows' Officer*) Mr Philip Arundel (*as above*)

CHURCHES
Advisory Committee for the Care of Churches (*Chairman*) Mr Robert Aagaard, The Manor House, High Birstwith, Harrogate HG3 2LG; (*Secretary*) Mr Philip Arundel (*as above*)
Church Buildings Committee Mr Philip Arundel (*as above*)
Redundant Churches Uses Committee Mr Philip Arundel (*as above*)

EDUCATION
Director of Education Mr Ian Mackenzie, The Castle CE School, Stockwell Rd, Knaresborough HG5 0JN
Tel: (01423) 869839
Religious Education Adviser (*Richmond, Wensley and Ripon Deaneries*) Revd Shirley Griffiths, Vicarage, East Cowton, Northallerton DL7 0BN   *Tel:* (01325) 378230
(*Leeds Archdeaconry and Harrogate Deanery*) Miss Janet Newell, High Mistels, High View, Burnt Yates, Harrogate HG3 3ET
Tel: (01423) 771683
Development Education Worker Miss S. Reardon, 30 Ebberston Place, Leeds LS6 1AV   *Tel:* 0113–278 6208

MINISTRY AND TRAINING
Director of Training Canon James Bell, 12 Clotherholme Rd, Ripon HG4 2DA
 Tel and Fax: (01765) 604835
Post-Ordination Training Canon James Bell (*as above*)
Director of Ordinands Revd Penny Driver, The School House, Berrygate Lane, Sharow, Ripon HG4 5BJ *Tel:* (01765) 607017
Children's Work Adviser Mrs Carol Glen, Mallard View, Flawith Rd, Tholthorpe, York YO6 2JL *Tel:* (01347) 838017
Youth Work Adviser Capt Nic Sheppard, 7 Loxley Grove, Westherby LS22 7YG
 Tel: (01937) 585440
Warden, Readers' Association Revd Paul Tudge, Vicarage, 1 Scotland Close, Horsforth, Leeds LS18 5SG *Tel:* 0113–258 2433
 Fax: 0113–228 1057
Officer for Local Ministry Revd Stephen Brown, Ripley Rectory, Harrogate HG3 3AY *Tel:* (01423) 770147
Adviser for Non-Stipendiary Ministry Revd Dr David Peat, 12 North Grange Mews, Leeds LS6 2EW *Tel:* 0113–275 3179
Convenor of Advisory Group on Christian Healing Canon Rachel Stowe, Preston Cottage, East Cowton, Northallerton DL7 0BD *Tel* and *Fax:* (01325) 378173

LITURGICAL
Chairman The Dean of Ripon (*as above*)
Secretary Revd Paul Summers, Rectory, Kirkby Overblow, Harrogate HG3 1HD
 Tel and *Fax:* (01423) 872314

MISSIONARY AND ECUMENICAL
Dioc Missioner Vacancy
World Mission Officer Revd Peter Roberts, Vicarage, Church Lane, Collingham, Wetherby LS22 5AU *Tel:* (01937) 573975
Ecumenical Officer Canon Terence Munro, St Mark's Vicarage, St Mark's Ave, Leeds LS2 9BN *Tel:* 0113–245 4893
ACUPA Link Officer Vacancy
Sri-Lanka Companion Link Officer Revd David Paton-Williams, Rectory, Bedale DL8 1AF *Tel:* (01677) 422103

SOCIAL RESPONSIBILITY
Chairman The Dean of Ripon
Social Responsibility Officer Vacancy
Social Responsibility Office Leeds Church Institute, Leeming House, Vicar Lane, Leeds LS2 7JF *Tel:* 0113–234 3533
Community Chaplain for People with Learning Difficulties Revd Robert Brooke, 51 St James Approach, Leeds LS14 6JJ
 Tel: 0113–273 1396
Racial Justice Officer Vacancy
World Development Representative Revd Susan Whitehouse, Vicarage, Carperby, Leyburn DL8 4DQ *Tel:* (01969) 663235

COMMUNICATIONS
Communications Committee Revd John Carter, 7 Blenheim Court, Harrogate HG2 9DT *Tel:* (01423) 530369
 Fax: (01423) 538557
 e-mail: jhgcarter@aol.com
Press Officer Revd John Carter (*as above*)
Editor of Dioc Directory Mr Philip Arundel (*as above*)

DIOCESAN RECORD OFFICES
County Record Office, County Hall, Northallerton DL7 8DF (*County Archivist* Mr M. Y. Ashcroft) *Tel:* (01609) 3123; Leeds Archives Department, Chapeltown Rd, Sheepscar, Leeds LS7 3AP (*Leeds City Archivist* Mr William Connor)
 Tel: 0113–214 5814
 Fax: 0113–214 5815

STEWARDSHIP
Stewardship Adviser Mr Paul Winstanley, Dioc Office

AREA DEANS
ARCHDEACONRY OF RICHMOND
Harrogate (Acting) Revd Paul Summers, Rectory, Kirkby Overblow, Harrogate HG3 1HD *Tel:* (01423) 872314
Richmond Revd Peter Midwood, Rectory, Ronaldkirk, Barnard Castle DL12 9EE
 Tel: (01833) 650202
Ripon Revd Simon Talbott, Vicarage, Westerns Lane, Markington, Harrogate HG3 3PB *Tel:* (01765) 677123
Wensley Revd Clive Malpass, Vicarage, Askrigg, Leyburn DL8 3HZ
 Tel: (01969) 650301

ARCHDEACONRY OF LEEDS
Allerton Revd Stephen Jarratt, Vicarage, Wood Lane, Leeds LS7 3QF
 Tel: 0113–268 3072
Armley Revd Tim Lipscomb, Armley Vicarage, Wesley Rd, Leeds LS12 1SR
 Tel: 0113–263 8620
Headingley Revd Michael Cross, Headingley Vicarage, 16 Shire Oak Rd, Leeds LS6 2DE *Tel:* 0113–275 1526
Whitkirk Revd Alan Payne, Rectory, Kippax, Leeds LS25 7HF *Tel:* 0113–286 2710

DIOCESE OF ROCHESTER

Founded in 604. Kent west of the Medway, except for one parish in the south west (CHICHESTER); the Medway Towns; the London boroughs of Bromley and Bexley, except for a few parishes (SOUTHWARK); one parish in East Sussex.

Population 1,188,000 Area 542 sq m
Stipendiary Clergy 234 Benefices 192
Parishes 216 Churches 264

BISHOP (106th)
Rt Revd Michael Nazir-Ali PH D, Bishopscourt, Rochester, Kent ME1 1TS [1995]
Tel: (01634) 842721
Fax: (01634) 831136
[Michael Roffen:]
Chaplain Revd Paul Williams
Tel: (01634) 814439

SUFFRAGAN BISHOP
TONBRIDGE Rt Revd Brian Smith, Bishop's Lodge, 48 St Botolph's Rd, Sevenoaks, Kent TN13 3AG [1993]
Tel: (01732) 456070
Fax: (01732) 741449
e-mail: sevenoaks@clara.net

CATHEDRAL CHURCH OF CHRIST AND THE BLESSED VIRGIN MARY
Dean Very Revd Edward Shotter, The Deanery, Rochester, Kent ME1 1TG [1989]
Tel: (01634) 844023 (Home and Office)
(01634) 843366 (Cathedral Office)
Fax: (01634) 401410
Cathedral Office Cathedral Office, Garth House, The Precinct, Rochester, Kent ME1 1SX   *Tel:* (01634) 843366
Canons Residentiary
Vice-Dean Canon Edward Turner, Prebendal House, King's Orchard, The Precinct, Rochester, Kent ME1 1TG [1981]
Tel: (01634) 842756 (Office)
Fax: (01634) 843674
Canon Pastor Canon Jonathan Meyrick, 2 King's Orchard, The Precinct, Rochester, Kent ME1 1TG [1998] *Tel:* (01634) 841491
Canon Evangelist Ven Norman Warren, The Archdeaconry, Rochester, Kent ME1 1SX [1989] *Tel:* (01634) 842527
Precentor Canon John Armson, Easter Garth, King's Orchard, The Precinct, Rochester, Kent ME1 1SX [1989]
Tel: (01634) 406992
Cathedral Comptroller and Lay Canon Mr Christopher Hebron, Cathedral Office
Cathedral Organist and Director of Music Mr Roger Sayer, 7 Minor Canon Row, Rochester, Kent ME1 1ST *Tel:* (01634) 400723

ARCHDEACONS
ROCHESTER Ven Norman Warren, The Archdeaconry, Rochester, Kent ME1 1SX [1989] *Tel:* (01634) 842527
TONBRIDGE Ven Judith Rose, 3 The Ridings, Blackhurst Lane, Tunbridge Wells, Kent TN2 4RU [1996] *Tel:* (01892) 520660
BROMLEY Ven Garth Norman, 6 Horton Way, Farningham, Kent DA4 0DQ [1994]
Tel: (01322) 864522

CONVOCATION (MEMBERS OF THE HOUSE OF CLERGY OF THE GENERAL SYNOD)
Dignitaries in Convocation
The Dean of Rochester
The Archdeacon of Bromley
Proctors for Clergy
Revd John Banner
Canon Peter Lock
Canon Gordon Oliver
Ven Judith Rose

MEMBERS OF THE HOUSE OF LAITY OF THE GENERAL SYNOD
Mr James Cheeseman
Mrs Helen Jennings
Mr Ernie Mann
Mr Gerald O'Brien
Mrs Lesley Still
Mr David Webster

DIOCESAN OFFICERS
Dioc Secretary Mr Peter Law, St Nicholas Church, Boley Hill, Rochester, Kent ME1 1SL *Tel:* (01634) 830333
Fax: (01634) 829463
Chancellor of Diocese His Honour Judge Michael Goodman, Parkside, Dulwich Common, London SE21 7EU
Tel: 0181–693 3564
Registrar of Diocese and Bishop's Legal Secretary Mr Michael Thatcher, Registry Chambers, The Old Deanery, Dean's Court, London EC4V 5AA
Tel: 0171-593 5110
Fax: 0171-248 3221

DIOCESAN ORGANISATIONS
Diocesan Office St Nicholas Church, Boley Hill, Rochester, Kent ME1 1SL
Tel: (01634) 830333
Fax: (01634) 829463
e-mail: rochdiooff@cableinet.co.uk

ADMINISTRATION
Assistant Secretary Mr David Gater, Dioc Office
Assistant Secretary Mrs Penny Law, Dioc Office
Dioc Synod (Chairman, House of Clergy) Canon Peter Lock, Vicarage, 9 St Paul's Square, Bromley, Kent BR2 0XH *Tel:* 0181-460 6275; *(Chairman, House of Laity)* Mr David Webster, 5 Rosehill Walk, Tunbridge Wells, Kent TN1 1HL *Tel:* (01892) 526055; *(Secretary)* Mr Peter Law, Dioc Office
Board of Finance (Chairman) Mr Ian Fawkner, 13 Lyndhurst Drive, Sevenoaks, Kent TN13 2HD; *(Secretary)* Mr Peter Law *(as above)*; *(Dioc Treasurer)* Mr Dennis Barden, Dioc Office
Pastoral Committee Revd Brenda Hurd, Dioc Office
Board of Patronage Mrs Penny Law *(as above)*
Designated Officer Vacancy
Trusts Mrs Louise Kirby, Dioc Office

CHURCHES
Advisory Committee for the Care of Churches (Chairman) Canon Michael Hodge, Rectory, Rectory Drive, Bidborough, Tunbridge Wells, Kent TN3 0UL *Tel:* (01892) 528081; *(Administrator)* Mrs Sue Haydock, Dioc Office
Redundant Churches Uses Committee Revd Brenda Hurd *(as above)*

EDUCATION
Education Office Deanery Gate, The Precinct, Rochester, Kent ME1 1SJ
Tel: (01634) 843667
Fax: (01634) 843674
e-mail: education@rochester.anglican.org
Board of Education (Chairman) Canon David Herbert, Vicarage, Bickley Park Rd, Bickley, Bromley BR1 2BE
Acting Secretary and Director of Education Dr Diane Greenwood, Educ Office
Schools Adviser Dr Diane Greenwood *(as above)*
Assistant Director of Education (Parishes) Capt Neil Thomson, Educ Office
Financial Administrator Mr John Constanti, Educ Office
Children's Work Adviser Sister Jacqui Hill, Educ Office

MINISTRY
Advisory Council for Ministry and Training (*Chairman*) The Bishop of Tonbridge (*as above*); (*Secretary and Director of Training*) Canon Gordon Oliver, Dioc Office
Lay Ministry Adviser Revd Dr Jeremy Ive, Dioc Office
Director of Ordinands Canon Paul Longbottom, Vicarage, Butchers Hill, Shorne, Gravesend, Kent DA12 3EB
Tel: (01474) 822239
Associate Director of Ordinands Revd Elizabeth Walker, Rectory, 266 Rochester Rd, Burham, Rochester, Kent ME1 3RJ
Tel: (01634) 666862
Ministry Development Officer Revd Anne Dyer, Dioc Office
Director of Continuing Ministerial Education Canon Gordon Oliver (*as above*)
Readers' Association (*Warden*) Mr John Field, Dioc Office
Clerical Registry and Dioc Retirement Officer Revd Brian Pearson, St Placid's, 32 Swan St, West Malling, Kent ME19 6LP
Tel: (01732) 848462

LITURGICAL
Chairman Revd Paul Wright, Rectory, 1 Claremont Crescent, Crayford, Kent DA1 4RJ   Tel: (01322) 522078
Secretary Revd Jonathan Watson, Vicarage, 44A Colyers Lane, Erith, Kent DA8 3NP
Tel: (01322) 332809

MISSIONARY AND ECUMENICAL
Council for Mission and Unity (*Chairman*) The Archdeacon of Rochester; (*Secretary*) Revd Heather Turner, Rectory, Borough Green Rd, Wrotham, Kent TN15 7RA
Tel: (01732) 882211

PRESS, PUBLICITY AND PUBLICATIONS
Communications Officer Revd Christopher Stone, The Flat, Bishopscourt, Rochester, Kent ME1 1TS   Tel: (01634) 404343
Fax: (01634) 402793

DIOCESAN RECORD OFFICES
Kent Archives Office, County Hall, Maidstone, Kent ME14 1XH Tel: (01622) 671411; Archives Office, Civic Centre, Strood, Rochester, Kent   Tel: (01634) 727777

SOCIAL RESPONSIBILITY
Canterbury and Rochester Dioc Joint Council for Social Responsibility (*Senior Adviser*) Canon David Grimwood, 60 Marsham St, Maidstone, Kent ME14 1EW
Tel: (01622) 755014 *and* 686814
Dioc Committee for the Deaf (*Chairman*) Ven Judith Rose (*as above*)
Industrial Chaplain Revd Noel Beattie, 181 Maidstone Rd, Chatham, Kent ME4 6JG
Tel: (01634) 844867

RURAL DEANS
ARCHDEACONRY OF ROCHESTER
Cobham Revd James Tipp, Vicarage, St Katherine's Lane, Snodland, Kent ME6 5EH   Tel: (01634) 240232
Dartford Revd David Kitley, Vicarage, 67 Shepherds Lane, Dartford, Kent DA1 2NS
Tel: (01322) 220036
Gillingham Revd Paul Harvey, Vicarage, 27 Gillingham Green, Gillingham, Kent ME7 2RL   Tel: (01634) 850529
Gravesend Revd Clifford Goble, Rectory, Hook Green Rd, Southfleet, Kent DA13 9NQ   Tel: (01474) 833252
Rochester Revd Christopher Collins, Luton Rectory, Capstone Rd, Chatham, Kent ME5 7PN   Tel: (01634) 843780

Strood Revd David Low, Vicarage, Vicarage Lane, Hoo, Rochester, Kent ME3 9BB
Tel: (01634) 250291

ARCHDEACONRY OF BROMLEY
Beckenham Canon Douglas Redman, Vicarage, 37 Kingswood Rd, Shortlands, Bromley, Kent BR2 0HG
Tel: 0181–460 4989
Bromley Canon Peter Lock, Vicarage, 9 St Paul's Square, Bromley, Kent BR2 0XH
Tel: 0181–460 6275
Erith Revd David Springthorpe, Vicarage, 93 Pelham Rd, Barnehurst, Bexleyheath, Kent DA7 4LY   Tel: (01322) 523344
Orpington Revd Paul Miller, Vicarage, 46 World's End Lane, Green Street Green, Orpington, Kent BR6 6AG
Tel: (01689) 852905
Sidcup Revd Nicholas Kerr, Vicarage, 64 Days Lane, Sidcup, Kent DA15 8JR
Tel: 0181-300 1508

ARCHDEACONRY OF TONBRIDGE
Malling Revd Dr Brian Stevenson, Vicarage, 138 High St, West Malling, Kent ME19 6NE   Tel: (01732) 842245
Paddock Wood Canon Dennis Winter, Vicarage, 169 Maidstone Rd, Paddock Wood, Tonbridge, Kent TN12 6DZ
Tel: (01892) 833917
Sevenoaks Revd Dr Brian Godfrey, Rectory, Chevening Rd, Sundridge, Sevenoaks, Kent TN14 6AB   Tel: (01959) 563749
Shoreham Vacancy
Tonbridge Revd Robert Bawtree, Vicarage, 194 Tonbridge Rd, Hildenborough, Kent TN11 9HR   Tel: (01732) 833596
Tunbridge Wells Revd Francis Cumberlege, Vicarage, 1 St Mark's Rd, Tunbridge Wells, Kent TN2 5LT   Tel: (01892) 526069

DIOCESE OF ST ALBANS

Founded in 1877. Hertfordshire, except for a small area in the south (LONDON) and one parish in the west (OXFORD); Bedfordshire, except for one parish in the north (ELY) and one parish in the west (OXFORD); an area of Greater London.

Population 1,631,000   Area 1,116 sq m
Stipendiary Clergy 298   Benefices 238
Parishes 332   Churches 407

BISHOP (9th)
Rt Revd Christopher William Herbert, Abbey Gate House, St Albans, Herts AL3 4HD [1995]   Tel: (01727) 853305
Fax: (01727) 846715
[Christopher St Albans]

Chaplain Revd Derwyn Williams
Secretaries Mrs Mary Handford, Mrs Lynn Bridger

SUFFRAGAN BISHOPS
HERTFORD Rt Revd Robin Jonathan Norman Smith, Hertford House, Abbey Mill Lane, St Albans, Herts AL3 4HE [1990]
Tel: (01727) 866420
Fax: (01727) 811426
BEDFORD Rt Revd John Henry Richardson, 168 Kimbolton Rd, Bedford MK41 8DN [1994]   Tel: (01234) 357551
Fax: (01234) 218134

HONORARY ASSISTANT BISHOPS
Rt Revd and Rt Hon the Lord Runcie of Cuddesdon, 26A Jennings Rd, St Albans, Herts AL1 4PD
Rt Revd David John Farmbrough, St Michael Mead, 110 Village Rd, Bromham, Beds MK43 8HU [1993] Tel: (01234) 825042
Rt Revd Edwin Ronald Barnes, 14 Hall Place Gardens, St Albans, Herts AL1 3SP
Tel: (01727) 857764
Fax: (01727) 763025

CATHEDRAL AND ABBEY CHURCH OF ST ALBAN
Dean Very Revd Christopher Lewis PH D, The Deanery, Sumpter Yard, St Albans, Herts AL1 1BY [1994]   Tel: (01727) 852120
Cathedral Office The Chapter House, Sumpter Yard, St Albans, Herts AL1 1BY
Tel: (01727) 860780
Fax: (01727) 850944
e-mail: cathedra@alban.u-net.com
Web:
www.stalbansdioc.org.uk/cathedral/
Canons Residentiary
Canon Christopher Foster, (*Sub-Dean*),

The Old Rectory, Sumpter Yard, St Albans, Herts AL1 1BY [1994]
Tel: (01727) 854827
Canon Carl Garner, Holywell Close, 43 Holywell Hill, St Albans, Herts AL1 1HD [1984]   Tel: (01727) 854832
Canon Bill Ritson, 2 Sumpter Yard, St Albans, Herts AL1 1BY [1987]
Tel: (01727) 861744
Canon Michael Sansom PH D, 4D Harpenden Rd, St Albans, Herts AL3 5AB [1988]   Tel: (01727) 833777
Canon Anders Bergquist PH D, 7 Corder Close, St Albans, Herts AL3 4NH [1997]
Tel: (01727) 841116
Precentor Revd David Munchin, 1 The Deanery, Sumpter Yard, St Albans, Herts AL1 1BY [1996]   Tel: (01727) 855321
Chaplain Revd Dr Christopher Pines, Deanery Barn, Sumpter Yard, St Albans, Herts AL1 1BY [1997]   Tel: (01727) 854950
Cathedral Administrator Mr Nicholas Bates, Cathedral Office
Master of the Music Mr Andrew Lucas, 31 Abbey Mill Lane, St Albans, Herts AL3 4HA   Tel: (01727) 864780
Assistant Master of the Music and Director of the St Albans Abbey Girls' Choir Mr Andrew Parnell, 16 Glenferrie Rd, St Albans, Herts AL1 4JU Tel: (01727) 867818
Cathedral Education Officer Susanna Ainsworth, Education Centre, Sumpter Yard, St Albans, Herts AL1 1BY
Tel: (01727) 836223
Archaeological Consultant Prof Martin Biddle
Architect Mr Andrew Anderson

ARCHDEACONS
ST ALBANS Ven Richard Cheetham, 6 Sopwell Lane, St Albans, Herts AL1 1RR [1999] (*From March 1999*)
Tel: (01727) 857973
Fax: (01727) 837294
BEDFORD Ven Malcolm Lesiter, 17 Lansdowne Rd, Luton, Beds LU3 1EE [1993]   Tel: (01582) 730722
Fax: (01582) 877354
HERTFORD Ven Trevor Jones, St Mary's House, Church Lane, Stapleford, Hertford SG14 3NB [1997]   Tel: (01992) 581629
Fax: (01992) 558745

CONVOCATION (MEMBERS OF THE HOUSE OF CLERGY OF THE GENERAL SYNOD)
Dignitaries in Convocation
The Dean of St Albans
The Archdeacon of Bedford
Proctors for Clergy
Canon Brian Andrews
Revd Mark Bonney
Revd Christine Hardman
Canon Les Oglesby
Canon Patience Purchas
Canon Hugh Wilcox

MEMBERS OF THE HOUSE OF LAITY OF THE GENERAL SYNOD
Mr Anthony Archer
Dr Keith Barker
Mr Michael Catty
Mrs Anna de Lange
Mr Paul Godfrey
Mrs Shirley Jackson
Mr Philip Lovegrove
Mrs Christina Rees
Mr David Warner

DIOCESAN OFFICERS
Dioc Secretary Mr Lawrence Nicholls, Holywell Lodge, 41 Holywell Hill, St Albans, Herts AL1 1HE
Tel: (01727) 854532
Fax: (01727) 844469
e-mail: stalbans@cix.compulink.co.uk
Chancellor of Diocese His Honour the Worshipful Canon Rupert Bursell, Holywell Lodge, 41 Holywell Hill, St Albans, Herts AL1 1HD   Tel: (01727) 865765
Registrar of Diocese and Bishop's Legal Secretary Mr David Cheetham (*same address*)
Surveyor Mr William Handford, c/o 41 Holywell Hill, St Albans, Herts AL1 1HE
Tel: (01727) 854516

DIOCESAN ORGANISATIONS
Diocesan Office Holywell Lodge, 41 Holywell Hill, St Albans, Herts AL1 1HE
Tel: (01727) 854532
Fax: (01727) 844469
e-mail: stalbans@cix.compulink.co.uk

ADMINISTRATION
Dioc Synod (*Chairman, House of Clergy*) Canon Brian Andrews; (*Chairman, House of Laity*) Mr Nicholas Alexander; (*Secretary*) Mr Lawrence Nicholls, Dioc Office
Board of Finance (*Chairman*) Mr Philip Lovegrove, Vicarage, 159 Baldwins Lane, Croxley Green, Rickmansworth, Herts WD3 3LL Tel: (01923) 232387; (*Secretary*) Mr Lawrence Nicholls (*as above*)

Financial Secretary Mr Stephen Rider, Dioc Office
Estates Secretary Mrs Michèle Manders, Dioc Office
Board of Patronage Mr Roger Collor, Dioc Office
Designated Officers (Joint) Mr David Cheetham and Mr Lawrence Nicholls, Dioc Office
Pastoral Committee Mr Roger Collor (*as above*)
Trusts Mrs Emma Critchley, Dioc Office

CHURCHES
Advisory Committee for the Care of Churches (*Chairman*) Canon Neil Collings, Dioc Office; (*Secretary*) Mr Roger Collor (*as above*)

EDUCATION
Dioc Resource Centre Education Centre, Hall Grove, Welwyn Garden City, Herts AL7 4PJ   *Tel:* (01707) 332321   *Fax:* (01707) 373089
Director of Education Vacancy, Education Centre (*as above*)
Schools Adviser Mr Richard Butcher (*same address*)
Youth Officer Mr David Green (*same address*)
Children's Work Adviser Revd Andrew Pattman (*same address*)

MINISTRY
Director of Ordinands Canon Michael Sansom, 4D Harpenden Rd, St Albans, Herts AL3 5AB   *Tel:* (01727) 833777
Ministerial Development Officer Canon Anders Bergquist, Dioc Office
   Tel: (01727) 830802
Continuing Ministerial Education Officer Revd Dr Alan Winton, Dioc Office
   Tel: (01727) 830802
Adult Education Adviser Vacancy, Dioc Office   *Tel:* (01727) 830802
Bishop's Officer for Women's and Non-Stipendiary Ministry Canon Patience Purchas, Rectory, Church St, Wheathampstead, Herts AL4 8LR
   Tel and *Fax:* (01582) 834285
Board of Readers' Work (Hon Secretary) Mr Philip McDonough, 28 Washbrook Close, Barton-le-Cley, Beds MK45 4LF
   Tel: (01582) 881772

LITURGICAL
Chairman Canon Michael Sansom (*as above*)

MISSIONARY AND ECUMENICAL
Ecumenical Officer Revd Dr David Butler, 114 High St, Watton-at-Stone, Hertford SG14 3RZ   *Tel:* (01920) 831011

Board of Mission and Unity Mrs Carolyn Mercurio, Holy Saviour Vicarage, St Anne's Rd, Hitchin, Herts SG5 1QB
   Tel: (01462) 456140
Council for Partnership in World Mission Revd John Schild, Vicarage, Church Rd, Kings Walden, Hitchin, Herts SG4 8JX
   Tel: (01438) 871278
Workplace Ministry The Administrator, 41 Holywell Hill, St Albans, Herts AL1 1HE
   Tel: (01727) 869461

PRESS AND PUBLICATIONS
Dioc Communications Officer Capt Andrew Crooks, Dioc Office   *Tel:* (01727) 869506 (01582) 467247 (Home)
Editor of Dioc Directory Mr Lawrence Nicholls (*as above*)
Dioc Leaflet Mr Roy Watson, Dioc Office

DIOCESAN RECORDS OFFICES
County Hall, Hertford, Herts SG13 8DE (*County Archivist* Dr Kate Thompson) *Tel:* (01992) 555105; County Hall, Bedford MK42 9AP (*County Archivist* Kevin Ward)
   Tel: (01234) 63222, Ext 277

SOCIAL RESPONSIBILITY
Board for Social Responsibility (Adviser and Secretary) Revd Richard Wheeler, Dioc Office   *Tel:* (01727) 851748

STEWARDSHIP
Stewardship Development Officer Mr Nigel Guard, Dioc Office   *Tel:* (01727) 854532

RURAL DEANS
ARCHDEACONRY OF ST ALBANS
Aldenham Revd Grant Fellows, Vicarage, Church Field, Christchurch Crescent, Radlett, Herts WD7 8EE
   Tel: (01923) 856606
Berkhamsted Revd Richard Clarkson, Kingsmead, Gravel Path, Berkhampstead, Herts HP4 2PH   *Tel:* (01442) 873014
Hemel Hempstead Revd Paul Hughes, St John's Vicarage, 10 Charles St, Boxmoor, Hemel Hempstead, Herts HP1 1JH
   Tel: (01442) 255382
Hitchin Revd Frank Mercurio, Holy Saviour Vicarage, St Ann's Rd, Hitchin, Herts SG5 1QR   *Tel:* (01462) 456140
Rickmansworth Revd John Kingsley-Smith, Christ Church Vicarage, Chorleywood Common, Rickmansworth, Herts WD3 5SG   *Tel:* (01923) 282149
St Albans Revd Tony Hurle, St Paul's Vicarage, 7 Brampton Rd, St Albans, Herts AL1 4PN   *Tel:* (01727) 836810
   (01727) 846281 (Office)

Watford Revd John Brown, St Michael's Vicarage, 5 Mildred Ave, Watford, Herts WD1 7DY   *Tel:* (01923) 232460
Wheathampstead Revd Tom Purchas, Rectory, Church St, Wheathampstead, Herts AL4 8LR   *Tel:* (01582) 833144

ARCHDEACONRY OF BEDFORD
Ampthill Revd Norman Jeffery, Vicarage, 30 Church Rd, Woburn Sands, Milton Keynes MK17 8TG   *Tel:* (01908) 582581
Bedford Revd Trevor Maines, Vicarage, Goldington, Bedford MK41 0AP
   Tel: (01234) 355024
Biggleswade Canon Robert Sibson, Vicarage, Shortmead St, Biggleswade, Beds SG18 0AT   *Tel:* (01767) 312243
Dunstable Revd Graham Newton, Rectory, 8 Furness Ave, Dunstable, Beds LU6 3BN
   Tel: (01582) 664467
Elstow Revd Christopher Strong, Vicarage, Wootton, Bedford MK43 9HF
   Tel: (01234) 768391
Luton Revd Barry Etherington, Vicarage, 33 Felix Ave, Luton, Beds LU2 7LE
   Tel: (01582) 724754
Sharnbrook Revd Ian Arthur, Rectory, 81 High St, Sharnbrook, Bedford MK44 1PE
   Tel: (01234) 781444
Shefford Revd Ken Dixon, Rectory, 8 Rectory Close, Clifton, Shefford, Beds SG17 5EL   *Tel:* (01462) 850150

ARCHDEACONRY OF HERTFORD
Barnet Revd Roger Huddleston, Holy Trinity Vicarage, 18 Lyonsdown Rd, New Barnet EN5 1JE   *Tel:* 0181–449 0382
Bishop's Stortford Revd Clive Slaughter, Rectory, Vicerons Place, Thorley, Bishop's Stortford, Herts CM23 4EL
   Tel: (01279) 654955
Buntingford Revd Leslie Harman, Vicarage, 31 Baldock Rd, Royston, Herts SG8 5BJ   *Tel:* (01763) 246371 (Office)
   (01763) 243145 (Home)
Cheshunt Revd John Springbett, Vicarage, 11 Amwell St, Hoddesdon, Herts EN11 8TS   *Tel:* (01992) 462127
Hatfield Revd Jim Smith, Vicarage, 4 Bury Lane, Codicote, Hitchin, Herts SG8 8XT
   Tel: (01438) 820266
Hertford and Ware (Joint rural deans) Revd Graham Edwards, St Andrew's Rectory, 43 North Rd, Hertford SG14 1LZ
   Tel: (01992) 582726
Revd Barry Goodwin, Vicarage, 25 Hoddesdon Rd, Stanstead Abbots, Ware, Herts SG12 8EG   *Tel:* (01920) 870115
Stevenage Revd Melvyn Barnsley, Rectory, Cuttys Lane, Stevenage, Herts SG1 1UP
   Tel: (01438) 351631

DIOCESE OF ST EDMUNDSBURY AND IPSWICH

Founded in 1914. Suffolk, except for a small area in the north-east (NORWICH); one parish in Essex.

Population 590,000 Area 1,439 sq m
Stipendiary Clergy 175 Benefices 182
Parishes 443 Churches 479

BISHOP (9th)
Rt Revd (John Hubert) Richard Lewis, Bishop's House, 4 Park Rd, Ipswich, Suffolk IP1 3ST [1997] Tel: (01473) 252829
Fax: (01473) 232552
[Richard St Edm and Ipswich]

Bishop's Secretary Mrs Marion Crane (*same address*)

SUFFRAGAN BISHOP
DUNWICH Rt Revd Tim Stevens, 28 Westerfield Rd, Ipswich, Suffolk IP4 2UJ [1995]
Tel: (01473) 222276
Fax: (01473) 210303
Bishop's Secretary Mrs Kati Wakefield (*same address*)

CATHEDRAL CHURCH OF ST JAMES, BURY ST EDMUNDS
Provost Very Revd James Edgar Atwell, Provost's House, Bury St Edmunds, Suffolk IP33 1RS [1995] Tel: (01284) 754852
Cathedral Office Cathedral Office, Angel Hill, Bury St Edmunds, Suffolk IP33 1LS
Tel: (01284) 754933
Fax: (01284) 768655
Canons Residentiary
Precentor Canon Martin Shaw, 1 Abbey Precincts, Bury St Edmunds, Suffolk IP33 1RS [1989] Tel: (01284) 761982
e-mail: baritone@globalnet.co.uk
Chapter Clerk Canon Marion Mingins, 2 Abbey Precincts, Bury St Edmunds, Suffolk IP33 1RS [1993] Tel: (01284) 753396
Cathedral Chaplain Revd Richard Davey, Clopton Cottage, The Churchyard, Bury St Edmunds, Suffolk IP33 1RS
Tel: (01284) 755868
Clerk to the Administrative Chapter Mr Christopher Fowler, Cathedral Office
Arts and Visitors Officer Mr Charles Borthwick, Cathedral Office
Director of Music Mr Scott Farrell, Cathedral Office Tel: (01284) 725778

ARCHDEACONS
IPSWICH Ven Terry Gibson, 99 Valley Rd, Ipswich, Suffolk IP1 4NF [1984]
Tel: (01473) 250333
Fax: (01473) 286877
SUDBURY Ven John Cox, 84 Southgate St, Bury St Edmunds, Suffolk IP33 2BJ
Tel: (01284) 766796
Fax: (01284) 723163
SUFFOLK Ven Geoffrey Arrand, Glebe House, The Street, Ashfield cum Thorpe, Stowmarket, Suffolk IP14 6LX [1994]
Tel: (01728) 685497
Fax: (01728) 685969

CONVOCATION (MEMBERS OF THE HOUSE OF CLERGY OF THE GENERAL SYNOD)
The Archdeacon of Ipswich
Proctors for Clergy
Revd Graham Archer
Canon Colin Bevington
Canon Cedric Catton

MEMBERS OF THE HOUSE OF LAITY OF THE GENERAL SYNOD
Mrs Jenny Freeman
Mr Richard Simmons
Mr Tony Redman
Mr Peter Smith

DIOCESAN OFFICERS
Dioc Secretary Mr Nicholas Edgell, Diocesan House, Tower St, Ipswich, Suffolk IP1 3BG Tel: (01473) 211028
Fax: (01473) 232407
e-mail: dbf@stedmundsbury.anglican.org
Chancellor of Diocese The Honourable Mr Justice Blofeld, 20–32 Museum St, Ipswich, Suffolk IP1 1HZ
Registrar of Diocese and Bishop's Legal Secretary Mr James Hall, 20/32 Museum St, Ipswich, Suffolk IP1 1HZ
Tel: (01473) 232300
Fax: (01473) 230524

DIOCESAN ORGANISATIONS
Diocesan Office Diocesan House, Tower St, Ipswich, Suffolk IP1 3BG
Tel: (01473) 211028
Fax: (01473) 232407
e-mail: dbf@stedmundsbury.anglican.org

ADMINISTRATION
Dioc Secretary Mr Nicholas Edgell, Dioc House
Dioc Synod (*Chairman, House of Clergy*) Canon Cedric Catton, Vicarage, Exning, Newmarket CB8 7HS Tel: (01638) 577413; (*Chairman, House of Laity*) Mr Peter Smith, Lusaka House, Great Glemham, Saxmundham IP17 2DH Tel: (01728) 663466; (*Secretary*) Mr Nicholas Edgell, Dioc House
Board of Finance (*Chairman*) Brigadier Adam Gurdon, Burgh House, Burgh, Woodbridge, Suffolk IP13 6PU Tel: (01473) 735273; (*Secretary*) Mr Nicholas Edgell (*as above*)
Assistants Mr James Halsall, Mr Eric Brown, Mr Malcolm Green
Financial Controller Mrs Katy Reade, Dioc House
Dioc Surveyor Mr Tony Hatch, Dioc House
Board of Patronage Mr Nicholas Edgell (*as above*)
Pastoral Committee Mr Nicholas Edgell (*as above*)
Glebe and Investment Committee Mr Nicholas Edgell (*as above*)
Parsonages Committee Mr Eric Brown (*as above*)
Designated Officer Mr Nicholas Edgell (*as above*)

CHURCHES
Advisory Committee for the Care of Churches (*Chairman*) Mrs Hester Agate, The Old Rectory, Chattisham, Ipswich, Suffolk IP8 3PY Tel and Fax: (01473) 652306
(*Secretary*) Mr James Halsall (*as above*)
Church Buildings Committee (*Chairman*) The Hon Jill Ganzoni, Rivendell, Spring Meadow, Playford, Ipswich IP6 9ED
Tel: (01473) 624662
Secretary Mrs Brenda Fradd, Dioc House
Redundant Churches Uses Committee: (*Chairman*) The Hon Jill Ganzoni; (*Secretary*) Mr Nicholas Edgell (*as above*)

COUNSELLING
Adviser in Pastoral Care and Counselling Revd Harry Edwards, Rectory, Marlesford, Woodbridge IP13 0AT
Tel: (01728) 746747
e-mail: Harry@psalm23.demon.co.uk
Bishop's Adviser on Exorcism and Deliverance Revd Philip Gray, Vicarage, Mendlesham, Stowmarket IP14 5RS
Tel: (01449) 766359

St Edmundsbury and Ipswich

MINISTRY

Ministry Development Group (*Chairman*) The Bishop of Dunwich (*as above*)
Vocations Adviser Revd Michael Stone, Chanters Mead, School Rd, Coddenham, Ipswich IP6 9PS Tel: (01449) 760631
Continuing Ministerial Education 1–4 Revd Mark Sanders, Rectory, The Street, Framsden, Stowmarket, Suffolk IP14 6MG
 Tel: (01473) 890934
Dioc Director of Ordinands Canon Marion Mingins, 2 Abbey Precincts, Bury St Edmunds, Suffolk IP33 1RS
 Tel: (01284) 753396
Assistant Dioc Director of Ordinands Revd Mark Sanders (*as above*)
Principal of Ministry Scheme Canon Michael West PH D, c/o Dioc House
Officer for Local Non-Stipendiary Ministry Canon Roger Pallant, Rectory, Glebe Close, Sproughton, Ipswich IP8 3BQ
 Tel: (01473) 241078
Dioc Adviser for Women's Ministry Canon Sally Fogden, Rectory, Honington, Bury St Edmunds IP31 1RG Tel: (01359) 269265
Lay Education and Training Adviser Miss Elizabeth Moore, Dioc House
 Tel: (01473) 254263
Dioc Youth and Children's Advise Ms Jane Boyce, Dioc House Tel: (01473) 216944
Dioc Widows Officers Canon John and Mrs Marjorie Gore, 8 De Burgh Place, Clare, Sudbury CO10 8QL Tel: (01787) 278558
Clergy Retirement Officer Canon Dennis Pearce, 74 Hintlesham Drive, Orwell Green, Felixstowe IP11 8YL
 Tel: (01394) 279189

SCHOOLS

Dioc Director of Education Revd Clare Sanders, Dioc House Tel: (01473) 254263
Deputy Dioc Director of Education Mrs Barbara Rowe, Dioc House
Schools Administrator Mr Andrew Firth, Dioc House

LITURGICAL

Chairman The Bishop of St Edmundsbury and Ipswich
Secretary Very Revd Canon Stuart Morris, The Deanery, Hadleigh, Ipswich IP7 5DT
 Tel: (01473) 822218

MISSION AND SOCIAL RESPONSIBILITY

Mission Group (*Chairman*) The Archdeacon of Suffolk (*as above*)

Mission and Rural Affairs Adviser c/o Dioc Secretary
Stewardship Adviser c/o Mr Malcolm Green, Dioc House
Social Responsibility Adviser c/o Dioc Secretary
FLAME – Family Life and Marriage Education Mrs Kathy Blair, 59 Old Barrack Rd, Woodbridge IP12 4ER
 Tel: (01394) 382030
Suffolk Christian Resource Library Dioc House Tel: (01473) 213452

COMMUNICATIONS

Dioc Communications Officer Canon Simon Pettitt, Dioc House and 3 Crown St, Bury St Edmunds, Suffolk IP33 1QX
 Tel and *Fax*: (01284) 753866
 (0850) 480533 (Mobile)
 e-mail: canon@globalnet.co.uk
Editor of Dioc Directory Canon Simon Pettitt (*as above*)
Editor of 'The Church in Suffolk' Canon Simon Pettitt (*as above*)

DIOCESAN RECORD OFFICES

77 Raingate St, Bury St Edmunds, Suffolk IP33 2AR Tel: (01284) 352000 *Ext.* 2352; Gatacre Rd, Ipswich IP1 2LQ Tel: (01473) 264541; The Central Library, Lowestoft NR32 1DR Tel: (01502) 566325 *Ext.* 3308

SPIRITUALITY

Bishop's Adviser in Spirituality Canon Martin Shaw, 1 Abbey Precincts, Bury St Edmunds IP33 1RS Tel: (01284) 761982
Dioc Spiritual Director for Cursillo Revd Ian Morgan, Rectory, 74 Ancaster Rd, Ipswich IP2 9AJ Tel: (01473) 601895
Lay Director for Cursillo Mrs Christine Kreckler, 3 Pine Leys, Tollgate Lane, Bury St Edmunds IP32 6DF Tel: (01284) 763778

RURAL DEANS
ARCHDEACONRY OF IPSWICH

Bosmere Revd Roger Dedman, Vicarage, Vicarage Lane, Bramford, Ipswich, Suffolk IP8 4AE Tel: (01473) 741105
Colneys Canon Geoffrey Grant, Rectory, Nacton, Ipswich, Suffolk IP10 0HY
 Tel: (01473) 659232
Hadleigh Very Revd Canon Stuart Morris, The Deanery, Hadleigh, Ipswich, Suffolk IP7 5DT Tel: (01473) 822318

Ipswich Revd David Cutts, St Margaret's Vicarage, 32 Constable Rd, Ipswich IP4 2UW Tel: (01473) 253906
Samford Canon Roger Pallant, Rectory, Glebe Close, Sproughton, Ipswich IP8 3BQ Tel: (01473) 241078
Stowmarket Revd Nigel Hartley, Rectory, Woodland Close, Onehouse, Stowmarket IP14 3HL Tel: (01449) 614378
Woodbridge Revd Robert Clifton, Rectory, Orford, Woodbridge, Suffolk IP12 2NN
 Tel: (01394) 450336

ARCHDEACONRY OF SUDBURY

Clare Revd Edmund Betts, Rectory, 10 Hopton Rise, Hanchett Grange, Haverhill, Suffolk CB9 9FS Tel: (01440) 708768
Ixworth Revd David Mathers, Thurston Vicarage, Bury St Edmunds, Suffolk IP31 3RU Tel: (01359) 230301
Lavenham Revd Derrick Stiff, Rectory, Lavenham, Sudbury, Suffolk CO10 9SA
 Tel: (01787) 247244
Mildenhall Canon Geoffrey Smith, St Mary's Rectory, 5A Fitzroy St, Newmarket, Suffolk CB8 0JW
 Tel: (01638) 662448
Sudbury Revd Lawrence Pizzey, Rectory, Christopher Lane, Sudbury, Suffolk CO10 6AS Tel: (01787) 372611
Thingoe Revd David Underwood, St John's Vicarage, 37 Well St, Bury St Edmunds IP33 1EQ Tel: (01284) 754335

ARCHDEACONRY OF SUFFOLK

Beccles and South Elmham Canon Jonathan Falkner, Church House, Low St, Ilketshall St Margaret, Bungay, Suffolk IP35 1QZ
 Tel: (01986) 781345
Halesworth Revd Tony Norton, Vicarage, Church Lane, Spexhall, Halesworth, Suffolk IP19 0RQ
 Tel and *Fax*: (01986) 875453
Hartismere Revd Christopher Atkinson, Vicarage, 41 Castle St, Eye, Suffolk IP23 7AW Tel: (01379) 870277
Loes Canon Richard Addington Hall, Vicarage, Charsfield, Woodbridge, Suffolk IP13 7PY Tel: (01473) 37740
Saxmundham Canon Roger Smith, Rectory, Rectory Rd, Middleton, Saxmundham, Suffolk IP17 3NR
 Tel: (01728) 648421

DIOCESE OF SALISBURY

Founded in 1075, formerly Sherborne (AD 705) and Ramsbury (AD 909). Wiltshire, except for the northern quarter (BRISTOL); Dorset, except for an area in the east (WINCHESTER); a small area of Hampshire; a parish in Devon.

Population 840,000   Area 2,046 sq m
Stipendiary Clergy 239   Benefices 183
Parishes 451   Churches 577

BISHOP (77th)
Rt Revd David Stancliffe D LITT, South Canonry, 71 The Close, Salisbury, Wilts SP1 2ER [1993]   Tel: (01722) 334031
Fax: (01722) 413112
e-mail: 101324.1053@compuserve.com
[David Sarum]

AREA BISHOPS
SHERBORNE Rt Revd John Dudley Galtrey Kirkham, Little Bailie, Dullar Lane, Sturminster Marshall, Wimborne, Dorset BH21 4AD [1976]   Tel: (01258) 857659
Fax: (01258) 857961
RAMSBURY Vacancy

HONORARY ASSISTANT BISHOP
Rt Revd John Kingsmill Cavell, 5 Constable Way, West Harnham, Salisbury, Wilts SP2 8LN   Tel: (01722) 334352

CATHEDRAL CHURCH OF THE BLESSED VIRGIN MARY
Dean Very Revd Derek Richard Watson, The Deanery, 7 The Close, Salisbury, Wilts SP1 2EF [1996]
Cathedral Office 6 The Close, Salisbury SP1 2EF   Tel: (01722) 555110
Fax: (01722) 555155
Canons Residentiary
Precentor Canon Jeremy Davies, Hungerford Chantry, 54 The Close, Salisbury, Wilts SP1 2EL [1985]
Tel: (01722) 555179 (Home)
Office Dept of Liturgy and Music, Ladywell, 33 The Close, Salisbury SP1 2EJ
Tel: (01722) 555125
Fax: (01722) 555116
e-mail: jeremy@mcenery.demon.co.uk
Treasurer Canon June Osborne, 23 The Close, Salisbury, Wilts SP1 2EH [1995]
Tel: (01722) 555176
Fax: (01722) 555177
e-mail: OSBGOULD@aol.com
Chancellor Canon David Durston, 24 The Close, Salisbury, Wilts SP1 2EH [1992]
Tel: (01722) 555193
Fax: (01722) 323569

Chapter Clerk Brigadier Christopher (Kit) Owen, Cathedral Office
Tel: (01722) 555100
Fax: (01722) 555109
e-mail: CHAPTEROFF@aol.com
Director of Music Mr Simon Lole, Dept of Liturgy and Music (*as above*)

ARCHDEACONS
SHERBORNE Ven Paul Wheatley, Rectory, West Stafford, Dorchester, Dorset DT2 8AB [1991]   Tel: (01305) 264637
Fax: (01305) 260640
e-mail: 101543.3471@compuserve.com
DORSET Ven Geoffrey Walton, Vicarage, Witchampton, Wimborne, Dorset BH21 5AP [1982]   Tel: (01258) 840422
Fax: (01258) 840786
WILTS Ven Barney Hopkinson, Sarum House, High St, Urchfont, Devizes, Wilts SN10 4QH [1986]   Tel: (01380) 840373
Fax: (01380) 848247
e-mail: adsarum@compuserve.com
SARUM (Acting) Ven Barney Hopkinson (*as above*)

CONVOCATION (MEMBERS OF THE HOUSE OF CLERGY OF THE GENERAL SYNOD)
The Archdeacon of Wilts
Proctors for Clergy
Revd Christopher Brown
Revd Mary Crameri
Canon Jeremy Davies
Canon Barry Lomax

MEMBERS OF THE HOUSE OF LAITY OF THE GENERAL SYNOD
Mrs Rosemary Bassett
Mrs Mary Bordass
Mr Paul Boyd-Lee
Lt Col John Darlington
Mrs Jane Dibdin
Mrs Deirdre Ducker
Mr James Humphery
Mrs Anne Parry

DIOCESAN OFFICERS
Dioc Secretary Revd Karen Curnock, Church House, Crane St, Salisbury, Wilts SP1 2QB   Tel: (01722) 411922
Fax: (01722) 411990
Chancellor of Diocese His Honour Judge Samuel Wiggs, c/o Dioc Office
Registrar of Diocese and Bishop's Legal Secretary Mr Andrew Johnson, Minster Chambers, 42/44 Castle St, Salisbury, Wilts SP1 3TX   Tel: (01722) 411141
Registrar of Dorset Archdeaconry Mr John Arkell, Palladwr House, Bleke St, Shaftesbury, Dorset SP7 8AH   Tel: (01747) 521761

DIOCESAN ORGANISATIONS
Diocesan Office Church House, Crane St, Salisbury, Wilts SP1 2QB
Tel: (01722) 411922
Fax: (01722) 411990

ADMINISTRATION
Deputy Dioc Secretaries Mr John Voaden, Dioc Office and Mr Richard Trahair, Dioc Office   Tel: (01722) 411933
Dioc Synod (*Chairman, House of Clergy*) Canon Clive Cohen, Rectory, Winterslow, Salisbury SP5 1RE Tel: (01980) 862231; (*Chairman, House of Laity*) Mr Neil Whitton, Homanton Cottage, Salisbury Rd, Shrewton, Salisbury, Wilts Tel: (01980) 620433; (*Secretary*) Revd Karen Curnock, Dioc Office
Board of Finance (*Chairman*) Mr Hugh Privett, The Manor House, Marston Magna, Yeovil, Som BA22 8DW Tel: (01935) 850294; (*Secretary*) Revd Karen Curnock (*as above*); *Deputy Secretary:* Mr John Voaden (*as above*)
Property Secretary Mr Richard Trahair (*as above*)
Diocesan Surveyor Mr John Carley, Dioc Office   Tel: (01722) 411933
Pastoral Committee (*Secretary*) Mr John Voaden (*as above*)
Designated Officer Mr Andrew Johnson, Minster Chambers, 42/44 Castle St, Salisbury, Wilts SP1 3TX   Tel: (01722) 411141

CHURCHES
Advisory Committee for the Care of Churches (*Chairman*) The Dean, Cathedral Office (*as above*) (*Secretary*) Miss Carolann Johnson, Dioc Office   Tel: (01722) 321996
Redundant Churches Uses Committee and Furnishings Officer Mr Richard Trahair (*as above*)
Ringers' Association Mr Anthony Lovell-Wood, 11 Brook Close, Tisbury, Salisbury, Wilts   Tel: (01747) 871111

EDUCATION
Director of Education Mr Henry Head,

Audley House, Crane St, Salisbury, Wilts SP1 2QA Tel: (01722) 411977 Fax: (01722) 331159
Buildings and Trusts Officer Mr Simon Franklin (*same address*)
Adviser to Schools Mrs Ruth Eade (*same address*)
Youth and Children's Officer Young Sarum Team (*same address*)

MINISTRY

Secretary and Adviser on Continuing Ministerial Education Rev Sheila Watson, Dioc Office Tel: (01722) 411944
Director of Ordinands Canon Stanley Royle, South Canonry, 71 The Close, Salisbury SP1 2ER Tel: (01722) 334031

PARISH DEVELOPMENT

Adviser for Parish Development Revd Alan Jeans, Dioc Office Tel: (01722) 411955
Liturgical Revd Stephen Lake, Vicarage, St Aldhelm's Rd, Branksome, Poole, Dorset BH13 6BT Tel: (01202) 764420
Christian Stewardship Adviser Mr Chris Love, Dioc Office Tel: (01722) 411955
 e-mail: chris_love@compuserve.com

CHURCH AND SOCIETY

Ecumenical (Secretary) Revd Nigel LLoyd, Rectory, 19 Springfield Rd, Parkstone, Poole, Dorset BH14 0LG
  Tel: (01202) 748860
  e-mail: nigel@branksea.demon.co.uk
Adviser for Church and Society Revd Ian Woodward, Dioc Office
  Tel: (01722) 411966
Social Responsibility (Secretary) (*Wilts*) Mrs Kathleen Ben Rabha (*also Bristol Diocese and Ecumenical*), Dioc Office
  Tel: (01722) 411966
(*Dorset*) Revd Hazel Barkham URC (*Ecumenical*), The Croft, North Rd, Mere BA12 6HQ Tel: (01747) 816514

PRESS AND PUBLICATIONS

Communications (Secretary and Communications Officer) Mr Julian Hewitt, Dioc Office
  Tel: (01722) 411988
  0370 961629 (Mobile)

Editor The Sarum Link Mrs Jane Warner, Dioc Office Tel: (01722) 339447
Editor of Dioc Directory Mrs Miriam Darke, Dioc Office Tel: (01722) 411922
Editor of Dioc Handbook Dioc Secretary (*as above*)

DIOCESAN RECORD OFFICES

County Record Office, County Hall, Trowbridge, Wilts BA14 8JG (*Principal Archivist* Mr John D'Arcy) Tel: (01225) 713000, Ext 3500 (*For parishes in the Archdeaconries of Wilts and Sarum*); County Record Office, Bridport Rd, Dorchester, Dorset DT1 1RP (*County Archivist* Mr Hugh Jacques) Tel: (01305) 250550 (*For parishes in the County of Dorset*); County Record Office, 20 Southgate St, Winchester, Hants SO23 9EF (*County Archivist* Miss Rosemary Dunhill) Tel: (01962) 846154 (*For the few Salisbury Diocesan parishes situated in the County of Hampshire*)

RURAL DEANS

ARCHDEACONRY OF SHERBORNE

Dorchester Revd Ken Scott, Rectory, Church Lane, Frampton, Dorchester, Dorset DT2 9NL Tel: (01300) 320429
Lyme Bay Revd John Atkinson, Rectory, Church St, Burton Bradstock, Bridport, Dorset DT6 4QS Tel: (01308) 897359
Sherborne Canon Eric Woods, Vicarage, Abbey Close, Sherborne, Dorset DT9 3LQ
  Tel: (01935) 812452
Weymouth Canon Keith Hugo, Wyke Regis Rectory, 1 Portland Rd, Weymouth, Dorset DT4 9ES Tel: (01305) 784649

ARCHDEACONRY OF DORSET

Blackmore Vale Revd William Ridding, Vicarage, Kington Magna, Gillingham, Dorset SP8 5EW Tel: (01747) 838494
Milton and Blandford Canon Gerald Squarey, Vicarage, Shaston Rd, Stourpaine, Blandford, Dorset DT11 8TA
  Tel: (01258) 480580

Poole Canon Victor Barron, Rectory, 51 Millham's Rd, Kinson, Bournemouth, Dorset BH10 7LJ Tel: (01202) 571996
Purbeck Canon Peter Hardman, Rectory, 19 Pound Lane, Wareham, Dorset BH20 4LQ Tel: (01929) 552684
Wimborne Revd Tony Watts, Rectory, 250 New Rd, West Parley, Wimborne Dorset BH22 8EW Tel: (01202) 873561

ARCHDEACONRY OF SARUM

Alderbury Revd Michael Gallagher, Vicarage, Barford Lane, Downton, Salisbury, Wilts SP5 3QA Tel: (01725) 510326
Avon Revd Malcolm Bridger, Rectory, 10 St James St, Ludgershall, Andover, Hants SP11 9QF Tel: (01980) 790393
Chalke Revd Michael Ridley, Rectory, Mill End, Damerham, Fordingbridge SP6 3HU
  Tel: (01725) 518642
Heytesbury Revd Michael Flight, Vicarage, Bitham Lane, Westbury, Wilts BA13 3BU
  Tel: (01373) 822209
Salisbury Revd Keith Robinson, Rectory, Tollgate Rd, Salisbury SP1 2JJ
  Tel: (01722) 335895
Wylye and Wilton Revd Bryan Thomas, Rectory, Steeple Langford, Salisbury, Wilts SP3 4NH Tel: (01722) 790337

ARCHDEACONRY OF WILTS

Bradford Canon Christopher Brown, Rectory, Union St, Trowbridge, Wilts BA14 8RU Tel: (01225) 755121
Calne Revd Peter Giles, Old Vicarage, Honeyhill, Wootton Bassett, Swindon SN3 7DY Tel: (01793) 852643
Devizes Canon John Record, Rectory, 39 Long St, Devizes, Wilts SN10 1NS
Marlborough Revd Henry Pearson, Rectory, 1 Rawlingswell Lane, Marlborough, Wilts SN8 1AU Tel: (01672) 512357
Pewsey Revd Nicolas Leigh-Hunt, Vicarage, 5 Eastcourt, Burbage, Marlborough, Wilts SN8 3AG Tel: (01672) 810258

DIOCESE OF SHEFFIELD

Founded in 1914. Sheffield; Rotherham; Doncaster, except for a few parishes in the south-east (SOUTHWELL); an area of North Lincolnshire; an area of south-eastern Barnsley.

Population 1,197,000   Area 576 sq m
Stipendiary Clergy 201   Benefices 157
Parishes 175   Churches 220

BISHOP (6th)
Rt Revd John (Jack) Nicholls, Bishopscroft, Snaithing Lane, Sheffield, S Yorks S10 3LG [1998] *Tel:* 0114–230 2170 *Fax:* 0114–263 0110
[Jack Sheffield]

Domestic Chaplain Canon Cedric Whiteman, 11 Thornbrook Close, Chapeltown, Sheffield S35 2BB *Tel:* 0114–245 7479

SUFFRAGAN BISHOP
DONCASTER Rt Revd Michael Gear, Bishop's Lodge, Hooton Roberts, Rotherham S65 4PF [1993] *Tel:* (01709) 853370 *Fax:* (01709) 852310

HONORARY ASSISTANT BISHOPS
Rt Revd Kenneth John Fraser Skelton, 65 Crescent Rd, Sheffield S7 1HN
Tel: 0114–255 1260
Rt Revd Kenneth Harold Pillar, 75 Dobcroft Rd, Millhouses, Sheffield S7 2LS
Tel: 0114–236 7902

CATHEDRAL CHURCH OF ST PETER AND ST PAUL
Provost Very Revd Michael Sadgrove, The Cathedral, Church St, Sheffield S1 1HA [1996] *Tel:* 0114–275 3434 *Fax:* 0114–278 0344
e-mail: provshef@aol.com
Canons Residentiary
Canon Trevor Page, The Cathedral [1982]
Ven Stephen Lowe, The Cathedral [1988]
Canon Christopher Smith, The Cathedral [1991]
Canon Jane Sinclair, The Cathedral [1993]
e-mail: shefflit@aol.com
Cathedral Administrator Mr Brian Watson, The Cathedral *e-mail:* sheffexec@aol.com
Master of the Music Mr Neil Taylor, The Cathedral *e-mail:* sheffmusic@aol.com
Asst Master of Music Vacancy, The Cathedral

ARCHDEACONS
SHEFFIELD Ven Stephen Lowe, 23 Hill Turrets Close, Ecclesall, Sheffield S11 9RE [1988] *Tel:* 0114–235 0191
Fax: 0114–235 2275
e-mail: 100737.634@compuserve.com
Office Diocesan Church House, 95–99 Effingham St, Rotherham S65 1BL
Tel: (01709) 512449
Fax: (01709) 512550
DONCASTER Ven Bernard Holdridge, Fairview House, 14 Armthorpe Lane, Doncaster DN2 5LZ [1994] *Tel:* (01302) 325787
Fax: (01302) 760493
Office Diocesan Church House (*as above*)

CONVOCATION (MEMBERS OF THE HOUSE OF CLERGY OF THE GENERAL SYNOD)
The Archdeacon of Sheffield
Proctors for Clergy
Revd Richard Atkinson
Revd Michael Breen
Revd James Forrester
Canon Jane Sinclair

MEMBERS OF THE HOUSE OF LAITY OF THE GENERAL SYNOD
Prof David McClean
Mrs Elizabeth Paver
Mr Jonathan Redden
Mrs Janet Vout

DIOCESAN OFFICERS
Dioc Secretary Mr Tony Beck, Diocesan Church House, 95–99 Effingham St, Rotherham S65 1BL *Tel:* (01709) 512368
Fax: (01709) 512550
e-mail: sheffield.diocese@ukonline.co.uk
Chancellor of Diocese Prof David McClean, 6 Burnt Stones Close, Sheffield S10 5TS
Tel: 0114–230 5794
Registrar of Diocese and Bishop's Legal Secretary Mrs Miranda Myers, Old Cathedral Vicarage, St James Row, Sheffield, S Yorks S1 1XA *Tel:* 0114–272 2061
Fax: 0114–270 0813 or 275 0243

DIOCESAN ORGANISATIONS
Diocesan Office Diocesan Church House, 95–99 Effingham St, Rotherham S65 1BL
Tel: (01709) 511116
Fax: (01709) 512550
e-mail: sheffield.diocese@ukonline.co.uk

ADMINISTRATION
Dioc Secretary Mr Tony Beck, Dioc Office
Tel: (01709) 512368
Deputy Secretary Miss Margaret Barlow, Dioc Office *Tel:* (01709) 512370
Property Manager Mr Brian Cook, Dioc Office *Tel:* (01709) 512445
Finance Officer Mr Roger Pinchbeck, Dioc Office *Tel:* (01709) 515877
Dioc Synod (Chairman, House of Clergy) Canon Gordon Taylor, Vicarage, 22 Clifton Gardens, Goole DN14 6AS *Tel:* (01405) 764259; *(Chairman, House of Laity)* Mrs Elizabeth Paver, 113 Warning Tongue Lane, Bessacarr, Doncaster DN4 6TB *Tel:* (01302) 530706; *(Secretary)* Mr Tony Beck (*as above*)
Board of Finance (Chairman) Mr John Biggin, 7 Ranmoor Crescent, Sheffield S10 3GU *Tel:* 0114–268 5880
Fax: 0114–230 4546
(Secretary) Mr Tony Beck (*as above*)
Pastoral Committee (Chairman) The Provost of Sheffield (*as above*); *(Secretary)* Miss Margaret Barlow (*as above*)
Redundant Churches Uses Committee (Chairman) Ven Stephen Lowe, Dioc Office *Tel:* (01709) 512449; *(Secretary)* Mr Brian Cook (*as above*)
Parsonages Committee (Chairman) Ven Bernard Holdridge (*as above*); *(Secretary)* Mr Brian Cook (*as above*)
Board of Patronage (Secretary) Mr David Wilson, 363 Fulwood Rd, Sheffield, S Yorks S10 3GE *Tel:* 0114–266 2066
Designated Officer Canon Cedric Whiteman, 11 Thornbrook Close, Chapeltown, Sheffield S30 4BB *Tel:* 0114–245 7479

CHURCHES
Advisory Committee for the Care of Churches (Chairman) Rt Revd Kenneth Skelton, 65 Crescent Rd, Sheffield S7 1HN *Tel:* 0114–255 1260; *(Secretary)* Miss Margaret Barlow (*as above*)

EDUCATION
Dioc Board of Education (Chairman) Ven Bernard Holdridge (*as above*); *(Secretary)* Mr Malcolm Robertson, Dioc Office
Tel: (01709) 512446
Director of Education Mr Malcolm Robertson (*as above*)
RE and Worship Adviser Revd Alan Parkinson, Dioc Office *Tel:* (01709) 512447

PARISH TRAINING
Training Committee (*Chairman*) The Bishop of Doncaster; (*Secretary*) Canon Peter Chambers, Dioc Office *Tel:* (01709) 515871
Director of Training Canon Peter Chambers (*as above*)
Lay Ministry Officer Mr John Bouch, Dioc Office *Tel:* (01709) 515871
Youth Outreach Officer Mr Tim Smithies, Dioc Office *Tel:* (01709) 512447
Children's and Youth Officer Mrs Bridget Fudger, Dioc Office *Tel:* (01709) 512447
Resources and Information Officer Dr Mary Kenchington, Dioc Office
  Tel: (01709) 512378

MINISTRY
Mission and Unity Committee (*Chairman*) The Bishop of Doncaster (*as above*); (*Secretary and Ecumenical Officer*) Revd Hilary Smart, Dioc Office *Tel:* (01709) 512448
Adviser in Evangelism Revd David Sherwin, Dioc Office *Tel:* (01709) 515874
Director of Ordinands Canon Trevor Page, 393 Fulwood Rd, Sheffield S10 3GE
  Tel: 0114–230 5707
Asst POT Officer Revd Mark Cockayne, St Polycarp's Vicarage, 33 Wisewood Lane, Sheffield S6 4WA
  Tel: 0114–266 1932
Bishop's Adviser on Ministry Vacancy
Bishop's Adviser on Women in Ministry Canon Sue Proctor, Rectory, 217 Nursery Rd, Dinnington, Sheffield S31 7QU
  Tel: (01909) 562335
Bishop's Adviser on Non Stipendiary Ministry Revd Bridget Brooke, 166 Tom Lane, Sheffield S10 3PG *Tel:* 0114–230 2147
Bishop's Adviser on Church Army Ministry Vacancy
Readers' Board (*Secretary*) Mr Stuart Carey, Corben House, 3 Station Rd, Hatfield, Doncaster DN7 6PQ *Tel:* (01302) 844936

PRESS AND PUBLICATIONS
Communications Officer Revd Dr Peter Bold, 40 Renecliffe Ave, Broom Valley, Rotherham S60 2RP *Tel:* (01709) 364729
  Fax: (01709) 363959
  e-mail: PEBold@aol.com
Editor of Dioc News Revd Peter Gascoigne, Bilham Vicarage, Churchfield Rd, Clayton, Doncaster DN5 7DH
  Tel and *Fax:* (01977) 643756
Editor of Dioc Year Book Mr Tony Beck, Dioc Office

DIOCESAN RECORD OFFICES
Sheffield City Archives, 52 Shoreham St, Sheffield S1 4SP *Tel:* 0114–273 4756 (*For parishes in the Archdeaconry of Sheffield*); Doncaster Archives, King Edward Rd, Balby, Doncaster DN4 0NA *Tel:* (01302) 859811 (*For parishes in the Archdeaconry of Doncaster*)

FAITH AND JUSTICE
Faith and Justice Committee (*Chairman*) Ven Stephen Lowe, Dioc Office
  Tel: (01709) 512449
Secretary Ms Rachel Ross, Dioc Office
  Tel: (01709) 512448
Social Responsibility Officer Ms Rachel Ross (*as above*)
Faith in the City Development Worker Dr Ian McCollough, Dioc Office *Tel:* (01709) 512448
Industrial Mission (*Senior Chaplain*) Canon Michael West, 21 Endcliffe Rise Rd, Sheffield S11 8RU *Tel:* 0114–266 1921
Office The Industrial Mission in South Yorkshire, Cemetery Rd Baptist Church, Napier St Entrance, Sheffield S11 8HA
  Tel: 0114–275 5865
Bishop's Adviser on Black Concerns Mrs Carmen Franklin, 13 Staindrop View, Chapeltown, Sheffield S30 4YS
  Tel: 0114–246 9650
Bishop's Rural Adviser Revd Philip Ireson, Rectory, Letwell, Worksop S81 8DF
  Tel: (01909) 730346
European Link Officer Canon Bob Fitzharris

STEWARDSHIP
Christian Giving Adviser Mr Derek Lane, Dioc Office *Tel:* (01709) 515875

RURAL DEANS
ARCHDEACONRY OF SHEFFIELD
Attercliffe Canon Richard Blackburn, Vicarage, Duke St, Mosborough, Sheffield S19 5DG *Tel:* 0114–248 6518
Ecclesall Revd David Williams, 51 Vicarage Lane, Dore, Sheffield S17 3GY
  Tel: 0114–236 3335
Ecclesfield Revd Tim Ellis, Vicarage, Everingham Rd, Sheffield S5 7LW
  Tel: 0114–243 6689
Hallam Revd Philip West, 214 Oldfield Rd, Stannington, Sheffield S6 6DY
  Tel: 0114–232 4490
Laughton Canon Sue Proctor, Rectory, 217 Nursery Rd, Dinnington, Sheffield S31 7QU *Tel:* (01909) 562335
Rotherham Revd John Wraw, Clifton Vicarage, 10 Clifton Crescent North, Rotherham S65 2AS *Tel:* (01709) 363082
Tankersley Canon Lewis Atkinson, Vicarage, Church St, Oughtibridge, Sheffield S30 3FU *Tel:* 0114–286 2317

ARCHDEACONRY OF DONCASTER
Adwick-le-Street Canon Bob Fitzharris, Vicarage, 3A High St, Bentley, Doncaster DN5 0AA *Tel* and *Fax:* (01302) 876272
  e-mail: 106517.1056@compuserve.com
Doncaster Revd John Barnes, Rectory, Church St, Armthorpe, Doncaster DN3 3AD *Tel:* (01302) 831231
Snaith and Hatfield Canon Gordon Taylor, Vicarage, 22 Clifton Gardens, Goole DN14 6AS *Tel:* (01405) 764259
Wath Canon Martin Baldock, Vicarage, Christchurch Rd, Wath upon Dearne, Rotherham, S63 6NW *Tel:* (01709) 873210
West Doncaster Revd Graham Marcer, Balby Vicarage, 6 Greenfield Lane, Doncaster DN4 0PT *Tel:* (01302) 853278
  e-mail: Graham.Marcer@btinternet.com

DIOCESE OF SODOR AND MAN

Founded in 447. The Isle of Man.

Population 72,000   Area 221 sq m
Stipendiary Clergy 22   Benefices 28
Parishes 27   Churches 42

BISHOP (79th)
Rt Revd Nöel Debroy Jones, The Bishop's House, Quarterbridge Rd, Douglas, Isle of Man IM2 3RF [1989]   Tel: (01624) 622108
    Fax: (01624) 672890
[Nöel Sodor and Man]
Domestic Chaplain Revd David Guest (*same address*)   Tel: (01624) 621547
Personal Secretary Mrs Joyce Jones (*same address*)

CATHEDRAL CHURCH OF ST GERMAN, PEEL
Dean The Bishop
Canons
Canon Brian Kelly, Cathedral Vicarage, Albany Rd, Peel, Isle of Man IM5 1JS [1980] *Tel:* (01624) 842608
Canon Hinton Bird PH D, Vicarage, Rushen, Port St Mary, Isle of Man IM9 5LP [1993]   *Tel:* (01624) 832275
Canon Duncan Whitworth, St Matthew's Vicarage, Alexander Drive, Douglas, Isle of Man IM2 3QN [1996]
    Tel: (01624) 676310
Canon Peter Robinson, St Paul's Vicarage, Walpole Drive, Ramsey, Isle of Man IM8 1NA [1998]   *Tel:* (01624) 812275
Chapter Clerk The Hon Christopher Murphy, c/o 26 The Fountains, Ramsey, Isle of Man IM8 1NN
    Tel and *Fax:* (01624) 816545

ARCHDEACON
ISLE OF MAN Ven Brian Partington, St George's Vicarage, 16 Devonshire Rd, Douglas, Isle of Man IM2 3RB [1996]
    Tel: (01624) 675430
    Fax: (01624) 616136

MANX CONVOCATION
(*Secretary*) Canon Hinton Bird PH D, Vicarage, Rushen, Port St Mary, Isle of Man IM9 5LP   *Tel:* (01624) 832275

CONVOCATION (MEMBERS OF THE HOUSE OF CLERGY OF THE GENERAL SYNOD)
The Archdeacon of Man
Proctor for the Clergy
Canon Hinton Bird PH D

MEMBER OF THE HOUSE OF LAITY OF THE GENERAL SYNOD
Dr Paul Bregazzi

DIOCESAN OFFICERS
Dioc Secretary The Hon Christopher Murphy, c/o 26 The Fountains, Ramsey, Isle of Man IM8 1NN
    Tel and *Fax:* (01624) 816545
Vicar-General and Chancellor of Diocese The Worshipful Clare Faulds, 30 Athol St, Douglas, Isle of Man IM1 1JB
    Tel: (01624) 676868
Registrar of Diocese and Bishop's Legal Secretary Mr Christopher Callow, 6 Hill St, Douglas, Isle of Man IM1 1EF
    Tel: (01624) 611211
    Fax: (01624) 675125
Dioc Architect Miss Karen Horncastle, Partington, Nixon and Kinrade, Drinkwater St, Douglas, Isle of Man IM1 1AT
    Tel: (01624) 628715

CHURCH COMMISSIONERS FOR THE ISLE OF MAN
The Lord Bishop
The Archdeacon of Man
Mrs Audrey Ainsworth
Mr H. Dawson
Revd Philip Frear
Revd Roderick Geddes
Revd Roger Harper
Mr P. Kelly
Mr Timothy Mann
Revd Michael Roberts
(*Secretary*) The Hon Christopher Murphy

DIOCESAN ORGANISATIONS
Diocesan Office c/o 26 The Fountains, Ramsey, Isle of Man IM8 1NN
    Tel and *Fax:* (01624) 816545

ADMINISTRATION
Dioc Synod (*Chairman, House of Clergy*) Canon Hinton Bird PH D, Vicarage, Rushen, Port St Mary, Isle of Man IM9 5LP *Tel:* (01624) 832275; (*Chairman, House of Laity*) Mr J. E. Noakes, St Jude, Quarterbridge Rd, Douglas, Isle of Man *Tel:* (01624) 628548; (*Secretary*) The Hon Christopher Murphy, Dioc Office
Board of Finance (*Chairman*): Revd Roger Harper, 16–18 St George's St, Douglas, Isle of Man IM1 1PL *Tel:* (01624) 624945; (*Secretary*) The Hon Christopher Murphy (*as above*)
Designated Officer Vacancy

CHURCHES
Advisory Committee for the Care of Churches (*Secretary*) Hon Christopher Murphy (*as above*)
Council of Church Music (*Secretary*) Vacancy

EDUCATION
Council for Education (*Secretary*) Mrs Beverley Wells, St Peter's Vicarage, Onchan, Isle of Man IM3 1BF   *Tel:* (01624) 675797
Director of Diocesan Institute Revd Malcolm Convery, Vicarage, Marown, Crosby, Isle of Man IM4 4BH
    Tel: (01624) 851378
Bishop's Youth Officer, Dioc Adviser for Children's Work and Religious Adviser in Education Revd Rod Geddes, Rectory, Village Rd, Andreas, Isle of Man IM7 1HH
    Tel: (01624) 880419
Adult Education Canon Peter Robinson, St Paul's Vicarage, Walpole Drive, Ramsey, Isle on Man IM8 1NA   *Tel:* (01624) 812275

MINISTRY
Dioc Director of Ordinands Canon John Sheen, Kentraugh Hill, Colby, Isle of Man IM9 4AU   *Tel:* (01624) 832406
Council for Health and Healing (*Bishop's Adviser*) Revd David Green, Vicarage, Maughold, Isle of Man IM7 1AS
    Tel: (01624) 812070
Bishop's Adviser for Non-Stipendiary Ministries Revd Neville Pilling, Morwenna, Athol Park, Port Erin, Isle of Man IM9 6ES
    Tel: (01624) 832382
Readers' Board (*Warden*) Revd John Gulland, Anchor House, Queen's Rd, Port St Mary, Isle of Man IM9 5ES *Tel:* (01624) 834548; (*Secretary*) Mr Paul Suckling, 20 Clybane Rd, Braddan, Isle of Man IM2 2LP   *Tel:* (01624) 629819

LITURGICAL
Bishop's Adviser Canon Duncan Whitworth, St Matthew's Vicarage, Alexander Drive, Douglas, Isle of Man IM2 3QN
    Tel: (01624) 676310

MISSIONARY AND ECUMENICAL
Council for Mission (*Secretary*) Mrs Anne Kean, 14 Barrule Park, Ramsey, Isle of Man IM8 2BN   *Tel:* (01624) 813984
Decade of Evangelism Officer Revd Nick Wells, St Peter's Vicarage, Onchan, Isle of Man IM3 1BF   *Tel:* (01624) 675797

Ecumenical Officer Revd William Martin, Vicarage, 56 Ard Reayrt, Ramsey Rd, Laxey, Isle of Man IM4 7QQ
Tel: (01624) 862050
ACORA Officer Mr Alan Matthews, Crosh Yvor, Ballachrink Crossing, Ballasalla, Isle of Man IM9 2AD   *Tel:* (01624) 822432

PRESS AND PUBLICATIONS
Communications Officer Revd David Guest, 62 Ballabrooie Way, Douglas, Isle of Man IM1 4AB   *Tel:* (01624) 621547
The Dioc Newspaper, Editor Mr Ian Faulds, 14 Douglas St, Peel, Isle of Man IM5 3LQ
Tel: (01624) 843102
Fax: (01624) 842325

Editor of Dioc Directory Mrs Anne Kean (*as above*)

DIOCESAN RECORD OFFICE
Further information can be obtained from the Manx Museum Library, Kingswood Grove, Douglas, Isle of Man IM1 3LY, *Archivist* Miss Miriam Critchlow
Tel: (01624) 675522

BOARD OF SOCIAL RESPONSIBILITY
Representative Mrs Wendy Fitch, Vicarage, Marathon Ave, Douglas, Isle of Man IM2 4JA   *Tel:* (01624) 611503

STEWARDSHIP
Christian Stewardship Adviser Mr John Guilford, Strathallan Rd, Douglas, Isle of Man IM2 4PN   *Tel:* (01624) 672001

RURAL DEANS
Castletown and Peel Canon Brian Kelly, Cathedral Vicarage, Albany Rd, Peel, Isle of Man IM5 1JS   *Tel:* (01624) 842608
Douglas Canon Duncan Whitworth, St Matthew's Vicarage, Alexander Drive, Douglas, Isle of Man IM2 3QN
Tel: (01624) 676310
Ramsey Revd David Green, Vicarage, Maughold, Isle of Man IM7 1AS
Tel: (01624) 812070

DIOCESE OF SOUTHWARK

Founded in 1905. Greater London south of the Thames, except for most of the London Boroughs of Bromley and Bexley (ROCHESTER), and a few parishes in the south-west (GUILDFORD); the eastern third of Surrey.

Population 2,358,000   Area 317 sq m
Stipendiary Clergy 392   Benefices 293
Parishes 303   Churches 378

BISHOP (9th)
Rt Revd Thomas Frederick Butler PH D, LLD, Bishop's House, 38 Tooting Bec Gardens, London SW16 1QZ [1998]
Tel: 0181–769 3256
Fax: 0181–769 4126
e-mail: bishops.house@dswark.org.uk
[Thomas Southwark]
Personal Assistant Revd Andrew Nunn (*same address*)
e-mail: andrew.nunn@dswark.org.uk
Secretary Miss Helen Mitchell (*same address*)
e-mail: helen.mitchell@dswark.org.uk

AREA BISHOPS
CROYDON Rt Revd Dr Wilfred Wood, St Matthew's House, 100 George St, Croydon, Surrey CR0 1PE [1985]
Tel: 0181–681 5496
Fax: 0181–686 2074
e-mail: bishop.wilfred@dswark.org.uk
KINGSTON Rt Revd Peter Price, Kingston Episcopal Area Office, Whitelands College, West Hill, London SW15 3SN [1997]
Tel: 0181–392 3742
Fax: 0181–392 3743
e-mail: bishop.peter@dswark.org.uk
WOOLWICH Rt Revd Colin Buchanan, 37 South Rd, Forest Hill, London SE23 2UJ [1996]
Tel: 0181–699 7771
Fax: 0181–699 7949
e-mail: bishop.colin@dswark.org.uk

HONORARY ASSISTANT BISHOPS
Rt Revd John Hughes, Hospital of the Holy Trinity, Block 6, Flat 2, North End, Croydon CR0 1UB [1987]
Tel: 0181–686 8313
Rt Revd Hugh Montefiore, White Lodge, 23 Bellevue Rd, London SW17 7EB [1987]
Tel: 0181–672 6697
Rt Revd Simon Phipps, Sarsens, Shipley, W Sussex RH13 8PX [1987]
Tel: (01403) 741354

CATHEDRAL AND COLLEGIATE CHURCH OF ST SAVIOUR AND ST MARY OVERIE
Provost Very Revd Colin Slee, Provost's Lodging, 51 Bankside, London SE1 9JE [1994]   Tel and Fax: 0171–928 6414 (Home)
Cathedral Office Montague Chambers, Montague Close, London SE1 9DA
Tel: 0171–407 3708
0171–407 2939 (Vestry)
Fax: 0171–357 7389
e-mail: cathedral@dswark.org.uk
Canons Residentiary
Vice-Provost Canon Roy White, Cathedral Office [1991]   Tel: 0171–735 8322 (Home)
Treasurer Canon David Painter, Trinity House, 4 Chapel Court, London SE1 1HW [1991]   Tel: 0171–403 8686 (Office)
0181–871 1118 (Home)
e-mail: david.painter@dswark.org.uk
Pastor Canon Helen Cunliffe, Cathedral Office [1995]   Tel: 0171–587 1831 (Home)
Chancellor Canon Jeffrey John, Trinity House, 4 Chapel Court, London SE1 1HW [1997]   Tel: 0171–403 8686 (Office)
0171–820 8079 (Home)
e-mail: jeffrey.john@dswark.org.uk
Missioner Canon Bruce Saunders, Trinity House, 4 Chapel Court, London SE1 1HW [1997]   Tel: 0171–403 8686 (Office)
0171–820 8376 (Home)
e-mail: bruce.saunders@dswark.org.uk
Succentor Revd John Paton, Cathedral Office [1998]
Chaplain Canon Roger Royle, Cathedral Office [1993]
Administrator Mrs Sarah King, Cathedral Office
Education Officer Miss Rachel Murray, Cathedral Office
Cathedral Organist Mr Peter Wright, Cathedral Office

ARCHDEACONS
CROYDON Ven Anthony Davies, St Matthew's House, 100 George St, Croydon CR0 1PE [1994]   Tel: 0181–681 5496
Fax: 0181–686 2074
e-mail: tony.davies@dswark.org.uk
LAMBETH Ven Richard Bird, Kingston Episcopal Area Office, Whitelands College, West Hill, London SW15 3SN [1988]
Tel: 0181–392 3742
Fax: 0181–392 3743
e-mail: kingston@dswark.org.uk
LEWISHAM Ven David Atkinson, 3A Court Farm Rd, Mottingham, London SE9 4JH [1996]   Tel: 0181–857 7982
e-mail: david.atkinson@dswark.org.uk
REIGATE Ven Martin Baddeley, St Matthew's House (*as above*) [1996]
e-mail: martin.baddeley@dswark.org.uk
SOUTHWARK Ven Douglas Bartles-Smith, 1A Dog Kennel Hill, East Dulwich, London SE22 8AA [1985]   Tel: 0171–274 6767
e-mail:
douglas.bartles-smith@dswark.org.uk
WANDSWORTH Ven David Gerrard, Kingston Episcopal Area Office (*as above*) [1989]
e-mail: david.gerrard@dswark.org.uk

CONVOCATION (MEMBERS OF THE HOUSE OF CLERGY OF THE GENERAL SYNOD)
Dignitaries in Convocation
The Provost of Southwark
The Archdeacon of Wandsworth
Proctors for Clergy
Revd Colin Boswell
Canon Bernice Broggio
Revd Stephen Burdett
Canon Jeffrey John D PHIL
Revd Geoffrey Kirk
Revd Peter Ronayne
Revd Jennifer Thomas

MEMBERS OF THE HOUSE OF LAITY OF THE GENERAL SYNOD
Mr Barry Barnes
Mr Mark Birchall
Miss Vasantha Gnanadoss
Mr Brian McHenry
Mrs Marion Simpson
Mr John Smallwood
Mr Tom Sutcliffe
Mr William Taylor

DIOCESAN OFFICERS
Dioc Secretary Mr Simon Parton, Trinity House, 4 Chapel Court, Borough High St, London SE1 1HW   Tel: 0171–403 8686
Fax: 0171–403 4770
e-mail: simon.parton@dswark.org.uk
Chancellor of Diocese The Worshipful Charles George, 2 Harcourt Buildings, Temple, London EC4Y 9DB
Tel: 0171–353 8415
Registrar of Diocese and Bishop's Legal Secretary Mr Paul Morris, Registry Chambers, The Old Deanery, London EC4V 5AA   Tel: 0171–593 5110
Fax: 0171–248 3221

DIOCESAN ORGANISATIONS
Diocesan Office Trinity House, 4 Chapel Court, Borough High St, London SE1 1HW   Tel: 0171–403 8686
                                  Fax: 0171–403 4770
       e-mail: trinity@dswark.org.uk

ADMINISTRATION
Dioc Synod (*Chairman, House of Clergy*) Canon Graham Corneck; (*Chairman, House of Laity*) Mr Brian McHenry; (*Secretary*) Mr Simon Parton, Dioc Office
South London Church Fund and Dioc Board of Finance (*Chairman*) Mr John Smallwood, The Willows, Parkgate Rd, Newdigate, Dorking, Surrey RH5 5AH *Tel*: (01306) 631457; (*Secretary*) Mr Simon Parton (*as above*)
Parsonages Board (*Secretary*) Mr Simon Parton (*as above*)
Pastoral Committee and Redundant Churches Uses Committee (*Secretary*) Mr Simon Parton (*as above*)
Chapter of Ministers in Secular Employment
Chapter Dean for Kingston Revd Dr Anne Townsend, 90 Augustus Rd, London SW19 5ER   Tel: 0181–785 7675
Chapter Dean for Croydon Vacancy
Chapter Dean for Woolwich Revd Adam Scott, 19 Blackheath Park, London SE3 9RW   Tel: 0181–852 3286
Designated Officer Mr Paul Morris, 35 Great Peter St, London SW1P 3LR
                                  Tel: 0171–828 9315

CHURCHES
Advisory Committee for the Care of Churches (*Chairman*) Mr J. Michael Davies c/o Trinity House (*as above*)
(*Secretary*) Mr Andrew Lane, Trinity House
       e-mail: andrew.lane@dswark.org.uk

EDUCATION
Board of Education (*Director*) Mrs Linda Borthwick, 48 Union St, London SE1 1TD
                                  Tel: 0171–407 7911
       e-mail: info@sdbe.demon.co.uk

BOARD FOR CHURCH IN SOCIETY
Chair The Bishop of Southwark
Vice Chair The Archdeacon of Southwark (*as above*)
Secretary Canon Bruce Saunders
Executive Officer Mr Paul Buxton
Office 1st Floor, Trinity House, 4 Chapel Court, London SE1 1HW
                       Tel: 0171–403 8686 Ext 212
                                  Fax: 0171–403 2242
       e-mail: bcs@dswark.org.uk
Canon Missioner for Church in Society Canon Bruce Saunders, Trinity House (*as above*)
Children's Officer Revd Kevin Parkes, Kingston Area Mission Team (*as above*)

Churches Community Care (*Woolwich*) Jill McKinnon, Trinity House   Ext 221
Community Development Adviser Ann Stricklen, Trinity House   Ext 217
Canon Chancellor, Theologian and Bishop's Adviser for Ministry Canon Jeffrey John, Trinity House
Dioc Director of Ordinands Canon David Painter, Trinity House   Ext 246
Faith in the City Officer The Archdeacon of Croydon (*as above*)
Housing and Homelessness Adviser Dr Patrick Logan, Trinity House   Ext 219
Industrial Mission Revd John Paxton (*Senior Chaplain*), SLIM, Christchurch Industrial Centre, 27 Blackfriars Rd, London SE1 8NY   Tel: 0171–928 3970
                                  Fax: 0171–928 1148
Inter-Faith Adviser Revd Andrew Wakefield, 47 Wilton Grove, London SW19 3QU
                                  Tel: 0181–542 1794
LNSM Training Revd Stephen Lyon (*Principal*), St Michael's Hall, Trundle St, London SE1 1QT   Tel: 0171–378 7506
                                  Fax: 0171–403 6497
Liturgical Committee Revd Dr John Thewlis (*Secretary*), 107 Westmount Rd, London SE9 1XX   Tel: 0181–850 3030
Ministry Development Officer Revd Geoff Mason, St Michael's Hall (*as above*)
Pastoral Care and Counselling Adviser Revd Susan Walrond-Skinner, 78 Stockwell Park Rd, London SW9 0DA
                                  Tel: 0171–733 8676
Race Relations Commission Vacancy (*Director*), St Michael's Hall (*as above*)
Reader Training Revd David Gatliffe (*Director*), 234 The Broadway, London SW19 1SB   Tel: 0181–542 1388
Warden of Readers Ven Martin Baddeley, St Matthew's House, 100 George St, Croydon CR0 1PE   Tel: 0171–681 5496
                                  Fax: 0181–686 2074
       e-mail: martin.baddeley@dswark.org.uk
Rural Ministry Adviser Revd John Goodden, Rectory, Starrock Lane, Chipstead, Surrey CR5 3QD   Tel: (01737) 552157
Southwark Pastoral Auxiliary Training Ms Joanna Cox, Croydon Area Mission Team, St Matthew's House, 100 George St, Croydon CR0 5NS   Tel: 0181–681 5496
                                  Fax: 0181–686 2074
Urban Ministry Adviser Mr Chris Chapman, St Michael's Hall (*as above*)
Urban Projects/CUF Adviser Ms Steph Blackwell, Trinity House   Ext 215
WelCare Service for Parents and Children Vacancy (*Director*), Trinity House   Ext 224
Youth Officer Capt Rayman Khan, Croydon Area Mission Team (*as above*)

COMMUNICATIONS
Director of Communications and Resources Wendy Robins, Dioc Office
                       Tel: 0171–403 8686 (Office)
       e-mail: wendy.robins@dswark.org.uk

Communications Officer, Bishop's Press Officer and Editor of Dioc Directory Enquiries to Mr Patrick Olivier, Dioc Office
                            0831 694021 (Mobile)

DIOCESAN RECORD OFFICES
London Metropolitan Archives, 40 Northampton Rd, London EC1R 0HB *Head Archivist* Dr Deborah Jenkins, *Tel*: 0171–332 3824 (*For Inner London Boroughs*)
Surrey Record Office, County Hall, Kingston-upon-Thames, Surrey KT1 2DN, *Archivist* Dr D. B. Robinson, *Tel*: 0181–541 9065 (*For Outer London Boroughs, Kent and Surrey*)

STEWARDSHIP
Director, Communications and Resources Wendy Robins, Dioc Office
Resources Officer Vacancy, Dioc Office

RURAL DEANS
ARCHDEACONRY OF SOUTHWARK
Bermondsey Revd Stuart Wilmot, Vicarage, 10 Thorburn Square, London SE1 5QH
                                  Tel: 0171–237 3950
Camberwell Revd Stephen Roberts, St George's Vicarage, 115 Wells Way, London SE5 7SZ   Tel: 0171–703 2895
Dulwich Revd Cecil Heatley, 173 Choumert Rd, London SE15 4AW
                            Tel: 0171–639 5072 (Home)
                            0171–732 3435 (Office)
Southwark and Newington Revd Grahame Shaw, St Paul's Vicarage, Lorrimore Square, London SE17 3QU
                            Tel: 0171–735 2947 (Home)
                            0171–735 3506 (Office)
                            Fax: 0171–639 7860

ARCHDEACONRY OF LAMBETH
Brixton Revd Lyle Dennen, Vicarage, 92 Vassall Rd, London SW9 6JA
                                  Tel: 0171–735 9340
Lambeth Revd Richard Truss, St John's Vicarage, 1 Secker St, London SE1 8UF
                            Tel: 0171–928 4470 (Home)
                            0171–633 9819 (Office)
Merton Revd Nigel Worn, Vicarage, Sherwood Park Rd, Mitcham, Surrey CR4 1NF
                                  Tel: 0181–764 1258
Clapham Revd David Houghton, 15 Elms Rd, Clapham Common, London SW4 9ER
                                  Tel: 0171–622 8703
Streatham Revd Jeffry Wilcox, 1 Becmead Ave, London SW16 1UH
                                  Tel: 0181–769 1216

ARCHDEACONRY OF REIGATE
Caterham Revd Michael Hart, Rectory, 5 Whyteleafe Rd, Caterham, Surrey CR3 5ER   Tel: (01883) 342062

Godstone Revd Clare Edwards, Bletchingley Rectory, Outwood Lane, Bletchingley, Surrey RH1 4LR
Tel: (01883) 743252
Reigate Revd Robert McLean, Vicarage, The Avenue, Tadworth, Surrey KT20 5AS
Tel: (01737) 813152

ARCHDEACONRY OF LEWISHAM
Deptford Canon Graham Corneck, St Nicholas Vicarage, 41 Creek Rd, London SE8 3BU
Tel: 0181–692 2749
East Lewisham Canon David Garlick, Vicarage, 48 Lewisham Park, London SE13 6QZ
Tel: 0181–690 1585
Greenwich Thameside Revd Dr Malcolm Torry, St George's Vicarage, 89 Westcombe Park Rd, London SE3 7RZ
Tel: 0181–305 2339 (Home)
0181–858 3006 (Office)

Greenwich South Revd John Neal, Vicarage, Sowerby Close, London SE9 6HB
Tel: 0181–850 2731
West Lewisham Canon John Ardley, 41 Trewsbury Rd, Sydenham, London SE26 5DP
Tel: 0181–778 3065

ARCHDEACONRY OF WANDSWORTH
Battersea Canon Peter Clark, Christ Church Vicarage, Candahar Rd, London SW11 2PU
Tel: 0171–228 1225
Kingston Revd Peter Holmes, 21 Wolsey Close, Kingston-upon-Thames, Surrey KT2 7ER
Tel: 0181–942 8330
Richmond and Barnes Revd Richard Ames-Lewis, Rectory, 25 Glebe Rd, London SW13 0DZ
Tel: 0181–878 6982
Tooting Canon Bernice Broggio, Holy Trinity Vicarage, 14 Upper Tooting Park, London SW17 7SW
Tel: 0181–672 4790

Wandsworth Revd Colin Pritchard, St Andrew's Vicarage, 22 St Andrew's Court, London SW18 3QF
Tel: 0181–946 4214

ARCHDEACONRY OF CROYDON
Croydon Addington Revd Arthur Quinn, Vicarage, 49 Shirley Church Rd, Shirley, Croydon CR0 5EF
Tel: 0181–654 1013
Croydon Central Revd Graham Derriman, 23A St Augustine's Ave, South Croydon CR2 6JN
Tel: 0181–688 2663
Croydon North Revd Patrick Washington, St Philip's Vicarage, 66 Pollards Hill North, London SW16 4NY
Tel: 0181–764 1812
Croydon South Revd Alan Wait, 84 Higher Drive, Purley, Surrey CR8 2HJ
Tel: 0181–660 3251
Sutton Canon David Lewis, Holy Trinity Vicarage, Maldon Rd, Wallington, Surrey SM6 8BL
Tel: 0181–647 7605

DIOCESE OF SOUTHWELL

Founded in 1884. Nottinghamshire; a few parishes in Doncaster.

Population 1,040,000   Area 847 sq m
Stipendiary Clergy 198   Benefices 184
Parishes 256   Churches 311

BISHOP (9th)
Rt Revd Patrick Burnet Harris, Bishop's Manor, Southwell, Notts NG25 0JR [1988]
Tel: (01636) 812112
Fax: (01636) 815401
e-mail: bishop.southwell@john316.com
[Patrick Southwell]

SUFFRAGAN BISHOP
SHERWOOD Rt Revd Alan Wyndham Morgan, Sherwood House, High Oakham Rd, Mansfield, Notts NG18 5AJ [1989]
Tel: (01623) 657491
Fax: (01623) 662526
e-mail: bishop.sherwood@john316.com

CATHEDRAL AND PARISH CHURCH OF THE BLESSED VIRGIN MARY
Provost Very Revd David Leaning, The Residence, Southwell, Notts NG25 0HP [1991]   *Tel* and *Fax:* (01636) 812593
Office The Minster Office, Trebeck Hall, Bishop's Drive, Southwell, Notts NG25 0JP   *Tel:* (01636) 812649
Fax: (01636) 815904
e-mail: minster.office@John316.com
Canons Residentiary
Precentor Canon Ian Collins, 5 Vicars' Court, Southwell, Notts NG25 0HP [1985]
Tel: (01636) 815056
Chancellor Canon Graham Hendy, 2 Vicar's Court, Southwell, Notts NG25 0HP [1997]   *Tel:* (01636) 813188,
Vicar Choral Revd John Wardle, 3 Vicars' Court, Southwell, Notts NG25 0HP
Tel: (01636) 813767
Cathedral Administrator Mr D. F. J. Mills, The Minster Office
Rector Chori Mr Paul Hale, 4 Vicars' Court, Southwell, Notts NG25 0HP
Tel: (01636) 812228

ARCHDEACONS
NOTTINGHAM Ven Gordon Ogilvie, 2B Spencer Ave, Mapperley, Nottingham NG3 5SP [1996]
Tel: (01636) 814490 (Office)
Fax: (01636) 815882
0115–967 0875 (Home)
Fax: 0115–967 1014 (Home)
NEWARK Ven David Hawtin, 4 The Woodwards, New Balderton, Newark, Notts NG24 3GG [1992]
Tel: (01636) 814490 (Office)
Fax: (01636) 815882
(01636) 612249 (Home)
Fax: (01636) 611952 (Home)

CONVOCATION (MEMBERS OF THE HOUSE OF CLERGY OF THE GENERAL SYNOD)
The Archdeacon of Newark
Proctors for Clergy
Revd Dr Francis Bridger
Revd Jeremy Fletcher
Revd Peter Hill
Revd Nigel Peyton

MEMBERS OF THE HOUSE OF LAITY OF THE GENERAL SYNOD
Dr Christina Baxter
Mr Andrew David
Dr John Holden
Mr Colin Slater

DIOCESAN OFFICERS
Dioc Secretary Mr Peter Prentis, Dunham House, Westgate, Southwell, Notts NG25 0JL   *Tel:* (01636) 814331
Fax: (01636) 815084
Chancellor of Diocese Worshipful John Shand, Dioc Office
Deputy Chancellor The Worshipful Simon Tonking, Dioc Office
Registrar of Diocese and Bishop's Legal Secretary Mr Christopher Hodson, Dioc Office
Dioc Surveyors (Parsonages) c/o Dioc Office

DIOCESAN ORGANISATIONS
Diocesan Office Dunham House, Westgate, Southwell, Notts NG25 0JL
Tel: (01636) 814331
Fax: (01636) 815084
e-mail: SDBF@JOHN316.com

ADMINISTRATION
Dioc Synod (Chairman, House of Clergy) Revd Peter Hill, Vicarage, 18 Crookdole Lane, Calverton, Nottingham NG14 6GF *Tel:* 0115–965 2552; *(Chairman, House of Laity)* Mr Grenville Gibson, 'Westering', 6 Cresta Gardens, Mapperley Rise, Nottingham NG3 5GD; *(Secretary)* Mr Peter Prentis, Dioc Office
Board of Finance (Hon Dioc Treas) Mr Patrick Bailey, Dioc Office; *(Secretary)* Mr Peter Prentis *(as above)*
Parsonages Board Mr Peter Prentis *(as above)*
Parsonages Officer Mr Michael Jeffrey *(Asst Secretary Property)*, Dioc Office
Glebe Committee Mr Michael Jeffrey *(as above)*
Pastoral Committee Mr Stephen Langford, Dioc Office
Designated Officer Christopher Hodson, Dioc Office
Redundant Churches Uses Committee (Chairman) The Archdeacon of Nottingham; *(Secretary)* Mr Stephen Langford *(as above)*
Dioc Board of Patronage Mr Peter Prentis *(as above)*

CHURCHES
Advisory Committee for the Care of Churches (Chairman) Revd Keith Turner, Rectory, Main St, Linby, Nottingham NG15 8AE *Tel:* 0115–963 2346; *(Secretary)* Mr Stephen Langford *(as above)*

EDUCATION
Dioc Director Mr Nigel Ladbury, Dioc Office   *Tel:* (01636) 814504
Schools (Inspector) Revd Anthony Shaw *(same address)*
(Administration) Mrs Brenda Greenland *(same address)*
Adult Work Adviser Revd Michael Allen *(same address)*
Youth Work Adviser Capt Denis Tully *(same address)*
Children's Work Adviser Mr Steven Pearce *(same address)*

MINISTRY
Director of Ordinands and Bishop's Research Officer Canon Ian Bunting, 8 Crafts Way, Southwell, Notts NG25 0BL
Tel and *Fax:* (01636) 813868
e-mail: i.bunting@john316.com

Adviser for Women's Ministry Canon Valerie Rampton, Vicarage, Baulk Lane, Kneesall, Newark, Notts
Director of Post-Ordination Training and Bishop's Adviser on Training Revd Dr Neil Burgess, Dioc Office
Dioc Ministry Development Adviser Revd Nigel Peyton, Rectory, Church St, Lambley, Notts NG4 4QP
Dioc Officer for Tourism Revd Anthony Tucker, Vicarage, Main St, Norwell, Notts NG23 6JT Tel: (01636) 636329
 e-mail: t.tucker@john316.com
Readers' Association (Secretary) Mr G. W. Richardson, The Limit, Sutton-cum-Lound, Retford, Notts DN22 8PN
 Tel: (01777) 705080
Warden of Readers and Director of Studies Canon Andrew Woodsford, Gamston Rectory, Retford, Notts DN22 0QB
 Tel: (0177 783) 706
 e-mail: woodsford@msn.com
Assistant Warden of Readers Revd Susan Spencer, 29 Marlock Close, Fiskerton, Notts NG25 0UB Tel: (01636) 830331
Chaplain to Retired Clergy Canon Charles Young, 9 The Paddocks, London Rd, Newark, Notts NG24 1SS
Clergy Widows Officer Revd Reg Hoye, 1 Whiteacre, Burton Joyce, Nottingham NG14 5BU Tel: 0115–931 2485

LITURGICAL
Liturgical Officer Revd Anthony St John Walker, St Saviour's Vicarage, 31 Richmond Rd, Retford, Notts DN22 6SJ
 Tel: (01777) 703800

MISSION
Chairman The Archdeacon of Nottingham
Secretary and Treasurer Mr Anthony Hustwayte, 3 Harvey's Field, Church St, Southwell, Notts NG25 0JD
Bishop's Adviser on Evangelism and Dioc Officer for the Millennium Revd Paul Morris, 39 Davies Rd, West Bridgford, Nottingham NG2 5JE Tel: 0115–981 1311
Assistant Dioc Adviser in Evangelism Revd David Rowe, 13 Rolleston Drive, Lenton Abbey, Nottingham NG7 1JS
 Tel: 0115–947 2777
Bishop's Ecumenical Officer Revd David Bignell, Edwalton Vicarage, Nottingham NG12 4AB Tel: 0115–923 2034

Ecumenical Officer for Derbyshire and Nottinghamshire Mrs Terry Garley, 64 Wyndale Drive, Ilkeston, Derbys DE7 4JO
Bishop's Adviser on Overseas Relations Revd Andrew Wigram, 2 Dobbin Close, Cropwell Bishop, Nottingham NG12 3GR
 Tel: 0115–989 3172

PRESS, PUBLICITY AND PUBLICATIONS
Communications Officer Mrs Rachel Farmer, Dioc Office
 Tel and Fax: (01636) 816276
 0411 214081 (Mobile)
Editor of Dioc Newspaper 'See' Mrs Rachel Farmer (*as above*)

DIOCESAN RECORDS OFFICE
Nottinghamshire Archives, County House, Castle Meadow Rd, Nottingham NG1 1AG, *Principal Archivist* Mr A. J. M. Henstock Tel: 0115–950 4524

SOCIAL RESPONSIBILITY
(*Chairman*) Canon Eric Forshaw
(*Secretary and Social Responsibility Officer*) Mrs Ruth Shelton, St Catharine's House, St Ann's Well Rd, Nottingham NG3 1EJ
 Tel: 0115–958 5517
Council for Family Care (*Director*): Mrs Muriel Weis, Warren House, Pelham Court, Pelham Rd, Nottingham NG5 1AP
 Tel: 0115–950 1805
 Fax: 0115–950 4959
(*Chairman*) Mr Grenville Gibson (*same address*)
Dioc Rural Officer Revd Michael Brock, Rectory, Main St, Epperstone, Notts NG14 6AG Tel: 0115–996 4220

STEWARDSHIP
Funding Advisers/Directors Mrs Carole Park, Mr Anthony Yates c/o Dioc Office

For details of other Diocesan Advisers and Chaplaincies please contact the Diocesan Office

RURAL DEANS
ARCHDEACONRY OF NEWARK
Bawtry Revd John Britton, Vicarage, Tickhill Rd, Harworth, Notts DN11 8PD
 Tel: (01302) 744157
Mansfield Revd Angela Smythe, Vicarage, Pleasley Hill, Mansfield, Notts NG19 7SZ
 Tel: (01623) 812390
Newark Revd Alistair Conn, Rectory, 1 Vicarage Close, Collingham, Newark, Notts NG23 7PQ Tel: (01636) 892317
Newstead Canon Fred Green, Rectory, Annesley Rd, Hucknall, Nottingham NG15 7DE Tel: 0115–963 2033
Retford Canon Andrew Woodsford, Gamston Rectory, Gamston, Retford, Notts DN22 0QB Tel: (01777) 838706
 e-mail: woodsford@msn.com
Worksop Revd Glyn Jones, St John's Vicarage, Shepherd's Ave, Worksop, Notts S81 0JD Tel: (01909) 489868
 e-mail: g.jones@john316.com

ARCHDEACONRY OF NOTTINGHAM
Beeston Revd Jonathan Smithurst, 46 Sandy Lane, Bramcote, Nottingham NG9 3GS Tel: 0115–922 6588
Bingham Canon George Barrodale, Rectory, Thurman Drive, Cotgrave, Nottingham NG12 3HT Tel: 0115–989 2223
Bingham South Revd Trevor Sisson, Keyworth Rectory, Keyworth, Nottingham NG12 5ED Tel: 0115–937 2017
Bingham West Revd Graham Pigott, The Parsonage, Boundary Rd, West Bridgford, Notts NG2 7BD Tel: 0115–923 3492
Gedling Revd Gordon Calthrop-Owen, Vicarage, Lingwood Lane, Woodborough, Nottingham NG14 6DX
 Tel: 0115–965 2250
Nottingham Central Revd Eileen McLean, 15 Hamilton Drive, The Park, Nottingham NG7 1DF Tel: 0115–924 3354
Nottingham North Revd John Walker, Carrington Vicarage, 6 Watcombe Circus, Nottingham NG5 2DT
 Tel: 0115–962 1291
Nottingham West Revd Allen Hart, St John's Vicarage, Graylands Rd, Nottingham NG8 4FD Tel: 0115–929 3320
Southwell Revd Peter Hill, Vicarage, Crookdole Lane, Calverton, Notts NG14 6GF Tel: 0115–965 2552
 e-mail: peter.hill@ichthus.dircon.co.uk

DIOCESE OF TRURO

Founded in 1877. Cornwall; the Isles of Scilly; one parish in Devon.

Population 484,000   Area 1,390 sq m
Stipendiary Clergy 123   Benefices 141
Parishes 225   Churches 313

BISHOP (14th)
Rt Revd William Ind, Lis Escop, Truro, Cornwall TR3 6QQ   Tel: (01872) 862657
Fax: (01872) 862037
[William Truro]

Domestic Chaplain Revd Robert Sellers, Vicarage, Devoran, Truro, Cornwall TR3 6PA   Tel: (01872) 863116 (Home)
(01872) 862657 (Office)

SUFFRAGAN BISHOP
ST GERMANS Rt Revd Graham Richard James, 32 Falmouth Rd, Truro, Cornwall TR1 2HX [1993]   Tel: (01872) 273190
Fax: (01872) 277883

CATHEDRAL CHURCH OF ST MARY
Dean Very Revd Michael Moxon, The Deanery, Lemon St, Truro, Cornwall TR1 2PE [1998]   Tel: (01872) 272661
Cathedral Office 21 Old Bridge St, Truro, Cornwall TR1 2AH   Tel: (01872) 276782
Fax: (01872) 277788
Canons Residentiary
Chancellor Canon Perran Gay, St Michael's House, 52 Daniell Rd, Truro, Cornwall TR1 2DA [1994]   Tel: (01872) 276491
e-mail: Perrangay@aol.com
Treasurer Canon Paul Mellor, Lemon Lodge, Lemon St, Truro, Cornwall TR1 2PE [1994]   Tel: (01872) 272094
Librarian Canon Peter Goodridge, 16 Crescent Rise, Truro, Cornwall TR1 3ER [1996]   Tel: (01872) 270940
Cathedral Administrator Mrs Bette Owen, Cathedral Office
Cathedral Organist Mr Andrew Nethsingha, Cathedral Office

ARCHDEACONS
BODMIN Ven Rodney Whiteman, Archdeacon's House, Cardynham, Bodmin, Cornwall PL30 4BL [1989]
Tel: (01208) 821614
Fax: (01208) 821602

CORNWALL Ven Trevor McCabe, Archdeacon's House, 3 Knights Hill, Kenwyn, Truro, Cornwall TR1 3UY [1988]
Tel: (01872) 272866
Fax: (01872) 242102

CONVOCATION (MEMBERS OF THE HOUSE OF CLERGY OF THE GENERAL SYNOD)
Dignitaries in Convocation
The Bishop of St Germans
The Archdeacon of Bodmin
Proctors for Clergy
Revd Robert Law
Canon Paul Mellor
Canon Tony Neal

MEMBERS OF THE HOUSE OF LAITY OF THE GENERAL SYNOD
Mrs Pat Brown
Mr Jeremy Dowling
Mr Terence Musson

DIOCESAN OFFICERS
Dioc Secretary Mr Ben Laite, Diocesan House, Kenwyn, Truro, Cornwall TR1 1JQ
Tel: (01872) 274351
Fax: (01872) 222510
Chancellor of Diocese The Worshipful Timothy Briden, 1 Temple Gardens, Temple, London EC4Y 9BB
Registrar of Diocese and Bishop's Legal Secretary Mr Martin Follett, Follett Stock, Malpas Rd, Truro, Cornwall TR1 1QH
Tel: (01872) 241700
Fax: (01872) 225052
Dioc Surveyor Mr Richard Thomas, Dioc House, Kenwyn, Truro, Cornwall TR1 1JQ
Tel: (01872) 274351

DIOCESAN ORGANISATIONS
Diocesan Office Diocesan House, Kenwyn, Truro, Cornwall TR1 1JQ
Tel: (01872) 274351
Fax: (01872) 222510

ADMINISTRATION
Dioc Synod and Bishop's Council (*Secretary*) Mr Ben Laite, Dioc Office
Dioc Synod (*Chairman, House of Clergy*) Canon Michael Warner, Rectory, 18 Fore St, Tregony, Truro TR2 5RN Tel: (01872) 530507; (*Chairman, House of Laity*) Mr Robert Foulkes, Beechwood, Lower Tremar, Liskeard, Cornwall PL14 5HF
Tel: (01579) 342821
Board of Finance (*Chairman*) Mr Graham Tyson, Dioc Office; (*Secretary*) Mr Ben Laite (*as above*)
Parsonages Committee Mr Ben Laite (*as above*)
Pastoral Committee Mr Ben Laite (*as above*)
Glebe Committee Mr Ben Laite (*as above*)
Board of Patronage Canon Maurice Friggens, Vicarage, St Cleer, Liskeard, Cornwall PL14 5DJ   Tel: (01579) 343240
Designated Officer Mr Ben Laite (*as above*)

CHURCHES
Advisory Committee for the Care of Churches (*Chairman*) Canon Alan Dunstan, 7 The Cresent, Truro, Cornwall TR1 3ES Tel: (01872) 279604; (*Secretary*) Canon Michael Warner, Dioc Office
Truro Diocesan Guild of Ringers (*President*) Revd F. M. Bowers; (*Gen Secretary*) Mr Robert Perry, 34 Cornubia Close, Truro TR1 1SA   Tel: (01872) 277117

EDUCATION AND TRAINING
Director and Secretary of Education Mr Julian Pykett, Dioc Office
Tel: (01872) 274352
Youth Officer Mrs Jacquie Price (*same address*)
RE Adviser Revd Frank Yates (*same address*)
Children's Adviser Revd Graham Barratt (*same address*)

BOARD OF MINISTRY
Director of Ministerial Training Canon Perran Gay, 52 Daniell Rd, Truro, Cornwall TR1 2DA   Tel: (01872) 276491
Director of Lay Training Preb Tim Gouldstone, Rectory, Tresillian, Truro, Cornwall TR2 4AA   Tel: (01872) 520431
Director of Ordinands The Bishop of St Germans (*as above*)
Director of Ordained Local Ministry Revd David Thurburn-Huelin, Dioc Office
Tel: (01872) 276766
Dioc Readers Rear Admiral Alec Weir, Tipton, St Kew Highway, Bodmin PL30 3ET
Tel: (01208) 84289
Clergy Retirement and Widows Officer Revd Peter Denny, Tralee, The Crescent, Truro, Cornwall TR1 3ES   Tel: (01872) 274492

LITURGICAL
Chairman The Bishop of Truro
Secretary Canon Perran Gay (*as above*)

COUNCIL FOR EVANGELISM AND UNITY
Chairman Ven Rodney Whiteman, Rectory, Cardynham, Bodmin, Cornwall PL30 4BL   Tel: (01208) 821614
    Fax: (01208) 821602
Joint Officers for Evangelism Revd Roger Medley, Vicarage, Linkinhorne, Callington, Cornwall PL17 7LY
    Tel: (01579) 62560
Revd Brian Anderson, Rectory, 31 Trevanion Rd, Wadebridge, Cornwall PL27 7NZ
    Tel: (01208) 812460
Officer for Unity Mrs Daphne Worraker, 12 Crescent Rise, Truro, Cornwall TR1 3ER
    Tel: (01872) 277134
World Church Committee (Chairman) Mrs Pam Miller, Chy-an-Garth, Tregowris, St Keverne, Helston, Cornwall TR12 6PT
    Tel: (01326) 280279

COUNCIL FOR SOCIAL RESPONSIBILITY
Adviser Mr Allan Chesney, 1 Oaklands, The Square, Week St Mary, Holsworthy, Devon EX22 6XH
    Tel and Fax: (01288) 341298

PRESS AND PUBLICATIONS
Dioc Communications Officer Mr Jeremy Dowling, Rosecare Villa Farm, St Gennys, Bude, Cornwall E23 0BG
    Tel: (01840) 230326
    Fax: (01288) 352786

Editor of Dioc News Leaflet Mr Jeremy Dowling (*as above*)
Editor of Dioc Directory Mr Ben Laite (*as above*)

DIOCESAN RECORDS
Diocesan Records Officer Mrs Christine North, County Archivist, County Hall, Truro TR1 3AY
    Tel: (01872) 322000

STEWARDSHIP
Christian Stewardship Adviser Mrs Sheri Sturgess, Dioc House
    Tel: (01872) 270162

RURAL DEANS
ARCHDEACONRY OF CORNWALL
St Austell Revd Malcolm Bowers, Vicarage, Church St, St Blazey, Par, Cornwall PL24 2NG
    Tel: (01726) 817665
Carnmarth North Revd Roger Bush, 53 Clinton Rd, Redruth, Cornwall TR15 2LP
    Tel: (01209) 215258
Carnmarth South Canon Roger Gilbert, Rectory, Albany Rd, Falmouth, Cornwall TR11 3RR
    Tel: (01326) 314176

Kerrier Revd Peter Walker, Vicarage, Pendeen Rd, Porthleven, Helston, Cornwall TR13 9AL
    Tel: (01326) 562419
Penwith Revd Andrew Couch, Vicarage, St Andrew's St, St Ives, Cornwall TR26 1AH
    Tel: (01736) 796404
Powder Preb Tim Gouldstone, Rectory, Tresillian, Truro, Cornwall TR2 4AA
    Tel: (01872) 520431
Pydar Revd Robert Law, Rectory, St Columb Major, Cornwall TR9 6AE
    Tel: (01637) 880252

ARCHDEACONRY OF BODMIN
East Revd Robert Oakes, Rectory, Liskeard Rd, Callington, Cornwall PL17 7DJ   Tel: (01579) 383341
Stratton Revd John Ayling, Rectory, Boscastle, Cornwall PL35 0DJ
    Tel: (01840) 250359
Trigg Major Revd Allan Brownridge, Rectory, Werrington, Launceston, Cornwall PL17 8TP
    Tel: (01566) 773925
Trigg Minor and Bodmin Revd Brian Anderson, Rectory, 31 Trevanion Rd, Wadebridge, Cornwall PL27 7NZ
    Tel: (01208) 812460
West Revd Brian McQuillen, St Martin's Rectory, Barbican Rd, Looe, Cornwall PL13 1NX   Tel: (01503) 263070

DIOCESE OF WAKEFIELD

Founded in 1888. Wakefield; Kirklees; Calderdale; Barnsley, except for an area in the south-east (SHEFFILED); a few parishes in North Yorkshire.

Population 1,077,000   Area 557 sq m
Stipendiary Clergy 172   Benefices 172
Parishes 189   Churches 241

BISHOP (11th)
Rt Revd Nigel Simeon McCulloch, Bishop's Lodge, Woodthorpe Lane, Wakefield WF2 6JL [1992]
Tel: (01924) 255349
Fax: (01924) 250202
e-mail: 113002.1417@compuserve.com
[Nigel Wakefield]

Bishop's Chaplain Canon Roy Clements (same address)
e-mail: 100612.1514@compuserve.com

SUFFRAGAN BISHOP
PONTEFRACT Rt Revd David Charles James, Pontefract House, 181A Manygates Lane, Wakefield WF2 7DR [1998]
Tel: (01924) 250781
Fax: (01924) 240490

CATHEDRAL CHURCH OF ALL SAINTS
Provost Very Revd George Nairn-Briggs, 1 Cathedral Close, Margaret St, Wakefield WF1 2DP [1997]
Tel: (01924) 210005
Fax: (01924) 210009
Cathedral Office Cathedral Office, Northgate, Wakefield WF1 1HG
Tel: (01924) 373923
Fax: (01924) 215054
Canons Residentiary
Vice-Provost Canon Richard Capper, 3 Cathedral Close, Margaret St, Wakefield WF1 2DP [1996]
Tel: (01924) 210007
Canon Precentor Canon Robert Gage, 4 Cathedral Close, Margaret St, Wakefield WF1 2DP [1997]
Tel: (01924) 210008
Chapter Clerk Mrs Linda Box, Cathedral Office
Cathedral Organist Mr Jonathan Bielby, Womack Cottage, Heath, Wakefield, WF1 5SN
Tel: (01924) 378841
Asst Organist and Director of the Cathedral Girls' Choir Miss Louise Marsh, Cathedral Office

ARCHDEACONS
HALIFAX Ven Richard Inwood, 2 Vicarage Gardens, Rastrick, Brighouse HD6 3HD [1995]
Tel: (01484) 714553
Fax: (01484) 711897
PONTEFRACT Ven Tony Robinson, 10 Arden Court, Horbury, Wakefield WF4 5AH [1997]
Tel: (01924) 276797
Fax: (01924) 261095
e-mail: awrobinson@arden.clara.net

CONVOCATION (MEMBERS OF THE HOUSE OF CLERGY OF THE GENERAL SYNOD)
The Archdeacon of Halifax
Proctors for Clergy
Canon Margaret Bradnum
Canon John Hudson
Canon John Hawley
Very Revd George Nairn-Briggs

MEMBERS OF THE HOUSE OF LAITY OF THE GENERAL SYNOD
Mr David Ashton
His Honour Judge John Bullimore
Mrs Mary Judkins
Mr Tim Slater
Mr Andrew Waude

DIOCESAN OFFICERS
Dioc Secretary Vacancy, Church House, 1 South Parade, Wakefield WF1 1LP
Tel: (01924) 371802
Fax: (01924) 364834
Chancellor of Diocese Chanc Peter Collier, 12 St Helens Rd, Dringhouses, York YO2 2HP
Registrar of Diocese and Bishop's Legal Secretary Mrs Linda Box, Bank House, Burton St, Wakefield WF1 2DA
Tel: (01924) 373467
Fax: (01924) 366234
Deputy Registrar Mr Julian Gill (same address)

DIOCESAN ORGANISATIONS
Diocesan Office Church House, 1 South Parade, Wakefield WF1 1LP
Tel: (01924) 371802
Fax: (01924) 364834

ADMINISTRATION
Dioc Secretary Vacancy, Church House
Dioc Synod (Chairman, House of Clergy) Revd Trevor Hicks, Vicarage, Wcmersley, Doncaster DN6 9BG *Tel:* (01977 620436; *(Chairman, House of Laity)* Mrs Mary Judkins, The Old Vicarage, 3 Church Lane, East Ardsley, Wakefield WF3 2LJ *Tel:* (01924) 826802; *(Secretary)* Vacancy
Board of Finance (Chairman) Mr Pamela Green, Church House; *(Secretary)* Vacancy
Secretary (Finance and Pastoral) Mr Ashley Ellis, Church House
Dioc Property Manager Mr Nick Shields, Church House
Secretary (Houses) Mr Peter Thomas, Church House
Pastoral Committee Mr Ashley Ellis (as above)
Dioc Trust Mr Ashley Ellis (as above)
Board of Patronage Mrs Linda Box, Bank House, Burton St, Wakefield WF1 2DA
Tel: (01924) 373467
Designated Officer Mrs Linda Box (as above)

CHURCHES
Advisory Committee for the Care of Churches Mrs Linda Box (as above)
Parish Development Officer Canon Richard Giles, St Thomas's Vicarage, 78 Bankfield Rd, Huddersfield HD1 3HR
Tel: (01484) 420660

EDUCATION
Director of Education Revd Ian Wildey, Church House
Board of Education (Chairman) Ven Richard Inwood; *(Secretary)* Revd Ian Wildey, Church House
Schools Manager Miss Anne Young, Church House
Parish Education Adviser (Children) Revd Betty Pedley, Church House

MINISTRY
Dioc Dean of Ministry and Director of Ordinands Revd Felicity Lawson, 24 Pledwick Lane, Sandal, Wakefield WF2 6DN
Director of Clergy Training and Wakefield Ministry Scheme Officer Revd Dr John Williams, Church House
Principal of Wakefield Ministry Scheme, Warden of Readers and Co-ordinator for Lay Ministry Canon Margaret Bradnum, Church House
Bishop's Adviser for Pastoral Care and Counselling Revd Christine Bullimore, Church House
Bishop's Officer for NSMs Revd Stephen Bradberry, Church House
Retired Clergy and Widows Officers Canon Roland Taylor, 57 Fair View, Carleton, Pontefract *Tel:* (01977) 796564
Revd John Gore, 16 Hepton Drive, Heptonstall, Hebden Bridge HX7 7LU
Tel: (01422) 842004

LITURGICAL
Secretary Revd Michael Rawson, Vicarage, 404 Spen Lane, Gomersall, Cleckheaton BD19 4LS *Tel:* (01274) 872131

MISSION AND UNITY
Ecumenical Officer (*West Yorks*) Dr Edmund Marshall, 14 Belgravia Rd, Wakefield WF1 3JP
Tel: (01924) 378310
e-mail: e.i.marshall@bradford.ac.uk
Assistant Officer (*South Yorks*) Revd Richard Jenkins, 33 Queens Drive, Barnsley S75 2PQ
Tel: (01226) 284775
Dioc Missioner and Bishop's Chaplain for Evangelism Revd Stephen Cottrell, Church House
Canon Missioner Canon John Holmes, Church House

SOCIAL RESPONSIBILITY
Bishop's Adviser for Social Responsibility Canon Ian Gaskell, Church House
Bishop's Adviser on Inter-Faith Issues, Community Relations and Diocese of Mara Link Officer Canon Bill Jones, 316 Huddersfield Rd, Mirfield WF14 9PY
Family Life and Marriage Education Officer Revd Richard Swindell, Church House
Homelessness Worker Julie Burnham, Church House
Bishop's Adviser for Industrial and Economic Affairs Revd Trevor Hicks, Vicarage, Womersley, Doncaster DN6 9BG
Tel: (01977) 620436

PRESS AND PUBLICATIONS
Communications Officer Ms Pippa Allott, Church House
Dioc Newspaper Revd Catherine Ogle, 3 Church St, Woolley, Wakefield WF4 2JU
Tel: (01226) 382550
Dioc Year Book (*Editor*) Vacancy
Editor of Dioc News and Publications Adviser Revd Michael Bootes, 1 Manor Farm Close, Kellington, Goole DN14 0PF
Tel: (01977) 662876
Fax: (01977) 663072
e-mail: mb@theoratory.demon.co.uk

DIOCESAN RECORDS OFFICE
County Archivist Mrs Ruth Harris, West Yorkshire Archive Service, Registry of Deeds, Newstead Rd, Wakefield WF1 2DE

DIOCESAN RESOURCES CENTRE
Childrens' Adviser Revd Betty Pedley, Church House

STEWARDSHIP
Christian Giving Adviser Graham Richards, Church House

RURAL DEANS
ARCHDEACONRY OF HALIFAX
Almondbury Revd Mark Thomas, 2 Westgate, Almondbury, Huddersfield HD5 8XE *Tel:* (01422) 256088
Brighouse and Elland Revd Martin Wood, Rectory, 50 Victoria Rd, Elland HX5 0QA
Tel: (01484) 713386

Calder Valley Canon Peter Calvert, Vicarage, Todmorden OL14 7BS
Tel: (01706) 813180
Halifax Canon Alastair Ross, Vicarage, Kensington Rd, Halifax HX3 0HN
Tel: (01422) 365477
Huddersfield Canon Ed Roberts, Holy Trinity Vicarage, 132 Trinity St, Huddersfield HD1 4DT
Tel: (01484) 422998
Kirkburton Revd Graham Whitcroft, Vicarage, 138 Wakefield Rd, Lepton, Huddersfield HD8 0LU
Tel: (01484) 602172

ARCHDEACONRY OF PONTEFRACT
Barnsley Canon John Hudson, The Clergy House, Church St, Royston, Barnsley S71 4QZ
Tel: (01226) 722410
Birstall Revd Dhoe Craig-Wild, St Andrew's Vicarage, 4 Lewisham St, Morley, Leeds LS27 0LA
Tel: 0113–252 3783
Chevet Revd John White, Vicarage, 3 Church Lane, Chapelthorpe, Wakefield WF4 3JB *Tel:* (01924) 255360
Dewsbury Revd Lindsay Dew, 51 Frank Lane, Thornhill, Dewsbury WF12 0JW
Tel: (01924) 465064
Pontefract Revd Trevor Hicks, Vicarage, Womersley, Doncaster DN6 9BG
Tel: (01977) 620436
Wakefield Revd Keith Williams, Vicarage, Church Lane, East Ardsley, Wakefield WF3 2JL *Tel:* (01924) 822184

DIOCESE OF WINCHESTER

Founded in 676. Hampshire, except for the south-eastern quarter (PORTSMOUTH), an area in the north-east (GUILDFORD), a small area in the west (SALISBURY) and one parish in the north (OXFORD); an area of eastern Dorset; the Channel Islands.

Population 1,214,000   Area 1,216 sq m
Stipendiary Clergy 247   Benefices 210
Parishes 304   Churches 407

BISHOP (96th)
Rt Revd Michael Charles Scott-Joynt, Wolvesey, Winchester, Hants SO23 9ND [1995] Tel: (01962) 854050
Tel and Fax: (01962) 842376
e-mail: michael.scott-joynt@dial.pipex.com
[Michael Winton:]

Bishop's Assistant Mr Stephen Adam (*same address*)

SUFFRAGAN BISHOPS
SOUTHAMPTON Rt Revd Jonathan Gledhill, Ham House, The Crescent, Romsey, Hants SO51 7NG [1996]
Tel: (01794) 516005
Fax: (01794) 830242
e-mail: jonathan.gledhill@dial.pipex.com
BASINGSTOKE Rt Revd Geoffrey Rowell, Bishopswood End, Kingswood Rise, Four Marks, Alton, Hants GU34 5BD [1994]
Tel: (01420) 562925
Fax: (01420) 561251
e-mail: geoffrey.rowell@dial.pipex.com

HONORARY ASSISTANT BISHOPS
Rt Revd Leslie Lloyd Rees, Kingfisher Lodge, 20 Arle Gardens, Alresford, Hants SO24 9BA [1987] Tel: (01962) 734619
Rt Revd Hassan Barnaba Dehqani Tafti, c/o Church House, 9 The Close, Winchester SO23 9LS Tel: (01962) 844644
Rt Revd John Austin Baker, Norman Corner, 4 Mede Villas, Kingsgate Rd, Winchester, Hants SO23 9QQ [1994]
Tel: (01962) 861388
Rt Revd Simon Hedley Burrows, 8 Quarry Rd, Winchester, Hants SO23 8JF [1994]
Tel: (01962) 881566
Rt Revd John Yates, 15 Abbotts Ann Rd, Harestock, Winchester SO22 6ND [1995]
Tel: (01264) 354996
Rt Revd Gordon Roe, 8 Eldon Rd, Bournemouth BH9 2RT [1997]
Tel: (01202) 535127

CATHEDRAL CHURCH OF THE HOLY TRINITY, AND OF ST PETER, ST PAUL AND OF ST SWITHUN
Dean Very Revd Michael Till, The Deanery, The Close, Winchester, Hants SO23 9LS [1996] Tel and Fax: (01962) 853738
e-mail: dean.of.winchester@dial.pipex.com
Cathedral Office 5 The Close, Winchester, Hants SO23 9LS Tel: (01962) 853137
Fax: (01962) 841519
e-mail: winchester.cathedral.office@dial.pipex.com
Canons Residentiary
Canon Keith Walker, 11 The Close, Winchester, Hants SO23 9LS [1987]
Tel: (01962) 864923
Ven John Guille, 1 The Close, Winchester, Hants SO23 9LS [1998]
Tel and Fax: (01962) 869374
Canon Philip Morgan, 8 The Close, Winchester, Hants SO23 9LS [1994]
Tel: (01962) 854771
Canon Charles Stewart, 5 The Close, Winchester, Hants SO23 9LS [1994]
Tel: (01962) 856236
Receiver General Mr Keith Bamber, Cathedral Office
Chapter Clerk Mr Julian Hartwell, Godwin Bremridge & Clifton, 12 St Thomas St, Winchester, Hants SO23 9HF
Tel: (01962) 841484
Fax: (01962) 841554
Cathedral Organist Mr David Hill, 10 The Close, Winchester, Hants SO23 9LS
Tel: (01962) 854392
Sub-Organist Mr Stephen Farr, Cathedral Office

ARCHDEACONS
WINCHESTER Ven Alan Clarkson, Vicarage, Church Corner, Burley, Ringwood, Hants BH24 4AP [1984] Tel: (01425) 402303
Fax: (01425) 403753
e-mail: alan.clarkson@dial.pipex.com
BASINGSTOKE Ven John Guille, 1 The Close, Winchester, Hants SO23 9LS [1998]
Tel: and Fax: (01962) 869374

CONVOCATION (MEMBERS OF THE HOUSE OF CLERGY OF THE GENERAL SYNOD)
Vacancy
Proctors for Clergy
Revd Dr Anne Barton
Revd Barry Fry
Ven John Guille
Revd Dr Richard Turnbull
Channel Islands
The Dean of Guernsey

MEMBERS OF THE HOUSE OF LAITY OF THE GENERAL SYNOD
Mr Peter Bray
Ms Christine Fry
Mr Richard Leyton
Dr Peter May
Dr Kathryn Morfey
Mrs Angela Southern
Mrs Margot Townsend
Channel Islands:
Ms Jane Bisson
Mr David Robilliard

DIOCESAN OFFICERS
Dioc Secretary Mr Ray Anderton, Church House, 9 The Close, Winchester, Hants SO23 9LS Tel: (01962) 844644
Fax: (01962) 841815
Chancellor of Diocese Chanc Christopher Clark, 3 Pump Court, Temple, London EC4Y 7AJ Tel: 0171–353 0711
Registrar of Diocese and Bishop's Legal Secretary Mr Peter White, 19 St Peter St, Winchester, Hants SO23 8BU
Tel: (01962) 844440
Fax: (01962) 842300

DIOCESAN ORGANISATIONS
Diocesan Office Church House, 9 The Close, Winchester, Hants SO23 9LS
Tel: (01962) 844644
Fax: (01962) 841815
e-mail: chsewinchester@clara.net

ADMINISTRATION
Asst Dioc Secretary (*Churches and Administration*) Mr Stephen Bowler, Church House
Asst Dioc Secretary (*Synod and Property*) Vacancy
Finance Manager and Asst Dioc Secretary Mr Stephen Collyer, Church House
Parish Resources Adviser Mr Roger Parsons, Church House
Dioc Synod (*Chairman, House of Clergy*) Canon Clifford Wright, Rectory, 44 Cheriton Rd, Winchester SO23 5AY Tel: (01962) 854849; (*Chairman, House of Laity*) Dr Katharine Morfey, 2 Royston Close, Southampton SO17 1TB Tel: (01703) 554396; (*Secretary*) Mr Ray Anderton, Church House; (*Asst Secretary*) Vacancy

Board of Finance (*Chairman*) Mr Robin Hodgson, Tara, Dean Lane, Winchester SO22 5RA *Tel:* (01962) 862119; (*Secretary*) Mr Ray Anderton (*as above*)
Property Committee Vacancy
Dioc Surveyor Mr Michael Hewin, Church House
Dioc Surveyor (*Schools*) Mr Trevor Samphier, Church House
Pastoral Committee Vacancy
Electoral Registration Officer Vacancy
Designated Officer Mr Stephen Bowler (*as above*)

CHURCHES
Advisory Committee for the Care of Churches (*Chairman*) Mr Nicholas Jonas, North House, St Peter's St, Bishop's Waltham, Southampton SO32 1AD
Tel: (01489) 892585
(*Secretary*) Mr Stephen Bowler (*as above*)

EDUCATION
Director of Education Revd Richard Lindley, Church House
RE Adviser Mrs Lilian Weatherley, Church House

MINISTRY AND FAITH DEVELOPMENT
Ministry Development
Director of Ministry Development (*inc CME and POT*) Canon John Cullen, Church House
Lay Ministry Adviser and Warden of Readers Revd Simon Baker, Church House
Lay Training Officers (*Basingstoke Archdeaconry*) Revd Michael Kenning, Rectory, North Waltham, Basingstoke RG25 2BQ
Tel and Fax: (01256) 397256
(*Winchester Archdeaconry*) Mrs Margaret Hounsham, 46 Augustine Rd, Drayton, Portsmouth PO6 1HZ
Tel: (01705) 382394
Adviser for Ordinands Vacancy
Vocations Adviser (*Convenor*) Vacancy
Clerical Registry Revd Dr Ronald Pugh, Church House
Faith Development
Director of Faith Development and Field Officer Winchester Archdeaconry (*Adults*) Revd Stephen Pittis, Church House
Faith Development Field Officer Basingstoke Archdeaconry (*Adults*) Revd Tim Humphrey, 19 Sainfoin Lane, Oakley, Basingstoke RG23 7HZ Tel: (01256) 782790
Basingstoke Archdeaconry (*Youth and Children*) Mr Nigel Argall, Church House
Winchester Archdeaconry (*Youth*) Mrs Mel McPherson, Church House
(*Children*) Miss Diana Lester, Church House

Partnership and Ecumenical
Partnership Committee (*Secretary*) Mr Stephen Bowler (*as above*)
Ecumenical Officer Revd John Pragnell, Copythorne Vicarage, Romsey Rd, Cadnam SO40 2NN Tel: (01703) 814769

LITURGICAL
Secretary Canon Charles Stewart, 5 The Close, Winchester SO23 9LS
Tel: (01962) 853137
Development and Research Officer for Liturgical Matters Revd Dr Anne Barton, Rectory, Wolverton, Tadley RG26 5RU
Tel: (01635) 298008

COMMUNICATIONS, PUBLICATIONS AND RESOURCES
Communications Officer Revd Caroline Baston, Rectory, 19 Petersfield Rd, Winchester SO23 8JD Tel: (01962) 853777
Fax: (01962) 841714
e-mail: caroline.baston@dial.pipex.com
Publications (*inc Dioc Directory*) Mr Ian Knight, Church House
Resource Centre (*Manager*) Mr Ian Knight (*as above*)
Dioc Newspaper (*Editor*) Miss Hazel Southam, Church House

DIOCESAN RECORD OFFICES
Hants Record Office, Sussex St, Winchester, Hants SO23 8TH (*Archivist* Miss Rosemary Dunhill) Tel: (01962) 846154; Southampton City Record Office, Civic Centre, Southampton SO14 7LY (*Archivist* Mrs Sue Woolgar) Tel: (01703) 832251

SOCIAL RESPONSIBILITY
Director of Social Responsibility Canon Chris Rich, Church House
Housing and Homelessness Adviser Mrs Audrey Hollingbery, Church House
Social and Community Work Team (*Leader*) Ms Marilyn Taylor, Church House
Voluntary Care Groups Advisers Mr Kevin Fray, Revd Helen Jesty and Ms Gillian Limb, Church House
World Development Education Adviser Mr Kevin Fray (*as above*)
Hampshire, Isle of Wight and Channel Islands Association for the Deaf (*Chaplain*) Revd John Studd, Fairbairn Centre for the Deaf, 18 Augustine Rd, Southampton SO14 0PL
Tel: (01703) 226803
Community Development Team (*Leader*) Mr Jeremy Coombe, 25 Church St, Romsey SO51 8BT Tel: (01794) 516456
Rural Officer Revd Tony Jardine, Farringdon Rectory, Alton GU34 3EE
Tel and Fax: (01420) 588398

RURAL DEANS
ARCHDEACONRY OF WINCHESTER
Bournemouth Revd Anthony Chambers, St James Vicarage, 12 Harewood Ave, Bournemouth, Dorset BH7 6NQ
Tel: (01202) 425918
Fax: (01202) 432118
Christchurch Revd John Williams, Vicarage, 33 Nea Rd, Highcliffe, Christchurch, Dorset BH23 4NB Tel: (01425) 272767
Eastleigh Revd Adrian Harbidge, Vicarage, Hursley Rd, Chandler's Ford, Eastleigh, Hants SO53 2FT
Tel: (01703) 252597
Lyndhurst Canon Michael Anderson, Vicarage, Stopples Lane, Hordle, Lymington, Hants SO41 0HX Tel: (01425) 614428
Romsey Revd Bruce Kington, Rectory, Braishfield, Romsey, Hants SO51 0PR
Tel: (01794) 368335
Southampton Canon Bruce Hartnell, Vicarage, 41 Station Rd, Sholing, Southampton SO19 8FN Tel: (01703) 448337

ARCHDEACONRY OF BASINGSTOKE
Alresford Revd Ryc Smith, Rectory, Preston Candover, Basingstoke, Hants RG25 2EE Tel: (01256) 389245
Alton Revd John Webb, Rectory, Bentworth, Alton, Hants GU34 5RB
Tel: (01420) 563218
Andover Revd Michael Harley, Vicarage, Hurstbourne Tarrant, Andover, Hants SP11 0AH Tel: (01264) 736222
Basingstoke Canon David Picton, Vicarage, Church Lane, Old Basing, Basingstoke, Hants RG24 7DJ Tel: (01256) 473762
Odiham Revd Neville Beamer, Vicarage, 99 Reading Rd, Yateley, Camberley, Surrey GU46 7LR Tel: (01252) 873133
Whitchurch Revd Martin Coppen, Vicarage, St Mary Bourne, Andover, Hants SP11 6AY Tel: (01264) 738308
Winchester Canon Robert Teare, Rectory, 22 St John's St, Winchester SO23 8HF
Tel: (01962) 863891

CHANNEL ISLANDS
Dean of Jersey Very Revd John Seaford, The Deanery, David Place, St Helier, Jersey, CI JE2 4TE Tel: (01534) 720001
Fax: (01534) 617488
Dean of Guernsey Very Revd Marc Trickey, The Rectory, La Grande Rue, St Martin's, Guernsey, CI GY4 6RR
Tel: (01481) 38303
Fax: (01481) 37710

DIOCESE OF WORCESTER

Founded 679. The eastern half of the County of Hereford and Worcester, except for a few parishes in the south (GLOUCESTER) and a few parishes in the north (BIRMINGHAM); all of Dudley; a few parishes in northern Gloucestershire.

Population 828,000   Area 671 sq m
Stipendiary Clergy 161   Benefices 123
Parishes 196   Churches 282

BISHOP (112th)
Rt Revd Peter Stephen Maurice Selby PH D, The Bishop's House, Hartlebury Castle, Kidderminster, Worcs DY11 7XX [1997] *Tel:* (01299) 250214
Fax: (01299) 250027
[Peter Wigorn:]

AREA BISHOP
DUDLEY Rt Revd Rupert William Noel Hoare PH D, Bishop's House, 366 Halesowen Rd, Cradley Heath, W Midlands B64 7JF [1993] *Tel:* 0121–550 3407
Fax: 0131–550 7340

HONORARY ASSISTANT BISHOPS
Rt Revd Derek Bond, Ambleside, 14 Worcester Rd, Evesham, Worcs WR11 4JU *Tel:* (01386) 446156
Rt Revd George Briggs, 1 Lygon Lodge, Newland, Malvern, Worcs WR13 5AX *Tel:* (01684) 572941
Rt Revd Kenneth Woollcombe, 19 Ashdale Ave, Pershore, Worcs WR10 1PL *Tel:* (01386) 556550

CATHEDRAL CHURCH OF CHRIST AND THE BLESSED VIRGIN MARY
Dean Very Revd Peter Marshall, The Deanery, 10 College Green, Worcester WR1 2LH [1997] *Tel:* (01905) 27821
e-mail: WorcesterDeanPJM@compuserve.com
Cathedral Office 10A College Green, Worcester WR1 2LH *Tel:* (01905) 28854
Fax: (01905) 611139
e-mail: worcestercathedral@compuserve.com
Canons Residentiary
Vice-Dean Canon David Thomas, The Chaplain's House, St Oswald's Close, The Tything, Worcester WR1 1HR [1987]
Tel: (01905) 616619
Ven Frank Bentley, Archdeacon's House, 56 Battenhall Rd, Worcester WR5 2BQ [1984] *Tel:* (01905) 764446

Canon Iain MacKenzie, 2 College Green, Worcester WR1 2LH [1989]
Tel: (01905) 25238
Precentor Revd Christine Owen, Cathedral Office
Steward and Chapter Clerk Mr Michael Lumley, Cathedral Office
Master of Choristers and Cathedral Organist Mr Adrian Lucas, Cathedral Office

ARCHDEACONS
WORCESTER Ven Frank Bentley, Archdeacon's House, 56 Battenhall Rd, Worcester WR5 2BQ [1984]
Tel: (01905) 764446
Office The Old Palace, Deansway, Worcester WR1 2JE *Tel:* (01905) 20537
Fax: (01905) 612302
DUDLEY Ven John Gathercole, 15 Worcester Rd, Droitwich, Worcs WR9 8AA [1987]
Tel and *Fax:* (01905) 773301

CONVOCATION (MEMBERS OF THE HOUSE OF CLERGY OF THE GENERAL SYNOD)
Dignitaries in Convocation
The Bishop of Dudley
The Archdeacon of Dudley
Proctors for Clergy
Canon Ray Adams
Revd Robert Jones
Revd Melvyn Smith

MEMBERS OF THE HOUSE OF LAITY OF THE GENERAL SYNOD
Prof Michael Clarke
Mr Harry Jeffery
Mr John Layton
Mr Peter Middlemiss

DIOCESAN OFFICERS
Dioc Secretary Mr Robert Higham, The Old Palace, Deansway, Worcester WR1 2JE
Tel: (01905) 20537
Deputy Chancellor of Diocese Mr Charles Mynors, 2 Harcourt Buildings, The Temple, London EC4Y 9DB
Tel: 0171–353 8415

Registrar of Diocese and Bishop's Legal Secretary Mr Michael Huskinson, Messrs March & Edwards, 8 Sansome Walk, Worcester WR1 1LN *Tel:* (01905) 723561
Fax: (01905) 723812
Dioc Surveyor Mr Jonathan Reeves, Fisher Hoggarth Estate Office, Dumbleton, Evesham, Worcs WR11 6TH
Tel: (01386) 881214

DIOCESAN ORGANISATION
Diocesan Office The Old Palace, Deansway, Worcester WR1 2JE *Tel:* (01905) 20537
Fax: (01905) 612302

ADMINISTRATION
Asst Dioc Secretary (*Finance*) Mr Stephen Lindner, Dioc Office
DAC Secretary Mr Stephen Bowyer, Dioc Office
Dioc Synod (*Chairman, House of Clergy*) Canon Michael Lewis, Rectory, 6 St Catherine's Hill, Worcester WR5 52EA *Tel:* (01905) 355119; (*Chairman, House of Laity*) Mr Alistair Findlay, Commissioner Cottage, Cowsden, Upton Snodsbury, Worcester WR7 4NX *Tel:* (01905) 381841; (*Secretary*) Mr Robert Higham, Dioc Office

RESOURCES BOARD
(*Chairman*) Mr Tony Prescott, Nestor House, Dymock Rd, Much Marcle, Hereford HR8 2NL *Tel:* (01531) 660699 (*Secretary*) Mr Robert Higham (*as above*)
Parsonages Board (*Chairman*) Revd David Hassell, Rectory, Bishampton, Pershore, Worcs WR10 2LT *Tel:* (01386) 4626648; (*Secretary*) Mr Stephen Lindner *as above*)
Investment and Glebe Committee (*Chairman*) Ven Frank Bentley, Archdeacon's House, 56 Battenhall Rd, Worcester WR5 2BQ *Tel:* (01905) 764446; (*Secretary*) Mr Stephen Lindner (*as above*)
Glebe Agent Mr Jonathan Reeves, Fisher Hoggarth Estate Office, Dumbleton, Evesham, Worcs WR11 6TH
Tel: (01386) 881214
Stewardship Committee (*Chairman*) Mr John Jones, Cymafon, 28 Avon Green, Wyre Piddle, Pershore WR10 6NJ
Tel: (01386) 552861
Stewardship and Resources Office Revd Mel Smith, Dioc Office
Pastoral Committee Mr Robert Higham (*as above*)
Board of Patronage Mr Robert Higham (*as above*)
Designated Officer Mr Robert Higham (*as above*)
Trust Mr Michael Huskinson, Messrs March & Edwards, 8 Sansome Walk, Worcester WR1 1LN *Tel:* (01905) 723561
Fax: (01905) 723812

CHURCHES

Advisory Committee for the Care of Churches (Chairman) Canon Michael Lewis *(as above)*
(Secretary) Mr Stephen Bowyer *(as above)*
Change Ringers Association Mr M. D. Fellows, 70A Hagley Rd, Stourbridge, W Midlands DY8 1QT　　Tel: (0138 43) 75320

EDUCATION

Board of Education (Chairman) Heather Haines, 33 Lyttelton Rd, Droitwich, Worcs WR9 7AB　　Tel: (01905) 774529
Director of Education Vacancy, Dioc Office
Tertiary Education Officer Revd David Gutteridge, Dioc Office
RE Adviser/Children's Officer Mr Robin Sharples, Dioc Office
Youth Officer Mr Alastair Langton, Dioc Office

TRAINING

Board for Ordained and Lay Development (Chairman) The Bishop of Dudley *(as above)*; *Secretary* Canon Peter Kerr, Rectory, Ombersley, Droitwich, Worcs WR9 0EW　　Tel: (01905) 620950
Adult Education and Ministerial Training Officer Canon Peter Kerr *(as above)*
Associate Officer Revd John Reader, Rectory, Elmley Lovett, Droitwich, Worcs WR9 0PU　　Tel: (01905) 251798
Local Ministry Officer Mr Martin Murphy, Dioc Office
Chaplaincy to People who are Deaf or Hard of Hearing: Chaplain Revd Paul Harrison, Vicarage, 16 Church Rd, Astwood Bank, Redditch, Worcs B69 6EH
　　Tel: (01527) 892489
Chaplaincy to People with Learning Difficulties: Chaplain Canon Hazel Hughes, Wribbenhall Vicarage, Trimpley Lane, Bewdley, Worcs DY12 1JJ　　Tel: (01299) 402196

MINISTRY

Dioc Director of Ordinands Canon John Green, Rectory, Madresfield, Malvern, Worcs WR13 5AB　　Tel: (01684) 574919
Convenor for Women's Ministry Canon Hilary Hanke, 25 Middleway Ave, Wordsley, Stourbridge DY8 5NB
　　Tel: (01384) 293350

Association of Readers Mr Roy Peacock, 44 Whitehall Rd, Stourbridge, W Midlands DY8 2JT　　Tel: (01384) 379972

LITURGICAL

Secretary Canon Guy Smith, Vicarage, 9 Sutton Park Rd, Kidderminster, Worcs DY11 6LE　　Tel and *Fax*: (01562) 822186

MISSION AND UNITY

Board for Mission (Chairman) Revd Robert Jones, St Barnabas Rectory, Church Rd, Worcester WR3 8NX
　　Tel and *Fax*: (01905) 23785
World Mission Officer Miss Catherine Graham, Dioc Office
Ecumenical Officer Revd Clifford Owen, Rectory, Clifton-on-Teme, Worcester WR6 6DJ　　Tel: (01886) 812483

PRESS AND PUBLICATIONS

Bishop's and Dioc Communications Officer Mrs Nicola Currie, St Stephen's Vicarage, 1 Beech Ave, Worcester WR3 8PZ
　　Tel: (01905) 454768
　　Fax: (01905) 755405
　　e-mail: nicola_currie@ecunet.org
Editor of the Dioc Directory Mr Robert Higham *(as above)*
Editor of Dioc News and Public Information Officer Mr Robert Higham *(as above)*

DIOCESAN RECORD OFFICES

St Helen's Church, Fish St, Worcester WR1 2HN *(County Archivist* Revd Anthony Wherry) Tel: (01905) 765921; Dudley Archives and Local History Dept, Mount Pleasant St, Coseley, W Midlands WV14 9JR *(Archivist* Mrs K. H. Atkins)
　　Tel: (01384) 812770

SOCIAL RESPONSIBILITY

Board for Social, Economic and Local Development
Chairman Canon Stephen Hutchinson, Vicarage, 34 South Rd, Stourbridge, W Midlands DY8 3YB
Secretary Alison Webster, Dioc Office
Social Responsibility Officer Alison Webster *(as above)*
Industrial Mission: Team Leader Canon Stephen Kendal, 15 St John's Ave, Kidderminster, Worcs DY11 6AT
　　Tel: (01562) 823929

Chaplaincy to Agriculture and Rural Life Revd John Willis, Glebe House, Grafton Flyford, Worcester WR7 4PG
　　Tel: (01905) 381460
　　Fax: (01905) 381110

RURAL DEANS

ARCHDEACONRY OF WORCESTER

Evesham Revd Harold Goddard, Rectory, Sedgeberrow, Evesham, Worcs WR11 6UE
　　Tel: (01386) 881291
Malvern Vacancy
Martley and Worcester West Revd Dr Michael Nott, Crown East Vicarage, Rushwick, Worcester WR2 5TU
　　Tel: (01905) 428801
Pershore Revd Ken Boyce, Fladbury Rectory, Pershore, Worcs WR10 2QW
　　Tel: (01386) 860356
Upton Revd Christopher Hardwick, Rectory, The Cross, Ripple, Tewkesbury, Glos GL20 6HA　　Tel: (01684) 592655
Worcester East Canon Michael Lewis, Rectory, 6 St Catherine's Hill, Worcester WR5 52EA　　Tel: (01905) 355119

ARCHDEACONRY OF DUDLEY

Bromsgrove Canon David Salt, St Stephen's Vicarage, 248 Birchfield Rd, Redditch, Worcs B97 4LZ　　Tel: (01527) 61543
Droitwich Revd Dennis Wight, Rectory, Fish House Lane, Stoke Prior, Bromsgrove, Worcs B60 4JT　　Tel: (01527) 832501
Dudley Revd Matthew Baynham, St Luke's Vicarage, Upper High St, Cradley Heath, Warley, W Midlands B64 5HX
　　Tel: (01384) 569940
Himley Revd Fred Trethewey, 5 Leys Rd, Brockmoor, Brierley Hill, W Midlands DY5 3UR　　Tel: (01384) 263327
Kidderminster Revd Geoffrey Shilvock, Vicarage, Kidderminster, Worcs DY11 5XD　　Tel: (01562) 851133
Stourbridge Canon Paul Tongue, Vicarage, 4 The Holloway, Amblecote, Stourbridge, W Midlands DY8 4DH
　　Tel: (01384) 394057
Stourport Revd Barry Gilbert, Vicarage, Stourport-on-Severn, Worcs DY13 9DD
　　Tel: (01299) 822041

DIOCESE OF YORK

Founded in 627. York; East Riding of Yorkshire; Kingston-upon-Hull; Redcar; Middlesbrough; the eastern half of North Yorkshire; Stockton-on-Tees, south of the Tees; a few parishes in Leeds.

Population 1,362,000 Area 2,661 sq m
Stipendiary Clergy 290 Benefices 277
Parishes 475 Churches 605

ARCHBISHOP (96th)
Most Revd and Rt Hon David Michael Hope, *Primate of England and Metropolitan*, Bishopthorpe Palace, Bishopthorpe, York YO23 2GE [1995]   Tel: (01904) 707021/2
Fax: (01904) 709204
e-mail: office@bishopthorpe.u-net.com
[David Ebor:]

Chaplain to the Archbishop Revd Michael Kavanagh
Private Secretary to the Archbishop Mrs Mary Murray

SUFFRAGAN BISHOPS
SELBY Rt Revd Humphrey Taylor, 10 Precentor's Court, York YO1 7EJ [1991]
Tel: (01904) 656492
Fax: (01904) 655671
e-mail: bishselby@clara.net
HULL Rt Revd Richard Frith, Hullen House, Woodfield Lane, Hessle HU13 0ES [1998]   Tel: (01482) 649019
Fax: (01482) 647449
WHITBY Rt Revd Gordon Bates, 60 West Green, Stokesley, Middlesbrough TS9 5BD [1983]   Tel: (01642) 710390
Fax: (01642) 710685

PROVINCIAL EPISCOPAL VISITOR
BEVERLEY Rt Revd John Scott Gaisford, 3 North Lane, Roundhay, Leeds LS8 2QJ [1994]   Tel: 0113–273 2003
0410 887756 (Mobile)
Fax: 0113–273 3002
e-mail: 101740,2725@compuserve.com

HONORARY ASSISTANT BISHOPS
Rt Revd Clifford Barker, 15 Oaktree Close, Strensall, York YO3 5TR [1991]
Tel: (01904) 490406
Rt Revd Ronald Graham Gregory Foley, Ramsey Cottage, 3 Poplar Ave, Kirkbymoorside, York YO6 6ES [1989]
Tel: (01751) 432439
Rt Revd David Galliford, Bishopsgarth, Maltongate, Thornton Le Dale YO18 7SA [1991]   Tel: (01751) 474605

Rt Revd Richard James Wood, 90 Park Lane, Cottingham HU16 5RX [1985]
Tel: (01482) 843928

CATHEDRAL CHURCH OF ST PETER
Dean Very Revd Raymond Furnell, The Deanery, York YO1 7JQ [1994]
Tel: (01904) 623608
Fax: (01904) 672002
Dean and Chapter Office Church House, Ogleforth, York YO1 7JN
Tel: (01904) 624426
Fax: (01904) 654604
Precentor and Chamberlain Canon Paul Ferguson, 2 Minster Court, York YO1 7JJ [1995]   Tel: (01904) 624965
Treasurer Canon Edward Norman PH D, 3 Minster Court, York YO1 7JJ [1995]
Tel: (01904) 625599
Chancellor and Librarian Canon John Toy, 4 Minster Yard, York YO1 7JD [1983]
Tel: (01904) 620877
Canon Residentiary Canon Ron Metcalfe, 5 Minster Yard, York YO1 7JD [1988]
Tel: (01904) 642542
High Steward The Earl of Halifax
Chapter Clerk Brigadier Peter Lyddon, Church House, Ogleforth, York YO1 7JN
Tel: (01904) 622774
Fax: (01904) 654604
Bursar Mr Martin Vevers, Church House, Ogleforth, York YO1 7JN
Tel: (01904) 656846
Master of the Music Mr Philip Moore, 1 Minster Court, York YO1 7JJ
Tel: (01904) 624426

ARCHDEACONS
YORK Ven George Austin, North Back House, Main St, Wheldrake, York YO19 6AG [1988]   Tel: (01904) 448509
Fax: (01904) 448002
e-mail: george.austin@virgin.net
EAST RIDING Ven Peter Harrison, Brimley Lodge, 27 Molescroft Rd, Beverley HU17 7DX [1998]   Tel: (01482) 881659
CLEVELAND Ven Christopher Hawthorn, Park House, Rosehill, Great Ayton, Middlesbrough TS9 6BH [1991]
Tel: (01642) 723221
Fax: (01642) 724137

CONVOCATION (MEMBERS OF THE HOUSE OF CLERGY OF THE GENERAL SYNOD)
Dignitaries in Convocation
The Bishop of Hull
The Dean of York
The Archdeacon of Cleveland
Proctors for Clergy
Revd Benjamin Hopkinson
Canon David Lickess
Revd Simon Stanley
Canon Glyn Webster
Revd John Weetman
Canon John Young

MEMBERS OF THE HOUSE OF LAITY OF THE GENERAL SYNOD
Mrs Bernadette Burbridge
Mr Martin Dales
Mrs Rachel Harrison
Mr Arthur Pollard
Mr John Porter
Mr Bryan Sandford
Mrs Carole Smith
Mr Ian Smith

DIOCESAN OFFICERS
Dioc Secretary Mr Colin Sheppard, Church House, Ogleforth, York YO1 7JE
Tel: (01904) 611696
Fax: (01904) 620375
Chancellor of Diocese His Honour Judge Thomas Coningsby, Leyfields, Elmore Rd, Chipstead, Surrey CR3 3SG
Registrar of Diocese and Archbishop's Legal Secretary Mr Lionel Lennox, The Registry, Stamford House, Piccadilly, York YO1 9PP   Tel: (01904) 623487
Fax: (01904) 611458
e-mail: denison.till@dial.pipex.com
Dioc Surveyors Messrs Ferrey and Mennim, 12 Minster Yard, York YO1 2HH
Tel: (01904) 624103
Fax: (01904) 626983

DIOCESAN ORGANISATIONS
Diocesan Office Church House, Ogleforth, York YO1 7JE   Tel: (01904) 611696
Fax: (01904) 620375

ADMINISTRATION
Dioc Synod (Chairman, House of Clergy) Canon Glyn Webster, 22 Markham Crescent, York YO3 7NS Tel: (01904) 453120; *(Chairman, House of Laity)* Mr Richard Liversedge, 1 Caledonia Park, Victoria Dock, Hull Tel: (01482) 588357; *(Secretary)* Mr Colin Sheppard, Church House
Assistant Dioc Secretary Ms Shirley Davies, Church House

Board of Finance (Chairman) Mr Bryan Sandford, Church House; *(Secretary)* Mr Colin Sheppard *(as above)*
Financial Secretary Mr David Fletcher, Church House
Parsonages Committee (Secretary) Mr Colin Sheppard *(as above)*
Pastoral Committee (Secretary) Mr Colin Sheppard *(as above)*
Designated Officer Mr Colin Sheppard *(as above)*
Property and Trust Committee Mr Colin Sheppard *(as above)*

CHURCHES

Advisory Committee for the Care of Churches (Secretary) Canon Edwin Newlyn, Vicarage, Goathland YO22 5AN
    Tel: (01947) 86227
Furnishings Officer Mrs Jean Nugent, c/o DAC Office *(same address)*
    Tel: (01947) 896339
Redundant Churches Uses Committee Mr Colin Sheppard *(as above)*

EDUCATION

Board of Education (Director) Revd Andrew Martlew, Church House
    e-mail: acm.yorkdbe@demon.co.uk
Dioc Advisers for Schools Mrs Sue Foster and Mrs Sue Holmes, Church House
Adviser for Children and Youth Work (East Riding) Mr Justin Fielder, 106 Maplewood Ave, Hull HU5 5YF
    Tel and *Fax:* (01482) 573740
Archbishop's Senior Adviser in Youth Work Vacancy

MINISTRY AND MISSION

Resources Consultant Vacancy
Secretary for Mission and Ministry Canon Ronald Metcalfe, 5 Minster Yard, York YO1 2JE
    Tel: (01904) 642542
Dean of Women's Ministry Revd Catherine Rowling, Vicarage, Ingleby Greenhow, Middlesbrough TS9 6LL
    Tel: (01642) 723947
Director of Ordinands Revd Michael Kavanagh, Bishopthorpe Palace, Bishopthorpe, York YO23 2GE
    Tel: (01904) 707021/2
Officer for NSMs Revd David Simon, 8 Melrose Park, Keldgate, Beverley HU17 8JL
    Tel: (01482) 862855
Readers' Association Mr Peter Bowes, 236 Westella Rd, Wast Ella, Hull HU10 7SF
    Tel: (01482) 656392
Director of Training Revd Michael Searle, Cavalino, Back Lane, Allerthorpe, York YO4 4RP
    Tel: (01759) 302544
Dioc Forum for Mission and Evangelism (Secretary) Revd Paul Wordsworth, St Thomas' Vicarage, 157 Haxby Rd, York YO3 7JL
    Tel: (01904) 652228

Ecumenical Adviser to the Diocese Vacancy
Ecumenical Council (Secretary) Vacancy

LITURGICAL

York Diocesan Liturgical Group The Dean of York

PRESS AND PUBLICATIONS

Archbishop's Media Adviser (National) Revd Rob Marshall, 33 rpm   *Tel:* 0181-450 1455
    0385 767594 (Mobile)
Communications Officer (Diocese) Vacancy
Editorial Committee of Dioc Handbook c/o Church House
Editor of Dioc Manual c/o Church House
Communications Officer (Broadcasting) Revd Margaret Cundiff, 37 Oaklands, Camblesforth, Selby YO8 8HH
    Tel: (01757) 618148
Dioc Magazine SEEN Editor Revd Simon Stanley, c/o Down Your Way Publishing Ltd, Windsor House, Green Park Business Centre, Sutton-in-the-Forest, York YO61 1ET   *Tel:* (01347) 811882
    Fax: (01347) 811886

DIOCESAN RECORD OFFICES

The Borthwick Institute, St Anthony's Hall, Peasholme Green, York YO1 2PW, *Director and Diocesan Archivist* Prof David Smith, *Tel:* (01904) 642315 *(For parish records in the Archdeaconry of York)*; Humberside County Record Office, County Hall, Beverley HU17 9BA *(County Archivist* Mr K. D. Holt) *Tel:* (01482) 867131, Ext 394 *(For parish records in the Archdeaconry of the East Riding)*; North Yorkshire County Record Office, County Hall, Northallerton DL7 8SG *(County Archivist* Mr M. Y. Ashcroft) *Tel:* (01609) 3123, Ext 455 *(For parish records in the Archdeaconry of Cleveland*)
*Parishes within the present county boundaries of Cleveland may, if they so wish, deposit their records in the Cleveland County Archives Dept, Exchange House, 6 Marton Rd, Middlesbrough TS1 1DB *(Archivist* Mr D. Tyrell)
    Tel: (01642) 248321

SOCIAL RESPONSIBILITY

Secretary for Social Action Mr David Mather, SRC Resource Centre, Central Methodist Church, St Saviourgate, York YO1 2NQ
    Tel: (01904) 631715

RURAL DEANS
ARCHDEACONRY OF YORK

Buckrose (Acting) Revd J. Woods, Vicarage, 2 Cromarty Cottages, Birdsall, Malton YO17 9NN
Bulmer and Malton Revd Bob Rogers, Vicarage, 17 The Mount, Malton, York YO17 0ND   *Tel:* (01653) 692089
Derwent Canon Geoffrey Hunter, Vicarage, Heslington, York YO1 5EE
    Tel: (01904) 410389

Easingwold Revd Tony Hart, Vicarage, Church Hill, Easingwold, York YO6 3JT
    Tel: (01347) 821394
New Ainsty Revd Richard Seed, Vicarage, Boston Spa, Wetherby LS23 5EA
    Tel: (01937) 842454
South Wold Revd David Cook, Vicarage, Holme-on-Spalding Moor, York YO4 4AG
    Tel: (01403) 860248
Selby Revd Gwynne Richardson, Rectory, Main St, Hillam, Leeds LS25 5HH
    Tel: (01977) 682357
York Canon Glynn Webster, 22 Markham Crescent, York YO3 7NS
    Tel: (01904) 632380

ARCHDEACONRY OF THE EAST RIDING

Beverley Revd David Hoskin, St Mary's Vicarage, 15 Molescroft Rd, Beverley HU17 7DX   *Tel:* (01482) 881437
Bridlington Revd Stephen Cope, Rudston Vicarage, Driffield YO25 0XA
    Tel: (01262) 420313
Harthill (Acting) Revd Robert Jones, Vicarage, Wetwang, Driffield YO25 9XT
    Tel: (01377) 236410
Holderness North Revd Martyn Dunning, Rectory, West St, Leven HU17 5LR
    Tel: (01964) 543793
Holderness South Revd Stuart Robinson, Rectory, Staithes Rd, Preston in Holderness, Hull HU12 8TB *Tel:* (01482) 898375
Howden Revd Ian Ellery, Minster Rectory, Howden, Goole DN14 7BL
    Tel: (01430) 430332
Kingston-upon-Hull Canon John Waller, Holy Trinity Vicarage, 66 Pearson Park, Hull HU5 2TQ   *Tel:* (01482) 342292
Scarborough Revd Christopher Humphries, Vicarage, Filey YO14 9AD
    Tel: (01723) 512745

ARCHDEACONRY OF CLEVELAND

Guisborough Revd Thomas Evans, Rectory, North Terrace, Skelton, Saltburn by the Sea TS12 2ES *Tel:* (01287) 650329
Helmsley Revd David Newton, Rectory, Ampleforth, York YO6 4DU
    Tel: (0439) 788264
Middlesbrough Revd David Hodgson, Ascension Vicarage, Penrith Rd, Berwick Hills, Middlesbrough TS3 7JR
    Tel: (01642) 244857
Mowbray Revd David Biles, Vicarage, Kilburn, York YO6 4AH *Tel:* (01347) 868234
Pickering Canon Francis Hewitt, Vicarage, Whitby Rd, Pickering YO18 7HD
    Tel: (01751) 472983
Stokesley Canon David Lickess, Vicarage, Hutton Rudby, Yarm TS15 0HY
    Tel: (01642) 700223
Whitby Revd Robert Lewis, Vicarage, Danby, Whitby YO21 2NQ
    Tel: (01287) 660388

GENERAL

PART 3

PART 3 CONTENTS

GENERAL INFORMATION 157
Addressing the Clergy 157
Archbishops of Canterbury and York 158
Bishops in the House of Lords 159
Chaplains in Her Majesty's Services 160
Forces Synodical Council 160
Chaplains in Higher Education 161
Chaplains in the Prison Service 164
Christian Aid 164
Church Army 165
Church Colleges of Higher Education 165
Church Urban Fund 166
Clergy Appointments Adviser 166
Conference Centres and Retreat Houses 167
Decade of Evangelism 170
Faculty Office and Special Marriage Licences 170
Hospice Movement 171
The Children's Hospice Movement 171
Marriage: Legal Aspects 172
Mothers' Union 172
Press: Church Newspapers 172
Schools, Church of England 172
Services Authorised and Commended 173
TV and Radio 176
Women's Ministry 178
Theological Colleges and Regional Courses 179

TABLES 182–89
Selected Church Statistics 181
Parochial Fees 190
Church Electoral Rolls 192

ROYAL PECULIARS, THE CHAPELS ROYAL, ETC. 193
Westminster Abbey 193
Windsor 194
Domestic Chaplains to HM The Queen 195
Chapels Royal 195
College of Chaplains 195
Royal Almonry 196
The Queen's Chapel of the Savoy 196
Royal Memorial Chapel, Sandhurst 197
The Royal Foundation of St Katharine 197
Deans of Peculiars 198
Preachers at the Inns of Court 198

RELIGIOUS COMMUNITIES 199
Anglican Religious Communities 199
Advisory Council on the Relations of Bishops and Religious Communities 199
Communities Consultative Council 200
Communities for Men 200
Communities for Women 202
Mixed Communities 207

GENERAL INFORMATION

Addressing the Clergy

Since the Lambeth Conference of 1968, at which styles of address were debated, there has been a trend towards simpler forms of address. Resolution 14 stated: 'The Conference recommends that the bishops, as leaders and representatives of a servant Church, should radically examine the honours paid to them in the course of divine worship, in titles and customary address, and in style of living, while having the necessary facilities for the efficient carrying on of their work.'

Whereas formerly a bishop would have been addressed as 'My Lord' and a dean as 'Mr Dean', it has become more usual to address a bishop in speech as 'Bishop' and a dean as 'Dean'. There is, however, a correct way to address clergy on an envelope, which is normally as follows:

Archbishop of Canterbury or York	The Most Revd and Rt Hon the Lord Archbishop of
Archbishop of another Province	The Most Revd the Lord Archbishop of
Bishop of London	The Rt Revd and Rt Hon the Lord Bishop of
Diocesan/Suffragan Bishop	*Either* The Rt Revd the Lord Bishop of
	or The Rt Revd the Bishop of
Assistant/Retired Bishop	The Rt Revd J.D. Smith (*or* John Smith)
Dean	The Very Revd the Dean of
Provost	The Very Revd the Provost of
Archdeacon	The Ven the Archdeacon of
Canon	The Revd Canon J.D. Smith (*or* John or Jane Smith)
Prebendary	The Revd Prebendary J.D. Smith (*or* John or Jane Smith)
Rural Dean	No special form of address (The Rev, the Revd Canon, etc)
Dean of Oxford/Cambridge College	No special form of address
Cleric also Professor	*Either* The Revd Professor J.D. Smith
	or Professor the Revd J.D. Smith
Canon also Professor	*Either* The Revd Canon Professor J.D. Smith
	or Professor the Revd Canon J.D. Smith
Cleric also Doctor	*Either* The Revd Dr J.D. Smith
	or The Revd J.D. Smith (degree)
Canon also Doctor	The Revd Canon J.D. Smith (degree)
Other Clergy/Priest/Deacon	The Revd J.D. Smith (*or* John or Jane Smith)

The following points should be noted particularly:
1. A diocesan or suffragan bishop has a title conferred on him by his consecration or subsequent translation, which he is entitled to hold until he resigns. He then reverts to his personal name, retaining the title 'Right Reverend'.
2. A dean, provost or archdeacon has a territorial title until he resigns. He then reverts to his personal name, and his title is 'Reverend' unless the rank of dean, provost or archdeacon emeritus has been awarded.
3. Retired archbishops properly go back to the status of a bishop but may be given as a courtesy the style of an archbishop.
4. A bishop holding office as a dean or archdeacon is addressed as The Rt Revd the Dean/Archdeacon of.
5. If a cleric's name or initials are unknown, he or she should be addressed as The Revd — Smith or the Revd Mr/Mrs/Miss/Ms Smith. It is never correct to refer to a cleric as 'The Reverend Smith' or 'Revd Smith'.
6. There is no universally accepted way of addressing an envelope to a married couple of whom both are in holy orders. We recommend the style 'The Revd A B and the Revd C D Smith'.

Archbishops of Canterbury and York

CANTERBURY

597 Augustine
604 Laurentius
619 Mellitus
624 Justus
627 Honorius
655 Deusdedit
668 Theodore
693 Beorhtweald
731 Tatwine
735 Nothelm
740 Cuthbeorht
761 Breguwine
765 Jaenbeorht
793 Æthelheard
805 Wulfred
832 Feologild
833 Ceolnoth
870 Æthelred
890 Plegmund
914 Æthelhelm
923 Wulfhelm
942 Oda
959 Ælfsige
959 Beorhthelm
960 Dunstan
c988 Athelgar
990 Sigeric Serio
995 Ælfric
1005 Ælfheath
1013 Lyfing
1020 Æthelnoth
1038 Eadsige
1051 Robert of Jumièges
1052 Stigand
1070 Lanfranc
1093 Anselm
1114 Ralph d'Escures
1123 William de Corbeil
1139 Theobald
1162 Thomas Becket
1174 Richard [of Dover]
1185 Baldwin
1193 Hubert Walter
1207 Stephen Langton
1229 Richard le Grant
1234 Edmund Rich
1245 Boniface of Savoy
1273 Robert Kilwardby
1279 John Peckham
1294 Robert Winchelsey
1313 Walter Reynolds
1328 Simon Mepeham
1333 John Stratford
1349 Thomas Bradwardine
1349 Simon Islip
1366 Simon Langham
1368 William Whittlesey
1375 Simon Sudbury
1381 William Courtenay
1396 Thomas Arundel[1]
1398 Roger Walden
1414 Henry Chichele
1443 John Stafford
1452 John Kemp
1454 Thomas Bourchier
1486 John Morton
1501 Henry Dean
1503 William Warham
1533 Thomas Cranmer
1556 Reginald Pole
1559 Matthew Parker
1576 Edmund Grindal
1583 John Whitgift
1604 Richard Bancroft
1611 George Abbot
1633 William Laud
1660 William Juxon
1663 Gilbert Sheldon
1678 William Sancroft
1691 John Tillotson
1695 Thomas Tenison
1716 William Wake
1737 John Potter
1747 Thomas Herring
1757 Matthew Hutton
1758 Thomas Secker
1768 Frederick Cornwallis
1783 John Moore
1805 Charles Manners Sutton
1828 William Howley
1848 John Bird Sumner
1862 Charles Thomas Longley
1868 Archibald Campbell Tait
1883 Edward White Benson
1896 Frederick Temple
1903 Randall Thomas Davidson
1928 Cosmo Gordon Lang
1942 William Temple
1945 Geoffrey Francis Fisher
1961 Arthur Michael Ramsey
1974 Frederick Donald Coggan
1980 Robert Alexander Kennedy Runcie
1991 George Leonard Carey

YORK

BISHOPS
625 Paulinus
[vacancy for 30 years]
664 Ceadda
669 Wilfrith I
678 Bosa[2]
705 John of Beverley
718 Wilfrith II

ARCHBISHOPS
c734 Ecgbeorht
767 Æthelbeorht
780 Eanbald I
796 Eanbald II
c812 Wulfsige
837 Wigmund
854 Wulfhere
900 Æthelbeald
c928 Hrothweard
931 Wulfstan I
958 Oscytel
971 Edwaldus
972 Oswald
992 Ealdwulf
1003 Wulfstan II
1023 Ælfric Puttoc
1041 Æthelric[3]
1051 Cynesige
1061 Ealdred
1070 Thomas I
1100 Gerard
1109 Thomas II
1119 Thurstan
1143 William Fitzherbert
1147 Henry Murdac[4]
1154 Roger of Pont l'Eveque
1191 Geoffrey Plantagenet
1215 Walter de Gray
1256 Sewal de Bovill
1258 Godfrey Ludham
1266 Walter Giffard
1279 William Wickwane
1286 John le Romeyn
1298 Henry Newark
1300 Thomas Corbridge
1306 William Greenfield
1317 William Melton
1342 William Zouche
1352 John Thoresby
1374 Alexander Neville
1388 Thomas Arundel
1396 Robert Waldby
1398 Richard le Scrope
1407 Henry Bowet
1426 John Kemp
1452 William Booth
1465 George Nevill
1476 Lawrence Booth
1480 Thomas Rotherham (or Scot)
1501 Thomas Savage
1508 Christopher Bainbridge
1514 Thomas Wolsey
1531 Edward Lee
1545 Robert Holgate
1555 Nicholas Heath
1561 Thomas Young
1570 Edmund Grindal
1577 Edwin Sandys
1589 John Piers
1595 Matthew Hutton
1606 Tobias Matthew
1628 George Montaigne
1629 Samuel Harsnett
1632 Richard Neile
1641 John Williams
1660 Accepted Frewen
1664 Richard Sterne
1683 John Dolben
1688 Thomas Lamplugh
1691 John Sharp
1714 William Dawes
1724 Lancelot Blackburn
1743 Thomas Herring
1747 Matthew Hutton
1757 John Gilbert
1761 Robert Hay Drummond
1777 William Markham
1808 Edward Venables Vernon Harcourt
1847 Thomas Musgrave
1860 Charles Thomas Longley
1863 William Thomson
1891 William Connor Magee
1891 William Dalrymple Maclagan
1909 Cosmo Gordon Lang
1929 William Temple
1942 Cyril Foster Garbett
1956 Arthur Michael Ramsey
1961 Frederick Donald Coggan
1975 Stuart Yarworth Blanch
1983 John Stapylton Habgood
1995 David Michael Hope

---

[1] On 19 October 1399 Boniface IX annulled Arundel's translation to St Andrews and confirmed him in the see of Canterbury.
[2] Wilfrith was restored to office in 686 and Bosa in 691.
[3] Ælfric Puttoc was restored in 1042.
[4] William Fitzherbert was restored in 1153.

Bishops in the House of Lords

The Archbishops of Canterbury and York and the Bishops of London, Durham and Winchester always have seats in the House of Lords. The twenty-one other seats are filled by diocesan bishops in order of seniority. In the case of Bishops awaiting seats, the order of seniority is shown (1), (2), (3) etc.

The Bishop of Sodor and Man and the Bishop of Gibraltar in Europe are not eligible to sit in the House of Lords.

	Election as Diocesan Bishop confirmed	Translated to present See	Entered House of Lords
Canterbury (Most Revd & Rt Hon G. L. Carey)	1987	1991	1991
York (Most Revd & Rt Hon D. M. Hope)	1985	1995	1990
London (Rt Revd & Rt Hon R. J. C. Chartres)	1995		1996
Durham (Rt Revd M. Turnbull)	1988	1994	1994
Winchester (Rt Revd M. C. Scott-Joynt)	1995		1996
Bath and Wells (Rt Revd J. L. Thompson)	1991		1997
Birmingham (Rt Revd M. Santer)	1987		1994
Blackburn (Rt Revd A. D. Chesters)	1989		1995
Bradford (Rt Revd D. J. Smith)	1992		1997
Bristol (Rt Revd B. Rogerson)	1985		1990
Carlisle (Rt Revd I. Harland)	1989		1996
Chelmsford (Rt Revd J. F. Perry)	1996		(6)
Chester (Rt Revd P. Forster)	1996		(8)
Chichester (Rt Revd E. W. Kemp)	1974		1979
Coventry (Rt Revd C. Bennetts)	1997		(14)
Derby (Rt Revd J. S. Bailey)	1995		(4)
Ely (Rt Revd S. W. Sykes)	1990		1996
Exeter (Rt Revd G. H. Thompson)	1985		1990
Gloucester (Rt Revd D. E. Bentley)	1993		1998
Guildford (Rt Revd J. Gladwin)	1994		(2)
Hereford (Rt Revd J. K. Oliver)	1990		1997
Leicester (Vacancy)			
Lichfield (Rt Revd K. N. Sutton)	1984		1989
Lincoln (Rt Revd R. M. Hardy)	1987		1993
Liverpool (Rt Revd J. S. Jones)	1998		(15)
Manchester (Rt Revd C. J. Mayfield)	1993		1997
Newcastle (Rt Revd J. M. Wharton)	1997		(12)
Norwich (Rt Revd P. J. Nott)	1985		1991
Oxford (Rt Revd R. D. Harries)	1987		1993
Peterborough (Rt Revd I. P. M. Cundy)	1996		(7)
Portsmouth (Rt Revd K. Stevenson)	1995		(3)
Ripon (Rt Revd D. N. de L. Young)	1977		1984
Rochester (Rt Revd M. Nazir-Ali)	1994		(1)
St Albans (Revd C. W. Herbert)	1995		(5)
St Edmundsbury and Ipswich (Rt Revd J. H. R. Lewis)	1996		(9)
Salisbury (Rt Revd D. S. Stancliffe)	1993		1997
Sheffield (Rt Revd J. Nicholls)	1997		(13)
Southwark (Rt Revd T. F. Butler)	1991	1998	1997
Southwell (Rt Revd P. B. Harris)	1988		1996
Truro (Rt Revd W. Ind)	1997		(10)
Wakefield (Rt Revd N. S. McCulloch)	1992		1997
Worcester (Rt Revd P. S. M. Selby)	1997		(11)

General Information

Chaplains in Her Majesty's Services

ROYAL NAVY
Chaplains of all denominations are employed in many parts of the world, ashore and afloat in capital ships, squadrons of frigates and destroyers, Royal Marine Commandos, hospitals, Naval Colleges, Royal Naval Air Stations, HM Naval Bases and Training Establishments. Apart from conducting the customary services in their ships, units or establishments, for which all the necessary facilities are provided, chaplains find numerous opportunities for extending the work of the Church through pastoral contacts with families and dependents, as well as being 'friend and adviser of all on board'. They are given particular opportunity to teach the Christian faith to young people in Training Establishments. In-Service training for all Royal Naval Chaplains is carried out at the Armed Forces Chaplaincy Centre, Amport House, Andover, Hants SP11 8BG. Christian Leadership Courses for all service personnel are provided at the centre during the year. The Anglican Church in the Royal Navy is served by 46 priests and is very much a part of the Anglican Communion with the Single Service and Tri-Service Synodical structures. The Senior Anglican Chaplain in the Royal Navy is granted the ecclesiastical dignity of Archdeacon by the Archbishop of Canterbury. The Archbishop is the Ordinary for all service chaplains and grants ecclesiastical licences to all Anglican chaplains on the Active List. The Royal Navy is an Equal Opportunities employer and applications for entry from both male and female priests under 39 are always welcome. Full particulars concerning the entry of Anglican Chaplains can be obtained from the Archdeacon for the Royal Navy, Ven Simon Golding, Room 201, Victory Building, HM Naval Base, Portsmouth PO1 3LS
Tel: (01705) 727904

ARMY
There is a definite Establishment of Chaplains, Church of England, Church of Scotland, Roman Catholic, Methodist and United Board (United Reformed Church and Baptist). This Establishment is governed by the strength of the Army. Chaplains of all denominations (except Roman Catholic) are administered by the Chaplain General assisted by the Deputy Chaplain General at the Ministry of Defence (Army), and through Senior Chaplains at the Headquarters of Commands/Districts at home and overseas. The Chaplain General (the present holder of the office is a Church of Scotland Minister) is responsible to the 2nd Permanent Under-Secretary of State for the general well-being of the Department. The religious training of the Army is an integral part of military life. Regular periods of Religious Instruction/Discussion are provided. The Armed Forces Chaplaincy Centre is situated at Amport and the Royal Army Chaplains' Department Depot at Netheravon. These centres serve the double purpose of a spiritual home for all chaplains, and as training centres for all ranks, with different courses to develop leaders, refresh churchmen, or inform enquirers. Courses for military personnel are also held at centres overseas. *The Chaplain General* Revd Dr Victor Dobbin. *Deputy Chaplain General* Ven John Holliman. Ministry of Defence Chaplains (Army), Trenchard Lines, Upavon, Wiltshire SN9 6BE
Tel: (01980) 615802
Fax: (01980) 615800

ROYAL AIR FORCE
From the foundation of the Royal Air Force, Chaplains have been proud to minister to the needs of servicemen and women and their families, in peace and war. The Chaplains' Branch of the Royal Air Force offers a real challenge and a rewarding ministry to young priests who have the necessary qualities, initiative and enthusiasm. The Royal Air Force is a large body of men and women drawn from every corner of Britain and from every stratum of society. There is a continuing need for clergy to minister to these men and women and the Royal Air Force understands and supports this ministry. Chaplains are commissioned by Her Majesty the Queen to provide for the moral and spiritual needs of all Service personnel and their families. This care is unlimited, and extends wherever members of the Royal Air Force are called to serve. Further details concerning Chaplaincy in the Royal Air Force can be obtained from: The Chaplain-in-Chief (RAF), Ministry of Defence, P & T Command HQ, RAF Innsworth, Gloucester GL3 1EZ
Tel: (01452) 712612 Ext 5032
For a list of **Chaplains to Her Majesty's Services** see *Crockford*

Forces Synodical Council

President The Archbishop of Canterbury
Senior Vice-President Rt Revd John Kirkham (*Bishop of Sherborne and the Archbishop of Canterbury's Episcopal Representative to Her Majesty's Forces*)
Clergy Vice-President Vacancy
Lay Vice-President Wing Commander Chris Hill

Secretary Revd John Green, c/o Armed Forces Chaplaincy Centre, Amport House, Amport, Andover, Hants SP11 8PG
Tel: (01705) 727901
Fax: (01705) 727112
The Forces Synodical Council was first convened in 1990. In 1997 it will have thirty-six elected members, six clergy

and six lay members from the Royal Navy, Army and the Royal Air Force, and nine ex-officio members. The Council carries out many of the responsibilities of a diocesan synod and is the highest tier of the synodical structure within the Armed Forces. The Council gives the clergy and laity of the Services the opportunity to contribute their ideas and opinions, and to make decisions pertinent to the life of the Church in the Armed Forces. Each Service has an elected Archdeaconry Synod, and elected representation at chaplaincy level is to Chaplaincy Councils. The three archdeacons represent the Armed Forces, as ex-officio members, on General Synod.

Chaplains in Higher Education

Note: Only one name is given for each institution, many of which have several chaplains.

UNIVERSITIES

Aston Revd Thomas Pyke, The Chaplaincy Suite, Lawrence Tower, Aston University, Aston Triange, Birmingham B4 7ET Tel: 0121–359 6531 Ext 4059

Bath Revd Jonathan LLoyd, The Chaplaincy Centre, University of Bath, Claverton Down, Bath, Avon BA2 7AY Tel: (01225) 826458

Birmingham Revd Andrew Gorham, Anglican Chaplaincy, St Francis' Hall, Edgbaston Park Rd, Birmingham B15 2TT Tel: 0121–416 7000

Bournemouth Revd Dr Anne Dawtry, Bournemouth University, Wallisdown Rd, Poole, Dorset BH12 5BB Tel: (01202) 524111 Ext 5383

Bradford Revd Michael Harrison, Anglican Chaplaincy, Michael Ramsey House, 2 Ashgrove, Bradford, W Yorks BD7 1BN Tel: (01274) 727034

Brighton Revd Anthony Cane, The Chaplaincy, Cockcroft Building, Lewes Rd, Moulsecoomb, Brighton, E Sussex BN2 4GJ Tel: (01273) 642955

Bristol Revd Dr Angus Stuart, Ecumenical Chaplaincy Centre, 1 Priory Rd, Clifton, Bristol BS8 1TX Tel: 0117–928 8823

Brunel Revd Maureen Whitcombe, The Meeting House, Brunel University, Uxbridge UB8 3PH Tel: (01895) 203308

Cambridge Colleges
Christ's Revd Owen Spencer-Thomas Tel: (01223) 334922
Churchill Vacancy Tel: (01223) 336218
Clare (Acting Dean) Revd Jo Bailey Wells Tel: (01223) 333240
Corpus Christi Revd Dr Mark Pryce Tel: (01223) 338002
Downing Revd Bruce Kinsey Tel: (01223) 334810
Emmanuel Revd Jeremy Caddick Tel: (01223) 334264
Fitzwilliam Revd Ben Quash Tel: (01223) 332013
Girton Revd Jeremy Clark-King Tel: (01223) 338956

Gonville and Caius Revd Jack McDonald Tel: (01223) 332408
Jesus Revd Timothy Jenkins (Dean) Tel: (01223) 339303
King's Revd Dr George Pattison Tel: (01223) 331248
Magdalene Revd Hueston Finlay Tel: (01223) 332129
Newnham Revd Dr Nicholas Cranfield Tel: (01223) 335775
Pembroke Canon Brian Watchorn Tel: (01223) 338147
Peterhouse Revd Dr Graham Ward Tel: (01223) 338217
Queens' Revd Dr Jonathan Holmes Tel: (01223) 335545
Robinson Revd Hugh Shilson-Thomas Tel: (01223) 339140
St Catharine's Revd Dr David Goodhew Tel: (01223) 338346
St Edmund's Revd Dr Michael Robson (Dean) Tel: (01223) 336123
St John's Revd Dr Andrew Macintosh Tel: (01223) 338709
Selwyn Revd Dr Nicholas Cranfield Tel: (01223) 335875
Sidney Sussex Revd Ellen Clark-King Tel: (01223) 338870
Trinity (Dean) Revd Dr Arnold Browne Tel: (01223) 338563
Trinity Hall Revd Dr Charles Elliott Tel: (01223) 332525
Wolfson Canon Christine Farrington Tel: (01223) 335900

University of Central England in Birmingham Revd Michael Harris, The Chaplaincy, Student Services, Baker Building, Perry Barr, Birmingham B42 2SU Tel: 0121–331 5345

Central Lancashire Revd Bill Turner, University of Central Lancashire, Corporation St, Preston PR1 2HE Tel: (01772) 892615

City University Vacancy, The City University, St John's St, London EC1V 4PB Tel: 0171–477 8000

Coventry Revd Carolyn Kennedy, The Chaplaincy, Coventry University, Priory St, Coventry CV1 5FB Tel: (01203) 838315

De Montfort Revd Jane Curtis, Chaplaincy & Centre for Religions, Newarke Close, Leicester LE1 9BH Tel: 0116–255 1551 Ext 8599

Derby Revd David Heslop, University of Derby, Kedlestone Rd, Derby DE22 1GB Tel: (01332) 622222

Durham Colleges
Collingwood and Grey Revd Benedick de la Mare
　　　　　　　　　　　　　　　Tel: 0191–374 4563
Hatfield Revd David Glover　　Tel: 0191–374 3163
St Aidan's Revd Robert Thomson　Tel: 0191–374 3269
St Chad's Revd Dr Joseph Cassidy (Acting)
　　　　　　　　　　　　　　　Tel: 0191–374 3362
St Hild and St Bede Revd Alan Bayes　Tel: 0191–374 3069
St John's Vacancy　　　　　　Tel: 0191–374 3579
St Mary's Revd Margaret Parker　Tel: 0191–384 2700
Trevelyan and Van Mildert Revd Kenneth Anderson
　　　　　　　　　　　　　　　Tel: 0191–374 3770
University Revd Charles Yeats　Tel: 0191–374 3868

East Anglia Revd Garth Barber, The Chaplaincy, University of East Anglia, Norwich NR4 7TJ
　　　　　　　　　　　　　　　Tel: (01603) 592166

East London Revd John Richardson, c/o Student Services Centre, Romford Rd, Stratford, London E15 4LZ
　　　　　　　　　　　　　　Tel: 0181–590 7722 Ext 4450

Essex Revd Dr Ian Kenway, Multifaith Chaplaincy Centre, University of Essex, Wivenhoe Park, Colchester, Essex CO4 3SQ　　　　Tel: (01206) 872098

Exeter Revd Dr Jeremy Law, Dept of Theology, Queen's Building, University of Exeter, The Queen's Drive, Exeter EX4 4QE　　　　　Tel: (01392) 264240

Greenwich Revd Lou Gale, Greenwich University, Wellington St, Woolwich, London SE18 6PF
　　　　　　　　　　　　　　Tel: 0181–331 8150

Hertfordshire Revd George Bolt (Ecumenical), University of Hertfordshire, Hatfield Campus, College Lane, Hatfield, Herts AL10 9AB　Tel: (01707) 284456

Huddersfield Vacancy, The Chaplaincy Centre, University of Huddersfield, Queensgate, Huddersfield HD1 3DH　　　　　　　　　　Tel: (01484) 472090

Hull Vacancy, Anglican Chaplaincy, 13 Salmon Grove, Hull, Humberside HU6 7SX　Tel: (01482) 493251

Humberside Revd Rodney Ward, The Chaplaincy, Student Services, Grimsby College, Nun's Corner, Grimsby DN34 5BQ　　　　　Tel: (01482) 440550 Ext 5066

Keele Revd Catherine Lack, The Chapel, Keele University, Keele, Staffs ST5 5BG
　　　　　　　　　　　　　　Tel: (01782) 621111 Ext 7163

Kent Revd Stephen Laird, Chaplaincy, Keynes College, University of Kent, Canterbury, Kent CT2 7NP
　　　　　　　　　　　　　　Tel: (01227) 764000 Ext 7491

Kingston Vacancy (Ecumenical), Room 7, Kenry House, Kingston University, Kingston-upon-Thames KT2 7LB
　　　　　　　　　　　　　　Tel: 0181–547 7311

Lancaster Revd Di Williams, The Chaplaincy Centre, Lancaster University, Bailrigg, Lancaster LA1 4YW
　　　　　　　　　　　　　　Tel: (01524) 594071

Leeds Revd Dr Simon Robinson, Emmanuel Institute, Leeds University, Leeds LS2 9JT　Tel: 0113–233 5070

Leeds Metropolitan Revd Dr Mike Benwell, Chaplaincy Centre, Leeds Metropolitan University, Calverley St, Leeds LS1 3UE　　　Tel: 0113–283 2600 Ext 3522

Leicester Revd Ian McIntosh, The Gatehouse, University Rd, Leicester LE1 7RH　　Tel: 0116–285 6493

Liverpool Vacancy, Anglican Chaplaincy, Mulberry Court, Mulberry St, Liverpool L7 7EZ
　　　　　　　　　　　　　　Tel: 0151–794 3302/03

Liverpool John Moores Revd Robert Dickinson, Ecumenical Chaplaincy, Roscoe Court, 4 Rodney St, Liverpool L1 2TP　　　　　Tel: 0151–231 3171

London Guildhall University Revd William Taylor, The Chaplaincy, Calcutta House, Old Castle St, London E1 7NT　　　　　　Tel: 0171–320 1379

London Colleges
Senior Chaplain Revd Stephen Williams
　　　　　　　　　　　　　　Tel: 0171–387 0670
Bedford/Royal Holloway Revd Andrew Taylor, Royal Holloway and Bedford New College, Egham Hill, Egham, Surrey TW20 0EX　Tel: (01784) 443070/950
Goldsmith's Vacancy, Lewisham Way, New Cross, London SE14 6NW　　Tel: 0171–919 7171
Imperial College: School of Medicine Revd Alistair McCollum, 1 Porchester Gardens, London W2 3LA
　　　　　　　　　　　　Tel: 0171–229 5089/0171–594 9600
King's (Dean) Revd Dr Richard Burridge, King's College, Strand, London WC2R 2LS　Tel: 0171–873 2333/2063
London School of Economics Revd Neil Nicholls, Houghton St, Aldwych, London WC2A 2AE　Tel: 0171–955 7965
Queen Mary and Westfield Revd David Peebles, Queen Mary and Westfield College, Mile End Rd, London E1 4NS　　　　　　Tel: 0171–775 3179
St Bartholomew's & QMW Hospital Medical Schools Revd David Peebles　　　　Tel: 0181–980 1204
St George's Hospital Medical School The Anglican Chaplain　Tel: 0181–672 9944 Ext 55298
West London Institute of Higher Education Revd David Wilson　　　　　　Tel: 0181–568 8741 Ext 2655

Loughborough Vacancy, Edward Herbert Building, Loughborough, Leics LE11 3TU　Tel: (01509) 223740

Luton Revd Catherine Bell, University of Luton, Park Square, Luton, Beds LU1 3JU *Tel:* (01582) 21867/453236

Manchester Revd Peter Hewis, St Peter's House, Precinct Centre, Oxford Rd, Manchester M13 9GH
Tel: 0161–273 1465

Manchester Metropolitan Revd Ian Gomersall, Student Services, All Saints, Manchester M15 6BH
Tel: 0161–247 3496/0161–273 1465

Middlesex Revd Dr Martin Eggleton (Ecumenical), Middlesex University, Student Services Area, Enfield Campus, Queensway, Enfield, Middx *Tel:* 0181–362 5162

Newcastle Revd Roger Mills, The Chaplaincy, University of Newcastle, Newcastle upon Tyne NE1 7RU
Tel: 0191–222 6341

Nottingham Canon Ian Tarrant, 3 Wortley Hall Close, Nottingham University, University Park, Nottingham NG7 2RD *Tel:* 0115–951 3927

Nottingham Trent Revd Trevor Hatton, The Chaplaincy, City Site, Burton St, Nottingham NG1 4BU
Tel: 0115–941 8418 Ext 2305

North London Revd Jonathan Clark, University of North London, Holloway Rd, London N7 8DB
Tel: 0171–753 7038

Northumbria at Newcastle Revd Andrew Shipton, Chaplaincy, Student Services, Ellison Buildings, Ellison Place, Newcastle upon Tyne NE1 8ST *Tel:* 0191–222 1679

Oxford Colleges
All Souls Revd Prof John McManners *Tel:* (01865) 279368
Balliol Revd Douglas Dupree *Tel:* (01865) 277777
Brasenose Revd Richard Smail *Tel:* (01865) 277833
Christ Church Revd Ralph Williamson
Tel: (01865) 276236
Corpus Christi Revd Dr Judith Maltby
Tel: (01865) 276722
Exeter Revd David Marshall *Tel:* (01865) 279610
Green Dr David Cook (Baptist) *Tel:* (01865) 274785
Harris Manchester Revd Peter Hewis *Tel:* (01865) 271006
Hertford Revd Michael Chantry *Tel:* (01865) 279400
Jesus Revd Andrew Moore *Tel:* (01865) 279757
Keble Revd John Davies *Tel:* (01865) 272787
Lady Margaret Hall Revd Alan Doig *Tel:* (01865) 274386
Lincoln Revd Robin Griffiths-Jones *Tel:* (01865) 279800
Magdalen Revd Dr Michael Piret *Tel:* (01865) 276027
Mansfield Revd Dr Catherine Middleton
Tel: (01865) 270999
Merton Revd Mark Everitt *Tel:* (01865) 276365

New Revd Robert Harnish *Tel:* (01865) 279541
Nuffield Revd Dr Margaret Yee (URC)
Tel: (01865) 278567
Oriel Revd Nigel Biggar *Tel:* (01865) 276580
Pembroke Revd Dr John Platt *Tel:* (01865) 276426
Queen's Revd Peter Southwell *Tel:* (01865) 279143
Regent's Park Revd Dr Jane Shaw *Tel:* (01865) 288120
St Catherine's Revd Hugh White *Tel:* (01865) 271700
St Edmund Hall Revd Duncan MacLaren
Tel: (01865) 279021
St Hilda's Canon Brian Mountford *Tel:* (01865) 243806
St Hugh's Revd Jeremy Gilpin *Tel:* (01865) 274900
St John's Revd Elizabeth Carmichael *Tel:* (01865) 277351
St Peter's Revd Christopher Jones *Tel:* (01865) 278900
Somerville Revd Sabine Akire *Tel:* (01865) 270600
Trinity Revd Trevor Williams *Tel:* (01865) 279886
University Revd Bill Sykes *Tel:* (01865) 276663
Wadham Revd Giles Fraser *Tel:* (01865) 277905
Westminster Revd Martin Groves *Tel:* (01865) 246644
Worcester Revd Peter Doll *Tel:* (01865) 278371

Oxford Brookes Revd Andrew Coleby, 46 Lower Rd, Chinnor, Oxon OX9 4DO *Tel:* (01865) 354052

Plymouth Revd Barry Hallett (Ecumenical), University of Plymouth, Drake Circus, Plymouth PL4 8AA
Tel: (01752) 232261

Portsmouth Revd Fiona Stewart-Darling, The Chaplaincy, Nuffield Centre, St Michael's Rd, Portsmouth PO1 2ED *Tel:* (01705) 843157/876453

Reading Revd Graham Rainey, The Chaplaincy Centre, Park House Lodge, University of Reading, Whiteknights, PO Box 217, Reading, Berks RG6 2AH
Tel: (01734) 318797

Salford Revd Janet Fife, University of Salford, Salford, Lancs M5 4WT *Tel:* 0161–745 5000 Ext 4660

Sheffield Revd Cheryl Collins, The Chaplaincy Office, The Octagon, University of Sheffield S10 2TN
Tel: 0114–282 4956

Sheffield Hallam Revd Sandra Howes (Ecumenical), Sheffield Hallam University, City Campus, Pond St, Sheffield S1 1WB *Tel:* 0114–253 2139

Southampton Revd David Simpson, The Chaplaincy Centre, The University, 52 University Rd, Southampton SO17 1BJ *Tel:* (01703) 558126

South Bank Revd Frank Hung, South Bank University, Borough Rd, London SE1 0AA
Tel: 0171–928 8989 Ext 2781

Staffordshire Revd Arthur Hughes, Chaplaincy, Staffordshire University, College Rd, Shelton, Stoke-on-Trent ST4 2DE *Tel:* (01782) 744531 Ext 3273

General Information

Sunderland Vacancy, University of Sunderland, Langham Tower, Ryhope Rd, Sunderland SR2 7EE
Tel: 0191–515 2939

Surrey Revd Robin Harvey, University of Surrey, Guildford, Surrey GU2 5XH   *Tel:* (01483) 300800 Ext 2754

Sussex Revd Gavin Ashenden, The Meeting House, University of Sussex, Falmer, Brighton BN1 9QN
Tel: (01273) 678217

Teesside Revd Philip Ashdown, The Chaplaincy, University of Teesside, Middlesbrough, Cleveland TS1 3BA
Tel: (01642) 342264

Thames Valley Revd Jeremy Hurst, Chaplaincy Office, Thames Valley University at Slough, Wellington St, Slough SL1 1YG   *Tel:* (01753) 542068

Warwick Revd Mark Bratton, The Chaplaincy Centre, University of Warwick, Coventry CV4 7AL
Tel: (01203) 523519

Westminster Revd Jonathan Brewster, Staff and Student Centre, 104/108 Bolsover St, London W1P 7HF
Tel: 0171–911 5050

West of England, Bristol Canon Shaun Darley, University of the West of England, The Octagon, Coldharbour Lane, Frenchay, Bristol BS16 1QY
Tel: 0117–976 2172

Wolverhampton Preb Geoffrey Wynne, The Chaplaincy Centre, The University, Wolverhampton WV1 1SB
Tel: (01902) 25747

York Revd John Robertson, University of York, Heslington, York YO1 5DD   *Tel:* (01904) 433131

COLLEGES AND INSTITUTES OF HIGHER EDUCATION

Bolton Institute Revd Gary Lawson, Bolton Institute of Higher Education, Deane Rd, Bolton BL3 5AB
Tel: (01204) 528851 Ext 3080

For **Church Colleges of Higher Education** *see* page 165

Chaplains in the Prison Service

The Prison Service Chaplaincy provides Chaplains for all HM Prisons in England and Wales. It works within the Prison Service part of the Home Office, and the responsibilities of the Chaplain General and his headquarters colleagues include the giving of advice to ministers and officials about policy decisions with a religious or ethical dimension. In addition Chaplains are recruited, trained, deployed and supported in their work of providing for the religious needs of prisoners, giving opportunities for worship, evangelism and instruction, and offering a pastoral ministry at times of crisis and opportunity. Chaplains are also involved in facilitating the observance of other faiths.

All prisons have an Anglican, a Roman Catholic and a Methodist Chaplain; the headquarters team includes senior representatives of all three denominations.

The Bishop to Prisons
Rt Revd The Bishop of Lincoln, Bishop's House, Eastgate, Lincoln LN2 1QQ   *Tel:* Lincoln (01522) 534701

Chaplain General
Ven David Fleming, Prison Service Chaplaincy, Room 709, Abell House, John Islip St, London SW1P 4LH
Tel: 0171–217 5817

Assistants Chaplain General
Revd Thomas Johns, Prison Service Chaplaincy, Room 715, Abell House, John Islip St, London SW1P 4LH
Tel: 0171–217 2024

Revd Bob Payne, Revd Peter Taylor, Prison Service Chaplaincy, PO Box 349, Gaol Square, Stafford ST16 3DL
Tel: (01785) 213456

For a list of **Prison Chaplains** *see Crockford.*

Christian Aid

In a world where 500 million people suffer from chronic malnutrition and 2.4 billion have no adequate sanitation, organisations like Christian Aid play a vital role in helping poor communities to overcome their poverty.

Christian Aid is the official agency of the British and Irish churches – including the Church of England – and as such is one of the largest church relief agencies in Europe. But both at home and overseas it also works with people of other faiths or none who share its concerns.

The agency's income in 1997/98 was nearly £38 million. A substantial amount of its general income is received through the annual Christian Aid Week collections, to be held from May 12–18 in 1999. It spends under 12 per cent of the money it raises on fundraising and administration. More than 80 per cent is spent on tackling poverty overseas.

It funds projects in more than 70 countries worldwide, standing by the poor whether they are digging wells or fighting famine, building homes or growing crops, learning to read or writing about human rights abuses, healing the wounds of war or preventing the spread of illness.

Money spent overseas is passed to local partner organisations which ensures that it is spent where local people need it most. Christian Aid has no permanent offices abroad, believing that poor communities are best placed to devise and run their own projects and solve their own problems. Channelling money through partners is an effective and respectful way of giving the poor the means to help themselves.

In Sri Lanka, for example, Christian Aid funds Gami Seva Sevana, a farm training centre which teaches teenage apprentices to grow a wide range of crops using only natural, organic manure and pesticides. In Uganda, it supports the Rukararwe Partnership Workshop for Rural Development, which helps farmers to earn a living from crafts without destroying their country's own dwindling forests. In Jamaica the Small Projects Assistance Team, also supported by Christian Aid, is helping farmers to reduce dependence on banana exports by growing crops such as bread-fruit and plantain, and training them in livestock and poultry rearing.

Prevention of hunger is better than cure, but Christian Aid is also active in emergencies, sending money to provide food, shelter, medicine and transport when floods, famine, earthquakes or war strike.

The agency's education work in the UK and Ireland accounts for up to ten per cent of its income. This is because Christian Aid recognises the role of richer countries in creating the conditions that keep people poor. It believes that education and campaigning can help people to understand the root causes of poverty and encourage action by politicians and the public to remove them. Its 1996–2000 campaign, Change the Rules, looks at the impact on poor people of the unfair terms of trade and international debt, and promotes alternative international strategies to end world poverty.

Director Dr Daleep Mukarji, Inter-Church House, 35–41 Lower Marsh, London SE1 7RL   *Tel:* 0171–620 4444
Fax: 0171–620 0719

Church Army

Church Army Evangelists share the Christian faith through words and action and equip others to do the same. Over 400 full-time evangelists and 350 further staff are devoted to a wide range of service in Anglican churches, projects and teams throughout the British Isles.

Church Army trains and sends evangelists to work in five areas of focus.

Area Evangelism providing training and resources for groups of churches.

Children and Young People introducing the Christian message in new and fresh ways.

Church Planting providing expertise and resources to establish new congregations.

Homeless People helping churches and communities support those in need.

Older People recognising the gifts of older people and communicating the Gospel to them in practical ways.

President The Archbishop of Canterbury.
Chief Secretary Capt Philip Johanson, Church Army Headquarters, Independents Rd, Blackheath, London SE3 9LG   *Tel:* 0181–318 1226
Fax: 0181–318 5258
e-mail: information@churcharmy.org.uk

Principal Revd David Jeans, Wilson Carlile College of Evangelism, 50 Cavendish St, Sheffield S3 7RZ
Tel: 0114–278 7020
Fax: 0114–279 5863
e-mail: trainingcollege@sheffieldcentre.org.uk

Church Colleges of Higher Education

Canterbury *Christ Church College*, North Holmes Rd, Canterbury, Kent CT1 1QU *Tel:* (01227) 767700; Principal: Professor Michael Wright; Dean of Chapel: Revd Dr Brian Kelly, 1 St Martin's Cottages, St Martin's Priory, North Holmes Rd, Canterbury, Kent CT1 1QU
Tel: (01227) 767700 Ext 33

Cheltenham *Cheltenham and Gloucester College of Higher Education*, PO Box 220, The Park Campus, The Park, Cheltenham GL50 2QF *Tel:* (01242) 532701; Principal: Miss J. O. Trotter; Chaplain: Revd Graham Pollitt

Chester *University College Chester*, Cheyney Rd, Chester CH1 4BJ *Tel:* (01244) 375444 Ext 2305; Principal: Professor Tim Wheeler; Chaplain: Revd Michael French

Lancaster *St Martin's College*, Bowerham, Lancaster LA1 3JD *Tel:* (01524) 384562/1; Principal: Prof Christopher Carr; Chaplain: Revd Michael Everitt

Lincoln *Bishop Grosseteste College*, Lincoln LN1 3DY *Tel:* (01522) 527347; Principal: Mrs Eileen Baker; Chaplain: Revd Stuart Foster

Liverpool **Liverpool Hope University College*, Hope Park, Liverpool L16 9JD *Tel:* 0151–291 3243; Pro-Rector: Revd Dr R. J. Elford; Chaplain: Revd Liz Leaver

London **Roehampton Institute*, Whitelands College, West Hill, London SW15 3SN *Tel:* 0181–392 3000; Principal: Revd David Peacock; Chaplain: Revd David Hart

Plymouth *The College of St Mark and St John*, Derriford Rd, Plymouth PL6 8BH *Tel:* (01752) 636829 Ext 5701: Principal: Dr John Rea; Chaplain: Revd Karl Freeman

Winchester *King Alfred's College*, Sparkford Rd, Winchester SO22 4NR *Tel:* (01962) 827222; Principal: Professor John Dickinson; Chaplain: Revd Dr Anne Barton

York *The University College of Ripon and York St John*, Lord Mayor's Walk, York YO3 7EX *Tel:* (01904) 656771; Principal: Professor Robin Butlin; Chaplains: Revd Gregory Hoyland and Revd David Paton-Williams

*These colleges are constituent members of ecumenical federal Institutes of Higher Education.

College in a Special Relationship with the Church of England
Bognor/Chichester *The Chichester Institute of Higher Education*, Bishop Otter Campus, College Lane, Chichester PO19 4PE *Tel:* (01243) 816050; Director: Dr Philip Robinson; Chaplain: Revd Simon Griffiths

Church Urban Fund

Chairman
The Archbishop of Canterbury

Vice-Chairman
Mr Stephen O'Brien

Other Trustees
Mrs Elaine Appelbee, Mr Mark Cornwall-Jones, Mr Richard Farnell, Ven Granville Gibson, Revd Eileen Lake, Mrs Ruth McCurry, Mr Alan McLintock, Mr Michael Mockridge, Canon John Stanley

Chief Executive
Mrs Angela Sarkis
Office 2 Great Peter St, London SW1P 3LX
Tel: 0171–898 1000
Fax: 0171–799 1829

The Fund supports practical action for justice in disadvantaged and marginalised communities by awarding grants for local projects and by working in partnership with others to inform the wider debate on urban regeneration. The Fund aims to help the Church better understand the needs and gifts of people living in urban priority areas, and develop and implement a range of sustainable responses that take full account of local resources and potential.

The Fund was born out of the landmark *Faith in the City* report, and since allocating its first grant in 1988 has awarded more than £29 million to over 1,500 projects. Grants are awarded for work in such categories as community development, social care, youth and education, housing and homelessness, evangelism and interfaith efforts, and opening up church buildings for community use.

Application to the Fund is made through the local diocese. However, the national office is happy to respond to initial enquiries and can provide details of the appropriate diocesan contact.

The Fund is grateful for the continuing support of parishes and individuals who have contributed to its work.

Clergy Appointments Adviser

The Adviser has been appointed by the Archbishops of Canterbury and York to assist clergy, both from overseas and in England, to find suitable new appointments, and also to assist patrons and others responsible for making appointments to find suitable candidates. The Adviser has the responsibility to assist beneficed and unbeneficed clergy, men and women, together with deaconesses and accredited lay workers. The Adviser produces a list of vacancies for incumbencies, team posts, assistant curates and specialised ministries. The list is available free of charge. Those seeking advice should contact: Revd John Lee, Clergy Appointments Adviser, Fielden House, Little College St, London SW1P 3SH *Tel:* 0171–898 1897/8
Fax: 0171–898 1899
e-mail: caa@clara.net

Conference Centres and Retreat Houses

CONFERENCE CENTRES

ASHBURNHAM PLACE	Ashburnham Place, Battle, E Sussex TN33 9NF *Tel:* (01424) 892244 *Fax:* (01424) 892243 *e-mail:* ashburnham@compuserve.com (*Administrator:* Mrs Jennifer Oldroyd)
HAYES CONFERENCE CENTRE	Hayes Conference Centre, Swanwick, Derbyshire DE55 1AU *Tel:* (01773) 602482 *Fax:* (01773) 540841 (*Manager:* Mr Peter Anderson) *e-mail:* peter@ cct.org.uk *Web:* http://www.cct.org.uk
HENGRAVE HALL	Hengrave Hall Centre, Bury St Edmunds, Suffolk IP28 6LZ *Tel:* (01284) 701561 *Fax:* (01284) 702950 *e-mail:* co-ordinator@ hengravehallcentre.org.uk *Web:* http://hengravehallcentre.org.uk
HIGH LEIGH CONFERENCE CENTRE	High Leigh Conference Centre, Lord St, Hoddesdon, Herts EN11 8SG *Tel:* (01992) 463016 *Fax:* (01992) 446594 *Web:* www.cct.org.uk (*Manager:* Mr Ian Andrews)
LEE ABBEY	Lee Abbey Fellowship, Lynton, Devon EX35 6JJ *Tel:* (01598) 752621 *Fax:* (01598) 752619 *e-mail:* payne@leeabbey.org.uk (*Warden:* Revd Bob Payne)
SCARGILL HOUSE	Scargill House, Kettlewell, Skipton, N Yorks BD23 5HU *Tel:* (01756) 760234 *Fax:* (01756) 760499 *e-mail:* Scargill.house@dial.pipex.com (*Warden:* Revd Keith Knight)

RETREAT HOUSES

The following is a list of diocesan conference centres and retreat houses including some run by religious communities. For details of accommodation for individual retreats *see* Religious Communities page 199, or contact the National Retreat Association, The Central Hall, 256 Bermondsey St, London SE1 3JJ *Tel:* 0171–357 7736 whose journal *Vision* is published annually in December.

BATH AND WELLS	Abbey House, Chilkwell St, Glastonbury, Som BA6 8DH (*Retreat House*) *Tel:* (01458) 831112 (*Warden:* David Hill)
	Community of St Francis, Compton Durville Manor House, South Petherton TA13 5ES *Tel:* (01460) 40473
BLACKBURN	Whalley Abbey, Whalley, Clitheroe, Lancs BB7 9SS *Tel:* (01254) 822268 *Fax:* (01254) 824227 (*Warden*: Revd Christopher Sterry; *Manager:* Mrs Dinah Critchley)
BRADFORD	Parcevall Hall, Appletreewick, Skipton, N. Yorks BD23 6DG *Tels:* (0175 672) 213 and 283 *Fax:* (01756) 720656 (*Warden:* Miss Florence Begley)
CARLISLE	Carlisle Diocesan Conference House, Rydal Hall, Ambleside, Cumbria LA22 9LX *Tel:* (0153 94) 32050 *Fax:* (0153 94) 34887 (*Warden:* Revd Michael Kitchener)
CHELMSFORD	Diocesan House of Retreat, Pleshey, Chelmsford, Essex CM3 1HA *Tel:* (01245) 237251 (*Warden:* Canon John Howden)

CHESTER	Chester Diocesan Conference Centre, Foxhill, Frodsham, Cheshire WA6 6XB *Tel:* (01928) 733777 (*Wardens:* Mr & Mrs Ian Cameron)
	The Retreat House, 11 Abbey Square, Chester CH1 2HU *Tel:* (01244) 321801 (*Warden:* Sister Margaret CHN)
CHICHESTER	Monastery of the Holy Trinity, Crawley Down, Crawley, W Sussex RH10 4LH *Tel:* (01342) 712074
	Neale House Conference Centre, Moat Rd, East Grinstead, W Sussex RH19 3LB *Tel:* (01342) 312552
	St Margaret's Convent, St John's Rd, East Grinstead, W Sussex RH19 3LE *Tel:* (01342) 323497
COVENTRY	Coventry Diocesan Retreat House, Offchurch, Leamington Spa, Warks CV33 9AS *Tel:* (01926) 423309 (*Wardens:* Revd Michael and Revd Sharon Simpson)
DERBY/SOUTHWELL	Morley Retreat and Conference House, Morley, Derby DE7 6DE *Tel:* (01332) 831293 (*Warden:* Revd J. A. Heslop)
DURHAM	*See* entry for NEWCASTLE
ELY	Bishop Woodford House, Barton Road, Ely, Cambs CB7 4DX *Tels:* (01353) 663039 (Office); 665065 (Warden's Residence); and 662746 (Visitors).
	The Community of the Resurrection, St Francis' House, Hemingford Grey, Huntingdon PE18 9BJ *Tel:* (01480) 462185
EXETER	Mercer House, Exwick Road, Exeter EX4 2AT *Tel:* (01392) 219609 *Fax:* (01392) 218758 (*Warden:* Mr Graeme and Mrs Janet Williams)
GLOUCESTER	Glenfall House, Mill Lane, Charlton Kings, Cheltenham, Glos GL54 4EP *Tel:* (01242) 583654 *Fax:* (01242) 251314 (*Warden:* Vacancy)
GUILDFORD	St Columba's House, Maybury Hill, Woking, Surrey GU22 8AB *Tel:* (01483) 766498
	House of Bethany, Tilford Rd, Hindhead, Surrey GU26 6RB *Tel:* (01428) 604578
HEREFORD	Bishop Mascall Centre, Lower Galdeford, Ludlow, Shropshire SY8 2RU *Tel:* (01584) 873882. (*Director:* Revd Graham Earney)
LEICESTER	Launde Abbey, East Norton, Leicestershire LE7 9XB *Tel:* (01572) 717254 (*Warden:* Revd Graham Johnson)
LICHFIELD	Lichfield Diocesan Retreat and Conference Centre, Shallowford House, Norton Bridge, Stone, Staffs ST15 0NZ *Tel:* (01785) 760233 *Fax:* (01785) 760390 (*Warden:* Mr David Rowlands)
LINCOLN	Edward King House, The Old Palace, Lincoln LN2 1PU *Tel:* (01522) 528778 *Fax:* (01522) 527308 (*Warden:* Revd Alex Adkins)
LONDON	The Royal Foundation of Saint Katharine, 2 Butcher Row, London E14 8DS *Tel:* 0171–790 3540 *Fax:* 0171–702 7603 (*Master:* Prebendary Ronald Swan)
NEWCASTLE/DURHAM	Shepherd's Dene, Riding Mill, Northumberland NE44 6AF *Tel:* (01434) 682212. (*Warden:* Mr David Bennell)

NORWICH	Horstead Centre, Norwich NR12 7EP *Tels:* (01603) 737215 (*Office*); (01603) 737674 (*Guests*) (*Warden:* Mrs Valerie Khambatta)
	All Hallows Convent, Ditchingham, Bungay NR35 2DT *Tel:* (01986) 892749
OXFORD	Priory of Our Lady, Priory Lane, Burford OX18 4SQ *Tel:* (01993) 823605/823141
	Clewer Spirituality Centre, Convent of St John Baptist, Hatch Lane, Windsor SL4 3QR *Tel:* (01753) 850618
	St Mary's Convent, Wantage OX12 9DJ *Tel:* (012357) 20170
PETERBOROUGH	Ecton House, Ecton, Northampton NN6 0QE *Tel:* (01604) 406442 (*Warden:* Vacancy)
SALISBURY	Sarum College, 19 The Close, Salisbury SP1 2EE *Tel:* (01722) 424800 *Fax:* (01722) 338508 *e-mail:* 00635.63@compuserve.com (*Director:* Canon Bruce Duncan)
	Society of St Francis, The Friary, Hilfield, Dorchester DT2 7BE *Tel:* (01300) 341345 *Fax:* (01300) 341293
	St Denys Retreat Centre, 2 Church St, Warminster BA12 8PG *Tel:* (01985) 214824
SHEFFIELD	Whirlow Grange Conference Centre, Ecclesall Road South, Sheffield, S Yorks S11 9PZ *Tels:* 0114–236 3173 (Office) and 236 1183 (Visitors) (*General Manager:* Mr Jonathon Green)
SOUTHWARK	Wychcroft, Bletchingley, Redhill, Surrey RH1 4NE. *Tel:* (01883) 743041 (*Bookings Secretary:* Mr Chris Archer)
	The Community of Sisters of the Church, St Michael's Convent, 56 Ham Common, Richmond TW10 7JH *Tel:* 0181–9408711/948 2502
SOUTHWELL	*See* entry for DERBY.
TRURO	Community of the Epiphany, Copeland Court, Kenwyn, Truro, Cornwall TR1 3DU *Tel:* (01872) 272249
WAKEFIELD	Community of the Resurrection, Mirfield, W Yorks WF14 0BN *Tel:* (01924) 497596 *Fax:* (01924) 492738
	Community of St Peter, Horbury, W Yorks WF4 6BB *Tel:* (01924) 272181 *Fax:* (01924) 261225
WINCHESTER	Old Alresford Place, Old Alresford, Hants *Tel:* (01962) 732518 (*Director:* Canon Terry Pinner, *Warden:* Mrs Penny Matthews)
	Alton Abbey, Beech, Alton, Hants GU34 4AP *Tel:* (01420) 562145/ 563575
WORCESTER	Holland House, Cropthorne, nr Pershore, Worcs WR10 3NB (*Retreat House*) *Tel:* (01386) 860330 (*Warden:* Mr Peter Middlemiss)
YORK	York Diocesan House, Wydale Hall, Brompton-by-Sawdon, Scarborough, N Yorks YO13 9DG *Tel:* (01723) 85270 (*Warden:* Mr Peter Fletcher)
	St Oswald's Pastoral Centre, Woodlands Drive, Sleights, Whitby, N Yorks YO21 1RY *Tel:* (01947) 810496

Decade of Evangelism

The Lambeth Conference recommended that the closing years of this millennium should be 'a "Decade of Evangelism" during which, in co-operation with other Christians, there should be a renewed and united emphasis on making Christ known to the people of his world'. The General Synod of the Church of England endorsed this recommendation at its meeting in York in 1989.

To affirm, encourage and resource this initiative, the Board of Mission has three Decade staff, Canon Robert Warren (National Officer for Evangelism), Miss Janice Price (Mission and Evangelism Secretary), and Mr Alan Tuddenham (Decade Administrator), who work closely with the Diocesan Missioners and Advisers on Evangelism. The Officers also work in partnership with their colleagues in other churches, the ACC, the Missionary Societies, Churches Together in England, and other evangelistic organisations in this country. Their work and the strategy for the work of evangelism in and beyond the Decade of Evangelism are shaped and encouraged by the Mission, Evangelism and Renewal Committee, a sub-committee of the Board of Mission which is chaired by the Bishop of Wakefield, and draws its membership from a broad cross-section of the traditions within the Church of England.

SPRINGBOARD
Springboard – Lambeth Palace, London SE1 7JU
Administrative Office 4 Station Yard, Abingdon, Oxon
OX14 3LD   Tel: (01235) 553722
                       Fax: (01235) 553922
           e-mail: springboard.UK@btinternet.com

Director Martin Cavender
Administrator Martin Hayward
Archbishops' Adviser in Evangelism Canon Michael Green
Springboard Team
Revd Angela Butler (Priest-in-Charge of Chipperfield, Herts)
Revd Stephen Cottrell
Revd James Lawrence (Team Evangelist, CPAS)

Working to the vision, 'to encourage, renew and mobilize the church for evangelism', Springboard is the joint initiative of the Archbishops of Canterbury and York. Working alongside the Diocesan Missioners and others, it is an additional resource for dioceses and parishes throughout the country, and in the wider Anglican Communion. Receiving its policy from the Archbishops, the strategy for work is set by an 18 member executive representing all the Anglican Church traditions. The core Springboard Team works alongside others in a widening network of evangelists, missioners, teachers and other practitioners holding to a three stranded cord of 'spirituality – evangelism – and apologetics'. Always working ecumenically, and across the traditions of the Church, Springboard is available at the invitation of dioceses, deaneries and parishes to support and encourage the existing work; to help unlock potential; and to help increase the effectiveness of the Church in evangelism and mission. Strategic elements of the work include Diocesan Travelling Schools, Long Courses in evangelism, conferences, CME/POT and other leadership training, conferences, work in theological colleges, and parish, deanery and area missions.

Faculty Office and Special Marriage Licences

The Faculty Office of the Archbishop of Canterbury, otherwise known as The Court of Faculties, exercises on behalf of the Archbishop the dispensing powers that he has by virtue of the Ecclesiastical Licences Act of 1533. These comprise the appointment of Notaries Public, the granting of degrees, and the granting of marriage licences. The right to grant a Special Licence for marriage at any convenient time or place in England or Wales is unique to the Archbishop, and this jurisdiction is sparingly exercised and good cause must always be shown why a more normal preliminary to Anglican marriage cannot be used. Marriage with any other preliminary must be solemnized between 8am and 6pm, and although a Special Licence could omit this requirement, that will only in practice be done in a case of serious illness.

The more common need for a Special Licence is the parties' desire to marry in a building not normally authorised for Anglican marriage, or in a parish where they cannot satisfy the residence requirements. Even in the last case cause must be shown, normally in the form of a real connection with the parish or church in question; the *Special Licence procedure is not intended to enable parties to choose a church building on aesthetic or sentimental grounds.*

More detailed guidance on the grounds that may be considered sufficient for the granting of a Special Licence may always be sought from the Faculty Office by letter or telephone.

Special arrangements may sometimes be made in a genuine emergency. In such cases the clergy or the couple concerned should first contact the Diocesan Registrar, Archdeacon, or diocesan or area Bishop. If unable to resolve the difficulty himself he will make arrangements for the Faculty Office to be approached.

Orders made by the Master of the Faculties prescribe from time to time fees which are to be charged for applications for Special Licences. The fee is currently £120.00.

The Faculty Office is open to telephone and personal callers between 10am and 4pm Monday to Friday, except on certain days around Easter and Christmas.
Office 1 The Sanctuary, Westminster, London SW1P 3JT
Tel: 0171–222 5381 Ext 2262

Hospice Movement

The word 'Hospice' was first used from the fourth Century onwards when Christian orders welcomed travellers, the sick and those in need. It was first applied to the care of dying patients by Mme Jeanne Garnier who founded the Dames de Calvaire in Lyon, France in 1842. The modern hospice movement, however, with its twin emphases on medical and psychosocial enquiry, dates from the founding of St Christopher's Hospice by Dame Cicely Saunders in 1967. Since 1967, 'Hospice' has become a worldwide philosophy adapting to the needs of different cultures and settings – hospital, hospice and community – and is established in six continents.

Hospice and palliative care is the active, total care of patients whose disease no longer responds to curative treatment, and for whom the goal must be the best quality of life for them and their families. Palliative medicine is now a distinct medical speciality in the UK. It focuses on controlling pain and other symptoms, easing suffering and enhancing the life that remains. It integrates the psychological and spiritual aspects of care, to enable patients to live out their lives with dignity. It also offers support to families, both during the patient's illness and their bereavement. It offers a unique combination of care in hospices and at home.

Although hospice care is principally for patients with advanced cancer, many services will consider patients with other terminal illnesses such as HIV/AIDS, motor neurone disease or other neurological illnesses. Hospice and palliative care is free of charge regardless of whether it is provided by a voluntary hospice, Macmillan Service, Marie Curie Cancer Care, Sue Ryder Home or by an NHS service. The criteria for admission are based on medical, social and emotional need. Referral to a hospice or palliative care service (including inpatient and home care nursing services) is normally arranged by the patient's own GP or hospital doctor. Further information on hospice care in the UK and overseas and a *Directory of Hospice and Palliative Care Services* (on receipt of a large SAE and 64p stamp) is available from the Hospice Information Service, 51–59 Lawrie Park Rd, Sydenham, London SE26 6DZ
Tel: 0181–778 9252
Fax: 0181–776 9345

The Children's Hospice Movement

The Children's Hospice Movement grew out of a recognition that families with children with life-limiting illnesses usually want to look after their children at home once hospital no longer seems appropriate. The strain and loneliness can be very great, especially when the illness is slow and progressive. The children's hospices are small and as much like home as possible, places where children and their families can come to stay from time to time, much in the way that people have a holiday occasionally or go to stay with friends and relatives.

In other societies the existence of the close-knit extended family and the greater involvement of the local community provide a kind of support which is generally lacking in contemporary British society. Using the extended family as their model, children's hospices have a role, outside the immediate family, to be alongside, offering friendship, support and practical help, however protracted, throughout the child's illness and during the terminal phase and the months and years of bereavement that follow.

The children's hospices offer respite care, accompanied or unaccompanied, terminal care and bereavement care. In some cases, home care is also offered. New referrals are not normally accepted over the age of 16. No charge is made to families.

Details of individual hospices for adults and children can be obtained from the Hospice Information Service at the above address.

For details of the **Association of Hospice Chaplains** *see* page 221.

Marriage: Legal Aspects

A comprehensive statement of the law and information on related matters is available from the Faculty Office of the Archbishop of Canterbury. Copies of *Anglican Marriage in England and Wales – A Guide to the Law for Clergy* were sent to incumbents and licensed clergy of the Church of England and the Church in Wales in 1992.

Further copies are available by post, price £2.00, from: The Faculty Office, 1 The Sanctuary, Westminster, London SW1P 3JT

For details of **Special Marriage Licences** see the entry for the Faculty Office, page 170.

Mothers' Union

The Mothers' Union is an Anglican organisation which promotes the well-being of families worldwide. This is done through developing prayer and spiritual growth in families, studying and reflecting on family life and its place in society and resourcing members to take practical action to improve conditions for families, both nationally and in the communities in which they live. It has over 750,000 members thoughout the world, and is organised locally into branches attached to a local church It works extensively overseas throughout the Anglican Communion. It has a quarterly magazine *Home and Family*.

World Wide President Lady Eames

Chief Executive Mrs Angela Ridler

Office Mary Sumner House, 24 Tufton St, London SW1P 3RB
Tel: 0171–222 5533
Fax: 0171–222 1591
e-mail: mu@themothersunion.org
Web: http://www.the mothersunion.org

Press

CHURCH TIMES
Established 1863. An independent weekly newspaper which reports on the Anglican Church worldwide. As well as full news coverage, it includes comment and opinion on matters of the day; general features; clergy appointments and resignations; obituaries; reviews of the latest books, music and art; with classified advertisements. Goes to press on Wednesday; published on Friday; price 50p; annual subscription on application. *Editor* Mr Paul Handley. *Office* 33 Upper St, London N1 0PN
Tel: 0171–359 4570
Fax: 0171–226 3073/3051
Subscriptions: *Tel:* (01502) 711171
Fax: (01502) 711585

CHURCH OF ENGLAND NEWSPAPER
A weekly newspaper which aims to provide a full, objective and lively coverage of Christian news from Britain and overseas. Contents include general features, book reviews, the latest clergy appointments, a weekly theology page and comment on current issues. Goes to press on Tuesday; published Friday; price 50p (annual subscription £36.00). *Editor* C. M. Blakely. *Office* The Church of England Newspaper, 10 Little College St, London SW1P 3SH
Tel: 0171–976 7760
Fax: 0171–878 1548
Subscriptions: *Tel:* 0171–878 1510
Fax: 0171–976 0783

ENGLISH CHURCHMAN
Church of England newspaper (established 1843), incorporating St James's Chronicle (1766). Protestant and evangelical. News, various features, diocesan round-up, book reviews, correspondence and church calendar. Published fortnightly, Fridays, price 30p. *Editor* Dr Napier Malcolm. *Office* 22 Lesley Ave, Canterbury, Kent CT1 3LF
Tel: (01227) 781282
Fax: (01934) 712520
e-mail: nama@kpws.demon.co.uk

Schools, Church of England

Throughout the country there are 4,774 Church of England schools within the maintained system of education, together with a number of schools in the private sector which are able to claim strong connection with the Church. The term 'Church of England School' is at present properly applicable only to voluntary aided, controlled, special agreement and grant maintained Church of England schools which are funded through the local Education Authority and the Department for Education as part of the national schools system, whilst still retaining their position as autonomous educational charities. New legislation in 1998 will change the nomenclature and status of controlled, special agreement and grant maintained Church of England schools.

All such schools lie within the responsibilities of the Diocesan Boards of Education. They provide education for 904,000 children and young people and represent a major investment on the part of the Church of England in the national education system. In addition to these schools there are many independent schools, founded on trusts which provide that worship and religious teaching taking place in them shall be of a Church of England character. These include many of the well-known public schools and grammar schools of ancient foundation, some of which are associated with Cathedrals or other major Churches.

In recent years, Government legislation has created and continues to create a number of changes both in the framework within which all schools are required to operate and also in the arrangements for their administration. Such changes challenge the governors and staff of Church schools to establish clear policies which indicate how they express their understanding of their role as Church of England schools in their particular circumstances. In this task the schools are supported by the staff of the Diocesan Boards of Education as stipulated by the DBE Measure and by the work of the General Synod Board of Education and the National Society, which provides a range of publications and other resources. The National Society has also established training courses for inspectors of Church schools under section 23 of the School Inspection Act 1996. Details of these courses and of the publications and support service provided by the National Society and the General Synod Board of Education can be obtained from their offices, whose address is given elsewhere in the Year Book. Details of individual schools may be obtained from the Diocesan Directors of Education in the case of maintained schools or in *The Church of England Schools and Colleges Handbook* (published by The School Government Publishing Company), and in the case of independent schools from the *Public and Preparatory Schools Year Book* (published by A & C Black).

Services Authorized and Commended

Public worship in the Church of England is a matter governed by law.

Canon B2 provides that the General Synod may approve forms of service with or without time limit. Services thus approved are alternative to those of *The Book of Common Prayer*. The power given to General Synod under Canon B2 derives from the Worship and Doctrine Measure 1974.

Canon B4 provides that the Convocations, the Archbishops in their provinces or the Bishops in their dioceses may approve forms of service for use on occasions for which *The Book of Common Prayer* or *Authorized Alternative Services* do not provide.

Canon B5 (paragraph 2) allows discretion to any minister where no other provision has been made under Canons B1 or B4, to use other forms of service which are considered suitable. If questions are raised as to whether such forms of service are suitable the decision rests with the Bishop.

Authorized Alternative Services are those approved by the General Synod under Canon B1 (for fuller details *see* page 175).

Commended Services are those which the Bishops corporately have judged to be 'suitable' either for approval under Canon B4 or for use in the contexts envisaged in Canon B5 (for fuller details *see* page 176).

The forms of service currently *authorized* for use in public worship (as at 1 January 1999) are:

The Book of Common Prayer – authorized without time limit.

The Alternative Service Book 1980 and *Ministry to the Sick* – authorized until 31 December 2000.

Series 1 Solemnization of Matrimony, Series 1 Burial Services – authorized until 31 December 2000.

Series 2 Baptism and Confirmation – authorized until 31 December 2000.

Further Alternative Rules to Order the Service together with an Additional Alternative Lectionary – authorized until 31 December 2000.

A Service of the Word – authorized until 31 December 2000.

Affirmations of Faith – authorized until 31 December 2000.

Common Worship, Calendar, Lectionary and Collects – authorized until further resolution of the General Synod.

Common Worship, Initiation Services – authorized until further resolution of the General Synod.

A leaflet entitled *Public Worship in the Church of England* is issued on the authority of the Standing Committee of the

General Information

General Synod. The Sixth edition, published in 1994, takes account of the revision of the liturgical canons and the authorization of *A Service of the Word*. It is a guide for both clergy and laity, available from Church House Bookshop, 31 Great Smith St, London SW1P 3BN, price 50p (by post 75p).

A further leaflet entitled *A Brief Guide to Liturgical Copyright* deals with the procedures for local reproduction. It provides guidance on preparing local texts and information about copyright requirements. The current edition (October 1997) is available price £1.50 from Church House Bookshop.

AUTHORIZED ALTERNATIVE SERVICES
AUTHORIZED BY GENERAL SYNOD UNTIL 31 DECEMBER 2000

a) *The Alternative Service Book 1980* containing
The Calendar and Rules to Order the Service
General Notes
Sentences
Morning Prayer and Evening Prayer
Prayers for Various Occasions
Holy Communion Rite A
Holy Communion Rite B
Initiation Services

Corresponding separate editions

ASB 10 Morning and Evening Prayer
ASB 12 Evening Prayer
ASB 20 Holy Communion Rite A
ASB 22 Holy Communion Rite B†
ASB 31 Baptism of Children (card)
ASB 35 Thanksgiving for the Birth of a Child/or after Adoption (card)
ASB 40 Confirmation

The Marriage Service
Funeral Services

ASB 50 Marriage Service
ASB 60 Funeral Services (large format)
ASB 62 Funeral Services (standard format)

The Ordinal
Sentences, Collects and Readings
Tables of Psalms, Readings and Sunday Themes

ASB 87 Collects
Collects (Traditional Language) for use with Rite B†

b) Ministry to the Sick (1983)
ASB 70
contains Communion with the Sick (Rite A and Rite B), The Laying on of Hands with Prayer, and Anointing, A Commendation at the Time of Death, Prayers for Use with the Sick

ASB 71 Ministry to the Sick (card) (Distribution of Communion Rite A, Laying on of Hands)
ASB 73 (Rite A) Holy Communion at Home
ASB 74 (Rite B)† (or in Hospital) (cards)

c) Series 1 Solemnization of Matrimony†
Series 1 Burial Services†

d) Series 2 Baptism and Confirmation†

AS 152 Matrimony
AS 160 Burial Services (standard format)
AS 162 Burial Services (large format)

e) Further Alternative Rules to Order the Service together with an Additional Alternative Lectionary (these are for use with the Prayer Book).

f) A Service of the Word } published together
Affirmations of Faith }

AUTHORIZED BY GENERAL SYNOD UNTIL FURTHER RESOLUTION OF THE SYNOD

g) Common Worship – Calendar, Lectionary and Collects
Selections of this material are also contained in:

h) Common Worship: Collects and Post Communion Prayers for Sundays and Festivals

i) Common Worship: Advent 1997 to Advent 1998 (The first in a series of annual publications)

j) Common Worship: Initiation Services

AUTHORIZED BY THE ARCHBISHOPS OF CANTERBURY AND YORK, WITHOUT TIME LIMIT, FOR USE IN THEIR RESPECTIVE PROVINCES

k) A Service for Remembrance Sunday

†These services are in traditional language.

General Information

COMMENDED SERVICES
COMMENDED BY THE HOUSE OF BISHOPS OF THE GENERAL SYNOD

Services of Prayer and Dedication after Civil Marriage (1985)

Lent, Holy Week, Easter: Services and Prayers* (1986)
   Night Prayer: A Service for Late Evening (from the above, published separately† (1987))

Funeral Service for a Child dying near the time of birth (1989)

Ministry at the Time of Death (1991)

The Promise of His Glory: Services and Prayers for the Season from All Saints to Candlemas† (1991)
NOTE The suggested Calendar and Lectionaries appended to the above are now subsumed in a revised form in the newly authorized calendar and lectionary.

Patterns for Worship (1995) (this incorporates texts commended by the House of Bishops and the authorised A Service of the Word and Affirmations of Faith)

VERSIONS OF THE BIBLE AND OF THE PSALMS

The following may be used in Book of Common Prayer services (with the permission of the PCC) instead of the Authorized Version of the Bible and the Psalter in *The Book of Common Prayer*:

Bible	Psalters
Revised Version	Revised Psalter
Revised Standard Version	The Liturgical Psalter (The Psalms
New English Bible	a New Translation for Worship)
Jerusalem Bible	
Good News Bible	
(Today's English Version)	

NOTE: Any version of the Bible or Psalter may be used with alternative services.

TV and Radio

BBC LOCAL RADIO
There are thirty-nine BBC local radio stations in counties and cities throughout England. Each station is responsible for its own religious broadcasting and some have religious advisory panels. Religious programmes are often presented and produced by local clergy and lay people who observe the editorial policy of the BBC. For details of stations, contact the BBC Regions' Press Office
Tel: 0171–765 2795

BBC RELIGIOUS BROADCASTING DEPARTMENT
Arranges a wide variety of religious broadcasts for transmission in the BBC's television service, local radio, the five domestic radio services and the World Service. The aims of religious broadcasting are (1) to seek to reflect the worship, thought and action of the principal religious traditions represented in the UK, recognising that those traditions are mainly, though not exclusively, Christian; (2) to seek to present to viewers and listeners those beliefs, ideas, issues and experiences in the contemporary world which are evidently related to a religious interpretation or dimension of life; and (3) to seek also to meet the religious interests, concerns and needs of those on the fringe of, or outside, the organised life of the religious bodies. On matters of policy the Corporation is advised by a representative Central Religious Advisory Committee which also acts as adviser to the ITC. *Head of Religious Broadcasting* Revd Ernest Rea, BBC, Room 5038, Oxford Rd, Manchester M60 1SJ

CENTRAL RELIGIOUS ADVISORY COUNCIL
CRAC advises the BBC and the ITC on policy matters relating to religion. Its membership is drawn from the

major Christian traditions and world faiths represented in the United Kingdom. CRAC can be contacted c/o the BBC or ITC.

CHURCHES' ADVISORY COUNCIL FOR LOCAL BROADCASTING
CACLB is an ecumenical body with charitable status established in 1967 for the advancement of the Christian religion through broadcasting on radio and television. It is a formal network of CCBI. Its council is drawn from the Church of England, Roman Catholic Church, Methodist, Baptist, United Reformed, Evangelical Alliance, Salvation Army, Free Churches' Council, CCBI, Churches Together in England, Church of Ireland, Churches Together in Wales, and ACTS (Scotland), with representatives of the BBC, Independent Television Commission, Radio Authority, Association of Christians in Local Broadcasting, Churches Media Trust, and Christian broadcast training organisations. *President* Rt Revd Nigel McCulloch, Bishop of Wakefield. *Chairman* Revd Dr Leslie Griffiths. *Gen Secretary* Mr Jeff Bonser, PO Box 124, Westcliff-on-Sea, Essex SS0 0QU   *Tel:* (01702) 348369
Fax: (01702) 305121
e-mail: office@caclb.org.uk
Web: http://www.caclb.org.uk

FOUNDATION FOR CHRISTIAN COMMUNICATION LTD (CTVC)
Major producer and co-producer of religious television programmes. Distributes television programmes worldwide. Training courses are held in the use of radio and television and in personal communication. Television and sound studios fitted to full broadcast standard and post-production facilities. All are available for hire. A large video distribution service is available on request. Catalogue available. *Director* Revd Barrie Allcott, Hillside Studios, Merry Hill Rd, Bushey, Watford, Herts WD2 1DR   *Tel:* 0181–950 4426/7
Fax: 0181–950 1437
e-mail: ctvc@ctvc.co.uk
web: http://www.ctvc.co.uk

INDEPENDENT RADIO
Under the Broadcasting Act 1990, the Radio Authority is charged with regulating all sound broadcasting services which are provided in the United Kingdom by persons other than the BBC. The Act requires the Radio Authority to publish codes giving guidance on a range of programme matters, (including religious broadcasts), advertising and sponsorship. Complaints about the content of any religious broadcast on an Independent Radio station should be addressed to the station concerned, or to the Radio Authority, Holbrook House, 14 Great Queen St, London WC2B 5DG   *Tel:* 0171–430 2724

INDEPENDENT TELEVISION COMMISSION
The Independent Television Commission was established under the Broadcasting Act 1990 to regulate all non-BBC television services in the United Kingdom including the terrestrial channels, ITV, Channel 4, Channel 5, and services on satellite and cable television. Further details from Ms Rachel Viney, Religious Broadcasting Officer, ITC, 33 Foley St, London W1P 7LB   *Tel:* 0171–306 7848

INDEPENDENT TELEVISION, RELIGIOUS PROGRAMMES ON
Religious Broadcasting on Independent Television includes programmes which are carried by the entire ITV network; programmes on Channels 4 and 5; items on the breakfast service, and programmes made by individual ITV companies for their own regional audiences. Most of the ITV network religious programmes are shown on Sundays. Regional religious programmes, usually transmitted during the week, though not exclusively so, include documentary series, religious magazine programmes and short reflective slots.

Anglican Advisers to the ITV Companies:
ANGLIA TELEVISION Revd Philip Spence, 7 Minster Precincts, Peterborough PE1 1XS   *Tel:* (01733) 64899
CENTRAL INDEPENDENT TELEVISION Mrs A. M. Gatford, 72 Pastures Hill, Littleover, Derby DE3 7BB
Tel: (01332) 512700
Rt Revd John Saxby, Bishop's House, Corvedale Rd, Halford, Craven Arms, Shropshire SY7 9BT
Tel: (01588) 673571
BORDER TELEVISION Revd Christopher Morris, Vicarage, Lanercost, Brampton, Cumbria CA8 2HQ
Tel: (01697) 72478
CHANNEL TELEVISION Revd Marc Trickey, St Martin's Rectory, Grande Rue, Guernsey   *Tel:* (01481) 38303
GRAMPIAN TELEVISION Revd Emsley Nimmo, St Margaret's House, Gallowgate, Aberdeen AB1 1EA
Tel: (01224) 644969
GRANADA TELEVISION Rt Revd David Bonser, 4 Sandfield Drive, Lostock, Bolton BL6 4DU   *Tel:* (01204) 843400
HTV WEST Rt Revd Peter Firth, 7 Ivywell Rd, Bristol BS9 1NX   *Tel:* (01904) 634531
LONDON WEEKEND TELEVISION Revd Perry Butler, c/o LWT, Southbank Television Centre, London SE1 9TL
Tel: 0171–261 3434
MERIDIAN BROADCASTING c/o Revd Ray Short, 36–38 Southampton St, London SE1 9RD
TYNE TEES TELEVISION Canon Peter Strange, St Nicholas Cathedral, Newcastle upon Tyne NE1 1PF
Tel: 0191–232 1939
ULSTER TELEVISION Rt Revd Dr James Mehaffey, The See House, Culmore Rd, Londonderry   *Tel:* (01504) 51206

WESTCOUNTRY TELEVISION c/o Sue Bannister, Westcountry Television, Langage Science Park, Plymouth, Devon PL7 5BG
Mr Jeremy Dowling, Rosecare Villa Farm, St Gennys, Bude EX23 0BG *Tel:* (01840) 230326
YORKSHIRE TELEVISION Revd Martin Short, 30 Newall Hall Park, Otley, W Yorks LS21 2RD *Tel:* (01943) 465071

SANDFORD ST MARTIN (CHURCH OF ENGLAND) TRUST

A registered charity founded 1978 to support excellence in broadcast programmes concerned with religion and spiritual values, and to encourage Christian participation and interest in radio and television. The Trust makes five awards annually for outstanding programmes concerned with religion. These awards are given to radio and television in alternate years. The Trust was initially provided from an Anglican source but its scope is ecumenical. The Trust has sponsored a number of consultations and courses including, in 1995, a seminar with the Farmington Institute for teachers of religious education and writers and producers working in religious broadcasting. As a result of this consultation, the Trust made a further series of awards in 1997 for outstanding programmes in the specific field of religious education, which will be made again in 1999. *Chairman* Very Revd Michael Mayne. *Hon Secretary* Dr Robert Towler, Room 644, Church House, Great Smith St, London SW1P 3NZ
Tel: 0171–898 1574
Fax: 0171–898 1581

WORLD ASSOCIATION FOR CHRISTIAN COMMUNICATION (WACC)

WACC is an organisation of corporate and personal members who wish to give high priority to Christian values in the world's communication and development needs. It is not a council or federation of churches. The majority of members are communication professionals from all walks of life. Others include partners in different communication activities, and representatives of church and agencies. It funds communication activities which reflect regional interests, and encourages ecumenical unity among communicators. As a professional organisation, WACC serves the wider ecumenical movement by offering guidance on communication policies, interpreting developments in communications worldwide, discussing the consequences which such developments have for churches and communities everywhere but especially in the Third World, and assisting the training of Christian communicators. It publishes *Action*, a newsletter ten times a year, and the quarterly journal *Media Development*. It has 860 members in 115 countries. UK members include the Anglican Communion Office, BBC Religious Programmes Dept, The Foundation for Christian Communication, Council for World Mission, Feed the Minds, Church of England Communications Unit, Independent Television Commission, and SPCK. *Gen Secretary* Revd Carlos A. Valle, 357 Kennington Lane, London SE11 5QY
Tel: 0171–582 9139
Fax: 0171–735 0340
e-mail: wacc@gn.apc.org
web: http://www.oneworld.org/wacc

Women's Ministry

Women and men may be ordained Priest or Deacon, licensed as Accredited Lay Worker or admitted as Reader. Under the Priests (Ordination of Women) Measure 1993 and Canon C4B, women may be ordained priest and are eligible for appointment to most offices in the Church of England. There is no provision for women to become Bishops. Under Canon C 21 a Deacon who has been ordained for more than six years may now be appointed as Canon residentiary of a Cathedral.

Theological Colleges and Regional Cources

THEOLOGICAL COLLEGES

Addresses and Telephone Numbers	Diocese	Principle or Warden	Fees p.a.£
Cranmer Hall (St John's College), Durham DH1 3RJ 0191–374 3579	Durham	Mr David Day Revd Dr Steven Croft (Warden)	7,020
College of the Resurrection, Mirfield, W Yorks WF14 0BW (01924) 490441	Wakefield	Revd Christopher Irvine	4,341
Oak Hill Theological College, Southgate, London N14 4PS 0181–449 0467 *Fax:* 0181–441 5996	London	Revd Dr David Peterson	7,299
The Queen's College, Somerset Rd, Edgbaston, Birmingham B15 2QH (Ecumenical) 0121–454 1527 *Fax:* 0121–454 8171 *e-mail:* Queens-College@compuserve.com	Birmingham	Revd Peter Fisher	7,257
Ridley Hall, Cambridge CB3 9HG (01223) 741080 *Fax:* (01223) 741081	Ely	Revd Graham Cray	7,443
Ripon College, Cuddesdon, Oxford OX44 9EX (01865) 874404	Oxford	Revd John Clarke	7,101
St John's College, Bramcote, Nottingham NG9 3DS 0115 925 1114 *Fax:* 0115 943 6438	Southwell	Dr Christina Baxter	7,320
St Stephen's House, 16 Marston St, Oxford OX4 1JX (01865) 247874 *Fax:* (01865) 794338 *e-mail:* dgmoss@ermine.ox.ac.uk	Oxford	Revd Dr Jeremy Sheehy	7,020
Trinity College, Stoke Hill, Bristol BS9 1JP 0117 968 2803 *Fax:* 0117 968 7470 *e-mail:* principal@trinity-bris.ac.uk	Bristol	Canon David Gillett	7,290
Westcott House, Jesus Lane, Cambridge CB5 8BP (01223) 741000 *Fax:* (01223) 741002	Ely	Revd Michael Roberts	7,425
Wycliffe Hall, Oxford OX2 6PW (01865) 274200 *Fax:* (01865) 274215	Oxford	Revd Dr Alister McGrath	7,122
Theological Institute of the Scottish Episcopal Church, Old Coates House, 32 Manor Place, Edinburgh EH3 7EB *Tel:* 0131–220 2272 *Fax:* 0131–220 2294 *e-mail:* tisec@scotland.anglican.org	Edinburgh	Canon Rosemary Nixon	N/A
St Michael's College, Llandaff, Cardiff CF5 2YJ (01222) 563379 *Fax:* (01222) 576377 *e-mail:* stmichaels@nildram.co.uk	Llandaff	Revd Dr John Holdsworth	N/A

REGIONAL COURSES

Address and Telephone Number	Principal or Director
Carlisle and Blackburn Diocesan Training Institute Church House, West Walls, Carlisle, Cumbria CA3 8UE (01228) 522573	Revd Tim Herbert
East Anglian Ministerial Training Course EAMTC Office, 5 Pound Hill, Cambridge CB3 0AE (01223) 741026 *Fax:* (01223) 741027	Canon Joy Tetley PH D
East Midlands Ministry Training Course Block D, Cherrytree Buildings, The University Park, Nottingham NG7 2RD 0115 951 4854 *Fax:* 0115–951 4817 *e-mail:* emmtc@nottingham.ac.uk	Revd Michael Taylor
North East Oecumenical Course Regional office: Carter House, Pelaw Leazes Lane, Durham DH1 1TB 0191–384 8317 *Fax:* 0191–384 7529	Canon Trevor Pitt
Northern Ordination Course Luther King House, Brighton Grove, Rusholme, Manchester M14 5JP 0161–225 6668 *Fax:* 0161–248 9201 *e-mail:* office@noc1.u-net.com	Canon Michael Williams
North Thames Ministerial Training Course Chase Side, Southgate, London N14 4PS 0181–364 9442 *Fax:* 0181–364 8889	Vacancy

General Information

St Albans and Oxford Ministry Course Diocesan Church House, North Hinksey, Oxford OX2 0NB (01865) 208260	Revd Dr Mike Butterworth
South East Institute for Theological Education Deanery Gate, The Precinct, Rochester, Kent ME1 1SJ (01634) 832299	Revd Alan Le Grys
Southern Theological Education and Training Scheme 19 The Close, Salisbury, Wilts SP1 2EE (01722) 412996 *Fax:* (01722) 424811 *e-mail:* STETS.ac.uk	Revd Dr Christopher Cocksworth
South West Ministry Training Course SWMTC Office, Petherwin Gate, North Petherwin, Launceston PL15 8LW *Tel:* (01566) 785545 *Fax:* (01566) 785749	Revd Dr David Hewlett
West Midlands Ministerial Training Course Queen's Birmingham, Somerset Rd, Edgbaston, Birmingham B15 2QH 0121–452 2604	Revd Dr Dennis Stamps
West of England Ministerial Training Course 7c College Green, Gloucester GL1 2LX *Tel* and *Fax:* (01452) 300494	Revd Dr Richard Clutterbuck

ORDAINED LOCAL MINISTRY SCHEMES RECOGNISED BY THE HOUSE OF BISHOPS

Address and Telephone Number	Principal or Director
Canterbury LNSM Scheme, Diocesan House, Lady Wootton's Green, Canterbury, Kent CT1 1NQ (01227) 459401 *Fax:* (01227) 450964	Vacancy
Carlisle LNSM Scheme, Church House, West Walls, Carlisle, Cumbria CA3 8UE (01228) 22573	Revd Tim Herbert
Gloucester LNSM, 4 College Green, Gloucester GL1 2LX (01452) 410022 *Fax:* (01452) 382905	Mrs Caroline Pascoe (Dioc Local Ministry and OLM Officer)
Guildford Diocesan Ministry Course, Vicarage, 5 Burwood Rd, Hersham, Surrey KT12 4AA *Tel:* (01932) 269343 *Fax:* (01932) 230274 *e-mail:* hazel@nickhaze.demon.co.uk	Revd Hazel Whitehead
Hereford Local Ministry Scheme, The Cottage, Bishop Mascall Centre, Lower Galdeford, Ludlow, Shropshire SY8 1RZ (01584) 872334 *Fax:* (01584) 877945	Preb Gill Sumner
Lichfield LNSM, Backcester Lane, Lichfield WS13 6JH (01543) 411550 *Fax:* (01543) 411552 *e-mail:* lichmin@cix.co.uk	Preb David Sceats
Lincoln OLM Scheme, The Forum, Church House, Lincoln LN2 1PU (01522) 528886 *Fax:* (01522) 512717 *e-mail:* lincolndio@claranet.co.uk	Revd Kathryn Windslow
Liverpool OLM Scheme, Rectory, Halsall Rd, Halsall, Ormskirk, Lancs L39 8RN (01704) 841202	Canon Peter Goodrich
Manchester LNSM Scheme, Church House, 90 Deansgate, Manchester M3 2GJ 0161–832 5785 *Fax:* 0161–832 1466	Revd Wendy Bracegirdle
Newcastle LNSM Scheme, Denewood, Clayton Rd, Jesmond, Newcastle NE2 1TL 0191 281 9943/1452 or 0191–263 7922 *Fax:* 0191–281 1452	Canon Richard Bryant
Norwich LNSM, Emmaus House, 65 The Close, Norwich NR1 4DH (01603) 611196	Canon Malory Makower D PHIL
Oxford LNSM, SAOMC, Diocesan Church House, North Hinksey, Oxford OX2 0NB (01865) 208260	Revd Dr Mike Butterworth
St Edmundsbury and Ipswich Local Ministry Scheme, Diocesan House, 13 Tower St, Ipswich IP1 3BG (01473) 211028	Canon Michael West PH D
Southwark OLM Scheme, Diocese of Southwark Ministry Development Dept, St Michael's Church Hall, Trundle St, London SE1 1QT 0171–378 7506 *Fax:* 0171–403 6497 *e-mail:* trundlest@dwark.org.uk	Revd Stephen Lyon
Truro LNSM, Diocesan House, Kenwyn, Truro TR1 3DU (01872) 276766/274351 *Fax:* (01872) 222510	Revd David Thurburn-Huelin

Selected Church Statistics

The following pages contain a selection of tables reprinted from *Church Statistics*, (published as General Synod Misc Paper 514) and *Statistics of Licensed Ministers* (published as General Synod Misc Paper 520).

Please note that in Tables D to I the following definitions apply:-

Income

Total planned giving	– net covenants including regular Gift Aid donations and non-covenanted planned giving
Total direct giving	– planned giving plus church collections and boxes.
Other voluntary income	– all other voluntary income for ordinary expenditure excluding direct giving and income tax on covenants. e.g. fund-raising events, net profit on magazine/bookstall, sundry donations.
Total voluntary income	– direct giving plus income tax on covenants plus other voluntary income.

Expenditure

Total charitable donations – payments by parochial church councils to:
- (a) the recognised missionary societies, or other overseas missions, diocesan associations, Diocesan Mission Councils.
- (b) Christian organisations primarily concerned with relief and development.
- (c) payments to home missions and other Church societies and organisations, (including the Church Urban Fund).
- (d) payments to other charities which are secularly based.

Please also note that:
1. Many figures in these tables have been rounded, and that in general totals, percentages and averages were calculated before rounding. Hence row and column totals will not always agree exactly with the sum of the stated amounts.
2. Among the 13,000 parishes of the Church of England there are a number of Local Ecumenical Projects in some (around 300) of which there is a congregation and a ministry shared between the Church of England and certain other churches. In such circumstances it is not always possible (or indeed desirable) to isolate the Anglican component of the congregation. The parochial membership figures will therefore include a small element which may appear also in the statistics of other churches.
3. Where figures are not available for any reason, 'n.a.' appears in the tables.

General Information

A Distribution of Full Time Stipendiary Diocesan Clergy

(Actual and according to the deployment formula)

			December 31st 1997 Actual	Share	Number over under (-) share	Percent over under (-) share	*
1	Bath and Wells	C	251	236	15	6.4%	(5)
2	Birmingham	C	205	212	-7	-3.3%	(32)
3	Blackburn	Y	249	238	11	4.6%	(9)
4	Bradford	Y	122	123	-1	-0.8%	(26)
5	Bristol	C	154	154	0	0.0%	(19)
6	Canterbury	C	174	175	-1	-0.6%	(22)
7	Carlisle	Y	165	157	8	5.1%	(7)
8	Chelmsford	C	424	449	-25	-5.6%	(36)
9	Chester	Y	292	294	-2	-0.7%	(25)
10	Chichester	C	347	320	27	8.4%	(4)
11	Coventry	C	149	147	2	1.4%	(16)
12	Derby	C	200	192	8	4.2%	(11)
13	Durham	Y	241	246	-5	-2.0%	(30)
14	Ely	C	161	157	4	2.5%	(13)
15	Exeter	C	268	273	-5	-1.8%	(29)
16	Gloucester	C	168	165	3	1.8%	(15)
17	Guildford	C	207	179	28	15.6%	(1)
18	Hereford	C	117	126	-9	-7.1%	(38)
19	Leicester	C	170	172	-2	-1.2%	(28)
20	Lichfield	C	374	375	-1	-0.3%	(21)
21	Lincoln	C	229	251	-22	-8.8%	(41)
22	Liverpool	Y	255	255	0	0.0%	(19)
23	London	C	551	527	24	4.6%	(10)
24	Manchester	Y	324	316	8	2.5%	(14)
25	Newcastle	Y	159	166	-7	-4.2%	(34)
26	Norwich	C	200	225	-25	-11.1%	(43)
27	Oxford	C	447	445	2	0.4%	(18)
28	Peterborough	C	161	174	-13	-7.5%	(39)
29	Portsmouth	C	116	129	-13	-10.1%	(42)
30	Ripon	Y	162	161	1	0.6%	(17)
31	Rochester	C	234	215	19	8.8%	(3)
32	St. Albans	C	298	300	-2	-0.7%	(24)
33	St. Edms & Ipswich	C	175	177	-2	-1.1%	(27)
34	Salisbury	C	239	248	-9	-3.6%	(33)
35	Sheffield	Y	201	195	6	3.1%	(12)
36	Sodor and Man	Y	22	20	2	10.0%	(2)
37	Southwark	C	392	370	22	5.9%	(6)
38	Southwell	Y	198	189	9	4.8%	(8)
39	Truro	C	123	134	-11	-8.2%	(40)
40	Wakefield	Y	172	183	-11	-6.0%	(37)
41	Winchester	C	247	255	-8	-3.1%	(31)
42	Worcester	C	161	162	-1	-0.6%	(23)
43	York	Y	290	307	-17	-5.5%	(35)
Totals Province of Canterbury (C)			6,942	6,944	-2	0.0%	
Totals Province of York (Y)			2,852	2,850	3	0.1%	
Totals CHURCH OF ENGLAND			9,794	9,794			

*   The set of figures in brackets gives the magnitude, in descending order, of the figures immediately

B Non-Stipendiary Ministers and Church Army Evangelists 1997

Ref. No.	Diocese		Non-stipendiary Clergy men	women	total	Local Non-stipendiary Clergy men	women	total	Church Army men	women	total
1	Bath and Wells	C	25	11	36				2	2	4
2	Birmingham	C	22	7	29				2	2	4
3	Blackburn	Y	14	8	22				5	1	6
4	Bradford	Y	12	3	15				4	3	7
5	Bristol	C	27	9	36				1	1	2
6	Canterbury	C	30	13	43				2	1	3
7	Carlisle	Y	19	10	29				1		1
8	Chelmsford	C	31	41	72				8	3	11
9	Chester	Y	24	12	36				2	1	3
10	Chichester	C	55	16	71				6	4	10
11	Coventry	C	12	7	19				6	1	7
12	Derby	C	26	10	36				3	3	6
13	Durham	Y	21	10	31				3		3
14	Ely	C	31	11	42				7	2	9
15	Exeter	C	34	20	54				10		10
16	Gloucester	C	32	11	43				4	3	7
17	Guildford	C	27	11	38	5	3	8	2		2
18	Hereford	C	18	8	26				1	1	2
19	Leicester	C	31	15	46				3	1	4
20	Lichfield	C	22	11	33				6	6	12
21	Lincoln	C	23	6	29	13	5	18	1		1
22	Liverpool	Y	21	1	22				6	3	9
23	London	C	81	20	101				11	6	17
24	Manchester	Y	29	9	38	19	10	29	6	4	10
25	Newcastle	Y	13	13	26						
26	Norwich	C	19	9	28	15	7	22	2	1	3
27	Oxford	C	131	40	171				10	8	18
28	Peterborough	C	14	6	20				3	2	5
29	Portsmouth	C	30	17	47				2		2
30	Ripon	Y	11	5	16				4	4	8
31	Rochester	C	24	13	37				3	2	5
32	St. Albans	C	55	35	90				8	3	11
33	St. Edms & Ipswich	C	23	13	36	11	5	16	1	1	2
34	Salisbury	C	28	18	46	4	4	8	3		3
35	Sheffield	Y	14	3	17				16	4	20
36	Sodor and Man	Y	7		7				1		1
37	Southwark	C	86	29	115	14	7	21	14	7	21
38	Southwell	Y	28	19	47				3	1	4
39	Truro	C	24	8	32	2	2	4	3		3
40	Wakefield	Y	11	6	17				7	1	8
41	Winchester	C	30	21	51				4		4
42	Worcester	C	16	13	29				3	3	6
43	York	Y	18	7	25				6	1	7
Totals Province of Canterbury (C)			1,007	449	1,456	64	33	97	131	63	194
Totals Province of York (Y)			242	106	348	19	10	29	64	23	87
Totals CHURCH OF ENGLAND			1,249	555	1,804	83	43	126	195	86	281

C Licensed Readers 1997

Ref. No.	Diocese		Admissions during year men	Admissions during year women	Number licensed at 31 December 1997 men		Number licensed at 31 December 1997 women		Number in training at 31 December 1997 men	Number in training at 31 December 1997 women
1	2		3	4	5		6		7	8
1	Bath and Wells	C	9	9	157	(54)	91	(18)	14	10
2	Birmingham	C	8	7	102	(21)	78	(4)	11	13
3	Blackburn	Y	4	4	113	(26)	67	(5)	20	21
4	Bradford (a)	Y	5	2	67	(18)	36	(6)	9	16
5	Bristol	C	6	5	81	(22)	60	(6)	8	10
6	Canterbury	C	4	8	97	(18)	69	(7)	7	18
7	Carlisle	Y	2	5	81	(27)	46	(6)	11	11
8	Chelmsford	C	5	16	191	(39)	129	(12)	20	16
9	Chester	Y	23	22	255	(37)	144	(4)	45	38
10	Chichester	C	8	3	147	(56)	73	(11)	15	9
11	Coventry	C	4	5	90	(22)	39	(6)	9	18
12	Derby	C	14	5	155	(11)	99	(4)	19	22
13	Durham	Y	6	4	89	(18)	38	(4)	22	12
14	Ely	C	5	6	95	(10)	44	(5)	19	31
15	Exeter	C	4	4	95	(53)	48	(14)	23	27
16	Gloucester (a)	C	10	7	117	(46)	91	(13)	8	6
17	Guildford	C	9	6	119	(17)	55	(4)	21	20
18	Hereford	C	3	5	45	(12)	40	(4)	4	7
19	Leicester	C	7	8	108	(27)	70	(10)	7	8
20	Lichfield	C	11	7	274	(49)	150	(6)	11	11
21	Lincoln	C	10	6	92	(30)	66	(2)	17	25
22	Liverpool	Y	11	6	192	(19)	115	(4)	26	29
23	London	C	9	4	125	(28)	74	(5)	23	24
24	Manchester	Y	6	4	161	(42)	67	(9)	8	11
25	Newcastle	Y	5	3	58	(12)	45	(5)	14	6
26	Norwich	C	9	8	144	(21)	100	(9)	30	25
27	Oxford	C	12	19	218	(39)	136	(14)	30	26
28	Peterborough	C	7	3	69	(11)	38	(1)	12	14
29	Portsmouth	C	4	2	57	(7)	34	(3)	22	21
30	Ripon	Y	1	1	59	(17)	47	(2)	8	14
31	Rochester	C	9	14	186	(46)	97	(10)	18	30
32	St. Albans	C	6	11	122	(41)	86	(8)	32	39
33	St. Edms & Ipswich	C	10	2	112	(38)	74	(11)	24	25
34	Salisbury	C	7	3	107	(39)	64	(13)	12	15
35	Sheffield	Y	11	14	123	(0)	69	(0)	13	18
36	Sodor and Man	Y	1	0	13	(0)	7	(1)	0	0
37	Southwark (b)	C	0	0	203	(37)	105	(13)	38	45
38	Southwell	Y	10	10	155	(30)	110	(10)	27	20
39	Truro	C	3	2	55	(24)	37	(8)	4	2
40	Wakefield	Y	7	8	103	(13)	75	(3)	15	34
41	Winchester	C	11	13	113	(54)	59	(12)	24	20
42	Worcester	C	0	9	80	(14)	42	(2)	9	11
43	York	Y	10	7	137	(37)	96	(11)	14	16
Totals Province of Canterbury (C)			204	197	3,556	(886)	2,148	(235)	491	548
Totals Province of York (Y)			102	90	1,606	(296)	962	(70)	232	246
Totals CHURCH OF ENGLAND			306	287	5,162	(1,182)	3,110	(305)	723	794
Comparable figures for 1996 :-										
Totals Province of Canterbury (C)			178	241	3,540	(860)	2,038	(195)	527	591
Totals Province of York (Y)			74	93	1,602	(273)	917	(63)	238	251
Totals CHURCH OF ENGLAND			252	334	5,142	(1,133)	2,955	(258)	765	842

NOTES:
1. Figures in brackets in cols 5 and 6 refer to the additional number of Readers with Permission to Officiate and active Emeriti.
2. (a) denotes a change in retirement arrangements at age 70 as from 1996.
3. (b) indicates that Southwark has changed its admissions from the end of the second year of training to the end of the third year of training.

Selected Financial Comparisons
1964 to 1996

D Covenanted planned giving to Parochial Church Councils:
Contributors, amounts and average weekly rates

		Actual		In real terms of 1996*	
Year	Subscribers under covenants 000s	Covenanted giving: net subscriptions £ 000s	Weekly average per subscriber £	Covenanted giving: net subscriptions £ 000s	Weekly average per subscriber £
1	2	3	4	5	6
1964	126	2,113	0.32	22,722	3.47
1970	168	3,325	0.38	27,445	3.14
1980	362	17,692	0.94	40,382	2.15
1990	405	71,130	3.38	86,132	4.09
1991	403	77,902	3.71	89,105	4.25
1992	403	86,617	4.14	95,495	4.56
1993	405	95,301	4.52	103,430	4.91
1994	405	103,745	4.93	109,939	5.23
1995	404	111,045	5.28	113,721	5.41
1996	404	118,111	5.62	118,111	5.62

E Uncovenanted planned giving to Parochial Church Councils:
Contributors, amounts and average weekly rates

		Actual		In real terms of 1996*	
Year	Uncovenanted planned giving subscribers 000s	Uncovenanted planned giving: subscriptions £ 000s	Weekly average per subscriber £	Uncovenanted planned giving: subscriptions £ 000s	Weekly average per subscriber £
1	2	3	4	5	6
1964	1,029	7,198	0.13	77,404	1.45
1970	800	6,348	0.15	52,397	1.26
1980	529	13,748	0.50	31,380	1.14
1990	326	23,565	1.39	28,535	1.68
1991	326	26,243	1.55	30,016	1.77
1992	317	29,212	1.77	32,206	1.95
1993	311	31,257	1.93	33,924	2.10
1994	304	32,845	2.08	34,806	2.20
1995	298	34,401	2.22	35,231	2.27
1996	290	35,032	2.32	35,032	2.32

F Direct giving to Parochial Church Councils:

	Actual		In real terms of 1996*	
Year	Total Direct Giving £ 000s	Weekly average per Electoral Roll Member £	Total Direct Giving £ 000s	Weekly average per Electoral Roll Member £
1	2	3	4	5
1964	14,961	0.11	160,883	1.15
1970	15,847	0.12	130,803	1.00
1980	51,521	0.55	117,597	1.25
1990	141,076	1.94	170,829	2.35
1991	152,549	2.04	174,486	2.33
1992	164,854	2.17	181,751	2.40
1993	175,898	2.29	190,903	2.49
1994	187,468	2.44	198,659	2.58
1995	197,163	2.58	201,915	2.65
1996	205,417	3.06	205,417	3.06

General Information

G Total voluntary income of Parochial Church Councils

	Actual		In real terms 1996*	
Year	Total Voluntary Income £ 000s	Weekly average per Electoral Roll Member £	Total Voluntary Income £ 000s	Weekly average per Electoral Roll Member £
1	2	3	4	5
1964	20,033	0.14	215,425	1.54
1970	22,110	0.17	182,498	1.39
1980	72,798	0.77	166,161	1.76
1990	195,193	2.69	236,359	3.26
1991	212,974	2.85	243,600	3.26
1992	230,005	3.03	253,581	3.34
1993	246,050	3.21	267,038	3.48
1994	262,886	3.42	278,580	3.62
1995	275,388	3.61	282,025	3.69
1996	288,358	4.30	288,358	4.30

H Total ordinary income of Parochial Church Councils

	Total Ordinary Income	
Year	Actual £000s	In real terms of 1996* £000s
1	2	3
1964	22,108	237,738
1970	26,396	217,875
1980	85,880	196,021
1990	237,385	287,449
1991	256,796	293,723
1992	273,546	301,584
1993	287,421	311,938
1994	307,598	325,961
1995	327,531	335,424
1996	344,897	344,897

I Charitable giving and total ordinary expenditure by Parochial Church Councils

	Actual £ 000s		In real terms of 1996* £ 000s	
Year	Total Charitable Donations	Total Ordinary Expenditure	Total Charitable Donations	Total Ordinary Expenditure
1	2	3	4	5
1964	2,173	21,711	23,367	233,469
1970	2,593	28,038	21,403	231,428
1980	8,480	77,849	19,356	177,690
1990	24,573	227,314	29,755	275,255
1991	25,945	250,704	29,676	286,755
1992	26,366	270,365	29,069	298,077
1993	24,990	289,447	27,122	314,137
1994	25,814	307,698	27,355	326,068
1995	25,154	320,197	25,760	327,914
1996	25,361	338,671	25,361	338,671

NOTES ON TABLES D to I
1. Figures for cathedrals and their daughter churches are not included.
2. * i.e. adjusted by the Retail Price Index to reflect 1996 purchasing power.

J Marriages in England 1981–1994

	Number of marriages solemnised			Marriages solemnised in Church of England as a proportion per 1,000 marriages	
	Church of England*	with religious ceremonies	all marriages	with religious ceremonies	all marriages
1981	111,819	168,182	332,213	665	337
1982	110,511	166,305	323,137	665	342
1983	110,348	165,720	324,443	666	340
1984	111,248	167,761	330,012	663	337
1985	110,121	166,330	327,241	662	337
1986	111,476	168,417	328,411	662	339
1987	114,958	172,245	332,233	667	346
1988	112,184	168,535	329,183	666	341
1989	112,612	168,869	327,244	667	344
1990	109,369	163,634	312,712	668	350
1991	97,446	145,889	290,118	668	336
1992	96,828	145,418	294,962	666	328
1993	91,214	137,457	283,326	664	322
1994	86,143	130,500	275,531	660	313

* Figures exclude Isle of Man (Sodor and Man Diocese) and Channel Islands (part of Winchester Diocese) together with a small number of Church of England parishes in Wales.

K Combinations of Previous Marital Condition in England and Wales 1994

Marital condition	Church of England & Church in Wales	with religious ceremonies	all marriages
All	90,703	138,956	291,069
Bachelor marrying:			
Spinster	81,584	110,568	174,200
Widow	396	611	1,472
*Divorced woman	2,083	7,288	30,405
Widower marrying:			
Spinster	400	637	1,387
Widow	939	1,534	3,278
*Divorced woman	249	832	3,694
*Divorced man marrying:			
Spinster	3,399	10,233	30,745
Widow	209	704	3,130
*Divorced woman	1,444	6,549	42,758

* no record is kept of whether the previous partner is still alive.

Source: *Marriage and Divorce statistics, 1994.* Crown Copyright 1997. Reproduced by permission of the Controller of HMSO and the Office for National Statistics.

Note: 1994 is the latest year for which these data are available.

General Information

L   Baptisms 1996

Ref. No.	Diocese	Live births 1996	Infants under one year of age	Infant baptism rates per 1,000 live births	Children aged 1 to 12 years	All other persons
1	2	3	4	5	6	7
1	Bath and Wells	8,900	2,800	316	740	200
2	Birmingham	20,400	2,700	130	970	150
3	Blackburn	15,800	4,200	269	870	140
4	Bradford	9,100	1,400	156	360	80
5	Bristol	11,500	2,300	202	620	160
6	Canterbury	9,400	2,700	288	880	190
7	Carlisle	5,400	2,600	484	370	60
8	Chelmsford	35,800	5,200	144	1,950	370
9	Chester	18,400	5,300	287	1,200	240
10	Chichester	15,900	4,200	264	1,470	280
11	Coventry	9,200	2,100	226	620	130
12	Derby	11,600	2,800	243	710	130
13	Durham	17,200	5,100	297	920	100
14	Ely	7,200	2,100	294	590	150
15	Exeter	11,400	3,200	282	900	260
16	Gloucester	7,000	2,400	343	630	180
17	Guildford	11,400	3,200	279	1,010	160
18	Hereford	3,100	1,400	445	370	60
19	Leicester	11,000	2,000	180	550	130
20	Lichfield	24,500	5,900	242	1,600	250
21	Lincoln	10,500	4,500	431	850	190
22	Liverpool	19,300	4,900	254	1,350	170
23	London	50,400	4,200	83	1,980	560
24	Manchester	26,000	5,100	197	1,510	230
25	Newcastle	8,700	2,500	289	480	80
26	Norwich	8,600	2,300	270	660	150
27	Oxford	27,000	6,800	253	1,700	350
28	Peterborough	9,500	2,000	214	620	150
29	Portsmouth	8,300	1,900	232	600	90
30	Ripon	9,400	2,200	237	620	110
31	Rochester	15,500	3,300	214	1,200	220
32	St. Albans	21,800	4,200	194	1,510	330
33	St. Edms & Ipswich	6,800	1,800	272	550	110
34	Salisbury	9,300	3,300	354	640	190
35	Sheffield	14,400	3,900	271	920	150
36	Sodor and Man	800	300	346	70	20
37	Southwark	34,900	4,500	128	1,970	340
38	Southwell	12,500	2,600	210	830	170
39	Truro	5,100	1,500	292	410	100
40	Wakefield	14,000	3,100	225	840	130
41	Winchester	14,100	4,300	309	1,140	230
42	Worcester	9,900	2,900	290	770	100
43	York	15,700	5,300	335	1,040	170
	Totals Province of Canterbury	430,200	92,700	215	28,190	5,900
	Totals Province of York	186,700	48,700	261	11,370	1,840
	Totals CHURCH OF ENGLAND	616,900	141,400	229	39,560	7,740

NOTES : 1. Figures for cathedrals are included.
2. The information in columns 4, 6 and 7 was extracted from the 1996 parochial returns. Data in columns 3 and 5 are based on statistics obtained from the Office for National Statistics (ONS).
3. The figures in columns 6 and 7 have in general been rounded to the nearest 10. Other roundings in the table are to the nearest 100.

M Confirmations 1996

Ref. No.	Diocese	Services	Males	Females	Totals
1	2	3	4	5	6
1	Bath and Wells	63	343	452	795
2	Birmingham	56	304	515	819
3	Blackburn	123	953	1,270	2,223
4	Bradford	33	189	273	462
5	Bristol	68	249	388	637
6	Canterbury	72	396	555	951
7	Carlisle	67	297	438	735
8	Chelmsford	131	591	1,070	1,661
9	Chester	121	544	859	1,403
10	Chichester	125	676	1,042	1,718
11	Coventry	67	253	423	676
12	Derby	42	293	495	788
13	Durham	67	369	638	1,007
14	Ely	34	249	381	630
15	Exeter	82	366	562	928
16	Gloucester	60	317	519	836
17	Guildford	76	381	603	984
18	Hereford	51	197	236	433
19	Leicester	46	163	285	448
20	Lichfield	164	725	1,097	1,822
21	Lincoln	85	338	502	840
22	Liverpool	93	619	993	1,612
23	London	163	745	1,229	1,974
24	Manchester	107	662	1,070	1,732
25	Newcastle	66	163	282	445
26	Norwich	15	243	360	603
27	Oxford	251	1,049	1,310	2,359
28	Peterborough	37	306	487	793
29	Portsmouth	39	111	175	286
30	Ripon	60	206	420	626
31	Rochester	71	407	623	1,030
32	St. Albans	102	535	793	1,328
33	St. Edms & Ipswich	63	225	338	563
34	Salisbury	78	490	765	1,255
35	Sheffield	96	216	419	635
36	Sodor and Man	23	35	85	120
37	Southwark	107	617	1,133	1,750
38	Southwell	37	273	497	770
39	Truro	65	159	288	447
40	Wakefield	69	267	426	693
41	Winchester	103	448	595	1,043
42	Worcester	70	251	424	675
43	York	138	459	774	1,233
Province of Canterbury		2,386	11,427	17,645	29,072
Province of York		1,100	5,252	8,444	13,696
CHURCH OF ENGLAND		3,486	16,679	26,089	42,768

NOTE Confirmations in the Armed Forces are not included.

TABLE OF PAROCHIAL FEES

From 1 January 1999

Prepared by the Church Commissioners under the Ecclesiastical Fees Measure 1986
Authorised by the Parochial Fees Order 1998

	Fee payable towards stipend of incumbent (See Note 2) £	Fee payable to Parochial Church Council £	Total fee payable £
BAPTISMS			
Certificate issued at time of baptism	8.00	—	8.00
Short certificate of baptism given under Section 2, Baptismal Registers Measure 1961	6.00	—	6.00
MARRIAGES			
Publication of banns of marriage	9.00	5.00	14.00
Certificate of banns issued at time of publication	8.00	—	8.00
Marriage service	58.00	69.00	127.00
(Marriage certificate – See Note 6)			
FUNERALS AND BURIALS			
Service in church			
Funeral service in church	35.00	29.00	64.00
Burial in churchyard following on from service in church	—	115.00	115.00
Burial in cemetery or cremation following on from service in church (See Note 3(iii))	—	—	NIL
Burial of body in churchyard on separate occasion (See Notes 3(iii))	23.00	115.00	138.00
Burial of cremated remains in churchyard on separate occasion	23.00	35.00	58.00
Burial in cemetery on separate occasion (See Note 3(iii))	23.00	—	23.00
No service in church			
Service in crematorium or cemetery (See Note 3(i))	64.00	—	64.00
Burial of body in churchyard (See Notes 3(iv))	23.00	115.00	138.00
Burial of cremated remains in churchyard (See Notes 3(iv))	23.00	35.00	58.00
Certificate issued at time of burial (See Note 3(v))	8.00	—	8.00
MONUMENTS IN CHURCHYARDS			
Erected with consent of incumbent under Chancellor's general directions –			
Small cross of wood	4.00	8.00	12.00
Small vase not exceeding 305mm × 203mm (12" × 8" × 8")	8.00	16.00	24.00
Tablet, erected horizontally or vertically and not exceeding 533mm × 533mm (21" × 21"), commemorating person cremated	14.00	28.00	42.00
Any other monument	33.00	65.00	98.00
(the above fees to include the original inscription)			
Additional inscription on existing monument (See Note 4)	23.00	—	23.00
SEARCHES IN CHURCH REGISTERS, ETC.			
Searching registers of marriages for period before 1 July 1837 (See Note 5) (for up to one hour)	8.00	5.00	13.00
(for each subsequent hour or part of an hour)	6.00	5.00	11.00
Searching registers of baptisms or burials (See Note 5) (including the provision of one copy of any entry therein) (for up to one hour)	8.00	5.00	13.00
(for each subsequent hour or part of an hour)	6.00	5.00	11.00
Each additional copy of an entry in a register of baptisms or burials	8.00	5.00	13.00
Inspection of instrument of apportionment or agreement for exchange of land for tithes deposited under the Tithe Act 1836	6.00	—	6.00
Furnishing copies of above (for every 72 words)	6.00	—	6.00

'EXTRAS'

The fees shown in this table are the statutory fees payable. It is stressed that the figures do not include any charges for extras such as music (e.g. organist, choir), bells, flowers and special heating, which are fixed by the Parochial Church Council.

Published by
The Church Commissioners
1 Millbank, LONDON SW1P 3JZ

NOTES

1 Definitions
The definitions in the Order include the following:
'Burial' includes deposit in a vault and the interment or deposit of cremated remains.
'Churchyard' includes the curtilage of a church and a burial ground of a church whether or not immediately adjoining such church.
'Cemetery' means a burial ground maintained by a burial authority.
'Monument' includes a headstone, cross, kerb, border, vase, chain, railing, tablet, flatstone, tombstone or monument or tomb of any other kind.

2 Incumbent's Fee
In general, this fee is paid as part of the stipend. It is not in addition to it. The stipend level is determined by the diocese.

3 Funerals and Burials
(i)   No fee is payable in respect of a burial of a still-born infant, or for the funeral or burial or an infant dying within one year after birth.
(ii) The fees prescribed by this table for a funeral service in any cemetery or crematorium are mandatory except where a cemetery or crematorium authority has itself fixed different charges for these services, in which case the authority's charges apply.
(iii) The fee for a burial in a churchyard on a *separate occasion* applies when burial does not follow on from a service in church.
(iv) If a full funeral service is held at the graveside in a churchyard the incumbent's fee is increased to that payable where the service is held in church.
(v)   The certificate issued at the time of burial is a copy of the entry in the register of burials kept under the Parochial Registers and Records Measure 1978.

4 Monuments in Churchyards
The fee for an additional inscription on a small cross of wood, a small vase or a tablet not exceeding 533mm × 533mm shall not exceed the current fee payable to the incumbent for the erection of such a monument.

5 Searches in Church Registers
The search fee relates to a particular search where the approximate date of the baptism, marriage or burial is known. The fee for a more general search of a church register would be negotiable.

6 Fee for Marriage Certificate
The following fees are currently payable to the incumbent under the Registration of Births, Deaths and Marriages (Fees) Order 1996: certificate of marriage —
    at registration £3.50; subsequently £6.50.
These fees may be increased from 1 April 1999.

Church Electoral Rolls

C.B.F. ref nos	Dioceses	Numbers on Church Electoral Rolls 1989	Numbers on Church Electoral Rolls 1994
(1)	(2)	(3)	(4)
	PROVINCE OF CANTERBURY		
1	Bath and Wells	53,777	49,082
2	Birmingham	21,433	20,832
5	Bristol	23,322	22,971
6	Canterbury	23,515	21,910
8	Chelmsford	59,082	60,111
10	Chichester	72,247	67,101
11	Coventry	23,308	20,718
12	Derby	25,759	24,533
14	Ely	26,961	24,386
15	Exeter	42,932	39,147
16	Gloucester	32,040	29,862
17	Guildford	40,140	34,140
18	Hereford	22,802	20,665
19	Leicester	22,327	19.181
20	Lichfield	62,306	58,961
21	Lincoln	40,213	32,850
23	London	49,307	47,775
26	Norwich	34,935	32,042
27	Oxford	66,736	64,923
28	Peterborough	23,244	22,518
29	Portsmouth	22,015	21,687
31	Rochester	39,524	36,669
32	St Albans	61,271	54,402
33	St Edms. and Ipswich	28,614	27,808
34	Salisbury	54,317	51,190
37	Southwark	51,651	50,718
39	Truro	25,028	21,254
41	Winchester	45,195*	43,470*
42	Worcester	22,323	24,173
44	Europe	10,284	10,158
	Totals, Province of Canterbury	**1,126,608**	**1,055,580**
	PROVINCE OF YORK		
3	Blackburn	63,587	47,797
4	Bradford	16,992	15,542
7	Carlisle	34,015	27,980
9	Chester	55,386	56,563
13	Durham	39,240	32,420
22	Liverpool	42,324	38,655
24	Manchester	47,550	42,658
25	Newcastle	20,978	20,802
30	Ripon	29,358	26,814
35	Sheffield	24,768	24,938
36	Sodor and Man	3,923	3,359
38	Southwell	24,053	22,341
40	Wakefield	29,604	28,025
43	York	42,826	42,039
	Totals, Province of York	**474,604**	**429,933**
	GRAND TOTALS	**1,601,212**	**1.485,513**

*This figure excludes the Channel Islands

(5)

1. QUALIFICATION
In 1919–20 a new system of Church Government was set up. The electoral basis was the roll which had to be prepared in each parish and there have been only small changes in qualifications for entry since that time. The present rule provides that a person may apply for entry if he/she (i) is baptised; (ii) is a member of the Church of England or another Church of the Anglican Communion or Church in Communion with the Church of England; (iii) is sixteen or over and (iv) is resident in the parish or if not so resident, has habitually attended public worship in the parish during a period of six months prior to enrolment.

2. REVISION
Church electoral rolls are revised annually, the names of those no longer qualified being removed and the names of other applying being added. The system is not always effective in establishing a realistic roll as insufficient care may be taken in revision. Another important factor is that any person who is baptised and resident has a right to claim membership of the Church of England and entry on the roll regardless of whether he/she attends services or otherwise shows interest in Church affairs. The names of persons within this category cannot be removed without their consent.

3. NEW ROLLS
The Church Representation Rules attached to the Synodical Government Measure 1969 required that in 1972 for the first time existing rolls should come to an end, and that thereafter new rolls should be prepared every six years. The fourth preparation of new rolls was in 1990 and the fifth took place in 1996.

4. INTERPRETATION
It is impossible to draw any accurate conclusions from the figures on either the total membership of the Church or the practising membership for the following reasons:
(1) The roll is an electoral roll not a membership roll. No member need apply for entry unless he/she wishes to exercise certain rights.
(2) Any resident may have his/her name entered on the new roll regardless of whether he/she is a practising member.
(3) Since 1974 a person may have his/her name on any number of rolls if he/she is properly qualified. Previously he/she could be enrolled in two parishes, but not more.
(4) Persons under the age of seventeen were not eligible until the qualifying age was reduced to sixteen as from 1 May 1980.
(5) While parishes are urged to inform qualified practising Church members of their rights, it is likely that there are considerable differences in the steps taken and energy with which they are pursued.
But having mentioned these caveats the figures are of interest.
The figures for 1989 and 1994 are those certified in those years by the secretaries of diocesan synods: the numbers of members elected to the House of Laity of the General Synod are based on these figures.

ROYAL PECULIARS, THE CHAPELS ROYAL, ETC.

Westminster Abbey

Description of Arms. Azure, a cross patonce between 5 martlets or; on a chief or France and England quarterly on a pale, between two roses, gules, seeded and barbed proper.

COLLEGIATE CHURCH OF ST PETER
The collegiate church of St Peter in Westminster, usually called Westminster Abbey, is a Royal Peculiar, and, as such, it is extra-provincial as well as extra-diocesan and comes directly under the personal jurisdiction of Her Majesty The Queen, who is the Visitor.

Throughout medieval times it was the Abbey Church of a great Benedictine Monastery, which was in existence at Westminster before the Norman Conquest. After the dissolution of the monastery in 1540 it became increasingly a great national shrine, where famous writers, poets, statesmen and leaders in the Church and State are buried. It is the Coronation Church, and in it also take place from time to time Royal weddings and many services on great occasions of a National or Commonwealth character. Daily, the Holy Communion is celebrated and Morning and Evening Prayers are said or sung.

DEAN
Very Revd Wesley Carr PH D, The Deanery, Westminster [1997]   Tel: 0171–222 2953

SUB-DEAN
Canon Anthony Harvey DD, 3 Little Cloister SW1P 3PL [1987]   Tel: 0171–222 4174

RECTOR OF ST MARGARET'S
Vacancy: correspondence c/o The Chapter Office, 20 Dean's Yard, Westminster Abbey SW1P 3PA

CANONS OF WESTMINSTER
Archdeacon and Lector Theologiae Canon Anthony Harvey DD (*as above*) [1982]

Steward Canon David Hutt, 5 Little Cloister, SW1P 3PL [1995]   Tel: 0171–222 6939

Treasurer Canon Michael Middleton, 8 Little Cloister, SW1P 3PL [1997]   Tel: 0171–222 5791
One vacancy

PRECENTOR
Revd Dominic Fenton, 7 Little Cloister SW1P 3PL [1995]
Tel: 0171–222 4023

CHAPLAIN AND SACRIST
Revd John Townend, 4B Little Cloister, SW1P 3PL [1998]   Tel: 0171–222 1386

PRIEST VICARS
Revd John Pedlar
Revd Roger Holloway
Revd Philip Chester
Revd Peter Cowell
Revd Dr Paul Bradshaw
Revd Huw Mordecai

PASTORAL ASSISTANT
Sister Hilary Markey CSMV

LAY OFFICERS
High Steward The Lord Blake of Braydeston, Norfolk

Deputy High Steward The Rt Worshipful the Lord Mayor of Westminster

High Bailiff and Searcher of the Sanctuary The Lord Weatherill

Deputy High Bailiff Rear Admiral Kenneth Snow

Chapter Clerk and Receiver General Vacancy, The Chapter Office, 20 Dean's Yard, Westminster Abbey SW1P 3PA
Tel: 0171–222 5152

Registrar Mr S. J. Holmes (*same address*)

Organist and Master of the Choristers Vacancy, correspondence c/o The Chapter Office

Surveyor of the Fabric Mr D. R. Buttress, 2b Little Cloister, SW1P 3PL   Tel: 0171–222 5801

Legal Secretary Mr C. L. Hodgetts, Thomas Eggar & Son, East Pallant, Chichester, Sussex PO19 1TS
Tel: (01243) 786111

Auditor Mr D. Hunt, Binder Hamlyn, 20 Old Bailey, London EC4M 7BH   Tel: 0171–489 9000

Librarian Dr T. Trowler, The Library, Westminster Abbey, London SW1P 3PL   Tel: 0171–222 5152

Headmaster of the Choir School Mr R. P. Overend, Dean's Yard, London SW1   *Tel:* 0171–222 6151

Keeper of the Muniments Dr R. Mortimer, The Muniments Room and Library, Westminster Abbey, London SW1 3PL   *Tel:* 0171–222 5152

Windsor

Description of Arms. The shield of St George, argent a cross gules, encircled by the Garter

THE QUEEN'S FREE CHAPEL OF ST GEORGE WITHIN HER CASTLE OF WINDSOR

A ROYAL PECULIAR

Founded by Edward III in 1348 and exempt from diocesan and provincial jurisdictions, the College of St George is a self-governing secular community of priests and laymen, the first duty of which is to celebrate Divine Service daily on behalf of the Sovereign, the Royal House and the Order of the Garter. Its present Chapel was founded by Edward IV in honour of Our Lady, St George and St Edward in 1475 and, with the cloisters and buildings annexed, is vested in the Dean and Canons. In it the Eucharist, Mattins and Evensong are sung or said daily and are open to all.

The Order of the Garter has its stalls and insignia in the Quire, where Knights and Ladies Companions are installed by the Sovereign. Beneath the Quire – the scene of many Royal funerals – are vaults in which lie the bodies of six monarchs. Elsewhere in the Chapel are the tombs of four others.

The College has its own school, where it maintains twenty-four choristerships. It also awards an organ scholarship. A house for conferences has been established under the name of St George's House.

THE VISITOR
The Lord Chancellor

DEAN
Rt Revd David Conner, The Deanery, Windsor Castle, Windsor, Berks SL4 1NJ [1998]   *Tel:* (01753) 865561

CANONS
Precentor Canon John White, 8 The Cloisters, Windsor Castle [1982]   *Tel:* (01753) 860409

Treasurer Canon Barry Thompson, 4 The Cloisters, Windsor Castle [1998]   *Tel:* (01753) 864142

Steward Canon Laurence Gunner, 6 The Cloisters, Windsor Castle [1996]   *Tel:* (01753) 866313

Chaplain in the Great Park Canon John Ovenden, Chaplain's Lodge, Windsor Great Park, Windsor, Berks [1998]   *Tel:* (01784) 432434

MINOR CANONS
Succentor and Dean's Vicar Revd Alan Gyle, 3 The Cloisters, Windsor Castle [1994]   *Tel:* (01753) 868680
Revd Trevor Harvey, 12 The Cloisters, Windsor Castle [1987]   *Tel:* (01753) 842086

LAY OFFICERS
Chapter Clerk Lt Col Nigel Newman, Chapter Office, The Cloisters, Windsor Castle [1990]   *Tel:* (01753) 865538

Organist and Master of the Choristers Mr Jonathan Rees-Williams, 23 The Cloisters, Windsor Castle [1991]   *Tel:* (01753) 864529

Clerk of Accounts Mr Stanford Robinson, Chapter Office, The Cloisters   *Tel:* (01753) 861419

Clerk of Works Mr Fred Wilson, Clerk of Works Office, The Cloisters   *Tel:* (01753) 860824

Archivist and Librarian Dr Eileen Scarff, The Aerary, The Cloisters   *Tel:* (01753) 857942 *or* 865538

Verger Mr David Wilson, 22 Horseshoe Cloister, Windsor Castle   *Tel:* (01753) 859218

Headmaster, St George's School Revd Roger Marsh, St George's School, Windsor Castle   *Tel:* (01753) 865553

Warden, St George's House Prof Alfred Smyth, St George's House, Windsor Castle   *Tel:* (01753) 861341

Domestic Chaplains to HM The Queen

Buckingham Palace Revd William Booth
Windsor Castle The Dean of Windsor

Sandringham Canon George Hall

Chapels Royal

The Chapel Royal is the body of Clergy, Singers and Vestry Officers appointed to serve the spiritual needs of the Sovereign – in mediaeval days on Progresses through the Realm as well as upon the battlefields of Europe, as at Agincourt. Its ancient foundation is first-century with the British Church: its latter day choral headquarters have been at St James's Palace since 1702 along with the Court of St James. Since 1312 the Chapel Royal has been governed by the Dean who, as the Ordinary, also exercises, along with the Sub-Dean, jurisdiction over the daughter establishments of Chapels Royal at the Tower of London and at Hampton Court Palace. Members of the public are welcome to attend Sunday and weekday services as advertised.

The Chapel Royal conducts the Service of Remembrance at the Cenotaph in Whitehall, with a Forces Chaplain in company, and combines with the choral establishment of the host Abbey or Cathedral on the occasion of Royal Maundy, under the governance of the Lord High Almoner and Sub-Almoner. Each Member of the College of thirty-six Chaplains to The Queen, headed by the Clerk and Deputy Clerk of the Closet, is required by Warrant to preach with the Chapel Royal once a year, and are visibly distinguished, along with the Chapel Royal, Forces and Mohawk Chaplains, by the wearing of red cassocks.

Dean of the Chapels Royal
The Bishop of London

Sub-Dean
Revd William Booth
Chapel Royal, St James's Palace, London SW1

CHAPEL ROYAL, ST JAMES'S AND THE QUEEN'S CHAPEL, ST JAMES'S

Priests in Ordinary
Revd Richard Bolton

Revd Stephen Young

Deputy Priests
Revd Paul Abram
Revd Hugh Mead
Canon Michael Moore
Revd Mark Oakley
Revd Timothy Thornton

HAMPTON COURT PALACE
East Molesey, Surrey *Tel:* 0181–977 2762

Chaplain
Canon Michael Moore

H. M. TOWER OF LONDON
(includes the Chapels Royal of St John the Evangelist and St Peter ad Vincula.)

Chaplain
Revd Paul Abram

THE ROYAL CHAPEL OF ALL SAINTS, WINDSOR GREAT PARK

This is a Private Chapel and the property of the Crown within the grounds of the Royal Lodge. Attendance is restricted to residents and employees of the Great Park.

Chaplain
Revd John Ovenden, Chaplain's Lodge, Windsor Great Park, Windsor, Berks *Tel:* (01784) 432434

College of Chaplains

The position of Royal Chaplain is a very ancient one. The College of Chaplains, the members of which as such must not be confused with the Priests in Ordinary, preach according to a Rota of Waits in the Chapels Royal. The College comprises the Clerk of the Closet (who presides), the Deputy Clerk of the Closet, and thirty-six Chaplains. When a vacancy in the list of Chaplains occurs, the Private Secretary to The Queen asks the Clerk of the Closet to suggest possible names to Her Majesty. The duties of the Clerk of the Closet include the presentation of Bishops to Her Majesty when they do homage before taking possession of the revenues of their Sees; and he also examines theological books whose authors desire to present copies to The Queen. He preaches annually in the Chapel Royal, St James's Palace.

CLERK OF THE CLOSET
The Bishop of Derby (Rt Revd Jonathan Bailey)

DEPUTY CLERK OF THE CLOSET
Revd William Booth

CHAPLAINS TO THE QUEEN
Revd David Adams
Ven Douglas Bartles-Smith
Ven Frank Bentley
Canon Michael Benton
Canon Andrew Bowden
Canon Raymond Brazier
Canon Eric Buchanan
Revd David Burgess
Canon Peter Calvert
Canon Rex Chapman
Canon Anthony Chesterman
Revd Robert Clarke
Canon James Colling
Canon Alan Craig

Canon Christine Farrington
Ven David Fleming
Canon Roger Gilbert
Canon Donald Gray
Canon George Hall
Canon Ian Hardaker
Revd John Haslam
Canon Colin Hill
Canon Glyndwr Jones
Canon Marion Mingins
Canon Brian Osborne
Ven Keith Pound
Revd John Priestley
Revd John Robson
Ven Ian Russell
Canon Ivor Smith-Cameron
Canon John Stanley
Canon John Sykes
Canon Lionel Webber
Canon David Wheaton

Extra Chaplains
Canon Anthony Caesar
Canon Eric James
Canon Gerry Murphy
Revd John Stott
Preb Austen Williams
Ven Edwin Ward

Royal Almonry

The Royal Almonry dispenses The Queen's charitable gifts and is responsible for the Royal Maundy Service each year, at which Her Majesty distributes Maundy money to as many men and as many women pensioners as the years of her own age.

HIGH ALMONER
Rt Revd Nigel McCulloch (*Bishop of Wakefield*)

SUB-ALMONER
Revd William Booth
Chapel Royal, St James's Palace, London SW1

The Queen's Chapel of the Savoy

Savoy Hill, Strand, London WC2R 0DA
Tel: 0171–836 7221

CHAPEL OF THE ROYAL VICTORIAN ORDER
The Queen's Chapel of the Savoy is the Chapel of Her Majesty the Queen in right of her Duchy of Lancaster, and the Queen appoints the Chaplain. It is, therefore, a 'free' Chapel not falling within any ecclesiastical jurisdiction.

On the occasion of his Coronation in 1937, the late King George VI commanded that the 16th century Chapel of the Savoy should be placed at the disposal of the Victorian Order and be regarded by members as their Chapel. Membership of the Order is an honour in the personal gift of the Sovereign. By the Queen's appointment the present Chaplain is also Chaplain of the Order.

In 1958 were added an Ante-Chapel, a Robing Room for the Queen and a Chaplain's Room. A new three manual Walker organ was presented to the Chapel by the Queen in 1965.

Members of the public are most welcome to attend the Services on Sundays (11.00 a.m.) and weekdays with the exception of those for special or official occasions. The Chapel uses the Book of Common Prayer and has a particularly fine musical tradition with a choir of men and boys.

CHAPLAIN
Revd John Robson, Chaplain of the Royal Victorian Order [1989]   *Tel* and *Fax:* 0171–379 8088

MASTER OF MUSIC
Mr Philip Berg

VERGER
Mr Phillip Chancellor   *Tel:* 0171–836 7221

HONORARY WARDENS
Mr Colin Brough
Mr William Culver
Mr Randall Edwards
Dr Roy Palmer
Sir Walter Verco
Mr Stephen White

Royal Memorial Chapel Sandhurst

Camberley, Surrey GU15 4PQ

The Royal Memorial Chapel Sandhurst, the Domestic Chapel of the Royal Military Academy Sandhurst is also the Memorial Chapel of the Officers of the Army.

Built in 1879 it was considerably enlarged between 1919 and 1921 (though some work was not completed until 1937) as a Memorial to all Sandhurst-trained Officers who gave their lives in the First World War.

Following the Second World War, the names of all officers of the Armies of the British Commonwealth who died in that conflict were inscribed on a Roll of Honour. A page of this book is turned at the commencement of the main Sunday service.

A Book of Remembrance containing the names of all former cadets who have been killed or died whilst serving since 1947 is kept in the Chapel of Remembrance, sometimes referred to as the South Africa Chapel.

All services are normally open to the public on application for a pass.

CHAPLAIN
Revd Alan Brown

CHOIRMASTER AND ORGANIST
Mr Christopher Connett

CONSTITUTION OF THE CHAPEL COUNCIL
Maj-Gen A. G. Denaro (*Chairman*); Maj-Gen T. J. Granville-Chapman; Revd Dr V. Dobbin, Chaplain-General; General Sir Robert Ford; Gen Sir William Jackson; Gen Sir John Mogg; Maj-Gen J. D. Stokoe; Revd A. J. Brown *Treasurer:* Maj J. C. Preston, Academy Administrative Officer; *Hon Secretary:* Brig M. C. Owen

The Royal Foundation of St Katharine in Ratcliffe

Butcher Row, London E14 8DS   *Tel:* 0171–790 3540
                                      Fax: 0171–702 7603

The Royal Foundation of St Katharine was originally founded by Queen Matilda in about 1147 and was situated for nearly seven centuries adjacent to the Tower of London. One of the oldest charities in the United Kingdom, the Foundation is now located in Stepney, East London. Its purpose is to maintain a Christian centre providing prayer, conferences, retreats and counselling and also to work locally in the East London community. It is able to offer hospitality to those doing research or on sabbatical, as well as to visitors from the church overseas.

Her Majesty Queen Elizabeth The Queen Mother is Patron of the Royal Foundation of St Katharine. The Chapter consists of a Master and a number of resident lay people.

MEMBERS OF THE COURT
The Viscount Churchill (*Chairman*)
Mr Benjamin Hanbury (*Treasurer*)
The Bishop of London
The Lord Holderness
Preb Ronald Swan
Dame Frances Campbell-Preston
Mrs Alison Mayne
Lady Ailsa O'Brian

CLERK TO THE COURT
Mr S. J. Northcott, 10 Great James St, London WC1N 3DQ
                                      Tel: 0171–831 9661
                                      Fax: 0171–405 4101

MASTER
Preb Ronald Swan

Deans of Peculiars

The few present-day Deans of Peculiars are the residue of some 300 such office-holders in the medieval period, when the granting of 'peculiar' status, fully or partially exempting a jurisdiction from episcopal control, was commonly employed by Popes and others to advance the interests of a particular institution, or limit the power of the bishops. Unlike the Royal Peculiars, the Deaneries had little in common, and the privileges and duties of the individual posts ranged from nominal to significant. Most of the special provisions were brought to an end in the nineteenth century. But each Peculiar has interesting light to throw on a phase of Anglican or national history.

Battle   Very Revd William Cummings [1991]
Bocking   Very Revd Philip Need (Bocking, Essex) [1996]
                Very Revd Stuart Morris (Hadleigh, Suffolk) [1994]
Guernsey and its Dependencies
                         Very Revd Marc Trickey [1995]
Jersey   Very Revd John Seaford [1993]
Stamford   Rt Revd Alastair Redfern [1998]

Preachers at The Inns of Court

THE TEMPLE
Master: Canon Joseph Robinson
Reader: Revd A. H. Mead

LINCOLN'S INN
Canon W. B. Norman

GRAY'S INN
Revd Roger Holloway

RELIGIOUS COMMUNITIES

Anglican Religious Communities

The roots of the Religious Life can be traced back to the Early Church in Jerusalem, and the subsequent traditions such as the Benedictines, Franciscans, etc, were flourishing in England until the Reformation when all were suppressed.

Most Anglican Communities were founded in the last century as a result of the Oxford Movement. There are now over sixty different Communities in the British Isles and throughout the Anglican Communion. Some are very small. Some have over eighty members.

Religious Communities are formed by men and women who feel called to seek God and live out their baptismal vows in a particular way under vows. There are some 1,200 Anglican men and women living this life in the United Kingdom.

PRAYER AND WORK
Each Community has its own history and character, some follow one of the traditional Rules, and others those written by more recent founders, but all have one thing in common: their daily life based on the work of prayer and living together centred in their Daily Office and the Eucharist. The work grows from the prayer, depending on the particular Community and the gifts of its members.

Some Communities are 'enclosed'. The members do not normally go out, but remain within the convent or monastery and its grounds, seeking and serving God through silence and prayer, study and work. Other Communities share the basic life of prayer and fellowship and may also be involved in work outside the Community.

HOSPITALITY
Most Community houses offer a place where people can go for a time of Retreat, either alone or with a group, for a day, several days, or occasionally for longer periods of time. They offer a place of quiet to seek God, grow in prayer and find spiritual guidance.

THE CALLING
People who feel called to the Religious Life and who wish to apply to a Community are usually aged between 21 and 45. They normally need to be physically and psychologically robust. Academic qualifications are not essential. There is a training period of about three years before any vows are taken.

Those who are considering a vocation are advised to visit Community houses to experience their particular ethos: further information is available from the houses or general enquiries may be made to The Communities Consultative Council at the address below.

Advisory Council on the Relations of Bishops and Religious Communities

This Council, to serve the two Provinces, is responsible to the Archbishops and the House of Bishops. Its functions are: (1) to advise Bishops upon (*a*) questions arising about the charters and rule of existing Communities, (*b*) the establishment of new Communities, (*c*) matters referred to it by a diocesan bishop; (2) to advise existing Communities or their Visitors in any matters that they refer to it; (3) to give guidance to those who wish to form Communities. The Chairman and Convenor of the Council must be a diocesan bishop appointed by the Archbishops of Canterbury and York. The Council consists of at least 13 members, 3 of whom are nominated by the Bishops and 10 elected by the Communities. Up to 5 additional members may be co-opted. The present membership is: *Chairman:* The Bishop of Bradford; *3 Members nominated by the House of Bishops:* The Archbishop of York, the Bishop of Oxford, vacancy; *10 Members elected by the Communities:* Abbot Basil Matthews OSB, Father Christopher Lowe CR, Brother Damian SSF, Father Gregory CSWG, Sister Margaret Angela CSJD, Sister Alison OHP, Sister Lillian CSA, Mother Mary Jean CHN, Sister Pamela CAH, Sister Tessa SLG; one co-opted member: Sister Elizabeth Mary CSD; Father Anthony Maggs CRL (RC Observer). *Hon Pastoral Secretary* Revd David Platt, 1 Saxons Way, Didcot, Oxon OX11 9RA *Tel:* (01235) 814729 *Fax:* (01235) 811590

Administrative Secretary Miss Jane Melrose, General Synod Office, Church House, Great Smith St, London SW1P 3NZ *Tel:* 0171–898 1379

Communities Consultative Council

The Communities Consultative Council was set up in 1975. It consists of elected representatives from all Anglican Religious Communities who have houses in this country. The Council exists to promote co-operation and exchange of ideas between Religious Communities as well as providing general and vocational information about Communities and the Religious Life. To this end, the Council have produced a range of literature which is available upon receipt of an A4 SAE (31p stamp). The leaflets include a brief introduction to the Religious Life, vocation, associates, etc together with material for the annual Day of Prayer for Vocations to the Religious Life (Trinity 5). The *Anglican Religious Communities Year Book* is published by Canterbury Press (£4.99 plus 75p p&p). *Chair:* Sister Elizabeth Mary CSD, St Margaret's Church, Barking, Essex IG11 8AS   *Tel:* 0181-594 1736

Communities for Men

BENEDICTINE COMMUNITY OF ELMORE ABBEY
Church Lane, Speen, Newbury, Berks RG14 1SA
Tel: (01635) 33080

Abbot Dom Basil Matthews

Visitor Rt Revd Rowan Williams (*Bishop of Monmouth*)

Founded 1914. 1926–87 Nashdom Abbey. From 1987 Elmore Abbey. Resident community 11 monks. Oblate confraternity over 350. Various pastoral works undertaken including retreats. Fine theological library.

BENEDICTINE COMMUNITY OF THE PRIORY OF OUR LADY, BURFORD
See **Mixed Communities** page 207.

COMMUNITY OF OUR LADY AND ST JOHN
Alton Abbey, Alton, Hants GU34 4AP
Tel: (01420) 562145/563575
Fax: (01420) 561691

Abbot Rt Revd Dom Giles Hill

Visitor Rt Revd Michael Scott-Joynt (*Bishop of Winchester*)

Founded 1884. A community of Benedictine monks which undertakes retreats. Guest accommodation for men and women (24 single rooms, 2 twin rooms). Other work includes the manufacture of altar wafers. Commissions accepted for painting of icons. The Seamen's Friendly Society of St Paul is managed from the Abbey. Day conference facilities and residential groups welcome: contact the Guestmaster.

COMMUNITY OF THE GLORIOUS ASCENSION
Lamacraft Farm, Start Point, Kingsbridge, Devon
TQ7 2NG   *Tel:* (01548) 511474

Prior Bro Simon CGA

Visitor Rt Revd Edward Holland (*Bishop of Colchester*)
Founded 1960, the brothers, lay and clerical, are called to unite a working life outside their Priories with a monastic community life.

COMMUNITY OF THE RESURRECTION
House of the Resurrection, Mirfield, W Yorks WF14 0BN
Tel: (01924) 494318
Fax: (01924) 490489

Superior Fr Crispin Harrison CR

Visitor Most Revd David Hope (*Archbishop of York*)

Founded 1892, it undertakes teaching (theological college), retreats, missions and missionary works. *Theological College:* College of the Resurrection, Mirfield, W. Yorks WF14 0BW. *Tel:* (01924) 490441; *Fax:* (01924) 492738. *The Mirfield Centre:* co-ordinates the College of the Resurrection, the Northern Ordination Course (Eastern wing) and the Faith in Community Project. *Address:* Mirfield Centre, College of the Resurrection, Mirfield, W Yorks WF14 0BW *Tel:* (01924) 481911 *Fax:* (01924) 492735 *Retreat House:* St Francis House, Hemingford Grey, Huntingdon, Cambs PE18 9BJ. *Tel:* (01480) 462185. *Branch Houses:* St Michael's Priory, 14 Burleigh St, London WC2E 7PX. *Tel:* 0171–379 6669; *Fax:* 0171–240 5294. *Overseas:* St Peter's Priory, PO Box 991, Southdale 2135, S. Africa. *Tel:* 00 27 11 434 2504; *Fax:* 00 27 11 434 4556

THE COMMUNITY OF THE SERVANTS OF THE WILL OF GOD
Monastery of the Holy Trinity, Crawley Down, Crawley, W Sussex RH10 4LH   *Tel:* (01342) 712074

Father Superior Revd Fr Gregory CSWG

Visitor Rt Revd Eric Kemp (*Bishop of Chichester*)

Founded 1953 for men (clerical and lay). Women are now received also. Contemplative. Retreats and conferences. Monastery of Christ the Saviour, 23 Cambridge Rd, Hove, E Sussex BN3 1DE   *Tel:* (01273) 726698

Prior Revd Fr Brian CSWG. Contemplative: Fostering ministry and mission of urban church; providing an opportunity for men and women to live a monastic life within this urban setting.

EWELL MONASTERY
Water Lane, West Malling, Kent ME19 6HH

Prior Revd Fr Aelred Arnesen

Visitor Rt Revd Richard Llewellin (*Bishop of Dover*)

Founded 1966. An Anglican Cistercian order for men.

ORATORY OF THE GOOD SHEPHERD
See **Organisations** p. 246

THE SOCIETY OF ST FRANCIS
The Brothers of the First Order, founded in 1922, engage in active work especially in the areas of the poor and underprivileged. Three Friaries (at Hilfield, Glasshampton and Alnmouth) have a ministry with guests and retreatants. The other centres of work are principally within a city context from which the brothers engage in various active ministries. Some work with educational institutions, conducting retreats and with parishes continues.

There are four Provinces: Europe, the Pacific Islands, America and Australia/New Zealand.

Minister General Brother Daniel SSF

Protector General Rt Revd Richard Appleby (*Bishop of the Northern Territory*)

Minister, European Province Brother Damian SSF, Alverna, 110 Ellesmere Rd, Gladstone Park, London NW10 1JS
Tel and *Fax*: 0181-452 7285

Asst Minister Brother Samuel SSF

Bishop Protector, Europe Rt Revd Michael Scott-Joynt (*Bishop of Winchester*)

Houses: Hilfield *Tel:* (01300) 341345, Cambridge *Tel:* (01223) 353903; Glasshampton *Tel:* (01299) 896345; Plaistow *Tel:* 0171-476 5189; Paddington *Tel:* 0171-723 9735; 10 Halcrow St, Stepney *Tel:* 0171-247 6233; Gladstone Park *Tel:* 0181-452 7285; Alnmouth *Tel:* (01665) 830213; Birmingham *Tel:* 0121-411 1276; Belfast *Tel:* (01232) 351480; Edinburgh *Tel:* 0131-228 3077; and Glasgow *Tel:* 0141-550 1202

Minister, Australia and New Zealand Province Brother Colin Wilfred SSF. *Houses:* Brisbane (QLD), Stroud (NSW), Auckland

Pacific Islands Province
Regional Minister, Papua New Guinea Brother Clifton Henry SSF. *Houses:* Goroka, Haruro, Lae, Katerada, Siomoromoro

Regional Minister, Solomon Islands Brother Andrew Manu SSF. *Houses:* Auki, Hautambu, Honiara, Kira Kira, Kohimarama, Vanga Point

Minister, American Province Brother Justus Richard SSF. *Houses:* Long Island, San Francisco, New York.

The Society comprises a First Order for men (see above) and women (Community of St Francis), called to the Franciscan life under the vows of poverty, chastity and obedience; a Second Order of enclosed sisters (Order of St Clare); and a Third Order for ordained and lay people.

SOCIETY OF ST JOHN THE EVANGELIST
St Edward's House, 22 Gt College St, Westminster, London SW1P 3QA. *Tel:* 0171-222 9234

Superior General Revd James Naters SSJE

Visitor Rt Revd Dominic Walker (*Bishop of Reading*)

Founded 1866, for men, clerical and lay. Engaged in retreats, missions and educational work.

Houses: The Anchorhold, Paddockhall Rd, Haywards Heath, Sussex RH16 1HN, *Tel:* (01444) 452468; The Priory, 228 Iffley Rd, Oxford OX4 1SE. *Tel:* (01865) 248116

SOCIETY OF THE SACRED MISSION
1 Linford Lane, Milton Keynes MK15 9AB
Tel: (01908) 234546

Director Fr Christopher Myers SSM

Visitor Most Revd Richard Holloway (*Bishop of Edinburgh*)

Founded 1893. A religious community engaged in educational, pastoral and missionary work.

The Society is divided into Provinces:

Province of Europe
Provincial Fr Douglas Brown SSM
Houses: 1 Linford Lane, Milton Keynes MK15 9AB *Tel, Fax* and *Answering Service:* (01908) 234546; St Antony's Priory, 77 Claypath, Durham DH1 1QT *Tel:* 0191-384 3747, *Fax:* 0191-384 4939; 90 Vassall Rd, Kennington, London SW9 6JA *Tel:* 0171-582 2040, *Fax:* 0171-582 6640.

Southern Province
Provincial Fr Christopher Myers SSM
Houses: St John's Priory, 14 St John's St, Adelaide, S Australia 5000; St Michael's Priory, 75 Watsons Rd, Diggers Rest, Victoria 3427; PO Box 1579, Maseru 100, Lesotho, Southern Africa

Communities for Women

BENEDICTINE COMMUNITY OF ST MARY AT THE CROSS
Convent of St Mary at the Cross, Priory Field Drive, Edgware, Middx HA8 9PZ Tel: 0181–958 7868
Fax: 0181–958 1920

Abbess Mother Mary Therese Zelent OSB

Visitor Rt Revd Brian Masters (*Bishop of Edmonton*)

Founded in 1866; caring for disabled people throughout its history. This work, now including the care of frail elderly people, continues today in Henry Nihill House, a modern residential/nursing home. The community gives priority to prayer and worship in the Divine Office and Eucharist and its ministry of intercession. A growing number of people and parishes are united in the community's prayer through its 'Prayer Link'. Easily accessible from the M1 and A1, it offers an excellent day conference centre, guest accommodation for rest or retreat, and space for Quiet Days. The monastic experience can be shared by women wishing to take 'Time Out' for up to three months.

BENEDICTINE COMMUNITY OF ST MARY'S ABBEY
West Malling, Kent ME19 6JX Tel: (01732) 843309

Abbess Sister Mary John Marshall OSB

Visitor Rt Revd John Waine

Founded 1891. Monastic community with a guest house in the grounds.

BENEDICTINE COMMUNITY OF THE PRIORY OF OUR LADY, BURFORD
See **Mixed Communities** page 207

COMMUNITY OF ALL HALLOWS
All Hallows Convent, Ditchingham, Norfolk
Postal Address Bungay, Suffolk NR35 2DT
Tel: (01986) 892749
Fax: (01986) 892731

Superior Revd Mother Sheila CAH

Visitor Rt Revd Peter Nott (*Bishop of Norwich*)

Founded 1855. Augustinian Visitation Rule. Work and Houses at Ditchingham:
(1) The Convent: as above
(2) All Hallows House: Guests and retreats
Tel: (01986) 892840.
(3) Holy Cross House: Guests and retreats
Tel: (01986) 894092.
(4) St Mary's Lodge: Silent house for self-catering retreats Tel: (01986) 892731.
(5) St Gabriel's Retreat and Conference Centre: 100 residential and 200 day visitors
Tel: (01986) 892133; 892749 (*Bookings*).
(6) St Michael's House: Conferences and retreats
Tel: (01986) 895749.
(7) St Raphael's: available for self-catering groups who are happy with dormitory accommodation
Tel: (01986) 892133.
(8) Day Nursery – up to 20 children
Tel: (01986) 895091
(9) All Hallows Country Hospital (accommodates 30 patients) Tel: (01986) 892728.
(10) Adele House: 38 Bed Nursing Home (including EMI patients) Tel: (01986) 892643.
(11) Spiritual Direction and Retreat Work.

In Norwich:
(12) All Hallows, Rouen Road, Norwich NR1 1QT Tel: (01603) 624738. Guests accepted for retreats, quiet weekends, etc. Situated near Julian Shrine (run by CSP Sisters).
(13) The Little Portion, Norwich NR3 1BU Tel: (01603) 628087. Support for women and families under stress. Ministry in Norwich Cathedral, and elsewhere as necessary and possible.

COMMUNITY OF REPARATION TO JESUS IN THE BLESSED SACRAMENT
Convent of St John Baptist, Hatch Lane, Windsor, Berks SL4 3QR Tel: (01753) 850618

Superior Revd Mother Jane Olive CSJB

Visitor Rt Revd Richard Harries (*Bishop of Oxford*)

Founded 1869. Work with the elderly.

COMMUNITY OF ST ANDREW
St Andrew's House, 2 Tavistock Rd, Westbourne Park, London W11 1BA Tel: 0171–229 2662

Superior Revd Mother Donella CSA

Visitor Rt Revd Richard Chartres (*Bishop of London*)

Founded 1861. Full membership of the Community consists of professed sisters who are ordained, or who, though not seeking ordination, serve in other forms of diaconal ministry, such as the caring professions. Present number is 11.

The fundamental ministry is the offering of prayer and worship, evangelism, pastoral work and hospitality. This is carried out through parish and specialised ministry.

COMMUNITY OF ST CLARE
St Mary's Convent, Freeland, Witney, Oxon OX8 8AJ
Tel: (01993) 881225

Superior Sister Paula OSC

Bishop Protector Rt Revd Michael Scott-Joynt (*Bishop of Winchester*)

Founded 1950. Second Order of Society of St Francis. Contemplative and enclosed.

COMMUNITY OF ST DENYS
Sarum College, 19 The Close, Salisbury SP1 2EE
Tel: (01722) 339761

Superior Revd Mother Frances Anne CSD

Visitor Rt Revd David Stancliffe (*Bishop of Salisbury*)

Founded 1879. Undertakes mission work in the UK, adult teaching, parish work, retreats. Three sisters are priests.

Branches: St Denys Retreat House, 2/3 Church St, Warminster BA12 8PG *Tel:* (01985) 214824; St Margaret's Centre, The Broadway, Barking, Essex IG11 8AS *Tel:* 0181–591 5567; Sarum College, 19 The Close, Salisbury, SP1 2EE *Tel:* (01722) 339761. There are two other houses in Warminster.

COMMUNITY OF ST FRANCIS
Founded 1905, the sisters of the First Order of the Society of St Francis engage in active ministries: evangelistic, caring, conferences, retreats, spiritual direction, and hospitality. Some sisters who live in urban areas engage in paid part-time work. Some sisters live a life of contemplative solitude as hermits.

There are two provinces: European with a New Zealand region, and American.

Minister General Sister Teresa CSF, Newcastle-under-Lyme   *Tel and Fax:* (01782) 611180

Minister Provincial, European Province Sister Joyce CSF, Brixton   *Tel and Fax:* 0181–674 5344

Visitor Rt Revd Michael Scott-Joynt (*Bishop of Winchester*)

Houses:
1. 43 Endymion Rd, Brixton, London SW2 2BU
   Tel: 0181–671 9401
2. St Francis Convent, Compton Durville, South Petherton, Somerset TA13 5ES   *Tel:* (01460) 240473
   Fax: (01460) 242360
3. Greystones St Francis, First Ave, Porthill, Newcastle-under-Lyme, Staffs ST5 8QX   *Tel:* (01782) 636839
4. 10 Halcrow St, Stepney, London E1 2EP
   Tel and Fax: 0171–247 6233
5. St Francis House, 113 Gillott Rd, Birmingham B16 0ET
   Tel: 0121–454 8302
   Fax: 0121–455 9784

Deputy Minister Provincial, New Zealand Region Sister Maureen CSF, 33 Carlton Gore Rd, Auckland 1, New Zealand

Minister Provincial, American Province Sister Pamela Clare CSF, 3743 Cesar Chavez St, San Francisco CA 94110, USA

COMMUNITY OF ST JOHN BAPTIST
Convent of St John Baptist, Hatch Lane, Windsor, Berks SL4 3QR   *Tel:* (01753) 850618

Superior Mother Jane Olive CSJB

Visitor Rt Revd Richard Harries (*Bishop of Oxford*)

Chaplain Revd Lister Tonge

Founded 1852 to honour and worship Almighty God and to serve him in works of charity. Runs a Retreat/Spirituality Centre and undertakes care of the aged, mission and parish work. Church Embroidery. *Tel:* (01753) 861924. Responsible for St John's Convent Home (for mentally handicapped women), *Tel:* (01753) 850618 and St Anne's House, Windsor (for elderly women) *Tel:* (01753) 865757

COMMUNITY OF ST JOHN THE DIVINE
St John's House, 652 Alum Rock Rd, Birmingham, W Midlands B8 3NS   *Tel:* 0121–327 4174

Superior Mother Christine CSJD

Visitor Rt Revd Mark Santer (*Bishop of Birmingham*)

Founded in 1848. The ethos of the community covers all aspects of health, healing, reconciliation and wholeness in its widest context. The community is at the beginning of an exploration, considering how Religious (committed for life) and Lay people (committed for a set period) could form Christian community and share their lives together. The community's life is based on prayer from which the different expressions of ministry flow. Within the House there is an important ministry of listening and hospitality, and larger facilities for more day group activities are planned. Outisde the House, members of the community are involved with local ministries where they feel called.

COMMUNITY OF ST LAURENCE
Convent of St Laurence, Field Lane, Belper, Derby DE56 1DD.   *Tel:* (01773) 822585/823390

Superior Mother Jean Mary CSL

Visitor Rt Revd Jonathan Bailey (*Bishop of Derby*)

Founded 1874. The house is available for parish weekends, teaching weekends, conferences and Quiet Days. Guests taken for limited periods, including Christmas and Easter. Parish visiting.

COMMUNITY OF ST MARY THE VIRGIN
St Mary's Convent, Challow Rd, Wantage, Oxon OX12 9DJ   *Tel:* (01235) 763141

Superior Mother Barbara Claire CSMV

Visitor Rt Revd Richard Harries (*Bishop of Oxford*)

Founded 1848. The Sisters work in England, India and South Africa.

England
1. St Mary's Convent. (Retreats for individuals and groups; Printing Press; Studio and Workshop.)
2. St Peter's Bourne, 40 Oakleigh Park South, London N20 9JN *Tel:* 0181–445 5535. (Retreats for individuals and groups.)
3. 4 Hilton Rd, Leeds LS8 4HB *Tel:* (0113) 262 7681
4. 366 High St, Smethwick B66 3PD *Tel:* 0121–558 0094
5. St Katharine's House, Ormond Rd, Wantage OX12 8EA *Tel:* (01235) 762739 (Home for the Elderly.)
6. St Mary's Lodge, Challow Rd, Wantage OX12 9DH *Tel:* (01235) 767112

India
Christa Prema Seva Ashram, Shivajinagar, Pune 411005, Maharashtra, India (Ecumenical; inter-faith dialogue.)

South Africa
3 Keurboom Ave, Omega Park, Brakpan 1541, South Africa *Tel:* 00 2711 740 9156

COMMUNITY OF ST PETER

St Peter's Convent, Maybury Hill, Woking, Surrey GU22 8AE *Tel:* (01483) 761137

Superior Mother Margaret Paul CSP

Visitor Rt Revd John Gladwin (*Bishop of Guildford*)

Founded 1861. A house for retreats and conferences was opened 1968 within the convent grounds. Guests, men and women, taken all year round.

COMMUNITY OF ST PETER, HORBURY

St Peter's Convent, Dovecote Lane, Horbury, Wakefield, W Yorks WF4 6BB *Tel:* (01924) 272181

Superior Mother Robina CSPH

Visitor Rt Revd Nigel McCulloch (*Bishop of Wakefield*)

Benedictine in spirit. Undertakes a variety of pastoral ministries and retreat work.

COMMUNITY OF THE COMPANIONS OF JESUS THE GOOD SHEPHERD

Convent of St John Baptist, Hatch Lane, Windsor, Berks SL4 3QR *Tel:* (01753) 850618
  Fax: (01753) 869989

Superior Mother Ann Verena CJGS

Visitor Rt Revd Richard Cartwright

Founded 1920. Undertakes work with the elderly, lay and LNSM training, quiet days and retreats, spiritual direction.

COMMUNITY OF THE EPIPHANY

Copeland Court, Truro, Cornwall TR1 3DR
  Tel: (01872) 722249

Administrator Delma Byrom

Visitor Rt Revd Bill Ind (*Bishop of Truro*)

Founded 1883. Thirteen single bedrooms available for retreatants. Private retreats can be arranged. Organised day retreats are held during the year. Day conferences can now be catered for. Details on application to the Administrator.

COMMUNITY OF THE GLORIOUS ASCENSION

Prasada, Quartier Subrane, Montauroux, 83440, France
  Tel: 00 334 94 47 74 26

Prioress Sister Jean CGA

The sisters are called to unite a monastic community life with work alongside other people. At Prasada they welcome visitors who seek a peaceful environment in which to find refreshment. Guests have the opportunity to use the chapel for private prayer and to join the sisters for Eucharist and Divine Office.

COMMUNITY OF THE HOLY CROSS

Holy Cross Convent, Rempstone Hall, Rempstone, Nr Loughborough LE12 6RG *Tel:* (01509) 880336
  Fax: (01509) 881812

Mother Superior Revd Mother Mary Luke CHC

Visitor Rt Revd Eric Kemp (*Bishop of Chichester*)

Founded in 1857 for mission work but later adopted the Rule of St Benedict. All the work, centred on the daily celebration of the Divine Office and the Eucharist, is done within the Enclosure.

The Sisters produce and send out two series of leaflets of devotional and spiritual content, one concerning Unity between Christians, and a wider ecumenism, and the other Prayer and Faith, reflecting the mission of the Church in the world. A variety of prayer and greeting cards are also produced by the Sisters. The Community provides for Quiet Days for individuals and groups, and there is limited residential accommodation for those wishing to make longer retreats.

COMMUNITY OF THE HOLY FAMILY

The Gatehouse, St Mary's Abbey, West Malling, Kent ME19 6LP *Tel:* (01732) 849016

Superior Mother Kathleen Mary CHF

Visitor Rt Revd Eric Kemp (*Bishop of Chichester*)

From January 1997, the Community continues its life in the Gatehouse of Malling Abbey. It is anticipated that the spirit of the educational work begun by the Foundress, Mother Agnes Mason, at the beginning of this century, will still be continued in the eastern end of the diocese of Chichester through the operation of the Mother Agnes Trust which undergirds the Community of the Holy Family. The charity in the future will seek to provide a theological library and an extensive educational resource centre.

COMMUNITY OF THE HOLY NAME
Convent of the Holy Name, Morley Rd, Oakwood, Derby DE21 4QZ *Tel:* (01332) 671716
Fax: (01332) 669712

Superior Revd Mother Jean Mary CHN

Visitor Rt Revd David Smith (*Bishop of Bradford*)

Founded 1865. Undertakes mission and retreat work. Guests received. *Branch Houses:* Holy Name House, Ambleside Rd, Keswick, Cumbria CA12 4DD *Tel:* (01768) 772998; St Michael's House, 53 Wimborne Rd, Radford, Nottingham NG7 5PD *Tel:* 0115–978 5101; 88 Braunston Rd, Oakham, Rutland LE15 6LE *Tel:* (01572) 770287; 6 St Peter's Court, 398 Woodborough Rd, Nottingham NG3 4JF *Tel:* 0115–960 8794; Cottage 5, Lambeth Palace, London SE1 7JU *Tel:* 0171–928 5407.

The Community also has charge of the Retreat House, 11 Abbey Square, Chester *Tel:* (01244) 321801

Overseas: Lesotho: Convent of the Holy Name, PO Box LR 43, Leribe; CHN Mission House, PO Box MS 87, Maseru; St Stephen's Mission, PO Box MH 90, Mohale's Hoek, Lesotho. *Zululand:* Convent of the Holy Name, Kwa Magwaza, P/B 806, Melmoth, RSA; St Vincent's Mission, P/B 675, Nqutu 3135, RSA; St Luke's Mission, PO Box 175, 3950 Nongoma, RSA; Usuthu Mission, PO 8, via Luyengo, Swaziland; St Cyprian's Parish, Box 216, Nkandla, RSA; 14 Web Castle Way, Castle Hill, Marbe Ray 4037, RSA.

Moçambique: CP 120, Maputo, Moçambique.

COMMUNITY OF THE PRESENTATION
St Francis House, 113 Gillott Rd, Birmingham B16 0ET
Tel: 0121–454 8302

Founded 1927.

All enquiries care of the Community of the Presentation at the above address.

COMMUNITY OF THE SACRED PASSION
Mother House: Convent of the Sacred Passion, Lower Rd, Effingham, Leatherhead, Surrey KT24 5JP
Tel: (01372) 457091

Superior Mother Gloria CSP

Visitor Rt Revd Ian Brackley (*Bishop of Dorking*)

Founded 1911. An order which combines prayer and mission work in varying forms. A house opened in Walsall in 1981 and in the autumn of 1983 in the parish of St John the Divine, Kennington. Since 1991 three sisters have been living and working next to the Julian Shrine in Norwich. The Community withdrew from Tanzania in June 1991, leaving behind a community of more than ninety Tanzanian women known as the Community of St Mary.

COMMUNITY OF THE SERVANTS OF THE CROSS
Marriott House, Tollhouse Close, Chichester, W Sussex PO19 3EZ *Tel:* (01243) 781620

Superior Mother Angela CSC

Visitor Vacancy

Warden Canon Keith Hobbs

Augustinian Rule.

COMMUNITY OF THE SISTERS OF THE LOVE OF GOD
Convent of the Incarnation, Fairacres, Oxford OX4 1TB
Tel: (01865) 721301/2

Superior Revd Mother Rosemary SLG

Visitor Rt Revd Richard Harries (*Bishop of Oxford*)

Founded 1906 and has a modern rule based on monastic principles and Carmelite spirituality. Membership, with Oblature and Associations for men and women. *Function:* The contemplative life. It offers hospitality for private retreats. The SLG Press publishes pamphlets and books on spirituality and prayer.

Other Convents: Convent of St Mary and the Angels, Woodland Ave, Hemel Hempstead, Herts HP1 1RG *Tel:* (01442) 256989; Bede House, Staplehurst, Tonbridge, Kent TN12 0HQ (with its solitaries) *Tel:* (01580) 891262; St Isaac's Retreat, PO Box 93, Opononi, Northland, New Zealand.

FRANCISCAN SERVANTS OF JESUS AND MARY
Posbury St Francis, Crediton, Devon EX17 3QG
Tel: (01363) 772304

Superior Mother Hilary FSJM

Visitor Rt Revd John Richards (*Bishop of Ebbsfleet*)

Founded 1930; its work consists of a life of prayer, work and hospitality; guests are received and retreats conducted between Easter and October.

ORDER OF THE HOLY PARACLETE
St Hilda's Priory, Sneaton Castle, Whitby, N Yorks YO21 3QN Tel: (01947) 602079
Fax: (01947) 820854
e-mail: ohppriorywhitby@btinternet.com

Superior Sister Judith OHP

Visitor Most Revd David Hope (*Archbishop of York*)

Founded 1915 and based on Rule of St Benedict. Main undertaking: prayer, pastoral work, children's hospice, retreats, conferences, missions, parish work.

Residential Centre: Sneaton Castle Centre, Whitby, N Yorks YO21 3QN Tel: (01947) 600051
Fax: (01947) 603490
e-mail: sneaton@globalnet.co.uk

Accommodation and facilities for large and small groups for parish activities, conferences and educational courses.

Branch Houses: Beach Cliff, 14 North Promenade, Whitby, N Yorks YO21 3JX *Tel:* (01947) 601968; St Oswald's Pastoral Centre, Woodlands Drive, Sleights, Whitby, N Yorks YO21 1RY *Tel:* (01947) 810496; The Abbey Cottage, Rievaulx, York YO62 5LB *Tel:* (01439) 798209; 7 Minster Yard, York YO1 7JD *Tel:* (01904) 620601; St Michael's House, 15 Portman St, Belgrave, Leicester LE4 6NZ *Tel:* 0116–266 7805; Martin House, Grove Rd, Clifford, Wetherby, W Yorks LS23 6TX *Tel:* (01937) 843449; 21 Honey Green Rd, Flat 5, Dundee DD4 8BD *Tel:* (01328) 509206.

Overseas: Swaziland: PO 1272, Manzini: Industrial Training Centres and other development work, diocesan youth work. *Republic of S Africa:* St Benedict's Retreat House, PO Box 27, Rosettenville, 2130 *Ghana:* PO Box 594, Accra, Training for Lay Ministry.

ST MARY'S CONVENT
Burlington Lane, Chiswick, London W4 2QE
Tel: 0181–994 4641
Fax: 0181–994 2156

Superior Sister Jennifer Anne SSM

Visitor Vacancy

Has a Residential Home for elderly retired ladies; and Nursing Home for those needing full-time nursing care.

See Society of St Margaret, East Grinstead, below.

ST SAVIOUR'S PRIORY
18 Queensbridge Rd, London E2 8NS
Tel and Fax: 0171–739 6775 (Revd Mother)
0171–739 9976 (Sisters)

Superior Sister Elizabeth SSM

Visitor Rt Revd Dominic Walker (*Bishop of Reading*)

Convent of the Society of St Margaret, working as staff members in various parishes, in schools, with the homeless etc; retreats and individual spiritual direction. The Priory has a few guest rooms and facilities for individual private retreats as well as excellent facilities for small group meetings.

SISTERS OF BETHANY
7 Nelson Rd, Southsea, Hants PO5 2AR
Tel: (01705) 833498

Superior Mother Gwenyth SSB

Visitor Rt Revd Kenneth Stevenson (*Bishop of Portsmouth*)

Founded 1866 for hospitality, retreat work and praying for Christian Unity. The Sisters are available for leading quiet days and retreats, as spiritual directors, and also to give talks on prayer. People are welcome to come individually or as groups to spend time in silence and prayer. It is possible to accommodate a few residential guests or groups of up to 24 for the day.

SISTERS OF CHARITY
St Elizabeth's House, Longbrook St, Plympton St Maurice, Plymouth PL7 1NL Tel: (01752) 336112

Superior Revd Mother Mary Theresa SC

Visitor Rt Revd John Garton (*Bishop of Plymouth*)

Founded 1869. The Rule is based on that of St Vincent de Paul. Undertakes care of those in need, young or old; parish work, missions, retreats. *Branch Houses:* St Vincent's Nursing Home, Plympton St Maurice, Plymouth PL7 3NE *Tel:* (01752) 336205. Parish work in Sunderland and Plymouth. 6 North View, Castletown, Sunderland SR5 3AF; 81 Fore St, Plympton St Maurice, Plymouth PL7 3NE *Tel:* (01272) 345918. *Overseas:* The Convent of the Sisters of Charity and Holy Spirit Retreat and Conference Center, 701 Park Place, PO Box 818, Boulder City, Nevada, 89005 USA.

SISTERS OF THE CHURCH
(Regd Charity: Church Extension Association Inc)
St Michael's Convent, Ham Common, Richmond, Surrey TW10 7JH Tels: 0181–940 8711 *and* 0181–948 2502
Fax: 0181–332 2927

Superior Sister Anita CSC

Visitor Rt Revd Peter Selby (*Bishop of Worcester*)

Founded 1870. Has a two-fold ethos of worship and active mission. Undertakes group and private retreats and workshops; chaplaincy, educational and pastoral work, hospitality. *Branch Houses:* St Gabriel's, 27A Dial Hill Rd, Clevedon, Avon BS21 7HL *Tel:* (01275) 872586; 82 Ashley Rd, St Paul's, Bristol BS6 5NT *Tel:* (0117) 941 3268; 112 St Andrew's Rd North, St Annes-on-Sea, Lancs

FY8 2JQ *Tel:* (01253) 728016; 10 Furness Rd, West Harrow, Middx HA2 0RL *Tel:* 0181–423 3780 and in Australia, Canada, Solomon Islands.

SOCIETY OF ALL SAINTS SISTERS OF THE POOR
All Saints Convent, St Mary's Rd, Oxford OX4 1RU
Tel: (01865) 249127
Fax: (01865) 726547

Superior Mother Helen ASSP

Visitor Rt Revd Robert Runcie

Founded in London 1851. Works of the Society:
(1) St John's Home for the elderly, St Mary's Rd, Oxford OX4 1QE *Tel:* (01865) 247725.
(2) Helen House, a hospice for children, 37 Leopold St, Oxford OX4 1QT *Tel:* (01865) 728251.
(3) Church Embroidery Department
Tel: (01865) 248627.
(4) Small Guest House. Enquiries regarding visits and private retreats welcomed.
(5) The Porch. A drop-in centre for the homeless
Tel: (01865) 728545.
(6) All Saints House, 82 Margaret St, London W1N 8LH
Tel: 0171–637 7818

SOCIETY OF ST MARGARET
St Margaret's Convent, St John's Rd, East Grinstead, W Sussex RH19 3LE *Tel:* (01342) 323497

Superior Mother Raphael Mary SSM

Visitor Rt Revd Eric Kemp (*Bishop of Chichester*)

Founded 1855 and undertakes nursing work, runs guest and retreat houses and a home for the aged, and in Sri Lanka a retreat house and a children's home.
Neale House Conference Centre *Tel:* (01342) 312552.
Branch Houses: St Mary's Convent and Nursing Home, Burlington Lane, Chiswick, London W4 2QE (guest house for elderly ladies and nursing home for geriatric and handicapped ladies), *Tel:* 0181–994 4641.

Overseas: St Margaret's Convent, Polwatte, Colombo 3, Sri Lanka, and St John's Home, Moratuwa, Sri Lanka.

Independent Convents of the Society: St Margaret's Convent, 17 Spital, Aberdeen, AB24 3HT *Tel:* (01224) 632648. St Saviour's Priory, Queensbridge Rd, London E2 8NS (*see* p. 206) *Tel:* 0171–739 6775. Priory of Our Lady, Walsingham, Norfolk, NR22 6ED *Tel:* (01328) 820340. St Margaret's Convent, 17 Highland Park St, Roxbury, MA 02119, USA.

SOCIETY OF THE HOLY TRINITY
Ascot Priory, Ascot, Berks SL5 8RT

Superior Mother Cecilia SHT

Founded 1845. Order based on Poor Clares. Contemplative. St Michael's and St Gabriel's Retreat House, self-catering. Day conference facilities available.

SOCIETY OF THE PRECIOUS BLOOD
Burnham Abbey, Lake End Rd, Taplow, Maidenhead, Berks SL6 0PW *Tel:* (01628) 604080

Superior The Revd Mother SPB

Visitor Rt Revd Richard Harries (*Bishop of Oxford*)

Founded 1905 and based on rule of St Augustine. Contemplative and exists for the purpose of perpetual intercession for the Church and for the world. *Branch House:* St Pega's Hermitage, Peakirk, Peterborough *Tel:* (01733) 252219. *Overseas:* Independent daughter House, Priory of Our Lady Mother of Mercy, Masite, PO Box MS 7192, Maseru 100, Lesotho; Dependent House: St Monica's House of Prayer, 46 Green St, West End, Kimberley 8301, Cape, RSA.

Mixed Communities

BENEDICTINE COMMUNITY OF THE PRIORY OF OUR LADY, BURFORD
Burford Priory, Priory Lane, Burford, Oxon OX18 4SQ
Tel: (01993) 823605

Prior Brother Stuart Burns OSB

Visitor Rt Revd James Thompson (*Bishop of Bath and Wells*)

Founded in 1941 from Wantage under its official title 'The Society of the Salutation of Mary the Virgin', this is a monastic community living under the Rule of St Benedict. In 1987 it formally opened its novitiate to men as well as women, and since then has evolved as a mixed monastery. The Community has oblates and a Friends' Association.

The nuns and monks seek to support themselves by a variety of work including printing, writing, icon mounting and retreat work. They do not normally undertake work outside the Priory but are concerned to develop a life of prayer and hospitality which is open to all. Guests are accommodated in the Guest House and are welcome to share in the life and worship of the Community. Day groups and small residential groups are also welcome.

ORGANISATIONS

PART 4

Classified List of Organisations included in this Section

Animal Welfare
Anglican Society for the Welfare of Animals
Animal Christian Concern
Christian Consultative Council for the Welfare of Animals

Art, Architecture
Art and Christianity Enquiry
Christian Arts
Ecclesiological Society
Friends of Friendless Churches
Historic Churches Preservation Trust
York Glaziers' Trust

Bellringing
Ancient Society of College Youths
Central Council of Church Bell-Ringers
Society of Royal Cumberland Youths

Bible Study
Bible Reading Fellowship
Bible Society
Scripture Gift Mission
Scripture Union
Vacation Term for Biblical Study

Blind People
Blind, Royal National Institute
Blind, St John's Guild for
Guild of Church Braillists

Church Buildings
Friends of Friendless Churches
Greater Churches Group
Historic Churches Preservation Trust
Incorporated Church Building Society
Marshall's Charity
Vergers, Church of England Guild of

Church Societies — General
ABWON
Additional Curates Society
Affirming Catholicism
Anglican Association
Anglican Evangelical Assembly
Association of English Cathedrals
Cathedral Administration and Finance Association
Cathedral and Church Shops Association
Catholic Group in General Synod
Catholic League
Church Pastoral Aid Society
Church Society
Church Union
Churches' Advertising Network
Modern Churchpeople's Union
Open Synod Group
Parish and People
Protestant Reformation Society
Society for the Maintenance of the Faith

Church Societies — Specific
Anglican Fellowship in Scouting and Guiding
Baptismal Reform Movement
Christian Evidence Society
Church of England Record Society
Church House Deaneries Group
Ecumenical Society of the Blessed Virgin Mary
Forward in Faith
Guild of St Helena
Guild of St Leonard
Guild of Servants of the Sanctuary
Lord's Day Observance Society
Movement for the Reform of Infant Baptism
Reform
Royal Martyr Church Union
St Aidan Trust
Society of King Charles the Martyr
Society of Mary
Third Province Movement

Clergy Associations
Association of Black Clergy
Association of Hospice Chaplains
Association of Ordinands and Candidates for Ministry
College of Health Care Chaplains
Company of Mission Priests
English Clergy Association
Federation of Catholic Priests
Lesbian and Gay Clergy Consultation
MSF Clergy Section
Oratory of the Good Shepherd
Retired Clergy Association
School Chaplains' Conference
Society of the Holy Cross
Society of Ordained Scientists
See also **Professional Groups**

Consultancy
Christians Abroad
Church and Community Trust
Grubb Institute

Co-ordinating Bodies
Anglican Voluntary Societies Forum
Church of England Evangelical Council
Churches' Group on Funeral Services
Churches' Main Committee
Evangelical Alliance
Religious Education Council of England and Wales
Universities and Colleges Christian Fellowship of Evangelical Unions

Counselling
Lesbian and Gay Christian Movement
Magdalene Fellowship
Relate
True Freedom Trust

Deaf People
British Deaf Association
Deaf People, Royal Association in Aid of
Deaf, Royal National Institute
National Deaf Church Conference

Defence, Disarmament, Pacifism
Anglican Pacifist Fellowship
Commonwealth War Graves Commission
Council on Christian Approaches to Defence and Disarmament

Diocesan Associations see pages 260–61

Drama
Actors' Church Union
Radius

Ecumenism
Anglican and Eastern Churches Association
Anglican–Lutheran Society
Christians for Europe
Churches' Group on Funeral Services
Churches' Main Committee
Fellowship of St Alban and St Sergius
Harold Buxton Trust
International Ecumenical Fellowship
Nikaean Club
Order of Christian Unity
Society of St Willibrord

Education
Archbishop's Examination in Theology
Association of Church College Trusts
Christian Education Movement
Church Schools Company
Corporation of SS Mary and Nicolas
Culham College Institute
Lincoln Theological Institute for the Study of Religion and Society
Mirfield Centre
North of England Institute for Christian Education
Religious Education Council of England and Wales
Royal Alexandra and Albert School
Royal Asylum of St Ann's Society

Family
Care Trust
Family Life and Marriage Education Network
Family Welfare Association
Fellowship of St Nicholas
St Michael's Fellowship

Finance
Anglican Stewardship Association
Christian Ethical Investment Group
Ecclesiastical Insurance Group

Ecumenical Council for Corporate Responsibilty
Fidelity Trust Ltd

Grant-Making Bodies
Church of England Clergy Stipend Trust
EFAC Bursary Scheme
Newton's Trust
Pilgrim Trust
Queen Victoria Clergy Fund
See also **Welfare**

Interfaith, Religions
Council of Christians and Jews
INFORM
Inter Faith Network for the United Kingdom
World Congress of Faiths

Libraries see pages 262–4

Marriage
Anglican Marriage Encounter
Broken Rites
Family Life and Marriage Education Network
Magdalene Fellowship
Relate

Medicine, Health, Healing
Acorn Christian Healing Trust
Association of Hospice Chaplains
Burrswood
Christian Medical Fellowship
Churches' Council for Health and Healing
College of Health Care Chaplains
Crowhurst Christian Healing Centre
Fellowship Charitable Foundation
Guild of Health
Guild of Pastoral Psychology
Guild of St Barnabas
Guild of St Raphael
Harnhill Centre of Christian Healing
Pilsdon Community
Richmond Fellowship for Community Mental Health
St Luke's Hospital for the Clergy

Ministry
Diaconal Association of the Church of England
Diakonia

Distinctive Diaconate
Edward King Institute for Ministry Development
MODEM
Royal Naval Lay Readers' Society

Ministry, Women
Anglican Group Educational Trust
Li Tim-Oi Foundation
Society for the Ministry of Women in the Church
WATCH

Mission
Bible Society
Careforce
Christian Witness to Israel
Church Pastoral Aid Society
Church's Ministry among Jewish People
Greenbelt Festivals
London City Mission
Mersey Mission to Seamen
Message
Missions to Seamen
Romsey House
Scripture Gift Mission
Scripture Union in Schools
Society for Promoting Christian Knowledge
Soldiers' and Airmen's Scripture Readers Association
Student Christian Movement
Trinitarian Bible Society
United Society for Christian Literature
Universities and Colleges Christian Fellowship of Evangelical Unions

Mission Overseas
Africa Inland Mission International
All Nations Christian College
Bush Brotherhoods
Crosslinks
Church Mission Society
College of the Ascension
Crowther Hall
Feed the Minds
Foreign Missions Club
Intercontinental Church Society
Interserve
Korean Mission Partnership
Leprosy Mission
Melanesian Mission
Mid-Africa Ministry

New England Company
OMF International Ltd
Overseas Bishoprics Fund
Oxford Mission
Papua New Guinea Church Partnership
Reader Missionary Studentship Association
South American Mission Society
Southern Africa Church Development Trust
Tearfund
United Society for the Propagation of the Gospel
World Vision

Music
Archbishops' Certificate in Church Music
Choir Benevolent Fund
Choir Schools Association
Church Music Society
Gregorian Association
Guild of Church Musicians
Hymn Society of Great Britain and Ireland
Jubilate Hymns
Morse-Boycott Bursary Fund
Plainsong and Medieval Music Society
Royal College of Organists
Royal School of Church Music

Ordination Candidate Funds
(General)
St Aidan's College Charity

Overseas
Womenaid International
Centre for International Briefing
Christianity and the Future of Europe
Christians Abroad
Christians for Europe
Churches' Commission on Overseas Students
European Christian Industrial Movement
United Nations Association
World Vision

Patronage Trusts see pages 264–6

Prayer, Meditation, Retreats
Archway
Association for Promoting Retreats
Confraternity of the Blessed Sacrament
Guild of All Souls
Julian Meetings
Julian of Norwich, Shrine of Lady
National Retreat Association
Servants of Christ the King
Society of Retreat Conductors
Women's World Day of Prayer

Professional Groups
Actors' Church Union
Anglican Association for Social Responsibility
Association of Christian Teachers
Association of Christian Writers
Association of Ordinands and Candidates for Ministry
Chaplains' Conference
Christian Arts
Christians at Work
Church Computer Users Group
Church House Deaneries' Group
Church Schoolmasters' and School Mistresses' Benevolent Institution
Deans' and Provosts' Conference
Deans' and Provosts' Vergers' Conference
Ecclesiastical Law Society
Guildford Diocese Productions
Guild of Pastoral Psychology
Homes for Retired Clergy
Industry Churches Forum
Librarians' Christian Fellowship
MSF Clergy Section
Society of Retreat Conductors
Vergers, Church of England Guild of
See also **Clergy Associations**

Publishing, Print Media
Bray Libraries
Feed the Minds
National Christian Education Council
Rebecca Hussey's Book Charity
Scripture Union
Society for Promoting Christian Knowledge
Trinitarian Bible Society
United Society for Christian Literature

Renewal
Anglican Renewal Ministries
Keswick Convention
SOMA

Research
Arthur Rank Centre
Care Trust
Christian Research
Churches' Fellowship for Psychical and Spiritual Studies
Institute for the Study of Christianity and Sexuality
Keston Institute
Rural Theology Association
St George's House, Windsor
Urban Theology Unit
William Temple Foundation

Rural Affairs
Arthur Rank Centre
Rural Theology Association

Scholarship and Science
Alcuin Club
Canterbury and York Society
Henry Bradshaw Society
Latimer House
Philip Usher Memorial Fund
Public Record Office
Pusey House
Society for Liturgical Study
Society for Old Testament Study
Society of Ordained Scientists
Vacation Term for Biblical Study
Victoria Institute

Social Concern
Age Concern England
Careforce
Changing Attitude
Christian Socialist Movement
Church Action with the Unemployed
Church Housing Trust
English Churches Housing Group
Evangelical Christians for Racial Justice
Lesbian and Gay Christian Movement
Metropolitan Visiting and Relief Association
National Viewers' and Listeners' Association
Order of Christian Unity
Pilsdon Community
St Pancras Housing

Organisations 213

Samaritans
Shaftesbury Society
Social Concern

Training
Administry
Anglican Marriage Encounter
Anglican Stewardship Association
Association of Church Fellowships
Catechumenate Network
Christians at Work
Clinical Theology Association
College of Preachers
GFS Platform for Young Women
Industry Churches Forum
National Christian Education Council
Student Christian Movement
Time Ministries International
William Temple Foundation

Travel, Pilgrimage
Pilgrim Adventure
Walsingham, Shrine of Our Lady of

Welfare
Almshouses, National Association of
Becker's Charity
Bromley and Sheppard's Colleges
Came's Charity
Charterhouse
Church Moral Aid Association
Church of England Soldiers', Sailors' and Airmen's Clubs
Church of England Soldiers', Sailors' and Airmen's Housing Association
Church Schoolmasters' and School Mistresses' Benevolent Institution
Clergy Holidays Society
Community Housing and Therapy
Compassionate Friends
Corporation of the Sons of the Clergy
Crosse's Charity
Diocesan Institutions of Chester, Manchester, Liverpool and Blackburn
DGAA – Homelife
Family Welfare Association
Friends of the Clergy Corporation
Friends of the Elderly
Homes for Retired Clergy
House of St Barnabas in Soho
KeyChange
Langley House Trust
MACA – Partners in Mental Health
Mayflower Family Centre
Mrs Ashton's Charity
Partis College
Pyncombe Charity
Richards Charity
RPS Rainer
St Michael's Fellowship
Samaritans
Seamen's Friendly Society of St Paul
Society for the Assistance of Ladies in Reduced Circumstances
Society for the Relief of Poor Clergymen
Society of Mary and Martha
Toc H
YMCA
Young Women's Christian Association

Worship
Alcuin Club
Praxis
Prayer Book Society

Youth
Barnardo's
Boys' Brigade
Campaigners
Cathedral Camps
Children's Society
Church Lads' and Church Girls' Brigade
Crusaders
Fellowship of St Nicholas
Frontier Youth Trust
Girls' Brigade
Guides Association
Lee Abbey Household Communities
Lee Abbey International Students' Club
London Union of Youth Clubs
RPS Rainer
St Christopher's Fellowship
Scout Association
Shaftesbury Homes and 'Arethusa'
William Temple House

ORGANISATIONS

The following list of societies and organisations with importance for the Church of England includes many that are specifically Anglican, others that are inter-denominational, and others without religious affiliation.
   The inclusion of an organisation is for the purposes of information and is not to be taken as implying acceptance of the objects of the organisation by the Editor and Publishers of the Year Book or by the General Synod.
   A classified list of organisations is provided in the preceding pages. **Diocesan Associations** (in support of overseas provinces and dioceses), **Libraries**, and **Patronage Trusts** are grouped together at the end of the section. See also Part 3 General Information.

Acorn Christian Healing Trust
Founded in 1983 by Bishop Morris Maddocks and his wife Anne to see the Church and nation renewed in the service of Christ the Healer, believing that every person has the right to receive the best care and attention that will enable them to grow into wholeness. Acorn offers all Christian churches a variety of teaching and training resources in Christian healing. Many of these are conducted at Whitehill Chase, Acorn's resource centre in Hampshire, which also holds a weekly open day every Tuesday (10.30 am–3.00 pm) in conjunction with a service of healing. Other components of the Trust's ministry are the Christian Listener Project, which trains people in learning how to offer the gift of listening; the Apostolate, which is the teaming together of someone trained in professional health care with a person with pastoral skills, who together offer care to the whole person; and the training of resource advisers in healing in all major denominations, demonstrating the Trust's commitment to working within the structure of the churches. *Patron:* The Archbishop of Canterbury *Director:* Revd Russ Parker, Whitehill Chase, High St, Bordon, Hants GU35 0AP
Tel: (01420) 478121
Fax: (01420) 478122

Action for Biblical Witness to Our Nation
ABWON was founded 1984 to urge within the Church of England a practical allegiance to and proclamation of biblical theology and morality by upholding the divinity of Christ and his uniqueness as the only way of salvation in all discussions of other faiths and by reaffirming biblical teaching on the sinfulness of fornication, adultery and homosexual practice, whilst encouraging a compassionate approach to those tempted in these areas. *Director:* Revd Tony Higton, Emmanuel Church, Main Rd, Hawkwell, Hockley, Essex SS5 4NR   *Tel:* (01702) 543514
Fax:(01702) 543554
e-mail: TonyHigton@compuserve.com

Actors' Church Union
Founded 1899, members and associates serve those engaged in the performing arts through their interest, their action – often in association with other related bodies – and their prayers. Additionally, more than two hundred honorary chaplains serve all members of the profession in theatres, studios and schools at home and overseas. As well as spiritual counsel and practical advice, material help is given when possible. Through the Children's Charity, for example, funds are available for theatrical parents facing difficulties with the costs of their children's education. *President:* Rt Revd Frank Sargeant *Senior Chaplain:* Canon Bill Hall, St Paul's Church, Bedford St, Covent Garden, London WC2E 9ED
Tel: 0171–836 5221

Additional Curates Society
Founded in 1837 to help maintain additional curates in poor and populous parishes and especially in new areas. The society also fosters vocations to the priesthood. *Chairman:* Ven Bernard Holdridge *Secretary:* Revd Stephen Leach, Gordon Browning House, 8 Spitfire Rd, Birmingham, W Midlands B24 9PB   *Tel:* 0121–382 5533
Fax: 0121–382 6999

Administry
Good management, co-ordination, organisation and leadership are all necessary if the Church is to be effective in its mission. Administry serves churches by helping them organise and co-ordinate their activities. We provide a unique service: publications to give fresh ideas to PCCs and groups, training events for leaders and church members, and consultancy to help churches organise and grow. *Executive Director:* Rob Norman, PO Box 57, St Albans, Herts AL1 3DT   *Tel:* (01727) 856370
Fax: (01727) 843765
e-mail: administry@ibm.net

Affirming Catholicism
A movement within the Church of England and the Anglican Communion, formed in 1990. 'The object of the Foundation shall be the advancement of education in the doctrines and the historical development of the Church of England and the Churches of the wider Anglican Communion, as held by those professing to stand within

Organisations   215

the catholic tradition' (extracted from the Trust Deed). Its purposes are to promote theological thinking about the contemporary implications of Catholic faith and order; to further the spiritual growth and development of clergy and laity; to organise or support lectures, conferences and seminars; to publish or support books, tracts, journals and other educational material; to provide resources for local groups meeting for purposes of study and discussion. *Secretary:* Elizabeth Field, Affirming Catholicism, St Luke's Centre, 90 Central St, London EC1V 8AQ
Tel: 0171–253 1138
Fax: 0171–253 1139

Africa Inland Mission International
An evangelical, inter-denominational and international Mission founded in 1895. It has 750 members working in fourteen countries in Africa and the adjacent islands. The Mission's main aims are to take the gospel to people who have so far been unevangelised and to assist churches to grow strong though it is also involved in other forms of compassionate work. It has particular interest in the training of leaders and plans to increase its work in urban areas and with children. *International Director:* Dr Fred Beam *UK Director:* Revd Timothy Alford, 2 Vorley Rd, Archway, London N19 5HE *Tel:* 0171–281 1184
e-mail: africa.mission@ukonline.co.uk

Age Concern England
(The National Council on Ageing)
The centre of a network of over 1100 independent local Age Concern groups serving the needs of elderly people with help from over 250,000 volunteers. Age Concern England's Governing Body also includes representatives of 95 national organisations and works closely with Age Concern Scotland, Cymru and Northern Ireland. Age Concern groups provide a wide range of services which can include visiting, day care, clubs and specialist services for physically and mentally frail elderly people. Age Concern England supports and advises groups through national Field Officers and a variety of grant schemes. Other work includes training, information, campaigning, and the provision of services such as insurance, tailored to meet the needs of older people. Research is promoted through the Age Concern Institute of Gerontology at King's College. Publications include the annual *Your Rights* and *Your Taxes and Savings* for Pensioners. *Director General:* Sally Greengross, Astral House, 1268 London Rd, London SW16 4ER *Tel:* 0181–679 8000
Fax: 0181–679 6069
e-mail: ace@ace.org.uk
Web: http://www.ace.org.uk/

Alcuin Club
Founded 1897 to promote liturgical studies, the club has a long record of publishing works of liturgical scholarship and more practical publications. It continues to publish Liturgical Studies (jointly with Grove Books) and Collections; new series of handbooks and monographs are planned. The Club organises occasional conferences. Members receive some publications free, others at special rates. *President:* The Bishop of Chichester *Chairman:* Canon Donald Gray *Secretary:* Revd Dr Martin Dudley *Enquiries:* Revd Tim Barker, Alcuin Club, The Parsonage, Church St, Spalding PE11 2PB *Tel:* (01775) 722675
Fax: (01775) 710273
e-mail: tr.barker@cwcom.net

All Nations Christian College
The College came into existence in 1971 following the merger of three Bible Colleges. Whilst interdenominational in character, many of its staff and students are members of the Anglican Communion. Several of the staff are licensed readers and two are ordained Anglicans, including the Principal. The College exists to train students primarily for cross-cultural ministries. The 185 students are mainly post-graduates and follow a two-year theological course incorporating missiological and pastoral lectures. There is also practical training in church work and the development of technical skills appropriate to developing countries. In addition to its own Diploma and Certificate, the College also offers a two-year BA in Biblical and Cross-cultural Studies and a one-year Postgraduate Diploma/MA in Missiology, validated by Open University. Candidates can be accepted for doctoral studies. Many of the students are married and about half are from overseas. A day nursery is provided whilst parents attend lectures. *For details of courses apply to:* The Admissions Secretary, ANCC, Easneye, Ware, Herts SG12 8LX
Tel: (01920) 461243
Fax: (01920) 462997
e-mail: mailbox@allnations.ac.uk
Web: http://www/allnations.ac.uk

Almshouse Association
(National Association of Almshouses)
Is concerned with the preservation and extension of over 1,750 member Almshouse Trusts. A number of major almshouses have a resident Anglican chaplain, or appoint Anglican clergy as Master or Custos of the Foundation. It advises members on any matters concerning almshouses and the welfare of the elderly and aims to promote improvements in almshouses, to promote study and research into all matters affecting almshouses, and to make grants or loans to members. It also keeps under review existing and proposed legislation affecting almshouses and when necessary takes action, and encourages the provision of almshouses. *Exec Ctee Chairman:* Lady Benson *Director:* Anthony Leask, Billingbear Lodge, Wokingham, Berks RG11 5RU *Tel:* (01344) 452922
Fax: (01344) 862062

Ancient Society of College Youths
Established 1637. The College Youths take into member-

ship distinguished and respected bellringers from the British Isles and overseas, wherever English change-ringing is practised. From its headquarters in the City of London the society meets a number of obligations to provide ringers for and maintain the bells of particular churches, and runs a charitable fund that contributes to maintenance costs. *Secretary:* Mr Antony Kench, 40D Cornwall Gardens, London SW7 4AA
Tel: 0171–937 9559
Fax: 0171–938 4786
e-mail: ark@globalnet.co.uk

Anglican and Eastern Churches Association
Founded 1864 to promote mutual understanding of, and closer relations between, the Orthodox, Oriental and Anglican Churches. *Presidents:* Archbishop Gregorios of Thyateira and the Bishop of London. *Chairman:* Revd John Salter *General Secretary:* Revd Philip Warner, St Mark's Vicarage, St Mark's Rd, Teddington, Middx TW11 9DE *Tel:* 0181–977 4067
e-mail: aeca@ssmkjb.demon.co.uk

Anglican Association
Founded in 1969, incorporating the Anglican Society founded 1924, to insist on theological integrity and to maintain the identity of the Church of England, it is traditionalist in both doctrine and liturgy. The Association publishes its own journal the *Anglican Catholic*. *President:* Canon Prof Roy Porter *General Secretary and Treasurer:* Robin Davies, 22 Tyning Rd, Winsley, Bradford on Avon, Wilts BA15 2JJ *Tel:* (01225) 862965

Anglican Association for Social Responsibility
Established in 1985 as a support for its members who work in social responsibility, social work and social projects. The association, which welcomes members from other churches in related fields, provides opportunities for professional development. Regional groups meet regularly to share and support each other in their work. Among other facilities open to members are an annual conference, a national newsletter, retreats, consultations and seminars. *President:* The Bishop of Guildford *Secretary:* Jackie Boys, Diocesan House, 109 Dereham Rd, Easton, Norwich NR9 5ES
Tel: (01603) 881385

Anglican Evangelical Assembly
The Assembly is organised each year by the Church of England Evangelical Council in pursuance of its aim to consult with the evangelical constituency within the Church of England and to foster leadership. Membership is broadly representative of evangelicalism within the dioceses of the Church of England, and of other evangelical interests in the Church such as societies and theological colleges. *President:* The Bishop of Southwell *Chairman:* Preb Richard Bewes *Exec Officer:* Mr Frank Knaggs, PO Box 93, Heaton, Newcastle upon Tyne NE6 5WL *Tel and Fax:* 0191–240 2084
e-mail: CEEC@cableinet.co.uk

Anglican Fellowship in Scouting and Guiding
Founded in 1983 at the request of guiders, scouters and clergy. Its aims are to support leaders and clergy in the religious aspects of the Promise and Law and the training programme in Scouting and Guiding, and to maintain links with other Guide/Scout religious guilds and fellowships in order to foster ecumenical understanding. Individual membership is open to persons aged 15 years or over who are members of the Scout and Guide movements, or others (e.g. clergy) who are sympathetic to the aims of Guiding and Scouting. Collective membership is available for Scout Groups and Guide Units (which do not have to be church sponsored), and for Anglican churches. *Secretary:* Mrs June Davies, 31 Loseley Rd, Farncombe, Godalming GU7 3RE *Tel:* (01483) 428876

Anglican Group Educational Trust
Formed in 1973 to assist women engaged in theological studies or work within the Church of England and to carry out such other legally charitable purposes for the advancement of the Ministry of Women within the Church of England as the Trustees shall from time to time decide. The Trust currently awards scholarships for women clergy who wish to study abroad as part of their career development or sabbatical leave. Applications for the Roxburgh Scholarships for 2000 will be considered in September 1999. Application forms and details of the Trust may be obtained from the *Chair:* Canon Joy Tetley, c/o EAMTC Office, 5 Pound Hill, Cambridge CB3 0AE

Anglican Marriage Encounter
Anglican Marriage Encounter is a voluntary organisation which offers residential and non-residential programmes for married and engaged couples to review and deepen their relationship by developing a compelling vision for their marriage, and providing the communication skills to support this. *Episcopal adviser:* Rt Revd Michael Scott-Joynt *Lay Executive couple:* Dr & Mrs P. J. Cox, 5 Hillside Way, Welwyn, Herts AL6 0TY *Tel:* (01438) 715337

Anglican Pacifist Fellowship
Founded 1937. Members pledged to renounce war and all preparation to wage war and to work for the construction of Christian peace in the world. Bi-monthly Newsletter *Challenge*. *Chairman:* Revd Sidney Hinkes *Hon Secretary:* Dr Tony Kempster, 11 Weavers End, Hanslope, Milton Keynes MK19 7PA *Tel:* (01908) 510642
e-mail: Kempster@compuserve.com

Anglican Renewal Ministries
Established in 1980 to encourage charismatic renewal in the Church of England. Produces training courses for

churches and groups and runs residential and one-day conferences in various parts of the country and a quarterly magazine *Anglicans for Renewal*. *Director:* Revd John Leach, 42 Friar Gate, Derby DE1 1DA
Tel: (01332) 200175
Fax: (01332) 200185
e-mail: ARMDerby@aol.com
Web: http://www.members.aol.com/ARMDerby

Anglican Society for the Welfare of Animals
Founded 1972, for the purpose of including the whole creation in the redemptive love of Christ and especially for prayer, study and action on behalf of animals. *President:* Rt Revd John Austin Baker *Chairman:* Rt Revd Dominic Walker OGS *Treasurer:* Revd Kenneth Hewitt *Correspondence Secretary:* Mrs S. J. Chandler, The Old Toll Gate, Hound Green, Hook, Hants RG27 8LQ
Tel: (01189) 326586

Anglican Stewardship Association
A registered charity formed to promote the ideals of responsible ownership and giving amongst Christians and the Church. The association's aim is to assist Christians at parish, deanery and diocesan level to address issues of money and wealth-handling and thus to make full use of all the latent resources of the Church so that its mission may be fully developed. *General Secretary:* Mrs Carol Sims, 71 Dee Banks, Chester CH3 5UX
Tel: (01244) 341996
Fax: (01244) 400338
e-mail: peter@patent.u-net.com

Anglican Voluntary Societies Forum
Founded in 1980 to promote understanding and co-operation between the Voluntary Societies and the Boards and Councils of the General Synod. To be eligible for membership, societies must be Anglican, national, and involved in mission. The Forum meets two or three times a year to discuss matters of mutual concern. *Chairman:* Mrs Daphne Cook (Chairman of the Trustees of Family Life and Marriage Education). *Secretary:* Mr Robert Wellen, General Synod Office, Church House, Great Smith St, London SW1P 3NZ *Tel:* 0171–898 1371
Fax: 0171–898 1369
e-mail: synod@church-house-coe-london.org.uk

Anglican-Lutheran Society
Founded in 1984 to pray for the unity of the Church and especially the Anglican and Lutheran Communions; to encourage opportunities for common worship, study, friendship and witness; to encourage a wider interest in and knowledge of the Anglican and Lutheran traditions and contemporary developments within them. The society publishes a newsletter, *The Window*, organises conferences, lectures and other events. *Co-Presidents:* Rt Revd David Tustin and Rt Revd Erik Vikstrom. *Co-Moderators:* Revd Ronald T. Englund and Rt Revd Gordon Roe. *Secretary:* Mrs Valerie Phillips, 8 Eldon Rd, Bournemouth, Dorset BH9 2RT *Tel:* (01202) 535127

Animal Christian Concern
Founded 1985 with the following aims: (1) to express the view that cruelty of any kind is incompatible with Jesus Christ's teachings of love, that love is indivisible and that cruelty towards any sentient creature is a breach of love; (2) to hold services for Animal Welfare; (3) to oppose such practices as animal experimentation, intensive farming, fur trade and blood sports. *President:* Most Revd Alwyn Rice Jones, Archbishop of Wales. *Patrons:* Revd Lord Soper, Very Revd John Southgate, Monsignor Michael Buckley, Rt Revd John Austin Baker. *Co-ordinator:* Mrs May Tripp, PO Box 70, Leeds LS18 5UX
Tel: 0113–258 3517

Archbishop's Examination in Theology
(leading to the Lambeth Diploma of Student in Theology (S Th))
Founded 1905 to provide a means of scholarly theological study. Originally for women, but opened to men in 1944, it can be taken by thesis, for suitably qualified candidates, or by examination. A limited number of candidates with good theological qualifications may register for a Lambeth MA by thesis. *Hon Director:* Rt Revd Geoffrey Rowell *Hon Secretary:* Canon Martin Kitchen, 3 The College, Durham DH1 3EQ *Tel:* 0191–384 2415

Archbishops' (Canterbury and Westminster) Certificate in Church Music
Founded 1961 to provide a minimum qualification for church organists, choirmasters, cantors and instrumentalists. Now fully ecumenical. *Information from General Secretary:* Mr John Ewington, Guild of Church Musicians, Hillbrow, Godstone Rd, Bletchingley, Surrey RH1 4PJ *Tel* and *Fax:* (01883) 741854

Archway
Anglican Retreat and Conference House Wardens' Association. Promotes the use of retreat and conference houses as a vital contribution to the life and development of Church and community. *Secretary:* Mr Peter Fletcher, Wydale Hall, Brompton by Sawdon, Scarborough, N Yorks YO13 9DG *Tel:* (01723) 859270
Fax: (01723) 859702

Art and Christianity Enquiry (ACE)
Begun in 1991 ACE draws together all for whom the visual arts are vital in their understanding, teaching and practice of the faith. Now a charitable trust, it organises lectures, undertakes research, energises, encourages. Quarterly bulletin by subscription, complimentary copy on request. *Director:* Revd Tom Devonshire Jones, 4 Regent's Park Rd, London NW1 7TX
Tel and *Fax:* 0171–482 3006

Arthur Rank Centre

Established 1972 as a collaborative venture between the Churches, the Royal Agricultural Society of England and the Rank Foundation. It is fully ecumenical and recognised as the rural focus and resource centre for churches nationally. It provides the secretariat for the Churches' Rural Group, a representative ecumenical body which is a network of the Churches Together in England and of the Council of Churches in Britain and Ireland. It runs clergy courses especially for those recently appointed to rural areas. Members of staff are peripatetic and are available for consultations and local conferences. The Diocesan Rural Officers meet regularly with the Church of England Rural Officer who is a member of staff. It is also concerned with rural community issues and with farming and environmental matters. Recent initiatives have been the Rural Stress Information Network, the National Churches Tourism Group, the Church and Community Fund, study panels on the ethics of land ownership and animal welfare. It also produces material for rural churches including the magazine *Country Way*. *Director:* Revd John Clarke, Arthur Rank Centre, National Agricultural Centre, Stoneleigh Park, Warws CV8 2LZ
Tel: (01203) 696969
Fax: (01203) 414808
e-mail: arthur.rank.centre@virgin.net
Web: http://freespace.virgin.net/arthur_rank.centre

Association for Promoting Retreats

Founded in 1913 to foster the growth of the spiritual life in the Anglican Communion by the practice of retreats. Welcomes as members all Christians in sympathy with this aim. Membership by subscription for individuals, parishes and retreat houses. The APR is one of the six retreat groups which form the National Retreat Association (*see* separate entry). *Administrator:* Paddy Lane, The Central Hall, 256 Bermondsey St, London SE1 3UJ
Tel: 0171–357 7736
Fax: 0171–357 7724

Association of Black Clergy

Founded 1982 to provide support for each other, identification of issues of social justice and theological reflection upon them, and action in the community and church which will be a sign of the association's commitment to 'kingdom' principles. *Chairman:* Revd Charles Lawrence *Secretary:* Revd Theo Samuel *Facilitator:* Canon Ivor Smith-Cameron, 100 Prince of Wales Drive, London SW11 4BD
Tel and *Fax:* 0171–622 3809

Association of Christian Teachers

Formed in 1971 from three existing Christian teacher organisations to unite Christians in education and to work at bringing Christian insights and values into education at all levels and into every subject. ACT runs a variety of courses on educational subjects for teachers, administrators, parents and church leaders at its study centre, Stapleford House. ACT is represented on the Religious Education Council and has been actively involved in the current debate about religious education as well as wider issues in education. It publishes a magazine, *ACT NOW, The Journal of Education and Christian Belief*, the RE resource magazine *Digest*, and other specialist publications. It has fifty local groups and regularly organises education conferences. It is in partnership with the Stapleford Centre for Educational Research, Training and Resources. *General Secretary:* Mr Richard Wilkins, ACT, 94A London Rd, St Albans, Herts AL1 1NX
Tel: (01727) 840298

Association of Christian Writers

A group of Christians who wish to serve God in the field of writing. Some members are professional writers, others part time and many are beginners in different areas of writing. Three writers' days a year are held and many local groups meet regularly. Members receive a quarterly magazine and a manuscript criticism service is available. *Administrator:* Warren Crawford, 73 Lodge Hill Rd, Farnham, Surrey GU10 3RB
Tel and *Fax:* (01252) 715746
e-mail: admacw@dial.pipex.com
Web: http://dspace.dial.pipex.com/admacw

Association of Church College Trusts

In 1979 the Association of Church College Trusts was established as a loosely knit organisation to facilitate an exchange of information and co-operation. It meets every six months. The Church College Trusts were formed following the closure of their respective Colleges of Education. They are autonomous, answerable only to the Charity Commission; their financial management policies are such that they are required both to sponsor present work from their income and also to ensure that their capital is maintained at a level that can finance similar levels of work in the future. In the last 18 years they have been involved in helping individual teachers, students and others, sponsoring corporate projects in part or in total, and aiding schools, colleges and church educational activities. They also maintain certain residual college functions relating to former students and staff such as keeping records, giving references and holding reunions. The individual Trusts are:

ALL SAINTS EDUCATIONAL TRUST
Personal awards to teachers, intending teachers, students in dietetics. Not assisted-school pupils, students in counselling, engineering, law, medicine, ordination, social work. Corporate awards – imaginative new projects which will enhance the Church's contribution to higher

and further education. Date for applications 31 January each year.
Correspondent: Mr Alfred Bush, St Katherine Cree Church, 86 Leadenhall St, London EC3A 3DH   *Tel:* 0171-283 4485
Fax: 0171–283 2920

CULHAM EDUCATIONAL FOUNDATION
The Trust gives mainly personal grants not exceeding £1000 to practising Anglicans who are pursuing personal study or undertaking projects or research primarily relating to RE in schools. Consideration is also given to similar type of work relating to parish and church school education and, for Anglican clergy, to general school issues.
Correspondent: Mrs S. Thirkettle, The Malthouse, 60 East St Helen St, Abingdon, Oxon OX14 5EB
Tel: (01235) 520458
Fax: (01235) 535421
e-mail: enquiries@culham.ac.uk

HOCKERILL EDUCATIONAL FOUNDATION
Applications considered from persons seeking teaching qualifications – the priority subject being Religious Education. Counselling courses or clergy in full time parochial ministry are not considered.
Correspondent: Mr D. J. Newman, 'Ingrebourne', 51 Pole Barn Lane, Frinton-on-Sea, Essex CO13 9NQ
Tel: (01255) 676509
Fax: (01255) 851529

ST GABRIEL'S TRUST
The object of the Trust is the advancement of higher and further education in Religious Education. Grants are made to foster good practice in RE teaching.
Correspondent: Mr P. M. Duffell, Ladykirk, 32 The Ridgeway, Enfield, Middx EN2 8QH   *Tel:* 0181-363 6474

KESWICK HALL CHARITY
The Trustees' spending gives priority to their own initiatives, but they also give grants in response to personal or corporate applicants for research or study in Religious Education. Within this field, they give priority to teachers or student teachers and to work in East Anglia.
Correspondent: Mrs H. Herrington, School of Education and Professional Development, University of East Anglia, Norwich NR4 7TJ   *Tel:* (01603) 505975
e-mail: a.m.miller@uea.ac.uk

ST LUKE'S COLLEGE FOUNDATION
The foundation is a Church of England Trust set up to promote Religious Education. Grants are awarded for research projects, work, producing publications and higher degrees in this field.
Correspondent: Dr P. S. Uzzell, 35 Argyll Rd, Exeter EX4 4RX   *Tel:* (01392) 276825

ST MARY'S COLLEGE TRUST
The Trust's annual income is normally committed to supporting the Welsh National Centre for Religious Education and the Anglican Chaplaincy at the University of Wales, Bangor. As a result, grants to individuals and other institutions are only awarded in very exceptional circumstances.
Correspondent: Mr Gwilym T. Jones, Chwarel Plas, Llangefni, Anglesey, Gwynedd   *Tel:* (01248) 382934
Fax: (01248) 372187

FOUNDATION OF ST MATTHIAS
Considers applications for grants for higher and further education, priority being given to residents of Bristol, Bath and Wells, and Gloucester dioceses and to courses with a teaching/RE element. Second degrees are not normally considered.
Correspondent: Mrs V. Prater, Diocesan Church House, 23 Great George St, Bristol BS1 5QZ   *Tel:* 0117–921 4411.

SARUM ST MICHAEL EDUCATIONAL CHARITY
Further and higher education – preference given to those living or working in the diocese of Salisbury.
Correspondent: Mrs Diana Arundale, 13 New Canal, Salisbury, Wilts SP1 2AA   *Tel:* (01722) 422296

ST HILD AND ST BEDE TRUST
The Trust's annual income is restricted to the advancement of higher and further education in the dioceses of Durham and Newcastle and is presently committed to supporting the North of England Institute for Christian Education, the North East Religious Learning Resources Centre, several lectureships, chaplaincies (in particular the chaplaincy in the College of St Hild and St Bede), scholarships, libraries and a demonstration school.
Correspondent: Mrs Mary Gullick, c/o The College of St Hild and St Bede, University of Durham, Durham DH1 1SZ
Tel: 0191–374 3083

ST PETER'S SALTLEY TRUST
The Trust's annual income is committed to initiating, supporting and evaluating locally based projects in adult theological education, further education and RE development in schools. The Trust's area of benefit comprises the region covered by the Anglican dioceses of Birmingham, Coventry, Hereford, Lichfield, and Worcester. The Trust does not make grants to individuals for research or continuing education purposes.
Correspondent: Mrs J. E. Jones, Grays Court, 3 Nursery Rd, Edgbaston, Birmingham B15 3JX   *Tel:* 0121–427 6800

ST CHRISTOPHER'S COLLEGE TRUST
Correspondent: Mr D. Grimes, The National Society, Church House, Great Smith St, London SW1P 3NZ
Tel: 0171–898 1492
Fax: 0171–898 1520
e-mail: ns@natsoc.demon.co.uk

Please note that applications have to be made to the individual Trusts concerned and not centrally through the Association.

SECRETARY TO THE ASSOCIATION OF CHURCH COLLEGE TRUSTS
Revd Dr John Gay, Director, Culham College Institute, 60 East Saint Helen St, Abingdon, Oxon OX14 5EB
Tel: (01235) 520458
e-mail: enquiries@culham.ac.uk

Association of Church Fellowships
Founded 1963. Sponsored by clergy and laity to meet a growing need in this country and overseas to encourage and enable the laity to take their full part in the life and work of the Church in open groups and in co-operation with existing groups. *Patrons:* Archbishops of Canterbury and York *National Chairman:* Canon Stanley Owen, Bickenhill House, 154 Lode Lane, Solihull, W Midlands B91 2HP   Tel: 0121–704 9281

Association of English Cathedrals
Established in 1990 and authorised by the Administrative Chapters of the Anglican Cathedrals as their representative organisation, the AEC deals with governmental agencies, the General Synod, and their constituent bodies and the Churches' Main Committee on behalf of the English cathedrals, provided only that it cannot commit any individual cathedral chapter to a specific decision. It monitors the negotiations resulting from the Archbishops' Commission on Cathedrals. Membership consists of one representative of each Administrative Chapter. *Chairman:* Very Revd Raymond Furnell, Dean of York *Secretary:* Very Revd Edward Shotter, The Deanery, Rochester, Kent ME1 1TG   Tel: (01634) 844023
Fax: (01634) 401410

Association of Hospice Chaplains
The Association of Hospice Chaplains seeks to promote the provision of good pastoral and spiritual care in hospice and palliative care units. It offers training and support for clergy involved (whether on a full-time or part-time basis) by means of advice about appointments, induction, and training courses. St Columba's Hospice, Edinburgh and St Christopher's Hospice, Sydenham both provide courses for chaplains newly appointed, and many hospices offer placements and courses which form part of pre- and post-ordination training. The Association monitors professional developments within the constituency of palliative care, and maintains a networking relationship with the College of Health Care Chaplains. It also offers a three-day residential training course for practising chaplains each spring (usually at All Saints Pastoral Centre, London Colney). Enquiries are welcome via the Chaplain's Office, St Christopher's Hospice, 51–59 Lawrie Park Rd, Sydenham, London SE26 6DZ *Hon Secretary:* Revd John Casselton, St Elizabeth's Hospice, 565 Foxhall Rd, Ipswich IP3 8LX

Association of Ordinands and Candidates for Ministry
Founded in 1968, AOCM currently represents over one thousand ordinands from all of the Anglican theological colleges, courses, schemes and institutes in England, Ireland, Scotland and Wales. At three conferences per year, representatives from these institutions meet to discuss issues related to theological training. The Chair of AOCM, who is a member of the ABM Board, communicates the conclusions of these conferences to those who make decisions affecting ordinands. The Association publishes *Training for Ministry*, an annual handbook for ordinands. *Chairperson:* Dr Meg Gilley, Dunelm Mount, 36 Western Hill, Durham DH1 4RJ   Tel: 0191–384 1504
e-mail: meg.gilley@zetnet.co.uk

Baptismal Reform Movement
See **MORIB** page 244.

Barnardo's
Founded 1866. Barnardo's works with over 30,000 children, young people, and their families. The charity finds its inspiration in the Christian faith and its work is enriched and shared by people of other faiths and philosophies. Barnardo's operates as a separate charity in the Republic of Ireland, Australia and New Zealand. Working in partnership with local authorities, parents, voluntary agencies and churches, Barnardo's runs over 285 community based services which include: fostering and adoption, day care, family support services, youth and community work and services for young people with physical and learning difficulties. *Chair of Council:* Revd D. Gamble *Senior Director:* Mr Roger Singleton, Tanners Lane, Barkingside, Essex IG6 1QG
Tel: 0181–550 8822

Becker's (Mrs) Charity for Clergy
Founded 1852 to provide relief, either generally or individually, to clergy of the United Church of England and Ireland retired through sickness or age and who are in conditions of need, hardship or distress. Grants of money or providing or paying for items, services or facilities, not exceeding £50 p.a. at the discretion of the Trustees. *Chairman:* Senior of the four trustees *Secretary:* Mr A. P. Newman, 71 Eastfield Ave, Weston, Bath BA1 4HH
Tel: (01225) 424229

Bible Reading Fellowship
Founded 1922 to encourage and promote growth in the knowledge of God through devotional Bible reading and study. Provides daily Bible readings, study materials and resources for Advent, Lent, Confirmation, Prayer and Spirituality, for both individual and group use. BRF's

Organisations

Barnabas imprint provides resources for children under the age of 11. *President:* Rt Revd Lord Coggan *Chairman:* The Bishop of Southwell *Chief Exec:* Mr Richard Fisher, Peter's Way, Sandy Lane West, Oxford OX4 5HG
Tel: (01865) 748227
Fax: (01865) 773150
e-mail: enquiries@brf.org.uk

Bible Society
Bible Society is committed to changing attitudes, changing minds, and opening people's hearts to the Bible by developing campaigning programmes to highlight the relevance of the Bible in today's world. The Society aims to tune into twenty-first-century culture and use dynamic formats and media to communicate the Scriptures both at home and overseas. *Chief Exec:* Mr Neil Crosbie, Bible Society, Stonehill Green, Westlea, Swindon, Wilts SN5 7DG
Tel: (01793) 418100
Fax: (01793) 418118
e-mail: corpcom@bfbs.org.uk

Blind, Royal National Institute for the (RNIB)
RNIB is Britain's largest organisation working on behalf of blind and partially sighted people. It runs over sixty different services for blind people. It aims to improve the quality of life of all visually impaired people by promoting the same opportunities and choices that sighted people enjoy – in education, training, employment, health and leisure. To achieve this RNIB provides a wide range of practical services, advice, information and special equipment. RNIB runs schools for blind children of all abilities. It equips people for work by offering training and advice on special equipment to employers and employees. RNIB designs and sells specially adapted equipment and games, and publishes a wide range of material in Braille, Moon and on tape. It runs Braille and tape libraries, including the well-known RNIB Talking Book Service. It also runs residential care homes, holiday hotels and rehabilitation centres. Research into the prevention of blindness, and into the needs of visually impaired people, is also a part of RNIB's work. *President:* His Grace the Duke of Westminster *Chairman:* Mr John Wall *Director-General:* Mr Ian Bruce, 224 Great Portland St, London W1N 6AA
Tel: 0171–388 1266

Blind, St John's Guild for the
Founded 1919 to bring blind and partially sighted people more closely into the life of the Church. There are twenty-five branches in the UK meeting regularly to share in worship, fellowship and friendship. A quarterly magazine *The Church Messenger* in Braille, Moon and on tape is produced and a newsletter three times a year in Braille, Moon, Tape, Large print and print. A Residential Home is maintained at St Albans. The Guild administers the Braille Bible Reading Fellowship. *Warden:* Revd Graeme Hands *General Secretary:* Margaret Chambers,

8 St Raphaels Court, Avenue Rd, St Albans, Herts AL1 3EH
Tel: (01727) 864076

Boys' Brigade
Founded 1883 for the advancement of Christ's Kingdom among boys and the promotion of habits of obedience, reverence, discipline, self-respect and all that tends towards a true Christian manliness. *Brigade Secretary:* Mr Sydney Jones, Felden Lodge, Felden, Hemel Hempstead, Herts HP3 0BL
Tel: (01442) 231681
e-mail: felden@boys-brigade.org.uk
Web: http://www.boys.brigade.org.uk

Bray Libraries
Assist the establishment of small libraries within parochial, deanery or diocesan groups in UK and overseas, where there is significant Anglican participation. Financed by subscriptions and a trust fund substantially augmented by a grant from SPCK. *Contact:* The Project Co-ordinator, SPCK Worldwide, Holy Trinity Church, Marylebone Rd, London NW1 4DU
Tel: 0171–387 5282
Fax: 0171–387 3411
e-mail: spckww@spck.org.uk
Web: http://www.spck.org.uk

British Deaf Association
The British Deaf Association was founded over one hundred years ago and is the Association of the Deaf people of this country, liaison being maintained through its Area Councils and some 178 local branches. It is principally concerned with the welfare and needs of people most profoundly affected by deafness, those who were born deaf or who were deafened in childhood. Provides services and information on sign language, interpreters, citizen and community advocacy, youth, and health promotion. Publishes a monthly magazine. Holidays are organised. *Chairman:* Mr A. Murray Holmes *Chief Exec:* Jeff McWhinney, 38 Victoria Place, Carlisle, Cumbria CA1 1HU
Tel: (01228) 48844 (Voice/text)
Fax: (01228) 41420

Broken Rites
Formed in 1983, Broken Rites is an independent association of divorced and separated wives of Anglican clergy and ministers of Non-Established Churches, living in the United Kingdom. We affirm the Christian ideal of life-long marriage. We welcome the support of everyone who is in sympathy with our aims, which are to support one another with sympathy and understanding and practical help where possible; to continue to draw the attention of the Churches to the problems of ex-wives of the clergy; and to promote a more vivid awareness among Christian people of the increasing incidence of clergy marriage breakdown and the implications for the witness of the Church and its teaching on marriage. *Chairman:* Mrs

Wendy Catley *Hon Secretary:* Christine McMullen, 114 Brown Edge Rd, Buxton, Derbys SK17 7AB
Tel: (01298) 73997
e-mail: christin@noc6.u-net.com

Bromley and Sheppard's Colleges

Bromley College was founded in 1666 to provide houses for clergy widows and Sheppard's College in 1840 to provide houses for unmarried daughters of clergy widows, who had lived with their mothers at Bromley College. Houses in both colleges have been converted into flats and widows/widowers of clergy, retired clergymen and their spouses, divorced and separated spouses of clergy or retired clergy of the Church of England, the Church in Wales, the Scottish Episcopal Church or the Church of Ireland may now be admitted. Unmarried daughters or stepdaughters of a deceased former resident may also apply. Contact the *Chaplain/Clerk to the Trustees:* Chaplain's Office, Bromley & Sheppard's Colleges, London Rd, Bromley, Kent BR1 1PE
Tel: 0181–460 4712

Burrswood

Christian Centre for Health Care and Ministry Burrswood was founded by Dorothy Kerin who received a commission from God to 'heal the sick, comfort the sorrowing and give faith to the faithless'. The Dorothy Kerin Trust is a registered charity, administered by a board of trustees. The main buildings, set in beautiful surroundings, comprise a Christian non-surgical hospital with 35 beds for short-term inpatient care and an interdisciplinary team of resident doctors, nurses, physiotherapists and counsellors; a church with two resident chaplains which is fully integrated with the hospital and has healing services open to the public four times a week; a guest/retreat house with single and twin rooms, sleeping 15; a physio and hydrotherapy complex for inpatients and outpatients, a medical and counselling outpatient facility and a conference centre for up to 40 delegates. *Director:* Dr Gareth Tuckwell *Senior Chaplain:* Revd Michael Fulljames, Burrswood, Groombridge, nr Tunbridge Wells, Kent TN3 9PY
Tel: (01892) 863637
(Enquiries) (01892) 863818 (Admissions)
Fax: (01892) 863623

Bush Brotherhoods

Founded 1897 to preach the Gospel and administer the Sacraments to members of the Anglican Communion in the Outback of Australia. *President:* The Bishop of Rockhampton *Secretary:* Revd C. N. Lavender, 25 Holme Cottages, The Great Hospital, Norwich, Norfolk NR1 4EL
Tel: (01603) 665524

Came's Charity for Clergymen's Widows

Founded to provide small pensions to benefit clergy widows who are wanting. *Apply:* The Clerk Worshipful Company of Cordwainers, Eldon Chambers, 30 Fleet St, London EC4Y 1AA
Tel: 0171–353 4309
Fax: 0171–583 4931

Campaigners

Founded 1922 this Christian youth organisation is committed to providing a modern local church structured programme, catering for the mental, physical and spiritual needs of young people in an exciting relevant way. Campaigners teach the Bible and the Gospel, not only in word but also through practical activity and relationship building pursuits. Further details from the *Director General:* Revd Kenneth Argent, Campaigner House, Colney Heath, Herts AL4 0NQ
Tel: (01727) 824065

Canterbury and York Society

Founded 1904 for the printing of bishops' registers and other ecclesiastical records. *Jt Presidents:* The Archbishops of Canterbury and York. *Chairman:* Prof D. M. Smith *Secretary:* Prof Christopher Harper-Bill, 15 Cusack Close, Twickenham, Middx TW1 4TB
Tel: 0181–892 0500

CARE Trust

CARE (Christian Action Research and Education) is a registered charity concerned to promote and defend Christian family values, particularly marriage and the sanctity of life. As an interdenominational evangelical charity, it is a resource centre for all who wish to strengthen marriage and the family, to see a strong Christian influence in national education and to create compassionate parallel programmes directed towards those who are in need. CARE Campaigns is an associated body concerned more directly with changes in the law. Other departments include Caring Services, CARE for Education, CARE for Europe, CARE for Life, and Ethics Development Initiative and an international department. *Exec Director:* Mr Charles Colchester, 53 Romney St, London SW1P 3RF
Tel: 0171–233 0455
Fax: 0171–233 0983
e-mail: mail@care.org.uk
Web: http://www.care.org.uk

Careforce

Founded in 1980 to serve churches and Christian projects by recruiting volunteers age 18 to 25 to spend a year in the UK and Eire engaged in youth and outreach ministries in local churches, serving homeless people, the elderly, those with difficult family situations, those with addiction difficulties, and those with learning difficulties or physical disability. *Director:* Revd Ian Prior, 577 Kingston Rd, London SW20 8SA
Tel: 0181–543 8671
Fax: 0181–540 0113
e-mail: enquiry@careforce.co.uk
Web: http://www.careforce.co.uk

Catechumenate Network

The network promotes the use of the Catechumenate – the Adult Way to Faith – by means of training, seminars

and the exchange of information about the preparation of adults for baptism and confirmation. Publications include a parish Starter Pack. Membership is open to individuals (lay or ordained), parishes, chaplaincies and diocesan organisations. The Adult Way to Faith emphasises welcome, accompanied journey into faith, celebration of stages of commitment and a strong ministry for lay people with experience of Christian community, as outlined in *On the Way*. The Catechumenate Network is ecumenical in approach and is a founder member of the international network incorporating Roman Catholic, Anglican and Presbyterian traditions. *Contact:* Canon Peter Ball, Whittonedge, Whittonditch Rd, Ramsbury, Wilts SN8 2PX
Tel and *Fax:* (01672) 520259

Cathedral and Church Shops Association
The Cathedral and Church Shops Association provides a forum for the exchange of information amongst its members. It arranges an annual conference and trade fair in November and sponsors meetings of staff from cathedral and church shops in different areas of the country each spring. It also gives advice and assistance for the setting up and running of church shops from experienced shop managers. Membership is open to the staff of any shop operating within, or associated with, a cathedral or church and which is open for trading for five or six days a week all the year or during the visitor season of the area which it serves. *Chairman:* Mr John Simmons *Secretary:* Mrs Gill Green, Cathedral Enterprises (St Albans) Ltd, St Albans Cathedral, St Albans AL1 1BY
Tel: (01727) 864738
Fax: (01727) 850944
e-mail: cathedra@alban.u-net.com
Web: http://www.stalbansdioc.org.uk/cathedral/

Cathedral Camps
Organises working summer holidays for young people between 16 and 30, though most are under 25, at cathedrals and large churches in Britain. Volunteers help to conserve and restore parts of these ancient buildings which might well be neglected otherwise. The sort of work available varies enormously. It is unskilled, but often demanding. It offers the privilege of close contact with magnificent buildings and with those who work full-time there. Volunteers are asked to contribute £45.00 towards the cost of the camp, though bursaries are available. Accommodation and food are basic, but the enthusiasm and comradeship generated by a week together overcomes most hardships. There are no religious expectations or restrictions, but most have had some contact with the Church in its different traditions. Volunteers come from Britain and Europe, as well as other parts of the world. There is a heavy demand for places. *Chairman:* Robert Aagaard *Administrator and Booking Secretary:* Shelley Bent, 16 Glebe Ave, Flitwick, Beds MK45 1HS
Tel: (01525) 716237
e-mail: Cathedralcamps@compuserve.com
Web: http://www.summerfield-group.co.uk/cathedralcamps

Cathedrals Administration and Finance Association (CAFA)
In 1975 cathedral administrators and treasurers began, as a body, to exchange information on all matters touching on best practice and the most effective administration of the English Anglican cathedrals. The association now enjoys a valued link with the Association of English Cathedrals for which organisation it undertakes research as needed. There is an annual conference and regular regional meetings. *Chairman:* Canon David Mead *Admin Secretary:* Mr Jamie Milford, Church Commissioners, 1 Millbank, London SW1P 3JZ
Tel: 0171–898 1000

Catholic Group in General Synod
The Catholic Group consists of those on General Synod committed to the catholic, traditional and orthodox voice in the Church of England. It seeks to make a positive contribution to all debates and especially where Catholic faith and order are involved. It welcomes both the ARCIC discussions and dialogue with the Orthodox churches. The group maintains that ethical teaching which scripture and tradition have consistently upheld. It is not averse to change where contemporary church life demands it, but stands firm on a Gospel that is based on God's revelation of Himself as Father, Son and Holy Spirit. Members represent a variety of practice within the doctrinal framework. *Chairman:* Ven Robin Ellis *Secretary:* Mrs Anne Williams, 30 Blackhills Terrace, Horden, Co Durham SR8 4LJ
Tel: 0191–586 7238

Catholic League
Founded in 1913 with the aim of promoting fellowship among Catholics. Its special objects are the union of all Christians with the Apostolic See of Rome, the spread of the Catholic Faith, and the deepening of the spiritual lives of the members. It is governed by a Priest Director, the General Secretary and a Council of elected members. Further details from the *General Secretary:* Mr Geoffrey Wright, 205 Merlin House, Napier Rd, Enfield, Middx EN3 4QN
Tel: 0181–805 5107
Fax: 0181–292 4520

Central Council of Church Bell Ringers
Founded 1891. Its aims are to promote the ringing of church bells, to represent the ringing exercise to the world at large and to provide expert information and advice to ringers, church authorities and the general public on all matters relating to bells and bell ringing. *President:* Mrs Jane Wilkinson *Hon Secretary:* Mr Christopher

Rogers, 50 Cramhurst Lane, Witley, Godalming, Surrey GU8 5QZ *Tel* and *Fax:* (01428) 682790

Centre for International Briefing
The Centre, which occupies Farnham Castle, is an independent organisation founded in 1953. Its purpose is to help men and women who have been recruited to work overseas by Government, the private sector or the Churches, to gain a deeper understanding and appreciation of the societies and aspirations of the peoples of the countries in which they are to be resident with the aim that they may live and work among them successfully. Financial assistance to cover some part of course fees, in the form of bursaries, is available to missionary and charitable organisations. *Director:* Mr David Ellison, Farnham Castle, Farnham, Surrey GU9 0AG *Tel:* (01252) 721194
Fax: (01252) 711283
e-mail: cib.farnham@dial.pipex.com
Web: http://www.cibfarnham.com

Charterhouse
(Sutton's Hospital)
Founded 1611. Residence and care for bachelors and widowers of limited means, retired from the services, business or the professions. *Apply to:* The Master, Charterhouse, London EC1M 6AH *Tel:* 0171–253 9503

Children's Society
A voluntary organisation of the Church of England and the Church in Wales. Established in 1881, the Society is one of Britain's leading children's charities with over 90 projects throughout England and Wales. The Society not only works alongside some of the country's most vulnerable children and young people, it actively campaigns for the rights of all children in the UK. The Society works with children with disabilities and their families; runaways, out on the streets, afraid and in danger; children and families living in some of Britain's most deprived areas; teenagers just out of children's homes with no family of their own to turn to. The Society relies on the prayers and support of Church members to carry out this important work. *Chairman:* The Bishop of Bath and Wells *Chaplain Missioner:* Revd John Bradford *Chief Exec:* Mr Ian Sparks, Edward Rudolf House, Margery St, London WC1X 0JL *Tel:* 0171–837 4299
Fax: 0171–837 0211
e-mail: communications@the.childrens.society.org.uk
Web: http://www.the-childrens-society.org.uk

Choir Benevolent Fund
Founded 1851. A registered Friendly Society for subscribing Cathedral and Collegiate Lay Clerks and Organists. *Trustees:* The Deans of St Paul's, Westminster and Windsor. *Secretary:* Mr Roland Tatnell, Foxearth Cottage, Frittenden, Cranbrook, Kent *Tel:* (01580) 712825

Choir Schools Association
Founded 1919 to promote the welfare of cathedral, collegiate and parish church choir schools. In 1985 it set up a bursary trust to help children from low income families become choristers. *Chairman:* Mr C. Brown *Administrator:* Mrs Wendy Jackson, CSA, The Minster School, Deangate, York YO1 7JA *Tel:* (01904) 624900

Christian Aid
See page 164.

Christian Alliance
See **KeyChange** page 241.

Christian Arts
An association of artists, architects, designers, craftsmen and women and all involved in the arts who are committed Christians and wish to explore and deepen their relationship between their faith and the arts. Its activities include holding exhibitions and an annual conference. An illustrated journal is published quarterly. *Contact:* Revd Michael Day, 40 Thistlewaite Rd, London E5 0QQ
Tel: 0181–985 8568

Christian Education Movement
(Incorporating Student Christian Movement in Schools and Institute of Christian Education)
Founded in 1965, a servicing and support agency for teachers concerned with education from a Christian perspective, especially religious education. Provides professional development for teachers of religious education, inter-school conferences to explore beliefs and values in the contemporary world, and regular mailings for primary and secondary schools, libraries and resource centres. The Professional Council For Religious Education circulates curriculum material (including examinations) ideas and information to RE specialists and non-specialists and in-service training guidelines. Publications: *The British Journal of Religious Education*, *RE Today*, and a wide variety of professional papers and class room material. *President:* Lady Margaret Parkes *Chairman:* Revd Dr Kenneth Wilson *General Secretary:* Revd Dr Stephen Orchard, Royal Buildings, Victoria St, Derby DE1 1GW
Tel: (01332) 296655
Fax: (01332) 343253
e-mail: cem@cem.org.uk

Christian Ethical Investment Group
Founded in 1988 as a voluntary pressure group to promote a stronger ethical investment policy in the Church of England. In April 1996 it adopted a constitution with the following objects: (1) to promote an awareness and study of ethical investment issues within the Christian Churches and organisations in Britain and Ireland. This to be both by individual church members and by congregations, parishes, dioceses, national bodies and other equivalent structures; (2) to encourage the development of clearly stated theologically based ethical investment

policy by Church bodies with financial investment responsibilities; (3) to promote personal and corporate responsibility through the active and responsible use of shareholder action and other appropriate ways in order to encourage a Christian approach to business and economic activity. The CEIG does not seek to promote a specific line on any particular ethical issue and is not able to offer financial advice. The Group works closely with the Ethical Investment Research Service (EIRIS) and the Ecumenical Council for Corporate Responsibility (ECCR). Membership is open to all who can support the objects. Subscription £10 p.a. for individuals and £50 p.a. for financial institutions. *Chair:* Mr Mike Tyrrell *Secretary:* Canon Bill Whiffen, 90 Booker Ave, Bradwell Common, Milton Keynes MK13 8EF *Tel and Fax:* (01908) 677466

Christian Evidence Society
Founded 1870 for the study, proclamation and defence of the Christian faith. *President:* The Archbishop of Canterbury *Chairman:* Canon Donald Gray *Administrator:* Revd Eric Britt, 3 Hylands Close, Barnston, Great Dunmow, Essex CM6 1LG *Tel:* (01371) 876039
e-mail: eric.b@netchannel.co.uk

Christian Medical Fellowship
Founded 1949 (1) to unite Christian doctors in seeking the highest attainable standards of Christian and professional conduct; (2) to increase in the medical profession faith in Christ and the acceptance of his ethical teaching and (3) to support the work of Christian medical missionaries throughout the world. *President:* Dr Antony Wing *General Secretary:* Dr Andrew Fergusson, 157 Waterloo Rd, London SE1 8XN *Tel:* 0171–928 4694
Fax: 0171–620 2453
e-mail: cmfuk@compuserve.com
Web: http://www.cmf.org.uk

Christian Research
Christian Research serves churches and church leaders by researching and publishing trends in today's society, such as in the *UK Christian Handbook, Religious Trends* and *World Churches Handbook*. Members receive *Quadrant – 'Information to Steer By'* – six times a year. Christian Research helps Christian leaders turn data into decisions by providing relevant data, running regular seminars on *Priorities, Planning and Paperwork, Know Yourself, Know Your Team,* and *Interpretation of Data*. Please ask for details. *Chairman:* Chris Radley *Exec Director:* Dr Peter Brierley, Vision Building, 4 Footscray Rd, Eltham, London SE9 2TZ *Tel:* 0181–294 1989
Fax: 0181–294 0014
e-mail: 100616.1657@compuserve.com

Christian Socialist Movement
Formed in 1960. Encourages Christians to work for a democratic socialist order of society as the political expression of their faith, and to make Christian values a significant influence upon the socialist movement. Publications: *Christian Socialist* (quarterly) and the annual Tawney Lectures. *President:* Revd Lord Soper *Chairman:* Chris Bryant *Contact:* Eric Wright, 36 Cross Flats, Leeds LS11 7BG *Tel:* (0113) 270 5756

Christian Witness to Israel
(formerly Barbican Mission to the Jews and International Society for Evangelisation of the Jews)
Founded in 1889 and 1842 to preach the Gospel to the Jews. *Chief Exec Officer:* Revd John Ross, 166 Main Rd, Sundridge, Sevenoaks, Kent TN14 6EL
Tel: (01959) 565955
Fax: (01959) 565966
e-mail: cwi@cwi.org.uk
Web: http://www.cwi.org.uk

Christianity and the Future of Europe
CAFE is an independent ecumenical association set up in 1989 and registered as a charity. It is a 'body in association' of the Council of Churches of Britain and Ireland. Its objectives are the promotion of education, research, and public reflection on the issues that arise for the Christian churches of Britain from the continuing evolution of a European identity. Its Council includes corresponding secretaries in Ireland, Scotland and Wales. It functions in association with the Lincoln Theological Institute in the University of Sheffield and has links with similar bodies and church organisations in mainland Europe. Help is offered for parish twinnings. *Director:* Revd Prof Kenneth Medhurst, Lincoln Theological Institute, University of Sheffield, 36 Wilkinson St, Sheffield S10 2GB
Tel: 0114–222 6399
Fax: 0114 276 3973
e-mail: Lincoln@Sheffield.ac.uk
Web: http://www.shef.ac.uk/~lti/

Christians Abroad
An ecumenical organisation for people of any faith or none seeking work overseas in development or mission. Provides an information and advice service for individuals including free booklet, a vacancy bulletin and guidance interviews, as well as a recruitment and selection programme for Christian professionals on behalf of overseas employers. *General Secretary:* Mr Colin South, Christians Abroad, 1 Stockwell Green, London SW9 9HP
Tel: 0171–346 5950
Fax: 0171–346 5955
e-mail: wse@cabroad.org.uk

Christians at Work
Founded in 1942 to bring together Christians to work for the extension of Christ's kingdom in the world of business and industry. To encourage active evangelism and fellowship. To provide information, literature and other facilities. To help Christians who stand alone in their

place of work and to provide a means whereby young Christians starting work may be strengthened in their faith. *Contact:* 148 Railway Terrace, Rugby, Warws CV21 3HN *Tel:* (01788) 579738

Christians for Europe
An ecumenical group which aims to strengthen links with the European Community; to foster studies; to educate public opinion, especially in the Christian community and so to bring the Judeo-Christian inheritance to bear upon the problems and opportunities and structures of today; to undertake particular projects in the field of research, of publications, of local friendship links, and in other appropriate ways; to co-operate with the European Movement and with ecumenical organisations based in Brussels and Strasbourg. *Hon Secretary:* Miss Diana Garnham, Europe House, 1A Whitehall Place, London SW1A 2HA

Church Action with the Unemployed
Formed in 1981, an ecumenical organisation supported by the leaders of the main Churches in Great Britain. Its objective is to help and encourage churches in their ministry with unemployed people by the promotion of Unemployment Sunday (last Sunday before Lent) and by the provision and distribution of information outlining different ways in which local churches can support and sustain unemployed people. *Chairman:* Canon Frank Scuffham *Contact:* Ms Catherine Smyth, 45B Blythe St, London E2 6LN *Tel:* 0171–729 9990
Fax: 0171–256 1072

Church and Community Trust
An independent organisation that offers guidance and information to local churches concerning the more effective use of their resources – buildings, money, people – for worshipping God and serving the community. *Coordinator:* Pam Nicholls, Napier Hall, Hide Place, London SW1P 4NJ *Tel and Fax:* 0171–976 6347

Church Computer Users Group
An independent, non-profit making, charity seeking to support all in the churches who are exploring the use of computers and their associated technology for the glory of God and the work of the Church. It publishes a newsletter *Church Computer* three times a year and the *Church Computer Directory of Software* annually. It frequently appears at Christian Resources Exhibitions and has organised its own Church Computer Roadshows throughout the country. *Patron:* The Archbishop of Canterbury *Correspondence:* c/o CCUG, 15 Cricklewood Drive, Halesowen B62 8SN

Church House Deaneries' Group
The Church House Deaneries' Group exists to stimulate local and national consideration of the developing role of the deanery, to encourage an informal network for the exchange of information about deanery thinking and deanery initiatives, and to realise the mission opportunities of deaneries. Every two years since 1988 it has held a national conference about deaneries. It has very close links with Parish and People which resources deaneries with printed material (*see* separate entry). *Chairman:* Canon Peter Croft *Chairman National Conference:* Canon Colin Hill *Secretary:* Canon Graham Corneck, 41 Creek Rd, London SE8 3BU *Tel:* 0181–692 2749

Church Housing Trust
Formed by the Church Housing Association in 1984. As a Christian organisation it takes positive action to provide better facilities, opportunities and futures for homeless people whilst promoting a wider national understanding of the difficulties faced by those in housing need. It raises funds nationally for the establishment, equipping, organising, furnishing and maintenance of housing, hostel and other accommodation. Church Housing Trust reaches the elderly, students, single people, families and the physically and mentally ill who are unable by reason of poverty, sickness, age or youth to make adequate provision for themselves. *Chairman:* Alan Foster *Chief Exec:* Jan Bunstead, Sutherland House, 70–78 West Hendon Broadway, London NW9 7BT *Tel:* 0181–202 3458
Fax: 0181–202 1440
e-mail: CHT@dial.pipex.com
Web: http://www.charitynet.org/~cht

Church Lads' and Church Girls' Brigade
This uniformed and exclusively Anglican organisation has more than a century of experience of serving the Church. Parish based and with the requirement that all officers are communicants, it offers a unique and effective means of extending Christ's Kingdom among children and young people. Fun and friendship are its hallmarks so helping its members develop as balanced Christians in a modern society. *President:* The Archbishop of Canterbury *Governor:* Major General Sir Desmond Langley *General Secretary:* Wing Commander Stewart Cresswell, National Headquarters, 2 Barnsley Rd, Wath upon Dearne, Rotherham S63 6PY *Tel:* (01709) 876535
Fax: (01709) 878089

Church Mission Society
CMS, founded in 1799, is 'an association of people united in obedience to the call of God to proclaim the Gospel in all lands and to gather the people of all races into the fellowship of Christ's Church'. Today's mission partners serve in a wide range of posts in twenty-seven countries in Africa, Asia, Eastern Europe and Britain. They go at the invitation of Churches within the Anglican Communion, of United Churches and of ecumenical

Organisations 227

interdenominational agencies. Today the society works in partnership with local churches, sharing in evangelism, leadership and theological training, church growth and community development. CMS is a voluntary membership society set within the Anglican Communion. Members affirm that they will commend the Gospel, inform themselves and pray regularly for mission, and use their time and money responsibly as God's gifts. A budget of about £5 million a year is needed to maintain and expand this work. The staff in this country includes a team of area secretaries representing CMS to the dioceses of Britain. Publications include YES with *Prayer Paper* published four times a year; *Christians in Contact*, a tape magazine programme with notes, published ten times a year; the *General Secretary's CMS Newsletter* and a range of audio-visual materials. CMS has sister societies in Ireland, Australia and New Zealand. (*See also* Crowther Hall CMS Training College and Mid-Africa Ministry (CMS)) *President:* Lady Brentford *General Secretary:* Diana Witts, Partnership House, 157 Waterloo Rd, London SE1 8UU
Tel: 0171–928 8681
Fax: 0171–401 3215
e-mail: info@cms-uk.org

Church Music Society

Founded 1906. The society is a leading publisher of all types of Church music, and has consistently served the Church of England since the beginning of the century. An annual lecture and other events for members pursue further aims of advancing knowledge of the art of Church music and its historical perspective. OUP has recently been re-appointed the Society's publisher. Details of membership and activities are available from the Secretary. *Chairman:* Ian Curror *Hon Secretary:* Simon Lindley, 8 The Chandlers, The Calls, Leeds LS2 7EZ
Tel and *Fax:* 0113–234 1146

Church of England Clergy Stipend Trust

Founded 1952 to augment stipends of parochial clergy, normally through Diocesan Boards of Finance. *Chairman:* Mr Anthony G. Trower, 6 New Square, Lincoln's Inn, London WC2A 3RP *Tel:* 0171–831 6292

Church of England Evangelical Council

Founded 1960 to (1) bring together evangelical leaders of the Church of England for mutual counsel and discussion (2) seek to reach a common mind on the issues of the day and when appropriate to reveal their findings to the Church and nation (3) encourage those societies and individuals in a position to do so to increase the evangelical contribution to the Church of England (4) assist in such work throughout the Anglican Communion. It organises an annual assembly, the Anglican Evangelical Assembly, to help further its aims. *President:* The Bishop of Southwell *Chairman:* Preb Richard Bewes *Exec Officer:* Mr Frank Knaggs, PO Box 93, Heaton, Newcastle upon Tyne NE6 5WL *Tel* and *Fax:* 0191–240 2084
e-mail: CEEC@cableinet.co.uk

Church of England Record Society

Founded in 1991 with the object of promoting interest in and knowledge of the history of the Church of England from the sixteenth century onwards, the Society publishes primary material of national significance for Church history. It aims to produce one volume each year, set against an annual subscription of £20 (individuals), and £30 (institutions). *Exec Secretary:* Miss Melanie Barber, Lambeth Palace Library, London SE1 7JU
Tel: 0171–928 6222
Fax: 0171–928 7932

Church of England Soldiers', Sailors' and Airmen's Clubs (1891)

A registered charity which, since its foundation in 1891, has maintained Clubs at home and abroad for HM Forces and their dependants, whatever their religious denomination. The work of the Association now encompasses rented housing for elderly ex-Service people or their widows/widowers. The Association also helps other charities to build sheltered housing for ex-service people, working in parallel with its sister organisation, CESSA Housing Association. Donations always welcomed. *General Secretary:* Cdr Tom O'Rourke, Head Office, 1 Shakespeare Terrace, High St, Portsmouth, Hants PO1 2RH
Tel: (01705) 829319

Church of England Soldiers', Sailors' and Airmen's Housing Association Ltd (1972)

Registered with the Housing Corporation to provide rented sheltered accommodation for elderly ex-Service people or their widows/widowers of all denominations. Construction costs were provided partly by Government grants, but donations are always welcome to help fund further homes. *Chief Exec:* Cdr Tom O'Rourke, 1 Shakespeare Terrace, High St, Portsmouth, Hants PO1 2RH
Tel: (01705) 829319

Church Pastoral Aid Society

CPAS was founded in 1836, and today resources local churches and their leaders for mission and evangelism in the UK and Ireland. It offers a comprehensive evangelism service for local church needs. It helps churches become missionary congregations through leadership support including grants for additional leaders, patronage of over five hundred benefices, professional ministry advice, support for lay leaders. Young people, children and families are served by over four thousand church-based youth and children's groups, residential ventures for young people and resources for church-based work with families. CPAS publishes biblically based resources from

video-based training courses to workbooks on important themes of ministry. *General Director:* Canon Brian Pearson, CPAS, Athena Drive, Tachbrook Park, Warwick CV34 6NG
Tel: (01926) 334242
Fax: (01926) 337613
e-mail: info@cpas.org.uk
Web: http://www.cpas.org

Church Schoolmasters' and School Mistresses' Benevolent Institution
Founded 1857 for the relief of financial distress among past and present members of the Church of England in the teaching profession. Provides a Dual Registered Home catering for both residential and nursing care on a 24-hour basis. *President:* The Bishop of London *Chairman:* Mr R. G. Whitwell *Secretary:* Mr D. J. F. Godfrey, Glen Arun, 9 Athelstan Way, Horsham, Sussex RH13 6HA
Tel: (01403) 253881

Church Schools Company
Founded 1883 to provide a sound general education for girls and boys, with religious instruction in accordance with the principles of the Church of England. Schools at Southampton, Guildford, Surbiton, Caterham, Hull, Lincoln, and Sunderland. Clergy bursaries available. *Chairman:* Lady Prior *Chief Exec:* Mr Ewan Harper, Church Schools House, Titchmarsh, Kettering, Northants NN14 3DA
Tel: (01832) 735105
Fax: (01832) 734760

Church Society
Formed in 1950 by the amalgamation of the Church Association and National Church League which was founded in 1835, continues to seek to maintain the evangelical and reformed faith of the Church of England, based upon the authority of Holy Scripture (see Canon A5) and the foundational doctrines of the Thirty-nine Articles and the Book of Common Prayer. Publishes a journal *Churchman* and a quarterly broadsheet *Cross+Way*. The Society publishes books, booklets and leaflets on current issues and organises conferences and public meetings. Patronage is administered through the Church Society Trust. (*See also Patronage Trusts*) *President:* The Viscount Brentford *Chairman:* Revd Donald Allister *Director:* Revd David Phillips, Dean Wace House, 16 Rosslyn Rd, Watford, Herts WD1 7EY   *Tel:* (01923) 235111 (24 Hours)
Fax: (01923) 800362
e-mail: 106522.1537@compuserve.com

Church Union
Founded in 1859, at the time of the 'Oxford Movement', to promote catholic faith and order, it continues this work today by providing support and encouragement to those lay people and priests who wish to see catholic faith, order, morals and spirituality maintained and upheld, and who wish to promote catholic unity. The Union runs Faith House Bookshop (Christian books, cards and sacristry supplies), publishes books, tracts, and a biannual theological journal, *The Tufton Review* produces a quarterly magazine, the *Church Observer*, and has full-time staff who can advise on matters liturgical, legal and musical. *President:* Rt Revd Eric Kemp, Bishop of Chichester *Chairman:* Rt Revd Lindsay Urwin, Bishop of Horsham Faith House, 7 Tufton St, London SW1P 3QN
Tel: 0171–222 6952
Fax: 0171–976 7180

Church Urban Fund
See page 166.

Church Welfare Association (Incorporated)
(formerly the Church Moral Aid Association)
Founded 1851. Gives financial aid to Church projects assisting and supporting women and children in need of residential care and/or moral support. *Chairman:* Miss Joan Watts *Secretary:* Mr D. J. Boddington, 15 Marina Court, Alfred St, Bow, London E3 2BH

Church's Ministry Among Jewish People
Founded 1809 as London Society for Promoting Christianity among the Jews, to take the Christian Gospel to Jewish people. *President:* Rt Revd John Taylor *Chairman:* Revd Tony Higton *General Director:* Vacancy, 30c Clarence Rd, St Albans, Herts AL1 4JJ
Tel: (01727) 833114
Fax: (01727) 848312
e-mail: 100731.2227@compuserve.com

Churches Commission on Overseas Students
The national ecumenical co-ordinating agency for concern towards all students from abroad. *Chair:* Dr Gwenda Thompson *Exec Secretary:* Ms Gillian Court, 1 Stockwell Green, London SW9 9HP
Tel: 0171–737 1101
Fax: 0171–346 5955

Churches Main Committee
Founded 1941, and registered as a charity in 1966, to advance the charitable work, whether religious or otherwise, of the Churches by furthering their common interests in secular matters relating to that work, other than education; to give advice to the Churches on these matters; to conduct negotiations and take such action as may be thought fit; to act as a liaison body between the Churches and the machinery of Government. *Chairman:* The Bishop of London *Secretary:* Mr Derek Taylor Thompson *Asst Secretary:* Mrs Betty Cracknell, Fielden House, Little College St, London SW1P 3SH
Tel: 0171–898 1878; 0171–222 4984
Fax: 0171–898 1899

Churches' Advertising Network
A professional group of Christians from all traditions co-operating to develop the professional use of advertising

as part of the churches' communication and outreach. CAN seeks free or low cost poster space and radio airtime from leading media owners, which it uses on behalf of the churches. All members give their services free. *Secretary:* Revd Martin Short, 30 Newall Hall Park, Otley, Leeds LS21 2RD *Tel:* (01943) 465071
Fax: (01943) 467269
e-mail: can@coin.org.uk

Churches' Council for Health and Healing
British Churches of all denominations and the main medical bodies, including the British Medical Association and the Royal Colleges, are officially represented on the Council, together with the guilds and fellowships of healing which work within the Churches' ministry of healing on a basis of mutual understanding and co-operation with the medical profession. It acts as a centre for co-ordinating activities and distributing appropriate material as part of the regular work of the churches. *President:* The Archbishop of Canterbury *Secretary:* Dr Rachel Rosser, St Luke's Hospital for the Clergy, 14 Fitzroy Square, London W1P 6AH *Tel:* 0171–388 7903

Churches' Fellowship for Psychical and Spiritual Studies
Founded 1953 to study the psychic and spiritual and their relevance to Christian faith and life. *President:* Canon Michael Perry *Chairman:* Prebendary Michael Shrewsbury *General Secretary:* Mr Julian Drewett, The Rural Workshop, South Rd, North Somercotes, Louth, Lincs LN11 7PT *Tel* and *Fax:* (01507) 358845

Churches' Group on Funeral Services at Cemeteries and Crematoria
Formed in 1980 by the mainstream Churches in England and Wales to co-ordinate their policies in connection with the pastoral and administrative aspects of funeral services at cemeteries and crematoria and to represent the Churches at national level in joint discussions with public and private organisations on any matters relating to ministry at such funerals. Publications sponsored by the Group include a handbook of funeral procedures, *Funerals and Ministry to the Bereaved* (Church House Publishing, second edition 1989), intended for use by clergy, funeral directors and cemetery and crematorium staff; and two joint funeral service books (The Canterbury Press, Norwich), one for use in England (1986 and 1994) the other for use in Wales (1987); *The Role of the Minister in Bereavement: Guidelines and Training Suggestions* (Church House Publishing, 1989); and a leaflet entitled *Questions Commonly Asked About Funerals* (1994). Reports of the Group's conferences on *The Role of a Minister at a Funeral* (1991) *Bereavement and Belief* (1993) and *Clergy and Cremation Today* (1995) are available on application from the General Synod Office, Church House, London SW1P 3NZ (price £2.75) as is a bibliography, *Death, Dying and Bereavement. Guidelines for Best Practice of Clergy at Funerals* (1997) (price £3.95 inc VAT) is also available. The Group keeps in close touch with the main organisations concerned with funeral provision and bereavement counselling. *Chairman:* Rt Revd Geoffrey Rowell *Hon Secretary:* Revd Michael Bray *Asst Secretary:* Mr David Hebblethwaite, Church House, Great Smith St, London SW1P 3NZ *Tel:* 0171–898 1364
Fax: 0171–898 1369
e-mail: synod@church-house-coe-london.org.uk

Clergy Holidays Society
Founded in 1978 to assist clergy who wish to arrange holiday locums or exchanges; and also to assist clergy and Licensed Church Workers who wish to arrange inexpensive holidays in Britain. *Director:* Revd A. C. Grieve, 11 Crabgate Lane, Skellow, Doncaster DN6 8LE
Tel: (01302) 337101

Clinical Theology Association
Founded in 1962. The core activity of the Association is seminars in pastoral care and pastoral counselling which are directed by authorised tutors and widely available in the UK. Seminars are designed to promote self-awareness which is needed for effective pastoral work, and to teach the theory and practice of pastoral counselling with reference to the assumptions, values and meanings of the Christian faith. Further information about Clinical Theology education and training may be obtained from the *General Director:* Revd Peter van de Kasteele, St Mary's House, Church Westcote, Oxford OX7 6SF
Tel: (01993) 830209

College of Health Care Chaplains
Founded 1992 as a result of the merger of the Hospital Chaplains' Fellowship and the National Association of Whole-Time Hospital Chaplains. An inter-denominational, inter-faith body based on a federation of branches formed on the boundaries of Regional Health Authorities in England together with branches in North Wales, South Wales and Scotland. The College concerns itself with all matters of interest to clergy and laity working in health care establishments and aims to promote and safeguard the work of the Church in such establishments. Holds an annual residential study course. Issues regular journals and newsletters. The College is an autonomous section of the Manufacturing, Science and Finance Union (MSF). *President:* Revd Peter Page *Contact:* Chaplain's Office, Addenbrooke's Hospital, Box 105, Hills Rd, Cambridge CB2 9QQ *Tel:* (01223) 217769

College of Preachers
Founded 1960 to help, encourage and stimulate those engaged in the ministry of preaching. Conducts training

courses for clergy and lay preachers on an ecumenical basis. *Chairman:* The Bishop of Durham *Director:* Revd Dr Eric Young, 81 North Rd, Bourne, Lincs PE10 9BT
Tel and *Fax:* (01778) 422929

Commonwealth War Graves Commission
Founded 1917. Responsible for marking and maintaining in perpetuity the graves of those of Commonwealth Forces who fell in the 1914–18 and 1939–45 Wars and for commemorating by name on memorials those with no known grave. *President:* HRH The Duke of Kent. *Chairman:* The Secretary of State for Defence in the United Kingdom. *Enquiries:* Legal Adviser and Solicitor, 2 Marlow Rd, Maidenhead, Berks SL6 7DX *Tel:* (01628) 634221 *Fax:* (01628) 771208

Community Housing and Therapy
CHT runs educational and therapeutic residential programmes for people with mental health problems. It educates in a practical and in psychological way. Clients learn practical living skills and learn to become emotionally and intellectually articulate members of a community. Through dialogue with others, CHT's clients gain the confidence to become integrated citizens. *Chief Exec:* Mr Stephen Hawkins *Director of Social Work:* Mr John Gore, Bishop Creighton House, 378 Lillie Rd, London SW6 7PH *Tel:* 0171–384 1939

Company of Mission Priests
Founded 1940. An association of male priests of the Anglican Communion who, wishing to consecrate themselves wholly to the Church's mission, keep themselves free from the attachments of marriage and family, and endeavour to encourage and strengthen each other by mutual prayer and fellowship, sharing the vision of St Vincent de Paul of a priesthood dedicated to service. *Warden:* Canon Michael Shields, Flat 14, Bromley College, London Rd, Bromley, Kent BR1 1PE *Tel:* 0181–464 7906

Compassionate Friends
A nationwide organisation of bereaved parents and their families offering friendship and understanding to others similarly bereaved. Personal and group support. Quarterly newsletter, annual conferences, postal book library and a range of leaflets. *Pastoral Coordinator:* Simon Bees *Office Administrator:* Jon Gilbody, 53 North St, Bristol BS3 1EN *Tel:* 0117–953 9639 (Helpline)
0117–966 5202 (Admin)
Fax: 0117–966 5202

Confraternity of the Blessed Sacrament
Founded 1862 to honour Jesus Christ our Lord in the Blessed Sacrament; to make mutual eucharistic intercession and to encourage eucharistic devotion. *Superior-General:* Revd Timothy Bugby *Secretary General:* Revd Dr Lawson Nagel, Aldwick Vicarage, 25 Gossamer Lane, Bognor Regis, W Sussex PO21 3AT *Tel:* (01243) 262049
e-mail: lnagel@netcomuk.co.uk
Web: http://www.netcomuk.co.uk/~lnagel/cbs.html/

Corporation of SS Mary and Nicolas (The Woodard Schools)
Founded by Canon Nathaniel Woodard in 1848 to promote education in the doctrines and principles of the Church of England. The Corporation now runs some twenty-three schools and a further fifteen schools are affiliated to the Corporation. *President:* The Bishop of Blackburn *Registrar:* Mr Peter Beesley, 1 The Sanctuary, London SW1P 3JT *Tel:* 0171–222 5381
Fax: 0171–222 7502
e-mail: 106102.1723@compuserve.com

Corporation of the Sons of the Clergy
(Trustees for the Clergy Orphan Corporation)
Founded 1655. Incorporated by Royal Charter 1678. For helping clergy of the Anglican Communion in the UK, Eire and Anglican missionaries abroad providing they are sponsored by a UK based missionary society. The Corporation can also help widows and widowers of such clergy, their separated or divorced wives, and the dependent children of any of the above. Help can also be given to unmarried daughters of pensionable age. Grants are not made for holidays or the purchase or running of cars. *President:* The Archbishop of Canterbury *Registrar:* Mr Christopher Leach, 1 Dean Trench St, London SW1P 3HB *Tel:* 0171–799 3696 and 0171–222 5887
Fax: 0171–233 1913

Council of Christians and Jews
Founded 1942 to combat all forms of religious and racial intolerance, to promote mutual understanding and goodwill between Christians and Jews, and to foster co-operation in educational activities and in social and community service. Sixty local branches in the UK. *Presidents:* The Archbishop of Canterbury, the Cardinal Archbishop of Westminster, the Moderator of the Church of Scotland, the Moderator of the Free Churches' Council, the Archbishop of Thyateira and Great Britain and the Chief Rabbi. *Director:* Sister Margaret Shepherd, Drayton House, 30 Gordon St, London WC1H 0AN
Tel: 0171–388 3322
Fax: 0171–388 3305
e-mail: ccjuk@aol.com
Web: http://www.jcrelations.com

Council on Christian Approaches to Defence and Disarmament
CCADD was established in 1963 by the Rt Rev Robert Stopford, then Bishop of London, to study problems relating to defence and disarmament within a Christian

context. The British Group of CCADD comprises Christians of different traditions, varying vocations and specialisations and political views, with a range of responsibilities, governmental and non-governmental. CCADD seeks to bring an ethical viewpoint to bear on disarmament and arms control and related issues and to this end the British Group has always stressed the importance of dialogue between official and non-official bodies. *President:* The Bishop of Oxford *Chairman:* Sir Arthur Hockaday *Admin Secretary:* Miss Vera Plumb, CCADD, St Bride Foundation Institute, Bride Lane, London EC4Y 8EQ
Tel: 0171–583 4145

Crosse's Charity
Provides small annuities for widows of clergymen of the Church of England. Preference given to those, who from age, ill-health, accident or infirmity are unable to maintain themselves by their own exertions. *For form of application please apply to:* Clerks to Trustees, Hinckley Birch & Brown, 20 Saint John St, Lichfield, Staffs WS13 6PD
Tel: (01543) 262491

Crosslinks
Founded 1922 as the Bible Churchmen's Missionary Society (BCMS). Crosslinks is an international evangelical Anglican mission agency with the slogan *God's Word to God's World.* It supports and encourages churches through the exchange of mission and study partners and is a full member of the Partnership for World Mission. Mission partners work in East, North and South Africa, Zimbabwe, Spain, Portugal, France and Asia as well as among those of other faiths in the UK. *President:* Revd Dr C. Wright *General Secretary:* Revd Roger Bowen, 251 Lewisham Way, London SE4 1XF *Tel:* 0181–691 6111
Fax: 0181–694 8023
e-mail: crosslinks@pro-net.co.uk

Crowhurst Christian Healing Centre
Opened in 1928. Guests come for a few days or up to two weeks for rest, renewal, healing prayer and ministry in peaceful and beautiful surroundings. The daily programme revolves around Christ-centred worship, Holy Communion and twice-weekly healing services. Courses on the healing ministry and creative courses are also available. *Apply to the:* Secretary, Crowhurst Christian Healing Centre, The Old Rectory, Crowhurst, Battle, E Sussex TN33 9AD *Tel:* (01424) 830204
Fax: (01424) 830053

Crowther Hall CMS Training College
Crowther Hall is one of three colleges for training in mission which, together with seven others, make up the Selly Oak Colleges at Birmingham. All CMS long-term Mission Partners spend from three to nine months in preparation for service abroad. Students from overseas (including several involved in the Centre for Anglican Communion Studies, CEFACS) spend three terms studying in different departments in Selly Oak. Leasow House offers facilities for Mission Partners on leave, sabbaticals, retreats and small conferences. *Principal:* Revd George Kovoor, Crowther Hall, Selly Oak, Birmingham B29 6QT
Tel: 0121–472 4228
Fax: 0121–471 2662

Crusaders
A well-established youth movement working with churches and Christians of all main denominations to show the relevance of Jesus Christ to young people between the ages of 4 and 18. The backbone of this national organisation is the regular youth group which has a mix of Bible teaching through active learning, games, outings, holidays, local and national activities. It aims to help churches with their youth outreach strategies and provides teaching resources, activity materials, an extensive Leadership Training Programme, a Leaders' magazine, short term service opportunities, over forty adventure holidays for young people each summer, backed up by a team of Area workers, a Head Office Team and Book Centre in St Albans. There are three residential centres available to schools and youth groups. *Director:* Vacant, Crusaders, 2 Romeland Hill, St Albans, Herts AL3 4ET *Tel:* (01727) 855422
Fax: (01727) 848518
e-mail: email@crusaders.org.uk
Web: http://www.crusaders.org.uk

Culham College Institute
This is a research, development, and information agency working in the fields of Church schools, Church colleges, and RE. It is managed by the Culham Educational Foundation and arose out of the closure of a Church of England college of education. It has established a national system of networking, collaborative activity, and project management. Current collaboration includes work with the Jerusalem Trust, the St Gabriel's Trust, the All Saints Trust, British Telecom and the school broadcasting departments of the BBC and Channel 4. The Association of Church College Trusts has its base at Culham. *Director:* Revd Dr John Gay, 60 East St Helen St, Abingdon, Oxon OX14 5EB *Tel:* (01235) 520458
Fax: (01235) 535421
e-mail: enquiries@culham.ac.uk
Web: http://www.culham.ac.uk

Deaf People, Royal Association in Aid of
(formerly The Royal Association in Aid of the Deaf and Dumb)
Founded 1841 to promote the spiritual, social and general welfare of deaf people. Works in the dioceses of London, Chelmsford, Guildford, Rochester and Southwark. *Patron:* HM The Queen. *President:* The Archbishop of Canterbury. *Vice-Presidents:* The Bishops of London,

Rochester, Southwark, Guildford and Chelmsford. *Chairman:* Mr Maurice Hawker, 27 Old Oak Rd, Acton, London W3 7HN
Tel: 0181–743 6187
Fax: 0181–740 6551

Deaf People, Royal National Institute for
The RNID is the largest charity representing the 8.7 million deaf and hard of hearing people in the UK. As a membership charity, it aims to achieve a radically better quality of life for deaf and hard of hearing people by campaigning and lobbying to change laws and government policies, by providing information and raising awareness of deafness, hearing loss and tinnitus, by running training courses and consultancy on deafness and disability, offering communication services including sign language interpreters. It trains interpreters, lipspeakers and speech-to-text operators. It seeks lasting change in education for deaf children and young people and runs employment programmes to help deaf people into work. It provides residential and community services for deaf people with special needs. Other areas of work include the provision of equipment and products for deaf and hard of hearing people and social, medical and technical research. *Chairman:* Mr David Livermore *Chief Exec:* Mr James Strachan, 19–23 Featherstone St, London EC1Y 8SL
Tel: 0870–6050 123
0870–6033 007 (Text)
Fax: 0171–296 8199

Deans' and Provosts' Conference
The Deans' and Provosts' Conference is the meeting together (three times annually) of those who preside over their Cathedral Chapters to reflect upon Cathedral issues of particular concern to Deans and Provosts in their public and cathedral roles. *Chairman:* The Dean of Wells *Treasurer:* The Dean of Exeter *Secretary:* The Provost of Blackburn, Provost's Office, Cathedral Close, Blackburn BB1 5AA
Tel: (01254) 51491
e-mail: provost@blackburn.ce.u-net.com

Deans' and Provosts' Vergers' Conference
Founded in 1989 to bring together Head Vergers who are employed in that capacity by a Dean or Provost and Chapter of the Church of England. The Conference enables members to communicate with each other, exchange and discuss ideas of common interest and to have regular contact with the Deans and Provosts Conference. The Head Vergers of the forty-two English Cathedrals, Westminster Abbey and St George's Windsor are eligible for membership. *Chairman:* Mr W. Ross *Secretary:* Mr Paul Timms, Southwark Cathedral, Montague Close, London SE1 9DA
Tel: 0171–633 0433 (Home)
0171–407 2939 (Office)

DGAA – Homelife
Founded 1897 as the Distressed Gentlefolk's Aid Association to alleviate need and distress by giving financial help to people of professional or similar background of either sex of British or Irish nationality, irrespective of religious denomination, and to provide and maintain nursing and residential accommodation. *Chairman:* Billy Carbutt *Acting Chief Exec:* A. M. P. Leaver, 1 Derry St, London W8 5HY
Tel: 0171–396 6700
Fax: 0171–396 6739

Diaconal Association of the Church of England
DACE is a professional association for Diaconal Ministers (deacons, accredited lay workers, and Church Army officers) working in the Church of England, established in 1988 to succeed the Deaconess Committee and the Anglican Accredited Lay Workers Federation. Associated membership is also open to priests, students in training for ministry, and diaconal ministers working in other provinces in the UK. DACE exists to promote the distinctive (permanent) diaconate and other diaconal ministries in the Church of England, support all nationally recognised diaconal ministers, and consider the theological and practical implications of diaconal ministry within the total ministry of the Christian church, in partnership with other agencies and denominations. *Secretary:* Capt Neil Thomson, 95 Ballens Rd, Lordswood, Chatham, Kent ME5 8PA
Tel: 07020 960520
e-mail: secretary@dace.societies.anglican.org
Web: http://www.societies.anglican.org/dace

Diakonia
Founded in 1947 to link the various European deaconess associations, it is now a 'World Federation of Diaconal Associations'. It concerns itself with the nature and task of 'Diakonia' and encourages deaconesses, deacons, and lay people doing diaconal work. It also furthers ecumenical relations between the diaconal associations in other countries. The Diaconal Association of the Church of England is a member. There is a Diakonia *UK Liaison Group* which also includes representatives from the Methodist Diaconal Order, the Church of Scotland Diaconate and the Deaconesses of the Presbyterian Church in Ireland. *UK representative on International Exec Committee:* Miss Jane Martin, 12A Carnoustie Court, Ardler, Dundee DD2 3RB
Tel: (01382) 813786

Diocesan Institutions of Chester, Manchester, Liverpool and Blackburn
For the relief of widows and orphans of clergymen who have officiated in their last sphere of duty in the Archdeaconries of Chester, Macclesfield, Manchester, Rochdale, Liverpool, Warrington or Blackburn. *For further details please apply to:* Canon James Colling, Rectory, Warrington, Cheshire WA1 2TL
Tel: (01925) 635020

Distinctive Diaconate
An unofficial Church of England centre which serves to promote the diaconate as one of the historic orders of the

Church's ministry by sharing information about current developments through the newsletters *Distinctive Diaconate News* and *Distinctive News of Women in Ministry*. Lambeth's *Mission and Ministry* report recommended the sharing of experiences with the diaconate within the Anglican Communion and suggested using Distinctive Diaconate. *Editor:* Revd Sr Teresa, CSA, St Andrew's House, 2 Tavistock Rd, Westbourne Park, London W11 1BA
Tel: 0171–229 2662 Ext 24
Fax: 0171–792 5993
e-mail: sister.teresa@dlondon.org.uk

Distressed Gentlefolk's Aid Association
See **DGAA – Homelife**, page 233.

Ecclesiastical Insurance Group
Founded 1887 to offer specialist insurance for church property and personal policies for clergy and laity. Grants to English dioceses are made. The Company also provide Life insurance including Pensions, Mortgages, Free Standing AVC and Ethical Unit Trusts. (Total grants made for Church objectives are 29 million. In the last five years alone grants for churches and charitable purposes have amounted to 14.3 million.) *Chairman:* Mr M. A. Cornwall-Jones. *Managing Director:* Mr Graham Dodswell. *Branch Offices: Birmingham:* Berwick House, 35 Livery St, Birmingham B3 2PB; *Bristol:* Kings Court, King St, Bristol BS1 4EE; *Cambridge:* Abbeygate House, 164–167 East Rd, Cambridge CB1 1DB; *Cardiff:* Riverside House, 31 Cathedral Rd, Cardiff CF1 9HB; *Manchester:* Lincoln House, 1 Brazennose St, Manchester M2 5FJ; *Southampton:* Adyar House, 32 Carlton Crescent, Southampton SO15 2YP; *East Grinstead:* Kings House, 13/21 Cantelupe Rd, E Grinstead, W Sussex RH19 3BE; *Edinburgh:* 55 North Castle St, Edinburgh EH2 3QA; *Harrogate:* 7 Cambridge Rd, Harrogate, N Yorks HG1 1PB; *London:* 19/21 Billiter St, London EC3M 2RY. *Head Office:* Beaufort House, Brunswick Rd, Gloucester GL1 1JZ
Tel: (01452) 528533
Fax: (01452) 423557
e-mail: gbeigmkg@ibmmail.com
Web: http://www.ecclesiastical-insurance.co.uk

Ecclesiastical Law Society
Founded in 1987 to promote the study of ecclesiastical law, through the education of office bearers and practitioners in the ecclesiastical courts, the enlargement of knowledge of ecclesiastical law among clergy and laity of the Anglican Communion, and assistance in matters of ecclesiastical law to the General Synod, Convocations, Bishops and Church dignitaries. *President:* The Bishop of Chichester *Chairman:* Dr Frank Robson *Secretary:* Mr Peter Beesley, 1 The Sanctuary, London SW1P 3JT
Tel: 0171–222 5381

Ecclesiological Society
St Andrew-by-the Wardrobe, Queen Victoria St, London EC4V 5DE. Founded as the Cambridge Camden Society in 1839. Studies the arts, architecture and liturgy of the Christian Church by meetings, tours and publications. *President:* Donald Buttress *Contact:* Paul Velluet, 9 Bridge Rd, St Margaret's, Twickenham, Middx TW1 1RE

Ecumenical Council for Corporate Responsibility
ECCR was set up in 1989 to study and research the corporate responsibility of the Churches' investments and the companies in which those investments are held, with special reference to those which are transnational corporations. ECCR is an ecumenical body with membership from many different denominations, societies, religious orders and other Church organisations. Its membership is approaching 200 corporate bodies and individuals. It has the status of a Body in Association with the Council of Churches for Britain and Ireland and it is structured as a company limited by guarantee, registered in England and Wales. *Co-ordinator:* Revd Crispin White, PO Box 4317, Bishop's Stortford CM22 7GZ
Tel: (01279) 718274
Fax: (01279) 718097
e-mail: ECCR@GEO2.poptel.org.uk

Ecumenical Society of the Blessed Virgin Mary
Founded in London in 1967, 'to advance the study at various levels of the place of the Blessed Virgin Mary in the Church under Christ and to promote ecumenical devotion'. *Patrons:* Cardinal Basil Hume, Lord Runcie, Archbishop Gregorios of Thyateira, Revd Dr John Newton. *Secretary:* Mr Joe Farrelly, 11 Belmont Rd, Wallington, Surrey SM6 8TE
Tel: 0181–647 5992

Edward King Institute for Ministry Development
Founded in 1986 for clergy, ministers and lay people who are concerned to improve their understanding and practice of ministry. The Institute promotes consultations in which the aim is to work for realistic, planned change; produces a journal *Ministry*, three times a year; keeps a library of working papers and the publications of the Alban Institute. *Hon Directors:* Canon Les Oglesby and Canon Robin Greenwood. *Hon Secretary:* Mrs V. Tyler, Church House, Churchyard, Hitchin, Herts SG5 1HP
Tel: (01462) 452758

EFAC Bursary Scheme
see **Studylink** – EFAC International Training Partnership, page 255.

English Churches Housing Group
Formed in 1991 by the merger of the Church Housing Association and the Baptist Housing Association. Manages 10,000 self-contained homes and 60 supported housing schemes with space for 2,000 people. Offers a wide range of housing from general needs to sheltered

schemes for elderly people and supported housing schemes for single homeless people. ECHG's subsidiary company, Heritage Care, provides domiciliary care to enable people with daily care needs to live independently in the community. *Chairman:* Mr Tim Richmond *Chief Exec:* Caroline White, Sutherland House, 70–78 West Hendon Broadway, London NW9 7BT *Tel:* 0181–203 9233 *Fax:* 0181–203 0092

English Clergy Association
Recently revived, formerly the Parochial Clergy Association, founded 1938, sustains in fellowship all Clerks in Holy Orders in their vocation and ministry within the Church of England, promoting in every available way the good of English parish and cathedral life and the welfare of clergy. Related Trustees give discretionary clergy holiday grants upon application to the Hon Almoner. The Association seeks to foster the independence of the clergy whether in freehold office or not, and broadly supports the patronage system. Publishes *Parson and Parish* Journal. *Patron:* Chancellor June Rodgers *Chairman:* Revd John Masding, The Old School, Norton Hawkfield, Bristol BS39 4HB *Tel* and *Fax:* (01275) 830017 *e-mail:* masding@msn.com

European Christian Industrial Movement (Bridgebuilders)
Founded in June 1975, firstly to remind peoples of the Christian Gospel and its full implications in the new technological society with its multinational groups, and secondly to help build the many bridges of trust, understanding and co-operation that are necessary, not only between the peoples of the nations but also between the many opposing sections of each community. (Associated with The Bridge Builders, Rue Gachard 35, B-1050, Brussels). *Secretary General:* Mr Tom Chapman, Barrowdale, Stainton with Adgarley, Barrow-in-Furness, Cumbria LA13 0NW *Tel:* (01229) 63743

Evangelical Alliance
Founded 1846 as a representative body for evangelical Christians to promote evangelical unity and truth and represent evangelical concern to government and media. Co-ordinates corporate activity in evangelism, theological issues and social involvement. *President:* Sir Fred Catherwood *General Director:* Revd Joel Edwards, Whitefield House, 186 Kennington Park Rd, London SE1 14BT *Tel:* 0171–207 2100 *Fax:* 0171–207 2150 *e-mail:* London@eauk.org *Web:* http://www.eauk.org

Evangelical Christians for Racial Justice
Originally the Evangelical Race Relations Group, the name was changed in 1984 to reflect an increasing commitment to positive action to combat racism. ECRJ now offers a radical biblical critique of both Church and society in the area of *racial justice*. It is based on a nationwide, multi-racial membership and aims to support its members at a local level as well as address issues on a national canvas. The journal *Racial Justice* is published three times a year. *Co-chairs of Exec Committee:* Beverley Thomas and Peter Hobson, 109 Homerton High St, London E9 6DL *Tel:* 0181–985 2764

Family Life and Marriage Education Network
A church network launched in 1990. Most dioceses are now involved, and there are links with other churches and agencies. FLAME aims to co-ordinate, support and sustain the work of Family Life and Marriage Education at present done in dioceses of the Church of England and to act as a network for the exchange of information and expertise. It also aims to encourage good practice and to initiate new projects where needed. It has developed from the work of the Family Life Education Advisory Group since 1972 and the House of Bishops' Marriage Education Panel between 1984 and 1988. Contact can be made through Diocesan Boards for Social Responsibility, Boards of Education and, where they are already appointed, Family Life Education Officers and through FLAME. *Chairman of Trustees:* Mrs Daphne Cook, All Saints Vicarage, 20 Burcot Lane, Bromsgrove, Worcs B60 1AE *Tel:* (01527) 579849

Federation of Catholic Priests
A federation of diocesan associations of priests in communion with the See of Canterbury who have undertaken to live in accordance with Catholic doctrine and practice. It exists for mutual support in propagating, maintaining and defending such doctrine and practice and for the deepening of the spiritual life of members. *Chairman:* Revd Scott Anderson *Secretary General:* Prebendary Brian Tubbs, Vicarage, Palace Place, Paignton TQ3 3AU *Tel:* (01803) 559059 *e-mail:* FATHER_TUBBS@compuserve.com

Feed the Minds
Grant-making charity established in 1964 which supports Christian literature and communication, literacy, and theological education in developing countries and Eastern Europe. Feed the Minds is interdenominational, and 22 British and Irish missionary societies and Churches are member bodies. *Chair:* Mr John Clark *Director:* Dr Alwyn Marriage, Albany House, 67 Sydenham Rd, Guildford GU1 3RY *Tel:* (01483) 888580 *Fax:* (01483) 888581 *e-mail:* feedtheminds@gn.apc.org

Fellowship of St Alban and St Sergius
Founded 1928. An unofficial body which fosters understanding and friendship between Eastern Orthodox and

Western Christians. *Presidents:* Lord Runcie and Archbishop Gregorios of Thyateira and Great Britain. *General Secretary:* Revd Stephen Platt, 1 Canterbury Rd, Oxford OX2 6LU *Tel:* (01865) 552991 *Fax:* (01865) 316700 *e-mail:* stephen.platt-albanandsergius@btinternet.com *Web:* http://www.btinternet.com/~sobornost

Fellowship of St Nicholas
Founded in 1939 to provide a loving Christian home for children. We now provide a Children's Centre including after school and holiday play schemes, plus a range of groups, supporting parents and providing artistic activities for children, and a Funbus project. *Chairman:* Mrs Mollie Green *Director:* Mr Tony Cox, 10 Carisbrooke Rd, St Leonards-on-Sea, E Sussex TN38 0JS
Tel: (01424) 423683/443358
Fax: (01424) 460446

Fidelity Trust Limited
Founded 1908 for the holding of trusteeships of real and personal property for Church and charitable purposes. *Chairman:* Bernard Moss *Director and Secretary:* Revd David Maudlin, Keeley House, 22–30 Keeley Rd, Croydon, Surrey CR0 1TE *Tel:* 0181–661 6081

Foreign Missions Club
Founded 1893 to provide accommodation for missionaries and other Christian guests visiting the metropolis. *Manager:* Mr David Littlehales, 26 Aberdeen Park, London N5 2BJ *Tel:* 0171–226 2663
Fax: 0171–704 1853

Forward in Faith
Founded in November 1992, Forward in Faith exists to support all who in conscience are unable to accept the ordination of women to the priesthood or the episcopate. It seeks an ecclesial structure which will continue the orders of bishop and priest as the church has received them. It offers support to all who need it via a national and local network. It is governed by an elected council, drawn from the members of its National Assembly, which meets annually. It publishes the monthly journal *New Directions*, the quarterly newspaper *Forward Plus* and a variety of catechetical material. *Chairman:* The Bishop of Fulham *Director:* Mr Stephen Parkinson, Faith House, 7 Tufton St, London SW1P 3QN
Tel: 0171–976 0727
Fax: 0171–976 0737
e-mail: forwardinfaith@compuserve.com

Friends of Friendless Churches
Founded 1957 to preserve churches and chapels of architectural or historic interest. Now owns 20 redundant places of worship in England and Wales. *Patron:* The Marquess of Anglesey *President:* Lord Blake *Chairman:* Prof R. Brunskill *Hon Secretary:* Mr John Bowles *Hon Director:* Mr Matthew Saunders, St Ann's Vestry Hall, 2 Church Entry, London EC4V 5HB *Tel:* 0171–236 3934
Fax: 0171–329 3677

Friends of the Clergy Corporation
This charity gives financial and other assistance to (1) the clergy of the Anglican Communion, and (2) any widow or other dependant of such persons, who may be in financial necessity or distress, wherever they may be. Grants are made to cover many kinds of emergency including debts, bereavement or illness; also for removals, school clothing, holidays, etc. Pensions are paid to certain widows and elderly unmarried daughters of clergymen. Administers the assets of the former Curates Augmentation Fund. *Enquiries to:* The Secretary, The Friends of the Clergy Corporation, 27 Medway St, London SW1P 2BD *Tel:* 0171–222 2288
Fax: 0171–233 1244

Friends of the Elderly
Founded 1905. A voluntary society administering homes for elderly professional people and a welfare department giving general help to elderly people of any background. *President:* HRH The Princess Margaret, Countess of Snowdon. *Chief Exec:* Sally Levett, 40–42 Ebury St, London SW1W 0LZ *Tel:* 0171–730 8263
Fax: 0171–259 0154

Frontier Youth Trust
Founded 1964. Provides training, resources information, support and association for Christians working with disadvantaged young people in the community, whether church based, unattached or within the youth and community service, particularly in urban/industrial areas. *Secretary:* Mr Michael Eastman, 4th Floor, 70–74 City Rd, London EC1Y 2BJ *Tel:* 0171–336 7744
Fax: 0171–324 9900
e-mail: frontier@fyt.org.uk

FWA (Family Welfare Association)
Founded 1869. Provides social work and social care services for families and individuals including special housing services. Administers Trust Funds which give financial grants to individuals. Provides information to students through the Educational Grants Advisory Service. *Chief Exec:* Helen Dent, 501/505 Kingsland Rd, Dalston, London E8 4AU *Tel:* 0171–254 6251

GFS Platform for Young Women
A world-wide charity committed to supporting and protecting vulnerable young women. The work in this coun-

try is increasingly directed to helping young disadvantaged women who are homeless and generally at risk. Eight inner city shared housing schemes provide over 350 secure bed-spaces. 200 voluntary support groups meet regularly. Five community projects provide education and support for young women and young unsupported mothers and their children. *Chief Exec:* Mrs Hazel Crompton, 126 Queen's Gate, London SW7 5LQ
Tel: 0171–589 9628
Fax: 0171–225 1458
e-mail: platform@gfs.u-net.com
Web: hppt://www.tabor.co.uk/gfs/

Girls' Brigade
An international inter-denominational youth organisation having as its aim 'to help girls to become followers of the Lord Jesus Christ and through self-control, reverence and sense of responsibility to find true enrichment of life'. *National Secretary:* Mrs Sylvia Bunting, Girls' Brigade House, Foxhall Rd, Didcot, Oxon OX11 7BQ
Tel: (01235) 510425
Fax: (01235) 510429

Greater Churches Group
The group was founded in 1991 as an informal association of non-cathedral churches which, by virtue of their great age, size, historical, architectural or ecclesiastical importance, display many of the characteristics of a cathedral, also fulfil a role which is additional to that of a normal parish church. Its aims are to provide help and mutual support in dealing with the special problems of running a 'cathedral-like' church within the organizational and financial structure of a parish church, to enhance the quality of parish worship in such churches and to promote wider recognition of the unique position and needs of churches in this category. The group also serves as a channel of communication for other organisations wishing to have contact with churches of this type. *Hon Secretary:* Mr Marcus Ashman, 12 Colston Parade, Bristol BS1 6RA   *Tel* and *Fax:* 0117–929 1487

Greenbelt Festivals
Organises an annual Christian arts festival which takes place in the grounds of Deene Park, a stately home in Northamptonshire. Average audience figures are between fifteen and twenty thousand, most of whom camp for the five-day event held over the August Bank Holiday. There is one large open-air venue which hosts nightly concerts and the main communion service on Sunday morning. There are also tented venues for music, seminars, theatre, film, an art gallery, workshops, resources, cafes and shops. The event is interdenominational but a recent survey has shown that the largest denominational presence is Anglican. *Chair:* Dot Reid *General Manager:* Andy Thornton, The Greenhouse, Hillmarton Rd, London N7 9HE   *Tel* and *Fax:* 0171–700 5765
e-mail: lukeswarm@msn.com

Gregorian Association
Founded 1870 to spread reliable information on Plainsong and to promote its use; to demonstrate its suitability to the English language by means of services and holding lectures and conferences; to provide expert advice and instruction on the use of Plainsong. *President:* The Archbishop of Canterbury *General Secretary:* Mr Grey Macartney, 26 The Grove, Ealing, London W5 5LH
Web: http://www.beaufort.demon.co.uk/chant.htm

Grubb Institute
The Grubb Institute's central aim is to contribute to the well-being of society. It is committed to explore ways in which the Christian faith and theology can be a resource for understanding society and for generating the hope that society needs. The Institute pursues these aims by engaging with individuals, groups and institutions through advisory work training assignments, applied social research and evaluations. It focuses on the interaction between leadership, management, organisation and vocation. Its starting point is the working experience of those in the situation, analysing this by using scientific disciplines based on a psycho-dynamic and systematic approach, in dialogue with theology. It considers that the task of the Church is to create conditions for the transformation of society and works with clergy and lay people to bring them about. Since 1969 it has worked with churches, religious orders and Christian agencies in many different parts of the world. *Director of Development:* Miss Jean Hutton, The Grubb Institute, Cloudesley St, London N1 0HU   *Tel:* 0171–278 8061
Fax: 0171–278 0728
e-mail: GrubbUK@aol.com

Guides Association
Founded 1910. Open to all girls and women between 5 and 65 years regardless of race, faith or any other circumstance, who are willing to make The Promise and endeavour to keep The Guide Law. Its purpose is to enable girls to mature into confident, capable and caring women determined, as individuals, to realise their potential in their career, home and personal life, and willing as citizens to contribute to their community and the wider world. *President:* HRH The Princess Margaret, Countess of Snowdon. *Chief Guide:* Miss Bridget Towle *Chief Exec:* Vacancy, 17/19 Buckingham Palace Rd, London SW1W 0PT   *Tel:* 0171–834 6242
e-mail: chq@guides.org.uk

Guild of All Souls
Founded 1873 as an intercessory guild, caring for the dying, the dead and the bereaved. Open to members of

the Church of England and Churches in communion with her. Chantry chapel at Walsingham and at St Stephen's, Gloucester Rd, London. Patron of 39 livings. *President:* The Bishop of Richborough *General Secretary:* Charles Brown, St Katharine Cree Church, 86 Leadenhall St, London EC3A 3DH   Tel: 0171–621 0098

Guild of Church Braillists
The Guild consists of a group of people who give their services to help blind readers by transcribing a variety of religious literature into Braille. Requests are welcome from individual readers for books, special services, etc. All other productions are sent to the National Library for the Blind or the Library of the RNIB. For further details contact the *Secretary:* Mrs Mabel Owen, 321 Feltham Hill Rd, Ashford, Middx TW15 1LP   Tel: (01784) 258040

Guild of Church Musicians
See **Archbishops' Certificate in Church Music** page 218.

Guild of Health
Founded in 1904 to further the Church's Ministry of Healing through prayer, sacrament and visiting the sick, and by co-operation with Christian doctors, nurses and other members of the healing team. It publishes a quarterly magazine *Way of Life*. *President:* Vacancy *General Secretary:* Revd Antonia Lynn, Guild of Health, Edward Wilson House, 26 Queen Anne St, London W1M 9LB
Tel: 0171–580 2492

Guild of Pastoral Psychology
The Guild offers a meeting ground for all interested in the relationship between religion and depth psychology, particularly the work of C. G. Jung and his followers. Depth psychology has contributed many new insights into the meaning of religion and its symbols and their relevance to everyday life. The Guild has monthly lectures in central London, a day conference in London in the Spring and a three-day Summer conference at Oxford. Further information and details of membership available from *Administrator:* Nicola Stanley, PO Box 1107, London W3 6ZP   Tel: 0181–993 8366

Guild of Servants of the Sanctuary
Founded 1898 to raise the spiritual standard of Servers, to promote friendship among them and to encourage attendance at Holy Communion in addition to times of duty. *Patrons:* The Archbishops of Canterbury, York and Wales. *Warden:* Rev David Moore, Vicarage, St Ives, Huntingdon, Cambs PE17 4DH. *Secretary General:* Mr Roy Cresswell, 20 Doe Bank Rd, Ocker Hill, Tipton, W Midlands DY4 0ES   Tel: 0121–556 2257

Guild of St Barnabas
Founded 1876 to be a fellowship of nurses within the Church of England. Membership is now open to all who are qualified or training in the health care professions and who are committed members of the Anglican Church, or of other churches in communion with it. The Guild aims to encourage the development of the spiritual life of members who are trying to witness to their Christian commitment through their professional practice. Members, both active and retired, support one another through prayer and caring friendship. *President:* Mrs B. M. Baer *Organising Secretary:* Mrs Mary Morrow, 16 Copperwood, Ashford, Kent TN24 8PZ
Tel: (01233) 635334

Guild of St Helena
Founded in 1875, the guild offers Christian fellowship and charitable giving to wives, families and members of the armed forces. *President:* Lady Cowan *Warden:* Mrs Sarah-Jane Gilchrist *Chief Secretary:* Mrs Janice Carson, Guild of St Helena, Wellington Barracks, Birdcage Walk, London SW1E 6HQ   Tel: 0171–414 3461

Guild of St Leonard
The Guild, with a membership of about 750, publishes a quarterly Intercession Paper. The Annual Eucharist and General Meeting are held in the autumn, usually in a prison chapel. *Warden:* Rt Revd Lloyd Rees *Chaplain and Secretary:* Revd Peter Walker OGS, The Chaplain's Office, HMP Moorland, Bawtry Rd, Hatfield Woodhouse, Doncaster DN7 6BW   Tel: (01302) 351500

Guild of St Raphael
Founded 1915 to work for the restoration of the Ministry of Healing as part of the normal function of the Church, by preparing the sick for all ministries of healing, by teaching the need of repentance and faith, by making use of the Sacraments of Healing and by Intercession. *Contact:* General Secretary, The White House, Holy Island, Northumberland TD15 3SR   Tel: (01289) 389302
e-mail: straphael@enterprise.net

Guildford Diocese Productions
Established at Grayswood Studio in 1975 as a communications centre for the benefit of churches and church groups primarily to make video, audio and audio visual presentations. The studio is also used by charitable, educational and commercial concerns at a local, national and international level. A primary objective is to enable Christians to communicate the Gospel for themselves by putting professional training equipment and editorial decisions into their own hands. GDP also produces and sells a range of videos including programmes for evangelism, stewardship, deaf people, and education. *President:* The Bishop of Guildford *Chairman:* Ven Mark Wilson *Director:* Canon Geoffrey Curtis, Grayswood Studio, The Vicarage, Clammer Hill, Grayswood, Surrey GU27 2DZ   Tel: (01428) 644208
Fax: (01428) 656684

Harnhill Centre of Christian Healing
A resource centre for the ministry of Christian Healing through counselling, prayer, quiet days, teaching courses and Christian Healing Services. The Centre provides residential accommodation. *Chairman:* Mr Angus Baillie-Hamilton *Chaplain/Warden:* Revd Paul Springate, Harnhill Manor, Cirencester, Glos GL7 5PX *Tel:* (01285) 850283
Fax: (01285) 850519

Harold Buxton Trust
Founded 1919 by the Rev Harold Buxton, late Bishop of Gibraltar, who had a particular concern for international ecumenism. The Trust's main focus is to promote mutual understanding and interchange between the Anglican, Roman Catholic and Orthodox Churches, particularly through the support of study and exchange visits to and from churches in Eastern Europe, the former Soviet Union and the Middle East. The trustees meet twice a year (May and November) to allocate grants. Further details and application form available from the *Secretary:* Mrs Pat Philips, c/o SPCK, Holy Trinity Church, Marylebone Rd, London NW1 4DU *Tel:* 0171–387 5282
Fax: 0171–388 2352
e-mail: pphillips@spck.org.uk

Henry Bradshaw Society
Founded 1890 for printing liturgical texts from manuscripts and rare editions of service books, etc. For available texts, apply to the *Secretary:* Dr David Chadd, School of Music, University of East Anglia, Norwich NR4 7TJ
e-mail: d.chadd@uea.ac.uk

Historic Churches Preservation Trust
Founded 1953 to assist with the preservation of historic churches of any Christian denomination whose parishioners are unable to commission essential repairs without outside financial help. *Patron:* HM The Queen *Chairman of Trustees:* Lord Nicholas Gordon Lennox *Secretary:* Wing Cdr Michael Tippen, Fulham Palace, London SW6 6EA
Tel: 0171–736 3054

Homes for Retired Clergy
BEAUCHAMP COMMUNITY, NEWLAND, MALVERN
Home for retired people, clerical or lay, either sex. Unfurnished, single and double flats available from time to time. Apply to the *Administrator to Trustees*, Beauchamp Community, Newland, Malvern, Worcs WR13 5AX
Tel: (01684) 562100

COLLEGE OF ST BARNABAS, LINGFIELD, SURREY
Permanent homes for 40 retired clergy with limited accommodation for married couples. Sick Bay-Resident Nursing Staff, for residents falling ill. Next to Dormans Station. *Apply:* The Warden, College of St Barnabas, Blackberry Lane, Lingfield, Surrey RH7 6NJ
Tel: (01342) 870260

House of St Barnabas in Soho
Founded 1846, provides accommodation for 34 single homeless women aged 18–70 who have low care needs such as marital breakdown or domestic troubles. All meals are provided and help is given to find permanent accommodation. *Warden:* Ms Anne Woodhouse, 1 Greek St, Soho, London W1V 6NQ *Tel:* 0171–437 1894

Hymn Society of Great Britain and Ireland
Founded in 1936 to encourage the study of hymns, both words and music; to raise the standard of hymn singing and to encourage a more discerning use of hymns. The Society publishes a Bulletin four times a year, and there is a three-day Annual Conference. Further information and details of membership from the *Secretary:* Revd Geoffrey Wrayford, 7 Paganel Rd, Minehead, Somerset TA24 5ET, Sutton Coldfield B76 9ES *Tel and Fax:* (01643) 703530

Incorporated Church Building Society
Founded 1818 as the 'Incorporated Society for promoting the Enlargement, Building and Repairing of Churches and Chapels' in the Anglican dioceses of England and Wales. A charity wholly dependent on voluntary giving, which makes interest free loans to Anglican churches in need of repair. Since 1963 the Society has been managed by the Historic Churches Preservation Trust. *President:* The Archbishop of Canterbury *Secretary:* Wing Cdr Michael Tippen, Fulham Palace, London SW6 6EA
Tel: 0171–736 3054

Industry Churches Forum
Founded 1918 as successor to the Navvy Mission (1877), and incorporating the Christian Social Union. ICF is a nationwide network which provides support for Christians who want to apply their faith in fresh and creative ways in the everyday working world, especially in industry and commerce. ICF aims to: Bring the concerns and opportunities of the world of work to the attention of clergy and congregations so that they will be alert to the scope for prayer and Christian action. Ensure that the relationship between faith, work and worship receives proper attention in Church life. Promote Christian training, counselling and prayer support for members of the congregation in their working vocations. Arrange special services of thanksgiving and prayer for industry and commerce. ICF is ecumenical and has close links with other groups and agencies involved with the Church's mission to industry and commerce. Membership is open to all. *Acting Secretary:* Terry Drummond, ICF, St Matthew House, 100 George St, Croydon CR0 1PE
Tel: 0181–656 1644

INFORM
(Information Network Focus on Religious Movements)
INFORM is a non-sectarian organisation, started in 1988

with funding from the Home Office, the Church of England and other main-line Churches. Further support has been received from the Wates and Nuffield Foundations, Smith's Charity and the Sainsbury family trusts. Its primary aims are to collect and to disseminate accurate, up-to-date information about new religious movements (or 'cults'), and to put inquirers in touch with a network of people and organisations with specialist knowledge. It will also put people in touch with a further, complementary, network of people or organisations that can advise or counsel those who are experiencing difficulties because of their own, a friend's or a relative's involvement in one of the movements. *Chairman:* Prof Eileen Barker, Houghton St, London WC2A 2AE
Tel: 0171–955 7654
Fax: 0171–955 7679
e-mail: INFORM@LSE.ac.uk

Institute for the Study of Christianity and Sexuality
Launched 1989, ISCS aims to promote an understanding of sexuality and its theological meaning through widening the previously narrow sexuality debate and offering new thinking on sexuality and gender issues. *Enquiries and donations to:* The Secretary, ISCS, Oxford House, Derbyshire St, London E2 6HG   *Tel:* 0171–739 1249

Inter Faith Network
Established in 1987 to encourage contact and dialogue at all levels between different faith communities in the United Kingdom. It aims to advance public knowledge and mutual understanding of the teaching, traditions and practices of the different faith communities in Britain, including an awareness of their distinctive features and of their common ground, and to promote good relations between persons of different faiths. *Co-chairs:* Mr Om Parkash Sharma and Rt Revd Roy Williamson. *Director:* Mr Brian Pearce, 5–7 Tavistock Place, London WC1H 6SN
Tel: 0171–388 0008
Fax: 0171–387 7968

Intercontinental Church Society
Founded 1823. ICS, an evangelical Anglican mission society, has served English speakers around the world and now operates permanent and seasonal chaplaincies in Europe and permanent chaplaincies in North Africa, the Middle East, the South Atlantic and South America. It ministers through its permanent chaplaincy congregations to those of any nationality and background who speak English. ICS sends over one hundred clergy annually to operate seasonal chaplaincies in Europe, ministering to holiday makers, including senior citizens on Thomson *Young at Heart* Holidays. ICS also publishes the *Directory of English-speaking Churches Abroad* (next edition due early 1999). *President:* Viscount Brentford *International Director:* Canon John Moore, 1 Athena Drive, Tachbrook Park, Warwick CV34 6NL   *Tel:* (01925) 430347
Fax: (01925) 330238
e-mail: icsint@compuserve.com

International Ecumenical Fellowship
Founded Fribourg 1967. Its aim is to 'seek in fellowship to serve the will of God and unite the People of God, by hearing the Word of God, declaring the praise of God and breaking the Bread of God unto the Glory of God'. Regions of the IEF have been established in Britain, Holland, Germany, France, Spain, Belgium, the USA, Poland and the Czech Republic. *Chairman of British Region:* Mrs Mardi Hall *Secretary:* Miss June Foster, Dryfe View, Boreland, Lockerbie DG11 2LH

Interserve
(formerly BMMF International)
Founded 1852. An international and interdenominational mission. Evangelical in its basis, it has five hundred personnel serving the peoples of South and Central Asia, the Middle East and also among ethnic groups in Britain. Personnel are involved in many different ministries – all with the common aim of sharing Good News of Jesus Christ in word and action. Those with professional training are welcomed, both long and short-term periods of service, to fill a wide range of vacancies. *Chairman:* Mr Alastair Watson *National Director:* Mr Richard Clark, 325 Kennington Rd, London SE11 4QH   *Tel:* 0171–735 8227
Fax: 0171–587 5362
e-mail: isewi@isewi.globa net.co.uk

Jubilate Hymns
An association of authors and musicians formed in 1974 for the purpose of publishing material for contemporary worship: *Hymns for Today's Church, Church Family Worship, Carols for Today, Carol Praise, Let's Praise!* 1 and 2, *Prayers for the People, Psalms for Today, Songs from the Psalms, The Dramatised Bible, The Wedding Book, Hymns for the People, World Praise* 1 and 2. *Chairman:* Rt Revd Michael Baughen *Secretary:* David Peacock *Copyright Manager:* Mrs M. Williams, 4 Thorne Park Rd, Chelston, Torquay TQ2 6RX   *Tel:* (01803) 607754
Fax: (01803) 605682
e-mail: JubilateMW@aol.com

Julian Meetings
A network of contemplative prayer groups, begun in Britain in 1973. There are now about three hundred groups in the UK and some in Australia, South Africa and the USA. Ecumenical. *Contact:* Yvonne Walker, 5 Fernbrook Drive, Harrow, Middx HA2 7EE

Julian of Norwich, Shrine of Lady
The cell of Julian of Norwich, a chapel attached to St

Julian's Church, Norwich, stands on the site where the 14th-century anchoress wrote her book *Revelations of Divine Love*. There is accommodation in the convent of the Community of the Sacred Passion beside the Church. Quiet days and retreats can be arranged. The Julian Centre where there is a bookstall and library of spirituality, welcomes visitors and pilgrims (open weekdays 11am–4pm summer; 11am–3pm winter). Large parties and those wanting overnight accommodation must book in advance. *Booklist and mail order books:* The Julian Centre, Rouen Rd, Norwich NR1 1QT
Tel: (01603) 767380 (hours as above)
Accommodation and visits: Sister in Charge, All Hallows House, Rouen Rd, Norwich NR1 1QT Tel: (01603) 624738

Keston Institute
The centre for the study of religion and church-state relations in the postcommunist and communist world. Founded in 1970 following a request by persecuted Ukranian Christians, Keston defends the right to believe by publishing information and research in a weekly e-mail news bulletin *Keston News Service*, a bimonthly magazine *Frontier* and a quarterly academic journal *Religion, State & Society*. Keston maintains offices in Oxford and Moscow and its staff are frequently cited in the international news media. Its unique archive and library are used by believers, scholars, government departments, the news media and visitors from all over the world. *Director:* Canon Michael Bourdeaux, 4 Park Town, Oxford OX2 6SH Tel: (01865) 311022
Fax: (01865) 311280
e-mail: keston.institute@keston.org
Web: http://www.keston.org

Keswick Convention
Founded 1875 to promote personal, practical and scriptural holiness. *Chairman:* Mr Jonathan Lamb *Convention Secretary:* Mr Mark Smith, The Keswick Convention Centre, Skiddaw St, Keswick, Cumbria CA12 4BY
Tel: (0176 87) 72589

KeyChange
(formerly Christian Alliance)
Established 1920. Offers care, acceptance and Christian community to people in need through the provision of residential care for frail elderly people and supported accommodation for young homeless people. *Chief Exec:* David Shafik, 5 St George's Mews, 43 Westminster Bridge Rd, London SE1 7JB Tel: 0171–633 0533
Fax: 0171–928 1872
e-mail: info@keychange.org.uk
Web: http://www.keychange.org.uk

Korean Mission Partnership
Founded 1889 to support the Anglican Church in Korea.

Hon Secretary and Treasurer: Miss Eilene Hassall, Lewis Cottage, The Palace, Hereford HR4 9BJ
Tel: (01432) 274238

Langley House Trust
Founded in 1958 the Langley House Trust, a national Christian charity, provides care and rehabilitation for ex-offenders to work towards crime-free independence and integration into normal society. The Trust aims to help ex-offenders to address their physical, emotional, mental and spiritual needs. It currently runs 12 residential homes and six move-on projects scattered across the UK providing different types of accommodation for varying needs including drug rehabilitation, mental disorder and alcohol related offending. *Chairman:* Colin Honey *Chief Exec:* John Adams *Contact:* Paul Langley, PO Box 181, Witney, Oxon OX8 6WD Tel and Fax: (01993) 774075

Latimer House
Founded 1959 to promote from an evangelical standpoint theological research and scholarly writing on current Church questions. *Chairman of the Council:* Dr Derek Scales *Warden:* Revd Nigel Atkinson, 131 Banbury Rd, Oxford OX2 7AJ Tel: (01865) 513879
Fax: (01865) 513879

Lee Abbey Household Communities
There are three household communities based in Urban Priority Areas in Birmingham, Blackburn, and Bristol. Community members live under a common rule of life and seek to be involved in their local community and church. *Contact:* Ven Alan Smith, Archdeacon's House, 39 The Brackens, Clayton, Newcastle-under-Lyme, Staffs ST5 4JL Tel: (01782) 663066
Fax: (01782)711165

Lee Abbey International Students' Club
Founded in 1964 by the Lee Abbey Fellowship as a ministry to students of all nationalities, the Club provides long and short-term hostel accommodation for students of all faiths or none and is served by a Christian community, many of whom are young people. Applications are invited from anyone interested in joining the community, residing as a student or staying as a holiday-maker when students are away. *Warden:* Revd David Weekes, Lee Abbey International Students' Club, 57/67 Lexham Gardens, London W8 6JJ Tel: 0171–373 7242
Fax: 0171–244 8702

Leprosy Mission
Founded 1874 (1) to minister in the name of Jesus Christ to the physical, mental and spiritual needs of sufferers from leprosy (2) to assist in their rehabilitation and (3) to work towards the eradication of leprosy. *Exec Director:*

Revd J. A. Lloyd, Goldhay Way, Orton Goldhay, Peterborough PE2 5GZ   *Tel:* (01733) 370505
Fax: (01733) 370960
e-mail: TLMEW@cityscape.co.uk

Lesbian and Gay Christian Movement
LGCM has four principal aims: to encourage fellowship, friendship and support among lesbian and gay Christians through prayer, study and action; to help the whole Church examine its understanding of human sexuality and to work for positive acceptance of gay relationships; to encourage members to witness to their Christian faith within the gay community and to their convictions about human sexuality within the Church; to maintain and strengthen links with other gay Christian groups both in Britain and elsewhere. An extensive network of local groups exists and a wide range of resources are available. *Secretary:* Revd Richard Kirker, LGCM, Oxford House, Derbyshire St, Bethnal Green, London E2 6HG
Tel: 0171–739 1249
0171–739 8134 (Counselling Helpline)
Fax: 0171–739 1249
e-mail: lgcm@churchnet.ucsm.ac.uk

Lesbian and Gay Clergy Consultation
The national support organisation for gay and lesbian clergy and ordinands in the Anglican Churches of Great Britain. It holds six-monthly meetings offering a safe environment to meet in. It also seeks to act as a forum for educational dialogue within the Church, and to represent the concerns of gay and lesbian clergy and ordinands to the House of Bishops and the wider Church. *Convenor:* Revd Colin Coward, 11 Murfett Close, Wimbledon, London SW19 6QB   *Tel:* 0181–788 1384
e-mail: CCMCoward@aol.com

Li Tim-Oi Foundation
Perpetuates the name of the first Anglican woman priest. It was founded on the 50th anniversary of her priesting on 25 January 1944. It provides bursaries to help women in the majority world of the 'South' train for Christian work, lay or ordained, in their own countries. It welcomes enquiries for help from, or on behalf of, candidates who are members of Anglican dioceses or of United Churches in communion with Canterbury, but only exceptionally for those seeking training at institutions in the 'North'. Requests for help, particularly from Africa, are already outstripping funds available. Thus all donations from parishes and individuals are put to good use. *Patrons:* Lord Coggan, Lord Runcie, Bishop Penny Jamieson of Dunedin, the Archbishop of Canterbury and Bishop K. H. Ting. *Chair:* Canon Ruth Wintle *Secretary:* Revd Christopher Hall, The Knowle, Deddington, Banbury OX15 0TB   *Tel* and *Fax:* (01869) 338225
e-mail: achall@mail.globalnet.co.uk

Librarians' Christian Fellowship
Constituted 1976 to provide opportunities for Christian librarians to consider issues in librarianship from a Christian standpoint, and to promote opportunities for presenting the Christian faith to people working in libraries of all kinds. *Hon Secretary:* Graham Hedges, 34 Thurlestone Ave, Ilford, Essex IG3 9DU   *Tel:* 0181–599 1310
e-mail: fm128@viscount.org.uk
Web: http://churchnet.ucsm.ac.uk/lcf/lcfhome.htm

Lincoln Theological Institute for the Study of Religion and Society
Inaugurated in 1997, the Institute is a research and teaching unit of the University of Sheffield, specialising in the study of religion and society. The Institute focuses on postgraduate and postdoctoral research and works on funded projects that benefit society, churches and higher education by applying theological insights to issues of common concern. There are also courses and lectures open to the public and resources for lay people and clergy. The Lincoln Theological Institute originated from Lincoln Theological College, founded as an ordination training college in 1874. The Institute has an extensive library, developed since 1874, containing approximately 20,000 volumes on theology and related subjects, as well as an extensive periodical collection and works of reference. The library has been fully computerised to allow for flexible searching and retrieval. Visitors are welcome. For further information and library subscription details contact the Administrator/Librarian. *Director:* Dr Martyn Percy *Administrator/Librarian:* Caroline Dicker, 36 Wilkinson St, Sheffield S10 2GB   *Tel:* 0114–222 6399
Fax: 0114–276 3973
e-mail: C.Dicker@Sheffield.ac.uk
Web: http://www.shef.ac.uk/~lti/

London City Mission
Founded 1835 to extend the knowledge of the Gospel among the inhabitants of London and its vicinity. Interdenominational. *Chairman:* David Houghton *General Secretary:* Revd James McAllen, Nasmith House, 175 Tower Bridge Rd, London SE1 2AH   *Tel:* 0171–407 7585
Fax: 0171–403 6711
e-mail: lcm.uk@btinternet.com

London Union of Youth Clubs
A long established voluntary association of youth organisations in the Greater London area. Brings skills and resources to voluntary and statutory youth clubs and groups, and provides a London resource for work with young women. *Chief Exec:* Mark Wakefield, 64 Camberwell Rd, London SE5 0EN   *Tel:* 0171–701 6366
e-mail: name@youthworklondon.demon.co.uk
Web: http://www.youthworklondon

Lord Wharton's Charity
Founded 1696 to distribute Bibles and other religious books to children and young people of all denominations in all counties of the United Kingdom and Northern Ireland. *Clerk to the Trustees:* Mrs B. Edwards, 30 Prentis Rd, London SW16 1QD Tel: 0181–769 1924

Lord's Day Observance Society (Inc)
Founded 1831 to preserve Sunday as the national day of rest and to promote its observance as the Lord's Day for worship and Christian service. *President:* Mr J. Neville Knox *Secretary:* Mr John G. Roberts, Unit 3, Epsom Business Park, Kiln Lane, Epsom, Surrey KT17 1JF
Tel: (01372) 728300
Fax: (01372) 722400
e-mail: ldos.dayone@ukonline.co.uk

MACA – Partners in Mental Health
MACA provides a wide range of quality community-based services for people with mental health needs and their carers. Its facilities offer care which is appropriate to each individual and is designed to encourage their independence and self-respect. MACA develops new services in conjunction with Health and Social Services organisations to meet the needs of local communities. These include: supported accommodation and community support; day care and social clubs; employment training; carer support; services for offenders with mental health needs; and information and training services. MACA is registered with CCETSW to offer assessment for NVQs in care and special needs housing. *Chairman:* Mr J. Birney *Chief Exec:* Gilbert Hitchon, 25 Bedford Square, London WC1B 3HW Tel: 0171–436 6194
Fax: 0171–637 1980

Marshall's Charity
Founded 1627. Makes grants for (1) building, purchasing or modernising parsonages of the Church of England or the Church in Wales. (2) repairs to churches in Kent, Surrey and Lincolnshire. *Clerk to the Trustees:* Mr Richard Goatcher, Marshall House, 66 Newcomen St, London SE1 1YT Tel: 0171–407 2979

Mayflower Family Centre
A local church and community centre in Canning Town in the East End of London. Activities include groups for all ages, sports facilities, pensioners' luncheon club, advice desk, youth work, worship and Christian teaching. Three hostels, a launderette/coffee bar, charity shop and workshops. The centre offers residential facilities and ministry to those in need. The Mayflower Family Centre, Vincent St, London E16 1LZ Tel: 0171–476 1171
Fax: 0171–511 1019

Melanesian Mission
Founded in 1849 to preach the Gospel and to teach and care for the sick in the Solomon Islands and Vanuatu (then the Diocese of Melanesia). Its present function is to support by prayer, interest, alms, and staff when necessary, the Church of the Province of Melanesia formed in 1975. *Chairman:* The Bishop of Bristol *General Secretary:* Revd Peter Fox, Harpsden Rectory, 2 Harpsden Way, Henley-on-Thames, Oxon RG9 1NL Tel: (01491) 573401
Fax: (01491) 579871
e-mail: CMelanesUK@aol.com

Mersey Mission to Seamen
Founded 1855 for the spiritual and temporal welfare of seafarers frequenting Merseyside. *Chairman:* Mr L. A. Holder *Chapl Supt:* Revd G. John Simmons, Colonsay House, 20 Crosby Rd South, Liverpool, Merseyside L22 1RQ Tel: 0151–920 3253
Fax: 0151–928 0244
e-mail: liverangel@aol.com
Web: http://netministries.org/see/charmin/CH01395

Message
Founded 1969 by Miss Norah Coggan. Message is 'the service offered by local groups of churches through the medium of two-minute recorded telephone talks explaining the Good News of Jesus Christ as revealed in the Bible'. *President:* The Archbishop of Canterbury *Chairman:* Mr Michael Graves *National Admin Secretary:* Mrs Rita Hatch, 6 Darnley Rd, Woodford Green, Essex IG8 9HU Tel: 0181–504 4134

Metropolitan Visiting and Relief Association
Founded 1843 for promoting the relief of destitution in London and for improving the conditions of the poor. It aims to assist the clergy of the Church of England in the Metropolitan area (1) in giving financial help in their parishes (2) to help them in constructive social work by providing financial help for cases where permanent good results may be expected (3) to assist clergy who co-operate with other Agencies engaged in social work (4) to assist some married ordinands' families. Family Welfare Assn, 501/505 Kingsland Rd, Dalston, London E8 4AU Tel: 0171–249 6636

Mid-Africa Ministry (CMS)
(formerly Ruanda Mission)
Founded in 1921 and working in partnership with the Anglican Church in South West Uganda, Rwanda, Burundi and Democratic Republic of Congo through theological training, medical, educational, agricultural and technical work. *Chairman:* Revd David Applin *General Secretary:* Revd Robert de Berry, Partnership House, 157 Waterloo Rd, London SE1 8UU Tel: 0171–261 1370
Fax: 0171–401 2910
e-mail: mid_africa_ministry@compuserve.com

Mirfield Centre

Co-ordinates the combined resources of the College of the Resurrection, the Northern Ordination Course (Eastern Wing) and the Faith in Community Project, with the support of the Community of the Resurrection, to make them available for building up the whole people of God in the area of the West Yorkshire Ecumenical Council and beyond. *Director:* Bridget Rees, The Mirfield Centre, College of the Resurrection, Mirfield, W Yorks WF14 0BW
Tel: (01924) 481911
Fax: (01924) 492738
e-mail: brees@mirfield.co.uk

Missions to Seamen

Anglican missionary society which supports and links the Anglican Church's ministry to seafarers of all races and creeds in ports throughout the world. It has full-time staff and/or seafarers' centres in over 100 ports, honorary chaplains in over 200 others. In many ports it works in close co-operation with Christian societies of other denominations, and it is a member of the International Christian Maritime Association. *President:* HRH The Princess Royal *Secretary General:* Canon Glyn Jones *Justice and Welfare Secretary:* Canon Ken Peters *Ministry Secretary:* Canon Bill Christianson, St Michael Paternoster Royal, College Hill, London EC4R 2RL
Tel: 0171–248 5202
Fax: 0171–248 4761
e-mail: flyingangel@mtslondon.demon.co.uk

MODEM

(Managerial and Organisational Disciplines for the Enhancement of Ministry)
MODEM encourages the exchange of managerial and organisational skills between the workplace and the churches. It aims to set the agenda for management/ministry issues so that by the year 2000 the values and disciplines of those engaged in the management of secular and church organisations will be mutually recognised and respected. Corporate, group or congregational, and individual members of MODEM are able to share in the developing network of those offering, or needing, experience and resources. MODEM publishes a register for the exchange of skills. Its members are encouraged to combine to offer specialised information, courses or topical consultations. It is associated with the Edward King Institute in the publication of the Journal *Ministry*. *Trustees:* Mr Raymond Clarke, Rt Revd Christopher Mayfield, Professor Gillian Stamp, Canon Norman Todd, Mr Roger Young. *Chairman:* Mr Alan Harpham *Membership information:* MODEM, Carselands, Woodmancote, Henfield, W Sussex BN5 9SS
Tel and *Fax:* (01273) 493172
Web: http://churchnet.ucsm.ac.uk/modem/

Modern Churchpeople's Union

Founded 1898. A society within the Church of England and the Anglican Communion for the advancement of liberal Christian thought. MCU embraces the spirit of freedom and informed enquiry, seeks to involve the Christian faith in an ongoing search for truth by interpreting traditional doctrine in the light of present day understanding. Publishes a quarterly journal *Modern Believing*. It sponsors and encourages like-minded organisations as well as the setting up of local groups and conferences to foster dialogue and exchange views. Holds an annual conference on contemporary issues. MCU affirms a comprehensive Church of England, respects other churches and is prepared to learn from other world religions and concerned people. *President:* Rt Revd John Saxbee *General Secretary:* Revd Nicholas Henderson, MCU Office, 25 Birch Grove, London W3 9SP
Tel: 0181–932 4379
Fax: 0181–993 5812
e-mail: modchurchunion@btinternet.com
Web: http://www.mcm.co.uk/modchurchunion

Morse-Boycott Bursary Fund

(formerly St Mary-of-the-Angels Song School Trust)
Founded 1932 originally as a parochial Choir School but from 1935 to 1970 served the Church at large and now takes the form of Bursaries for boys at Cathedral choir schools. *Administrator:* The Communar, Cathedral Office, Royal Chantry, Cathedral Cloisters, Chichester PO19 1PX
Tel: (01243) 782595

Mothers' Union

See page 172.

Movement for the Reform of Infant Baptism (MORIB)

MORIB has four aims: to bring an end to the practice of indiscriminate infant baptism; to demonstrate that baptism is the sacrament instituted by Christ for those becoming members of the visible Church; to seek the reform of the Canons and rules of the Church of England in line with the above stated aims; to promote within the Church of England debate and review of the biblical, theological, pastoral and evangelistic aspects of Christian initiation. *President:* Rt Revd Colin Buchanan, *Chairman:* Revd Clifford Owen *Secretary:* Mrs Carol Snipe, 18 Taylors Lane, Lindford, Bordon, Hants GU35 0SW
Tel: (01420) 477508

Mrs Frances Ashton's Charity

Provides grants of variable amounts for needy clergymen of the Church of England, serving or retired, and the widows or widowers of such clergy. Completed applications are required by 1st June for the annual distribution in September. *Details from:* The Receiver, Mrs Barbara Davis, Charities Aid Foundation, Kings Hill, West Malling, Kent ME19 4TA
Tel: (01732) 520081
e-mail: bdavis@caf.charitynet.org

MSF Clergy and Church Workers
The Clergy Section of the Manufacturing, Science and Finance union was set up in 1994 in response to the needs of clergy for a professional association with the facilities and support of a modern trade union. Membership is wholly ecumenical and open to all who work in the service of the churches and other faiths, throughout the United Kingdom and Ireland. The section's name has been changed recently to reflect its growing membership among lay workers, as well as ordained ministers. MSF itself is Britain's third largest union, with almost 500,000 members, and the clergy and church workers are part of its voluntary sector. *Chair:* Revd W. F. Ward *Exec Chair:* Revd Hazel Barkham *Communications:* Revd Stephen Trott *National Secretary:* Dr Chris Ball, MSF Centre, 33–37 Moreland St, London EC1V 8BB
Tel: 0171–505 3000
Fax: 0171–505 3282
e-mail: ballc@msf.org.uk

National Christian Education Council
(Incorporating International Bible Reading Association) An ecumenical body concerned with development and training in Christian education in the church. Publishers of books and visual aids covering all aspects of Christian education. *General Secretary:* Revd John Gear, 1020 Bristol Rd, Selly Oak, Birmingham B29 6LB
Tel: 0121–472 4242
Fax: 0121–472 7575
e-mail: ncec@netlink.co.uk

National Deaf Church Conference
Founded in 1967 by the late Canon Tom Sutcliffe, who was himself deaf. It is the national forum for delegates from the Deaf Church and meets twice yearly for weekend and day conferences where the spiritual and social issues facing the Church of England are discussed. The main objective is to make the general public aware that deaf Christians are not isolated worshipping communities, but part of the whole Church. It works closely with the Advisory Board of Ministry Committee for Ministry among Deaf People. *Chair:* Revd Vera Hunt, 27 Redriff Close, Maidenhead, Berks SL6 4DJ

National Retreat Association
Comprising these Christian retreat groups – Association for Promoting Retreats, Baptist Union Retreat Group, Methodist Retreat Group, National Retreat Movement (RC), Quaker Retreat Group, United Reformed Church Silence and Retreat Network. Offers information and resources about retreats to both the would-be and the seasoned retreatant, co-ordinates training opportunities in the field of retreat giving and spiritual direction, promotes the work of retreat houses and encourages regional activity. *The Vision*, an ecumenical journal listing retreat houses in Britain and Ireland and their programmes is published annually (1999 edition £4.80 inc p&p). Other literature is also available, send for publications list. *Exec Officer:* Paddy Lane, The Central Hall, 256 Bermondsey St, London SE1 3UJ
Tel: 0171–357 7736
Fax: 0171–357 7724

New England Company
A charity founded 1649 and is the senior English missionary society. *Governor:* Mr T. C. Stephenson *Treasurer:* Viscount Bridgeman *Secretary:* Mrs Jenny Carter, The Bower House, Clavering, Saffron Walden, Essex CB11 4QR
Tel: (01799) 550212
Fax: (01799) 550169

Newton's Trust
Established to provide assistance to widows or unmarried daughters of deceased clergymen and to divorced or separated wives of clergymen of the Church of England. Applications are considered by the grants committee appointed by the Trustees, and one time cash grants are made at their discretion. *Chairman:* Mr Dale Bridgewater *Secretary:* Mr C. Tomlinson, 19A The Close, Lichfield, Staffs WS13 7LD
Tel: (01543) 306100
Fax: (01543) 306109
e-mail: lich.cath@virgin.net

Nikaean Club
Founded 1925 to exercise hospitality on behalf of the Archbishop of Canterbury to Christians of non-Anglican traditions. *Chairman:* Sir Peter Marshall *Guestmaster:* Canon Richard Marsh *Hon Secretary:* Miss Josephine Pollard, Lambeth Palace, London SE1 7JU
Tel: 0171–928 8282
Fax: 0171–261 9836
e-mail: Jo.Pollard@lampal.clara.net

North of England Institute for Christian Education
Founded in 1981 as an ecumenical foundation managed by a board representing the educational interests of the Churches, universities and other educational institutions in the North East of England. Its primary objective is to create links, at both the theoretical and practical level, between Christian theology and education so as to contribute, mainly by research projects, towards the further education of those with a responsibility for teaching the Christian faith. *Director:* Revd Prof Jeff Astley, NEICE, Carter House, Pelaw Leazes Lane, Durham DH1 1TB
Tel: 0191–384 1034; 0191–374 2000 Ext 7807
Fax: 0191–384 7529
e-mail: Jeff.Astley@durham.ac.uk

OMF International (UK)
(formerly China Inland Mission)
Founded 1865 to preach the Christian message in East Asia and to establish the Church there. *Contact:* Guido

Braschi, Station Approach, Borough Green, Sevenoaks, Kent TN15 8BG
Tel: (01732) 887299
Fax: (01732) 887224
e-mail: gbraschi@omf.org.uk
Web: http://www.omf.org.uk

Open Synod Group

The objects of the Group are the promotion and advancement of the Christian religion. Its particular emphasis is working through the synodical structures for the growth of unity between all the Churches and the renewal of the life and organisation of the Church of England. Membership is open to all Christians but will be of particular interest to serving or one-time members of the General Synod, of any Diocesan or Deanery Synod, and of any PCC (PCCs are also eligible for corporate membership). The Group meets during each Group of Sessions of the General Synod. It publishes a magazine twice a year and holds a national conference every two or three years. There are several diocesan branches. *President:* The Bishop of Bristol *Chairman:* Canon Richard Atkinson *Secretary:* Dr Carole Cull, 6 Forndon Close, Lower Earley, Reading RG6 3XR *Tel:* (01189) 617923

Oratory of the Good Shepherd

Founded in 1913 at Cambridge University. The Oratory is a Society of professed priests and brothers working in five provinces, Britain, USA, Southern Africa, Canada and Australia. Oratorians are Regulars and bound together by a common Rule and discipline. They do not normally live together in community but meet for Chapter and are resident each year for the Oratory Retreat and General Chapter. Members include bishops, parish priests, lecturers, and missionaries. There is a noviciate before temporary profession after which life vows may be taken. The Rule of the Oratory requires celibacy, a regular account of spending and direction of life. In addition, 'Labour of the Mind' is a characteristic of the Oratory and members are expected to spend time in study. Attached to the Oratory are Companions, lay, ordained, married and single, who keep a Rule of Life and are part of the Oratory family. *English Provincial:* Rt Revd Lindsay Urwin OGS *Secretary General:* Fr Michael Bootes OGS, Vicarage, 1 Manor Farm Close, Kellington, Goole DN14 0PF *Tel:* (01977) 662876
Fax: (01977) 663072
e-mail: mb@theoratory.demon.co.uk

Order of Christian Unity

Christians from all churches who care about Christian values in the family, medical ethics, Christian education and the media, and who provide specialist back-up in the form of information and literature. *President:* Rt Revd Maurice Wood *Chairman:* James Bogle, Christian Unity House, 58 Hanover Gardens, London SE11 5TN
Tel: 0171–735 6210
Fax: 0171–582 1174

Ordination Candidate Funds (General)

ANGLO-CATHOLIC ORDINATION CANDIDATES' FUND
Secretary: Revd C. W. Danes, 31 Oakley Rd, Bocking, Braintree, Essex CM7 5QS

BRISTOL CLERICAL EDUCATION SOCIETY
Grants of up to £200 to ordinands and, occasionally, to clergy undertaking in-service training, for specific and exceptional items. *Secretary:* Revd Paul Denyer, Director of Ordinands, Vicarage, Kington Langley, Chippenham, Wilts SN15 5NJ *Tel:* (01249) 750231

CHURCH PASTORAL AID SOCIETY MINISTERS IN TRAINING FUND
Grants for men and women, married or single, in training for ordained or accredited ministry; for evangelical candidates only. *Vocation and Ministry Adviser:* Revd James Ambrose, CPAS Ministry and Vocation Unit, Athena Drive, Tachbrook Park, Warwick CV34 6NG
Tel: (01926) 334242

CLEAVER ORDINATION CANDIDATES' FUND
An academic trust to assist ordinands, clergy pursuing recognised courses of post-graduate study, and parochial clergy on approved study leave. Candidates must belong to the Catholic tradition within the Anglican Communion. Preference may be given to graduates of British universities. There is no permanent office, the Clerk of the time being working from his home address. *Apply:* Revd Dr Peter Lynn, Clerk to the Cleaver Trustees, Vicarage, Firle, Lewes, E Sussex BN8 6NP *Tel:* (01273) 858227

ELLAND SOCIETY ORDINATION FUND
Grants are made to applicants who are Evangelical in conviction, who are in training, and who must spend their first two years of ministry in the Province of York. Grants are usually made to help in cases of special need. *Apply:* Revd Tony Bowering, Vicarage, 2 Sunderland St, Tickhill, Doncaster DN11 9QJ *Tel:* (01302) 742224

LADY PEEL LEGACY TRUST
A small charity making grants to ordinands of catholic tradition. *Apply:* Prebendary James Trevelyan, Rectory, Honiton, Devon EX14 8BH

Overseas Bishoprics' Fund

Founded 1841 to assist towards the endowment and maintenance of bishoprics in any part of the world and to act as trustees of episcopal endowment funds. *Chairman:* Mr John Smallwood. *Hon Sec:* Mr John Clark, c/o PWM, Partnership House, 157 Waterloo Rd, London SE1 8XA *Hon Clerk:* Mr Terry Dawson, Central Board of Finance, Church House, Great Smith St, London SW1P 3NZ
Tel: 0171–928 8681

Oxford Mission
Founded 1880. The Oxford Mission consists of two Religious Communities, the Brotherhood and Sisterhood of the Epiphany and the Christa Sevika Sangha. Has houses in India and Bangladesh. Their work is pastoral, medical and educational and is carried on in the Dioceses of Calcutta and Dhaka. *India:* Father James Stevens (on loan from the diocese of Calcutta) and Sister-in-Charge, Sister Florence SE; *Bangladesh:* Rev Fr Francis Pande BE and Revd Mother Susila CSS. *Secretary:* Mrs Mary Marsh, PO Box 86, Romsey, Hants SO51 8YD
Tel and *Fax:* (01794) 515004

Papua New Guinea Church Partnership
Founded 1891 as the New Guinea Mission to give support to the Diocese of New Guinea in prayer, by sending staff and raising money. In 1977, when the Province of Papua New Guinea was inaugurated, the name of the mission was changed to Papua New Guinea Church Partnership in order to be more descriptive of the work. Staff serve in governmentally approved teaching, health and training posts; an annual block grant of £12,000 goes to the Provincial budget and audited accounts are sent to the UK. Unless new money is found this level of support cannot be maintained beyond the millenium. *President:* The Archbishop of York *Chairman:* Dr James Harper *General Secretary:* Chris Luxton, PNG Church Partnership, Partnership House, 157 Waterloo Rd, London SE1 8XA
Tel: 0171–928 8681
Fax: 0171–928 2371

Parish and People
Founded 1949 and was instrumental in effecting a quiet revolution in popularising the parish communion. In 1963 it merged with the Keble Conference Group and spearheaded movements towards team ministry, synodical government and church unity. It has continued to promote new life in the Anglican denomination, and publishes a range of stimulating material for parishes and deaneries in order to enable growth from the grass roots up of a lively, open, people's church in which lay ministry can blossom. In 1988 it took *Partners* under its wing, thus widening its interests to include publications on evangelism. In 1989 it set up the Deanery Resource Unit which provides a bi-annual mailing to over 200 deaneries which includes the well-established *Deanery Exchange* broadsheet, together with copies of books, pamphlets and briefings on matters of deanery concern. The unit works in cooperation with the Church House Deaneries Group. *Contact:* Revd Jimmy Hamilton-Brown, The Old Mill, Spetisbury, Blandford Forum, Dorset DT11 9DF
Tel and *Fax:* (01258) 453939
e-mail: PandPeople@aol.com

Partis College
Founded 1825 to provide accommodation (house) for ladies who are communicant members of the Church of England with low incomes. Also small Residential Care Home. The College was founded for the widows or daughters of clergymen, HM forces and other professions. *Chairman:* Ven John Burgess *Bursar:* Major Max Young, 1 Partis College, Newbridge Hill, Bath BA1 3QD
Tel: (01225) 421532

Philip Usher Memorial Fund
Founded 1948. Grants annual scholarships to Anglican priests, deacons or ordinands, preferably under 35 years of age, to study in a predominantly Orthodox country. Applications not later than 31 December for the following year. *Chairman:* The Archbishop of Canterbury *Hon Secretary of the Exec Ctee:* Administrative Secretary, CCU, Church House, Great Smith St, London SW1P 3NZ
Tel: 0171–898 1472
e-mail: Jan.ayres@chho.u-net.com

Pilgrim Adventure
Founded in 1987, Pilgrim Adventure provides a selection of *Pilgrim Journeys* for people who like to travel off the beaten track. Hill walking, island hopping and worship in out of the way places are all part of the experience. Pilgrim Adventure is Anglican based and ecumenical in outlook. *Patrons:* Rt Revd Richard Rutt, Very Revd Horace Dammers. *Chair:* David Gleed *Enquiries:* The Secretary, Pilgrim Adventure, 120 Bromley Heath Rd, Downend, Bristol BS16 6JJ
Tel: 0117–957 3997
Web: http://www.yell.co.uk/sites/pilgrim-adventure-uk/

Pilgrim Trust
Founded 1930 by the late Edward S. Harkness of New York with a sum of £2 million. The Trustees give grants to charities or recognised public bodies concerned with social welfare, art and learning and preservation. Current priorities for social welfare projects include the diversion of young people away from crime and substance misuse, the support of those with mental illness living as part of the community and the housing and rehabilitation of the long-term homeless. Grants are also offered to projects which seek to widen access to the arts and for the preservation of historic buildings. Block grants are given to the Council for the Care of Churches and the Historic Churches Preservation Trust for the repair and conservation of parish churches. *Director:* Miss Georgina Nayler, Fielden House, Little College St, London SW1P 3SH
Tel: 0171–222 4723

Pilsdon Community
The Pilsdon Community is dedicated to the ideals of the Christian gospel in the context of community living and open hospitality. The community at any one time will comprise of six to eight community members (leadership) and their children, about 25 guests (staying from

one month to several years), up to six visitors (staying one day to two weeks) and up to eight wayfarers (staying up to three days). Many of the guests have experienced a crisis in their lives (e.g. mental breakdown, alcoholism, drug addiction, marital breakdown, abuse, homelessness, prison, drop out of school or college, asylum seeking etc.). Pilsdon provides a working therapeutic environment of communal living, manual work, creative opportunities (pottery, art, crafts, music etc.) recreation, worship and pastoral care, to rebuild peoples' lives, self-respect, confidence and faith. Founded in 1958 by an Anglican priest, the community occupies an Elizabethan manor house and its outbuildings and smallholding of ten acres, six miles from the sea near Lyme Regis. The community life is inspired by the monastic tradition and the Little Gidding Community built around families. The worship and spirituality is Anglican and sacramental, but ecumenical in membership and all faiths and none as well as all races and cultures are welcome. Membership, guest and visitor enquiries should be made to the *Warden:* Revd Peter Barnett, Pilsdon Community, Pilsdon Manor, Pilsdon, Bridport, W Dorset DT6 5NZ
Tel: (01308) 868308
Fax: (01308) 868161
e-mail: pilsdon@btinternet.com
Web: http://www.btinternet.com/~pilsdon

Plainsong and Mediaeval Music Society
Formed 1888 to promote the study and appreciation of plainsong and mediaeval music; to arrange the printing, publication and sale of facsimiles, transcriptions, musical texts and studies; and to promote lectures and performances thereof. Publishes an annual scholarly journal. *Secretary:* Dr Stephen Farmer, Magdalene College, Cambridge CB3 0AG

Praxis
Founded 1990, Praxis is sponsored by the Liturgical Commission, the Alcuin Club and the Grove Group for the Renewal of Worship. Its aims are to enrich the practice and understanding of worship in the Church of England; to serve congregations and clergy in their exploration of God's call to worship; and to provide a forum in which different worshipping traditions can meet and interact. Praxis events include day meetings in London and the regions, residential conferences and national consultations. In 1997 Praxis, together with the ecumenical Institute for Liturgy and Mission at Sarum College in Salisbury, appointed a National Education Officer to help promote education in worship at every level. *Chairman:* Canon Stephen Oliver *National Education Officer:* Revd Mark Earey *Secretary:* Vacancy, St Matthew's House, 20 Great Peter St, London SW1P 2BU
Tel: 0171–222 3704
e-mail: paec@stmw.globalnet.co.uk
Web: http://www.sarum.ac.uk

Prayer Book Society
Founded in 1975 to uphold the worship and doctrine of the Church of England as enshrined in the Book of Common Prayer. The Society has a branch in every diocese of the Church of England and affiliated branches in Ireland, Scotland and Wales. Journals are published quarterly, also a quarterly newsletter, and the Society publishes other material of a critical or educational kind, related to the Book of Common Prayer. The Society encourages the use of the Book of Common Prayer as a major element in the worshipping life of the Church of England and seeks to spread knowledge and love of the 1662 Prayer Book. *Patron:* The Bishop of London *Chairman:* Anthony Kilminster *Hon Secretary:* Mrs Elaine Bishop, St James Garlickhythe, Garlick Hill, London EC4V 2AL
Tel: (01923) 824278

Protestant Reformation Society
Founded 1827 to study the doctrine and theology of the English Reformers and to promote the religious principles of the English Reformation. *Secretary:* Dr D. A. Scales, PO Box 47, Ramsgate, Kent CT11 9XB
Tel: (01843) 580542

Public Record Office
Records of central government and courts of law from the Norman Conquest (Domesday Book) to the recent past (for example, the Suez Campaign). Ruskin Ave, Kew, Richmond, Surrey TW9 4DU *Tel:* 0181–876 3444
Web: http://www.pro.gov.uk

Pusey House, Oxford
Founded 1884 to continue the work of Dr Pusey, academic and pastoral, in Oxford. *Principal:* Revd Philip Ursell, Pusey House, Oxford OX1 3LZ *Tel:* (01865) 278415

Pyncombe Charity
Income about £5,000 applied to assist needy serving clergymen in financial difficulties due to illness or other special circumstances within the family. Applications to be made through the Bishop. *Secretary:* Mr Ian Billinge, The Old Rectory, Crowcombe, Taunton, Som TA4 4AA
Tel: (01984) 618287
Fax: (01984) 618416
e-mail: BILLINGEIL@MSN.COM

Queen Victoria Clergy Fund
Founded 1897 to raise money towards the support of Church of England parochial clergy. Apart from one particular endowment, all the Fund's income is disbursed annually in block grants to dioceses specifically for the help of the clergy. *Chairman:* Bryan Sandford *Secretary:* Colin Menzies, Church House, Great Smith St, London SW1P 3NZ *Tel:* 0171–898 1310

Radius
(The Religious Drama Society of Great Britain)
Founded 1929 to encourage drama which throws light on the human condition. Assists and brings together those who create drama as a means of Christian understanding. Maintains an extensive lending library, publishes a quarterly magazine, organises summer schools, workshops and play writing competitions. Also publishes 'Radius Plays'. *Patrons:* The Archbishop of Canterbury, Dame Judi Dench. *Contact:* The Secretary, Radius Office, Christ Church and Upton Chapel, 1A Kennington Rd, London SE1 7QP   *Tel:* 0171–401 2422

Reader Missionary Studentship Association
Founded 1904 to offer financial assistance to Readers training as priests for service in the Church overseas. *Chairman:* Mr G. E. Crowley *Hon Treasurer:* Miss M. Brown *Hon Secretary:* Mrs Anne Ward, 3 Churchill Rd, Wells, Somerset BA5 3HZ   *Tel:* (01749) 671409

Rebecca Hussey's Book Charity
Established 1714 to give grants of religious and useful books to institutions in the United Kingdom. *Clerk to the Trustees:* Mrs Anne Butters, 21 Erleigh Rd, Reading RG1 5LR   *Tel:* 0118–987 1845

Reform
An evangelical network of clergy and laity in churches throughout the country. It came into being in 1993 and has campaigned for biblical integrity. It holds regular conferences, has over 1500 members and is currently establishing a Reform Fellowship of Churches. It has published a number of booklets on matters relating to biblical teaching on doctrine and morality within the Church of England. *Chairman:* Revd Philip Hacking *Administrators:* Jonathan and Fiona Lockwood, Reform, PO Box 1183, Sheffield S10 3YA
Tel and *Fax:* 0114–230 9256
e-mail: reform@legend.co.uk
Web: http://www.reform.org.uk

Relate
(formerly National Marriage Guidance Council)
Offers counselling and psychosexual therapy to those who seek advice with adult couple relationships, whether married or not. Relate also publishes a wide range of helpful literature available from its bookshop. There are 126 Relate Centres – to contact your nearest consult the local telephone directory. *Chief Exec:* Sarah Bowler, Herbert Gray College, Little Church St, Rugby, Warws CV21 3AP   *Tel:* (01788) 573241
Fax: (01788) 535007

Religious Education Council of England and Wales
The Council was formed in 1973 and is open to national organisations which have a special interest in the teaching of religious education in schools and colleges. The present membership of forty organisations includes representation from the main Christian denominations, the World Faiths, the British Humanist Association and the main educational bodies with professional RE interests. *Chair:* Mr Ian Wragg *Secretary:* Dr Stephen Orchard, CEM, Royal Buildings, Victoria St, Derby DE1 1GW
Tel: (01332) 296655
Fax: (01332) 343253
e-mail: cem@cem.org.uk

Retired Clergy Association
Founded 1927 to act as a bond of friendship in prayer and mutual help to retired clergy. Membership at 31 December 1997 was 3,170. There are local branches in Bexhill, Birmingham, Blackburn, Bournemouth, Bristol, Bury St Edmunds, Cambridge, Canterbury, Cheltenham, Chester, Chichester, Eastbourne, East Devon, Ely, Harrogate, Henfield, Hereford, Huntingdonshire, Isle of Wight, Lancaster, Leamington, Ludlow, Norwich, Oxford, Portsmouth (Mainland), Ripon, Rochester, Scarborough and Filey, Shrewsbury, Southampton, Stockport, Wells, West London, Weston-super-Mare, Winchester and Alresford, Worcester, Worthing and York. *Chairman:* Rt Revd Derek Bond *Hon Secretary:* Mr Kenneth Lightfoot, 12 Clouston Rd, Farnborough, Hants GU14 8PN   *Tel:* (01252) 546486

Rev Dr George Richards' Charity
Founded 1837 to financially assist clergy of the Church of England forced to retire early due to ill-health. Widows and dependants can also apply for assistance. *Secretary:* Mr David Newman, 51 Pole Barn Lane, Frinton-on-Sea, Essex CO13 9NQ   *Tel:* (01255) 676509
Fax: (01255) 851529

Richmond Fellowship for Community Mental Health
Established in 1959 to provide residential care services for people with mental health problems, and to promote understanding of mental health issues and human relations in the wider community. It now operates more than seventy residential, supported housing, day care and workscheme services for people with mental health, substance misuse and/or socio-emotional problems throughout the UK. Richmond Fellowship Training and Consultancy Services run an extensive programme of short courses on mental health, group work, supervision and management, which are open to those working in the care field. In addition, Training and Consultancy Services run an RSA Diploma in Post Traumatic Stress Counselling. *For further information contact:* The Richmond Fellowship, 8 Addison Rd, Kensington, London W14 8DJ
Tel: 0171–603 6373
Fax: 0171–602 8652

Royal Alexandra and Albert School
Founded in 1758, a voluntary-aided junior and secondary school providing boarding education for boys and girls aged 8–16 who are without one or both parents or who would benefit from boarding education because of home circumstances. Only boarding fees payable and bursaries available. Exceptional facilities. *President:* HRH The Duchess of Gloucester *Contact:* Foundation Secretary, Gatton Park, Reigate, Surrey RH2 0TW
Tel: (01737) 642576

Royal Asylum of St Ann's Society
The Society, founded in 1702, offers grants towards the expenses of educating children, from the age of 11, at boarding or day schools. Most, but not all, of those aided are children of clergy of the Church of England, however, in the first instance clergy should approach the Corporation of the Sons of the Clergy. The Society welcomes collections, donations and legacies towards this purpose. *President:* The Dean of Westminster *Chairman:* Mr Hugh Baddeley *Secretary:* Mr David Hanson, King Edward's School Witley, Petworth Rd, Wormley, Surrey GU8 5SG

Royal College of Organists
Founded 1864, Incorporated by Royal Charter 1893, 'to promote the art of organ-playing and choir training'. Holds lectures, recitals and master-classes nationwide. Examinations for Fellowship, Associateship, and Diploma in Choral Teaching. Membership open to all who take an interest in the work and profession of the organist and in organ music. *Patron:* HM The Queen *President:* Mr Martin Neary *Senior Exec:* Mr Alan Dear, 7 St Andrew St, Holborn, London EC4A 3LQ *Tel:* 0171–936 3606 (Admin)
0171–936 4321 (Library)
Fax: 0171–353 8244
Web: http://www.rco.org.uk

Royal Martyr Church Union
Founded 1906 to promote the restoration of King Charles's name to its proper place in the worldwide Church's Calendar and maintain the principles of Faith, Loyalty and Liberty for which he died and bring together descendants of cavalier officers and men, and anyone interested in Caroline history. *Chairman:* Hubert Wandesford Fenwick *Hon Secretary:* Ronald Miller of Pittenweem, The Priory, Pittenweem, Fife KY10 2LJ

Royal Naval Lay Readers' Society
Founded 1860. Licensed Readers assist in the work of the Anglican Church amongst the men and women of the Royal Navy and their families. In ships at sea and in naval establishments ashore they work alongside Naval Chaplains in the furtherance of the Christian faith and the welfare of the Navy's people. The society is dependent financially on voluntary contributions for the maintenance of its work. *Treasurer:* Mrs Stella Crawford, Room 203, Victory Building, HM Naval Base, Portsmouth, Hants PO1 3LS *Tel:* (01705) 727902

Royal School of Church Music
Music has a vital part to play in our worship. The RSCM aims to promote the use of music in worship by providing the musical and educational resources to train, develop and inspire clergy, church musicians and congregations of all denominations. A particularly important part of the RSCM's work over the last sixty years has centred on young people. Through holiday courses, training schemes, awards and festivals, the RSCM will continue to provide for tomorrow's Church. Appointed the official music agency for the Church of England from April 1996. *President:* The Archbishop of Canterbury *Chairman:* Sir David Harrison *Director General:* Professor John Harper, Cleveland Lodge, Westhumble, Dorking, Surrey RH5 6BW *Tel:* (01306) 877676
Fax: (01306) 887260
e-mail: cl@rscm.com
Web: http://www.rscm.com

RPS Rainer
(The Royal Philanthropic Society, incorporating the Rainer Foundation) A national voluntary organisation, founded in 1788, working primarily with young people at risk to delinquency, homelessness and abuse, through several community-based projects, some in partnership with local authorities and other voluntary organisations. Particular services include aftercare projects and bail support schemes, youth information, accommodation and support to young people on release from young offender institutions, youth training and employment schemes. *Patron:* HRH Prince Philip The Duke of Edinburgh *Chair:* Norman Warner *Chief Exec:* Don Coleman, Rectory Lodge, High St, Brasted, Westerham, Kent TN16 1JF *Tel:* (01959) 578200
Fax: (01959) 561891
e-mail: RPSCharity@aol.com

Rural Theology Association
Founded 1981 to provide a forum for the rural churches and to focus for the Church at large the distinctive ways and needs and contributions of the rural. Its aims are to study the gospel and develop theology in a rural setting, to encourage the development of patterns of ministry and mission appropriate to the countryside today, and to discover ways of living in the countryside which embody a Christian response to the world. *President:* Revd Prof Leslie Francis *Chairman:* Revd Eric Ashby *Secretary :* Revd Geoff Platt, Brecklands Cottage, Brecklands Green, North Pickenham, Swaffham PE37 8LG
Tel: (01760) 441581

Samaritans
A registered charity, founded in 1953 at St Stephen, Walbrook, EC4, which provides confidential and emotional support to people in crisis. The Samaritans is available, 24 hours a day, for anyone passing through crisis and at risk of suicide. It aims to provide society with a better understanding of suicide and the value of expressing feelings that may lead to suicide. Local branches can be found in the phone book under S or call 0345 90 90 90 (local rate) or write to Chris, PO Box 9090, Stirling FK8 2SA. *Chief Exec:* Simon Armson, 10 The Grove, Slough, Berks SL1 1QP
Tel: (01753) 532713
Fax: (01753) 819004
e-mail: jo@samaritans.org

School Chaplains' Conference
An association for anyone, ordained and lay, involved in Christian ministry in state and independent schools. *President:* Rt Revd Paul Barber, Bishop of Brixworth *Chairman:* Revd Richard Warden *Secretary:* Revd Stephen Burgess, c/o The Chaplain, Wycombe Abbey School, High Wycombe, Bucks HP11 1PE
Tel: (01494) 520381

Scout Association
Founded 1907 to encourage the physical, intellectual, social, and spiritual development of young people so that they may take a constructive place in society. Membership 700,000 of which a third are in Scout Groups sponsored by Anglican churches. *Chief Scout:* W. George Purdy *Contact:* Programme and Training Dept, The Scout Association, Gilwell Park, Chingford, London E4 7QW
Tel: 0181–524 5246
Fax: 0181–498 5329
e-mail: ukgilscout@aol.com

Scripture Gift Mission Inc
Founded 1888 to promote evangelism by means of the Scriptures. *Chairman:* Kenneth Griffiths *International Director:* Mr Hugh Davies, Radstock House, 3 Eccleston St, London SW1W 9LZ
Tel: 0171–730 2155

Scripture Union
Scripture Union seeks to make the Christian faith known to children, young people and families and to support the Church through resources, Bible reading and training. SU's work in Britain includes schools work, Bible ministries, publishing, training, evangelism, holidays and missions, family ministry and Frontier Youth Trust (supporting Christians working with young people outside the Church). Scripture Union is active in more than one hundred countries. *Chief Exec:* Peter Kimber, 207–209 Queensway, Bletchley, Milton Keynes MK2 2EB
Tel: (01908) 856000
Fax: (01908) 856111
e-mail: postmaster@scriptureunion.org.uk
Web: http://www.scripture.org.uk

Scripture Union in Schools
Works to establish, encourage and resource a voluntary Christian presence in Primary and Secondary schools through term-time work and holiday activities. *Head of Dept:* Mr Emlyn Williams, 207–209 Queensway, Bletchley, Milton Keynes MK2 2EB
e-mail: schools@scriptureunion.org.uk
Web: http://www.scripture.org.uk

Seamen's Friendly Society of St Paul
Trust administered by Alton Abbey, able to offer financial assistance to merchant sailors. *Contact:* The Abbot, Alton Abbey, Beech, Alton, Hants GU34 4AP
Tel: (01420) 562145/563575
Fax: (01420) 561691

Servants of Christ the King
Founded 1942 by Canon Roger Lloyd of Winchester. A movement of groups or 'Companies' of Christians who seek to develop a corporate life by praying together in silence, with disciplined discussion. They actively wait upon God to be led by the Holy Spirit, and undertake to do together any work which they are given by him to do. *Enquirers' Correspondent:* Mrs S. Wilsdon, Well Cottage, The Street, Kilmington, Axminster, Devon EX13 7RW
Tel: (01297) 34142

Shaftesbury Homes and *Arethusa*
Founded 1843 to house and educate homeless children in London, the society continues its work with 12 housing projects including residential children's homes, bedsitter projects, a home for vulnerable young mothers and babies, and a careers and education service giving the support essential in enabling young people to find their way back into society with confidence. It also provides the challenges of sail training in the ocean-going training ketch Arethusa and provides opportunities for children from the inner-city to swim, canoe, sail and climb at the Arethusa Venture Centre on the Medway, developing self confidence and a sense of achievement. *Director:* Capt Neil Baird-Murray, 3 Rectory Grove, London SW4 0EG
Tel: 0171–720 8709
Fax: 0171–720 2516

Shaftesbury Society
Shaftesbury exists to enable people in great need to achieve security, self-worth and significance and through this to show Christian care in action. It provides care and education services to people with learning and/or physical disabilities, and support for people who are poor or disadvantaged. *Chief Exec:* F. M. Beckett, The Shaftesbury Society, 16–20 Kingston Rd, London SW19 1JZ
Tel: 0181–239 5555
Fax: 0181–239 5580

Social Concern
(formerly the Church of England National Council for Social Aid, Church of England Temperance Society and Police Court Missionaries)
Social Concern – an independent charity raising its own funds – works to promote social justice and reconciliation and to protect the vulnerable in society. It seeks to identify unmet needs and help develop services and support to meet them. Currently it is focusing on two areas: (1) restorative justice – a process for bringing together all the parties involved in an offence to decide jointly how to deal with what has happened and how to face the future. Social Concern organises conferences and workshops to publicise new developments in this field at home and overseas; (2) educational material for schools – on topics such as gambling, to help young people gain a greater understanding of the pressures on them. In addition, Social Concern as a campaigning organisation responds to Government consultations and works with other groups in this field. It also acts as a resource and information centre for students and others. *Presidents:* The Archbishops of Canterbury and York *Chairman:* Rt Revd Colin Docker *Director:* Peter Carlin, Montague Chambers, Montague Close, London SE1 9DA   Tel: 0171–403 0977
Fax: 0171–403 0799
e-mail: info@social-concern.demon.co.uk

Society for Liturgical Study
Founded 1978. The Society promotes liturgical study and research, and holds a conference in alternate years. Membership is interdenominational and is open by invitation to persons involved in teaching liturgy, or in research in this field, or holding official appointments with responsibility for liturgy and worship. *Secretary:* Dr Martin Stringer, Dept of Theology, University of Birmingham, Edgbaston, Birmingham B15 2TT

Society for Old Testament Study
Founded 1917 as a society for OT Scholars in Britain and Ireland. Scholars not resident in the British Isles may also become members. Two meetings to hear and discuss papers are arranged annually. The Society also publishes its annual *Book List* and is involved in other publishing activities. It maintains links with OT scholars throughout the world, particularly the Dutch-Flemish OT Society with which it holds joint meetings every three years. Candidates for membership must be proficient in Hebrew and be proposed by two existing members. *Hon Secretary:* Dr Katharine Dell, The Divinity School, St John's St, Cambridge CB2 1TW   Tel: (01223) 332586
Fax: (01223) 332582
e-mail: kjd24@cam.ac.uk

Society for Promoting Christian Knowledge
Founded in 1698, SPCK is the oldest Anglican missionary society and seeks to support the work of the Church in every part of the world through the production and distribution of Christian literature and other communication resources. SPCK has three areas of activity: SPCK Publishing produces books to help Christians understand and deepen their faith, and provides resources for worship and evangelism. Under its four imprints – SPCK, Triangle, Lynx Communications and Sheldon Press – the Society has numerous titles in print and international distribution, which make it one of the largest and most active Christian publishers in Britain. SPCK Bookselling is one of Britain's largest chain of Christian bookshops, with thirty-three shops located throughout England and Wales. Through these shops the Society sells a wide range of new and secondhand Christian books. The shops aim to encourage people to read and learn more about the Christian faith. They support local churches by providing ready access to Christian books and other church requisites. Parishes are further assisted through co-operation in book agency schemes and by the provision of bookstalls at conferences and other major church events. Special discounts are made available to those training for full time ministry. SPCK Worldwide assists the development of Christian publishing and bookselling throughout the world and provides literature and other resources for education, worship and the training of church leaders in many countries. SPCK Worldwide's activities include the making of book grants to ordinands and theological libraries, the provision of capital and equipment to enable churches to establish publishing facilities in their own countries, the translation and production of liturgical material in indigenous languages, and the development of a wide range of Christian communications projects. These projects are dependent upon the voluntary giving of parishes and individuals, all such gifts being used directly in project work, with costs carried by the Society's endowment income. Projects are supported in over 120 countries and many are carried out in co-operation with other missionary agencies as well as local churches. *President:* The Archbishop of Canterbury *Chairman of the Governing Body:* General Sir Hugh Beach *General Secretary:* Paul Chandler, Holy Trinity Church, Marylebone Rd, London NW1 4DU
Tel: 0171–387 5282
Fax: 0171–388 2352
e-mail: spck@spck.org.uk
Web: http://www.spck.org.uk

Society for the Assistance of Ladies in Reduced Circumstances
Founded by the late Miss Edith Smallwood in 1886. Assistance is given to ladies of British nationality living alone on low incomes domiciled in the British Isles. A registered charity, solely dependent on voluntary contributions. *Patron:* Her Majesty The Queen *Apply:* The Secretary, Lancaster House, 25 Hornyold Rd, Malvern, Worcs WR14 1QQ   Tel: (01684) 574645

Society for the Maintenance of the Faith
Founded in 1873 the society presents, or shares in the presentation of, priests to over eighty benefices. As well as its work as a patronage body the society aims to promote Catholic teaching and practice in the Church of England at large. *Secretary:* Revd Paul Conrad, Christ Church Vicarage, 10 Cannon Place, London NW3 1EJ
Tel: 0171–435 6784

Society for the Ministry of Women in the Church
Founded 1929, the aim of this ecumenical society is to win support for the conviction that women as well as men should be eligible for ordination to the full ministry of word and sacrament by means of a *Newsletter* and meetings. With more churches ordaining women, it encourages the working together for the ministry of the whole people of God and fosters initiatives and exchanges experiences in the areas of women's ministry, lay and ordained. It encourages the deployment of women in a wider spectrum of ministries and keeps in touch with other organisations that have similar aims. *President:* Dr Pauline Webb *Exec Chair:* Revd Sister Teresa CSA *Membership Secretary and Editor:* Revd Dr Janet Wootton, 19A Compton Terrace, Islington, London N1 2UN
Tel: 0171–354 3631
Fax: 0171–354 3989
e-mail: janet.wootton@ukonline.co.uk

Society for the Relief of Poor Clergymen
Founded 1788 to aid evangelical ministers and their dependants in times of financial distress due to sickness, bereavement or other difficulties. c/o CPAS, Athena Drive, Tachbrook Park, Warwick CV34 6NG
Tel: (01926) 334242
e-mail: srpc@cpas.org.uk

Society of King Charles the Martyr
Founded 1894 to promote a wide observation of January 30, the day of the martyrdom of King Charles I in 1649, and work for the reinstatement of this day in the Kalendar of the Churches of the Anglican Communion. *President:* Revd Edward Thompson *Chairman:* Robin Davies, 22 Tyning Rd, Winsley, Bradford on Avon, Wilts BA15 2JJ
Tel: (01225) 862965

Society of Mary
Founded 1931 to promote devotion to Our Lady; mainly an Anglican society but welcomes members from other churches of a Catholic tradition. *President and Superior General:* Vacancy *Secretary:* Mr Richard North, 11 Larkfield Rd, Farnham, Surrey GU9 7DB   *Tel:* (01252) 722095

Society of Mary and Martha
An independent ecumenical charity providing support for people in Christian ministry and/or their spouses. Sheldon is a converted farm in the Teign Valley run by a lay community. It welcomes guests taking part in programme events such as *12,000–mile Service* weeks, family holidays, reading weeks, retreats, workshops, seminars and quiet days. It also offers hospitality and support to people needing an emergency bolt-hole or a safe place at a time of stress or crisis. Enquiries by letter or telephone welcome. *Warden:* Carl Lee *Administrator:* Sarah Horsman, Sheldon, Dunsford, Exeter EX6 7LE
Tel and *Fax:* (01647) 252752

Society of Ordained Scientists
Founded 1987. A dispersed order for ordained scientists, men and women. Members aim to offer to God, in their ordained role, the work of science in the exploration and stewardship of creation, to express the commitment of the Church to the scientific enterprise and their concern for its impact on the world and to support each other in their vocation. *Visitor:* Rt Revd Rupert Hoare, Bishop of Dudley. *Warden:* Canon Maureen Palmer *Secretary:* Revd Dr Richard Hills, Stamford Cottage, 47 Old Rd, Mottram, Hyde, Cheshire SK14 6LW   *Tel:* (01457) 763104

Society of Retreat Conductors
Founded in 1923 for the training of Retreat Conductors, the building of Retreat Houses and the conducting of retreats on traditional lines. *Administrator:* Vacant, Stacklands Retreat House, West Kingsdown, nr Sevenoaks, Kent TN15 6AN   *Tel:* (01474) 852247

Society of Royal Cumberland Youths
Bell ringing society founded in 1747. Its headquarters are at St Martin in the Fields and the society is responsible for ringing at a number of London churches. The society has a worldwide membership, promoting high standards among proficient change ringers. *Master:* Alan Regin *Hon Secretary:* Linda M. Garton, Thriplow House West, 36 Middle Street, Thriplow, Royston, Herts SG8 7RD
Tel: (01763) 208171
Web: http://www.hblock.demon.co.uk/

Society of St Willibrord
(The Anglican and Old Catholic Society of St Willibrord) Founded 1908 to promote friendly relations between the Anglican and Old Catholic Churches, including the fullest use of the full Communion established between them in 1931. *Presidents:* The Bishop of Gibraltar in Europe and the Bishop of Haarlem, Holland. *Exec Secretary:* Revd Ivor Morris, Vicarage, 57 Maltese Rd, Chelmsford CM1 2PB
Tel and *Fax:* (01245) 353914

Society of the Holy Cross (SSC)
Founded 1855 for priests (850 members) 'to maintain and extend the Catholic faith and discipline and to form a special bond of union between Catholic clergy'. *Provinces:* European Union, Australasia, Canada, Africa, USA. *Master General:* Canon Michael Shields *International*

Editor: Revd Stephen Bond, 58 rue Albert Vincon, 44570 Certe, Loire Atlantique, France   *Tel:* 00 33 40 459217

Soldiers' and Airmen's Scripture Readers Association

Founded 1838 to present the claims of Christ to the men and women serving in the Army and later the RAF, to promote interdenominational Christian fellowship among them and to encourage individual serving Christians to witness to their comrades. *Chairman:* Brigadier Ian Dobbie *General Secretary:* Lt Col Malcolm Hitchcott, Havelock House, Barrack Rd, Aldershot, Hants GU11 3NP   *Tel:* (01252) 310033
Fax: (01252) 350722
e-mail: hq@sasra.org.uk

SOMA – Sharing of Ministries Abroad

Founded 1978 to serve the renewal of the Church throughout the world, particularly in the Anglican Communion. SOMA now has eight centres in different parts of the world. Its work includes the provision of teams for ministry, mainly in the Two-Thirds World; welcoming teams and individuals for ministry in parishes (in the UK or other home countries); and international leadership conferences. A newsletter *SHARING*, is published three times a year. *SOMA International Chairman:* Revd David Harper *SOMA UK Director:* Revd Don Brewin, PO Box 6002, Heath and Reach, Leighton Buzzard LU7 0ZA
Tel: (01525) 237953
Fax: (01525) 237954
e-mail: SOMAUK@compuserve.com

South American Mission Society

(Incorporating the Spanish and Portuguese Church Aid Society)
Founded 1844 to make known the Gospel of the Lord Jesus Christ to the people of Latin America and the Iberian Peninsula and continuing in active partnership now with their mission priorities. *General Secretary:* Rt Revd David Evans, Allen Gardiner House, 12 Fox Hill, Birmingham B29 4AG   *Tel:* 0121–4722616
Fax: 0121–472 7977
e-mail: 106313.3712@compuserve.com

Southern Africa Church Development Trust

Founded 1960 to inform, encourage concern for and involvement in the Church in Southern Africa. Supports projects for building village churches, education, clergy and lay training, and medical work. Publishes a quarterly bulletin of information and projects which is sent to all subscribers. *President:* Mr Martin Kenyon *Director:* Miss Joan Antcliff, Little Court, Pound Lane, Shaldon, Devon TQ14 0HA   *Tel:* (0162 687) 2726

St Aidan Trust

Established 1994 for the healing of the lands through men, women and children who draw inspiration from the Celtic saints. Its three aims are: to restore the memory, landmarks, witness and experience of the Celtic Church in ways that relate to God's purposes today; to research the history, beliefs, lifestyle, evangelism and relationship to cultural patterns of the Celtic church, and how they apply to the renewal of today's church and society; to resource through an Order of St Aidan with a Way of Life, Soul Friends and vocational guidance. Organises conferences, seminars and retreats. Produces liturgies suitable for personal and corporate worship. *Chair of Trustees:* The Bishop of Coventry *Development Officer:* Revd Ray Simpson, Red Hill Farm, Snitterfield, Stratford on Avon CV37 0PQ   *Tel:* (01789) 731427

St Aidan's College Charity

Founded in 1980 with the funds of the former St Aidan's Theological College, Birkenhead, the Charity exists to assist ordinands to meet the cost of their theological training and the support of their dependants. Limited grants may also be available towards the cost of In-Service Training for clergy. Grants to Ordinands are considered by the trustees annually in November, and applications must reach the Clerk to the Trustees by 15 September. Applications for in-service training grants must reach the Clerk by 31 March for consideration at the Trustees' April meeting. *Chairman:* Canon John Bowers *Enquiries to:* The Clerk to the Trustees, St Aidan's College Charity, Diocesan House, Raymond St, Chester CH1 4PN
Tel: (01244) 379222

St Christopher's Fellowship

Formed by the amalgamation of The Fellowship of St Christopher (founded 1929) and Homes for Working Boys in London (founded 1870). Provides two projects in the London area for young people of both sexes, all races and creeds, preparing to leave local authority care, from 16–21 years of age and one project for severely (including sexually) abused children aged 4–10. A further support project for young care leavers operated in partnership with the London Borough of Richmond on Thames opened in September 1994. Also provides accommodation in twenty-nine shared houses offering supported housing to 200 young single homeless people aged 17–22. The Fellowship also operates a forty bedspace nightshelter in partnership with London Borough of Hammersmith and Fulham and a short life hostel for nine homeless young people in partnership with the London Borough of Ealing. *Chairman:* Mr Brian Blackler *Director:* Mrs Ann Hithersay, 217 Kingston Rd, Wimbledon, London SW19 3NL   *Tel:* 0181–543 3619
Fax: 0181–544 1633

St George's House, Windsor Castle

Founded 1966. A residential study centre, under the direction of a Council of which the Dean and Canons are *ex*

officio members, to provide opportunity of study and discussion by clergy and laity. Ecumenical and inter-faith stances enjoined by Trust Deed. Internal clergy and secular interfaces programme, but also available for events sponsored by complementary outside organisations. It has accommodation for about thirty-six people. *Chairman:* The Dean of Windsor *Vice-Chairman:* HRH The Duke of Edinburgh *Contact:* The Warden, St George's House, Windsor Castle, Windsor, Berks SL4 1NJ
Tel: (01753) 861341
Fax: (01753) 832115

St Luke's Hospital for the Clergy
A surgical and medical hospital for the clergy, their spouses, widows, and dependent children, monks and nuns, deaconesses, ordinands, Church Army staff, and overseas missionaries. Over 150 leading London consultants give their services free of charge. Treatment is entirely free. The usual referral letter from a patient's doctor should be sent to the Medical Officer at the Hospital. *President:* The Archbishop of Canterbury *Chairman:* Ven Derek Hayward *Contact:* The General Secretary, 14 Fitzroy Square, London W1P 6AH   Tel: 0171-388 4954

St Michael's Fellowship
Runs five Residential Family Support Units in South London to offer protection and prevention to children by working in partnership with parents. Works with adolescent single mothers, one or two parent families with special needs such as drug/alcohol misuse, psychiatric illness, learning disabilities, history of abuse, and families who have been separated. *Director:* Mrs Sue Pettigrew, 53A Clapham High St, London SW4 7TH
Tel: 0171-622 6322
Fax: 0171-622 6323

St Pancras Housing
Founded 1924 by Rev Basil Jellicoe, this charitable association provides housing and support for families, single people and those with special needs in nearly 4,500 flats and houses in N London and Hertfordshire. *President:* The Bishop of London *New Business Manager:* Lucy Nuttall, St Richard's House, 110 Eversholt St, London NW1 1BS   Tel: 0171-209 9287
Fax: 0171-209 9223

Student Christian Movement
An ecumenical movement founded in 1889, it offers an intelligent and liberal approach to the challenges and questions of the Christian faith. It also offers support and empowerment to students in nearly seventy affiliated groups and chaplaincies across Britain, holds regular national conferences, produces a variety of resources for study, worship and publishes the journal *Movement.* It is affiliated to the World Student Christian Federation.

SCM, Westhill College, 14–16 Weoley Park Rd, Selly Oak, Birmingham B29 6LL   Tel: 0121-471 2404
Fax: 0121-414 1251
e-mail: scm@charis.co.uk
Web: http://www.charis.co.uk/scm

Studylink – EFAC International Training Partnership
Started in 1965 as part of the work of the Evangelical Fellowship in the Anglican Communion, and renamed Studylink in 1996. Provides bursaries to ordained nationals who are potential leaders in Anglican churches overseas to enable them to undertake further academic study at theological colleges in the United Kingdom. Financial support comes from evangelical parishes in England, who also offer hospitality and parish experience to the partners. *Chairman:* Revd Howard Peskett *Secretary:* Mr Peter LeRoy, 8 Brook Cottage, Lower Barton, Corston, Bath BA2 9BA   Tel: (01225) 873023
Fax: (01225) 873871
e-mail: a.leroy@clara.net

Tearfund
Formed by the Evangelical Alliance in 1968, Tearfund works through local and national churches and other Christian organisations in relieving poverty and distress in Christ's name in over one hundred countries throughout the world. Its wide-ranging ministry includes provision of funds for relief and development projects, the support of technical and administrative personnel, the sponsorship of students and children, of young adults undertaking vocational training and the sale of Tearcraft handicrafts. *Gen Director:* Doug Balfour, 100 Church Rd, Teddington, Middx TW11 8QE   Tel: 0181-977 9144
0845 355 8355 (Enquiries)
Fax: 0181-943 3594
e-mail: enquiry@tearfund.dircon.co.uk
Web: http://www.tearfund.org

Third Province Movement
The object of the Third Province Movement, which was started in November 1992, is to advocate, and eventually secure, the establishment within the Church of England of an autonomous province for all those, whatever their churchmanship, who in conscience cannot accept the ordination of women to the priesthood and other liberal developments. It also advocates a realignment on the same principle within the whole Anglican Communion. *Chairman:* Mrs Margaret Brown, Luckhurst, Mayfield, E Sussex TN20 6TY   Tel: (01435) 873007

Time Ministries International
The Time Strategy for development of the local church stresses unity of vision leading to the formation of ministry teams for evangelism, intercession, pastoral and practical work. The foundation workbook, for leaders and

members, *Called to Serve*, is used by over 1000 churches worldwide. Time also places an emphasis on a balanced eschatology. *Directors:* Revd Tony Higton (Chairman), Mrs Patrica Higton (Executive), Emmanuel Church, Hawkwell, Hockley, Essex SS5 4NR *Tel:* (01702) 543514
Fax: (01702) 543554
e-mail: TonyHigton@compuserve.com

Toc H
Founded 1915, Toc H fights to break down barriers by challenging individuals' preconceptions of others and the divisions which exist in society. While its work is based on Christian principles, all faiths and none are recognised and accepted. Toc H works with people from all walks of life, tackling social problems such as loneliness, isolation and deprivation through an approach which focuses on self-help and taking responsibility for oneself and the local community. *Enquiries to the:* Director, Toc H Central Services, 1 Forest Close, Wendover, Bucks HP22 6BT *Tel:* (01296) 623911
Fax: (01296) 696137

Trinitarian Bible Society
Founded in 1831 to circulate faithful Protestant translations of the Word of God. *General Secretary:* Mr Paul Rowland, Tyndale House, Dorset Rd, London SW19 3NN
Tel: 0181–543 7857
Fax: 0181–543 6370
e-mail: trinitarian.bible.society@ukonline.co.uk
Web: http://biz.ukonline.co.uk/trinitarian.bible.society/contents

True Freedom Trust
An interdenominational counselling and teaching ministry on homosexuality and related issues, for the Church and people seeking Christian counsel. It believes that the Bible forbids homosexual acts. It supplies resources, speakers and organises conferences to help the Church overcome fear and prejudice and act with understanding and love in a biblical and Christ-like way. *Chairman:* Mr Walter Hurst *Director and Founder:* Mr Martin Hallett, PO Box 3, Upton, Wirral, Merseyside L49 6NY
Tel: 0151–653 0773
Fax: 0151–653 7036
e-mail: martin@tftrust.u-net.com
Web: http://www.tftrust.u-net.com

United College of the Ascension
(USPG and Methodist Church)
Founded 1923 within the Selly Oak Colleges' federation, for training missionaries, the College is a community of people from many nations, cultures and religious traditions, who are studying within the Selly Oak federation in preparation for mission, and other church-related and educational work, overseas and in the UK. The college offers short courses and sabbaticals for the church in Britain. An international centre for Anglican Communion Studies began in September 1992 in association with the CMS College, Crowther Hall. *Responsible body:* USPG and the Methodist Church. *Principal:* Canon Andrew Wingate, United College of the Ascension, Weoley Park Rd, Birmingham B29 6RD *Tel:* 0121–472 1667
Fax: 0121–472 4320

United Nations Association of Great Britain and Northern Ireland
UNA is a grassroots membership organisation, independent of the United Nations and of government, which supports the UN and its family of agencies and programmes. It lobbies, educates and informs government, members of both houses of Parliament, the media and the general public to encourage the UK to use its position as a permanent member of the UN Security Council to the best advantage of the whole world community. Though any UN issue is of interest to UNA it concentrates its energies on three main areas – sustainable development, UN and conflict, and refugees and human rights. It works with schools and universities to develop understanding of the UN and internationalism, in particular by means of Model United Nations General Assemblies (MUNGA). In 1998, UNA will be focusing on the 50th Anniversary of the Universal Declaration of Human Rights. UNA International Service sends qualified volunteers to work with partners in developing countries. UNA fundraises for UNICEF and the UN High Commissioner for Refugees. *Director:* Mr Malcolm Harper, 3 Whitehall Court, London SW1A 2EL
Tel: 0171–930 2931
Fax: 0171–930 5893
e-mail: una_uk@compuserve.com

United Society for Christian Literature
Founded 1799 for the production of Christian literature for home and overseas. Today through Feed the Minds it also assists churches overseas in the translation, production, selling and distribution of Christian literature. *President:* Dr Pauline Webb *Chairman:* Mr John Clark *Secretary:* Dr Alwyn Marriage, Albany House, 67 Sydenham Rd, Guildford GU1 3RY *Tel:* (01483) 888580
Fax: (01483) 888581
e-mail: feedtheminds@gn.apc.org

United Society for the Propagation of the Gospel
USPG was formed in 1965 by the merger of SPG, which had been in existence since 1701, and the Universities' Mission to Central Africa, founded in response to Livingstone's call in 1857. The Cambridge Mission to Delhi (1877) merged in 1968. USPG is a voluntary society based in the Church of England and serving Anglican and united churches in mission in about twenty Provinces (or their equivalent), in about forty countries, including the United Kingdom, Northern Ireland and Eire. The Society serves the church in East, Central, Southern and West

Africa, islands of the Indian and Atlantic Oceans, the West Indies, India, Pakistan, East Asia and South America. The Society is firmly committed to the principles of mission in partnership as devised by the Anglican Consultative Council and the Partnership for World Mission. These include commitment to consultation, transparency, sharing and justice. The Society budgets over £1 million in grants to overseas churches. USPG continues to put high value on the movement of people between partner churches. The growing Bursaries Programme enables church people, lay and ordained, to get leadership training in countries other than their own, and also to contribute to local mission in the country where they train. A local bursaries scheme has also been established to enable people to train within their own countries. About 105 USPG people serve churches outside the British Isles as missionaries as well as about thirty people on short-term placements. Opportunities for people to explore a part of the World Church for six to twelve months are offered under the Experience Exchange Programme. Root Groups provide the opportunity for small communities of young people to explore mission alongside local churches for a year. Training in mission takes place at USPG's College of the Ascension, part of the Selly Oak Federation of Colleges in Birmingham. During 1996/7 the Society undertook a strategic review to seek to form strategies for the next five years leading up to the celebrations for its Tercentenary in the year 2001. The Society has a budget of £4 million and looks forward to generosity of giving particularly in the light of the Synod's decision to recommend that all parishes make contributions of 5% to the Anglican World Mission Agencies. *President:* The Archbishop of Canterbury *Chairman of Council:* Rt Revd Richard Llewellin *Secretary:* Rt Revd Mano Rumalshah, Partnership House, 157 Waterloo Rd, London SE1 8XA *Tel:* 0171–928 8681 *Fax:* 0171–928 2371

Universities and Colleges Christian Fellowship
(formerly Inter-Varsity Fellowship of Evangelical Unions)
Is the co-ordinating body for the interdenominational evangelical student 'Christian Unions' in Britain and Ireland. Founded in 1928 by fourteen University CUs, there are now groups in all universities, most other HE institutions and many FE colleges in the Britain. The aim is to be a Christian witness in the student world, the work being based on expressing orthodox Christian belief in the contemporary scene. Regional staff workers support and encourage groups. The publishing arm is the Inter-Varsity Press. The academic research arms are Tyndale House in Cambridge and the Whitefield Institute in Oxford. *Office:* 38 De Montfort St, Leicester LE1 7GP
Tel: 0116–255 1700
Fax: 0116–255 5672
e-mail: enquiries@uccf.org.uk

Urban Theology Unit
Founded 1969 (1) to develop new insights of theology derived from the life of the city; (2) to create a community of clergy and laity concerned to discover relevant forms of ministry and action within urban areas; (3) to help people discover their vocation in relation to Gospel calls. Conducts Urban Priority Area Ministry Courses; a Master and Doctor of Ministry programme (MMin, DMin, degree awarded by Sheffield University); courses for MA, MPhil and PhD in Contextual, Urban and Liberation theologies; a Study Year in Sheffield leading to Diploma in Theology and Mission; basic ministerial training leading to a Diploma or Bachelor degree in Ministry and Theology, (BMinTh); and two-year in-service Diploma in Community Ministry; Conferences and Consultations on Church and Urban Mission. Ecumenical. Publishes various books on urban issues. *Chairperson:* Revd Raymond Goadby *Director:* Revd Inderjit Bhogal *Administrator:* Mr Peter Colby, Pitsmoor Study House, 210 Abbeyfield Rd, Sheffield, S Yorks S4 7AZ
Tel and *Fax:* 0114–243 5342

Vacation Term for Biblical Study
The Vacation Term for Biblical Study is a Summer School held each summer at St Anne's College, Oxford, primarily devoted to the study of the Bible and related subjects. The aim is to enable people of all ages, occupations and denominations to become acquainted with contemporary scholarship. *Chairman:* Dr Barbara Spensley *Further details are available from:* Mrs Elizabeth Lee, 13 Oxford Rd, Dewsbury, W Yorks WF13 4LN *Tel:* (01924) 467319
e-mail: http://www.web$wise.com

Vergers, Church of England Guild of
Founded in 1932 for the spiritual and social benefit of all Vergers, full or part-time. Help and advice is given on request to those seeking assistance with a problem relating to their vocation and ministry. Provides a comprehensive Training Scheme, which is available to all members, each student being under the guidance of an Area Tutor. The scheme is scrutinised by an internal and an independent external panel of assessors. The Annual Residential Training Conference takes place at a College or University which is regarded as an integral part of the Training Scheme. *General Secretary:* Ian Griffiths, 14 Pennington Court, 245 Rotherhithe St, London SE16 1FT
Tel: 0171–231 6888
e-mail: iangensec@btinternet.com

Victoria Institute
(or Philosophical Society of Great Britain)
Founded 1865 to enquire into the relationship between the Christian revelation and modern scientific research. Publishes *Faith and Thought Bulletin* and jointly with Christians in Science, *Science and Christian Belief. President:*

Dr D. J. E. Ingram *Secretary:* Mr Brian Weller, 41 Marne Ave, Welling, Kent DA16 2EY *Tel* and *Fax:* 0181–303 0465

Walsingham, Shrine of Our Lady of
Founded in 1061 in response to a vision, destroyed in 1538, restored in 1922 by Revd A. Hope Patten, Vicar of Walsingham. Since 1931, when it was moved from the parish church, the Shrine has contained the image of Our Lady of Walsingham together with the Holy House. The House represents the home in Nazareth where the Blessed Virgin Mary and St Joseph cared for Jesus in his formative years. Nowadays Walsingham is England's premier place of pilgrimage. It is administered by a College of Guardians. There are facilities for pilgrims to be accommodated and cared for. Special facilities are available for receiving sick and handicapped people. There is also a full-time Education Office who will facilitate visits for schools and other young people's groups. Information is available from the *Administrator:* Revd M. Warner, The College, Walsingham, Norfolk NR22 6EF
Tel: (01328) 820266

WATCH (Women and the Church)
Founded in 1996. WATCH provides a forum for promoting women's ministry in the Church of England, based on a vision of the Church as a community of God's people where, regardless of gender, justice and equality prevail. *Chair:* Christina Rees, Churchfield, Pudding Lane, Barley, Royston, Herts SG8 8JX *Tel:* (01763) 848472
Fax: (01763) 848774

William Temple Foundation
Founded in 1947, as a research and training centre focussing on the links between theology, the economy and urban mission practice. The Foundation works with practitioners in industrial mission, community work, social responsibility etc. to deepen the social and theological analysis of contemporary society and to develop innovative responses. There is a particular concern for the perspectives of people marginalised by current economic trends. The Foundation works closely with churches and practitioners across Europe especially the Work and Economy Network in the European Churches. Foundation staff contribute to training programmes for Industrial Mission, community work etc. and to post-graduate teaching in the University of Manchester. It produces regular papers and the quarterly journal *Foundations* available on subscription. *Contact:* Revd Malcolm Brown, William Temple Foundation, Manchester Business School, Manchester M15 6PB *Tel:* 0161–275 6534
Fax: 0161–272 8663
e-mail: ECG.WEN@MCR1.poptel.org.uk

William Temple House
Residence for students from overseas and the United Kingdom, men and women of all nationalities and faiths, where they can exercise responsibility and develop spiritually in a learning by experience situation. Under the Management of International Students Club (Church of England) Ltd. Registered Charity. *Enquiries to:* The Warden, 29 Trebovir Rd, London SW5 9NQ
Tel: 0171–373 6962
Fax: 0171–341 0003

Women's World Day of Prayer
Founded in America in 1887 (Britain 1930–34) to unite Christian women in prayer by means of services held on the first Friday in March each year, by fostering local inter-denominational prayer groups meeting throughout the year and to give financial support to charitable educational projects and the Christian literature societies. *President:* Mrs Joan Hannon *Chairman:* Mrs Olive Linyard *Admin Secretary:* Mrs Lynda Lynam, WWDP, Commercial Rd, Tunbridge Wells, Kent TN1 2RR
Tel and *Fax:* (01892) 541411

World Congress of Faiths
Founded 1936 to promote mutual understanding and promote a spirit of fellowship between people of different religious traditions. The current programme explores issues arising out of religious pluralism. WCF works to explain and reconcile religious conflict and the tensions between the different faith communities. Conferences and lectures are arranged, the journal *World Faiths Encounter* is published three times a year and a newsletter *One Family*. *President:* Professor Keith Ward. *Chairman:* Revd Marcus Braybrooke *Editor:* Revd Alan Race *Hon Secretary:* Shahin Bekhradnia, World Congress Of Faiths, 2 Market St, Oxford OX1 3EF *Tel:* (01865) 202751
Fax: (01865) 202746

World Vision
Formed in London in 1979, World Vision UK is part of the international World Vision partnership and is a major UK relief and development agency. World Vision is at work in over 100 countries in Africa, Asia, Eastern Europe, Latin America, and the Middle East. It is involved in partnering churches and other non-governmental organisations in projects ranging from relief work in Rwanda to income generation projects in Bangladesh. *Exec Director:* Mr Charles Clayton, 599 Avebury Boulevard, Milton Keynes MK9 3PG *Tel:* (01908) 841000
Fax: (01908) 841001
e-mail: peter_scott@wvi.org

YMCA
Founded 1844 to promote the physical, intellectual and spiritual well-being of young people. *President:* Lord Judd *Secretary:* Mr E. Thomas, National Council of YMCAs, 640 Forest Rd, London E17 3DZ
Tel: 0181–520 5599
e-mail: 11352.3504@compuserve.com

York Glaziers' Trust
Established 1967 by the Dean and Chapter of York and the Pilgrim Trust (i) to conserve and restore the stained glass of York Minster; (ii) to conserve, restore and advise on all stained glass or glazing of historic or artistic importance, in any building whether religious or secular, public or private; (iii) to establish and maintain within the City of York a stained glass workshop dedicated to the training and employment of conservators and craftsmen specialising in the preservation of glass of historic and artistic importance; and (iv) to encourage public interest in the preservation of stained glass, to collaborate with educational institutions and to assist with scientific and art historical research into stained and painted glass. Advice should always be sought when considering treatment of glass of artistic or historic value. The Trust welcomes enquiries from all sources. It offers a full advisory service and will compile comprehensive condition reports. *Chairman:* The Dean of York *Secretary:* Penelope Winton, 6 Deangate, York YO1 2JA   *Tel:* (01904) 622676

Young Women's Christian Association of Great Britain
The YWCA of Great Britain strives for social justice and equality for young women through its work as a membership movement and as a youth work organisation. It is a registered social landlord and offers the single largest provision of shared and supported housing specifically for young women in the country. It aims to provide a platform for young women to be heard and to contribute to debate on issues affecting young women at local, national and international levels. *President:* Mrs Sheila Brain *Chief Exec:* Ms Gill Tishler, YWCA Headquarters, Clarendon House, 52 Cornmarket House, Oxford OX1 3EJ   *Tel:* (01865) 304200
Fax: (01865) 204805

Diocesan Associations

Arctic Fellowship	Miss M. Dean 81 Kerrysdale Ave Leicester LE4 7GN Tel: 0116–266 8664	**Diocese of the North Eastern Caribbean and Aruba Association**	Canon Robert Eke 77 Hangleton Way Hove E Sussex BN3 8AF Tel and Fax: (01273) 421443
Association of the Dioceses of Singapore and West Malaysia	Revd Ann Bucknall 20 St Margaret's Rd Lichfield Staffs WS13 7RA Tel: (01543) 257382	**Egypt Diocesan Association**	Lady Morris 26 Bickerton Rd Headington Oxford OX3 7LS Tel and Fax: (01865) 761461
Belize Church Association	Mrs Daphne Russell Moorcroft Cassington Oxford OX8 1DL Tel: (01865) 881288	**Fellowship of the Maple Leaf** (*Supports the work of the Church in Canada, particularly in the Prairie and Western Provinces*)	Canon John Williams 2 Fox Spring Rise Edinburgh EH10 6NE
Borneo Mission Association	Canon Alan Burn 8 Purleigh Ave Lyppard Habington Worcester WR4 0DX Tel: (01905) 25575	**Friends of the Church in India**	Revd Barrie Scopes 100 Prince of Wales Drive London SW11 4BD Tel: 0171–622 3809
Central Tanganyika Diocesan Association	Miss S. M. Horsman 15 Woodstock Ave Harold Park Romford Essex Tel: (01708) 345691 e-mail: shorsman@ema.co.uk	**Friends of the Diocese of Cyprus and the Gulf**	Mrs Mary Banfield Garden Corner Old London Rd Mickleham Surrey RH5 6DL Tel and Fax: (01372) 373912
Church of Burma Association	Mrs Nita Sharpley 6 Parklands Swan Lane London N20 0PW Tel: 0181–446 1970	**Friends of the Diocese of Iran**	Mrs Eleanor Ashton 104 Pelham Rd Wimbledon London SW19 1PA Tel: 0181–543 1167
Church of Ceylon Association	Revd John Elliott 14 Victoria St Loughborough Leics LE11 2EN Tel: (01509) 263365	**Friends of the Diocese of Uruguay**	Revd Charles Bradshaw St James' Vicarage Birstall Leicester LE4 4DJ Tel: 0116–267 4517 Fax: 0116–267 6329
Congo Church Association	Mrs Rosemary Peirce 70 Yarnells Hill Oxford OX2 9BG Tel: (01865) 721330	**Guyana Diocesan Association**	Mr J. R. Chee-a-tow 13E Courtleet Drive Erith Kent DA8 3NB Tel: (0132 24) 42897

Hong Kong Anglican Church Association	Mrs Ann Hart The Old Bank House 25 London Rd Beaconsfield Bucks HP9 2HN *Tel:* (01494) 674911	**Rockhampton Auxiliary**	Mr F. G. Bellhouse Park Cottage Halstead Lane Knockholt Sevenoaks Kent TN14 7JF *Tel:* (01959) 533187
Jerusalem and the Middle East Church Association	Mrs Vanessa Wells 1 Hart House The Hart Farnham Surrey GU9 7HA *Tel:* (01252) 726994 *Fax:* (01252) 735558	**Sierra Leone Inter-Diocesan Association**	Mrs Elfreda Taylor 18 Dovedale Ave Clay Hall Ilford Essex IG5 0QF
		Sudan Church Association	Mrs Sara Taffinder 69 Poynders Rd Clapham London SW4 8PL *Tel:* 0181–671 1974
Kenya Church Association	Miss Jean Breckenridge 35 Parliament Hill London NW3 2TA *Tel:* 0171–794 7557	**Transvaal, Zimbabwe and Botswana Association**	Mrs Pat Dutton Pevers Farm Martins Lane Kirkstead Green Norfolk NR15 1ED *Tel* and *Fax:* (01508) 550638
Lesotho Diocesan Association	Canon Ron Tovey 86 Kings Rd Oakham Leics LE15 6PD *Tel:* (01572) 770628	**Uganda Church Association**	Mr David Thomson 37 Murray Rd Northwood Middx HA6 2YP *Tel:* (01923) 827015
Mozambique and Angola Anglican Association	Miss Joan Antcliff Little Court Pound Lane Shaldon Devon TQ14 0HA *Tel:* (01626) 872726	**Willochran Association**	Revd Roger Jones Vicarage Wiston Haverfordwest Pembs SA62 4PL *Tel:* (01437) 731266 *e-mail:* rjones4330@aol.com
Nigeria Fellowship	Dr Rena Partridge 55 Hipwell Court Olney Bucks MK46 5QB *Tel:* (01234) 240018	**Windward Islands Diocesan Association**	Mrs Mary Anderson 115 Broadfield Rd Catford London SE6 1TJ *Tel:* 0181–461 1775
North Queensland Auxiliary in England	Canon Leslie Buffee 46 Stone Bridge Way Faversham Kent ME13 7SB *Tel:* (01795) 535790	**Zululand Swaziland Association**	Canon Edgar Ruddock Rectory St Peter's Close Stoke-on-Trent Staffs ST4 1LP *Tel* and *Fax:* (01782) 845287 *e-mail:* edrud@cix.co.uk
Province of the Indian Ocean Support Association	Mrs Judith Hepper 61 Queens Rd Alton Hants GU34 1JG		

Diocesan Associations

Libraries

Canterbury

Cathedral Library
Cathedral House
The Precincts
Canterbury
Kent CT1 2EH

Cathedral Librarian Mrs Sheila Hingley

Archivist Dr Michael Stansfield

Tel: (01227) 463510 (Archives)
(01227) 458950 (Library)
Fax: (01227) 762897
e-mail: catlib@ukc.ac.uk
(library)

50,000 volumes with large collections of manuscripts.

Durham

Dean and Chapter Library
The College
Durham
DH1 3EH

Librarian Canon Prof David Brown

Deputy Librarian Mr Roger Norris

Tel: 0191–386 2489

Open: 0900–1300; 1415–1700 hours Mon–Fri

Search room open pm only

40,000 printed books including 70 incunabula, 360 manuscripts 6th–16th centuries. Other MS collections include Hunter, Sharp, Raine, Surtees, Ian Ramsey, early music. Meissen Library of German Theology (approx 20,000 books donated by the EKD).

Lambeth

Lambeth Palace Library
London
SE1 7JU

Librarian and Archivist Dr Richard Palmer

Deputy Librarian and Archivist Miss Melanie Barber

Tel: 0171–928 6222
Fax: 0171–928 7932

Open: 1000–1700 hours Mon–Fri
Closed Public Holidays and ten days at Christmas and Easter.

Main library for the history of the Church of England, open for public use since 1610. 200,000 printed books, 4,000 manuscripts 9th–20th centuries. Registers and correspondence of Archbishops of Canterbury 12th–20th centuries. Records of Province of Canterbury, Lambeth Conferences, Bishops of London, and papers of churchmen, statesmen and organisations within the Church of England. Manuscripts and printed books earlier than 1850 from Sion College Library.

Partnership House

Partnership House
Mission Studies Library
157 Waterloo Rd
London
SE1 8XA

Librarian Mr Colin Rowe

Tel: 0171–928 8681
Fax: 0171–928 3627
e-mail:
c.rowe@mailbox.ulcc.ac.uk

Open: 0930–1700 hours Mon–Fri
Closed Public Holidays
Books also lent by post

25,000 volumes, 400 periodicals. Post-1945 collections of the former Church Missionary Society and United Society for the Propagation of the Gospel missionary libraries. Pre-1946 books from the CMS Library (the CMS Max Warren collection).

Pusey House Pusey House Oxford OX1 3LZ	*Custodian* Revd William Davage *Tel:* (01865) 278415 Open: 0915–1245; 1400–1645 Mon–Fri 0915–1245 Sat During Full Term Contact the Custodian for Vacation opening times	100,000 volumes. Includes Dr Pusey's Library (a theological library specialising in Patristics, Church History and Liturgy) and the library from St Augustine's College, Canterbury (a theological library specialising in Church of England and the Anglican Communion).
St Deiniol's St Deiniol's Residential Library Hawarden Nr Chester Flintshire CH5 3DF	*Warden and Chief Librarian* Revd Peter Francis *Tel:* (01244) 532350 *Fax:* (01244) 520643 *e-mail:* deiniol.visitors@btinternet.com	200,000 plus volumes, including 50,000 pamphlets. Theology, Biblical Studies, Spirituality, Liturgy, 19th century Ecclesiastical and Secular History, Bishop Moorman Franciscan Library, and all areas of the Arts/Humanities. Residential accommodation for 47 people. Bursaries for clergy and students. Financial assistance for Sabbaticals. Scholarship grants for research and writing for higher degrees or publication, meeting the entire cost of the stay at St Deiniol's.
St Paul's The Library St Paul's Cathedral London EC4M 8AE	*Librarian* Mr Jo Wisdom *Tel:* 0171–246 8345 *Fax:* 0171–246 8325	Re-established after the Great Fire of 1666, the library is strong in theology, ecclesiastical history, and sermons, especially of 17th and 18th centuries. Special collections include early printed Bibles; St Paul's Cross sermons; 19th century theological tracts. The archive of Dean and Chapter is deposited at Guildhall Library, Aldermanbury, London EC2P 2EJ.
Sion College	The library has closed. The older books (–1850) were transferred to Lambeth Palace Library. The bulk of the balance of the collection is in the library of King's College, London.	50 current periodicals. Biblical studies, philosophy, Anglican theology, church history, biography and liturgy. Special collections include Sion College Port Royal Library, Industrial Christian Fellowship Library, and extensive pamphlet collections.

United Society for the Propagation of the Gospel Rhodes House Library South Parks Rd Oxford OX1 3RG	*Librarian* Mr John Pinfold *Tel:* (01865) 270909 *Fax:* (01865) 270912 *e-mail:* rhodes.house.library @bodley.ox.ac.uk Written application necessary before first visit.	The Society's library to 1944 and archival material. Extensive collections from the 19th century, back holdings of missionary journals.
Westminster Abbey Westminster Abbey Library London SW1P 3PA	*Librarian* Dr Tony Trowles *Keeper of the Muniments* Dr R. Mortimer *Tel:* 0171–222 5152 *Fax:* 0171–222 6391 Open: 1000–1300, 1400–1645 hours Mon–Fri, appointments desirable	14,000 volumes (16th–18th century), 70,000 archives (monastic history 8th–16th century, Abbey records to present day).
York Minster York Minster Library Dean's Park York YO1 2JD	*Sub-Librarian* Bernard Barr *Archivist* Mrs Louise Hampson *Tel:* (01904) 625308 (01904) 611118 (Archives & MSS) *Fax:* (01904) 611119 Open: 0900–1700 hours Mon–Thur; 0900–1200 Fri	120,000 volumes. Extensive collections of manuscripts, incunables, prints, music, photographs, Civil War tracts; archives of Dean and Chapter from medieval times.

See also main Organisations section

Patronage Trusts

Church Pastoral Aid Society Patronage Trust	*Secretary* Revd David Field CPAS, Athena Drive Tachbrook Park Warwick CV34 6NG *Tel:* (01926) 334242 *Fax:* (01926) 337613 *e-mail:* mpowell@cpas.org.uk	A Trust holding Rights of Presentation to a number of benefices. Administered by the Church Pastoral Aid Society.
Church Patronage Trust	*Secretary* Revd Kenneth Habershon Truckers Ghyll Horsham Rd, Handcross W Sussex RH17 6DT *Tel:* (01444) 400274	A Trust holding the Rights of Presentation to a number of benefices. Evangelical tradition.

Church Society Trust	*Secretary* J. M. Lindeck Dean Wace House 16 Rosslyn Rd Watford, Herts WD1 7EY *Tel:* (01923) 235111 (24 hrs) *Fax:* (01923) 800362 e-mail: 106522,1537@compuserve.com	Patron of more than one hundred livings.
Church Trust Fund Trust	*Secretary* Revd David Field CPAS, Athena Drive Tachbrook Park Warwick CV34 6NG *Tel:* (01926) 334242 *Fax:* (01926) 337613 *e-mail:* mpowell@cpas.org.uk	A Trust holding Rights of Presentation to a number of benefices. Administered by the Church Pastoral Aid Society.
Guild of All Souls	*General Secretary* Charles Brown Guild of All Souls St Katharine Cree Church 86 Leadenhall St London EC3A 3DH *Tel:* 0171–621 0098	Patron of 39 livings of catholic tradition.
Hulme Trustees	*Secretary* Mr Jonathan Shelmerdine, Taylor, Kirkman and Mainprice, Solicitors, 205 Moss Lane, Bramhall, Stockport SK7 1BA *Tel:* 0161–439 8228	A Trust holding the Rights of Presentation to a number of benefices.
Hyndman's (Miss) Trustees	*Administrative Secretary* Mrs Ann Brown 6 Angerford Ave Sheffield S8 9BG *Tel* and *Fax:* 0114–255 1945	Patronage Trust. Varied Churchmanship.
Martyrs Memorial and Church of England Trust	*Secretary* Revd David Field CPAS, Athena Drive Tachbrook Park Warwick CV34 6NG *Tel:* (01926) 334242 *Fax:* (01926) 337613 *e-mail:* mpowell@cpas.org.uk	A Trust holding Rights of Presentation to a number of benefices. Administered by the Church Pastoral Aid Society.
Peache Trustees	*Secretary* Revd Kenneth Habershon Truckers Ghyll Horsham Rd, Handcross W Sussex RH17 6DT *Tel:* (01444) 400274	A Trust holding the Rights of Presentation to a number of benefices. Evangelical tradition.

Simeon's Trustees	*Administrative Secretary* Mrs Ann Brown 6 Angerford Ave Sheffield S8 9BG *Tel* and *Fax:* 0114–255 1945	Holds and administers the patronage of those livings in the Church of England which belong to the Trust on the principles laid down in Charles Simeon's Charge.
Society for the Maintenance of the Faith	*Secretary* Revd Paul Conrad Christ Church Vicarage 10 Cannon Place London NW3 1EJ *Tel:* 0171–435 6784	Administers patronage and promotes Catholic teaching and practice.

The Anglican and Porvoo Communions

Part 5

PART 5 CONTENTS

THE ANGLICAN COMMUNION 271

The Lambeth Conference 272
The Anglican Communion Office 274
The Anglican Consultative Council 275
The Anglican Centre in Rome 276

CHURCHES AND PROVINCES OF THE ANGLICAN COMMUNION 277

Anglican Church in	Aotearoa, New Zealand and Polynesia 277
Anglican Church of	Australia 278
Episcopal Anglican Church of	Brazil 281
Church of the Province of	Burundi 282
Anglican Church of	Canada 283
Church of the Province of	Central Africa 285
Anglican Church of the	Central American Region 287
Church of the Province of	the Congo 287
	Hong Kong Sheng Kung Hui 288
Church of the Province of the	Indian Ocean 288
Church of	Ireland 289
Anglican Communion in	Japan 293
Episcopal Church in	Jerusalem and the Middle East 294
Anglican Church of	Kenya 294
Anglican Church of	Korea 296
Church of the Province of	Melanesia 296
Anglican Church of	Mexico 297
Church of the Province of	Myanmar 297
Church of the Province of	Nigeria 298
Anglican Church of	Papua New Guinea 301
Episcopal Church in the	Philippines 302
Church of the Province of	Rwanda 302
	Scottish Episcopal Church 303
Church of the Province of	South East Asia 304
Church of the Province of	Southern Africa 305
Anglican Church of the	Southern Cone of America 307
Church of the Province of the	Sudan 308
Anglican Church of	Tanzania 309
Church of the Province of	Uganda 310
Episcopal Church in the	United States of America 312
Church in	Wales 318
Church of the Province of	West Africa 321
Church in the Province of the	West Indies 322

Other Churches and Extra-Provincial Dioceses 323
Regional Councils 325

UNITED CHURCHES IN FULL COMMUNION 326

The Church of Bangladesh *326*
The Church of Ceylon *326*
The Church of North India *327*
The Church of Pakistan *328*
The Church of South India *329*

THE HOLY CATHOLIC CHURCH IN CHINA 332

OTHER CHURCHES IN COMMUNION WITH THE CHURCH OF ENGLAND 335

Old Catholic Churches *335*
Philippine Independent Church *335*
Mar Thoma *336*

MAPS OF THE CHURCHES AND PROVINCES OF THE ANGLICAN COMMUNION 337

THE PORVOO COMMUNION 353

Nordic Lutheran Churches *355*
Baltic Lutheran Churches *359*
Non-signatory Churches *361*

THE ANGLICAN COMMUNION

There are nearly 70 million members of the Anglican household of 38 self-governing churches made up of about 500 dioceses, 30,000 parishes and 64,000 individual congregations in a total of 164 countries. While the Anglican Communion does not rank among the biggest groupings of Christians it is, after the Roman Catholic Church, arguably the most widespread.

The Anglican Communion has developed in two stages. During the first stage, which began in the seventeenth century, Anglicanism was established by colonisation in countries such as Australia, Canada, New Zealand, Southern Africa and the USA. In the early days of expansion a somewhat remote control was exercised by the Bishops of London. After the American War of Independence Samuel Seabury of Connecticut, USA was consecrated in Scotland as the first bishop of the Anglican Communion outside the British Isles. Soon this precedent was followed by the Church in Canada and then India, Australia, New Zealand and South Africa.

The second stage began just over a century ago. During that era Anglican churches were planted all over the world as a result of the missionary work of the churches in England, Ireland, Scotland, and Wales which were joined in this task by the churches formed in the previous two centuries. Most of these churches became constitutionally independent in the period following the second world war, usually ahead of the attainment of political independence. In regions which are large, diverse, and the population of Anglicans is perceived as too small to support a Province, a useful halfway house has been found in the development of regional councils such as the Council of the Churches of East Asia.

Anglican churches uphold and proclaim the catholic and apostolic faith, based on Scripture and creeds, interpreted in the light of Christian tradition, scholarship and reason. Following the teachings of Jesus Christ, the Churches are committed to the proclamation of the good news of the gospel to the whole creation.

By baptism, in the name of the Father, Son and Holy Spirit, a person is made one with Christ and received into the Church.

Central to worship for Anglicans is the celebration of the Holy Eucharist (also called the Holy Communion, the Lord's Supper, the Mass). In this offering of prayer and praise are recalled the life, death and resurrection of Christ, through the proclamation of the Word and celebration of the Sacrament.

Worship is at the very heart of Anglicanism. Its styles vary from the simple to the elaborate, from Evangelical to Catholic, from charismatic to traditional or indeed from a combination of these various traditions. The Book of Common Prayer, in its various revisions throughout the Communion, gives expression to the comprehensiveness found within the Church whose principles reflect, since the time of Elizabeth I, a *via media* in relation to other Christian traditions.

Other rites include Confirmation, Holy Orders, Reconciliation, Marriage and Anointing of the Sick.

Almost everywhere Anglican Churches are self-supporting. Only a small percentage of income is transferred from richer to less affluent churches. Many of the member churches of the Anglican Communion are to be found in the so-called developing or 'Third' world. It is estimated that 3,000 persons are added to membership each day through birth, baptism or conversion. The fastest growing areas are in the global south.

For over 200 years there has been a process of decentralisation which has led to flexibility and a capacity for indigenisation and involvement in local ecumenical negotiations and projects. This leaves open the possibility of loss of identity. But to compensate for this the Anglican Communion has developed a number of institutions which have ensured cohesion and communication. The oldest and most important of these is the Lambeth Conference. The 1968 Lambeth Conference agreed to the formation of the Anglican Consultative Council which brings together clergy and lay as well as episcopal representatives once every two or three years. More recently there have been regular meetings of Primates – senior bishops and archbishops from each member church.

The Churches of the Anglican Communion are linked by affection and common loyalty. They are in full communion with the See of Canterbury and thus the Archbishop of Canterbury, in his person, is a unique focus of Anglican unity. He calls the once-a-decade Lambeth Conference, is Chairman of the meeting of Primates and is President of the Anglican Consultative Council.

The Secretary General of the Anglican Communion, aided by a permanent Secretariat staff, assists the Archbishop of Canterbury in servicing the Lambeth Conference and meetings of the Primates and thereby exercises a vital co-ordinating role.

During recent years, in addition to local ecumenical negotiations and projects, the Anglican Communion has been engaged in international dialogues with a number of major churches including the Roman Catholic Church, the Lutheran World Federation, the Orthodox Churches, and the World Alliance of Reformed Churches. Through the Faith and Order Commission of the World Council of Churches it has also been engaged in a multilateral dialogue process which has resulted in the publication of the Faith and Order Document *Baptism, Eucharist and Ministry*.

Outstanding features within the Anglican Communion in the past 25 years are the constitution of many new autonomous provinces in Africa, Asia and Latin America and the emergence of the Anglican Consultative Council. These are both parts of a bigger process of transition and maturing whereby relationships within the Communion have progressed in becoming a family of varied but essentially equal members within the Body of Christ. The family is interdependent. There is still need for the small, the poor, the weak to receive help from the stronger and richer, because the responsibilities of the Communion and the mission of the whole family is one and interdependent in the Body of Christ.

OUR CHURCHES
The present list of member churches or Provinces, and of councils, is:

- The Church of the Province of Aotearoa, New Zealand and Polynesia
- The Anglican Church of Australia
- The Episcopal Church of Brazil
- The Episcopal Church of Burundi
- The Anglican Church of Canada
- The Church of the Province of Central Africa
- The Anglican Church of the Central American Region
- The Church of Ceylon (Sri Lanka)
- The Anglican Church of the Congo
- The Church of England
- Hong Kong Sheng Kung Hui
- The Church of the Province of the Indian Ocean
- The Church of Ireland
- The Anglican Communion in Japan (Nippon Sei Ko Kai)
- The Episcopal Church in Jerusalem and the Middle East
- The Anglican Church of Kenya
- The Anglican Church of Korea
- The Church of the Province of Melanesia
- The Anglican Church of Mexico
- The Church of the Province of Myanmar
- The Church of the Province of Nigeria
- The Anglican Church of Papua New Guinea
- The Philippine Episcopal Church
- The Lusitanian Church of Portugal
- The Episcopal Church of Rwanda
- The Scottish Episcopal Church
- The Church of the Province of South East Asia
- The Church of the Province of Southern Africa
- The Anglican Church of the Southern Cone of America
- The Spanish Reformed Episcopal Church
- The Church of the Province of the Sudan
- The Anglican Church of Tanzania
- The Church of Uganda
- The Episcopal Church in the United States of America
- The Church in Wales
- The Church of the Province of West Africa
- The Church in the Province of the West Indies

In addition: The Churches of Bangladesh, Pakistan, North and South India

The Lambeth Conference

It could be said that the Lambeth Conference has its origin in 1865 when, on 20 September, the Provincial Synod of the Church of Canada unanimously agreed to urge the Archbishop of Canterbury and the Convocation of his province to find a means by which the bishops consecrated within the Church of England and serving overseas could be brought together for a General Council to discuss issues facing them in North America, and elsewhere. Part of the background for this request was a serious dispute about the interpretation and authority of the Scriptures which had arisen in Southern Africa between Robert Gray, Archbishop of Cape Town, and Bishop Colenso, Bishop of Natal.

Notwithstanding the opposition of a significant number of the bishops in England, Archbishop Longley invited Anglican bishops to their first Conference together at Lambeth Palace on 24 September 1867 and the three following days.

Seventy-six bishops finally accepted the invitation and the Conference was called to order and met in the Chapel of Lambeth Palace. A request to use Westminster Abbey for a service was not granted.

Of the 76 bishops attending the first Lambeth Conference the distribution was the following:

England	– 18 bishops
Ireland	– 5 bishops
Scotland	– 6 bishops
Colonial and Missionary	– 28 bishops
United States	– 19 bishops

It was made clear at the outset that the Conference would have no authority of itself as it was not competent to make declarations or lay down definitions on points of doctrine. But the Conference was useful in that it explored many aspects of possible inter-Anglican co-operation and by providing common counsel it inaugurated a practical way in which the unity of the faith of the Church could be maintained. The Conference did not take any effective action regarding the issues raised by

Bishop Colenso but its far-reaching impact can be seen in the fact that it was the precursor of the Lambeth Conference which we know today.

In 1878 the second Lambeth Conference was convened by Archbishop Tait and 100 bishops attended. The heavy agenda included 'Modern forms of infidelity'. It marked another milestone in the growth of the relationship of diverse parts of the Anglican Communion and reinforced the value of the meeting of Anglican bishops to share their common experience.

One hundred and forty-five bishops attended the Lambeth Conference of 1888 called by Archbishop Benson. Meeting at Lambeth Palace in the Library, its agenda addressed such contemporary issues as intemperance, purity, divorce, care of immigrants, and socialism. More important for the ongoing life of the Church itself, the agenda concerned itself with the issues of Oecumenism. In 1886 the House of Bishops of the Episcopal Church in the United States of America, meeting in Chicago, had devised a formula which provided a basic framework of recognition of 'authentic' Christian tradition. This formula, known as the Chicago Quadrilateral, was a statement, from the Anglican standpoint, of the essentials for a reunited Christian church. The four main elements were as follows:

1. The Holy Scriptures of the Old and New Testaments, as 'containing all things necessary to Salvation', and as being the rule and ultimate standard of Faith.
2. The Apostles' Creed, as the baptismal symbol; and the Nicene Creed, as the sufficient statement of the Christian Faith.
3. The two Sacraments ordained by Christ himself – Baptism and the Supper of Our Lord ministered with unfailing use of Christ's words of institution, and of the elements ordained by him.
4. The Historic Episcopate.

The 1888 Conference, taking this statement, promulgated the first of several successive versions of what has become known as the Lambeth Quadrilateral. It is this Lambeth Quadrilateral which has been one of the major contributions of the Anglican Communion to the evolving search for unity between the churches which is at the heart of the ecumenical movement.

The 1897 Lambeth Conference was attended by 194 bishops and presided over by Archbishop Frederick Temple. There were two main matters of interest: first, the Conference warmly commended the concept of deaconesses; and, secondly, it asked for the establishment of a consultative committee which was to be the direct ancestor of the Anglican Consultative Council.

The Conference of 1908 with Archbishop Davidson in the chair was attended by 242 bishops and concerned itself with the issues of the Ministry of Healing, the possible revision of the Prayer Book, and the supply and training of the clergy.

The Lambeth Conference should have convened again in 1918 but this was postponed due to the outbreak of the Great War. Much had changed in the way in which many people understood the world around them when the next Conference met in 1920. This Conference, attended by 252 bishops, was dominated by the subject of Church Unity. The celebrated 'Appeal to All Christian People' which was promulgated at the 1920 Conference invited other churches to accept episcopacy as the indispensable precondition for their unity with Anglicans. Developing from the consideration of the 1897 Conference there was also greater sympathy for a more prominent role for women in the governing and in the ministry of the Church. The 1920 Conference addressed itself to the issue of contraception and rejected its use outright.

The 1930 Conference was presided over by Archbishop Cosmo Lang, 307 bishops in attendance. It proved to be a very crowded occasion in the Lambeth Palace Library. The momentum towards Church Unity in South India found support, encouraging Anglicans in the Indian subcontinent to enter seriously into discussions related to a United Church in India.

Archbishop Geoffrey Fisher presided over two Conferences – 1948 attended by 349 bishops and 1958 attended by 310 bishops. By 1948 the Church of South India was an accomplished fact. In 1958 the proposal for a United Church of North India was welcomed. Nuclear disarmament was an issue in 1958 with the majority being in favour of disarmament, and the report on the family was a milestone with its sensitive treatment of the subject of contraception within marriage. The 1958 Conference approved the appointment of the first Anglican Executive Officer, thus assisting in the evolution both of the role of the Archbishop of Canterbury and of inter-Anglican structures. This was also the first Conference in which wives of the bishops were taken into account in the planning and organisation.

The Conference of 1968, under Archbishop Ramsey, was attended by 462 bishops. With this Conference it was no longer possible to meet at Lambeth Palace and the Conference was thus convened in the Church Assembly Hall at Church House, Westminster. Preparatory papers were offered to members of the Conference written by expert consultants and some 35 committees prepared the work for the final report. The issue of the ordination of women came forward and a proposed constitution for the establishment of the Anglican Consultative Council was agreed to. With the 1968 Conference the Lambeth Conferences became the modern phenomenon that we know them to be today with more extensive preparation, more committee work, and more concern for communication both between the churches and with the general public.

Another change of venue was to find the 1978 Conference meeting residentially in the University of Kent at Canterbury under Archbishop Coggan. Living and worshipping together gave a new community dynamic to the Conference. Again, preparatory work was a key element in the deliberations of the Conference and an important factor in this was the development of the work and role of the Anglican Consultative Council whose full Standing Committee was present for the Conference. Among the important and controversial issues on the agenda of the 1978 Conference were the ordination of women to the priesthood, the training of bishops, human rights, and the evolving Inter-Anglican bodies.

In 1988, the Conference was again held at the University of Kent at Canterbury, under the chairmanship of Archbishop Runcie. The Conference began on Sunday 17 July with a great opening service at Canterbury Cathedral and concluded on Sunday 7 August with a great closing service again in Canterbury Cathedral. The Conference resolved to set up several Inter-Anglican bodies: a Commission on the Ordination of Women to the Episcopate and on the implications of such ordinations for relations between the Churches of the Anglican Communion; an Advisory Body on Prayer Book Revision; an Inter-Faith Committee which would offer guidelines towards establishing a common approach to people of other faiths on a Communion-wide basis; a Commission on Anglican-Oriental Orthodox relations; conversations with the World Methodist Council and the Baptist World Alliance with a view to the beginning of international dialogues with these two traditions. The report of the Lambeth Conference 1988, *The Truth Shall Make You Free*, is published by Church House Publishing, price £8.50.

The Lambeth Conference 1998 was held in Canterbury, convened by Archbishop George Carey. Some 800 bishops attended. Reports are in preparation.

OTHER MEANS OF CONSULTATION
A second field of communication has been the Pan-Anglican Congresses. These have been held in London in 1908, in Minneapolis, USA in 1954 and in Toronto, Canada in 1963. Normally held at a time midway between Lambeth Conferences, the Congress, though like the Conference in having no executive authority, is distinguished from it by the presence of clerical and lay representatives from all the dioceses in the Communion.

Apart from the value of persons meeting one another, these Congresses have played a lesser role than the Lambeth Conferences and have had less influence. A significant contribution, though, to Anglican self-understanding came from the 1963 Congress. This was the concept of Mutual Responsibility and Interdependence in the Body of Christ. Unfortunately it became popularly identified solely with finance and projects, whereas it describes admirably the proper relationships within a worldwide family of autonomous churches.

The third step in forwarding the process of inter-Anglican consultation and common action was taken in 1958, when the Lambeth Conference of that year recommended 'that a full time Secretary of the Advisory Council on Missionary Strategy should be appointed by the Archbishop of Canterbury with the approval of the Advisory Council' and then went on to say, 'This Officer would collect and disseminate information, keep open lines of communication and make contact when necessary with responsible authority.' This official became known as the **Anglican Executive Officer**. The appointment was first held by Bishop Stephen Bayne of the United States who established the practice of travelling widely and personally meeting the Church in many parts of the world. Bishop Ralph Dean of Canada succeeded him and also acted as Episcopal Secretary to the 1968 Lambeth Conference. In 1969 he was succeeded by Bishop John Howe.

The 1968 Lambeth Conference called for the setting up of an **Anglican Consultative Council** (*see below*). The Council would come into being if two-thirds of the provinces of the Anglican Communion gave their consent. By the end of 1969 all had expressed their approval, and so the Council, asked for by the whole Anglican Communion, came into being. Canon Samuel Van Culin of the USA served as Secretary General until retiring in 1994.

The Lambeth Conference of 1978 requested that **Primates'** meetings should be set up to enable regular consultation between the Primates of the Anglican Communion. The first meeting took place in Ely, England in November/December 1979. The second meeting took place in Washington DC, USA in April/May 1981, the third was in Limuru, Kenya in October 1983, the fourth in Toronto, Canada in March 1986, the fifth in Larnaca, Cyprus in April/May 1989, the sixth in Ireland in April 1991, the seventh with the ACC in Cape Town, and the eighth in Windsor, England in 1995. The 1997 meeting was held in Jerusalem.

The Anglican Communion Office

Secretary General Canon John L. Peterson

Anglican Communion Office Partnership House, 157 Waterloo Rd, London SE1 8UT
Tel: 0171–620 1110
Fax: 0171–620 1070

The Anglican Consultative Council

MEMBERSHIP

The Archbishop of Canterbury is President and the Council chooses its own Chairman and Secretary General, which appointment replaces the former one of Anglican Executive Officer.

Each province or member church chooses up to three members. There are also six co-opted members, two of whom shall be women and two under 28 years of age. The resulting membership, made up of bishops, clergy and lay people, is notable for its spread of nationalities and races.

FUNCTIONS

The Council meets every two or three years and its Standing Committee in the intervening years. Council meetings are held in different parts of the world.

True to the Anglican Communion's style of working, the Council has no legislative powers. It fills a liaison role, consulting and recommending, and at times representing the Anglican Communion. The functions of the Council are stated as follows:

1. To share information about developments in one or more provinces with the other parts of the Communion and to serve as needed as an instrument of common action.
2. To advise on inter-Anglican, provincial and diocesan relationships, including the division of provinces, the formation of new provinces and of regional councils and the problems of extra-provincial dioceses.
3. To develop as far as possible agreed Anglican policies in the world mission of the Church and to encourage national and regional churches to engage together in developing and implementing such policies by sharing their resources of manpower, money and experience to the best advantage of all.
4. To keep before national and regional churches the importance of the fullest possible Anglican collaboration with other Christian Churches.
5. To encourage and guide Anglican participation in the Ecumenical Movement and the ecumenical organisations; to co-operate with the World Council of Churches and the world confessional bodies on behalf of the Anglican Communion; and to make arrangements for the conduct of Pan-Anglican conversations with the Roman Catholic Church, the Orthodox Churches and other churches.
6. To advise on matters arising out of national or regional church union negotiations or conversations and on subsequent relations with united churches.
7. To advise on problems of inter-Anglican communication and to help in the dissemination of Anglican and ecumenical information.
8. To keep in review the needs that may arise for further study and, where necessary, to promote enquiry and research.

RECORD OF MEETINGS

FIRST MEETING,
LIMURU, KENYA 1971

SECOND MEETING,
DUBLIN, IRELAND 1973

THIRD MEETING,
TRINIDAD 1976

FOURTH MEETING,
LONDON, ONTARIO, CANADA 1979

FIFTH MEETING,
NEWCASTLE UPON TYNE, ENGLAND 1981

SIXTH MEETING OF THE COUNCIL, BADAGRY, NIGERIA 1984
Sections:
1. Mission and Ministry: Evaluation of Mission (Mission Audit); Mission Strategy and Ministry.
2. Dogmatic and Pastoral Matters: Anglican/Roman Catholic Marriages; Polygamy; Christian Marriage and Family Life; Relations with Islam.
3. Ecumenical Relations: Steps Towards Unity; International Dialogues; World Council of Churches; and Church of England in South Africa.
4. Christianity and the Social Order: Social Issues; Peace; Refugees; Family; and United Nations.

SEVENTH MEETING OF THE COUNCIL, SINGAPORE 1987
Sections:
1. Mission and Ministry: Mission Agencies; New Mission Issues and Strategy Advisory Group; Renewal of the Church in Mission; Ordination of Women to the Priesthood and the Episcopate.
2. Dogmatic and Pastoral Concerns: Inter-Anglican Theological and Doctrinal Commission; Inter-Faith Relations; Christian Initiation; Anglican Communion Liturgical Commission.
3. Ecumenical Relations: Emmaus Report (which refers to dialogues with other churches); Anglican-Roman Catholic International Commission (ARCIC); Baptism, Eucharist and Ministry (BEM); United Churches in Full Communion.
4. Christianity and the Social Order: Peace and Justice; The Family; South Africa; AIDS.

The report of the meeting, *Many Gifts, One Spirit*, was published by Church House Publishing for the ACC, price £4.50.

EIGHTH MEETING OF THE COUNCIL, WALES 1990
Sections:
1. Spirituality and Justice.
2. Mission, Culture and Human Development.
3. Evangelism and Communication.
4. Unity and Creation.

The report of the meeting, *Mission in a Broken World*, with an overview by the editor – a new feature – was published by Church House Publishing for the ACC, price £6.50.

FIRST JOINT MEETING OF THE COUNCIL AND THE PRIMATES, CAPE TOWN, SOUTH AFRICA 1993
Working groups:
1. Running the Family.
2. Mission and Evangelism.
3. Dynamics of Communion.

The report, *A Transforming Vision*, was published by Church House Publishing for the ACC/Primates price £7.50, alongside a video and magazine, *Anglican World*.

TENTH MEETING OF THE COUNCIL, PANAMA 1996
Theme: Witnessing as Anglicans in the Third Millennium.
Sections:
1. Looking to the Future in Worship.
2. Looking to the Future in Ministry.
3. Looking to the Future in Relation to Society.
4. Looking to the Future in Communicating Our Beliefs.

Hearings: Human Sexuality, Jerusalem, Islam, United Nations.

The report, *Being Anglican in the Third Millennium*, was published by Morehouse Publishing.

The next ACC meeting will be in 1999 in Scotland.

PUBLICATIONS
The Anglican Cycle of Prayer
The Essential Guide to the Anglican Communion
Anglican World magazine

The Anglican Centre in Rome

The Metropolitans of the Anglican Communion endorsed the establishment of the Anglican Centre in Rome in April 1966. This followed consultations among representatives of the several Churches of the Anglican Communion on action for the furtherance of Christian Unity and considering the prospect for renewed fellowship and co-operation between Anglicans and Roman Catholics in particular, held out by the Second Vatican Council and by the historic visit of the Archbishop of Canterbury to Rome in March 1966.

The purposes of the Centre are:

1. To provide a meeting place and opportunities for clergy and seriously interested laity of the Anglican Communion, and those of other Christian denominations, particularly Roman Catholic, to come together for discussion, worship and prayer for the achievement of Christian Unity.
2. To provide a focal point for Anglican collaboration with the various agencies of the Roman Catholic Church and in particular its Council for Promoting Christian Unity.
3. To provide a library of Anglican history, theology and liturgy for the use of students, theologians and churchmen of all Christian denominations.
4. To give all possible help to Anglican scholars who wish to work in Rome and to aid them in meeting and working with those in Rome.
5. To sponsor various activities including lectures, seminars and discussion groups to elucidate Anglicanism and its relation to the thinking and practice of Roman Catholic and other theologians.
6. To provide information and, as appropriate, publicity concerning the Churches of the Anglican Communion, the Anglican Centre, and its objectives, programmes and activities.
7. To provide a base where the appointees of the several Anglican Churches may pursue co-ordinated discussions on appropriate lines of action for promoting unity, with the Roman Catholic Church and others.

The Centre publishes a quarterly magazine *CENTRO*, and organises seminars, including the ROMESS Summer School, open to clergy and laity with a genuine interest in ecumenism. The Centre's library is open from 0900–1230 Monday to Friday, except holidays.

The activities of the Centre are governed by a governing body, and a director.

Director and Archbishop of Canterbury's Counsellor on Vatican Affairs Canon Bruce Ruddock, The Anglican Centre in Rome, Palazzo Doria, Piazza Collegio Romano 2, 00186 Rome, Italy   *Tel:* +39–06–678–0302
                                Fax: +39–06–678–0674

FRIENDS OF THE ANGLICAN CENTRE IN ROME
Founded in 1984 to enlist support both through prayer and financial assistance for the work of the Centre.

President The Archbishop of Canterbury

Chairman The Bishop of Chichester

Vice-Chairman Revd Sir Derek Pattinson

Chairman, English Friends Revd Sir Derek Pattinson, 4 Strutton Court, Great Peter St, London SW1P 2HH.

CHURCHES AND PROVINCES OF THE ANGLICAN COMMUNION

AUTONOMOUS CHURCHES AND PROVINCES IN COMMUNION WITH THE SEE OF CANTERBURY

Anglican Church in Aotearoa, New Zealand and Polynesia

The Anglican Church in Aotearoa, New Zealand and Polynesia, formerly known as the Church of the Province of New Zealand (commonly called The Anglican Church), was established as an autonomous Church in full communion with the Church of England when its Constitution was accepted in 1857.

A revised Constitution adopted in May 1992 allows freedom and responsibility to implement worship and mission in accordance with the culture and social conditions within the units of the three equal partners that make up the Church – Te Pihopatanga o Aotearoa, the dioceses in New Zealand, and the Diocese of Polynesia.

Primate and Archbishop of New Zealand
Most Revd John Campbell Paterson (*Bishop of Auckland*)

Co-presiding Bishops
Rt Revd Whakahuihui Vercoe (*Bishop of Aotearoa*)
Rt Revd Jabez Leslie Bryce (*Bishop of Polynesia*)

General Secretary and *Treasurer* Mr Robin Nairn, PO Box 885, Hastings   Fax: 06–878 7905

THEOLOGICAL COLLEGES
College of the Southern Cross, 202 St John's Rd, Remuera, Auckland 5 (Serves both Anglicans and Methodists. *Administrative Manager* Ms Carol Anne Sensicle)
Fax: 09–521 2420

Te Rau Kahikatea College Maori Theological College, 202 St John's Rd, Auckland 5 (*Te Ahorangi /Dean* Ms J. Te Paa)

College of the Diocese of Polynesia, 202 St John's Rd, Remuera, Auckland 5 (*Principal* Ven W. Halapua)

College House, 100 Waimairi Rd, Christchurch 4 (*Principal* Dr A. Stockley)

Selwyn College, 560 Castle St, Dunedin (*Warden* Revd Philip Richardson)

The two last named cater for pre-ordination or post-graduate studies.

AOTEAROA
Bishop Rt Revd Whakahuihui Vercoe, PO Box 146, Rotorua, New Zealand   Fax: 07–348 6091
e-mail: mvercoe@aot.org.nz

Bishop in Tai Tokerau Rt Revd Waiohau Rui Te Haara, PO Box 25, Paihia   Fax: 09–402 6663
e-mail: bishop@pih.ang.org.nz

Bishop in Tai Rawhiti Rt Revd William Brown Turei, PO Box 1128, Napier   Fax: 06–835 7465

Bishop in Te Upoko O Te Ika Rt Revd Muru Walters, 11 Hobson Crescent, Levin   Fax: 04–479 8513
e-mail: muruwalters@compuserve.com

Bishop in Te Waipounamu Rt Revd John Robert Kuru Gray, PO Box 10086, Christchurch   Fax: 03–389 0912

AUCKLAND
Bishop Rt Revd John Campbell Paterson (*Primate and Presiding Bishop of the Anglican Church in Aotearoa, New Zealand* and *Polynesia and Bishop of Auckland*), PO Box 37–242, Parnell, Auckland   Fax: 09–303 3321
e-mail: 100400.2636@compuserve.com

CHRISTCHURCH
Bishop Rt Revd Dr David John Coles, PO 4438, Christchurch   Fax: 03–372 3357
e-mail: david.coles@p3.terrier.chch.planet.org.uk

DUNEDIN
Bishop Rt Revd Dr Penelope Ann Bansall Jamieson, PO Box 5445, Dunedin   Fax: 03–477 4932
e-mail: pennydn@earthlight.co.nz

NELSON
Bishop Rt Revd Derek Lionel Eaton, Bishopdale, PO Box 100, Nelson   Fax: 03–548 2125
e-mail: +derek@nn.ang.org.nz

POLYNESIA
Bishop in Rt Revd Jabez Leslie Bryce, Bishop's House, Box 35 GPO, Suva, Fiji Islands   Fax: 679 302 687

Assistant Bishop Rt Revd V. M. Hala'api'api (*same address*)
Fax: 679 302 152

WAIAPU
Bishop Rt Revd Murray John Mills, 8 Cameron Terr, PO Box 227, Napier, Hawkes Bay *Fax:* 06–835 0680
e-mail: murray.waiapu@hb.ang.org.nz

Bishop in the Bay of Plenty Rt Revd George Howard Douglas Connor, 60 Judea Rd, Tauranga *Fax:* 07–577 0684
e-mail: georgebop@ang.org.nz

WAIKATO
Bishop Rt Revd David John Moxon, PO Box 21, Hamilton,
Waikato *Fax:* 07–838 0050
e-mail: davidm@wave.co.nz

WELLINGTON
Bishop Rt Revd Dr Thomas John Brown, PO Box 12–046, Wellington *Fax:* 04– 449 1360
e-mail: 100401.320@compuserve.com

Assistant Bishop Rt Revd Brian Ruane Carrell, PO Box 442, Palmerston North *Fax:* 06–359 3264
e-mail: BrianCarrell@compuserve.com

Anglican Church of Australia

The Church came to Australia with the 'First Fleet', which largely comprised convicts and associated military personnel, in 1788. This community was ministered to by the Chaplain, Revd Richard Johnson. The whole continent of Australia formed an archdeaconry of the Diocese of Calcutta in 1824 but in 1836 Broughton was consecrated the first Bishop of Australia and soon after, in 1842, a second diocese, that of Tasmania, was formed. Five years later, three more dioceses were created, and the Bishop of Australia became the Bishop of Sydney. At the same time Broughton was made Metropolitan of the Province of Australia which included the New Zealand and the Australian dioceses.

The first General Synod of Australia was convened in 1872 when the number of dioceses had grown to ten, and in the early years of the twentieth century the Church had divided itself into four ecclesiastical provinces which correspond generally to the States of New South Wales, Victoria, Queensland and Western Australia. The Province of South Australia was formed by the General Synod in May 1973. There are now 23 dioceses, seven in New South Wales, four in Queensland, three in Western Australia, three in South Australia, and Tasmania is an extraprovincial diocese. The Diocese of the Northern Territory was formed in 1968 and the Diocese of The Murray in 1969. The Diocese of Papua New Guinea had been part of the Province of Queensland since its formation, but following proposals authorised by the General Synod in May 1973 and the independence of the country, a separate province was formed in February 1977. In 1996 the Diocese of North Queensland was enlarged to include the Diocese of Carpentaria, which ceased to exist.

From 1854 Acts of Parliament had been passed in various state legislatures constituting the Church of England in those states as a voluntary organisation and granting the Church local autonomy. But on 1 January 1962 the Constitution of the Church of England in Australia came into force, having first been approved by the 25 diocesan synods and given legal force and effect by suitable Acts passed by the six State Parliaments. The General Synod is required to meet at least once every four years. The Primate is elected from among the diocesan bishops by an Electoral College of bishops, clergy and laity. The name change from the Church of England in Australia to the Anglican Church of Australia took effect from 24 August 1981.

Australia occupies a significant position in the south-west Pacific and south-east Asian region. A large country geographically, she has a comparatively small population. Her 17 million people occupy a fertile south-eastern and south-western crescent of a continent of almost 3,000,000 square miles.

The descendants of the original Australians, the Aborigines and Torres Strait Islanders, number 350,500 or 1.9 per cent of the total population. Bishop Arthur Malcolm, an aboriginal Australian, plays a leading role in aboriginal concerns. Bishop Ted Mosby, a Torres Strait Islander, was consecrated in 1997. Constitutional changes to the General Synod have been initiated to give indigenous people direct representation on the General Synod. One quarter of Australians were born in another country, and the multi-cultural nature of the population can be gauged from the fact that more than half of this group were born in non-English-speaking countries.

The Anglican Church of Australia plays its role as a member of the Christian Conference of Asia and of the Council of the Church of East Asia. The Church has strengthened her links of partnership in New Guinea, Melanesia and Polynesia, which were traditional areas of missionary interests. Japan is Australia's largest trading partner.

Primate of the Anglican Church of Australia
Most Revd Keith Rayner (*Archbishop of Melbourne*)

General Secretary of the General Synod Revd Dr B. N. Kaye

Hon Treasurer Mr Adrian Scarra

General Synod Office Box Q190, QVB Post Office, New South Wales 1230 *Fax:* 02 9264–6552

THE ANGLICAN THEOLOGICAL COLLEGES
Anglican Institute of Theology and Religious Education, Cnr Hardy and Leura St, Nedlands, WA6009 (*Director* Revd Dr J. Dunhill) *Fax:* 08–9386 8327

Institute of Theological Education, PO Box 535, Boronia, Vic 3155 (*Director* Revd Trevor Smith)
Fax: 03–9761 2344

Moore Theological College, 1 King St, Newtown, NSW 2042 (*Principal* Canon Peter Jensen) *Fax:* 02–9577 9988
e-mail: admin@moore.usyd.edu.au

Nungalinya College, PO Box 40371, Casuarina, NT 0811 (*Principal* Wali Fejo) *Fax:* 08–8927 2332

Ridley College, 106 The Avenue, Parkville, Vic 3052 (*Principal* Revd Dr Graham Cole) *Fax:* 03–9387 5099

St Barnabas Theological College, 34 Lipsett Terrace, Brooklyn Park, SA 5032 (*Principal* Revd Dr Scott Cowdell)
Fax: 08–8416 8450
e-mail: barbara.dalton@flinders.edu.au

St Francis Theological College, 233 Milton Rd, PO Box 1261, Milton Qld 4064 (*Principal* Canon James McPherson) *Fax:* 07–3369 4691
e-mail: stfrancis@docnet.org.au

St John's College Ministry Centre, PO Box 71, Morpeth, NSW 2321 (*Principal* Canon Ann McElligott)
Fax: 02–4934 5170
e-mail: annep@bigpond.com

St Mark's National Theological Centre, 15 Blackall St, Barton, ACT 2600 (*Director* Dr Stephen Pickard)
Fax: 02–6273 4067
e-mail: cdundon@csu.edu.au

Trinity College Theological School, Royal Parade, Parkville, Vic 3052 (*Director* Vacancy) *Fax:* 03–9347 1610

Wollaston Theological College, Wollaston Rd, Mt Claremont, WA 6010 (*Principal* Revd Roger Sharr)
Fax: 08–9385 3364
e-mail: rsharr@central.murdoch.edu.au

CHURCH PAPERS
The Adelaide Church Guardian 16 page magazine containing Archbishop's letter and wide news coverage. *Editorial Offices* Church Office, 44 Currie St, Adelaide, SA 5000.

The Melbourne Anglican 12 page diocesan newspaper for Melbourne, including news from Bendigo and Wangaratta. *Director* A.I.O., Cathedral Buildings, Flinders Lane, Melbourne 3000.

Anglican Encounter 8 page newspaper of Newcastle Diocese, containing diocesan and Australian news. *Editorial Offices* PO Box 817, Newcastle 2300.

Church News 8 page, small newspaper format, from Tasmania Diocese, containing wide comment. *Editorial Offices* GPO Box 784 H, Hobart 7001.

Southern Cross 16 page newspaper of Sydney Diocese, containing diocesan, national and world news, letter from the Archbishop. *Editorial Offices* Box Q190, Queen Victoria PO, Sydney 2000.

Anglican Messenger 16 page newspaper based in Perth, containing news from North West Australia and Bunbury. *Editorial Offices* GPO Box W2067, Perth 6001.

The Dioceses of Ballarat, Bathurst, Brisbane, Rockhampton, Gippsland, Canberra and Goulburn, Willochra and North Queensland also produce monthly magazines/Bishop's newsletters, with mainly diocesan and parochial news.

PROVINCE OF NEW SOUTH WALES
Metropolitan Most Revd Harry (Richard Henry) Goodhew (*Archbishop of Sydney*)

ARMIDALE
Bishop Rt Revd Peter Chiswell, Bishopscourt, PO Box 198, Armidale, NSW 2350 *Fax:* 02–6772 9261
e-mail: diocarm@northnet.com.au

BATHURST
Bishop Rt Revd Bruce Winston Wilson, Bishopscourt, PO Box 23, Bathurst, NSW 2795 *Fax:* 02–6332 2772

CANBERRA AND GOULBURN
Bishop Rt Revd George Victor Browning, The Anglican Registry, GPO Box 1981, Canberra, ACT 2601
Fax: 02–6247 6829
e-mail: gbrowning@fc.accnet.net.au

Assistant Bishop Rt Revd Richard Randerson (*same address*)
e-mail: richard.randerson@fc.accnet.net.au

GRAFTON
Bishop Rt Revd Philip James Huggins, Bishopsholme, PO Box 4, 37 Victoria St, Grafton, NSW 2460
Fax: 02–6643 1814
e-mail: angdio@hotkey.net.au

NEWCASTLE
Bishop Rt Revd Roger Adrian Herft, Bishop's Registry, PO Box 817, 250 Darby St, Newcastle, NSW 2300
Fax: 02–4926 1968
e-mail: roher@bigpond.com

RIVERINA
Bishop Rt Revd Bruce Quinton Clark, PO Box 10, Narrandera, NSW 2700 *Fax:* 02–6929 2903
e-mail: riverina.diocese@accnet.net.au

Churches and Provinces: Australia

SYDNEY
Archbishop Most Revd Harry (Richard Henry) Goodhew (*Archbishop of Sydney, Metropolitan of the Province of NSW*), PO Box Q190, QVB Post Office, NSW 2000
Fax: 02–9265 1504
e-mail: res@glebeaust.com.au

Assistant Bishops
Rt Revd Raymond George Smith (*Bishop of Liverpool*) (*same address*)
Fax: 02–9261 4485
e-mail: mpj@glebeaust.com.au

Rt Revd Dr Paul William Barnett (*Bishop of North Sydney*) (*same address*)
Fax: 02–9419 6761

Rt Revd Peter R. Watson (*Bishop of South Sydney*) (*same address*)
Fax: 02–9265 1543

Rt Revd Reg Piper (*Bishop of Wollongong*), 74 Church St, Wollongong 2500
Fax: 02–4228 4296

Rt Revd Dr Brian King (*Bishop of Parramatta*), PO Box 1443, Parramatta, NSW 2124
Fax: 02–9633 3636

PROVINCE OF QUEENSLAND
Metropolitan Most Revd Peter John Hollingworth (*Archbishop of Brisbane*)

BRISBANE
Archbishop Most Revd Peter John Hollingworth (*Archbishop of Brisbane, Metropolitan of Queensland*), Bishopsbourne, Box 421, GPO, Brisbane 4001, Queensland
Fax: 07–3832 5030
e-mail: archbishops.office@docnet.org.au

Assistant Bishops
Rt Revd Ronald John Chantler Williams (*same address*)
e-mail: bishopsoffice@docnet.org.au

Rt Revd John Ashley Noble (*same address*)
e-mail: janoble@gil.com.au

Rt Revd Raymond Bruce Smith, Box 2600, Toowoomba, Queensland 4350
Fax: 07–4632 6882
e-mail: toowoomba.office@docnet.org.au

NORTH QUEENSLAND
Bishop Rt Revd Clyde Wood, Diocesan Registry, Box 1244, Townsville, Queensland 4810
Fax: 07–4721 1756
e-mail: clyde.wood@accnet.net.au

Assistant Bishops
Rt Revd Ted Mosby (*Bishop in the Torres Strait Islands*) (*same address*)

Rt Revd Ian Campbell Stuart, PO Box 235, Charters Towers, Queensland 4820
Fax: 07–4787 3049
e-mail: assg@httech.com.au

Rt Revd Arthur Malcolm, 6 Loridin Drive, Brinsmead Glen, Cairns, Queensland 4870
Fax: 089- 480 585

THE NORTHERN TERRITORY
Bishop Rt Revd Richard Franklin Appleby, PO Box 2950, Darwin, NT 0801
Fax: 08–8941 7446
e-mail: dio.nt@taunet.net.au

ROCKHAMPTON
Bishop Rt Revd Ronald Francis Stone, PO Box 6158, Central Queensland Mail Centre, Rockhampton, Queensland 4702
Fax: 07–4922 4562
e-mail: bishop@anglicanrock.org.au

PROVINCE OF SOUTH AUSTRALIA
Metropolitan Most Revd Ian Gordon Combe George (*Archbishop of Adelaide*)

ADELAIDE
Archbishop Most Revd Ian Gordon Combe George (*Archbishop of Adelaide, Metropolitan of the Province of South Australia*), 26 King William Rd, N Adelaide, S Australia 5006
Fax: 08–8305 9399
e-mail: ian.george@accnet.net.au

Assistant Bishop Rt Revd Phillip John Aspinall (*same address*)
e-mail: anglade@comtech.net.au

THE MURRAY
Bishop Rt Revd Graham Howard Walden, PO Box 269, Murray Bridge, S Australia 5253
Fax: 085–325 760

WILLOCHRA
Bishop Rt Revd William David Hair McCall, Bishop's House, PO Box 96, Gladstone, S Australia 5473
Fax: 08–8662 2027
e-mail: David.McCall@fc.accnet.net.au

PROVINCE OF VICTORIA
Metropolitan Most Revd Keith Rayner (*Archbishop of Melbourne*)

BALLARAT
Bishop Rt Revd David Silk, PO Box 89, Ballarat, Victoria 3350
Fax: 03–5333 2982
e-mail: annagndio@lin.cbl.com.au

BENDIGO
Bishop Rt Revd Raymond David Bowden, PO Box 2, Bendigo, Victoria 3550
Fax: 03–5441 2173

GIPPSLAND
Bishop Rt Revd Arthur Jones, PO Box 28, Sale, Victoria 3850
Fax: 03–5144 7183

MELBOURNE
Archbishop Most Revd Keith Rayner (*Archbishop of Melbourne, Metropolitan of the Province of Victoria and Primate*),

The Anglican Centre, 209 Flinders Lane, Melbourne, Victoria 3000
Fax: 03–9650 2184
e-mail: keithrayner@accnet.net.au

Assistant Bishops
Rt Revd Andrew St John (*Bishop in Geelong*), The Bishop's House, 364 Shannon Ave, Newtown, Victoria 3220
Fax: 03–5222 2378
e-mail: astjohn@pipeline.com.au

Rt Revd James Alexander Grant, St Paul's Cathedral Bldg, Flinders Lane, Melbourne, Victoria 3000
Fax: 03–9650 2184

Rt Revd John Warwick Wilson (*same address*)

Rt Revd Andrew William Curnow (*same address*)
e-mail: bishop@nthregion.org.au

Rt Revd John Craig Stewart (*same address*)
e-mail: jcstew@ozemail.com.au

WANGARATTA
Bishop Rt Revd David Farrer, PO Box 457, Wangaratta 3676
Fax: 03–5722 1427
e-mail: dwang@w140.aone.net.au

PROVINCE OF WESTERN AUSTRALIA
Metropolitan Most Revd Peter Frederick Carnley (*Archbishop of Perth*)

BUNBURY
Bishop Rt Revd Hamish Thomas Jamieson, Bishopscourt, PO Box 15, Bunbury 6231, W Australia
Fax: 08–9791 2300
e-mail: bishop@diocese.altu.net.au

NORTH-WEST AUSTRALIA
Bishop Rt Revd Anthony Howard Nicholls, PO Box 171, Geraldton, W Australia 6530
Fax: 08–9964 2200
e-mail: dnwa@wn.com.au

(*Regional Bishop for the Kimberley*), PO Box 158, Broome, W Australia 6725
Fax: 091–93 5482

PERTH
Archbishop Most Revd Peter Frederick Carnley (*Archbishop of Perth and Metropolitan of the Province of Western Australia*), GPO Box W2067, Perth, W Australia 6001
Fax: 08–9325 6741

Assistant Bishops
Rt Revd Gerald Edward Beaumont (Goldfields Region), PO Box 439, Kalgoorlie, W Australia 6430
Fax: 08–9091 2757
e-mail: gebart@ludin.com.au

Rt Revd David Owen Murray, Anglican Church Office, 26 Queens St, Freemantle, W Australia 6160
Fax: 08–9336 3374
e-mail: srbishop@iinet.net.au

Rt Revd Brian George Farran, PO Box 42, Joondalup, W Australia 6919
Fax: 08–9300 0893
e-mail: plusbrian@bigpond.com

EXTRA-PROVINCIAL DIOCESE
TASMANIA
Bishop Rt Revd Phillip Keith Newell, GPO 748H, Hobart, Tasmania 7001
Fax: 03–6223 8968

The Episcopal Anglican Church of Brazil
(Igreja Episcopal Anglicana Do Brasil)

The Episcopal Anglican Church of Brazil was founded by two students from the Virginia Seminary who arrived in 1889. Two years later three new recruits arrived. Missions and schools were established in the south of the country where the majority of Christians live. In 1950 the Missionary District was divided into three dioceses. Fifteen years later the Brazilian Church became autonomous from ECUSA and became the nineteenth autonomous province of the Anglican Communion.

This Anglican province covers all the territory of the Federal Republic of Brazil, and was inaugurated on 25 April 1965. There were British chaplaincies in Central, South Central and Northern Brazil. Due to its enormous geographical area, Brazil is a country of great contrasts. The nation is facing serious economic and social problems where the foreign debt and the low standard of living of 80 per cent of people are the context where the Church is called to witness and to perform its mission today.

The Partners in Mission Consultation in April 1990 decided to appoint three priorities for the next years: education, service and expansion.

As all over Latin America, the Anglican Communion has an important contribution to make to the spiritual life of the Brazilian people as a Church both catholic and reformed. The Synod of the Church meets every three years. In the meantime it functions through the Executive Council of the Synod which meets twice a year.

Theological education in Brazil is supervised by a National Board, with clerical or lay representation from each diocese. The national Seminary has a unique role in clergy and lay training today but several dioceses have their own theological centres to prepare lay leaders and auxiliary ministers.

Some church schools and social institutions are run by the dioceses in the south where most church members live. The Northern Diocese is an increasing work and Brasilia is a missionary diocese inaugurated in 1985.

CHURCH PAPER

A monthly church journal in Portuguese, *Estandarte Cristão*, published since 1893, which contains general articles and news about the life of the Church at local, national and international level. This journal is the main channel of the Communication Department of the Church. *Editor/Editorial offices:* Revd Renato Raatz, Caixa Postal 11510, Cep 90841–970, Porto Alegre, RS, Brazil.

Primate Most Revd Glauco Soares de Lima (*Bishop of São Paulo*)

Provincial Secretary Revd Mauricio de Andrade, Caixa Postal 11510, Cep 90841–970, Porto Alegre, RS, Brazil
Fax: 55–051–336 5087
e-mail: m_andrade@conex.com.br

Provincial Treasurer Mr Ricardo Hallbarg Luiz (*same address*)

BRASILIA
Bishop Rt Revd Almir dos Santos, Caixa Postal 00515, Cep 70359–970 Brasilia, DF, Brazil   *Fax:* 55–061–243 8074
e-mail: familia.santos@nutecnet.com.br

PELOTAS
Bishop Rt Revd Luiz Osório Pires Prado, Caixa Postal 791, Cep 96001–970, Pelotas, RS, Brazil
Fax: 55–0532–22 1347
e-mail: dprado@conesul.com.br

RECIFE
Bishop Rt Revd Edward Robinson de Barros Calvalcanti, Caixa Postal 04704, Cep 51012–970, Recife, PE, Brazil
Fax: 55–081–325 2089

RIO DE JANEIRO
Bishop Rt Revd Sydney Alcoba Ruiz, Av Rio Branco 277/907-Centro, CEP 20047–900, Rio de Janeiro, RJ, Brazil
Fax: 55–021–220 2705

SÃO PAULO
Archbishop Most Revd Glauco Soares de Lima (*Primate of the Episcopal Church of Brazil*), Rua Com Elias Zarzur, 1239, CEP 04736–002 São Paulo, SP, Brazil
Fax: 55–011–246 2180
e-mail: rgovier@ecunet.org

SOUTH WESTERN BRAZIL
Bishop Rt Revd Jubal Pereira Neves, Caixa Postal 98, CEP 97001–970, Santa Maria, RS, Brazil
Fax: 55–055–223 1196
e-mail: jneves@sm.conex.com.br

SOUTHERN BRAZIL
Bishop Rt Revd Orlando Santos de Oliveira, Caixa Postal 11504, Cep 90870–970, Porto Alegre, RS, Brazil
Fax: 55–051–336 3531
e-mail: oso@hotnet.net

The Church of the Province of Burundi

Primate Most Revd Ndayisenga (*Archbishop of Burundi*)

Provincial Secretary Vacancy, BP 2098, Bujumbura, Burundi

THEOLOGICAL COLLEGES
Canon Warner Memorial College, Eglise Episcopale du Burundi, EEB Buye, BP 94 Ngozi, Burundi

Kosiya Shalita Interdiocesan Theological College and Bible School, EEB Matana, DS 12, Bujumbura, Burundi

BUJUMBURA
Bishop Rt Revd Pie Ntukamazina, BP 1300, Bujumbura, Burundi   *Fax:* 257 229 275

BUYE
Bishop Most Revd Samuel Ndayisenga (*Archbishop of Burundi and Bishop of Buye*), EEB Buye, BP 94, Ngozi, Burundi   *Fax:* 257 030 2317

GITEGA
Bishop Rt Revd Jean Nduwayo, BP 23, Gitega, Burundi

MAKAMBA
Bishop Rt Revd Martin Blaise Nyaboho, BP 96, Makamba, Burundi   *Fax:* 257 229 129

MATANA
Bishop Rt Revd Bernard Ntahoturi, BP 447, Bujumbura, Burundi   *Fax:* 257 22 9129

The Anglican Church of Canada

Primate of The Anglican Church of Canada
Most Revd Michael G. Peers, 600 Jarvis St, Toronto, Ontario, M4Y 2J6 *Fax:* 416 924 0211
e-mail: primate@national.anglican.ca

Offices of the General Synod and of its Departments Anglican Church of Canada, 600 Jarvis Street, Toronto, ON M4Y 2J6 *Fax:* 416 968 7983

UNIVERSITIES AND COLLEGES OF THE ANGLICAN CHURCH OF CANADA
British Columbia
Vancouver School of Theology*, 6000 Iona Dr, Vancouver, BC V6T 1L4 (*Principal* Revd Dr William J. Phillips)

Manitoba
Henry Budd College for Ministry, Box 2518, The Pas MB R9A 1M3 (*President* Canon Fletcher Stewart)
St John's College, 400 Dysart Rd, Winnipeg MB R3T 2M5 (*Acting Warden* Dr Janet Harkine)

Newfoundland
Queen's College, Prince Philip Dr, St John's NF A1B 3R6 (*Principal* Revd Boyd Morgan)

Northwest Territories
Arthur Turner Training School, c/o 4910 51st St, Box 1454, Yellowknife, NT X1A 2P1
Nova Scotia Atlantic School of Theology*, 640 Francklyn St, Halifax, NS B3H 3B5 (*President* Revd Dr Gordon MacDermid)

Ontario
Canterbury College, 172 Patricia Rd, Windsor ON N9B 3B9 (*Principal* Revd Dr David T. A. Symons)
Huron College, 1349 Western Rd, London, ON N6G 1H3 (*Principal* Dr David G. Bevan)
Renison College, Westmount Rd N., Waterloo, ON N2L 3G4 (*Principal* Dr Gail Brandt)
Thorneloe College, Ramsey Lake Rd, Sudbury, ON P3E 2C6 (*Provost* Dr Donald Thompson)
Trinity College, 6 Hoskin Ave, Toronto, ON M5S 1H8 (*Dean of Divinity* Dr Donald Wiebe)
Wycliffe College, 5 Hoskin Ave, Toronto, ON M5S 1H7 (*Principal* Revd Michael J. Pountney)

Quebec
Bishop's University, PO Box 5000, Lennoxville, PQ J1M 1Z7
Montreal Diocesan Theological College, 3473 University St, Montreal, PQ H3A 2A8 (*Principal* Revd Dr John Simons)

Saskatchewan
College of Emmanuel and St Chad, 1337 College Dr, Saskatoon, SK S7N 0W6 (*Principal* Canon William Christensen)

*Ecumenical

CHURCH PAPERS
Anglican Journal/Journal anglican Tabloid format, national church paper under management of a Board of Trustees appointed by General Synod. It circulates as an insert for a number of diocesan publications. Issued monthly except July and August. *Editorial offices:* 600 Jarvis St, Toronto, ON M4Y 2J6.
Ministry Matters published three times a year by the Information Resources Dept of General Synod. Intended primarily for clergy and lay leaders.

The dioceses of the Anglican Church of Canada are grouped in four ecclesiastical provinces, each with a metropolitan archbishop. Each province and diocese has its own synod.

The first General Synod of the Anglican Church of Canada was held in 1893. General Synod now meets every three years, comprising the archbishops, the bishops and elected clergy and lay representatives of all the dioceses.

Work of General Synod between sessions is carried out under the authority of the Council of General Synod, which meets semi-annually. National headquarters are at 600 Jarvis Street, Toronto, Ontario M4Y 2J6. Here the work of administration, planning and programme is carried out, and the Primate also makes it his headquarters.

PROVINCE OF BRITISH COLUMBIA AND YUKON
Metropolitan Most Revd David P. Crawley (*Archbishop of Kootenay*)

BRITISH COLUMBIA
Bishop Rt Revd R. Barry R. Jenks, 912 Vancouver St, Victoria, BC V8V 3V7 *Fax:* 250 386 4013
e-mail: bishop@acts.bs.ca

CALEDONIA
Bishop Rt Revd John E. Hannen, PO Box 278, Prince Rupert, BC V8J 3P6 *Fax:* 250 624 4299
e-mail: BISHOP_HANNEN@ecunet.org

CARIBOO
Bishop Rt Revd James D. Cruikshank, 5–618 Tranquille Rd, Kamloops, BC V2B 3H6 *Fax:* 250 376 1984
e-mail: DIOCESE_OF_CARIBOO@ecunet.org

KOOTENAY
Archbishop Most Revd David P. Crawley (*Archbishop of Kootenay and Metropolitan of the Ecclesiastical Province of British Columbia and Yukon*), 1876 Richter St, Kelowna, BC V1Y 2M9 *Fax:* 250 762 4150
e-mail: DIOCESE_OF_KOOTENAY@ecunet.org

NEW WESTMINSTER
Bishop Rt Revd Michael C. Ingham, Suite 580, 401 West Georgia St, Vancouver BC V6B 5A1 *Fax:* 604 684 7017
e-mail: MICHAEL_INGHAM@ecunet.org

YUKON
Bishop Rt Revd Terrence O. Buckle, PO Box 4247, Whitehorse, Yukon Y1A 3T3 *Fax:* 403 667 6125

PROVINCE OF CANADA
Metropolitan Most Revd Arthur Peters (*Archbishop of Nova Scotia*)

CENTRAL NEWFOUNDLAND
Bishop Rt Revd Edward F. Marsh, 34 Fraser Rd, Gander, NF A1V 2E8 *Fax:* 709 256 2396
e-mail: bishop_marsh@ecunet.org

EASTERN NEWFOUNDLAND AND LABRADOR
Bishop Rt Revd Donald F. Harvey, 19 King's Bridge Rd, St John's NF A1C 3K4 *Fax:* 709 576 7122
e-mail: don_harvey@ecunet.org

FREDERICTON
Bishop Rt Revd George C. Lemmon, 115 Church St, Fredericton, NB E3B 4C8 *Fax:* 506 460 0520
e-mail: diocfton@nbnet.ab.ca

Coadjutor Bishop Rt Revd William J. Hockin (*same address*)

MONTREAL
Bishop Rt Revd Andrew S. Hutchison, 1444 Union Ave, Montreal, QC H3A 2B8 *Fax:* 514 843 3221
e-mail: bishopscourt@ibm.net

Assistant Bishop Rt Revd Russell Hatton (*same address*)

NOVA SCOTIA
Bishop Most Revd Arthur G. Peters (*Archbishop of Nova Scotia and Metropolitan of the Ecclesiastical Province of Canada*), 5732 College St, Halifax, NS B3H 1X3
Fax: 902 425 0717
e-mail: diocese@fox.nstn.ca

Suffragan Bishop Rt Revd Frederick J. Hiltz (*same address*)

QUEBEC
Bishop Rt Revd A. Bruce Stavert, 31 rue des Jardins, Quebec, PQ G1R 4L6 *Fax:* 418 692 3876
e-mail: diocese_of_quebec@sympatico.ca

WESTERN NEWFOUNDLAND
Bishop Rt Revd Leonard Whitten, 13 Cobb Lane, Corner Brook, NF A2H 2V3 *Fax:* 709 639 1636
e-mail: dsown@nf.sympatico.ca

PROVINCE OF ONTARIO
Metropolitan Most Revd Percy R. O'Driscoll (*Archbishop of Huron*)

ALGOMA
Bishop Rt Revd Ronald C. Ferris, Box 1168, Sault Ste Marie, ON P6A 5N7 *Fax:* 705 946 1860

HURON
Archbishop Most Revd Percy R. O'Driscoll (*Archbishop of Huron and Metropolitan of the Ecclesiastical Province of Ontario*), 903–255 Queens Ave, London, ON N6A 5R8
Fax: 519 673 4151
e-mail: huron@wwdc.com

Bishop Suffragan Rt Revd C. Robert Townshend (*same address*)

MOOSONEE
Bishop Rt Revd Caleb J. Lawrence, Box 841, Schumacher, ON P0N 1G0 *Fax:* 705 360 1120
e-mail: moosonee@ntl.sympatico.ca

NIAGARA
Bishop Rt Revd D. Ralph Spence, 252 James St North, Hamilton, ON L8R 2L3 *Fax:* 905 527 1281
e-mail: adatri@niagara.anglican.org

ONTARIO
Bishop Rt Revd Peter R. Mason, 90 Johnson St, Kingston, ON K7L 1X7 *Fax:* 613 547 3745
e-mail: pmason@ontario.anglican.ca

OTTAWA
Bishop Rt Revd John A. Baycroft, 71 Bronson Ave, Ottawa ON K1R 6G6 *Fax:* 613 232 7088
e-mail: jbaycroft@magmacom.com

TORONTO
Bishop Rt Revd Terence E. Finlay, 135 Adelaide St East, Toronto, ON M5C 1L8 *Fax:* 416 363 3683
e-mail: finlay@tap.net

Bishops Suffragan
Rt Revd Douglas C. Blackwell, 63 Glen Dhu Drive, Whitby, Ontario L1R 1K3 *Fax:* 905 668 8216
e-mail: BishopB@yesic.com

Rt Revd J. Taylor Pryce, Aurora Conference Centre, 162 St John's Sideroad West, Aurora, Ontario L4G 3G8
Fax: 905 727 4937

Rt Revd Michael H. H. Bedford-Jones, St Paul's, L'Amoreaux, 3333 Finch Ave East, Scarborough, Ontario M1W 2R9　　　　　　　　　　　　　　*Fax:* 416 497 4103
e-mail: mbj@total.net

Rt Revd Ann E. Tottenham, 256 Sheldon Ave, Etobicoke, Ontario M8W 4X8　　　　　　　*Fax:* 416 503 8229
e-mail: cvalley@tap.net

PROVINCE OF RUPERT'S LAND
Metropolitan Most Revd J. Barry Curtis (*Archbishop of Calgary*)

THE ARCTIC
Bishop Rt Revd Christopher Williams, Box 1454, 4910 51st St, Yellowknife, NWT X1A 2P1　　　*Fax:* 867 873 8478
e-mail: CHRIS_WILLIAMS@ecunet.org

Suffragan Bishop Rt Revd Paul Idlont, Box 2219, Iqaluit, NWT XOA 0H0　　　　　　　　　*Fax:* 867 979 7814

ATHABASCA
Bishop Rt Revd John R. Clarke, Box 6868, Peace River, AB T8S 1S6　　　　　　　　　　　　*Fax:* 403 624 2365

BRANDON
Bishop Rt Revd Malcolm A. W. Harding, 341–13th St, Brandon, MB R7A 4P8　　　　　　*Fax:* 204 727 4135
e-mail: bishopbdn@galaxy.mb.ca

CALGARY
Bishop Most Revd J. Barry Curtis (*Archbishop of Calgary and Metropolitan of the Ecclesiastical Province of Rupert's Land*), 3015 Glencoe Rd SW, Calgary, AB T2S 2L9
Fax: 403 243 2182
e-mail: diocese@telusplanet.net

Assistant Bishop Rt Revd Gary F. Woolsey, St Peter's Anglican Church, 903–75th Avenue SW, Calgary, AB T2V 0S7　　　　　　　　　　　　　*Fax:* 403 255 0752
e-mail: gwoolsey@cadvision.com

EDMONTON
Bishop Rt Revd Victoria Matthews, 10033 84th Ave, Edmonton, AB T6E 2G6　　　　　*Fax:* 403 439 6549
e-mail: bishopv@freenet.edmonton.ab.ca

KEEWATIN
Bishop Rt Revd Gordon W. Beardy, 915 Ottawa St, Keewatin, ON P0X 1C0　　　　　　　　*Fax:* 807 547 3356

QU'APPELLE
Bishop Rt Revd Duncan D. Wallace, 1501 College Ave, Regina SK S4P 1B8　　　　　　　*Fax:* 306 352 6808
e-mail: quappelle@sk.sympatico.ca

RUPERT'S LAND
Bishop Rt Revd Patrick V. Lee, 935 Nesbitt Bay, Winnipeg, MB R3T 1W6　　　　　　　　　*Fax:* 204 452 3915
e-mail: diocese@escape.ca

SASKATCHEWAN
Bishop Rt Revd Anthony J. Burton, Box 1088, Prince Albert, SK S6V 5S6　　　　　　　　*Fax:* 306 764 5172
e-mail: burton@sk.sympatico.ca

Bishop Suffragan Rt Revd Charles J. Arthurson, Box 96, Lac La Ronge, SK S0J 1L0

SASKATOON
Bishop Rt Revd Thomas O. Morgan, PO Box 1965, Saskatoon, SK S7K 3S5　　　　　　　*Fax:* 306 665 0244
e-mail: diocese.stoon@sk.sympatico.ca

The Church of the Province of Central Africa

The province covers Botswana, Malawi, Zimbabwe and Zambia. It was inaugurated in 1955. The province's first archbishop was the great missionary bishop of Mashonaland, Edward Paget, who resigned in March 1957. The second archbishop was James Hughes, who was first Bishop of Matabeleland. The third archbishop was Oliver Green-Wilkinson, Bishop of Zambia, who was elected in 1962. After his accidental death in 1970, the Most Revd Donald Seymour Arden, Bishop of Southern Malawi became the fourth archbishop. He resigned in September 1980 and was succeeded by the Most Revd Walter Paul Khotso Makhulu, Bishop of Botswana.

The countries forming the province are very different. Zimbabwe, formerly Rhodesia, is relatively highly industrialised with a population of nine million people.

Malawi is almost entirely rural with a population of eight million people and it is densely populated.

Zambia has a population of seven million people. Zambia produces much of the world's copper.

Botswana's main industry has been cattle ranching. But there are now rich diamond, copper and nickel mines. It has a population of about 1.2 million people and is sparsely populated.

The constitution of the province is similar to that of provinces in other parts of Africa, but, unlike most of them, it has a movable archbishopric. A recent development has been the creation of territorial councils in countries where there are more than one diocese. Although the Zambian Anglican Council and the Anglican Council of Malawi have extensive administrative and financial powers, the Anglican Council of Zimbabwe is purely consultative.

Each country faces its own problems. Zimbabwe, now an independent state, is still experiencing problems of social adjustment after independence.

Zambia and Botswana suffer the difficulties of rapid industrialisation, contrasting with the underdevelopment of the thinly populated areas.

In Malawi, where farming is the main source of livelihood, 30 per cent of adult males are away at any given time as migrant labourers in other countries, often with disastrous results on family life.

HISTORY OF THE ANGLICAN CHURCH IN MALAWI

The first Anglican missionary was Bishop Charles Mackenzie, leader of the Universities' Mission to Central Africa. His party arrived together with David Livingstone in 1861, but was withdrawn in 1863 following Bishop Mackenzie's death. A fresh start was made on Zanzibar Island in the same year, and in 1882 William Johnson and Charles Janson reached Lake Nyasa (now Lake Malawi). Twelve days later Janson died. His companion carried on for another 46 years, operating from Likoma Island on Lake Nyasa.

FORMATION OF DIOCESES

In the 1950s the new Diocese of South West Tanganyika and the northern half of the Diocese of Lebombo were formed out of the work of the eastern lakeshore. On Malawi's attainment of independence in 1964 the Diocese of Nyasaland changed its name to Diocese of Malawi. In 1971 the diocese was divided into two – Diocese of Lake Malawi and Diocese of Southern Malawi.

HISTORY OF THE ANGLICAN CHURCH IN ZIMBABWE

The Church in Zimbabwe dates from the pioneer missionary journey in 1888 of Bishop Knight-Bruce of Bloemfontein. Concerted work began in 1891 when the Diocese of Rhodesia was created with Knight-Bruce as its first bishop. He was assisted by a small band of trained African catechists, one of whom was Bernard Mizeki, who was martyred five years later. Bernard Mizeki is commemorated in the calendars of Central and South Africa provinces.

The Diocese of Southern Rhodesia became part of the Church of the Province of South Africa, and included part of Botswana and Moçambique. The Diocese of Matabeleland was formed in 1953.

In 1981 the Diocese of Manicaland was formed out of Mashonaland, and The Lundi formed out of Matabeleland.

ZAMBIAN ANGLICAN HISTORY

The Church in Zambia dates back to 1910 when Bishop John Hine, previously Bishop of Nyasaland and Zanzibar, started pioneer work in what was then Northern Rhodesia. The formation of the Diocese of Northern Rhodesia marked the jubilee of the UMCA. One of the first priests to join Bishop Hine was Leonard Kamungu, Nyasaland's first indigenous priest.

Kamungu died at Msoro three years later. He is also commemorated in the calendar of the province. The diocese changed its name to Zambia when Northern Rhodesia changed its name to Zambia in 1964. For its last nineteen years the diocese was led by Bishop Oliver Green-Wilkinson, who became the third archbishop. Shortly after his accidental death in 1970, the country was divided into three dioceses – Lusaka, Central Zambia and Northern Zambia.

THE ANGLICAN CHURCH IN BOTSWANA

The Diocese of Botswana was formed in 1972. Before then it was divided between Kimberley and Kuruman in South Africa and Matabeleland in Southern Rhodesia. The diocese is having a hard task in trying to reach the people who are sparsely scattered over a wide area and with poor communications.

Archbishop of the Province Most Revd Walter P. K. Makhulu (*Bishop of Botswana*)

Acting Provincial Secretary Revd Richard J. Chance, PO Box 769, Gaborone, Botswana   *Fax:* 352075

Provincial Treasurer Mr Simon Thomas, Accounting Services Pty Ltd, PO Box 1229, Gaborone, Botswana

ANGLICAN THEOLOGICAL COLLEGES
National Anglican Theological College of Zimbabwe (Ecumenical Institute of Theology), 11 Thornburg Ave, Groombridge, Mount Pleasant, Harare, Zimbabwe

Zomba Theological College, PO Box 130, Zomba, Malawi (jointly with the Presbyterian Church of Central Africa)

St John's Seminary, Mindolo, PO Box 21493, Kitwe, Zambia

CHURCH PAPERS
Link Monthly newspaper for the Dioceses of Mashonaland and Matabeleland giving news and views of the dioceses. *Editorial Offices* Link Board of Management, PO Box UA7, Harare City.

A Mpingo (previously *Ecclesia*) Monthly duplicated magazine for the Dioceses of Southern Malawi and Lake Malawi giving news and views of the dioceses. *Editor* Revd Bernard Njakare, c/o Chilema Lay Training Centre, PO Chilema, Malawi.

Epifania Triennial magazine for the province published by the Archbishop's Office. *Editor* Provincial Secretary.

BOTSWANA
Bishop Most Revd Walter P. K. Makhulu (*Bishop of Botswana and Archbishop of the Province of Central Africa*), PO Box 769, Gaborone, Botswana *Fax:* 313 015
e-mail: acenter@info.bw

CENTRAL ZAMBIA
Bishop Rt Revd Clement Williard Hlanya Shaba, PO Box 70172, Ndola, Zambia *Fax:* 02 615 954

CENTRAL ZIMBABWE
Bishop Rt Revd Titus Zhenje, PO Box 25, Gweru, Zimbabwe

EASTERN ZAMBIA
Bishop Rt Revd John Osmers, PO Box 510154, Chipata, Zambia *Fax:* 062 21 294
e-mail: josmers@zamnet.zm

EASTERN ZIMBABWE
Bishop Rt Revd Elijah Masuko, 115 Herbert Chitepo St, Mutare, Zimbabwe *Fax:* 020 63076

HARARE
Bishop Rt Revd Jonathan Siyachitema, Bishopsmount Close, PO Box UA7, Harare, Zimbabwe *Fax:* 04 700 419

LAKE MALAWI
Bishop Rt Revd Peter Nathaniel Nyanja, PO Box 30349, Lilongwe 3, Malawi *Fax:* 731 966

LUSAKA
Bishop Rt Revd Leonard Jameson Mwenda, Bishop's Lodge, PO Box 30183, Lusaka, Zambia *Fax:* 01 262 379

MATABELELAND
Bishop Rt Revd Theophilus Naledi, PO Box 2422, Bulawayo, Zimbabwe *Fax:* 09 68353

NORTH MALAWI
Bishop Rt Revd Jackson Biggers, Box 120, Mzuzu, Malawi
e-mail: biggers@malawi.net

NORTHERN ZAMBIA
Bishop Rt Revd Bernard Malango, PO Box 20173, Kitwe, Zambia *Fax:* 02 224 778

SOUTHERN MALAWI
Bishop Rt Revd James Tengatenga, P/Bag 1, Chilema, Zomba, Malawi *Fax:* 531 243
e-mail: jtengatenga@unima.wn.apc.org

The Anglican Church of the Central American Region

(Iglesia Anglicana de la Region Central de America)

COSTA RICA
Bishop Rt Revd Cornelius Joshua Wilson, Apartado 2773, 1000 San José, Costa Rica *Fax:* 253 8311
e-mail: amiecr@sol.racsa.co.cr

EL SALVADOR
Bishop Rt Revd Martin de Jesus Barhona Pascacio, 47 Avenida Sur, 723 Col. Flor Blanca, Apartado Postal (01), 274 San Salvador, El Salvador *Fax:* 223 7952
e-mail: martinba@gbm.net

GUATEMALA
Bishop Rt Revd Armando Guerra-Soria, Apartado 58A, Guatemala City, Guatemala *Fax:* 472 0764
e-mail: diocesis@infovia.com.gt

NICARAGUA
Bishop Rt Revd Sturdie Downs, Apartado 1207, Managua, Nicaragua *Fax:* 02 226 701

PANAMA
Bishop Rt Revd Clarence W. Hayes-Dewar, Box R, Balboa, Republic of Panama *Fax:* 262 2097
e-mail: Iglesia.episcopal.pma@ecunet.org

The Church of the Province of the Congo

The Anglican Church was established in the Congo in 1896 by Canon Apolo Kivebulaya, an evangelist from Uganda who was based in Boga-Zaïre (now the Congo). In 1954 the Anglican Church was able to reach the Shaba (now Katanga) region, but it was not until the 1970s that large parts of the Congo were evangelised.

Following independence, the Church began to expand and form dioceses as part of the Province of Uganda, Burundi, Rwanda and Boga-Zaïre. During the PIM Consultation held in Kigali in 1989, it was proposed that Zaïre should form a new province. This was approved by the Anglican Consultative Council. The Rt Revd Byankya Njojo was elected first archbishop and the new province was inaugurated on 30 May 1992. On 30 May 1996 the province celebrated the centenary of the Anglican Church in Congo, culminating in the opening of the new diocese of Kindu in January 1997. The name of the province was changed in 1997.

Archbishop of the Province Most Revd Patrice Byankya Njojo, CAC-Boga, PO Box 21285, Nairobi, Kenya

Provincial Secretary Revd Molanga Botola, CAC-Bunia, PO Box 21285, Nairobi, Kenya

Provincial Treasurer Mr Philip Bingham, CAC-Boga, PO Box 21285, Nairobi, Kenya

THEOLOGICAL COLLEGE
The Anglican Theological Seminary, CAC-Bunia, PO Box 21285, Nairobi, Kenya

BOGA
Bishop Most Revd Patrice Byankya Njojo (*Archbishop of Zaïre and Bishop of Boga*), CAC-Boga, PO Box 21285, Nairobi, Kenya

BUKAVU
Bishop Rt Revd Fidèle Balufuga Dirokpa, CAC-Bukavu, PO Box 53435, Nairobi, Kenya

Assistant Bishop Rt Revd Peter Donald Dawson, CAZ-Kindu, PO Box 53435, Nairobi, Kenya

KATANGA
Bishop Rt Revd Isingoma Kahwa, EAZ-Lubumbashi, c/o United Methodist Church, PO Box 22037, Kitwe, Zambia

KINDU
Bishop Rt Revd Zacharie Masimango Katanda, CAC-Kindu, PO Box 53435, Nairobi, Kenya
e-mail: angkindu@antenna.nl

KISANGANI
Bishop Rt Revd Sylvestre Tibafa Mugera, CAC-Kisangani, BP 861, Kisangani, Dem Rep Congo

Assistant Bishop Rt Revd Antoine Mavatikwa Kany, c/o CAC-Kinshasa, BP 16482, Kinshasa 1, Dem Rep Congo
Fax: 884 008

NORD KIVU
Bishop Rt Revd Methusela Musubaho Munzenda, CAC-Butembo – Zaire, PO Box 21285, Nairobi, Kenya
Fax: 871 1661121

Hong Kong Sheng Kung Hui

The province of the Hong Kong Sheng Kung Hui was founded in the autumn of 1998, consisting of the dioceses of Hong Kong Island, Western Kowloon, Eastern Kowloon and the missionary area of Macau. At present there are 44 congregations, over 120 nurseries, kindergartens, primary and secondary schools, a theological college, a college affiliated with the University of Hong Kong and over 80 social service agencies operating within the province.

Primate Most Revd Peter Kwong Kong-kit, Bishop's House (*Bishop of Hong Kong Island*), 1 Lower Albert Rd, Hong Kong *Fax:* 2525 2537

Bishop of Eastern Kowloon Rt Revd Louis Tsui (*same address*) *Fax:* 2711 1609

Bishop of Western Kowloon Rt Revd Thomas Soo (*same address*) *Fax:* 2783 0799

The Church of the Province of the Indian Ocean

Archbishop of the Province Most Revd Remi Rabenirina (*Bishop of Antananarivo*)

Provincial Secretary Revd Bery Rakotoarimanana, c/o Évêché Anglican, Ambohimanoro, 101 Antananarivo, Madagascar

Chancellor/Registrar of the Province Maître Bernard Georges, PO Box 44, Victoria, Mahé, Seychelles
Fax: 248 224296

Dean of the Province Rt Revd Keith Benzies (*Bishop of Antsiranana*)

ANGLICAN THEOLOGICAL COLLEGES
St Paul's College, Ambatohararana, Merimandroso, Ambohidratrimo, Madagascar (*Warden* Revd Vincent Rakotoarisoa)

St Paul's College, Rose Hill, Mauritius (*Warden* Vacancy)

St Philip's Theological College, La Misère, Seychelles (*Diocesan Trainer* Mr Neville Marston)

CHURCH MAGAZINES
Newsletters of Province of the Indian Ocean Support Assn, *Editor* Mrs M. Woodward, Vicarage, Old Town, Brackley, Northants NN13 7BZ; *Seychelles Diocesan Magazine* – a quarterly newspaper covering diocesan events and containing articles of theological and other interest; *Magazine du Diocese de Maurice* – a quarterly newspaper covering diocesan events and containing articles of theological and ecumenical interest.

ANTANANARIVO
Bishop Most Revd Remi Rabenirina, Évêché Anglican, Lot VK57 ter, Ambohimanoro, 101 Antananarivo, Madagascar   *Fax:* 020 226 1331

ANTSIRANANA
Bishop Rt Revd Keith John Benzies, Évêché Anglican, BP 278, 201 Antsiranana, Madagascar

MAHAJANGA
Bishop Rt Revd Jean-Claude Andrianjafimanana, BP 169, Mahajanga 401, Madagascar
e-mail: eemdmaha@dts.mg

MAURITIUS
Bishop Rt Revd Luc Rex Donat, Bishop's House, Phoenix, Mauritius   *Fax:* 230 697 1096
e-mail: diocese_mauritius@ecunet.org

SEYCHELLES
Bishop Rt Revd French Chang-Him, PO Box 44, Victoria, Mahé, Seychelles   *Fax:* 248 224 296

TOAMASINA
Bishop Rt Revd Donald Westwood Smith, Évêché Anglican, BP 531, Toamasina 501, Madagascar

The Church of Ireland

The Primate of All Ireland and Metropolitan Most Revd Robert Henry Alexander Eames (*Archbishop of Armagh*)

Hon Secretaries of the General Synod
Clerical Very Revd Herbert Cassidy, The Library, Abbey St, Armagh, Co Armagh BT61 7DY   *Tel:* (01861) 523142
Fax: (01861) 524177

Ven Gordon Linney, St Paul's Vicarage, Silchester Rd, Glenageary, Co Dublin   *Tel:* 01–2801616
Fax: 01–2809459

Lay Mr E. W. R. Cookman, Orchard Lodge, Raphoe, Co Donegal   *Tel:* (074) 45212
Fax: (074) 45212

Mr S. R. Harper, Cramer's Grove, Kilkenny, Co Kilkenny
Tel: (056) 22842/160
Fax: (056) 63449

Assistant Secretary of the General Synod Ms Valerie Beatty

Chief Officer and Secretary of the Representative Church Body Mr Robert Sherwood

Central Office of the Church of Ireland Church of Ireland House, Church Ave, Rathmines, Dublin 6
Tel: 01–4978422
Fax: 01–4978821

THEOLOGICAL COLLEGE
The Church of Ireland Theological College, Braemor Park, Rathgar, Dublin 14, which conducts courses in conjunction with the School of Hebrew, Biblical and Theological Studies, Trinity College, Dublin (*Principal* Canon John Bartlett)   *Tel:* 01–4923506/4923274
Fax: 01–4923082

CHURCH PAPER
Church of Ireland Gazette Weekly. Deals with items of general interest to the Church of Ireland in a national context and also contains news from the various dioceses and parishes together with articles of a more general nature. *Editor/Editorial offices* Canon Cecil Cooper, 36 Bachelor's Walk, Lisburn, Co Antrim BT28 1XN
Tel: (01846) 675743
Fax: (01846) 675743

The Irish Church Act 1869 provided that from 1 January 1871, the statutory union between the Churches of England and Ireland should be dissolved and that the Church of Ireland should cease to be established by law. To prepare the ground for the future government of the Church of Ireland, a General Convention was held in 1870 when it was declared 'that a General Synod of the Church of Ireland, consisting of the archbishops and bishops, and of representatives of the clergy and laity, shall have chief legislative power therein, and such administrative power as may be necessary for the Church, and consistent with its episcopal constitution'.

The General Synod consists of two Houses, the House of Bishops and the House of Representatives. The archbishops and bishops for the time being constitute the

House of Bishops. The House of Representatives is composed of 216 clerical and 432 lay representatives, elected triennially by the various diocesan synods. Both Houses sit together in General Synod. While either House may sit separately, and the House of Bishops does so from time to time, there has never been a separate meeting of the House of Representatives. Legislation must be passed by both Houses, and in the House of Representatives a vote by orders may be demanded, in which case a majority of both clerical and lay representatives is required. To make any liturgical change a vote by orders must always be taken, and a two-thirds majority of each order is necessary.

Each diocesan synod consists of the clergymen of the diocese and of lay synodsmen elected triennially by the registered vestrymen of each parish in the proportion of two (or up to five) to each clergyman officiating therein. The diocesan synod, subject to the control of the General Synod, administers the temporalities of the diocese, and it makes provision for the appointment of a Diocesan Council to carry on the financial and other business of the diocese.

The Select Vestry of each parish consists of the officiating clergymen, two churchwardens (one nominated by the incumbent and one elected), two glebewardens (appointed in like manner) and not more than twenty other persons. It is the executive body, and it controls parochial funds.

An incumbent of a parish is nominated by a Board of Nomination, which consists of the bishop (chairman), four clergymen and one layman appointed by the diocesan synod, and four laymen elected by the parish.

The Archbishop of Armagh is elected by the House of Bishops from its own number. Other episcopal elections are made by an electoral college, presided over by the Metropolitan, and comprising three representatives of the House of Bishops and representatives of all the dioceses in the province, the vacant diocese having twenty-four representatives (twelve clerical and twelve lay) and each other diocese having four representatives (two clerical and two lay).

Under the Irish Church Act, all church property was, subject to certain interests then existing, vested in the Commissioners of Church Temporalities, created by that Act, who carried out all the transactions which the Act required. As all the ecclesiastical corporations were dissolved by the Act, it was necessary to create a corporate body to take over from the Commissioners the property and monies transferred to the disestablished Church. Thus, the Representative Church Body was incorporated in 1870 as trustee of the property and funds then transferred or subsequently acquired. It consists of the archbishops and bishops, one clerical and two lay representatives of each of the dioceses or united dioceses, and twelve co-opted members. Its recent Reports show that its assets now amount to over IR£292m.

PROVINCE OF ARMAGH

ARMAGH

Archbishop Most Revd Robert Henry Alexander Eames, The See House, Cathedral Close, Armagh, Co Armagh BT61 7EE *Tel:* (01861) 522 851 (Home)
(01861) 527 144 (Office)
Fax: (01861) 527 823
e-mail: archbishop@armagh.anglican.org

Secretary of Diocesan Council Mr Richard McConnell, Church House, 46 Abbey St, Armagh, Co Armagh BT61 7DZ *Tel:* (01861) 522 858
Fax: (01861) 510 596

CATHEDRAL CHURCH OF ST PATRICK, Armagh
Dean Very Revd Herbert Cassidy, The Library, Abbey Street, Armagh BT61 7DY *Tel:* (01861) 523142
Fax: (01861) 524177

CLOGHER

Bishop Rt Revd Brian Desmond Anthony Hannon, The See House, Fivemiletown, Co Tyrone BT75 0QP
Tel: (013655) 21 265
Fax: (013655) 22 299

Secretary of Diocesan Council Very Revd Thomas Moore, The Deanery, 10 Augher Rd, Clogher, Co Tyrone BT76 0AD *Tel* and *Fax:* (016625) 48235

CATHEDRAL CHURCHES OF ST MACARTAN, Clogher, and ST MACARTIN, Enniskillen
Dean Very Revd Thomas Moore (*as above*)

CONNOR

Bishop Rt Revd James Edward Moore, Bishop's House, 113 Upper Rd, Greenisland, Carrickfergus, Co Antrim BT38 8RR *Tel:* (01232) 863 165
Fax: (01232) 364 266

Secretary of Diocesan Council Mr Neil Wilson, Diocesan Office, Church of Ireland House, 61–67 Donegall St, Belfast BT1 2QH *Tel:* (01232) 322268/323188
Fax: (01232) 321635

CATHEDRAL CHURCH OF ST SAVIOUR, Lisburn
Dean Very Revd Frederick Rusk, 15 Harberton Park, Belfast BT9 6TW *Tel:* (01232) 667753

CATHEDRAL CHURCH OF ST ANNE, Belfast
(Cathedral of the United Dioceses of Down and Dromore and the Diocese of Connor)
Dean Very Revd John Shearer, The Deanery, 5 Deramore Drive, Belfast BT9 5JQ *Tel:* (01232) 660980 (Home)
(01232) 328332 (Cathedral)
Fax: (01232) 238855

DERRY AND RAPHOE
Bishop Rt Revd James Mehaffey, The See House, 112 Culmore Rd, Londonderry, Co Derry BT48 8JF
Tel: (01504) 351206 (Home)
(01504) 262440 (Office)
Fax: (01504) 352554

Secretary of Diocesan Council G. Kelly, Diocesan Office, London St, Londonderry, Co Derry BT48 6RQ
Tel: (01504) 262440

CATHEDRAL CHURCH OF ST COLUMB, Derry
Dean Very Revd William Wright Morton, The Deanery, 30 Bishop St, Londonderry, Co Derry BT48 6PP
Tel: (01504) 262746

CATHEDRAL CHURCH OF ST EUNAN, Raphoe
Dean Very Revd Stephen White, The Deanery, Raphoe, Lifford, Co Donegal
Tel: (074) 45226

DOWN AND DROMORE
Bishop Rt Revd Harold Creeth Miller, The See House, 32 Knockdene Park South, Belfast BT5 7AB
Tel: (01232) 471973
Fax: (01232) 650584
e-mail: bishop@down.anglican.org

Secretary of Diocesan Council Mr Neil Wilson, Diocesan Office, Church of Ireland House, 61–67 Donegall St, Belfast BT1 2QH
Tel: (01232) 322268/323188

CATHEDRAL CHURCH OF THE HOLY AND UNDIVIDED TRINITY, Down
Dean Very Revd John Dinnen, 17 Dromore Rd, Hillsborough, Co Down BT26 6HS
Tel and *Fax:* (01846) 682366

CATHEDRAL CHURCH OF CHRIST THE REDEEMER, Dromore
Dean Very Revd David Chillingworth, Seagoe Rectory, 8 Upper Church Lane, Portadown, Craigavon, Co Armagh BT63 5JE
Tel: (01762) 332538 (Home)
Tel and *Fax:* (01762) 350583 (Office)

KILMORE, ELPHIN AND ARDAGH
Bishop Rt Revd Michael Hugh Gunton Mayes, The See House, Cavan
Tel: (049) 31336
Fax: (049) 62829
e-mail: bishop@kilmore.anglican.org

Secretaries of Diocesan Councils Revd Eileen O'Reilly, Rectory, Cootehill, Co Cavan (*Kilmore*) *Tel:* (049) 52004 *Fax:* (049) 56321; Canon Ian Gallagher, Rectory, Drumcliffe, Co Sligo (*Elphin and Ardagh*)
Tel and *Fax:* (071) 63125

CATHEDRAL CHURCH OF ST FETHLIMIDH, Kilmore
Dean Very Revd David Godfrey, The Deanery, Danesfort, Kilmore, Cavan
Tel: (049) 31918

CATHEDRAL CHURCH OF ST MARY THE VIRGIN AND ST JOHN THE BAPTIST, Sligo
Dean Very Revd Stuart McGee, Cathedral Rectory, Strandhill Rd, Sligo
Tel: (071) 62263

TUAM, KILLALA AND ACHONRY
Bishop Rt Revd Richard Henderson, Bishop's House, Knockglass, Crossmolina, Co Mayo
Tel: (096) 31317
Fax: (096) 31775
e-mail: bishop@tuam.anglican.org

Secretary of Diocesan Council Mrs Heather Sherlock, Stonehall House, Ballisodare, Co Sligo
Tel: (071) 67280
Fax: (071) 30264

CATHEDRAL CHURCH OF ST MARY, Tuam
Dean Very Revd Ian Corbett, The Rectory, Deanery Place, Cong, Co Mayo
Tel and *Fax:* (092) 46017

CATHEDRAL CHURCH OF ST PATRICK, Killala
Dean Very Revd Edward Ardis, Rectory, Ballina, Co Mayo
Tel: (096) 21654

PROVINCE OF DUBLIN
CASHEL, WATERFORD, LISMORE, OSSORY, FERNS AND LEIGHLIN
Bishop Rt Revd John Robert Winder Neill (*Bishop of Cashel and Ossory*), The Palace, Kilkenny, Co Kilkenny
Tel: (056) 21 560
Fax: (056) 64 399
e-mail: bishop@cashel.anglican.org

Secretaries of Diocesan Councils Mrs Denise Hughes, Diocesan Office, St Canice's Library, Kilkenny (*Cashel, Ossory and Leighlin*) *Tel:* (056) 61910 (Office); (056) 27248 (Home) *Fax:* (056) 64399; Mrs Joan Deacon, Garranvabbey, The Rower, Thomastown, Co Kilkenny (*Ferns*)
Tel: (051) 423637

CATHEDRAL CHURCH OF ST JOHN THE BAPTIST AND ST PATRICK'S ROCK, Cashel
Dean Very Revd Phillip Knowles, The Deanery, Cashel, Co Tipperary
Tel: (062) 61232

CATHEDRAL CHURCH OF THE BLESSED TRINITY (CHRIST CHURCH), Waterford
Dean Very Revd Peter Barrett, The Deanery, 41 Grange Park Rd, Waterford, Co Waterford
Tel and *Fax:* (051) 74119

CATHEDRAL CHURCH OF ST CARTHAGE, Lismore
Dean Very Revd James Healey, The Deanery, The Mall, Lismore, Co Waterford
Tel and *Fax:* (058) 54137

CATHEDRAL CHURCH OF ST CANICE, Kilkenny
Dean Very Revd Norman Lynas, The Deanery, Kilkenny
Tel: (056) 21516
Fax: (056) 51817

CATHEDRAL CHURCH OF ST EDAN, Ferns
Dean Very Revd Leslie Forrest, The Deanery, Ferns, Co Wexford   *Tel:* (054) 66124

CATHEDRAL CHURCH OF ST LASERIAN, Leighlin
Dean Vacancy

CORK, CLOYNE AND ROSS
Bishop Rt Revd Robert Alexander Warke, The Palace, Bishop St, Cork, Co Cork   *Tel:* (021) 316114
Fax: (021) 273 437

Secretary of Diocesan Council Mr Wilfred Baker, St Nicholas House, 14 Cove St, Cork, Co Cork   *Tel:* (021) 272262
Fax: (021) 968467

CATHEDRAL CHURCH OF ST FIN BARRE, Cork
Dean Very Revd Michael Jackson, The Deanery, 9 Dean St, Cork   *Tel* and *Fax:* (021) 964742

CATHEDRAL CHURCH OF ST COLMAN, Cloyne
Dean Very Revd George Hilliard, The Deanery, Midleton, Co Cork   *Tel:* (021) 631449
Fax: (021) 964742

CATHEDRAL CHURCH OF ST FACHTNA, Ross
Dean Very Revd Christopher Peters, The Deanery, Rosscarbery, Co Cork   *Tel:* (023) 48166

DUBLIN AND GLENDALOUGH
Archbishop Most Revd Walton Newcombe Francis Empey (*Archbishop of Dublin, Bishop of Glendalough, Primate of Ireland and Metropolitan*), The See House, 17 Temple Rd, Milltown, Dublin 6   *Tel:* 01–4977849
Fax: 01–4976355

Secretary of Diocesan Council Mr Keith Dungan, Diocesan Office, Church of Ireland House, Church Ave, Rathmines, Dublin 6   *Tel:* 01–4966981
Fax: 01–4972865

CATHEDRAL CHURCH OF THE HOLY TRINITY
(commonly called CHRIST CHURCH)
Cathedral of the United Dioceses of Dublin and Glendalough, Metropolitan Cathedral of the United Provinces of Dublin and Cashel
Dean Very Revd John Paterson, The Deanery, St Werburgh St, Dublin 8   *Tel:* 01–4781797 (Home)
01–6778099 (Cathedral)
Fax: 01–6798991

THE NATIONAL CATHEDRAL AND COLLEGIATE CHURCH OF ST PATRICK, Dublin
(The 'National Cathedral of the Church of Ireland having a common relation to all the dioceses of Ireland')

Dean and Ordinary Very Revd Maurice Evan Stewart, The Deanery, Upper Kevin St, Dublin 8
Tel: 01–4543428 (Home)
01–4754817 (Cathedral)
01–4539472 (Office)
Fax: 01–4546374

LIMERICK, ARDFERT, AGHADOE, KILLALOE, KILFENORA, CLONFERT, KILMACDUAGH AND EMLY
Bishop Rt Revd Edward Flewett Darling (*Bishop of Limerick and Killaloe*), Bishop's House, North Circular Rd, Limerick   *Tel:* (061) 451532
Fax: (061) 451100
Mobile: 087–2221700
e-mail: bishop@limerick.anglican.org

Secretary of Diocesan Council Canon Joseph Condell, St Cronan's Rectory, Roscrea, Co Tipperary
Tel: (0505) 21725
Fax: (0505) 21993

Assistant Secretary Canon Robert Warren, St John's Rectory, Ashe St, Tralee, Co Kerry   *Tel:* (066) 22245
Fax: (066) 29004
Mobile: 088–521133

CATHEDRAL CHURCH OF ST MARY, Limerick
Dean Very Revd Maurice Sirr, The Deanery, 7 Kilbane, Castletroy, Limerick   *Tel:* (061) 338697
Fax: (061) 332158
Mobile: 088–541121

CATHEDRAL CHURCH OF ST FLANNAN, Killaloe
Dean Very Revd Nicholas Cummins, The Deanery, Killaloe, Co Clare   *Tel* and *Fax:* (061) 376687

CATHEDRAL CHURCH OF ST BRENDAN, Clonfert
Dean Very Revd Nicholas Cummins (*as above*)

MEATH AND KILDARE
Bishop Most Revd Richard Lionel Clarke, Bishop's House, Moyglare, Maynooth, Co Kildare   *Tel:* 01–6289354
Fax: 01–6289696
e-mail: bishop@meath.anglican.org

Secretary of Diocesan Council Mrs Karen Seaman, Rivendell, Temple Mills, Celbridge, Co Kildare
Tel: 01–6275352
Fax: 01–6270749

CATHEDRAL CHURCH OF ST PATRICK, Trim
Dean of Clonmacnoise Very Revd Andrew Furlong, St Patrick's Deanery, Trim, Co Meath
Tel and *Fax:* (046) 36698

CATHEDRAL OF ST BRIGID, Kildare
Dean Very Revd Robert Townley, Dean's House, Curragh Camp, Co Kildare
Tel: (045) 441654

The Anglican Communion in Japan
(Nippon Sei Ko Kai)

In 1859 the American Episcopal Church sent two missionaries to Japan, and some years later the Church of England and the Church in Canada shared in the work. A general Anglican Synod took place in 1887 and the Constitution and Canons which formed the Nippon Sei Ko Kai were adopted.

The Biennial General Synod is the final authority. Between Synods administration is in the hands of the Provincial Office and an Executive Provincial Standing Committee. The Primate is elected by General Synod from among the active diocesan bishops for a two-year renewable term and also serves as Chairman of the House of Bishops and of the General Synod and Executive Standing Committee.

To strengthen its co-ordinating role among the eleven dioceses, the Provincial Office has undergone a restructuring process and now has five secretaries under the General Secretary to be responsible for: Mission, External PIM, Communications, Finance and General Affairs.

There are 57,407 baptised Christians (among whom are 29,504 active communicants) organised into 318 churches and preaching stations served by 345 clergy and lay workers in all areas of Japan. In addition the following related institutions are part of the total mission of the NSKK: *Religious Orders:* 2; *Hospitals, clinics:* 9; *Social Welfare:* 30; *Kindergartens:* 117; *Nurseries:* 35; *Primary and Middle Schools:* 11; *Secondary Schools:* 8; *Junior Colleges:* 5; *Universities:* 5; *Nursing:* 2; *Student Youth Centres:* 3; *Others:* 2.

THEOLOGICAL TRAINING
Central Theological College, 1–12–31 Yoga, Setagaya-ku, Tokyo 158–0097, for clergy and lay workers

Bishop Williams Theological School, Shimotachiuri-agaru, Karasuma Dori, Kamikyo-ku, Kyoto 602–8332

CHURCH NEWSPAPERS
Sei Ko Kai Shimbun Published on 20th of each month in Japanese. Usually eight pages, tabloid format. Subscription through the Provincial Office. Each diocese also has its own monthly paper.

NSKK News English language newsletter. Usually two pages. Published quarterly. Available through the Provincial Office.

Primate Most Revd John Makoto Takeda (*Bishop of Tokyo*)

Provincial Office Nippon Sei Ko Kai, 65 Yarai-cho, Shinjuku-ku, Tokyo 162–0805, Japan (Please use this address for all correspondence) *Fax:* 052 28 3175

General Secretary Revd Samuel Isamu Koshiishi

CHUBU
Bishop Rt Revd Francis Toshiaki Mori, 1–47 Yamawaki-cho, Showa-ku, Nagoya 466–0063 *Fax:* 052 731 6222

HOKKAIDO
Bishop Rt Revd Nathaniel Makoto Uematsu, Kita 15 jo, 20 Nishi 5-chome, Kita-ku, Sapporo 001–0015
Fax: 011 736 8377

KITA KANTO
Bishop Rt Revd James Toru Uno, 2–19–60–801 Mihara, Asaka-shi 351–0025 *Fax:* 08 648 0358

KOBE
Bishop Rt Revd John Junichiro Furumoto, 3–10–20 Nakayamate, Chuo-ku, Kobe 650–0011
Fax: 078 382 1095
e-mail: xpl0661@niftyserve.or.jp

KYOTO
Bishop Rt Revd Barnabas Mutsuji Muto, Shimotachiuri-agaru, Karasumadori, Kamikyo-ku, Kyoto 602–8332
Fax: 075 441 4238

KYUSHU
Bishop Rt Revd Joseph Noriaki Iida, 2–9–22 Kusagae, Chuo-ku, Fukuoka 810–0045 *Fax:* 092 771 9857

OKINAWA
Bishop Rt Revd David Shoji Tani, 101 Aza Yoshihara, Chatan-cho, Nakagami-gum, Okinawa 904–0105
Fax: 098 936 3019

OSAKA
Bishop Rt Revd Koichi Augustine Takano, 2–1–8 Matsuzaki-cho, Abeno-ku, Osaka 545–0053
Fax: 06 621 3097

TOHOKU
Bishop Rt Revd John Tadao Sato, 2–13–15 Kokubu-cho, Aoba-ku, Sendai 980–0803 *Fax:* 022 223 2349

TOKYO
Bishop Most Revd John Makoto Takeda, 3–6–18 Shibakoen, Minato-ku, Tokyo 105–0011   *Fax:* 03 3433 8678
e-mail: jmtakeda@nskk.org

YOKOHAMA
Bishop Rt Revd Raphael Shiro Kajiwara, 14–57 Mitsusawa Shimo-cho, Kanagawa-ku, Yokohama 221–0852
Fax: 045 323 2763

The Episcopal Church in Jerusalem and the Middle East

The Jerusalem Bishopric was founded in 1841 and became an archbishopric, but not a province, in 1957. In January 1976 the Jerusalem Archbishopric came to an end and was replaced by the Episcopal Church in Jerusalem and the Middle East. This change in status was also marked by alterations in the diocesan arrangements. The Diocese of Jordan, Lebanon and Syria was rejoined to the Jerusalem Bishopric after being severed for 19 years. At the same time, Cyprus, Iraq and the Arabian Peninsula detached from the Jerusalem Bishopric and formed the new Diocese of Cyprus and the Gulf. The Diocese of Egypt, which had been suspended since 1958, revived with its own bishop in 1974. The Bishop in Egypt has jurisdiction over the Anglican Chaplaincies in Libya, Tunisia, Algiers, Ethiopia, Eritrea and Somalia. The Diocese of Iran is unchanged.

The Episcopal Church in Jerusalem and the Middle East is governed by a Central Synod representing the four dioceses of Jerusalem, Iran, Egypt and Cyprus and the Gulf. This Central Synod holds metropolitical authority and elects one of the four diocesan bishops to be President-Bishop for a term of five years. The President-Bishop may serve for two five-year terms.

The Cathedral Church of St George the Martyr in Jerusalem is the cathedral of the Diocese of Jerusalem. The cathedral has a special relationship to the entire Anglican Communion through its ministry to pilgrims.

St George's College, Jerusalem, is in partnership with the Anglican Communion. It presents the Bible in its setting through the 'Jerusalem Experience'.

THE CENTRAL SYNOD
President-Bishop Most Revd Ghais Abd El-Malik (*Bishop in Egypt with North Africa, Ethiopia, Somalia, Eritrea, and Djibouti*)

Provincial Secretary Rt Revd Riah Hanna Abu el-Assal (*Bishop Coadjutor in Jerusalem*), Christ Church, PO Box 75, Nazareth   *Fax:* 972–66–563649

Provincial Treasurer Rt Revd Clive Handford (*Bishop of Cyprus and the Gulf*), Diocesan Office, 2 Grigori Afxentiou St, PO Box 2075, Nicosia, Cyprus

The Jerusalem and the Middle East Church Association acts in support of the Episcopal Church in Jerusalem and the Middle East, the Central Synod and all four dioceses. *Secretary* Mrs Vanessa Wells, 1 Hart House, The Hart, Farnham, Surrey GU9 7HA   *Tel:* (0252) 726994
Fax: (0252) 735558

CYPRUS AND THE GULF
Bishop in Rt Revd Clive Handford, Diocesan Office, 2 Grigori Afxentiou St, PO Box 2075, Nicosia, Cyprus
Fax: 02 466 553
e-mail: bishop@spidernet.com.cy

EGYPT
Bishop in Most Revd Ghais Abd El-Malik (*President-Bishop of the Episcopal Church in Jerusalem and the Middle East*), Diocesan Office, PO Box 87, Zamalek, Cairo, Egypt
Fax: 02 340 8941
e-mail: diocese@intouch.com

IRAN
Bishop in Rt Revd Iraj Mottahedeh, PO Box 135, Postal Code 81465, Isfahan, Iran

JERUSALEM
Bishop in Rt Revd Riah Hanna Abu el-Assal, St George's Close, PO Box 19122, Jerusalem   *Fax:* 02 627 3847
e-mail: Riahasal@netvision.net.il

The Anglican Church of Kenya

In February 1969, the Provincial Synod of East Africa held in Dodoma decided to divide the Province of East Africa into the Province of Kenya and the Province of Tanzania. The Province of Kenya was inaugurated on 3 August 1970 when the Most Revd Festo Habakkuk Olang, formerly Bishop of Maseno North, was enthroned in All Saints' Cathedral, Nairobi, as Archbishop of Kenya and Bishop of Nairobi. On the same day the Archbishop of East Africa (the Most Revd Leonard Beecher) retired. Archbishop Olang retired as Archbishop of Kenya and Bishop of Nairobi in November 1979. The total number of Anglicans in the province is 2,290,000.

Primate Most Revd David Gitari (*Bishop of Nairobi*), PO Box 40502, Nairobi, Kenya   *Fax:* 2542 714750

Provincial Secretary Revd Enos Ashimala (*same address*)

Provincial Treasurer Mr Willaim Ogara, Corat Africa, PO Box 42593, Nairobi, Kenya   *Fax:* 2542 714750

THEOLOGICAL COLLEGES
St Paul's United Theological College (Ecumenical), PO Limuru, Kenya

Trinity College, PO Box 72430, Nairobi, Kenya (Centre for Theological Extension)

Carlile College for Theology and Business Studies, PO Box 72584, Nairobi, Kenya (*Principal* Revd Capt Tim Dakin)

BUNGOMA
Bishop Rt Revd Eliud Wabukala, PO Box 2392, Bungoma, Kenya

BUTERE
Bishop Rt Revd Horace Etemesi, PO Box 54, Butere, Kenya   *Fax:* 0333 20 038

ELDORET
Bishop Rt Revd Thomas Kogo, PO Box 3404, Eldoret, Kenya   *Fax:* 0321 33 477

EMBU
Bishop Rt Revd Moses Njue, PO Box 189, Embu, Kenya   *Fax:* 061 30 468

KAJIADO
Bishop Rt Revd Jeremiah John Mutua Taama, PO Box 203, Kajiado, Kenya   *Fax:* 0301 21 106

KATAKWA
Bishop Rt Revd Eliud Okiring Odera, PO Box 68, Amagoro, Kenya

KIRINYAGA
Bishop Rt Revd Daniel Munene Ngoru, PO Box 95, Kutus, Kenya   *Fax:* 0163 44 020
e-mail: ACK-Kirinyaga@thorntree.com

KITALI
Bishop Rt Revd Stephen Kewasis Nyorsok, PO Box 4176, Kitali, Kenya   *Fax:* 0325 31 387

KITUI
Bishop Rt Revd Benjamin N. P. Nzimbi, PO Box 1054, Machakos, Kenya   *Fax:* 0141 22 119

MACHAKOS
Bishop Rt Revd Joseph Mutie Kanuku, PO Box 282, Machakos, Kenya   *Fax:* 0145 20 178

MASENO NORTH
Bishop Rt Revd Simon M. Oketch, PO Box 416, Kakamega, Kenya   *Fax:* 0331 30 752

MASENO SOUTH
Bishop Rt Revd Francis Mwayi Abiero, PO Box 380, Kisumu, Kenya   *Fax:* 035 45219

MASENO WEST
Bishop Rt Revd Joseph Otieno Wasonga, PO Box 793, Siaya, Kenya   *Fax:* 0334 21483

MBEERE
Bishop Rt Revd Gideon G. Ireri, PO Box 122, Siakago, Kenya

MERU
Bishop Rt Revd Henry Paltridge, PO Box 446, Meru, Kenya

MOMBASA
Bishop Rt Revd Julius Robert Kalu Katoi, PO Box 80072, Mombasa, Kenya   *Fax:* 011 311 105

MOUNT KENYA CENTRAL
Bishop Rt Revd Julius Gatambo Gachuche, PO Box 121, Murang'a, Kenya   *Fax:* 0156 22 642

MOUNT KENYA SOUTH
Bishop Rt Revd Peter Njenja, PO Box 886, Kiambu, Kenya   *Fax:* 0154 22 408

MOUNT KENYA WEST
Bishop Rt Revd Alfred Chipman, PO Box 229, Nyeri, Kenya   *Fax:* 254 171 30214

MUMIAS
Bishop Rt Revd William Wesa Shikukule, PO Box 213, Mumias, Kenya

NAIROBI
Bishop Most Revd David Gitari (*Archbishop of Kenya and Bishop of Nairobi*), PO Box 40502, Nairobi, Kenya   *Fax:* 02 718 442
e-mail: dgitari@thorntree.com

NAKURU
Bishop Rt Revd Stephen Njihia Mwangi, PO Box 56, Nakuru, Kenya   *Fax:* 037 44 379

NAMBALE
Bishop Rt Revd Josiah Were, PO Box 4, Nambale, Kenya   *Fax:* 033 66 2407

NYAHURURU
Bishop Rt Revd Charles Gaikia Gaita, PO Box 926, Nayahururu, Kenya *Fax:* 037 44 379

SOUTHERN NYANZA
Bishop Rt Revd Haggai Nyang', PO Box 65, Homa Bay, Kenya *Fax:* 0385 220 56

TAITA TAVETA
Bishop Rt Revd Samson Mwaluda, PO Box 75, Voi, Kenya

THIKA
Bishop To be elected, PO Box 214, Thika, Kenya

The Anglican Church of Korea

On 29 September 1890 the Rt Revd John C. Corfe, who had been consecrated for Korea on 1 November 1889, arrived in the country which, apart from two Chinese Anglican lay evangelists who had arrived in 1880, had not known Anglican Christians. For the next 75 years the Diocese of Korea continued under him and four successive English bishops until on 27 May 1965 the first Korean bishop was consecrated. This coincided with the division of the diocese into that of Seoul, under the new Korean bishop, and Taejon under the last English bishop in Korea. Taejon had one more English bishop until 1 June 1974 when the new diocese of Pusan was detached from it and at the same time two Koreans were consecrated in Seoul, one for the Diocese of Taejon and one for the Diocese of Pusan. On 16 April 1993 when the Archbishop of Canterbury installed the newly elected Primate, the Most Revd Simon S. Kim, and handed over jurisdiction to him, the Anglican Church of Korea became a province of the Anglican Communion.

The 95 churches in the three dioceses are grouped into 66 parishes which in turn are grouped into eight archpresbyteries. There are 124 clergy apart from the diocesan bishops. There are four religious communities in the country: the Society of the Holy Cross, founded in 1925, which has its mother house in Seoul; the Daughters of St Francis, founded in 1988, which has its house in the Taejon Diocese; the Benedictine Society founded in Pusan Diocese in 1993; and the Korean Franciscan Brotherhood founded in 1994. There is an Anglican university where ordinands are trained in the Graduate School of Theology.

Primate Most Revd Matthew C. Chung (*Bishop of Seoul*)

Secretary General Revd Amos K. S. Kim, # 3 Chong-dong, Chung-ku, Seoul 100–120, Korea *Fax:* 82–2–737–4210
e-mail: anck@peacenet.or.kr
Web: http://anck.peacenet.or.kr

ANGLICAN UNIVERSITY
(*Songgonghoe Daehak*) # 1 Hand-dong, Kuro-ku, Seoul 152–140, Korea (*President* Revd Dr John Lee)
Fax: 82–2–737–4210

CHURCH PAPER
Songgonghoebo Fortnightly paper of the Anglican Church of Korea is the joint concern of all three dioceses. Newspaper format. Printed in Korean. Contains regular liturgical and doctrinal features as well as local, national and international church news.

PUSAN
Bishop Vacancy, Anglican Diocese of Pusan, PO Box 103, Tongrae, Pusan 607–061, Korea *Fax:* 051–553–9643

SEOUL
Bishop Most Revd Matthew C. Chung, Anglican Church of Korea, # 3 Chong-dong, Chung-ku, Seoul 100–120, Korea *Fax:* 02–723 2640
e-mail: bishop100@hosanna.net

TAEJON
Bishop Rt Revd Paul Hwan Yoon, Anglican Church, PO Box 22, Taejon 300–600, Korea *Fax:* 042–255–8918

The Church of the Province of Melanesia

The Church of the Province of Melanesia was formed in 1975 after 118 years' missionary association with the General Synod of the Church of the Province of New Zealand. The boundary of the province encompasses two sovereign island nations in the South Pacific – the Republic of Vanuatu, Solomon Islands, and the French Trust Territory of New Caledonia. It encircles a total area of approximately 2,000 square kilometres, much of which is covered by sea.

Beginning with an initial total of four dioceses, the scattered nature of the islands, the diversity of language and culture in Melanesian society, and a rapid increase in its congregations, have demanded a more focused approach, in terms of episcopal, pastoral and administrative oversight. This resulted in the creation of four more new dioceses, giving a total of eight. The youngest diocese, Central Solomons, was inaugurated on 4 May 1997.

Archbishop of the Province Most Revd Ellison L. Pogo (*Bishop of Central Melanesia*)

General Secretary Mr Nicholas Ma'aramo, Provincial Headquarters, PO Box 19, Honiara, Solomon Islands
Fax: (677) 21098

ANGLICAN THEOLOGICAL COLLEGE
Bishop Patteson Theological Centre, Kohimarama, PO Box 19, Honiara, Solomon Islands (trains students up to diploma standard) (*Principal* Revd Dr John Blyth)

BANKS AND TORRES
Bishop Rt Revd Charles W. Ling, PO Box 19, Sola, Vanualava, Torba Province, Republic of Vanuatu

CENTRAL MELANESIA
Bishop Most Revd Ellison L. Pogo (*Bishop of Central Melanesia and Archbishop of the Province*), Archbishop's House, PO Box 19, Honiara, Solomon Islands *Fax:* 21 098

CENTRAL SOLOMONS
Bishop Rt Revd Charles Koete, PO Box 52, Tulagi, Central Province, Solomon Islands *Fax:* 32 042

HANUATO'O
Bishop Rt Revd James P. Mason, c/o PO Kirakira, Makira/Ulawa Province, Solomon Islands *Fax:* 50 128

MALAITA
Bishop Rt Revd Dr Terry M. Brown, Bishop's House, PO Box 7, Auki Malaita, Solomon Islands *Fax:* 40 027

TEMOTU
Bishop Rt Revd Lazarus Munamua, Bishop's House, Luesalo, Lata, Santa Cruz, Solomon Islands *Fax:* 53 092

VANUATU
Bishop Rt Revd Michael H. Tavoa, Bishop's House, PO Box 238, Luganville, Santo, Vanuatu *Fax:* 36 026
e-mail: DIOCESE_OF_VANUATU@acunet.org

YSABEL
Bishop Rt Revd Walter Siba, Bishop's House, PO Box 6, Buala, Jejevo, Ysabel Province, Solomon Islands
Fax: 35 071

The Anglican Church of Mexico

Primate Most Revd Samuel Espinoza-Venegas (*Bishop of Western Mexico*)

Provincial Secretary Revd Benito Juárez-Martinez, Calle La Otra Banda # 40, Col. San Angel, Delegacion Alvaro Obregón, 01000 Mexico, D.F., Mexico *Fax:* 616–4063
e-mail: ofipam@planet.com.mx

CUERNAVACA
Bishop Most Revd Martiniano Garcia-Montiel, Apartado Postal 538, Admon 4, CP 62431 Cuernavaca, Morelos, Mexico *Fax:* 073 152870
e-mail: diovca@giga.com.mx

MEXICO
Bishop Rt Revd Sergio Carranza-Gomez, Ave San Jeronimo 117, Col S Angel, Deleg A Obregon 01000, Mexico DF *Fax:* 05 616 2205

NORTHERN MEXICO
Bishop Rt Revd German Martinez-Marquez, Simon Bolivar 2005 Nte, Colonia Mitras Centro, 64460 Monterrey, NL, Mexico *Fax:* 08 348 7362

SOUTHEASTERN MEXICO
Bishop Most Revd Claro Huerta-Ramos, Avenue de Las Americas, #73, Colonia Aguacatal, 91130, Xalapa, Veracruz, Mexico *Fax:* 028 14 43 87

WESTERN MEXICO
Bishop Most Revd Samuel Espinoza-Venegas (*Bishop of Western Mexico and Archbishop of the Province*), Francisco J. Gamba 255, Col. Sector Jaurez, 44100 Guadalajara, Jalisco, Mexico *Fax:* 03 615 4413

The Church of the Province of Myanmar

A Province of Myanmar was formed in 1970 with four dioceses: Rangoon (now Yangon), Mandalay, Hpa-an and Sittwe. This is a Church within the Anglican Communion and is an indigenous church. The Missionary Diocese of Myitkyina was inaugurated on 2 January 1988 and the Missionary Diocese of Toungoo on 1 January 1992. Both missionary dioceses became full dioceses in October 1993.

Archbishop of the Province Most Revd Andrew Mya Han (*Bishop of Yangon*)

Provincial Secretary Revd Saw Kenneth, 140 Pyidaungsu Yeiktha Rd, Dagon PO (11191), Yangon, Myanmar
Fax: 95 1251405

Provincial Treasurer Revd Peter Thein Maung (*same address*)

Secretary and Treasurer, Yangon Diocesan Trust Association Mr Stanley Peters (*same address*)

ANGLICAN THEOLOGICAL COLLEGES
Holy Cross Theological College, 104 Inya Rd, University PO (11041), Yangon, Myanmar (*Principal* Revd Saw Maung Doe)
Emmanuel Theological College, Mohnyin, Kachin State (*Principal* Bishop John Shan Lum)

CHURCH NEWSLETTER
The Province publishes a monthly 36-page *Newsletter*. *Editor and Manager* Mr Saw Peter Aye, Bishopscourt, 140 Pyidaungsu Yeiktha Rd, Dagon PO (11191), Yangon, Myanmar

HPA-AN
Bishop Rt Revd Daniel Hoi Kyin, Bishopscourt, Cathedral of St Peter, Bishop Gone, Hpa-an, Kayin State, Myanmar
Fax: 1 77 512

MANDALAY
Bishop Rt Revd Andrew Hla Aung, Bishopscourt, 22nd St 'C' Rd (between 85–86 Rd), Mandalay, Myanmar

MYITKYINA
Bishop Rt Revd John Shan Lum, Diocesan Office, Tha Kin Nat Pe Rd, Thida Ya, Myitkyina, Myanmar

SITTWE
Bishop Rt Revd Barnabas Theaung Hawi, St John's Church, Paletwa, Sittwe, Myanmar

Assistant Bishop Rt Revd Aung Tha Tun (*same address*)

TOUNGOO
Bishop Rt Revd Saw (John) Wilme, Diocesan Office, Nat Shin Naung Rd, Toungoo, Myanmar

YANGON
Bishop Most Revd Andrew Mya Han (*Bishop of Yangon and Archbishop of the Province*), 44 Prome Rd, Dagon PO (11191), Yangon, Myanmar
Fax: 01 251 405

Assistant Bishop Rt Revd Joseph Than Pe *Fax:* 01–77 512

The Church of the Province of Nigeria

The Province of Nigeria was formed by the division of the Province of West Africa in 1979. In 1997 it was divided into three provinces. For the previous history of the province *see* pages 321–2.

Archbishop Province I Most Revd Joseph A. Adetiloye (*Bishop of Lagos*)

Archbishop Province II Most Revd Benjamin Chukuemeka Nwankiti (*Bishop of Owerri*)

Archbishop Province III Most Revd Peter Jasper Akinola (*Bishop of Abuja*)

General Secretary Ven Samuel B. Akinola, 29 Marina, PO Box 78, Lagos, Nigeria

Provincial Treasurer Chief S. O. Adekunle, Church House, 29 Marina, PO Box 78, Lagos, Nigeria

Dean of the Province Rt Revd B. C. Nwankiti (*Bishop of Owerri*)

THEOLOGICAL COLLEGES
Immanuel College (Ecumenical), PO Box 515, Ibadan
Trinity College (Ecumenical), Umuahia, Imo State, Nigeria
Vining College, Akure, Ondo State, Nigeria
St Francis of Assisi College, Wusasa, Zaria, Nigeria

ABA (Province II)
Bishop Rt Revd Augustine Onyeyrichukwu Iwuagwu, Bishopscourt, 70/72 St Michael's Rd, PO Box 212, Aba, Nigeria

ABAKALIKI (Province II)
Bishop Rt Revd Benson C. Onyeibor, All Saints' Cathedral, PO Box 112, Abakaliki, Ebonyi State, Nigeria

ABUJA (Province III)
Bishop Most Revd Peter Jasper Akinola, Archbishop's Palace, PO Box 212, ADCP, Abuja, Nigeria
Fax: 09 523 0986
e-mail: abuja@anglican.skannet.com.ng

AKOKO (Province I)
Bishop Rt Revd Jacob O. K. Olowokure, PO Box 572, Ikare-Akoko, Ondo State, Nigeria

AKURE (Province I)
Bishop Rt Revd Emmanuel Bolanle Gbonigi, Bishopscourt, PO Box 1622, Akure, Nigeria   *Fax:* 034 241 572
e-mail: akdangc@akure.rcl.nig.com

ASABA (Province II)
Bishop Rt Revd Rowland Nwafo Nwosu, Bishopscourt, Cable Point, PO Box 216, Asaba, Delta State, Nigeria

AWKA (Province II)
Bishop Rt Revd Maxwell Samuel Chike Anikwenwa, Bishopscourt, Ifite Rd, PO Box 130, Awka, Anambra State, Nigeria   *Fax:* 046 550 052
e-mail: angawka@infoweb.abs.net

BAUCHI (Province III)
Bishop Rt Revd Laudamus Ereaku, Bishop's House, 2 Hospital Rd, PO Box 2450, Bauchi, Nigeria

BENIN (Province I)
Bishop Rt Revd Peter Onekpe, Bishopscourt, PO Box 82, Benin City, Edo State, Nigeria

CALABAR (Province II)
Bishop Rt Revd Wilfred George Ekprikpo, Bishopscourt, PO Box 74, Calabar, Cross River State, Nigeria
Fax: 088 220 835

DAMATURU (Province III)
Bishop Rt Revd Daniel Abu Yisa, PO Box 312, Damaturu, Yobe State, Nigeria

DIOCESE ON THE NIGER (Province II)
Bishop Rt Revd Jonathan Arinzechukwu Onyemelukwe, Bishopscourt, PO Box 42, Onitsha, Nigeria

DUTSE (Province III)
Bishop Rt Revd Yesufu Ibrahim Lumu, PO Box 15, Dutse, Jagawa State, Nigeria

EGBA (Province I)
Bishop Rt Revd Matthew Oluremi Owadayo, Bishopscourt, Onikolobo, PO Box 267, Ibara, Abeokuta, Nigeria

EGBU (Province II)
Bishop Rt Revd Emmanual Iheagwam, All Saint's Cathedral, PO Box 1967, Owerri, Imo State, Nigeria

EKITI (Province I)
Bishop Rt Revd Samuel Abe, Bishopscourt, PO Box 12, Ado-Ekiti, Nigeria

ENUGU (Province II)
Bishop Rt Revd Emmanuel O. Chukwuma, Bishop's House, PO Box 418, Enugu, Nigeria

IBADAN (Province I)
Bishop Rt Revd Gideon I. Olajide, Bishopscourt, Arigidi St, Bodija Estate, PO Box 3075, Ibadan, Nigeria
Fax: 02 810 1413
e-mail: bishop@ibadan.scannet.com

IFE (Province I)
Bishop Rt Revd Gabriel B. Oloniyo, Bishopscourt, PO Box 312, Ife-Ife, Osun State, Nigeria

IJEBU (Province I)
Bishop Vacancy, Bishopscourt, Ejirin Rd, PO Box 112, Ijebu-Ode, Nigeria

IKALE-ILAJE (Province I)
Bishop Rt Revd Joseph Akinyele Omoyajowo, Bishopscourt, Ikoya Rd, P M B 3, Ilutitun, Ondo State, Nigeria

ILESA (Province I)
Bishop Rt Revd Ephraim Adebola Ademowo, Bishopscourt, Oke-Oye, PO Box 237, Ilesa, Nigeria

JALINGO (Province III)
Bishop Rt Revd Tanimu Samari Aduda, PO Box 4, Jalingo, Taraba State, Nigeria

JOS (Province III)
Bishop Rt Revd Benjamin Argak Kwashi, Bishopscourt, PO Box 6283, Jos, Plateau State, Nigeria   *Fax:* 073 612 221
e-mail: argak.kasco@pinet.net

KABBA (Province I)
Bishop Rt Revd Solomon Olaife Oyelade, Bishopscourt, Obaro Way, PO Box 62, Kabba, Kogi State, Nigeria

KADUNA (Province III)
Bishop Rt Revd Josiah Idowu-Fearon, PO Box 72, Kaduna, Nigeria   *Fax:* 062 230 408
e-mail: 106101.2127@compuserve.com

KAFANCHAN (Province III)
Bishop Rt Revd William Weh Diya, Bishopscourt, 5b Jemma'a St, PO Box 29, Kafanchan, Kaduna State, Nigeria

KANO (Province III)
Bishop Rt Revd Zakka Lalle Nyam, Bishop's Court, PO Box 362, Kano, Nigeria   *Fax:* 064 647 816
e-mail: kano@anglican.skannetcom.nig

Churches and Provinces: Nigeria

KATSINA (Province III)
Bishop Rt Revd James S. Sekari Kwasu, Bishop's Lodge, PO Box 904, Katsina, Nigeria

KEBBI (Province III)
Bishop Rt Revd Edmund Efoyikeye Akanya, PO Box 701, Birnin Kebbi, Kebbi State, Nigeria   *Fax:* 068 21 179

KWARA (Province I)
Bishop Rt Revd Jeremiah Olagbamigbe A. Fabuluje, Bishopscourt, Fate Rd, PO Box 1884, Ilorin, Kwara State, Nigeria

LAGOS (Province I)
Bishop Most Revd Joseph Abiodun Adetiloye, T, 29 Marina, PO Box 13, Lagos, Nigeria   *Fax:* 01 263 6026
e-mail: bishop@rcl.nig.com

LOKOJA (Province I)
Bishop Rt Revd George Bako, PO Box 11, Lokoja, Kogi State, Nigeria   *Fax:* 058 220 5881

MAIDUGURI (Province III)
Bishop Rt Revd Emmanuel K. Mani, Bishopscourt, Off Lagos St, GRA PO Box 1693, Maiduguri, Borno State, Nigeria

MAKURDI (Province III)
Bishop Rt Revd Nathan Nyitar Inyom, Bishopscourt, PO Box 1, Makurdi, Nigeria   *Fax:* 044 533 349

MBAISE (Province II)
Bishop Rt Revd Cyril Chukwka Anyanwu, Bishopscourt, PO Box 10, Ife, Ezinihitte Mbaise, Imo State, Nigeria

MINNA (Province III)
Bishop Rt Revd Nathaniel Yisa, Bishopscourt, Dutsen Kura, PO Box 2469, Minna, Nigeria

THE NIGER DELTA (Province II)
Bishop Rt Revd Gabriel Pepple, Bishopscourt, PO Box 115, Port Harcourt, Rivers State, Nigeria

NIGER DELTA NORTH (Province II)
Bishop Rt Revd Samuel Onyuku Elenwo, PO Box 53, Port Harcourt, Nigeria

NNEWI (Province II)
Bishop Rt Revd Godwin Izundu Nmezinwa Okpala, c/o Bishopscourt (opposite Total Filling Station), PO Box 2630, Uruagu-Nnewi, Anambra State, Nigeria

NSUKKA (Province II)
Bishop Rt Revd Jonah Ilonuba, PO Box 516, Nsukka, Enugu State, Nigeria

OKE-OSUN (Province I)
Bishop Rt Revd Abraham O. Awosan, Bishopscourt, PO Box 251, Gbongan, Osun State, Nigeria

OKIGWE NORTH (Province II)
Bishop Rt Revd Alfred Nwaizuzu, PO Box 156, Okigwe, Imo State, Nigeria

OKIGWE SOUTH (Province II)
Bishop Rt Revd Bennett Okoro, Bishopscourt, Ezeoke Nsu, PO Box 235 Nsu, Ehime Mbano L.G.A., Imo State, Nigeria

ONDO (Province I)
Bishop Rt Revd Samuel O. Aderin, Bishopscourt, College Rd, PO Box 265, Ondo, Nigeria

ORLU (Province II)
Bishop Rt Revd Samuel Chukuma N. Ebo, Bishop's House Nkwerre, PO Box 260, Nkwerre, Imo State, Nigeria

OSUN (Province I)
Bishop Rt Revd Seth Oni Fagbemi, Bishopscourt, Isale-Aro, PO Box 285, Osogbo, Nigeria

OTURKPO (Province III)
Bishop Rt Revd Ityobee Ugede, St John's Cathedral, Depot Rd, PO Box 360, Oturkpo, Benue State, Nigeria

OWERRI (Province II)
Bishop Vacancy, Bishopscourt, Egbu, PO Box 31, Owerri, Imo State, Nigeria

OWO (Province I)
Bishop Rt Revd Peter A. Adebiyi, Bishopscourt, PO Box 472, Owo, Ondo State, Nigeria

REMO (Province I)
Bishop Rt Revd Elijah Oluremi Ige Ogundana, Bishopscourt, Ewusi St, PO Box 522, Sagamu, Ogun State, Nigeria

SABONGIDA ORA (Province I)
Bishop Rt Revd Albert Agbaje, Bishopscourt, PO Box 13, Sabongida Ora, Edo State, Nigeria

SOKOTO (Province III)
Bishop Rt Revd Joseph Akinfenwa, Bishop's Lodge, PO Box 3489, Sokoto, Nigeria

UGHELLI
Bishop Rt Revd Vincent O. Muoghereh, Bishopscourt, Ovurodawanre, PO Box 762, Ughelli, Delta State, Nigeria
Fax: 053 250 091

UKWA (Province II)
Bishop Rt Revd Uju Otuokwesiri Wachukwu Obinya, PO Box 20468, Aba, Nigeria

UMUAHIA (Province II)
Bishop Rt Revd Ugochuckwu Uwaoma Ezuoke, St Stephen's Cathedral Church Compound, PO Box 96, Umuahia, Nigeria

UYO (Province II)
Bishop Rt Revd Emmanuel E. Nglass, Bishopscourt, PO Box 70, Uyo, Akwa Ibom State, Nigeria   *Fax:* 085 200 451

WARRI (Province I)
Bishop Rt Revd Nathaniel Enuku, Bishopscourt, 17 Mabiaku Rd, GRA, PO Box 4571, Warri, Nigeria

WUSASA (Province III)
Bishop Rt Revd Ali Buba Lamido, Box 28, Wusasa Zaria, Nigeria

YEWA (Province I)
Bishop Rt Revd Timothy I. O. Bolaji, Bishopscourt, PO Box 484, Ilaro, Ogun State, Nigeria

YOLA (Province III)
Bishop Rt Revd Christian Ogochukwu Efobi, PO Box 601, Yola, Adamawa State, Nigeria

The Anglican Church of Papua New Guinea

After many years as part of the Australian Province of Queensland, Papua New Guinea became an independent province on 27 February 1977. The Anglican Church largely functions in rural areas where mountains and rainforest provide natural barriers to travel. There are some 100 parishes and the Church supports a similar number of community schools, three high schools and 25 health centres and aid posts. The province raises 60 per cent of its funding from within the country despite the fact that only 14 per cent of the population are in waged employment – the rest being subsistence farmers. The balance is made up from generous grants from the Anglican Board of Mission – Australia, the New Zealand Anglican Board of Mission and the UK-based Papua New Guinea Church Partnership.

Archbishop Most Revd James Ayong, PO Box 893, Mt Hagen, Western Highlands Province   *Fax:* 542 1181

General Secretary Dr Colin McArdle, PO Box 673, Lae, Morobe Province   *Fax:* 472 1852

Provincial Registrar Mr Martin Gardham, PO Box 893, Mt Hagen, Western Highlands Province   *Fax:* 542 1181

THEOLOGICAL COLLEGE
Newton Theological College, PO Box 162, Popondetta, Oro Province (*Principal* Revd Roderick MacDougall SSM)
Fax: 3297476

CHURCH PAPER
Family. Published three times a year. Editors Howard and Penny Gorringe, PO Box 26, Popondetta, Oro Province
Fax: 329 7476

AIPO RONGO
Bishop Most Revd James Simon Ayong, PO Box 893, Mt Hagen, Western Highlands Province   *Fax:* 542 1181

DOGURA
Bishop Rt Revd Tevita Talanoa, PO Box 19, Dogura, MBP
Fax: 641 1129

NEW GUINEA ISLANDS
Bishop Rt Revd Rhynold Ewaruba Sanana, PO Box 198, Kimbe, WNBP

POPONDOTA
Bishop Rt Revd Reuben Barago Tariambari, PO Box 26, Popondetta, Oro Province   *Fax:* 729 7474

PORT MORESBY
Bishop Rt Revd Michael George Hough, PO Box 6491, Boroko, NCD   *Fax:* 3232 493
e-mail: hough@dg.com.pg

Episcopal Church in the Philippines

The ECP began as a missionary district of the Episcopal Church of the United States of America (ECUSA) in 1901 with Charles Henry Brent as the first bishop. In 1965 it became a missionary diocese, divided into three dioceses in 1972 and became a province of the Anglican Communion on 1 May 1990 with five dioceses. It still receives a subsidy from ECUSA until 2007 with a programmed yearly reduction and envisions that by 2007 ECP will be a renewed church, fully self-supporting.

ECP began its missionary work in non-Christian communities or in communities where there were no other Christian churches. These communities are now 99 per cent Christian. This style of mission explains why the work of this Church is largely concentrated in indigenous communities and in mostly rural and marginal communities. It is now trying to reach out to the majority in the centres of population.

National Office The ECP Mission Center, 275 E Rodriguez Sr Blvd, Cathedral Heights, 112 Quezon City, Philippines

Mail Address PO Box 10321, Broadway Centrum, 1112 Quezon City, Philippines *Fax:* 721 1923
e-mail: ecp@phil.gn.apc.org

Prime Bishop Most Revd Ignacio Capuyan Solita (*same address*)

CENTRAL PHILIPPINES
Bishop Rt Revd Benjamin Gayno Botengan, PO Box 655, Manila 2800, Philippines *Fax:* 742–2143

NORTH CENTRAL PHILIPPINES
Bishop Rt Revd Joel A. Pachao, PO Box 137, 2600 Baguio City, Philippines *Fax:* 74–442–3638

NORTHERN LUZON
Bishop Rt Revd Renato M. Abibico, Bulanao, Tabuk, Kalinga-Apayao 3800, Philippines *Fax:* 721 1923

NORTHERN PHILIPPINES
Bishop Rt Revd Edward Pacyaya Malecdan, Diocesan Center, Bontoc, Mountain Province 0601, Philippines
Fax: 721 1923

Suffragan Bishop Rt Revd Miguel Paredes Yamoyam (*same address*)

SOUTHERN PHILIPPINES
Bishop Rt Revd James Buanda Manguramas, PO Box 113, Cotabato City 9600, Philippines *Fax:* 64 421 1703

The Church of the Province of Rwanda

Archbishop of the Province Most Revd Emmanuel Mbona Kolini

Dean of the Province Rt Revd Onesphore Rwaje (*Bishop of Byumba*)

Provincial Secretary Canon Andrew Kayizari, BP 2487, Kigali, Rwanda *Fax:* 250 73 213

BUTARE
Bishop Rt Revd Venuste Mutiganda, BP 225, Butare, Rwanda *Fax:* 250 30 504

BYUMBA
Bishop Rt Revd Onesphore Rwaje, BP 17, Byumba, Rwanda *Fax:* 250 64 242

CYANGUGU
Bishop Rt Revd Ken Barham, BP 52, Cyangugu, Rwanda
Fax: 01424 773 073
e-mail: BishopKen@compuserve.com

GAHINI
Bishop Rt Revd Alexis Bilindabagado, BP 22 Kigali, Rwanda *Fax:* 250 77 831

KIBUNGO
Bishop Rt Revd Prudence Ngarambe, EER Kibungo Diocese, BP 719, Kigali, Rwanda

KIGALI
Bishop Most Revd Emmanuel Mbona Kolini, BP 61, Kigali, Rwanda *Fax:* 250 73 213

KIGEME
Bishop Rt Revd Norman Kayumba, BP 67, Gikongoro, Rwanda *Fax:* 250 34 011

SHYIRA
Bishop Rt Revd John Rucyahana Kabango, BP 26, Ruhengeri, Rwanda *Fax:* 250 46 449

SHYOGWE
Bishop Rt Revd Jered Karimba, BP 27, Gitarama, Rwanda
Fax: 250 62 460

The Scottish Episcopal Church

The Episcopal Church was formerly the Established Church of Scotland. It was disestablished and disendowed in 1689 by King William III, who, almost entirely on political grounds, set up the Presbyterian Church in its place.

The disestablished Episcopal Church continued strongly until 1746 when, again for political reasons after the Jacobite rebellion, severe Penal Statutes were imposed upon all Episcopalians. These laws made it illegal for them to possess any churches or chapels; all public services were forbidden and Episcopalian clergy were not allowed to minister to more than five persons at a time, under penalties of imprisonment or banishment.

The laws continued in force until 1792. Under such conditions it is not remarkable that the persecuted Church dwindled in numbers until it became 'a shadow of a shade'. Nevertheless, throughout the whole period the bishops maintained their continuity and in 1784 gave the Episcopate to the American Church by the consecration, in an upper room in Aberdeen, of Bishop Seabury, its first bishop.

Today the Scottish Episcopal Church has seven diocesan bishops, one of whom is elected Primus by the others, about 190 stipendiary clergy, 180 non-stipendiary and 52,000 members, of whom 32,000 are communicants.

THEOLOGICAL COLLEGE
The Theological Institute of the Scottish Episcopal Church, Old Coates House, 32 Manor Place, Edinburgh EH3 7EB (*Director* Revd Rosemary Nixon)
Tel: 0131–220 2272
Fax: 0131–220 2294
e-mail: tisec@scotland.anglican.org

CHURCH NEWSPAPER
The Scottish Episcopalian 8 pages, 10 issues yearly. Newspaper format. *Editor* Mrs Nan Macfarlane, Edrington Mains Cottage, Foulden, By Berwick on Tweed TD15 1UZ
Tel: (01289) 386288
e-mail: episcopalian@scotland.anglican.org

GENERAL SYNOD
President The Primus Most Revd Richard Holloway (Bishop of Edinburgh)

Convener of Standing Committee Mr Gavin Gemmell, Baillie Gifford & Co, 1 Rutland Court, Edinburgh EH3 8EY

Secretary General Mr John Stuart, 21 Grosvenor Crescent, Edinburgh EH12 5EE
Tel: 0131–225 6357
Fax: 0131–346 7247
e-mail: secgen@scotland.anglican.org
office@scotland.anglican.org

Communications Officer Revd Jim Wynn-Evans (*same address*)
e-mail: press@scotland.anglican.org

Since 1982 the governing authority of the Episcopal Church has been the General Synod. This is an elected body of some 160 members which meets once a year.

The General Synod operates five principal Boards: Faith and Order, Mission, Administration, Information and Communication and a Board for Ministry. These in turn have pendant committees that work in particular areas.

The Church raises funds for social responsibility (including homes for the elderly), education, support of overseas partnership, clergy stipends, pensions, retirement housing and maintenance and development of buildings.

ABERDEEN AND ORKNEY
Bishop Rt Revd Bruce Cameron, Diocesan Centre, 39 King's Crescent, Aberdeen AB24 3HP
Tel: (01224) 636653
Fax: (01224) 636186
e-mail: office@aberdeen.anglican.org

Dean Very Revd Gerald Stranraer-Mull, Rectory, Ellon, Aberdeenshire AB41 9NP
Tel: (01358) 720366

ST ANDREW'S CATHEDRAL, Aberdeen
Provost Very Revd David Wightman, 15 Morningfield Rd, Aberdeen AB15 4AP
Tel: (01224) 314765
(01224) 640119 (Office)

ARGYLL AND THE ISLES
Bishop Rt Revd Douglas Cameron, The Pines, Ardconnel Rd, Oban PA34 5DR
Tel and Fax: (01631) 566912
e-mail: office@argyll.anglican.org

Dean Very Revd John Henry James Macleay, St Andrew's Rectory, Parade Rd, Fort William PH33 6BA
Tel: (01397) 702979

ST JOHN THE DIVINE CATHEDRAL, Oban
(the Cathedral of Argyll)
Provost Very Revd Allan Murray MacLean, Rectory, Ardconnel Terrace, Oban PA34 5DJ
Tel: (01631) 562323

COLLEGIATE CHURCH OF THE HOLY SPIRIT, Cumbrae
(the Cathedral of The Isles)
Clergy Rt Revd Douglas Cameron (*as above*)

BRECHIN
Bishop Rt Revd Neville Chamberlain, Bishop's Office, St Paul's Cathedral, 1 High St, Dundee DD1 1TD
Tel: (01382) 229230
Fax: (01382) 203446
e-mail: office@brechin.anglican.org

Dean Very Revd Robert William Breaden, 46 Seafield Rd, Broughty Ferry DD5 3AN   *Tel:* (01382) 477477

ST PAUL'S CATHEDRAL, Dundee
Provost Very Revd Miriam Byrne, Cathedral Office, 1 High St, Dundee DD1 1TD   *Tel:* (01382) 224486

EDINBURGH
Bishop Most Revd Richard Holloway, Diocesan Centre, 21A Grosvenor Crescent, Edinburgh EH12 5EL
Tel: 0131–538 7044
Fax: 0131–538 7088
e-mail: office@edinburgh.anglican.org

Dean Very Revd Timothy David Morris, The Rectory, Parsonage Rd, Galashiels TD1 3HS
Tel and *Fax:* (01896) 753118
e-mail: tim@parsonage.scotborders.co.uk

ST MARY'S CATHEDRAL, Edinburgh
Provost Very Revd Graham John Thomson Forbes, 8 Lansdowne Crescent, Edinburgh EH12 5EQ
Tel: 0131–225 2978
Fax: 0131–225 3181

GLASGOW AND GALLOWAY
Bishop Rt Revd Idris Jones, Diocesan Office, 5 St Vincent Place, Glasgow G1 2DH   *Tel:* 0141–221 5720/2694
Fax: 0141–221 7014
e-mail: bishop@glasgow.anglican.org

Dean Very Revd Dr Gregor Duncan, St Columba's Rectory, Aubery Crescent, Largs KA30 8PR
Tel: (01475) 673143
Fax: (01475) 676020

ST MARY THE VIRGIN CATHEDRAL, Glasgow
Provost Very Revd Griff Dines, St Mary's Cathedral, 300 Great Western Rd, Glasgow G4 9JB
Tel and *Fax:* 0141–339 6691
e-mail: provost@glasgow.anglican.org

MORAY, ROSS AND CAITHNESS
Bishop Rt Revd Gregor Macgregor, Diocesan Office, 11 Kenneth St, Inverness IV3 5NR
e-mail: office@moray.anglican.org

Dean Very Revd Michael Francis Hickford, The Parsonage, 4 Castle St, Dingwall IV15 9HU   *Tel:* (01349) 862204

ST ANDREW'S CATHEDRAL, Inverness
Provost Very Revd Malcolm Grant, 15 Ardross St, Inverness IV3 5NS   *Tel:* (01463) 233535

ST ANDREWS, DUNKELD AND DUNBLANE
Bishop Rt Revd Michael Henley, Diocesan Office, 28A Balhousie St, Perth PH1 5HJ   *Tel:* (01738) 443173
Fax: (01738) 443174
e-mail: office@standrews.anglican.org

Dean Very Revd Alfred Ian Watt, 33 Stirling Rd, Milnathort KY13 9XS   *Tel:* (01577) 865711

ST NINIAN'S CATHEDRAL, Perth
Provost Very Revd Kevin Gerhard Franz, 40 Hay St, Perth PH1 5HS   *Tel:* (01738) 626874

The Church of the Province of South East Asia

Primate Most Revd Moses Tay (*Bishop of Singapore*)

THEOLOGICAL COLLEGES
House of the Epiphany, PO Box No 347, 93704 Kuching, Sarawak, Malaysia (*Warden* Revd Aeries Sumping Jingan)

Trinity College, 7 Mount Sophia, Singapore 0922 (interdenominational)

St Peter's Hall, residential hostel for Anglican students (*Warden* Revd Soon Soo Kee)

Seminari Theoloji Malaysia (STM), Xavier's Hall, 133 Jalan Gasing, 46000 Petaling Jaya, Malaysia (*Principal* Revd Hwa Yung)

KUCHING
Bishop Rt Revd Made Katib, Bishop's House, PO Box 347, 93704 Kuching, Sarawak, Malaysia   *Fax:* 082 426 488
e-mail: bkg@pc.jaring.my

SABAH
Bishop Rt Revd Datuk Ping Chung Yong, Rumah Bishop, Jalan Tangki, PO Box 10811, 88809 Kota Kinabalu, Sabah, Malaysia *Fax:* 088 245 942
e-mail: pcyong@pc.jaring.my

Assistant Bishop Rt Revd Chen Fah Yong, Good Shepherd Church, WDT No 254, 90009 Sandakan, Sabah, Malaysia
Fax: 089 271 862
e-mail: cogs@tm.net.my

SINGAPORE
Bishop Most Revd Moses Tay, Bishopsbourne, 4 Bishopsgate, Singapore 249970 *Fax:* 479 5482
e-mail: province@livingstreams.org.sg

Assistant Bishop Rt Revd John Tan (*same address*)
e-mail: johntan@livingstreams.org.sg

WEST MALAYSIA
Bishop Rt Revd Datuk Cheng Ean Lim, Rumah Bishop, 14 Pesiaran Stonor, 50450 Kuala Lumpur, Malaysia
Fax: 03 201 3225
e-mail: diocese@tm.net.my

Assistant Bishop Rt Revd Moses Ponniah, St Christopher's Church, 5 Jalan Mustaffa, 80100 Johor Bahru, Malaysia
Fax: 07 224 3054
e-mail: prteo@pl.jaring.my

The Church of the Province of Southern Africa

EXTRACT FROM THE CONSTITUTION OF THE CHURCH OF THE PROVINCE OF SOUTHERN AFRICA
'The Provincial Synod of this Church ... shall be the Legislative Body of the Church of this Province; and every enactment of the said Provincial Synod shall be a Law and Rule of the Church of this Province in those matters to which it may pertain.

'Provided that the Provincial Synod of the Church of this Province shall be subordinate to the higher authority of a General Synod of the Churches of the Anglican Communion, to which this Province shall be invited to send representatives, whenever such General Synod shall be convened.' – Article II.

The Provincial Synod meets normally every three years. Every diocese sends representatives, clerical and lay, in proportion to the number of clergy in the diocese. No enactment can be made without majority votes in the three houses of Bishops, Clergy and Laity. Diocesan synods may meet more often. The diocesan synod 'shall resemble, as far as possible, the Provincial Synod in its constitution and mode of procedure, but may not make regulations contrary to those of the Provincial Synod'.

The election of the bishop of any diocese ... 'shall be by an Elective Assembly (if the number of Priests licensed in such diocese be not less than ten). When the number of Priests licensed in any diocese is less than ten, the Bishop shall be elected by the Bishops of the Province'.

The 23 dioceses in the Church of the Province extend beyond the Republic of South Africa and fall under many varying administrations. There can, of course, in these circumstances be little common ground in detailed policy making, and it is not therefore to be expected that beyond very broad lines of natural justice the Church can make any general pronouncements which will be relevant to its work. The Church's frequent protests regarding various aspects of apartheid in the Republic are well known.

The Church's work in the Province falls under the following administrations: The Republic of South Africa, the Foreign and Commonwealth Office (St Helena and Tristan da Cunha); Moçambique (Lebombo and Niassa); the Republic of Namibia; the Kingdom of Lesotho; the Kingdom of Swaziland.

Primate Most Revd Winston Njongonkulu Ndungane (*Archbishop of Cape Town*)

Provincial Executive Officer Canon Peter Gunning, Khotso House, Marshall St, Johannesburg
Fax: 001 8365782

THEOLOGICAL COLLEGE
The College of the Transfiguration, PO Box 77, Grahamstown 6140 (*Warden* Revd Luke Pato)

CHURCH PAPER
Anglican Update, Bishopscourt, Cape Town 7700

BLOEMFONTEIN
Bishop Rt Revd Patrick Glover, PO Box 411, Bloemfontein 9300 *Fax:* 51 447–5874
e-mail: rabdsc@global.co.za

Bishop Suffragan Vacancy

CAPE TOWN
Archbishop Most Revd Njongonkulu Winston Hugh Ndungane, (*Archbishop of Cape Town and Metropolitan of Southern Africa*), 16–20 Bishopscourt Drive, Claremont, Cape 7700 *Fax:* 21 761–4193
e-mail: archbish@cpsa.org.za

Bishops Suffragan
Rt Revd Mervyn Edwin Castle, PO Box 633, Kasselsvlei 7533 *Fax:* 21 951–4314
e-mail: mcastle@cpsa.org.za

Rt Revd Edward Mackenzie, 39 Paradise Rd, Newlands, 7700 *Fax:* 21 23–5782
e-mail: emackenz@cpsa.org.za

Rt Revd John Christopher Gregorowski, PO Box 1932, Cape Town 8001 *Fax:* 21 451 571
e-mail: tablebay@cpsa.org.za

CHRIST THE KING
Bishop Rt Revd Peter John Lee, PO Box 1653, Rosettenville 2130 *Fax:* 11 435 2868
e-mail: dioctk@cpsa.org.za

GEORGE
Bishop Rt Revd Donald Frederick Harker, PO Box 227, George 6530, Cape Province *Fax:* 44 873 5680
e-mail: dharker@intekom.co.za

GRAHAMSTOWN
Bishop Rt Revd David Patrick Hamilton Russell, PO Box 162, Grahamstown, Cape Province 6140
Fax: 46 622 5231
e-mail: bpgtn@intekom.co.za

Bishop Suffragan Rt Revd Bethlehem Nepece, PO Box 1772, Queenstown 5320 *Fax:* 451 82 874
e-mail: bishopnopece@intekom.co.za

HIGHVELD
Bishop Rt Revd David Albert Beetge, PO Box 563, Brakpan 1540 *Fax:* 11 740 9156
e-mail: dbeetge@cpsa.org.za

JOHANNESBURG
Bishop Rt Revd Duncan Buchanan, PO Box 1131, Johannesburg 2000 *Fax:* 11 333–3053
e-mail: jhbishop@cpsa.org.za

KIMBERLEY AND KURUMAN
Bishop Rt Revd Itumeleng Baldwin Moseki, PO Box 45, Kimberley 8300 *Fax:* 531 812 730
e-mail: opswartz@cpsa.org.za

KLERKSDORP
Bishop Rt Revd David Cecil Tapi Nkwe, PO Box 11417, Klerksdorp 2570 *Fax:* 18 462–4939
e-mail: dnkwe@wn.apc.org

LEBOMBO
Bishop Rt Revd Dinis Salomão Sengulane, CP 120, Maputo, Moçambique *Fax:* 1 40–1093
e-mail: libombo@zebra.uem.mz

LESOTHO
Bishop Rt Revd Andrew Thabo Duma, PO Box 87, Maseru 100, Lesotho *Fax:* 266 310 161
e-mail: jandjgay@lesloff.com

NAMIBIA
Bishop Rt Revd Nehemiah Shihila Hamupembe, PO Box 57, Windhoek, Namibia *Fax:* 61 225 903

Bishop Suffragan Rt Revd Petrus Hilukiluah (*same address*)

NATAL
Bishop Rt Revd Michael Nuttall, PO Box 899, Pietermaritzburg 3200 *Fax:* 331 948 785
e-mail: mnuttall@cpsa.org.za

Bishops Suffragan
Rt Revd Rubin Phillip, PO Box 47439, Greyville 4023
Fax: 31 309 6963
e-mail: rphillip@cpsa.org.za

Rt Revd Matthew M. Makhaye, PO Box 463, Ladysmith 3370 *Fax:* 361 24 949

NIASSA
Bishop Rt Revd Paulino Tomas Manhique, CP 264, Lichinga, Niassa, Moçambique *Fax:* 9258 71–2336
e-mail: anglican-niassa@maf.org

BISHOP FOR THE ORDER OF ETHIOPIA
Rt Revd Sigqibo Dwane, PO Box 46803, Glosderry, Cape 7702 *Fax:* 21 7797 3039

PORT ELIZABETH
Bishop Rt Revd Eric Pike, PO Box 7109, Newton Park 6055
Fax: 41 352 049
e-mail: epike@cpsa.org.za

PRETORIA
Bishop Rt Revd Johannes Seoka, PO Box 1032, Pretoria 0001 *Fax:* 12 322 9411
e-mail: ptabish@cpsa.org.za

Bishop Suffragan Rt Revd Robin Briggs, PO Box 137, White River 1240 *Fax:* 13 750 0773
e-mail: robin.briggs@cpsa.org.za

ST HELENA
Bishop Rt Revd John Harry Gerald Ruston, PO Box 62, Island of St Helena, South Atlantic Ocean *Fax:* 290 4330

ST JOHN'S
Bishop Rt Revd Jacob Zambuhle Dlamini, PO Box 163, 1 Callaway St, Umtata, Transkei *Fax:* 471 22 895

ST MARK THE EVANGELIST
Bishop Rt Revd Rollo Philip John Le Feuvre, PO Box 643, Pietersburg 0700 *Fax:* 152 297 0408
e-mail: stmarks@pixie.co.za

SWAZILAND
Bishop Rt Revd Lawrence Bekisia Zulu, PO Box 118, Mbabane, Swaziland *Fax:* 268 46 759

UMZIMVUBU
Bishop Rt Revd Geoffrey Francis Davies, PO Box 644, Kokstad 4700 *Fax:* 37 727 4117
e-mail: mzimvubu@cpsa.org.za

ZULULAND
Bishop Rt Revd Anthony Mdletshe, PO Box 147, Eshowe 3815 *Fax:* 354 42 047
e-mail: zulld@cpsa.org.za

THE ORDER OF ETHIOPIA is a body which in August 1900 approached and petitioned the archbishop and the bishops of the Church of the Province for a share in the graces and mercies which God has bestowed upon his Catholic Church, viz. valid episcopate and priesthood. The Order is an integral part of the Church of the Province of Southern Africa and adheres to its liturgy, rites and discipline. Its priests are trained at Anglican theological colleges.

The Order is independent and manages its own affairs.

All Order churches are open to all people without distinction of race or colour.

The Order has a Constitution approved by the Provincial Synod. The annual Conference is its legislative body. The Provincial Synod of 1979 made provision for a bishop for the Order who is recognised as a bishop of the province and who also acts as Provincial of the Order. The Rt Revd Sigqibo Dwane was consecrated first bishop in April 1983. The Archbishop of Cape Town is the Visitor.

The Order works chiefly in the Dioceses of Cape Town, George, Port Elizabeth, Grahamstown, St John's (Transkei), Johannesburg, Kimberley and Kuruman and Natal.

The Anglican Church of the Southern Cone of America

In 1974 the Archbishop of Canterbury gave over his metropolitical authority for the Dioceses of Chile, Peru and Bolivia; Argentina and Eastern South America; and Paraguay, Northern Argentina to the Consejo Anglicano Sud-Americano (CASA). Brazil, though already a separate province, joined CASA as an associate member. The Diocese of Peru and Bolivia was formed in 1978.

In 1981 final approval was given to the constitution and canons of the proposed new province of the Anglican Church of the Southern Cone of America. The inauguration took place in Buenos Aires, Argentina on 29–30 April 1983. The province now comprises the dioceses of Argentina, Bolivia, Chile, Northern Argentina, Paraguay, Peru, and Uruguay.

Presiding Bishop Rt Revd Maurice Sinclair, Casilla de Correo 187, CP 4400, Salta, Argentina *Fax:* 87–31–2622
e-mail: sinclair@salnet.com.ar

Provincial Secretary Sr Rolando Dalmas, Reconquista 522, 11000 Montevideo, Uruguay

Provincial Treasurer Sr Teodosio Rivas, Casilla 1124, Asunción, Paraguay

THEOLOGICAL EDUCATION
Planned and carried out by a Theological Education Commission which selects candidates, applies grants and sets courses of study, some of which are led by clergy of the diocese. Some students follow courses of theological training 'by extension' and others attend ecumenical seminaries.

ARGENTINA
Bishop Rt Revd David Leake, CC. 4293, 1000 Correo Central, Argentina *Fax:* 1 331 0234
e-mail: diocesisanglibue@arnet.com.ar

BOLIVIA
Bishop Rt Revd Gregory Venables, Casilla 9574, La Paz, Bolivia *Fax:* 2 371 414
e-mail: bpgreg@megalink.com

CHILE
Bishop Rt Revd Colin Frederick Bazley, Casilla 50675, Correo Central, Santiago, Chile *Fax:* 2 639 4581
e-mail: cbazley@red6.mic.cl

Coadjutor Bishop Rt Revd Hector Zavola (*same address*)
e-mail: tzavala@red6.mic.cl

Assistant Bishop Rt Revd Abelino Apeleo, Casilla de Correo 26-D, Temuco, Chile *Fax:* 45 211 130

NORTHERN ARGENTINA
Bishop Rt Revd Maurice Sinclair (*Bishop of Northern Argentina and Primate of the Province of the Southern Cone of America*), Casilla de Correo 187, CP 4400, Salta, Argentina
Fax: 87 312 622
e-mail: sinclair@salnet.com.ar

Assistant Bishops
Rt Revd Humberto Axt (*same address*)

Rt Revd Mario Lorenzo Mariño, Casilla 19, 3636 Ingeniero Juárez, Formosa, Argentina

PARAGUAY
Bishop Rt Revd John Ellison, Iglesia Anglicana Paraguya, Casilla de Correo 1124, Asunción, Paraguay
Fax: 21 214 328
e-mail: butellis@pla.net.py

PERU
Bishop Rt Revd Harold William Godfrey, c/o Apartado 18–1032 Miraflores, Lima 18, Peru *Fax:* 1 445 3044
e-mail: godfrey@telematic.com.pe

URUGUAY
Bishop Rt Revd Migel Tamayo Zaldivar, CC 6108, Montevideo, CP11000, Uruguay *Fax:* 2 916 251
e-mail: mtamayo@netgate.com.uy

The Church of the Province of the Sudan

In 1974 the Diocese of the Sudan, formerly part of the Jerusalem Archbishopric, reverted to the sole jurisdiction of the Archbishop of Canterbury as an extra-provincial diocese while awaiting the setting up of the new Province of the Sudan. The province, consisting of four new dioceses, was inaugurated in October 1976.

Archbishop Vacancy, c/o PO Box 52802, Nairobi, Kenya

Provincial Secretary Revd Nelson K. Nyumbe, PO Box 110, Juba, Sudan

Acting Provincial Treasurer Mr Joel Lupin (*same address*)

THEOLOGICAL COLLEGE
Bishop Gwynne College, Juba. Equatoria (*Principal* Canon Micah Laila Dawidi)

CHURCH NEWS LETTER
News Letter of the Episcopal Church of the Sudan Monthly. Covers news of the whole province. *Editor* PO Box 47429, Nairobi, Kenya

BOR
Bishop Rt Revd Nathaniel Garang, c/o NSCC, PO Box 52802, Nairobi, Kenya

CUEIBET
Bishop Rt Revd Reuben Macir Makoi, c/o CEAS, PO Box 40870, Nairobi, Kenya *Fax:* 02–570 807

EL OBEID
Bishop Rt Revd Ismail Abudigin Kawo Gibreil, PO Box 65, Omdurman, Sudan

EZZO
Bishop Rt Revd Benjamin Ruati, c/o NSCC, PO Box 52802, Nairobi, Kenya *Fax:* 447 015

IBBA
Bishop Rt Revd Levi Hassan Nzakara, c/o PO Box 110, Juba, Sudan

JUBA
Archbishop Vacancy, PO Box 110, Juba, Sudan

KADUGULI AND NUBA MOUNTAINS
Bishop Rt Revd Peter Kuthurdu Elbersh Kowa, c/o PO Box 65, Omdurman, Sudan

KAJO-KEJI
Bishop Rt Revd Manasseh Dawidi Binyi, c/o NSCC, PO Box 52802, Nairobi, Kenya

KHARTOUM
Bishop Rt Revd Bulus Idris Tia, PO Box 65, Omdurman, Sudan

LAINYA
Bishop Rt Revd Eliaba Ladu Menesona, c/o PO Box 110, Juba, Sudan

LUI
Bishop Vacancy, PO Box 3364, Khartoum, Sudan

MALAKAL
Bishop Rt Revd Kedhekia Mabior, c/o NSCC, PO Box 52802, Nairobi, Kenya

MARIDI
Bishop Rt Revd Joseph Marona, PO Box 676, Arua, Uganda *Fax:* 447 015

MUNDRI
Bishop Rt Revd Eluzai Gima Munda, PO Box 110, Juba, Sudan

PORT SUDAN
Bishop Rt Revd Yousif Abdalla Kuku, PO Box 278, Red Sea State, Sudan

REJAF
Bishop Rt Revd Michael Lugor, PO Box 110, Juba, Sudan

RENK
Bishop Rt Revd Daniel Deng Bul Yak, PO Box 1532, Khartoum, Sudan

ROKON
Bishop Elect Rt Revd Francis Loyo, PO Box 60837, Nairobi, Kenya

RUMBEK
Bishop Rt Revd Gabriel Roric Jur, PO Box 65, Omdurman, Sudan
Fax: 11 777 100

TORIT
Bishop Rt Revd Wilson Arop Ogwok Ocheng, c/o Church of Uganda, PO Box 14123, Kampala, Uganda
Fax: 41 254 423

WAU
Bishop Rt Revd Henry Cuir Riak, All Saint's Cathedral, PO Box 135, Khartoum, Sudan

YAMBIO
Bishop Vacancy, c/o NSCC, PO Box 52802, Nairobi, Kenya

YEI
Bishop Rt Revd Seme L. Solomona, c/o PO Box 370, Arua, Uganda

YIROL
Bishop Rt Revd Benjamin Mangar Mamur, c/o All Saint's Cathedral, PO Box 3364, Khartoum, Sudan

The Anglican Church of Tanzania

Following the Provincial Synod's decision at Dodoma in February 1969 to divide the Province of East Africa into the Province of Kenya and the Province of Tanzania, the Province of Tanzania was inaugurated on 5 July 1970. Beginning with nine dioceses, the province now has 16 dioceses representing two inherited churchmanships: evangelical and anglo-catholic.

Archbishop Most Revd Donald Leo Mtetemela (*Bishop of Ruaha*), PO Box 1028, Iringa, Tanzania
Fax: 64 2479

Dean Rt Revd Gerald Mpango, PO Box 13, Kasulu, Tanzania

Provincial Secretary Canon Mkunga Mtingele, PO Box 899, Dodoma, Tanzania

Provincial Treasurer Mr John Maligana, PO Box 2, Mpwapwa, Tanzania

Provincial Registrar Mr Dominic Mbezi, PO Box 103, Dodoma, Tanzania

THEOLOGICAL COLLEGES
St Philip's Theological College, PO Box 26, Kongwa, Tanzania (*Acting Principal* Revd Boniface Kwangu)

St Mark's Theological College, PO Box 25017, Dar es Salaam, Tanzania (*Principal* Canon Lawrence Mnubi)

CHURCH NEWSPAPER
Sauti ya Jimbo Quarterly newspaper in Swahili and English containing diocesan, provincial and world church news. *Editor* c/o Provincial Secretary

CENTRAL TANGANYIKA
Bishop Rt Revd Godfrey Mdimi Mhogolo, PO Box 15, Dodoma, Tanzania
Fax: 61 320 004
e-mail: mhogolo@maf.org

Assistant Bishop Rt Revd John Ball (*same address*)

DAR ES SALAAM
Bishop Rt Revd Basil Sambano, PO Box 25016, Ilala, Dar es Salaam, Tanzania
Fax: 51 153 042

KAGERA
Bishop Rt Revd Edwin Nyamubi, PO Box 18, Ngara, Tanzania
Fax: 871 176 0266

MARA
Bishop Rt Revd Hilkia Omindo, PO Box 131, Musoma, Tanzania
Fax: 68 662 414
e-mail: MaraCPT@maf.org

MASASI
Bishop Rt Revd Patrick Mwachiko, Private Bag, PO Masasi, Mtwara, Tanzania

MOROGORO
Bishop Rt Revd Dudley Mageni, PO Box 320, Morogoro, Tanzania
e-mail: phunter@maf.org

MOUNT KILIMANJARO
Bishop Rt Revd Simon Makundi, PO Box 1057, Arusha, Tanzania
e-mail: dmk@marie.gn.apc.org

MPWAPWA
Bishop Rt Revd Simon Chiwanga, PO Box 2, Mpwapwa, Tanzania

RIFT VALLEY
Bishop Rt Revd Alpha Mohamed, PO Box 16, Manyoni, Tanzania   Fax: 61 324 565

RUAHA
Bishop Most Revd Donald Leo Mtetemela (*Bishop of Ruaha and Archbishop of the Province*), PO Box 1028, Iringa, Tanzania   Fax: 64 2479

RUVUMA
Bishop Rt Revd Stanford Abraham Shauri, PO Box 1, Liuli, Mbinga, Tanzania

SOUTH-WEST TANGANYIKA
Bishop Rt Revd John Mwela, PO Box 32, Njombe, Tanzania

TABORA
Bishop Rt Revd Francis Nzaganya Ntiruka, PO Box 1408, Tabora, Tanzania   Fax: 62 4899

VICTORIA NYANZA
Bishop Rt Revd John Changae, PO Box 278, Mwanza, Tanzania

WESTERN TANGANYIKA
Bishop Rt Revd Gerard Mpango, PO Box 13, Kasulu, Tanzania   Fax: 695 3434

ZANZIBAR AND TANGA
Bishop Rt Revd John Acland Ramadhani, PO Box 35, Korogwe, Tanzania   Fax: 61 324 565

The Church of the Province of Uganda

Another long history of devoted missionary work and Christian expansion from which martyrdoms have not been absent led to the formation, in April 1961, of the Church of Uganda, Rwanda and Burundi. The Archbishop of Canterbury inaugurated the province on 16 April 1961. Boga-Zaïre was added in 1972. The province consisted of 23 dioceses, ten of which formerly comprised the old Diocese of Uganda, seven formerly comprised the Diocese of the Upper Nile and six were in Rwanda, Burundi and Boga-Zaïre.

In May 1980 the new Province of Burundi, Rwanda and Zaïre was inaugurated, leaving 17 dioceses of Bukedi, Bunyoro-Kitara, Busoga, East Ankole, Kampala, Karamoja, Kigezi, Lango, Madi and West Nile, Mbale, Mityana, Namirembe, Northern Uganda, Ruwenzori, Soroti, West Ankole and West Buganda in the Province of Uganda.

In recent years new dioceses have been formed from the original ones bringing the present total to 27.

Archbishop of the Province Most Revd Livingstone Mpalanyi-Nkoyoyo (*Bishop of Kampala*)

Provincial Secretary Canon George K. Tibeesigwa

Provincial Treasurer Mr J. E. Sentongo

Primatial and Provincial Headquarters PO Box 14123, Kampala, Uganda

THEOLOGICAL COLLEGES
Bishop Tucker Theological College, PO Box 4, Mukono (*Principal* Revd E. Maari)

Bishop Balya College, PO Box 368, Fort-Portal (*Principal* Revd Y. Kule)

Canon Barham Divinity College, PO Box 3, Kabale (*Principal* Canon Kamagara)

Mityana Theological Training College, PO Box 102, Mityana (*Principal* Revd Mukasa-Mutambuze)

Ngora Diocesan Training Centre, PO Box 1, Ngora (*Principal* Revd S. Amuret)

Namugongo Martyrs Seminary, PO Box 20183, Lugogo, K'la (*Principal* Revd S. Sekadde)

Aduku Diocesan Theological College, PO Aduku, Lira (*Principal* Revd S. O. Obura)

Kabwohe College, PO Kabwohe, Mbarara (*Principal* Revd Y. R. Buremu)

Ringili College, PO Box 370, Arua (*Principal* Revd P. Nigo)

CHURCH PAPER
The New Century Published monthly. Contains diocesan, provincial and world church news and items of general interest. *Editorial and business office* PO Box 6246, Kampala, Uganda

BUKEDI
Bishop Rt Revd Nicodemus Engwalas-Okille, PO Box 170, Tororo, Uganda

BUNYORO-KITARA
Bishop Rt Revd Wilson Nkuna Turumanya, PO Box 20, Hoima, Uganda   Fax: 465 40 399

BUSOGA
Vicar-General Revd Christopher George Palacas, PO Box 1658, Jinja, Uganda　　　　　　　　*Fax:* 43 20 547

CENTRAL BUGANDA
Bishop Rt Revd George Sinabulya, PO Box 1200, Karoni-Gomba, Mpigi, Uganda　　　　　　*Fax:* 41 242 724

EAST ANKOLE
Bishop Rt Revd Elisha Kyamugambi, PO Box 14, Mbarara, Ankole, Uganda

KAMPALA
Bishop Most Revd Livingstone Mpalanyi-Nkoyoyo (*Archbishop of Uganda and Bishop of Kampala*), PO Box 14123, Kampala, Uganda　　　　　　*Fax:* 41 251 925

Assistant Bishop Rt Revd Eliphaz Maari, PO Box 335, Kampala, Uganda　　　　　　　　*Fax:* 41 342 601

KARAMOJA
Bishop Rt Revd Peter Lomongin, c/o MAF, PO Box 1, Kampala, Uganda

KIGEZI
Bishop Rt Revd George Katwesigye, PO Box 14123, Kampala, Uganda　　　　　　　　*Fax:* 486 22 447

KINKIZI
Bishop Rt Revd John Ntegyereize, PO Box 77, Karuhinda, Rukungiri, Uganda

KITGUM
Bishop Rt Revd Macleord Baker Ochola II Ameda Mollo, PO Box 187, Kitgum, Uganda

LANGO
Bishop Rt Revd Melchizedek Otim, PO Box 6, Lira, Uganda

LUWERO
Bishop Rt Revd Evans Mukasa Kisekka, PO Box 125, Luwero, Uganda　　　　　　　　*Fax:* 41 610 132

MADI AND WEST NILE
Bishop Rt Revd Enock Lee Drati, PO Box 370, Arua, Uganda

MBALE
Bishop Rt Revd Israel Wanambisi Koboyi, Bishop's House, PO Box 473, Mbale, Uganda

MITYANA
Bishop Rt Revd Wilson Mutebi, PO Box 102, Mityana, Uganda

MUHABURA
Bishop Rt Revd Ernest Shalita, Church of Uganda, PO Box 22, Kisoro, Uganda

MUKONO
Bishop Rt Revd Michael Senyimba, PO Box 39, Mukono, Uganda

NAMIREMBE
Bishop Rt Revd Samuel Balagadde Ssekkadde, PO Box 14297, Kampala, Uganda

NEBBI
Bishop Rt Revd Henry Orombi, PO Box 27, Nebbi, Uganda

NORTH KIGEZI
Bishop Rt Revd John Kahigwa, PO Box 23, Rukungiri, Uganda

NORTH MBALE
Bishop Rt Revd Nathan Muwombi, Bishop's House, PO Box 1837, Mbale, Uganda　　　　　*Fax:* 41 254 576

NORTHERN UGANDA
Bishop Rt Revd Nelson Onono-Onweng, PO Box 232, Gulu, Uganda　　　　　　　　*Fax:* 250 828

RUWENZORI
Bishop Rt Revd Eustace Kamanyire, Bishop's House, PO Box 37, Fort Portal, Uganda　　　*Fax:* 493 22 636

SOROTI
Bishop Rt Revd Geresom Ilukor, PO Box 107, Soroti, Uganda

SOUTH RWENZORI
Bishop Rt Revd Zebedee Masereka, PO Box 142, Kasese, Uganda　　　　　　　　*Fax:* 483 44 450
　　　　　　e-mail: bishopmase@uge.healthnet

WEST ANKOLE
Bishop Rt Revd William Magambo, PO Box 140, Bushenyi, Uganda　　　　　　　　*Fax:* 485 21 304

WEST BUGANDA
Bishop Rt Revd Christopher Senyonjo, PO Box 242, Masaka, Uganda

The Episcopal Church in the United States of America

Presiding Bishop Most Revd Frank Tracy Griswold III

President, House of Deputies Dr Pamela Chinnis

Executive Officer, The General Convention and Secretary, The Executive Council Vacancy

Secretary, House of Bishops Rt Revd Mary Adelia McLeod

Offices of the Episcopal Church and its Departments Episcopal Church Center, 815 Second Ave, New York, NY 10017

NATIONAL SEMINARIES
California
Bloy Episcopal School of Theology, 1325 N. College Ave, Claremont, CA 91711 (*Dean* Very Revd J. H. Olson)
Church Divinity School of the Pacific, 2451 Ridge Rd, Berkeley, CA 94709 (*Dean* Very Revd Charles Perry)

Connecticut
Berkeley Divinity School at Yale University, 363 St Ronan St, New Haven, CT 06511 (*Dean* Mr William Franklin)

Illinois
Seabury-Western Theological Seminary, 2122 Sheridan Rd, Evanston, IL 60201 (*Dean* Vacancy)

Kentucky
The Episcopal Theological Seminary in Kentucky, 544 Sayre Ave, Lexington, KY 40508 (*Dean* Rt Revd Don A. Wimberly)

Massachusetts
Episcopal Divinity School, 99 Brattle St, Cambridge, MA 02138 (*Dean* Very Revd William Rankin)

New York
Bexley Hall, Rochester Center for Theological Studies, 1110 South Goodman St, Rochester, NY 14620 (*Dean* Very Revd William H. Peterson)
George Mercer Jr Memorial School of Theology, 65 4th Garden City, NY 11530 (*Dean* Very Revd Lloyd A. Lewis)
The General Theological Seminary of the Protestant Episcopal Church in the United States, 175 Ninth Ave, New York, NY 10011 (*Dean* Rt Revd Craig Anderson)

Philadelphia
Trinity Episcopal School for Ministry, 311 Eleventh St, Ambridge, PA 15003 (*Dean* Rt Revd William Frey)

Tennessee
School of Theology of the University of the South, Sewanee, TN 37375 (*Dean* Very Revd Guy E. Lytle, III)

Texas
The Episcopal Theological Seminary of the Southwest, PO Box 2247, Austin, TX 78768 (*Dean* Very Revd D. McDonald)

Virginia
Virginia Theological Seminary, Alexandria, VA 22304 (*Dean* Very Revd Richard Reid)

Wisconsin
Nashotah House, Nashotah, WI 53058 (*Provost* Very Revd Gary Kriss)

CHURCH PAPERS
Episcopal Life An independently edited, officially sponsored monthly newspaper published by The Domestic and Foreign Missionary Society of the Episcopal Church, 815 Second Ave, New York NY10017, upon authority of the General Convention of the Protestant Episcopal Church in the USA.

The Living Church Weekly magazine. *Editorial and Business Offices* 407 E. Michigan St, Milwaukee, WI 53202. Contains news and features about Christianity in general and the Episcopal Church in particular.

ALABAMA (Province IV)
Bishop Rt Revd Robert Oran Miller, Carpenter House, 521 N. 20th St, Birmingham AL 35203   Fax: 205 715 2066
  e-mail: DioAla@aol.com

Coadjutor Bishop Rt Revd Henry Nutt Parsley Jr (*same address*)

ALASKA (Province VIII)
Bishop Rt Revd Mark Lawrence MacDonald, 1205 Denali Way, Fairbanks, Alaska 99701–4178   Fax: 907 456 6552
  e-mail: mark.macdonald@ecunet.org

ALBANY (Province II)
Bishop Rt Revd Daniel William Herzog, 62 So. Swan St, Albany NY 12210   Fax: 518 436 1182
  e-mail: dherzog@christcom.net

ARIZONA (Province VIII)
Bishop Rt Revd Robert Reed Shahan, 114 West Roosevelt St, Phoenix AZ 85003   Fax: 602 495 6603
  e-mail: ROBERT_SHAHAN@ecunet.org

ARKANSAS (Province VII)
Bishop Rt Revd Larry Earl Maze, Cathedral House, PO Box 164668, Little Rock AR 72216   Fax: 501 372 2147
e-mail: Bishopmaze@aol.com

ATLANTA (Province IV)
Bishop Rt Revd Frank Kellogg Allan, 2744 Peachtree Rd, NW Atlanta GA 30363   Fax: 404 261 2515
e-mail: fallan@mindspring.com

Assistant Bishop Rt Revd Onell Soto (same address)
e-mail: pbisposoto@aol.com

BETHLEHEM (Province III)
Bishop Rt Revd Paul Victor Marshall, 333 Wyandotte St, Bethlehem PA 18015   Fax: 610 691 1683
e-mail: Paul.Marshall@ecunet.org

CALIFORNIA (Province VIII)
Bishop Rt Revd William Edwin Swing, 1055 Taylor St, San Francisco CA 94108   Fax: 415 673 9268
e-mail: bishop@diocal.org

Assisting Bishops Rt Revd George Richard Millard, 1812 Sandhill Rd, 311, Palii Altu CA 14304–2136; Rt Revd John R. Wyatt, 1204 Chelsa Way, Redwood City CA 44061

*CENTRAL ECUADOR (Province IX)
Bishop Rt Revd Jose Neptali Larrea-Moreno, Av Amazonas 4430 Y Villalengua, Piso 7 Oficina 708, Edificio Banco Amazonas, Quito, Ecuador   Fax: 2 252 226

CENTRAL FLORIDA (Province IV)
Bishop Rt Revd John Howe, Diocesan Office, 1017 E Robinson St, Orlando, Florida 32801–2023   Fax: 407 872 006
e-mail: bcf3@aol.com

Assistant Bishop Rt Revd Hugo Pina-Lopez (same address)
Fax: 407 872 0096

Assisting Bishop Rt Revd Reginald Hollis

CENTRAL GULFCOAST (Province IV)
Bishop Rt Revd Charles Farmer Duvall, Box 13330, Pensacola, Florida 32591–3330   Fax: 904 434 8577
e-mail: staff@diocgc.org

CENTRAL NEW YORK (Province II)
Bishop Rt Revd David Joslin, 310 Montgomery St, Suite 200, Syracuse NY 13202–2093   Fax: 315 478 1632

CENTRAL PENNSYLVANIA (Province III)
Bishop Rt Revd Michael Whittington Creighton, 221 N. Front St, Box 11937, Harrisburg PA 17108–1937
Fax: 717 236 6448
e-mail: bishopcpa@aol.com

CHICAGO (Province V)
Bishop Vacancy, 65 E. Huron St, Chicago IL 60611
Fax: 312 787 4534

Bishop Suffragan Rt Revd William W. Wiedrich (same address)

*COLOMBIA (Province IX)
Bishop Rt Revd Bernardo Merino-Botero, Apartado Aereo 52964, Bogota 2, Colombia SA   Fax: 1 288 3248

COLORADO (Province VI)
Bishop Rt Revd William Winterrowd, 1300 Washington St, Denver CO 80203   Fax: 303 837 1311

Assisting Bishops Rt Revd William Davidson, Rt Revd William H. Wolfrum

CONNECTICUT (Province I)
Bishop Rt Revd Clarence Coleridge, 1335 Asylum Ave, Hartford CT 06105–2295   Fax: 860 523 1410

Bishop Suffragan Rt Revd Andrew Donnan Smith (same address)   e-mail: adsmith@ctdiocese.org

DALLAS (Province VII)
Bishop Rt Revd James Monte Stanton, 1630 Garrett St, Dallas TX 75206   Fax: 214 826 5968
e-mail: jmsdallas@aol.com

DELAWARE (Province III)
Bishop Rt Revd Wayne Parker Wright, 2020 Tatnall St, Wilmington DE 19802   Fax: 302 656 7342
e-mail: wright@delanet.com

*DOMINICAN REPUBLIC (Province IX)
Bishop Rt Revd Julio Cesar Holguin Khoury, Apartado 764, Calle Santiago No 114, Santo Domingo, Dominican Republic   Fax: 809 686 6354
e-mail: h.rkhoury@codetel.net.do

EAST CAROLINA (Province IV)
Bishop Rt Revd Clifton Daniel, PO Box 1336, Kinston NC 27803   Fax: 919 523 5272
e-mail: diocese.ec@coastalnet.com

Assisting Bishop Rt Revd C. Charles Vaché

EAST TENNESSEE
Bishop Rt Revd Robert Tharp, 401 Cumberland Ave, Knoxville, Tennessee 37902–2302   Fax: 615 521 2905
e-mail: rtharp@conc.tels.net

EASTERN MICHIGAN
Bishop Rt Revd Edward Max Leidel Jr, Diocesan Office, 4611 Swede Ave, Midland, Michigan 48642–3861
Fax: 517 835 6302
e-mail: ed.leidel@ecunet.org

EASTERN OREGON (Province VIII)
Bishop Rt Revd Rustin Ray Kimsey, PO Box 620, The Dalles, Oregon 97058 *Fax:* 541 298 7875
 e-mail: rustin@gorge.net

EASTON (Province III)
Bishop Rt Revd Martin Gough Townsend, Box 1027, Easton MD 21601 *Fax:* 410 763 8259
 e-mail: MARTIN_TOWNSEND@ecunet.org

EAU CLAIRE (Province V)
Bishop Rt Revd William Charles Wantland, 510 So. Farwell St, Eau Claire WI 54701 *Fax:* 715 835 9212
 e-mail: w750dec@aol.com

EL CAMINO REAL (Province VIII)
Bishop Rt Revd Richard L. Shimpfky, Box 1903 Monterey, CA 93940 *Fax:* 408 394 7133
 e-mail: saltig@aol.com

EUROPE, CONVOCATION OF AMERICAN CHURCHES IN
Bishop Rt Revd Jeffery William Rowthorn, 23 Avenue George V, 75008 Paris, France *Fax:* 1 4723 9530
 e-mail: rowthorn@american-cath.assoc.fr

FLORIDA (Province IV)
Bishop Rt Revd Stephen Hays Jecko, 325 Market St, Jacksonville FL 32202 *Fax:* 904 355 1934
 e-mail: bfl7@crci.net

FOND DU LAC (Province V)
Bishop Rt Revd Russell Edward Jacobus, PO Box 149, Fond du Lac WI 54936–0149 *Fax:* 920 921 8761
 e-mail: plusruss@vbe.com

FORMOSA
See Missionary Diocese of Taiwan

FORT WORTH (Province VII)
Bishop Rt Revd Jack Leo Iker, 6300 Ridglea Place, Suite 1100, Fort Worth, Texas 76116 *Fax:* 817 738 9955
 e-mail: jliker@dfw.net

GEORGIA (Province IV)
Bishop Rt Revd Henry Irving Loutitt Jr, 611 E Bay St, Savannah GA 31401–1296 *Fax:* 912 236 2007

*HAITI (Province II)
Bishop Rt Revd Jean Zache Duracin, Eglise Episcopale d'Haiti, PO Box 1309, Port-au-Prince, Haiti
 Fax: 57 3412
 e-mail: epihaiti@globalsud.net

HAWAII (Province VIII)
Bishop Rt Revd Richard Sui On Chang, Diocesan Office, 229 Queen Emma Sq, Honolulu HI 96813–2304
 Fax: 808 538 7194
 e-mail: rsoc@aloha.net

*HONDURAS (Province IX)
Bishop Rt Revd Leopold Frade, Apartado Postal 586, San Pedro Sula, Honduras CA *Fax:* 556 6467
 e-mail: episcopal@mayanet.hn

IDAHO (Province VIII)
Bishop Rt Revd John Stuart Thornton, PO Box 936, Boise ID 83701 *Fax:* 208 345 9735

Bishop Coadjutor Rt Revd Harry Bainbridge (*same address*)
 e-mail: bishopb@micron.net

INDIANAPOLIS (Province V)
Bishop Rt Revd Catherine Elizabeth Maples Waynick, 1100 W. 42nd St, Indianapolis IN 46208
 Fax: 317 926 5456
 e-mail: hob929@aol.com

IOWA (Province VI)
Bishop Rt Revd Christopher Epting, 225 37th St, Des Moines IA 50312 *Fax:* 515 277 0273
 e-mail: BISHOP.EPTING@ecunet.org

KANSAS (Province VII)
Bishop Rt Revd William Smalley, Bethany Place, 833–35 Polk St, Topeka KS 66612 *Fax:* 913 235 2449
 e-mail: wsmalley@espicopal-ks.org

KENTUCKY (Province IV)
Bishop Rt Revd Edwin Funsten Gulick, 600 East Main St, Louisville KY 40202 *Fax:* 502 587 8123
 e-mail: TGULICK@ecunet.org

LEXINGTON (Province IV)
Bishop Rt Revd Don Adger Wimberly, PO Box 610, Lexington KY 40586 *Fax:* 606 231 9077

LITORAL DIOCESE OF ECUADOR (Province IX)
Bishop Rt Revd Alfredo Morante-Arevalo, Box 0901–5250, Amarilis Fuentes entre V Trusillo, y La 'D', Guayaquil, Equador *Fax:* 4 443 088

LONG ISLAND (Province II)
Bishop Rt Revd Orris Walker Jr, 36 Cathedral Ave, Garden City, NY 11530 *Fax:* 516 248 4883
 e-mail: dioceseli@aol.com

Bishop Suffragan Rt Revd Rodney Rae Michel (*same address*)

LOS ANGELES (Province VIII)
Bishop Rt Revd Frederick Houk Borsch, Box 2164, Los Angeles CA 90051 *Fax:* 213 482 5304
 e-mail: Bishop@ladiocese.org

Bishop Suffragan Rt Revd Chester L. Talton (*same address*)
e-mail: suffragan@ladiocese.org

LOUISIANA (Province IV)
Bishop Rt Revd Charles Edward Jenkins III, 1623 Seventh St, New Orleans LA 70115–4111   Fax: 504 895 6637
e-mail: revchuck@worldnet.att.net

MAINE (Province I)
Bishop Rt Revd Chilton Abbie Richardson Knudsen, Loring House, 143 State St, Portland ME 04101
Fax: 207 773 0095
e-mail: Chilton_knudsen@ecunet.org

MARYLAND (Province III)
Bishop Rt Revd Robert Wilkes Ihloff, 4 East University Parkway, Baltimore MD 21218   Fax: 410 554 6387
e-mail: rihloff@ang-md.org

Bishop Suffragan Rt Revd John Leslie Rabb (*same address*)

MASSACHUSETTS (Province I)
Bishop Rt Revd Thomas Shaw SSJE, Society of St John the Evangelist, 980 Memorial Drive, Cambridge, MA 02138
Fax: 617 482 8431

Bishop Suffragan Rt Revd Barbara Harris, 138 Tremont St, Boston MA 02111   Fax: 617 482 8431
e-mail: BARBARA.HARRIS@ecunet.org

MICHIGAN (Province V)
Bishop Rt Revd Stewart Wood, 4800 Woodward Ave, Detroit MI 48201   Fax: 313 831 0259
e-mail: stewwood@aol.com

MILWAUKEE (Province V)
Bishop Rt Revd Roger J. White, 804 E. Juneau Ave, Milwaukee WI 53202   Fax: 414 272 7790
e-mail: MILWAUKEE.DIOCESE@ecunet.org

MINNESOTA (Province VI)
Bishop Rt Revd James Louis Jelinek, 1730 Clifton Place, Suite 201, Minneapolis MN 55403   Fax: 6112 871 0552
e-mail: JIM.JELINEK@ecunet.org

MISSISSIPPI (Province IV)
Bishop Rt Revd Alfred Clark Marble Jr, PO Box 23107, Jackson MS 39225–3107   Fax: 601 354 3401

MISSOURI (Province V)
Bishop Rt Revd Hays Rockwell, 1210 Locust St, St Louis MO 63103   Fax: 314 231 3373
e-mail: bishop@missouri.anglican.org

MONTANA (Province VI)
Bishop Rt Revd Charles I. Jones, 515 North Park Ave, Helena MT 59601   Fax: 406 442 2238
e-mail: CI_JONES@ecunet.org

NAVAJOLAND AREA MISSION (Province VIII)
Bishop Rt Revd Steven Tsosie Plummer, Box 720, Farmington, New Mexico 87499   Fax: 435 672 2369

NEBRASKA (Province VI)
Bishop Rt Revd James Edward Krotz, 200 N. 62nd St, Omaha NB 68132–6357   Fax: 402 558 0094
e-mail: Diocese_of_Nebraska@ecunet.org

NEVADA (Province VIII)
Bishop Rt Revd Stewart C. Zabriskie, 2100 S. Maryland Parkway, Suite 4, Las Vegas NV 89104
Fax: 702 737 6488
e-mail: diocese.of.nevada@ecunet.org

NEW HAMPSHIRE (Province I)
Bishop Rt Revd Douglas E. Theuner, 63 Green St, Concord NH 03301   Fax: 603 225 7884
e-mail: DOUGLAS.THEUNER@ecunet.org

NEW JERSEY (Province II)
Bishop Rt Revd Joe Morris Doss, 808 W. State St, Trenton NJ 08618   Fax: 609 394 9546
e-mail: JOE.MORRIS.DOSS@ecunet.org

NEW YORK (Province II)
Bishop Rt Revd Richard Frank Grein, Synod House, 1047 Amsterdam Ave, Cathedral Heights, New York NY 10025
Fax: 212 932 7312
e-mail: cybersexton@dioceseny.org

Coadjutor Bishop Rt Revd Mark Sean Sisk (*same address*)
e-mail: MarkSisk@worldnet.att.net

Bishops Suffragan
Rt Revd Walter Decoster Dennis (*same address*)
Fax: 212 316 7405

Rt Revd Catherine S. Roskam, Region Two Office, 55 Cedar St, Dobbs Ferry, NY 10522   Fax: 914 693 0407
e-mail: Glenregli@aol.com

NEWARK (Province II)
Bishop Rt Revd John Shelby Spong, 31 Mulberry St, Newark NJ 07102   Fax: 923 622 3503
e-mail: cmsctm@aol.com

Bishop Suffragan Rt Revd Jack Marston McKelvey (*same address*)   Fax: 973 622 3503
e-mail: BpJackM@aol.com

Bishop Coadjutor Rt Revd John Palmer Croneberger, Highwood Ave and Engle, Tenafly, NJ 07670

NORTH CAROLINA (Province IV)
Bishop Rt Revd Robert Carroll Johnson Jr, PO Box 17025, Raleigh NC 27619–7025   Fax: 919 787 0156
    e-mail: DIOCESE.OF.NC@ecunet.org

Bishop Suffragan Rt Revd James Gary Gloster (*same address*)

NORTH DAKOTA (Province VI)
Bishop Rt Revd Andrew Hedtler Fairfield, 33600 25th St (Box 10337), Fargo ND 58106–0337   Fax: 701 232 3077

NORTHERN CALIFORNIA (Province VIII)
Bishop Rt Revd Jerry Lamb, Box 161268, Sacramento CA 95816   Fax: 916 442 6927
    e-mail: bishopjal@aol.com

NORTHERN INDIANA (Province V)
Bishop Rt Revd Francis C. Gray, Cathedral House, 117 N. Lafayette Blvd, South Bend, Indiana 46601
    Fax: 219 287 7914

NORTHERN MICHIGAN (Province V)
Bishop Rt Revd Thomas Kreider Ray, 131 E. Ridge St, Marquette MI 49855   Fax: 906 228 7171

NORTHWEST TEXAS (Province VII)
Bishop Rt Revd C. Wallis Ohl Jr, The Episcopal Church Center, 1802 Broadway, Lubbock TX 79408
    Fax: 806 472 0641
    e-mail: wallisohl@hub.ofthe.net

NORTHWESTERN PENNSYLVANIA (Province III)
Bishop Rt Revd Robert Deane Rowley, 145 W. 6th St, Erie PA 16501   Fax: 814 454 8703
    e-mail: ROBERT_ROWLEY@ecunet.org

OHIO (Province V)
Bishop Rt Revd J. Clark Grew II, 2230 Euclid Ave, Cleveland OH 44115–2499   Fax: 216 771 9252
    e-mail: bishop@dohio.org

Bishop Suffragan Rt Revd Arthur Benjamin Williams Jr (*same address*)   Fax: 216 623 0735
    e-mail: bishsuff@diohio.org

OKLAHOMA (Province VII)
Bishop Rt Revd Robert Moody, 924 N. Robinson, Oklahoma City OK 73102   Fax: 405 232 4912

OLYMPIA (Province VIII)
Bishop Rt Revd Vincent Warner Jr, Box 12126, Seattle WA 98102   Fax: 206 325 4631

Assisting Bishop Rt Revd Sandford Z. K. Hampton (*same address*)   *e-mail:* shampton@olympia.anglican.org

OREGON (Province VIII)
Bishop Rt Revd Robert Louis Ladehoff, PO Box 467, Lake Oswego OR 97034–0467   Fax: 503 636 5616
    e-mail: robertl@diocese-oregon.org

PENNSYLVANIA (Province III)
Bishop Rt Revd Charles E. Ellsworth Bennison Jr, 240 South Fourth St, Philadelphia PA 19106
    Fax: 215 627 7750
    e-mail: cbenni4455@aol.com

Bishop Suffragan Rt Revd Franklin Turner (*same address*)

PITTSBURGH (Province III)
Bishop Rt Revd Robert William Duncan Jr, 325 Oliver Ave, Pittsburgh PA 15222–2467   Fax: 412 471 5591
    e-mail: duncan@pgh.anglican.org

QUINCY (Province V)
Bishop Rt Revd Keith Ackerman, 3601 N. North St, Peoria, IL 61604   Fax: 309 688 8229
    e-mail: quincy8@ocslink.com

RHODE ISLAND (Province I)
Bishop Rt Revd Geralyn Wolf, 275 N. Main St, Providence RI 02903
    Fax: 401 331 9430

RIO GRANDE (Province VII)
Bishop Rt Revd Terence Kelshaw, 4304 Carlisle NE, Albuquerque NM 87107–4811   Fax: 505 883 9048
    e-mail: tkelshaw@aol.com

ROCHESTER (Province II)
Bishop Rt Revd William George Burrill, 935 East Ave, Rochester NY 14607   Fax: 716 473 3195
    e-mail: BILL.BURRILL@ecunet.org

SAN DIEGO (Province VIII)
Bishop Rt Revd Gethin Benwil Hughes, 2728 Sixth Ave, San Diego CA 92103–6397   Fax: 619 291 8362
    e-mail: SEE_SANDIEGO@ecunet.org

SAN JOAQUIN (Province IV)
Bishop Rt Revd John-David Mercer Schofield, 4159 E. Dakota Ave, Fresno CA 93726   Fax: 209 244 4832
    e-mail: s.joaquin@genie.geis.com

SOUTH CAROLINA (Province IV)
Bishop Rt Revd Edward L. Salmon Jr, Box 20127, Charleston SC 29413–0127   Fax: 803 723 7628
    e-mail: elsalmon@dioceseofsc.org

Suffragan Bishop Rt Revd William J. Skilton (*same address*)
e-mail: bskilton@dioceseofsc.org

SOUTH DAKOTA (Province VI)
Bishop Rt Revd Creighton Robertson, 500 S. Main St, Sioux Falls, South Dakota 57104–6814
Fax: 605 336 6243
e-mail: CREIGHTON_ROBERTSON@ecunet.org

SOUTHEAST FLORIDA (Province IV)
Bishop Rt Revd Calvin Onderdonk Schofield Jr, 525 NE 15 St, Miami FL 33132   Fax: 305 375 8054
e-mail: DioseF@aol.com

Bishop Suffragan Rt Revd John L. Said (*same address*)
e-mail: BishopSaid@aol.com

SOUTHERN OHIO (Province V)
Bishop Rt Revd Herbert Thompson, 412 Sycamore St, Cincinnati OH 45202   Fax: 513 421 0315

Bishop Suffragan Rt Revd Kenneth Price Jr, 125 E. Broad St, Columbus OH 43215   Fax: 614 461 1015
e-mail: BishopKen@aol.com

SOUTHERN VIRGINIA (Province III)
Bishop Rt Revd Frank Vest Jr, 600 Talbot Hall Rd, Norfolk VA 23505   Fax: 804 440 5354
e-mail: fhvest@southernvirginia.anglican.org

Coadjutor Bishop Rt Revd David Conner Bane Jr, 6603 Caroline St, Norfolk VA 23505   e-mail: dcbjr@aol.com

Assistant Bishop Rt Revd Donald P. Hart
e-mail: DON.HART@ecunet.org

SOUTHWEST FLORIDA (Province IV)
Bishop Rt Revd John Bailey Lipscomb, PO Drawer 491, St Petersburg FL 33731   Fax: 813 821 9254
e-mail: jlipscom@dioceseswfla.org

Assisting Bishop Rt Revd Telesforo Alexander Isaac (*same address*)

SOUTHWESTERN VIRGINIA (Province III)
Bishop Rt Revd Frank Neff Powell, PO Box 2279, Roanoke VA 24009–2279   Fax: 540 343 9114
e-mail: NEFF_POWELL@ecunet.org

SPOKANE (Province VIII)
Bishop Rt Revd Frank J. Terry, 245 E. 13th Ave, Spokane WA 99202   Fax: 509 747 0049

SPRINGFIELD (Province V)
Bishop Rt Revd Peter Hess Beckwith, 821 S. 2nd St, Springfield IL 62704–2694   Fax: 217 525 1877

*TAIWAN (Province VIII)
Bishop Rt Revd John Chien, 1–105–7 Hangchow, South Rd, Taipei, Taiwan 10044, Republic of China
Fax: 02 396 2014
e-mail: skhtpe@msiz.hinet.net

TENNESSEE (Province IV)
Bishop Rt Revd Bertram Nelson Herlong, 1 LeFleur Bld, Suite 107, 50 Vantage Way, Nashville, TN 37228–1504
Fax: 615 251 8010
e-mail: bishop@mail.episcopaldiocese-tn.org

TEXAS (Province VII)
Bishop Rt Revd Claude E. Payne, 3203 W. Alabama St, Houston TX 77098   Fax: 713 520 5723
e-mail: cepayne@neosoft.com

Bishops Suffragan
Rt Revd William Sterling (*same address*)

Rt Revd Leopoldo J. Alard (*same address*)
e-mail: ebpleo@aol.com

UPPER SOUTH CAROLINA (Province IV)
Bishop Rt Revd Dorsey Felix Henderson Jr, 1115 Marion, Columbia SC 29201   Fax: 803 799 5119
e-mail: dioceseusc@aol.com

UTAH (Province VIII)
Bishop Rt Revd Carolyn Tanner Irish, 80 S. 300 E. St, PO Box 3090, Salt Lake City UT 84110–3090
Fax: 801 322 5096

VERMONT (Province I)
Bishop Rt Revd Mary Adelia Rosamond McLeod, 5 Rock Point Rd, Burlington VT 05401–2735   Fax: 802 860 1562
e-mail: vtbishop3@aol.com

*VIRGIN ISLANDS (Province II)
Bishop Rt Revd Theodore Athelbert Daniels, PO Box 10437, St Thomas, VI 00801   Fax: 340 777 8485
e-mail: tad@aol.com

VIRGINIA (Province III)
Bishop Rt Revd Peter James Lee, 110 W. Franklin St, Richmond VA 23220   Fax: 804 644 6928

Assistant Bishop Rt Revd Robert P. Atkinson (*same address*)

Bishops Suffragan
Rt Revd F. Clayton Matthews, 8100 Three Chopt Rd, Suite 102, Richmond, Virginia 23229   Fax: 804 282 6008
e-mail: F_CLAYTON_MATTHEWS@ecunet.org

Rt Revd David Colin Jones, 6043 Burnside Landing Drive, Burke, Virginia 22015   Fax: 703 823 9524
e-mail: DAVID_COLIN_JONES@ecunet.org

Churches and Provinces: United States of America

WASHINGTON (Province III)
Bishop Rt Revd Ronald Hayward Haines, Episcopal Church House, Mount St Alban, Washington DC 20016
Fax: 202 364 6605
e-mail: rhaines@cathedral.org

Bishop Suffragan Rt Revd Jane Holmes Dixon (*same address*)

WEST MISSOURI (Province VII)
Bishop Rt Revd John Clark Buchannan, PO Box 413227, Kansas City MO 64141–3227 Fax: 816 471 0379
e-mail: wemy42c@prodigy.com

Bishop Coadjutor Rt Revd Barry Robert Howe (*same address*) *e-mail:* 105646.1226@compuserve.com

WEST TENNESSEE (Province IV)
Bishop Rt Revd James Coleman, 692 Poplar Ave, Memphis TN 38105 Fax: 901 526 1555
e-mail: edwt1@magibox.net

WEST TEXAS (Province VII)
Coadjutor Bishop Rt Revd James Edward Folts, PO Box 6885, San Antonio TX 78209 Fax: 210 822 8779

Bishop Suffragan Rt Revd Robert Boyd Hibbs (*same address*) *e-mail:* bphibbs@aol.com

WEST VIRGINIA (Province III)
Bishop Rt Revd John Smith, PO Box 5400, Charlestown WV 25361–5400 Fax: 304 343 3295
e-mail: jhswv@ecunet.org

WESTERN KANSAS (Province VII)
Bishop Rt Revd Vernon Edward Strickland, PO Box 2507, Salina KS 67402–2507 Fax: 913 825 0974

WESTERN LOUISIANA (Province IV)
Bishop Rt Revd Robert Hargrove Jr, PO Box 2031, Alexandria, Louisiana 71301 Fax: 318 442 8712

WESTERN MASSACHUSETTS (Province I)
Bishop Rt Revd Gordon P. Scruton, 37 Chestnut St, Springfield MA 01103 Fax: 413 746 9873
e-mail: BishopWMA@aol.com

WESTERN MICHIGAN (Province V)
Bishop Rt Revd Edward Lee Jr, The Cathedral, 2600 Vincent Ave, Portage MI 49024–5653 Fax: 616 381 7067
e-mail: diowestmi@aol.com

WESTERN NEW YORK (Province II)
Bishop Rt Revd David Charles Bowman, 1114 Delaware Ave, Buffalo NY 14209 Fax: 716 881 1724
e-mail: DAVID.BOWMAN@ecunet.org

WESTERN NORTH CAROLINA (Province IV)
Bishop Rt Revd Robert Hodges Johnson, Box 369, Vance Ave, Black Mountain NC 28711 Fax: 828 669 2756
e-mail: bishopwnc@compuserve.com

WYOMING (Province VI)
Bishop Rt Revd Bruce Caldwell, 104 South Fourth St, Laramie WY 82070 Fax: 307 742 6782

EXTRA-PROVINCIAL, PROVINCE IX
PUERTO RICO
Bishop Rt Revd David Alvarez-Velazquez, PO Box 902, Saint Just Sta., St Just, PR 00978, Puerto Rico
Fax: 787 761 0320

VENEZUELA
Bishop Rt Revd Orlando de Jesús Guerrero, Apartado 49–143, Avenue Caroni 100, Colinas de Bello Monte, Caracas 1042-A, Venezuela Fax: 02 751 3180

* Missionary Diocese

The Church in Wales

The Church in Wales was disestablished and partially disendowed by the Welsh Church Acts 1914 and 1919, which came fully into force on 1 April 1920. On that date the new Province of Wales was created.

The province is practically co-terminous with Wales. It comprises six dioceses: St Asaph, Bangor, St Davids, Llandaff, Monmouth, and Swansea and Brecon. There are 14 archdeaconries and 578 incumbencies in the province. There are at present about 700 stipendiary and 80 non-stipendiary clerics.

THE GOVERNING BODY
President Most Revd Alwyn Rice Jones (*Archbishop of Wales*)

Clerical Secretary Vacancy

Secretary General and Lay Secretary Mr David McIntyre, 39 Cathedral Rd, Cardiff CF1 9XF Tel: (01222) 231638

The Welsh Church Acts enabled the bishops, clergy and laity of the Church in Wales to appoint a legislative body with power to frame constitutions and regulations for the general management and good government of the Church and the property and affairs thereof whether as a whole or according to dioceses. The Church in Wales set up a Governing Body for the whole province consisting of the three orders of bishops, clergy and laity. The Governing Body has a membership of 356 representing the six dioceses.

The order of bishops consists of the archbishop and the diocesan bishops; the order of clergy consists of the deans and archdeacons *(ex officio)* and 15 members elected by each of the six diocesan conferences; and the order of the laity consists of 30 lay persons elected by each of the six diocesan conferences. In addition there are 15 clerical and 30 lay members co-opted and 14 members *ex officio*.

Its President is the Archbishop; it has two ordinary meetings annually and such other special meetings as may be necessary. Its powers are very wide and its decisions are binding upon all members of the Church. At its first session it passed the following resolution:

'The Governing Body does hereby accept the Articles, Doctrinal Statements, Rites, and Ceremonies, and save in so far as they may be necessarily varied by the Welsh Church Act 1914, the formularies of the Church of England as accepted by that Church and set forth in or appended to the Book of Common Prayer of the Church of England.'

THE REPRESENTATIVE BODY OF THE CHURCH IN WALES

Chairman Mr Richard Parkinson, 42 Victoria Rd, Penarth CF64 2HY

Secretary General Mr David McIntyre, 39 Cathedral Rd, Cardiff CF1 9XF　　　　　　Tel: (01222) 231638

Provision was made in the Welsh Church Acts for the setting up of a Representative Body of the Church in Wales with power, *inter alia*, to hold property for any of the uses and purposes of the bishops, clergy and laity of the Church in Wales.

The Representative Body was incorporated by Royal Charter on 24 April 1919. It bears somewhat the same relation to the Governing Body as the Central Board of Finance bears to the General Synod of the Church of England. It is subject to the order and control of the Governing Body, but this does not mean that everything it does has to be confirmed by the Governing Body in order to make it effective. Its powers are mainly financial and administrative; it has certain statutory obligations; it has authority to do certain things under its charter; by Chapter III of the Constitution it is enabled to carry through sales, purchases, leases, investments, etc., and it has further powers under schemes approved from time to time by the Governing Body.

All churches, most churchyards, parsonages, and other church properties are vested in the Representative Body. It is expected to initiate financial reforms and to make recommendations accordingly for the approval of the Governing Body.

The stipends of the bishops and dignitaries are paid by the Representative Body. It also pays substantial grants towards stipends of beneficed clergy and assistant curates; it pays the pensions of retired clergy and clergy widows and makes grants for the benefit of widows, orphans and dependants of deceased clergy. It administers funds out of which parsonage houses in the province are kept in good repair.

Archbishop Most Revd Alwyn Rice Jones, Esgobty, St Asaph, Clwyd LL17 0TW　　　　Tel: (01745) 583503
　　　　　　　　　　　　　　　　Fax: (01745) 584301

Assistant Bishop Rt Revd David Thomas, Bodfair, 3 White's Close, Belmont Rd, Abergavenny NP7 5HZ
　　　　　　　　　　　　　　　　Tel: (01873) 858780
　　　　　　　　　　　　　　　　Fax: (01873) 858269

Secretary General and Archbishop's Registrar Mr David McIntyre, 39 Cathedral Rd, Cardiff CF1 9XF
　　　　　　　　　　　　　　　　Tel: (01222) 231638

Archbishop's Media Officer Revd David Williams (*same address*)

THEOLOGICAL COLLEGE
St Michael's Theological College, Llandaff, Cardiff CF5 2YJ (*Warden* Revd Dr John Holdsworth)
　　　　　　　　　　　　　　　　Tel: (01222) 563379

CHURCH PAPER
Welsh Church Life Monthly publication in English. 16 pages. Contains general items of parish interest and articles on current church matters together with a children's page, editorial and news of diocesan clergy movements. *Editor* Revd Madalaine Brady, Diocesan Centre, Cathedral Close, Bangor LL57 1RL　　Tel: (01248) 354350

BANGOR

Bishop Rt Revd Barry Cennydd Morgan, Ty'r Esgob, Bangor LL57 2SS　　　　　　　Tel: (01248) 362895
　　　　　　　　　　　　　　　　Fax: (01248) 254 866

Chancellor His Honour Judge David Davies, 10 Dee Hills Park, Chester CH3 5AR

Registrar Mrs Hilary Morgan, Diocesan Centre, Cathedral Close, Bangor LL57 1RL　　Tel: (01248) 354999

Secretary of Diocesan Board of Finance Ms Stella Schultz, Bangor Diocesan Board of Finance, Diocesan Centre, Cathedral Close, Bangor LL57 1RL　　Tel: (01248) 354999

CATHEDRAL CHURCH OF ST DEINIOL, Bangor, Gwynedd
Dean Very Revd Trevor Evans, The Deanery, Cathedral Precinct, Bangor LL57 1LH　　Tel: (01248) 370693

LLANDAFF
Bishop Vacancy, Llys Esgob, The Cathedral Green, Llandaff, Cardiff CF5 2YE　　　*Tel:* (01222) 562400

Chancellor His Hon Norman Francis, 2 The Woodlands, Lisvane, Cardiff CF4 5SW

Registrar Mr David Lambert, Diocesan Registry, 9 The Chantry, Llandaff, Cardiff CF5 2NN　*Tel:* (01222) 823510

Secretary of Diocesan Board of Finance Mr Michael Beasant, Llandaff Diocesan Board of Finance, Heol Fair, Llandaff, Cardiff CF5 2EE　　　　　　*Tel:* (01222) 578899

CATHEDRAL CHURCH OF ST PETER AND ST PAUL, Llandaff, Cardiff
Dean Very Revd John Rogers, The Deanery, The Cathedral Green, Llandaff, Cardiff CF5 2YF
　　　　　　　　　　　　　Tel: (01222) 561545

MONMOUTH
Bishop Rt Revd Rowan Douglas Williams, Bishopstow, 91A Stow Hill, Newport NP9 4EA　*Tel:* (01633) 263510
　　　　　　　　　　　　　Fax: (01633) 259946

Chancellor His Honour Judge Philip Price, 23 Ty Draw Rd, Roath, Cardiff CF2 5HB

Registrar Mr Nigel Williams, Diocesan Registry, 7 Clytha Park Rd, Newport NP9 1SE　　*Tel:* (01633) 244933

Secretary of Diocesan Board of Finance Mr Richard Tarran, Diocesan Office, 64 Caerau Rd, Newport NP9 4HJ
　　　　　　　　　　　　　Tel: (01633) 267490

CATHEDRAL CHURCH OF ST WOOLOS, Newport
Dean Very Revd Richard Fenwick, The Deanery, Stow Hill, Newport NP9 4ED　　　*Tel:* (01633) 263338

ST ASAPH
Archbishop Most Revd Alwyn Rice Jones, Esgobty, St Asaph LL17 0TW　　　　　*Tel:* (01745) 583503
　　　　　　　　　　　　　Fax: (01745) 584301

Chancellor Chanc John Rogers, 15 St Peter's Square, Ruthin LL15 1AA

Registrar Mr David Hooson, Diocesan Registry, High St, St Asaph LL17 0RF　　　　*Tel:* (01745) 583393

Secretary of Diocesan Board of Finance Mr Christopher Seaton, St Asaph Diocesan Board of Finance, High St, St Asaph LL17 0RD　　　　　*Tel:* (01745) 582245

CATHEDRAL CHURCH OF ST ASAPH, St Asaph, Denbighshire
Dean Very Revd Kerry Goulstone, The Deanery, St Asaph LL17 0RL　　　　　　*Tel:* (01745) 583597

ST DAVIDS
Bishop Rt Revd David Huw Jones, Llys Esgob, Abergwili, Carmarthen SA31 2JG　　　*Tel:* (01267) 236597
　　　　　　　　　　　　　Fax: (01267) 223046

Chancellor His Hon Michael Evans, The Old Rectory, Reynoldston, Swansea SA3 1AD

Registrar Mr Basil Richards, Diocesan Registry, 4 St Mary St, Carmarthen, Dyfed SA31 1TN　*Tel:* (01267) 236426

Secretary of Diocesan Board of Finance Mr Vincent Lloyd, Diocesan Office, Abergwili, Carmarthen, Dyfed SA31 2JG
　　　　　　　　　　　　　Tel: (01267) 236145

CATHEDRAL CHURCH OF ST DAVID AND ST ANDREW, St Davids, Pembrokeshire
Dean Very Revd Wyn Evans, The Deanery, St Davids SA62 6RH　　　　　　*Tel:* (01437) 720202

SWANSEA AND BRECON
Bishop Vacancy, Ely Tower, Brecon LD3 9DE
　　　　　　　　　Tel and *Fax:* (01874) 622008

Hon Assistant Bishops
Rt Revd Benjamin Vaughan, 4 Caswell Drive, Newton, Swansea SA3 4RJ
Rt Revd Eryl Stephen Thomas, 17 Orchard Close, Gilwern, Abergavenny NP7 0EN

Chancellor Chanc Leolin Price, Moor Park, Llanbedr, Crickhowell NP8 1SS

Registrar Mr Timothy Davenport, Diocesan Registry, 8A High St, Brecon LD3 7AL　　*Tel:* (01874) 625151

Secretary of Diocesan Board of Finance Mr Huw Thomas, Swansea and Brecon Diocesan Centre, Cathedral Close, Brecon LD3 9DP　　　　　　*Tel:* (01874) 623716

CATHEDRAL CHURCH OF ST JOHN THE EVANGELIST, Brecon, Powys
Dean Very Revd Geraint Hughes, The Deanery, Cathedral Close, Brecon LD3 9DP　　　　*Tel:* (01874) 623344

The Church of the Province of West Africa

On 17 April 1951, with the consent of the Archbishop of Canterbury and according to Articles submitted by him after consultation with the dioceses concerned, the diocesan bishops of five West African dioceses holding mission from the see of Canterbury 'solemnly decreed and declared' that their dioceses were by their 'act and determination united in the Province of West Africa with the intention that its organisation should be developed in accordance with the Articles hereinafter contained as a Province of the Catholic Church in full communion with the Church of England and with the Anglican Communion of Churches'.

The Archbishop of Canterbury relinquished his metropolitical jurisdiction under the Articles, retaining certain powers during an interim period until a full Provincial Synod with three Houses of Bishops, Clergy and Laity should be brought into being and the Constitution and canons be completed and approved.

The Synod of the three Houses met for the first time in November 1957, following the Crowther centenary celebrations of the Niger Mission. The Synod then made arrangements to prepare its Constitution and canons. At its second meeting in Lagos in August 1962 the Constitution was finally passed and met with the approval of the Archbishop of Canterbury on 1 March 1963, the date on which it came into effect.

The Articles make special provision for the Provincial Synod of the Church of the province to have power to divide the Church into separate provinces related to one another within the Church; to admit new dioceses; and to authorise the creation of Missionary Dioceses or Missionary Areas. In 1952 the former diocese of Lagos was divided into four dioceses of Lagos, Ibadan, Ondo-Benin and the missionary diocese of Northern Nigeria. The diocese of the Niger Delta was separated from the diocese on the Niger which was further divided by the creation of the diocese of Owerri. In January 1962, a new diocese of Benin was created taking part of its territory from the diocese on the Niger and part from the diocese of Ondo-Benin, now the diocese of Ondo. In 1967 the diocese of Ekiti was formed out of part of Ondo diocese and in August 1970, the diocese of Enugu was formed out of part of the diocese on the Niger. In January 1972, the diocese of Aba was formed out of part of the diocese of the Niger Delta. On 17 June 1973 the archdeaconry of Kumasi was formally inaugurated as a diocese with the Rt Revd John Benjamin Arthur as bishop and a further two dioceses were formed in November 1974 in Nigeria, Kwara, from parts of Ibadan and Ondo dioceses, and Ilesha from Ibadan diocese. Two further dioceses were inaugurated in August 1976 from parts of Lagos diocese, Ijebu and Egba-Egbado. In August 1977, the diocese of Asaba was inaugurated from part of Benin diocese, and the diocese of Liberia was received as an associate diocese of the Province.

In February 1979, the new Province of Nigeria was inaugurated comprising the dioceses of Aba, Asaba, Benin, Egba-Egbado, Ekiti, Enugu, Ibadan, Ijebu, Ilesha, Kwara, Lagos, the diocese on the Niger, the Niger Delta, Northern Nigeria, Ondo and Owerri.

The dioceses of Accra, Kumasi, Liberia, Gambia and Guinea and Sierra Leone continued in the Province of West Africa.

On 17 August 1981 the new missionary diocese of Bo, formed out of Sierra Leone, was inaugurated, sponsored financially by the Church of the Province of West Africa and the diocese of Freetown (formerly Sierra Leone). In the same year the four new dioceses of Cape Coast, Koforidua, Sekondi and Sunyani/Tamale were formed from parts of Accra and Kumasi dioceses.

On 18 March 1982 the diocese of Liberia was admitted into full membership of the Province in St George's Cathedral, Freetown, Sierra Leone by Archbishop Lemaire. On 1 August 1985 the diocese of Guinea was inaugurated and its first bishop consecrated on 20 April 1986. On 22 February 1997 the unitary diocese of Sunyani/Tamale was reconstituted as two separate and autonomous dioceses.

Archbishop and Primate of the Province of West Africa Most Revd Robert Okine (*Bishop of Koforidua*)

Dean of the Province of West Africa Rt Revd Edward W. Neufville (*Bishop of Liberia*)

Episcopal Secretary of the Province of West Africa Rt Revd Solomon Tilewa Johnson (*Bishop of The Gambia*)

Provincial Secretary Mr B. A. Tagoe, PO Box 8, Accra, Ghana

Provincial Treasurer Mrs S. O. Thompson, PO Box 900, Freetown, Sierra Leone

THEOLOGICAL COLLEGES
Ghana
Trinity College (Ecumenical), PO Box 48, Legon
St Nicholas Anglican Theological College, PO Box A 162, Cape Coast, Ghana

Liberia
Cuttington University College, Suacoco, PO Box 10–0277, 1000 Monrovia 10, Liberia

Sierra Leone
Theological Hall, PO Box 128, Freetown

ACCRA
Bishop Rt Revd Justice Ofei Akrofi, Bishopscourt, PO Box 8, Accra, Ghana　　　　　　　　　*Fax:* 021 669 125

BO
Bishop Rt Revd Samuel Sao Gbonda, PO Box 21, Bo, Southern Province, Sierra Leone
　　　　　　　　　Fax: 022 251 306 (via Ghana)

CAPE COAST
Bishop Rt Revd Kobina Adduah Quashie, Bishopscourt, PO Box A 233, Adisadel Estates, Cape Coast, Ghana
　　　　　　　　　Fax: 042 2637

FREETOWN
Bishop Rt Revd Julius Olotu Prince Lynch, Bishopscourt, PO Box 537, Freetown, Sierra Leone
　　　　　　　　　Fax: 022 251 306 (via Ghana)

GAMBIA
Bishop Rt Revd Solomon Tilewa Johnson, Bishopscourt, PO Box 51, Banjul, The Gambia, West Africa
　　　　　　　　　Fax: 373 803
　　　　　　e-mail: 106617.1404@compuserve.com

GUINEA
Bishop Vacancy, BP 105, Conakry, Guinea

KOFORIDUA
Bishop Most Revd Robert Garshong Allotey Okine (*Archbishop and Primate of the Province of West Africa*), PO Box 980, Koforidua, Ghana　　　　　*Fax:* 021 669 125

KUMASI
Bishop Rt Revd Edmund Yeboah, Bishop's House, PO Box 144, Kumasi, Ghana　　　　　　*Fax:* 051 24 117

LIBERIA
Bishop Rt Revd Edward Neufville, PO Box 10–0277, 1000 Monrovia 10, Liberia　　　　　　　*Fax:* 227 519

SEKONDI
Bishop Rt Revd Theophilus S. A. Annobil, PO Box 85, Sekondi, Ghana　　　　　　　*Fax:* 021 669 125

SUNYANI
Bishop Rt Revd Thomas Ampah Brient, PO Box 23, Sunyani, Ghana　　　　　　　　*Fax:* 061 7203
　　　　　　　　e-mail: Deegyab@IGHMail.Com

TAMALE
Bishop Rt Revd Emmanuel Arongo, PO Box 110, Tamale NR, Ghana　　　　　　　　　*Fax:* 071 22849

The Church in the Province of the West Indies

The West Indies became a self-governing province of the worldwide Anglican Communion in 1883. It comprises two mainland dioceses, one in Central and the other in South America, and six island dioceses. A ninth, Venezuela, was created in 1973, but left the province in 1982 to join the Ninth Province of ECUSA.

The dioceses are for the most part able to meet their recurrent expenditure, but rely to a large extent on aid from the Partner Churches and Missionary Societies for developmental work. Such help is likely to be needed for some time to come.

Two theological seminaries, Codrington College in Barbados and the United Theological College of the West Indies (UTCWI) in Jamaica, are being used to train personnel for an indigenous ministry. Great emphasis is being placed on this development, but there is still the need for expatriate clergy to help meet the staffing requirements in some of the dioceses. The idea of a supplementary or auxiliary ministry was introduced in the 1960s to help meet the demands of an expanding society.

With the exception of Trinidad and Guyana which have large Muslim and Hindu populations, West Indians are for the most part at least nominally Christian; and the phenomenon of island dioceses and the scattered nature of settlements make the provision of pastoral care in most cases both difficult and costly.

The Church in the West Indies was a part of the Church of England until it became a self-governing province and as such it was 'established'. Disestablishment came in most cases with self-government, but the Church has inherited an overall pastoral responsibility not unlike that of the Church of England. This has created a situation which severely taxes all available resources.

The fact that the province is self-governing and entirely free from outside administrative control gives the Church a strong advantage in the territories which have now achieved political independence. What the whole province now needs is a substantial increase in its resources to strengthen its witness and extend its mission, particularly in the light of the steady influx of fundamentalism from North America.

The province values the Partners-in-Mission exercise throughout the Anglican Communion and sees it as a real understanding of mutual sharing for the building up of the Church around the world.

In 1986 the Provincial Synod decided to set up a Secretariat in the See of the Archbishop. Consequently, the Provincial Secretariat was established in Antigua on

1 May 1987, with the appointment of the Administrative Assistant to the Archbishop.

Archbishop of the Province Most Revd Orland Lindsay (*Bishop of North Eastern Caribbean and Aruba*), Bishop's Lodge, PO Box 23, St John's, Antigua, WI   *Fax:* 462 2090
e-mail: diocesneca@candw.ag

Administrative Assistant to the Archbishop Mr O. W. Flax (*same address*)

Provincial Secretariat PO Box 23, St John's, Antigua, WI   *Fax:* 462 2090

Provincial Secretary Rt Revd Drexel Gomez (*Bishop of Nassau and the Bahamas*), PO Box N-7107, Nassau, Bahamas   *Fax:* 242 322 7943

THEOLOGICAL SEMINARIES
Codrington College, St John, Barbados (*Principal* Canon Noel Titus)

United Theological College of the West Indies, PO Box 136, Golding Ave, Kingston 7, Jamaica (*Anglican Warden* Canon Ralston (Roy) Smith)

BARBADOS
Bishop Rt Revd Rufus Theophilus Broome, Leland, Philip Drive, Pine Gardens, St Michael, Barbados
Fax: 426 0871
e-mail: mandeville@sunbeach.com

BELIZE
Bishop Rt Revd Sylvestre Donato Romero-Palma, Bishopsthorpe, PO Box 535, Southern Foreshore, Belize City, Belize   *Fax:* 02 76 898
e-mail: bzediocese@btl.net

GUYANA
Bishop Rt Revd Randolph George, Austin House, 49 High St, Georgetown 1, Guyana   *Fax:* 02 64 183

JAMAICA
Bishop Rt Revd Neville de Souza, Church House, 2 Caledonia Ave, Kingston 5, Jamaica   *Fax:* 968 0618

Bishops Suffragan
Rt Revd Herman Victor Spence (*Bishop of Kingston*) (*same address*)   *e-mail:* sspence@toj.com

Rt Revd William Arthur Murray (*Bishop of Mandeville*), PO Box 159, Mandeville, Jamaica   *Fax:* 962 3225

Rt Revd Alfred Charles Reid (*Bishop of Montego Bay*), PO Box 346, Montego Bay, St James, Jamaica

NASSAU AND THE BAHAMAS
Bishop Rt Revd Drexel W. Gomez, Addington House, PO Box N-7107, Nassau, Bahamas   *Fax:* 242 322–7943

NORTH EASTERN CARIBBEAN AND ARUBA
Bishop Most Revd Orland Lindsay (*Archbishop of the West Indies and Bishop of North Eastern Caribbean and Aruba*), Bishop's Lodge, PO Box 23, St John's, Antigua
Fax: 462 2090
e-mail: diocesneca@candw.ag

Bishop Coadjutor Rt Revd Leroy Errol Brooks (*same address*)   *Fax:* 264 497 3012

TRINIDAD AND TOBAGO
Bishop Rt Revd Rawle Douglin, Hayes Court, 21 Maraval Road, Port of Spain, Trinidad   *Fax:* 628 1319
e-mail: red@trinidad.net

WINDWARD ISLANDS
Bishop Rt Revd Sehon Goodridge, Bishop's Court, Montrose, PO Box 502, St Vincent   *Fax:* 809 456 2591

Other Churches and Extra-Provincial Dioceses

BERMUDA (Anglican Church of Bermuda)
This is an extra-provincial diocese under the metropolitical jurisdiction of the Archbishop of Canterbury.

Bishop Rt Revd Ewen Ratteray, Bishop's Lodge, PO Box HM 769, Hamilton HM CX, Bermuda   *Fax:* 441 296 0592

Diocesan Office PO Box HM 769, Hamilton HM CX, Bermuda   *Fax:* 441 292 5421

Archdeacon Ven Dr Arnold Hollis, Sandys Rectory, 3 Middle Rd, Somerset Bridge, Sandys SB-02
Fax: 441 234 2723

EPISCOPAL CHURCH OF CUBA
(Iglesia Episcopal de Cuba)
The Episcopal Church of Cuba is under a Metropolitan Council in matters of Faith and Order composed of the Primate of Canada, the Archbishop of the West Indies and the President-Bishop of the Episcopal Church's Province IX.

Bishop Rt Revd Jorge Perera Hurtado, Calle 6, No 273 Vedado, Habana 4, 10400 Cuba   *Fax:* 07 3332 93

THEOLOGICAL COLLEGE
Seminario Evangelico de Teologica, Aptdo. 149, Matan-

zas (Interdenominational, run in co-operation with the Methodist and Presbyterian Churches).

CHURCH PAPER
Heraldo Episcopal Published quarterly. Contains diocesan, provincial and world news, homiletics, devotional and historical articles.

FALKLAND ISLANDS

In 1977 the Archbishop of Canterbury resumed episcopal jurisdiction over the Falkland Islands and South Georgia which his predecessor, Dr Michael Ramsey, relinquished in 1974 in favour of CASA. The Archbishop of Canterbury (Most Revd George Carey) made his first pastoral visit to the Falklands in 1992 to celebrate the centenary of Christ Church Cathedral.

Rector Revd Alistair McHaffie, The Deanery, Stanley, Falkland Islands, South Atlantic   *Fax:* 010–500–21842
e-mail: deanery@horizon.co.uk

LUSITANIAN CHURCH
(Portuguese Episcopal Church)
Bishop Rt Revd Dr Fernando da Luz Soares, Secretaria Diocesana, Apartado 392, P-4430 Vila Nova de Gaia, Portugal   *Fax:* 351 2 3752016
e-mail: ilcae@mail.telepac.pt

The 'Lusitanian Church, Catholic Apostolic Evangelical', its full name, was organised at a Synod on 8 March 1880, presided over by Bishop Riley, who had just been consecrated Bishop for the Church in Mexico by the American Episcopal Church. The Synod consisted of Roman Catholic priests and chosen laymen, who because of doctrinal problems had left the Roman Church and had formed congregations in and around Lisbon, using a Portuguese translation of the 1662 English Prayer Book in their services. It was definitely stated at the Synod that they intended to continue faithful to Anglican Faith and Order. A Constitution was approved and Bishop Riley asked to present to the Anglican Episcopate their decisions and their wish to have a bishop.

Until 1958 the Lusitanian Church (Lusitania being the ancient name for what is now Portugal), never succeeded in having a bishop of its own. During these years a group of three bishops of the Church of Ireland had formed a 'Council of Bishops' which acted as a Metropolitical Authority and provided the necessary episcopal ministrations (confirmations and ordinations). This Council of Bishops was unofficial because the Church of Ireland as a Church was not involved in it, although the Irish Church Authorities raised no objections.

In the late 1950s the American Episcopal Church became interested in the Iberian Churches and a Lusitanian bishop was finally consecrated in 1958. In 1961, the American Church established a Concordat of full Communion with the Lusitanian Church under the terms of the 'Concordat of Bonn'. In 1963 it was followed by the Church of Ireland and the Church of England, and later on by many other provinces of the Anglican Communion.

The bishops of the Union of Utrecht (Old Catholic Communion) established a similar concordat, and two Old Catholic bishops took part with Anglican bishops in the consecration of the second Lusitanian bishop, the Rt Revd Dr Luis Pereira.

As a result of a 'Partners in Mission Consultation' for the Iberian Churches in March 1978, a recommendation was made that a formal application should be made to the Archbishop of Canterbury requesting integration into the Anglican Communion as a member of full right.

The subject was brought up by the Archbishop of Canterbury at the Primates' Committee during the 1978 Lambeth Conference when it was asked that a Commission should be appointed to study the subject. According to the report of this Commission, the Primates, at their meeting in November 1979, approved unanimously the integration of the Lusitanian Church as a member of full right of the Anglican Communion, and that it should be an extra-provincial diocese under the Metropolitical Authority of the Archbishop of Canterbury, in his capacity as the focus of unity of the Anglican Communion throughout the world, and as President of both the Lambeth Conference and of the Anglican Consultative Council.

The integration took effect on 5 July 1980, at St Paul's Cathedral, Lisbon when the Document of Integration was read by Dr Henry Chadwick (Chairman of the Commission) before being delivered into the hands of Bishop Pereira. The Archbishop of Canterbury was represented by Bishop John Howe, General Secretary of the Anglican Consultative Council.

Since 1991 the Lusitanian Church has been a co-opted member of the Anglican Consultative Council by invitation of the ACC's Standing Committee at its meeting in April 1991 in Ireland. The representative of the Lusitanian Church on that Council is the diocesan bishop, Rt Revd Dr Fernando Soares, who is now also a member of the ACC's Standing Committee.

SPANISH REFORMED EPISCOPAL CHURCH
Bishop Rt Revd Carlos López-Lozano, Beneficiencia 18, 28004 Madrid   *Fax:* 091 594 4572

This Church was built up, consciously seeking to follow the traditions of Anglican teaching and order, under the leadership of the former Roman Catholic priest Juan Bautista Cabrera. The Bishop of Mexico visited Spain in 1880 and accepted the congregations under his pastoral care. In 1894 Juan Bautista Cabrera was consecrated as the first bishop by the Bishop of Meath, in the Church of Ireland, which had agreed to accept metropolitan authority over the Church.

Following the report of a commission appointed by the Archbishop of Canterbury full communion between the Church of England and the Spanish Episcopal Reformed Church was established in 1963 by the Convocations of Canterbury and York.

In 1978 the Spanish Episcopal Reformed Church, together with the Lusitanian Church of Portugal, applied to the Archbishop of Canterbury for full integration into the Anglican Communion. A commission set up by the Primates' Committee under the chairmanship of the Revd Prof Henry Chadwick produced its report for the Archbishop of Canterbury in October 1979. It recommended that the request for full integration into the Anglican Communion be agreed to and that the Church should be an extra-provincial diocese under the Metropolitical Authority of the Archbishop of Canterbury. The Report was approved by the Archbishop of Canterbury and had the unanimous support of the Meeting of Anglican Primates in November 1979.

The inaugural service to effect the integration took place at the Cathedral Church in Madrid on 2 November 1980. The Archbishop of Canterbury was represented by Bishop Ross Hook, His Grace's Chief of Staff.

Regional Councils

CONFERENCE OF THE ANGLICAN PROVINCES OF AFRICA
At the Conference of the Anglican Archbishops of Africa in July 1977 it was decided to set up in its place the regional Conference of the Anglican Provinces of Africa. CAPA meets every two years and each province (Burundi, Rwanda, Zaïre, Central Africa, the Indian Ocean, Jerusalem and the Middle East, Kenya, Nigeria, Southern Africa, Sudan, Tanzania, Uganda and West Africa) is represented by its archbishop or his episcopal representative, one clergyman and one layperson. CAPA's purposes include conferring on matters concerning the Churches in the rapidly changing continent of Africa, sharing experience, and considering opportunities for joint and ecumenical action. CAPA's first meeting took place in September 1979 in Malawi and the second in Nairobi, Kenya in July 1987.

Chairman Rt Revd French Chang-Him (*Bishop of Seychelles*)

Secretary Revd Severin Ndayizeye, PO Box 20017, Nairobi, Kenya　　　　　　　　　　　　*Fax:* 2–714 750

THE SOUTH PACIFIC ANGLICAN COUNCIL
The Council now comprises the Province of Melanesia, the Province of Papua New Guinea, and the Diocese of Polynesia.

Chairman Rt Revd Elison Pogo (*Primate of the Church of Melanesia*), Archbishop's House, PO Box 19, Honiara, Solomon Islands　　　　　　　　　　　*Fax:* 21 098

Secretary Rt Revd Jabez Bryce (*Bishop of Polynesia*), PO Box 35, Suva, Fiji　　　　　　　　　　　*Fax:* 302 503

UNITED CHURCHES IN FULL COMMUNION

CHURCHES RESULTING FROM THE UNION OF ANGLICANS WITH CHRISTIANS OF OTHER TRADITIONS

The population of the countries of South Asia is over 1,000 million and these Churches cover the whole area. The total Christian population is around 22–23 million and Christians of many different traditions, ranging from ancient oriental to pentecostal, are to be found here.

The region is undergoing rapid social, economic and political change. There is also a resurgence of some of the great world religions. Although there is a great deal of industrialisation and there have been 'green revolutions' in the agricultural sector in many countries there is still a tremendous inequality in the distribution of wealth and income.

In spite of the relatively small numbers of Christians, the churches have grown steadily and have been responsible for many initiatives in education, medical work and community development. Their influence is out of all proportion to their size.

The Church of England continues to relate to these churches mainly through its mission agencies: CMS, USPG, SPCK and Crosslinks. In addition, the Oxford Mission, the Dublin University Mission to Chota Nagpur and the Religious Communities are doing valuable work. Support in money and personnel also comes from churches in Canada, from CMS in Australia and New Zealand, from the USA, Holland, Germany, Scandinavia, Japan and Singapore.

The Churches themselves are involved in the training and sending of mission personnel both inside and outside India, including the sending of mission partners to the UK.

Mission partners from the Church of England work under the authority of the local church or institution to which they have been sent.

The Church of North India, the Church of South India and Mar Thoma Syrian Church of Malenkara are in full communion with each other and are members of a joint council to further and deepen their unity.

Since 1988, these churches have become full members of the Lambeth Conference and the Anglican Consultative Council. Their moderators also attend the meetings of Anglican Primates.

The Church of Bangladesh

Originally the Church of Bangladesh was part of the Church of Pakistan. After independence in 1971 only one diocese, that of Dhaka, was left. More recently, the new diocese of Kushtia has been created. Total membership is approximately 13,000.

DHAKA
Bishop Most Revd Barnabas Dwijen Mondal (*Moderator COB*), St Thomas's Church, 54 Johnson Rd, Dhaka 1100
Fax: 02 238 218

THEOLOGICAL COLLEGE
St Andrew's Theological College, St Thomas's Church Compound, 54 Johnson Rd, Dhaka 1100, Bangladesh (*Principal* Revd Bart Baak)

KUSHTIA
Bishop Rt Revd Michael Baroi, Kushtia, Diocesan Office, 94 N S Rd, Thanapara, Kushtia

The Church of Ceylon

(Sri Lanka)

Ecumenical action takes two forms. One is collaborating with the National Christian Council in which the Anglicans, Methodists, Baptists, Dutch Reformed Church, the Salvation Army, the Church of South India (Jaffna diocese) and the Presbytery of Lanka are engaged. Closer contact with the Roman Catholic Church is also a possibility.

The mission outreach of the dioceses is progressing satisfactorily and with the rural deaneries renewed for action there are signs of growth both in depth and outreach.

The sad disturbances in the country that go on unabated leave much cause for deep sorrow. Movement in certain parts is quite difficult and the retarding of work from this cannot be ignored. Intense prayer and work for the removal of the present disputes and the restoration of reconciliation with justice and mercy are crying needs.

The Church meanwhile retains the title The Church of Ceylon and the two Anglican dioceses are:

COLOMBO
Bishop Rt Revd Kenneth Michael James Fernando, Bishop's House, 358/2 Bauddhaloka Mawatha, Colombo 7, Sri Lanka *Fax:* 01 684 811
e-mail: bishop@eureka.lk

KURUNAGALA
Bishop Rt Revd Andrew Kumarage, Bishop's House, Kandy Rd, Kurunagala, Sri Lanka *Fax:* 037 22 191

THEOLOGICAL COLLEGE
Theological College of Lanka, Pilimatalawa, nr Kandy, Sri Lanka

The Church of North India

The united Church of North India was inaugurated on 29 November 1970 after many years of prayerful preparation. Six churches joined the united Church. They were: the Church of India, Pakistan, Burma and Ceylon (Anglican); the United Church of Northern India (Presbyterian and Congregational); the Council of the Baptist Churches in Northern India; the Church of the Brethren; the Disciples of Christ; and the Methodist Church (British and Australasian Conferences). According to ACC records, the total membership is approximately 1,400,000.

The officers of the Synod of the Church of North India are:

Moderator Most Revd Dhirendra Kumar Mohanty (*Bishop of Cuttack*)

Deputy Moderator Rt Revd Vinod Peter (*Bishop of Nagpur*)

General Secretary Dr Vidya Sagar Lall, CN1, 16 Pandit Pant Marg, New Delhi 110 001

Treasurer Mr Enos Das Pradhan (*same address*)

CHURCH PAPER
The North India Church Review The official monthly magazine of the CNI. Contains articles, reports, diocesan news, world news and letters. *Editorial Office* 16 Pandit Pant Marg, New Delhi 110001

The dioceses in the CNI are:

AGRA
Bishop Rt Revd Morris Andrews, Bishop's House, St Paul's Church Compund, 4/116-B Church Rd, Civil Lines, Agra 282002 UP *Fax:* 0562 350244

AMRITSAR
Bishop Rt Revd Anand Chandu Lal, 26 R. B. Prakash Chand Rd, Amritsar 143001 *Fax:* 0183 222910

ANDAMAN AND NICOBAR ISLANDS
Bishop Rt Revd Edmund Matthew, Cathedral Church Compound, House No. 1, Staging Post, Car Nicobar, 744 301, Andaman and Nicobar Islands

BARRACKPORE
Bishop Rt Revd Brojen Malakar, Bishop's Lodge, 86 Middle Rd, Barrackpore 743101, W. Bengal

BHOPAL
Bishop Rt Revd Manohar Singh, 7 Old Sehore Rd, Indore, 452001 MP

BOMBAY
Bishop Rt Revd Baiju Gavit, St John's House, Duxbury Lane, Colaba, Bombay 400005 *Fax:* 022 206 0248

CALCUTTA
Bishop Rt Revd Dinesh Chandra Gorai, Bishop's House, 51 Chowringhee Rd, Calcutta, WB 700071
Fax: 033 2426340

CHANDIGARH
Bishop Rt Revd Joel Vidyasagar Mal, Bishop's House, Mission Compound, Brown Rd, Ludhiana, 141008 Punjab

CHOTA NAGPUR
Bishop Rt Revd Zechariah James Terom, Bishop's Lodge, PO Box 1, Church Rd, Ranchi, 834001 Bihar

CUTTACK
Bishop Most Revd Dhirendra Kumar Mohanty (*Moderator CNI*), Bishop's House, Madhusudan Rd, Cuttack 753 001, Orissa Fax: 0671 602 206

DELHI
Bishop Rt Revd Karam Masih, Bishop's House, 1 Church Lane, Off North Ave, New Delhi 110 001
e-mail: stmartin@del3.vsnl.net.in

DURGAPUR
Bishop Rt Revd Onil Kumar Tirkey, Bishop's House, PO Box No 20, S. E. Railway, Bankura 722 101, W. Bengal
Fax: 0343 5123

EASTERN HIMALAYAS
Bishop Rt Revd Gerald Andrews, Diocesan Centre, Gandhi Rd, Darjeeling 734 101, W. Bengal Fax: 0354 52 208

GUJARAT
Bishop Rt Revd Vinod Kumar Malaviya, Bishop's House, Ellis Bridge, Ahmedabad 380 006, Gujarat State
Fax: 0272 6561 950

JABALPUR
Bishop Rt Revd Sunil Cak, Bishop's House, 2131 Napier Town, Jabalpur, MP 482 001 Fax: 0761 322 109

KOLHAPUR
Bishop Rt Revd MacDonald Claudius, Bishop's House, EP School Compound, Kolhapur 416 003, Maharashtra
Fax: 0231 654 832

LUCKNOW
Bishop Rt Revd Anil Stephen, Bishop's House, 25 Mahatma Gandhi Marg, Allahabad, UP 211011
Fax: 0532 623 324

NAGPUR
Bishop Rt Revd Vinod Peter (*Deputy Moderator CNI*), Cathedral House, Civil Lines, Sadar, Nagpur 440 001, Maharashtra Fax: 0712 523 089

NASIK
Bishop Rt Revd George Ambatoo Ninan, Bishop's House, 1 Outram Rd, Tarakpur, Ahmednagar, 414 001 Maharashtra Fax: 0241 28 682

NORTH EAST INDIA
Bishop Rt Revd Purely Lyndoh, Bishop's Kuti, Shillong 1, Meghalaya 793 001 Fax: 0364 223 155

PATNA
Bishop Rt Revd Philip Phembuar Marandih, Bishop's House, Christ Church Compound, Bhagalpur 812 001, Bihar Fax: 0641 400 314

PHULBANI
Bishop-in-Charge Most Revd D. K. Mohanty (*Moderator CNI*), Mission Compound, POG, Udayagari, Dist Phulbani, Orissa 762 100

RAJASTHAN
Bishop Rt Revd Emmanual Christopher Anthony, 63/X, Savitri Girls' College Rd, Civil Lines, Ajmer 305 001, Rajasthan

SAMBALPUR
Bishop Rt Revd Lingaraj Tandy, Mission Compound, Balangir 767 001, Orissa

The Church of Pakistan

The united Church of Pakistan was inaugurated on 1 November (All Saints' Day) 1970. Four churches joined the united Church: the Church of India, Pakistan, Burma and Ceylon (Anglican); the United Methodist Church of two Conferences, the Indus River Conference and the Karachi Conference; the United Presbyterian Church in Pakistan, Sialkot Church Council in West Pakistan and Rajshahi Church Council in Bangladesh; Pakistan Lutheran Church. There are eight dioceses in the Church: Faisalabad, Hyderabad, Karachi, Lahore, Multan, Peshawar, Raiwind and Sialkot. According to ACC records, total membership is approximately 700,000.
The officers of the Synod of the Church of Pakistan are:

Moderator Rt Revd Samuel Azariah (*Bishop of Raiwind*)

Deputy Moderator Rt Revd John Samuel (*Bishop of Faisalabad*)

General Secretary Vacancy

Treasurer Sardar Hassan Ghauri, SAS Accountant, 26-Sarhad Colony, Ram Dass Gate, Peshawar, Pakistan

ARABIAN GULF
Bishop for Rt Revd Azad Marshall, PO Box 3192, Gulberg-1, Lahore, Punjab 54660 Fax: 042 5220 591

FAISALABAD
Bishop Rt Revd John Samuel (*Deputy Moderator COP*), Bishop's House, PO Box 27, Mission Rd, Gojra Distt Toba Tek Sing, Faisalabad   *Fax:* 0411 4651 274

HYDERABAD
Bishop Rt Revd S. K. Dass, 27 Liaquat Rd, Civil Lines, Hyderabad 71000, Sind   *Fax:* 0221 28 772
e-mail: hays@hyd.infolink.net.pk

KARACHI
Bishop Vacancy, Bishop's House, Trinity Close, Karachi 0405

LAHORE
Bishop Rt Revd Alexander John Malik, Bishopsbourne, Cathedral Close, The Mall, Lahore 54000
Fax: 042 722 1270

MULTAN
Bishop Rt Revd John Victor Mall, 113 Qasim Rd, PO Box 204, Multan Cantt

PESHAWAR
Bishop Rt Revd Munawar Kenneth Rumalshah, Diocesan Centre, 1 Sir-Syed Rd, Peshawar 25000, North West Frontier Province   *Fax:* 091 277 499

RAIWIND
Bishop Rt Revd Samuel Azariah (*Moderator COP*), 17 Warris Rd, PO Box 2319, Lahore 3, Pakistan
Fax: 042 757 7255

SIALKOT
Bishop Rt Revd Samuel Pervez Sant Masih, Lal Kothi, Barah Patthar, Sialkot 2, Punjab   *Fax:* 0432 264 828

The Church of South India

The Church of South India was inaugurated in September 1947, by the union of the South India United Church (itself a union of churches of the Congregational and Presbyterian/Reformed traditions), the four Southern dioceses of the Church of India, Burma and Ceylon (Anglican) and the Methodist Church in South India. The four Anglican dioceses were acting in accordance with the permission given by the General Council of the CIBC in 1945.

The basis of the Constitution of the Church of South India is the Lambeth Quadrilateral, the historical episcopate being accepted in a constitutional form. From 1947 all ordinations have been by bishops.

In the Basis of Union the uniting churches:

(i) acknowledged each other's ministries 'to be real ministries of the Word and Sacrament';
(ii) agreed that 'all the ministers of the uniting Churches will from the inauguration of the union be recognised as equally ministers of the united Church without distinction or difference';
(iii) accepted the rule that 'every ordination of presbyters shall be performed by the laying on of hands of the bishops and presbyters, and all consecrations of bishops shall be performed by the laying on of hands at least of three bishops'.

Resolutions of the Lambeth Conference of 1968 and the Anglican Consultative Council of 1971 advised Anglican Churches and provinces to re-examine their relation to the Church of South India with a view to entering into full communion with that Church.

In July 1972 the General Synod reconsidered the relations between the Church of England and the Church of South India. The General Synod passed the following resolution:

'This Synod, recognising that the Church of South India is an episcopally ordered Church and believing it to hold all the essentials of the Christian Faith, requests the House of Bishops to consider how the Church of England and the Church of South India can now be joined in a relationship of full communion.'

The General Synod also gave provisional approval to certain amendments to the resolutions about the Church of South India which had been passed by the Convocations in 1955. Following the passing of Canon B15A the General Synod proposed the repeal of two of the 1955 resolutions which concerned members of the Church of South India communicating in the Church of England. The General Synod also proposed the removal of the clause in the 1955 resolutions which permitted bishops or episcopally ordained presbyters of the Church of South India to celebrate the Holy Communion in a church of the Church of England only if they were willing to celebrate exclusively in Anglican churches.

The main limitation which now remains on establishing closer relations with the Church of South India is that the four presbyters of that Church who have not been episcopally ordained cannot celebrate the Holy Communion, or hold office, in the Church of England without amendment to the Act of Uniformity, the Preface of the Ordinal and the Canons. The Church of South India has a few women presbyters.

According to the ACC, total membership is 2 million.

The main mission agencies in Great Britain support work in the Church of South India. Further information on the Church of South India will be given on application to the Friends of the Church in India, Hon Secretary (UK),

Revd Barrie Scopes/Mrs Joy Martin, and Treasurer, Revd Charles Watson, c/o Livingstone House, 12 Carteret St, London SW1H 9DL.

The officers of the Synod of the Church of South India are:

Moderator Most Revd Vasant P. Dandin (*Bishop in Karnataka North*) *Fax:* 044 852 3528

Deputy Moderator Rt Revd William Moses (*Bishop in Coimbatore*)

Hon Treasurer Mr Frederick William, CSI Centre, 5 Whites Rd, Royapettah, Madras 600041, S India

General Secretary Prof George Koshy (*same address*)

CHURCH PAPERS
The South India Churchman Monthly. Contains articles, reports and news from the dioceses. *Editor* CSI Communications Dept, 1–2–288/31 Damalguda, Hyderabad, 29, AP, India; *Agent in UK* Mrs D. Elton, The Rectory, Great Ellingham, Norfolk NR17 1LD. Subscription £1.00 per annum.
Pilgrim Published by The Friends of the Church in India (London) in Feb and Aug. Subscription (minimum) 50p per annum. Contains news, letters from CSI and CNI and prayer topics.

COIMBATORE
Bishop in Rt Revd William Moses (*Deputy Moderator CSI*), Bishop's House, Coimbatore 641018, T N 1
Fax: 044 852 3528

DORNAKAL
Bishop in Rt Revd Rajarathnam Allu, Bishop's House, Cathedral Compound, Dornakal, Andhra Pradesh 506 381

EAST KERALA
Bishop in Rt Revd Joseph Samuel Kunnumpurathu, Bishop's House, Melukavumattom P.O. Kottayam 686 652, Kerala State *Fax:* 0482 291 044

JAFFNA
Bishop in Rt Revd Dr Subramaniam Jabanesan, Bishop's House, 39 Fussels Lane, Colombo 6, Sri Lanka
Fax: 01 584 836

KANYAKUMARI
Bishop in Rt Revd Messiadhas Kesari, CSI Diocesan Office, 71A Dennis St, Nagercoil 629 001
Fax: 04652 31 295

KARIMNAGAR
Bishop in Rt Revd Sanki John Theodore, Bishop's House, PO Box 40, Karimnagar 505 001, Andhra Pradesh

KARNATAKA CENTRAL
Bishop in Rt Revd Vasanthkumar Suputhrappa, Diocesan Office, 20 Third Cross, CSI Compound, Bangalore 560 027, Karnataka

KARNATAKA NORTH
Bishop in Rt Revd Dr Vasant P. Dandin (*Moderator CSI*), Bishop's House, Haliyal Rd, Dharwad 508 008, Karnataka State *Fax:* 044 852 3528

KARNATAKA SOUTH
Bishop in Rt Revd Christopher Lazarus Furtado, Bishop's House, Balmatta, Mangalore 575 001 *Fax:* 0824 425 042

KRISHNA-GODAVARI
Bishop in Rt Revd Prakasa Rao Babu Deva Thumaty, Bishop's House, Bishop Azariah High School Compound, Vijayawada, 520010 AP *Fax:* 0866 476 007

MADHYA KERALA
Bishop in Rt Revd Sam Mathew Valiyathottathil, Bishop's House, Cathedral Rd, Kottayam 686 001, Kerala State

MADRAS
Bishop in Rt Revd Masilamani Azariah, Diocesan Office, PO Box 4914, 226 Cathedral Rd, Madras 600 086, Tamil Nadu *Fax:* 044 827 0608

MADURAI-RAMNAD
Bishop in Rt Revd Thavaraj David Eames, CSI New Mission Compound, Thirumangalam 625 706, Madurai District, Tamil Nadu

MEDAK
Bishop in Rt Revd Badda Peter Sugandhar, Bishop's Annexe, 145 MacIntyre Rd, Secunderabad 500 003, Andhra Pradesh *Fax:* 040 867297

NANDYAL
Bishop in Vacancy, Bishop's House, Nandyal RS, Kurnool Dist AP 518502 *Fax:* 08514 42 255

NORTH KERALA
Bishop in Rt Revd P. G. Kuruvilla, Diocesan Office, PO Box 104, Shoranur 679 121 Kerala State

RAYALASEEMA
Bishop in Rt Revd Chowtipalli Bellam Moses Fredrick, Bishop's House, CSI Compound, Gooty, Andhra Pradesh 515 401

SOUTH KERALA
Bishop in Rt Revd John Wilson Gladstone, Bishop's House, LMS Compound, Trivandrum 695 033, Kerala State *Fax:* 0471 316 439

TIRUNELVELI
Bishop in Rt Revd Jason S. Dharmaraj, Bishopstowe, Box 18, Palayamkottai, Tirunelveli 627 002, Tamil Nadu
Fax: 0462 574 525

TRICHY-TANJORE
Bishop in Rt Revd Daniel James Srinivasan, PO Box 31, 8 V.O.C. Rd, Tiruchirapalli 620 001, Tamil Nadu

VELLORE
Bishop in Rt Revd R. Trinity Bhaskeran, Ashram Bungalow, 13 Filterbed Rd, Vellore, N Arcot Dt. 632 001
Fax: 01416 27490

Bishops without diocesan charge Rt Revd C. S. Sundaresan, c/o CSI Synod Office; Rt Revd Pereji Solomon, c/o The Bishop of the Dornakal Diocese; Rt Revd C. Selvamony; Rt Revd B. Prabhudas; Rt Revd G. B. Devasahayam; Rt Revd G. S. Luke; Rt Revd W. V. Karl; Rt Revd K. E. Gill; Rt Revd B. G. Prasada Rao; Rt Revd T. B. Benjamin; Rt Revd N. D. Ananda Rao Samuel; Rt Revd S. Daniel Abraham; Rt Revd Dr Sundar Clarke; Rt Revd Dr M. C. Mani; Rt Revd P. John; Rt Revd Sam Ponniah; Rt Revd K.C. Seth; Rt Revd I. Jesudasan; Rt Revd K. Michael John; Rt Revd Dr P. Victor Premasagar; Rt Revd K. E. Swamidas; Rt Revd H. S. Thanaraj; Rt Revd D. Pothirajulu; Rt Revd L. V. Azariah

Note: The bishops in the Church of South India are designated as 'The Rt Revd the Bishop in –' *not* 'of' and sign with their individual names.

THE HOLY CATHOLIC CHURCH IN CHINA

(Chung Hua Sheng Kung Hui)

The Chung Hua Sheng Kung Hui was an important denomination in China and its history dates back to the mid-nineteenth century. Today the CHSKU, as a separate denomination, no longer exists in the People's Republic of China, except for Hong Kong which returned to Chinese sovereignty on 1 July 1997. Under the formula 'one country – two systems' Hong Kong keeps its autonomy for 50 years, including the religious situation. The same will apply to Macao which will be returned by Portugal to China in 1999.

On the Chinese mainland the Protestant churches, with few exceptions, have entered into a post-denominational phase under the China Christian Council. A united church is in the process of being created and Christians of Anglican inspiration are very much a part of this process. Bishops K. H. Ting and Stephen Wang, now in their old age, are retiring from active leadership of the China Christian Council.

Although the CHSKU does not exist any more, many former Anglicans still share a strong spiritual affinity with other Anglican Churches on matters of belief and liturgical tradition. As the Chinese Protestant Church develops its own ecclesiology and forms of worship, the Anglican traditions will no doubt contribute to a richer synthesis.

The Chung Hua Sheng Kung Hui owes its beginnings to the prayers and the men and women of six member Churches of the Anglican Communion:

1. The American Church, through its Department of Missions: work was begun in 1844, when the first bishop, Wm J. Boone, arrived in Shanghai, commissioned as 'Bishop of China'. The work extended up the valley of the Yangtze River, and three dioceses were founded, Kiangsu, Hankow and Anking.
2. The Church of England, through its missionary societies:
   (*a*) The CMS also began work in 1844, and in 1849 George Smith was consecrated Bishop of Victoria, Hong Kong, with jurisdiction over all British Anglican work in China and Japan. CMS did most of its work south of the Yangtze, and the Dioceses of Victoria, Hong Kong; Fukien; Chekiang; Kwangsi-Hunan; Yun-Kwei; and Szechwan were founded, the last being subsequently divided into the Dioceses of Eastern and Western Szechwan.
   (*b*) The Society for the Propagation of the Gospel in Foreign Parts in 1874 opened work in northern China, and the Dioceses of North China and Shantung were founded.
   (*c*) The Church of England Zenana Mission worked in several CMS dioceses, and the BCMS later opened work in the south and west.
   (*d*) The Anglican portion of the China Inland Mission worked in East Szechwan.
3. The Church of England in Canada, through its Missionary Society, founded the Diocese of Honan in 1909.
4. The Church of Ireland, through the Dublin University Mission, worked in association with the CMS in Fukien.
5. and 6. The Churches of Australia and New Zealand, through their Boards of Mission, worked in association with the Dioceses of Shantung and North China respectively. The CMS of Australia and Tasmania also worked in a number of dioceses.

Shensi, established in 1934 as the missionary diocese of the CHSKH, later became one of the fourteen regular dioceses of the Church.

In 1912 eleven dioceses were in being and in that year was held the first General Synod, with its House of Bishops and House of Delegates (clerical and lay). The Constitution was approved in 1915; and three years later came the election, confirmation and consecration of the first Chinese bishop, T. S. Sing, as Assistant Bishop of Chekiang. Additions to the Chinese episcopate followed, until by 1947 the majority of the House of Bishops were Chinese.

At the General Synod in that year the Rt Revd Lindel Tsen was elected Chairman of the House of Bishops, and after his resignation because of ill-health the Rt Revd Chen Chien-tsun was elected in his place.

In 1949 the People's Republic of China was established in Beijing and it became obvious that western missionaries were no longer a help to the Chinese Church in the new situation. In 1950 there was a general withdrawal which included the remaining western bishops. They were replaced by Chinese colleagues who were elected and consecrated according to the Canons of the CHSKU. The Anglican Church in China, with most of the other

[Note: For the sake of continuity, the Wade-Giles romanization for Chinese localities and dioceses is retained for this historical section. The new system of pin-yin for Chinese names will be used for the period after 1949.]

churches in that country, adopted the principles of the Three-Self Movement – self-support, self-government and self-propagation. The old diocese of Victoria, Hong Kong was divided into South China and Hong Kong and Macao, which for the time being is associated with the Council of the Churches of South East Asia.

After the establishment of the People's Republic, contacts with the churches outside China became few and sporadic. Nevertheless, between 1955 and 1963 there were a limited number of visits in both directions. Outstanding among these were the visits of Bishop K. H. Ting of Chekiang to England in 1956; and in the same year visits to China of the Bishop of Hong Kong and subsequently of a delegation from the Australian Church led by the late Primate of Australia, the Most Revd H. W. K. Mowll.

With the outbreak of the Great Proletarian Cultural Revolution in China in 1966, contacts with churches outside China became very difficult. All the churches were closed and most church leaders were imprisoned or sent to work in factories or in the countryside. It was only after the death of Mao Zedong in 1976 and the downfall of the extreme left that organised religious activities returned to normal. In 1979 churches began to reopen and in 1980 the National Christian Conference was held. Besides the reconstituting of the Three-Self Movement, a significant new development was the creation of the China Christian Council to take charge of the internal affairs of the Church. In the mid-1980s the China Christian Council decided the time was ripe to take a new ecumenical step forward and declared that the Protestant Church in China had entered a post-denominational phase although a few churches remained outside and the process did not involve the Roman Catholic Church.

The Church in China has gone through a period which can only be described as an experience of death and resurrection. In spite of the sufferings and difficulties the number of Christians is greater than ever before. In 1949 there were 700,000 Protestant Christians and three million Roman Catholics. The official figure today is ten million plus Protestants and six million Catholics; other estimates put the figure much higher. Under the direction of the China Christian Council more than 30,000 churches and meeting points are now open for worship. More than ten million Bibles have been printed, not only in Chinese but also in a few ethnic languages. Some 2,000 students have graduated from 13 theological training centres and about 1,000 are currently in ministerial training. The Nanjing Theological Seminary has a graduate school which trains teachers in theology; a new Centre for Theological Research was established in 1996, and sends out more than 30,000 copies of a bi-monthly set of training materials for the use of volunteer evangelists.

International relationships have also been established. Bishop K. H. Ting visited the USA and Canada in 1979. A Chinese Christian delegation, composed of Catholics and Protestants, took part in the first Christian conference on China in Montreal in 1980. In 1981 Bishop Ting and others attended a conference in Hong Kong sponsored by the Christian Conference of Asia during which they were able to be present at the consecration of the new Anglican Bishop of Hong Kong, Peter Kwong.

This was followed by many mutual visits including the churches in Britain. In October 1982 a Chinese delegation visited Britain and Ireland at the invitation of the British Council of Churches. Lord Runcie, the Archbishop of Canterbury at the time, made a private visit to China in the same year, and in December 1983 he led a BCC delegation of 20 representatives of the British churches to China. The present Archbishop of Canterbury, Dr George Carey, visited China in 1994 and other bishops in 1995 and 1996. Chinese bishops were also invited to the Lambeth Conference.

The Council of Churches for Britain and Ireland, taking over from the British Council of Churches, continue to develop the relations with China. Regular exchanges take place. Those worth mentioning include delegations of women's groups, youth groups, theological students as well as theological educators. The British and Irish churches also co-operate with the Amity Foundation, a church-sponsored development agency, in areas of social service, rural development and English-language teaching. Every year several Amity English teachers are sent to various colleges in China. Since 1996 a British person has been seconded to the Hong Kong office of the Amity Foundation.

The suppression of the pro-democracy movement in June 1989 has cast a shadow on this encouraging development. Other factors, such as the perceived threat from the fast growth of the Christian churches and the collapse of Marxist regimes in Eastern Europe and Russia, contribute to a tighter policy of political and ideological control. Religious freedom is generally respected but the practical implementation of religious policy is governed by a stricter set of regulations. Non-official groups are under pressure to accept the regulations.

The relations between the Church in China and the churches in the UK are facilitated by the China Department of the Churches' Commission for Mission. The latter is a section of the Council of Churches of Britain and Ireland (CCBI). The China Department is a continuation of the ecumenical *China Study Project* which was established in 1972 by the leading missionary societies, including Anglican organisations such as the CMS, USPG and the Archbishop's China Appeal Fund. In 1987 it was integrated into the British Council of Churches. The latter passed a resolution in 1988 and appealed to its member churches to respond ecumenically to the post-denominational challenge of the Protestant Church in China by renouncing bilateral relations with China on

The Holy Catholic Church in China

a denominational basis. This challenge has taken on a new dimension since the Roman Catholic Church of England, Wales and Scotland joined the CCBI in 1990.

The Friends of the Church in China, an ecumenical association which works closely with the China Department of CCBI, takes a more grassroots approach in relation to Christians in China. It publishes a popular newssheet on China and organises a yearly visit to Chinese churches.

China Department/CCBI, Inter-Church House, 35–41 Lower Marsh, London SE1 7RL. *Tel:* 0171–620 4444. The Secretary is Mr Edmond Tang.

Friends of the Church in China, 49 Pages Lane, Muswell Hill, London N10 1QB. Its Chairman is Dr Martin Conway and the Secretary is the Revd David Mullins.

OTHER CHURCHES IN COMMUNION WITH THE CHURCH OF ENGLAND

Old Catholic Churches of the Union of Utrecht

The Old Catholic Churches are a family of nationally organised churches which bound themselves together in the Union of Utrecht in 1889. Most of them owe their origin to Roman Catholics who were unable to accept the decrees of the First Vatican Council in 1870 and left the communion of that Church. The Archbishopric of Utrecht (from which the other Old Catholic Churches derived their episcopal orders) has been independent of Rome since the eighteenth century following a complex dispute involving papal and capitular rights of nomination and accusations of Jansenism. For many years the Latin Mass continued in use, though all the Old Catholic Churches now worship in the vernacular. Their rites stand within the Western tradition, though with various 'Eastern' features.

By the acceptance of the Bonn Agreement on 20 and 22 January 1932, the Convocation of Canterbury established full communion with the Old Catholic Churches by means of the following resolutions:

'That this House approves of the following statements agreed on between the representatives of the Old Catholic Churches and the Churches of the Anglican Communion at a Conference held at Bonn on 2 July 1931:

1. Each Communion recognises the catholicity and independence of the other and maintains its own.
2. Each Communion agrees to admit members of the other Communion to participate in the Sacraments.
3. Intercommunion does not require from either Communion the acceptance of all doctrinal opinion, sacramental devotion, or liturgical practice characteristic of the other, but implies that each believes the other to hold all the essentials of the Christian Faith.

'And this House agrees to the establishment of Intercommunion between the Church of England and the Old Catholics on these terms.'

An Anglican–Old Catholic International Coordinating Council has been established.

AUSTRIA
Bishop Rt Revd Bernhard Heitz, Schottenring 17/1/3/12, A–1010 Vienna

CROATIA
(Bishopric vacant)

CZECH REPUBLIC
Bishopric Rt Revd Dusan Hagbol, Cirkve Starokatolicke V CSFR, Hladkor 3, CZ–16900, Prague 6

GERMANY
Bishop Rt Revd Joachim Vobbe, Gregor Mendelstrasse 28, 53115 Bonn, Germany

NETHERLANDS
Archbishop Most Revd Antonius Jan Glazemaker (Archbishop of Utrecht and President of the International Bishops' Conference), Kon Wilhelminalaan, 3, NL–3818HN Amersfoort

POLAND (The Polish National Catholic Church)
Prime Bishop Most Revd Wiktor Wysoczanski, ul. Balanowa 7, PL-02–635 Warsaw

SWITZERLAND
Bishop Rt Revd Hans Gerny, Willadingweg 39, CH–3006 Bern

USA (Polish National Catholic Church of America and Canada)
Prime Bishop Most Revd John Swantek, 115 Lake Scranton Rd, Scranton PA18505, USA

Philippine Independent Church

The Philippine Independent Church is in part the result of the Philippine revolution against Spain in 1896 for religious emancipation and Filipino identity. It was formally established in 1902, declaring its independence from the Roman Catholic Church but seeking to remain loyal to the Catholic Faith. It now derives its succession from the Protestant Episcopal Church in the United States of America (and therefore from Anglican sources), with which full communion was established in September 1961.

It has a membership of approximately four million followers, 28 dioceses with 50 bishops, 600 regular church

Other Churches in Communion

buildings and 2,000 village chapels served by about 600 priests.

Following the report of a Commission appointed by the Archbishop of Canterbury, full communion on the basis of the Bonn Agreement was established between the Church of England and the Philippine Independent Church in 1963 by the Convocations of Canterbury and York. It is in full communion with all the member Churches in the Anglican Communion.

The Philippine Independent Church is very active in its ecumenical relations. It is the most senior member in the National Council of the Churches in the Philippines, a member of the Council of Churches in East Asia, a member of the Christian Churches in Asia, and ar active member of the World Council of Churches.

Supreme Bishop (*Obispo Maximo*) Most Revd Alberto Ramento, 1500 Taft Avenue, Ermita, Manila, Philippines 2801

Mar Thoma

During the latter part of the nineteenth century the Syrian Orthodox Church of Malabar divided into two over the issues of autonomy from the Patriarchate of Antioch and the removal of non-biblical features from teaching and worship, the latter issue being a result of the influence of Anglican missionaries of the Church Missionary Society who had been working in Malabar since the beginning of the century. The larger section (which itself has subsequently divided into the Indian Orthodox and Jacobite Churches) chose closer links with Antioch and remained 'unreformed'; the smaller group which eventually adopted the name of Mar Thoma Syrian Church of Malabar rejected Patriarchal authority and undertook a conservative revision of its rites, removing elements (such as the invocation of saints) which were felt not to be scriptural in origin. The general form of Mar Thoma worship remains Orthodox. Its episcopal succession derives from the Patriarchate of Antioch.

The former CIPBC (Church of India, Pakistan, Burma and Ceylon) had partial intercommunion with the Mar Thoma Church from 1937 until 1961 when a Concordat of Full Communion was established. The Mar Thoma Church is now in full communion with the united churches in India and Pakistan. With the Church of South India and the Church of North India it has formed a Joint Council to facilitate co-operation in mission and theological and social issues. The Mar Thoma Church has stated its desire to preserve its eastern traditions and is not willing to merge with the two western-derived united churches. Several Anglican provinces have recently entered into a relationship of full communion with the Mar Thoma Church, and others are in the process of doing so. The Church of England established communion with the Mar Thoma Church in 1974.

In 1989 the Metropolitan of the Malabar Independent Syrian Church of Thozhiyoor (a small 'unreformed' Syrian Orthodox Church in communion with the Mar Thoma Church) visited England and expressed his willingness to extend eucharistic hospitality to members of the Church of England.

THE MAR THOMA SYRIAN CHURCH
Most Revd Dr Alexander Mar Thoma
Metropolitan
Poolatheen
Tiruvalla 689 101
Kerala
South India

THE MALABAR INDEPENDENT SYRIAN CHURCH
Most Revd Joseph Mar Koorilose
Thozhiyur
680 520 Trichur (Dt)
Kerala
South India

Maps of the Churches and Provinces of the Anglican Communion

MAPS

1. The Church of **England**; The Church of **Ireland**
   The **Scottish** Episcopal Church; The Church in **Wales**

2. The Anglican Church of **Australia**
   The Anglican Church of **Papua New Guinea**

3. The Anglican Church in **Aotearoa, New Zealand and Polynesia**
   The Church of the Province of **Melanesia**

4 & 5. The Episcopal Church in the **United States of America**
   The Anglican Church of the **Central American Region**
   The Episcopal Anglican Church of **Brazil**; The Episcopal Church of **Cuba**;
   The Church in the Province of the **West Indies**; The Anglican Church of **Mexico**
   The Anglican Church of the **Southern Cone of America**

6. The Anglican Church of **Canada**

7. The Church of the Province of **Central Africa**
   The Church of the Province of the **Indian Ocean**
   The Church of the Province of **Southern Africa**

8. Anglican Church of **Kenya**
   Anglican Church of **Tanzania**

9. The Church of the Province of **Burundi**
   The Church of the Province of **Rwanda**
   The Church of the Province of the **Sudan**
   The Church of the Province of **Uganda**
   The Church of the Province of **Congo**

10. The Church of the Province of **Nigeria**

11. Anglican Communion **Japan**
    The Episcopal Church in **Jerusalem and the Middle East**
    The Church of the Province of **West Africa**

12. The Church of **North India**; The Church of **South India**
    The Church of **Pakistan**; The Church of **Ceylon**
    The Church of **Bangladesh**

13. The Anglican Church of **Korea**; The Church of the Province of **Myanmar**
    The Episcopal Church in the **Philippines**
    The Church of the Province of **South East Asia**
    Hong Kong Sheng Kung Hui

The maps of the Anglican Communion which follow have been supplied by Barbara Lawes of The Mothers' Union. She will be happy to hear of any changes which need to be made.

© *The Mothers' Union 1998*

Maps of the Anglican Communion

MAP 1

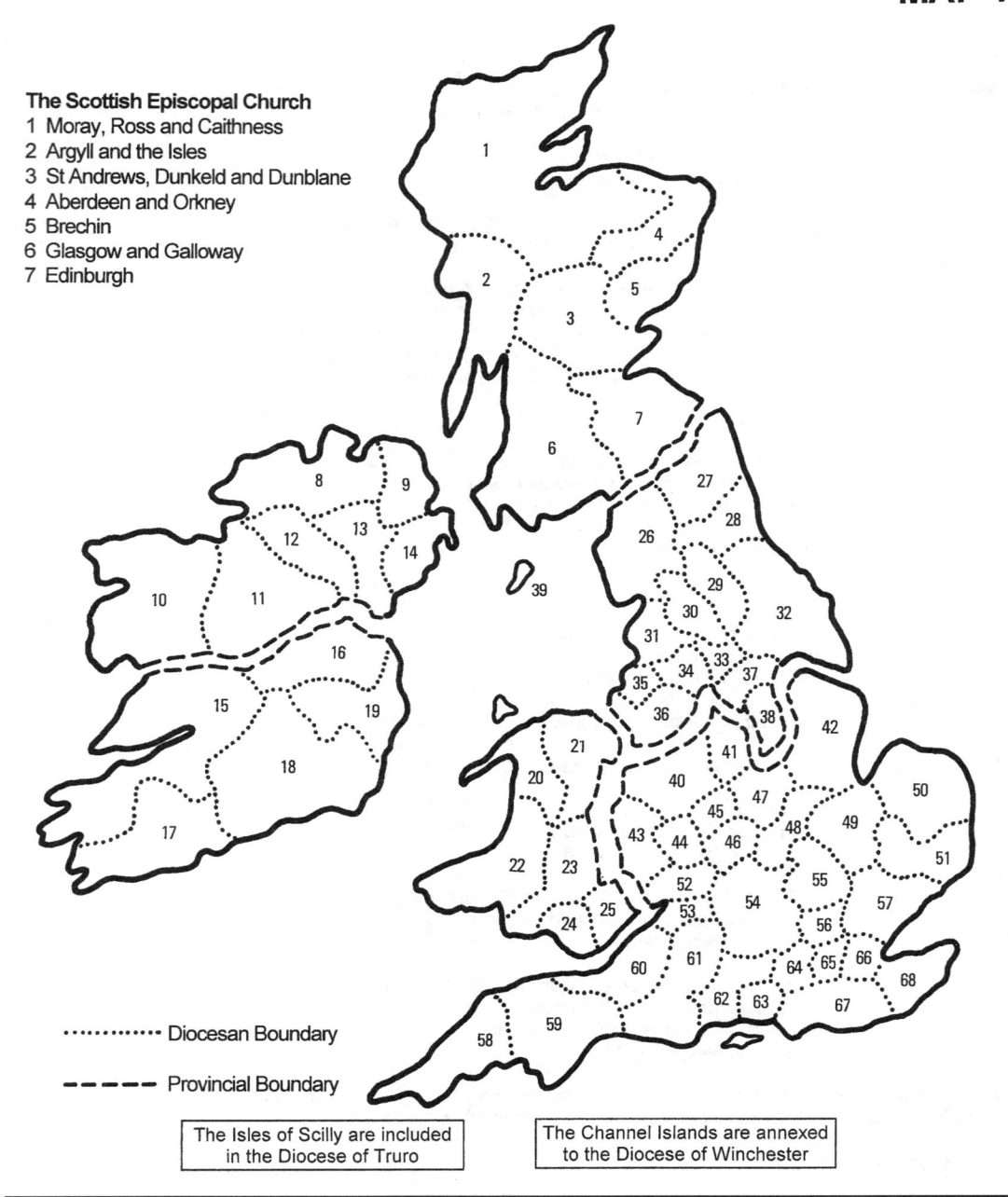

The Scottish Episcopal Church
1. Moray, Ross and Caithness
2. Argyll and the Isles
3. St Andrews, Dunkeld and Dunblane
4. Aberdeen and Orkney
5. Brechin
6. Glasgow and Galloway
7. Edinburgh

.... Diocesan Boundary

– – – – – Provincial Boundary

| The Isles of Scilly are included in the Diocese of Truro | The Channel Islands are annexed to the Diocese of Winchester |

338 Anglican and Porvoo Communions

The Church of Ireland
Province of Armagh
8 Derry and Raphoe
9 Connor
10 Tuam, Killala and Achonry
11 Kilmore, Elphin and Ardagh
12 Clogher
13 Armagh
14 Down and Dromore

Province of Dublin
15 Limerick and Killaloe
16 Meath and Kildare
17 Cork, Cloyne and Ross
18 Cashel and Ossory
19 Dublin and Glendalough

The Church in Wales
20 Bangor
21 St Asaph
22 St Davids
23 Swansea and Brecon
24 Llandaff
25 Monmouth

The Church of England
Province of York
26 Carlisle
27 Newcastle
28 Durham
29 Ripon
30 Bradford
31 Blackburn
32 York
33 Wakefield
34 Manchester
35 Liverpool
36 Chester
37 Sheffield
38 Southwell
39 Sodor and Man

Province of Canterbury
40 Lichfield
41 Derby
42 Lincoln
43 Hereford
44 Worcester
45 Birmingham
46 Coventry
47 Leicester
48 Peterborough
49 Ely
50 Norwich
51 St Edmundsbury and Ipswich
52 Gloucester
53 Bristol
54 Oxford
55 St Albans
56 London
57 Chelmsford
58 Truro
59 Exeter
60 Bath and Wells
61 Salisbury
62 Winchester
63 Portsmouth
64 Guildford
65 Southwark
66 Rochester
67 Chichester
68 Canterbury
Diocese in Europe

Extra - Provincial Dioceses
Bermuda
Lusitanian Church
Spanish Reformed Episcopal Church

Falkland Islands

Maps of the Anglican Communion

MAP 2

PAPUA NEW GUINEA

The Anglican Church of Australia

Province of Western Australia
1 North West Australia
2 Perth
3 Bunbury

Province of South Australia
4 Willochra
5 Adelaide
6 The Murray

Province of Queensland
7 The Northern Territory
8 North Queensland
9 Rockhampton
10 Brisbane

Province of New South Wales
11 Riverina
12 Bathurst
13 Armidale
14 Grafton
15 Newcastle
16 Sydney
17 Canberra and Goulburn

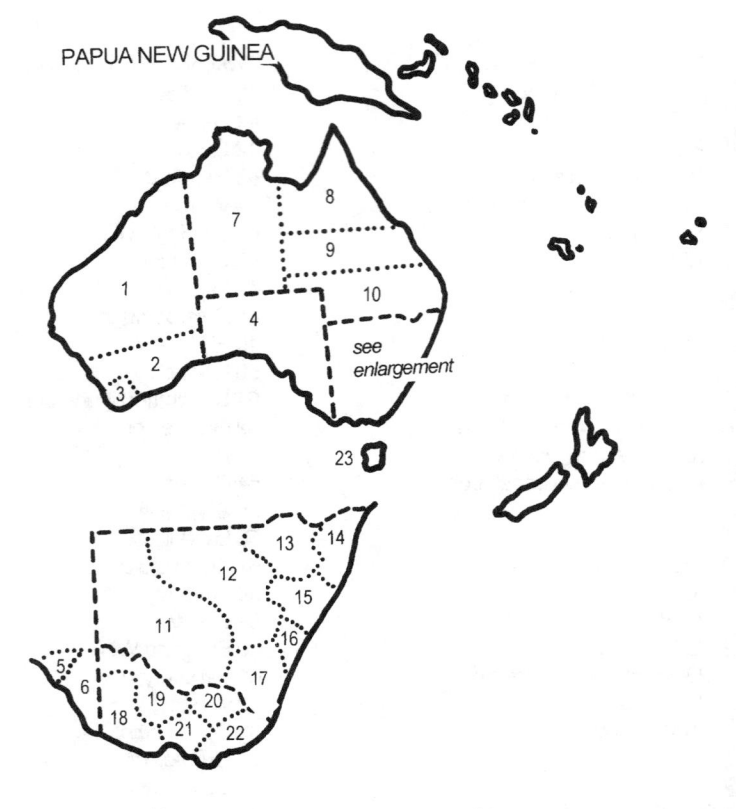

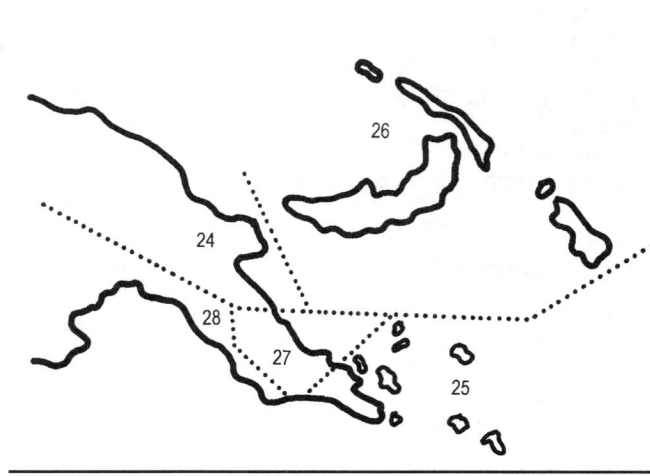

Province of Victoria
18 Ballarat
19 Bendigo
20 Wangaratta
21 Melbourne
22 Gippsland

23 Tasmania *(extra-provincial)*

The Anglican Church of Papua New Guinea
24 Aipo Rongo
25 Dogura
26 New Guinea Islands
27 Popondota
28 Port Moresby

MAP 3

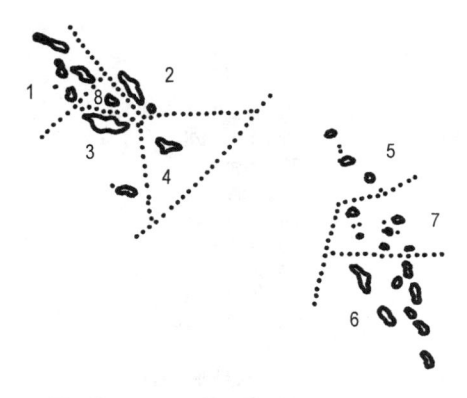

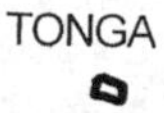

FIJI

TONGA

The Province of Melanesia
1. Ysabel
2. Malaita
3. Central Melanesia
4. Hanuato'o
5. Temotu
6. Vanuatu
7. Banks and Torres
8. Central Solomons

The Province of Aotearoa, New Zealand and Polynesia
9. Auckland
10. Waikato
11. Waiapu
12. Wellington
13. Nelson
14. Christchurch
15. Dunedin
16. Polynesia

Bishopric of Aotearoa
A. Hui Amorangi ki te Tai Tokerau
B. Hui Amorangi ki te Manawa o te Wheke
C. Hui Amorangi ki te Tairawhiti
D. Hui Amorangi ki te Upoko o te Ika
E. Hui Amorangi ki te Waipounamu

— · — · — Bishopric of Aotearoa

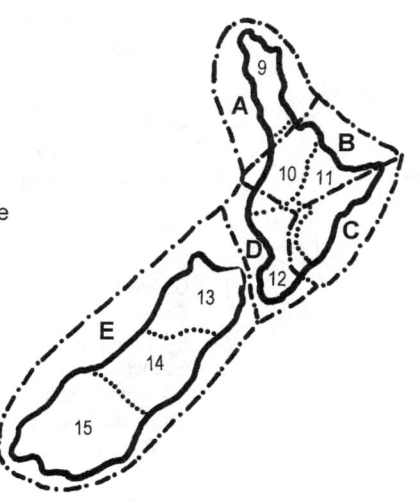

ANGLICAN AND PORVOO COMMUNIONS

Maps of the Anglican Communion

The Episcopal Church of the United States of America

Province I
1 Connecticut
2 Maine
3 Massachusetts
4 New Hampshire
5 Rhode Island
6 Vermont
7 Western Massachusetts

Province II
8 Albany
9 Central New York
10 Long Island
11 New Jersey
12 New York
13 Newark
14 Rochester
15 Western New York
Haiti (*see map 5*)
Virgin Islands (*see map 5*)
Convocation of American Churches in Europe

Province III
16 Bethlehem
17 Central Pennsylvania
18 Delaware
19 Easton
20 Maryland
21 Northwestern Pennsylvania
22 Pennsylvania
23 Pittsburgh
24 Southern Virginia
25 Southwestern Virginia
26 Virginia
27 Washington
28 West Virginia

Province IV
29 Alabama
30 Atlanta
31 Central Florida
32 Central Gulf Coast
33 East Carolina
34 East Tennessee
35 Florida
36 Georgia
37 Kentucky
38 Lexington
39 Louisiana
40 Mississipi
41 North Carolina
42 South Carolina
43 Southeast Florida
44 Southwest Florida
45 Tennessee
46 Upper South Carolina
47 West Tennessee
48 Western North Carolina

Province V
49 Chicago
50 Eau Claire
51 Fond du Lac
52 Indianapolis
53 Michigan
54 Milwaukee
55 Missouri
56 Northern Indiana
57 Northern Michigan
58 Ohio
59 Quincy
60 Southern Ohio
61 Springfield
62 Western Michigan
63 Eastern Michigan

Province VI
64 Colorado
65 Iowa
66 Minnesota
67 Montana
68 Nebraska
69 North Dakota
70 South Dakota
71 Wyoming

Province VII
72 Arkansas
73 Dallas
74 Fort Worth
75 Kansas
76 Northwest Texas
77 Oklahoma
78 Rio Grande
79 Texas
80 West Missouri
81 West Texas
82 Western Kansas
83 Western Louisiana

Province VIII
84 Arizona
85 California
86 Eastern Oregon
87 El Camino Real
88 Idaho
89 Los Angeles
90 Navajoland
91 Nevada
92 Northern California
93 Olympia
94 Oregon
95 San Diego
96 San Joaquin
97 Spokane
98 Utah
Hawaii
Alaska (*see map 6*)
Taiwan (*see map 13*)

MAP 4

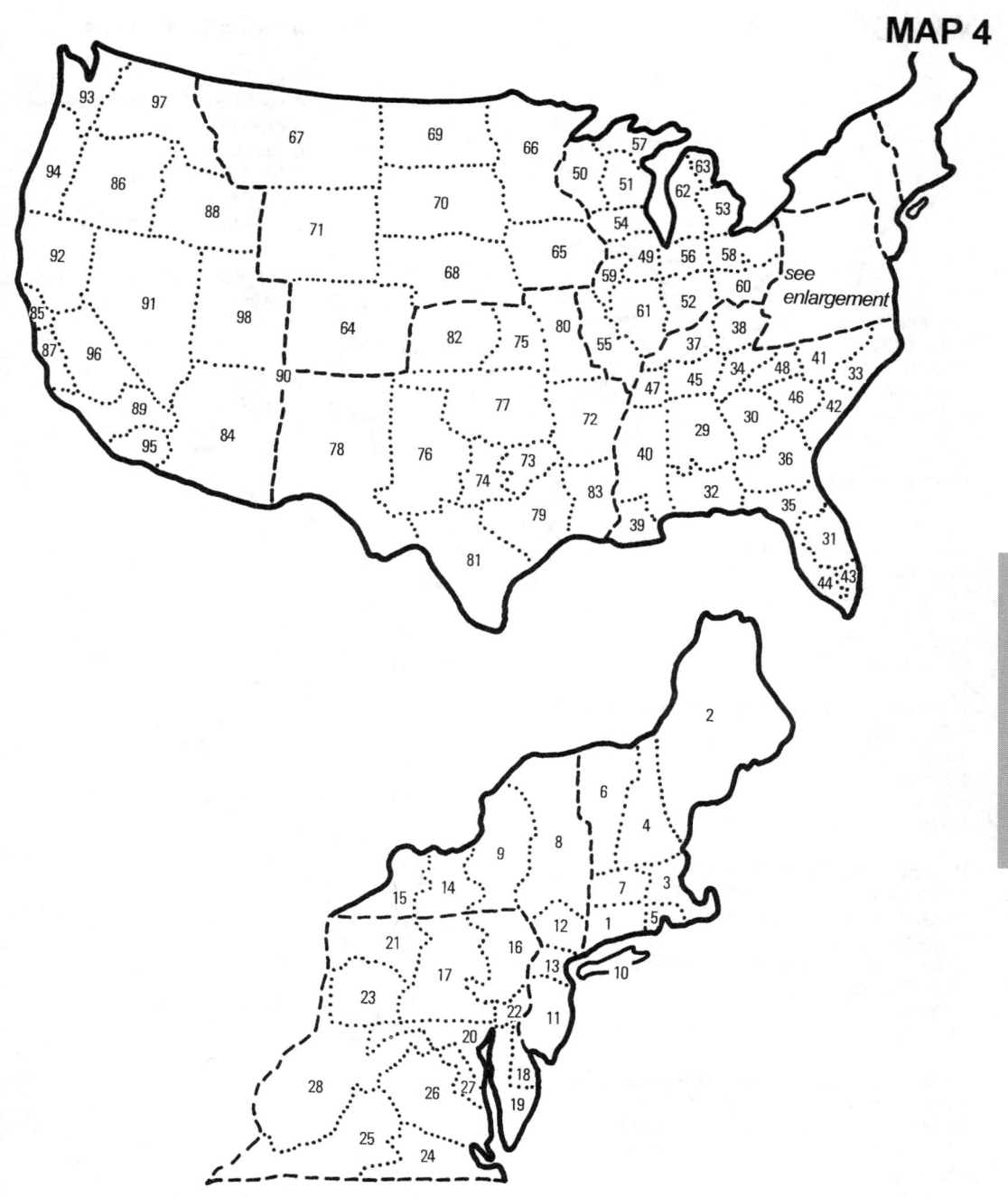

ANGLICAN AND PORVOO COMMUNIONS

Maps of the Anglican Communion 343

MAP 5

Province of the West Indies
32 Belize
33 Jamaica
34 North Eastern Caribbean & Aruba
35 Windward Islands
36 Barbados
37 Trinidad and Tobago
38 Guyana
39 Nassau and the Bahamas

The Episcopal Church of Cuba
(Autonomous diocese)
40 Cuba

Province IX
2 Honduras
6 Litoral
7 Ecuador
8 Colombia
9 Dominican Republic
11 Puerto Rico (Ex-Prov)
12 Venezuela (Ex-Prov)
Europe (Convocation of American Churches)

The Anglican Church of Mexico
13 Western Mexico
14 Northern Mexico
15 Mexico
16 Cuernavaca
17 Southeastern Mexico

The Anglican Church of the Central American Region
1 Guatemala
3 El Salvador
4 Nicaragua
5 Panama
10 Costa Rica

The Anglican Episcopal Church of Brazil
18 Rio de Janeiro (formerly Central Brazil)
19 Recife (formerly Northern Brazil)
20 Southern Brazil
21 São Paulo (formerly South Central Brazil)
22 Southwestern Brazil
23 Brasilia
24 Pelotas

Anglican Church of the Southern Cone of America
25 Argentina
26 Chile
27 Northern Argentina
28 Paraguay
29 Peru
30 Uruguay
31 Bolivia

FALKLAND ISLANDS

344   Anglican and Porvoo Communions

MAP 6

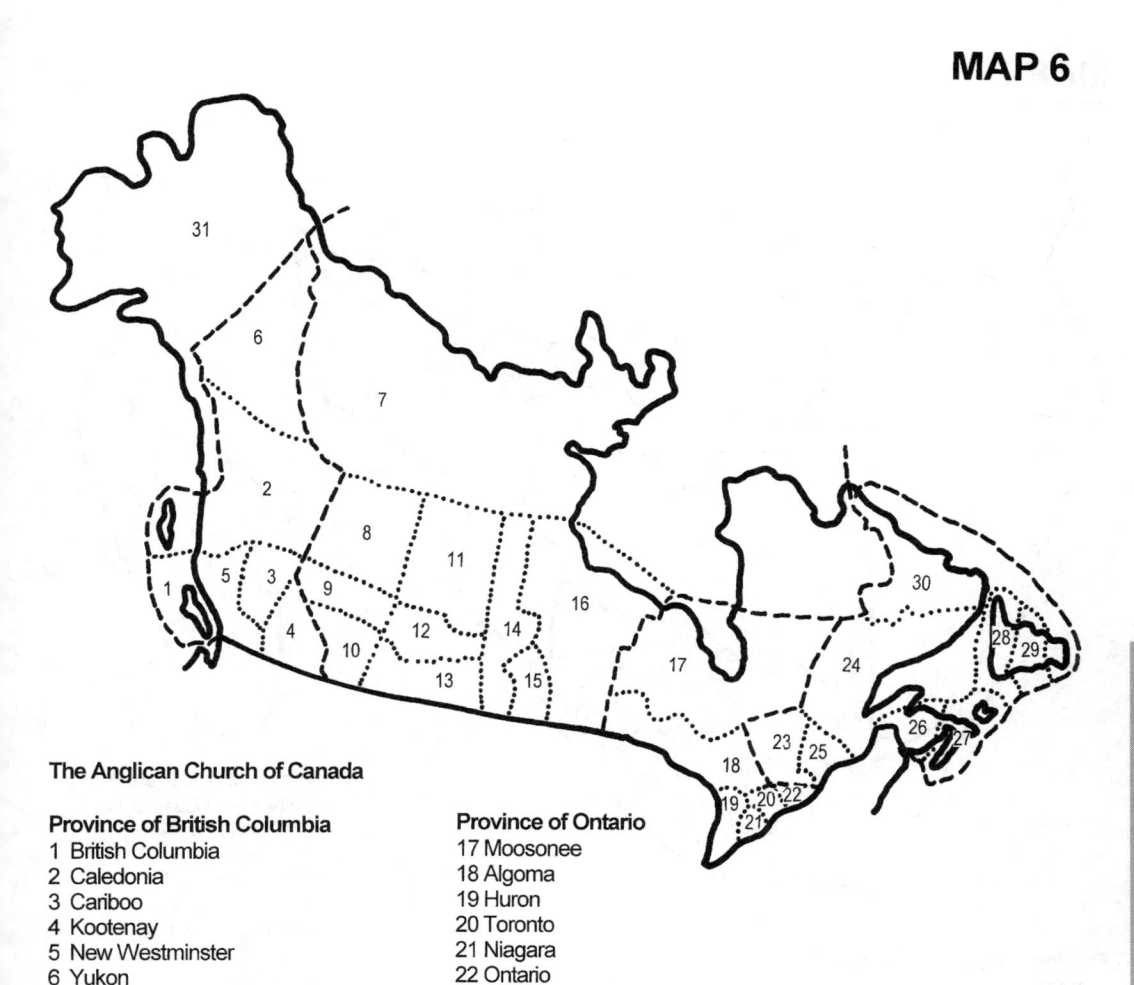

The Anglican Church of Canada

Province of British Columbia
1 British Columbia
2 Caledonia
3 Cariboo
4 Kootenay
5 New Westminster
6 Yukon

Province of Rupert's Land
7 Arctic
8 Athabasca
9 Edmonton
10 Calgary
11 Saskatchewan
12 Saskatoon
13 Qu'Appelle
14 Brandon
15 Rupert's Land
16 Keewatin

Province of Ontario
17 Moosonee
18 Algoma
19 Huron
20 Toronto
21 Niagara
22 Ontario

Province of Canada
23 Ottawa
24 Quebec
25 Montreal
26 Fredericton
27 Nova Scotia
28 Western Newfoundland
29 Central Newfoundland
30 Eastern Newfoundland and Labrador

31 Alaska *(in Province VIII of ECUSA)*

ANGLICAN AND PORVOO COMMUNIONS

Maps of the Anglican Communion   345

MAP 7

Angola is at present an Archdeaconry of the Diocese of Lebombo

Province of Southern Africa
1 Niassa
2 Lebombo
3 St Mark the Evangelist
4 Pretoria
5 Highveld
  (formerly South Eastern Transvaal)
6 Christ the King
7 Johannesburg
8 Klerksdorp
9 Kimberley and Kuruman
10 Namibia
11 Cape Town
12 George
13 Port Elizabeth
14 Grahamstown
15 St John's
16 Umzimvubu
17 Bloemfontein
18 Natal
19 Zululand
20 Lesotho
21 Swaziland
  St Helena
  Order of Ethiopia

Province of Central Africa
22 Northern Zambia
23 Central Zambia
24 Lusaka
25 Eastern Zambia
26 Lake Malawi
27 Northern Malawi
28 Southern Malawi
29 Harare
30 Manicaland
31 Central Zimbabwe
32 Matabeleland
33 Botswana

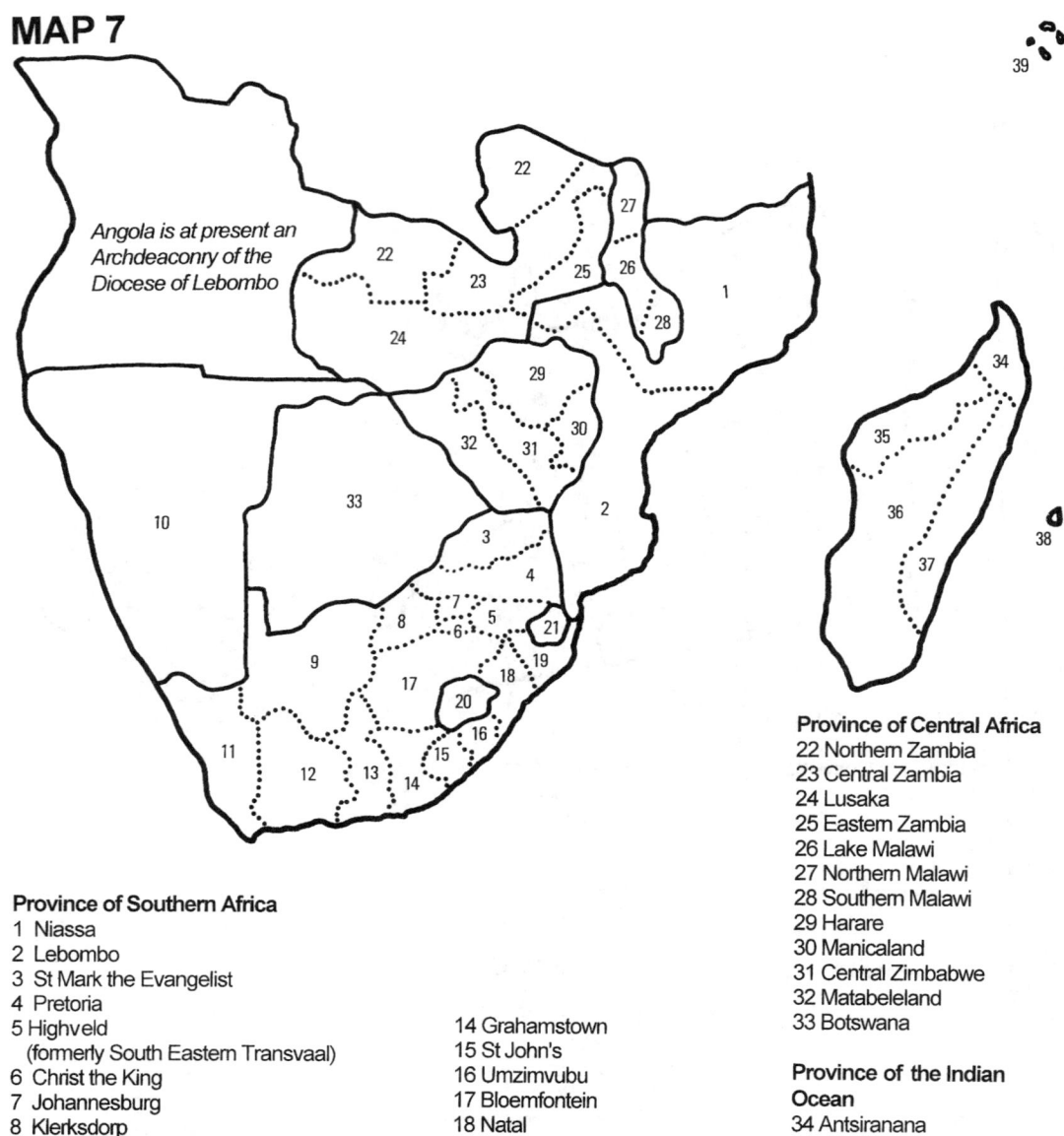

Province of the Indian Ocean
34 Antsiranana
35 Mahajanga
36 Antananarivo
37 Toamasina
38 Mauritius
39 Seychelles

346   Anglican and Porvoo Communions

MAP 8

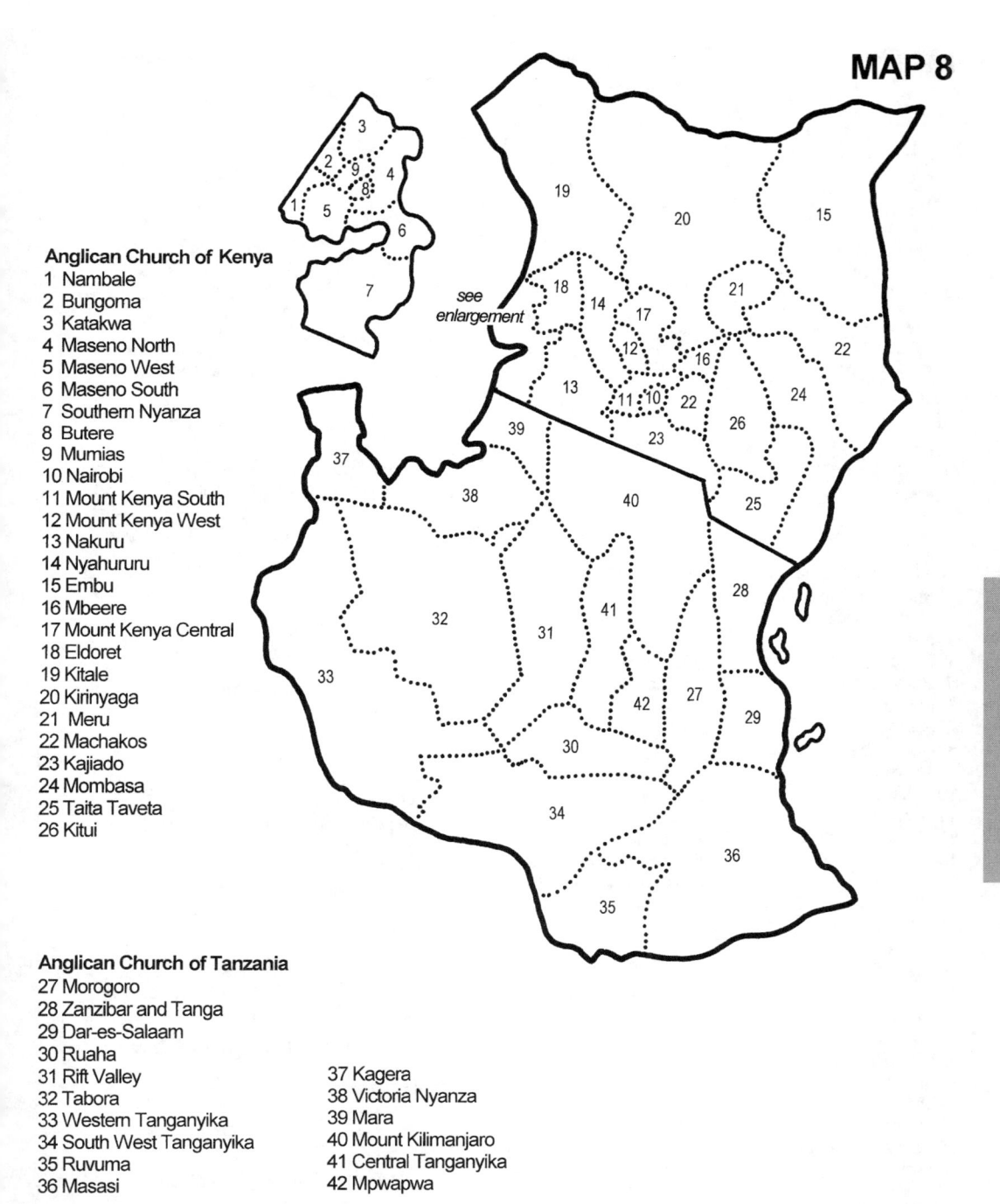

Anglican Church of Kenya
1 Nambale
2 Bungoma
3 Katakwa
4 Maseno North
5 Maseno West
6 Maseno South
7 Southern Nyanza
8 Butere
9 Mumias
10 Nairobi
11 Mount Kenya South
12 Mount Kenya West
13 Nakuru
14 Nyahururu
15 Embu
16 Mbeere
17 Mount Kenya Central
18 Eldoret
19 Kitale
20 Kirinyaga
21 Meru
22 Machakos
23 Kajiado
24 Mombasa
25 Taita Taveta
26 Kitui

Anglican Church of Tanzania
27 Morogoro
28 Zanzibar and Tanga
29 Dar-es-Salaam
30 Ruaha
31 Rift Valley
32 Tabora
33 Western Tanganyika
34 South West Tanganyika
35 Ruvuma
36 Masasi
37 Kagera
38 Victoria Nyanza
39 Mara
40 Mount Kilimanjaro
41 Central Tanganyika
42 Mpwapwa

ANGLICAN AND PORVOO COMMUNIONS

Maps of the Anglican Communion

MAP 9

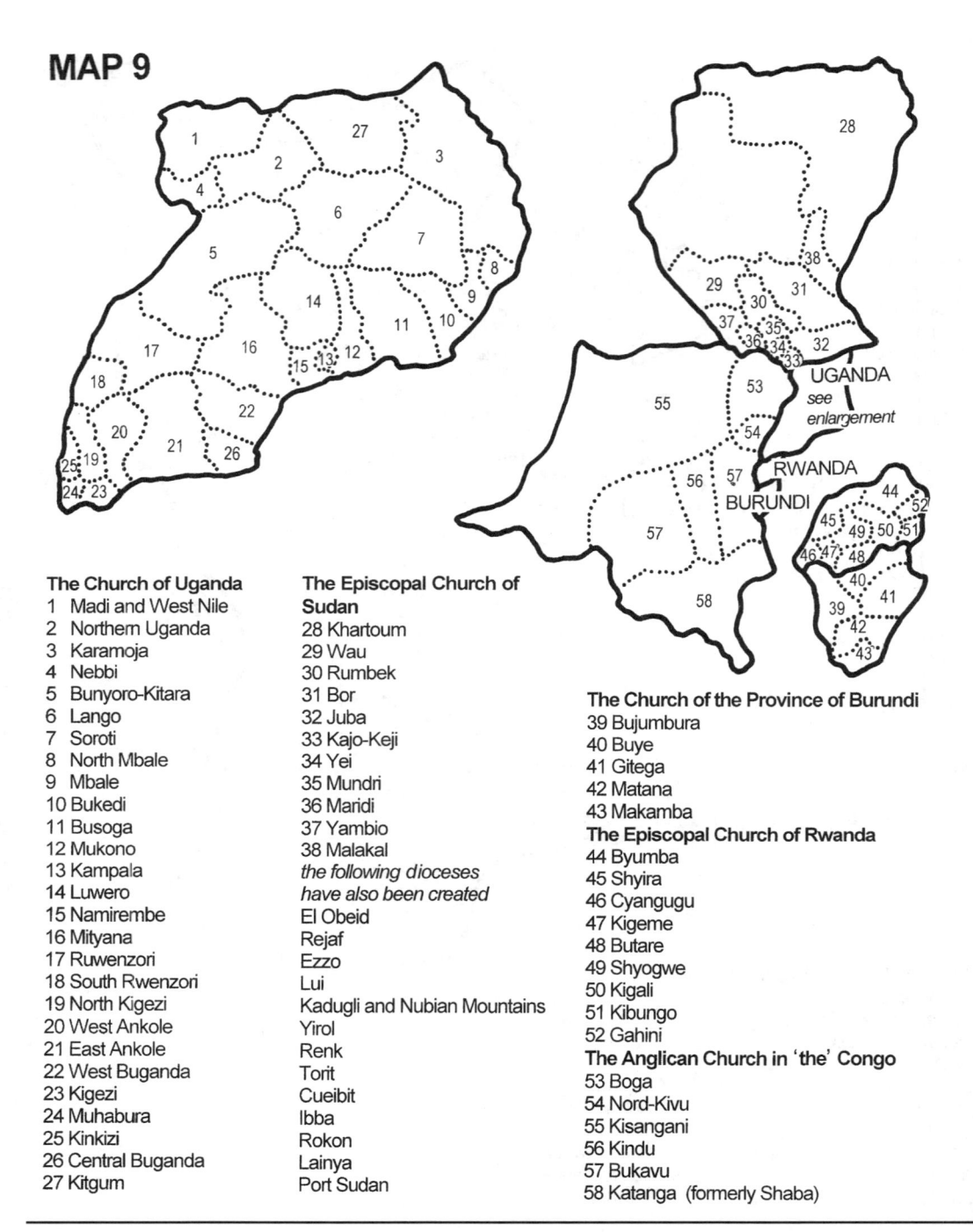

The Church of Uganda
1. Madi and West Nile
2. Northern Uganda
3. Karamoja
4. Nebbi
5. Bunyoro-Kitara
6. Lango
7. Soroti
8. North Mbale
9. Mbale
10. Bukedi
11. Busoga
12. Mukono
13. Kampala
14. Luwero
15. Namirembe
16. Mityana
17. Ruwenzori
18. South Rwenzori
19. North Kigezi
20. West Ankole
21. East Ankole
22. West Buganda
23. Kigezi
24. Muhabura
25. Kinkizi
26. Central Buganda
27. Kitgum

The Episcopal Church of Sudan
28. Khartoum
29. Wau
30. Rumbek
31. Bor
32. Juba
33. Kajo-Keji
34. Yei
35. Mundri
36. Maridi
37. Yambio
38. Malakal

the following dioceses have also been created
El Obeid
Rejaf
Ezzo
Lui
Kadugli and Nubian Mountains
Yirol
Renk
Torit
Cueibit
Ibba
Rokon
Lainya
Port Sudan

The Church of the Province of Burundi
39. Bujumbura
40. Buye
41. Gitega
42. Matana
43. Makamba

The Episcopal Church of Rwanda
44. Byumba
45. Shyira
46. Cyangugu
47. Kigeme
48. Butare
49. Shyogwe
50. Kigali
51. Kibungo
52. Gahini

The Anglican Church in 'the' Congo
53. Boga
54. Nord-Kivu
55. Kisangani
56. Kindu
57. Bukavu
58. Katanga (formerly Shaba)

Anglican and Porvoo Communions

MAP 10

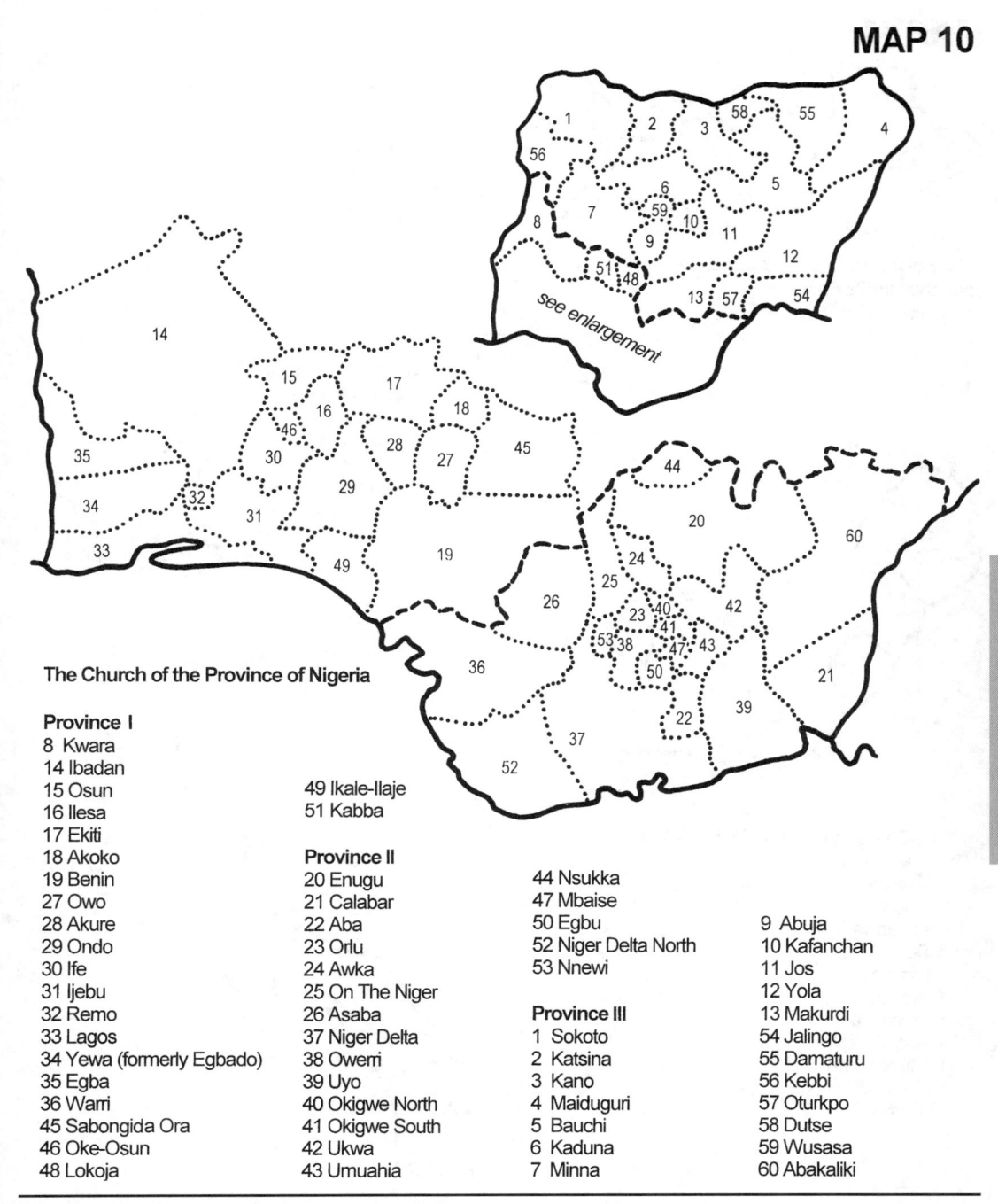

The Church of the Province of Nigeria

Province I
8 Kwara
14 Ibadan
15 Osun
16 Ilesa
17 Ekiti
18 Akoko
19 Benin
27 Owo
28 Akure
29 Ondo
30 Ife
31 Ijebu
32 Remo
33 Lagos
34 Yewa (formerly Egbado)
35 Egba
36 Warri
45 Sabongida Ora
46 Oke-Osun
48 Lokoja
49 Ikale-Ilaje
51 Kabba

Province II
20 Enugu
21 Calabar
22 Aba
23 Orlu
24 Awka
25 On The Niger
26 Asaba
37 Niger Delta
38 Owerri
39 Uyo
40 Okigwe North
41 Okigwe South
42 Ukwa
43 Umuahia
44 Nsukka
47 Mbaise
50 Egbu
52 Niger Delta North
53 Nnewi

Province III
1 Sokoto
2 Katsina
3 Kano
4 Maiduguri
5 Bauchi
6 Kaduna
7 Minna
9 Abuja
10 Kafanchan
11 Jos
12 Yola
13 Makurdi
54 Jalingo
55 Damaturu
56 Kebbi
57 Oturkpo
58 Dutse
59 Wusasa
60 Abakaliki

Maps of the Anglican Communion

ANGLICAN AND PORVOO COMMUNIONS

MAP 11

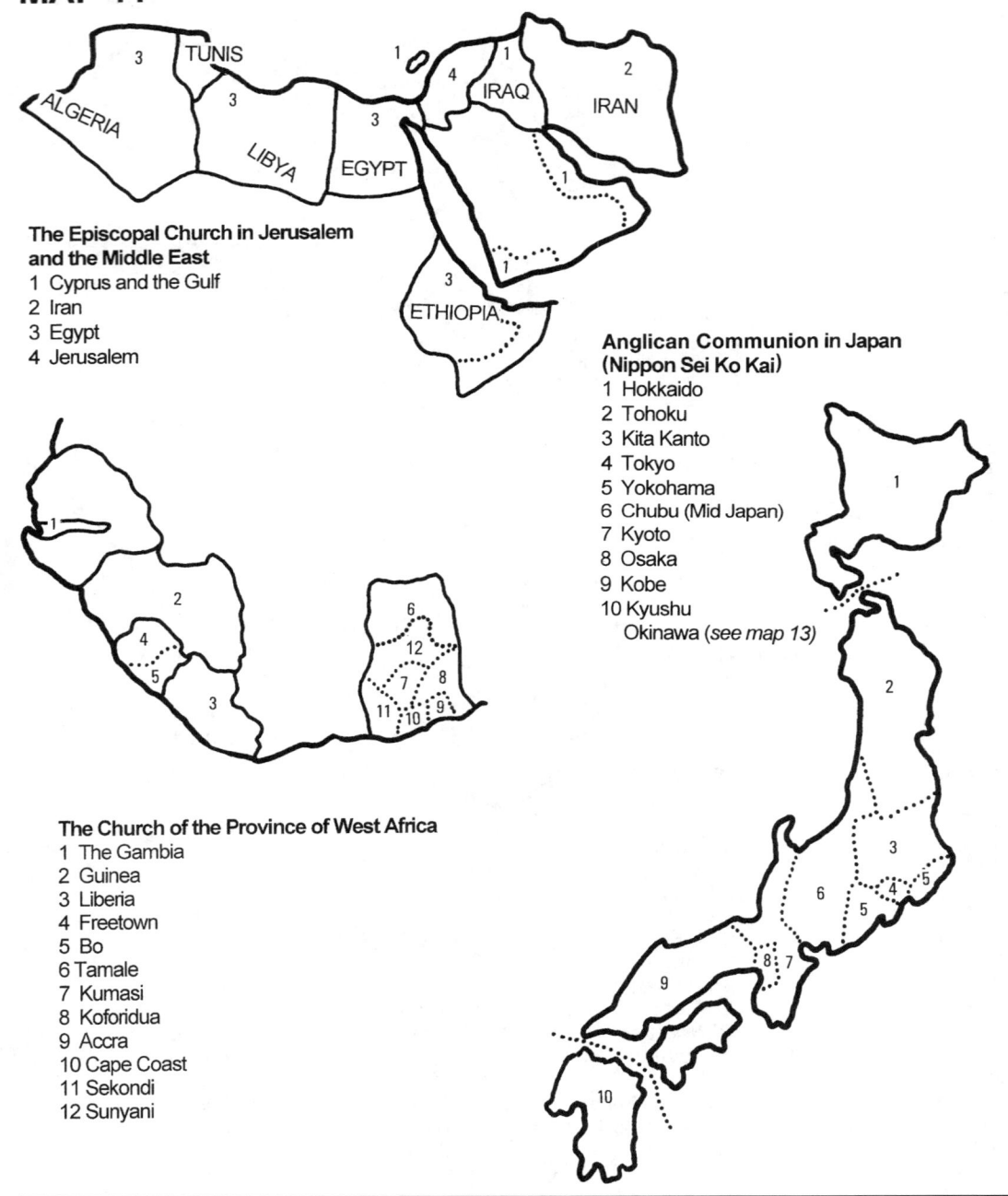

The Episcopal Church in Jerusalem and the Middle East
1. Cyprus and the Gulf
2. Iran
3. Egypt
4. Jerusalem

Anglican Communion in Japan (Nippon Sei Ko Kai)
1. Hokkaido
2. Tohoku
3. Kita Kanto
4. Tokyo
5. Yokohama
6. Chubu (Mid Japan)
7. Kyoto
8. Osaka
9. Kobe
10. Kyushu
    Okinawa (see map 13)

The Church of the Province of West Africa
1. The Gambia
2. Guinea
3. Liberia
4. Freetown
5. Bo
6. Tamale
7. Kumasi
8. Koforidua
9. Accra
10. Cape Coast
11. Sekondi
12. Sunyani

Anglican and Porvoo Communions

MAP 12

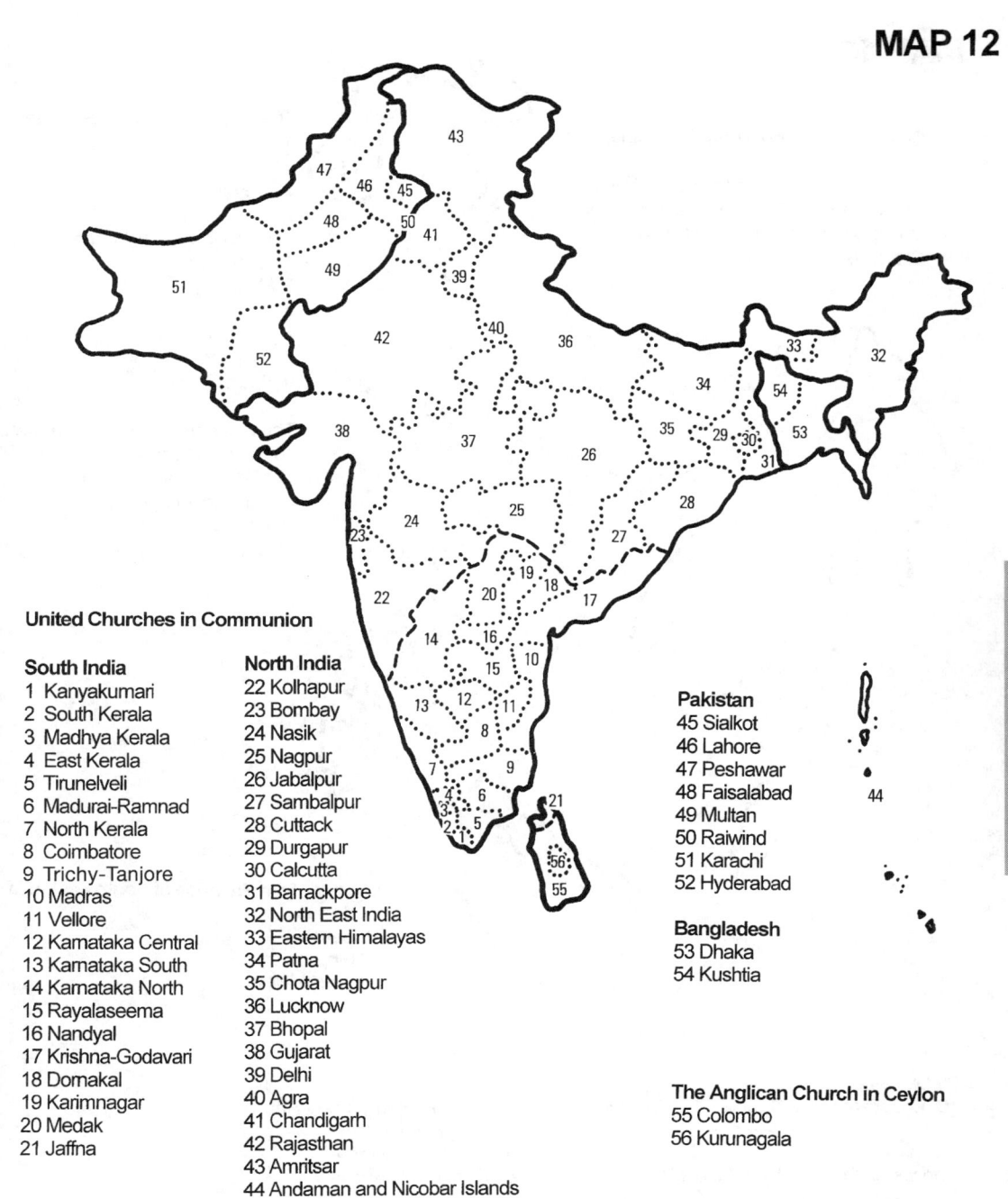

United Churches in Communion

South India
1 Kanyakumari
2 South Kerala
3 Madhya Kerala
4 East Kerala
5 Tirunelveli
6 Madurai-Ramnad
7 North Kerala
8 Coimbatore
9 Trichy-Tanjore
10 Madras
11 Vellore
12 Karnataka Central
13 Karnataka South
14 Karnataka North
15 Rayalaseema
16 Nandyal
17 Krishna-Godavari
18 Domakal
19 Karimnagar
20 Medak
21 Jaffna

North India
22 Kolhapur
23 Bombay
24 Nasik
25 Nagpur
26 Jabalpur
27 Sambalpur
28 Cuttack
29 Durgapur
30 Calcutta
31 Barrackpore
32 North East India
33 Eastern Himalayas
34 Patna
35 Chota Nagpur
36 Lucknow
37 Bhopal
38 Gujarat
39 Delhi
40 Agra
41 Chandigarh
42 Rajasthan
43 Amritsar
44 Andaman and Nicobar Islands

Pakistan
45 Sialkot
46 Lahore
47 Peshawar
48 Faisalabad
49 Multan
50 Raiwind
51 Karachi
52 Hyderabad

Bangladesh
53 Dhaka
54 Kushtia

The Anglican Church in Ceylon
55 Colombo
56 Kurunagala

ANGLICAN AND PORVOO COMMUNIONS

Maps of the Anglican Communion

MAP 13

Chung Hua Sheng Kung Hui (China)

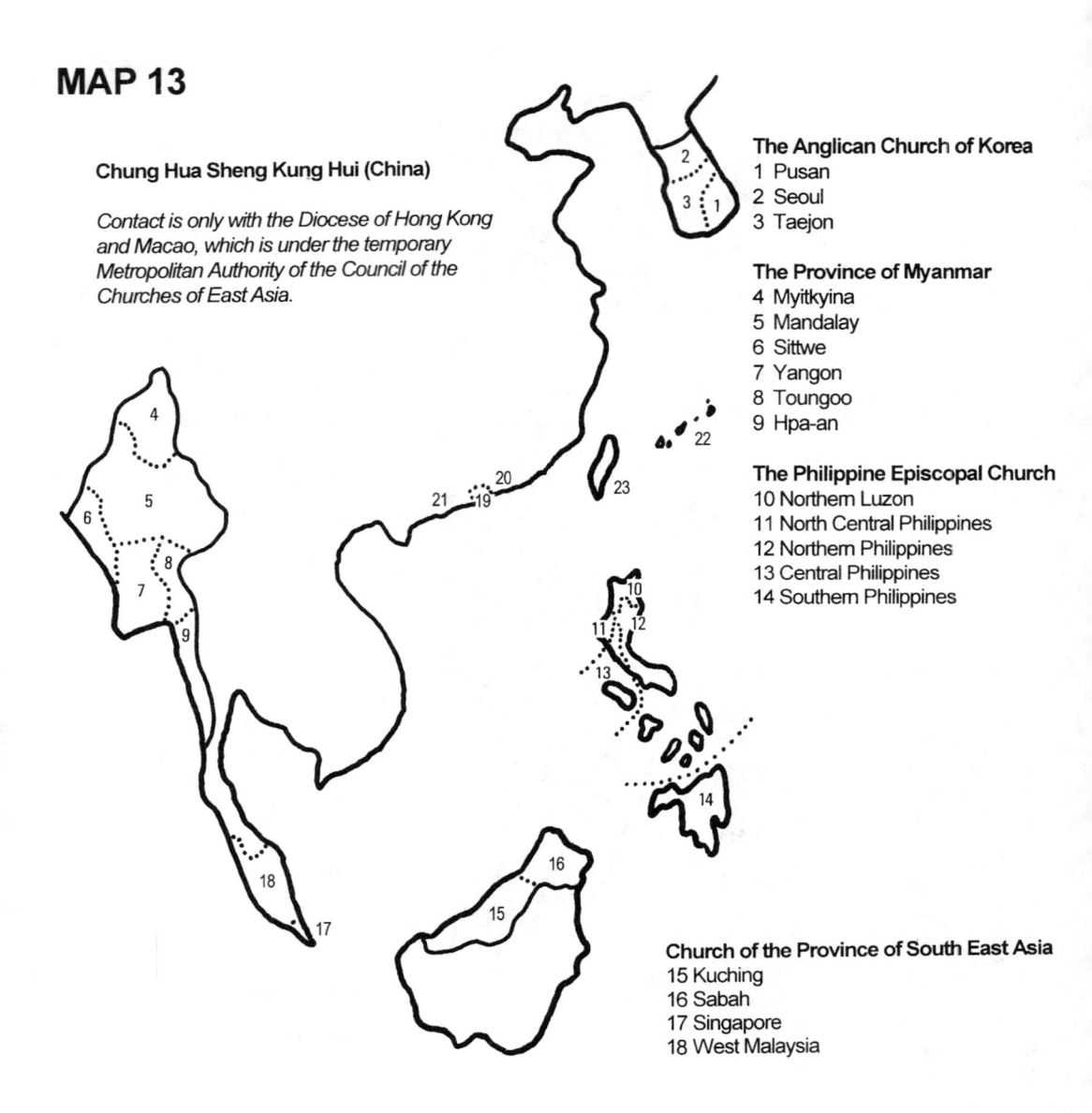

Contact is only with the Diocese of Hong Kong and Macao, which is under the temporary Metropolitan Authority of the Council of the Churches of East Asia.

The Anglican Church of Korea
1 Pusan
2 Seoul
3 Taejon

The Province of Myanmar
4 Myitkyina
5 Mandalay
6 Sittwe
7 Yangon
8 Toungoo
9 Hpa-an

The Philippine Episcopal Church
10 Northern Luzon
11 North Central Philippines
12 Northern Philippines
13 Central Philippines
14 Southern Philippines

Church of the Province of South East Asia
15 Kuching
16 Sabah
17 Singapore
18 West Malaysia

22 Okinawa
(Diocese in the Holy Catholic Church of Japan)

23 Taiwan
(Diocese in Province VIII of ECUSA)

Hong Kong Sheng Kung Hui
19 Hong Kong Island
20 Eastern Kowloon
21 Western Kowloon

THE PORVOO COMMUNION

In October 1992 representatives of the four British and Irish Anglican churches, the five Nordic Lutheran churches and the three Baltic Lutheran churches met in Finland for the fourth and final plenary session of their formal Conversations, which had commenced in 1989. They agreed *The Porvoo Common Statement*, named after Porvoo Cathedral, in which they had celebrated the Eucharist together.

The Common Statement recommended that the participating churches jointly make the Porvoo Declaration, bringing them into communion with each other. This involves common membership, a single, interchangeable ministry and structures to enable the churches to consult each other on significant matters of faith and order, life and work. The implementation of the commitments contained in the Declaration is co-ordinated by the Porvoo Agreement Contact Group.

In 1994 and 1995 the Declaration was approved by the four Anglican churches, four of the Nordic Lutheran churches and two of the Baltic Lutheran churches. The General Synod's final approval of the Declaration in July 1995, following a reference to the diocesan synods, was by overwhelming majorities in each House. The Danish bishops announced in August 1995 that none of them was able to approve the Declaration, and the Evangelical-Lutheran Church of Latvia has not yet reached its decision. The Declaration was signed in the autumn of 1996 at services in Trondheim (Norway), Tallinn (Estonia) and Westminster Abbey.

The Nordic Lutheran churches are the historic national churches of their respective countries. At the Reformation, when they adhered to Lutheranism, they continued to be episcopally ordered, retaining the historic sees. In Sweden and Finland the succession of the laying on of hands at episcopal consecration was unbroken, whereas in Denmark, Norway and Iceland this was not the case. The Estonian and Latvian Lutheran churches are similarly their countries' historic national churches, which became Lutheran at the Reformation. Only in the northern part of Estonia was episcopacy retained, and there only until 1710, but it was restored in both Estonia and Latvia in the twentieth century, the bishops being consecrated in the historic succession. The Lithuanian Lutheran Church, which is now a small minority church, adopted episcopacy in historic succession in 1976.

The Porvoo Agreement supersedes earlier separate agreements dating from the 1920s, 1930s and 1950s with the churches concerned (except the Lithuanian Lutheran Church). These provided for mutual eucharistic hospitality and (with the Swedish, Finnish, Estonian and Latvian churches) mutual participation in episcopal consecrations. Because of the Soviet occupation of the Baltic States, however, it was only in 1989 and 1992 respectively that it was possible for an Anglican bishop to participate in a Latvian and an Estonian consecration for the first time.

The Porvoo Declaration commits the signatory churches 'to regard baptized members of all of our churches as members of our own'. It also means that clergy ordained by bishops of the signatory churches are placed in the same position with regard to ministry in the Church of England as those ordained by Anglican bishops overseas.

The text of the Porvoo Common Statement is available as CCU Occasional Paper No. 3 (£2.85 inc. p&p) and in *Together in Mission and Ministry. The Porvoo Common Statement with Essays on Church and Ministry in Northern Europe* (Church House Publishing, 1993), which also contains fuller information on the history of the churches and the earlier agreements. Further information can be found on The Porvoo Page: The Homepage of the Porvoo Communion: www.svkyrkan.porvoo.

The Porvoo Agreement Contact Group
Co-Chairmen Rt Revd John Neill (*Bishop of Cashel and Ossory*); Rt Revd Dr Erik Vikström (*Bishop of Porvoo*)

Co-Secretaries Revd Dr Johan Dalman (Church of Sweden); Dr Colin Podmore (Church of England Council for Christian Unity – *see* p. 16)

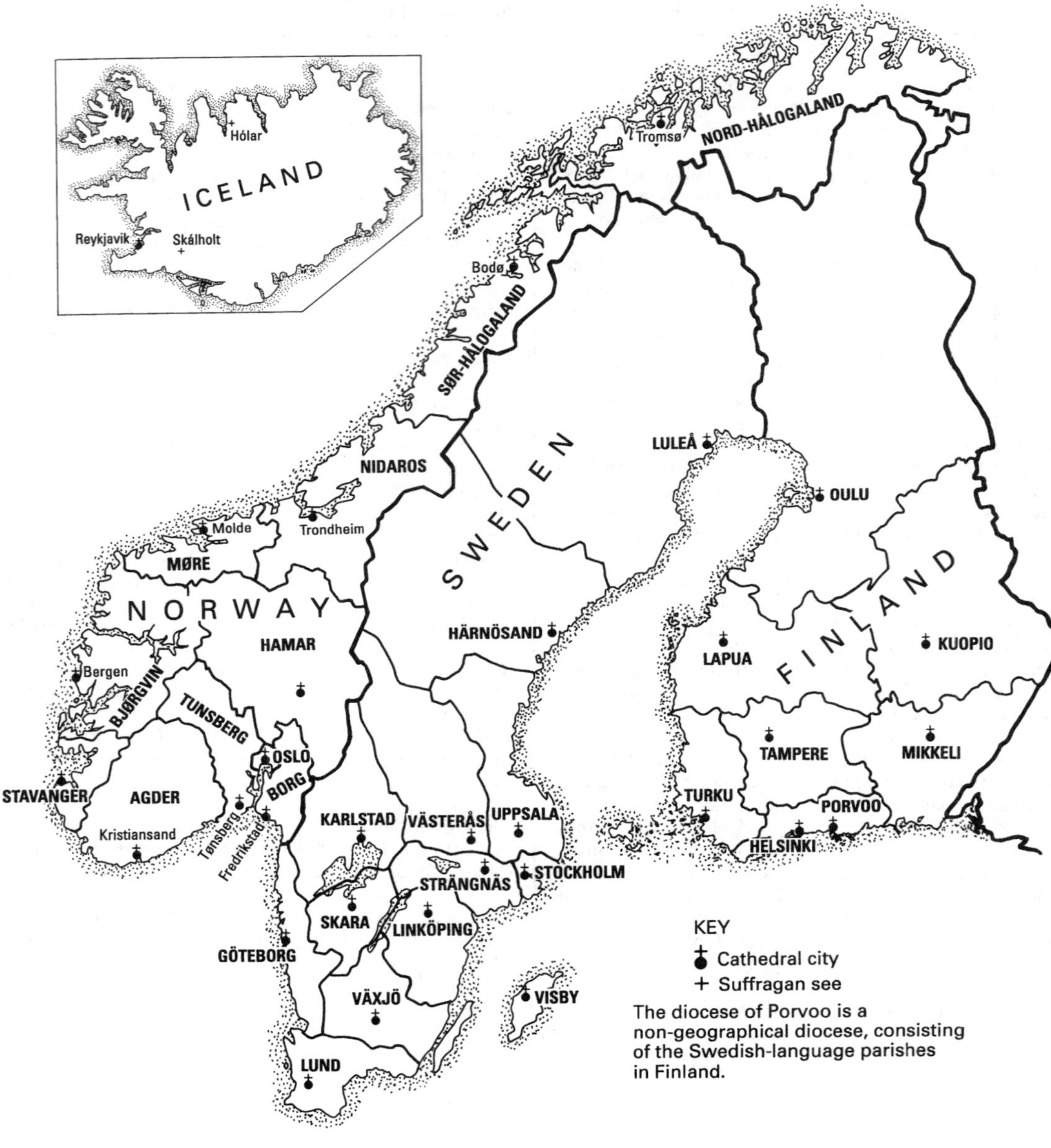
ICELAND
Hólar
Reykjavik
Skálholt
NORD-HÅLOGALAND
Tromsø
Bodø
SØR-HÅLOGALAND
NIDAROS
Trondheim
Molde
MØRE
NORWAY
HAMAR
Bergen
BJØRGVIN
TUNSBERG
OSLO
BORG
STAVANGER
AGDER
Kristiansand
Tønsberg
Fredrikstad
SWEDEN
LULEÅ
HÄRNÖSAND
KARLSTAD
VÄSTERÅS
UPPSALA
STOCKHOLM
STRÄNGNÄS
SKARA
LINKÖPING
GÖTEBORG
VÄXJÖ
VISBY
LUND
FINLAND
OULU
LAPUA
KUOPIO
TAMPERE
MIKKELI
TURKU
PORVOO
HELSINKI
KEY
Cathedral city
Suffragan see
The diocese of Porvoo is a non-geographical diocese, consisting of the Swedish-language parishes in Finland.

NORDIC LUTHERAN CHURCHES

The Evangelical-Lutheran Church of Finland

The first bishop in the Finnish Church was St Henrik, the Apostle of Finland. According to tradition, St Henrik was an Englishman who accompanied the Swedish king on a military expedition to south-western Finland in 1155 and was martyred there the following year. From the middle of the thirteenth century until 1809 Finland was part of Sweden, and until the Reformation it formed a single diocese (Turku) in the Province of Uppsala.

In 1554 the Swedish king appointed the Finnish Lutheran Reformer Mikael Agricola (d. 1557) as Bishop of Turku, at the same time founding a second Finnish see, Viipuri (eventually transferred to Tampere). In addition to translating the New Testament and parts of the Old into Finnish, Mikael Agricola compiled the first hymnal, liturgy and ritual in Finnish. He is regarded as the father of Finnish as a written language.

A wave of revivals, beginning in the eighteenth century, gave rise in the nineteenth to four mass movements. These remained within the Church of Finland and are still influential on its life today.

In 1809 Finland was annexed by Russia. As a result, the Finnish Church became entirely independent of the Church of Sweden, and from 1817 the Bishop of Turku was styled Archbishop. Finland finally gained its independence in 1917.

Today, 86 per cent of Finns are members of the Church of Finland, while only 4 per cent are members of other churches. The Church of Finland is a 'folk church' (as is the Orthodox Church). The framework for its life is set by the Ecclesiastical Act. Amendments to this state law can only be proposed by the Synod, and Parliament can accept or reject but not amend such proposals. The Church is governed by the Synod, the Ecclesiastical Board and the Bishops' Conference. Although the archbishop is only *primus inter pares* of the Finnish bishops, he is the President of the Synod and chairs both the Bishops' Conference and the Ecclesiastical Board.

Porvoo Agreement Contact Revd Dr Juhani Forsberg, Department for International Relations, Satamakatu 11, Box 185, FIN-00161 Helsinki *Tel:* 00 358–9 1802 290
Fax: 00 358–9 1802 230

HELSINKI
Bishop Rt Revd Dr Eero Huovinen, Diocesan Chapter, PL 142, FIN-00121 Helsinki *Tel:* 00 358–9 601 095
Fax: 00 358–9 605 408

KUOPIO
Bishop Rt Revd Dr Wille Riekkinen, Diocesan Chapter, PL 42, FIN-70101 Kuopio *Tel:* 00 358–17 261 3800
Fax: 00 358–17 261 3836

LAPUA
Bishop Rt Revd Dr Jorma Laulaja, Diocesan Chapter, PL 60, FIN-62101 Lapua *Tel:* 00 358–6 438 8623
Fax: 00 358–6 437 4214

MIKKELI
Bishop Rt Revd Dr Voitto Huotari, Diocesan Chapter, PL 122, FIN-50101 Mikkeli *Tel:* 00 358–15 151 390
Fax: 00 358–15 151 003

OULU
Bishop Rt Revd Dr Olavi Rimpiläinen, Diocesan Chapter, PL 85, FIN-90101 Oulu *Tel:* 00 358–8 311 4654
Fax: 00 358–8 311 0659

PORVOO
[The Diocese of Porvoo (Borgå) is a non-geographical Swedish-language diocese.]
Bishop Rt Revd Dr Erik Vikström, Diocesan Chapter, PB 30, FIN-06101 Borgå *Tel:* 00 358–19 524 5155
Fax: 00 358–19 585 705

TAMPERE
Bishop Rt Revd Dr Juha Pihkala, Diocesan Chapter, PL 53, FIN-33201 Tampere *Tel:* 00 358–3 223 1960
Fax: 00 358–3 212 9493

TURKU
Archbishop of Turku and Finland Vacancy, PL 60, FIN-20501 Turku *Tel:* 00 358–2 251 6500
Fax: 00 358–2 251 6541

Bishop of Turku Rt Revd Dr Ilkka Kantola (*same address*)

The Evangelical-Lutheran Church of Iceland

Christianity was adopted at Thingvellir by decree of the legislature in the year 1000. The ancient Icelandic sees of Skálholt and Hólar were founded in 1055 and 1106 respectively. Having previously been under the jurisdiction of Bremen and Lund, from 1153 Iceland belonged to the Province of Nidaros (Trondheim). Part of the Kingdom of Norway from 1262, Iceland eventually came under Danish rule. The Lutheran Reformation was introduced in 1541. From this time onwards until 1908 (with one exception in the late eighteenth century), Icelandic bishops were consecrated by the Bishops of Sealand (Copenhagen).

The two Icelandic sees were united in 1801, but in 1909 they were revived as suffragan sees. Iceland gained its independence from Denmark in 1918, becoming a republic in 1944.

A new church law came into effect on 1 January 1998, granting the church a considerable autonomy from the state. The Church Assembly is its highest organ of the church. Today, around 90 per cent of the Icelandic population are members of the Church of Iceland.

Porvoo Agreement Contact Revd Baldur Kristjánsson,
Háaleiti, 815 Thorlákshöfn
    Tel: 00 354–562 1500
    Fax: 00 354–551 3284
    e-mail: baldurkr@centrum.is

The Church of Iceland comprises a single diocese, with two suffragan bishops in the ancient sees of Hólar and Skálholt.

Bishop of Iceland Most Revd Karl Sigurbjörnsson, Laugavegur 31, 150 Reykjavík
    Tel: 00 354–562 1500
    Fax: 00 354–551 3284
    e-mail: biskup@ismennt.is

Bishop of Skálholt Rt Revd Sigurður Sigurðarson, Skálholti biskupshúsi, 801 Selfoss
    Tel: 00 354–486 8972
    Fax: 00 354–486 8975

Bishop of Hólar Rt Revd Bolli Þorir Gústavsson Hólum, biskupssetri, 551 Sauðákrókur   *Tel:* 00 354 453 6593

The Church of Norway

From around AD 1000 Christianity was brought to Norway by missionaries both from the British Isles and from Germany. Central to the Christianizing of Norway was King Olav Haraldsson. After his death in 1030 he was venerated as St Olave, and his shrine in Nidaros Cathedral (Trondheim) was a centre of pilgrimage. Episcopal sees were established in Nidaros, Bergen, Oslo (by 1100), and in Stavanger (1125) and Hamar (1153). Part of the Province of Lund from 1103, Norway became a separate province when Nidaros was raised to an archiepiscopal see in 1153. In addition to the five Norwegian sees, the Province of Nidaros also included six further dioceses covering Iceland, the Faeroes, Greenland, the Shetland and Orkney Islands, the Hebrides and the Isle of Man. Under Olav IV (1380–87) Norway was united with Denmark.

The Norwegian Reformation of 1537 was imposed by the new King of Denmark, Christian III, with little evidence of popular enthusiasm. New bishops ('Superintendents') were ordained to the sees of Nidaros, Bergen and Stavanger by Johannes Bugenhagen, the Superintendent of Wittenberg, in 1537, and Bugenhagen's Danish Church Order was extended to Norway in 1539. Of the pre-Reformation bishops, Bishop Hans Rev of Oslo alone accepted the Reformation, and returned to his see (to which that of Hamar had been united) as Superintendent in 1541. The diocesan structure had been retained, with four of the five historic sees, and the term 'Bishop' soon replaced its Latin synonym 'Superintendent', but until recent years neither Bishop Rev nor any other bishop consecrated in the historic succession of the laying on of hands participated in the consecration of future bishops. Nidaros ceased to be an archiepiscopal see, Oslo replacing it *de facto* as the senior Norwegian see.

In the eighteenth and nineteenth centuries, pietist movements became influential, but they remained within the Church of Norway, the membership of which still amounts to 88 per cent of the population. During the German occupation of 1940–45, the Church was a focus of resistance under the leadership of Bishop Eivind Berggrav of Oslo (1884–1959). In 1993 Rosemarie Köhn became the Church of Norway's first (and so far only) woman bishop, when the Norwegian government appointed her Bishop of Hamar.

The Church of Norway has an 86-member General Synod, consisting of the 77 members of the eleven diocesan councils (including the bishops), three members representing clergy, laity and lay employees, three non-voting representatives of the theological faculties and three Sami representatives. Its executive is the 15-member National Council, which has a lay chairman. Related central bodies include the Bishops' Conference, the Council on Foreign Relations, the Sami Church Council and a doctrinal commission. Church legislation still requires parliamentary approval. The King of Norway remains the Church's constitutional head, and the government retains powers over the Church, exercised through the Ministry of the Church, Education and Research.

Porvoo Agreement Contact Vacancy, Council on Ecumenical and International Relations, PO Box 5816, Majorstua, N-0308 Oslo 3   *Tel:* 00 47–22 93 27 93
    Fax: 00 47–22 93 28 28/29

AGDER
Bishop Vacancy, Diocesan Centre, Gyldenloves gate 9, N-4611 Kristiansand
Tel: 00 47–38 02 27 33
Fax: 00 47–38 02 92 50

BJØRGVIN
Bishop Rt Revd Ole Hagesæther, Diocesan Centre, Kalvedalsveien 45A, N-5018 Bergen
Tel: 00 47–55 30 64 70
Fax: 00 47–55 30 64 85
e-mail: bjoergvin.biskop:kirken.no

BORG
Bishop Rt Revd Ole Chr. M. Kvarme, PO Box 403, N-1601 Fredrikstad
Tel: 00 47–69 30 79 00
Fax: 00 47–69 31 01 74
e-mail: borg.bdr@kirken.no

HAMAR
Bishop Rt Revd Rosemarie Köhn, Folkestadgt, 52, N-2300 Hamar
Tel: 00 47–62 53 01 11
Fax: 00 47–62 52 92 71
e-mail: hamar.bdr@kirken.no

MØRE
Bishop Rt Revd Odd Bondevik, Diocesan Centre, Julsundveien 30, N-6400 Molde
Tel: 00 47–71 25 06 70
Fax: 00 47–71 25 06 71
e-mail: moere.bdr@kirken.no
[The Bishop of Møre has been elected as *Praeses* of the Bishops' Conference.]

NIDAROS
Bishop Rt Revd Finn Wagle, Archbishop's House, N-7013 Trondheim
Tel: 00 47–73 53 91 00
Fax: 00 47–73 53 91 11
e-mail: nidaros.bdr@kirken.no

NORD-HÅLOGALAND
Bishop Rt Revd Ola Steinholt, PO Box 790, N-9001 Tromsø
Tel: 00 47–77 60 39 60/61
Fax: 00 47–77 68 00 87
e-mail: nord-haalogaland.bdr@kirken.no

OSLO
Bishop Rt Revd Gunnar Staalsett, PO Box 9307, Gronland, N-0135 Oslo
Tel: 00 47–22 19 37 00
Fax: 00 47–22 68 28 92
e-mail: oslo.biskop@kirken.no

SØR-HÅLOGALAND
Bishop Rt Revd Øystein Larsen, PO Box 374, N-8001 Bodø
Tel: 00 47–75 52 55 73
Fax: 00 47–75 52 39 33
e-mail: soer-haalogaland.bdr@kirken.no

STAVANGER
Bishop Rt Revd Dr Ernst Oddvar Baasland, Diocesan Centre, Eiganesveien 113, N-4009 Stavanger
Tel: 00 47–51 84 62 70
Fax: 00 47–51 84 62 71
e-mail: stavanger.biskop@kirken.no

TUNSBERG
Bishop Rt Revd Sigurd Osberg, PO Box 1253, Trudvang, N-3105 Tønsberg
Tel: 00 47–33 31 73 00
Fax: 00 47–33 31 40 11
e-mail: tunsberg.bdr@kirken.no

The Church of Sweden

The first to preach the gospel in Sweden was St Ansgar (801–65), the first Archbishop of Hamburg-Bremen, but it was in the eleventh century that the systematic conversion of Sweden was begun, largely by missionaries from England. From 1104 the new Swedish dioceses formed part of the Nordic Province of Lund (which was Danish until 1658), but only until 1164, when Uppsala was raised to an archiepiscopal see. The most celebrated figure of the mediaeval Swedish Church was St Birgitta of Vadstena (1303–73), foundress of the Brigittine Order.

Under the Lutheran Reformers Olaus Petri (1493–1552) and his brother Laurentius (d. 1573), who became the first Lutheran archbishop in 1531, the Swedish Reformation was gradual, and moderate in character. The Augsburg Confession was adopted in 1593.

The eighteenth and nineteenth centuries saw both latitudinarian and pietist movements, and in the earlier twentieth century a strong high-church movement developed. Archbishop Nathan Söderblom (1866–1931), one of the leading figures of the Ecumenical Movement, used the concept of 'evangelical catholicity' to describe the Church of Sweden's position. In 1997 Christina Odenberg became the Church of Sweden's first (and so far only) woman bishop, when she was appointed Bishop of Lund.

The Church of Sweden is governed by a General Synod with 251 members and a 15-member Central Board (chaired by the Archbishop), together with the Bishops' Conference. The bishops attend the Synod, but are not members of it, although they have all the rights of members except the right to vote. They are ex officio members of the Synod Committee on Church Doctrine. A complete separation of Church and State will be effected in the year 2000. Some 87 per cent of Swedish citizens are members of the Church of Sweden.

Porvoo Agreement Contact Revd Dr Johan Dalman, Church of Sweden, S-75170 Uppsala *Tel:* 00 46–18 169 573 *Fax:* 00 46–18 169 538

GÖTEBORG
Bishop Rt Revd Dr Lars Eckerdal, Stiftskansliet, Box 11937, S-404 39 Göteborg *Tel* and *Fax:* 00 46–31 771 30 30

HÄRNÖSAND
Bishop Rt Revd Dr Karl-Johan Tyrberg, Stiftskansliet, Box 94, S-871 22 Härnösand *Tel:* 00 46–611 254 00 *Fax:* 00 46–611 134 75

KARLSTAD
Bishop Rt Revd Dr Bengt Wadensjö, Stiftskansliet, Box 186, S-651 05 Karlstad *Tel:* 00 46–54 17 24 00 *Fax:* 00 46–54 17 24 70

LINKÖPING
Bishop Rt Revd Dr Martin Lind, Stiftskansliet, Box 2056, S-580 02 Linköping *Tel:* 00 46–13 24 26 00 *Fax:* 00 46–13 12 03 40

LULEÅ
Bishop Rt Revd Rune Backlund, Stiftskansliet, Stationsgatan 40, S-972 32 Luleå *Tel:* 00 46–920 447 00 *Fax:* 00 46–920 447 27

LUND
Bishop Rt Revd Christina Odenberg, Stiftskansliet, Box 32, S-221 00 Lund *Tel:* 00 46–46 35 87 00 *Fax:* 00 46–46 18 49 48

SKARA
Bishop Rt Revd Lars-Göran Lönnermark, Malmgatan 14, S-532 00 Skara *Tel:* 00 46–511 262 00 *Fax:* 00 46–511 262 70

STOCKHOLM
Bishop Rt Revd Caroline Krook, Stiftskansliet, Box 2016, S-103 11 Stockholm *Tel:* 00 46–8 781 01 00 *Fax:* 00 46–8 24 75 75

STRÄNGNÄS
Bishop Rt Revd Dr Jonas Jonson, Stiftskansliet, Box 84, S-645 22 Strängnäs *Tel:* 00 46–152 242 00 *Fax:* 00 46–152 242 45

UPPSALA
Archbishop Most Revd Dr Karl Gustav Hammar, S-751 70 Uppsala *Tel:* 00 46–18 16 95 00 *Fax:* 00 46–18 16 96 25

Bishop Rt Revd Dr Tord Harlin, Box 1314, S-751 43 Uppsala *Tel:* 00 46–18 68 07 00 *Fax:* 00 46–18 12 45 25

VÄSTERÅS
Bishop Rt Revd Dr Claes-Bertil Ytterberg, Stiftskansliet, V Kyrkogatan 9, S-722 15 Västerås *Tel:* 00 46–21 17 85 00 *Fax:* 00 46–21 12 93 10

VÄXJÖ
Bishop Rt Revd Anders Wejryd, Östrabo, S-352 39 Växjö *Tel:* 00 46–470 77 38 00 *Fax:* 00 46–470 72 95 50

VISBY
Bishop Rt Revd Dr Biörn Fjärstedt, Stiftskansliet, Box 1334, S-621 24 Visby *Tel:* 00 46–498 21 05 70 *Fax:* 00 46–498 21 01 03

Further information about the history of the Nordic Lutheran churches and of their relations with the Church of England can be found in Lars Österlin, *Churches of Northern Europe in Profile. A Thousand Years of Anglo-Nordic Relations* (Norwich, 1995).

BALTIC LUTHERAN CHURCHES

The Estonian Evangelical-Lutheran Church

The conversion of Estonia to Christianity began at the end of the tenth century, and the first known bishop was consecrated in 1165. The mission was prosecuted by the Brethren of the Sword, an order founded in 1202 which merged with the Teutonic Order in 1237. In 1219 the Danes conquered the northern area and founded the capital Reval (Tallinn), which became an episcopal see within the Province of Lund. Further sees were established at Dorpat (Tartu) in 1224 and Hapsal (Saare-Lääne) in 1227, within the Province of Riga, the capital of Livonia, which included the southern part of modern Estonia. In some areas secular authority was in the hands of the bishops, while in others the Teutonic Order held sway. The entire area was very much under German dominance.

The Lutheran movement reached Estonia in 1523, and as early as the following year an assembly in Reval decided to adhere to the Reformation. Later in the century, however, the twin provinces of Estonia and Livonia became divided between neighbouring powers. Most of Estonia placed itself under Swedish rule in 1561, but Denmark ruled the island of Oesel (Saarema) from 1560 to 1645 and Livonia was annexed by Poland from 1561 to 1621. In Swedish Estonia, the Church was governed by a bishop and consistory, but Danish ecclesiastical law was introduced in Oesel, while Livonia came under the influence of the Counter-Reformation. Superintendents, rather than bishops, were appointed for these areas after they came under Swedish rule (in 1621 and 1645).

In 1710 both provinces came under Russian rule. In Estonia the office of bishop was replaced with that of superintendent. The consistories were chaired by laymen. In 1832 the Lutheran churches of all three Baltic provinces were united with Russia's German-speaking Lutheran Church into a Russian Lutheran Church, with a General Consistory in St Petersburg. Each province (and – until 1890 – Reval, Oesel and Riga separately) had its own General superintendent and consistory. The University of Dorpat (Tartu), originally founded in 1632, was refounded in 1802. As the only Protestant theological faculty in the Russian Empire, it was of great importance.

Throughout the period up to 1918 the clergy were German, like the ruling elite. The Moravian Church, which was active in Estonia and Livonia from 1736, enjoyed considerable influence over the Estonian peasantry, and by 1854 there were 276 Moravian prayer halls. However, the Moravian authorities blocked the development of this movement into a separate Moravian Church, and the Moravians' adherents remained within the Lutheran Church.

In 1918 Estonia and the Estonian northern part of Livonia became an independent state. The Church too became independent. It remained united, having both German and Estonian clergy and members. The office of bishop was immediately restored, the first bishop being consecrated in 1921 by the Archbishop of Uppsala and a Finnish bishop.

Estonia's independent existence lasted little more than twenty years, however. In 1940 it was occupied by the Red Army. German occupation followed, but Soviet rule was restored in 1944. Archbishop Kópp, who had remained unconsecrated because the war prevented bishops from other countries travelling to Estonia, went into exile with 70 other clergy and members of congregations. Of the clergy who remained, one third were eventually deported to Siberia. Not until 1968 was it possible for an archbishop to be consecrated.

In 1988, Estonia began to move towards independence, which was achieved in 1991. This was accompanied by a remarkable blossoming of church life. The Theological Faculty at Tartu, which had been dissolved by the Soviet authorities, was reopened.

The Estonian Evangelical-Lutheran Church is governed by a General Synod, the executive organ of which is the six-member Consistory.

Porvoo Agreement Contact Dr Alar Laats, Consistory of the EELC, Kirikuplats 3, EE-10130-Tallinn
Tel: 00 372–6 27 73 50
Fax: 00 372–6 27 73 52

Archbishop of Estonia Most Revd Jaan Kiivit, Consistory of the EELC, Kirikuplats 3, EE-10130-Tallinn
Tel: 00 372–6 27 73 50
Fax: 00 372–6 27 73 52

The Evangelical-Lutheran Church of Lithuania

Not until 1387 was an episcopal see established in Vilnius, following the baptism the previous year of Grand Duke Jogaila (whose coronation as King of Poland inaugurated a union lasting until 1795), and it was 1418 before the inhabitants of German-dominated Samogitia (covering much of present-day Lithuania) were forced to accept baptism.

A Lutheran congregation was founded in Vilnius as

early as 1521, but persecution forced the Lithuanian Reformer Martin Mazvydas to flee to Königsberg. In time the Lithuanian nobility established the Reformed faith on their estates, while the numerous German merchants and craftsmen established Lutheran congregations in the towns from the 1550s. Until the early nineteenth century, the Lutheran Church continued to be a German and urban minority church. Sigismund Vasa (1587–1632) successfully restored Roman Catholicism as the religion of the people, and subsequent anti-protestant policies meant that by 1775, when religious freedom was granted, just 30 Reformed and five Lutheran congregations remained (except those in Prussian-ruled Tauragé/Tauroggen).

In 1795 most of Lithuania was ceded to Russia, and Lithuania's Lutheran congregations were placed under the Consistory of Courland (now southern Latvia). Immigration of Lutheran Letts, Germans and Lithuanians from East Prussia produced new Lutheran congregations, especially in the countryside. The pastors (only nine in 1918) were all Germans.

At independence in 1918, Lithuania's population included 75,000 Lutherans, of whom roughly 30,000 were Germans, 30,000 Lithuanians and 15,000 Letts. In 1920 separate synods had to be formed for the three linguistic groups, and for much of the inter-war period tension between them paralysed the Lutheran Church. By 1939, however, there were 55 congregations with 33 pastors. To these should be added the separate Lutheran Church of the Prussian *Memelgebiet*, which Lithuania annexed in 1923. By 1939 this had 135,000 members (the majority German) in 32 parishes, served by 39 pastors.

Lithuanian Lutheranism was soon to be decimated. In 1941, following the 1940 Soviet annexation of Lithuania, most of the German population, together with a large number of Lithuanian Lutherans, emigrated to Germany. In Memelland and the Vilnius area, both reintegrated into Lithuania and thus the Soviet Union in 1945, the picture was even more stark. All but 30,000 inhabitants fled, while the pastor of the historic Lutheran church in Vilnius emigrated with his entire congregation.

A provisional Lutheran Consistory found itself responsible for 20,000 Lithuanians and Letts in Lithuania proper, together with just 15,000 Lithuanians in Klaipéda (Memelland). There were no pastors in Klaipéda and only six in the rest of the country, three of whom were soon banished to Siberia. After Stalin's death in 1953 and a first post-war synod in 1955, the structures of church life were gradually restored, but several thousand more Protestants emigrated between 1957 and 1965. At a second synod in 1970, Jonas Kalvanas, the only pastor left who had studied theology at university (he was ordained in 1940), was elected to chair the Consistory. It was with his consecration as Bishop by the Archbishop of Estonia in 1976 that his church gained the historic episcopate. He was succeeded in 1995 by his son and namesake, in whose consecration the Bishop of Tonbridge shared.

In 1992 the Lutheran Church had 41 congregations, with about 15,000 communicant members and twelve clergy (including deacons).

Porvoo Agreement Contact Revd Darius Petkunas, Simonaitytes 18–21, LIT-5814 Klaipeda
Tel: 00 370–6 220 409
Fax: 00 370–6 258 270
e-mail: petkunas@usa.net

Bishop of the Evangelical-Lutheran Church of Lithuania
Rt Revd Jonas Kalvanas, Bretkuno 13, LIT-5900 Taurage
Tel: 00 370–46 53 451

NON-SIGNATORY CHURCHES

The Church of Denmark

In August 1995 the bishops of the fifth Nordic Lutheran church, the Church of Denmark, announced that they were not able to approve the Porvoo Declaration. Its provisions therefore do not apply to that church. At meetings held under the Porvoo Agreement, the Church of Denmark is represented by observers.

However, an agreement providing for mutual eucharistic hospitality between the Church of England and the Church of Denmark (approved by the churches in 1954 and 1956 respectively) remains in force.

Observer at meetings of the Porvoo Agreement Contact Group Revd Ane Hjerrild, Council on Inter-Church Relations, Vestergade 8, 1 DK-1456 Copenhagen K
Tel: 00 45–33 114488
Fax: 00 45–33 119588
e-mail: interchurch@folkekirken.dk

Bishop of Copenhagen Rt Revd Erik Norman Svendsen, Nørregade 11, DK-1165 Copenhagen
Tel: 00 45–33 13 35 08
Fax: 00 45–33 14 39 69

The Evangelical-Lutheran Church of Latvia

The Church of Latvia has not yet voted on the Porvoo Declaration.

Porvoo Agreement Contact The Archbishop

Archbishop of Riga and Latvia Most Revd Jānis Vanags, M. Pils iéla 4, LV-1050 Riga
Tel: 00 371–722 6057
Fax: 00 371–782 0041

There are also Anglican chaplaincies in most of the countries covered by the Porvoo Agreement. These belong to the Archdeaconry of Scandinavia and Germany within the Diocese in Europe. A leaflet giving details is available from the Diocesan Office of the Diocese in Europe, *see below*.

A directory of English-speaking churches abroad is available from Intercontinental Church Society, 1 Athena Drive, Tachbrook Park, Warwick CV34 6NL. New edition available early 1999.
Tel: (01926) 430347
Fax: (01926) 330238
e-mail: icsint@compuserve.com

Continental Anglican churches are listed in the *Diocesan Directory* of the Diocese of Gibraltar in Europe, available from the Diocesan Office, 14 Tufton St, Westminster, London SW1P 3QZ
Tel: 0171–976 8001
Fax: 0171–976 8002

ECUMENICAL

PART 6

PART 6 CONTENTS

ECUMENICAL CANONS *365*

EVANGELICAL CHURCH IN GERMANY *365*

CHURCHES TOGETHER IN ENGLAND *366*

INTERMEDIATE COUNTY BODIES AND AREA ECUMENICAL COUNCILS *367*

COUNCIL OF CHURCHES FOR BRITAIN AND IRELAND *371*

CHURCHES' COMMISSION ON MISSION *374*

CHURCHES' COMMISSION FOR RACIAL JUSTICE *375*

SCOTLAND, WALES AND IRELAND *375*

CHURCHES IN BRITAIN AND IRELAND: ADDRESSES *377*

CONFERENCE OF EUROPEAN CHURCHES *378*

WORLD COUNCIL OF CHURCHES *379*

REGIONAL CONFERENCES *384*

ECUMENICAL

The Church of England is committed to the search for full, visible unity with other Christian churches, and to the bodies which promote this at the local, intermediate, national, European and world levels. The Council for Christian Unity acts, on behalf of the Standing Committee, as the principal channel of communication between the General Synod and the national and international bodies.

ECUMENICAL CANONS
Canon B43 (Of Relations with Other Churches) and Canon B44 (Of Local Ecumenical Projects) encourage and make provision for sharing in worship with other churches. Full details are given in *The Ecumenical Relations Code of Practice* (Church House, 1989) and Supplement (CCU, 1997, 50p). The following churches in England have been designated by the Archbishops of Canterbury and York as churches to which the Church of England (Ecumenical Relations) Measure, and thus Canons B43 and B44, apply: The Baptist Union, The Methodist Church, The Moravian Church, The Roman Catholic Church in England and Wales, The United Reformed Church, The Congregational Federation, The International Ministerial Council of Great Britain, The Lutheran Council of Great Britain, The Greek Orthodox Archdiocese of Thyateira and Great Britain, The Council of African and Afro-Caribbean Churches, The Free Church of England, The Southam Road Evangelical Church Banbury, The Assemblies of God in Great Britain and Ireland, The New Testament Church of God, the Russian Orthodox Church, the Church of Scotland (presbyteries in England).

The Evangelical Church in Germany

The Evangelical Church in Germany (Evangelische Kirche in Deutschland – EKD) is a Communion of 25 member churches (mostly *Landeskirchen* or territorial churches). Of these ten are Lutheran (eight of them forming the United Evangelical Lutheran Church – VELKD), one is purely Reformed, one is predominantly Reformed and twelve are United (seven forming the Evangelical Church of the Union – EKU, which is the twenty-fifth member church). In many of the United churches the Lutheran tradition predominates.

In November 1988 the General Synod welcomed the Meissen Common Statement, *On the Way to Visible Unity*, which called for a closer relationship between the Church of England and the German Evangelical Churches. The Meissen Declaration, which it recommended, was approved by the General Synod in July 1990 without dissent, and solemnly affirmed and proclaimed an Act of Synod on 29 January 1991. The Meissen Declaration makes provision for the Church of England and the Evangelical Church in Germany to live in closer fellowship with one another (though not yet with interchangeable ministries) and commits them to work towards the goal of full visible unity. The member churches of the EKD have been designated as churches to which the Ecumenical Canons apply (*see* **Ecumenical Canons**).

The Meissen Commission (the Sponsoring Body for the Church of England – EKD Relations) exists to oversee and encourage relationships (*see* Council for Christian Unity). Fuller information is contained in *The German Evangelical Churches* (CCU Occasional Paper No 1 – £2.95 + 35p p&p) and Anglo-German Ecumenical Links: An Information Pack (£1 inc. p&p). The text of the Meissen Agreement can be found in *The Meissen Agreement: Texts* (CCU Occasional Paper No 2 – £2.10 inc. p&p). These are all available from the Council for Christian Unity.

Chairman of the EKD Council Präses Manfred Kock (*Präses of the Evangelical Church in the Rhineland*)

German Co-Secretary of the Meissen Commission OKR Paul Oppenheim, EKD Kirchenamt, Postfach 21 02 20, D–30402 Hannover, Germany   *Tel:* (00 49) 511 2796 127
Fax: (00 49) 511 2796 725
e-mail: ekd@ekd.de

Churches Together in England

Churches Together in England is in association with the Council of Churches for Britain and Ireland. Its basis is as follows:

> Churches Together in England unites in pilgrimage those Churches in England which, acknowledging God's revelation in Christ, confess the Lord Jesus Christ as God and Saviour according to the Scriptures, and, in obedience to God's will and in the power of the Holy Spirit, commit themselves:
>
> – to seek a deepening of their communion with Christ and with one another in the Church, which is his body; and
> – to fulfil their mission to proclaim the Gospel by common witness and service in the world
>
> to the glory of the one God, Father, Son and Holy Spirit.

The Presidents of Churches Together in England are: The Archbishop of Canterbury, the Cardinal Archbishop of Westminster, Revd Dr Kathleen Richardson, and Rowena Loverance, who meet together quarterly.

It has 23 Member Churches: Baptist Union of Great Britain, Cherubim and Seraphim Council of Churches, Church of England, Church of Scotland, Congregational Federation, Council of African and Afro-Caribbean Churches, Council of Oriental Orthodox Christian Churches, Free Churches' Council; Greek Orthodox Church, Ichthus Christian Fellowship, Independent Methodist Churches, International Ministerial Council of Great Britain, Joint Council for Anglo-Caribbean Churches, Lutheran Council of Great Britain, Methodist Church, Moravian Church, New Testament Assembly, Religious Society of Friends, Roman Catholic Church, Russian Orthodox Church, Salvation Army, United Reformed Church, Wesleyan Holiness Church.

The Religious Society of Friends has membership under a clause designed for 'any Church or Association of Churches which on principle has no credal statements in its tradition'.

All substantive decisions are taken by these Member Churches.

The Seventh Day Adventist Church is an Observer.

Churches Together in England encourages its Member Churches to work together nationally, and provides various means for this purpose. There is an *Enabling Group*, which meets three times a year. There is a *Forum* of 300 members, which meets every other year (next in July 1999). Its Moderator is Mrs Terry Garley and its Deputy Moderator The Ven David Hawtin.

There are 13 *Co-ordinating Groups* (*see below*).

There are also a large number of informal or as yet not formally recognised groups and networks.

Churches Together in England encourages its Member Churches to work together locally. To enable this most counties and metropolitan areas have established ecumenical councils and officers, whose task is to foster and encourage all sorts of ecumenical work locally within their areas. The main task of the two Field Officers (*see below*) is to support those working in counties and metropolitan areas.

Churches Together in England publishes an ecumenical news bulletin, *Pilgrim Post*, six times a year.

General Secretary Revd Bill Snelson, Churches Together in England, Inter-Church House, 35–41 Lower Marsh, London SE1 7RL *Tel:* 0171–523 2009 *Fax:* 0171–928 5771

Administration Officer Mrs Judith Lampard (*same address*)

Field Officer North & Midlands Mrs Jenny Carpenter, Churches Together in England, Crookesmoor Valley Methodist Church, Crookesmoor Road, Sheffield S6 3FQ *Tel:* 0114–268 2151 *Fax:* 0114–266 8731

Field Officer South Revd Roger Nunn, Churches Together in England, Room 517, Baptist House, 129 Broadway, Didcot OX11 8XD *Tel:* (01235) 511622 *Fax:* (01235) 817539

CO-ORDINATING GROUPS

GROUP FOR LOCAL UNITY
Secretary Mrs Jenny Carpenter (*address see above*)

GROUP FOR EVANGELISATION
Secretary Revd Roger Whitehead, The Manse, 116 High St, Harrold, Beds MK43 7BJ *Tel:* (01234) 721127

CHRISTIAN ADULT LEARNING MEETING
Secretary Tony McCaffrey, St Mary's University College, Waldegrave Rd, Twickenham TW1 4SX *Tel:* 0181–240 4196

CHURCHES JOINT EDUCATION POLICY COMMITTEE
Miss Gillian Wood, Free Church Council, 27 Tavistock Square, London WC1H 9HH *Tel:* 0171–387 8413

CHURCHES COMMITTEE FOR HOSPITAL CHAPLAINCY
Secretary Revd Christine Pocock, Free Church Council, 27 Tavistock Square, London WC1H 9HH *Tel:* 0171–387 8413

CHURCHES COMMUNITY WORK ALLIANCE
Secretary Revd Brian Ruddock, 36 Sandygate, Wath-upon-Dearne, Rotherham S63 7LW

ENGLISH CHURCHES YOUTH SERVICE
Secretary Peter Ball, Church House, Great Smith St, London SW1P 3NZ Tel: 0171–898 1506

THEOLOGY AND UNITY GROUP
Secretary Revd Bill Snelson (*address see above*)

CHURCHES RURAL GROUP
Secretary Revd John Clarke, Arthur Rank Centre, The National Agricultural Centre, Stoneleigh Park, Warws CV8 2LZ

CHURCHES TOGETHER FOR FAMILIES
Secretary Pauline Butcher, FCC, 27 Tavistock Square, London WC1H 9HH Tel: 0171–387 8413

CHURCHES MILLENNIUM GROUP
Executive Secretary Revd Stephen Lynas, Church House, Great Smith St, London SW1P 3NZ Tel: 0171–898 1436

INDEM (Group for Mission in Industry and the Economy) Paul Fuller, Pump Hill Cottage, Donington Rd, South Willingham, Lincs LN8 6NJ

SPIRITUALITY GROUP
Secretary Judith Lampard (*as above*)

WOMEN'S CO-ORDINATING GROUP
Secretary

There are also five *Agencies*:

CHURCHES ADVISORY COUNCIL FOR LOCAL BROADCASTING
General Secretary Mr Jeff Bonser, PO Box 124, Westcliff on Sea, Essex SS0 0QU Tel: (01702) 348369

CHRISTIAN ENQUIRY AGENCY
Secretary Phillip Clements-Jewery, Inter-Church House, 35–41 Lower Marsh, London SE1 7RL
 Tel: 0171–620 4444

CHRISTIAN AID
Director Dr Daleep Mullarji, PO Box 100, London SE1 7RL
 Tel: 0171–620 4444

CAFOD
Director Mr Julian Filochowski, 2 Romero Close, Stockwell Rd, London SW9 9TY Tel: 0171–733 7900

OPPORTUNITIES FOR VOLUNTEERING
Secretary Mr Malcolm Smart, Inter-Church House, 35–41 Lower Marsh, London SE1 7RL Tel: 0171–620 4444

The following are *Bodies in Association* with Churches Together in England: Afro-West Indian United Council of Churches, Association of Interchurch Families, Bible Society, Christians Aware, College of Preachers, Fellowship of Prayer for Unity, Focolare Movement, Iona Community, National Association of Christian Communities and Networks, National Retreat Association, Student Christian Movement, Young Men's Christian Association, Young Women's Christian Association.

The address of the Focolare Movement is Mari Ponticaccia, 62 King's Ave, London SW4 8BH. For other addresses, *see* page 373 (under CCBI) or the **List of Organisations** (pages 209–266).

Intermediate County Bodies and Area Ecumenical Councils

Avon (Area of Greater Bristol)
Churches Together in Greater Bristol
Executive Secretary

Revd Brian Scott
St Nicholas House
Lawford's Gate
Bristol BS5 0RE
Tel: 0117 954 2133

Avon (South)
see **Somerset**

Bedfordshire
Churches Together in Bedfordshire
Ecumenical Officer
(also Hertfordshire)

Revd Dr David Butler
114 High St
Watton-at-Stone
Herts SG14 3RZ
Tel: 01920 426829

Berkshire
Churches Together in Berkshire
County Ecumenical Officer

Revd Phil Abrey
51 Galsworthy Drive
Caversham Park
Reading RG4 0PR
Tel: 01734 475152

Birmingham, Greater
Birmingham Churches Together
General Secretary

Revd Mark Fisher
Carrs Lane Church Centre
Birmingham B4 7SX
Tel: 0121–643 6603

Buckinghamshire
(except Milton Keynes)
Buckinghamshire Ecumenical Council
County Ecumenical Officer

Canon Derek Palmer
124 Bath Rd
Banbury
Oxon OX16 0TR
Tel: 01295 268201

Intermediate County Bodies

Cambridgeshire
Cambridgeshire
  Ecumenical Council
County Ecumenical Officer

Revd Frank Fisher
Stapleford Vicarage
Cambridge CB2 5BG
Tel: 01223 842150

Cheshire
Churches Together in
  Cheshire
County Ecumenical Officer

Canon Michael Rees
5 Abbey Green
Chester CH1 2JH
Tel: 01244 347500

Cleveland (North)
see **Durham**

Cleveland (South)
see **Yorkshire (North)**

Cornwall
Churches Together in
  Cornwall
Secretary

Revd Gerald Burt
138 Bodmin Rd
Truro
Cornwall TR1 1RB
Tel: 01872 273154

Cumbria
Churches Together in
  Cumbria
County Ecumenical Officer

Revd Andrew Dodd
Church House
West Walls
Carlisle CA3 8UE
Tel: 01228 22573

Derbyshire
Churches Together in
  Derbyshire
Secretary

Mr Colin Garley
64 Wyndale Drive
Ilkeston, Derbyshire
DE7 4JG
Tel: 0115 932 9402

Counties Ecumenical Officer
for Derbyshire and
Nottinghamshire

Mrs Terry Garley
64 Wyndale Drive
Ilkeston, Derbyshire
DE7 4JG
Tel: 0115 932 9402

Devon
Christians Together in
  Devon
County Ecumenical Officer

Revd John Bradley
Grenville House
Whites Lane
Torrington, Devon EX38 8DS
Tel: 01805 625059

Dorset
Churches Together in
  Dorset
County Ecumenical Officer

Mrs Val Potter
22 D'Urberville Close
Dorchester
Dorset DT1 2JT
Tel: 01305 264416

Durham (and North
Cleveland)
Durham Church
  Relations Group
  (DCRG)
Secretary

Canon John Hancock
St Michael's Vicarage
Westoe Rd
South Shields NE33 3PJ
Tel: 0191–425 2074

Essex
Essex Churches
  Consultative Council
County Ecumenical Officer
  (also London, Barking
  Area Church Leaders'
  Group)

Revd David Hardiman
349 Westbourne Grove
Westcliff on Sea
Essex SS0 0PU
Tel and *Fax:* 01702 342327

Gloucestershire
(and North Avon)
Gloucestershire Churches
  Together
County Ecumenical Officer

Revd Dr David Calvert
151 Tuffley Ave
Gloucester GL1 5NP
Tel: 01452 301347

Hampshire (and Isle of
Wight and Channel
Islands)
Churches Together in
  Hampshire and the
  Isle of Wight
Area Ecumenical Officer

Dr Paul Rolph
71 Andover Rd
Winchester SO22 6AU
Tel: 01962 862574

Herefordshire
Churches Together in
  Herefordshire
Secretary

Mrs Anne Double
Malvern View
Garway Hill, Orcop
Hereford HR2 8EZ
Tel: 01981 580495

Hertfordshire
Churches Together in
  Hertfordshire
Ecumenical Officer
  (also Bedfordshire)

Revd Dr David Butler
114 High St
Watton-at-Stone
Herts SG14 3RZ
Tel: 01920 426829

Hull and East Yorkshire
Churches Together in
  Kingston-upon-Hull
  and East Yorkshire (KEY)
Secretary

Revd David Perry
Skirlaugh Vicarage
Hull HU11 5HE
Tel: 01964 562259

Isle of Man
Churches Together in Man
Secretary

Revd Stephen Caddy
The Manse
11 Bayr Grianagh
Castletown
Isle of Man IM9 1HN
Tel: 01624 822541

Jersey Christians Together in Jersey	Revd Fred Noden The URC Manse Sion St John Jersey JE3 4FL *Tel:* 01534 861386	**London** **Hackney, Islington,** **Tower Hamlets** East London Church Leaders' Group *Secretary*	Revd Pauline Barnett The Manse Bethnal Green London E2 9JP *Tel:* 0181–980 5278

Kent
Churches Together in
   Kent
County Ecumenical Officer
   (including London
   Boroughs of Bexley and
   Bromley)
	Revd Michael Cooke
	St Lawrence Vicarage
	Stone St, Seal
	Sevenoaks
	Kent TN15 0LQ
	Tel: 01732 761766
		London
		Brent, Ealing, Harrow,
		Hillingdon
		Churches Together in
		   North West London
		Convenor
			Mr Bill Boyd
			20 Radnor Ave
			Harrow
			Middx HA1 1SB
			Tel and *Fax:* 0181–427 3418

Lancashire Churches Together in Lancashire *County Ecumenical Officer*	Revd Donald Parsons 45 Alder Drive Hoghton Preston PR5 0AS *Tel:* 01254 852860	**London** **Hammersmith, Fulham,** **Hampton, Hounslow,** **Kensington, Chelsea,** **Spelthorne, Richmond** **(north of the Thames)** Churchlink West *Convenor*	Mr Tom Flynn 30 Glencairn Drive Ealing London W5 1RT *Tel:* 0181–248 9947

Leicestershire
Churches Together in
   Leicester
Secretary
	Mr Jonathan Cryer
	Church House
	St Martin's East
	Leicester LE1 5FX
	Tel: 0116–262 7445
	Fax: 0116–253 2889
		London
		(South of the Thames)
		Croydon, Greenwich,
		Kingston, Lambeth,
		Lewisham, Merton,
		Richmond, Southwark,
		Sutton, Wandsworth
		Churches Together in
		   South London
		Secretary
			Sister Liz Grant
			Sisters of St Andrew
			St Peter's House
			308 Kennington Lane
			London SE11 5HY
			Tel: 0171–587 0087

All Lincolnshire Churches Together in All Lincolnshire *Ecumenical Officer*	Revd John Cole Pelham House Little Lane Wrawby Brigg DN20 8RW *Tel:* 01652 657484		
		Manchester (Greater) Greater Manchester Churches Together *County Ecumenical Officer*	Sister Maureen Farrell FCJ St Peter's House Oxford Rd Manchester M13 9GH *Tel:* 0161–273 5508 *Fax:* 0161–272 7172

London
Barking and Dagenham,
Havering, Newham,
Redbridge and
Waltham Forest
Barking Area Church
   Leaders' Group
Secretary
   (also Essex Churches
   Consultative Council)
	Revd David Hardiman
	349 Westbourne Grove
	Westcliff on Sea
	Essex SS0 0PU
	Tel: 01702 342327
		Merseyside
		Merseyside and Region
		   Churches' Ecumenical
		   Assembly (MARCEA)
		Ecumenical Officer
			Revd Anthony Hodgetts
			Friends Meeting House
			65 Paradise St
			Liverpool L1 3BP
			Tel: 0151–709 0125

London
Enfield, Haringey,
Camden, East Barnet
North London Church
   Leaders' Group
Secretary
	Revd Dr Philip Morgan
	1 Ellesmere Ave
	Mill Hill
	London NW7 3EX
	Tel: 0181–959 7246
		Milton Keynes
		Milton Keynes Christian
		   Council
		Ecumenical Moderator
			Revd Murdoch Mackenzie
			c/o Church of Christ the
			   Cornerstone
			300 Saxon Gate West
			Central Milton Keynes
			MK9 2ES
			Tel: 01908 230655

Intermediate County Bodies

Norfolk
Norfolk Churches Together
Executive Officer

Revd Robin Hewetson
The Rectory, Marsham
Norwich NR10 5PP
Tel: 01263 733249

Northamptonshire
Northamptonshire Ecumenical Council
Executive Secretary

Mrs Christine Nelson
4 The Slade
Daventry
Northants NN11 4HH
Tel: 01327 705803

Northumberland (and Tyne & Wear north of the Tyne)
Newcastle Church Relations Group
Secretary

Revd Gordon Shaw
Pinehurst
Wansbeck Rd
Ashington
Northumberland NE63 8JE
Tel: 01670 812137

Nottinghamshire
Churches Together in Nottinghamshire
Secretary

Mr Alan Langton
35 Aylesham Ave
Woodthorpe View, Arnold
Nottingham NG5 6PP
Tel: 0115 926 9090

Counties Ecumenical Officer for Derbyshire and Nottinghamshire

Mrs Terry Garley
64 Wyndale Drive
Ilkeston
Derbyshire
DE7 4JG
Tel: 0115 932 9402

Oxfordshire
Oxfordshire Ecumenical Council
Executive Secretary

Revd Dr Graeme Smith
Westminster College
Oxford OX2 9AT
Tel: 01865 247644
Fax: 01865 251847

Peterborough
Greater Peterborough Ecumenical Council

Mr Frank Smith
61 Hall Lane
Werrington
Peterborough PE4 6RA
Tel: 01733 321245 (Home)
     01733 51915 (Office)

Shropshire (not Telford)
Churches Together in Shropshire
Secretary

Mr Ged Cliffe
Fern Villa
Four Crosses
Llanymynech
SY22 6PR
Tel: 01691 831374

Somerset
Somerset Churches Together
Ecumenical Officer

Mr Robin Dixon
12 Lawson Close
Saltford, Bristol BS18 3LB
Tel: 01225 872903

Staffordshire
Staffordshire Plus Ecumenical Council
Secretary

Revd Donald Brockbank
66 Heritage Court
Lichfield
WS14 9ST
Tel: 01543 417179

Suffolk
Suffolk Churches Together
Ecumenical Officer

Canon Colin Bevington
Bishop's House
4 Park Rd
Ipswich IP1 3ST
Tel: 01473 252829

Surrey
Churches Together in Surrey
Ecumenical Co-ordinator

Mrs Rosemary Underwood
The Parish Centre
Station Approach
Stoneleigh, Epsom
Surrey KT19 0QZ
Tel and *Fax:* 0181-394 0536

Sussex
Sussex Churches
Ecumenical Officer

Revd Terry Stratford
14 Ledgers Meadow
Cuckfield
W. Sussex RH17 5EB
Tel: 01444 456588

Swindon
Churches Together in Swindon
Secretary

Anne Doyle
16 Sherwood Ave
Melksham
Wilts SN12 7HJ
Tel: 01225 704748

Telford
Telford Christian Council
Development Officer

Revd David Lavender
Parkfield, Park Avenue
Madeley, Telford TF7 5AB
Tel: 01952 585731

Tyne & Wear (South)
see **Durham**

Tyne & Wear (North)
see **Newcastle Church Relations Group**

Warwickshire
Coventry & Warwickshire Ecumenical Council
Ecumenical Officer

Revd David Rowland
59 Tiverton Drive
Nuneaton CV11 6YJ
Tel: 01203 352551

West Midlands
West Midlands Region Churches Forum
General Secretary

Revd Mark Fisher
Carrs Lane Church Centre
Birmingham B4 7SX
Tel: 0121–643 6603

Wiltshire
Wiltshire Churches Together
Secretary

Anne Doyle
16 Sherwood Avenue
Melksham, Wilts
SN12 7HJ
Tel: 01225 704748

Worcester
Dudley and Worcestershire Ecumenical Council (OWEC)
Ecumenical Officer

Revd Clifford Owen
The Rectory
Clifton-upon-Teme
Worcester WR6 6DJ
Tel: 01886 812483

Yorkshire (North)
divided into three Regional Ecumenical Forums:
South Teeside,
North York Moors, Vale of York

North York Moors

Mrs Rachel Harrison
The Vicarage
Glaisdale
Whitby
N. Yorks YO21 2PL

South Teeside

Tel: 01947 897214

Vale of York

Jean Abbey
The Manor
Moss End Farm
Hawkhills
Easingwold
York YO6 3EW
Tel: 01347 838593

Yorkshire (South)
Churches Together in South Yorkshire
Ecumenical Development Officer

Mr Colin Brady
Crookes Valley Methodist Church
Crookesmoor Rd
Sheffield S6 3FQ
Tel: 0114 266 6156

Yorkshire (West)
West Yorkshire Ecumenical Council (WYEC)

Dr Stephanie Rybak
WYEC
62 Headingley Lane
Leeds LS6 2BU
Ecumenical Officer
Tel: 0113 274 7912
Fax: 0113 224 9998

The Council of Churches for Britain and Ireland

Office Inter-Church House, 35–41 Lower Marsh, London SE1 7RL
Tel: 0171–620 4444
Fax: 0171–928 0010
e-mail: gensec@ccbi.org.uk
Web: www.ccbi.org.uk

Presidents
Revd Io Smith
Revd Hugh Davidson
Most Revd A. R. Jones
H.E. Cardinal Thomas Winning
Mrs Gillian Kingston
Revd David Staple

Hon Treasurer Dr Jeremy Gerhard

General Secretary Revd John Reardon

The Council of Churches for Britain and Ireland (CCBI) is a fellowship of churches in Britain and Ireland which 'confess the Lord Jesus Christ as God and Saviour according to the Scriptures and therefore seek to fulfil together their common calling to the glory of the one God, Father, Son and Holy Spirit'. CCBI was inaugurated in September 1990 as the successor to the British Council of Churches as a result of an Inter-Church Process through which, over several years, the member churches explored their common calling and grew closer together in co-operation and commitment.

The Council, which is an Associated Council of Churches of the World Council of Churches and the Conference of European Churches, co-ordinates the work of the member churches and bodies in association in Britain and Ireland which are themselves grouped together in Churches Together in England, CYTUN (Churches Together in Wales), ACTS (Action of Churches Together in Scotland) and Irish ecumenical bodies, particularly the Irish Council of Churches.

The Council works through an Assembly meeting every two years and a Church Representatives' Meeting,

meeting at least twice each year. The Church of England members of the CRM are the Rt Revd Barry Rogerson, Mr Philip Mawer, Mrs Margaret Swinson and the Revd Sam Philpott. Ultimately authority for the Council is rooted in the decision-making bodies of the participating churches and the different patterns of authority in the churches are reflected in the balance between the meetings of CCBI. These meetings of CCBI give direction to the Council and are the means by which the churches decide on work which can appropriately be done together and the priority to be placed on such work. CCBI is financed by the member churches and bodies in association and by other donations.

The Week of Prayer for Christian Unity is observed each year from 18 to 25 January. The leaflets are available from September each year from CCBI Publications. Other ecumenical publications and a catalogue may be obtained from CCBI Publications, Inter-Church House, 35–41 Lower Marsh, London SE1 7RL.

CCBI works in co-operation with agencies which undertake work entrusted to them by the churches. In particular there is a very close relationship with Christian Aid, CAFOD and SCIAF, three overseas agencies sponsored by the member churches of the Council. Other agencies are One World Week, Christians Abroad and the Churches Commission on Overseas Students.

There is a provision in CCBI's constitution for the emergence of Commissions through which the churches will co-operate on particular aspects of work which they have decided to undertake together. The first Commission was the Churches' Commission on Mission which grew out of the work of the Conference for World Mission. The further Commissions for Racial Justice and Inter-Faith Relations have also been established. The decisions about recognising Commissions are taken by the Church Representatives' Meeting, and the integration of their work into the wider work of the churches is partly the responsibility of the Co-ordinating Secretaries. Commissions, to qualify for establishment within CCBI, must be supported by the churches with appropriate financing, staffing and other resourcing.

The most common method of working is through Networks of formal and informal organisations and groupings that help to develop the witness of the churches and whose work and insights are made available to the churches together through CCBI's Co-ordinating Secretaries.

SCHEDULE OF REPRESENTATION
The schedule of representation in the Council is as follows:

Full Members Baptist Union of Great Britain, 12; Cherubim & Seraphim Council of Churches, 2; Church in Wales, 8; Church of England, 45; Church of Ireland, 12; Church of Scotland, 30; Congregational Federation, 2; Council of African & Afro-Caribbean Churches, 3; Council of Oriental Orthodox Christian Churches, 3; Free Churches' Council, 2; Greek Orthodox Church, 5; Independent Methodist Churches, 2; International Ministerial Council of Great Britain, 2; Joint Council for Anglo-Caribbean Churches, 2; Lutheran Council of Great Britain, 2; Methodist Church, 20; Methodist Church in Ireland, 3; Moravian Church, 2; New Testament Assembly, 2; Presbyterian Church of Wales, 6; Religious Society of Friends, 3; Roman Catholic Church in England and Wales, 40; Roman Catholic Church in Scotland, 20; Russian Orthodox Church, 2; Salvation Army (British Territory), 5; Scottish Episcopal Church, 3; Scottish Congregational Church, 3; Serbian Orthodox Church, 3; Undeb yr Annibynwyr Cymraeg (Union of Welsh Independents), 5; United Free Church of Scotland, 2; United Reformed Church, 12; Wesleyan Holiness Church, 2.

Bodies in Association Action of Christians Against Torture, 1; Afro-West Indian United Council of Churches, 1; Association of Centres of Adult Theological Education, 1; Associations of Interchurch Families in Britain and Ireland, 1; Centre for Black and White Christian Partnership, 1; Christian Council on Ageing, 1; Christian Education Movement, 1; Christianity and the Future of Europe, 1; Church Action on Poverty, 1; Churches Council for Health and Healing, 1; Churches' East West European Relations Network, 1; Ecumenical Council for Corporate Responsibility, 1; Feed the Minds, 1; Fellowship of Prayer for Unity, 1; Fellowship of St Alban and St Sergius, 1; Iona Community, 1; Irish School of Ecumenics, 1; Living Stones, 1; National Association of Christian Communities & Networks, 1; National Christian Education Council, 1; New Assembly of Churches, 1; YMCA, 1; YWCA, 1.

Associate Members Roman Catholic Church in Ireland, 2; Seventh Day Adventist Church, 2.

STAFF
General Secretary Revd John Reardon

Co-ordinating Secretaries Revd Dr Colin Davey (*Church Life*); Vacancy (*Public Affairs*); Mr Paul Renshaw (*International Affairs*)

Associate Secretary Revd Jean Mayland (*Community of Women and Men*)

Churches' Commission on Mission Revd Donald Elliott (*Commission Secretary*); Mr Edmond Tang (*China*); Mr Simon Barrow (*Associate Commission Secretary*)

Churches' Commission for Racial Justice Revd Arlington Trotman (*Associate Secretary*); Apostle James Ozigi (*Projects Fund*)

Churches' Commission for Interfaith Relations Canon Christopher Lamb, Church House, Great Smith St, London SW1P 3NZ   *Tel:* 0171–898 1477

BODIES IN ASSOCIATION

ACTION OF CHRISTIANS AGAINST TORTURE
Mr Ken Smith, 35 North Hill, Highgate, London N6 4BD

AFRO-WEST INDIAN UNITED COUNCIL OF CHURCHES
Revd Eric Brown, Arcadian Gardens, High Rd, Wood Green, London N22 5AA   *Tel:* 0181–888 9427

ASSOCIATION OF CENTRES OF ADULT THEOLOGICAL EDUCATION
Helen Stanton, The Old Deanery, Wells, Somerset BA5 2UG   *Tel:* 01749 670777

ASSOCIATIONS OF INTERCHURCH FAMILIES IN BRITAIN AND IRELAND
Ruth Reardon, Inter-Church House, 35–41 Lower Marsh, London SE1 7RL   *Tel:* 0171–620 4444

CENTRE FOR BLACK AND WHITE CHRISTIAN PARTNERSHIP
Rt Revd Joseph Aldrad, Centre for Black and White Christian Partnership, Selly Oak Colleges, Birmingham B29 6LQ   *Tel:* 0121–472 7952
Fax: 0121–472 2400

CHRISTIAN COUNCIL ON AGEING
Mrs Margaret Young, Epworth House, Stuart St, Derby DE1 2EQ   *Tel* and *Fax:* (01335) 390484

CHRISTIAN EDUCATION MOVEMENT
Revd Dr Stephen Orchard, Royal Buildings, Victoria Street, Derby DE1 1GW   *Tel:* (01332) 296655

CHRISTIANITY AND THE FUTURE OF EUROPE
Revd Prof Kenneth Medhurst, c/o Lincoln Theological Institute, 36 Wilkinson St, Sheffield S10 2LB
Tel: 0114–276 3973

CHURCH ACTION ON POVERTY
The Co-ordinator, Central Buildings, Oldham Street, Manchester M1 1JT   *Tel:* 0161–236 9321

CHURCHES COUNCIL FOR HEALTH AND HEALING
Dr Rachel Rosser, St Luke's Hospital for the Clergy, 14 Fitzroy Square, London W1P 6AH   *Tel:* 0171–388 7903

CHURCHES' EAST WEST EUROPEAN RELATIONS NETWORK
Dr Philip Walters, 81 Thorney Leys, Witney, Oxon OX8 7AY   *Tel:* 01993 77178

ECUMENICAL COUNCIL FOR CORPORATE RESPONSIBILITY
Revd Crispin White, PO Box 4317, Bishop's Stortford, Herts CM22 7EZ   *Tel:* (01279) 718274

FEED THE MINDS
Dr Alwyn Marriage, Albany House, 67 Sydenham Rd, Guildford GU1 3RY   *Tel:* (01483) 888580

FELLOWSHIP OF PRAYER FOR UNITY
Revd Paul Renyard, 29 Ramley Rd, Pennington, Lymington, Hants SO41 8LH   *Tel:* (01590) 672646

FELLOWSHIP OF ST ALBAN AND ST SERGIUS
Revd Stephen Platt, 1 Canterbury Rd, Oxford OX2 6LU
Tel: (01865) 52991

IONA COMMUNITY
Revd Norman Shanks, Pearce Institute, Govan, Glasgow G51 3UU   *Tel:* 0141–445 4561
Fax: 0141–445 4295

IRISH SCHOOL OF ECUMENICS
Pamela Stotter, Milltown Park, Dublin 6, Ireland
Tel: 00–3531 2698607

LIVING STONES
Revd Dr Michael Prior, St Mary's College, Strawberry Hill, Twickenham TW1 4SX   *Tel:* 0181–892 0051

NATIONAL ASSOCIATION OF CHRISTIAN COMMUNITIES AND NETWORKS
Revd Stanley Baxter, Holyrood House with Thorpe House, 10 Sowerby Rd, Sowerby, Thirsk YO7 1HX
Tel: (01845) 522580

NATIONAL CHRISTIAN EDUCATION COUNCIL
General Secretary, 1020 Bristol Rd, Selly Oak, Birmingham B29 6LB   *Tel:* 0121–472 4242
Fax: 0121–472 7575

NEW ASSEMBLY OF CHURCHES
Revd Carmel Jones, 15 Oldridge Rd, London SW12 8PL
Tel: 0181–673 0595

WILLIAM TEMPLE FOUNDATION
Revd Malcolm Brown, Manchester Business School, Manchester M15 6PB   *Tel:* 0161–275 6534

YOUNG MEN'S CHRISTIAN ASSOCIATION
Mr Tony Malcolm, YMCA Christian and Spiritual Development Unit, Colman House, Station Rd, Knowle B93 0HL   *Tel:* 01564 730229

YOUNG WOMEN'S CHRISTIAN ASSOCIATION
Ms Gill Tishler (*Gen Secretary*), YWCA Headquarters, Clarendon House, 52 Cornmarket St, Oxford OX1 3EJ

For addresses of Full Members *see* pages 377–8.

The Council of Churches for Britain and Ireland

The Churches' Commission on Mission

Moderator Revd Dr Janet Wootton

Deputy Moderator Mr John Clark

Secretaries
Revd Donald Elliott (*Commission Secretary*)
Mr Edmond Tang (*China*)
Mr Simon Barrow (*Associate Commission Secretary*)

Office Inter-Church House, 35–41 Lower Marsh, London SE1 7RL
Tel: 0171–620 4444
Fax: 0171–928 0010

The Conference of Missionary Societies in Great Britain and Ireland was founded in 1912 as an outcome of the Edinburgh World Missionary Conference, and has been the centre of co-operative consultation, planning and common action among missionary agencies in Britain. In 1978 the Conference became a Division of the British Council of Churches, with the title of 'Conference for World Mission'.

With the termination of the British Council of Churches, much of the Conference's work has been taken up through the Churches' Commission on Mission of the Council of Churches for Britain and Ireland.

The Commission assists the churches and mission bodies to relate together to missionary and evangelistic work in all overseas areas, particularly through regional and national ecumenical councils, and to bring that work to bear on mission education and evangelism in Britain and Ireland. To that end, the Commission assists the churches in their organising of ecumenical forums with a broad agenda on specific world regions and mission tasks, including health care overseas. It works closely with the churches' aid and development agencies and relates especially to the relevant units of the World Council of Churches. The Commission is financed according to negotiated formulae by the participating bodies and from some special sources. Its total budget for 1998 was £256,000. Some bodies additionally contribute through the Commission to specific joint projects (e.g. China work, ecumenical bursaries, research on missionary congregations).

The following organisations have been providing resource persons for particular forums of the Commission:

Board of Mission (C of E) – Mission Theology
Church of Scotland – Middle East
Methodist Church – Pacific, and India Relations
Medical Missionaries of Mary – Overseas Health Care
Presbyterian Church of Wales – Asia
South American Missionary Society – Caribbean and Latin America
Union of Welsh Independents – Europe
United Society for the Propagation of the Gospel – International Encounter

PARTICIPATING BODIES
Most Full Members of, and some Bodies in Association with, the Council of Churches for Britain and Ireland (*see* page 371).
(N.B. Missionary and evangelistic societies of the Church of England working through PWM participate through Church of England representation – *see* page 21.)

In addition:

BAPTIST MISSIONARY SOCIETY
PO Box 49, Didcot, Oxon OX11 8XA
Revd Dr Alistair Brown

CATHOLIC FUND FOR OVERSEAS DEVELOPMENT
2 Romero Close, Stockwell Rd, London SW9 9TY
Mr Julian Filochowski

CATHOLIC INSTITUTE FOR INTERNATIONAL RELATIONS
Unit 3, Canonbury Yard, 190A New North Rd, London NW1 7BJ
Mr Ian Linden

CENTRE FOR BLACK AND WHITE CHRISTIAN PARTNERSHIP
Selly Oak Colleges, Bristol Rd, Birmingham B29 6LQ
Bishop Joe Aldred

CHRISTIAN AID
35–41 Lower Marsh, London SE1 7RL
Dr Daleep Mukarji

CHRISTIANS ABROAD
1 Stockwell Green, London SW9 9HP
Colin South

CHRISTIANS AWARE
Bishop's House, 38 Tooting Bec Gardens, London SW16 1QZ
Mrs Barbara Butler

CHRISTIAN EDUCATION MOVEMENT
Royal Buildings, Victoria St, Derby DE1 1GW
Revd Dr Stephen Orchard

CHURCHES' COMMISSION ON OVERSEAS STUDENTS
1 Stockwell Green, London SW9 9HP
Ms Gillian Court

FEED THE MINDS
Albany House, 67 Sydenham Rd, Guildford, Surrey GU1 3RY
Dr Alwyn Marriage

GRASSROOTS
Luton Industrial College, Chapel St, Luton LU1 2SL
Dr David Cowling

INTERSERVE (UK)
325 Kennington Rd, London SE11 4QH
Mr Richard Clark

IRISH MISSIONARY UNION
Orwell Park, Rathgar, Dublin 6, Ireland
Fr Tom Kiggins

LEPROSY MISSION INTERNATIONAL
80 Windmill Rd, Brentford, Middx TW8 0GA
Mr Trevor Durston

QUAKER PEACE AND SERVICE
Friends House, Euston Rd, London NW1 2BJ
Andrew Clark

SCHOOL OF MISSION AND WORLD CHRISTIANITY
Selly Oak Colleges, Birmingham B29 6LE
Revd Dr Andrew Kirk

WORLD CONFERENCE (THE BOYS' BRIGADE ETC)
Church House, Belfast, Northern Ireland BT1 6DW
Eric Woodburn

YMCA
Colman House, Station Rd, Knowle, Solihull B93 0HL
Mr Tony Malcolm

The Churches' Commission for Racial Justice

Moderator Prebendary Theo Samuel

Deputy Moderators Ms Maryanne Ure, Ms Pat White

Associate Secretary Mr Arlington Trotman

Executive Secretary for the Racial Justice Fund Senior Apostle James Ozigi

Office Inter-Church House, 35–41 Lower Marsh, London SE1 7RL
Tel: 0171–620 4444
Fax: 0171–928 0010
e-mail: ccrj@ccbi.org.uk

The Churches' Commission for Racial Justice (CCRJ) is a Commission of the Council of Churches for Britain and Ireland, and reports annually to the CCBI. It has been formed by the churches themselves to monitor trends in race relations in British society, to encourage the exchange of information among the churches regarding these trends and, in conjunction with the churches' own committees responsible for race issues, to co-ordinate a response.

It manages the Ecumenical Racial Justice Fund, supported mainly by Christian Aid, the Church Urban Fund, the Catholic Association for Racial Justice and the Methodist Church which funds local and national groups, and organisations combating racism or overcoming racial discrimination. Its policy is decided by a Commission of 25 representatives from CCBI member churches, including those of African, African Caribbean and Asian origin.

Scotland, Wales and Ireland

ACTION OF CHURCHES TOGETHER IN SCOTLAND
Scottish Churches House, Dunblane, Perthshire FK15 0AJ
Tel: (01786) 823588
Fax: (01786) 825844

General Secretary Revd Maxwell Craig

Convenor of Central Council Most Revd Richard Holloway

ACTS is nine Scottish churches working together in the cause of Christ's kingdom. It embraces what the church and Christian people plan to do together in Scotland. It has a Central Council to enable this wider pilgrimage and action. It has three Commissions: Unity, Faith and Order; Mission, Evangelism and Education; Justice, Peace, Social and Moral Issues.

Member Churches Church of Scotland, Methodist Church, Religious Society of Friends, Roman Catholic Church in Scotland, Salvation Army (Scottish Territory), Scottish Congregational Church, Scottish Episcopal Church, United Free Church of Scotland, United Reformed Church.

Associate Members Christian Aid, Feed the Minds (Scotland), Iona Community, Lutheran Council of Great Britain, National Bible Society of Scotland, Orthodox Church, Scottish Catholic International Aid Fund, Student Christian Movement, World Day of Prayer, YMCA, YWCA.

Observer Unitarian Church.

CYTUN: CHURCHES TOGETHER IN WALES
President Vacancy

General Secretary Gethin Abraham Williams, 11 St Helen's Rd, Swansea SA1 4AL
Tel: (01792) 460876
Fax: (01792) 469391

The objects of CYTUN are the advancement of the Christian religion and of any other purposes which are charitable according to the law of England and Wales.

CYTUN shall seek to further its objects by (1) gathering together the churches in Wales in all the richness of their present diversity so that they can learn from and value each other's traditions in a parity of esteem; (2) offering the churches the opportunity to enter into a new commitment to reflect together theologically on matters of faith, order and ethics; to pray together and to learn to appreciate each other's pattern of prayer; to work together, sharing resources and presenting the gospel in word and action; (3) seeking to help the churches to arrive at a common mind so that they might become more fully united in faith, communion, pastoral care and mission; (4) acting as a body which enables the churches themselves to reach their decisions in the context of common study, prayer and worship; (5) enabling the churches to do together whatever they can.

Member Churches The Salvation Army, The Presbyterian Church of Wales, Covenanted Baptist Churches in Wales, The United Reformed Church, The Methodist Church, The Roman Catholic Church, The Church in Wales, The Congregational Federation, The Union of Welsh Independents, The Baptist Union of Wales, Religious Society of Friends.

Observers The Lutheran Council of Great Britain, The Orthodox Churches in Wales, The Seventh Day Adventist Church.

Bodies in Association Bible Society, Cardiff Centre for Christian Adult Education, Christian Education Movement, Enfys, Fellowship of Reconciliation, Free Church Council for Wales, Free Churches' Federal Council for England and Wales, Student Christian Movement, Sunday Schools Council for Wales, National Association of Christian Communities and Networks, National Retreat Association, Women's World Day of Prayer, YWCA.

Agencies Christian Aid, CAFOD, Christians against Torture, Churches' National Housing Coalition, Welsh Council on Alcohol and Drugs

CYTUN also works in close collaboration with Enfys: The Commission of the Covenanted Churches in Wales.

CYTUN functions through the following structures:
(a) GYMANFA (The Assembly) meeting once every three/four years and as broadly representative as possible of the life of the churches in Wales at all levels.
(b) The Council meeting three times annually on which senior representatives of the churches will serve as well as those who are representative of the diversity of the life of the churches.

A recent review has led to the discontinuation of the three Commissions. Consultations are currently underway to explore other patterns of collaboration in specialist fields, through regular meetings of denominational officers and short-term working groups on specialist topics.

THE IRISH COUNCIL OF CHURCHES
Inter-Church Centre, 48 Elmwood Ave, Belfast BT9 6AZ
Tel: (01232) 663145
Fax: (01232) 381737
e-mail: Icpep@unite.co.uk
Web: www.unite.co.uk/customers/Icpep

President Revd Edmund Mawhinney

Vice-President Revd Dr Ian Ellis

Hon Treasurer Miss Hazel McMillan

General Secretary Dr David Stevens

Administrative Secretary Mrs Florence Pyper

From 1906 the Presbyterian and Methodist Churches had a joint committee for united efforts. In 1910 the General Assembly of the Presbyterian Church invited other evangelical churches to set up similar joint committees with it. The Church of Ireland accepted and by 1911 the joint committee of these two churches was in action. Following a recommendation of the 1920 Lambeth Conference, these joint committees developed in 1922 into the United Council of Christian Churches and Religious Communions in Ireland by the inclusion of most of its present constituents. In 1966 the United Council changed its name to the Irish Council of Churches. The Council employed its first full-time secretary in April 1972.

The Irish Council of Churches is constituted by Christian Communions in Ireland willing to join in united efforts to promote the spiritual, physical, moral and social welfare of the people and the extension of the rule of Christ among all nations and over every region of life.

Member Churches The Church of Ireland, The Greek Orthodox Church, Lifelink Network of Churches, The Lutheran Church in Ireland, The Methodist Church in Ireland, The Irish District of the Moravian Church, The Non-Subscribing Presbyterian Church of Ireland, The Presbyterian Church in Ireland, The Salvation Army (Ireland Division), The Religious Society of Friends in Ireland.

The Council consists of 71 members appointed by the Member Churches, together with the Heads of the Member Churches and up to ten co-opted members, the General Secretary, Treasurer and immediate Past President of the Council. It meets twice a year. The Member Churches appoint an Executive Committee which is responsible for the day-to-day affairs of the Council.

The work of the Council is structured into two Boards: Inter-Church Affairs (including the Child in the Church group, ICC Women's Link, and local ecumenical activity) and Overseas Affairs (including World Mission and Christian Aid). Every member of the Council can be a member of a Board.

The Council puts considerable emphasis on peace and reconciliation work. A peace programme has been developed since July 1978 in conjunction with the Irish Commission for Justice and Peace, and materials for schools and adult Bible study guides have been produced.

More information about the Council's work can be obtained from the Annual Report (available free).

Churches in Britain and Ireland: Addresses

FULL MEMBERS OF CCBI

BAPTIST UNION OF GREAT BRITAIN
Revd David Coffey (*General Secretary*), Baptist House, 129 Broadway, Didcot, Oxon OX11 8RT
Tel: (01235) 512077
Fax: (01235) 811537

CHERUBIM AND SERAPHIM COUNCIL OF CHURCHES (UK)
Most Senior Apostle J. A. Odufona, 57 Endymion Rd, London SW2 2BU *Tel:* 0181–671 0144

CHURCH IN WALES
Mr David McIntyre (*Secretary General*), 39 Cathedral Rd, Cardiff, S. Glam CF1 9XF *Tel:* (01222) 231638
Fax: (01222) 387835

CHURCH OF ENGLAND
Mr Philip Mawer (*Secretary General of the General Synod*), Church House, Great Smith St, London SW1P 3NZ
Tel: 0171–898 1360
Fax: 0171–799 2714

CHURCH OF IRELAND
Mr David Meredith, The Chief Officer, Representative Body, Church of Ireland House, Upper Rathmines, Dublin 6, Eire *Tel:* 0001–4978 422
Fax: 0001–4978 821

CHURCH OF SCOTLAND
Revd Dr F. A. J. Macdonald, 121 George St, Edinburgh EH2 4YN *Tel:* 0131–225 5722
Fax: 0131–226 6121

CONGREGATIONAL FEDERATION
Pastor Graham Adams, 4 Castle Gate, Nottingham NG1 7AS *Tel:* (0115) 941 3801
Fax: (0115) 948 0902

COUNCIL OF AFRICAN AND AFRO-CARIBBEAN CHURCHES
Most Revd Fr Olu Abiola, 31 Norton House, Sidney Rd, London SW9 0UJ *Tel:* 0171–274 5589

COUNCIL OF THE ORIENTAL ORTHODOX CHRISTIAN CHURCHES
Rt Revd Yegishe Gizirian, The Armenian Vicarage, Iverna Gardens, London W8 6BR *Tel:* 0171–937 0152

FREE CHURCHES' COUNCIL
Revd Geoffrey Roper (*Secretary*), 27 Tavistock Place, London WS1H 9HH *Tel:* 0171–387 0150

GREEK ORTHODOX CHURCH
The Most Revd Archbishop Gregorios, 5 Craven Hill, London W2 3EN *Tel:* 0171–723 4787
Fax: 0171–224 9301

INDEPENDENT METHODIST CHURCHES
Mr John M. Day (*General Secretary*), Old Police House, Croxton, Stafford ST1 6PE *Tel:* (0163 082) 671

INTERNATIONAL MINISTERIAL COUNCIL OF GREAT BRITAIN
Revd Sheila Douglas, 55 Tudor Walk, Watford, Herts WD2 4NY *Tel:* (01923) 239266

JOINT COUNCIL FOR ANGLO-CARIBBEAN CHURCHES
Revd Esme Beswick, 141 Railton Rd, London SE24 0LT
Tel: 0171–737 6542
Fax: 0171–733 2821

LUTHERAN COUNCIL OF GREAT BRITAIN
Very Revd Robert Patkai, Lutheran Church House, 8 Collingham Gardens, London SW5
Tel and *Fax:* 0181–904 2849

METHODIST CHURCH
Revd Nigel Collinson (*Secretary of the Conference*), 25 Marylebone Rd, London NW1 5JR *Tel:* 0171–486 5502
Fax: 0171–233 1295

METHODIST CHURCH IN IRELAND
Revd Dr Edmund Mawhinney (*Secretary of the Conference*), 3 Upper Malone Rd, Belfast BT9 6TD
Tel: (01232) 324554
Fax: (01232) 2399467

MORAVIAN CHURCH
Revd W. J. McOwat (*Secretary Provincial Board*), 5 Muswell Hill, London N10 3TJ   *Tel:* 0181–883 3409
Fax: 0181–442 0112

NEW TESTAMENT ASSEMBLY
Revd Io Smith, 5 Wallrod Rd, London E11 1DQ
Tel: 0181–539 2755

PRESBYTERIAN CHURCH OF WALES
Revd Dafydd Owen, Presbyterian Church of Wales, 53 Richmond Rd, Cardiff CF2 3UP   *Tel:* (01222) 494913
Fax: (01222) 464293

RELIGIOUS SOCIETY OF FRIENDS
Elsa Dicks (*Recording Clerk*), Friends House, Euston Rd, London NW1 2BJ   *Tel:* 0171–387 3601
Fax: 0171–388 1977

ROMAN CATHOLIC CHURCH IN ENGLAND AND WALES
Rt Revd Mgr Arthur Roche, 39 Eccleston Square, London SW1V 1PD   *Tel:* 0171–630 8220
Fax: 0171–630 5166

ROMAN CATHOLIC CHURCH IN SCOTLAND
Rt Revd Mgr Henry Docherty, 64 Aitken St, Airdrie, Lanarkshire ML6 6LT   *Tel:* (01236) 764061
Fax: (01236) 762489

RUSSIAN ORTHODOX CHURCH
The Most Revd Metropolitan Anthony of Sourozh, Cathedral of the Assumption and All Saints, Ennismore Gardens, London SW7 1NH   *Tel:* 0171–584 0096

SALVATION ARMY (British Territory)
Commissioner Dinsdale Pender, 101 Queen Victoria St, London EC4P 4EP   *Tel:* 0171–236 5222
Fax: 0171–236 6272

SCOTTISH CONGREGATIONAL CHURCH
Revd John Arthur (*Secretary*), PO Box 189, Glasgow G1 2BX   *Tel:* 0141–332 7667
Fax: 0141–332 8463

SCOTTISH EPISCOPAL CHURCH
Mr John Stuart (*Secretary*), 21 Grosvenor Cresc, Edinburgh EH12 5EE   *Tel:* 0131–225 6357
Fax: 0131–346 7247

SERBIAN ORTHODOX CHURCH
Very Revd Milenko Zebic, 131 Cob Lane, Bournville, Birmingham B30 1QE   *Tel:* 0121–458 5273
Fax: 0121–458 4986

UNDEB YR ANNIBYNWYR CYMRAEG
(UNION OF WELSH INDEPENDENTS)
Revd Derwyn Jones (*Secretary*), 11 Heol Sant Helen, Swansea SA1 4AL   *Tel:* (01792) 652542
Fax: (01792) 650647

UNITED FREE CHURCH OF SCOTLAND
Revd John Fulton (*Secretary*), 11 Newton Place, Glasgow G3 7PR   *Tel:* 0141–332 3435

UNITED REFORMED CHURCH
Revd Anthony Burnham (*General Secretary*), 86 Tavistock Place, London WC1H 9RT   *Tel:* 0171–916 2020
Fax: 0171–916 2021

WESLEYAN HOLINESS CHURCH
Revd Kecious Gray, Holyhead Rd, Handsworth, Birmingham B21 0LA   *Tel:* 0121–520 7849

ASSOCIATE MEMBERS
ROMAN CATHOLIC CHURCH IN IRELAND
Revd Aidan O'Boyle, Iona, 65 Newry Rd, Dundalk, Co. Louth   *Tel:* 00353 423 8087
Fax: 042–33575

SEVENTH DAY ADVENTIST CHURCH
Revd Denys Baildam, 3 Hardy Green, Wellington Chase, Crowthorne, Berks RG45 7QR   *Tel:* (01344) 772027

Conference of European Churches

Moderator Metropolitan Jérémie Caligiorgis

Vice-Moderator Oberkirchenrätin Rut Rohrandt

Deputy Vice-Moderator Prof Dr Jean-Marc Prieur

General Secretary Revd Dr Keith Clements, PO Box 2100, 150 Route de Ferney, 1211 Geneva 2, Switzerland
Tel: 791 61 11
Fax: 791 62 27

Born in the era of the 'cold war' some 30 years ago, the CEC emerged into a fragmented and divided continent. Thus it was that churches of Eastern and Western Europe felt one priority of their work to be promoting international understanding – building bridges. This the CEC has consistently tried to do, always insisting that no 'iron curtain' exists among the churches.

The supreme governing body of the Conference is the Assembly. Here all 123 member churches are represented. The first Assembly was in 1959 and further

Assemblies were held in 1960, 1962, 1964, 1967, 1971, 1974, 1979, 1986, 1992 and 1997.

The CEC initiated the European Ecumenical Assembly 'Peace with Justice' held in Basel in May 1989, co-sponsored with the Council of European Bishops' Conferences (Roman Catholic). A second European Ecumenical Assembly was held in Graz, Austria, in 1997 with the theme 'Reconciliation: Gift of God and Source of New Life'.

The 40-member Central Committee oversees the implementation of the decisions of the Assembly. A Presidium, drawn from the Central Committee, acts as the Executive Council of the Conference.

The Secretariat ensures the continuity of the activities of CEC. It consists of 10.5 staff: the General Secretary and secretaries responsible for finance and administration; communications and information; and in Unity, Mission and Service, and Witness in Church and Society.

Publications include occasional papers, and *Monitor*, a quarterly news-sheet.

World Council of Churches

The Church of England has taken its full share in the international ecumenical movement since the Edinburgh Conference of 1910. In 1998 the General Synod made a grant of £117,200 to the General Budget of the World Council of Churches.

Presidium Prof Anne-Marie Aagaard; Bishop Vinton Anderson; The Hon Revd Leslie Boseto; Ms Priyanka Mendis; Revd Eunice Santana; His Holiness Pope Shenouda; Dr Aaron Tolen

Moderator of Central Committee His Holiness Aram I, Catholicos of Cilicia (Armenian Apostolic Church (Cilicia), Lebanon)

Vice-Moderators
Ephorus Dr S. A. E. Nababan (Batak Protestant Christian Church, Indonesia); Pastor Nélida Ritchie (Evangelical Methodist Church of Argentina)

General Secretary Revd Dr Konrad Raiser (Evangelical Church in Germany)

Office 150 route de Ferney, 1211 Geneva 2, Switzerland
Tel: 00–41–22–791 61 11
Telex No: 415 730 OIK CH
Fax: 00–41–22 791 03 61
Cable: Oikoumene Geneva
e-mail: info@wcc-coe.org

The World Council of Churches was brought into formal existence by a resolution of its first Assembly at Amsterdam in 1948.

At the New Delhi Assembly in 1961, the first basis of the World Council – 'a fellowship of Churches which accept our Lord Jesus Christ as God and Saviour' – was amended as follows:

> The World Council of Churches is a fellowship of Churches which confess the Lord Jesus Christ as God and Saviour according to the Scriptures, and therefore seek to fulfil together their common calling to the glory of the one God, Father, Son and Holy Spirit.

In the amended constitution, accepted by the Nairobi Assembly in 1975, the functions of the Council are as follows:

1 to call the churches to the goal of visible unity in one faith and in one eucharistic fellowship expressed in worship and in common life in Christ, and to advance towards that unity in order that the world may believe;
2 to facilitate the common witness of the churches in each place and in all places;
3 to support the churches in their worldwide missionary and evangelistic task;
4 to express the common concern of the churches in the service of human need, the breaking down of barriers between people, and the promotion of one human family in justice and peace;
5 to foster the renewal of the churches in unity, worship, mission and service;
6 to establish and maintain relations with national councils and regional conferences of churches, world confessional bodies and other ecumenical organisations;
7 to carry on the work of the world movements for Faith and Order and Life and Work and of the International Missionary Council and the World Council of Christian Education.

The constitution also states, in regard to the authority of the World Council:

> The World Council shall offer counsel and provide opportunity for united action in matters of common interest.
> It may take action on behalf of constituent churches only in such matters as one or more of them may commit to it and only on behalf of such churches.
> The World Council shall not legislate for the churches; nor shall it act for them in any manner except as indicated above or as may hereafter be specified by the constituent churches.

The WCC is governed by an Assembly of Member Churches, a Central Committee, and by an Executive Committee. Assemblies have been held as follows:

1. AMSTERDAM, 1948 – theme: 'Man's Disorder and God's Design'
2. EVANSTON, 1954 – theme: 'Christ the Hope of the World'
3. NEW DELHI, 1961 – theme: 'Jesus Christ, the Light of the World'
4. UPPSALA, 1968 – theme: 'Behold, I Make All Things New'
5. NAIROBI, 1975 – theme: 'Jesus Christ Frees and Unites'
6. VANCOUVER, 1983 – theme: 'Jesus Christ the Life of the World'
7. CANBERRA, 1991– theme: 'Come, Holy Spirit – Renew the Whole Creation'
8. HARARE 1998 – theme: 'Turn to God – Rejoice in Hope'

The Central Committee elected by the Seventh Assembly includes two members of the Church of England: Rt Revd Barry Rogerson (*Bishop of Bristol*) and Mrs Maryon Jägers. At its first full meeting in September 1991, one of its tasks was to approve some reorganisation within the present structure of the Council to enable it to carry out the programmes called for by the Assembly using a more co-ordinated and flexible style of work.

Theological reflection and analysis is central to the task of the WCC and must therefore undergird all its programmes.

WCC programmes are approved by a range of committees, commissions and advisory groups whose membership is drawn from the Council's member churches. The work of the Council is carried out through the General Secretariat and four Programme Units, as follows:

The General Secretariat includes the Office of the General Secretary, and Offices for Church and Ecumenical Relations, Interreligious Relations, Communication; the Ecumenical Institute, Bossey; Programme Co-ordination, and Finance and Administration.

PROGRAMME UNIT I: UNITY AND RENEWAL
Brings together the concern for the search for Ecclesial Unity – Faith and Order; Lay participation towards Inclusive Community; Worship and Spirituality; and Ecumenical Theological Education.

PROGRAMME UNIT II: CHURCHES IN MISSION, HEALTH EDUCATION, WITNESS
Focuses on Mission and Evangelism in Unity; Gospel and Cultures; CMC – Churches' Action for Health; Education for all God's People; Community and Justice.

PROGRAMME UNIT III: JUSTICE, PEACE AND CREATION
Brings together concerns relating to Justice, Peace and the Integrity of Creation (JPIC) a conciliar process; Programme to Combat Racism; Women; Youth: International Affairs (CCIA); Economy, Ecology and Sustainable Society (ECOS).

PROGRAMME UNIT IV: SHARING AND SERVICE
Is concerned with the Sharing of Ecumenical Resources; Understanding Diakonia; Meeting Urgent Human Need: Emergencies, Refugees; Advocacy and Action with the Poor, Equipping and Linking Churches in Service.

The World Council has 332 member churches, including 33 which are associated. Almost every Church of the Anglican Communion is included, together with Orthodox churches and all the main Protestant traditions. The Roman Catholic Church is not in membership but has sent official observers to all main World Council meetings since 1960. It is a full member of the Faith and Order Commission of the World Council.

WCC MEMBER CHURCHES, ASSOCIATE MEMBER CHURCHES AND ASSOCIATE COUNCILS

* Associate member church.
** Associate council.
† Names and locations of churches are given according to information available to the WCC at the time of publication. The name of the country appears in square brackets where it is not obvious from the name of the church. Geographical references are provided only where they are necessary to identify the church or when they indicate the location of headquarters of churches with regional or world membership.
The mention of a country in this list does not imply any political judgement on the part of the WCC.

AFRICA
African Christian Church and Schools [Kenya]
African Church of the Holy Spirit [Kenya]*
African Israel Church, Nineveh [Kenya]
African Protestant Church [Cameroon]*
Anglican Church of Kenya
Anglican Church of Tanzania
Botswana Christian Council**
Christian Council of Churches in Madagascar (FFKM)**
Christian Council of Ghana**
Christian Council of Tanzania**
Christian Council of Zambia**
Church of Christ in Congo
 – Baptist Community of Western Congo
 – Community of Disciples of Christ
 – Episcopal Baptist Community
 – Evangelical Community
 – Mennonite Community
 – Presbyterian Community
Church of Christ – Light of the Holy Spirit [Congo]
Church of Jesus Christ in Madagascar
Church of Jesus Christ on Earth by His Messenger Simon Kimbangu [Congo]
Church of the Brethren in Nigeria
Church of the Lord Aladura [Nigeria]
Church of the Province of Burundi
Church of the Province of Central Africa [Botswana]
Church of the Province of Nigeria
Church of the Province of Rwanda
Church of the Province of Southern Africa [South Africa]
Church of the Province of the Indian Ocean [Seychelles]
Church of the Province of Uganda
Church of the Province of West Africa [Ghana]
Council of Christian Churches in Angola**
Council of Churches in Namibia**
Council of Churches in Sierra Leone**
Council of Swaziland Churches**
Ecumenical Council of Christian Churches of Congo**
Episcopal Church of the Sudan
Ethiopian Evangelical Church Mekane Yesus
Ethiopian Orthodox Tewahedo Church
Evangelical Church of Cameroon
Evangelical Church of Gabon
Evangelical Church of the Congo
Evangelical Congregational Church in Angola
Evangelical Lutheran Church in Southern Africa [South Africa]
Evangelical Lutheran Church in the Rep. of Namibia
Evangelical Lutheran Church in Tanzania
Evangelical Lutheran Church in Zimbabwe
Evangelical Pentecostal Mission of Angola
Evangelical Presbyterian Church, Ghana
Evangelical Presbyterian Church in South Africa
Evangelical Presbyterian Church of Togo
Evangelical Reformed Church of Angola

Gambia Christian Council**
Kenya Evangelical Lutheran Church*
Lesotho Evangelical Church
Liberian Council of Churches**
Lutheran Church in Liberia
Malagasy Lutheran Church
Methodist Church, Ghana
Methodist Church in Kenya
Methodist Church in Togo
Methodist Church in Zimbabwe
Methodist Church, Nigeria
Methodist Church of Southern Africa [South Africa]
Methodist Church, Sierra Leone
Moravian Church in Southern Africa [South Africa]
Moravian Church in Tanzania
Native Baptist Church of Cameroon
Nigerian Baptist Convention
Presbyterian Church in Cameroon
Presbyterian Church in the Sudan
Presbyterian Church of Africa [South Africa]
Presbyterian Church of Cameroon
Presbyterian Church of East Africa [Kenya]
Presbyterian Church of Ghana
Presbyterian Church of Mozambique*
Presbyterian Church of Nigeria
Presbyterian Church of Rwanda
Presbyterian Church of Southern Africa [South Africa]
Presbyterian Community of Kinshasa [Congo]
Presbytery of Liberia*
Protestant Church of Algeria*
Protestant Methodist Church of Benin
Protestant Methodist Church, Ivory Coast
Reformed Church in Zambia
Reformed Church in Zimbabwe
Reformed Church of Equatorial Guinea*
Reformed Presbyterian Church in Southern Africa [South Africa]
Sudan Council of Churches**
The South African Council of Churches**
Uganda Joint Christian Council**
Union of Baptist Churches of Cameroon
United Church of Zambia
United Congregational Church of Southern Africa [South Africa]
United Evangelical Church 'Anglican Communion in Angola'*
Uniting Reformed Church in Southern Africa
Zimbabwe Council of Churches**

ASIA
Anglican Church in Aotearoa, New Zealand and Polynesia
Anglican Church of Australia
Anglican Communion in Japan
Associated Churches of Christ in New Zealand
Bangladesh Baptist Sangha
Baptist Union of New Zealand
Batak Christian Community Church [Indonesia]*

Batak Protestant Christian Church [Indonesia]
Bengal–Orissa–Bihar Baptist Convention [India]*
China Christian Council
Christian Church of Central Sulawesi [Indonesia]
Christian Church in East Timor (GKTT)
Christian Evangelical Church in Minahasa [Indonesia]
Christian Protestant Angkola Church [Indonesia]
Christian Protestant Church in Indonesia
Church of Bangladesh*
Church of Ceylon [Sri Lanka]
Church of Christ in Thailand
Church of North India
Church of Pakistan
Church of South India
Church of the Province of Myanmar
Churches of Christ in Australia
Communion of Churches in Indonesia**
Conference of Churches in Aotearoa – New Zealand**
Council of Churches of Malaysia**
East Java Christian Church [Indonesia]
Episcopal Church in the Philippines
Evangelical Christian Church in Halmahera [Indonesia]
Evangelical Christian Church in Irian Jaya [Indonesia]
Evangelical Church of Sangir Talaud [Indonesia]
Evangelical Methodist Church in the Philippines
Hong Kong Christian Council**
Hong Kong Council of the Church of Christ in China
Indonesian Christian Church (GKI)
Indonesian Christian Church (HKI)
Javanese Christian Churches [Indonesia]
Kalimantan Evangelical Church [Indonesia]
Karo Batak Protestant Church [Indonesia]
Korean Christian Church in Japan*
Korean Methodist Church
Malankara Orthodox Syrian Church [India]
Maori Council of Churches in Aotearoa [New Zealand]**
Mar Thoma Syrian Church of Malabar [India]
Methodist Church in India
Methodist Church in Malaysia
Methodist Church in Singapore*
Methodist Church of New Zealand
Methodist Church [Sri Lanka]
Methodist Church, Upper Burma [Myanmar]
Myanmar Baptist Convention
Myanmar Council of Churches**
National Christian Council in Japan**
National Christian Council of Sri Lanka**
National Council of Churches in Australia**
National Council of Churches in India**
National Council of Churches in Korea**
National Council of Churches in the Philippines**

World Council of Churches 381

National Council of Churches of Singapore**
Nias Protestant Christian Church [Indonesia]
Orthodox Church in Japan
Pasundan Christian Church [Indonesia]
Philippine Independent Church
Presbyterian Church in Taiwan
Presbyterian Church in the Republic of Korea
Presbyterian Church of Aotearoa New Zealand
Presbyterian Church of Korea
Presbyterian Church of Pakistan
Protestant Christian Church in Bali* [Indonesia]
Protestant Church in Indonesia
Protestant Church in Sabah [Malaysia]
Protestant Church in South-East Sulawesi [Indonesia]
Protestant Church in the Moluccas [Indonesia]
Protestant Church in Western Indonesia
Protestant Evangelical Church in Timor [Indonesia]
Samavesam of Telugu Baptist Churches [India]
Simalungun Protestant Christian Church [Indonesia]
Toraja Church [Indonesia]
United Church of Christ in Japan
United Church of Christ in the Philippines
United Evangelical Lutheran Churches in India
Uniting Church in Australia

CARIBBEAN
Church in the Province of the West Indies [Antigua]
Council of Churches of Cuba**
Jamaica Baptist Union
Jamaica Council of Churches**
Methodist Church in Cuba*
Methodist Church in the Caribbean and the Americas [Antigua]
Moravian Church, Eastern West Indies Province [Antigua]
Moravian Church in Jamaica
Moravian Church in Surinam
Presbyterian Church in Trinidad and Tobago
Presbyterian Reformed Church in Cuba*
St Vincent and the Grenadines Christian Council**
United Church of Jamaica and the Cayman Islands
United Protestant Church [Netherlands Antilles]*

EUROPE
Action of Churches Together in Scotland**
Armenian Apostolic Church
Autocephalous Orthodox Church in Poland
Baptist Union of Denmark
Baptist Union of Great Britain
Baptist Union of Hungary
Bulgarian Orthodox Church
Catholic Diocese of the Old Catholics in Germany
Christian Council of Sweden**
Church in Wales
Church of England
Church of Greece
Church of Ireland
Church of Norway
Church of Scotland
Church of Sweden
Churches Together in England**
Council of Christian Churches in Germany**

Council of Churches for Britain and Ireland**
Council of Churches in the Netherlands**
Cytun: Churches Together in Wales**
Czechoslovak Hussite Church
Ecumenical Council of Churches in Austria**
Ecumenical Council of Churches in the Czech Republic**
Ecumenical Council of Churches in Hungary**
Ecumenical Council of Churches in the Slovak Republic**
Ecumenical Council of Churches in Yugoslavia**
Ecumenical Council of Denmark**
Ecumenical Patriarchate of Constantinople [Turkey]
Estonian Evangelical Lutheran Church
European Continental Province of the Moravian Church [Netherlands]
Evangelical Baptist Union of Italy*
Evangelical Church in Germany
Church of Lippe
Evangelical Church in Baden
Evangelical Church in Berlin – Brandenburg
Evangelical Church in Hesse and Nassau
Evangelical Church in Württemberg
Evangelical Church of Anhalt
Evangelical Church of Bremen
Evangelical Church of Hesse Electorate – Waldeck
Evangelical Church of the Palatinate
Evangelical Church of the Province of Saxony
Evangelical Church of the Rhineland
Evangelical Church of the Silesian Oberlausitz
Evangelical Church of Westphalia
Evangelical Lutheran Church in Bavaria
Evangelical Lutheran Church in Brunswick
Evangelical Lutheran Church in Oldenburg
Evangelical Lutheran Church in Thuringia
Evangelical Lutheran Church of Hanover
Evangelical Lutheran Church of Mecklenburg
Evangelical Lutheran Church of Saxony
Evangelical Lutheran Church of Schaumburg – Lippe
Evangelical Reformed Church in Bavaria and Northwestern Germany
North Elbian Evangelical Lutheran Church
Pomeranian Evangelical Church
Evangelical Church of Czech Brethren [Czech Republic]
Evangelical Church of the Augsburg and Helvetic Confessions [Austria]
Evangelical Church of the Augsburg Confession in Poland
Evangelical Church of the Augsburg Confession in Romania
Evangelical Church of the Augsburg Confession in the Slovak Republic
Evangelical Church of the Augsburg Confession of Alsace and Lorraine [France]
Evangelical Lutheran Church in the Kingdom of the Netherlands
Evangelical Lutheran Church in Denmark
Evangelical Lutheran Church of Finland
Evangelical Lutheran Church of France
Evangelical Lutheran Church of Iceland
Evangelical Lutheran Church of Latvia
Evangelical Methodist Church of Italy
Evangelical Presbyterian Church of Portugal*
Evangelical Synodal Presbyterial Church of the Augsburg Confession in Romania
Finnish Ecumenical Council **

Greek Evangelical Church
Latvian Evangelical Lutheran Church Abroad [Germany]
Lusitanian Catholic Apostolic Evangelical Church [Portugal]*
Lutheran Church in Hungary
Mennonite Church [Germany]
Mennonite Church in the Netherlands
Methodist Church [UK]
Methodist Church in Ireland
Mission Covenant Church of Sweden
Moravian Church in Great Britain and Ireland
Netherlands Reformed Church
Old Catholic Church of Austria
Old Catholic Church of Switzerland
Old Catholic Church of the Netherlands
Old Catholic Mariavite Church in Poland
Orthodox Autocephalous Church of Albania
Orthodox Church of the Czech Lands and Slovakia
Orthodox Church of Slovakia [Slovak Republic]
Orthodox Church of Finland
Polish Catholic Church in Poland
Polish Ecumenical Council**
Presbyterian Church of Wales
Reformed Christian Church in Slovakia [Slovak Republic]
Reformed Christian Church in Yugoslavia
Reformed Church in Hungary
Reformed Church of Alsace and Lorraine [France]
Reformed Church of France
Reformed Church in Romania
Reformed Churches in the Netherlands
Remonstrant Brotherhood [Netherlands]
Romanian Orthodox Church
Russian Orthodox Church
Scottish Congregational Church
Scottish Episcopal Church
Serbian Orthodox Church [Yugoslavia]
Silesian Evangelical Church of the Augsburg Confession [Czech Republic]
Slovak Evangelical Church of the Augsburg Confession in Yugoslavia
Spanish Evangelical Church
Spanish Reformed Episcopal Church*
Swiss Protestant Church Federation
Union of Welsh Independents
United Free Church of Scotland
United Protestant Church of Belgium
United Reformed Church in the United Kingdom
Waldensian Church [Italy]

LATIN AMERICA
Anglican Church of the Southern Cone of America [Argentina]
Baptist Association of El Salvador*
Baptist Convention of Nicaragua
Bolivian Evangelical Lutheran Church*
Christian Biblical Church [Argentina]*
Christian Reformed Church of Brazil
Church of God [Argentina]*
Church of the Disciples of Christ [Argentina]*
Episcopal Anglican Church of Brazil
Evangelical Church of Lutheran Confession in Brazil
Evangelical Church of the River Plate [Argentina]
Evangelical Lutheran Church in Chile
Evangelical Methodist Church in Bolivia*

Evangelical Methodist Church in Uruguay*
Evangelical Methodist Church of Argentina
Evangelical Methodist Church of Costa Rica*
Free Pentecostal Mission Church of Chile
Methodist Church in Brazil
Methodist Church of Chile*
Methodist Church of Mexico
Methodist Church of Peru*
Moravian Church in Nicaragua
National Council of Christian Churches in Brazil**
Pentecostal Church of Chile
Pentecostal Mission Church [Chile]
Salvadorean Lutheran Synod*
United Evangelical Lutheran Church [Argentina]*
United Presbyterian Church of Brazil*

MIDDLE EAST
Armenian Apostolic Church [Lebanon]
Church of Cyprus
Coptic Orthodox Church [Egypt]
Episcopal Church in Jerusalem and the Middle East
Greek Orthodox Patriarchate of Alexandria and All Africa [Egypt]
Greek Orthodox Patriarchate of Antioch and All the East [Syria]
Greek Orthodox Patriarchate of Jerusalem
Holy Apostolic Catholic Assyrian Church of the East [Iraq]
National Evangelical Synod of Syria and Lebanon [Lebanon]
Syrian Orthodox Patriarchate of Antioch and All the East [Syria]
Synod of the Evangelical Church of Iran
Synod of the Nile of the Evangelical Church [Egypt]

Union of the Armenian Evangelical Churches in the Near East [Lebanon]

NORTH AMERICA
African Methodist Episcopal Church [USA]
African Methodist Episcopal Zion Church [USA]
American Baptist Churches in the USA
Anglican Church of Canada
Canadian Council of Churches**
Canadian Yearly Meeting of the Religious Society of Friends
Christian Church (Disciples of Christ) [Canada]
Christian Church (Disciples of Christ) [USA]
Christian Methodist Episcopal Church [USA]
Church of the Brethren [USA]
Episcopal Church [USA]
Estonian Evangelical Lutheran Church Abroad [Canada]
Evangelical Lutheran Church in America
Evangelical Lutheran Church in Canada
Hungarian Reformed Church in America [USA]
International Council of Community Churches [USA]
International Evangelical Church [USA]
Moravian Church in America (Northern Province)
Moravian Church in America (Southern Province)
National Baptist Convention of America
National Baptist Convention, USA, Inc.
National Council of the Churches of Christ in the USA**
Orthodox Church in America
Polish National Catholic Church [USA]

Presbyterian Church in Canada
Presbyterian Church (USA)
Progressive National Baptist Convention, Inc. [USA]
Reformed Church in America
Religious Society of Friends: Friends General Conference and Friends United Meeting [USA]
United Church of Canada
United Church of Christ [USA]
United Methodist Church [USA]

PACIFIC
Church of the Province of Melanesia [Solomon Islands]
Congregational Christian Church in American Samoa
Congregational Christian Church in Samoa
Cook Islands Christian Church
Evangelical Church in New Caledonia and the Loyalty Isles [New Caledonia]
Evangelical Church of French Polynesia
Evangelical Lutheran Church of Papua New Guinea
Kiribati Protestant Church
Methodist Church in Fiji
Methodist Church in Samoa
Methodist Church in Tonga
National Council of Churches of American Samoa**
Papua New Guinea Council of Churches**
Presbyterian Church of Vanuatu
Tonga National Council of Churches**
Tuvalu Christian Church
United Church in Papua New Guinea
United Church in the Solomon Islands
United Church of Christ – Congregational in the Marshall Islands

Regional Conferences

ALL AFRICA CONFERENCE OF CHURCHES
General Secretary Revd José Belo Chipenda, Waiyaki Way, PO Box 14205, Westlands, Nairobi, Kenya

Founded 1963.

CHRISTIAN CONFERENCE OF ASIA
General Secretary Bishop John Victor Samuel (Church of Pakistan)

Central Office Pak Tin Village, Mei Tin Rd, Shatin, N.T., Hong Kong *Fax:* 852 721 6007

Founded 1959.

CARIBBEAN CONFERENCE OF CHURCHES
General Secretary Revd Dr Monrelle T. Williams, PO Box 616, Bridgetown, Barbados, WI *Fax:* (246) 427-2681

Founded 1973.

CONFERENCE OF EUROPEAN CHURCHES
See page 378.

LATIN AMERICAN COUNCIL OF CHURCHES
(Consejo Latinoamericano de Iglesias (CLAI))

President Dr Walter Altmann, Rua Martin Lutero 358, Sao Leopoldo/ R. S. B. R. 93030-120, Brasil
Tel and *Fax:* 5551-5926835
e-mail: waltmann@plug-in.com.br

General Secretary Mr Felipe Adolf, Casilla 17-08 8522, Quito, Ecuador *Fax:* 5932-553996
e-mail: felipe@clai.ecuanex.net.ac

MIDDLE EAST COUNCIL OF CHURCHES (MECC)
HQ address PO Box 5376, Beirut, Lebanon
Fax: 09-515621

Liaison Office PO Box 4259, Limassol, Cyprus
Fax: 357-5-324496

General Secretary Revd Dr Riad Jarjour (*same address*)

Founded 1962, reorganised 1974, Nicosia. Member Churches: Eastern Orthodox, Oriental Orthodox, Catholic, Episcopal and Evangelical Churches.

PACIFIC CONFERENCE OF CHURCHES
Moderator Revd Reuben Magekon

Acting General Secretary Revd Valamotu Palu, PCC Secretariat, 4 Thurston St, Suva, Fiji *Fax:* (679) 303205

PART 7

WHO'S WHO

Abbrevations used in the biographies

pt	part time
Aber	Aberdeen
ABM	Advisory Board of Ministry
Abth	Aberystwyth
ACA	Associate of the Institute of Chartered Accountants
ACC	Anglican Consultative Council
ACCM	Advisory Council for the Church's Ministry
ACIB	Associate of the Chartered Institute of Bankers
ACIS	Associate of the Institute of Chartered Secretaries and Administrators
ACORA	Archbishops' Commission on Rural Areas
ACP	Associate of the College of Preceptors
ACU	Actors Church Union
ACS	Additional Curates Society
AD	Area Dean
Adn	Archdeacon
Adnry	Archdeaconery
AHA	Area Health Authority
AIA	Associate of the Institute of Actuaries
Aid	Aidan
AIMLS	Associate of the Institute of Medical Laboratory Sciences
AKC	Associate of King's College, London
ALAM	Associate of the London Academy of Music
ALCD	Associate of the London College of Divinity
ALCM	Associate of the London College of Music
Ant	Anthony
APF	Anglican Pacifist Fellowship
APMI	Associate of the Pensions Management Institute
APR	Association for Promoting Retreats
ARAM	Associate of the Royal Academy of Music
ARCIC	Anglican-Roman Catholic International Commission
ARCM	Associate of the Royal College of Music
ARCO(CHM)	Associate of the Royal College of Organists with Diploma in Choir Training
ARICS	Associate of the Royal Institute of Chartered Surveyors
ASA	Associate of the Society of Actuaries
ATII	Associate Member of the Institute of Taxation
AYPA	Anglican Young People's Assembly
B & W	Bath and Wells
BAGUPA	Bishop's Advisory Group on UPA's
BCC	British Council of Churches
BCL	Bachelor of Civil Law
B COMM	Bachelor of Commerce
BD	Bachelor of Divinity
BDS	Bachelor of Dental Surgery
BM	Board of Mission
BMU	Board for Mission and Unity
BNC	Brasenose College
BRF	Bible Reading Fellowship
BS	Bachelor of Surgery/Science
BSR	Board for Social Responsibility
Bt	Baronet
C	Curate
C and YP	Children and Young People
C-in-c	Curate-in-charge
CA	Church Army
CA	Member of the Institute of Chartered Accountants of Scotland
CAB	Citizens Advice Bureau
CACLB	Churches Advisory Council for Local Broadcasting
Carl	Carlisle
CB	Companion of the Order of the Bath
CBF	Central Board of Finance
CCBI	Council of Churches in Britain and Ireland
CCC Cam	Corpus Christi College Cambridge
CCC	Council for the Care of Churches
C CHEM	Certified Chemist
CCHH	Churches Council for Health and Healing
CCU	Council for Church Unity
CD	Conventional District
CEC	Conference of European Churches
CECC	Church of England Committee for Communications
CEIG	Christian Ethical Investment Group
CEMS	Church of England Men's Society
C ENG	Chartered Engineer
CERC	Church of England Record Centre
CERT SPECIAL EDUC MGT	Certificate in Special Education Management
CERT TH	Certificate in Theology
CF	Chaplain to the Forces
CF(TA)	Chaplain to the Forces (Territorial Army)
CFE	College of Further Education
Ch	Christ
CH B	Bachelor of Surgery
Ch Ch	Christ Church
Ch Hosp	Christ's Hospital
Ch(s)	Church(es)
Chan	Chancellor
Chr	Christian
CME	Continuing Ministerial Education
CMEAC	Committee for Minority Ethnic Anglican Concerns
CMJ	Church's Ministry Among the Jews
CMS	Church Mission Society or Church Music Society
CND	Campaign for Nuclear Disarmament

Who's Who 387

C PHYS	Chartered Physicist of the Institute of Physics
CQSW	Certificate of Qualification in Social Work
CR	Community of the Resurrection
CRAC	Central Religious Advisory Committee of the BBC and ITA
CRC	Central Readers Council
CSA	Community of Saint Andrew
CSC	Community of Sisters of the Church
CSMV	Community of Saint Mary the Virgin
CSO	Central Statistical Office
CSR	Council for Social Responsibility
C STAT	Chartered Statistician
CTE	Churches Together in England
CU	Church Union
CUF	Church Urban Fund
CYFA	Church Youth Fellowships Association
DA	Diploma in Anaesthetics
DAA	Diploma in Archive Administration
DAC	Diocesan Advisory Committee
DACE	Diaconal Association of the Church of England
DASS	Diploma in Applied Social Studies
Dav	David
DBF	Diocesan Board of Finance
D CH	Doctor of Surgery
DCH	Diploma in Child Health
DCL	Doctor of Civil Law
DCO	Diocesan Communications Officer
DDO	Diocesan Director of Ordinands
DDS	Doctor of Dental Surgery
DHA	District Health Authority
DIC	Diploma of Imperial College
DIP AD	Diploma in Advertising
DIP AD ED	Diploma in Advanced Education
DIP EE	Diploma in Electrical Engineering
DIP HE	Diploma in Higher Education
DIP L & A	Diploma in Liturgy and Architecture
DIP LIB	Diploma of Librarianship
DIP N	Diploma in Nursing
DIP PE	Diploma in Physical Education
DIP RJ	Diploma in Retail Jewellery
DIP SOC STUDY	Diploma in Social Study
DIP SOC WORK	Diploma in Social Work
DIP SP ED	Diploma in Special Education
DIP TH	Diploma in Theology
DIPTP	Diploma in Town Planning
DL	Deputy Lieutenant
D MIN	Doctor of Ministry
Dn	Deacon
DN	Diploma in Nursing
Dny	Deanery
Dny Syn	Deanery Synod
D OBSTRCOG	Diploma in Obstetrics, Royal College of Obstetricians and Gynaecologists
Doct	Doctrine
DPA	Diploma in Public Administration
DPS	Diploma in Pastoral Studies
DRCOG	Diploma of the Royal College of Obstetricians and Gynaecologists
Dss	Deaconess
DTM&H	Diploma in Tropical Medicine and Hygiene
DTPH	Diploma in Tropical Public Health
DTS	Diploma in Theological Studies
E	East
ECUSA	Episcopal Church of the United States of America
Edm	Edmund
EFAC	Evangelical Fellowship in the Anglican Communion
EIG	Ecclesiastical Insurance Group
EKD	Evangelische Kirche Deutschland
EUR ING	European Engineer
Ev	Evangelist
FAC	Fabric Advisory Committee
FBIM	Fellow British Institute of Management
FC INST M	Fellow of the Chartered Institute of Marketing
FCA	Fellow of the Institute of Chartered Accountants
FCCA	Fellow of the Chartered Association of Certified Accountants
FCII	Fellow of the Chartered Insurance Institute
FCMA	Fellow of the Institute of Cost and Management
FCO	Foreign and Commonwealth Office
FCP	Fellow of the College of Preceptors
FDSRCS	Fellow in Dental Surgery of the Royal College of Surgeons of England
FHSM	Fellow, Institute of Health Service Management
FIA	Fellow of the Institute of Actuaries
FIAA	Fellow of the Institute of Actuaries of Australia
FIBMS	Fellow, Institute of Biomedical Sciences
FIED	Fellow of the Institute of Engineering Designers
FIHT	Fellow of the Institution of Highways and Transportation
FIPD	Fellow of the Institute of Personnel Directors
FIWSC	Fellow of the Institute of Wood Science
FKC	Fellow of King's College, London
FLAME	Family Life and Marriage Education
FOAG	Faith and Order Advisory Group
FPMI	Fellow of the Pensions Management Institute
FRCA	Fellow of the Royal College of Anaesthetists
FRCO	Fellow of the Royal College of Organists
FRCS ED	Fellow of the Royal College of Surgeons of Edinburgh

FRCS ENG	Fellow of the Royal College of Surgeons of England
FRGS	Fellow of the Royal Geographical Society
FRHIST S	Fellow of the Royal Historical Society
FRICS	Fellow of the Royal Institute of Chartered Surveyors
FRIPHH	Fellow of the Royal Institute of Public Health and Hygiene
FROCG	Fellow of the Royal College of Obstetricians and Gynaecologists
FRS	Fellow of the Royal Society
FRSA	Fellow of the Royal Society of Arts
FRSC	Fellow of the Royal Society of Chemistry
FRSL	Fellow of the Royal Society of Literature
FSA	Fellow of the Society of Antiquaries
FSCA	Fellow of the Royal Society of Company and Commercial Accountants
H	Holy
HA	Health Authority
HCC	Hospital Chaplaincies Council
HMDC	Her Majesty's Detention Centre
IBA	Independent Broadcasting Authority
ICS	Intercontinental Church Society
IDC	Inter-Diocesan Certificate
IMEC	Initial Ministerial Education Committee
in-c	in-charge
IOM	Isle of Man
IPR	Institute of Public Relations
K	King(s)
LDSRCS	Licentiate in Dental Surgery of the Royal College of Surgeons
LEP	Local Ecumenical Project
LIM	Licentiate of the Institute of Metals
LLD	Doctor of Laws
LLAM	Licentiate of the London Academy of Music and Dramatic Art
Llan	Llandaff
LLM	Master of Laws
LRAM	Licentiate of the Royal Academy of Music
LRCP	Licentiate of the Royal College of Physicians
LTCL	Licentiate of the Trinity College of Music, London
L TH	Licentiate in Theology
M	Member
MAFF	Ministry for Agriculture Fisheries and Food
MB	Bachelor of Medicine
MBC	Metropolitan Borough Council
MBCS	Member of the British Computer Society
MBIM	Member of the British Institute of Management
MCIM	Member of the Chartered Institute of Marketing
MCT	Member of the Association of Corporate Treasurers
MICE	Member of the Institution of Civil Engineers
MIEE	Member of the Institution of Electrical Engineers
MIM	Member of the Institute of Metals
MIMGT	Member of the Institute of Management
M INST D	Member of the Institute of Directors
M INST P	Member of the Institute of Physics
M INST R	Member of the Institute of Refrigeration
MIPD	Member of the Institute of Personnel and Development
MIPR	Member of the Institute of Public Relations
MJI	Member of the Institute of Journalists
MRCGP	Member of the Royal College of General Practitioners
MRCS	Member of the Royal College of Surgeons
MRTPI	Member of the Royal Town Planning Institute
MSF	Manufacturing, Science and Finance Union
N	North
NACRO	National Association for the Care and Rehabilitation of Offenders
NAHT	National Association of Headteachers
NCA	National Certificate in Agriculture
NCEC	National Christian Education Council
NDA	National Diploma in Agriculture
NDD	National Diploma in Design
NFF	National Froebel Foundation
NNEB	Nursery Nurse Examination Board
NS	National Service
NSM	Non Stipendiary Minister/Ministry
NT	New Testament
NTMTC	North Thames Ministerial Training Course
OCF	Officiating Chaplain to the Forces
OGS	Order of the Good Shepherd
OHP	Order of the Holy Paraclete
OM	Order of Merit
OU	Open University
PACTA	Professional Associate of the Clinical Theology Association
Perm	Permission
P-in-c	Priest-in-charge
POT	Post Ordination Training
PPS	Personal Private Secretary
Prec	Precentor
Pres	President
PROs	Public Relations Officers
PWM	Partnership for World Mission
QHC	Queen's Honorary Chaplain
R	Rector or Royal
RAChD(TA)	Royal Army Chaplains' Department (Territorial Army)
RCHME	Royal Commission on Historical Monuments

RD	Rural Dean
Red	Redundant
RGN	Registered General Nurse
RHM	Rank Hovis McDougall
RIBA	Royal Institute of British Architects
RICS	Royal Institute of Chartered Surveyors
RM	Registered Midwife
RMA	Royal Military Academy
RMN	Registered Mental Nurse
RN	Royal Navy
RSCM	Royal School of Church Music
S	South
SAMS	South American Mission Society
SC D	Doctor of Science
SOAS	School of Oriental and African Studies
SPI	Society of Practitioners of Insolvency
SSC	Society of the Holy Cross
SSF	Society of Saint Francis
SST	Society for the Study of Theology
St	Saint
St As	Saint Asaph
STB	Bachelor of Theology
STETS	Southern Theological Education Training Scheme
STH	Scholar in Theology
STL	Reader of Sacred Theology
STM	Master of Theology
Succ	Succentor
Suff	Suffragan
TD	Territorial (Officers') Decoration
TEC	Training and Enterprise Council
TM	Team Ministry or Team Minister
TR	Team Rector
TV	Team Vicar
UPAs	Urban Priority Areas
USCL	United Society for Christian Literature
UWIST	University of Wales Institute of Science and Technology
V	Vicar
W	West
w	with
WWDP	Women's World Day of Prayer

WHO'S WHO

A Directory of General Synod members, together with those suffragan bishops, deans, provosts and archdeacons who are not members of General Synod, and principal staff members of the General Synod, Church Commissioners and Lambeth Palace, and Church Commissioners who are not members of General Synod. General Synod members are distinguished by the date of their membership, printed in bold type, which follows the diocese or appointment and precedes the date of birth. Dates of membership of those who are no longer Synod members are indicated in italic. All details are fully accurate at the time of going to press.

AAGAARD, Mr Robert
Manor House, High Birstwith, Harrogate, N Yorks HG3 2LG [RIPON] **1995–** *b* 27 Jun 1932; *educ* Gresham's Sch Holt; Managing Dir Robert Aagaard Ltd Antiques 1960–80, Consultant 1980–95; Dir Aagaard-Hanley Ltd Fibrous Plasterers 1970–80, Consultant from 1980; Partner R & FC Aagaard Designers and Decorators of Historic House Interiors from 1980; Founder and Chmn Cathl Camps from 1980; Consultant Robert Aagaard & Co Period Chimneypieces and Marble Processing from 1995; M Cathls Fabric Commn for England; Chmn Ripon DAC; M Ripon Cathl Fabric Adv Ctee; M Bradf Cathl Fabric Adv Ctee; M Dioc Redundant Chs Uses Ctee; M Dioc Worship Ctee; M Dioc Rural Min Grp
Tel: (01423) 770385
Fax: (01423) 770714

ACWORTH, Ven Dick (Richard Foote)
Old Rectory, Croscombe, Wells, Som BA5 3QN [ARCHDEACON OF WELLS] *1980–95,* **1998–** *b* 19 Oct 1936; *educ* St Jo Sch Leatherhead; SS Coll Cam; Cuddesdon Th Coll; C St Etheldreda's Fulham 1963; All SS and Martyrs, Langley 1964–66; C St Mary Bridgwater 1966–69; V Yatton 1969–81; R Yatton Moor 1981; P-in-c St Jo Ev 1981–84; St Mary Magd Taunton 1981–85; V St Mary Magd Taunton 1985–93; Adn of Wells from 1993
Tel: (01749) 342242
Fax: (01749) 330060

ADAMS, Mrs Marian, BA
Church Commissioners, 1 Millbank, London SW1P 3JZ [PROPERTY ACCOUNTANT, CHURCH COMMISSIONERS] *b* 21 Oct 1957; *educ* Henry Box Sch Witney; Leeds Univ; Property Accountnt Ch Commrs from 1996
Tel: 0171–898 1677
Fax: 0171–222 0653
e-mail: marian.adams@chucomm.org.uk

ADAMS, Canon Ray (Raymond) Michael, BD, ALCD
Ipsley Rectory, Icknield St, Ipsley, Redditch, Worcs B98 0AN [WORCESTER] **1990–** *b* 4 Dec 1941; *educ* Gravesend Tech Sch; Lon Univ; Lon Coll of Div; C Holy Trin Old Hill Worc 1967–73; TR Ipsley from 1973; Hon Can Worc Cathl from 1984; Grp Chmn Redditch Grp Min from 1985; M Gen Syn Revision Ctee The Service of the Word; M Calendar, Lectionary and Collects Revision Ctee; Appeal Panel Proctor under 1983 Pastl Measure; M Bp's Coun and Stg Ctee; M Dioc Liturg Ctee; Bp's Selector; ABM Selector; M Dioc Patronage Bd
Tel: (01527) 523307

ADCOCK, Mr Roger Anthony, MA, PGCE, FBIM
The Barn, North Sidborough, Loxbeare, Tiverton, Devon EX16 8BY [EXETER] **1985–** *b* 21 Mar 1927; *educ* Win Coll Quirister Sch; Ardingly Coll; St Cath's Coll Cam; St Edm Hall Ox; McGill Univ Montreal; Asst Master Southend High Sch 1952–55; Hd of History Marlborough Gr Sch 1955–59; Warden Comberton Village Coll 1959–64; Hdmaster Wells Blue Sch 1964–68; Hd of Educ Bede Coll Dur 1968–71; Prin Coll of St Matthias Bris 1971–78; Asst Co-ord Gov Tr Devon CC 1990–94; Sec Nat Govs Coun; M Dioc Syn; Rdr
Tel: (01884) 881361
Fax: (01884) 881534
e-mail: roger.adcock@ngc.co.uk

AINSWORTH, Revd Michael Ronald, LLM, MA
Rectory, Walkden Rd, Worsley, Manchester M28 2WH [MANCHESTER] **1995–** *b* 18 Jun 1950; *educ* K Edw VII Gr Sch Sheff; K Coll Lon; Trin Hall Cam; Westcott Ho Th Coll; C St Paul Scotforth 1975–78; Chapl St Martin Coll Lanc 1978–82; Chapl and Tutor Nn Ord Course 1982–89; R St Chris Withington 1989–94; TR Worsley TM from 1994; Bps' Inspector of Th Colls and Courses; M CCC; Dioc Moderator of Rdr Tr; M Dioc Worship Ctee; M DAC; M Dioc Red Chs Uses Ctee
Tel and *Fax:* 0161–790 2362

ALLAN, Mrs Kate (Kathleen Mabel), T CERT
19 Beech Rd, Stockton Heath, Warrington WA4 6LT [CHESTER] **1990–** *b* 23 Mar 1935; *educ* Blackburn High

Sch for Girls; Cartrefle Teacher Coll, Wrexham; Open Univ; Secondary School teacher 1955–88; Rtd; Open Univ Student; M Bp's Coun; M Dioc CSR; Lay Chair Gt Budworth Dny Syn   Tel: (01925) 266331

ALLEN, Ven Geoffrey Gordon
Ijsselsingel 86, 6991 ZT Rheden, Netherlands [ARCHDEACON IN NORTH-WEST EUROPE] *b* 14 May 1939; *educ* Alton Co Sec Sch; K Coll Lon; Sarum Th Coll; C St Mary Langley 1966–70; Miss to Seamen Tilbury 1970–72; Schiedam 1972–74; Port Chapl Antwerp and OCF 1974–78; Chapl Tildonk 1974–78; Chapl St Mary Rotterdam and Sen Chapl Miss to Seamen 1978–82; Chapl Pernis 1982–83; Assoc Chapl The Hague, Voorschoten and Leiden 1983–93; Warden to Rdrs dio of Eur 1983–95; Chapl E Netherlands from 1993; Adn in NW Europe from 1993; Canon Brussels Pro Cathl from 1993; Chmn Angl Netherlands Area Coun from 1983; P-in-c Haarlem from 1995
Tel: 00–31–26–4953800
Fax: 00–31–26–4954922
e-mail: 106362.1337@compuserve.com

ANDERSON, Canon Rosemary Ann, BA
St John's Vicarage, Carrhill Rd, Mossley, Ashton-under-Lyne OL5 0BL [MANCHESTER] **1990–** *b* 7 Nov 1936; *educ* Lyme Regis Gr Sch; Ex Univ; Nn Ord Course; Par Dn NSM St Paul Oldham 1986–89; Bp's Adv for Women's Min 1988–94; P-in-c St Jo Roughtown from 1993   *Tel:* (01457) 832250
e-mail: revand@surfaid.org

ANDREWS, Canon Brian Keith, MA
Vicarage, High St, Abbots Langley, Herts WD5 0AS [ST ALBANS] **1995–** *b* 8 May 1939; *educ* Alleyns Sch; Keble Coll Ox; Coll of Resurr Mirfield; C Isle of Dogs, Poplar 1964–68; TV St Mary Hemel Hempstead 1968–79; RD Watford 1988–94; V Abbots Langley from 1979; Hon Can St Alb Cathl from 1994; M Gov Body St Alb and Ox Min Course from 1994; Chmn Dioc Assisted Self Appraisal Scheme 1990–96; Chmn Dioc Ho of Clergy from 1993; M Gov Body Ripon Coll Cuddesdon from 1996
Tel: (01923) 263013
Fax: (01923) 261795

APPELBEE, Mrs Elaine, BA, CQSW
168 Highfield Lane, Keighley, W Yorks BD21 2HU [BRADFORD] **1990–** *b* 9 Jun 1954; *educ* Lanc Girls' Gr Sch; Bradf Univ; Social Worker Lynfield Mount Hospital 1977–78; Community Worker Bradf Social Services 1979–86; Senior Community Worker Bradf dio 1987–91; Bp's Officer for Church in Society Bradf dio from 1992; M BSR; M CMEAC
Tel: (01535) 671377

ARCHER, Mr Anthony William, LL B, ACA
Manor End, Little Gaddesden, Berkhamsted, Herts HP4 1PL [ST ALBANS] **1993–** *b* 17 Jan 1953; *educ* St Edw Sch Ox; Birm Univ; Mgment Consultant Ray & Berndtson from 1995; M ABM from 1994; M Recruitment Strategy Working Party; Regional Adv for Alpha Course   *Tel:* (01442) 843249 (Home)
0171–233 8888 (Office)
e-mail: awarcher@compuserve.com

ARCHER, Revd Graham John, B SC, AIMLS, DIP TH, DPS
2 Blyford Way, Orwell Green, Felixstowe, Suffolk IP11 8FW [ST EDMUNDSBURY AND IPSWICH] **1995–** *b* 13 Jun 1958; *educ* Cam High Sch for Boys; Hill Rd Sixth Form Coll; Lanc Univ; Nottm Univ; St Jo Coll Nottm; C St Matt Ipswich 1985–89; Min Cavendish Community Ch Walton 1989–95; P-in-c Walton from 1995; Chapl Felixstowe Gen Hosp from 1996; Chapl Bartlet Hosp from 1996
Tel and *Fax:* (01394) 274284 (Home)
(01394) 282204 (Office)
e-mail: Ccchurch@btinternet.com

ARNOLD, Very Revd John Robert, MA
The Deanery, Durham DH1 3EQ [DEAN OF DURHAM] **1980–** *b* 1 Nov 1933; *educ* Ch Hosp; SS Coll Cam; Westcott Ho Th Coll; C H Trin Millhouses, Sheff 1960–63; Sir Henry Stephenson Fell Sheff Univ 1962–63; Angl Chapl and Vis Lect Southn Univ 1963–72; Sec BMU 1972–78; Dean of Rochester 1978–89; Dean of Durham from 1989; M Central Ctee Conf of Eur Chs from 1993, Pres and Chmn 1993–97; M CCU   *Tel:* 0191–384 7500
Fax: 0191–386 4267

ARRAND, Ven Geoffrey William, BD, AKC
Glebe House, The Street, Ashfield cum Thorpe, Stowmarket, Suffolk IP14 6LX [ARCHDEACON OF SUFFOLK] *b* 24 Jul 1944; *educ* Scunthorpe Gr Sch; K Coll Lon; St Boniface Warminster; C Washington 1967–70; C S Ormsby Grp 1970–73; TV Gt Grimsby TM 1973–79; TR Halesworth 1979–85; Dean of Bocking 1985–94; R Hadleigh w Layham and Shelley 1985–94; RD Hadleigh 1986–94; Hon Can St Eds Cathl from 1991; Adn of Suffolk from 1994   *Tel:* (01728) 685497
Fax: (01728) 685969

ASHENDEN, Revd Gavin Roy Pelham, LL B, BA, M TH
42 New Rd, Shoreham by Sea BN43 6RA [UNIVERSITIES, SOUTH] **1995–** *b* 3 Jun 1954; *educ* K Sch Cant; Bris Univ; Heythrop Coll Lon; Oak Hill Th Coll; C St Jas w Ch Ch Bermondsey 1980–83; TV All SS Sanderstead 1983–89; Dir Aid to Russian

Christians 1982–89; Coun M Keston Inst from 1983; Vc-Chmn from 1992; Chapl and Lect Sussex Univ from 1989; M CCU; Delegate to WCC
Tel: (01273) 606755 (Office)
(01273) 453277 (Home)
Fax: (01273) 453277
e-mail: G.Ashenden@Sussex.ac.uk

ASHTON, Mr David
2 Manor Drive, Battyeford, Mirfield, W Yorks WF14 0ER [WAKEFIELD] **1972–** *b* 2 Jul 1941; *educ* Warw Rd Junior Sch; Dewsbury and Batley Tech Sch; Kitson Eng Coll; Br Telecom Grp Logistics Service Centre Operations Mgr (NE and Midlands Zone); M Bp's Coun; Chmn Ho of Laity Dioc Syn; Vc-Pres Dioc Syn; M Dioc Pastl Ctee
Tel: (01924) 497996
e-mail: ashtond@boat.bt.com

ASKEW, Prebendary Richard George, MA, DIP TH
The Abbey Rectory, Redwood House, Trossachs Drive, Bathampton, Bath BA2 6RP [BATH AND WELLS] **1985–90, 1995–** *b* 16 May 1935; *educ* Harrow; BNC Ox; Ridley Hall Th Coll; C St Mary Chesham 1964–66; C St Matt and St Jas Mossley Hill Liv 1966–67; Chapl Ox Pastorate 1967–72; Asst Chapl BNC Ox 1967–71; R St Giles and St Geo Ashtead 1972–83; Dioc Adv on Miss and Min Sarum 1983–90; Can Res and Treas Sarum Cathl 1983–90; R Bath Abbey from 1990; Preb Wells Cathl from 1992; M Bp's Coun
Tel: (01225) 464930 (Home)
(01225) 422462 (Office)
Fax: (01225) 429990

ASTON, Bishop of [SUFFRAGAN, BIRMINGHAM] Rt Revd John Michael Austin, BA
Strensham House, 8 Strensham Hill, Moseley, Birmingham B13 8AG b 4 Mar 1939; *educ* Worksop Coll; St Edm Hall Ox; St Steph Ho Ox; C St Jo E Dulwich 1964–68; St Jas Cathl Chicago USA 1968–69; Warden Pemb Ho Miss Walworth 1969–76; Soc Resp Adv St Alb 1976–84; Dir Lon Dioc BSR 1984–92; Bp of Aston from 1992
Tel: 0121–428 2228
Fax: 0121–428 1114

ATKIN, Dr Susan Anne Jennifer, BA, PH D
3 St Bride Court, Colchester, Essex CO4 4PQ [CHELMSFORD] **1995–** *b* 2 Aug 1948; *educ* Qu Eliz Girls' Gr Sch Barnet; Reading Univ; Admin Trainee Min of Defence 1973–75; Admin Asst City Univ 1975–78; Asst Registrar City Univ 1978–83; Dep Registrar City Univ 1983–86; Dep Registrar York Univ 1986–90; Planning Officer Essex Univ from 1990; M Dioc Syn from 1995
Tel: (01206) 854976 (Home)
(01206) 872422 (Office)
Fax: (01206) 872164 (Office)
e-mail: saja@essex.ac.uk

ATKINSON, Ven David John, B SC, PH D, M LITT, MA
3A Court Farm Rd, Mottingham, London SE9 4JH [ARCHDEACON OF LEWISHAM] *b* 5 Sep 1943; *educ* Maidstone Gr Sch; K Coll Lon; Bris Univ; Tyndale Hall Th Coll; Tchr Maidstone Tech High Sch 1968–69; C St Pet Halliwell Bolton 1972–74; Sen C St Jo Harborne Birm 1974–77; Libr Latimer Ho Ox 1977–80; Lect and Chapl CCC Ox 1980–93; Fell CCC Ox 1984–93; Can Res S'wark Cathl 1993–96; Exam Chapl 1993–96; Adn of Lewisham from 1996; M Dioc Bd for Ch in Society; M Dioc Syn; M Bp's Coun
Tel: 0181–857 7982 (Home)
0171–403 8696 (Office)
Fax: 0181–2449 0350(Home)
0171–403 4770 (Office)
e-mail: david.atkinson@dswark.org.uk

ATKINSON, Mrs Janet Mary, MA
548 Yarm Rd, Eaglescliffe, Stockton-on-Tees, Cleveland TS16 0BX [DURHAM] **1985–** *b* 4 Sep 1932; *educ* Huyton Coll; St Anne's Coll Ox; Tchr St Leon Sch St Andr 1954–55; Hartlepool Coll of Further Educ (pt) 1979–84; pt Lect WEA from 1979; JP; M CBF; M CBF Exec; M CBF Staff Ctee; M Dios Commn; Ch Commr from 1993; M CE Pensions Bd from 1994; M DBF; M Bp's Coun
Tel: (01642) 782292

ATKINSON, Mr Roger Douglas, MA, LLM
115 Eastbrook Rd, Lincoln LN6 7EW [LINCOLN] **1990–** *b* 24 Dec 1938; *educ* Haileybury Coll; Selw Coll Cam; Solicitor from 1965; Partner Andrew & Co Solicitors Linc from 1969; HM Coroner for Linc from 1994
Tel: (01522) 683209
Fax: (01522) 546713

ATKINSON, Canon Richard William Bryant, MA
Rotherham Vicarage, 2 Heather Close, Rotherham S60 2TQ [SHEFFIELD] **1991–** *b* 17 Dec 1958; *educ* St Paul's Sch Lon; Magd Coll Cam; Ripon Coll Cuddesdon; C Abingdon w Shippon 1984–87; TV Sheff Manor Par 1987–91; Hon M of Staff Ripon Coll Cuddesdon 1987–92; TR Sheff Manor Par 1991–96; V All SS Rotherham from 1996; Dep Chair N Br Housing Assn; Chair Open Syn Grp from 1997; M CBF; M CTE and CCBI; Hon Can Sheff Cathl from 1998; M Central Ch Fund Ctee
Tel: (01709) 364341 (Home)
(01709) 364737 (Office)

ATWELL, Very Revd James Edgar, MA, TH M, BD
The Provost's House, Bury St Edmunds, Suffolk IP33 1RS [PROVOST OF ST EDMUNDSBURY] *b* 3 Jun 1946; *educ* Dauntsey's Sch; Ex Coll Ox; Harvard Univ; Cuddesdon Th Coll; C St Jo E Dulwich 1970–74; C Gt St Mary Cam 1974–77; Chapl Jes Coll Cam

1977–81; V Towcester w Easton Neston 1981–95; RD Towcester 1983–91; Provost of St Eds from 1995
Tel: (01284) 754852 (Home)
(01284) 754933 (Office)
Fax: (01284) 768655

AUSTIN, Ven George (Bernard), BA
North Back House, Main St, Wheldrake, York YO19 6AG [ARCHDEACON OF YORK] *1970–95 b* 16 Jul 1931; *educ* Bury High Sch; St D Coll Lamp; Chich Th Coll; C St Pet Chorley 1955–57; C St Clem's Notting Hill Lon 1957–60; Asst Chapl Univ of Lon 1960; C Priory Ch of St Pet Dunstable 1961–64; V St Mary's, Eaton Bray 1964–70; V St Pet Bushey Heath 1970–88; Assmbly of BCC 1974–83; M Angl/Lutheran Jt Wrkng Grp 1975; Delegate WCC Vancouver 1983, Canberra 1991; Chmn of CBF Staff Ctee 1975–88; Adn of York from 1988; Ch Commr 1978–95; M Bd of Govs 1981–95; M CBF 1970–88, 1991–95; M Coun Forward in Faith
Tel: (01904) 448509
Fax: (01904) 448002
e-mail: george.austin@virgin.net

AVIS, Prebendary Paul David Loup, BD, PH D
Church House, Great Smith St, London SW1P 3NZ [SECRETARY, COUNCIL FOR CHRISTIAN UNITY] *1990–95 b* 21 Jul 1947; *educ* St Geo Monoux Gr Sch Walthamstow; Lon Univ; Westcott Ho Th Coll; C S Molton Grp 1975–80; V Stoke Canon, Polimore w Huxham, Rewe w Netherexe 1980–88; Sub Dean Ex Cathl from 1996; Dir Centre for Study of the Christian Church from 1996; Sec CCU from 1998; Vc-Chmn FOAG from 1994; Chmn Ho of Clergy Ex Dioc Syn from 1996
Tel: 0171–898 1470

AXTELL, Mrs Jessie Mary, BA, PGCE
15 Berwick Ave, Heaton Mersey, Stockport SK4 3AA [MANCHESTER] **1995–** *b* 5 May 1934; *educ* Market Bosworth Dixie Gr Sch; Bedf Coll Lon; Inst of Educ Lon; Classics Tchr Eothen Sch Caterham 1956–59; Classics Tchr Prescot Girls' Gr Sch 1959–61; Miss CMJ Iran 1962–78; Admin Sec Nn Ord Course 1979–98; M Dioc Children and Young People's Ctee; M Dioc Worship Ctee
Tel and Fax: 0161–432 5943
e-mail: ronaxtell@compuserve.com

AYERS, Revd Paul Nicholas, MA
Vicarage, Vicarage Drive, Pudsey LS28 7RL [BRADFORD] **1995–** *b* 26 Sep 1961; *educ* Bradf Gr Sch; St Pet Coll Ox; Trin Coll Bris; C St Jo Bapt Clayton 1985–88; C StAndr Keighley 1988–91; V St Cuth Wrose 1991–97; V St Lawr and St Paul Pudsey from 1997
Tel: 0113–256 4197

BADDELEY, Ven Martin James, MA
89 Nutfield Rd, South Merstham, Redhill, Surrey RH1 3HD [ARCHDEACON OF REIGATE] *b* 10 Nov 1936; *educ* St Pet Sch York; Keble Coll Ox; Makerere Univ Coll of E Africa; Linc Th Coll; C St Matt Stretford 1962–65; M Staff Linc Th Coll 1965–69; Chapl Fitzw Coll Cam 1969–74; Fell 1972–74; Chapl New Hall Cam 1969–74; Res Can Roch Cathl 1974–80; Prin S'wark Ord Course 1980–94; Jt Prin SE Inst for Th Educ 1994–96; Adn of Reigate from 1996
Tel: (01737) 642375
e-mail: martin.baddeley@dswark.org.uk

BAINES, Mr Gerald Charles, B COM, FCA
1 Millbank, London SW1P 3JZ [ACCOUNTANT, CHURCH COMMISSIONERS] *b* 27 Jul 1939; *educ* Ipswich Sch; Leeds Univ; On staff of Ch Commrs from 1973; Accountant from 1993
Tel: 0171–898 1680

BAINES, Revd Nicholas, BA
Vicarage, 128 Hallfields Lane, Rothley, Leicester LE7 7NG [LEICESTER] **1995–** *b* 13 Nov 1957; *educ* Holt Comp Sch Liv; Bradf Univ; Trin Coll Bris; C St Thos Kendal 1987–91; C H Trin Leic 1991–92; V Rothley from 1992; M PWM; M Dioc Syn; M Bd of Patronage; M Vacancy in See Ctee; M Spiritual Direction Working Grp; M Bp's Th Issues Grp; RD Goscote; M Cathl Provisional Coun from 1998
Tel: 0116–230 2241
e-mail: baines@leicester.anglican.org

BAKER, Canon Robert Mark, BA
Rectory, 73 The Street, Brundall, Norwich NR13 5LZ [NORWICH] **1985–** *b* 20 Jun 1950; *educ* Northgate Gr Sch Ipswich; Bris Univ; St Jo Coll Nottm; C Ch Ch Portswood 1976–80; R Brundall, Braydeston and Postwick from 1980; Ch Commr from 1992, Bd of Govs from 1995; Hon Can Nor Cathl from 1993; Exam Chapl to Bp of Nor
Tel: (01603) 715136

BAKER WILBRAHAM, Sir Richard, BT, DL
Rode Hall, Scholar Green, Cheshire ST7 3QP [CHURCH COMMISSIONER] *b* 5 Feb 1934; *educ* Harrow Sch; J. Henry Schroder Wagg & Co Ltd 1954–89; Chmn Bibby Line Grp Ltd 1992–97; Dep Chmn Brixton Estate plc; Dep Chmn Grosvenor Estate Holdings; Dir Majedie Investments plc; Ch Commr from 1994, Assets Ctee from 1994, Bd of Govs from 1995; Gov Man Metropolitan Univ from 1998
Tel: (01270) 882961

BAMPFYLDE, Mr Stephen John, MA
35 Old Queen St, London SW1H 9JA [APPOINTED MEMBER, ARCHBISHOPS' COUNCIL] *b* 31 Mar 1952; *educ* Portsm Gr Sch; Jes Coll Cam; Civil Servant 1973–80; Managing Dir Saxon Bampfylde Hever from 1986; Apptd M Abps' Coun from 1999
Tel: 0171–799 1433
Fax: 0171–222 0489

BANKS, Revd Norman, MA
St Paul's Vicarage, 53 Grosvenor Drive, Whitley Bay, Tyne and Wear NE26 2JR [NEWCASTLE] **1990–** *b* 4 Apr 1954; *educ* Wallsend Gr Sch; Oriel Coll Ox; St Steph Ho Th Coll; C Ch Ch w St Ann Newcastle 1982–84; C-in-c St Ann 1984–87; P-in-c Ch Ch w St Ann 1987–90; V Tynemouth St Paul Cullercoats from 1990
Tel: 0191–252 4916

BANNER, Revd John William, BA
63 Claremont Rd, Tunbridge Wells, Kent TN1 1TE [ROCHESTER] **1995–** *b* 4 Jun 1936; *educ* Prenton Sch Birkenhead; Liv Coll of Building Tech; Tyndale Hall Th Coll; C St Leon Bootle 1964–67; C St Jas Wigan 1967–70; Gen Sec Scripture Union 1970–72; V Ch Ch Norris Green Liv 1972–82; V H Trin w Ch Ch Tunbridge Wells from 1982; M Dioc Parsonages Ctee; M Dioc Pastl Ctee; M DBF; M Dioc Syn
Tel and *Fax:* (01892) 526644

BANTING, Ven (Kenneth) Mervyn Lancelot Hadfield, MA
5 The Boltons, Wootton Bridge, Ryde, Isle of Wight PO33 4PB [ARCHDEACON OF THE ISLE OF WIGHT] **1998–** *b* 8 Sep 1937; *educ* Tonbridge Sch; Pemb Coll Cam; Cuddeson Th Coll; Asst Chapl Win Coll 1965–70; C St Fran Leigh Park 1970–73; TV Highfield Hemel Hempstead 1973–79; V Goldington 1979–88; RD Bedford 1984–87; V St Cuth Portsea 1988–96; RD Portsm 1994–96; Adn of the Isle of Wight from 1996
Tel and *Fax:* (01983) 884432

BARKER, Dr Keith, B SC, PH D, C ENG, MIM, FRSA
36 Tring Rd, Dunstable, Beds LU6 2PT [ST ALBANS] **1995–** *b* 10 Sep 1941; *educ* Scunthorpe Tech High Sch; N Lindsey Tech Coll; Nottm Univ; Birm Univ; Tech Asst Appleby-Frodingham Steel Co 1965–66; Research Assoc Birm Univ 1966–69; Asst Tchr Long Eaton Gr Sch 1969–73; Hd of Mathematics Pingle Sch Swadlincote 1973–76; Dep Hdmaster Greenhead Gr Sch Keighley 1977–84; Hdmaster Queensbury Sch Dunstable 1985–93; Rtd *Tel:* (01582) 607163

BARKING, Bishop of [AREA BISHOP, CHELMSFORD]
Rt Revd Roger Frederick Sainsbury, MA
Barking Lodge, 110 Capel Rd, Forest Gate, London E7 0JS **1985–88, 1996–** *b* 2 Oct 1936; *educ* High Wycombe R Gr Sch; Jes Coll Cam; Clifton Th Coll; C Ch Ch Spitalfield 1960–63; Missr Shrewsbury Ho Liv 1963–74; P-in-c St Ambrose w St Tim Everton 1967–74; Warden Mayflower Family Centre Canning Town 1974–81; P-in-c St Luke Victoria Dock 1978–81; Alderman Lon Boro Newham 1976–78; V Walsall 1981–87; R Walsall TM 1987–88; Adn of W Ham 1988–91; Chmn Frontier Youth Trust Trustees 1987–92; Bp of Barking from 1991; Chmn Trustees Children in Distress from 1995; Chmn Bps Urban Panel from 1996; M CCBI Balkans Working Grp from 1994; Vc-Chair Lon Chs Grp from 1998; Co-Chair BSR Community and Urban Affairs Ctee from 1998
Tel and *Fax:* 0181–478 2456 (Home)
Tel: 0181–514 6044 (Office)
Fax: 0181–514 6049 (Office)
e-mail: bishoproger@chelmsford.anglican.org

BARNES, Mr Barry Karl
30 Junction Rd, S Croydon, Surrey CR2 6RB [SOUTHWARK] **1995–** *b* 11 May 1946; *educ* Selhurst Gr Sch; Solicitor; Chmn Croydon YMCA Housing Assoc from 1993; M Legal Aid Commn from 1996
Tel: 0181–686 5179 (Home)
0181–681 6116 (Office)
Fax: 0181–686 9776 (Office)

BARTLES-SMITH, Ven Douglas Leslie, MA
1A Dog Kennel Hill, East Dulwich, London SE22 8AA [ARCHDEACON OF SOUTHWARK] *educ* Shrewsbury Sch; St Edm Hall Ox; Wells Th Coll; C St Steph Rochester Row 1963–68; C-in-c St Mich w Em and All So Camberwell 1968–72; V 1972–75; V St Luke Battersea 1975–85; RD Battersea 1981–85; Adn of S'wark from 1985; Chapl to HM The Queen from 1996
Tel: 0171–274 6767
Fax: 0171–274 0899
e-mail: douglas.bartles-smith@dswark.org.uk

BARTON, Ven (Charles) John Greenwood, ALCD
Birmingham Diocesan Office, 175 Harborne Park Rd, Birmingham B17 0BH [ARCHDEACON OF ASTON] *b* 5 Jun 1936; *educ* Battersea Gr Sch; Lon Coll of Div; Asst C St Mary Bredin, Cant 1963–66; V Whitfield w W Langdon 1966–75; V St Luke's Redcliffe Square, Lon and AD Chelsea 1975–83; Chief Broadcasting Offcr 1983–90; M Coun Corp of Ch Ho; Adn of Aston from 1990; Can Res Birm Cathl from 1990
Tel: 0121–454 5525 (Home)
0121–427 5141 (Office)
0976 747535 (Mobile)
Fax: 0121–455 6085 (Home)
0121–428 1114 (Office)

BARTON, Revd Dr (Margaret) Anne, MA, D PHIL
Rectory, Wolverton, Tadley, Hants RG26 5RU [WINCHESTER] **1995–** *b* 22 Feb 1954; *educ* Nottm High Sch for Girls; St Anne's Coll Ox; Selw Coll Cam; Ridley Hall Th Coll; C Burley 1990–94; Chapl K Alfred's Coll Win from 1994; Sec Dioc Liturg Ctee
Tel: (01962) 827246 (Office)
Tel and *Fax:* (01635) 298008 (Home)
e-mail: anneba@patrol.i-way.co.uk (Home)
anne.barton@wkac.ac.uk (Office)

BASINGSTOKE, Bishop of [SUFFRAGAN, WINCHESTER] Rt Revd (Douglas) Geoffrey Rowell, MA, PH D, DD
Bishopswood End, Kingswood Rise, Four Marks, Alton, Hants GU34 5BD b 13 Feb 1943; *educ* Eggar's Gr Sch Alton; Win Coll; CCC Cam; Cuddesdon Th Coll; Asst Chapl and Hastings Rashdall Student New Coll Ox 1968–72; Hon C St Andr Headington 1968–72; Fell, Chapl and Tutor in Th Keble Coll Ox 1972–94, Emer Fell from 1994; Univ Lect in Th 1977–94; M Liturg Commn 1980–90; Gov Pusey Ho Ox from 1979, Pres from 1995; M Gov Body SPCK 1984–94 and from 1997; Hon Dir Abp's Exam in Th from 1986; Can and Preb Chich Cathl from 1981; M Angl-Oriental Orthodox Internat Forum from 1985, Angl Co-Chmn from 1996; Conservator Mirfield Cert in Pastl Th 1987–93; M Coun Management St Steph Ho Ox from 1988; M Doct Commn 1990–95, Consultant from 1996; Bp of Basingstoke from 1994; CE Rep on CCBI from 1995; Vis Prof Chich Inst (Sch of Religion and Th) from 1996
Tel: (01420) 562925
Fax: (01420) 561251
e-mail: geoffrey.rowell@dial.pipex.com

BASSETT, Mrs Rosemary Louise
Hengistbury, Winterbourne Steepleton, Dorset DT2 9LQ [SALISBURY] 1990– b 11 Aug 1942; *educ* City of Lon Sch for Girls; Housewife; M Bp's Coun
Tel: (01305) 889466

BASSHAM, Ms Sallie, B SC
4 Pen-y-Ghent View, Horton-in-Ribblesdale, N Yorks BD24 0HE [BRADFORD] 1995– b 19 Mar 1947; *educ* Qu Eliz Gr Sch Hexham; Salford Univ; Mathematics Lect Univ of Salford; M ABM from 1996; Chair Dioc Adv Coun for Min and Tr; Lay Chair Bowland Dny Syn
Tel: (01729) 860 446 (Home)
0161–295 4905 (Office)
Fax: 0161–295 5559
e-mail: S.Bassham@cms.salford.ac.uk

BATH AND WELLS, Bishop of, Rt Revd James Lawton Thompson, MA, FCA, DD
The Palace, Wells, Som BA5 2PD **1985–** b 11 Aug 1936; *educ* Dean Close Sch Cheltenham; Em Coll Cam; Cuddesdon Th Coll; Hon Fell Qu Mary Coll Lon; Hon Fell Em Coll Cam; Hon D Litt E Lon Poly; Hon DD Ex; 2nd Lt 3rd R Tank Regiment 1959–61; C E Ham 1966–68; Chapl Cuddesdon Th Coll 1968–71; R Thamesmead Dio S'wark 1971–78; Bp of Stepney 1978–91; Chmn Urban Learning Foundation -1991; Jt Chmn Interfaith Network UK 1987–1992; Bp of B & W from 1991; Chmn Social Policy Ctee BSR 1990–96; Chmn Social, Economic and Industrial Ctee BSR 1996–97; Chmn Childrens Soc from 1997; Pres R Bath and W of England Soc from 1997; Commis to Bp of Namibia
Tel: (01749) 672341
Fax: (01749) 679355
e-mail: bishop@bathwells.anglican.org

BAXTER, Dr Christina Ann, BA, PH D
St John's College, Chilwell Lane, Bramcote, Nottingham NG9 3DS [SOUTHWELL] 1985– b 8 Mar 1947; *educ* Walthamstow Hall Sevenoaks; Dur Univ; Bris Univ; Hd Relig Studies John Leggott Sixth Form Coll; Dur Research Student and pt staff M St Jo Coll Dur; Prin St Jo Coll Nottm; M Gen Syn Stg Ctee 1985–95; Vc-Chmn Ho of Laity 1990–95; Chmn Ho of Laity from 1995; M ACC from 1993; M Doct Commn
Tel: 0115–922 4087 (Home)
0115–925 1114 (Office)
Fax: 0115–943 6438

BAXTER, Mrs Margaret Ann, BA
76A Brownedge Rd, Lostock Hall, Preston, Lancs PR5 5AD [BLACKBURN] 1990– b 27 Jan 1942; *educ* Weston-super-Mare Gr Sch; Nottm Univ; Homerton Coll Cam; RE Tchr Chatteris Cambs 1964–65; Navrongo, Ghana 1965–70; pt Tutor Sierra Leone Th Hall 1977–83; Dir Rdr Tr Blackb dio 1990–93; Asst Dioc Dir of Tr from 1993; Author
Tel: (01772) 493789
e-mail: mabaxter@wavenet.uk.co

BEAL, Dr John Frank, PH D, BDS, LDSRCS
Oakroyd, 4 North Park Rd, Leeds LS8 1JD [RIPON] 1995– b 21 Jul 1942; *educ* Finchley Co Gr Sch; R Dental Hosp; Lon Univ; Birm Univ; Lect in Dental Health Birm Univ 1968–76; Sen Dental Officer Avon AHA (Teaching) 1977–79; Area Dental Officer Birm AHA 1979–83; Hon Lect in Community Dental Health Leeds Univ from 1983; Consultant in Dental Public Health Leeds HA from 1983; Regional Dental Adv N Yorks NHS Exec from 1991; JP; M HCC from 1996; M Dioc BMU 1990–93; M Bp's Coun from 1993
Tel: 0113–294 8795
Fax: 0113–295 2152 (Office)

BEAVER, Revd Dr William Carpenter II, BA, D PHIL, ABC
Church House, Great Smith St, London SW1P 3NZ [DIRECTOR OF COMMUNICATIONS FOR THE CHURCH OF ENGLAND] b 17 Sep 1945; *educ* St Jo Military Sch Salina, Kansas; Colorado Coll; Wolfson Coll Ox; St Steph Ho Ox; Exec Dir Ox Development Records Project 1977–80; Sen Rep J Walter Thompson 1980–83; Dir of Publicity Barnardo's 1983–89; Grp Dir of Public Affairs Pergamon AGB Research Internat 1989–91; Grp Dir Corporate Affairs NatWest 1991–92; NSM St Jo the Divine Kennington 1980–95; Dir of Marketing The Industrial Soc 1992–97; NSM St Mary

Redcliffe Bris from 1995; NSM St Andr Avonmouth 1995–97; Dir of Communications for C of E from 1997
Tel: 0171–898 1462
Fax: 0171–898 1461
e-mail: cofecommsunit@cix.compulink.co.uk

BEDFORD, Bishop of [SUFFRAGAN, ST ALBANS] **Rt Revd John Henry Richardson,** MA
168 Kimbolton Rd, Bedford MK41 8DN b 11 Jul 1937; *educ* Winchester Coll; Trin Hall Cam; Cuddesdon Th Coll; C Stevenage 1963–66; C St Mary Eastbourne 1966–68; V St Paul Chipperfield 1968–75; V St Mary Rickmansworth 1975–86; RD Rickmansworth 1977–86; V St Mich Bishop's Stortford 1986–94; Bp of Bedford from 1994
Tel: (01234) 357551
Fax: (01234) 218134

BEDI, Prof Raman, BDS, M SC, DDS, FDSRCS, DIP HE
Oak Cottage, 12 Manor Way, Potters Bar, Herts EN6 1EL [BIRMINGHAM] **1995–** *b* 20 May 1953; *educ* Headlands Sch Swindon; Bris Univ; Trin Coll Bris; Dir WHO Collaborating Centre for disability, culture and oral health; Head Nat Centre for Transcultural Oral Health; M BSR; Co-Chair Community and Urban Affairs Ctee BSR
Tel: 0171–915 2314
Fax: 0171–915 1233
e-mail: R.Bedi@eastman.ucl.ac.uk

BEER, Ven John Stuart, MA
Rectory, Hemingford Abbots, Huntingdon PE18 9AN [ARCHDEACON OF HUNTINGDON] *b* 15 Mar 1944; *educ* Roundhay Sch Leeds; Pemb Coll Ox; Westcott Ho Th Coll; C St Jo Knaresborough 1971–74; Fell and Chapl Fitzw Coll and New Hall Cam 1974–80; R Toft w Caldecote and Childerley and Harwick 1980–87; V Grantchester 1987–97; DDO, Dir of POT and Rdr Tr 1987–97; Hon Can Ely Cathl from 1989; Chmn Cathl Pilgrims Assoc Conference 1986–96; M Ethics Ctee Dunn Nutrition Unit from 1985; Adn of Huntingdon from 1997; Co-DDO and Dir POT from 1997; M Bp's Coun; Dioc Pastl Ctee; Communications Ctee; Bd of Patronage; Vacancy-in-See Ctee; Dioc Bd of Educ; DAC
Tel: (01480) 469856
Fax: (01480) 496073
e-mail: archdeacon.huntingdon@ely.anglican.org

BEHENNA, Mrs Margaret Rose, BA, M ED, PGCE
Windjammer, Holcombe Rd, Teignmouth, Devon TQ14 8UP [EXETER] **1995–** *b* 10 Feb 1938; *educ* Heathfield Ho High Sch Cardiff; Bris Univ; Ex Univ; Dep Prin Teignmouth Community Coll 1979–88; Dioc Dir of Educ 1988–96
Tel and Fax: (01626) 774124

BELL, Mr Stuart, MP
Church Commissioners, 1 Millbank, London SW1P 3JZ [SECOND CHURCH ESTATES COMMISSIONER] **1997–** *b* 16 May 1938; *educ* Hookergate Gr Sch Durham; Gray's Inn Lon; Barrister-at-Law; MP for Middlesbrough from 1983; PPS to Rt Hon Roy Hattersley 1983–84; Front bench spokesperson N Ireland 1984–87; Vc-Chair Inter-Parliamentary Union Exec British Grp 1991–94; Vc-Chair British Irish Inter-Parliamentary Body 1990–92; Front bench spokesperson trade and industry 1992–97; Second Ch Estates Commr from 1997
Tel: 0171–898 1000
Fax: 0171–898 1131

BENTLEY, Ven Frank W. H., AKC
Archdeacon's House, 56 Battenhall Rd, Worcester WR5 2BQ [ARCHDEACON OF WORCESTER] *1986–95 b* 4 Mar 1934; *educ* Yeovil Sch; K Coll Lon; C Shepton Mallet 1958–62; R Kingsdon w Podymore Milton, C-in-c Yeovilton 1962–66; R Babcary 1964–66; V Wiveliscombe 1966–76; RD Tone 1973–76; V St Jo-in-Bedwardine Worc 1976–84; RD Martley and Worc W 1979–84; Hon Can Worc Cathl from 1981; Adn of Worc and Can Res Worc Cathl from 1984; Chapl to HM The Queen from 1994
Tel: (01905) 764446 (Home)
(01905) 20537 (Office)
Fax: (01905) 612302

BERRY, Prof Anthony John, B SC, M PHIL, PH D, DIC
24 Leafield Rd, Disley, Stockport, Cheshire SK12 2JF [CHESTER] **1994–** *b* 22 Aug 1939; *educ* Bath Univ; Imp Coll Lon; Seattle Univ; Man Univ; Aerodynamicist Br Aircraft Corp 1962; Aerodynamics Engineer The Boeing Co Seattle 1965–69; Rsch Fell 1971–73, Lect 1973–86, Sen Lect 1986–95 in Management Development Man Univ; Prof Sheff Hallam Univ from 1995; M Bp's Coun; M DBF; M Dioc Syn; Rdr
Tel: (01663) 762393
e-mail: A.J.BERRY@shu.ac.uk

BERRY, Very Revd Peter Austin, BA, B TH, MA, HON DD
The Provost's House, 16 Pebble Mill Rd, Birmingham B5 7SA [PROVOST OF BIRMINGHAM] **1990–** *b* 27 Apr 1935; *educ* Solihull Sch; Keble Coll Ox; St Steph Ho Th Coll; Bp's Chapl Community Relations Cov Cathl 1963–70; Midlands Regional Officer CRC 1970–73; Can Res Cov Cathl 1973–77; Vc Provost of Cov 1977–85; Chmn Race Pluralism Ctee BSR 1985–88; M Sen Appts Ctee 1987–92; Provost of Birm from 1986; Hon Fell Cov Univ; M Cathl Statutes Commn from 1987; Ch Commr
Tel: 0121–236 6323 (Office)
0121–472 0709 (Home)
Fax: 0121–212 0868

BEVERLEY, Bishop of [PROVINCIAL EPISCOPAL VISITOR: YORK] **Rt Revd John Scott Gaisford,** BA, MA
3 North Lane, Roundhay, Leeds LS8 2QJ 1975–94, 1994–

95 *b* 7 Oct 1934; *educ* Burnage Gr Sch Man; St Chad's Coll Dur; Asst C St Hilda Audenshaw 1960–62; Asst C Bramhall 1962–65; V St Andr Crewe 1965–86; Asst Warden of Rdrs for Dio 1967–81; RD Nantwich 1974–86; Hon Can Ches Cathl 1980–86; Chmn Ho of Clergy Dioc Syn 1983–85; Adn of Macclesfield 1986–94; Ch Commr 1986–94; Wrdn of Rdrs 1986–94; M CE Pensions Bd 1982–97; Vc-Chmn Housing and Resid Care Ctee; Trustee Churches Conservation Trust from 1989; Bp of Beverley from 1994
Tel: 0113–273 2003
0410 887756 (Mobile)
Fax: 0113–273 3002
e-mail: 101740,2725@compuserve.com

BEVINGTON, Canon Colin Reginald, ALCD
44 Thorney Rd, Capel St Mary, Ipswich IP9 2LH [ST EDMUNDSBURY AND IPSWICH] **1995–** *b* 1 Jan 1936; *educ* Monkton Combe Sch; Lon Coll of Div; C St Budeaux Devonport 1963–65; C Ch Ch Attenborough w Chilwell 1965–68; R Benhall w Sternfield 1968–74; P-in-c Snape 1973–74; V St Steph Selly Hill 1974–81; P-in-c St Wulstan Selly Oak 1980–81; V St Steph and St Wulstan Selly Park 1981–88; Dioc Ecum Officer from 1988; Adv on Miss 1988–95; Co Ecum Officer from 1990; Hon Can St Eds Cathl from 1993; Chapl to Bp of St Eds and Ips from 1995; M Dioc Syn   *Tel:* (01473) 310069 (Home)
(01473) 252829 (Office)
Fax: (01473) 232552 (Office)

BIRCHALL, Mr Mark Dearman, MA
3 Melrose Rd, London SW18 1ND [SOUTHWARK] **1980–** *b* 26 Jul 1933; *educ* Eton; Trin Coll Ox; Stockbroker 1956–82; Rtd; Vc-Chmn Evang Alliance; Rdr; Trustee Ridley Hall and Wycliffe Hall   *Tel:* 0181–265 9736
e-mail: mdbirchall@aol.com

BIRD, Ven (Colin) Richard (Bateman), MA
Home: 7 Hoadly Rd, Streatham, London SW16 1AE
Office: Whitelands Coll, West Hill, London SW15 3SN
[ARCHDEACON OF LAMBETH] *b* 31 Mar 1933; *educ* privately; Co Tech Coll Guildf; Selw Coll Cam; Cuddesdon Th Coll; C St Mark's Cathl George 1958–61; C St Sav Claremont Cape Town 1961–64; C N Suburbs Pretoria 1964–66; R Tzaneen w Duiwelskloof and Phalaborwa 1966–70; C Limpsfield, in-c St Andr 1970–75; V St Cath Hatcham 1975–88; RD Deptford 1980–85; Hon Can S'wark 1983–88; Exam Chapl 1978–88; Adn of Lambeth from 1988; Bp of S'wark's Adv for Hosp Chaplaincy; P-in-c St Sav Brixton Hill 1989–94   *Tel:* 0181–392 3742 (Office)
0181–769 4384 (Home)
Fax: 0181–392 3743
e-mail: kingston@dswark.org.uk

BIRD, Revd David Ronald, BA, L TH
St Giles Vicarage, Spring Gardens, Northampton NN1 1LX [PETERBOROUGH] **1995–** *b* 14 Aug 1955; *educ* K Edw VI Gr Sch Nuneaton; York Univ; Westhill Coll Birm; St Jo Coll Nottm; Youth Worker All So Clubhouse Lon 1977–80; Community Centre Warden Nottm City Coun 1980–83; C Kinson TM 1986–90; R Thrapston 1990–97; V St Giles Northn from 1997; M Bp's Coun from 1994; Chmn CPAS from 1996
Tel: (01604) 634060
e-mail: drbird1408@aol.com

BIRD, Canon (Frederick) Hinton, MA, BD, M ED, PH D, PGCE
Rushen Vicarage, Port St Mary, Isle of Man IM9 5LP [SODOR AND MAN] **1995–** *b* 30 Jun 1938; *educ* Pontywaun Gr Sch Risca; St Edm Hall Ox; St D Coll Lamp; C Mynyddislwyn Monmouth 1965–67; Min Can St Woolos Cathl Newport 1967–70; Chapl Anglo-American Coll Faringdon 1970–71; Head of RE Folkestone Tech High Sch 1972–75; Head of RE Caerleon Comp Sch 1975–82; V Rushen from 1982; Chmn Ho of Clergy Dioc Syn; Sec Manx Convocation; M DBF, Stg Ctee, Legisl Ctee, Vacancy in See Ctee   *Tel:* (01624) 832275

BIRKENHEAD, Bishop of [SUFFRAGAN, CHESTER]
Rt Revd Michael Laurence Langrish, B SOC SC, BA, MA
Bishop's Lodge, 67 Bidston Rd, Birkenhead, Wirral L43 6TR **1985–** *b* 1 Jul 1946; *educ* K Edward Sch Southn; Birm Univ; Fitzw Coll Cam; Ridley Hall Th Coll; C Stratford-upon-Avon 1973–76; Chapl Rugby Sch 1976–81; V Offchurch and DDO 1981–87; Exam Chapl to Bp of Cov 1982–89; Chmn ACCM Vocations Ctee 1984–91; TR Rugby 1987–93; Chmn Ho of Clergy Dioc Syn 1988–93; Hon Can Cov Cathl 1990–93; Bp of Birkenhead from 1993; M BAGUPA 1996–98; M Urban Bps' Panel from 1996; M BSR Community and Urban Affairs Ctee from 1998
Tel: 0151–652 2741
Fax: 0151–651 2330
e-mail: bpbirkenhead@clara.net

BIRMINGHAM, Bishop of, Rt Revd Mark Santer, MA
Bishop's Croft, Old Church Rd, Harborne, Birmingham B17 0BG **1985–** *b* 29 Dec 1936; *educ* Marlboro Coll; Qu Coll Cam; Westcott Ho Th Coll; Tutor Cuddesdon Coll 1963–67; Asst C Cuddesdon 1963–67; Fell and Dean Clare Coll Cam 1967–72 (and Tutor 1968–72); Asst Lect in Div Univ of Cam 1968–72; Prin Westcott Ho Cam 1973–81; M Angl-Orthodox Jt Doctrinal Commn 1974–82; Area Bp of Kensington 1981–87; Bp of Birm from 1987; Co-Chmn ARCIC from 1983;

M Doct Commn from 1997; M Coun NACRO from 1984; Hon Fell Clare Coll Cam from 1987; Qu Coll Cam from 1991
Tel: 0121–427 1163
Fax: 0121–426 1322

BISHOP, Ven Anthony Peter, L TH, M PHIL, FRSA
Ministry of Defence, RAF Innsworth, Gloucester GL3 1EZ [CHAPLAIN-IN-CHIEF, RAF] **1998–** *b* 24 May 1946; *educ* Gravesend Gr Sch; Lon Coll of Div; St Jo Coll Nottm; C St Geo Beckenham 1971–75; Chapl RAF 1975–91; Asst Chapl--Chief 1991–98; Chapl-in-Chief from 1998
Tel: (01452) 712612 Ext 5030
Fax: (01452) 510828

BISSON, Ms Jane Victoria
Glenhaven, La Rocque, Grouville, Jersey JE3 9BB [WINCHESTER-CHANNEL ISLANDS] **1995–** Bank Manager

BLACK, Canon Neville, MBE, DMS, DASHE
445 Aigburth Rd, Liverpool L19 3PA [LIVERPOOL] **1995–** *b* 25 Apr 1936; *educ* Bootle Gr Sch; Liv Poly; Oak Hill Th Coll; C St Ambrose w St Tim Everton 1964–69; P-on-c St Geo Everton 1969–71; V 1971–81; Project Officer Evang Urban Tr Project 1974–81; Dir Dioc Grp for Urban Min and Leadership 1984–95; TR St Luke in the City from 1981; M Bp's Coun 1984–89; Chmn Dioc Ho of Clergy 1991–98
Tel: 0151–427 9803
01399–727–640 (Pager)
Fax: 0151–494 0736

BLACKBURN, Bishop of, Rt Revd Alan David Chesters, BA, MA
Bishop's House, Ribchester Rd, Blackburn BB1 9EF **1975–** *b* 26 Aug 1937; *educ* Elland Gr Sch; St Chad's Coll Dur; St Cath's Coll Ox; St Steph Ho Th Coll; C St Anne Wandsworth Lon 1962–66; Chapl Tiffin Sch Kingston-u-Thames 1966–72; Hon C St Richard's Ham 1967–72; R Brancepeth 1972–84; Dioc Dir Educ 1972–84; Adn of Halifax 1985–89; Bp of Blackb from 1989; Ch Commr from 1983; Bd of Govs from 1992; Pres Woodard Corp from 1993; M Countryside Commn from 1995
Tel: (01254) 248234
Fax: (01254) 246668
e-mail: bishop.blackburn@ukonline.co.uk

BLACKMORE, Dr David Richard, MA, D PHIL
Coniston, Newton Lane, Chester CH2 2HJ [CHESTER] **1980–** *b* 16 Dec 1938; *educ* Whitgift Sch S Croydon; CCC Ox; UMIST; Rsch Associate UMIST 1963–69; Rsch Scientist Wood River (Illinois) Shell Development Co 1973–75; Sen Prin Scientist Shell Rsch Ltd, Thornton, Rtd 1997; Rdr; Lay Chmn Dioc Syn; Lay Chmn Ches Dny
Tel: (01244) 323494
e-mail: blackmore@virtual-chester.com

BLADON, Mr Keith Victor, B COMM, FCA
11 Salisbury Ave, Tupsley, Hereford HR1 1QG [HEREFORD] **1995–** *b* 29 Mar 1933; *educ* K Geo V Sch Southport; Liv Univ; Partner Thorne Widgery Chartered Accountants 1966–88, Man Partner 1985–88; Business Consultancy 1988–93; JP; Dep Chmn Herefs Bench from 1998; Chmn Herefs Youth Court Panel 1995–97; M Dioc Syn from 1986; Chmn Ho of Laity from 1995; M Bp's Coun; M DBF, Chmn 1990–95; M Ch Commrs Dioc Consultative Grp 1993–95; M CBF and Exec Ctee from 1995; Rdr
Tel: (01432) 272402 (Home)
(01432) 355335 (Office)

BLAKE, Mrs Katy Vivian, LL B
106 Cooks Close, Bradley Stoke, Bristol BS32 0BB [BRISTOL] **1995–** *b* 6 Jan 1960; *educ* Cheltenham Bournside Sch; Reading Univ; Bris Poly; Articled Clerk to Solicitor Woodspring Distr Coun 1982–84; Asst Solicitor Cheltenham Boro Coun 1984–88; OFSTED trained Lay Inspector of Schs and Nat Soc trained denominational inspector; M Bd of Educ and Schs Ctee; M Dioc Fin Ctee; M Bp's Coun; M Dioc Bd of Educ
Tel: (01454) 617569
e-mail: ckdblake@zetnet.co.uk

BLAKEY, Revd Cedric Lambert, BA, MA, DPS
Derby Church House, Full St, Derby DE1 3DR [DERBY] **1995–** *b* 16 Aug 1954; *educ* Worksop Coll; Fitzw Coll Cam; St Jo Coll Nottm; C Cotmanhay 1979–83; C-in-c St Andr Blagreaves CD 1983–89; P-in-c Sinfin Moor 1984–89; V Heanor 1989–97; RD Heanor 1994–97; Chapl to Bp of Derby from 1997
Tel: (01332) 382233
e-mail: C.Blakey@btinternet.com

BOARDMAN, Revd Philippa Jane, MA
Vicarage, St Stephen's Rd, London E3 5JL [LONDON] **1994–** *b* 24 Mar 1963; *educ* Haberdashers' Aske's Sch for Girls; Jes Coll Cam; Ridley Hall Th Coll; C St Mary and St Steph Walthamstow 1990–93; Asst Pr St Mary of Eton Hackney Wick 1993–96; Dean of Women's Min Stepney Area from 1994; P-in-c St Paul w St Mark Old Ford from 1996
Tel and Fax: 0181–980 9020

BOLTON, Bishop of [SUFFRAGAN, MANCHESTER] **Rt Revd David Bonser,** MA, AKC
4 Sandfield Drive, Lostock, Bolton, Gtr Manchester BL6 4DU **1982–85** *b* 1 Feb 1934; *educ* Hillhouse Sec Sch Huddersfield; Univ of Man; K Coll Lon and St Boniface, Warminster; C St Jas Heckmondwike 1962–65; St Geo Sheff 1965–68; R St Clem Chorlton-cum-Hardy 1968–82; Bp's Ecum Offer 1973–81; Tutor, Extra Mural Dept Univ of Man 1977–82; Hon Can Man 1980–82; AD Hulme 1981–82; V St Chad Roch-

dale 1982–86; TR Rochdale 1986–91; Adn of Rochdale 1982–91; Bp of Bolton from 1991
Tel: (01204) 843400
Fax: (01204) 849652

BONE, Mr David Hugh, MA
3 Hardy Lane, Tockington, Bristol BS12 4LJ [BRISTOL] **1997–** *b* 18 Jan 1939; *educ* Harrow Co Boys' Gr Sch; Worc Coll Ox; Univ of Aston; Asst Tutor Kingsgate Coll (YMCA) Broadstairs 1957–59; Assembly Hand Joseph Lucas 1963–64; Tchr RE Classics Kettering Boys' Gr Sch 1965–67; Hd of Divinity Crypt Boys' Gr Sch Gloucester 1967–72; Student Counsellor Plymouth Poly 1972–74; Careers Adv UWE (formerly Bristol Poly) from 1975; M Dioc Syn from 1994; M Vacancy-in-See Ctee; Rdr from 1996
Tel: (01454) 614601
Fax: 0117–976 3819 (Office)

BONHAM, Revd Valerie, ALA
12 Wakelins End, Cookham, Berks SL6 9TQ [OXFORD] **1990–95, 1998–** *b* 26 Aug 1947; *educ* Wing Co Sec Sch; Coll of Librarianship Abth; St Alb and Ox Min Course; Bucks Co Library 1964–68 and 1970–72; Hillingdon Libraries 1972–75; E Berks AHA 1989–90; Par Dn St Mary Speen 1997–98; C H Trin Cookham-on-Thames from 1998; Hon Historian Community of St Jo B Clewer; M Lord's Prayer Revision Ctee 1998; M Berks Sub-ctee Ox Dioc Buildings Ctee; M Berks Chs Trust Exec Ctee

BONNEY, Revd Mark Philip John, MA, PGCE
Rectory, Berkhamsted, Herts HP4 2DH [ST ALBANS] **1995–** *b* 2 Mar 1957; *educ* Northgate Gr Sch Ipswich; St Cath Coll Cam; St Steph Ho Ox; C St Pet Stockton-on-Tees 1985–88; Chapl St Alb Abbey 1988–90; Prec St Alb Abbey 1990–92; V Eaton Bray w Edlesborough 1992–96; R Gt Berkhamsted from 1996
Tel: (01442) 864194

BOOTH, Miss Sue (Susan) Nancy
6 Fairoak Flats, Harrowby Drive, Newcastle, Staffs ST5 3JR [LICHFIELD] **1997–** *b* 15 May 1931; *educ* Ipswich High Sch; Birm Univ; Secretarial posts 1952–55; BBC Studio Manager, External Services 1955; Asst Overseas Instructor BBC Staff Tr 1959–68; Programme Tr Officer Zambia Broadcasting Corp 1965; Producer BBC Radio Stoke-on-Trent 1968; Freelance Broadcaster and Lect in Communications from 1978; Chmn Ecum Ctee Dioc BMU; M Black and White Together in Faith Ctee Lichf; Forum Elected M CTE Enabling Grp; Angl Rep Stg Ctee Staffs Plus Ecum Coun
Tel: (01782) 613855

BORDASS, Mrs (Elizabeth) Mary, T CERT
8 Bishop's Mead, Laverstock, Salisbury, Wilts SP1 1RU [SALISBURY] **1995–** *b* 9 Jan 1943; *educ* Ilkeston Gr Sch; Glouc Tr Coll; Tchr Home Economics/Food Tech 1964–73 and 1979–95; Hd of Dept from 1966; Made Redundant 1995
Tel: (01722) 336698

BOSWELL, Revd Colin John Luke
Brandon Lodge, Croydon Vicarage, 22 Bramley Hill, Croydon CR0 5EG [SOUTHWARK] **1998–** *b* 12 Jun 1947; *educ* Elliot Sch Putney; Sarum and Wells Th Coll; C H Trin Upper Tooting 1974–78; C St Phil Sydenham 1978–79; P-in-c St Helier 1979–83; Chapl St Helier Hosp 1979–83; R Caterham 1983–95; R Chaldon 1985–95; V St Jo Croydon from 1995; Borough Dean Croydon
Tel: 0181–688 1387 (Home)
0181–688 8104 (Office)
Fax: 0181–688 5877

BOWEN, Dr David Vaughan, MA, PH D, C CHEM, FRSC
30 Salisbury Rd, Canterbury, Kent CT2 7HH [CANTERBURY] **1990–** *b* 15 Jul 1945; *educ* Phillips Academy, Mass, USA; St Jo Coll Cam; Lon Univ; Instructor Wayne State Sch of Medicine 1970–72; Asst Prof Rockefeller Univ 1972–77; Sen Scientist Union Carbide Corp 1977–80; Head of Spectroscopy Pfizer Central Research, Sandwich 1980–93; Info Techn Consultant Pfizer from 1993
Tel: (01227) 453026
Fax: (01304) 616663
e-mail: David_Bowen@sandwich.pfizer.com

BOWEN, Mr John Ivor
Dept FGY, PO Box 99, Bracknell, Berks RG42 5NQ [OXFORD] **1995–** *b* 29 Dec 1942; *educ* Melbourne CE Sch Australia; City of Lon Sch; MIT USA; Man Dir Elex Systems from 1971; Lay Chmn Bracknell Dny Syn 1984–94; M Dioc Syn from 1985; M Bp's Coun; M DBF
Tel: (01344) 52933

BOWERING, Ven Michael Ernest
12 Rectory Park, Morpeth, Northumberland NE61 2SZ [ARCHDEACON OF LINDISFARNE] **1985–87, 1990–** *b* 25 Jun 1935; *educ* Barnstaple Gr Sch; Kelham Th Coll; C St Oswald Middlesbrough 1959–62; C Huntington w New Earswick 1962–64; V Brayton w Barlow 1964–72; RD Selby 1971–72; V Saltburn by the Sea 1972–81; Res Can York Minster and Sec for Miss and Evang 1981–87; Adn of Lindisfarne from 1987
Tel: (01670) 513207
Fax: (01670) 503837
e-mail: m.bowering@newcastle.anglican.org

BOWLER, Prebendary Kenneth Neville
70 Fulham High St, London SW6 3LG [LONDON] **1995–** *b* 14 Jan 1937; *educ* Ernest Bailey Gr Sch Matlock; K Coll Lon; St Boniface Th Coll Warminster; C Buxton 1961–67; R Sandiacre 1967–75; V Bedfont 1975–87;

AD Hounslow 1982–87; Preb St Paul's Cathl from 1985; V All SS Fulham from 1987
Tel: 0171–736 6301

BOYD-LEE, Mr Paul Winston Michael, BA, DIP TH
Manor Barn, Horsington, Templecombe, Som BA8 0ET [SALISBURY] **1991–** *b* 3 May 1941; *educ* Brighton Coll; Open Univ; Ex Univ; Theatre Manager Rank Organisation 1963–66; Credit Controller Internat Factors Ltd 1966–72; Self-employed publisher from 1972
Tel: (01963) 371137

BRACEGIRDLE, Canon (Cynthia) Wendy Mary, MA
Rectory, Parsonage Close, Salford M5 3GS [MANCHESTER] **1998–** *b* 2 Mar 1952; *educ* Qu Sch Ches; LMH Ox; Nn Ord Course; Tutor Nn Ord Course 1976–85; Asst Chapl Cen Man Hosps 1985–88; Prin Man Ordained Local Min Scheme from 1989; Hon Can Man Cathl from 1998; M ABM Working Party on LNSM 1996–98
Tel: 0161–872 0800 (Home)
0161–832 5785 (Office)
Fax: 0161–832 1466

BRADFORD, Bishop of, Rt Revd David James Smith, AKC
Bishopscroft, Ashwell Rd, Heaton, Bradford, W Yorks BD9 4AU **1973–80, 1983–87, 1992–** *b* 14 Jul 1935; *educ* Hertf Gr Sch; K Coll Lon; St Boniface Coll Warminster; C All SS Gosforth 1959–62; C St Fran High Heaton 1962–64; P-in-c St Mary Magd Long Benton 1964–68; V Longhirst w Hebron 1968–75; V St Mary Monkseaton 1975–82; V Felton 1982–83; Adn of Lindisfarne 1981–87; Bp of Maidstone 1987–92; Bp to the Forces 1990–92; Bp of Bradf from 1992
Tel: (01274) 545414
Fax: (01274) 544831
e-mail: bishbrad@nildram.co.uk

BRADLEY, Revd Peter David Douglas, B TH
Rectory, 1A College Rd, Up Holland, Skelmersdale WN8 0PY [LIVERPOOL] **1990–** *b* 4 Jun 1949; *educ* Brookfield Comp Sch; Nottm Univ; Ian Ramsey Coll; Linc Th Coll; C Up Holland 1979–83; V H Spirit Dovecot 1983–94; Sec Dioc Bd of Min 1983–88; Sec Grp for Urban Min and Leadership 1984–88; Asst Dir In-Service Tr 1988–89; Dir CME from 1989; TR Up Holland from 1994; M BM Mission at Home Ctee; M Dioc Bd of Min *Tel and Fax:* (01695) 622936

BRADNUM, Canon (Ella) Margaret, MA, PGCE
13 Boothtown Rd, Halifax, W Yorks HX3 6EU [WAKEFIELD] **1995–** *b* 5 Sep 1941; *educ* Abbey Sch Reading; St Hugh's Coll Ox; Lon Inst of Educ; Dss St Mary Illingworth 1969–72; Dss All SS Batley 1972–73; Lay Tr Officer 1977–82; Minl Tr Officer 1982–93; Warden of Rdrs from 1986; Co-ord Lay Tr from 1993; Prin Wakef Min Scheme from 1997
Tel: (01422) 321740

BRADWELL, Bishop of [AREA BISHOP, CHELMSFORD] **Rt Revd Laurie (Laurence Alexander) Green,** BD, AKC, STM, D MIN
Bishop's House, Orsett Rd, Horndon-on-the-Hill, Essex SS17 8NS b 26 Dec 1945; *educ* East Ham Gr Sch; K Coll Lon; New York State Univ; New York Th Seminary; St Aug Coll Cant; C St Mark Kingstanding Birm 1970–73; V St Chad Erdington 1973–83; Prin Aston Tr Scheme 1983–89; Hon C H Trin Birchfield 1984–89; TR All SS Poplar Lon 1989–93; Bp of Bradwell from 1993
Tel: (01375) 673806
Fax: (01375) 674222
e-mail: lauriegr@globalnet.co.uk
b.bradwell@chelmsford.anglican.org

BRAMHALL, Revd Eric, MA
All Saints' Vicarage, Childwall Abbey Rd, Liverpool L16 0JU [LIVERPOOL] **1995–** *b* 15 May 1939; *educ* Liv Inst High Sch for Boys; St Cath Coll Cam; Tyndale Hall Th Coll; C St Luke Eccleston St Helens 1963–66; C Em Bolton 1966–69; Hd of RE Wallasey Gr Sch 1969–74; V Ch Ch Aughton 1975–92; V All SS Childwall from 1992
Tel: 0151–737 2169

BRANDON, Mrs Beatrice, DMS
Clopton Manor, Clopton, Kettering, Northants NN14 3DZ [PETERBOROUGH] **1995–** *b* 28 May 1955; Design Consultant; M Dioc Pastl Ctee; M Vacancy-in-See Ctee; Lay Chmn Pet Dny Syn; M Bp's Coun and Stg Ctee; M Dioc Budget Review Grp; M Archbishops' Millennium Grp
Tel: (01832) 720346
Fax: (01832) 720446
e-mail: beatrice.brandon@btinternet.com

BRAY, Mr Peter, M INST R, MDT
4 Lupin Rd, Southampton SO16 3LB [WINCHESTER] **1995–** *b* 12 Jan 1936; *educ* Truro Sch; Swansea Univ; Southn Univ; Chmn Southn Sail Tr Assn Comm 1976–86; Managing Director Braeaire Ltd from 1980; Southn and Fareham Chamber of Trade and Ind, M Manufacturing Ctee and Educ and Tr Ctee from 1992
Tel: (01703) 556866 (Office)
(01703) 553070 (Home)
Fax: (01703) 322581

BREEN, Revd Michael James, MA, L TH
Rectory, 18A Hallam Gate Rd, Sheffield S10 5BT [SHEFFIELD] **1996–** *b* 13 Jun 1958; *educ* Oak Hill Th Coll; Cranmer Hall Dur; C St Martin Cam 1983–87; V All SS Clapham Park 1987–92; USA 1992–94; TR St Thos Crookes Sheff from 1994
Tel: 0114–268 6362

BREGAZZI, Dr Paul Kneen, MA, PH D, CERT ED
Ballachree, Ballaugh, Isle of Man IM7 5EB [SODOR AND MAN] **1990–** *b* 18 Oct 1935; *educ* K William's Coll Isle of Man; Ch Coll Cam; Nottm Univ; Univ of Wales; Asst Master Cheltenham Coll 1962–66 and 1971–79; Marine Biologist British Antarctic Survey 1967–71; Prin K William's Coll Isle of Man 1979–89; Rtd
Tel: (01624) 897715

BRENTFORD, Viscountess Gill (Gillian) Evelyn, OBE, FCA
Cousley Place, Wadhurst, E Sussex TN5 6HF [CHICHESTER] **1990–** *b* 22 Nov 1942; *educ* West Heath Sch; Ch Commr from 1991; Bd of Govs from1994; Lay Chmn Dioc Syn from 1992; M Crown Appts Commn from 1995; Joint Chair Springboard from 1996; Pres CMS from 1998
Tel: (01892) 783737
Fax: (01892) 784428
e-mail: 101563.2113@compuserve.com

BRETT, Canon Paul Gadsby, MA
Rectory, 41 Worrin Rd, Shenfield, Brentwood, Essex CM15 8DH [CHELMSFORD] **1993–** *b* 19 Feb 1941; *educ* Monkton Combe Sch; Wycliffe Hall Th Coll; C St Pet Bury 1965–68; Asst Ind Missr Man 1968–72; Sen Ind Chapl Kidderminster 1972–76; Asst Sec (Ind and Economic Affairs) Gen Syn BSR 1976–84; Res Can Chelmsf Cathl and Dir Social Resp Chelmsf 1985–94; M BSR from 1994; R Shenfield from 1994; Res Can Emer Chelmsf Cathl from 1994; M BM Rural Affairs Ctee from 1994; Ctee M Open Syn Grp 1994–96; Ctee M CEIG from 1995
Tel: (01277) 220360

BRIDGER, Revd Francis William, MA, PH D, DIP TH
St Mark's Vicarage, 37A Melbury Rd, Woodthorpe, Nottingham NG5 4PG [SOUTHWELL] **1998–** *b* 27 May 1951; *educ* Gravesend Sch for Boys; Pemb Coll Ox; Bris Univ; Trin Coll Bris; C St Jude Mildmay Grove and St Paul Canonbury 1978–82; Lect St Jo Coll Nottm 1982–90, Dir of Studies 1989–90, Assoc Lect 1990–92; V St Mark Woodthorpe from 1990; M Bp's Coun; Vc-Chair Bp's Strategy Ctee
Tel: 0115–926 7859
e-mail: fbridger@surfaid.org

BRIDGEWATER, Mr Allan, CBE, ACII, FIPD, CIMGT, FRSA
Linquenda, 447 Unthank Rd, Norwich NR4 7QN [EX-OFFICIO, CHAIRMAN, CHURCH OF ENGLAND PENSIONS BOARD] *b* 26 Aug 1936; *educ* Group Chief Exec Nor Union 1989–97; main Bd Dir 1985–97; Chmn Swiss Re UK Ltd and Swiss Re Life & Health UK Ltd; Chmn Divisional Bd for Swiss Re Life & Health from 1998; Dir Riggs Bank Europe from 1991
Tel and Fax: (01603) 455120

BRISTOL, Bishop of, Rt Revd Barry Rogerson, BA, LLD
Bishop's House, Clifton Hill, Bristol, Avon BS8 1BW **1982–** *b* 25 Jul 1936; *educ* Magnus Gr Sch Newark, Notts; Leeds Univ; Wells Th Coll; C St Hilda's S Shields 1962–65; C St Nic Bishopwearmouth Sunderland 1965–67; Lect Lich Th Coll 1967–71; Vc-Prin Lich Th Coll 1971–72; Lect Sarum-Wells Th Coll 1972–75; V St Thos Wednesfield Wolv 1975–78; TR Wednesfield 1979; Bp of Wolv 1979–85; Bp of Bris from 1985; M Faith & Order Commn WCC 1987–98; Chmn ACCM 1987–91; Chmn ABM 1991–93; M Cen Ctee WCC from 1991
Tel: 0117–973 0222
Fax: 0117–923 9670
e-mail: 106430.1040@compuserve.com

BRIXWORTH, Bishop of [SUFFRAGAN, PETERBOROUGH] **Rt Revd Paul Everard Barber,** MA
4 The Avenue, Dallington, Northampton NN5 7AN **1979–85** *b* 16 Sep 1935; *educ* Sherborne Sch; St Jo Coll Cam; Wells Th Coll; Asst C St Fran Westborough 1960–66; V St Mich Camberley w Yorktown 1966–73; V St Thos-on-the Bourne Farnham 1973–80; RD Farnham 1974–79; Hon Can Guildf 1980–89; Adn of Surrey 1980–89; Bp of Brixworth from 1989; Hon Can Pet Cathl from 1997; M Coun of the Coll of Preachers; Abp's Adv to Hdmasters' and Headmistresses' Conf from 1993
Tel: (01604) 759423
Fax: (01604) 750925

BROAD, Revd Hugh Duncan, NDA, CERT ED
St George's Vicarage, Grange Rd, Tuffley, Gloucester GL4 0PE [GLOUCESTER] **1995–** *b* 28 Oct 1937; *educ* Bishop's Castle Co High Sch Shropshire; Shropshire Inst of Agric; Hereford Coll of Educ; Bernard Gilpin Soc; Lichf Th Coll; C H Trin Hereford 1967–72; Tchr Bp of Heref's Blue Coat Sch 1972–74; C SS Peter and Paul Fareham 1974–76; V All SS and St Barn Hereford 1976–90; R St Kath Matson 1990–97; V St Geo Glouc and St Marg Whaddon from 1997; M Dioc Coun of Par Resources; M Crown Appts Commn from 1997; Convenor Affirming Catholicism Grp in Gen Syn from 1997
Tel: (01452) 520851
0831 808349 (Mobile)

BROADBENT, Ven Pete (Peter Alan), MA
247 Kenton Rd, Harrow, Middx HA3 0HQ [ARCHDEACON OF NORTHOLT] **1985–** *b* 31 Jul 1952; *educ* Merchant Taylors Sch Northwood; Jes Coll Cam; St Jo Coll Nottm; C St Nic Dur City 1977–80; C Em Holloway 1980–83; Chapl to N Lon Poly and Hon C St Mary Islington 1983–89; Bps Chapl for Miss in Stepney 1980–89; Councillor and Chair of Planning Lon Boro of Islington 1982–89; M Dioc Commn 1989–92;

M Panel of Chmn Gen Syn 1990–92; M CE Evang Coun 1984–95; Chair Vacancy-in-See Ctee Regulation Working Party 1991–93; M Gen Syn Stg Orders Ctee 1991–95; M Appointments Sub-Ctee 1992–95; V Trin St Mich Harrow 1989–95; AD Harrow 1994; Adn of Northolt from 1995; M CBF from 1991; M Gen Syn Stg Ctee from 1992; Chair Gen Syn Business Sub-Ctee from 1996; Chair Elections Review Grp from 1996; Chair Lon Dioc Bd for Schs from 1996; M Spring Harvest Exec
Tel: 0181–907 5941 (Home)
0181–907 5993 (Area Office)
Fax: 0181–909 2368
e-mail: pete@arch.northolt.demon.co.uk

BROGGIO, Canon Bernice, BA, BD, DIP SOC STUDY, CQSW
Holy Trinity Vicarage, 14 Upper Tooting Park, London SW17 7SW [SOUTHWARK] **1990–** *b* 4 Dec 1935; *educ* High Wycombe High Sch; Bedford Coll Lon; K Coll Lon; Glasgow Univ; Geography Tchr 1957–59; Company of St Francis 1960–63; Accredited Lay Worker Killingworth Newcastle 1966–70; Psychiatric Social Worker Nuffield Child Psychiatry Unit Newc 1972–77; Deputy Head Benton Grange (RC Residential) School 1977–80; Tm Mgr C and YP Residential Services Avon Co Coun 1980–88; NSM St Thos Newc 1972–80; NSM St Paul Bris 1981–88; C St Luke w H Trin Charlton 1988–95; Hon Can S'wark Cathl from 1995; V H Trin Upper Tooting from 1995; RD Tooting from 1996; M Dioc Bd of Ch and Society; M Open Syn Grp; M Ctee CEIG
Tel: 0181–672 4790

BROTHERTON, Mrs Daphne Margaret Yvonne, MA
4 Canon Lane, Chichester, W Sussex PO19 1PX [CHICHESTER] **1993–** *b* 27 Oct 1936; *educ* St Leon Sch St Andr Fife; St Hugh's Coll Ox; Economic Research 1958–64; Statistician w CSO in Trinidad 1965–67; Dir Caribbean Market Research Trinidad 1967–75; Housewife; M DBF; Trustee Cleaver Trust; Chmn Regnum Crossroads Scheme from 1995; Lay Chmn Chich Dny Syn from 1997
Tel: (01243) 779134
Fax: (01243) 536452

BROTHERTON, Ven John Michael, MA
4 Canon Lane, Chichester, W Sussex PO19 1PX [ARCHDEACON OF CHICHESTER] **1995–** *b* 7 Dec 1935; *educ* Hipperholme Sch Yorks; St Jo Coll Cam; Cuddesdon Th Coll; C St Nic Chiswick 1961–64; Inst of Educ Univ of Lon; Chapl Trin Coll Port of Spain, Trinidad 1965–69; R St Mich Diego Martin Trinidad 1969–75; V St Mary and St Jo Ox 1976–81; Chapl St Hilda's Coll Ox 1976–81; RD Cowley 1978–81; V St Mary Portsea 1981–91; Hon Can St Mich Cathl Kobe from 1986; Adn of Chich from 1991; Res Can Chich Cathl from 1991; Chmn Dioc Overseas Ctee from 1994; M Legal Adv Commn from 1996
Tel: (01243) 779134
Fax: (01243) 536452

BROWN, Mr Andrew Charles, B SC, FRICS
Church Commissioners, 1 Millbank, London SW1P 3JZ [CHIEF SURVEYOR, CHURCH COMMISSIONERS] *b* 30 Oct 1957; *educ* Ashmole Comp Sch; S Bank Poly; Healey & Baker 1981–84; St Quintin 1984–94; Chief Surveyor Ch Commrs from 1994
Tel: 0171–898 1634
Fax: 0171–898 1132

BROWN, Canon Christopher Francis
Rectory, Union St, Trowbridge, Wilts BA14 8RU [SALISBURY] **1993–** *b* 23 Apr 1944; *educ* Bridgemary Sch Gosport; Bernard Gilpin Soc Dur; Sarum Th Coll; C High Wycombe 1971–74; C Sherborne 1974–77; R Yarnbury 1977–82; R Portland 1982–88; RD Weymouth 1985–88; R St Jas Trowbridge from 1988; RD Bradford from 1994; Non Res Can Sarum Cathl from 1998
Tel: (01225) 755121

BROWN, Ven Gerald Arthur Charles, MA
Styrmansgatan 1, 11454, Stockholm, Sweden [ARCHDEACON OF SCANDINAVIA, DIOCESE IN EUROPE] *b* 24 Apr 1935; *educ* Alderman Newton's Sch Leic; CCC Cam; St Steph Ho Ox; C St Pet Wolverhampton 1960–66; V Trent Vale 1966–74; V St Andr Wolverhampton 1974–82; Chapl All SS Milan 1982–89; Chapl St Edmund Oslo and Adn of Scandinavia 1990–92; Chapl St Pet and St Sigrid Stockholm and Adn of Scandinavia from 1992; P-in-c Angl Chaplaincy Riga from 1994
Tel: 00–46–8–663–82–48

BROWN, Mrs Margaret Mary
Luckhurst, Mayfield, E Sussex TN20 6TY [CHICHESTER] **1985–** *b* 9 Nov 1934; *educ* Braemar Sch, Tunbridge Wells
Tel: (01435) 873007

BROWN, Mrs (Mary) Patricia, NFF T DIP
30 Chirgwin Rd, Tregolls, Truro, Cornwall TR1 1TT [TRURO] **1985–** *b* 31 Mar 1929; *educ* Truro Co Gr Sch; Maria Grey Coll of Educ; Kindergarten Mistress Bath High Sch 1950–54; Hd of Infant Dept Cardinham Co Primary Sch 1967–77; Hdmistress Lanlivery Primary Sch 1977–84; Rtd; Housewife; M Bp's Coun, Vacancy in See Ctee from 1985; M Dioc Bd of Educ from 1990; M Cathls Commn Follow Up Grp 1994–98; Lay Can Truro Cathl from 1992; M Cathls Measure Steering Grp 1996–98
Tel: (01872) 70350

BROWN, Canon Simon Nicolas Danton, MA
Rectory, The Precincts, Burnham, Slough, Berks SL1 7HU [OXFORD] **1995–** *b* 23 Feb 1937; *educ* Merchant Taylors Sch Northwood; Clare Coll Cam; S'wark Ord Course; Linc Th Coll; NS 1956–58; Youth Leader Bede Ho Bermondsey 1961–63; C Lambeth 1964–66; Warden LMH Settlement 1966–72; TV Southn City Cen 1972–79; R Gt Brickhill w Bow Brickhill and Lt Brickhill 1979–84; TR Burnham TM Slough from 1984; RD Burnham from 1988; Dioc Consultant for Dny Development from 1997; M Bp's Coun
Tel: (01628) 604173 (Home)
(01628) 664338 (Office)

BROWNE, Revd Dr Herman Beseah, BA, BD, AKC, D PHIL
Lambeth Palace, London SE1 7JU [ARCHBISHOP OF CANTERBURY'S ASSISTANT SECRETARY FOR ANGLICAN COMMUNION AND ECUMENICAL AFFAIRS] *b* 11 Mar 1965; *educ* St Patr Sch Monrovia; Cuttington Univ; K Coll Lon; Heythrop Coll; C N Lambeth 1990–91; Tutor Simon of Cyrene Th Inst 1990–96; Abp of Cant's Asst Sec for Angl Communion and Ecum Affairs from 1996
Tel: 0171–928 8282
Fax: 0171–401 9886
e-mail: hermanbrowne@lampal.clara.net

BROWNSELL, Prebendary John Kenneth, MA
All Saints' Vicarage, Powis Gardens, London W11 1JG [LONDON] **1995–** *b* 16 May 1948; *educ* Ashby de la Zouch Gr Sch; Hertf Coll Ox; Cuddesdon Th Coll; C All SS w St Columba Notting Hill 1973–74; C Notting Hill 1974–76; TV 1976–82; V from 1982; AD Kensington 1984–92; Preb St Paul's Cathl from 1992; Dir of Ords Kensington Area Lon dio; Commissary for Bp of Windward Islands; M Initiation Services Revision Ctee; M Legal Aid Commn
Tel: 0171–727 5919

BRUINVELS, Mr Peter Nigel Edward, LL B, FRSA, FCIM, MCIJ, MIPR
14 High Meadow Close, Dorking, Surrey RH4 2LG [GUILDFORD] **1985–** *b* 30 Mar 1950; *educ* St Jo Sch Leatherhead; Lon Univ; Inns of Court Sch of Law; MP Leic E 1983–87; Prin–Peter Bruinvels Associates –Media Management and Public Affairs Consultants from 1986; Company Dir and Author; M Dioc Syn and Dorking Dny Syn from 1979; Freeman of City of Lon 1980; M Dios Commn 1991–96; M Legislative Ctee 1991–96; News Broadcaster, Political Commentator and Freelance Journalist; Ch Commr from 1993, Pastl Ctee from 1993; OFSTED Denominational Schs RE Inspector from 1994; M DSS Child Support and Soc Security Appeals Tribunals from 1994; Non-Exec Dir Radio Mercury plc 1994–97; Managing Editor Bruinvels News & Media Press and Broadcasting Agents from 1993; M Dioc Bd of Educ from 1994; M Gen Syn Bd of Educ from 1996; Parliamentary Candidate for The Wrekin 1997; Co-opted Business M Surrey LEA; Pres Norwest Midlands Chartered Inst of Marketing 1997–98
Tel: (01306) 887082 (Home and Office)
0336 764440 (Pager)
07050 085 456 (Mobile)
Fax: (01306) 887082

BRYANT, Canon Mark Watts, BA
Stoke Rectory, 365A Walsgrave Rd, Coventry CV2 4BG [COVENTRY] **1998–** *b* 8 Oct 1949; *educ* St Jo Sch Leatherhead; St Jo Coll Dur; Cuddesdon Th Coll; C Addlestone 1975–79; C St Jo Studley, Trowbridge 1979–83, V 1983–88; Chapl Trowbridge CFE 1979–83; DDO and Dir Vocations and Tr, Cov 1988–96; Hon Can Cov Cathl from 1993; TR Cov Caludon from 1998
Tel and *Fax:* (01203) 635731

BRYANT, Canon Richard Kirk, MA, DIP TH
2 Burlington Court, Hadrian Park, Wallsend NE28 9YH [NEWCASTLE] **1995–** *b* 28 Apr 1947; *educ* Hillfoot Hey High Sch Liv; Ch Coll Cam; Nottm Univ; Cuddesdon Th Coll; C St Gabr Heaton 1972–75; C Morpeth 1975–78; P-in-c Ven Bede Benwell 1978–82; V Earsdon and Backworth 1982–93; V Wylam 1993–97; Dir Rdr Tr Course 1990–98; Dir of Tr for Local Min 1997–98; Prin Local Min Scheme and Rdr Tr Course from 1998; Hon Can Newc Cathl from 1997
Tel: 0191–263 7922
e-mail: bmt@newcastle.anglican.org

BRYANT, Mr William Wells, B SC, M SC
10 Bolters Lane, Banstead, Surrey SM7 2AR [GUILDFORD] **1995–** *b* 24 May 1931; *educ* Bungay Gr Sch; Dur Univ; Lon Univ; Philips Electronics (UK) 1954–71; Dep Dir Philips Electronics (Internat) 1972–76; Tech Dir Polygram (UK) 1977–87; Boro Coun from 1986; Non Exec M Mid-Surrey DHA 1989–95; Vc-Chmn E Surrey Health Commn 1995–96; M Dioc Syn from 1988; Lay Chmn Epsom Dny Syn 1989–96; M Bp's Coun from 1989; M Steering Grp Chs Together in Surrey from 1991; Chmn Surrey Health Care Chapl Adv Ctee from 1992; Chmn Dioc Ctee for Unity from 1996; M Dioc CSR from 1996; M CTE Forum and CCBI Assembly
Tel: (01737) 357053
e-mail: bryban@msn.com

BUCKINGHAM, Bishop of [AREA BISHOP, OXFORD] **Rt Revd Michael Arthur Hill**
Magnolia Cottage, 28 Church St, Great Missenden, Bucks HP16 0AZ 1995–98 b 17 Apr 1949; *educ* Wilmslow Gr Sch; NW Cheshire CFE; Man Coll of Commerce; Ridley Hall Cam; Fitzw Coll Cam; C St Mary Magd Addiscombe 1977–80; C St Paul Slough 1980–83; P-in-c St Leon Chesham Bois 1983–90; R 1990–92; RD Amersham 1989–92; Adn of Berks 1992–98; Bp of Buckingham from 1998
Tel: (01494) 862173
Fax: (01494) 890508
e-mail: bishopbucks@oxford.anglican.org

BULL, Dr John, B SC, PH D, EUR ING, C ENG, FIHT, FIWSC, MICE
Gable Ends, 11 Glebe Mews, Bedlington, Northumberland NE22 6LJ [NEWCASTLE] 1995– *b* 13 Oct 1944; *educ* Farnborough Gr Sch; Ches Coll of Educ; Univ Coll Cardiff; Tchr ILEA 1966–68; Engineer/Chartered Engineer Dur Co Coun 1974–79; Lect in Structural Engineering Newc Univ from 1979; M Dioc Syn from 1988; M Bp's Coun from 1988; Vc Pres Dioc Syn from 1994; Chmn Dioc Bd of Educ 1991–97; Lay Chmn Bedlington Dny Syn 1990–97
Tel: 0191–222 7924 (Office)
Fax: 0191–222 5833
e-mail: John.Bull@newcastle.ac.uk

BULLIMORE, His Honour Judge John Wallace MacGregor, LL B
137 Edge Lane, Thornhill, Dewsbury, W Yorks WF12 0HB [WAKEFIELD] 1970– *b* 4 Dec 1945; *educ* Qu Eliz Gr Sch Wakefield; Bris Univ; Circuit Judge from 1991; Chan Dio of Derby from 1980; Chan Dio of Blackb from 1990; Rdr from 1968; M Bp's Coun
Tel: (01924) 463911

BUNKER, Very Revd Michael
The Deanery, Peterborough PE1 1XS [DEAN OF PETERBOROUGH] *b* 22 Jul 1937; *educ* Benjamin Adlard Sch Gainsborough; Acton and Brunel Colls Lon; Oak Hill Th Coll; C St Jas Alperton 1963–66; C St Helen St Helens 1966–70; V St Matt Muswell Hill 1970–78; V St Jas w St Matt Muswell Hill 1978–92; Preb St Paul's Cathl 1990–92; Dean of Petrb from 1992
Tel: (01733) 562780
e-mail: deanb@f.tech.co.uk

BURBRIDGE, Mrs Bernadette Celina Genevieve, BA
14 Clifton Dale, York YO3 6LJ [YORK] 1990– *b* 17 Sep 1954; *educ* Camborne Gr Sch; LMH Ox; Broadcast Journalist
Tel: (01904) 658908

BURDETT, Revd Stephen Martin, AKC
St Faith's Vicarage, Red Post Hill, London SE24 9JQ [SOUTHWARK] 1990– *b* 21 Dec 1949; *educ* Abp Tenison's Gr Sch; K Coll Lon; St Aug Coll Cant; C St Pet Walworth 1974–77; C All SS Benhilton 1977–80; P-in-c St John Earlsfield 1980–83; V 1983–89; V St Faith N Dulwich from 1989; M Draft Churchwardens and Amending Canon 1995
Tel: 0171–274 1338 (Home)
0171–274 3924 (Office)

BURNHAM, Revd Andrew, MA, ARCO (CHM)
St Stephen's House, 16 Marston St, Oxford OX4 1JX [OXFORD] 1990– *b* 19 Mar 1948; *educ* S'well Minister Gr Sch; New Coll Ox; St Steph Ho Ox; Schoolmaster 1972–78; Freelance Conductor and Music Tchr 1978–85; NSM Clifton TM Nottm 1983–85; C Beeston 1985–87; V St Jo Ev Carrington 1987–94; Vc Prin St Steph Ho from 1995; M Steering Ctee Eucharistic Prayers 1995; M Steering Ctee Calendar and Lectionary 1996; M Liturg Commn from 1996; Gen Syn Rep NTMTC Coun from 1996; M Steering Ctee Amending Canon 22 1998; M Steering Ctee Pastl Rites 1998
Tel: (01865) 247874
Fax: (01865) 794338
e-mail: aburnham@ststephenshouse.demon.co.uk

BURNLEY, Bishop of [SUFFRAGAN, BLACKBURN] **Rt Revd Martyn William Jarrett,** BD, AKC, M PHIL
449 Padiham Rd, Burnley, Lancs BB12 6TE b 25 Oct 1944; *educ* Cotham Gr Sch Bris; K Coll Lon; St Boniface Th Coll Warminster; Hull Univ; C St Geo Bris 1968–70; C Swindon New Town 1970–74; P-in-c St Jos the Worker Northolt 1974–76; V 1976–81; V St Andr Uxbridge 1981–85; Selection Sec ACCM 1985–88; Sen Selection Sec ACCM 1989–91; V Our Lady and All SS Chesterfield 1991–94; Bp of Burnley from 1994
Tel: (01282) 423564
Fax: (01282) 835496

BURNLEY, Mrs Isobel Margaret, BA, DIP SP ED
41 Marsh Lane, Nantwich, Cheshire CW5 5HP [CHESTER] 1995– *b* 1 Apr 1938; *educ* Chelmsford Co High Sch; Tiffin Sch Kingston; Gipsy Hill Tr Coll; Crewe and Alsager Coll of HE; Open Univ; Tchr Special Educational Needs; M Bp's Coun; Rdr
Tel: (01270) 624521
e-mail: 100417.3613@compuserve.com

BURNS, Canon Edward Joseph, B SC, MA
Christ Church Vicarage, 19 Vicarage Close, Fulwood, Preston, Lancs PR2 8EG [BLACKBURN] 1970– *b* 16 May 1938; *educ* Baines Gr Sch Poulton-le-Fylde; Liv Univ; St Cath's Coll Ox; Wycliffe Hall Th Coll; C Leyland Parish Ch 1961–64; C Burnley Parish Ch 1964–67; V

St Jas Chorley, 1967–75; RD Preston 1979–86; V Ch Ch Fulwood from 1975; Hon Can Blackb Cathl from 1986; Bp of Blackb's Adv for Hosp Chapl 1989–94; M Hosp Chapl Coun from 1991; M Dioc Pastl Ctee from 1974; M Bp's Coun from 1979; M Dioc Bd of Patronage from 1987; M Dioc Syn from 1970; Vc-Pres Dioc Syn and Chmn Dioc Ho of Clergy from 1993 Tel: (01772) 719210

BURRIDGE, Revd Dr Richard Alan, MA, PH D, PGCE, DIP TH
King's College, Strand, London WC2R 2LS [UNIVERSITIES, LONDON] **1994–** *b* 11 Jun 1955; *educ* Bris Cathl Sch; Univ Coll Ox; Nottm Univ; St Jo Coll Nottm; Classics Master and Ho Tutor Sevenoaks Sch 1978–82; C SS Pet and Paul Bromley 1985–87; Chapl and pt Lect in Depts of Th and Classics & Ancient History Univ of Ex 1987–94; Dean of K Coll Lon from 1994; M Coun of Management St Jo Coll Nottm from 1986; M Coun of Reference Monarch Publications from 1992; M Bd of Studies N Thames Min Tr Course from 1994; Trustee Chr Evidence Soc from 1994; Chmn Eric Symes Abbott Memorial Fund from 1994; M Studiorum Novi Testamenti Societas from 1995; M SST from 1995; ABM External Examiner to SW Min Tr Course from 1995; Chmn ABM Educ Validatory Sub-Ctee; M IMEC ABM; M CECC; Commis to Bp of High Veld from 1996; M Adv Bd *Celebrate CE* magazine; Gen Syn Rep PIM Consultation to Province of W Africa from 1997
Tel: 0171–873 2333
Fax: 0171–873 2344
e-mail: richard.burridge@kcl.ac.uk

BURROWS, Mr Gerald David, B SC, M SC, T CERT
3 Hall Rd, Fulwood, Preston, Lancs PR2 4QD [BLACKBURN] **1990–** *b* 26 Dec 1942; *educ* Wellington Gr Sch; Univ Coll of N Wales, Bangor; Scientific Officer Rutherford High Energy Laboratory 1967–69; Lect Grimsby Coll of Technology 1969–71; Sen Lect Blackb Coll from 1971 Tel: (01772) 719159

BURY, Very Revd Nicholas Ayles Stillingfleet, MA
The Deanery, Miller's Green, Gloucester GL1 2BP [DEAN OF GLOUCESTER] *1990–96 b* 8 Jan 1943; *educ* K Sch Cant; Qu Coll Cam; Cuddesdon Th Coll; C Liv Par Ch 1968–71; Chapl Ch Ch Ox 1971–75; V St Mary Shephall Stevenage 1975–84; V St Pet-in-Thanet 1984–97; RD Thanet 1993–97; Dean of Gloucester from 1997 Tel: (01452) 524167
Fax: (01452) 300469

BUTTERFIELD, Revd David John, B MUS, DIP TH
25 Church Rd, Lilleshall, Newport, Shropshire TF10 9HE [LICHFIELD] **1990–** *b* 1 Jan 1952; *educ* Belle Vue Boys Gr Sch Bradf; R Holloway Coll Lon; St Jo Coll Nottm; C Ch Ch Southport 1977–81; Min St Thos CD Aldridge 1981–91; V St Mich Lilleshall w St Mary Sheriffhales from 1991; M BM 1995–96; RD Edgmond from 1997 Tel and Fax: (01952) 604281
e-mail: davidb1152@aol.com

BUTTERY, Revd Graeme, BA, MA
St Lawrence House, 84 Centenary Ave, South Shields, Tyne and Wear NE34 6SF [DURHAM] **1995–** *b* 24 Nov 1962; *educ* Dame Allan's Boys Sch Newc; York Univ; Newc Univ; St Steph Ho Th Coll; C Peterlee 1988–91; C Sunderland TM 1991–92; TV Sunderland TM 1992–94; V St Lawr the Martyr Horsley Hill from 1994; M Dioc Pastl Ctee; M Seahouses Hostel Management Ctee Tel: 0191–456 1747

BYRNE, Canon John Victor, FCA, L TH
St Jude's Vicarage, 7 Hereford Rd, Southsea, Hants PO5 2DH [PORTSMOUTH] **1995–** *b* 14 Nov 1947; *educ* John Lyon Sch Harrow; St Jo Coll Nottm; Chartered Accountant; C St Mark Gillingham 1973–76; C Cranham Park Chelmsf 1976–80; V Balderstone, Rochdale 1980–87; V St Jude Southsea from 1987; ABM Pastl Selector 1993–97; Dioc Adv for Renewal of Resources 1994–97; P-in-c St Pet Southsea from 1995; M Bp's Coun; M DBF; Hon Can Portsm Cathl from 1997; M Vacancy in See Ctee; Bp's Exam Chapl
Tel and Fax: (01705) 821071

CAMERON, The Worshipful Sheila Morag Clark, QC, MA
2 Harcourt Buildings, Temple, London EC4Y 9DB [EX-OFFICIO, VICAR-GENERAL OF THE PROVINCE OF CANTERBURY] **1983–** *b* 22 Mar 1934; *educ* Commonweal Lodge Sch Purley; St Hugh's Coll Ox; Barrister-at-Law; Official Prin Adnry of Hampstead 1968–86; Chan Chelmsf Dio from 1969; Chan Lon Dio from 1992; Chmn Eccles Judges Assn from 1997; M Legal Adv Commn from 1975; M Marriage Commn 1975–78; Chmn Abps' Grp on the Episcopate 1986–90; Boundary Commr Commn for England 1989–96; Vic-Gen Province of Cant from 1983; Recorder of Crown Court from 1985; M Coun on Tribunals 1986–90 Tel: 0171–353 8415
Fax: 0171–353 7622

CAMPBELL, Mrs Rosalind Irene, B SC
18 Eaglesfield, Hartford, Northwich, Cheshire CW8 1NQ [CHESTER] **1995–** *b* 4 May 1942; *educ* K Edw VI High Sch for Girls Birm; Birm Univ; Chemistry Tchr Redditch Co High Sch 1963–66; Crewe Co Gr Sch for

Girls 1966–68; Hd of Chemistry Northwich Girls Gr Sch 1968–75; Supply and pt Teaching from 1982
Tel: (01606) 75849
e-mail: GCampb1066@aol.com

CANTERBURY, Archbishop of, Most Revd and Rt Hon George Leonard Carey, BD, ALCD, M TH, PH D
Lambeth Palace, London SE1 7JU and The Old Palace, Canterbury, Kent CT1 2EE **1985–** *b* 13 Nov 1935; *educ* Bifrons Sec Mod Sch Barking; Lon Univ; Lon Coll of Div; C St Mary Islington 1962–66; Lect Oak Coll 1966–70; Lect St Jo Coll Nottm 1970–75; V St Nich Dur 1975–82; Prin Trin Th Coll Bris 1982–87; Bp of B & W 1987–91; Abp of Cant from 1991
Tel: 0171–928 8282
Fax: 0171–261 9836

CAPON, Dr Peter Charles, B SC, PH D, MBCS, C ENG
137 Birchfields Rd, Manchester M14 6PJ [MANCHESTER] **1995–** *b* 19 Jan 1944; *educ* Kimbolton Sch; Southn Univ; Cam Univ; Man Univ; Sen Lect in Computer Science Man Univ from 1976
Tel: 0161–225 5970
e-mail: pcc@cs.man.ac.uk

CARLISLE, Bishop of, Rt Revd Ian Harland
Rose Castle, Dalston, Carlisle CA5 7BZ **1975–85, 1989–** *b* 19 Dec 1932; *educ* Dragon Sch Ox; Haileybury Coll; Peterho Cam; Wycliffe Hall Th Coll; C Melton Mowbray 1960–63; V Oughtibridge Sheff 1963–72; M Wortley Rural Distr Coun 1969–73; V St Cuthb's Fir Vale Sheff 1972–75; P-in-c All SS Brightside 1973–75; RD Ecclesfield 1973–75; V Rotherham1975–79; RD Rotherham 1976–79; Adn of Doncaster 1979–85; Bp of Lanc 1985–89; Bp of Carl from 1989
Tel: (0169 74) 76274
Fax: (0169 74) 76550

CARR, Very Revd (Arthur) Wesley, MA, PH D
The Deanery, Westminster Abbey, London SW1P 3PA [DEAN OF WESTMINSTER] **1980–87, 1989–** *b* 26 Jul 1941; *educ* Dulwich Coll; Jes Coll Ox; Jes Coll Cam; Univ of Sheff; Ridley Hall Th Coll; C Luton 1967–71; Tutor Ridley Hall 1970–71; Chapl Ridley Hall 1971–72; Fell Univ of Sheff Biblical Studies 1972–74; Hon C Ranmoor 1972–74; Chapl Chelmsf Cathl 1974–78; Dep Dir Chelmsf Cathl Cen for Rsch and Tr 1974–82; Dir of Tr Dio of Chelmsf 1976–84; Select Prchr Ox Univ 1984–85; Can Res Chelmsf Cathl 1978–87; Hon Fell New Coll Edin 1986–94; Dean of Bris 1987–97; Dean of Westmr from 1997
Tel: 0171–222 2953
Fax: 0171–799 2464
e-mail: Dean@westminster-abbey.org

CARR, Mrs Katherine Mary, BA, PGCE
22 Frenchgate, Richmond, N Yorks DL10 7AG [RIPON] **1995–** *b* 7 Jun 1932; *educ* Richmond High Sch for Girls; Westf Coll Lon; Lon Univ Inst of Educ; Asst Mistress Burghley Primary Sch Lon 1953–55; Asst Mistress Parliament Hill Comp Sch 1955–59; Lect Darlington Coll of Educ 1959–60, 1969–72; Dep Hd Sedgefield Comp Sch 1972–80; Hd Woodham Comp Sch Newton Aycliffe 1980–90; Rtd; JP; M Dioc Syn; Lay Chmn Richmond Dny Syn; M Bp's Coun
Tel: (01748) 823253
(01748) 884216

CASSIDY, Ven George Henry, B SC, M PHIL
2 Amen Court, Warwick Lane, London EC4M 7BU [ARCHDEACON OF LONDON] **1995–** *b* 17 Oct 1942; *educ* Belfast High Sch; Qu Univ Belfast; Univ Coll Lon; Oak Hill Th Coll; C Ch Ch Clifton Bris 1972–75; V St Edyth Sea Mills Bris 1975–82; V St Paul Portman Sq Lon 1982–87; Adn of Lon and Can Res St Paul's Cathl from 1987
Tel: 0171–248 3312
Fax: 0171–489 8579
e-mail: archdeacon.london@dlondon.org.uk

CATTON, Canon (Cedric) Trevor, STH, DIP RJ, CERT M
Exning Vicarage, New River Green, Exning, Newmarket, Suffolk CB8 7HS [ST EDMUNDSBURY AND IPSWICH] **1995–** *b* 23 Mar 1936; *educ* Ipswich Sch; Wells Th Coll; In Retail Management 1956–70; C Solihull 1972–74; R Hawstead and Nowton w Stanningfield etc 1974–79; R Cockfield 1979–83; Dioc Stewardship Adv 1977–83; V St Martin Exning w Landwade from 1983; Chapl Newmarket Hosp from 1985; Hon Can St Eds Cathl from 1990   *Tel and Fax:* (01638) 577413

CATTY, Mr Michael Anthony, BA, M SC
78 Dryden Crescent, Stevenage, Herts SG2 0JH [ST ALBANS] **1992–** *b* 7 Jan 1942; *educ* St Paul's Sch Lon; Trin Coll Dublin; Open Univ; Secondary School Tchr from 1972; M Dioc BSR Exec from 1995; M Dioc Bd of Educ from 1997   *Tel:* (01438) 350033

CAWDRON, Mr Keith William
Baringo, 61 Burbo Bank Rd, Blundellsands, Liverpool L23 6TQ [LIVERPOOL] **1995–** *b* 3 Jan 1956; *educ* Stockport Gr Sch; Dur Univ; Civil Servant DES 1977–85; Admin and Research Officer to Abp of Cant 1985–87; Dioc Sec from 1987; Sec Dioc Syn, Bp's Coun and DBF; Rdr; M Coun CPAS
Tel: 0151–931 2098 (Home)
0151–709 9722 (Office)
Fax: 0151–709 2885

CHAMBERLAIN, Michael Aubrey, LL D, FCA
1 Waterloo Way, Leicester LE1 6LP [APPOINTED MEMBER, ARCHBISHOPS' COUNCIL] *b* 16 Apr 1939; *educ* Repton Sch; KPMG Peat Marwick 1974–93; Pres Inst of Chartered Accountants in England and Wales 1993–94; M Coun Leic Univ from 1996; Consultant KPMG; Chmn Leic DBF; Lay Can Leic Cathl; Apptd M Abps' Coun from 1999 *Tel:* 0116–256 6000
Fax: 0116–256 6050

CHANTRY, Revd Helen Fiona, B SC, BA
Rectory, Mill Lane, Great Barrow, Chester CH3 7JF [CHESTER] **1994–** *b* 10 Oct 1959; *educ* Arnold High Sch for Girls; Bradf Univ; Trin Coll Bris; Tchr Aylesbury Gr Sch; NSM Par Dn St Geo Hyde; Dioc Youth Offcr from 1992; NSM Assoc Priest St Bart Barrow from 1994 *Tel:* (01829) 740263

CHAPMAN, Ven Michael Robin, BA
Westbrook, 11 The Drive, Northampton NN1 4RZ [ARCHDEACON OF NORTHAMPTON] **1995–** *b* 29 Sep 1939; *educ* Ellesmere Coll; Leeds Univ; Coll of the Resurr Mirf; C St Columba Sunderland 1963–68; Chapl RN 1968–84; V Hale 1984–91; RD Farnham 1988–91; Adn of Northampton from 1991
Tel: (01604) 714015
Fax: (01604) 792016
e-mail: MichaelRChapman@compuserve.com

CHAPMAN, Canon Rex Anthony, BA, MA, DPS
1 The Abbey, Carlisle, Cumbria CA3 8TZ [CARLISLE] **1985–** *b* 2 Sep 1938; *educ* Leeds Gr Sch; Univ Coll Lon; St Edm Hall Ox; Birm Univ; Wells Th Coll; C St Thos Stourbridge 1965–68; Chapl Aber Univ 1968–78; Hon Can St Andr Cathl Aber 1976–78; Res Can and Dioc Dir Educ from 1978; M Gen Syn Bd of Educ and Chmn Schs Ctee 1990–96; M Nat Soc Stg Ctee 1983–97; ABM Selector; Chmn Dioc Ho of Clergy from 1996; Chapl to HM The Queen from 1997 *Tel:* (01228) 597614 (Home)
(01228) 538086 (Office)
Fax: (01228) 815409 (Office)

CHAPMAN, Revd Sally Anne, B SC, MA, PGCE
18 Heather Grove, Willenhall, West Midlands WV12 4BT [LICHFIELD] **1998–** *b* 6 Jan 1955; *educ* Kingswood Gr Sch; Lanchester Poly; Swansea Univ; Wolv Univ; Qu Coll Birm; C Glascote and Stonydelph TM Tamworth 1990–93; TV Short Heath from 1993; M Dioc Bd of Min 1991–97; M Dioc Bd of Educ from 1997 *Tel:* (01902) 631498
e-mail: r.chapman@connect-2.co.uk

CHATTERLEY, Mrs Dorothy, BA
Kalyan, The Banks, Seascale, Cumbria CA20 1QW [CARLISLE] **1985–** *b* 21 Dec 1932; *educ* Darwen Gr Sch; Man Univ; Tchr w CJGS Newbury 1954–56; Tchr Cumbria Educ Auth 1966–86; Rdr; Lay Chmn Calder Dny Syn 1990–96; Area Sec RSCM Cumbria 1986–97; M Coun Guild of Ch Musicians; M Gen Syn Stg Ctee and Appts Sub-Ctee from 1990; M Coun of Corp of Ch Ho from 1989; M CCBI and CTE from 1990; Lay Vc-Chmn Catholic Grp in Gen Syn 1990–94; CE Rep at Gen Assembly of Ch of Scotland 1993 and 1994; M EKD Consultations Sept 1993; M In Tune w Heaven follow up grp 1993; Ch Commr from 1993; Gen Syn Rep on RSCM Coun; Elected Delegate to CEC Graz 1997 and WCC Harare 1998; M CU Coun *Tel:* (019467) 28379

CHEESEMAN, Mr James Reginald
25 Lambarde Drive, Sevenoaks, Kent TN13 3HX [ROCHESTER] **1975–** *b* 2 Nov 1934; *educ* Sevenoaks Sch; Coll of St Mark and St Jo; Supply Staff Kent Educ Ctee 1954–55; Asst Tchr Midfield Prim Sch 1957–68; Dep Hdmaster Edgebury Prim Sch 1968–69; Chmn Ho of Laity Roch Dioc Syn 1976–79; M Gen Syn Bd of Educ 1981–91; Hdmaster Pet Hills' Sch Rotherhithe 1969–97; Rdr; Co-Chmn Sevenoaks Dny Syn 1976–96; Consultant Lect Porlock Hall; Sec Sevenoaks Dny Syn; Trustee Guild of All So; Treas Qu Victoria Clergy Fund from 1991; Lay Chmn Forward In Faith Roch *Tel:* (01732) 455718

CHELMSFORD, Bishop of, Rt Revd John Freeman Perry, M PHIL, L TH
Bishopscourt, Margaretting, Ingatestone, Essex CM4 0HD **1995–** *b* 15 Jun 1935; *educ* Mill Hill Sch; Lon Coll of Div; C Ch Ch Woking 1959–62; C Ch Ch Chorleywood 1962–63; V St Andr Chorleywood 1963–77; RD Rickmansworth 1972–77; Warden Lee Abbey 1977–89; RD Shirwell 1979–83; Bp of Southn 1989–96; Can Win Cathl from 1989; Bp of Chelmsf from 1996; M ABM Bps Ctee for Min from 1991; Chmn ABM Ctee for Min among Deaf People; Chmn Trustees of Burrswood; Chmn CCHH
Tel: (01277) 352001
Fax: (01277) 355374
e-mail: bishopjohn@chelmsford.anglican.org

CHESTER, Bishop of, Rt Revd Peter Robert Forster, MA, BD, PH D
Bishop's House, Abbey Square, Chester CH1 2JD **1985–91, 1996–** *b* 16 Mar 1950; *educ* Tudor Grange Gr Sch Solihull; Merton Coll Ox; Edin Univ; Edin Th Coll; C St Matt and St Jas Mossley Hill Liv 1980–82; Sen Tutor St Jo Coll Dur 1983–91; V Beverley Minster 1991–96; Bp of Ches from 1996
Tel: (01244) 350864
Fax: (01244) 314187

CHETWOOD, Mr Nigel John, B SC
15 Tretawn Gardens, Tewkesbury, Glos GL20 8EF [GLOUCESTER] **1985–** *b* 30 Jan 1939; *educ* Oswestry Gr Sch; Man Univ; M CPAS Coun; Purchasing Mgr Micro Circuit Engineering Ltd; Rdr   Tel: (01684) 292473
   e-mail: Nigel.Chetwood@ibm.net

CHICHESTER, Bishop of, Rt Revd Eric Waldram Kemp, DD, D LITT, D TH
The Palace, Chichester, W Sussex PO19 1PY **1970–** *b* 27 Apr 1915; *educ* Brigg Gr Sch; Ex Coll Ox; St Steph Ho Th Coll; St Luke Southn 1939–41; Lib Pusey Ho Ox 1941–46; Fell, Chapl, Tutor, Lect, Ex Coll Ox 1946–69; Dean of Worc 1969–74; Bp of Chich from 1974
   Tel: (01243) 782161
   Fax: (01243) 531332

CHRISTIE, Canon Thomas Richard, MA
Prebendal House, The Precincts, Peterborough PE1 1XX [PETERBOROUGH] **1970–73, 1975–90, 1993–** *b* 8 Aug 1931; *educ* Clifton Coll Bris; CCC Cam; Linc Th Coll; C St Mark Portsea 1957–60; C Cherry Hinton 1960–61; P-in-c St Jas Cherry Hinton CD 1961–66; V St Aug Wisbech 1966–73; V Whitstable 1973–80; Can Res Petrb Cathl from 1980; RD Petrb 1987–96; Chmn Ho of Clergy Dioc Syn; Vc-Pres SPCK; Warden Community of the Holy Cross; Prov En Div Woodard Corp from 1994   Tel: (01733) 569441
   Fax: (01733) 552465

CHURCHILL, Viscount Victor George Spencer, MA
CCLA Investment Management Ltd, St Alphage House, 2 Fore St, London EC2Y 5AQ [INVESTMENT MANAGER, CBF CHURCH OF ENGLAND FUNDS] *b* 31 Jul 1934; *educ* Eton; New Coll Ox; Morgan Grenfell & Co Ltd 1958–74; Invest Mgr Charities Official Invest Fund 1974–95; Dir Local Authorities Mutual Invest Trust 1978; Dir CCLA Investment Management Ltd 1988; Non-Exec Dir Charter European Trust, Schroder Split Fund and Foreign and Colonial Income Growth Trust   Tel: 0171–588 1815
   Fax: 0171–588 6291

CLARK, Mr John Guthrie
12 Ash Drive, Haughton, Stafford ST18 9EU [LICHFIELD] **1970–** *b* 9 Jun 1938; *educ* Slough Gr Sch; Wrekin Coll; Ches Dio Tr Coll; Tchr Dawley Sec Mod Sch 1960–65; Phoenix Comp Sch 1965–67; Wobaston Sec Mod Sch 1967–68; Aelfgar Comp Sch 1968–86; Hd of Relig and Socl Educ Hagley Park Comp Sch Rugeley 1986–93; M Dioc Pastl Ctee and Bp's Coun
   Tel: (01785) 780689

CLARK, Mr John Mullin, MA, PGCE
Partnership House, 157 Waterloo Rd, London SE1 8XA [PARTNERSHIP SECRETARY, BOARD OF MISSION] *b* 19 Apr 1946; *educ* St Paul's Sch; St Pet Coll Ox; Inst of Educ Lon; Publisher, Tehran, Iran 1967–80; CMS Regional Sec Middle East and Pakistan 1980–86; Communications Sec CMS 1987–91; Sec PWM from 1992; Partnership Sec Bd of Miss from 1992; Chmn Feed the Minds and USCL; Sec Overseas Bishoprics Fund; Chmn Friends of Dio of Iran
   Tel: 0171–928 8681
   e-mail: pwm@pwwm.clara.net

CLARKE, Canon (Hilary) James
Church House, Great Smith St, London SW1P 3NZ [SECRETARY, COMMITTEE FOR MINISTRY AMONG DEAF PEOPLE] *b* 9 Sep 1941; *educ* Sandbach Sch; St David's Coll Lampeter; St Steph Ho Th Coll; C Kibworth 1966–68; Chapl/Social Worker Leic and Co Miss for the Deaf 1968–71; Prin Officer, Chapl Ch Miss for Deaf Walsall and S Staffs 1971–73; Prin Officer, Chapl and Sec Leic Co Miss for the Deaf 1973–89; Sec Gen Syn Coun for the Deaf 1989–91; Ctee for Min among Deaf People from 1991
   Tel: 0171–898 1429 (Office)
   0116–255 7283 (Home)
   0850–144150 (Mobile)
   Fax: 0116 233 0839

CLARKE, Mrs (Margaret) Ann, T CERT, CERT SPECIAL EDUC MGT
St Saviour's and All Saints' Vicarage, 46 Manor Rd, Weston-super-Mare, Avon BS23 2SU [BATH AND WELLS] **1995–** *b* 7 Jul 1937; *educ* Hastings High Sch for Girls; St Gabriel's Coll Camberwell; Tchr Hailsham Co Primary Sch 1957–58; Bexhill C E Junior Sch 1958–62; Ch Ch Primary Sch St Leonards on Sea 1962–67; Tchr/Hd of Dept Fairmead Special Sch Yeovil 1972–80; Dep Hd 1980–92; Housewife; M Forward in Faith Dioc Assembly; Delegate to Forward in Faith Nat Assembly
   Tel and Fax: (01934) 623230

CLARKE, Prof Michael Gilbert, BA, MA, FIPD, FRSA
Millington House, 15 Lansdowne Crescent, Worcester WR3 8JE [WORCESTER] **1990–93, 1995–** *b* 21 May 1944; *educ* Qu Eliz Gr Sch Wakef; Sussex Univ; Lect in Politics Edin Univ 1969–75; Dep Dir Policy Planning Lothian Regional Coun 1975–81; Dir Local Government Tr Bd 1981–90; Chief Exec Local Government Management Bd 1990–93; Hd of Sch of Public Policy Birm Univ 1993–98; Pro-Vc-Chan Birm Univ from 1998; M Review of Synodical Government Ctee from 1995; M Gen Syn Panel of Chairmen from 1996
   Tel: (01905) 617634
   Fax: (01905) 29502

CLARKE, Revd Robert Sydney, MA, AKC
Fielden House, Little College St, London SW1P 3SH

[SECRETARY AND DIRECTOR OF TRAINING, HOSPITAL CHAPLAINCIES COUNCIL] *b* 31 Oct 1935; *educ* St Dunstan's Coll; K Coll Lon; St Boniface Th Coll Warminster; C St Mary Hendon 1965–69; C Langley Marish 1969–70; Chapl New Cross Hosp Wolv 1970–74; Chapl Herrison Hosp Dorchester 1974–80; Sen Chapl Westmr Hosp Lon and Westmr Medical Sch 1980–85; Chapl R Hants Co Hosp Win 1985–94; Sen Chapl Win HA 1988–94; Chapl to The Queen from 1987; Sec and Dir of Tr Hosp Chapl Coun from 1994
Tel: 0171–898 1892
Fax: 0171–898 1891

CLARKSON, Ven Alan Geoffrey, MA
Vicarage, Church Corner, Burley, Ringwood, Hants BH24 4AP [ARCHDEACON OF WINCHESTER] *1970–75, 1990–95 b* 14 Feb 1934; *educ* Sherborne Sch; Ch Coll Cam; Wycliffe Hall Th Coll; C Penn, W'hampton 1959–60; C St Oswald's Oswestry 1960–63; C Wrington w Redhill 1963–65; V Chewton Mendip w Emborough 1965–74; Dioc Ecum Officer 1965–75; V St Jo B Glastonbury w Godney 1974–84; C-in-c W Pennard and Meare 1981–84; C-in-c St Benedict Glastonbury 1982–84; Adn of Win from 1984; V Burley from 1984; Hon Can Win Cathl from 1984
Tel: (01425) 402303
Fax: (01425) 403753
e-mail: alan.clarkson@dial.pipex.com

COCKE, Dr Thomas Hugh, MA, PH D, FSA
15 Lyndewode Rd, Cambridge CB1 2HL [SECRETARY, COUNCIL FOR THE CARE OF CHURCHES] *b* 19 Feb 1949; *educ* Marlboro Coll; Pemb Coll Cam; Courtauld Inst Lon; Lect in Art Hist Man Univ 1973–76; Investigator of hist buildings RCHME 1976–90; Sec Coun for Care of Chs from 1990
Tel: 0171–898 1882
Fax: 0171–898 1881

COLCHESTER, Bishop of [AREA BISHOP, CHELMSFORD] **Rt Revd Edward Holland,** AKC
1 Fitzwalter Rd, Lexden, Colchester, Essex CO3 3SS b 28 Jun 1936; *educ* New Coll Sch Ox; Dauntsey's Sch, W Lavington; K Coll Lon; C H Trin Dartford 1965–69; C Jo Keble Mill Hill 1969–72; Prec Gib Cathl and Seamen's Missr 1972–74; Chapl in Naples 1974–79; V St Mark Bromley 1979–86; Chapl Bromley Hosp 1979–86; Suff Bp in Eur 1986–94; Bp of Colchester from 1994
Tel: (01206) 576648
Fax: (01206) 763868

COLMAN, Sir Michael Jeremiah, BT, LLD
1 Millbank, London SW1P 3JZ [FIRST CHURCH ESTATES COMMISSIONER] **1993–** *b* 7 Jul 1928; *educ* Eton; Dir Reckitt & Colman plc 1970–95; Chmn Reckitt & Colman plc 1986–95; Hon LL D Hull Univ 1993; First Ch Estates Commr from 1993; Coun M R Warrant Holders Assn from 1977 (Pres 1984–85); Assoc Trin Ho, M Lighthouse Bd from 1985, Younger Brother 1994; M Court Worshipful Co of Skinners from 1985 (Master 1991–92); M Gen Coun and Fin Ctee K Edw Hosp Fund for Lon from 1978; Dir UK Cen for Economic and Environmental Development 1985–96, Chmn from 1996; Special Trustee St Mary's Hosp from 1988; Trustee Allchurches Trust Ltd from 1994
Tel: 0171–898 1000

COLMER, Ven Malcolm John, M SC, BA
59 Sutton Lane South, London W4 3JR [ARCHDEACON OF MIDDLESEX] *b* 15 Feb 1945; *educ* R Gr Sch Guildf; Sussex Univ; Nottm Univ; St Jo Coll Nottm; C St Jo Egham 1973–76; C Chadwell St Mary 1976–79; V S Malling, Lewes 1979–85; V St Mary w St Steph Hornsey Rise 1985–87; TR Hornsey Rise Whitehall Park Tm 1987–96; AD Islington 1990–95; Adn of Middx from 1996; M Dioc Liturg Grp
Tel: 0181–994 8148
e-mail: archdeacon.middlesex@dlondon.org.uk

COMBES, Revd Roger Matthew, LL B
St Matthew's Rectory, St Matthew's Rd, St Leonards-on-Sea, E Sussex TN38 0TN [CHICHESTER] **1995–** *b* 12 Jun 1947; *educ* Sherborne Sch; K Coll Lon; Ridley Hall Th Coll; C St Paul Onslow Sq Lon 1974–77; C H Trin Brompton Lon 1976–77; C H Sepulchre Cam 1977–86; R St Matt St Leonards-on-Sea from 1986; M Bp's Coun from 1998; RD Hastings from 1998
Tel: (01424) 423790

CONINGSBY, Chancellor His Honour Judge Thomas Arthur Charles, QC, MA
Leyfields, Elmore Rd, Chipstead, Surrey CR3 3SG [VICAR-GENERAL OF YORK] **1970–** *b* 21 Apr 1933; *educ* Epsom Coll; Qu Coll Cam; Barrister 1957–92; Circuit Judge from 1992; Chmn Family Law Bar Assn 1988–90 (Sec 1986–88); M Gen Coun Bar 1988–90; M Supreme Court Procedure Ctee 1988–92; M Matrimonial Causes Rule Ctee 1985–89; Recorder from 1986; QC from 1986; Dep High Court Judge from 1988; M Legal Adv Commn from 1973; Chan York Dio from 1977; M Marriage Commn 1975; Lay Chmn Croydon Dny Syn 1979–80; Vic Gen of York from 1980; M Legal Offcrs Fees Adv Ctee 1982–93; Chan Petrb Dio from 1989; M Stg Ctee Ecclesiastical Judges Assn from 1989; M Gov Body SPCK 1990–92; M Ctee Eccles Law Soc from 1996
Tel: (01737) 553304

CONNER, Rt Revd David John, MA
The Deanery, Windsor Castle, Berks SL4 1NJ [DEAN OF WINDSOR] *b* 6 Apr 1947; *educ* Ex Coll Ox; St Steph Ho Th Coll; Hon C Summertown Ox 1971–76; Asst Chapl St Edw Sch Ox 1971–73; Chapl 1973–80; TV Wolvercote w Summertown 1976–80; Chapl Win

Coll 1980–87; V Gt St Mary w St Mich Cam 1987–94; RD Cam 1989–94; Bp of Lynn 1994–98; Dean of Windsor from 1998 *Tel:* (01753) 865561

CONWAY, Revd Stephen David, MA, BA, PGCE
Auckland Castle, Bishop Auckland, Co Durham DL14 7NR [DURHAM] **1995–** *b* 22 Dec 1957; *educ* Abp Tenison's Gr Sch Kennington; Keble Coll Ox; Selw Coll Cam; Westcott Ho Th Coll; C St Mary Heworth 1986–89; C St Mich w St Hilda Bishopwearmouth 1989–90; DDO 1989–94; Hon C St Marg Dur 1990–94; P-in-c St Mary Cockerton 1994–98, V from 1998; Sen Chapl and Press Officer to Bp of Dur and DCO from 1998 *Tel:* (01388) 835842 (Home)
(01388) 602576 (Office)

COOK, Revd John Richard Millward, BA
43 Park Walk, London SW10 0AU [LONDON] **1995–** *b* 3 Mar 1961; *educ* Repton Sch; St Jo Coll Dur; Wycliffe Hall Th Coll; C St Thos Brampton 1985–89; C St Pet Farnboro 1989–92; C and Dir of Tr All So Langham Place Lon 1992–98; V St Jo w St Andr Chelsea from 1998; M Selection Tm for Ord Min Cen Lon; M CCU *Tel* and *Fax:* 0171–352 1675

COOPER, Mr Alan, OBE, B ED
11 Ravensdale Gardens, Eccles, Manchester M30 9JD [MANCHESTER] **1970–** *b* 11 Mar 1927; *educ* St Andr Sch Eccles; Didsbury Coll of Educ; Liv Univ; Hdmaster; Councillor Eccles Boro Coun 1958–73; Mayor of Eccles 1972–73; Councillor Salford 1975–79; Lay Chmn Eccles Dny Syn; Chmn DBF; M Bp's Coun; Dep Vc-Chmn CBF; Ch Commr; JP
Tel: 0161–789 1514

CORMACK, Sir Patrick Thomas, MP, BA, FSA
The Lyons, Enville, Staffs DY7 5LD [LICHFIELD] **1995–** *b* 18 May 1939; *educ* St Jas Choir Sch Grimsby; Havelock Sch Grimsby; Hull Univ; Schmaster 1961–70; MP for S Staffs from 1970; M Ecclesiastical Ctee from 1970; Trustee Historic Chs Trust from 1972; Vis Lect Univ of Texas 1984; Vis Fell St Ant Coll Ox 1994–95; M Faculty Jurisdiction Commn; M R Commn on Hist Mss from 1980; M DBF *Tel:* 0171–219 5514

COSH, Mrs Margaret Allen
Church House, Aston Eyre, Bridgnorth, Shropshire WV16 6XD [HEREFORD] **1994–** *b* 15 Aug 1935; *educ* Lowther Coll Abergele; Liv Univ; Dio of Yukon 1963–65; Social Worker Shropshire Social Services 1984–94; Independent Practice Tchr from 1994; Lay Co-Chmn Bridgnorth Dny Syn 1987–93; M Dioc CSR; M Dioc Pastl Ctee *Tel* and *Fax:* (01746) 714248
e-mail: astoneyre@aol.com

COULTON, Very Revd Nicholas Guy, BD
The Cathedral Vicarage, 26 Mitchell Ave, W Jesmond, Newcastle upon Tyne NE2 3LA [PROVOST OF NEWCASTLE] **1985–90, 1998–** *b* 14 Jun 1940; *educ* Blundell's Sch Tiverton; Cuddesdon Th Coll; Lon Univ; C Pershore Abbey 1967–71; Chapl to Bp of St Alb 1971–75; V St Paul's Bedf 1975–90; pt Chapl Herts and Beds Ind Miss 1976–89; Hon Can St Alb Cathl 1989–90; V of Newc and Provost of St Nic's Cathl from 1990; Chmn NE Coun of Christians and Jews from 1991; Co Chapl Order of St Jo from 1994
Tel: 0191–281 6554 (Home)
0191–232 1939 (Office)
Fax: 0191–230 0735

COUSSMAKER, Canon (Colin Richard) Chad, MA, M SC
'Moscow', c/o F.C.O., King Charles St, London SW1A 2AH [EUROPE] **1988–** *b* 13 Apr 1934; *educ* K Edw VI Sch Lich; W'hampton Gr Sch; Worc Coll Ox; Chich Th Coll; Asst C St Luke Newtown Southn 1960–64; Asst C Ch Ch Reading (in-c St Agnes Whitley) 1964–67; Chapl Ch Ch w St Helena Istanbul and All SS Moda and Apokrisarios of the Abp of Cant to the Oecumenical Patriarch of Constantinople 1967–72; Chapl H Trin Sliema Malta 1972–77; Chapl St Boniface Antwerp 1977–93; Chapl St Andr Moscow and Apokrisarios of the Abp of Cant to the Patriarch of Moscow, to the Patriarch-Catholicos of Georgia, and to the Catholicos-Patriarch of Armenia from 1993; M CCU from 1992; M Dioc Syn from 1981
Tel and *Fax:* 00–7–095–229–0990

COVENTRY, Bishop of, Rt Revd Colin James Bennetts, MA
Bishop's House, 23 Davenport Rd, Coventry CV5 6PW **1998–** *b* 9 Sep 1940; *educ* Battersea Gr Sch; Jes Coll Cam; Ridley Hall Th Coll; C St Steph Tonbridge 1965–69; Chapl Ox Pastorate 1969–73; Chapl Jes Coll Ox 1973–79; V St Andr Ox 1979–90; Can Res Ches Cathl and DDO 1990–94; Bp of Buckm 1994–98; Bp of Cov from 1998 *Tel:* ((01203) 672244
Fax: (01203) 713271
e-mail: bishcov@clara.net

COX, Ven John Stuart, BA, MA
84 Southgate St, Bury St Edmunds, Suffolk IP33 2BJ [ARCHDEACON OF SUDBURY] **1990–95** *b* 13 Sep 1940; *educ* Judd Sch Tonbridge; Univ Coll of Rhodesia and Nyasaland; Ox Univ; Birm Univ; Fitzw Ho Cam; Wycliffe Hall Ox; C St Mary Prescot 1968–71; C St Geo Birmingham 1971–73; R 1973–78; Selection Sec ACCM 1978–83; DDO S'wark 1983–91; Can Res and

Treas S'wark Cathl 1983–91; V Roehampton 1991–95; Can Emer 1991; Adn of Sudbury from 1995
Tel: (01284) 766796
Fax: (01284) 723163

CRAMERI, Revd Mary Barbara, BD, AKC, PGCE
Vicarage, Wilcot, Pewsey, Wilts SN9 5NS [SALISBURY] **1995–** *b* 27 May 1944; *educ* Brentwood Co High Sch for Girls; K Coll Lon; Lon Univ Inst of Educ; Sn Dios Min Tr Scheme; Various teaching posts 1965–88; C SS Phil and Jas Whitton 1988–91; pt Par Dn Bemerton TM 1991–93; pt Core Staff M Sn Dios Min Tr Scheme 1991–93; Vc-Prin Sn Tr Scheme for Chr Min from 1993, Acting Prin 1996–97; Dep Dir STETS and Minl Formation Officer 1997–98; TV Pewsey and Swanborough from 1998
Tel and Fax: (01672) 562282

CREDITON, Bishop of [SUFFRAGAN, EXETER]
Rt Revd Richard Stephen Hawkins, MA, B PHIL
10 The Close, Exeter, Devon EX1 1EZ b 2 Apr 1939; *educ* Ex Coll Ox; Univ of Ex; St Steph Ho Th Coll; Asst C St Thos Ex 1963–66; TV Clyst Valley TM 1966–78; TV Central Ex TM, Bp's Offcr for Min and Jt Dir Exeter-Truro Min Tr Scheme 1978–81; DDO 1979–81; P-in-C Whitestone w Oldridge 1981–87; Adn of Totnes 1981–88; Bp of Plymouth 1988–96; Bp of Crediton from 1996
Tel: (01392) 273509
Fax: (01392) 431266

CROYDON, Bishop of [AREA BISHOP, SOUTHWARK]
Rt Revd Wilfred Denniston Wood, DD
Home: 53 Stanhope Rd, Croydon, Surrey CR0 5NS, Office: St Matthew's House, 100 George St, Croydon CR0 1PJ 1987–95 *b* 15 Jun 1936; *educ* Combermere Sch Barbados; Codrington Coll, Barbados; Provincial Th Coll of the W Indies; C St Steph w St Thos Shepherds Bush 1962–66; Hon C 1966–74; Bp of Lon's Offcr in Race Relations 1966–74; V St Laur Catford 1974–82; Hon Can of S'wark Cathl since 1977; RD E Lewisham 1977–82; Adn and Boro Dean of S'wark 1982–85; Bp of Croydon from 1985; Area Bp from 1991
Tel: 0181–686 1822 (Home)
0181–681 5496 (Office)
Fax: 0181–686 2074
e-mail: bishop.wilfrid@dswark.org.uk

CULL, Dr Carole Anne, B SC, PH D, M SC, C STAT (HON)
6 Forndon Close, Lower Earley, Reading, Berks RG6 3XR [OXFORD] **1985–87, 1990–** *b* 20 Oct 1947; *educ* Bexley Gr Sch; Liv Univ; Lucy Cavendish Coll Cam; Medical Statistician Radcliffe Infirmary Ox; Rdr; M CRC Exec 1989–94; Hon Editor 'The Reader' 1989–94; M ABM Ctee for Min Development and Deployment 1991–96; M Gov Body Sarum & Wells Th Coll 1992–94; M Revision Ctee Tm and Grp Min Measure; Sec Open Synod Grp from 1993; Chmn Reading Dusseldorf Chs Interchange 1994–97; M Dioc Coun for Min from 1994; M Revision Ctee Calendar, Lectionary and Collects; M CCU from 1996; M Liturg Commn from 1996; M Elections Review Grp from 1996; M Steering Ctee Lord's Prayer; M Steering Ctee The Service of The Word; M Statistics Review Grp
Tel: (01189) 617923 (Home)
(01865) 224080/248418 (Office)
Fax: (01865) 723884 (Office)
e-mail: carole@carl.ox.ac.uk
ukpds@ermine.ox.ac.uk

CUMMINGS, Very Revd William Alexander Vickery, MA
The Deanery, Battle, E Sussex TN33 0JY [DEAN OF BATTLE] *b* 6 Apr 1938; *educ* K Coll Sch Wimbledon; Ch Ch Ox; Wycliffe Hall Ox; C St John Leytonstone 1964–67; C Writtle 1967–71; R Stratton St Mary w St Mich and Wacton 1971–91; RD Depwade 1981–91; Hon Can Nor Cathl 1990; Can Emer from 1991; Dean of Battle from 1991
Tel: (01424) 772693

CURRALL, Dr Arnold Edward, MA, D PHIL
Kelsyke, Great Strickland, Penrith, Cumbria CA10 3DJ [CARLISLE] **1995–** *b* 1 Jul 1924; *educ* Warwick Sch; Reading Univ; Keble Coll Ox; Geology Lect Sheff Univ 1952–66; Warden Freemens Hall and Admin Castle Leazes Hall Newc Univ 1966–82; Rtd; M DBF; M DAC; M Bp's Coun; M Dioc Pastl Ctee; Lay Chmn Appleby Dny Syn
Tel: (01931) 712242
Fax: (01931) 712462

CURRIE, Mr (Gavin) Lewis Sinclair, CQSW
Chapel Cottage, Gills Lane, Rooksbridge, Som BS26 2TU [BATH AND WELLS] **1990–** *b* 22 Aug 1936; *educ* Geo Watson's Boys Coll Edin; Moray Ho Coll of Educ Edin; Dep Dir of Social Work W Isles Islands Coun Isle of Lewis 1979–83; Social Worker, Project Leader, Family Rehabilitation 1983–95; Rdr from 1987; pt Adoption Panel Administrator Som Co Coun; Rtd; Chmn Dioc Evang F'ship from 1992; Lay Chmn Axbridge Dny Syn from 1996; M Bp's Coun from 1996; Lay Vc-Pres Dioc Syn from 1997
Tel and Fax: (01934) 750676

DA-COCODIA, Mrs Louise Adassa, BEM, MA (HON)
9 Arliss Ave, Levenshulme, Manchester M19 2PD [MANCHESTER] **1990–** *b* 9 Nov 1934; *educ* Delrose High Sch Kingston, Jamaica; Sen Nurse Manager 1977–88; Self Employed Project Consultant; M ABM M Commn for Racial Justice; M Dioc Syn from 1989; Chair Dioc Establishment Ctee; Consultant to the Govts' Moss Side and Hulme Task Force 1991–95; Man City Magistrates Bench (JP) from 1990; Bd M

Cariocca Enterprises Ltd; Chairperson Arawak Walton Housing Assn; Chair Moss Side and Hulme Women's Action Forum; Non-exec M Man HA (Purchasing) Tel: 0161–224 0209

DALBY, Ven (John) Mark Meredith, MA, PH D
21 Belmont Way, Rochdale OL12 6HR [ARCHDEACON OF ROCHDALE] *1985–95 b* 3 Jan 1938; *educ* K Geo V Sch Southport; Ex Coll Ox; Nottm Univ; Ripon Hall Th Coll; C Hambleden 1963–68; C Fawley, Fingest, Medmenham and Turville 1966–68; V St Pet Spring Hill Birm 1968–75; RD Birm City 1973–75; Sec Ctee for Th Educ and Selection Sec ACCM 1975–80; Hon C All Hallows Tottenham 1975–80; TR Worsley 1980–91; RD Eccles 1987–91; Exam Chapl to Bp of Man from 1980; Hon Tutor Dept of Th Studies Man Univ 1985–91; Adn of Rochdale from 1991
Tel and *Fax:* (01706) 648640

DALES, Mr Martin Paul
Priory Cottage, Old Malton, N Yorks YO17 7HB [YORK] *1995– b* 27 Dec 1955; *educ* St Dunstan's Coll; Bretton Hall; Open Univ; Dep Hd, Housemaster and Dir of Music various schs 1976–94; Organist and Choirmaster from 1976; Broadcaster from 1976; Music Publisher from 1981; Media Relations, Educ and Tr Officer RSCM NE Yorks Area from 1994; Coun Malton Town Coun (Mayor 1991–92, 1996–97); Sch Gov; M Dioc Coun for Min and Tr
Tel and *Fax:* (01653) 600990

DARLINGTON, Lt Col John
32 The Close, Salisbury, Wilts SP1 2EJ [SALISBURY] *1990– b* 24 Sep 1932; *educ* St Jo Sch Leatherhead; Royal Tank Regiment 1950–86; Bursar Sarum and Wells Th Coll 1986–94; Bursar Sarum College 1994–96; M Dioc Bd of Min from 1991; Vocations Adv from 1992; Lay Can Sarum Cathl from 1997; M Close Chapter from 1998 *Tel:* (01722) 415622
Fax: (01722) 555105

DARLOW, Mr Stewart Francis, MA, PH D
6 Harboro Grove, Sale, Cheshire M33 5BA [CHESTER] *1990– b* 30 Apr 1934; *educ* Latymer Upper Sch Hammersmith; Jesus Coll Cam; Physics Dept UMIST 1959–89; Sen Lect 1973–89; Asst Dir of Laboratories 1983–89; Rtd; M CBF Exec Ctee; M Pastl Measure Appeal Tribunal Panel; Chmn DBF; Chmn Finance and Central Services Ctee; Bp's Coun; Benefice Trustee; Rdr *Tel:* 0161–973 4697

DAVID, Mr Andrew Morgan
1 Church House, Main St, Farnsfield, Newark, Notts NG22 8EY [SOUTHWELL] *1995– b* 27 May 1954; *educ* K Sch Roch; BBC Popular Music Lib Lon and Scotland 1972–75; Presenter/Producer BBC Radio Nottm 1975–87; Presenter/Reporter BBC TV Midlands 1987–91; Freelance Producer/Presenter/Director Corporate and Broadcast Video Films from 1991; Conference MC and Concert Compere; BBC Radio Nottm Sunday Breakfast Show Presenter from 1998; Organist and Dir of Music St Mich Farnsfield; Chair S'well Dioc Communications Ctee
Tel and *Fax:* (01623) 882831
0410 088353 (Mobile)
01426 108410 (Pager)

DAVIDSON, Mr Keith Thomas, LL B
The Poplars, Sandy Lane, Church Brampton, Northampton NN6 8AX [PETERBOROUGH] *1970– b* 12 Sep 1932; *educ* Whitgift Sch; Solicitor; Rdr
Tel: (01604) 233233 (Office)
(01604) 845489 (Home)

DAVIES, Canon Jeremy (David Jeremy Christopher), MA
Ladywell, 33 The Close, Salisbury SP1 2EJ [SALISBURY] *1993– b* 7 Jan 1946; *educ* Cathl Sch Llandaff; Hurstpierpoint Coll; CCC Cam; Westcott Ho Th Coll; C St Dunstan Stepney 1971–74; Chapl Qu Mary Coll Lon 1974–78; Chapl Univ Coll Cardiff 1978–85; Prec and Can Res Sarum Cathl from 1985 *Tel:* (01722) 323289
Fax: (01722) 330699
e-mail: djcdavies@aol.com

DAVIES, Ven Lorys Martin, JP, BA, ALCM
45 Rudgwick Drive, Brandesholme, Bury, Lancs BL8 1YA [ARCHDEACON OF BOLTON] *1998– b* 14 Jun 1936; *educ* Whitland Gr Sch; St David's Coll Lamp; Univ of Wales; Wells Th Coll; C St Mary Tenby 1959–61; Asst Chapl Brentwood Sch 1962–66; Chapl and Hd of Dept Solihull Sch 1966–68; V St Mary Moseley 1968–81; Can Res Birm Cathl 1981–92; DDO 1982–90; Chmn Dioc Ho of Clergy 1991–92; Adn of Bolton from 1992; Bp's Adv for Hosp Chapls from 1992; Chmn Stewardship Ctee from 1992; Wrdn of Rdrs from 1994 *Tel* and *Fax:* 0161–761 6117

DAVIES, Ven Tony (Vincent Anthony)
246 Pampisford Rd, S Croydon CR2 6DD, Office: St Matthew's House, 100 George St, Croydon CR0 1PE [ARCHDEACON OF CROYDON] *b* 15 Sep 1946; *educ* Green Lane Sec Mod Sch Leic; Brasted Th Coll; St Mich Coll Llan; C St Jas Owton Manor Hartlepool 1973–76; C St Faith Wandsw 1976–78; V 1978–81; V St Jo Walworth 1981–93; RD S'wark and Newington 1988–93; Adn of Croydon from 1994
Tel: 0181–688 2943 (Home)
0181–681 5496 (Office)
Fax: 0181–686 2074
e-mail: tony.davies@dswark.org.uk

DAVIS, Ven Alan Norman, BA
50 Stainburn Rd, Workington, Cumbria CA14 1SN
[ARCHDEACON OF WEST CUMBERLAND] *b* 27 Jul 1938; *educ* K Edw Sch Birm; Dur Univ; Lich Th Coll; C St Luke Kingstanding 1965–68; P-in-c St Paul Ecclesfield CD 1968–73; V St Paul Wordsworth Ave 1973–75; V St Jas and St Chris Shiregreen 1975–80; V Maltby 1980–81; TR Maltby TM 1981–89; Abp's Officer for UPAs 1990–92; P-in-c St Cuth w St Mary Carlisle and DCO 1992–96; Adn of W Cumberland from 1996; Chmn Dioc BSR *Tel:* (01900) 66190
Fax: (01900) 873021

DAWS, Mr Christopher William, MA, FCA, ATII, MCT
Church Commissioners, 1 Millbank, London SW1P 3JZ
[DEPUTY SECRETARY (FINANCE AND INVESTMENT), CHURCH COMMISSIONERS] *b* 31 Aug 1947; *educ* Win Coll; Trin Coll Cam; Coopers & Lybrand 1969–79; Cadbury Schweppes 1979–87; Dowty Grp 1987–92; Sycamore Holdings 1993; Dep Sec (Finance and Investment) Ch Commrs from 1994
Tel: 0171–898 1786

DE LANGE, Mrs Anna Margaret, BA, MA
20 Broadfields, Harpenden, Herts AL5 2HJ [ST ALBANS] **1995–** *b* 26 Jun 1950; *educ* Newbury Girls Gr Sch; Ex Univ; Sheff Univ; Hants Co Lib Service 1973–77; Staff M Administry 1987–92; Mother; Rdr and M Staff Tm St Andr Woodside from 1993; M Liturg Commn from 1996; M Coun St Jo Coll Nottm from 1996 *Tel:* (01582) 765342

DERBY, Bishop of, Rt Revd Jonathan Sansbury Bailey, MA
Office: Derby Church House, Full St, Derby DE1 3DR, Home: Bishop's House, 6 King St, Duffield, Belper, Derby DE56 4EU **1988–92, 1995–** *b* 24 Feb 1940; *educ* Quarry Bank High Sch Liv; Trin Coll Cam; Ridley Hall Th Coll; C Sutton St Helens 1965–68; C St Paul Warrington 1968–71; Warden, Marrick Priory 1971–76; V Wetherby 1976–82; Adn of Southend 1982–92; Bp of Dunwich 1992–95; Bp of Derby from 1995; Clerk of the Closet to HM The Queen from 1996
Tel: (01332) 346744 (Office)
(01332) 840132 (Home)
Fax: (01332) 295810 (Office)
(01332) 842743 (Home)
e-mail: bishopderby@clara.net

DEUCHAR, Canon Andrew Gilchrist, B TH
Lambeth Palace, London SE1 7JU [SECRETARY FOR ANGLICAN COMMUNION AFFAIRS] *b* 3 Jun 1955; *educ* R Hosp Sch Ipswich; Southn Univ; Sarum and Wells Th Coll; HM Diplomatic Service 1974–81; C SS Mich and Paul Alnwick 1984–88; TV S Wye Hereford 1988–90; Adv Cant and Roch Joint Dioc Coun for Social Responsibility 1990–94; Abp of Cant's Sec for Anglican Communion Affairs from 1994; Non Res Can Cant Cathl from 1995 *Tel:* 0171–928 8282
Fax: 0171–401 9886
e-mail: JJ76@dial.pipex.com

DEXTER, Canon Frank Robert
Vicarage, St George's Close, Newcastle upon Tyne NE2 2TF [NEWCASTLE] **1992–** *b* 2 Aug 1940; *educ* Isleworth Gr Sch; Cuddesdon Th Coll; C H Cross Fenham Newc 1968–71; C Whorlton 1971–73; V Ch Carpenter Pet 1973–80; V St Phil High Elswick 1980–85; P-in-c St Aug Newc 1985; RD Newc W 1981–85; RD Newc Cen 1985–86; V St Geo Jesmond from 1985; P-in-c St Hilda Jesmond 1995–98; M Bp's Coun; Chmn Ho of Clergy Dioc Syn from 1993; RD Newc Cen 1994–95 *Tel:* 0191–281 1628 (Home)
0191–281 1659 (Office)

DIBDIN, Mrs Jane Penelope
Hill Top, Park Rd, Bridport, Dorset DT6 5DA [SALISBURY] **1990–** *b* 25 Feb 1937; *educ* St Mich Sch Limpsfield; Froebel Educl Inst Roehampton; Tchr St Mary's Primary Sch Bridport 1958–60; JP from 1973; Trustee Pilsdon Community from 1996; M Sarum Dioc Bd for Ch and Society from 1997
Tel: (01308) 422980

DICKINSON, Ms Jill Susan, BA
34 Chesterfield Rd, St Andrew's, Bristol BS6 5DL [BRISTOL] **1990–** *b* 19 Jan 1958; *educ* Plymouth High Sch for Girls; Bris Univ; Tchr of RE *Tel:* 0117–942 9378

DONCASTER, Bishop of [SUFFRAGAN, SHEFFIELD]
Rt Revd Michael Frederick Gear, BA
Bishop's Lodge, Hooton Roberts, nr Rotherham S65 4PF
b 27 Nov 1934; *educ* Tiffin Boys Sch Kingston-upon-Thames; St Jo Coll Dur; Cranmer Hall Dur; C Ch Ch Bexleyheath 1961–64; C St Aldates Ox 1964–67; V St Andr Clubmoor Liv 1967–71; R Avondale Harare Zimbabwe 1971–76; Tutor Wycliffe Hall Ox 1976–80; R Macclesfield Tm Par 1980–88; RD Macclesfield 1984–88; Hon Can Ches Cathl from 1986; Adn of Ches 1988–93; Bp of Doncaster from 1993; Worldwide Chapl MU from 1996 *Tel:* (01709) 853370
Fax: (01709) 852310

DORCHESTER, Bishop of [AREA BISHOP, OXFORD]
Rt Revd Anthony Russell, D PHIL
Holmby House, Sibford Ferris, Banbury, Oxon OX15 5RG **1980–88** *b* 25 Jan 1943; *educ* Uppingham Sch; St Chad's Coll Dur; Trin Coll Ox; Cuddesdon Th Coll; C Hilborough Grp of Parishes 1970–73; V of Preston-on-Stour, Atherstone-on-Stour and Whitchurch 1973–88; Chapl Arthur Rank Centre (Nat Agric

Centre) 1973–82; Dir Arthur Rank Cen 1983–88; Can Th Cov Cathl 1977–88; Chapl to HM Queen 1983–88; Exam Chapl to Bp of Hereford 1983–88; M BMU 1986–88; Bp of Dorchester from 1988; Vc-Pres R Agric Soc of England from 1991; Commr Rural Development Commn from 1991
Tel: (01295) 780583
Fax: (01295) 788686
e-mail: bishopdorchester@oxford.anglican.org

DORKING, Bishop of [SUFFRAGAN, GUILDFORD]
Rt Revd Ian James Brackley, MA
Dayspring, 13 Pilgrims Way, Guildford, Surrey GU4 8AD 1990–95 b 13 Dec 1947; *educ* Westcliff High Sch; Keble Coll Ox; Cuddesdon Th Coll; C St Mary Magd w St Fran Lockleaze Bris 1971–74; Asst Chapl Bryanston Sch 1974–77; Chapl 1977–80; V St Mary E Preston Chich 1980–88; RD Arundel and Bognor 1982–87; TR St Wilfrid Haywards Heath 1988–96; RD Cuckfield 1989–95; Bp of Dorking from 1996
Tel: (01483) 570829
Fax: (01483) 567268
e-mail: bishop.ian@cofeguildford.org.uk

DOVER, Bishop of [SUFFRAGAN, CANTERBURY]
[NOT APPOINTED AT TIME OF GOING TO PRESS.]

DOW, Mrs Molly Patricia, MA, DIP TH
173 Willesden Lane, Brondesbury, London NW6 7YN [LONDON] **1985–92, 1995–** *b* 23 Sep 1942; *educ* N Lon Collegiate Sch; St Hilda's Coll Ox; pt Tchr Portway Comp Sch Bris 1966–67; pt Tchr Tonbridge Tech High Sch 1967–68; Rdr from 1970; Supply Tchr Mathematics Cov 1981–90; M Liturg Commn 1987–96
Tel: 0181–451 1242
0181–451 0189
Fax: 0181–451 4606
e-mail: molly.dow@btinternet.com

DOWLING, Mr Jeremy Nicholas, DIP ED
Rosecare Villa Farm, St Gennys, Bude, Cornwall EX23 0BG [TRURO] **1978–** *b* 6 Jul 1938; *educ* Claiesmore Sch Dorset; Ox Inst of Educ; DCO; Lay Can Truro Cathl; Smallholder; Radio and TV Interviewer/Commentator/Producer; Rdr
Tel: (01840) 230326
Fax: (01288) 352786

DRAPER, Ven Martin Paul, BA, B TH
7 rue Auguste-Vacquerie, 75116 Paris, France [ARCHDEACON OF FRANCE] *b* 22 Apr 1950; *educ* Arnold Co High Sch Nottm; Birm Univ; Southn Univ; Chich Th Coll; C St Mary Primrose Hill 1975–78; C St Matt Westmr 1979–84; Chapl St Geo Paris from 1984; Adn of France from 1994; Co-Chmn French ARC from 1984; M Abp of Cant's Ecum Adv Ctee from 1990; M Conversations between CE and French Lutheran and Reformed Chs from 1993
Tel: 00–33–1–47–20–22–51

DRIVER, Revd Penny (Penelope May)
7 Loxley Grove, Wetherby, W Yorks LS22 7YG [RIPON] **1995–** *b* 20 Feb 1952; *educ* Nn Ord Course; Dioc Youth Adv Newc 1986–88; C St Geo Cullercoats 1987–88; Dioc Youth Chapl Ripon from 1988
Tel: (01937) 585440

DRURY, Very Revd John Henry, BA, MA
The Deanery, Christ Church, Oxford OX1 1DP [DEAN OF CHRIST CHURCH, OXFORD] *b* 23 May 1936; *educ* Trin Hall Cam; Westcott Ho Th Coll; C St John's Wood Lon 1963–66; Chapl Down Coll Cam 1966–69; Chapl Ex Coll Ox 1969–73; Can Res Nor Cathl 1973–79; Vc-Dean Nor Cathl 1978–79; Lect Sussex Univ 1979–81; Dean K Coll Cam 1981–91; Dean Ch Ch Ox from 1991
Tel: (01865) 276162 (Home)
(01865) 276161 (Office)

DUCKER, Mrs Deirdre Ann Josephine, NDD
91 The Common, Broughton Gifford, Melksham, Wilts SN12 8ND [SALISBURY] **1990–** *b* 8 Jul 1935; *educ* Abbotts Hill Sch Hemel Hempstead; Chelsea Sch of Art, Lon Univ; Farel House, L'Abri Fellowship Switzerland; Graphic Artist; Fine Artist; Theatre Designer; Parish Coun; M Sarum dio Communications Tm and Press and Publications Ctee; M Dioc Ecum Tm; M Wilts Environmental Forum ctee; Bradf Dny Communications Offcr
Tel and Fax: (01225) 783330

DUDLEY, Bishop of [AREA BISHOP, WORCESTER]
Rt Revd Rupert William Noel Hoare, MA, PH D
Bishop's House, 366 Halesowen Rd, Cradley Heath, W Midlands B64 7JF **1995–** *b* 3 Mar 1940; *educ* Rugby Sch; Trin Coll Ox; Fitzw Ho Cam; Berlin Univ; Birm Univ; Westcott Ho Th Coll; C St Mary Oldham 1964–68; Lect Qu Coll Birm 1968–72; Can Th Cov Cathl 1970–75; R Resurr Man 1972–78; Can Res Birm Cathl 1978–81; Prin Westcott Ho Cam 1981–93; Bp of Dudley from 1993
Tel: 0121–550 3407
Fax: 0121–550 7340

DUNCAN, Ven John Finch, MBE, MA
122 Westfield Rd, Edgbaston, Birmingham B15 3JQ [ARCHDEACON OF BIRMINGHAM] **1990–** *b* 9 Sep 1933; *educ* Qu Eliz Gr Sch Wakefield; Univ Coll Ox; Cuddesdon Th Coll; C S Bank Middlesbrough 1959–61; Novice SSF 1961–62; C St Pet Birm 1962–65; Chapl Birm Univ 1965–76; V K Heath Birm 1976–85; Adn of Birm from 1985; M CBF
Tel: 0121–454 3402
Fax: 0121–455 6178

DUNWICH, Bishop of [SUFFRAGAN, ST EDMUNDSBURY AND IPSWICH] **Rt Revd Timothy John Stevens,** MA
28 Westerfield Rd, Ipswich, Suffolk IP4 2UJ 1987–95 *b* 31 Dec 1946; *educ* Chigwell Sch; Selw Coll Cam; Ripon Hall Th Coll; C E Ham TM 1976–79; TV St Alban Upton Park 1979–80; TR Canvey Island 1980–88; Bp of Chelmsf's Urban Offcr 1988–91; Adn of West Ham 1991–95; Bp of Dunwich from 1995
Tel: (01473) 222276
Fax: (01473) 210303

DURHAM, Bishop of, Rt Revd Michael Turnbull, MA, HON D LITT
Auckland Castle, Bishop Auckland, Co Durham DL14 7NR **1970–75, 1987–** *b* 27 Dec 1935; *educ* Ilkley Gr Sch; Keble Coll Ox; Cranmer Hall Dur; C Middleton 1960–61; C and Lect Luton Par Ch 1961–65; Dom Chapl to Abp of York and DDO 1965–69; R Heslington and Chapl Univ of York 1969–76; M BMU 1975–85; Chief Sec CA 1976–84; Adn of Roch and Can Res Roch Cathl 1984–88; Bp of Roch 1988–94; Chmn PWM 1990–94; Chmn BRF 1990–94; M BM 1990–94; Chmn Abps Commn on Organisation of CE; M Cathls Commn 1992–94; Chmn Coll of Preachers 1990–98; M Bd of Govs Ch Commrs; Vc-Chmn CBF; Bp of Dur from 1994; M Legislative Ctee; Select Preacher Univ of Ox 1996
Tel: (01388) 602576
Fax: (01388) 605264
e-mail: bishdur@btinternet.com

EATON, Revd Julie Elizabeth, DIP HE, SEN (G), SEN (M)
Vange Rectory, 782 Clay Hill Rd, Vange, Basildon, Essex SS16 4NG [CHELMSFORD] **1995–** *b* 22 Jun 1957; *educ* Beyton Sch Suffolk; Trin Coll Bris; C St Andr Gt Ilford 1989–92; C (NSM) Billericay and Little Burstead TM and pt Hosp Chapl 1992–95; Stipend full time from 1995, V from 1996; Bp's Co-ord for Ordained Women; Bp of Bradwell's Dny Voc Adv
Tel: (01268) 557332
Fax: (01268) 581574

EBBSFLEET, Bishop of [PROVINCIAL EPISCOPAL VISITOR: CANTERBURY] **Rt Revd Rt Revd Michael Alan Houghton,** BA, B TH, PGCE
8 Goldney Ave, Clifton, Bristol BS8 4RA b 14 Jun 1949; *educ* Harold Hill Gr Sch; Lanc Univ; Dur Univ; Chich Th Coll; C All Hallows Wellingborough 1980–84; V Jamestown St Helena 1980–84; Hon Can St Paul's Cathl St Helena from 1994; Tutor Coll of Ascension Selly Oak 1990; V St Pet Folkestone 1990–98; Bp of Ebsfleet from 1998
Tel: 0117–973 1752
Fax: 0117–973 1762

EDEBOHLS, Ven William Ernest
c/o All Saints' Church, Via Solferino 17, 20121 Milan, Italy [ARCHDEACON OF ITALY AND MALTA] Adn of Italy and Malta from 1998
Tel and Fax: 00–39–02–655–2258

EDMONTON, Bishop of [AREA BISHOP, LONDON]
[NOT APPOINTED AT TIME OF GOING TO PRESS.]

EDSON, Ven Michael, B SC, BA
13 Stoneygate Ave, Leicester LE2 3HE [ARCHDEACON OF LEICESTER] *b* 2 Sep 1942; *educ* Mansfield Tech Sch; Birm Univ; Leeds Univ; Coll of the Resurr Mirfield; C St Pet w H Trin Barnstaple 1972–77; TV Barnstaple Central 1977–82; V St Andr Roxbourne 1982–89; P-in-c St Paul Harrow 1987–89; AD Harrow 1985–89; Warden Lee Abbey 1989–94; Adn of Leic from 1994; Dioc Missr from 1996
Tel: 0116–270 4441
Fax: 0116–270 1091
e-mail: medson@leicester.anglican.org

ELENGORN, Mr Martin David, MA
1 Millbank, London SW1P 3JZ [PASTORAL AND REDUNDANT CHURCHES SECRETARY, CHURCH COMMISSIONERS] *b* 17 Sep 1944; *educ* Enfield Gr Sch; G & C Coll Cam; On staff of Ch Commrs from 1966; Pastl and Red Chs Sec from 1993
Tel: 0171–898 1741
e-mail: martin.elengorn@chucomm.org.uk

ELLIOTT, Ven Peter, MA
80 Moorside North, Fenham, Newcastle upon Tyne NE4 9DU [ARCHDEACON OF NORTHUMBERLAND] *b* 14 Jun 1941; *educ* Qu Eliz Gr Sch Horncastle; Hertf Coll Ox; Linc Th Coll; C All SS Gosforth 1965–68; C St Pet Balkwell 1968–72; V St Phil High Elswick 1972–80; V N Gosforth 1980–87; V Embleton w Rennington and Rock 1987–93; RD Alnwick 1989–93; Adn of Northumberland from 1993; M Eng Heritage Cathls and Chs Adv Ctee from 1998; M Heritage Forum from 1998
Tel: 0191–273 8245
Fax: 0191–226 0286

ELLIS, Mrs Anne
33 Leat Walk, Roborough, Plymouth, Devon PL6 7AT [EXETER] **1990–** *b* 27 Aug 1936; *educ* Eccles Gr Sch; Alsager Tr Coll; Dartington Coll of Arts; Asst Tchr and Head of Music in primary and secondary schools Lancs 1956–64; Notts 1964–67; Cambs 1967–82; Deputy Head Walkhampton C E Primary School Devon 1984–89; Housewife and Musician from 1990; M Nat Coun Forward in Faith
Tel: (01752) 793397
Fax: (01752) 774618

ELLIS, Revd Robert Albert, BD, AKC, DIP ED
The Pump House, Jacks Lane, Marchington, Uttoxeter, Staffs ST14 8LW [LICHFIELD] **1995–** *b* 8 Jul 1948; *educ* K Coll Lon; St Aug Coll Cant; Ch Ch Coll Cant; C Our Lady and St Nic w St Anne Liv 1972–76; P-in-c Meerbrook 1976–80; Producer Relig Progr BBC 1976–80; V All SS Highgate Lon 1980–81; P-in-c Longdon 1981–87; DCO from 1981; M CECC from 1995
Tel: (01283) 820732 (Home)
(01543) 306030 (Office)
Fax: (01543) 306039
e-mail: info@lichfield.anglican.org

ELLIS, Ven Robin Gareth, BCL, MA
33 Leat Walk, Roborough, Plymouth, Devon PL6 7AT [ARCHDEACON OF PLYMOUTH] **1980–82, 1994–** *b* 8 Dec 1935; *educ* Worksop Coll; Pemb Coll Ox; Chich Th Coll; Asst C St Pet Swinton 1960–63; Asst Chapl Worksop Coll 1963–66; V of Swaffham Prior w Reach, and Asst Dir of Educ Ely dio 1966–74; V St Aug Wisbech 1974–82; V St Paul Yelverton 1982–86; Adn of Plymouth from 1982; M Gen Syn Working Party on Clerical Discipline from 1995, Implementation Grp from 1997; Chmn Catholic Grp in Syn from 1995
Tel: (01752) 793397
Fax: (01752) 774618

ELLOY, Mr Jeremy Andrew
Church House, Great Smith St, London SW1P 3NZ [BUDGETING OFFICER/HEAD OF PLANNING, ARCHBISHOPS' COUNCIL] *b* 2 Nov 1951; *educ* Hove Gr Sch; Selw Coll Cam; On staff of Ch Commrs 1975–94; Seconded to CBF from 1994; Budgeting Officer/Administrative Sec CBF 1994–96; Dep Sec/Budgeting Officer 1996–98; Budgeting Officer/Hd of Planning Abps' Coun from 1999
Tel: 0171–898 1562

ELY, Bishop of, Rt Revd Stephen Whitefield Sykes, MA
The Bishop's House, Ely, Cambs CB7 4DW **1990–** *b* 1 Aug 1939; *educ* Bris Gr Sch; Monkton Combe Sch; St Jo Coll Cam; Harvard Univ; Ripon Hall Th Coll; Asst Lect Div Cam Univ 1964–68; Fell and Dean St Jo Coll Cam 1964–74; Lect 1968–74; Van Mildert Prof Dur Univ 1974–85; Can Res Dur Cathl 1974–85; Regius Prof Div Cam Univ 1985–90; Bp of Ely from 1990; Chmn Doct Commn from 1997
Tel: (01353) 662749
Fax: (01353) 669477
e-mail: bishop@ely.anglican.org

EPTON, Mrs Joy, CERT ED
Northolme Hall, Wainfleet PE24 4AE [LINCOLN] **1995–** *educ* King's Lynn High Sch for Girls; Hockerill Tchr Tr Coll; Cen Pres Girls' Friendly Soc 1990–96; World Chmn Girls' Friendly Soc 1993–96; JP; Angl Rep WWDP Ctee; Local Min Wainfleet Grp of Parishes; Dny Lay Chmn Calcethwaith and Candleshoe 1982–92

EUROPE, Bishop of Gibraltar in, Rt Revd John William Hind, BA
Bishop's Lodge, Church Rd, Worth, Crawley, W Sussex RH10 7RT **1993–** *b* 19 Jun 1945; *educ* Watford Gr Sch; Leeds Univ; Cuddesdon Th Coll; Asst Master Leeds Modern Sch 1966–69; Asst Lect K Alfred's Coll Win 1969–70; C Catford, Southend and Downham 1972–76; V Ch Ch Forest Hill 1976–82; P-in-c St Paul Forest Hill 1981–82; Prin Chich Th Coll 1982–91; Bursalis Preb Chich Cathl 1982–91; Bp of Horsham 1991–93; Chmn FOAG from 1991; Bp of Gibraltar in Europe from 1993; Consultant to CCU; M Ho of Bps Th Grp
Tel: (01293) 883051
Fax: (01293) 884479
e-mail: 101741.3160@compuserve.com

EUROPE, Suffragan Bishop in, Rt Revd Henry William Scriven, BA, DPS
Diocese in Europe, 14 Tufton St, London SW1P 3QZ b 30 Aug 1951; *educ* Repton Sch; Sheff Univ; St Jo Coll Nottm; C H Trin Wealdstone 1975–79; SAMS Argentina 1979–82; Assoc R Ch Ch Little Rock Arkansas 1982–83; SAMS w Spanish Episc Reformed Ch Salamanca Spain 1984–88, Madrid 1988–90; Chapl Br Embassy Ch St Geo Madrid 1990–95; Suff Bp in Europe from 1995
Tel: 0171–976 8001
Fax: 0171–976 8002
e-mail: henry@dioeurope.clara.net

EVANS, Rt Revd David Richard John, MA
12 Fox Hill, Birmingham B29 4AG [GENERAL SECRETARY, SAMS] *b* 5 Jun 1938; *educ* Ch Hosp; Cam Univ; Clifton Th Coll; C Ch Ch Cockfosters 1965–68; Asst Pr H Trin Lomas de Zamora Buenos Aires 1969–77; Gen Sec Asociacion Biblic Argentina Univ 1971–76; Pr Lima Peru 1977–78; Chapl Gd Shep Lima 1977–83; Bp of Peru 1978–88, and Bolivia 1982–88; Asst Bp Bradf 1988–93; Gen Sec SAMS from 1993; Internat Co-ordinator EFAC from 1989; Asst Bp Chich from 1994–97; Asst Bp Roch 1994–97; Asst Bp Birm from 1997; Focal Person of Latin American Forum CCOM from 1993; Co-ordinator S American Network PWM from 1995; M BM from 1995; Lic to officiate in Provinces of Cant and York
Tel: 0121–472 2616 (Office)
Tel and Fax: 0121–472 5731 (Home)
Fax: 0121–472 7977 (Office)
e-mail: SAMSGB@compuserve.com

EVANS, Ven Patrick Alexander Sidney
Archdeacon's House, Charing, Kent TN27 0LU [ARCH-DEACON OF MAIDSTONE] **1996–** *b* 28 Jan 1943; *educ* Clifton Coll; Linc Th Coll; C Lyonsdown 1973–76; C Royston 1976–78; V Gt Gaddesden and Dioc Stewardship Adv 1978–82; V Tenterden w Smallhythe 1982–89; RD W Charing 1988–89; DDO 1989–94; Adn of Maidstone from 1989; Chmn Dioc Bd of Miss 1994–96; Chmn Dioc Pastl Ctee from 1994; Chmn Cant and Roch CSR from 1996   *Tel:* (01233) 712294

EVENS, Ven Bob (Robert John Scott), DIP TH, ACIB
56 Grange Rd, Saltford, Bristol BS31 3AG [ARCH-DEACON OF BATH] *1994–95 b* 29 May 1947; *educ* Maidstone Gr Sch; Trin Coll Bris; C St Simon Southsea 1977–79; C St Mary Portchester 1979–83; V St Jo B Locks Heath 1983–95; RD Fareham 1993–95; Adn of Bath from 1995; Chmn Somerset Chs Together from 1996   *Tel:* (01225) 873609
    Fax: (01225) 874110
    e-mail: 113145.1175@compuserve.com

EXETER, Bishop of, Rt Revd (Geoffrey) Hewlett Thompson
The Palace, Exeter, Devon EX1 1HY **1985–** *b* 14 Aug 1929; *educ* Aldenham Sch; Trin Hall Cam; Cuddesdon Th Coll; C St Matt N'hampton 1954–59; V St Aug Wisbech 1959–66; V St Sav Folkestone 1966–74; Vc Chmn Community and Race Relns Unit Bd, BCC 1976–80; Chmn 1980–84; Bp of Willesden 1974–85; Chmn Home Ctee of BMU 1976–85; Bp of Ex from 1985; Chmn HCC 1991–97; M Ch Commr Ho Ctee 1985–95, Dep Chmn from 1994 and Dep Chmn Bishoprics Ctee 1985–97   *Tel:* (01392) 272362
    Fax: (01392) 430923

FARRELL, Mr (Michael Geoffrey) Shaun
1 Millbank, London SW1P 3JZ [FINANCIAL SECRETARY, ARCHBISHOPS' COUNCIL] *b* 27 Apr 1950; *educ* Gillingham Gr Sch; On staff of Ch Commrs from 1969; Stipends and Allocations Sec 1994–98; Fin Sec Abps' Coun from 1999   *Tel:* 0171–898 1795
    e-mail: shaun.farrell@chucomm.org.uk

FARRINGTON, Canon Christine Marion, BA, MA, DASS
St Mark's Vicarage, Barton Rd, Cambridge CB3 9JZ [ELY] **1985–93, 1995–** *b* 11 Jun 1942; *educ* Cheshunt Gr Sch; Lon Univ; Nottm Univ; Middx Poly; St Alb Minl Tr Scheme; Asst Libr 1960–62; Primary Sch Tchr 1962–65; Probation Officer 1967–71; Social Work Lect 1971–79; Sen Probation Officer 1979–86; Asst Prison Chapl and Asst Dir of Pastl Studies Linc Th Coll 1986–87; Dn Sarum Cathl and Dir Sarum Chr Centre 1987–93; Co-DDO and Dir of Women's Min from 1993; V St Mark Cam from 1996; Chapl to HM The Queen from 1998; M Dioc Adult Educ Coun; M Bp's Coun; M Bp's Tm   *Tel:* (01223) 363339

FELL, Canon Alan William, BA, MA, DIP TH
Vicarage, Loftus Hill, Sedbergh, Cumbria LA10 5SQ [BRADFORD] **1994–** *b* 27 Oct 1946; *educ* Man Gr Sch; Ball Coll Ox; Leeds Univ; Coll of the Resurr Mirfield; C Woodchurch Birkenhead 1971–74; C St Cross Clayton Man 1974–75; C St Marg Prestwich 1975–77; V St Thos Hyde 1977–80; R Tattenhall and Handley 1980–86; V Sedbergh, Cautley and Garsdale from 1986; M Bp's Coun; M Synodical Agenda Grp; M Dioc Adv Coun for Min and Tr; M DAC; Hon Can Bradf Cathl from 1996; Chmn Vacancy-in-See Ctee   *Tel:* (15396) 20283

FENWICK, Revd Dr John Robert Kipling, B SC, BA, M TH, PH D, S TH
Rectory, Rectory Close, Chorley, Lancs PR7 1QW [BLACKBURN] **1998–** *b* 17 Apr 1951; *educ* Nelson Thomlinson Gr Sch Wigton; Dur Univ; Nottm Univ; K Coll Lon; St Jo Coll Nottm; C Dalton-in-Furness 1977–80; Lect in Chr Worship Trin Coll Bris 1980–88; Abp of Cant's Asst Sec for Ecum Affairs 1988–92; R Chorley from 1992; M Revision Ctee Clergy Representation Rules (Amendment); Chmr. Dioc Chr Unity Ctee; Moderator Chs Together in Chorley
    Tel: (01257) 263114 (Home)
    (01257) 231360 (Office)
    Fax: (01257) 231374

FERGUSON, Mr John William
1 Millbank, London SW1P 3JZ [HEAD OF INFORMATION TECHNOLOGY AND OFFICE SERVICES, ARCHBISHOPS' COUNCIL] *b* 23 Dec 1947; *educ* Jo Watson's Sch Edin; Computer Services Manager Matthew Hall Grp –1981; Computer Services Manager Ch Commrs from 1981; Computer and Office Services Manager from 1994; Hd of Information Technology and Office Services Abps' Coun from 1998   *Tel:* 0171–898 1640
    e-mail: john.ferguson@chucomm.org.uk

FERNYHOUGH, Ven Bernard, BA
Rectory, 5 Nook Lane, Empingham, Rutland LE15 8PT [ARCHDEACON OF OAKHAM] *1980–95 b* 2 Sep 1932; *educ* Wolstanton Co Gr Sch; St D Coll Lamp; Prec Trinidad Cathl 1955–61; R Stoke Bruerne w Grafton Regis and Alderton 1961–67; RD Preston 1965–67; V Ravensthorpe (w E Haddon and Holdenby from 1968) 1967–77; V E Haddon 1967–68; RD Haddon 1968–70; RD Brixworth 1971–77; Non Res Can Petrb Cathl 1974–77; Can Res 1977–89; Adn of Oakham

from 1977; Non Res Can Petrb Cathl from 1989; P-in-c Empingham, Exton and Whitwell from 1995
Tel: (01780) 460345

FIELD, Mr Brian Hedley, FCP, DIP PE
'Shebri', 21 Fauchons Close, Bearsted, Maidstone, Kent ME14 4BB [CANTERBURY] 1980– *b* 12 Apr 1931; *educ* Leeds Gr Sch; St Jo Coll York; Tchr: 1954–55 Central Tech Sch Glouc; 1955–59 Intake Secondary Sch Leeds; 1959–65 Leeds Gr Sch; Dep Hdmaster Primrose Hill Sec Sch Leeds 1965–67; Area Yth Offcr Airedale and Wharfedale Divisions of the W Riding 1968–74; Sen Community Educ Offcr Leeds 1974–75; Co Yth and Community Service Offcr in Kent 1975–89; Rdr from 1955; Hon Sec CRC 1989–94; M Bd of Educ 1986–90; Ldr Crusader Sportsman's Holiday 1973–91; M Coll of Preachers Coun from 1991, M Exec Ctee from 1993; M CE Evang Coun from 1991; M CPAS Coun from 1991, M Stg Ctee from 1995; M Rdrs Adv Grp from 1992; M Abp's Coun (Cant) from 1992; Hon Sec Cant Dioc Assn of Rdrs 1994–98; M Ch Soc Coun from 1995; Vc-Chair Ch Soc Coun and Mgt Ctee from 1998
Tel: (01622) 730117

FILBY, Ven William Charles Leonard
The Archdeaconry, Itchingfield, W Sussex RH13 7NX [ARCHDEACON OF HORSHAM] 1975–90 *b* 21 Jan 1933; *educ* Ashford Co Gr Sch; Lon Univ; Oak Hill Th Coll; V H Trin Richmond 1965–71; V Bp Hannington Mem Ch Hove 1971–79; R Broadwater 1979–83; RD Worthing 1980–83; Hon Can of Chich Cathl 1981–83; Pres Chic Dio Ev Union 1978–84; Chmn Redcliffe Missry Tr Coll 1970–92; M Keswick Convention Coun 1973–90; Chmn Trustees Divine Healing Miss Crowhurst 1987–91; Adn of Horsham from 1983; Chmn Dioc Ctee for Miss and Renewal 1987–92; Chmn Sussex Chs Broadcasting Ctee 1984–95; Bp's Adv for Hosp Chapls 1986–97; Govnr St Mary's Hall, Brighton from 1984; Gov W Sussex Inst of Higher Educ from 1985; Chmn Dioc Ind Miss Adv Panel from 1989; Chmn Dioc ACORA Grp from 1997
Tel: (01403) 790315
Fax: (01403) 791153

FISHER, Mrs Nicolete Anne, BA
7 Northorpe Lane, Thurlby, Bourne, Lincs PE10 0HE [LINCOLN] 1995– *b* 10 Dec 1948; *educ* Croydon High Sch for Girls; Kent Univ; Research Asst St Thos Hosp Lon 1970–73; Personnel/Ind Relations Officer Perkins Engines 1973–80; pt Personnel Consultant RDA Consultancy 1988–90; pt Personnel Manager British Sugar 1990–91; pt Personnel Projects Manager Berisford from 1991; M Bp's Coun
Tel: (01778) 423959

FISHER, Mrs (Rita) Elizabeth, BA, M ED, PGCE
71 Farquhar Rd, Edgbaston, Birmingham B15 2QP [BIRMINGHAM] 1985– *b* 16 Nov 1946; *educ* Wolsingham Sch; Dur Univ; Ox Univ; Hull Univ; Tchr Newbury Girls' Gr Sch 1969–70; Tchr Pilgrim Sch Bedf 1970–72; Adult Educ Officer Linc Dio 1980–84; Asst Dir/Project Officer N England Inst for Chr Educ 1984–91; Dir of Studies NE Ord Course 1989–91; M Panel of Chairmen 1989–91; M ABM 1986–96; M Heref Commn from 1993; IMEC from 1994; M CCU from 1996; Vc-Chair CCU; Hon Moderator Abps' Diploma for Rdrs 1994–98; pt Lect; Chair Birm Dioc Bd of Educ; M Bp's Coun
Tel and Fax: 0121–452 2612

FLEMING, Ven David
'Fair Haven', 123 Wisbech Rd, Littleport, Cambs CB6 1JJ [CHAPLAIN GENERAL OF PRISONS AND ARCHDEACON] 1990– *b* 8 Jun 1937; *educ* K Edw VII Gr Sch King's Lynn; Kelham Th Coll; Asst C St Marg Walton-on-Hill Liv 1963–67; Attached Sandringham Grp of Chs 1967–68; V Gt Staughton and Chapl Gaynes Hall Borstal 1968–76; RD St Neots 1972–76; V Whittlesey 1976–85; P-in-c Pondersbridge 1983–85; Chmn Ho of Clergy Dioc Syn 1982–85; RD March 1977–82; V Wisbech St Mary 1985–88; Hon Can Ely Cathl from 1982; Adn of Wisbech 1985–93; Chapl Gen of HM Prisons and Adn of Prisons from 1993; Chapl to HM The Queen from 1995
Tel: (01353) 862498 (Home)
0171–217 5683 (Office)
Fax: 0171–217 5090 (Office)

FLETCHER, Canon Colin William, MA
7 The Cottages, Lambeth Palace, London SE1 7JU [DOMESTIC CHAPLAIN TO THE ARCHBISHOP OF CANTERBURY] *b* 17 Nov 1950; *educ* Marlborough Coll; Trin Coll Ox; Wycliffe Hall Th Coll; C St Pet Shipley 1975–79; Tutor Wycliffe Hall and C St Andr Ox 1979–84; V H Trin Margate 1984–93; RD Thanet 1988–93; Dom Chapl to Abp of Cant from 1993
Tel: 0171–928 8282
Fax: 0171–261 9836

FLETCHER, Revd Jeremy James, BA, MA, DIP TH
Vicarage, Mansfield Rd, Skegby, Notts NG17 3ED [SOUTHWELL] 1995– *b* 31 Jul 1960; *educ* Woodhouse Grove Sch Bradf; Univ Coll Dur; St Jo Coll Nottm; Eng Tchr Belper High Sch 1982–85; C All SS Stranton, Hartlepool 1988–91; Assoc Min St Nic Nottm 1991–94; P-in-c Skegby from 1994 and P-in-c Teversal from 1996; M Dioc Liturg Ctee; M Coun St Jo Coll Nottm; M Liturg Commn from 1998
Tel and Fax: (01623) 558800

FLETCHER, Mrs Sheila Evelyn, BA, DIP TH, CERT ED
11 Troarn Way, Chudleigh, Newton Abbot, Devon TQ13 0PP [EXETER] 1995– *b* 22 Oct 1946; *educ* Warlingham Sch; Leeds Univ; Nottm Univ; Ex Dioc FLAME Adv from 1989; Rdr from 1994; M Bp's Coun and Stg Ctee; M Dioc Syn; M FLAME Ctee
Tel and *Fax*: (01626) 853998

FOOTTIT, Ven Anthony Charles, MA
Ivy House, Whitwell St, Reepham, Norwich NR10 4RA [ARCHDEACON OF LYNN] 1995– *b* 28 Jun 1935; *educ* Lancing Coll; K Coll Cam; Cuddesdon Th Coll; C Wymondham 1961–64; TV Blakeney Grp 1964–71; TR Camelot Grp 1971–81; RD Cary 1979–81; St Hugh's Missr Lincs 1981–87; Hon Can Linc Cathl 1986–87; Adn of Lynn from 1987
Tel and *Fax*: (01603) 870340

FORRESTER, Revd James Oliphant, MA
Vicarage, 230 The Wheel, Ecclesfield, Sheffield S35 9ZB [SHEFFIELD] 1995– *b* 8 Oct 1950; *educ* Bradfield Coll; SS Coll Cam; Wycliffe Hall Th Coll; C St Jo Newland Hull 1976–80; C Fulwood Sheff 1980–87; V St Luke Lodge Moor 1987–90; V St Mary Ecclesfield from 1990; M Dioc Pastl Ctee *Tel*: 0114–257 0002

FOSTER, Revd Stephen Arthur
St Matthew's Vicarage, 99 Chatham St, Stockport SK3 9EG [CHESTER] 1998– *b* 7 Mar 1954; *educ* Coll of Resurr Mirfield; C H Trin Ches 1978–82; C St Paul w St Luke Tranmere 1982–83; V St Andr Grange 1983–88; V All SS Cheadle Hulme 1988–94; P-in-c St Matt Stockport from 1994; Asst DDO from 1996
Tel: 0161–480 5515

FOWELL, Revd Graham Charles, B TH
Vicarage, Lymer Rd, Oxley, Wolverhampton WV10 6AA [LICHFIELD] 1995– *b* 17 Dec 1948; *educ* Southn Univ; Chich Th Coll; C Clayton 1982–86; C Uttoxeter w Bramshall 1986–70; V Oxley from 1990
Tel: (01902) 783342

FOX, Ven Michael John, B SC
86 Aldersbrook Rd, Manor Park, London E12 5DH [ARCHDEACON OF WEST HAM] *b* 28 Apr 1942; *educ* Barking Abbey Gr Sch; Hull Univ; Mirfield Th Coll; C St Eliz Becontree 1966–70; C H Trin S Woodford 1970–72; V Ascen Victoria Docks 1972–76; V All SS Chelmsf 1976–88; P-in-c Ascen Chelmsf 1985–88; RD Chelmsf 1986–88; R St Jas Colchester 1988–93; Adn of Harlow 1993–96; Adn of W Ham from 1996 *Tel*: 0181–989 8557
Fax: 0181–530 1311

FRAYNE, Very Revd David, MA, DIP TH
The Provost's House, Preston New Rd, Blackburn BB2 6PS [PROVOST OF BLACKBURN] 1987–9C *b* 19 Oct 1934; *educ* Reigate Gr Sch; St Edm Hall Ox; Qu Coll Birm; C E Wickham 1960–63; P-in-c St Barn Downham 1963–67; V N Sheen 1967–73; R Caterham 1973–83; RD Caterham 1981–83; Hon Can S'wark Cathl 1982–83; Can Emer from 1983; V St Mary Redcliffe w Temple Bris and St Jo B Bedminster 1983–92; RD Bedminster 1986–92; Hon Can Bris Cathl from 1991; Prov of Blackb from 1992
Tel: (01254) 52502 (Home)
(01254) 51491 (Office)
Fax: (01254) 689666
e-mail: cathedra@blackburnce.u-net.com

FREEMAN, Mrs Jenifer Jane, SRN, SCM
Lavender Cottage, Harkstead, Ipswich, Suffolk IP9 1BN [ST EDMUNDSBURY AND IPSWICH] 1985– *b* 12 Dec 1937; *educ* St Brandon's Sch Clevedon; Staff Midwife Gosport 1961–62; Nat Childbirth Trust Tchr 1964–89; Lay Chmn Samford Dny Syn 1979–88; Wife and Mother; M Bp's Coun from 1983; M Dioc Patronage Ctee; Bp's Visitor; M Transitional Cathl Coun
Tel: (01473) 328381

FREEMAN, Canon Robert John, B SC, MA
Martyrs Vicarage, 17 Westcotes Drive, Leicester LE3 0QT [LEICESTER] 1998– *b* 26 Oct 1952; *educ* Cam High Sch; St Jo Coll Dur; Fitw Coll Cam; Ridley Hall Th Coll; C St Jo Blackpool 1977–81; TV Chigwell 1981–85; V Ch of the Martyrs Leic from 1985; Vc-Chair Leic City Challenge 1992–94; Chair ACUPA; Chair Dioc BM and SR; CUF Link Officer; M Dicc Bd of Educ; M Dioc Bd of Min; M DBF *Tel*: 0116–254 6162
e-mail: rjf@frmn.surfaid.org

FROST, Ven George, MA
24 The Close, Lichfield, Staffs WS13 7LD [ARCHDEACON OF LICHFIELD] 1988– *b* 4 Apr 1935; *educ* Westcliff High Sch; Hatf Coll Dur; Linc Th Coll; C Barking 1960–64; C-in-c Marks Gate CD 1964–70; V Tipton 1970–77; V Penn 1977–87; RD Trysull 1984–87; Preb Lich Cathl 1985–87; Adn of Salop and V Tong 1987–98; Adn of Lichf from 1998
Tel: (01543) 306145/6
Fax: (01543) 306147

FRY, Revd Barry James, ACIB
St Barnabas' Vicarage, 12 Rose Rd, Southampton, Hants SO14 6TE [WINCHESTER] 1990– *b* 8 May 1949; *educ* Ripon Coll Cuddesdon; C Highcliffe w Hinton Admiral 1983–87; V St Barn Southn from 1987; Regional Dean Forward in Faith E Wessex
Tel and Fax: (01703) 223107

FRY, Ms Christine Ann, BA, DIP SOC WORK
7 Merryfield, Chineham, Basingstoke RG24 8XW [WINCHESTER] **1995–** *b* 12 Jul 1964; *educ* Arden Sch Knowle; Solihull Sixth Form Coll; Southn Univ; Middx Poly; Family Court Welfare Officer from 1995
Tel: (01256) 474466

FULHAM, Bishop of [SUFFRAGAN, LONDON]
Rt Revd John Charles Broadhurst, STH, AKC
26 Canonbury Park South, London N1 2FN 1973–96 *b* 20 Jul 1942; *educ* Owen's Sch Lon; K Coll Lon; St Boniface Th Coll Warminster; C St Michael-at-Bowes 1966–70; P-in-c St Aug Wembley Pk 1970–75; V 1975–85; M Stg Ctee Ho of Clergy 1981–88; AD Brent 1982–85; AD Haringey E 1986–92; M Panel of Chairmen 1981–84; M Coun Corp of Ch Ho 1980–90; TR Wood Green 1985–96; Bp of Fulham from 1996; M Gen Syn Stg Ctee 1988–96; Pro-Prolocutor Conv of Cant 1990–96; Chmn Dioc Ho of Clergy 1986–96; M Legal Aid Commn 1991–96; M Fees Adv Commn 1991–96; Delegate WCC Canberra 1991; M ACC from 1991; M CTE; Delegate CEC Prague 1992; Nat Chmn Forward in Faith
Tel: 0171–354 2334
Fax: 0171–354 2335
e-mail: bpfulham@compuserve.com

FURNELL, Very Revd Raymond
The Deanery, York YO1 2JQ [DEAN OF YORK] **1989–** *b* 18 May 1935; *educ* Hinchley Wood Sch; Brasted Place and Linc Th Coll; C St Luke's Cannock 1965–69; V St Jas Clayton 1969–75; R Hanley TM and RD N Stoke 1975–1981; Prov of St Eds 1981–94; Dean of York from 1994; Chmn Assn of English Cathls
Tel: (01904) 623608
e-mail: rfurnell@compuserve.com

GARBETT, Mr (George) James, MA, MA (ED), PGCE
Annandale, 72 Scotforth Rd, Lancaster LA1 4SF [BLACKBURN] **1995–** *b* 20 Feb 1931; *educ* Blackpool Gr Sch; St Jo Coll Cam; Ball Coll Ox; Leeds Univ; English Master Bolton Sch 1958–67, Sen English Master 1964–67; Dean of Initial Tchr Educ St Martin's Coll Lancaster 1975–89, Asst Prin (Academic) 1989–93; Rdr from 1990; Rtd; M Dioc Syn; M Dioc Bd of Educ, Chmn Schs Ctee; Lay Chair Lancaster Dny Syn
Tel: (01524) 65746

GARDEN, Mr Ian Harrison, LL B
Old Church Cottage, 29 Church Rd, Rufford, Ormskirk, Lancs L40 1TA [BLACKBURN] **1995–** *b* 18 Jun 1961; *educ* Sedbergh Sch; Univ Coll of Wales Abth; Barrister from 1989; M Bp's Coun from 1996; M Legislative Ctee from 1996; M Initiation Services Revision Ctee; M Appeals Tribunal Panel Pastl Measure 1983 and Incumbents (Vacation of Benefices) Measure 1977; M Appeals Tribunal Panel Ord of Women (Financial Provisions) Measure 1993; Guardian, Nat Shrine of Our Lady Walsingham from 1996; M Crown Appts Commn from 1997
Tel: 0151–709 4222 (Office)
(01704) 821303 (Home)
Fax: 0151–708 6311

GARLICK, Revd Kay (Kathleen Beatrice), BA, CERT ED
Birch Lodge, Much Birch, Hereford HR2 8HT [HEREFORD] **1995–** *b* 26 Feb 1949; *educ* Prendergast Gr Sch Catford; Leeds Univ; Birm Univ; Glouc Sch of Min; Hon C Much Birch w Lt Birch, Much Dewchurch etc from 1990; Ecum Chapl Heref Sixth Form Coll from 1996
Tel: (01981) 540666

GARNETT, Ven David Christopher, BA, MA
The Old Parsonage, Taddington, Buxton, Derbys SK17 9TW [ARCHDEACON OF CHESTERFIELD] 1990–96 *b* 26 Sep 1945; *educ* Giggleswick Sch; Nottm Univ; Fitzw Coll Cam; Westcott Ho Th Coll; C Cottingham 1969–72; Chapl and Fell Selw Coll Cam 1972–77; Pastl Adv Newnham Coll Cam 1972–77; R Patterdale 1977–80; DDO Carlisle 1977–80; V Heald Green 1980–87; Chapl St Ann's Hospice 1980–87; R Christleton 1987–92; TR Ellesmere Port 1992–96; Adn of Chesterfield from 1996; Chmn Bp's Th Adv Grp 1987–93; Chmn Assn of Ch Fellowships from 1987–92
Tel: (01298) 85607
Fax: (01298) 85583

GATFORD, Ven Ian, AKC
72 Pastures Hill, Littleover, Derby DE23 7BB [ARCHDEACON OF DERBY] **1995–** *b* 15 Jun 1940; *educ* Drayton Manor Gr Sch Hanwell; K Coll Lon; St Boniface Coll Warminster; C St Mary Clifton Nottm 1967–71; TV H Trin Clifton 1971–75; V St Martin Sherwood 1975–84; Can Res Derby Cathl from 1984; Sub Provost Derby Cathl 1990–93; Adn of Derby from 1993
Tel: (01332) 382233 (Office)
(01332) 512700 (Home)
Fax: (01332) 292969 (Office)
(01332) 523332 (Home)

GATHERCOLE, Ven John Robert, MA
15 Worcester Rd, Droitwich, Worcs WR9 8AA [ARCHDEACON OF DUDLEY] **1995–** *b* 23 Apr 1937; *educ* Judd Sch Tonbridge; Fitzw Coll Cam; Ridley Hall Th Coll; C St Nic Dur 1962–66; C St Bart Croxdale 1966–70; Soc and Ind Adv to Bp of Dur 1967–70; Ind Chapl Worc 1970–87; RD Bromsgrove 1978–85; Tm Ldr Worc Ind Miss 1985–91; Hon Can Worc Cathl from 1980; Adn of Dudley from 1987; Chmn Dioc Ho of Clergy from 1991; M Elections Review Grp from 1997
Tel and Fax: (01905) 773301

GAWEDA, Mr Ian, AMCA, AMCT
101 Hampton Drive, Newport, Shropshire TF10 7RH [LICHFIELD] *1998– b* 1 Oct 1951; *educ* W Bromwich Gr Sch; William Booth Memorial Coll; Salvation Army Officer 1981–84; Asst Dioc Sec (Finance) from 1991 *Tel:* (01952) 820116

GERRARD, Ven David Keith Robin, BA
Home: 68 North Side, Wandsworth Common, London SW18 2QX; Office: Whitelands Coll, West Hill, London SW15 3SN [ARCHDEACON OF WANDSWORTH] *1993– b* 15 Jun 1939; *educ* Guildf R Gr Sch; St Edm Hall Ox; Linc Th Coll; C St Olave Woodberry Down 1963–66; C St Mary Primrose Hill 1966–69; V St Paul Newington 1969–79; V St Mark Surbiton 1979–89; Adn of Wandsworth from 1989; Ch Commr from 1995, M Pastl Ctee from 1996 *Tel:* 0181–392 3742 (Office)
Tel and Fax: 0181–874 5766 (Home)
Fax: 0181–392 3743 (Office)
e-mail: david.gerrard@dswark.org.uk

GIBSON, Ven (George) Granville
2 Etherley Lane, Bishop Auckland, Co Durham DL14 7QR [ARCHDEACON OF AUCKLAND] *1980– b* 28 May 1936; *educ* Qu Eliz Gr Sch Wakef; Barnsley Coll of Techn; Cuddesdon Th Coll; C St Paul Cullercoats 1971–73; TV Cramlington 1973–77; V St Clare Newton Aycliffe 1977–85; M Broadcasting Panel of CECC 1981–85; R St Mich w St Hilda Bishopwearmouth 1985–90; M Panel of Assessors York Conv 1980–90; M BSR 1987–90; Chmn Dioc Ho of Clergy 1985–91; RD Wearmouth 1985–93; R Sunderland TM 1990–93; M Communications Ctee 1991–93; M Bp's Coun; Hon Can Dur Cathl from 1988; Ch Commr from 1991, Bd of Govs from 1993, M Gen Purposes Ctee from 1993; Trustee Ch Urban Fund from 1991; Adn of Auckland from 1993; Chmn Dioc Pastl Ctee from 1993; Chmn DBF from 1995; M Conditions of Service Working Party 1992–95; M Panel of Assessors York Conv from 1995; Chmn CUF Grants Ctee from 1997 *Tel:* (01388) 451635
Fax: (01388) 607502
e-mail: vengg@gibven.demon.co.uk

GIBSON, Ven Terence Allen, MA
99 Valley Rd, Ipswich, Suffolk IP1 4NF [ARCHDEACON OF IPSWICH] *1990– b* 23 Oct 1937; *educ* Boston Gr Sch; Jes Coll Cam; Cuddesdon Th Coll; C St Chad, Kirkby, Liv 1963–66; Wrdn Cen 63 Kirkby 1966–75; Area Yth Chapl 1966–72; TV for Yth Work Kirkby 1972–75; R Kirkby 1975–84; RD Walton 1979–84; Adn of Suffolk 1984–87; Adn of Ipswich from 1987
Tel: (01473) 250333
Fax: (01473) 286877

GIDDINGS, Dr Philip James, MA, D PHIL
5 Clifton Park Rd, Caversham, Reading, Berks RG4 7PD [OXFORD] *1985– b* 5 Apr 1946; *educ* Sir Thomas Rich's Sch Glouc; Worc and Nuff Colls Ox; Lect in Public Admin Ex Univ 1970–72; Lect in Politics Reading Univ from 1972; Rdr; M Dioc Syn from 1974; M Bp's Coun from 1979; Lay Vc-Pres Dioc Syn from 1989; M BSR 1991–96, Exec Ctee 1992–96; M Crown Appts Commn 1992–97; M Gen Syn Panel of Chairmen 1995–96; Vc-Chmn Dioc Ho of Laity from 1995 *Tel:* (01189) 543892 (Home)
(01189) 318207 (Office)
Fax: (01189) 753833
e-mail: P.J.Giddings@reading.ac.uk

GILBERT, Mr Tom
104 Church Rd, Gorleston, Great Yarmouth NR31 6LS [NORWICH] *1998– b* 25 Apr 1934; *educ* Ruskin Coll Ox; Newc Univ; Social Responsibility Officer Nor BSR from 1981 *Tel:* (01493) 604220

GILLETT, Canon David Keith, BA, M PHIL
16 Ormerod Rd, Stoke Bishop, Bristol BS9 1BB [BRISTOL] *1985–88, 1990– b* 25 Jan 1945; *educ* Wellingborough Gr Sch; Leeds Univ; Oak Hill Th Coll; C St Luke Watford 1968–71; Sec Pathfinders and CYFA N Area 1971–74; Tutor and Dir of Extension Studies St Jo Coll Nottm 1974–79; Chr Renewal Centre Rostrevor Nn Ireland 1979–82; V St Hugh Lewsey Luton 1982–88; Prin Trin Coll Bris from 1988; Hon Can Bris Cathl from 1991; M BM 1991–96; M Inter Faith Consultancy Grp 1991–96; M ABM from 1995; M CMEAC from 1995 and Vocations Ctee from 1997
Tel: 0117–968 2803 (Office)
0117–968 2646 (Home)
Fax: 0117–968 7470
e-mail: david.gillett@trinity-bris.ac.uk

GILLINGHAM, Mr (George) Michael, B SC, AKC, PGCE
5 Feversham Way, Taunton, Som TA2 8SD [BATH AND WELLS] *1990– b* 15 Oct 1949; *educ* Weston-super-Mare Gr Sch; K Coll Lon; Tchr Bp Fox's Community Sch from 1971; M Bp's Coun; M Dioc Coun for Min
Tel: (01823) 270044
e-mail: bishfox@rmplc.co.uk

GILLINGS, Ven Richard John, BA
Vicarage, Robins Lane, Bramhall, Stockport SK7 2PE [ARCHDEACON OF MACCLESFIELD] *1980– b* 17 Sep 1945; *educ* Sale Co Gr Sch; St Chad's Coll Dur; Linc Th Coll; C St Geo Altrincham 1970–75; P-in-c St Thos Stockport 1975–77; R St Thos Stockport 1977–83 and P-in-c St Pet's Stockport 1978–83; R Priory Tm Par

Birkenhead 1983–93; RD Birkenhead 1985–93; Hon Can Ches Cathl 1992–94; V St Mich Bramhall from 1993; Adn of Macclesfield from 1994
Tel: 0161–439 2254
Fax: 0161–439 0878

GILPIN, Ven Richard Thomas
Blue Hills, Bradley Rd, Bovey Tracey, Newton Abbot TQ13 9EU [ARCHDEACON OF TOTNES] **1995–** *b* 25 Jul 1939; *educ* Ashburton Coll; Lich Th Coll; C Whipton 1963–66; C Tavistock and Gulworthy 1966–69; V 1973–91; V Swimbridge 1969–73; Preb Ex Cathl from 1982; Sub-Dean Ex Cathl from 1992; RD Tavistock 1987–90; DDO 1990–91; Adv for Voc and DDO 1991–96; Sub-Dean Ex Cathl 1992–96; Adn of Totnes from 1996
Tel: (01626) 832064
Fax: (01626) 834947

GLOUCESTER, Bishop of, Rt Revd David Edward Bentley, BA
Bishopscourt, Pitt St, Gloucester GL1 2BQ **1993–** *b* 7 Aug 1935; *educ* Gt Yarmouth Gr Sch; Leeds Univ; Westcott Ho Th Coll; C St Ambrose Bris 1960–62; C H Trin w St Mary Guildf 1962–66; R Headley, Bordon 1966–73; R Esher 1973–86; RD Emly 1977–82; Hon Can Guildf Cathl 1980–86; Chmn Guildf Dioc CSR 1980–86; Chmn Guildf Dioc Ho of Clergy 1977–86; Bp of Lynn 1986–93; Chmn ACCM Candidates Ctee 1987–93; M ABM and Bp's Ctee for Min from 1987; Bp of Glouc from 1993; Chmn ABM Min Development and Deployment Ctee from 1995; Vc-Chmn ABM from 1995
Tel: (01452) 524598
Fax: (01452) 310025
e-mail: bshpglos@star.co.uk

GNANADOSS, Miss Vasantha Berla Kirubaibai, B SC
242 Links Rd, London SW17 9ER [SOUTHWARK] **1990–** *b* 25 Jun 1951; *educ* Portsm S Gr Sch; Birkbeck Coll Lon; Solicitors Dept of Metropolitan Police Service
Tel: 0181–769 3515

GODFREY, Mr Paul Alexander, MA, PGCE
15 Irwin Rd, Bedford MK40 3UL [ST ALBANS] **1995–** *b* 3 May 1957; *educ* K Edw VI Sch Southn; St Edm Hall Ox; Scripture Union Evang from 1991
Tel: (01234) 342868
e-mail: paulg@scriptureunion.org.uk

GOLDIE, Ven David, MA
60 Wendover Rd, Aylesbury HP21 9LW [ARCHDEACON OF BUCKINGHAM] **1990–** *b* 20 Dec 1946; *educ* Glas Academy; Glas Univ; Fitzw Coll Cam; Westcott Ho Th Coll; C Ch Ch Swindon 1970–73; C Troon 1973–75; Mission Priest Irvine New Town and R Ardrossan 1975–82; Priest Missr Milton Keynes 1982–86; RD Milton Keynes 1986–90; V Ch the Cornerstone Milton Keynes 1986–98; Borough Dean Milton Keynes 1990–98; Chmn Ho of Clergy Dioc Syn 1991–98; M Local Unity Ctee from 1993; M CTE and CCBI from 1996; Adn of Buckingham from 1998
Tel: (01296) 423269
Fax: (01296) 397324
e-mail: archdbuc@oxford.anglican.org

GOLDING, Ven Simon Jefferies, QHC
Room 201, Victory Building, HM Naval Base, Portsmouth PO1 3LS [ARCHDEACON FOR THE ROYAL NAVY] **1997–** *b* 30 Mar 1946; *educ* Bp's Sch Poona; HMS Conway; Brasted Place Th Coll; Linc Th Coll; C Wilton 1974–77; Chapl RN from 1977; Chapl of the Fleet and Adn for the Royal Navy 1997–98; Adn for the Royal Navy from 1998
Tel: (01705) 727904
Fax: (01705) 727112

GOOD, Ven Kenneth Roy, BD, AKC
62 Palace Rd, Ripon, N Yorks HG4 1HA [ARCHDEACON OF RICHMOND] *b* 28 Sep 1941; *educ* Stamford Sch; K Coll Lon; St Boniface Coll Warminster; C St Pet Stockton on Tees 1967–70; Miss to Seamen Chapl Antwerp 1970–74; Kobe 1974–79; Asst Gen Sec Miss to Seamen 1979–85; Hon Can Kobe from 1985; V Nunthorpe 1985–93; RD Stokesley 1989–93; Adn of Richmond from 1993
Tel and Fax: (01765) 604342

GORE, Mr Philip, BA, M I MGT
12 Ellesmere Rd, Morris Green, Bolton BL3 3JT [MANCHESTER] **1985–** *b* 15 Nov 1957; *educ* Smithills Gr Sch Bolton; Hull Univ; Chmn Philip Gore (Bolton) Ltd from 1981; Dir Silverwood Forestry Ltd from 1991; pt Tutor and Lect; M Bp's Coun; DBF, Trust and Fin Ctee; M Dioc Bd of Min; M Parsonages and Ch Building Ctee; M Dioc Bd of Patronage; M Ch Soc Trust from 1998; Lay Chmn Deane Dny Syn from 1990; Chmn Makerfield Conservative Assn from 1992; M Dios Commn 1991–95; M Coun Ch Soc 1992–95; M BSR Exec from 1996; JP
Tel: (01204) 63798 (Home)
(01204) 363000 and 524262 (Office)
Fax: (01204) 659750
e-mail: 106071.2156@compuserve.com

GRANGER, Mrs Penelope Ruth, BA, CERT ED
88 Queen Edith's Way, Cambridge CB1 4PW [ELY] **1980–** *b* 14 Jul 1947; *educ* Nor High Sch for Girls; Univ of Sheff; Homerton Coll Cam; Postgraduate Student; M Gen Syn Stg Ctee 1985–90 and 1991–95;

Ch Commr 1983–98; M Ord of Women Steering Ctee 1987–94; M CCBI Assembly; M CTE Forum; M Coun Westcott Ho; Lay Vc-Pres Dioc Syn 1988–97; M Dioc Liturg Ctee   Tel: (01223) 246392
e-mail: p.r.granger@dial.pipex.com

GRANTHAM, Bishop of [SUFFRAGAN, LINCOLN] **Rt Revd Alastair Llewellyn John Redfern,** MA
Fairacre, 243 Barrowby Rd, Grantham, Lincs NG31 8NP b 1 Sep 1948; *educ* Bicester Sch; Ch Ch Ox; Trin Coll Cam; Westcott Ho Th Coll; C Tettenhall 1976–79; Lect in Ch Hist, Dir of Pastl Studies and Vc-Prin Ripon Coll Cuddesdon 1979–87; C All SS Cuddesdon 1983–87; Can Res Bris Cathl 1987–97; Can Theologian and Dir of Tr 1987–97; Moderator of Par Resource Tm 1995–97; M ABM Initial Minl Educ Ctee; Moderator Archbps Dip for Rdrs; Bp of Grantham from 1997; Dean of Stamford from 1998
Tel: (01476) 564722
Fax: (01476) 592468

GREENWOOD, Mr Nigel Desmond, M PHIL, M ED, C CHEM, FRSC, FIBMS, FRIPHH
47 Broomfield, Adel, Leeds LS16 7AD [RIPON] 1990– *b* 18 Oct 1944; *educ* Leeds Gr Sch; Leeds Univ; Leic Univ; Posts in Public Health Services and Further Educ – Leeds Public Health Dept 1962–68; Tobacco Research Coun 1968–69; United Leeds Hosps 1969–74; Wigston CFE 1974–77; Keighley Tech Coll 1978–80; Airedale and Wharfedale Coll 1981–95; Educ and Tr Consultant from 1995; M Gen Syn Bd of Educ and F and HE Ctee; Sch Gov; M Dioc Bd of Educ and F and HE Ctee; M Nn Ord Course Gov Coun
Tel: 0113–261 1438

GRIEVE, Dr (Annie) Sheila, MB, CH B
14 Moseley Rd, Cheadle Hulme, Cheshire SK8 5HJ [CHESTER] 1985– *b* 27 Mar 1937; *educ* Blackpool Collegiate Sch for Girls; Man Univ; General Practitioner (Man Family Practitioner Ctee)   *Tel:* 0161–485 2096

GRIMLEY, Very Revd Robert William, MA
The Deanery, 20 Charlotte St, Bristol BS1 5PZ [DEAN OF BRISTOL] *b* 26 Sep 1943; *educ* Derby Sch; Ch Coll Cam; Wadham Coll Ox; Ripon Hall Th Coll; C Radlett 1968–72; Chapl K Edw Sch Birm 1972–84; V St Geo Edgbaston 1984–97; Exam Chapl to Bp of Birm 1988–97; Vc-Chmn Dioc Pastl Ctee 1996–97; Dean of Bris from 1997; Bps' Inspector of Th Colls from 1998   *Tel:* 0117–926 2443 (Home)
0117–926 4879 (Office)
Fax: 0117–925 3678

GRIMSBY, Bishop of [SUFFRAGAN, LINCOLN] **Rt Revd David Tustin,** MA, DD
Bishop's House, Church Lane, Irby-on-Humber, Grimsby, N E Lincs DN37 7JR 1990– *b* 12 Jan 1935; *educ* Solihull Sch; Magd Coll Cam; Cuddesdon Th Coll; C Stafford 1960–63; Asst Gen Sec CE Coun on Foreign Relns and C St Dunstan-in-the-W Lon 1963–67; V St Paul Wednesbury 1967–71; V Tettenhall Regis 1971–79; RD of Trysull 1976–79; Bp of Grimsby from 1979; Can and Preb of Brampton in Linc Cathl from 1979; Chmn Angl/Lutheran Internat Commn 1986–98; Pres Angl-Lutheran Society from 1986; Chmn Conversations with German Evangelical Ch 1987–88; Chmn Conversations with Nordic/Baltic Lutheran Chs 1989–92; Chmn Porvoo Chs Contact Grp 1992–98; M CCU 1991–98; Chmn CCU 1992–98; M Joint Pastl Consultative Grp with RC Bishops from 1993
Tel: (01472) 371715
Fax: (01472) 371716

GRUNDY, Ven Malcolm Leslie, BA, AKC
Vicarage, Gisburn, Clitheroe, Lancs BB7 4HR [ARCHDEACON OF CRAVEN] 1998– *b* 22 Mar 1944; *educ* Sandye Place Sch; Mander Coll Bedf; K Coll Lon; Open Univ; St Boniface Th Coll Warminster; C St Geo Doncaster 1969–72; Chapl Sheff Ind Miss 1972–74; Sen Chapl 1974–80; Dioc Dir of Educ and Community Lon 1980–86; TR Huntingdon 1986–91; Hon Can Ely Cathl 1987–94; Dir AVEC 1991–94; Adn of Craven from 1994; Commis Owo, Nigeria from 1994
Tel: (01200) 445214
Fax: (01200) 445816
e-mail: adcraven@gisburn.u-net.com

GUILDFORD, Bishop of, Rt Revd John Warren Gladwin, MA, DIP TH
Willow Grange, Woking Rd, Guildford GU4 7QS 1990– *b* 30 May 1942; *educ* Hertford Gr Sch; Chu Coll Cam; St Jo Coll Dur; C St Jo the B Kirkheaton 1967–71; Tutor St Jo Coll Dur 1971–77; Director of Shaftesbury Project 1977–82; Sec to Gen Syn BSR 1982–88; Preb of St Paul's Cathl 1984–88; Provost of Sheff 1988–94; Bp of Guildf from 1994   *Tel:* (01483) 590500
Fax: (01483) 590501
e-mail: bishopjohn@cofeguildford.org.uk

GUILLE, Ven John Arthur, B TH, CERT ED
1 The Close, Winchester, Hants SO23 9LS [ARCHDEACON OF BASINGSTOKE] 1990– *b* 21 May 1949; *educ* Guernsey Gr Sch; Ch Ch Coll Cant; Southn Univ; Sarum and Wells Th Coll; C Chandlers Ford 1976–80; P-in-c St John Bournemouth 1980–83; P-in-c St Mich Bournemouth 1983–84; V St John w St Mich Bournemouth 1984–89; R St Andre de la Pommeraye

Guernsey 1989–90; Adn of Basingstoke from 1998; M Dioc Syn from 1977; M Guernsey LEA from 1990; Vc-Dean Guernsey 1996–98; M Dioc Policy and Programme Ctee from 1997
Tel and *Fax:* (01962) 869374

HALL, Revd (Alfred) Christopher, MA
The Knowle, Philcote St, Deddington, Banbury OX15 0TB [OXFORD] **1972–85, 1994–** *b* 10 Dec 1935; *educ* Bromsgrove Sch; Trin Coll Ox; Westcott Ho Th Coll; C St Cyprian Frecheville 1961–64; C St Jo Dronfield 1964–67; V St Matt Smethwick 1967–75; Can Res Man and Adult Educ Offcr 1975–83; World Development Offcr 1976–89; V St Pet Bolton 1983–90; Co-ordinator Chr Concern for One World from 1990; M BM from 1996; Sec Li Tim Oi Foundation; Sec Dioc World Development Advs Core Grp; Editor SYNEWS; M Dioc BSR and PWM; M Co Ecum Coun; Adv Christian Aid SE Asia; M Nat Coun World Development Movement
Tel and *Fax:* (01869) 338225
e-mail: achall@mail.globalnet.co.uk

HALL, Ven John Barrie
Tong Vicarage, Shifnal, Shropshire TF11 8PW [ARCHDEACON OF SALOP] *b* 27 May 1941; *educ* Sarum and Wells Th Coll; C St Edw Cheddleton 1984–88; V Rocester 1988–94; V Rocester and Croxden w Hollington 1994–98; RD Uttoxeter 1991–98; Adn of Salop and V Tong from 1998; M DBF; M DAC; M Dioc Pastl Ctee
Tel: (01902) 372622
Fax: (01902) 374021

HALL, Canon John Robert, BA
Church House, Great Smith Street, London SW1P 3NZ [GENERAL SECRETARY, BOARD OF EDUCATION AND NATIONAL SOCIETY] *1984–92 b* 13 Mar 1949; *educ* St Dunstan's Coll Catford; St Chad's Coll Dur; Cuddesdon Th Coll; Head of RE Malet Lambert High Sch Hull 1971–73; C St Jo the Divine Kennington 1975–78; P-in-c All SS S Wimbledon 1978–84; V St Pet Streatham 1984–92; Exam Chapl to Bp of S'wark 1988–92; M Gen Syn Bd of Educ 1991–92; Chmn FCP 1990–93; Dioc Dir of Educ Blackb 1992–98; Hon Can Blackb Cathl 1992–94 and from 1998; Res Can Blackb Cathl 1994–98; M Nat Soc Coun 1997–98; Gen Sec Bd of Educ and Nat Soc from 1998; *Tel:* 0171–340 0283
Fax: 0171–233 1094
e-mail: john.hall@boeangel.demon.co.uk

HALL, Mrs Viviane Maria, BA
The Knowle, Philcote St, Deddington, Banbury, Oxon OX15 0TB [OXFORD] **1994–** *b* 20 Jun 1937; *educ* Surbiton High Sch; Southn Univ; Housewife; CAB Adviser; M Dioc Buildings Ctee; Bp's Visitor
Tel and *Fax:* (01869) 338225
e-mail: achall@mail.globalnet.co.uk

HALSTEAD, Mrs Joy (Josephine Elizabeth Grace)
23 Heath Drive, Chelmsford, Essex CM2 9HB [CHELMSFORD] **1995–** *b* 28 Sep 1940; *educ* Holy Cross Convent, George, S Africa; Trustee Visitor John Henry Keene Memorial Homes from 1985; Lay Chmn Chelmsf N Dny; M Dioc Conf Management Ctee from 1989; M Bp's Coun from 1991; M Dioc Pastl Ctee from 1991; M Dioc Vacancy-in-See Ctee from 1991
Tel: (01245) 354924

HANDLEY, Ven (Anthony) Michael
40 Heigham Rd, Norwich NR2 3AU [ARCHDEACON OF NORFOLK] *1980–85, 1990–95 b* 3 Jun 1936; *educ* Spalding Gr Sch; Selw Coll Cam; Chich Th Coll; Asst C Thorpe Episcopi 1962–66; P-in-c Fairstead Estate, King's Lynn 1966–72; V Hellesdon 1972–81; RD Nor N 1979–81; Adn of Nor 1981–93; Adn of Norfolk from 1993
Tel: (01603) 611808
Fax: (01603) 618954

HANFORD, Revd (William) Richard, MA, BD, LLM
Ewell Vicarage, Church St, Ewell, Epsom, Surrey KT17 2AQ [GUILDFORD] **1990–** *b* 19 Nov 1938; *educ* Dyffryn Gr Sch Port Talbot; Keble Coll Ox; St Steph Ho Ox; C St Martin Roath 1963–66; C Llantwit Major 1967–68; Succ Llan Cathl 1968–72; Chapl Llan Coll of Educ 1969–72; Chapl RN 1972–76; Hon Chapl Gibraltar Cathl 1974–76; C St Pet Brighton 1977–78; Can Res and Prec Guildf Cathl 1978–83; Tutor and Lect in Liturgy Chich Th Coll 1980–86; V Ewell from 1983; M Cathls Fabric Commn for England from 1991; M Coun SE Inst for Th Educ from 1994
Tel: 0181–393 2643

HANNAFORD, Revd Dr Robert, B ED, MA, PH D
25 Goudhurst Close, Canterbury, Kent CT2 7TU [CANTERBURY] **1997–** *b* 20 Feb 1953; *educ* Tamar Sec Sch Plymouth; St Luke's Coll Ex; Ex Univ; St Steph Ho Ox; Sch Tchr 1977–78; C St Jas Ex 1980–83; St Luke's Chapl and Lect Ex Univ 1983–88; Tutor in Doct St Steph Ho Ox and M Th Faculty Ox Univ 1989–92; Sen Lect in RS Ch Ch Coll Cant from 1992; M CU Coun; Chmn CU Publications Ctee and Tufton Books; SE Regional V Soc of the Holy Cross
Tel: (01227) 784148 (Home)
(01227) 767700 Ext 2587 (Office)
Fax: (01227) 767531 (Office)
e-mail: r.hannaford@cant.ac.uk

HANSON, Mr Brian John Taylor, CBE, LLM, FRSA
Church House, Great Smith St, London SW1P 3NZ [REGISTRAR AND LEGAL ADVISER TO THE GENERAL SYNOD, JOINT REGISTRAR OF THE PROVINCES OF CANTERBURY AND YORK AND LEGAL ADVISER TO THE ARCHBISHOPS' COUNCIL] *b* 23 Jan 1939; *educ* Hounslow Coll; Law Society's Coll of Law; Univ of Wales; Solicitor (admitted 1963) and Ecclesiastical Notary; In private practice 1963–65; Solicitor w Ch Commrs from 1965; Asst Legal Adv Gen Syn 1970–75; Solicitor to Gen Syn 1975–77; Legal Adv to Gen Syn from 1977; Joint Registrar of the two Provinces from 1980; Registrar of the Conv of Cant from 1982; Legal Adv to the Abps' Coun from 1998; M Legal Adv Commn from 1980 (Sec 1970–86); Guardian, Nat Shrine of Our Lady of Walsingham from 1984; M Coun of St Luke's Hosp for Clergy from 1985; Fell Woodard Corp and Sch Govnr from 1987; M Coun of Ecclesiastical Law Soc from 1987; Gov Pusey Ho from 1993; Abp's Nominee on St Luke's Research Foundn from 1998; Chmn Chich Dioc Bd of Patronage from 1998
 Tel: 0171–898 1366 (Office)
 (01444) 881890 (Home)

HANSON, Mrs (Margaret) Faith, T CERT
Ivy House, Gressenhall, Dereham, Norfolk NR20 4EU [NORWICH] **1995–** *b* 18 Apr 1945; *educ* Derby High Sch; Whitelands Coll Lon; Rdr from 1992; Housewife
 Tel: (01362) 860339

HARDMAN, Revd Christine Elizabeth, B SC, M TH
Vicarage, Letchmore Rd, Stevenage, Herts SG1 3JD [ST ALBANS] **1998–** *b* 27 Aug 1951; *educ* Qu Eliz Girls' Gr Sch Barnet; City of Lon Poly; Westmr Coll Ox; St Alb Dio Minl Tr Scheme; Dss St Jo B Markyate 1984–87; C 1987–88; Course Dir St Alb Minl Tr Scheme 1988–96; V H Trin Stevenage from 1996; M Dioc Syn; M Bp's Coun
 Tel: (01438) 353229
 Fax: (01438) 314127
 e-mail: chris@hardman.demon.co.uk

HARDY, Mr Antony Scott
1 Millbank, London SW1P 3JZ [STOCK EXCHANGE INVESTMENTS MANAGER, CHURCH COMMISSIONERS] *b* 10 Feb 1940; On staff of Ch Commrs from 1988; Stock Exchange Investments Manager from 1992
 Tel: 0171–898 1122

HARDY, Mr Brian James, B SC, FCA
1 Millbank, London SW1P 3JZ [MANAGEMENT ACCOUNTANT, CHURCH COMMISSIONERS] *b* 27 Nov 1952; *educ* Jarrow Gr Sch; Hull Univ; On staff of Ch Commrs since 1988
 Tel: 0171–898 1667
 e-mail: brian.hardy@chucomm.org.uk

HARPER, Prebendary Horace Frederic
Dresden Vicarage, 22 Red Bank, Longton, Stoke-on-Trent, Staffs ST3 4EY [LICHFIELD] **1995–** *b* 25 Jan 1937; *educ* Wolv Gr Sch; Keele Univ; Lichf Th Coll; C Stoke-upon-Trent 1960–63; C Fenton 1963–66; V Ch Ch Coseley 1966–75; V Trent Vale 1975–88; V Dresden from 1988; P-in-c Normacot from 1994; Preb Lichf Cathl from 1996; M Dioc Syn; M Dioc Bd of Min; M Vacancy-in-See Ctee; Dny Vocations Adv; Sch Gov various schs from 1966
 Tel: (01782) 321257

HARRIS, Mr Jeremy Michael, BA, PGCE
Lambeth Palace, London SW1P 7JU [ARCHBISHOP OF CANTERBURY'S SECRETARY FOR PUBLIC AFFAIRS] *b* 31 Oct 1950; *educ* Sevenoaks Sch; Clare Coll Cam; Nottm Univ; Journalist and Broadcaster 1974–98; BBC Madrid Correspondent 1982–86; BBC Moscow Correspondent 1986–89; BBC Washington Correspondent 1990–95; Radio Presenter Radio 4 1995–98; Abp of Cant's Sec for Public Affairs from 1998
 Tel: 0171–928 8282 (Office)
 0171–749 5658 (Home)
 Fax: 0171–261 9836
 e-mail: jeremy.harris@lampal.clara.net

HARRIS, Mrs Pat (Patricia Ann), T DIP
Vicarage, Elm Rd, Stonehouse, Glos GL10 2NP [GLOUCESTER] **1985–** *b* 29 May 1939; *educ* St Julian's High Sch Newport; Trin Coll Carmarthen; Tchr; Dioc Pres MU 1980–85; Pres World Wide MU (Cen Pres) 1989–94; M Bp's Coun from 1985; MU Rep on Womens Nat Commn from 1994; Hon Fell Trin Coll Carmarthen from 1995; Awarded Cross of St Aug 1995; Vc-Chmn BM from 1996; M PWM Ctee; M CMEAC 1994–96; M Abps Bd of Examiners from 1996; M Coun BRF and Publications Ctee from 1997; Chmn Carl Dioc Infrastructure Review Grp 1997–98
 Tel and *Fax:* (01453) 822332

HARRISON, Ven Peter Reginald Wallace, BA
Brimley Lodge, 27 Moulscroft Rd, Beverley HU17 7DX [ARCHDEACON OF EAST RIDING] *b* 22 Jun 1939; *educ* Charterhouse; Selw Coll Cam; Ridley Hall Th Coll; C St Luke Barton Hill Bris 1964–69; Chapl Greenhouse Trust 1969–77; Dir Northorpe Hall Trust 1977–84; TR Drypool 1984–98; AD E Hull 1988–98; Hon Can York Minster from 1994; Adn of E Riding from 1998
 Tel: (01482) 881659

HARRISON, Dr Jamie (James Herbert), MB, BS, MRCGP, MA
5 Dunelm Court, South St, Durham DH1 4QX [DURHAM] **1995–** *b* 17 Sep 1953; *educ* Stockport Gr Sch;

Magd Coll Ox; K Coll Hosp Medical Sch Lon; General Medical Practitioner Durham City from 1990; M Coun St Jo Coll Dur; Rdr
Tel: 0191–384 8643 (Home)
0191–386 4285 (Office)
Fax: 0191–386 5934 (Office)

HARRISON, Mrs Rachel Elizabeth, NNEB
Vicarage, Glaisdale, Whitby, N Yorks YO21 2PL [YORK] **1995–** *b* 18 Feb 1953; *educ* Northn Sch for Girls; Northn CFE; NVQ Childcare Assessor; M Dioc Syn; Hon Sec Chs Together in N York Moors
Tel: (01947) 897214

HASELOCK, Canon Jeremy Matthew, BA, B PHIL, MA
27 The Close, Norwich NR1 4DZ [CHICHESTER] **1995–** *b* 20 Sep 1951; *educ* St Nic Gr Sch Northwood; York Univ; York Cen for Medieval Studies; St Steph Ho Ox; C St Gabr Pimlico 1983–86; C St Jas Paddington 1986–88; Dom Chapl to Bp of Chich 1988–91; V Boxgrove 1991–98; Dioc Liturg Adv Chich 1991–98; Preb of Fittleworth and Canon Chich Cathl from 1994; Can Res and Prec Nor Cathl from 1998; M Liturg Commn from 1996
Tel: (01603) 764383 (Office)
Tel and *Fax:* (01603) 619169 (Home)
e-mail: jeremy@haselock.force9.co.uk

HAWES, Ven Arthur John, BA, DPS, DIP L&A
Archdeacon's House, Northfield Rd, Quarrington, Lincs NG34 8RT [ARCHDEACON OF LINCOLN] *b* 31 Aug 1943; *educ* City of Ox High Sch for Boys; Birm Univ; UEA; Chich Th Coll; C St Jo Kidderminster 1968–72; P-in-c St Richard Droitwich 1972–76; R Alderford w Attlebridge and Swannington 1976–92; Chapl Hellesdon & Dav Rice Hosps and Yare Clinic 1976–92; RD Sparham 1981–91; Mental Health Act Commr for Eng and Wales 1986–94; Hon Can Nor Cathl 1988–95; R St Faith King's Lynn 1992–95; Chmn Dioc BSR 1990–95; Adn of Linc from 1995; Can and Preb Linc Cathl from 1995; Adv on Mental Health Matters to BSR Social Policy Ctee from 1989; Patron Mind from 1996; Pres Lincs Rural Housing Assn from 1998
Tel: (01529) 304348
Fax: (01529) 304354

HAWES, Revd Andrew Thomas, BA, MA
Vicarage, Church Lane, Edenham, Bourne, Lincs PE10 0LS [LINCOLN] **1995–** *b* 18 Dec 1954; *educ* De Aston Sch Market Rasen; Sheff Univ; Em Coll Cam; Westcott Ho Th Coll; C Gt Grimsby TM 1980–84; V Lutton w Gedney Drove End 1984–89; V Edenham w Witham-on-the-Hill from 1989; RD Beltisloe from 1997; Warden Edenham Regional Ho
Tel: (01778) 591358
e-mail: EdenhamRH@aol.com

HAWKER, Ven Alan Fort, BA, DIP TH, PACTA
2 Louviers Way, Swindon, Wilts SN1 4DU [ARCHDEACON OF SWINDON] **1990–** *b* 23 Mar 1944; *educ* Buckhurst Hill Co High Sch; Hull Univ; Clifton Th Coll; C St Leon Bootle 1968–71; C-in-c Em Fazakerley 1971–73; V St Paul Goose Green 1973–81; TR S Crawley TM 1981–98; Preb of Bury and Can Chich Cathl 1991–98; RD E Grinstead 1994–98; M CBF; Adn of Swindon from 1998; Chmn Working Grp on Clergy Discipline and Reform of Ecclesiastical Courts from 1994; M Gen Syn Stg Ctee from 1995; M Gen Syn Policy Ctee from 1995; M CBF Budget Ctee from 1995; M DBF; M Bp's Coun
Tel: (01793) 644556
Fax: (01793) 495352

HAWKER, Ven Peter John
St Andrew's, Promenadengasse 9, 8001 Zurich, Switzerland [ARCHDEACON IN SWITZERLAND, DIOCESE IN EUROPE] *b* 10 Jun 1937; *educ* Yeovil Gr Sch; Ex Univ; Wycliffe Hall Th Coll; Asst Chapl St Ursula Berne 1970–76; Chapl 1976–89; Lect Berne Univ 1976–89; Adn in Switzerland from 1986; Chapl St Andr Zurich from 1989
Tel: 00–41–1–261–22–41

HAWLEY, Revd John Andrew, BD, AKC, CERT TH
Rectory, 16A Oxford Rd, Dewsbury, W Yorks WF13 4JT [WAKEFIELD] **1996–** *b* 27 Apr 1950; *educ* Ecclesfield Gr Sch; K Coll Lon; Wycliffe Hall Th Coll; C H Trin Hull 1974–77; C Bradf Cathl 1977–80; V All SS Woodlands, Doncaster 1980–91; TR Dewsbury from 1991; Vc-Chmn Dioc BMU 1991–96; Chm Dioc Communications Grp from 1996;
Tel: (01924) 465491
(01924) 457057
Fax: (01924) 458124

HAWTHORN, Ven Christopher John, MA
Park House, Rosehill, Great Ayton, Middlesbrough TS9 6BH [ARCHDEACON OF CLEVELAND] **1987–90, 1995–** *b* 29 Apr 1936; *educ* Marlboro Coll; Qu Coll Cam; Ripon Hall Ox; C St Jas Sutton, York 1962–66; V St Nic Kingston-upon-Hull 1966–72; V Coatham 1972–79; V St Martin Scarborough 1979–91; RD Scarborough 1982–91; Can and Preb York Minster from 1987; Chmn NE Ord Course Coun from 1994; Adn of Cleveland from 1991; M CE Pensions Bd from 1998
Tel: (01642) 723221
Fax: (01642) 724137

HAWTIN, Ven David Christopher, MA
4 The Woodwards, New Balderton, Newark, Notts NG24 3GG [ARCHDEACON OF NEWARK] **1983–** *b* 7 Jun 1943; *educ* K Edw VII Sch Lytham St Annes; Keble Coll Ox; Wm Temple Th Coll, Rugby; Cuddesdon Th Coll; C St Thos Pennywell, Sunderland 1967–71; C St Pet's

Stockton 1971–74; P-in-c CD St Andr Leam Lane, Gateshead 1974–79; R Washington Grp Min and LEP 1979–88; ACCM Selector 1987–92; Dioc Ecum Officer Dur 1988–92; M BMU 1986–90; M BCC 1985–90; M CTE from 1990; M CTE Enabling Grp from 1991; Dep Moderator CTE Forum from 1995; M CCBI from 1990; Consultant to CCU 1991–96, M Local Unity Ctee from 1997; Chmn Dioc Bd of Educ from 1993; Chmn E Midlands Consortium for Tr and Educ for Min from 1996; Gen Syn Rep on Gov Body E Midlands Minl Tr Course from 1997; Adn of Newark from 1992   *Tel:* (01636) 814490 (Office)
(01636) 612249 (Home)
Fax: (01636) 815882 (Office)
(01636) 611952 (Home)

HEBBLETHWAITE, Mr (John) David, BA
Church House, Great Smith St, London SW1P 3NZ [ADMINISTRATIVE SECRETARY, GENERAL SYNOD] *b* 16 Aug 1944; *educ* Bradf Gr Sch; Nottm Univ; Birm Univ; On staff of Ch Commrs 1966–84 (seconded to Gen Syn 1977–79); Seconded to Gen Syn from 1984; Sec Liturg Commn; Sec Dios Commn; Sec Ho of Clergy; Sec Appts Sub Committee
Tel: 0171–898 1364

HEDGES, Mr Christopher, B SC
51 High St, Old Portsmouth, Hants PO1 2LU [PORTSMOUTH] **1990–** *b* 30 Sep 1958; *educ* Hreod Burna Sen High Sch, Swindon; Nottm Univ; Production Engineer 1980–84; Product Manager 1984–88; Tr Manager 1988–91; Househusband 1991–97; Civil Servant from 1997; M Bp's Coun
Tel: (01705) 731282
Fax: (01705) 366928
e-mail: hedges@newnet.co.uk

HENDERSON, Mr (Robin Alan) Louis, BA
Lambeth Palace, London SE1 7JU [PUBLIC AFFAIRS OFFICER TO THE ARCHBISHOP OF CANTERBURY] *b* 12 Nov 1949; *educ* Univ Coll Sch Hampstead; Merton Coll Ox; On staff of Ch Commrs from 1975; Seconded to ABM/Ho of Bps 1991–95; Sec to Bps' Inspectorate of Th Colls and Courses 1995–96; Seconded to Lambeth Palace 1995; Public Affairs Officer from 1995   *Tel:* 0171–928 8282
Fax: 0171–261 9836

HEREFORD, Bishop of, Rt Revd John Keith Oliver
The Bishop's House, The Palace, Hereford HR4 9BN **1980–85, 1990–** *b* 14 Apr 1935; *educ* Collyer's Sch Horsham; Westmr Sch; G & C Coll Cam; Westcott Ho Th Coll; C Hilborough Grp 1964–68; Chapl Eton Coll 1968–72; TR S Molton Grp 1973–82; TR Cen Ex 1982–85; Adn of Sherborne and P-in-c W Stafford w Frome Billett 1985–90; Bp of Heref from 1990; Chmn ABM from 1993   *Tel:* (01432) 271355
Fax: (01432) 343047

HERTFORD, Bishop of [SUFFRAGAN, ST ALBANS] **Rt Revd Robin Jonathan Norman Smith,** MA
Hertford House, Abbey Mill Lane, St Albans, Herts AL3 4HE *b* 14 Aug 1936; *educ* Bedf Sch; Worc Coll Ox; Ridley Hall Th Coll; C St Marg Barking 1962–67; Chapl Lee Abbey 1967–72; V St Mary Chesham 1972–80; RD Amersham 1970–82; R Gt Chesham 1980–90; Bp of Hertford from 1990
Tel: (01727) 866420
Fax: (01727) 811426

HESSELWOOD, Mr Anthony Peter, FCA
38 Bromley Rd, Shipley, W Yorks BD18 4DT [BRADFORD] **1995–** *b* 16 Nov 1949; *educ* Belle Vue Boys Sch Bradf; Partner Firth Parish Chartered Accountants from 1979; Chmn DBF from 1982; Hon Lay Can Bradf Cathl 1994–98; M Bp's Coun; Treas Scargill Ho
Tel: (01274) 585613 (Home)
(01484) 422560 (Office)
Fax: (01484) 513523 (Office)

HEWETSON, Ven Christopher, MA
8 Queen's Park Rd, Chester CH4 7AD [ARCHDEACON OF CHESTER] *b* 1 Jun 1937; *educ* Shrewsbury Sch; Trin Coll Ox; Chich Th Coll; V St Pet Didcot 1973–82; R Ascot Heath 1982–90; Chapl St Geo Sch Ascot 1985–88; RD Bracknell 1986–90; P-in-c E Trin Headington Quarry 1990–94; RD Cowley 1994; Adn of Chester from 1994   *Tel:* (01244) 675417
Fax: (01244) 681959

HIGGINBOTHAM, Mr John Eagle, MA
16 Holmfield Ave, Stoneygate, Leicester LE2 2BF [LEICESTER] **1995–** *b* 28 Feb 1933; *educ* Bradf Gr Sch; Trin Hall Cam; Leic Univ; Housemaster and Hd of Classics Lancing Coll 1957–80; Hdmaster Leic Gr Sch 1980–89; Lect (TESOL) Leic Univ 1990–92; Freelance Lect, Writer and Course Dir from 1992; M Dioc Bd of Educ 1982–89; Bp's Nominee on Dioc Syn from 1985; M Ecum Ctee Bp's Coun from 1989; Frank Fisher Fell for study of Angl-RC Relations 1989–90; M Friends of Ang Centre in Rome from 1990; Vc-Chmn Leic Dioc Prayer Book Soc from 1992; Chmn Leic Dioc Forward in Faith from 1993; M Coun Friends of the Diocese of Uruguay; Fell Woodard Corp from 1996; Dioc Rep Qu Victoria Clergy Fund from 1996; Dioc Rep CBF from 1997; M Friends of Dio of Gibraltar in Eur from 1997
Tel: 0116–270 9462

HIGGINS, Very Revd Michael John, LL B, PH D
The Deanery, The College, Ely, Cambs CB7 4DN [DEAN OF ELY] **1994–** *b* 31 Dec 1935; *educ* Whitchurch Gr Sch Cardiff; Birm Univ; Cam Univ; Harvard Univ; Ridley Hall Th Coll; C Ormskirk 1965–68; Selection Sec ACCM 1968–74; V Frome 1974–80; R Preston 1980–91; Dean of Ely from 1991   *Tel:* (01353) 667735
Fax: (01353) 665658

HIGTON, Revd Tony (Anthony Raymond), BD
Rectory, Hawkwell, Hockley, Essex SS5 4JY [CHELMSFORD] **1985–** *b* 23 Dec 1942; *educ* Long Eaton Gr Sch; Lon Univ; Oak Hill Th Coll; C Ch Ch Newark 1967–70; C St Barn Cheltenham 1970–75; R Hawkwell from 1975; Founder Action for Biblical Witness to Our Nation; Co-Director Time Ministries Internat; Chmn Coun CMJ   *Tel:* (01702) 203870 (Home)
Fax: (01702) 543544
e-mail: tonyhigton@compuserve.com

HILARY, Sister , CSMV, B MUS, DIP TH, DIP ED
Chapter Office, 20 Dean's Yard, London SW1P 3PA [RELIGIOUS COMMUNITIES, SOUTH, LAY] **1995–** *b* 11 Mar 1925; *educ* Barnsley High Sch; Birm Univ; St Anne's Coll Ox; Tchr UK 1947–49, 1952–56, 1963–69; S Africa 1958–63; Pastl Tm St Paul's Cathl from 1985; Pastl Asst Westmr Abbey from 1988
Tel: 0171–222 5152
0171–928 4844
Fax: 0171–233 2072

HILL, Revd Peter, B SC, M TH
Vicarage, 18 Crookdole Lane, Calverton, Nottingham NG14 6GF [SOUTHWELL] **1993–** *b* 4 Feb 1950; *educ* Bp Gore Gr Sch Swansea; Man Univ; Nottm Univ; Wycliffe Hall Ox; Sheetmetal worker 1971–72; Schoolteacher 1972–78; Dep Hd Beaches Primary Sch Sale 1978–81; C Porchester 1983–86; V Huthwaite 1986–95; P-in-c Calverton from 1995; RD S'well from 1997; Chair Dioc Ho of Clergy from 1997; M Bp's Coun; M Dioc Fin Ctee   *Tel:* 0115– 965 2552
e-mail: Peter.Hill@icthus.dircon.co.uk

HIND, Mr Timothy Charles, MA, FCII
Plowman's Corner, The Square, Westbury-sub-Mendip, Wells, Som BA5 1HJ [BATH AND WELLS] **1995–** *b* 10 Aug 1950; *educ* Watford Boys Gr Sch; St Jo Coll Cam; Various posts at AXA Sun Life Services from 1972; M Bp's Coun; Chmn Dioc Vacancy-in-See Ctee; M Dioc Bd of Educ 1995–97; M Board of Educ (Schs and Colls) 1995–97; M CE Pensions Bd; M CE Pensions Bd Investment and Finance Ctee 1996–97; Lay Chmn Axbridge Dny Syn 1984–91; M Dioc Bd of Patronage 1986–94; Vc-Chair Bd of Govs Kings of Wessex Community Sch 1996–99
Tel: (01749) 870356 (Home)
0117–989 9000 Ext 3631 (Office)
e-mail: Tim.Hind@sunlife.co.uk

HOARE, Sir Timothy Edward Charles Bt, OBE, MA
10 Belitha Villas, London N1 1PD [LONDON] **1970–** *b* 11 Nov 1934; *educ* Radley Coll; Worc Coll Ox; Birkbeck Coll Lon; Army NS; Staff M Pathfinders and CYFA 1958–64; Staff M St Helen's Bishopsgate 1964–69; M Ch Assembly 1960–70; M ACCM 1971–86; M Chadwick Commn on Ch and State; Chmn, Law of Marriage Grp; M Crown Appts Commn 1987–92; CE Delegate to WCC Canberra 1991; Personnel Consultant from 1970, Dir Career Plan Ltd; Dir New Metals and Chemicals Ltd; M Stg Ctee from 1981; M Sen Ch Appts Review Grp; Chmn Appts Sub-Ctee; Chmn Steering Grp on Clergy Conditions of Service; Treas Lon Dioc Fund; Chmn Dioc Ho of Laity; M Coun St Jo Coll Dur   *Tel:* 0171–607 7359 (Home)
0171–242 5775 (Office)

HODGE, Canon Michael Robert
Rectory, Rectory Drive, Bidborough, Tunbridge Wells, Kent TN3 0UL [SYNODICAL SECRETARY, CONVOCATION OF CANTERBURY] *1970–95 b* 24 Apr 1934; *educ* Rugby Sch; Pemb Coll Cam; Ridley Hall Th Coll; Asst C Ch Ch Harpurhey Man 1959; Asst C St Mark Layton Blackpool 1959–62; V Old St Geo Stalybridge 1962–67; V Cobham w Luddesdowne and Dode 1967–81; R Bidborough 1981–99; Chmn Dioc Ho of Clergy 1985–94; Chmn Dioc Bd of Patronage 1989–99; Chmn DAC 1991–99; Synodical Sec, Conv of Cant from 1995   *Tel* and *Fax:* (01892) 528081
e-mail: michaelh@braxton.ndirect.co.uk

HOLDAWAY, Revd Stephen Douglas, BA
Rectory, Westgate, Louth, Lincs LN11 9YE [LINCOLN] **1988–** *b* 3 Oct 1945; *educ* Hornchurch Gr Sch; Hull Univ; Ridley Hall Th Coll; C St Chris Thornhill Southn 1970–73; Ind Chapl Redditch and P-in-c St Phil Webheath 1973–78; Ind Chapl Linc 1978–93; Co-ordinator Linc City Centre Grp Min 1981–93; TR Louth from 1993; RD Louthesk from 1995
Tel: (01507) 603213
e-mail: Stephen.Holdaway@btinternet.com

HOLDEN, Dr John Thomas, B SC, PH D
199 Musters Rd, West Bridgford, Nottingham NG2 7DQ [SOUTHWELL] **1985–** *b* 8 Sep 1938; *educ* Chiswick Co Gr Sch; Man Univ; Dur Univ; Research Fell Johns Hopkins Univ 1963–64; Lect Univ of Nottm 1964–91; Vis Prof Northwestern Univ 1979; Sen Lect Univ of Nottm from 1991; M Dios Commn; M Bp's Coun
Tel: 0115–981 2043
e-mail: john.holden@nottingham.ac.uk

HOLDRIDGE, Ven Bernard Lee
Fairview House, 14 Armthorpe Lane, Doncaster DN2 5LZ [ARCHDEACON OF DONCASTER] *b* 24 Jul 1935; *educ*

Thorne Gr Sch; Lich Th Coll; C Swinton 1967–71; V St Jude Doncaster 1971–81; R Rawmarsh w Parkgate 1981–88; RD Rotherham 1986–88; V Worksop Priory 1988–94; Adn of Doncaster from 1994; Guardian Shrine of Our Lady of Walsingham from 1997
Tel: (01302) 325787
Fax: (01302) 760493

HOLE, Very Revd Derek Norman
The Provost's House, 1 St Martin East, Leicester LE1 5FX [PROVOST OF LEICESTER] *b* 5 Dec 1933; *educ* Public Cen Sch Plymouth; Linc Th Coll; C St Mary Magd Knighton Leic 1960–62; Chapl to Abp of Cape Town 1962–64; C St Nic Kenilworth 1964–67; R St Mary V Burton Latimer 1967–73; V St Jas Leic 1973–92; Hon Can Leic Cathl 1983–92; RD Christianity S 1983–92; Chapl to HM The Queen 1985–92; Chmn Dioc Ho of Clergy and Vc-Pres Dioc Syn 1986–94; Prov of Leic from 1992
Tel: 0116–262 5294
Fax: 0116–262 5295
01426 251511 (Pager)
e-mail: dnhole@leicester.anglican.org

HOLLIMAN, Ven John James, BA, QHC
Ministry of Defence Chaplains (Army), Trenchard Lines, Upavon, Wilts SN9 6BE [DEPUTY CHAPLAIN GENERAL AND ARCHDEACON TO THE ARMY] **1995–** *b* 12 Aug 1944; *educ* St D Coll Lamp; C Tideswell Derby 1967–71; CF from 1971; Dep Chapl Gen and Adn to the Army from 1995
Tel: (01980) 615802

HOLMES, Mr Nigel Craven, BA, PGCE
Woodside, Great Corby, Carlisle CA4 8LL [CARLISLE] **1985–** *b* 25 Jan 1945; *educ* Rossall Sch Fleetwood; Dur Univ; Joined BBC Radio 1968; BBC Radio Producer 1970–97; M CECC 1986–95; M CACLB from 1993; M BM from 1996; Rdr; Chmn Editorial Ctee CRC from 1997; Chmn Ho of Laity Dioc Syn from 1997
Tel: (01228) 560617
Fax: (01228) 562372
e-mail: nigel@gt-corby.demon.co.uk

HOOPER, Ven Michael Wrenford, BA
The Archdeacon's House, The Close, Hereford HR1 2NG [ARCHDEACON OF HEREFORD] **1993–** *b* 2 May 1941; *educ* Crypt Sch Glouc; St D Coll Lampeter; St Steph Ho Th Coll; C St Mary Bridgnorth 1966–70; V Minsterley and R Habberley 1970–81; R Leominster 1981–85; TR Leominster 1985–97; RD Leominster 1981–97; Adn of Heref from 1997; Can Res Heref Cathl from 1997
Tel: (01432) 272873

HOPGOOD, Mr Richard Simon, BA
Church House, Great Smith St, London SW1P 3NZ [DIRECTOR OF POLICY AND DEPUTY SECRETARY GENERAL, ARCHBISHOPS' COUNCIL] *b* 7 Oct 1952; *educ* Ch Hosp; Wadh Coll Ox; On staff of Ch Commrs from 1977; Dep Sec (Policy and Planning) 1994–98; Dir of Policy and Dep Sec Gen Abps' Coun from 1999
Tel: 0171–898 1787

HOPKINSON, Revd Benjamin Alaric, MA
Vicarage, 21 Thornton Rd, Stainton, Middlesbrough TS8 9BS [YORK] **1980–85, 1995–** *b* 24 Feb 1936; *educ* Marlboro Coll; Trin Coll Ox; Chich Th Col.; C St Luke Pallion, Sunderland 1961–66; C Ascen Bulawayo 1966–67; P-in-c St Pet Mmadinare, Botswana 1967–70; Urban and Ind Missr Selebi-Pikwe, Botswana 1970–73; Pr Missr Sherwood and Carrington 1974–77; V Lowdham w Gunthorpe and Caythorpe 1977–85; R Whitby 1985–95; V Stainton-in-Cleveland and Hilton-in-Cleveland from 1995; Chapl to Cleveland Constabulary; Chair Dioc CSR; M Dioc CMEAC
Tel and Fax: (01642) 590423

HOPKINSON, Ven Barney (Barnabas John), MA
Sarum House, High St, Urchfont, Devizes, Wilts SN10 4QH [ARCHDEACON OF WILTS] **1995–** *b* 11 May 1939; *educ* Em Sch; Trin Coll Cam; Linc Th Col.; C All SS and Martyrs Langley 1965–67; C Gt St Mary Cam 1967–70; Asst Chapl Charterhouse 1970–75; TV Preshute 1975–81; RD Marlborough 1977–81; TR Wimborne Minster and Holt 1981–86; RD Wimborne 1985–86; Adn of Sarum from 1986; P-in-c Stratford-sub-Castle 1987–98; Adn of Wilts from 1998
Tel: (01380) 840373
Fax: (01380) 848247
e-mail: adsarum@compuserve.com

HOPKINSON, Revd William Humphrey, B SC, MA, M SC, M PHIL
Diocesan House, Lady Woottons Green, Canterbury, Kent CT1 1NQ [CANTERBURY] **1990–94, 1997–** *b* 4 Jun 1948; *educ* Herbert Strutt Gr Sch Belper; Univ Coll Lon; Dur Univ; Nottm Univ; Man Poly; Cranmer Hall Th Coll; C Normanton 1977–80; C Sawley 1980–82; pt Tutor St Jo Coll Nottm 1981–82; V Birtles 1982–87; Dir Pastl Studies N Ord Course 1982–94; Dir of Course Development 1990–94; CME Officer and Dir POT Chester 1987–94; V St Mich Tenterden 1994–96; Dir Min and Tr from 1994 *Tel:* 0410 033575 (Mobile)
Fax: (01227) 450964
e-mail: hpknsn@surfaid.org

HORSFIELD, Prebendary Robert Alan, BA, MA
Vicarage, The Hurst, Cleobury Mortimer, Kidderminster, Worcs DY14 8EG [HEREFORD] **1994–** *b* 5 Sep 1938; *educ* Batley Gr Sch; Leeds Univ; Inst of Historical Research Lon; Coll of the Resurr Mirfield; C St Jas Lower Gornal 1963–66; C H Trin Bridlington Quay and Sewerby w Marton; P-in-c St Matt Fairfield 1968–73; R Scartho 1973–79; V Cleobury Mortimer w

Hopton Wafers from 1979, now R United Benefice; RD Ludlow 1989–96; Preb Heref Cathl from 1992; M Bp's Coun from 1989; M DBF and Exec Ctee 1989–98; M BM from 1997   *Tel and Fax:* (01299) 270264

HORSHAM, Bishop of [AREA BISHOP, CHICHESTER] **Rt Revd Lindsay Goodall Urwin,** OGS
21 Guildford Rd, Horsham RH12 1LU b 13 Mar 1956; *educ* Camberwell Gr Sch Victoria, Australia; Ripon Coll Cuddesdon; C St Pet Walworth 1980–83; V St Faith Red Post Hill 1983–88; Dioc Missr Chich 1988–93; Bp of Horsham from 1993; Nat Chmn CU from 1995; UK Provincial OGS from 1996
Tel: (01403) 211139
Fax: (01403) 217349
e-mail: bishhorsham@clara.net

HOULDING, Revd David Nigel Christopher, AKC
All Hallows' House, 52 Courthope Rd, London NW3 2LD [LONDON] **1995–** *b* 25 Jul 1953; *educ* K Sch Cant; K Coll Lon; St Aug Coll Cant; Lay Chapl Chr Medical Coll Vellore, S India 1976–77; C All SS Hillingdon 1977–81; C St Alb Holborn w St Pet Saffron Hill 1981–85; V St Steph w All Hallows Hampstead from 1985   *Tel:* 0171–267 7833
0171–267 6317

HOWDEN, Canon John Travis, RIBA
Vicarage, The Street, Pleshey, Chelmsford, Essex CM3 1HA [CHELMSFORD] **1997–** *b* 12 Oct 1940; *educ* Sevenoaks Sch; Beckenham Gr Sch; Regent St Poly Sch of Architecture; Sarum Th Coll; C St Matt Gillingham 1969–72; TV Banbury 1972–73; Producer BBC Radio 1973–81; Sen Tr Officer BBC Radio 1981–86; R Doddinghurst and V Mountnessing 1986–91; Warden Pleshey (Chelmsf Dioc Ho of Retreat) and P-in-c Pleshey from 1991; M Dioc Millennium Grp; Chair APR; Vc-Chair Nat Retreat Assoc; Dir Pleshey Course for Spiritual Directors
Tel: (01245) 237251
(01245) 237236
Fax: (01245) 237594

HUDSON, Mr John, BA, M ED, PGCE
4 The Brambles, Barrow, Clitheroe, Lancs BB7 9BF [BLACKBURN] **1990–** *b* 27 Jan 1935; *educ* Percy Jackson Gr Sch Adwick-le-Street; Sheff Univ; Univ of Alberta Canada; Sch Tchr 1958–65; Educational Administration 1965–92; Rtd   *Tel:* (01254) 824481

HUDSON, Miss Julia
Lambeth Palace, London SE1 7JU [ADMINISTRATIVE SECETARY, LAMBETH PALACE] On staff of Ch Commrs from 1977; Seconded as Asst Sec CUF 1988–91; Head of Personnel 1994–96; Admin Sec Lambeth Palace from 1996   *Tel:* 0171–928 8282

HUDSON, Canon (John) Leonard, AKC
The Clergy House, Church St, Royston, Barnsley, S Yorks S71 4QZ [WAKEFIELD] **1995–** *b* 10 Feb 1944; *educ* The Crossley and Porter Gr Sch Halifax; K Coll Lon; St Boniface Th Coll Warminster; C St Jo Bapt Dodworth 1967–70; Prec Wakef Cathl 1970–73; V St Sav Ravensthorpe 1973–80; V St Jo Bapt Royston from 1980; RD Barnsley from 1993; P-in-c St Jo Ev Carlton from 1990; Chmn DAC; Chmn Wakef Cathl FAC; Chmn Wakef Dioc Forward in Faith; Hon Can Wakef Cathl from 1997   *Tel:* (01226) 722410

HUGHES, Mr Howell Harris, MA, MSI (DIP)
Church Commissioners, 1 Millbank, London SW1P 3JZ [SECRETARY, CHURCH COMMISSIONERS] Sec to Ch Commrs from 1998   *Tel:* 0171–898 1785

HULL, Bishop of [SUFFRAGAN, YORK] **Rt Revd Richard Michael Cokayne Frith,** MA
Hullen House, Woodfield Lane, Hessle HU13 0ES **1995–98** *b* 8 Apr 1949; *educ* Marlboro Coll; Fitzw Coll Cam; St Jo Coll Nottm; C Mortlake w E Sheem 1974–78; TV Thamesmead 1978–83; TR Keynsham 1983–92; Adn of Taunton 1992–98; Bp of Hull from 1998
Tel: (01482) 649019
Fax: (01482) 647449

HULME, Bishop of [SUFFRAGAN, MANCHESTER] [NOT APPOINTED AT TIME OF GOING TO PRESS]

HUMPHERY, Mr James Hambrook
Pound Cottage, Middle Woodford, Salisbury, Wilts SP4 6NR [SALISBURY] **1993–** *b* 13 Dec 1954; *educ* Charterhouse; Mgr The Hill Drug Scheme Britain-Nepal Medical Trust 1973–75; M DBF from 1991; Lawyer from 1981   *Tel:* (01722) 412512

HUNT, Dr Matthew Noel Seyfang, MA, BM, B CH, MRCGP, DCH, DRCOG
49 Corby Ave, Lakeside, Swindon, Wilts SN3 1PR [BRISTOL] **1995–** *b* 21 Oct 1960; *educ* Dulwich Coll; Trin Coll Cam; Madg Coll Ox; Ho Surgeon Qu Eliz Hosp Birm 1985–86; Ho Physician Jo Radcliffe Hosp Ox 1986; GP Voc Trainee Swindon 1986–89; GP Prin Victoria Cross Surgery Swindon from 1990
Tel: (01793) 523928 (Home)
0973 155141 (Mobile)
Fax: (01793) 497526
e-mail: mnsh@compuserve.com

HUNTINGDON, Bishop of [SUFFRAGAN, ELY] **Rt Revd John Robert Flack,** BA
14 Lynn Rd, Ely, Cambs CB6 1DA **1994–97** *b* 30 May 1942; *educ* Hertf Gr Sch; Leeds Univ; Coll of Resurr Mirf; C St Bart Armley 1966–69; C St Mary Northn 1969–72; V Chapelthorpe 1972–81; V Ripponden

1981–85; V Brighouse 1985–92; TR 1988–92; RD Brighouse and Elland 1986–92; Hon Can Wakef Cathl 1989–97; Chmn Dioc Ho of Clergy 1988–92; Adn of Pontefract 1992–97; Bp of Huntingdon from 1997
Tel: (01353) 662137
Fax: (01353) 669357
e-mail: suffragan@ely.anglican.org

INGRAM, Mrs Joanna Mary
25 The Woodlands, Melbourne, Derbys DE73 1DP [DERBY] 1980– *b* 9 Sep 1950; *educ* Broxbourne Gr Sch; M CCC 1986–96; M CBF from 1990; M CBF Publishing Ctee; M Gen Syn Stg Orders Ctee from 1996; M Faculty Rules Ctee; M DBF; M DAC; Sec Dioc Min Ctee; M Dioc Bd of Patronage
Tel: (01332) 862548

INWOOD, Ven Richard Neil, MA, B SC, BA
2 Vicarage Gardens, Rastrick, Brighouse, W Yorks HD6 3HD [ARCHDEACON OF HALIFAX] 1985–95, 1997– *b* 4 Mar 1946; *educ* Burton-on-Trent Gr Sch; Univ Coll Ox; St Jo Coll Nottm; C Ch Ch Fulwood Sheff 1974–78; C (Dir of Pastoring) All So Langham Place 1978–81; V St Luke Bath 1981–89; R Yeovil w Kingston Pitney 1989–95; Preb Wells Cathl 1990–95; Ch Commr 1991–95; Hon Treas Simeon's Trustees/Hyndman Trust; Adn of Halifax from 1995; Chmn Coun St Jo Coll Nottm from 1998
Tel: (01484) 714553
Fax: (01484) 711897
e-mail: richard@inwoodr.surfaid.org

ISAAC, Canon David Thomas, BA
Education Office, Cathedral House, St Thomas St, Portsmouth, Hants PO1 2HA [PORTSMOUTH] 1995– *b* 20 Sep 1943; *educ* Rhondda Gr Sch; Univ Coll of Wales, Abth; Cuddesdon Th Coll; C Llandaff Cathl 1967–71; C St Mary Swansea 1971–73; Prov Youth Chapl Ch in Wales 1973–77; V Pontardawe 1977–79; Ripon Dioc Youth Officer 1979–83; Nat Youth Officer Gen Syn Bd of Educ 1983–90; Res Can and Dir of Educ Portsm from 1990
Tel: (01705) 822053
Fax: (01705) 295081

ISON, Revd Hilary Margaret, BA, DIP TH, DPS
12 The Close, Exeter EX1 1EZ [EXETER] 1995– *b* 4 Mar 1955; *educ* Bilston Girls High Sch; Leic Univ; St Jo Coll Nottm; Par Worker NSM SS Nic and Luke Deptford 1980–87; Dn NSM 1987–88; C NSM St Phil Cov 1988–90; Par Dn Rugby TM 1990–93; Chapl Ex and Distr Hospice from 1993; Chair Assoc of Hospice Chapls from 1997
Tel: (01392) 275745

JACKSON, Monsignor Michael Joseph, STL
Presbytery, Cawley Rd, Chichester, W Sussex PO19 1XB [ECUMENICAL REPRESENTATIVE (ROMAN CATHOLIC CHURCH)] 1998– *b* 13 Apr 1951; *educ* St Pet Sch Guildf; St Edm Coll Cam; Ven English Coll Rome; Asst Pr St Mary Worthing 1977–79; Lect in Th St Jo Seminary Wonersh 1979–85; Doctoral Student St Edm Coll Cam 1985–87; Sec Ctee for Chr Unity Catholic Bps' Conf of England and Wales 1988–96; RC Co-Sec English ARC 1988–92; Chmn Commissioning Ctee CTE 1989–90; Chair Enabling Grp CTE 1993–95; Par Pr Chichester from 1996
Tel: (01243) 782343
Fax: (01243) 782332

JACKSON, Mrs Shirley Angela
Batemans, Much Hadham, Herts SG10 6DA [ST ALBANS] 1985– *b* 23 Aug 1933; *educ* Herts and Essex High Sch for Girls; Insolvency Practitioner; Chair Bishop's Stortford Dny Pastl Ctee from 1983; M DBF from 1986; M Bp's Coun from 1986; M Property Ctee from 1989; M Glebe Ctee from 1989; Pres Trad Anglicans St Albs dio 1985–92; M CBF from 1988; Gov Whitelands Coll from 1989; M Educ Working Party from 1992; Gen Syn M MU Cen Coun 1990–95; M Coun and Publications and Publishing Ctee Soc of Practitioners of Insolvency; Fell SPI from 1994; M Environment Agency Adv Panel 1994–95; Chair SPI Smaller Practices Ctee from 1997; M Pensions Regulations Steering Ctee
Tel: 0171–430 2321
e-mail: sjackson@begbenor.co.uk

JACOB, Ven William Mungo, LL B, MA, PH D
4 Cambridge Place, London W8 5PB (Home), The Old Deanery, Dean's Court, London EC4V 5AA (Office) [ARCHDEACON OF CHARING CROSS AND ARCHDEACON AT LONDON HOUSE] *b* 15 Nov 1944; *educ* K Edw VII Sch King's Lynn; Hull Univ; Linacre Coll Ox; Edin Univ; Ex Univ; St Steph Ho Th Coll; C Wymondham 1970–73; Asst Chapl Ex Univ 1973–75; Dir of Pastl Studies Sarum and Wells Th Coll 1975–80; Vc-Prin 1977–80; Sec Ctee for Th Educ ACCM 1980–85; Warden Linc Th Coll 1986–96; Adn of Charing Cross and Adn at The Old Deanery from 1996
Tel: 0171–937 2560 (Home)
0171–248 6233 (Office)
e-mail: archdeacon.charingcross@dlondon.org.uk

JÄGERS, Mrs Maryon Patricia, SRN, SCM
Hoefbladhof 61, 3991 GG Houten, The Netherlands [EUROPE] 1985– *b* 22 Jan 1942; *educ* St Chris Sch; The Hall, Beckenham, Kent; Dioc Elector for Utrecht 1980–90; M Bp's Coun 1980–85; M Dioc Syn for Europe from 1985; M BM 1985–90; M and Vc-Chmn CCU and Exec Ctee from 1990; Lay Chmn Adnry NW Europe from 1989; M Conversations w German Evan Chs 1987–88; M Conversations w Nordic and Baltic Lutheran Chs 1989–92; Gen Syn Delegate to WCC Canberra 1991; M Cen Ctee WCC from 1991; M Gen Syn Panel of Chmn 1991; Lay Vc-Pres Dioc

Syn; M Dioc Vacancy-in-See Ctee from 1993; Lay Chmn Dioc Ho of Laity, M Stg Ctee; M Bp's Coun from 1995; M Gen Syn Stg Ctee from 1996; M Gen Syn Business Sub Ctee from 1996; Commiss to Bp of Ballarat Australia from 1996; Gen Syn Delegate to WCC Assembly Harare 1998 and Decade in Solidarity of Women Harare 1998   *Tel:* 0031–30 6371780
0655 858337 (Mobile)
Fax: 0031–30 6351034

JAMES, Dr Richard Hugh, M SC, MB, BS, FRCA, DTM&H, D OBSTRCOG, DA, AKC
36 Ridgeway, Oadby, Leicester LE2 5TN [LEICESTER] **1995–** *b* 21 Dec 1945; *educ* St Lawr Coll Ramsgate; K Coll Lon; K Coll Hosp; Medical Missry Burundi 1971–74; Tr Posts in Anaesthesia K Coll Hosp 1974–80; Consultant Anaesthetist Leic R Infirmary from 1980; M Dioc Syn from 1985   *Tel:* 0116–271 4596

JAMES, Mrs Sarah Alison Livingston
Canton House, New St, Painswick, Glos GL6 6XH [GLOUCESTER] **1985–** *b* 4 Aug 1938; *educ* St Leon Sch St Andrews Fife; Chmn *Home & Family* Editorial Ctee 1982–86; MU Dioc Pres (Roch) 1980–85; MU Cen Vc-Pres 1986–91, MU Trustee 1995–97; Chmn Dioc MU Money Advice Service from 1998; Dir Highway Journeys from 1998; Lay Chmn Bromley Dny Syn 1984–90; Rdr; Wrdn Rdrs Roch Dio 1989–95; Vc-Chair CRC from 1995; M ABM; Ctee for Min Among Deaf People   *Tel* and *Fax:* (01452) 812419

JARROW, Bishop of [SUFFRAGAN, DURHAM]
Rt Revd Alan Smithson, MA
The Old Vicarage, Hallgarth, Pittington, Durham DH6 1AB b 1 Dec 1936; *educ* Bradf Gr Sch; Qu Coll Ox; Qu Coll Birm; C Ch Ch Skipton 1964–68; C St Mary V w St Cross and St Pet Ox 1968–72; Chapl Qu Coll Ox 1969–72; Chapl Reading Univ 1972–77; V Bracknell 1977–84; Dir of Tr Inst Carl 1984–90; Can Res Carl Cathl 1984–90; Bp of Jarrow from 1990
Tel: 0191–372 0225
Fax: 0191–372 2326

JEFFERSON, Mr Timothy Paul, NCA
26 Allergate, Durham DH1 4ET [DURHAM] **1998–** *b* 18 Aug 1944; *educ* K Edw VII Sch Lytham; Lanc Coll of Agriculture; Dairy Farmer New Zealand 1979; Farm Manager Dur Coll of Agriculture 1980–89; Regional Manager (Internat Division) Milk Marketing Bd 1989–93; Manager (Internat Division) Pig Improvement Co 1993–94; Exec Officer Dur-Lesotho Link from 1994; M Dioc BMU; Ctee M Lesotho Dioc Assn
Tel: 0191–384 8385
Fax: 0191–386 2863
e-mail: TPJ@btinternet.com

JEFFERY, Mr Harry Ernest, B SC, FCA, FIIA
Stonetiles, Teddington, Tewkesbury, Glos GL20 8JA [WORCESTER] **1994–** *b* 1 Aug 1947; *educ* Cheltenham Gr Sch; N Glos Tech Coll; Reading Univ; Price Waterhouse & Co 1969–76; Lucas Industries plc 1976–87; Renishaw plc 1987–91; pt Longborough Holdings Ltd 1992–95; Chartered Accountant in Private Practice since 1991; M Bp's Coun
Tel: (01242) 620515
Fax: (01242) 620990

JENKINS, Ven David Thomas Ivor
Woodcroft, Levens, Kendal, Cumbria LA8 8NQ [ARCHDEACON OF WESTMORLAND AND FURNESS, SEC AND TREAS YORK CONV] **1978–85** *b* 3 Jun 1929; *educ* Maesteg Gr Sch; K Coll Lon; Asst C St Mark's Bilton, Rugby 1953–56; V St Marg Wolston, Cov 1956–61; Asst Dir of Relig Educ Dio Carl 1961–63; V St Barn Carl 1963–72; V St Cuth w St Mary Carl 1972–91; Hon Can of Carl 1975–91; Can Res Carl Cathl 1991–95; Sec Carl Dioc Syn and Bp's Coun 1972–95; Dioc Sec 1984–95; Sec DBF 1990–95; Sec and Treas Conv of York from 1986; Adn of Westmor and Furness from 1995; Hon Can Carl Cathl from 1995
Tel: (015395) 61281
Fax: (015395) 61217

JENNINGS, Ven David Willfred Michael, AKC
136 Broomfield Rd, Chelmsford CM1 1RN [ARCHDEACON OF SOUTHEND] **1997–** *b* 13 Jul 1944; *educ* Radley Coll; K Coll Lon; St Boniface Coll Warminster; C Walton Liv 1967–69; C Ch Ch Win 1969–73; V Hythe 1973–80; V St Edw Romford 1980–92; RD Havering 1985–92; Hon Can Chelmsf Cathl 1987–92; Adn of Southend from 1992   *Tel:* (01245) 258257
Fax: (01245) 250845
e-mail: a.southend@chelmsford.anglican.org

JENNINGS, Mrs Helen Marina, BA
14 Glenfield Rd, Banstead, Surrey SM7 2DG [ROCHESTER] **1995–** *b* 4 Jul 1973; *educ* Chatham Gr Sch; Univ of Kent; Post-Graduate Student; M Dioc Syn from 1995; M Bp's Coun and Stg Ctee from 1995; M CTE Forum from 1996; M CCU Local Unity Ctee from 1996; M Dioc Ecum Ctee from 1997; Delegate to WCC Forum 1998

JOHN, Canon Jeffrey Philip Hywel, MA, D PHIL
2 Harmsworth Mews, West Square, London SE11 4SQ [SOUTHWARK] **1995–** *b* 10 Feb 1953; *educ* Tonyrefall Gr Sch Rhondda; Hertf Coll Ox; BNC Ox; Magd Coll Ox; St Steph Ho Th Coll; C St Aug Penarth 1978–80; Asst Chapl Magd Coll Ox 1980–82; Chapl and Lect BNC Ox 1982–84; Fell and Dean of Div Magd Coll Ox 1984–91; V H Trin Eltham 1991–97; M Gen Syn Stg Ctee and Appts Sub Ctee from 1995; M Exec

Affirming Catholicism Grp in Gen Syn from 1995; Can Chan and Can Th S'wark Cathl and Bp's Adv for Min from 1997; M Dioc Syn; M Dioc Min Policy Ctee; Exam Chapl to Bp of Worc
Tel: 0171–403 8686 (Office)
Fax: 0171–403 4770
e-mail: jeffrey.john@dswark.org.uk

JOHNS, Mrs Sue (Susan Margaret), HNC, M PHIL
103 Greenways, Eaton, Norwich NR4 6PD [NORWICH] **1990–** *b* 20 Mar 1955; *educ* Thorpe Gr Sch; Nor City Coll; Leeds Univ; Analytical Chemist and Public Analyst 1973–80; Housewife and Mother; Food Scientist MAFF CSL Food Science Lab Nor
Tel: (01603) 455029 (Home)
(01603) 259350 (Office)
e-mail: s.johns@csl.gov.uk

JOHNSON, Revd Malcolm Arthur, MA
St Martin in the Fields, Trafalgar Square, London WC2N 4JJ [LONDON] **1985–** *b* 8 Sep 1936; *educ* Framlingham Coll; Dur Univ; Cuddesdon Th Coll; C St Mark Portsea 1962–67; Chapl Qu Mary Coll Lon 1967–74; AD City of Lon 1985–90; R St Botolph Aldgate 1974–92; Master R Found of St Katharine 1993–97; Master Emer 1997; Bp of Lon's Adv on Past Care and Counselling from 1997
Tel: 0171–930 0089
Fax: 0171–839 5163

JOHNSON, Mr Nigel Ian, B SC
Church Commissioners, 1 Millbank, London SW1P 3JZ [OFFICIAL SOLICITOR, CHURCH COMMISSIONERS] *b* 23 Sep 1954; *educ* Oundle Sch; Univ of Wales; Coll of Law; Solicitor in private practice 1980–84; Solicitor Cheltenham & Gloucester Building Soc 1984–95, Chief Solicitor 1987–95; Chief Solicitor Cheltenham & Gloucester plc 1995–97; Official Solicitor Ch Commrs from 1997
Tel: 0171–898 1712
Fax: 0171–898 1798
e-mail: nigel.johnson@chucomm.org.uk

JOHNSTON, Mrs Mary Geraldine, BA, AKC, MIPD
56 Fairlawn Grove, Chiswick, London W4 5EH [LONDON] **1995–** *b* 8 Jan 1939; *educ* Barking Abbey Sch; K Coll Lon; Personnel Dept ICI 1961–66; Personnel Admin and Employee Relations Singer Co New York 1966–68; American Express New York 1968–70; Asst Personnel Manager and Staff Dev Manager Guinness Overseas 1970–80; Housewife from 1980; M Dioc Vacancy-in-See Ctee; M Eccles Jurisdiction Panel of Assessors; M CBF Staff Ctee; M Coun Corp of Ch Ho
Tel: 0181–995 6427

JONES, Mr David Arthur
St Chad's Vicarage, Hillmorton Rd, Wood End, Coventry CV2 1FY [COVENTRY] **1995–** *b* 3 Aug 1936; *educ* Abingdon Sch; RMA Sandhurst; RAF Staff Coll Bracknell; Army Officer 1957–85 (Colonel); Assoc Dir Oxfam 1985–93; Assoc Dir Internat Alert 1995–97; Dioc Adv CUF and Dioc Development Fund; M Bp's Coun; M DBF
Tel: (01203) 612909
Fax: (01203) 622834

JONES, Mr (James) Allan
30 Pimbo Rd, Kings Moss, St Helens, Merseyside WA11 8RD [LIVERPOOL] **1990–** *b* 21 Jan 1950; *educ* Central Secondary Boys' Sch St Helens; St Helens Coll of Tech; Production Control Clerk 1966–84; Navigator for Emergency Doctor Service from 1987; M Liv Dioc Bd of Educ 1991–94; Vc-Chmn Liv Branch Prayer Book Soc 1991–95; Dioc Lay Co-ordinator Forward in Faith from 1993; M Dioc BSR and Exec Ctee from 1998
Tel: (01744) 893367

JONES, Very Revd Keith Brynmor, MA
The Deanery, Exeter EX1 1HT [DEAN OF EXETER] *b* 27 Jun 1944; *educ* Ludlow Gr Sch; Selw Coll Cam; Cuddesdon Th Coll; C Limpsfield w Titsey 1969–72; Dean's V St Alb Abbey 1972–76; P-in-c St Mich Borehamwood 1976–79; TV 1979–82; V St Mary le Tower Ipswich 1982–96; RD Ipswich 1993–95; Dean of Ex from 1996
Tel: (01392) 252891 (Office)
(01392) 272697 (Home)

JONES, Revd Robert George, BA, MA
St Barnabas Rectory, Church Rd, Worcester WR3 8NX [WORCESTER] **1995–** *b* 30 Oct 1955; *educ* K Edw Sch Birm; Hatf Coll Dur Univ; Ripon Coll Cuddesdon; Ecum Inst Bossey; C H Innocents Kidderminster 1980–84; V St Fran 1984–92; TR St Barn w Ch Ch Worc from 1992; M Dioc BM; DAC Adv; M Magdesburg Partnership Grp
Tel and Fax: (01905) 23785

JONES, Miss Susan Margaret Shirley, LL B
Church Commissioners, 1 Millbank, London SW1P 3JZ [DEPUTY OFFICIAL SOLICITOR, CHURCH COMMISSIONERS] *educ* Alice Ottley Sch Worc; Bris Univ; Official Deputy Solicitor Ch Commrs from 1993
Tel: 0171–898 1704
Fax: 0171–976 8473
e-mail: sue.jones@chucomm.org.uk

JONES, Ven Trevor Pryce, B ED, B TH
St Mary's House, Church Lane, Stapleford, Hertford SG14 3NB [ARCHDEACON OF HERTFORD] *b* 24 Apr 1948; *educ* Dial Stone Sch Stockport; St Luke's Coll Ex; Southn Univ; Sarum and Wells Th Coll; C St Geo Glouc 1976–79; Warden Bp Mascall Centre Ludlow and M Heref Dioc Educ Tm 1979–84; DCO 1981–96; Sec Heref-Nurnberg European Ecum Partnership 1982–87; M Bp's Coun 1987–87; M Dioc Ecum Ctee 1985–87, Chmn 1996–97; TR Heref S Wye TM 1984–

97; OCF 1985–97; M Dioc Pastl/Minl Ctee 1996–97; Adn of Hertford from 1997; Chmn St Alb and Ox Min Course from 1998 *Tel:* (01992) 581629 *Fax:* (01992) 558745
e-mail: ad-hert@stalbansdioc.org.uk

JUDD, Very Revd Peter Somerset Margesson, MA
Provost's House, 3 Harlings Grove, Waterloo Lane, Chelmsford CM1 1YQ [PROVOST OF CHELMSFORD] *b* 20 Apr 1949; *educ* Charterhouse Sch; Trin Hall Cam; Cuddesdon Th Coll; C St Phil w St Steph Salford 1974–76; Chapl Clare Coll Cam 1976–81; Acting Dean Clare Coll 1980–81; TV Burnham w Dropmore, Hitcham and Taplow 1981–88; V St Mary V Iffley 1988–97; RD Cowley 1995–97; R and Prov of Chelms from 1997 *Tel:* (01245) 354318 (Home)
(01245) 294492 (Office)
Fax: (01245) 294499
e-mail: provost@chelmsford.anglican.org

JUDKINS, Mrs Mary, BA, PGCE, MA
Old Vicarage, 3 Church Lane, East Ardsley, Wakefield WF3 2LJ [WAKEFIELD] **1995–** *b* 29 Mar 1951; *educ* Leominster Gr Sch; Bris Univ; St Mary's Coll Cheltenham; Open Univ; Tchr in Bris and E Grinstead 1984–94; Supply Tchr; Homemaker/Mother; Lay Chmn Dioc Syn; Gen Syn Rep SAMS
Tel: (01924) 826802
e-mail: elephantmj@aol.com

KAVANAGH, Revd Michael Lowther, CPSYCHOL, BA, M SC
Bishopthorpe Palace, Bishopthorpe, York YO2 1QE [DOMESTIC CHAPLAIN TO THE ARCHBISHOP OF YORK] *b* 24 Sep 1958; *educ* Beverley Gr Sch; York Univ; Newc Univ; Leeds Univ; Coll of Resurr Mirfield; C Boston Spa 1987–91; V St Nic Beverley 1991–97; RD Beverley 1995–97; Dom Chapl to Abp of York and DDO from 1997; Sec York Ord Candidates Coun; M Dioc Syn *Tel:* (01904) 707021
Fax: (01904) 709204
e-mail: office@bishopthorpe.u-net.com

KEATING, Mr Colin Henderson
Whitridge House, Kirkwhelpington, Newcastle upon Tyne NE19 2SA [NEWCASTLE] **1990–** *b* 24 Dec 1930; *educ* Leamington Gr Sch; Managing Dir Family Engineering Business 1960–87; M Bp's Coun; Dioc Funding Adv 1987–97; M Dioc Syn from 1987; M DBF from 1987; M Dioc Deployment Grp from 1993
Tel: (01830) 540363

KEENS, Mrs Penny (Penelope Jane)
7 Pound Close, Wicken, Milton Keynes MK19 6BN [OXFORD] **1998–** *b* 22 Mar 1941; *educ* Felixstowe Coll; Hon Sec Bucks Historic Chs Trust from 1996; Lay Chmn Milton Keynes Dny Syn 1979–90 and from 1993; M Bp's Coun; M Dioc Pastl, Buildings, and Communications Ctees; M Chr Giving Grp; M Bd of Patronage *Tel* and *Fax:* (01908) 571232

KENSINGTON, Bishop of [AREA BISHOP, LONDON]
Rt Revd Michael John Colclough, BA
19 Campden Hill Square, London W8 8JY b 29 Dec 1944; *educ* Stanfield Tech High Sch; Leeds Univ; Cuddesdon Th Coll; C St Werburgh Burslem 1971–75; C St Mary S Ruislip 1975–79; V St Anselm Hayes 1979–86; AD Hillingdon 1985–92; P-in-c St Marg Uxbridge 1986–88; P-in-c St Andr w St Jo Uxbridge 1986–88; TR Uxbridge 1988–92; Adn of Northolt 1992–94; PA to Bp of Lon 1994–96; Dep Priest-in-Ordinary to HM The Queen 1995–96; Bp of Kensington from 1996; Chmn Lon and S'wark Dios Prisons and Penal Concerns Grp *Tel:* 0171–727 9818
Fax: 0171–229 3651
e-mail: bishop.kensington@dlondon.org.uk

KEY, Revd Robert Frederick, BA, DPS
St Andrew's Vicarage, 46 Charlbury Rd, Oxford OX2 6UX [OXFORD] **1995–** *b* 29 Aug 1952; *educ* Alleyn's Sch Dulwich; Bris Univ; Oak Hill Th Coll; C St Ebbe Ox 1976–80; Min St Patr Wallington 1980–85; V Eynsham and Cassington 1985–91; V St Andr Ox from 1991; M Coun Wycliffe Hall from 1985
Tel: (01865) 311212 (Office)
(01865) 311695 (Home)
Fax: (01865) 311320

KILNER, Canon Fred (Frederick James), MA
St Mary's Vicarage, St Mary's St, Ely, Cambs CB7 4ER [ELY] **1995–** *b* 20 Jan 1943; *educ* Millfield Sch; Qu Coll Cam; Ridley Hall Th Coll; C St Paul Harlow 1970–74; P-in-c St Steph Cam 1974–79; R Milton 1979–94; Hon Can Ely Cathl from 1988; TR Ely TM 1994–96; TR from 1996; Sec Ridley Hall Coun; M Bp's Coun; M Dioc Fin Ctee *Tel:* (01353) 662308

KING, Revd Malcolm Stewart
St Martin's Vicarage, Westcott Rd, Dorking, Surrey RH4 3DP [GUILDFORD] **1990–** *b* 9 Mar 1956; *educ* Kingston Gr Sch; Sarum and Wells Th Coll; C Farnham 1980–83; C Chertsey 1983–86; Chapl St Pet Hosp Chertsey 1983–86; V St Paul Egham Hythe 1986–91; TR Cove 1991–98; RD Aldershot 1993–98; V St Martin Dorking w Ranmore from 1998; Chmn Dioc Ho of Clergy from 1997; M Iona Community; M Bp's Coun from 1985; M Dioc Bd of Educ from 1986; Assessor under Ecclesiastical Jurisdiction Measure; M Dioc Pastl Ctee; M Dioc Bd of Patronage
Tel: (01306) 882875 (Home)
(01306) 886830 (Office)

KING, Canon Philip David, MA
Church House, Great Smith St, London Sw1P 3NZ [SECRETARY, GENERAL SYNOD BOARD OF MISSION] *b* 6 May 1935; *educ* Ch Hosp; Keble Coll Ox; Tyndale Hall Th Coll; C H Trin Redhill 1960–63; C-in-c St Pat Wallington 1963–68; V Ch Ch Fulham 1968–74; Gen Sec SAMS 1974–86; NSM H Trin Wallington 1974–86; M BMU 1982–86; M ACC Miss Issues and Strategy Adv Grp 1982–86; Chair BMU Miss Th Adv Grp 1985–89; V Ch Ch Roxeth and St Pet Harrow 1986–89; Sec BMU 1989–91; NSM Em Northwood 1989–97; Sec BM from 1991   *Tel:* 0171–898 1468

KING, Major Patrick Whittenham
10 Bridewell St, Walsingham, Norfolk NR22 6BJ [NORWICH] **1990–** *b* 21 Aug 1937; *educ* Marlborough Coll; RMA Sandhurst; Rtd Army Officer; M Dioc Liturg Ctee from 1987; Guardian Shrine of Our Lady of Walsingham from 1991; Lay Vc-Chmn Burnham and Walsingham Dny Syn from 1995; Bp's Furnishings Officer from 1995; M Steering Ctee Chr Initiation Gen Syn Liturg Commn; Trustee Ox Movement Anniversary Appeal from 1996; M DAC from 1996; M Dioc Red Chs Ctee from 1996; M Dioc Ctee for the Deaf from 1997   *Tel:* (01328) 820709
Fax: (01328) 820098

KINGSTON, Bishop of [AREA BISHOP, SOUTHWARK]
Rt Revd Peter Bryan Price, CERT ED, DPS
24 Albert Drive, London SW19 6LS b 17 May 1944; *educ* Glastonbury Sch Morden; Redland Coll of Educ Bris; Oak Hill Th Coll; Heythrop Coll Lon; Asst Tchr Ashton Park Sch Bris 1966–70; Sen Tutor Lindley Lodge Young People's Centre 1970; Head of RE Cordeaux High Sch Louth 1970–72; Community Chapl and C Ch Ch Portsdown 1974–78; Chapl Scargill Ho 1978–80; V St Mary Magd Addiscombe 1980–88; Can Chan S'wark Cathl 1988–91; Gen Sec USPG 1992–97; M Miss Agencies Working Grp 1992–93; M Angl Commn on Miss 1993–96; Bp of Kingston from 1997; M BM; M PWM; M Ch Commn on Miss; M Miss Th Adv Grp; M Gov Body SPCK; Chmn The Manna Soc   *Tel:* 0181–392 3742
Fax: 0181–392 3743
e-mail: bishop.peter@dswark.org.uk

KINSON, Mrs Wendy Elizabeth, BA
The Old Laundry, Maer, Newcastle, Staffs ST5 5EF [LICHFIELD] **1995–** *b* 24 Feb 1953; *educ* Bp Blackhall Sch Ex; Sussex Univ; Citizens Advice Bureau Adv from 1993; M Bp's Coun   *Tel:* (01782) 680613

KIRK, Revd Geoffrey, BA
St Stephen's Vicarage, Cressingham Rd, London SE13 5AG [SOUTHWARK] **1996–** *b* 10 Dec 1945; *educ* Coll of Resurr Mirfield; C St Aid Leeds 1972–74; C St Mark w St Luke Marylebone 1974–76; C St Jo Kennington 1977–79; C St Jo w St Jas Kennington 1979–81; P-in-c St Steph and St Mark Lewisham 1981–87; V from 1987   *Tel:* 0181–318 1295

KNAGGS, Mr Frank Aylesbury
52 Huntcliffe Gardens, North Heaton, Newcastle upon Tyne NE6 5UD [NEWCASTLE] **1985–** *b* 2 Oct 1937; *educ* Felsted Sch; Rutherford Coll of Tech; Production and Commercial Engineer and Mgr in power generation and aerospace industries 1956–93; Exec Officer CEEC from 1997; M CCU and Exec Ctee; M Bp's Coun; M DBF; M Dioc Bd of Miss and Social Responsibilty; Chmn Cruddas Youth Worker Project; Elder Bethel Chr Fell Newc
Tel: 0191–265 9603 (Home)
Tel and *Fax:* 0191–240 2084 (Office)
e-mail: CEEC@cablenet.co.uk

KNARESBOROUGH, Bishop of [SUFFRAGAN, RIPON] **Rt Revd Frank Valentine Weston,** MA
16 Shaftesbury Ave, Roundhay, Leeds LS8 1DT 1985–95 *b* 16 Sep 1935; *educ* Ch Hospital; Qu Coll Ox; Lich Th Coll; C St Jo B Atherton 1961–65; Chapl Coll of the Ascen Selly Oak 1965–69, Prin 1969–76; Prin Edin Th Coll 1976–82; Adn of Ox and Can of Ch Ch 1982–97; Bp of Knaresborough from 1997   *Tel:* 0113–266 4800
Fax: 0113–266 5649
e-mail: Knaresborough@btinternet.com

KNIGHT, Very Revd Alec (Alexander Francis), MA
The Deanery, 12 Eastgate, Lincoln LN2 1QG [DEAN OF LINCOLN] 1995–98 *b* 24 Jul 1939; *educ* Taunton Sch; Cath Coll Cam; Wells Th Coll; C Hemel Hempstead 1963–68; Chapl Taunton Sch 1968–74; Dir Bloxham Project 1975–81; Dir of Studies Aston Tr Scheme 1981–83; P-in-c Easton and Martyr Worthy 1983–91; Adn of Basingstoke 1990–98; Can Res Win Cathl 1991–98; Dean of Lincoln from 1998
Tel: (01522) 523608

KNOWLES, Very Revd Graeme Paul, AKC
The Deanery, Carlisle, Cumbria CA3 8TZ [DEAN OF CARLISLE] 1995–98 *b* 25 Sep 1951; *educ* Dunstable Gr Sch; K Coll Lon; St Aug Coll Cant; C St Peter-in-Thanet 1974–79; C and Prec Leeds Par Ch 1979–81; Chapl Prec Portsm Cathl 1981–87; V Leigh Park 1987–93; RD Havant 1990–93; Adn of Portsm 1993–98; Dean of Carl from 1998; M CCC, Vc-Chmn from 1996; Coun M RSCM from 1996   *Tel:* (01228) 523335

KNOWLES, Revd (Melvin) Clay, MA, DIP THEOL
St John's Rectory, Park Rd, Burgess Hill, W Sussex RH15 8HG [CHICHESTER] **1991–** *b* 4 Dec 1943; *educ* RE Lee High Sch; Stetson Univ, USA; Ex Univ;

Ripon Coll Cuddesdon; C Minchinhampton 1977–80; V Cathl Par St Helena 1980–82; TV Gd Shep Haywards Heath 1982–89; Adult Educ Adv Chich 1989–94; R St Jo w St Edw Burgess Hill from 1994
Tel: (01444) 232582

KOVOOR, Revd George Iype, BA, BD, MA
Crowther Hall, Weoley Park Rd, Selly Oak, Birmingham B29 6QT [BIRMINGHAM] 1995– *b* 6 Jun 1957; *educ* Airforce Public Sch; St Steph Coll Delhi Univ; Hindu Coll Delhi Univ; Serampore Univ; Nottm Univ; Union Bibl Sem Yavatmal; C Shanti Niwas Ch Faridabad 1980–82; Presbyter Santokh Majra Par Ch 1982–83; Hon Chapl to Indian Army and Airforce 1984–88; Presbyter St Paul Cathl Ambala 1984–88; Nat Youth Dir Ch of N India 1987–90; Chapl St Steph Hosp Delhi 1988–90; Min Derby Asian Chr Min Project 1990–94; Tutor Bibl Studies and Miss Crowther Hall 1994–97; Prin Crowther Hall and Miss Educ Dir CMS from 1997; M Dioc Syn from 1994
Tel: 0121–472 4228 (Office)
Tel and Fax: 0121–415 5738 (Home)

KUHRT, Ven Gordon Wilfred, BD
Church House, Great Smith St, London SW1P 3NZ, London SW1P 3NZ [DIRECTOR OF MINISTRY, ARCHBISHOPS' COUNCIL] 1986–96 *b* 15 Feb 1941; *educ* Colfe's Gr Sch; Lon Univ; Oak Hill Th Coll; RE Tchr 1963–65; C Illogan 1967–70; C Wallington 1970–73; V Shenstone 1973–79; V Em S Croydon 1979–89; RD Croydon Central 1981–86; Hon Can S'wark Cathl 1987–89; Th Lect Lon Univ Extra Mural Dept 1984–89; Adn of Lewisham 1989–96; M Ord of Women Steering Ctee 1987–93; M ABM 1990–96; M CCBI 1990–95; Sen Inspector of Th Colls and Courses 1988–96; Chief Sec ABM 1996–98; Dir of Min Abps' Coun from 1998; M CTE; Fell and M Coun Coll of Preachers; M Trustees *Anvil* Th Journal
Tel: 0171–898 1390
Fax: 0171–898 1419
e-mail: G.KUHRT@abmch.clara.net

LADDS, Mrs Roberta Harriet
St Michael's House, Hall Lane, St Michael's-on-Wyre, Preston PR3 0TQ [BLACKBURN] 1990– *b* 3 Jul 1942; *educ* Medway Tech High Sch; Medway Coll of Tech; Industrial Chemist Reed Internat 1959–65; Chmn Blackb MU Social Concern Dept 1988–91; M Dioc BSR; M Liturg Ctee; M Communications Ctee; CE Rep CTE from 1990; Housewife; Clergy wife
Tel: (01995) 679242

LADDS, Ven Robert Sidney, SSC, B ED, LRSC, FCS
St Michael's House, Hall Lane, St Michael's-on-Wyre, Preston PR3 0TQ [ARCHDEACON OF LANCASTER] *b* 15 Nov 1941; *educ* Swanley Sch; NW Kent Coll; Ch Ch Coll Lon Univ; Cant Sch of Min; C St Leon Hythe 1980–83; R St Jo B Bretherton 1983–91; Chapl Bp Rawstorne Sch 1983–86; Bp's Chapl for Min 1986–90; Bp of Blackb Audit Officer 1990–91; R Preston 1991–97; Adn of Lanc from 1997
Tel: (01995) 679242

LAIRD, Mrs Margaret Heather, BA, FRSA
Keysoe Vicarage, Bedford, Beds MK44 2HW [EX-OFFICIO, THIRD CHURCH ESTATES COMMISSIONER] 1980– *b* 29 Jan 1933; *educ* Truro High Sch; Westf Coll Lon; K Coll Lon; Div Mistress Grey Coat Hosp Westmr 1955–59; Div Mistress Newquay Gr Sch 1959–61; Div Mistress St Albans High Sch 1961–62; Hd of Relig Studies The Dame Alice Harpur Sch Bedf 1970–89; Third Ch Estates Commr from 1989; M ABM from 1989; ABM Bp's Selector from 1990; M CE Pensions Bd 1989–98; Trustee Lambeth Palace Library from 1993; Gov Pusey Ho from 1993; M Allchurches Trust Ltd from 1994; Vc-Pres Soc for Maintenance of the Faith from 1995
Tel: 0171–222 7010

LAMBERT, Mr (Joseph) David, FIM, MCIPS
48 Broomleaf Rd, Farnham, Surrey GU9 8DQ [GUILDFORD] 1994– *b* 29 Apr 1935; *educ* Shoreham Gr Sch; Worc Coll Ox; Overseas Service 'A' Course; Distr Offcr/Distr Commr Kenya 1955–63; Production and Supplies Management posts in Electronics and Motor Industries 1963–71; Managment Services Dir Crosby Grp Ltd 1971–80; Head of Information Systems Meyer Internat plc 1980–94; Rtd; Treas Nat Soc from 1991; Vol Adv Citizens Advice Bureau; M CBF 1994–95; M Ch Ho Publishing Ctee from 1993; M DBF from 1994, DBF Exec Ctee from 1997;
Tel: (01252) 722161
Fax: (01252) 737152
e-mail: 106431.457@compuserve.com

LAMMY, Mr David Lindon, LL B, LL M
43 Fetter Lane, London EC4 1JU [APPOINTED MEMBER, ARCHBISHOPS' COUNCIL] *b* 19 July 1972; *educ* K Sch Peterb; SOAS Lon Univ; Harvard Law Sch; Barrister-at-Law, Lincoln's Inn; Called to the Bar 1995; Apptd M Abps' Coun from 1999
Tel: 0171–284 0001

LANCASTER, Bishop of [SUFFRAGAN, BLACKBURN]
Rt Revd (Geoffrey) Stephen Pedley, MA
Vicarage, Shireshead, Forton, Preston PR3 0AE 1985–90 *b* 13 Sep 1940; *educ* Marlborough Coll; Qu Coll Cam; Cuddesdon Th Coll; C Our Lady and St Nic Liv 1966–69; C H Trin Cov 1969–71; P-in-c Kitwe, N Zambia 1971–77; V St Pet Stockton-on-Tees 1977–88; R Whickham 1988–93; Can Res Dur Cathl 1993–98; Bp of Lanc from 1998; Chair Dioc BMU; Chair Dioc Liturg Coun
Tel: (01524) 799900
Fax: (01524) 799901

LANCASTER, Miss Patricia Margaret, DIP ED, BA
8 Vectis Rd, Alverstoke, Gosport, Hants PO12 2QF
[CHURCH COMMISSIONER] *b* 22 Feb 1929; *educ* Southn Univ; Lon Univ; Hdmistress St Mich Sch Burton Park 1962–73; Hdmistress Wycombe Abbey Sch 1973–89; Ch Commr, M Houses Ctee 1989–95, M Bishoprics Ctee from 1995, M Red Chs Ctee 1991–96; Co-opted Bd of Govs from 1995; Sch Gov
Tel: (01705) 583189

LANDSBERT, Mr Terry (Terence) Carl, FCA
Coigne House, 57 Hurst Lane, Cumnor, Oxford OX2 9PR [OXFORD] 1985– *b* 21 Dec 1936; *educ* St Albans Sch; Rank Xerox 1972–74; Finance Dir Lake & Elliot Ltd 1974–76; PA Internat Management Consultants 1976–82; Sec Ox DBF 1982–98; M CBF 1985–98; M Cen Ch Fund from 1986
Tel: (01865) 863165

LANGLEY, Canon Myrtle Sarah, MA, BD, PH D, H DIP ED, FRAI, IDC
Rectory, Long Marton, Appleby-in-Westmorland, Cumbria CA16 6BN [CARLISLE] 1998– *b* 24 Oct 1939; *educ* Colaiste Moibhi Shankill, Co Dublin; C of I Tr Coll/Dubin Univ; Bris Univ; Dalton Ho Bris; Teaching Ireland 1959–64; Teaching Kenya 1966–73; Tutor and Course Leader Trin Coll Bris 1974–82; Dioc Missr and Asst Padgate TM Liv 1982–87; Dioc Dir of Chr Development for Miss and Co-ord of Tr Liv 1987–89; Hon Lect Faculty of Th Man Univ; Prin Carl and Blackb Dioc Tr Inst 1990–98; P-in-c Long Marton w Dufton and Milburn from 1998; M Dioc Syn; M Vacancy in See Ctee
Tel: (017683) 61269

LANGSTAFF, Ms Bridget Jane, RGN, RM, DN, B SC
East Wing, Bishop's Croft, Old Church Rd, Harborne, Birmingham B17 0BE [BIRMINGHAM] 1990– *b* 18 Jul 1954; *educ* Thorpe Ho Sch Norwich; Norwich High Sch; Middx Hosp Lon; John Radcliffe Hosp Ox; Birm Poly; Distr Nurse S Birm Health Authority 1986–94; Nurse Practitioner for the Homeless from 1994
Tel: 0121–427 2295

LARKIN, Canon Peter John, ALCD
Rectory, 9 Seymour Drive, Mannamead, Plymouth, Devon PL3 5BG [EXETER] 1993– *b* 29 Apr 1939; *educ* Qu Eliz Sch Crediton; Leic Coll of Art and Tech (Sch of Textiles); Lon Coll of Div; C Liskeard 1962–64; C St Andr Rugby 1964–67; Organising Sec Bp of Cov's Call to Mission 1967–68; V Kea Truro 1968–78; Sec Dioc Coun for Miss and Unity 1968–78; P-in-c St Jo Bromsgrove 1978–81; R St Matthias Torquay 1981–97; Can Sokoto dio Nigeria 1991–98; R N Sutton TM Plymouth from 1997; Can Kaduna Nigeria from 1998
Tel and *Fax:* (01752) 663321

LASH, Very Revd Archimandrite Ephrem
Monastery of SS Peter and Paul, Normanby, Whitby, N Yorks YO22 4PS [ECUMENICAL REPRESENTATIVE (ORTHODOX CHURCH)] 1995–

LAW, Revd Robert Frederick, HNC, DIP TH
Rectory, St Columb Major, Cornwall TR9 6AE [TRURO] 1995– *b* 12 Jan 1943; *educ* St Aid Birkenhead; C Bengeo 1969–72; C Sandy 1972–76; P-in-c St Ippolyts and Chapl Lister Hosp Stevenage 1976–81; Chapl Jersey Grp of Hosps 1981–84; V Crowan w Godolphin 1984–92; RD Kerrier 1990–92; R St Columb Major w St Wenn from 1992; RD Pydar from 1996
Tel: (01637) 880252
0468 820310 (Mobile)
Fax: (01637) 820310

LAYTON, Mr John Keith, LIM, MIM
50 Wall Well, Hasbury, Halesowen, W Midlands B63 4SJ [WORCESTER] 1995– *b* 7 Aug 1944; *educ* Grp Quality/Techical Manager Folkes Forgings Ltd; M Bp's Coun and Stg Ctee; M Vacancy in See Ctee; Jt Lay Chmn Dudley Dny Syn from 1986
Tel: 0121–550 2362

LEACH, Mr Robert, FCCA, FIPPM
19 Chestnut Ave, Stoneleigh, Epsom, Surrey KT19 0SY [GUILDFORD] 1995– *b* 19 Nov 1949; *educ* Glyn Gr Sch Ewell; Financial Author from 1986; M CBF from 1996; M CE Pensions Bd 1996–97; M Dioc Syn from 1990; Lay Chmn Epsom Dny Syn from 1996; Dir and Trustee CE Newspaper from 1992, Chmn from 1997
Tel: 0181–224 5695/6
Fax: 0181–393 6413
e-mail: 106234.3636@compuserve.com

LEANING, Very Revd David
The Residence, Southwell, Notts NG25 0HP [PROVOST OF SOUTHWELL] 1984–91 *b* 18 Aug 1936; *educ* Brigg Gr Sch Lincs; Keble Coll Ox; Lich Th Coll; Asst C Gainsborough, Lincs 1960–65; (P-in-c Mortor and East Stockwith 1963–65); R Warsop w Sookholme 1965–76; V Kington w Huntington 1976–80, RD Kington Weobley 1976–80; Adn of Newark 1980–91; Prov of Southwell from 1991; Warden Community of St Laur, Belper 1984–96; Chmn ABM Selection Confs 1988–96
Tel: (01636) 812649 (Office)
Tel and *Fax:* (01636) 812593 (Home)
Fax: (01636) 815904 (Office)

LEE, Revd John, B SC, M SC, M INST GA
Fielden House, Little College St, London SW1P 3SH [CLERGY APPOINTMENTS ADVISER] *b* 21 Oct 1947; *educ* St Dunstan's Coll Catford; Univ Coll Swansea; Inst of Grp Analysis Lon; Ripon Hall Th Coll; Research Scientist R Australian Navy Research Laboratory

Sydney 1971–73; pt Nursing Auxiliary Chu Hosp Ox 1973–75; C Cockett 1975–78; P-in-c St Teilo Cockett 1976–78; Pr/Counsellor St Botoloph Aldgate 1978–84; Hon Psychotherapist Dept of Psychological Medicine St Bart's Hosp Lon 1980–86; Course Consultant St Albs Minl Tr Scheme 1980–85; P-in-c Chiddingstone w Chiddingstone Causeway 1984–89; R 1989–98; Tutor in Individual and Grp Psychotherapy Dept of Psychological Medicine St Bart's Medical Sch 1987–92; Staff Consultant Richmond Fellowship 1989–98; Psychotherapist and Grp Analyst in private practice 1987–98; Clergy Appointments Adv from 1999 Tel: 0171–898 1897/8
Fax: 0171–898 1899

LEICESTER, Bishop of
[NOT APPOINTED AT TIME OF GOING TO PRESS.]

LEIGH, Mr John Roland, MA, ATII
Robin Hood Cottage, Blue Stone Lane, Mawdesley, Ormskirk, Lancs L40 2RG [BLACKBURN] **1995–** *b* 11 Mar 1933; *educ* Winchester Coll; K Coll Cam; Partner/Dir Rathbone Bros plc 1963–93; Dir The Greenbank Trust Ltd 1969–81; Dir Albany Investment Trust plc 1979–95; Rtd; M CBF from 1995; M CBF Investment Ctee from 1996; M Nat Soc Investment Ctee; Dir Nat Soc Enterprises Ltd; Chmn The Hulme Trust
Tel: (01704) 822641
Fax: (01704) 822691

LENNOX, Mr Lionel Patrick Madill, LL B
Provincial and Diocesan Registry, Stamford House, Piccadilly, York YO1 9PP [REGISTRAR, PROVINCE OF YORK] *educ* St Jo Sch Leatherhead; Birm Univ; Solicitor from 1973; In private practice 1973–80; Asst Legal Adv Gen Syn 1981–87; Sec Abp of Cant's Grp on Affinity 1982–84; Sec Bp of Lon's Grp on Blasphemy 1981–87; Sec Legal Adv Commn 1986–89; Registrar Province and Dio York and Registrar York Conv from 1987 and Solicitor in private practice; M Legal Adv Commn from 1987; Notary Public from 1992; M Ecclesiastical Rule Ctee from 1992; Trustee Yorks Hist Chs Trust Tel: (01904) 623487
Fax: (01904) 611458
e-mail: denison.till@dial.pipex.com

LEROY, Mr Peter John, MA, CERT ED
8 Brook Cottage, Lower Barton, Corston, Bath BA2 9BA [BATH AND WELLS] **1975–85, 1995–** *b* 17 Jun 1944; *educ* Monkton Combe Sch; Qu Coll Cam; Asst Master, Head of History and Housemaster Radley Coll 1967–84; Hdmaster Monkton Combe Jun Sch 1984–94; Vc-Chmn Incorp Assn of Prep Schs 1993–94; Sec Studylink EFAC Internat Tr Partnership from 1995; Area Rep for Jt Educl Trust from 1994; M Bd of Educ Schs Ctee; M Scripture Union Coun; Rdr from 1997 Tel: (01225) 873023
Fax: (01225) 873871
e-mail: a.leroy@clara.net

LESITER, Ven Malcolm Leslie, MA
17 Lansdowne Rd, Luton LU3 1EE [ARCHDEACON OF BEDFORD] **1985–** *b* 31 Jan 1937; *educ* Cranleigh Sch; Selw Coll Cam; Cuddesdon Th Coll; C St Marg Eastney Portsm 1963–66; TV St Paul Highfield Hemel Hempstead 1966–73; V Leavesden 1973–88; RD Watford 1981–88; Chmn St Alb Dioc Minl Tr Scheme 1980–83; V Radlett 1988–93; Adn of Bedf from 1993; M Clergy Conditions of Service Steering Grp; M Ch Grp on Funeral Services at Cemeteries and Crematoria Tel: (01582) 730722
Fax: (01582) 877354

LEWES, Bishop of [AREA BISHOP, CHICHESTER] Rt Revd Wallace Parke Benn, BA, DIP TH
Bishop's Lodge, 16A Prideaux Rd, Eastbourne BN21 2NB b 6 Aug 1947; *educ* St Andr Coll Dublin; Univ Coll Dublin; Univ of Lon; Trin Coll Bris; C St Mark New Ferry, Wirral 1972–76; C St Mary Cheadle 1976–82; V St Jas the Great Audley 1982–87; V St Pet Harold Wood 1987–97; pt Chapl Harold Wood Hosp 1987–96; Bp of Lewes from 1997; M Dioc Syn; M Dioc Staff Tm; Bp's Coun; M DBF; Bp w oversight for Youth and Children's Work Tel: (01323) 648462
Fax: (01323) 641514
e-mail: Wallace@lewes.clara.net

LEWIS, Very Revd Christopher Andrew, BA, PH D
The Deanery, St Albans, Herts AL1 1BY [DEAN OF ST ALBANS] **1985–88, 1995–** *b* 4 Feb 1944; *educ* Marlboro Coll; Bris Univ; CCC Cam; Westcott Ho Th Coll; Episc Th Sch Cam Mass; C Barnard Castle 1973–76; Tutor Ripon Coll Cuddesdon 1976–81; Dir Ox Inst for Ch and Soc 1976–79; P-in-c Aston Rowant and Crowell 1978–81; Vc Prin 1981–82; V Spalding 1982–87; Can Res Cant Cathl 1987–94; Dir Minl Tr Cant dio 1989–94; Dean of St Alb from 1994; Chmn Inspections Working Party Ho of Bps Ctee on Inspections Tel: (01727) 852120
Fax: (01727) 850944
e-mail: cathedra@alban.u-net.com

LEWIS, Very Revd Richard, MA
The Dean's Lodging, 25 The Liberty, Wells, Som BA5 2SZ [DEAN OF WELLS] **1984–** *b* 24 Dec 1935; *educ* R Masonic Sch; Fitzw Coll Cam; Ripon Hall Ox; C Hinckley 1960–63; C Sanderstead (in-c St Edm) 1963–66; V All SS S Merstham 1967–72; V H Trin S Wimbledon 1972–79; V St Barn Dulwich and Fndtn

Chapl Alleyn's Coll 1979–90; Exam Chapl to Bp of S'wark; Dean of Wells from 1990   *Tel:* (01749) 670278
Fax: (01749) 679184
e-mail: deanwels@welscathedra.u-net.com

LEYTON, Mr Richard Charles, MBCS
Dormer Cottage, 49 Chilbolton Ave, Winchester, Hants SO22 5HJ [WINCHESTER] **1995–** *b* 7 Nov 1944; *educ* Pet Symonds Sch Win; IS Management Consultant Digital Equipment Co from 1987; M CBF from 1995; Gen Syn Rep Ch Army Bd; M DBF, M Bp's Coun; Rdr; Lay Chmn Winchester Dny Syn
Tel: (01962) 863046
Fax: (01962) 841471
e-mail: leyton@mail.dec.com

LICHFIELD, Bishop of, Rt Revd Keith Norman Sutton, MA, D UNIV, D LITT
Bishop's House, 22 The Close, Lichfield, Staffs WS13 7LG **1984–** *b* 23 Jun 1934; *educ* Woking and Battersea Gr Schs; Jes and St Jo Colls Cam; Ridley Hall Th Coll; C St Andr Plymouth 1959–62; Chapl St Jo Coll Cam 1962–68; Tutor and Chapl of Bp Tucker Th Coll Uganda 1968–73; Prin Ridley Hall Th Coll 1973–78; Bp of Kingston-upon-Thames 1978–84; Bp of Lich from 1984; Chmn BMU 1989–91; Chmn BM 1991–94; Pres Qu Coll Birm 1986–94; Visitor Simon of Cyrene Th Inst from 1992; Vc Pres CMS from 1995
Tel: (01543) 306000
Fax: (01543) 306009

LICKESS, Canon David Frederick, BA
Vicarage, Hutton Rudby, Yarm, N Yorks TS15 0HY [YORK] **1985–** *b* 3 Oct 1937; *educ* Scarborough High Sch; Dur Univ; St Chad's Coll Dur; C Howden Minster 1965–70; V Rudby-in-Cleveland w Middleton from 1970; Non-res Can York Minster from 1990; M CCU from 1991; M CCBI & CTE from 1990; CE Rep to Methodist Conf 1993 and 1994; RD Stokesley from 1993; M CCBI Ch Representatives Meeting 1996; M CTE Enabling Grp 1996–97
Tel: (01642) 700223

LILLEY, Revd Christopher Howard, DIP CM, FCA, FTII
Vicarage, North St, Middle Rasen, Market Rasen, Lincs LN8 3TS [LINCOLN] **1996–** *b* 11 Oct 1951; *educ* K Sch Grantham; St Jo Coll Nottm; Hon C Skegness 1985–93; C Gt Limber w Brocklesby 1993–96; P-in-c Middle Rasen Grp 1996–97; R Middle Rasen Grp from 1997; M DBF; Ch Commr from 1997
Tel: (01673) 842249

LINCOLN, Bishop of, Rt Revd Robert Maynard Hardy, MA, DD
Bishop's House, Eastgate, Lincoln LN2 1QQ **1987–** *b* 5 Oct 1936; *educ* Qu Eliz Gr Sch Wakef; Clare Coll Cam; Cuddesdon Th Coll; Asst C All SS & Martyrs Langley 1962–65; Fell and Chapl Selw Coll Cam 1965–72; V All SS Borehamwood 1972–75; P-in-c Aspley Guise and Dir of St Alb's Dio Minl Tr Scheme 1975–80; R Aspley Guise w Husborne Crawley and Ridgmont 1980; Bp of Maidstone 1980–87; Bp to HM Prisons from 1985; Bp of Linc from 1987
Tel: (01522) 534701
Fax: (01522) 511095

LITTEN, Mr Julian William Sebastian, FSA
Vicarage, St Barnabas Rd, Walthamstow, London E17 8JZ, and 11 Hampton Court, Nelson St, King's Lynn PE30 5DX [CHELMSFORD] **1985–** *b* 6 Nov 1947; *educ* St Pet Collegiate Sch, Wolverhampton; NE Lon Poly; Cardiff Univ; Dept of Public Affairs Victoria and Albert Museum Lon; Court of Fells, Sec of the Faith from 1984; Chmn Portsm Cathl FAC from 1988; M Cathl Fabric Commn from 1991; M Westmr Abbey Architectural Adv Panel from 1993; Trustee Buildings Crafts and Conservation Trust from 1993; Chmn Ch Maintenance Trust from 1997; Trustee Mausolea and Monuments Trust from 1997; Trustee Traditional Buildings Trust from 1998
Tel: 0181–521 5523
(01553) 766643

LIVERPOOL, Bishop of, Rt Revd James Stuart Jones, BA, PGCE
Bishop's Lodge, Woolton Park, Liverpool L25 6DT **1995–** *b* 18 Aug 1948; *educ* Duke of York's Military Sch Dover; Ex Univ; Wycliffe Hall Th Coll; C Ch Ch Clifton 1982–90; V Em S Croydon 1990–94; Bp of Hull 1994–98; Bp of Liv from 1998
Tel: 0151–421 0831
Fax: 0151–428 3055

LLEWELLIN, Rt Revd (John) Richard Allan, MA
Lambeth Palace, London SE1 7JU [BISHOP AT LAMBETH (HEAD OF STAFF)] *1992–95 b* 30 Sep 1938; *educ* Clifton Coll; Law Soc Sch of Law; Fitzwm Coll Cam; Westcott Ho Th Coll; C Radlett 1964–68; C Johannesburg Cathl 1968–71; V Waltham Cross 1971–79; R Harpenden 1979–85; Bp of St Germans 1985–92; Bp of Dover 1992–99; Bp at Lambeth (Head of Staff) from 1999
Tel: 0171–928 8282
Fax: 0171–261 9836
e-mail: llewellin@clara.net

LLOYD, Ven (Bertram) Trevor, MA
Stage Cross, Whitemoor Hill, Bishop's Tawton, Barnstaple, N Devon EX32 0BE [ARCHDEACON OF BARNSTAPLE] **1991–** *b* 15 Feb 1938; *educ* Highgate Sch; Hertf Coll Ox; Clifton Th Coll; C Ch Ch Barnet 1964–69; V H Trin Wealdstone 1970–84; P-in-c St Mich Harrow

Weald 1980–84; V Trin St Mich Harrow 1984–89; AD Harrow 1977–82; Adn of Barnstaple from 1989; M Liturg Commn from 1981; M CBF from 1991; M CBF Publishing Ctee from 1991; M CCC from 1992; Preb of Ex Cathl from 1991; M Liturg Publishing Grp from 1995; M Gen Syn Stg Ctee 1996–98; M Policy Ctee 1996–98; M Chs Main Ctee from 1996; Chapl to Syn; Chmn SW Children's Hospice; Chmn Dioc Adult Tr Ctee; Chmn Dioc Liturg Ctee
Tel: (01271) 375475
Fax: (01271) 377934

LOCK, Canon Peter Harcourt D'Arcy, AKC
Vicarage, 9 St Paul's Square, Bromley, Kent BR2 0XH [ROCHESTER] **1980–** *b* 2 Aug 1944; *educ* Kingston Gr Sch; K Coll Lon; St Boniface Warminster; C St Jo B Meopham 1968–72; C St Matt Wigmore w All SS Hempstead1972–73; C Parish of S Gillingham 1973–77; R All SS Hartley 1977–83; R Fawkham and Hartley 1983–84; V H Trin Dartford 1984–93; Hon Can Roch Cathl from 1990; V St Pet & St Paul Bromley from 1993; RD Bromley from 1996; M Bp's Coun from 1994; Chmn Dioc Ho of Clergy from 1996; M Revision Ctee Eucharistic Prayers
Tel: 0181–460 6275 (Home)
0181–464 5244 (Office)
Fax: 0181–460 3732 (Office)

LOCKE, Mr Geoff
Narnia II, 88 Ravenscliffe Rd, Kidsgrove, Stoke-on-Trent ST7 4HX [LICHFIELD] **1985–90, 1995–** *b* 17 Feb 1943; *educ* Woodhouse Gr Sch Finchley; Lon Univ; Derby Univ; Telecommunications Traffic Superintendent Post Office 1963–68; Asst Prin Min to Tech 1968–69; Teaching 1969–71; Tutor Stoke-on-Trent Sixth Form Coll 1971–76; St Jo Coll Nottm 1977; CPAS NW Eng Youth Work Co-ord 1978–80; Educationist; M W Midl Min Tr Course Ctee 1986–90; M Revision Ctee Dioc Bds of Educ Measure 1987–90; Rdr; M CEEC Exec; Vc-Chmn Dioc Bd of Educ; Lay Chmn Dioc Syn; M Bd of Educ and Further and Higher Educ Ctee; M CMEAC; Chmn Evang Grp in Gen Syn; Lecturer
Tel: (01782) 785544
Fax: (01782) 785588

LOMAX, Canon Barry Walter John, STH
Rectory, 2 Portman Place, Deer Park, Blandford Forum, Dorset DT11 7DG [SALISBURY] **1994–** *b* 26 Dec 1939; *educ* W Taring High Sch Worthing; Worthing CFE; Lon Coll of Div; C St Nic Sevenoaks 1966–71; C Ch Ch Southport 1971–73; V St Matt Bootle 1973–78; P-in-c St Andr Litherland 1976–78; V St Jo New Boro and Leigh 1978–94; Hon Can Sarum Cathl from 1991; R Blandford Forum and Langton Long from 1994
Tel: (01258) 480092

LONDON, Bishop of, Rt Revd and Rt Hon Richard John Carew Chartres, MA, BD, DD
The Old Deanery, Dean's Court, London EC4V 5AA
1995– *b* 11 Jul 1947; *educ* Hertf Gr Sch; Trin Coll Cam; Cuddesdon Th Coll; Linc Th Coll; C St Andr Bedford 1973–75; Bp's Dom Chapl 1975–80; Chapl to Abp of Cant 1980–84; P-in-c St Steph w St Jo Westmr 1984–85; V 1986–92; DDO 1985–92; Prof Div Gresham Coll 1986–92; Six Preacher Cant Cathl 1991–96; Bp of Stepney 1992–95; Bp of London from 1995; Chmn Chs Main Ctee; Chmn Ch Heritage Forum
Tel: 0171–248 6233
e-mail: bishop.london@dlondon.org.uk

LOVEGROVE, Mr Canon Philip Albert, LL B, LLM
159 Baldwins Lane, Croxley Green, Herts WD3 3LL [ST ALBANS] **1977–** *b* 15 Aug 1937; *educ* Pet Symonds' Win; K Coll Lon; Investment Banker and Financial Consultant from 1962; Ch Commr from 1983; Chmn St Alb DBF from 1970; M Bp's Coun from 1970; M Gen Syn Stg Ctee 1980–85 and from 1990; Lay Can St Albs Cathl from 1998
Tel: (01923) 232387 (Home)
0171–600 4800 (Office)
Fax: 0171–600 4622 (Office)

LOVELESS, Mrs Jill (Gillian Margaret), BA, DL
Springfield House, Dyers Lane, Slindon, Arundel, W Sussex BN18 0RE [CHICHESTER] **1990–** *b* 1 Dec 1932; *educ* Hawnes Sch Beds; Westf Coll Lon; Birm Univ; Child Care Officer Middx Co Coun 1957–60; Adoption Social Worker; Dioc Assn for Family Social Work 1976–81; JP from 1974; Chmn Arundel Bench 1990–95; Lay Chmn Arundel & Bognor Dny Syn 1993–96; M Bp's Coun
Tel: (01243) 814356

LOWATER, Mr Peter Alexander, MA
Lower Gubbles, Hook Lane, Warsash, Southampton SO31 9HH [PORTSMOUTH] **1994–** *b* 30 Nov 1935; *educ* R Masonic Sch; Lay Can Portsm Cathl from 1984; Chmn DBF from 1991; Nurseryman
Tel: (01489) 572156

LOWE, Ven Stephen Richard, B SC
Sheffield Diocesan Church House, 95–99 Effingham St, Rotherham S65 1BL [ARCHDEACON OF SHEFFIELD] **1990–** *b* 3 Mar 1944; *educ* Leeds Gr Sch; Reading Sch; Lon Univ; Ripon Hall Th Coll; C St Mich Angl/Methodist Ch Gospel Lane Birm 1968–72; P-in-c Woodgate Valley CD 1972–75; TR E Ham 1975–88; Chelmsf Dioc Urban Officer 1986–88; Hon Can Chelmsf Cathl from 1985; Adn of Sheff from 1988; Ch Commr from 1992, M Bishoprics Ctee from 1991, M Bd of Govs from 1994; Trustee Ch Urban Fund

1991–97, Chmn Grants Ctee from 1993; M BAGUPA 1993–96; M CCBI 1991–96; M CBF Exec 1993–96; M Gen Syn Staff Ctee 1991–96; M Abps' Commn on Organisation of CE 1994–95; Chair Dioc Social Resp Ctee from 1995; Chair Dioc Faith in the City Ctee; Chair Yorkshire/Humberside Regions Adv Coun for BBC 1992–96; M English Nat Forum of BBC 1994–96
Tel: (01709) 512449
0850 599178 (Mobile)
Fax: (01709) 512550
e-mail: 100737.634@compuserve.com

LOWSON, Ven Christopher, M TH, STM, AKC
5 Brading Ave, Southsea, Hants PO4 9QJ [ARCHDEACON OF PORTSMOUTH] *b* 3 Feb 1953; *educ* Newc Cathl Schl; Consett Gr Sch; K Coll Lon; St Aug Coll Cant; Pacific Sch of Religion Berkeley California; Heythrop Coll Lon; C St Mary Richmond 1977–82; P-in-c H Trin Eltham 1982–83, V 1983–91; Chapel Avery Hill Coll 1982–85; Chapl Thames Poly 1985–91; V Petersfield and R Buriton 1991–99; RD Petersfield 1995–99; Vis Lect Portsm Univ from 1998; Adn of Portsm from 1999 *e-mail:* lowson@surfaid.org

LOWMAN, Canon David Walter, BD, AKC
25 Roxwell Rd, Chelmsford, Essex CM1 2LY [CHELMSFORD] **1995–** *b* 27 Nov 1948; *educ* Crewkerne Gr Sch; K Coll Lon; St Aug Coll Cant; Civil Servant 1966–70; C Notting Hill TM 1975–78; C St Aug w St Jo Kilburn 1978–81; Selection Sec and Voc Adv ACCM 1981–86; TR Wickford and Runwell 1986–93; DDO, Lay Min Adv and NSM Officer from 1993; Hon Can Chelmsf Cathl from 1993; M ABM Min Development and Deployment Ctee from 1990; M Dioc Syn from 1986; Chmn Dioc Ord Adv Ctee; Coun M N Thames Min Tr Course; E Anglian Min Course; SE Inst for Th Educ; Coun M Oak Hill Th Coll
Tel: (01245) 264187
Fax: (01245) 348789
e-mail: ddo@chelmsford.anglican.org

LUDLOW, Bishop of [SUFFRAGAN, HEREFORD] **Rt Revd John Charles Saxbee,** BA, PH D
The Bishop's House, Corvedale Rd, Craven Arms, Shropshire SY7 9BT **1985–94** *b* 7 Jan 1946; *educ* Cotham Gr Sch Bris; Bris Univ; Dur Univ; Cranmer Hall Dur; C Em w St Paul Plymouth 1972–76; V St Phil Weston Mill 1976–81; TV Cen Ex 1981–87; Dir SW Minl Tr Course 1981–92; Preb of Ex Cathl 1988–92; Adn of Ludlow from 1992; Bp of Ludlow from 1994; M Springboard Exec from 1996; Pres Modern Churchpeople's Union from 1997; Religious Adv to Central TV from 1997 *Tel:* (01588) 673571
Fax: (01588) 673585

LYNN, Bishop of [SUFFRAGAN, NORWICH]
[NOT APPOINTED AT TIME OF GOING TO PRESS.]

MACKENZIE, Revd Murdoch, MA, BD
31 Milesmere, Two Mile Ash, Milton Keynes MK8 8DP [ECUMENICAL REPRESENTATIVE, UNITED REFORMED CHURCH] **1998–** *b* 23 Feb 1938; *educ* Birkenhead Sch; Hertf Coll Ox; New Coll Edin; Presbyter Madras, Ch of S India 1966–78; Ch of Scotland 1978–81; Hallwood Par LEP Runcorn 1981–88; Carrs Lane Church Centre URC Birm 1988–96; Ecum Moderator Milton Keynes Chr Coun from 1996 *Tel:* (01908) 265053
Fax: (01908) 200216

MacLEAY, Revd Angus Murdo, BA, MA, M PHIL
Vicarage, Houghton, Carlisle, Cumbria CA6 4HZ [CARLISLE] **1995–** *b* 10 Jun 1959; *educ* Vyne Sch Basingstoke; Qu Mary's 6th Form Coll Basingstoke; Univ Coll Ox; Wycliffe Hall Th Coll; Solicitor 1982–85; C H Trin Platt 1988–92; V Houghton w Kingmoor from 1992 *Tel:* (01228) 810076

MAGOWAN, Revd Alistair James, B SC, DIP HE
Vicarage, Vicarage Rd, Egham, Surrey TW20 9JN [GUILDFORD] **1995–** *b* 10 Feb 1955; *educ* K Sch Worc; Leeds Univ; Trin Coll Bris; C St Jo Bapt Owlerton 1981–84; C St Nic Dur 1984–89; Chapl St Aid Coll Dur 1984–89; V St Jo Bapt Egham from 1989; RD Runnymede from 1993; Chmn Dioc Bd of Educ from 1996 *Tel:* (01784) 432066

MAIDSTONE, Bishop of [SUFFRAGAN, CANTERBURY] **Rt Revd Gavin Hunter Reid,** BA
Bishop's House, Pett Lane, Charing, Ashford, Kent TN27 0DL **1985–92, 1995–** *b* 24 May 1934; *educ* Roan Sch for Boys Greenwich; K Coll Lon; Oak Hill Th Coll; C St Paul E Ham 1960–63; C Rainham (P-in-c St Jo and St Matt S Hornchurch) 1963–66; Publications Sec CPAS 1966–71; NSM St Barn Cray 1967–71; Editorial Sec USCL 1971–74; M CRAC 1979–84; Dir of Evang CPAS 1974–90; Seconded Nat Dir Miss England 1982–85; Seconded Project Dir Miss 89 1988–89; M BMU 1986–90; Consultant Missr CPAS 1990–92; M BM 1991–92; Stg Ctee 1989–92; NSM St Jo Woking 1972–92; BM Decade of Evang Adv 1990–92; Bp of Maidstone from 1992; Chmn Abps' Adv Grp for the Millenium from 1995; Consultant to BM from 1997
Tel: (01233) 712950
Fax: (01233) 713543

MANCHESTER, Bishop of, Rt Revd Christopher John Mayfield, BA, MA, DIP TH, M SC
Bishopscourt, Bury New Rd, Manchester M7 0LE **1981–85, 1992–** *b* 18 Dec 1935; *educ* Sedbergh Sch; G and C Coll Cam; Linacre Ho Ox; Wycliffe Hall Th Coll; Cranfield Inst of Techn; C St Martin-in-the-Bullring

Birm 1963–67; Lect St Martin-in-the-Bullring Birm 1967–71; V St Mary's Luton 1971–80; RD Luton 1974–79; Adn of Bedford 1979–85; Bp of Wolverhampton 1985–93; Chmn Inter-Faith Consultative Grp 1988–95; Bp of Man from 1993; Chmn CRC from 1995
Tel: 0161–792 2096 (Office)
0161–792 1779 (Home)
Fax: 0161–792 6826

MANN, Mr Ernie (Ernest George), DIP EE, C ENG, MIEE
39 Windyridge, Gillingham, Kent ME7 3BB [ROCHESTER] **1995–** *b* 18 Nov 1936; *educ* Sheerness Tech Sch; Medway Coll of Tech; City Univ; Chartered Elect Eng and Mgr SEEBoard 1960–93; Inter Soc Administrator Abbeyfield Soc Ltd from 1993; Lay Chmn Gillingham Dny Syn from 1989; M Dioc Syn from 1990; M Bp's Coun from 1994; M Dioc Pastl Ctee; M Dioc Bd of Patronage
Tel: (01634) 304893

MANSELL, Revd Clive Neville Ross, LL B, DIP HE
Rectory, Kirklington, Bedale, N Yorks DL8 2NJ [RIPON] **1995–** *b* 20 Apr 1953; *educ* City of Lon Sch; Leic Univ; Coll of Law; Trin Coll Bris; Solicitor (no longer practising); C Gt Malvern Priory 1982–85; Min Can Ripon Cathl 1985–89; R Kirklington w Burneston, Wath and Pickhill from 1989; M Revision Ctee on the Draft Churchwardens Measure from 1996; M Legal Aid Commn from 1996; Ch Commr from 1997; M Revision Ctee on Draft Amending Canon No 22; M Dioc Bd of Educ; M Dioc Parsonages Bd; M Dioc Bd of Patronage; M Dioc Rural Min Grp; lately M Dioc Budget Review Ctee; Tutor Dioc Rdrs Tr Course; M Ecclesiastical Law Soc
Tel: (01845) 567429

MARGARET SHIRLEY, Sister, OHP
St Hilda's Priory, Sneaton Castle, Whitby, N Yorks YO21 3QN [RELIGIOUS COMMUNITIES NORTH, LAY] **1990–** *b* 10 Jul 1934; *educ* Herts and Essex High Sch; Bp Otter Coll Chichester; Teaching in UK 1955–58, 1960–66; Teaching in Swaziland and Zimbabwe 1966–82; Lay tr and par work in Zimbabwe 1982–89; Par Worker Ch Ch Lancaster 1991–93; Asst Warden of Retreat House from 1995
Tel: (01943) 602079
Fax: (01947) 820454

MARSH, Ven (Francis) John, BA, D PHIL, CERT TH, ARCO, ARCM, ATCL
19 Clarence Park, Blackburn BB2 7FA [ARCHDEACON OF BLACKBURN] **1990–96, 1997–** *b* 3 Jul 1947; *educ* Beckenham and Penge Gr Sch; York Univ; Oak Hill Th Coll; Selw Coll Cam; C St Matt Cambridge 1975–78; C Ch Ch Pitsmoor Sheff 1979–81; C St Thos Crookes 1981–85; V Ch Ch S Ossett 1985–96; RD Dewsbury 1993–96; Adn of Blackb from 1996; M Coun RSCM; Chmn Trustees Angl Renewal Ministries
Tel: (01254) 262571
Fax: (01254) 263394
e-mail: vendocjon@aol.com

MARSH, Mr Harry (Henry Arthur)
5 Vicarage Lane, Great Baddow, Chelmsford CM2 8HY [CHELMSFORD] **1994–** *b* 18 Feb 1943; *educ* Wirral Gr Sch; Inspector of Taxes from 1961; M Bp's Coun; M DBF; M Dioc Pastl Ctee; M CPAS Coun
Tel: (01245) 478038

MARSH, Canon Richard St John Jeremy, MA, PH D
Lambeth Palace, London SE1 7JU [SECRETARY FOR ECUMENICAL AFFAIRS TO THE ARCHBISHOP OF CANTERBURY] *b* 23 Apr 1960; *educ* Trin Sch of John Whitgift; Keble Coll Ox; Dur Univ; Mirfield Th Coll; C Grange St Andr Runcorn 1985–87; Chapl and Solway Fell Univ Coll Dur; Asst Sec for Ecum Affairs to the Abp of Cant 1992–95; Sec from 1995; Can Dio of Gibraltar in Eur from 1995; Non Res Can Cant Cathl from 1998
Tel: 0171–898 1232
Fax: 0171–401 9886
e-mail: richard.marsh.lambeth.palace@dial.pipex.com

MARSHALL, Canon Geoffrey Osborne, BA
24 Kedleston Rd, Derby DE22 1GU [DERBY] **1995–** *b* 5 Jan 1948; *educ* Repton Sch; Dur Univ; Mirf Th Coll; C Waltham Cross 1973–76; C Digswell 1976–78; P-in-c Ch Ch Belper and Milford 1978–86; V Spondon 1986–93; RD Derby N 1990–95; Res Can and Sub Provost Derby Cathl from 1993; DDO from 1995; Chair E Midlands Min Tr Course from 1998; M Dioc Bd of Min
Tel: (01332) 343144 (Home)
(01332) 341201 (Office)
Fax: (01332) 203991 (Office)
e-mail: Geoffrey@canonry.demon.co.uk

MARSHALL, Very Revd Peter Jerome
The Deanery, 10 College Green, Worcester WR1 2LH [DEAN OF WORCESTER] *b* 10 May 1940; *educ* McGill Univ Montreal; Westcott Ho Th Coll; C St Mary E Ham 1963–66; C St Mary Woodford 1966–71; C-in-c S Woodford 1966–71; V St Pet Walthamstow 1971–81; Dep Dir of Tr Chelmsf dio 1981–84; Can Res Chelmsf Cathl 1981–85; Dioc Dir of Tr Ripon dio 1985–97; Can Res Ripon Cathl 1985–97; Dean of Worc from 1997
Tel: (01905) 27821 (Home)
(01905) 28854 (Office)
Fax: (01905) 61139
e-mail: WorcesterDeanPJM@compuserve.com

MARSHALL, Mrs Sonia Margaret Cecilia, BA
135c Eastgate, Deeping St James, Peterborough PE6

8RB [LINCOLN] 1995– *b* 26 Mar 1949; *educ* Nuneaton High Sch for Girls; Westf Coll Lon; Various posts in personal taxation – Inland Revenue 1971–73; Barclays Bank Trust Co 1973–76; Thornton Baker Chartered Accountants 1976–79; Rdr from 1991; Tutor Dioc Rdrs Tr Course from 1995; M Dioc Liturg Ctee from 1996 *Tel* and *Fax*: (01778) 346420

MARTIN, Revd Penny (Penelope Elizabeth), MA
St Mary's Vicarage, 89 Front St, Sherburn Village, Durham DH6 1HD [DURHAM] **1992–** *b* 23 Oct 1944; *educ* Croydon High Sch; Cranmer Hall Dur; St Jo Coll Dur; Dss Seaham w Seaham Harbour 1986–87; Par Dn 1987–89; Par Dn Cassop cum Quarrington 1989–93; C Sherburn w Pittington in plurality w Shadforth 1993–95; V from 1995 *Tel*: 0191–372 0374

MARTINEAU, Revd Jeremy Fletcher, BD, AKC
Arthur Rank Centre, National Agricultural Centre, Stoneleigh Park, Warws CV8 2LZ [NATIONAL RURAL OFFICER] *b* 18 Mar 1940; *educ* Linc Gr Sch; Nottm Univ; K Coll Lon; C St Paul Jarrow 1966–73; Bp's Ind Adv 1966–73; P-in-c Raughton Head 1973–80; Chapl to Agric Carl 1973–80; Social and Ind Adv Bris 1980–90; Joint Sec ACORA 1987–90; Abps' Rural Officer from 1990–93; Nat Rural Officer from 1994
Tel: (01926) 812130 (Home)
Tel and *Fax*: (01203) 696460 (Office)
e-mail: J.Martineau@midnet.com

MASTERS, Mr Keith William, MB, CH B, FRCOG
378 Birmingham Rd, Walsall, W Midlands WS5 3NX [LICHFIELD] **1994–** *b* 5 Apr 1938; *educ* K Edw Sch Birm; Birm Univ Medical Sch; GP Prin Minehead 1963–65; Medical Offcr (Obstetrics) Uganda 1965–72; Consultant Obstetrician Br Birth Survey 1973–75; Consultant Adv on Maternity Care in the World 1973–85; Consultant Adv to World Bank on Maternal/Child Health/ Family Planning 1975–86; Consultant Obstetrician and Gynaecologist Walsall Hosp NHS Trust from 1973; Rdr; ABM Pastl Selector from 1987 *Tel*: (01922) 23828
Fax: (01922) 649075

MAWER, Mr Philip John Courtney, MA, DPA, FRSA
Church House, Great Smith St, London SW1P 3NZ [SECRETARY GENERAL OF THE ARCHBISHOPS' COUNCIL AND THE GENERAL SYNOD] *b* 30 Jul 1947; *educ* Hull Gr Sch; Edin Univ; Home Office 1971–89; Prin Private Sec to Home Sec 1987–89; Under Sec Cabinet Office 1989–90; Lay Chmn Reading Dny Syn and M Ox Dioc Syn 1984–86; Sec Gen of the Gen Syn from 1990; Sec Gen of Abps' Coun from 1998; M Steering Ctee CCBI and of the Enabling Grp CTE; M Gov Body SPCK; Non-Exec Dir EIG; Patron Ch Housing Trust *Tel*: 0171–898 1360
e-mail: philip.mawer@synod.clara.net

MAY, Dr Peter George Robin, MRCS, LRCP, MRCGP
41 Westridge Rd, Southampton, Hants SO17 2HP [WINCHESTER] **1985–** *b* 29 Oct 1945; *educ* R Free Hosp Medical Sch; Ho Officer Northallerton Hosp 1973–74; Travelling Sec UCCF 1974–77; Senior Ho Officer Southn Gen Hosp 1977–79; GP Shirley Health Centre Southn from 1980; M BM from 1991
Tel: (01703) 558931

MAYOSS, Father Aidan (Anthony), CR, BA
St Michael's Priory, 14 Burleigh St, London WC2E 7PX [RELIGIOUS COMMUNITIES IN CONVOCATION, NORTH] **1993–** *b* 5 Mar 1931; *educ* Haberdashers' Askes Sch; Leeds Univ; Coll of the Resurr Mirfield; C Meir Stoke-on-Trent 1957–62; CR from 1964; Angl Chapl Univ of Stellenbosch 1973–76; Chapl Lon Univ 1976–78; Bursar CR 1983–90; Dir Fraternity of the Resurr from 1990; M ABM *Tel*: 0171–379 6669
Fax: 0171–240 5294

McCABE, Ven (John) Trevor, RD, BA, DIP TH
Archdeacon's House, 3 Knights Hill, Kenwyn, Truro TR1 3UY [ARCHDEACON OF CORNWALL] *b* 26 Jan 1933; *educ* Falmouth Gr Sch; Nottm Univ; Ox Univ; Wycliffe Hall Th Coll; C Compton Gifford 1959–63; P-in-c St Martin, St Steph and St Laur 1963–66; V Capel 1966–71; V Scilly Isles 1971–81; Res Can Bris Cathl 1981–83; V Manaccan w St Anthony and St Martin 1983–96; RD Kerrier 1987–90 and 1994–96; Hon Can Truro Cathl from 1993; Adn of Cornwall from 1996; Chmn Cornwall and Isles of Scilly Learning Disabilities NHS Trust from 1990 *Tel*: (01872) 272866
Fax:(01872) 242102

McCLEAN, Prof (John) David, CBE, QC, DCL
6 Burnt Stones Close, Sheffield, S Yorks S10 5TS [SHEFFIELD] **1970–** *b* 4 Jul 1939; *educ* Qu Eliz Gr Sch Blackb; Magd Coll Ox; Prof of Law Univ of Sheff from 1973; Vc-Chmn Ho of Laity 1979–85; Chmn 1985–95; Chmn Legal Adv Commn; Rdr; Chan Sheff dio from 1992; Chan Newc dio from 1998
Tel: 0114–230 5794
e-mail: j.d.McClean@Sheffield.ac.uk

McHENRY, Mr Brian Edward, MA
216 Friern Rd, E Dulwich, London SE22 0BB [SOUTHWARK] **1980–85, 1987–** *b* 12 Dec 1950; *educ* Dulwich Coll; New Coll Ox; Barrister; Government Legal Service from 1978; Sen Civil Service Lawyer from 1996; Rdr; Lay Chmn Dulwich Dny Syn 1987–91; Lay Chmn Dioc Syn 1988–96 and from 1997; M Gen Syn Stg Ctee 1990–95; M Stg Orders Ctee 1988–90;

Chmn Stg Orders Ctee from 1991; M Legislative Ctee 1981–85 and 1991–95; M Panel of Chairmen 1990 and from 1996; M Crown Appts Commn from 1997; CE Delegate Porvoo Leaders Consultation 1998
Tel: 0181–693 1226 (Home)
Fax: 0181–516 6305 (Home)

McMULLEN, Mrs Christine Elizabeth, BA, DIP AD ED
114 Brown Edge Rd, Buxton, Derbys SK17 7AB [DERBY] **1990–** *b* 9 Mar 1943; *educ* St Helena Sch Chesterfield; Homelands Sch Derby; R Holloway Coll Lon; Tchr of RE and English 1979–87; Mgr Salcare Drop-In Centre 1987–93; Rdr from 1986; M Coun Trin Coll Bris from 1991; M Womens Inter Ch Coun from 1991; Nat Co-ordinator FLAME 1992–96; Tutor and Dir of Pastl Studies Nn Ord Course from 1994; M BM from 1993, M BM Exec from 1996; Sec Broken Rites; M CMEAC from 1996
Tel: (01298) 73997
Fax: (01298) 72448
e-mail: christin@noc6.u-net.com

MELLOR, Canon (Kenneth) Paul, BA, MA
Lemon Lodge, Lemon St, Truro, Cornwall TR1 2PE [TRURO] **1994–** *b* 11 Aug 1949; *educ* Ashfield Sch; Southn Univ; Leeds Univ; Cuddesdon Th Coll; C St Mary V Cottingham 1973–76; C All SS Ascot 1976–80; V St Mary Magd Tilehurst 1980–85; V Menheniot 1985–94; RD E Wivelshire 1990–94; Hon Can Truro Cathl 1990–94; Can Treas Truro Cathl from 1994; Vc Chmn Dioc Liturg Ctee; M Bp's Coun; M DBF
Tel: (01872) 276782 (Office)
(01872) 272094 (Home)
Fax: (01872) 277788

MENON, Mr Vijay
97 Marlborough Gdns, Upminster, Essex RM14 1SR [CHELMSFORD] **1970–** *b* 21 Aug 1930; *educ* St Thos Sch Kerala State, India; St Thos Coll Madras Univ India; Poplar Tech Coll Lon; S Shields Marine Coll Co Dur; Jnr Eng Mogul Lines 1952–55; Fourth Eng to Chief Eng Officer Admiralty 1956–60; Chief Eng Officer Stephenson Clarks Newc 1961; Senr Eng Surveyor, Lloyds Register Lon from 1961; Former M Stg Ctee and Miss Op Ctee CMS; M Coun Crosslinks; M Coun CPAS; M CEEC; M Coun Ch Soc; Rtd for full-time Chr Preaching/Teaching; On staff St Helens Bishopsgate Lon from 1988; M Br Nuclear Soc; Fell Inst Marine Engs
Tel: (01708) 501592

MENZIES, Mr Colin Douglas Livingstone, MA, FRSA
Church House, Great Smith St, London SW1P 3NZ [SECRETARY, CORPORATION OF THE CHURCH HOUSE] *b* 8 Apr 1944; *educ* Glenalmond Coll; Keble Coll Ox; Christian Salvesen plc Edin 1971–84; RICS Edin 1984–86; City admin and recruitment 1986–90; Sec to Corp of Ch Ho from 1990
Tel: 0171–898 1310

METCALF, Ven Robert Laurence, BA, DIP TH
38 Menlove Ave, Allerton, Liverpool L18 2EF [ARCHDEACON OF LIVERPOOL] *b* 18 Nov 1935; *educ* Oldershaw Gr Sch Wallasey; St Jo Coll Dur; Cranmer Hall Dur; C Ch Ch Bootle 1962–65; C St Luke Farnworth in-c St Jo 1965–67; V St Cath Wigan 1967–75; R H Trin Wavertree 1975–94; Chapl Liv Blue Coat Sch 1975–94; Chapl R Sch for Visually Handicapped 1975–94; DDO 1982–94; Hon Can Liv Cathl from 1988; Adn of Liv from 1994
Tel: 0151–724 3956
01426 187327 (Pager)
Fax: 0151–729 0587

METCALFE, Mrs Elizabeth Mavis Dorothy, BA
11 Lismore St, Carlisle, Cumbria CA1 2AH [CARLISLE] **1987–** *b* 5 Mar 1935; *educ* Hemel Hempstead Gr Sch; K Coll Lon; Tchr Sydenham Girls' High Sch 1957–60; Carlisle and Co High Sch for Girls 1960–65; Trin Sch Carlisle 1972–94; Rtd; M Dioc Syn from 1981; M Bp's Coun from 1988; M Dioc Bd of Educ 1981–93; M Dioc Coun for Min with Deaf and Hard-of-Hearing People from 1991; M Dioc Bd for Min and Tr from 1995; M ABM Ctee for Min among Deaf People from 1997
Tel: (01228) 22977

METHUEN, Very Revd John Alan Robert, MA
The Minster House, Ripon, N Yorks HG4 1PE [DEAN OF RIPON] *b* 14 Aug 1947; *educ* Eton Coll Choir Sch; St Jo Sch Leatherhead; BNC Ox; Cuddesdon Th Coll; C Fenny Stratford and Water Eaton TM Milton Keynes 1971–74; Asst Chapl Eton Coll 1974–77; P-in-c St Jas Dorney 1974–77; Warden Dorney Parish-Eton Coll Project Conf Centre 1974–77; V St Mark Reading 1977–83; R The Ascension Hulme 1983–95; Dean of Ripon from 1995; Chair Dioc BSR; Chair Dioc Music Ctee; Chair Dioc Worship Ctee; M Cathls Liturgy Grp; Ch Commr; Lect Swan Hellenic Tours; Writer and Dir Chr Educ Videos
Tel: (01765) 603615
Fax: (01765) 603462
e-mail: postmaster@riponcathedral.org.uk

MICHELL, Mrs Lesley Violet, MA
Vicarage, Church Rd, Rainford, St Helens, Merseyside WA11 8H [LIVERPOOL] **1990–** *b* 3 Sep 1943; *educ* Talbot Heath Sch Bournemouth; Girton Coll Cam; Tchr Lawrence Weston Comp Sch Bris 1965–66; pt Lect Prescot CFE 1980–85; Dioc Pres MU 1989–94; Rdr from 1995; Home Tutor for children w special needs from 1996; N Area Co-ord BRF Reps from 1997
Tel: (01744) 882200

MIDDLEMISS, Mr Peter James, BA (THEOL)
Vine Cottage, Kennel Bank, Cropthorne, Pershore, Worcs WR10 3NB [WORCESTER] 1990– b 25 Jul 1943; educ Carlton le Willows Sch Notts; Man Univ; Birm Univ; Chapl to Overseas Students Man Univ 1967–76; Par Educ Adv St Bart and St Chris Haslemere 1976–77; Warden Morley Retreat and Conference Centre Derby and S'well 1977–83; Warden Holland House Retreat, Conference and Laity Centre Worc dio from 1983; Trustee Saltley Trust; M Exec APR; M Exec Ecum Assn of Academies and Laity Centres in Europe; M Bd of Educ and Vol and Continuing Educ Ctee   Tel: (01386) 860330
Fax: (01386) 861208

MIDDLETON, Bishop of [SUFFRAGAN, MANCHESTER] **Rt Revd Stephen Squires Venner,** BA, MA
The Hollies, Manchester Rd, Rochdale, Lancs OL11 3QY 1985–94 b 19 Jun 1944; educ Hardye's Sch Dorchester; Birm Univ; Linacre Coll Ox; Lon Inst of Educ; St Steph Ho Th Coll; C St Pet Streatham 1968–71; Hon C St Marg Streatham Hill 1971–72; Hon C Ascen Balham 1972–74; V St Pet Clapham and Bp's Chapl to Overseas Students 1974–76; V St Jo Trowbridge 1976–82; V H Trin Weymouth 1982–94; M Dorset LEA 1982–94; Chmn Dioc Bd of Educ Sarum 1989–94; RD Weymouth 1988–94; Non-Res Can Sarum Cathl 1989–94; Chmn Ho of Clergy Dioc Syn 1993–94; M Gen Syn Bd of Educ from 1985, Chmn VCE Ctee from 1997; Bp of Middleton from 1994; Chmn Dioc Bd of Educ from 1994; Co-Chmn CE/Moravian Contact Grp   Tel: (01706) 358550
Fax: (01706) 354851
e-mail: Stephen.Venner@btinternet.com

MILLS, Mr David John
51 Greenways, Over Kellet, Carnforth, Lancs LA6 1DE [CARLISLE] 1985– b 19 Feb 1937; Civil Servant 1968; Probation Service from 1968; Senior Probation Officer; Rdr; Bp's Selector ABM; M Dioc Bd of Educ and Youth Ctee   Tel: (01524) 732194

MITCHELL, Mr Alan Bryce, BA, MA, M SC
Church House, Great Smith Street, London SW1P 3NZ [PUBLISHING MANAGER, CHURCH HOUSE PUBLISHING AND NATIONAL SOCIETY] b 30 Sep 1957; educ Man Gr Sch; St Andr Univ; Leic Poly; Nottm Univ; Loughb Univ; Editor Macmillan Press 1987–88; Commissioning Editor HarperCollins 1988–91; Editor Nat Society 1991–94; Publishing Mgr Church House Publishing and National Society from 1994
Tel: 0171–898 1450
Fax: 0171–898 1449
e-mail: amitchell@chp.u-net.com

MITCHELL, Canon (David) George, EA
Vicarage, Church Ave, Warmley, Bristol BS30 5JJ [BRISTOL] 1995– b 5 Jul 1935; educ Methodist Coll Belfast; Qu Univ Belfast; Sarum Th Coll; C Westbury-on-Trym 1961–64; C Cricklade w Latton 1954–68; V St Jo Fishponds 1968–77; TR E Bris 1977–87; V Warmley, Syston and Bitton from 1987; Chmn Ho of Clergy Dioc Syn; M Bp's Coun; M Bd of Dirs DBF
Tel: 0117–967 3965

MONBERG, Revd Ulla Stefan, BA
11 Ormonde Mansions, 106 Southampton Row, London WC1B 4BP [LONDON] 1995– b 16 Jul 1952; educ Oregaard Sch Copenhagen; Copenhagen Univ; Oregon Univ; Westcott Ho Th Coll; C St Jas Piccadilly 1990–94; Area Dir of Ords and Dean of Women's Min and Sec Board for Women Candidates in Lon dio from 1994; Assoc V St Jo Hyde Park from 1995
Tel: 0171–242 7533

MONCKTON, Mrs Joanna Mary
Stretton Hall, Stafford ST19 9LQ [LICHFIELD] 1990– b 31 May 1941; educ Oxton Ho Sch Kenton Exeter; High Sheriff of Staffordshire 1995–96; Dir Penk Ltd; Housewife; M Bp's Coun   Tel: (01902) 850288

MOORE, Canon John Richard
14 Grange Mews, Beverley Rd, Leamington Spa CV32 6PX [COVENTRY] 1970–75, 1985–88, 1995– b 15 Feb 1935; educ Worthing High Sch for Boys; Lon Coll of Div; C Em Northwood 1959–63; V Burton Dassett 1963–67; Youth Chapl Cov dio 1967–71; Dir Lindley Educ Trust 1971–82; TR Kinson 1982–88; Gen Dir CPAS 1988–96; Dir Intercontinental Ch Soc from 1996; M BM   Tel: (01926) 470636 (Home)
(01926) 430347 (Office)
Fax: (01926) 330238
e-mail: Johnrmoore@compuserve.com/
Icsint@compuserve.com

MORFEY, Dr Kathryn Margaret Victoria, LL B, MA, PH D
2 Royston Close, Southampton SO17 1TB [WINCHESTER] 1990– b 26 May 1942; educ Stourbridge Co High Sch; Cam Univ; Southn Univ; Lect in Economics Bris Univ 1963–64; Southn Univ 1967–69; Qualified as Solicitor 1980; Solicitor in Private Practice from 1980; Partner 1985–91; M Legal Adv Commn 1991–93; M Cathl Fabric Commn 1991–96; Gov K Alfred's Coll of HE from 1992; M Cathl Statutes Commn from 1996; M Pastl Measure 1983 Appeals Panel from 1996; M Ord of Women (Financial Provisions) Measure 1993 Appeals Panel from 1996; Chair Ho of Laity Dioc Syn from 1997   Tel: (01703) 554396

MORGAN, Mr David Geoffrey Llewelyn
25 Newbiggen St, Thaxted, Great Dunmow, Essex CM6 2QS [CHELMSFORD] 1990– *b* 1 Mar 1935; *educ* St Jo Sch Leatherhead; Sen Partner Duffields Solicitors Chelmsford from 1962; Company Dir; M CBF and Investment Adv Ctee; Vc-Chmn Dioc Bd of Patronage; M Dioc Pasl Ctee, Fin Ctee and Clergy Ho Ctee from 1988; M Bp's Coun from 1993; Trustee Victoria Clergy Fund from 1989; Vc-Chmn CU Coun; Chmn Dioc CU
Tel: (01371) 830132

MORGAN, Mrs Heather Margaret, BA
40 Countess Wear Rd, Exeter EX2 6LR [EXETER] 1995– *b* 15 Jul 1953; *educ* Arnold High Sch for Girls Blackpool; Ex Univ; Solicitor; Pres Mental Health Review Tribunals; Section 13 Insp Ch Schs; M Ex Cathl Community Ctee and M Liturgy Working Party; M Bp's Coun; M Dioc Bd of Educ; M Dioc Communications Ctee; Lay Chmn Christianity Dny Syn
Tel: (01392) 877623
Fax: (01392) 876344

MORGAN, Mrs Susan Deirdre, BA, FIPD, MHSM
Church House, Great Smith St, London SW1P 3NZ [DIRECTOR OF HUMAN RESOURCES, ARCHBISHOPS' COUNCIL] *b* 7 Apr 1956; *educ* Dame Alice Harpur Sch Bedford; N Lon Poly; Asst Personnel Officer NW Thames Regional Health Authority 1978–80; Personnel Officer Charing Cross Hosp 1980–83; Sen Personnel Officer W Essex Health Authority 1983–85, Dep Dir of Personnel 1985–91; Dir of Personnel Essex and Herts Health Services 1991–94; Dir Human Resources and Commercial Services Princess Alexandra Hosp NHS Trust Harlow 1994–97; Employers' rep on the Employment Tribunals for Eng and Wales from 1992; Personnel Dir CBF 1997–98; Dir of Human Resources to Abps' Coun from 1998
Tel: 0171–898 1565

MORIARTY, Mrs Rachel Milward, MA, M TH
22 Westgate, Chichester, W Sussex PO19 3EU [CHICHESTER] 1995– *b* 22 Mar 1935; *educ* Bedf High Sch; St Hugh's Coll Ox; K Coll Lon; Sen Classics Tchr in Lon schs; M Lon Dioc Syn and Ctees; Tutor in Ch Hist Chich Th Coll 1990–94; Lect Univ Southn Sch of Th and Relig from 1994; Research Fell/Lect in Th K Alfred's Coll Win and Tutor Southn Univ ACE; Chair of Govs Bp Luffa CE School (Tech Coll) Chich; M Chich Dioc Syn from 1991; M Dioc European Ecum Ctee from 1992; Adult Ed Bd of Studies; Lay Chmn Chich Dny Syn 1992–97; M CCU from 1996; Moderator Guildf LNSM Scheme
Tel and Fax: (01243) 789985
e-mail: moriartyrm@aol.com

MORRIS, Mr David Douglas, FCMA
Church House, Great Smith St, London SW1P 3NZ [FINANCE AND ADMINISTRATIVE SECRETARY, MINISTRY DIVISION] *b* 11 Dec 1944; *educ* Perth Academy; Government Official various posts 1964–91; Dir of Finance Inst of Child Health Lon 1991–96; Fin and Admin Sec Min Division from 1995
Tel: 0171–898 1392
e-mail: david.morris@abmch.clara.net

MORRIS, Very Revd Stuart Collard, AKC
The Deanery, Hadleigh, Ipswich IP7 5DT [DEAN OF BOCKING] *b* 17 Oct 1943; *educ* Bris Cathl Sch; K Coll Lon; St Boniface Th Coll Warminster; C Hanham 1967–71; C Whitchurch 1971–74; P-in-c Wapley W Codrington and Dodington 1974–77; P-in-c Westerleigh 1974–77; P-in-c Holdgate w Tugford 1977–82; P-in-c Abdon w Clee St Marg 1977–82; R Diddlebury w Bouldon and Munslow 1977–82; P-in-c Sotterley, Willingham, Shadingfield, Ellough etc 1982–87; RD Beccles and S Elmham 1983–94; Hon Can St Eds Cathl from 1987; V H Trin w St Mary Bungay 1987–94; P-in-c Hadleigh, Layham and Shelley 1994–96; RD Hadleigh from 1994; Dean of Bocking from 1994; R Hadleigh, Layham, Shelley, Hintlesham and Chattisham from 1996
Tel: (01473) 822218
e-mail: smorris743@aol.com

MORRISON, Ven John Anthony, BA, MA
Archdeacon's Lodging, Christ Church, Oxford OX1 1DP [ARCHDEACON OF OXFORD] 1980–90, 1998– *b* 11 Mar 1938; *educ* Haileybury Coll; Jes Coll Cam; Chich Th Coll; C St Pet Birm 1964–68; St Mich Ox 1968–74; Chapl Linc Coll Ox 1968–74; V Basildon 1974–82; RD Bradfield 1978–82; V Aylesbury 1982–89; RD Aylesbury 1985–89; TR Aylesbury 1989–90; Adn of Buckingham 1990–98; P-in-c Princes Risborough w Ilmer 1996–97; Adn of Ox and Res Canon Ch Ch from 1998
Tel: (01865) 204440
Fax: (01865) 204465
e-mail: archoxf@oxford.anglican.org

MOSES, Very Revd John Henry, BA, PH D
The Deanery, 9 Amen Court, London EC4M 7BU [DEAN OF ST PAUL'S] 1985– *b* 12 Jan 1938; *educ* Ealing Gr Sch; Univ of Nottm; Trin Hall Cam; Linc Th Coll; Visiting Fell Wolfs Coll Cam 1987; Asst C St Andr Bedf 1964–70; R Cov East TM 1970–77; Exam Chapl to Bp of Cov 1972–77; RD Cov East 1973–77; Adn of Southend 1977–82; Prov of Chelmsf 1982–96; Dean of St Paul's from 1996; Ch Commr from 1988; M Stg Ctee from 1996; Vc-Chmn USPG from 1997; M ACC from 1998
Tel: 0171–236 2827
Fax: 0171–332 0298

MOXON, Very Revd Michael Anthony, LVO, BD, MA
The Deanery, Lemon St, Truro, Cornwall TR1 2PE
[DEAN OF TRURO] 1985–90 *b* 23 Jan 1942; *educ* Merchant Taylors' Sch; Heythrop Coll Lon; Sarum Th Coll; C Kirkley St Pet Lowestoft 1970–74; Min Can St Paul's Cathl 1974–81; Sacrist 1977–81; Warden of Coll of Min Canons 1979–81; V Tewkesbury w Walton Cardiff 1981–90; Can of Windsor and Chapl in the Great Park 1990–98; Chapl to HM The Queen 1986–98; M CCC 1985–90; Dean of Truro and R St Mary Truro from 1998
Tel: (01872) 272661 (Home)
(01872) 276782 (Office)
Fax: (01872) 277883 (Office)

MULLINS, Revd Peter Matthew, MA, M PHIL
1 St Giles Ave, Lincoln LN2 4PE [LINCOLN] 1995– *b* 12 May 1960; *educ* Berkhamsted Sch; Ch Ch Ox; Irish Sch of Ecumenics; Qu Coll Birm; C Caversham and Mapledurham 1984–88; TV Old Brumby Linc 1989–94; Clergy Tr Adv Linc from 1994
Tel: (01522) 528199
e-mail: peter.mullins@virgin.net

MUNRO, Ms Josile Wenus, B SC, DTS
89 Brougham Rd, London E8 4PD [LONDON] 1994–95, 1997– *b* 28 Apr 1963; *educ* Haggerston Girls Sch; Kingsway Princeton Coll; S Bank Poly; Prin Trading Standards Officer from 1994; M Bp's Coun; Trustee Lon Dioc Fund; Coun M N Thames Min Tr Course; Bp's Selector; Lay Chair Hackney Dny Syn; Vc-Chair Area Bp's Coun
Tel: 0171–254 5577

MUSSON, Mr Terence Robert, HND
Worthen Farm, Pyworthy, Holsworthy, Devon EX22 6LQ [TRURO] 1995– *b* 10 Jul 1940; *educ* Grantham Boys Central Sch; Caythorpe Coll; Self Employed Farmer from 1962; Company Chairman 1981–90
Tel: (01288) 381585
Tel and *Fax:* (01288) 381464
e-mail: TMUSSON@AOL.COM

NAGEL, Mrs Mary Philippa, B ED
Aldwick Vicarage, 25 Gossamer Lane, Bognor Regis, W Sussex PO21 3AT [CHICHESTER] 1990– *b* 8 Mar 1954; *educ* Worthing High Sch; Lon Univ; Section 23 Inspector of Schs
Tel and *Fax* (01243) 262049
e-mail: lnagel@netcomuk.co.uk

NAIRN-BRIGGS, Very Revd George Peter, AKC
1 Cathedral Close, Margaret St, Wakefield WF1 2DP [PROVOST OF WAKEFIELD] 1980–87, 1990– *b* 5 Jul 1945; *educ* Slough Tech High Sch; K Coll Lon; St Aug Coll Cant; C St Laur Catford 1970–73; C St Sav Raynes Park 1973–75; V Ch the King Salfords 1975–81; V St Pet St Helier 1981–87; Bp's Adv for Soc Resp Wakef 1987–97; Can Res Wakef Cathl 1992–97; Provost of Wakef from 1997; M Bp's Senior Staff Meeting; M BSR; M BSR Exec Ctee; Dep Prolocutor York Conv; M BSR Working Party on the Family 1992–95; M Bps' Adv Grp on UPAs; M Gen Syn Stg Orders Ctee 1993–95; Assessor York Conv; M Third National Consultation Planning Grp 1993–95
Tel: (01924) 210005 (Home)
(01924) 373923 (Office)
Fax: (01924) 210009 (Home)
(01924) 215054 (Office)

NAPPIN, Miss Patricia, MA
7 Mavis Walk, Tollgate Rd, Mid Beckton, London E6 5TL [CHELMSFORD] 1975– *b* 17 Dec 1934; *educ* City of Bath Girls' Sch; Whitelands Coll Putney; Bris Univ; Open Univ; Tchr Lozells JM & I Sch Birm 1958–59; Tchr Southdown Inf Sch Bath 1959–70; Exch Tchr USA 1965–66; CE Prim Sch Barking, Hd Infs' Dept 1970–73; Hd Tchr Henry Green Infs' Sch Dagenham 1973–80; Hd Wm Bellamy Infs' Sch Dagenham 1980–Dec 87; Co Commr in Guiding for the London-over-the-Border Co 1978–87; Hd Becontree Prim Sch Dagenham 1988–97; Rdr; Chmn Ho of Laity Dioc Syn 1988–97; Dep Hon Sec CRC from 1997
Tel: 0171–474 0222

NEAL, Canon Anthony Terrence, BA, CERT ED
Rectory, Forth-an-Tewennow, Phillack, Hayle, Cornwall TR27 4QE [TRURO] 1990– *b* 11 Jan 1942; *educ* Germains Co Sec Sch Chesham; Open Univ; Leeds Univ; Bernard Gilpin Soc Dur; Chich Th Coll; C St Hilda Leeds 1968–73; Chapl and Head of RE Abbey Grange CE High Sch Leeds 1973–81; Dioc RE Adv Truro and P-in-c St Erth 1981–84; Childrens Officer 1985–87; Stewardship Adv 1987–88; V St Erth from 1984; Hon Can Truro Cathl from 1994; P-in-c Phillack w Gwithian, Gwinear and St Elwyn Hayle 1994–96; TR Godrevy TM from 1996
Tel: (01736) 753541 (Home)
(01736) 754866 (Office)
Fax: (01736) 755235

NEED, Very Revd Philip, AKC
The Deanery, Bocking, Braintree, Essex CM7 5SR [DEAN OF BOCKING] *b* 28 Apr 1954; *educ* Carlton-le-Willows Gr Sch; K Coll Lon; Chich Th Coll; C Ch Ch and St Jo Clapham 1977–80; C All SS Luton w St Pet 1980–83; V St Mary Magd Harlow 1983–89; P-in-c St Phil Chaddesden 1989–91; Dom Chapl to Bp of Chelmsf 1991–96; Dean and R St Mary Bocking from 1996
Tel: (01376) 324887
(01376) 553092
e-mail: philip.need@virgin.net

NEIL-SMITH, Mr (Noel) Jonathan, MA
Church House, Great Smith St, London SW1P 3NZ
[ADMINISTRATIVE SECRETARY, GENERAL SYNOD] *b* 5 Oct 1959; *educ* Marlboro Coll; St Jo Coll Cam; On staff of Ch Commrs from 1981; Bishoprics Offcr 1994–96; Seconded to Gen Syn from 1997; Asst Sec Ho of Bps 1997–98; Acting Sec Ho of Bps from 1998
Tel: 0171–898 1373
Fax: 0171–898 1369
e-mail: jonathan.neil.smith@synod.clara.net

NENER, Canon (Thomas) Paul Edgar, MB, CH B, FRCS ED, FRCS
St John's Vicarage, 2 Green Lane, Tuebrook, Liverpool L13 7EA [LIVERPOOL] **1990–** *b* 11 Sep 1942; *educ* Liverpool Inst High Sch; Liv Univ Medical Sch; Coll of Resurr Mirfield; C Warrington 1980–83; V St Jas the Great Haydock 1983–95; V St Jo Tuebrook, Liv from 1995; Hon Can Liv Cathl from 1995; Chmn Dioc Healing Panel; ABM Selector; Subwarden Guild of St Raphael
Tel: 0151–228 2023

NEWCASTLE, Bishop of, Rt Revd (John) Martin Wharton, MA
Bishop's House, 29 Moor Rd South, Gosforth, Newcastle upon Tyne NE3 1PA **1998–** *b* 6 Aug 1944; *educ* Ulverston Gr Sch; Dur Univ; Linacre Coll Ox; Ripon Hall Ox; C St Pet Birm 1972–75; C St Jo B Croydon 1975–77; Dir of Pastl Studies Ripon Coll Cuddesdon 1977–83; Exec Sec Bd of Min and Tr Bradf dio 1983–91; Can Res Bradf Cathl and Bp's Officer for Min and Tr 1992; Bp of Kingston-upon-Thames 1992–97; Bp of Newc from 1997
Tel: 0191–285 2220
Fax: 0191–284 6933
e-mail: Bishop@newcastle.anglican.org

NEWSUM, Mr Jeremy Henry Moore, B SC, ARICS
Priory House, Swavesey, Cambs CB4 5QJ [CHURCH COMMISSIONER] *b* 4 Apr 1955; *educ* Rugby Sch; Reading Univ; Chief Exec Grosvenor Estate Holdings; Ch Commr from 1993, Assets Ctee from 1993
Tel: (01954) 232084

NOËL, Mr Marcel Paul, MA
7 Canterbury Rd, Wolverhampton, W Midlands WV4 4EQ [LICHFIELD] **1985–90, 1991–** *b* 19 Mar 1920; *educ* Em Sch Lon; St Cath Coll Ox; RAF (Flt-Lt) 1941–46; Schmaster Wolverhampton Gr Sch Head of Maths for Science 1948–81; Rdr from 1984; Examiner in Maths GCSE 1981–93
Tel: (01902) 335238

NORMAN, Ven Garth, BA, DIP TH, MA, M ED, PGCE
6 Horton Way, Farningham, Kent DA4 0DQ [ARCHDEACON OF BROMLEY] **1995–** *b* 26 Nov 1938; *educ* Henry Mellish Gr Sch Nottm; St Chad's Coll Dur; UEA; C St Anne Wandsw 1963–66; TV Trunch 1966–71; TR Trunch 1971–83; RD Repps 1975–83; Prin Chiltern Chr Tr Scheme 1983–87; Dioc Dir of Tr Roch 1988–94; Adn of Bromley from 1994
Tel: (01322) 864522

NORMAN, Revd Michael John, LL B
St Saviour's Rectory, Claremont Rd, Bath, Somerset BA1 6LX [BATH AND WELLS] **1995–** *b* 17 Aug 1959; *educ* Dr Challoner's Gr Sch; Southn Univ; Wycliffe Hall Th Coll; C St Jo Woodley 1985–89; C Uphill 1989–92; TV St Barn Uphill 1992–98; R St Sav Bath w Swainswick and Woolley from 1998; M DBF; M Dioc Renewal Grp
Tel: (01225) 311637

NORWICH, Bishop of, Rt Revd Peter John Nott, BA, MA
Bishop's House, Norwich, Norfolk NR3 1SB **1975–77, 1985–** *b* 30 Dec 1933; *educ* Bris Gr Sch; Dulwich Coll; RMA Sandhurst; Fitzw Ho Cam; Westcott Ho Th Coll; C Harpenden Herts 1961–64; Chapl Fitzw Coll Cam 1964–69, Fell 1967–69; Hon Fell 1993; Chapl New Hall Cam 1966–69; R Beaconsfield 1969–77; Bp of Taunton 1977–85; Bp of Norwich from 1985
Tel: (01603) 629001
Fax: (01603) 761613

NUGEE, Mr Edward George, MA, TD, QC
Wilberforce Chambers, 8 New Square, Lincoln's Inn, London WC2A 3QP [CHURCH COMMISSIONER] *b* 9 Aug 1928; *educ* Radley Coll; Worc Coll Ox; Barrister-at-Law 1955; QC 1977; Ch Commr from 1989, Bd of Govs from 1993
Tel: 0171–306 0102
Fax: 0171–306 0095
e-mail: enuguee@wilberforce.co.uk

O'BRIEN, Mr Gerald Michael, B SC, DMS
Chestnuts, 14 Oakhill Rd, Sevenoaks, Kent TN13 1NP [ROCHESTER] **1980–85, 1987–** *b* 4 Nov 1948; *educ* Dulwich Coll; Bris Univ; Dir of Communications, Crosslinks; M CEEC 1988–92, 1996–
Tel: (01732) 453894
e-mail: gerry@crosslinks.org

OAKLEY, Mrs Irene May, T CERT
11 High Hamsterley Rd, Rowlands Gill, Tyne and Wear NE39 1HD [DURHAM] **1995–** *b* 8 Dec 1929; *educ* Witney Gr Sch; Erdington Gr Sch; St Mary's Coll Cheltenham; Asst Tchr in various schs 1950–59 and 1974–88; Rtd; M Dioc Parsonages Ctee 1988–97; M Bp's Coun and Stg Ctee 1992–97
Tel: (01207) 542360

OFFER, Ven Clifford Jocelyn, BA, FRSA
26 The Close, Norwich, Norfolk NR1 4DZ [ARCHDEACON OF NORWICH] *b* 10 Aug 1943; *educ* K Sch Cant; Ex Univ; Westcott Ho Th Coll; C Bromley 1969–74; TV Southn City Cen 1974–83; TR Hitchin

1983–94; Chmn Nor Dioc Bd of Min 1994–98; Adn of Nor, Can Res and Libr Nor Cathl from 1994; Warden of Rdrs from 1994; Chmn Nor Course Management Ctee from 1998 *Tel:* (01603) 630525
Fax: (01603) 661104

OGILVIE, Ven Gordon, MA, BD, ALCD
2B *Spencer Ave, Mapperley, Nottingham NG3 5SP* [ARCHDEACON OF NOTTINGHAM] **1990–96** *b* 22 Aug 1942; *educ* Hillhead High Sch Glasgow; Glasgow Univ; Lon Univ; Lon Coll of Div; C Ashtead 1967–72; V St Jas New Barnet 1972–80; Dir Pastl Studies Wycliffe Hall Ox 1980–87; TR St Paul Harlow Town Centre w St Mary Little Parndon 1987–96; Chapl Princess Alexandra Hosp Harlow 1988–96; Chmn Harlow Grp Min 1989–96; Chmn Dioc Ho of Clergy 1994–96; Adn of Nottm from 1996; Chmn Grove Books Ltd; M Simeon's Trustees; M CEEC from 1974 *Tel:* 0115–967 0875 (Home)
(01636) 814490 (Office)
Fax: 0115–967 1014 (Home)
(01636) 815822 (Office)

OGLESBY, Canon Leslie Ellis, MA, M PHIL
Derwent House, 21 West Hill, Hitchin, Herts SG5 2HZ [ST ALBANS] **1995–** *b* 24 Sep 1946; *educ* K Sch Pontefract; Univ Coll Ox; City Univ Lon; Wesley Ho Cam; Fitzw Coll Cam; Ripon Coll Cuddeson; C St Mary Shephall Stevenage 1978–80; V Markyate Street 1980–87; Dir St Alb Minl Tr Scheme 1980–87; Dir Continuing Minl Educ 1987–94; Hon Can St Alb Cathl from 1993; TR Hitchin TM and V St Mary from 1994; Inspector Ho of Bps Panel of Inspectors of Colls and Courses; Gen Syn Rep USPG Coun; M Bp's Coun; M Dioc Syn; Hon Dir Edw King Inst for Min Development; Chmn Verulam Ho Fund Trust; Trustee Grassroots Programme Luton
Tel: (01462) 434017

OLDHAM, Mr Gavin David Redvers, MA
Ashfield House, St Leonards, Tring, Herts HP23 6NP [OXFORD] **1995–** *b* 5 May 1949; *educ* Eton; Trin Coll Cam; Wedd Durlacher Mordaunt 1975–86, Partner 1984–86; Secretariat Barclays De Zoete Wedd (BZW) 1984–88; Chief Exec Barclayshare Ltd 1986–89, Chmn 1989–90; Chmn/Chief Exec The Share Centre Ltd from 1990; M Exec CEIG
Tel: (01442) 829100 (Office)
(01494) 758348 (Home)
Fax: (01442) 891191
e-mail: gavin@share.co.uk

OLIVER, Ven John Michael, BA
Archdeacon's Lodge, 2 Halcyon Hill, Leeds LS7 3PU [ARCHDEACON OF LEEDS] **1992–** *b* 7 Sep 1939; *educ* Ripon Gr Sch; St David Coll Lamp; Ripon Hall Ox; C St Pet Harrogate 1964–67; C St Pet Bramley Leeds 1967–72; V St Mary Harrogate 1972–78; V Beeston 1978–92; Ecum Officer Leeds 1981–86; Hon Can Ripon Cathl 1986–92; RD Armley 1986–92; Adn of Leeds from 1992 *Tel and Fax:* 0113–269 0594

OLIVER, Canon Thomas Gordon, L TH, B TH, DIP AD ED
18 Kings Ave, Rochester, Kent ME1 3DS [ROCHESTER] **1995–** *b* 25 May 1948; *educ* Whinney Hill Sec Mod Sch Dur; Dur Johnson Gr Tech Sch; Lon Coll of Div; St Jo Coll Nottm; C St Jo the Divine Thorpe Edge 1972–76; C St Mark Woodthorpe 1976–80; V All SS Huthwaite 1980–85; Dir Past Studies St Jo Coll Nottm 1985–94; Dioc Dir of Tr from 1994
Tel: (01634) 830333 (Office)
(01634) 841232 (Home)

OSBORNE, Revd Hayward John, MA, PGCE
St Mary's Vicarage, 18 Oxford Rd, Moseley, Birmingham B13 9EH [BIRMINGHAM] **1998–** *b* 16 Sep 1948; *educ* Sevenoaks Sch; New Coll Ox; Westcott Ho Th Coll; C St Pet and St Paul Bromley 1973–77; TV Halesowen 1977–83; TR St Barnabas Worc 1983–88; V St Mary Moseley from 1988; AD Moseley from 1994 *Tel:* 0121–449 1459

OWEN, The Hon and Rt Worshipful Sir John Arthur Dalziel, DCL, MA, BCL, LLM
Bickerstaff Farmhouse, Idlicote, Shipston-on-Stour, Warws CV36 5DT [DEAN OF THE ARCHES AND AUDITOR OF THE CHANCERY COURT OF YORK] **1970–** *b* 22 Nov 1925; *educ* Solihull Sch; BNC Ox; Univ of Wales; High Court Judge; Dean of the Arches and Auditor of Chancery Court of York from 1980

OWEN, Dr Peter Russell, B SC, D PHIL, C PHYS, EUR PHYS, M INST P, FRAS
11 The Downs, Blundellsands Rd West, Liverpool L23 6XS [LIVERPOOL] **1995–** *b* 29 Mar 1947; *educ* Southend High Sch for Boys; Birm Univ; Sussex Univ; Lect/Sen Lect R Military Coll of Science 1970–84; Sen Lect Liv John Moores Univ from 1985; Lay Chmn Sefton Dny Syn *Tel:* 0151–931 2251
e-mail: p.r.owen@livjm.ac.uk

OXFORD, Bishop of, Rt Revd Richard Douglas Harries, DD, FKC, FRSL
Diocesan Church House, North Hinksey, Oxford OX2 0NB **1987–** *b* 2 Jun 1936; *educ* Wellington Coll; Selw Coll Cam; Cuddesdon Th Coll; C St Jo Hampstead 1963–69; Chapl Westf Coll Lon 1967–69; Tutor Wells Th Coll 1969–71; Warden, Wells, Sarum and Wells Th Coll 1971–72; V All SS Fulham 1972–81; Dean K Coll Lon 1981–87; Bp of Ox from 1987; M ACC; M

Bd Christian Aid; Chmn Coun of Christians and Jews; Chair BSR from 1996   *Tel:* (01865) 244566
Fax: (01865) 790470
e-mail: bishopoxon@oxford.anglican.org

OZANNE, Ms Jayne Margaret, MA
21 Rockley Rd, London W14 0BT [APPOINTED MEMBER, ARCHBISHOPS' COUNCIL] *b* 13 Nov 1968; *educ* The Ladies' Coll Guernsey; St Jo Coll Cam; Dir of Communications and Trustee Susannah Trust; Marketing Consultant from 1998; Apptd M Abps' Coun from 1999   *Tel:* 0171–602 2787
Fax: 0171–603 2924
e-mail: jayneozanne@freenet.co.uk

PAGE, Canon Michael John, BD, AKC
Vicarage, Langley Rd, Winchcombe, Cheltenham GL54 5QP [GLOUCESTER] **1998–** *b* 11 Oct 1942; *educ* High Wycombe Tech High Sch; K Coll Lon; St Boniface Th Coll Warminster; C Rawmarsh w Parkgate 1967–72; P-in-c Holy Cross Gleadless Valley 1972–74, TR 1974–77; V Lechlade 1977–86; RD Fairford 1981–86; Hon Can Glouc Cathl from 1991; V Winchcombe from 1986; RD Winchcombe from 1994
Tel: (01242) 602368
Fax: (01242) 602067

PAGE, Mrs Sue (Susan Margaret Brinley)
The Greyhound, Back St, Reepham, Norfolk NR10 4SJ [NORWICH] **1984–** *b* 4 May 1941; *educ* St Paul's Girls Sch; Rose Bruford Coll of Speech and Drama; Actress; M Bp of Willesden's Commn 1968–72; M Abp's Commn on Ch Music 1989–92; M Ctee for Communications from 1991; Tchr of Drama; Voice Tutor; Lect in Communication Skills; Speaker at Confs and Retreats; Rdr   *Tel:* (01603) 870886

PAGET-WILKES, Ven Michael Jocelyn James, ALCD, NDA
10 Northumberland Rd, Leamington Spa, Warws CV32 6HA [ARCHDEACON OF WARWICK] *b* 11 Dec 1941; *educ* Dean Close Sch Cheltenham; Harper Adams Agric Coll; Lon Coll of Div; C All SS Wandsworth 1969–74; V St Jas Hatcham 1974–82; V St Matt Rugby 1982–90; Adn of Warwick from 1990
Tel: (01926) 313337 (Home)
(01203) 674328 (Office)

PAKENHAM-WALSH, Mr John, CB, QC, MA
Crinken, Weydown Rd, Haslemere, Surrey GU27 1DS [STANDING COUNSEL TO THE GENERAL SYNOD] *b* 7 Aug 1928; *educ* Bradfield Coll; Univ Coll Ox; Crown Counsel Hong Kong 1953–57; Parl Counsel Federation of Nigeria 1958–61; Home Office 1961–87; Stg Counsel to Gen Syn from 1988   *Tel:* (01428) 642033

PARKER, Miss Diane Elizabeth Alice, DASS, CQSW
246 Bloomfield Rd, Blackpool, Lancs FY1 6QG [BLACKBURN] **1985–** *b* 4 Aug 1936; *educ* Wyggeston Sch Leic; Liv Univ; Asst Chief Probation Offcr Lancs 1979–94; Rtd; Vc-Chair Dioc Ho of Laity from 1991; Rdr from 1991; Chmn Bay Housing Assn from 1995; M Gov Body APF from 1995; M Vacancy-in-See Legislation Working Party; M Churchwardens Measure Steering and Revision Ctee; M Panel of Chairmen 1996–97; Bp's Adv for Child Protection from 1996; Lay Chmn Blackpool Deanery Syn from 1997   *Tel* and *Fax:* (01253) 766038

PARRY, Mrs Elisabeth Anne
The Cottage, 13 Holton Heath, Poole, Dorset BH16 6JT [SALISBURY] **1992–** *b* 28 Feb 1933; *educ* Queensmount Sch Bournemouth; Sch Gov; Lay Co-Chmn Purbeck Dny Syn; Sec to Bp of Sherborne from 1977; M Exec Wessex Autistic Soc   *Tel:* (01202) 625383 (Home)
(01258) 857659 (Office)

PARTINGTON, Ven Brian Harold
St George's Vicarage, 16 Devonshire Rd, Douglas, Isle of Man IM2 3RB [ARCHDEACON OF THE ISLE OF MAN] **1996–** *b* 31 Dec 1936; *educ* St Aidan's Coll Birkenhead; C Barlow Moor 1963–66; C Deane 1966–68; V Patrick IOM 1968–96; Bp's Youth Chapl 1968–77; RD Peel 1976–96; P-in-c St Jo German 1977–78, V 1978–96; P-in-c Foxdale 1977–78, V 1978–96; Can St German's Cathl 1985–96; Adn of the Isle of Man from 1996; V St Geo and St Barn Douglas from 1996; Chmn DAC; M Isle of Man Ch Commrs; M DBF, Stg Ctee, Legislative Ctee, Vacancy in See Ctee and Communications Ctee   *Tel:* (01624) 675430
Fax: (01624) 616136
e-mail: arch-sodor@mcb.net

PAVER, Mrs Elizabeth Caroline, ACP, CERT ED, FRSA
113 Warning Tongue Lane, Bessacar, Doncaster DN4 6TB [SHEFFIELD and APPOINTED MEMBER, ARCHBISHOPS' COUNCIL] **1991–** *b* 26 Nov 1944; *educ* Doncaster Girls High Sch; St Mary's Coll Cheltenham; In Primary Educ 28 years; Headtchr Crags Rd Nurs/Inf Sch 1976–80; Hdtchr Askern Nurs/Inf Sch Littlemoor 1980–86; Hdtchr Intake Nursery and First Sch Doncaster from 1986; M Nat Coun NAHT from 1991; M Panel of Chmn Gen Syn; Lay Chmn Dioc Syn; M Bp's Coun; M Dioc Bd of Educ Tr Ctee; Apptd M Abps' Coun from 1999   *Tel:* (01302) 530706
Fax: (01302) 360811

PEAKE, Ven (Simon) Jeremy Brinsley, MA
Thugutstrasse 2/12, A 1020 Vienna, Austria [ARCHDEACON OF THE AEGEAN AND DANUBE] *b* 21 Oct 1930; *educ* Eton Coll; Worc Coll Ox; St Steph Ho Ox; C St Andr Eastbourne 1957–60; C Ch the King Claremont

Cape, S Africa 1960–61; R All SS Woodstock Cape S Africa 1961–65; R Gd Shep Maitland Cape S Africa 1965–69; R Kalulushi Zambia 1969–71; Chapl Mindolo Ecum Foundn Kitwe Zambia 1971–77; Chapl Athens 1977–87; Chapl Vienna from 1987; Adn of the Aegean and Danube from 1995
Tel: 00–43–1–663–920–9264 (Office)
Tel and *Fax:* 00–43–1–720–7973 (Home)

PENRITH, Bishop of [SUFFRAGAN, CARLISLE] **Rt Revd Richard Garrard,** BD, AKC, M I MGT
Holm Croft, Castle Rd, Kendal, Cumbria LA9 7AU **1995–** *b* 24 May 1937; *educ* Northn Gr Sch; K Coll Lon; St Boniface Warminster; C Woolwich Par Ch 1961–66; C Gt St Mary Cam 1966–68; Chapl/Lect Keswick Hall Coll of Educ Nor 1968–74; Prin Ch Army Tr Coll 1974–79; Can Chan S'wark Cathl and Dir of Clergy In-Service Tr 1979–87; Can St Eds and Adv for Clergy Tr 1987–91; Adn of Sudbury 1991–94; Bp of Penrith from 1994; M BM and Miss Th Adv Grp from 1996; Chmn Coun Carl and Blackb Dioc Tr Inst from 1997; M Bp's Coun; M Dioc Syn; Chair Dioc Bd for Min and Tr; M DBF; M Bd for Par Miss and Development
Tel: (01539) 727836
Fax: (01539) 734380

PERHAM, Very Revd Michael Francis, MA
The Provost's House, 9 Highfield Rd, Derby DE22 1GX [PROVOST OF DERBY] **1989–92, 1993–** *b* 8 Nov 1947; *educ* Hardye's Sch Dorchester; Keble Coll Ox; Cuddesdon Th Coll; C St Mary Addington 1976–81; Chapl to Bp of Win 1981–84; TR Oakdale, Poole 1984–92; Can Res and Prec Nor Cathl 1992–98; Vc-Dean 1995–98; Prov of Derby from 1998; M Liturg Commn from 1986; M Cathls Fabric Commn from 1996; Author; Chmn Cathls Liturg Grp
Tel and *Fax:* (01332) 342971 (Home)
Tel: (01332) 341201 (Office)
Fax: (01332) 203991 (Office)
e-mail: Derby.Cathedral@btinternet.com

PERRY, Ms Lesley
Lambeth Palace, London SE1 7JU [SECRETARY FOR BROADCASTING, PRESS AND COMMUNICATIONS TO THE ARCHBISHOP OF CANTERBURY] *b* 1 Apr 1952; *educ* Scarborough Girls High Sch; K Coll Lon; Br Coun Offcr 1975–87; Head of Public Affairs, R Inst of Internat Affairs 1987–91; Sec for Broadcasting, Press and Communications to the Abp of Cant from 1991
Tel: 0171–928 8282 (Office)
0171–373 3085 (Home)

PETERBOROUGH, Bishop of, Rt Revd Ian Patrick Martyn Cundy, MA
Bishop's Lodgings, The Palace, Peterborough, Cambs PE1 1YA **1996–** *b* 23 Apr 1945; *educ* Monkton Combe Sch; Trin Coll Cam; Tyndale Hall Th Coll; C Ch Ch New Malden 1969–73; Tutor Oak Hill Th Coll 1973–77; TR Mortlake w E Sheen 1978–83; Warden Cranmer Hall St Jo Coll Dur 1983–92; Bp of Lewes 1992–96; Bp of Petrb from 1996; Chmn CCU from 1998
Tel: (01733) 562492
Fax: (01733) 890077

PETERSON, Canon John Louis, BA, TH D, DD, DCL
Anglican Consultative Council, Partnership House, 157 Waterloo Rd, London SE1 8UT [SECRETARY GENERAL, ANGLICAN CONSULTATIVE COUNCIL] *b* 17 Dec 1942; *educ* Concordia Univ; Harvard Univ; Instructor Seabury Western Th Seminary 1972–73; Adjunct Prof 1973–75; Assoc St Aug Wilmette 1976; Can Th Christ the King Cathl Kalamazoo; Hon Can Cathl Ch of Ch the King Kalamazoo from 1982; V St Steph Plainwell 1976–82; Angl Centre in Rome 1988–91; Consultant Ibru Centre Nigeria from 1990; Dean St Geo Coll Jerusalem 1983–94; Hon Can St Geo Cathl Jerusalem from 1994; Sec Gen ACC from 1995; Hon Can Cant Cathl from 1995; M Gov Body Angl Centre in Rome from 1995
Tel: 0171–620 1110
Fax: 0171–620 1070
e-mail: John.l.peterson@anglicancommunion.org

PETTY, Very Revd John Fitzmaurice, MA, HON D LITT
7 Priory Row, Coventry CV1 5ES [PROVOST OF COVENTRY] *b* 9 Mar 1935; *educ* K Sch Bruton; RMA Sandhurst; Trin Hall Cam; Cuddesdon Th Coll. C St Cuth Fir Vale Sheff 1966–69; P-in-c Bp Andrewes' Ch St Helier Estate 1969–75; V St Jo Hurst Ashton-under-Lyne 1975–88; AD Ashton-under-Lyne 1983–87; Hon Can Man Cathl 1986–88; Provost of Cov Cathl from 1988
Tel: (01203) 227597
Fax: (01203) 631448
e-mail: prov@coventrycathedral.org.uk

PEYTON, Revd Nigel, MA, BD, STM
Rectory, Lambley, Nottingham NG4 4QP [SOUTHWELL] **1995–** *b* 5 Feb 1951; *educ* Latymer Sch Lon; Edin Univ; Union Th Seminary New York; Edin Th Coll; Chapl St Paul Cathl Dundee 1976–82; P-i-r-c All So Invergowrie 1979–85; V All SS Nottm 1985–91; P-in-c H Trin Lambley from 1991; Dioc Min Development Adv from 1991; Bps' Educ Selector; Exec Officer Dioc Bd of Min and Pastl Ctee; JP
Tel: 0115–931 3531 (Home)
(01636) 814331 (Office)
Fax: (01636) 815084
e-mail: SDBF@John316.com

PHILPOTT, Prebendary Samuel
St Peter's Vicarage, Wyndham Square, Plymouth, Devon PL1 5EG [EXETER] **1990–** *b* 6 Feb 1941; *educ* R Naval

Hosp Sch Holbrook; Kelham Th Coll; C St Mark Swindon 1965–70; C St Martin Torquay 1970–73; TV All SS Exmouth 1973–76; V Shaldon 1976–78; V St Pet Plymouth from 1978; RD Plymouth Devonport 1985–91 and from 1995; Preb of Ex Cathl from 1991; M DBF; M Dioc Bd of Educ; M Dioc Pastl Ctee; M Dioc Vacancy-in-See Ctee; M Bp's Coun; M Dioc Children and Young People's Ctee; Chair Icthus Community Projects; Chair Ship Hostel Plymouth; M Nat Coun Forward in Faith; M CCBI and CTE Enabling Grp *Tel:* (01752) 222007 *Fax:* (01752) 257973

PHYTHIAN, Mr George, B SC (AGRIC), DIP ED, T CERT
2 Shaftesbury Place, Scotforth, Lancaster LA1 4PZ [BLACKBURN] **1991–** *b* 17 Jul 1927; *educ* Upholland Gr Sch; Reading Univ; Asst Master Soham Gr Sch 1952–55; Head of Agric/Horticulture Worthing Tech High Sch 1955–60; Sen Master Pershore High Sch 1960–66; Hdmaster Ripley St Thos High Sch Lancaster 1966–91; Rtd; Rdr from 1954; M Dioc Syn; M Dioc Pastl Ctee; Sch Gov *Tel:* (01524) 65460

PICKFORD, Mr Christopher John, BA, DAA, FSA
Church of England Record Centre, 15 Galleywall Rd, South Bermondsey, London SE16 3PB [DIRECTOR, CHURCH OF ENGLAND RECORD CENTRE] *b* 2 Jun 1952; *educ* K Sch Worc; Leic Univ; Univ Coll Lon; Trainee Archivist Leics 1973–74; Asst Archivist Heref and Worc CC 1975–77; Asst Archivist Beds CC 1978–86; County Archivist Beds 1986–98; Dir CE Record Centre from 1998; M St Albs DAC 1986–91; M CCC Bells Sub-Ctee 1985–90; Bells Adv Birm DAC 1992–98 *Tel:* 0171–231 1251 Ext. 4183 *Fax:* 0171–231 5243
e-mail: chris-pickford@chucomm.org.uk

PITHERS, Canon Brian Hoyle
Vicarage, 63 Michaelson Ave, Torrisholme, Morecambe LA4 6SF [BLACKBURN] **1989–** *b* 6 Jun 1934; *educ* Rochdale High Sch; Chich Th Coll; C SS Pet and Paul Wisbech 1966–70; V Fenstanton 1970–75; V Hilton 1970–75; V St Matt Havergham Eaves 1975–85; P-in-c H Trin Habergham Eaves 1978–85; V St Matt w H Trin Habergham Eaves 1985–86; TR Ribbleton from 1986; V Ascen and St Martin Torrisholme from 1992; M BM 1990–97; M CBF 1990–95; M Cen Stewardship Ctee 1990–95; M Chs Commn on Miss 1994–95; M Gov Body Carl Dioc Tr Inst from 1993; Hon Can Blackb Cathl from 1997
Tel: (01524) 413144
e-mail: canonbrian@msn.com

PITTS, Revd Eve (Evadne Ione)
19 Elmcroft Ave, Bartley Green, Birmingham B32 4LZ [BIRMINGHAM] **1990–** *b* 23 Dec 1950; *educ* Coltesmore Sec Sch; Qu Coll Birm; C St Mich Bartley Green from 1989 *Tel:* 0121–422 1436

PLATTEN, Very Revd Stephen George, B ED
The Deanery, The Close, Norwich, Norfolk NR1 4EG [DEAN OF NORWICH] **1997–** *b* 17 May 1947; *educ* Stationers' Company's Sch; Lon Univ Inst of Educ; Trin Coll Ox; Cuddesdon Th Coll; C Headington 1975–78; Chapl and Tutor Linc Th Coll 1978–82; DDO and Minl Tr and Can Res Portsm Cathl 1982–89; Sec for Ecum Affairs to Abp of Cant 1990–95; Dean of Nor from 1995 *Tel:* (01603) 218308
Fax: (01603) 766032
e-mail: dean@cathedral.org.uk

PLYMOUTH, Bishop of [SUFFRAGAN, EXETER] **Rt Revd John Henry Garton,** MA
31 Riverside Walk, Tamerton Foliot, Plymouth PL5 4AQ *b* 3 Oct 1941; *educ* Tudor Grange Gr Sch Solihull; RMA Sandhurst; Worc Coll Ox; Cuddesdon Th Coll; Commissioned in R Tank Regiment 1962; CF Guards Depot Pirbright 1969–70, RMA Sandhurst 1970–72; N Ireland 1972–73; Lect Linc Th Coll 1973–78; TR Cov E 1978–86; Prin Ripon Coll Cuddesdon 1986–96; V Cuddesdon 1986–96; Hon Can Worc Cathl 1987–96; Bp of Plymouth from 1996
Tel: (01752) 769836
Fax: (01752) 769818

POLKINGHORNE, Canon Dr John Charlton, KBE, MA, PH D, SC D, FRS, DD
74 Hurst Park Ave, Cambridge CB4 2AF [UNIVERSITIES, CAMBRIDGE] **1990–** *b* 16 Oct 1930; *educ* Perse Sch Cam; Trin Coll Cam; Westcott Ho Th Coll; Prof of Mathematical Physics Cam Univ 1968–79; V Blean 1984–86; Dean Trin Hall Cam 1986–89; Pres Qu Coll Cam 1989–96; Fell Qu Coll Cam from 1996; Can Th Liv from 1994; M BSR from 1990
Tel and *Fax:* (01223) 360743

POLLARD, Prof Arthur, BA, B TH, BD, B LITT, D LITT
Sand Hall, North Cave, Brough, E Yorks HU15 2LA [YORK] **1990–** *b* 22 Dec 1922; *educ* Clitheroe R Gr Sch; Leeds Univ; Linc Coll Ox; Lect and Sen Lect Man Univ 1949–67; Prof of English Hull Univ 1967–84, Dean of Faculty of Arts 1976–78; Consultant Prof of English, Univ of Buckm 1983–89; Councillor, Alderman, Leader Congleton Boro Coun 1952–67; Co Councillor Humberside Co Coun (Educ Spokesman Conservative Grp) 1979–96; M E Riding Coun and Educ Spokesman from 1995; M Funding Agency for Schs 1996–98; M Gen Syn Bd of Educ and Schs Ctee from 1991, Chmn from 1996; M Abp's Coun 1991–97; M Dioc Bd of Educ 1990–93; Rdr from 1951 *Tel:* (01430) 422202 (Home)
(01482) 885011 (Office)
Fax: (01430) 424890

PONTEFRACT, Bishop of [SUFFRAGAN, WAKEFIELD] **Rt Revd David Charles James,** B SC, BA, PH D
Pontefract House, 181A Manygates Lane, Wakefield WF2 7DR 1985–90 b 6 Mar 1945; *educ* Nottm High Sch; Ex Univ; Nottm Univ; St Jo Coll Nottm; C Ch Ch Portswood 1973–76; C Goring-by-Sea 1976–78; Chapl UEA Nor 1978–82; V Ecclesfield 1982–90; RD Ecclesfield 1987–90; V Ch Ch Portswood 1990–98; Hon Can Win Cathl 1998; Bp of Pontefract from 1998
Tel: (01924) 250781
Fax: (01924) 240490

POPE, Mr John Henry William
6 Hawthylands Rd, Hailsham, E Sussex BN27 1EU [CHICHESTER] 1997– *b* 8 Aug 1945; *educ* Roan Sch for Boys; Woolwich Poly; Rtd   *Tel:* (01323) 841613

PORTER, Mr John Albert
165 Newland Park, Hull HU5 2DX [YORK] 1995– *b* 10 Oct 1941; *educ* Scarborough Boys High Sch; RAF Coll Cranwell; Computer Consultant; M Abp's Coun; Lay Chmn Hull Dny Syn; M DBF
Tel and *Fax:* (01482) 346284
e-mail: John_Porter@japorter.karoo.co.uk

PORTSMOUTH, Bishop of, Rt Revd Kenneth William Stevenson, MA, PH D, DD, FR HIST S
Bishopsgrove, 26 Osborn Rd, Fareham, Hants PO16 7DQ 1995– *b* 9 Nov 1949; *educ* Edin Academy; Edin Univ; Southn Univ; Man Univ; Sarum and Wells Th Coll; C Grantham 1973–76; Lect Boston Par Ch 1976–80; pt Lect Linc Th Coll 1975–80; Chapl and Lect Man Univ 1980–86; TV Whitworth Man 1980–82; TR 1982–86; Vis Prof Univ of Notre Dame Indiana 1982; ABM Selector 1982–92; R H Trin w St Mary Guildf 1986–95; Chmn Anglo-Nordic-Baltic Th Conf from 1997; M Doct Commn from 1996; Bp of Portsm from 1995
Tel: (01329) 280247
Fax: (01329) 231538

PRITCHARD, Ven John Lawrence, MA, M LITT
29 The Precincts, Canterbury, Kent CT1 2EP [ARCHDEACON OF CANTERBURY] *b* 22 Apr 1948; *educ* Arnold Sch Blackpool; St Pet Coll Ox; Ridley Hall Th Coll; St Jo Coll Dur; C St Martins-in-the-Bull Ring Birm 1972–76; Dioc Youth Officer B & W 1976–79; V St Geo Wilton 1980–88; Dir Pastl Studies Cranmer Hall and St Jo Coll Dur 1989–93; Warden Cranmer Hall 1993–96; Adn of Cant and Can Res Cant Cathl from 1996
Tel: (01227) 463036
Fax: (01227) 785209

PURCHAS, Canon (Catherine) Patience Ann, BA
Rectory, Church St, Wheathampstead, St Albans, Herts AL4 8AD [ST ALBANS] 1990– *b* 23 Mar 1939; *educ* St Alb Girls Gr Sch; St Mary's Coll Dur; St Alb Minl Tr Scheme; Relig Educ Resource Centre 1980–81; Relig Broadcasting Chiltern Radio 1981–87; Hon Dss Wheathampstead from 1987; Sec to Dioc Bd of Min 1987–93; Bp's Officer for Women's and NSM from 1993; Pro-Prolocutor Lower Ho Conv of Cant from 1994; M Gen Syn Stg Ctee from 1996; Author; Broadcaster
Tel: (01582) 833144 (Home)
Tel and *Fax:* (01582) 834285 (Office)

PYBUS, Mr Roy
22 Beaclair Rd, Wavertree, Liverpool L15 6XG [LIVERPOOL] 1995– *b* 3 Nov 1941; *educ* Liv Inst High Sch; Univ Coll Lon; Solicitor admitted 1966
Tel and *Fax:* 0151-722 9792

PYE, Mr Christopher Charles, BA, M SC
140 Hinckley Rd, St Helens, Merseyside WA11 9JY [LIVERPOOL] 1985–90, 1992– *b* 21 Apr 1946; *educ* Grange Park Sch St Helens; Open Univ. Technologist in Glass Industry from 1963; Occupational Hygienist; Lay Chmn St Helens Dny Syn from 1986; Lay Chmn Dioc Syn from 1991   *Tel:* (01744) 609506

RADFORD, Mrs Jennifer, MA
Poplar Farm, Hognaston, Ashbourne, Derbys DE6 1PR [DERBY] 1990– *b* 30 Oct 1937; *educ* Arnold High Sch Blackpool; Girton Coll Cam; Head of English Lemrose Sch Derby 1974–77; Head of English Zahra Sch Muscat, Oman 1981–83; Co Councillor Derbys 1989–97; M Derbys Dales Distr Coun from 1995; Educ Consultant in Eng and RE and Insp of Schs
Tel and *Fax:* (01335) 370143

RADFORD, Mr Roger George, AIA
7 Little College St, London SW1P 3SF [SECRETARY AND TREASURER TO THE CHURCH OF ENGLAND PENSIONS BOARD] *b* 17 Mar 1944; *educ* City of Lon Sch; Clerical, Medcl and Gen Life Assur Soc to May 1984; Dep Sec to Pensions Bd May-Sept 1984; Sec and Treas from Oct 1984
Tel: 0171–898 1807
Fax: 0171–898 1801

RAMSBURY, Bishop of [AREA BISHOP, SALISBURY] [NOT APPOINTED AT TIME OF GOING TO PRESS.]

RANDOLPH-HORN, Revd David Henry, BA, CQSW
The Inner Cities Religious Council, Floor 4/K10, Eland House, Bressenden Place, London SW1E 5DU [SECRETARY, INNER CITIES RELIGIOUS COUNCIL] *b* 15 Sep 1947; *educ* Stamford Sch; Nottm Univ; Keele Univ; Qu Coll Birm; C St Paul Hamstead Birm 1982–84; V St Jas Aston 1984–94; Sec Inner Cities Religious

Coun from 1994; C Holy Trin and St Aug of Hippo Harrow Green from 1997 *Tel:* 0171–890 3704 (Office) 0181–257 1162 (Home) *Fax:* 0171–890 3709 *e-mail:* drhorn@detrreegell.demon.co.uk

RATCLIFF, Ven David William, DIP AD ED
Styrmansgatan 1, S-114 54 Stockholm, Sweden [ARCH-DEACON OF SCANDINAVIA AND GERMANY] *b* 3 Nov 1937; *educ* Cant Cathl Choir Sch; St Mich Sch Ingoldisthorpe; K Coll Lon; Lon Univ Extra-Mural Dept; Edin Th Coll; C St Aug S Croydon 1962–65; P-in-c St Fran Selsdon 1965–69; V St Mary Milton Regis 1969–75; Adult Educ and Lay Tr Adv Cant dio 1975–91; Hon Min Can Cant Cathl 1975–91; Hon Pres Ecum Assoc Adult Educ in Eur 1982–88; M Internat Ctee German Evang Kirchentag from 1983; R American Episc Par Ch the King Frankfurt from 1991; Adn of Scandinavia and Germany from 1996; Hon Can Gibraltar Cathl from 1996; Chmn Commn on Min of the Baptised (ECUSA in Eur); Representative at Gen Convention of ECUSA 1994 and 1997
Tel: 46–8–663–8248
Fax: 46–8–663–8911
e-mail: anglican.church@telia.com

RAWES, Dr James Charteris Lea, MA, MB, B CHIR, D OBST RCOG, D CH
Falcons, Little Easton, Dunmow, Essex CM6 2JH [CHELMSFORD] 1995– *b* 16 Nov 1929; *educ* Marlboro Coll; Jes Coll Cam; St Thos Hosp Lon; USPG Miss List (Central and S Africa) 1960–66; GP 1966–90; pt GP and Nursing Homes Sch Adv N Essex HA 1991–95; Gov Helena Romanes Sch Dunmow 1971–94, Chmn 1988–94; Rtd 1990; USPG Gen Ctee and HealthAdv Grp 1969–82 and from 1993 *Tel:* (01371) 872640

RAZZALL, Revd Charles Humphrey, MA, BA
Holy Trinity Vicarage, 46 Godson St, Oldham OL1 2DB [MANCHESTER] 1995– *b* 7 May 1955; *educ* St Paul's Sch Lon; Worc Coll Ox; Qu Coll Cam; Westcott Ho Th Coll; C Catford and Downham TM 1979–83; V St Hilda w St Cyprian Crofton Park 1983–87; Dioc UPA Officer Man 1987–92; TV Oldham and AD Oldham from 1992; M BSR Community and Urban Affairs Ctee *Tel:* 0161–627 1540

READ, Revd Charles William, BA, PGCE, M PHIL
Vicarage, Great Cheetham St East, Higher Broughton, Salford M7 4UH [MANCHESTER] 1997– *b* 4 Feb 1960; *educ* K Edw VI Sch Lichf; Man Univ; Man Poly; St Jo Coll Nottm; Head of RS Audenshaw High Sch 1982–86; C Oldham Tm Min 1988–90; C St Clem Urmston 1990–93; Assoc Min Crawshawbooth and Goodshaw 1993–94; P-in-c St Jas and St Clem Broughton 1994–96; TV Broughton from 1996; M Dioc Syn; M Dioc Worship Ctee from 1991; M Dioc Bd of Min from 1995; M Editorial Bd Dioc Magazine 1990–94; Dir Grove Books from 1992; Hon Lect Regents Th Coll from 1994 *Tel:* 0161–792 1208

READE, Ven Nicholas Stewart, BA, DIP TH
27 The Avenue, Lewes BN7 1QT [ARCHDEACON OF LEWES AND HASTINGS] 1995– *b* 9 Dec 1946; *educ* Eliz Coll Guernsey; Leeds Univ; Coll of the Resurr Mirfield; C St Chad Coseley 1973–75; C-in-c H Cross Bilbrook and C Codsall 1975–78; V St Pet Upper Gornal and Chapl Burton Rd Hosp Dudley 1978–82; V Mayfield 1982–88; RD Dallington 1982–88; V and RD Eastbourne 1988–97; Chmn Dioc Liturg Ctee 1989–97; Can and Preb Chich Cathl from 1990; Adn of Lewes and Hastings from 1997; M Bp's Coun from 1989; Chmn Dioc Bd of Patronage from 1992; Vc-Pres Dioc Syn and Chmn Ho of Clergy from 1997
Tel: (01273) 479530
Fax: (01273) 476529

READING, Bishop of [AREA BISHOP, OXFORD] **Rt Revd Dominic (Edward William Murray) Walker,** OGS, AKC, MA, D LITT
Bishop's House, Tidmarsh Lane, Tidmarsh, Reading RG8 8HA b 28 Jun 1948; *educ* Plymouth Coll; K Coll Lon; Heythrop Coll Lon; C St Faith Wandsworth 1972–73; Dom Chapl to Bp of S'wark 1973–76; R Newington 1976–85; RD S'wark and Newington 1980–85; V Brighton 1985–97; RD Brighton 1985–97; Can and Preb Chich Cathl 1985–97; Superior OGS 1990–96; Bp of Reading from 1997 *Tel:* 0118–984 1216
Fax: 0118–984 1218
e-mail: bishopreading@oxford.anglican.org

REDDEN, Mr Jonathan Francis, MB, BS, FRCS ENG, FRCS ED (ORTH)
Tofield House, Carr Lane, Wadworth, Doncaster DN11 9AR [SHEFFIELD] 1989– *b* 21 Feb 1947; *educ* Loughb Gr Sch; St Bart Hosp Medical Coll Lon Univ; Senior Registrar Edin 1977–81; Lect Orthopaedic Surgery Wellington Medical Sch New Zealand; Consultant Orthopaedic Surgeon Doncaster R Infirmary from 1981 *Tel:* (01302) 853829

REDMAN, Mr Anthony James, B SC, FRICS
The Cottage, Great Livermere, Bury St Edmunds, Suffolk IP31 1JG [ST EDMUNDSBURY AND IPSWICH] 1989– *b* 1 May 1951; *educ* Walton on Thames Sec Mod Sch; Surbiton Gr Sch; Reading Univ; Chartered Building Surveyor; Conservation accredited; Rdr from 1976; M Dioc Property Ctee 1983–97; M Ecclesiastical Architects and Surveyors Assn Exec from 1988; Pres 1993–94; M CCC from 1991, Jt Vc-Chair (Conservation) from 1996; M CCC Publications Sub-Ctee 1991–95; Surveyor of Fabric St Edm Cathl from 1992;

M Exec Ctee Suffolk Hist Chs Trust 1993–97; Chmn RICS Conservation Skills Panel from 1998; M St Albs DAC from 1998   *Tel:* (01359) 269335
(01284) 760421
Fax: (01284) 704734
e-mail: whitcp@globalnet.co.uk

REED, Revd Keith Andrew, BA
25 Marylebone Rd, London NW1 5JR [ECUMENICAL REPRESENTATIVE (METHODIST CHURCH)] **1995–** *b* 26 Jul 1939; *educ* Bradf Gr Sch; Bris Univ; Didsbury Th Coll Bris; M Dursley and Stonehouse 1963–65; Huddersfield (West) 1965–71; Leeds (Headingley) 1971–80; York (North) 1980–95; Asst Sec of Conf and Ecum Officer from 1995   *Tel:* 0171–486 5502
Fax: 0171–224 1510

REES, Mrs Christina (Henking Muller), MA
Churchfield, Pudding Lane, Barley, Royston, Herts SG8 8JX [ST ALBANS] **1990–** *b* 6 Jul 1953; *educ* Hampton Day Sch; Pomona Coll; Wheaton Graduate Sch; K Coll Lon; Researcher IBA 1980; Asst Public Relations Offcr The Childrens Society 1985–87; Writer from 1980; Broadcaster from 1990; M Crown Appts Commn 1995; M Steering Ctee and Initiation Services Revision Ctee from 1996; M CECC from 1996; M ABM from 1996; Chair WATCH (Women and the Church); M Dioc Bd for Chr Development
Tel: (01763) 848472
(01763) 848822
Fax: (01763) 848774
e-mail: chrisrees@xc.org

REES, Revd (Vivian) John (Howard), MA, LL B, M PHIL
36 Cumnor Hill, Oxford OX2 9HB [OXFORD] **1995–** *b* 21 Apr 1951; *educ* Skinners' Sch Tunbridge Wells; Southn Univ; Ox Univ; Leeds Univ; Wycliffe Hall Ox; Solicitor (Admitted 1975); C Moor Allerton TM 1979–82; Chapl and Tutor Sierra Leone Th Hall, Freetown 1983–86; Ptnr Winckworth and Pemberton Solicitors from 1986; Treas Eccles Law Soc from 1995; Joint Registrar Ox Dio from 1998; Dep Registrar Prov of Cant from 1998; Legal Adv ACC from 1998   *Tel:* (01865) 865875
Fax: (01865) 726274
e-mail: johnrees@mailbox.rmplc.co.uk

REESE, Prebendary John David, CERT ED
Tupsley Vicarage, 107 Church Rd, Hereford HR1 1RT [HEREFORD] **1997–** *b* 29 Apr 1949; *educ* Handsworth Gr Sch; Coll of St Mark and St Jo; Ripon Coll Cuddesdon; C St Mary and All SS Kidderminster 1976–81; V S Johor Malaysia 1982–85; V Bp's Castle w Mainstone 1985–91; RD Clun Forest 1987–91; V Tupsley w Hampton Bp from 1991; RD Heref City from 1996; M Dioc Bd of Educ; M Dioc Pastl and Minl Ctee   *Tel:* (01432) 274490

REID, Very Revd (William) Gordon, MA
The Deanery, Bomb House Lane, Gibraltar [DEAN OF GIBRALTAR] *b* 28 Jan 1943; *educ* Galashiels Academy; Edin Univ; Keble Coll Ox; Cuddesdon Th Coll; C St Salvador Edin 1967–69; Chapl Sarum Th Coll 1969–72; R St Mich and All SS Edin 1972–84; Provost Inverness Cathl 1984–87; Chapl St Nic Ankara, Turkey 1987–89; Chap St Pet and St Seigfrid Stockholm 1989–92; V Gen Dio in Eur 1992–98; Adn in Eur 1996–98; Dean of Gibraltar from 1998
Tel: 00–350–78377 (Home)
00–350–75745 (Office)
Fax: 00–350–78463 (Office)

REISS, Ven Robert Paul, MA
Archdeacon's House, New Rd, Wormley, Godalming, Surrey GU8 5SU [ARCHDEACON OF SURREY] **1990–** *b* 20 Jan 1943; *educ* Haberdashers' Aske's Sch Hampstead; Trin Coll Cam; Westcott Ho Th Coll; C St John's Wood 1969–73; Asst Missr Rajshahi Miss Dacca Bangladesh 1973; Chapl Trin Coll Cam 1973–78; Selection Sec ACCM 1978–85; Sen Selection Sec 1983–85; TR Grantham 1986–96; RD Grantham 1991–96; Adn of Surrey from 1996; Chmn ABM Wrkg Party on Minl Review; M PWM 1993–96; M Bd of Educ from 1994; Chmn Bd of Educ F and HE Ctee from 1995   *Tel:* (01428) 682563
Fax: (01428) 682993
e-mail: bob.reiss@cofeguildford.org.uk

REPTON, Bishop of [SUFFRAGAN, DERBY]
[NOT APPOINTED AT TIME OF GOING TO PRESS.]

RHODES, Revd David Grant, BA, CERT TH, DIP AD ED
111 Potternewton Lane, Leeds LS7 3LW [RIPON] **1995–** *b* 4 Apr 1943; *educ* Huddersfield New Coll; Ex Univ; Sarum Th Coll; Journalist 1960–69; C Mirfield 1972–75; V St Thos Batley 1975–80; Adult Educ Officer Wakef 1976–79; Journalist and NSM St Jo Huddersfield 1982–86; Dir BRF 1986–87; V Roberttown 1987–94; Originator of Prayer Lights Min from 1989; NSM St Martin Potternewton from 1995; pt Project Worker w Faith in Leeds One City Project from 1994   *Tel:* 0113–274 2021
Tel and *Fax:* 0113–262 7247

RICHARDSON, Mr Colin
379 Chester Rd, Hartford, Northwich, Cheshire CW8 1QR [CHESTER] **1995–** Dep Headteacher

RICHARDSON, Very Revd John Stephen, BA, M INST D
The Provost's House, 1 Cathedral Close, Bradford, W Yorks BD1 4EG [PROVOST OF BRADFORD] 1993– *b* 2 Apr 1950; *educ* Haslingden Gr Sch; Southn Univ; St Jo Coll Nottm; C Bramcote 1974–78; C Radipole and Melcombe Regis 1977–80; P-in-c Stinsford, Winterborne Came w Whitcombe 1980–83; Asst Dioc Missr Sarum 1980–83; V Ch Ch Nailsea 1983–90; Dioc Adv on Evang B & W 1986–90; M Coun St Jo Coll Nottm 1988–94; V and Provost Bradf Cathl from 1990; Trustee and Vc-Chmn Acorn Chr Healing Trust from 1990; Trustee Spennithorne Home of Healing and Holy Rood Ho from 1991; Bp's Selector ABM 1992–96; M BM from 1996; M Evang Alliance Exec from 1994; M Spring Harvest Coun from 1998
Tel: (01274) 777722
(01274) 777727
Fax: (01274) 777730

RICHBOROUGH, Bishop of [PROVINCIAL EPISCOPAL VISITOR, CANTERBURY] **Rt Revd Edwin Barnes,** MA
14 Hall Place Gardens, St Albans, Herts AL1 3SP 1975–78, 1985–87, 1990–95 *b* 6 Feb 1935; *educ* Plymouth Coll; Ox Univ; Cuddesdon Th Coll; C St Mark North End Portsm 1960–64; C All SS Woodham Guildf 1964–67; R Farncombe 1967–78; V All SS Hessle 1978–87; Prin St Steph Ho 1987–95; M Gen Syn Stg Ctee 1993–95; M ABM 1990–95; Hon Can Ch Ch Ox 1994–95; CCBI Rep and CTE Enabling Grp 1994–95; Bp of Richborough from 1995; Pres Guild of All So from 1996; Asst Bp and Hon Can St Albs from 1997
Tel: (01727) 857764
Fax: (01727) 763025

RILEY, Very Revd Ken (Kenneth Joseph), BA, MA
1 Booth Clibborn Court, Park Lane, Manchester M7 4PJ [DEAN OF MANCHESTER] 1995– *b* 25 Jun 1940; *educ* Holywell Gr Sch; Univ Coll of Wales Aberystwyth; Linacre Coll Ox; Wycliffe Hall Th Coll; C Em Fazakerley 1964–66; Chapl Brasted Place Coll 1966–69; Chapl Oundle Sch 1969–74; Chapl Liv Univ 1974–83; V Mossley Hill 1975–83; RD Childwall 1982–83; Dioc Warden of Rdrs 1980–83; Can Res Liv Cathl 1983–93 (Treas 1983–87; Prec 1987–93); Dean of Man from 1993
Tel: 0161–833 2220
Fax: 0161–839 6226

RINGROSE, Ven Hedley Sidney, BA
The Sanderlings, Thorncliffe Drive, Cheltenham GL51 6PY [ARCHDEACON OF CHELTENHAM] 1990– *b* 29 Jun 1942; *educ* W Oxfordshire Coll; Open Univ; Sarum Th Coll; C Bishopston 1968–71; C Easthampstead 1971–75; V St Geo Gloucester w Whaddon 1975–88; RD Gloucester City 1983–88; V Cirencester w Watermoor 1988–98; RD Cirencester 1989–97; Hon Can Glouc Cathl 1986–98; Chmn Dioc Bd of Patronage 1990–98; Chmn Dioc Ho of Clergy 1994–98; Adn of Cheltenham from 1998; Reserved Can Glouc Cathl from 1998; Chmn Dioc Bd of Educ from 1998
Tel: (01242) 522923
Fax: (01242) 235925

RIPON, Bishop of, Rt Revd David Nigel de Lorentz Young, MA
Bishop Mount, Ripon, N Yorks HG4 5DP 1977– *b* 2 Sep 1931; *educ* Wellington Coll; Ball Coll Ox; Wycliffe Hall Th Coll; C All Hallows Allerton Liv 1959–62; C St Mark Hamilton Terr St Jo Wood Lon 1962–63; CMS Missnry 1963–67; Dir Dept Buddhist Studies Lanka Th Coll 1965–67; Lect in Buddhist Studies Man Univ 1967–70; V Burwell Ely 1970–75; Adn of Huntingd 1975–77; Bp of Ripon from 1977; Chmn Gen Syn Bd of Educ and Nat Soc from 1994
Tel: (01765) 602045
Fax: (01765) 600758

RIPPETH, Mrs Ione
11 The Ridge, Ryton, Tyne and Wear NE40 3LN [DURHAM] 1995– *b* 1940; Lect and Counsellor
Tel: 0191–413 3920

RISDON, Revd John Alexander, DIP TH
Stapleton Rectory, 21 Park Rd, Stapleton, Bristol BS16 1AZ [BRISTOL] 1995– *b* 5 Jul 1942; *educ* Churcher's Coll Petersfield; Lon Bible Coll; Clifton Th Coll; C St Jo W Ealing 1968–72; C St Pet Heref 1972–74; Hon C Ch Ch Bromley 1974–77; Ord Candidates Sec CPAS 1974–77; TV H Trin Cheltenham 1977–86; R H Trin Stapleton from 1986; M Bp's Coun; Dir DBF; M Coun Trin Coll Bris; M Dioc Pastl Ctee
Tel: 0117–958 3858

ROBILLIARD, Mr David John
Le Petit Gree, Torteval, Guernsey GY8 0RD [WINCHESTER-CHANNEL ISLANDS] 1998– *b* 22 Nov 1952; *educ* Guernsey Gr Sch for Boys; Clearing and Internat Banking 1969–82; Her Majesty's Dep Greffier 1982–87; Prin Asst Chief Exec Guernsey Civil Service 1987–94; Hd of External and Constitutional Affairs States of Guernsey from 1994; M Dioc Vacancy in See Ctee; Sec Guernsey Dny
Tel: (01481) 264344

ROBINSON, Ven Anthony William, CERT ED
10 Arden Court, Horbury, Wakefield WF4 5AH [ARCHDEACON OF PONTEFRACT] 1995–97 *b* 25 Apr 1956; *educ* Bedf Modern Sch; Bedf Coll of HE; Sarum and Wells Th Coll; C St Paul Tottenham 1982–85; TV Resurr Leic 1985–89, TR 1989–97; RD Christianity N 1992–

97; Hon Can Leic Cathl from 1994; M CBF 1995–97; M CMEAC 1996–97; Adn of Pontefract from 1997
Tel: (01924) 276797
Fax: (01924) 261095
e-mail: awrobinson@arden.clara.net

ROBINSON, Ven (John) Kenneth, BD, AKC
Rua da Ginjeira, Lote 5, Alcoitao, 2765 Estoril, Portugal [ARCHDEACON OF GIBRALTAR] *b* 17 Dec 1936; *educ* Balshaw's Gr Sch Leyland; K Coll Lon; St Boniface Th Coll Warminster; C Poulton-le-Fylde 1962–65; C Lanc Priory 1965–66; Chapl St Jo Sch Singapore 1966–68; V H Trin Colne 1968–70; Dir of Educ Windward Islands 1970–74; V St Luke Skerton 1974–81; Area Sec (E Anglia) USPG 1981–91; Min Can St Eds Cathl 1982–91; Chapl Gtr Lisbon from 1991; Adn of Gibraltar from 1994
Tel and *Fax:* 00–3511–469 2303

ROBOTTOM, Mr Peter Gordon, MA, DIPTP, MRTPI, MIMGT
38B Whittingehame Gardens, Brighton, E Sussex BN1 6PU [CHICHESTER] **1985–** *b* 6 Feb 1946; *educ* Solihull Sch; Jes Coll Ox; Birm Poly; Planning Asst Staffs Co Coun 1967–70; Asst Planner/Prin Asst Planner Ox City Coun 1970–73; Dep City Planning Officer Ox City Coun 1973–83; Boro Planning Officer Brighton Boro Coun 1983–91; Sen Housing and Planning Inspector The Planning Inspectorate from 1991; M Coun Corp of Ch Ho from 1989; Lay Chmn Brighton Dny Syn from 1990; M Bp's Coun from 1991; M Dios Commn from 1991   *Tel:* (01273) 559172 (Home)
(01273) 557537 (Office)

ROBSON, Dr Frank Elms, OBE, DCL
16 Beaumont St, Oxford OX1 2LZ and 2 Simms Close, Stanton St John, Oxford OX9 1HB [JOINT REGISTRAR OF THE PROVINCE OF CANTERBURY] *b* 14 Dec 1931; *educ* K Edw VI Gr Sch Morpeth; Selw Coll Cam; Solicitor; Registrar Ox Dio; Sec Ox Dioc Syn; Joint Registrar, Province of Cant from 1982; Vc-Chmn Legal Adv Commn; Chmn Ecclesiastical Law Soc
Tel: (01865) 241974

ROCHESTER, Bishop of, Rt Revd Michael James Nazir-Ali, BA, B LITT, M LITT, PH D
Bishopscourt, Rochester, Kent ME1 1TS **1994–** *b* 19 Aug 1949; *educ* St Paul's Sch Karachi; St Patr Coll Karachi; Karachi Univ; Fitzw Coll Cam; St Edm Hall Ox; Univ of N S Wales; Ridley Hall Th Coll; Tutorial Supervisor Th Cam Univ 1974–76; C H Sepulchre and All SS Cam 1974–76; Sen Tutor Karachi Th Coll 1976–81; Provost of Lahore Cathl 1981–84; Bp of Raiwind 1984–86; Asst to Abp of Cant and Dir in Residence Ox Cen for Miss Studies 1986–89; Co-ord of Studies and Ed Lambeth Conf 1988; Hon C St Giles and SS Phil and Jas w St Marg Ox 1986–89; Gen Sec CMS 1989–94; Asst Bp S'wark 1989–94; Can Th Leic 1992–94; Sec Abp's Commn on Communion and Women in the Episcopate from 1988; M Bd of Chr Aid 1988–97; M CCBI 1991–95; M ARCIC II from 1991; M BM from 1991, Chmn Miss Th Adv Grp from 1992; Bp of Roch from 1994; M Lambeth Conf Design Grp from 1994; M Ho of Bps' Theol Grp from 1996; M Urban Bps' Panel from 1996; Vis Prof of Th and Rel Studies Univ of Greenwich from 1996; M Human Fertilization and Embryology Authority from 1998; Chmn Trin Coll Bris Coun
Tel: (01634) 842721
Fax: (01634) 831136

RONAYNE, Revd Peter Henry
Vicarage, 6 Chatsworth Way, London SE27 9HR [SOUTHWARK] **1995–** *b* 8 Jul 1934; *educ* Oak Hill Th Coll; C St Mary Chesham 1966–69; C H Trin Worthing 1969–74; V St Leon w St Mich Shoreditch 1974–82; P-in-c Norood 1982–85; V from 1985; RD Streatham 1987–91   *Tel:* 0181–670 2706

RONE, Ven Jim (James), FSCA
Archdeacon's House, 24 Cromwell Rd, Ely, Cambs CB6 1AS [ARCHDEACON OF WISBECH] **1995–** *b* 28 Aug 1935; *educ* Skerry's Coll Liv; St Steph Ho Ox; Fin Officer Ox dio 1973–79; C Stony Stratford 1980–82; V St Pet and St Mary Magd Fordham 1982–89; R St Nic Kennett 1982–89; Res Can Ely Cathl 1989–95, Can Treas 1992–95; Adn of Wisbech from 1995; M CBF; M Corp of Ch Ho; M Bp's Coun; DBF; Pastl Ctee; Houses Ctee; Investments Ctee; Bd of Educ; Chmn Dioc Coun for Social Aid; DAC; Bp's Adv on Hosp Chaplaincies; Chmn Dioc Rural Min Grp; Chmn Schs Exec Bd of Educ   *Tel:* (01353) 662909
Fax: (01353) 662056
e-mail: archdeacon.wisbech@ely.anglican.org

ROSE, Ven (Kathleen) Judith, BD, DIP TH, IDC, NDD
3 The Ridings, Tunbridge Wells, Kent TN2 4EU [ARCHDEACON OF TONBRIDGE] **1975–80, 1980–81, 1987–** *b* 14 Jun 1937; *educ* Sexey's Gr Sch Blackford Som; Seale Hayne Agric Coll; St Mich Ho Ox; Lon Bible Coll; Par Wrkr Rodbourne Cheney Swindon 1966–71; Dss St Geo Leeds 1973–81; Chapl Bradf Cathl 1981–85; Min resp St Paul Parkwood S Gillingham 1986–90; RD Gillingham 1988–90; Personal Chapl to Bp of Roch, Bp's Offcr for Ordained Women and Assoc Dir of Ords 1990–95; Acting Adn of Tonbridge and Assoc DDO 1995–96; Adn of Tonbridge from 1996; M Clergy Conditions of Service Steering Grp; M Crown Appts Commn; M Bp's Coun; M Dioc Pastl Ctee; M DAC; M Dioc Parsonages Ctee; Simeon Trustee   *Tel* and *Fax:* (01892) 520660

ROYLE, Mr Timothy Lancelot Fanshawe, FC INST M
Icomb Place, Nr Stow-on-the-Wold, Cheltenham, Glos [GLOUCESTER] 1985– *b* 24 Apr 1931; *educ* Harrow; Rdr from 1959; Ch Commr 1967–82; MD Hogg Robinson Grp 1953–82; Chmn Control Risks Grp 1974–91; Chmn Berry Palmer Lyle 1983–91; Chmn Lindley Educl Trust 1970–98; Chmn Chr Weekly Newspapers 1976–98; Dir Well Marine Reinsurance Brokers from 1976; Trustee ICS, Wycliffe Hall Ox, Ridley Hall Cam; M Abp's Legal Commn 1966; M DBF; M Bp's Coun; M Revision Ctee Draft Incumbents (Vacation of Benefices) (Amendment) Measure; Trustee Charinco; Charishare; Dir Imperio Grp UK from 1993; Chmn Hill and Fenley from 1994; Chmn Fanshawe Somerset from 1996
Tel: (01451) 830231
0171–373 3092
Fax: (01451) 832450
e-mail: TROYLE@aol.com

RUDDOCK, Ms Beverley Elaine, M SC, BA, PGCE, RGN, SCM
Joydene, Murrell Hill Lane, Binfield, Berks RG42 4DA [OXFORD] 1995– *b* 14 Jan 1947; *educ* Ardenne High Sch Jamaica; Reading Univ; Univ Coll Lon; Midwifery Sister until 1982; pt FE Coll Tchr 1985–87; Primary Tchr 1988–90; Educ Psychologist from 1991; Sen Educ Psychologist from 1998

RUOFF, Mrs Alison Laura, SRN, SCM, DN
The White House, 75 Crossbrook St, Cheshunt, Herts EN8 8LU [LONDON] 1995– *b* 1 Nov 1942; *educ* Sutton Coldfield Girls High Sch; Nightingale Sch of Nursing, St Thos Hosp; Br Hosp for Mothers and Babies; Nursing Inst Worc; VSO India 1961–62; Asst Dir of Nursing Internat Grenfell Assn Newfoundland 1968–70; Admin Sister St Thos Hosp Grp 1970–72; Nursing Officer/Sen Nursing Officer Univ Coll Hosp 1972–74; Housewife; JP from 1979 Cheshunt and E Herts Bench, M Family Panel; Vc-Chmn Herts Magistrates' Assn; M Coun Nat Magistrates' Assn; M Bp's Coun; M CEEC; M HCC; regular contributor to Premier Radio
Tel: (01992) 623113
e-mail: Alison.Ruoff@dlondon.org.uk

RUSSELL, Ven (Harold) Ian Lyle, BD, ALCD
9 Armorial Rd, Coventry CV3 6GH [ARCHDEACON OF COVENTRY] 1970–75, 1985– *b* 17 Oct 1934; *educ* Epsom Coll; Lon Univ; Lon Coll of Div; C Iver 1960–63; C-in-c St Luke Lodge Moor Fulwood 1963–67; V Chapeltown Sheff 1967–75; RD Tankersley 1973–75; V St Jude Mapperley 1975–89; AD Nottm Cen 1986–89; Hon Can S'well Cathl 1988–89; M Hosp Chapl Coun 1986–96; Adn of Cov from 1989; M CE Pensions Bd from 1991, Vc-Chmn from 1998; M Coun St Jo Th Coll; Chmn Dioc Ho of Clergy from 1991; M Ethical Investment Working Grp from 1996; Chaplain to HM The Queen from 1997
Tel: (01203) 417750 (Home)
(01203) 674328 (Office)
Fax: (01203) 691760

RUSSELL, Ven Norman Atkinson, MA, BD
Foxglove House, Love Lane, Donnington, Newbury, Berks RG13 2JG [ARCHDEACON OF BERKSHIRE] *b* 7 Aug 1943; *educ* R Belfast Academical Inst; Chu Coll Cam; Lon Coll of Div; C Ch Ch w Em Clifton 1970–74; C Ch Ch Trent Park Enfield 1974–77; R Harwell w Chilton 1977–84; P-in-c Gerrards Cross 1984–88; P-in-c Fulmer 1985–88; R Gerrards Cross and Fulmer 1988–98; Hon Can Ch Ch Ox 1995–98; RD Amersham 1996–98; Adn of Berks from 1998; M Dioc BSR; M Dioc Ctee for Racial Justice
Tel: (01635) 552820
Fax: (01635) 522165
e-mail: archdber@oxford.anglican.org

SADGROVE, Very Revd Michael, MA
The Cathedral, Sheffield S1 1HA [PROVOST OF SHEFFIELD] *b* 13 Apr 1950; *educ* Univ Coll Sch Lon; Ball Coll Ox; Trin Coll Bris; Lic to Offic Ox dio 1975–76; Lect OT Sarum & Wells Th Coll 1977–82; Vc-Prin 1980–82; V Alnwick 1982–87; Can Res, Prec and Vc-Provost Cov Cathl 1987–95; Provost of Sheff from 1995; Bps' Inspector of Th Colls and Courses; M Cathls Fabric Commn for Eng
Tel: 0114–275 3434
Fax: 0114–278 0244
e-mail: msadgrove@aol.com

SADLER, Ven Anthony Graham, MA
The Archdeacon's House, 10 Paradise Lane, Pelsall, Walsall, W Midlands WS3 4NH [ARCHDEACON OF WALSALL] *b* 1 Apr 1936; *educ* Bp Vesey's Gr Sch Sutton Coldfield; Qu Coll Ox; Lichf Th Coll; C St Chad Burton-upon-Trent 1962–65; V Rangemore and Dunstall 1965–72; V Abbots Bromley 1972–79; V Pelsall 1979–90; RD Walsall 1982–90; P-in-c Uttoxeter, Bramshall, Gratwich, Marchington, Marchington Woodlands, Kingstone, Checkley, Stramshall and Leigh 1990–97; R Uttoxeter 1997; Preb of Lichf Cathl 1987–97; Hon Can Lichf Cathl from 1997; Adn of Walsall from 1997
Tel: (01922) 445353
Fax: (01922) 445354

SADLER, Mr Anthony John, MA, CIPD
Fielden House, Little College St, London SW1P 3SH [ARCHBISHOPS' APPOINTMENTS SECRETARY] *b* 2 Oct 1938; *educ* Bedf Sch; Magd Coll Cam; Personnel Mgr Hawker Siddeley Aviation 1964–68; Personnel Mgr Rank Audio Visual Ltd 1968–72; Personnel Dir

RHM General Products Ltd 1972–75; Asst Personnel Controller Rank Org 1975–78; Employee Relations Mgr Lloyds Bank Internat 1978–83; Chmn S Lon Ind Miss 1980–82; Dir, Grp Human Resources, Minet plc 1983–92; Chmn S'wark Welcare Centenary Appeal Ctee 1993–95; Abps' Appointments Sec from 1996   *Tel:* 0171–898 1875; 0171–233 0393 or 0171–222 7010 Ext 4033
Fax: 0171–976 0487
e-mail: ajsadler@asa.clara.net

SALISBURY, Bishop of, Rt Revd David Staffurth Stancliffe, MA, D LITT
South Canonry, 71 The Close, Salisbury, Wilts SP1 2ER **1985–** *b* 1 Oct 1942; *educ* Westmr Sch; Trin Coll Ox; Cuddesdon Th Coll; C St Bart's Armley, Leeds 1967–70; Chapl Clifton Coll Bris 1970–77; Can Res of Portsm, DDO and Dioc Lay Min Adv 1977–82; Prov of Portsm 1982–93; Bp of Sarum from 1993; M Liturg Commn from 1986, Chmn from 1993; M Cathls Fabric Commn from 1991   *Tel:* (01722) 334031
Fax: (01722) 413112
e-mail: 101324.1053@compuserve.com

SANDERS, Mr William Ashton, MA
Nine Chimney House, Balsham, Cambridge CB1 6ES [ELY] **1995–** *b* 20 Nov 1934; *educ* Kingswood Sch; Ex Coll Ox; Public Relations Officer The Stock Exchange 1965–75; Sec Zululand Swaziland Assn 1977–96; Appeal Dir Angl Cen in Rome from 1996; M CCC from 1996; M Dioc Syn; M Dioc Coun for Miss and Unity; Asst Sec Bp's Coun; Sec Dioc Bd of Patronage; M Cambs Ecum Coun
Tel: (01233) 893063
Fax: (01223) 890846

SANDFORD, Mr Bryan Moile, CBE, M SC, MIEE
Lanterns, 54 Thames Ave, Guisborough, Cleveland TS14 8AF [YORK] **1970–** *b* 3 Jun 1934; *educ* Man Gr Sch; Man Univ; Loughb Univ; Chartered Eng; Registered Safety Practitioner; Managing Dir Lantern Safety Services from 1989; Chmn DBF; M CBF; M CBF Exec; M Abps Commn on the Organisation of the CE; Chmn Dioc Commn; Chmn Qu Victoria Clergy Fund; Chmn Consultative Grp of DBF Chmn and Secs; Rdr   *Tel* and *Fax:* (01287) 632442

SASSER, Revd Howell Crawford, BA, MA
Rua do Campo Alegre 640–5D, 4150 Porto, Portugal [EUROPE] **1998–** *b* 25 Jul 1937; *educ* High Sch Florida USA; Maryland Univ; Geo Mason Univ Virginia; Westmr Coll Ox; Washington Dioc Course; Asst Chapl US Forces Germany 1977–80; Chapl Ch Ch Mogadishu Somalia 1981–83; Asst to Provost St Paul Cathl Nicosia 1984–87; Asst Chapl St Paul Athens 1989–92; Chapl St Jo Montreux 1992–97; Chapl St Jas Porto from 1997   *Tel* and *Fax:* 00351–2–609 1006

SAUNDERS, Mrs Sheila Constance
4 Edmonds Drive, Ketton, Stamford, Lincs PE9 3TH [PETERBOROUGH] **1995–** *b* 25 Apr 1935; *educ* Rye Gr Sch; Leic Domestic Science Tchr Tr Coll; Sec Dioc Miss Coun 1986–92; Chmn MU Dioc Educ Dept 1980–86; Vc Pres Dioc MU from 1992; M Dioc Bd on Min from 1993   *Tel* and *Fax:* (01780) 720228

SCHOFIELD, Prebendary Rodney, MA
West Monkton Rectory, Taunton, Som TA2 8QT [BATH AND WELLS] **1990–** *b* 21 Mar 1944; *educ* St Albs Sch; St Jo Coll Cam; Bris Univ; St Pet Coll Ox; St Steph Ho Ox; C St Mary Northn 1971–76; V Irchester 1976–84; Warden Lelapa La Jesu Sem Lesotho and Dir of POT Lesotho dio 1984–86; R W Monkton from 1986; DDO from 1989; M Dioc Coun for Min; M Bp's Coun; M Board of Studies SW Minl Tr Scheme; M Bd of Govs STETS   *Tel* and *Fax:* (01823) 412226

SCREECH, Revd Royden, BD, AKC
Church House, Great Smith St, London SW1P 3NZ [SENIOR SELECTION SECRETARY, MINISTRY DIVISION] *b* 15 May 1953; *educ* Cotham Gr Sch Bris; K Coll Lon; St Aug Coll Cant; C St Cath Hatcham 1976–80; V St Ant Nunhead 1980–87; P-in-c St Silas Nunhead 1983–87; RD Camberwell 1983–87; V St Edw New Addington 1987–94; ABM Selection Sec and LNSM Co-ordinator 1994–96; Sen Selection Sec ABM 1997–98; Sen Selection Sec Min Division from 1999; Staff M Min Division; Sec to Vocation, Recruitment and Selection Ctee   *Tel:* 0171–898 1402
Fax: 0171–898 1419

SEAFORD, Very Revd John Nicholas, BA
The Deanery, David Place, St Helier, Jersey, Channel Islands JE2 4TE [DEAN OF JERSEY] **1993–95** *b* 12 Sep 1939; *educ* Radley Coll; Dur Univ; St Chad's Coll Dur; C Bush Hill Park 1968–71; C Stanmore Win 1971–73; V Chilworth w N Baddesley 1973–78; V Highcliffe w Hinton Admiral 1978–93; RD Christchurch 1990–93; Hon Can Win Cathl from 1993; Dean of Jersey and R St Helier from 1993; M States of Jersey from 1993   *Tel:* (01534) 720001
Fax: (01534) 617488

SEDGWICK, Mrs Margaret Anne
187 Rugby Road, Binley Woods, Coventry CV3 2AY [COVENTRY] **1992–** *b* 7 Jul 1937; *educ* Chislehurst & Sidcup Tech High Sch; Rolle Coll; Leeds Univ; Asst Mistress Chislehurst & Sidcup Tech High Sch 1959–66; Hd of Relig Studies Qu Mary Sixth Form Coll Basingstoke 1972–74; Sen Tchr Coundon Court Sch

Cov 1974–77; Dep Hdteacher Cov Blue Coat CE Sch 1977–92; Asst Dioc Educ Offcr (Vol) 1993–98; Rdr; M Gen Syn Bd of Educ 1994–96; M Dioc Bd of Educ; M Dioc Syn; M Dioc Rdrs Course Ctee; M Bd of Management NCEC *Tel:* (01203) 542805

SELBY, Bishop of [SUFFRAGAN, YORK] **Rt Revd Humphrey Vincent Taylor**, MA
10 Precentor's Court, York YO1 2EJ b 5 Mar 1938; *educ* Harrow; Cam Univ; Lon Univ; Coll of Resurr Mirfield; C St Kath N Hammersmith 1963–64; C St Mark Notting Hill 1964–66; R St Pet Lilongwe, Malawi 1967–71; Chapl Bp Grosseteste Coll Linc 1972–74; Sec for Chaplaincies in Higher Educ Gen Syn Bd of Educ 1974–80; Sec Miss Programmes USPG 1980–84; Sec USPG 1984–91; Bp of Selby from 1991; M BSR from 1996 and Chmn Internat and Development Affairs Ctee from 1996; Chmn NHS Exec N and Yorks Adv Ctee on Spiritual Care and Chaplaincy from 1997 *Tel:* (01904) 656492
Fax: (01904) 655671
e-mail: bishselby@clara.net

SHAW, Mr (Robert) Martin
Windmill Farm, Willingale, Ongar, Essex CM5 0SS [CHURCH COMMISSIONER] *b* 17 Jan 1941; *educ* Shrewsb Sch; Ox Univ; Managing Dir Baring Asset Management Ltd; Ch Commr from 1994, M Assets Ctee

SHEFFIELD, Bishop of, Rt Revd Jack (John) Nicholls
Bishopscroft, Snaithing Lane, Sheffield S10 3LG b 16 Jul 1943; *educ* Bacup and Rawtenstall Gr Sch; K Coll Lon; Warminster Th Coll; C St Clem w St Cyprian Ordsall 1967–69; C All SS and Martyrs Langley 1969–72; V 1972–78; Dir of Pastl Studies Coll of Resurr Mir 1978–83; Can Res Man Cathl 1983–90; Bp of Lanc 1990–97; Bp of Sheff from 1997
Tel: 0114–230 2170
Fax: 0114–263 0110

SHERBORNE, Bishop of [AREA BISHOP, SALISBURY] **Rt Revd John Dudley Galtrey Kirkham**
Little Bailie, Dullar Lane, Sturminster Marshall, Wimborne, Dorset BH21 4AD 1980–85 b 20 Sep 1935; *educ* Lancing Coll; Trin Coll Cam; Westcott Ho Th Coll; C St Mary le Tower Ipsw 1962–65; Chapl to Bp of Nor 1965–69; Chapl to Bp of New Guinea 1969–70; C Martin-in-the-Fields Lon and St Marg's Westmr 1970–72; Dom Chapl to Abp of Cant 1972–76; Bp of Sherborne from 1976; Abp's Adv to Headmasters' Conference 1990–93; Bp to the Forces from 1992
Tel: (01258) 857659
Fax: (01258) 857961

SHERWOOD, Bishop of [SUFFRAGAN, SOUTHWELL] **Rt Revd Alan Wyndham Morgan**
Sherwood House, High Oakham Rd, Mansfield, Notts NG18 5AJ 1980–89 b 22 Jun 1940; *educ* Boys Gr Sch Gowerton; St D Coll Lamp; St Mich Coll Llan; Asst C Llangyfelach w Morriston 1964–69; Asst C Cockett 1969–72; V St Barnabas, Cov E 1972–77; Bp's Offcr for Social Resp Cov Dioc 1978–83; Adn of Cov 1983–89; Bp of Sherwood from 1989
Tel: (01623) 657491
Fax: (01623) 662526
e-mail: bishop.sherwood@john316.com

SHOTTER, Very Revd Edward Frank, BA
The Deanery, Rochester, Kent ME1 1TG [DEAN OF ROCHESTER] *1994– b* 29 Jun 1933; *educ* Humberstone Foundation Sch Clee; Univ of Wales, Lampeter; St Steph Ho Ox; C St Pet Plymouth 1960–62; SCM Intercollegiate Sec Lon 1962–66; Chapl Univ of Lon 1969–89; Dir Studies Lon Medical Grp 1966–89; Dir Inst of Medical Ethics 1974–89; Preb St Paul's Cathl 1977–89; Dean of Roch from 1989; Chmn Medway Enterprise Agency from 1993; Chmn Medway Business Point from 1996; Chmn Kent Co Constabulary Ecum Chapl Ctee from 1993; Chmn Inst of Medical Ethics Working Party on Ethics of Prolonging Life and Assisting Death from 1993; Sec Assn of Eng Cathls from 1994; Chmn Greenwich Univ Research Ethics Ctee from 1995 *Tel:* (01634) 844023
Fax: (01634) 401410

SHREEVE, Ven David Herbert, MA
11 The Rowans, Baildon, Shipley, W Yorks BD17 5DB [ARCHDEACON OF BRADFORD] *1977–90, 1993–97 b* 18 Jan 1934; *educ* Southfield Sch Ox; St Pet Coll Ox; Ridley Hall Cam; Asst C St Andr Plymouth 1959–64; V St Anne Bermondsey 1964–71; V St Luke Eccleshill 1971–84; RD Calverley 1978–84; Chmn Ho of Clergy Bradf Dio 1979–84; Hon Can Bradf Cathl 1983–84; Adn of Bradf from 1984; M Dios Commn 1988–97; M CBF 1985–90 and 1995–97
Tel: (01274) 583735
Fax: (01274) 586184

SHREWSBURY, Bishop of [AREA BISHOP, LICHFIELD] **Rt Revd David Marrison Hallatt**, BA, MA
68 London Rd, Shrewsbury, Salop SY2 6PG 1990–94 b 15 Jul 1937; *educ* Birkenhead Sch; Southn Univ; St Cath Coll Ox; Wycliffe Hall Th Coll; C St Andr Maghull 1963–67; V All SS Totley 1967–75; TR St Jas and Em Didsbury 1975–89; Adn of Halifax 1989–94; Bp of Shrewsbury from 1994 *Tel:* (01743) 235867
Fax: (01743) 243296

SIDAWAY, Canon Geoffrey Harold
Vicarage, Church Lane, Bearsted, Maidstone, Kent ME14 4EF [CANTERBURY] **1995–** *b* 28 Oct 1942; *educ* Kelham Th Coll; C Beighton 1966–70; C All SS Chesterfield 1970–72; V St Bart Derby 1972–77; V St Martin Maidstone 1977–86; V Bearsted and Thurnham from 1986; RD Sutton from 1992; Hon Can Cant Cathl from 1994; Commis for Bp of Kinkizi Uganda from 1995; M Dioc Syn; M Abp's Coun *Tel* and *Fax:* (01622) 737135

SIMMONS, Mrs Hazel
16 Coanwood Drive, Cramlington, Northumberland NE23 6TL [NEWCASTLE] **1995–** Rtd Medical Laboratory Scientific Officer; M CMEAC; M Dioc Ctee for Interfaith and Ethnic Relations; Rdr
Tel: (01670) 739270
(01670) 730136

SIMMONS, Mr Richard
30 Laburnum Way, Nayland, Colchester CO6 4LG [ST EDMUNDSBURY AND IPSWICH] **1995–** Senior Manager

SIMPSON, Very Revd John Arthur
The Deanery, Canterbury, Kent CT1 2EP [DEAN OF CANTERBURY] *1981–86 b* 7 Jun 1933; *educ* Cathays High Sch Cardiff; Keble Coll Ox; Clifton Th Coll; C Leyton 1958–59; C Ch Ch Orpington 1959–62; Tutor Oak Hill Coll 1962–72; V Ridge 1972–79; DDO and Dir POT St Alb 1975–81; Hon Can St Alb Cathl 1977–79; Can Res of St Alb Cathl and P-in-c Ridge 1979–81; Adn of Cant and Can Res of Cant Cathl 1981–86; Dean of Cant from 1986 *Tel:* (01227) 765983 (Home)
(01227) 762862 (Office)

SIMPSON, Mrs Marion Elizabeth, B ED
West Little Place, Godstone, Surrey RH9 8LT [SOUTHWARK] **1990–** *b* 20 Dec 1933; *educ* Woodhouse Gr Sch Finchley; Lon Univ; Dispenser Boots the Chemists 1949–59; Mother at home 1959–70; Tchr Tr 1970–75; Sec Sch Teacher (Science and Maths) 1975–90; Supply Teacher 1990–94; Rtd; Rdr from 1981; Adnry Vocations Adv 1991–98; M Dios Commn from 1996; Unit Co-ord Prayer and Spirituality S'wark MU; Hon Treas WATCH from 1996 *Tel:* (01883) 742724

SINCLAIR, Canon Jane Elizabeth Margaret, MA, BA
The Cathedral Church of St Peter and St Paul, Church St, Sheffield S1 1HA [SHEFFIELD] **1995–** *b* 1 Mar 1956; *educ* Westonbirt Sch Tetbury; St Hugh's Coll Ox; Nottm Univ; St Jo Coll Nottm; Dss St Paul w St Jo Herne Hill and St Sav Ruskin Park 1983–86; Lect in Liturg and Chapl St Jo Coll Nottm 1986–93; Can Res and Prec Sheff Cathl from 1993; M Liturg Commn from 1986 *Tel:* 0114–279 9553 (Cathedral)
0114–255 7782 (Home)
Fax: 0114–278 0244
e-mail: Shefflit@aol.com

SKIDMORE, Mr David Paul, BA, MA
Church House, Great Smith St, London SW1P 3NZ [SECRETARY, GENERAL SYNOD BOARD FOR SOCIAL RESPONSIBILITY] *b* 11 Mar 1943; *educ* Ampleforth Coll; Nottm Univ; Univ of Pennsylvania; LSE; Lect Univ of York 1971–85; Social Resp Adv St Alb dio 1985–89; Sec Gen Syn BSR from 1989
Tel: 0171– 898 1521 (Office)
(01727) 868209 (Home)

SLATER, Mr Colin Stuart, FIPR
11 Muriel Rd, Beeston, Nottingham NG9 2HH [SOUTHWELL] **1990–** *b* 28 Feb 1934; *educ* Belle Vue Gr Sch Bradford; Chief Public Relations Officer Notts Co Coun 1969–87, Severn Trent Water 1987–89, Notts Co Cricket Club 1989–95; Chmr BBC Radio Nottm Adv Coun 1975–79; former Chmn Soc of Co PROs and IPR Local Gvt Grp; M Coun Inst of PR 1986–90; JP from 1977; Public Relations Consultant and freelance broadcaster from 1994; M Gen Syn Central Stewardship Ctee; M Bp's Coun, F & GP grp, Parish Giving Ctee *Tel* and *Fax:* 0115–925 7532

SLATER, Mr Timothy George
17 Wentworth St, Huddersfield HD1 5PX [WAKEFIELD] **1990–** *b* 1 Jan 1954; *educ* K James' Gr Sch Huddersfield; Cam Coll of Arts and Tech; Bretton Hall Coll; Head of Music All SS High Sch Huddersfield from 1979; M Bp's Coun; M Dioc Pastl Ctee; Lay Chair Huddersfield Dny Syn; M Liturg Commn from 1996 *Tel:* (01484) 518504

SLAUGHTER, Miss Ingrid Elizabeth, LL B
Church House, Great Smith St, London SW1P 3NZ [ASSISTANT LEGAL ADVISER, GENERAL SYNOD] *b* 3 Mar 1947; *educ* Ursuline High Sch Brentwood; K Coll Lon; Barrister; In practice at Chancery Bar 1970–74; Legal Dept Nat Coal Bd 1974–83; Official Solicitor's Dept Ch Commrs from 1983; Asst Legal Adv Gen Syn from 1987; Rdr *Tel:* 0171–898 1368
e-mail: ingrid.slaughter@synod.clara.net

SLEE, Very Revd Colin Bruce, BD, AKC
Provost's Lodging, 51 Bankside, London SE1 9JE [PROVOST OF SOUTHWARK] **1995–** *b* 10 Nov 1945; *educ* Ealing Gr Sch; K Coll Lon; St Aug Coll Cant; C St Fran Heartsease Nor 1970–73; C Gt St Mary Cam 1973–76; Chapl Girton Coll Cam 1973–76; Chapl and

Tutor K Coll Lon 1976–82; Sub Dean and Can Res St Alb 1982–94; Provost of S'wark from 1994
Tel and Fax: 0171–928 6414 (Home)
0171–407 3708 (Office)
Fax: 0171–357 7389 (Office)
e-mail: cathedra@dswark.org.uk
SleeBanks@aol.com (Home)

SMALLEY, Very Revd Dr Stephen Stewart, BD, MA, PH D
The Deanery, 7 Abbey St, Chester CH1 2JF [DEAN OF CHESTER] *b* 11 May 1931; *educ* Battersea Gr Sch; Jes Coll Cam; Ridley Hall Th Coll; Eden Th Sem USA; C St Paul Portman Sq Lon 1958–60; Chapl Peterho Cam 1960–63 (Acting Dean 1962–63); Select Prchr Univ of Cam 1963–64; Lect and Sen Lect Ibadan Univ, Nigeria 1963–69; Lect and Sen Lect Man Univ 1970–77; Wrdn St Anselm Hall 1972–77; Can Res and Prec Cov Cathl 1977–86; Vc-Prov 1986; M Abps' Doct Commn 1981–86; Dean of Ches from 1987; Author
Tel: (01244) 351380 (Home)
(01244) 324756 (Office)
Fax: (01244) 341110
e-mail: dean@chestercathedral.org.uk

SMALLWOOD, Mr John Frank Monton, CBE, MA
The Willows, Parkgate Rd, Newdigate, Dorking, Surrey RH5 5AH [SOUTHWARK] **1970–** *b* 12 Apr 1926; *educ* City of Lon Sch; RAF 1944–48; Peterho Cam; Ch Assembly 1965–70; Bank of England 1951–79; Dep Chief Accntnt 1974–79; ACC 1975–87; BCC 1987–90; M numerous Ctees and Commns 1971–95; CBF 1965–99 (Dep Vc-Chmn 1972–82); Ch Commr 1966–99 (Bd of Gvnrs and M Gen Purposes Ctee); City Parchl Fdn 1969–99 (Chmn 1981–92); Lambeth Palace Lib 1977–99; Overseas Bishoprics Fund 1978–99 (Chmn 1992–99); Stg Ctee 1971–95; Pensions Bd 1985–95; Chs Main Ctee 1987–95; Coun Corp of Ch Ho 1987–95; S'wark DBF 1962–2000 (Chmn 1975–2000); S'wark Ord Course Coun 1960–94 (Vc-Chmn 1980–94); Rdr from 1983
Tel: (01306) 631457

SMITH, Ven Alan Gregory Clayton, BA, MA
Archdeacon's House, 39 The Brackens, Clayton, Newcastle-under-Lyme ST5 4JL [ARCHDEACON OF STOKE-UPON-TRENT] *b* 14 Feb 1957; *educ* Trowbridge High Sch for Boys; Birm Univ; Wycliffe Hall Th Coll; C St Lawr Pudsey 1981–82, w St Paul 82–84; Chapl Lee Abbey 1984–90; Dioc Missr and Exec Sec Lichf Dioc BMU 1990–97; TV St Matt Walsall 1990–97; Adn of Stoke-upon-Trent from 1997; Chmn Bd of Lee Abbey Household Communities
Tel: (01782) 663066
Fax: (01782) 711165

SMITH, Mrs Carol Alice, RGN, RMN, SCM
11 School Lane, Fulford, York YO10 4LU [YORK] **1994–** *b* 2 Jan 1949; *educ* Elmslie Girls' Sch Blackpool; Middx Hosp; Derby City Hosp; Staff Nurse Middx Hosp 1971–72; Community Psychiatric Nurse Lon 1973; District Midwife Cheltenham 1977–79; Housewife and Mother 1980–93; Practice Nurse Stockton Hall Psychiatric Hosp York from 1993; Bank Psychiatric Nurse Bootham Hosp York from 1993
Tel: (01904) 643646
e-mail: IanRSmith@compuserve.com

SMITH, Mr Christopher John Addison, BA, FCA
60 Roseneath Rd, London SW11 6AQ [LONDON] **1995–** *b* 30 Mar 1949; *educ* St Pet Sch York; UEA; Price Waterhouse 1970–93, various trainee and management posts 1970–89, Human Resources Partner 1989–93; Gen Sec Lon dio from 1993; M CBF; M CBF Exec; M CBF Staff Ctee
Tel: 0171–932 1221 (Office)
Fax: 0171–932 1114

SMITH, Mr Ian Rodney, B ED, FCII, MIMGT
11 School Lane, Fulford, York YO10 4LU [YORK] **1990–** *b* 6 Mar 1948; *educ* Hyde Co Gr Sch Ches; Dur Univ; Tchr Fitzharry's Sch Abingdon 1970–71; Tchr Convent High Sch Stockport 1971–74; Personnel Management Eagle Star Insurance Co 1974–82; Personnel Management NEM Insurance Co 1982–84; CMS Area Co-ord Ripon and York dios from 1984 and CMS N Co-ord from 1998; Rdr; Hon Dioc Adviser in Evang from 1990; M BM from 1990; M PWM Ctee from 1996; M CECC from 1996
Tel: (01904) 659792
e-mail: IanRSmith'compuserve.com

SMITH, Revd Martin David, LTCL, BA, CERT TH
Rectory, 10 Stepping Lane, Rouen Rd, Norwich NR1 1PE [NORWICH] **1995–** *b* 10 Sep 1952; *educ* Selhurst Gr Sch; Trin Coll of Music Lon; Hull Univ; Cuddesdon Th Coll; C St Thos Brentwood 1978–80; C St Giles Reading 1980–91; R Colkirk w Oxwick w Pattesley, Whissonsett etc 1991–95; P-in-c St Pet Parmentergate w St Jo Nor from 1995
Tel: (01603) 622509
e-mail: frmartinsmith@clara.net

SMITH, Mr Peter Reg, FRICS
Lusaka House, Great Glemham, Saxmundham, Suffolk IP17 2DH [ST EDMUNDSBURY AND IPSWICH] **1993–** *b* 17 Apr 1946; *educ* K Edw VI Sch Southn; Coll of Estate Management; M Coun USPG from 1991; Chmn Dioc Overseas Miss Grp; Chmn Dioc Ho of Laity
Tel and Fax: (01728) 663466
e-mail: happy hackers@usa.net(Peter and Geraldine Smith)

SMITH, Revd William Melvyn, BD, AKC, PGCE
330 Hagley Rd, Pedmore, Stourbridge, W Midlands DY9 0RD [WORCESTER] **1995–** *b* 22 Feb 1947; *educ* Newc under Lyme High Sch; K Coll Lon; St Aug Coll Cant; C H Trin Wordsley 1971–73; Hon C Ch Ch Coseley 1973–74; C St Paul Wood Green Wednesbury, in-c St Luke Mesty Croft 1974–78; V St Chad Coseley 1978–91; RD Himley 1983–96; TR Wordsley 1991–96; Dioc Stewardship and Resources Officer from 1996
Tel: (01562) 720414 (Home)
(01562) 20537 (Office)

SODOR AND MAN, Bishop of, Rt Revd Noël Debroy Jones, CB, BA
Bishop's House, Quarterbridge Rd, Douglas, Isle of Man IM2 3RF **1984–** *b* 25 Dec 1932; *educ* W Monmouth Gr Sch; St D Coll Lamp; Wells Th Coll; C St Jas Tredegar 1955–57; C St Mark Newport 1957–60; V Kano Nigeria 1960–62; Chapl RN 1962–84; Chapl of the Fleet 1984–89; CB 1986; Bp of Sodor and Man from 1989
Tel: (01624) 622108
Fax: (01624) 672890

SOUTHAMPTON, Bishop of [SUFFRAGAN, WINCHESTER] **Rt Revd Jonathan Michael Gledhill,** BA, MA, BCTS
Ham House, The Crescent, Romsey, Hants SO51 7NG **1995–96** *b* 15 Feb 1949; *educ* Strode's Sch Egham; Keele Univ; Bris Univ; Trin Coll Bris; C All SS Marple 1975–78; P-in-c St Geo Folkestone 1978–83; V St Mary Bredin Cant 1983–96; Tutor/Lect Cant Sch of Min 1983–94; Tutor/Lect SE Inst for Th Educ 1994–96; RD Cant 1988–94; Hon Can Cant Cathl 1992–96; Bp of Southn from 1996; M Meissen Commn 1993–96
Tel: (01794) 516005
Fax: (01794) 830242
e-mail: jonathan.gledhill@dial.pipex.com

SOUTHERN, Mrs Angela Helen
Greystone House, Brackley Ave, Hartley Wintney, Hook, Hants RG27 8QX [WINCHESTER] **1990–** *b* 5 May 1944; *educ* St Helen and St Kath Sch Abingdon; K Coll Hosp Lon; Radiographer (not practising); M Canon B17 Revision Ctee
Tel: (01252) 842274

SOUTHWARK, Bishop of, Rt Revd Thomas Frederick Butler, M SC, PH D, LLD
Bishop's House, 38 Tooting Bec Gardens, London SW16 1QZ **1991–** *b* 5 Mar 1940; *educ* K Edw's Sch Five Ways Birm; Univ Leeds; Coll of the Resurr Mirf; Asst C St Aug Wisbech 1964–66; Asst C St Sav Folkestone 1966–67; Lect and Chapl Univ Zambia 1967–73; Chapl Univ Kent 1973–80; Six Preacher Cant Cathl 1980–84; Adn of Northolt 1980–85; Bp of Willesden 1985–91; Bp of Leic 1991–98; Bp of S'wark from 1998; Chmn BM from 1995
Tel: 0181–769 3256
Fax: 0181–769 4126
e-mail: bishops.house@dswark.org.uk

SOUTHWELL, Bishop of, Rt Revd Patrick Burnet Harris, MA
Bishop's Manor, Southwell, Notts NG25 0JR **1988–** *b* 30 Sep 1934; *educ* St Albans Sch; Keble Coll Ox; Clifton Th Coll; C St Ebbe's Ox 1960–63; Miss SAMS 1963; Adn of Salta 1970–73; Bp of N Argentina 1973–80; R Kirkheaton and Asst Bp Wakef 1981–85; Sec PWM and Asst Bp Ox 1986–88; Bp of S'well from 1988
Tel: (01636) 812112
Fax: (01636) 815401
e-mail: bishop.southwell@john316.com

SPENCER, Mrs Caroline Sarah, BA, PGCE
Little Eggarton, Godmersham, Canterbury, Kent CT4 7DY [CANTERBURY] **1995–** *b* 9 Sep 1953; *educ* Wycombe Abbey Sch; St Hilda's Coll Ox; Lon Univ Inst of Educ; Asst Tchr Hist Sydenham High Sch 1976–80; pt Tutor Westmr Tutors Ltd 1981–84; Mother and Vol Worker for Ch and Community from 1980; M CBF; M Abp's Coun; M DBF; M Dioc Bd of Miss; Chs Together in Kent;
Tel and *Fax:* (01227) 731170

ST ALBANS, Bishop of, Rt Revd Christopher William Herbert, BA
Abbey Gate House, Abbey Mill Lane, St Albans, Herts AL3 4HD **1995–** *b* 7 Jan 1944; *educ* Monmouth Sch; St D Univ Coll Lamp; Wells Th Coll; C Tupsley and Schoolmaster Bp's Sch Heref 1967–71; Adv in Relig Educ Heref 1971–76; Dir of Educ Heref 1976–81; V Bourne 1981–90; Dir of POT Guildf 1983–90; Adn of Dorking 1990–95; Bp of St Alb from 1995
Tel: (01727) 853305
Fax: (01727) 846715

ST EDMUNDSBURY AND IPSWICH, Bishop of, Rt Revd (John Hubert) Richard Lewis, AKC
Bishop's House, 4 Park Rd, Ipswich, Suffolk IP1 3ST **1987–92, 1997–** *b* 10 Dec 1943; *educ* Radley; K Coll Lon; St Boniface Coll Warminster; C Hexham 1967–70; Ind Chapl Newc 1970–77; DCO Dur 1977–82; Agric Chapl Heref 1982–87; Adn of Ludlow 1987–92; Bp of Taunton 1992–97; Chmn ABM Recruitment and Selection Ctee 1993–96; Bp of St Eds & Ips from 1997; Chmn BSR Social, Economic and Indust Affairs Ctee from 1998
Tel: (01473) 252829
Fax: (01473) 232552

ST GERMANS, Bishop of [SUFFRAGAN, TRURO] **Rt Revd Graham Richard James,** BA
32 Falmouth Rd, Truro, Cornwall TR1 2HX **1995–** *b* 19

Jan 1951; *educ* Northampton Gr Sch; Lanc Univ; Cuddesdon Th Coll; C Christ Carpenter Petrb 1975–78; C Digswell 1978–82; TV Digswell 1982–83; Selection Sec and Sec for CME ACCM 1983–85; Sen Selection Sec 1985–87; Chapl to Abp of Cant 1987–93; Bp of St Germans from 1993; Chmn Communications Offcrs Panel; Vc-Moderator Chs Commn for Inter-Faith Relations
Tel: (01872) 273190
Fax: (01872) 277883

STAFFORD, Bishop of [AREA BISHOP, LICHFIELD] **Rt Revd Christopher John Hill,** BD, AKC, M TH
Ash Garth, 6 Broughton Crescent, Barlaston, Stoke-on-Trent, Staffs ST12 9DD b 10 Oct 1945; *educ* Sebright Sch Worcs; K Coll Lon; C Tividale Lich 1969–73; C Codsall 1973–74; Abp's Asst Chapl on Foreign Relations 1974–81; Abp's Sec for Ecum Affairs 1981–89; Angl Sec ARCIC I and II 1974–91; Hon Can Cant-Cathl 1982–89; Chapl to HM The Queen 1987–96; Can Res and Prec St Paul's Cathl 1989–96; M CE-German Chs Conversations 1987–89; CE Nordic-Baltic Conversations 1989–93; Vc-Chair Ecclesiastical Law Soc from 1993; Chair Cathl Precs Conf 1994–96; Co-Chmn CE-French Protestant Conversations from 1993; M Legal Adv Ctee from 1991; Co-Chair Lon Soc Jews and Chrs 1991–96; M CCU 1991–96; Bp of Stafford from 1996; M FOAG from 1997; Co-Chair Meissen Th Conversations from 1998
Tel: (01782) 373308
Fax: (01782) 373705

STALEY, Revd (John) Colin George, MA
261 Oxford Rd, Macclesfield, Cheshire SK11 8JY [CHESTER] **1996–** *b* 18 Jun 1944; *educ* Nottm High Sch; Southn Univ Sch of Navigation; Hull Univ; Wycliffe Hall Th Coll; C Tinsley 1971–73; C Slaithwaite 1973–75; V St Andr and St Mary Wakef 1975–80; Warden Scargill Ho 1980–82; TV Macclesfield from 1982; Sen Ind Chapl from 1987; M Bp's Dioc Miss Grp
Tel: (01625) 423851 (Home)
(01625) 517681 (Office)
Fax: (01625) 517824

STANES, Ven Ian Thomas, B SC, MA
The Archdeaconry, 21 Church Rd, Glenfield, Leicester LE3 8DP [ARCHDEACON OF LOUGHBOROUGH] **1994–** *b* 29 Jan 1939; *educ* City of Bath Boys Sch; Sheff Univ; Linacre Coll Ox; Wycliffe Hall Th Coll; C H Apostles Leic 1965–69; V St David Broom Leys 1969–76; Warden Marrick Priory 1976–82; Offcer for Miss, Min and Evang Willesden Area Lon 1982–92; CME Officer Willesden Area Lon 1984–92; Preb St Paul's Cathl 1989–92; Adn of Loughb from 1992
Tel: 0116–231 1632
Fax: 0116–232 1593

STANIFORD, Revd Doris Gwendoline, SRN
All Souls House, 1 Church House Close, Southwick, Brighton BN42 2WQ [CHICHESTER] **1995–** *b* 29 Dec 1943; *educ* Gilmore Course; Par Worker 1978–80; Dss Hangleton Hove 1980–82; Dss Durrington 1982–87; Par Dn 1987–89; M Staff Chich Th Coll 1983–89; Dioc Vocations Adv 1987–97; Par Dn Crawley TM 1989–97; Chapl Crawley Gen Hosp 1989–97; Chapl St Cath Hospice 1992–97; Asst DDO and Adv on Womens Min from 1997; C-in-c All So Southwick from 1997
Tel: (01273) 594084

STANLEY, Canon John
Vicarage, Bluebell Lane, Huyton, Merseyside L36 7SA [LIVERPOOL] **1973–** *b* 20 May 1931; *educ* Birkenhead Sch; Tyndale Hall Th Coll; C All SS Preston 1956–60; C St Mark's St Helens 1960–63; V St Cuthb's Everton 1963–70; P-in-c St Sav 1969–70; V St Sav w St Cuthb's 1970–74; Chmn Dioc Ho of Clergy 1979–85; M BCC 1984–87; V Huyton from 1974; AD Huyton from 1989; Ch Commr from 1983; Bd of Govs from 1989; Hon Can Liv Cathl from 1987; Trustee Ch Urban Fund from 1987; Prolocutor York Conv from 1990; Chapl to H M The Queen from 1993
Tel: 0151–449 3900
0385 564519 (Mobile)
Fax: 0151–480 6002
e-mail: John.Stanley@btinternet.com

STANLEY, Revd Simon Richard
St Barnabas' Vicarage, Jubilee Terrace, Leeman Rd, York YO26 4YZ [YORK] **1998–** *b* 20 May 1944; *educ* Central Gr Sch Birm; Wells Th Coll; C St Lawr Cov 1969–71; C All SS Hessle 1971–75; P-in-c Flamborough 1975–80; R Dunnington 1980–92; P-in-c St Barnabas York and Producer/Presenter BBC Radio York from 1992
Tel: (01904) 654214
Fax: (01904) 670519

STAPLE, Revd David, OBE, MA, BD, FRSA
1 Althorp Rd, St Albans, Herts AL1 3PH [ECUMENICAL REPRESENTATIVE (BAPTIST UNION)] **1995–** *b* 30 Mar 1930; *educ* Watford Gr Sch; Ch Coll Cam; Wadham Coll Ox; Regent's Park Coll Ox; Assoc Min W Ham Cen Miss 1955–58; Min Llanishen Bapt Ch Cardiff 1958–74; Min Harrow Bapt Ch 1974–86; Gen Sec Free Ch Federal Coun 1986–96; Gen Sec Emer Free Ch Federal Coun from 1996; M CTE Enabling Grp 1990–96; M CCBI Steering Ctee 1990–96; M CCBI Ch Representatives Meeting from 1990; President CCBI from 1995
Tel: (01727) 810009
Fax: (01727) 867888

STEPNEY, Bishop of [AREA BISHOP, LONDON] Rt Revd John Mugabi Sentamu, BA, LL B, MA, PH D
63 Coborn Rd, Bow, London E3 2DB 1985–96 b 10 Jun 1949; *educ* Masooli, Kyambogo and Kitante Hill and Old Kampala Sch Uganda; Makerere Univ; Law Development Cen, Inns of Court, Uganda; Cam Univ; Ridley Hall Th Coll; Barrister-at-Law; Chief Magistrate 1971–72; Judge High Court of Uganda 1972–74; Asst Chapl Selw Coll Cam 1979; Chapl HM Remand Cen Latchmere Ho 1979–82; C St Andr Ham 1979–82; C St Paul Herne Hill 1982–83; P-in-c H Trin Tulse Hill; Par Priest St Matthias 1983–84; V H Trin Tulse Hill and St Matthias 1984–96; P-in-c St Sav Brixton 1987–89; Bp of Stepney from 1996; M NACRO Coun from 1986; M Abp's Adv Grp on UPAs from 1985; Pro-Prolocutor Conv of Cant 1990–94; Chmn CMEAC from 1990; M Decade of Evang Steering Grp from 1991; Prolocutor Conv of Cant 1994–96; M Police Liaison Grp Lambeth 1986–96; Coun M Family Welfare Assn from 1989; M Health Adv Ctee HM Prisons; M CTE Forum; Advisory M The Stephen Lawrence Judicial Inquiry 1997
Tel: 0181–981 2323
Fax: 0181–981 8015
e-mail: bishop.stepney@dlondon.org.uk

STEVENS, Mr Robin Michael, B SC
Church House, Great Smith St, London SW1P 3NZ [NATIONAL STEWARDSHIP OFFICER] *b* 30 Jun 1945; *educ* Chigwell Sch; Birm Univ; Marconi Communication Systems Ltd 1967–79; Engineering Project Supervisor Thames TV 1979–91; Chartered Engineer from 1978; Hon Stewardship Adv Chelmsf dio from 1982; Rdr from 1990; Cen Stewardship Offcr CBF 1992–98; Dep Sec 1996–98; Nat Stewardship Offcr from 1999
Tel: 0171–898 1540
e-mail: robin.stevens@coestewardship.clara.net

STEVENSON, Mr Trevor John Philip, AIA, APMI
33 Saxonbury Close, Crowborough, E Sussex TN6 1EA [CHICHESTER] **1985–** *b* 16 Aug 1931; *educ* Wyggeston Sch Leic; Royal Insurance Co 1949–59; Nat Provident Institution 1959–78; Asst Sec Life Offces Assn 1979–85; Asst Life Mgr Assoc of Br Insurers 1986–90; Exec Officer CEEC 1993–97; M Gen Syn Stg Ctee; M Gen Syn Policy Ctee; M Gen Syn Stg Orders Ctee; M CMEAC; Ch Commr, M Gen Purposes and Audit Ctee; M CBF: M CE Pensions Bd; Coun M CPAS, Ch Soc and Latimer Ho; M Dioc Bd of Patronage; M DBF Finance Ctee; Vc Chmn Dioc Parsonages Ctee; M Dioc Stipends Ctee   *Tel and Fax:* (01892) 655951

STEWART, Ms Dorothy Elaine, MA, BA, SRN, SCM, CERT ED
4 Cottingley Drive, Leeds LS11 0JG [RIPON] **1997–** *b* 30 May 1951; *educ* Man Metropolitan Univ, Bradf Univ; M CMEAC; M Dioc BMU
Tel: 0113–226 2392 (Home)
0161–237 2821 (Office)

STILL, Mrs Lesley (Lesley-Joy), BA
3 The Maples, 23 Broadwater Down, Tunbridge Wells, Kent TN2 5NL [ROCHESTER] **1995–** *b* 14 Mar 1936; *educ* Parkstone Girls' Gr Sch Poole; Southn Univ; Ch Ch Coll Cant; Sec Sch Tchr 1958–60; Exec Officer BT 1984–85; Manager BT Property 1985–88; Company Admin 1988–94; pt Ch Admin 1994–97
Tel: (01892) 526881

STOCKPORT, Bishop of [SUFFRAGAN, CHESTER] Rt Revd Geoffrey Martin Turner
Bishop's Lodge, Back Lane, Dunham Town, Altrincham WA14 4SG 1988–94 b 16 Mar 1934; *educ* Bideford Gr Sch; Sandhurst; Oak Hill Th Coll; C St Steph Tonbridge 1963–66; C St Jo Parkstone 1966–69; V St Pet Derby 1969–73; V Ch Ch Chadderton 1973–79; R St Andr Bebington 1979–93; Hon Can Ches Cathl 1989–93; RD North Wirral 1990–93; Adn of Chester 1993–94; Bp of Stockport from 1994
Tel: 0161–928 5611
Fax: 0161–929 0692

STONE, Revd Dr David Adrian, MA, BM, B CH
20 Collingham Rd, London SW5 0LX [LONDON] **1995–** *b* 18 Sep 1956; *educ* Raynes Park Gr Sch; Oriel Coll Ox; Wycliffe Hall Th Coll; C St Geo the Martyr Holborn 1988–91; C-in-c St Jude S Kensington 1991–93; V from 1993; Area Adv for Evang 1992–97; M Bp's Coun; M Dioc BSR 1993–95; M Lee Abbey Coun from 1995; Chmn Lon Dioc Evang Coun from 1997; AD Chelsea from 1996   *Tel and Fax:* 0171–373 1693
e-mail: david.stone@dlondon.org.uk

STORKEY, Dr Elaine
3A Farm Lane, Southgate, London N14 4PP [LONDON] **1987–** *educ* Ossett Gr Sch; Univ Coll of Wales Abth; McMaster Univ Ontario; York Univ; Tutor in Philosophy Man Coll Ox 1967–68; Rsch Fell in Sociology Stirling Univ 1968–69; Tutor Open Univ 1976–80; Visiting Lect Calvin Coll USA 1980–81; Covenant Coll USA 1981–82; Lect in Philosophy Oak Hill Th Coll 1982–87; Lect in Faculty of Social Science Open Univ 1987–91; Dir Inst for Contemporary Christianity 1992–98; Scriptwriter for BBC OU; M ACORA 1988–90; M Crown Appointments Commn 1990; Broadcaster BBC from 1987; Vc-Pres UCCF 1987–93; M Abps' Commn on Cathl 1992–94; M Lausanne Working Party on Th from 1992; M CRAC from 1993; Examiner Sociology of Religion Lon Univ from 1993; Trustee C of E Newspaper from 1994; Vc-

Pres Cheltenham and Glouc Coll of HE from 1994; M Forum for the Future from 1995; Vis Lect in Th K Coll Lon from 1996; M Orthodox-Evang Dialogue WCC from 1996; New Coll Scholar Univ of New S Wales Sydney 1997; BBC1 Advent Sermons 1997; Pres Tear Fund from 1997; M Working Party on Christian-Jewish Relations from 1998; Lambeth DD 1998
Tel: 0181–449 3034 (Home)
0171–629 3615 (Office)

SUTCLIFFE, Mr Tom (James Thomas), MA
12 Polworth Rd, Streatham, London SW16 2EU [SOUTHWARK] 1990– *b* 4 Jun 1943; *educ* Prebendal Sch Chich; Hurstpierpoint Coll; Magd Coll Ox; English teacher Purcell Sch 1964–65; Counter tenor lay-clerk Westmr Cathl 1966–70; Advertisement Manager and Editor *Music and Musicians* magazine 1968–73; Sub-editor, opera critic, feature writer *The Guardian* 1973–96; Opera Critic *The Evening Standard* from 1996; M CECC
Tel: 0181–677 5849 and 0181–677 7939
e-mail: tomsutcliffe@msn.com

SUTTON, Revd John, BA
Timperley Vicarage, 12 Thorley Lane, Timperley, Cheshire WA15 7AZ [CHESTER] 1994– *b* 22 Feb 1947; *educ* Man Gr Sch; St Jo Coll Dur; Ridley Hall Th Coll; C St Lawr Denton Man 1972–74; C-in-c 1974–76; R 1976–82; V St Thos High Lane 1982–88; V St Anne w St Fran Sale 1988–96; V Timperley from 1996; Chair BSR Central Services Ctee; Vc-Chair Dioc CSR from 1996
Tel: 0161–980 4330

SWAN, Prebendary Ronald Frederick, MA
Royal Foundation of St Katharine, 2 Butcher Row, London E14 8DS [LONDON] 1997– *b* 30 Jun 1935; *educ* St Cath Coll Cam; Coll of Resurr Mirfield; C Staveley 1961–66; Chapl Lon Univ 1966–72; C St Martin-in-the-Fields Lon 1972–77; V St Barn Ealing 1977–88; V St Steph Castle Hill Ealing 1981–88; AD Ealing E 1884–87; V St Mary Harrow 1988–97; AD Harrow 1989–94; Preb St Paul's Cathl from 1991; Master R Foundation of St Katharine from 1997
Tel: 0171–790 3540
Fax: 0171–702 7603

SWINDON, Bishop of [SUFFRAGAN, BRISTOL] **Rt Revd Michael David Doe,** BA
Mark House, Field Rise, Swindon SN1 4HP 1990–94 *b* 24 Dec 1947; *educ* Brockenhurst Gr Sch; Dur Univ; Ripon Hall Th Coll; C St Pet St Helier 1972–76; Hon C 1976–81; Youth Sec BCC 1976–81; Priest Missr Blackbird Leys LEP Oxford 1981–88; V 1988–89; RD Cowley 1987–89; Soc Resp Adv Portsm 1989–94; Can Res Portsm Cathl 1989–94; Bp of Swindon from 1994; M CCBI Assembly and CTE Enabling Grp/Forum from 1991; Episcopal Visitor to Dioc World Development Advisers from 1994; Chmn CCU Local Unity Ctee from 1995
Tel and *Fax:* (01793) 538654
e-mail: 106064.431@compuserve.com

SWINSON, Mrs Margaret Anne, BA, ACA, ATII
46 Glenmore Ave, Liverpool L18 4QF [LIVERPOOL] 1985– *b* 16 Dec 1957; *educ* Alice Ottley Sch Worc; Liv Univ; Accountant (Tax Specialist); Gen Syn Stg Ctee from 1991; M BSR 1990–95; Chair Race and Community Relations Ctee 1990–95; Trustee Ch Urban Fund 1987–97; M CCBI; CE Delegate to WCC Canberra 1991; M CBF from 1996
Tel: 0151–724 3533
e-mail: Maggie@Swinson.surfaid.org

TATTERSALL, Mr Geoffrey Frank, MA, QC
2 The Woodlands, Lostock, Bolton BL6 4JD [MANCHESTER] 1995– *b* 22 Sep 1947; *educ* Man Gr Sch; Ch Ch Ox; Barrister; Called to Bar Lincoln's Inn 1970; Bencher 1997; In practice Nn Circuit from 1970; Recorder Crown Court from 1989; QC from 1992; Called to Bar New South Wales 1992; SC from 1995; Judge of Appeal Isle of Man from 1997; Lay Chmn Bolton Dny Syn from 1993; Chmn Ho of Laity Dioc Syn from 1994; M Bp's Coun; M DBF and Trust and Fin Ctee
Tel: (01204) 846265
Fax: (01204) 849863

TAUNTON, Bishop of [SUFFRAGAN, BATH AND WELLS] **Rt Revd (Andrew John) Andy Radford**
Bishop's Lodge, Monkton Heights, West Monkton, Taunton, Som TA2 8LU b 26 Jan 1944; *educ* Kingswood Gr Sch Bris; Trin Coll Bris; C St Mary Shirehampton, Bris 1974–78; C St Pet Henleaze, Bris 1978–80; Producer Religious Programmes BBC Radio Bristol 1974–80; V St Barn w Englishcombe, Bath 1980–85; DCO Glouc 1985–93; Producer Religious Programmes Severn Sound Radio 1985–93; Hon Can Glouc Cathl from 1991; Development and Tr Officer Communications Unit Church House 1993–98; Abps' Adv for Bps' Min 1998; Bp of Taunton from 1998
Tel: (01823) 413526
Fax: (01823) 412805

TAYLOR, Mrs Diana Mary
Volis Farm, Hestercombe, Kingston St Mary, Taunton, Som TA2 8HS [BATH AND WELLS] 1993– *b* 24 Mar 1945; *educ* Scunthorpe Gr Sch; Harper Adams Agric Coll; Farmer; M BM Rural Affairs Ctee from 1993; Bp's Visitor; M Dioc CSR; M Gov Body SW Min Tr Course from 1996; M Pensions Measure Revision Ctee 1996; M Bp's Coun; M Dioc Rural Grp
Tel: (01823) 451545
Fax: (01823) 451701

TAYLOR, Mr John Anthony, RIBA
Church Commissioners, 1 Millbank, London SW1P 3JZ [SENIOR ARCHITECT, CHURCH COMMISSIONERS] Sen Architect Ch Commrs from 1978
Tel: 0171–898 1026
Fax: 0171–898 1011

TAYLOR, Ven Peter Flint, MA, BD
Glebe House, Church Lane, Sheering, Bishop's Stortford CM22 7NR [ARCHDEACON OF HARLOW] *b* 7 Mar 1944; *educ* Clifton Coll Bris; Qu Coll Cam; Lon Univ; Lon Coll of Div; C St Aug Highbury New Park 1970–73; C St Andr Plymouth 1973–77; V Ironville, Derby 1977–83; P-in-c Riddings 1982–83; R Rayleigh 1983–96; pt Chapl HM Young Offenders Inst and Prison Bullwood Hall 1985–90; RD Rochford 1989–96; Adn of Harlow from 1996; M Dioc Syn; M DBF; M Coun for Min; M Family Purse Revision Ctee and Sub-ctee
Tel: (01279) 734524
Fax: (01279) 734426
e-mail: A.Harlow@chelmsford.anglican.org

TAYLOR, Mr Bill (William) Henry, ACII, CIP
8 Poplar Gardens, New Malden, Surrey KT3 3DW [SOUTHWARK] **1996–** *b* 13 Oct 1932; *educ* Beverley Sch New Malden; Kingston Jun Tech Coll; 40 years in Insurance Industry, Yorks Ins Co Motor Underwriting, E W Payne/Sedgwick Insurance Brokers, UK and USA Reinsurance, Grp Tr Manager; Rtd/Tr Consultant; Rdr; M Dioc Pastl Ctee; Wandsworth Adny Pastl Ctee; M Dioc Ruridecanal Conf then Lay Chair Dny Syn
Tel: 0181–942 3596

TERESA, Revd Sister, CSA, BA, STB, PGCE, DD
St Andrew's House, 2 Tavistock Rd, Westbourne Park, London W11 1BA [RELIGIOUS COMMUNITIES IN CONVOCATION, SOUTH] **1995–** *b* 24 Apr 1936; *educ* Wellesley Coll; Harvard Univ; Ch Ch Coll Cant; California Sch for Deacons; Religious Sister from 1970; Tchr Burlington Danes Sch Lon 1974–76; Gen Sec World Congress of Faiths 1977–81; Asst to Abp's Sec for Ecum Affairs 1981–82; NT Lect S'wark Dioc Rdrs Course 1981–89; Ed and Admin Distinctive Diaconate from 1981; Ed *DIAKONIA News* from 1987; Ed Distinctive News of Women in Min from 1994; Chair Soc for Min of Women in the Church from 1994; Consultant at DIAKONIA Fifth Faith and Order World Conf Santiago 1993; CE delegate to Angl-Lutheran Internat Conversations special consultation on the diaconate 1995; M Calendar, Lectionary and Collects Revision Ctee 1996; M CCBI from 1996; M Extended Communion Revision Ctee 1998
Tel: 0171–229 2662 Ext 24
Fax: 0171–792 5993
e-mail: Sister.Teresa@dlondon.org.uk

TEWKESBURY, Bishop of [SUFFRAGAN, GLOUCESTER] **Rt Rev John Stewart Went,** MA
Green Acre, 166 Hempsted Lane, Gloucester GL2 5LG 1990–95 *b* 11 Mar 1944; *educ* Colchester R Gr Sch; Cam Univ; Oak Hill Th Coll; C Em Northwood 1969–75; V H Trin Margate 1975–83; Vc-Prin Wycliffe Hall Ox 1983–89; Adn of Surrey 1989–96; Bp of Tewkesbury from 1996
Tel: (01452) 521824
Fax: (01452) 505554
e-mail: bshptewk@star.co.uk

THAKE, Prebendary Terry (Terence), ALCD
Vicarage, Main Rd, Little Haywood, Stafford ST18 0TS [LICHFIELD] **1989–** *b* 10 Dec 1941; *educ* Hertf Gr Sch; Lon Coll of Div; Circulation Mgr CE Newspaper 1960–62; C Faringdon w Little Coxwell 1966–70; C Aldridge 1970–73; V Werrington and Chapl HMDC Werrington Ho 1973–82; TR Chell and Chapl Westcliffe Hosp 1982–94; RD Stoke North 1991–94; Jt Sec Dioc Syn 1988–95; V Colwich w Gt Haywood from 1994; Preb Lich Cathl from 1994; P-in-c Colton from 1995; Chmn Dioc Ho of Clergy from 1995; RD Rugeley from 1998
Tel and *Fax:* (01889) 881262
e-mail: Terry.Thake@bt.nternet.com

THETFORD, Bishop of [SUFFRAGAN, NORWICH] **Rt Revd Hugo Ferdinand de Waal,** BA, MA
Rectory Meadow, Bramerton, Norwich NR14 7DW *b* 16 Mar 1935; *educ* Tonbridge Sch; Pemb Coll Cam; Ridley Hall Cam; Munster Univ; C St Martin Birm 1960–64; P-in-c Dry Drayton 1964–68; R 1968–74; Chapl Pemb Coll Cam 1964–68; V St Jo Ev Blackpool 1974–78; Prin Ridley Hall Cam 1978–92 Bp of Thetford from 1992
Tel: (01508) 538251
Fax: (01508) 538371

THISELTON, Canon Prof Anthony Charles, BD, M TH, PH D, DD
South View Lodge, 390 High Rd, Chilwell, Nottingham NG9 5EG [UNIVERSITIES, NORTH] **1995–** *b* 13 Jul 1937; *educ* City of Lon Sch; K Coll Lon; Sheff Univ; Oak Hill Th Coll; C H Trin Sydenham 1960–63; Tutor Tyndale Hall Bris 1963–67; Sen Tutor 1967–70; Lect Bibl Studies Sheff Univ 1970–79; Sen Lect 1979–85; Prof Calvin Coll Grand Rapids 1982–83; Prin St Jo Coll Nottm 1985–88; Special Lect Th Nottm Univ 1986–88; Prin St Jo Coll and Cranmer Hall Dur 1988–92; Hon Prof Th Dur Univ 1992; Prof Chr Th Nottm Univ from 1992 and Hd of Th Dept from 1992; Can Th Leic Cathl from 1994; Edit Bd Bib Int (Leiden) from 1992; M Human Fertilization and Embryology Authority from 1995; M Doct Commn from 1996; Pres Soc for Study of Th 1998–2000
Tel and *Fax:* 0115–917 6392 (Home)
Tel: 0115–951 5852 (Office)
Fax: 0115–951 5887 (Office)
e-mail: mary-elmer@nottingham.ac.uk

THOMAS, Mrs Anahid Heleni
188 Castle St, Portchester, Fareham, Hants PO16 9QH
[PORTSMOUTH] 1995– *educ* Schmidts Girls Coll Jerusalem; Housewife; M Dioc Syn; M Dioc Coun for Miss and Unity; M Vacancy-in-See Ctee
Tel and *Fax*: (01705) 420416

THOMAS, Revd Jennifer Monica, IDC, DCM
Christ Church Vicarage, 20 Gaynesford Rd, Forest Hill, London SE23 2HQ [SOUTHWARK] 1998– *b* 26 Aug 1958; *educ* Burlington High Sch Jamaica; St Cath's Convent High Sch Jamaica; Woolwich Coll; Wilson Carlile Coll of Evang; SE Surrey Coll; CA Tr Coll; Sarum and Wells Th Coll; Par Ev St Ann's Bay Jamaica 1982; Par Ev Herne Hill 1988; C St Paul Wimbledon Park 1993–97; V Forest Hill from 1997
Tel: 0181–291 2382

THOMAS, Revd Dr Philip Harold Emlyn, MA, BD, PH D
Vicarage, Heighington, Co Durham DL5 6PP [DURHAM] 1997– *b* 23 Apr 1941; *educ* Univ of Cant NZ; Melbourne Coll of Divinity; Dur Univ; C H Trin Adelaide 1967–70; Warden Latimer Ho Christchurch NZ 1971–77; Chapl and Solway Fell Univ Coll Dur 1978–82; V Ngaio Wellington NZ 1982–84; V Heighington from 1984; RD Darlington from 1993; Bp's Inspector of Th Colls and Courses
Tel and *Fax*: (01325) 312134

THOMAS-BETTS, Dr Anna, MA, PH D
68 Halkingcroft, Langley, Slough, Berks SL3 7AY [OXFORD] 1990– *b* 1 Feb 1941; *educ* Christava Mahilalayam, Alwaye, S India; Madras Chr Coll, Madras Univ; Keele Univ; Lect in Physics Madras Chr Coll 1960–62; Post-Doctoral Rsch Asst Imp Coll Lon 1966–74; Lect in Geophysics Imp Coll Lon 1974–92; Sen Lect from 1992; M CCU 1991–96; M CBF from 1996
Tel: (01753) 822013 (Home)
0171–594 6430 (Office)
e-mail: a.thomas-bts@ic.ac.uk

TICEHURST, Mrs Carol Ann
57 Silver St, Coningsby, Lincoln LN4 4SG [LINCOLN] 1995– *b* 29 Dec 1938
Tel: (01526) 342076

TILL, Very Revd Michael Stanley, MA
The Deanery, The Close, Winchester, Hants SO23 9LS [DEAN OF WINCHESTER] 1986–96 *b* 19 Nov 1935; *educ* Brighton, Hove and Sussex Gr Sch; Linc Coll Ox; Westcott Ho Th Coll; C St Jo St Jo Wood Lon 1964–67; Chapl K Coll Cam 1967–70; Dean and Fell 1970–81; V All SS Fulham 1981–86; RD Hammersmith 1982–86; Adn of Cant 1986–96; Dean of Win from 1996
Tel and *Fax*: (01962) 853738
e-mail: dean.of.winchester@dial.pipex.com

TOMLINSON, Mr Arthur, B SC, M SC
4 Orchard Way, Congleton, Cheshire CW12 4PW [CHESTER] 1990– *b* 25 May 1930; *educ* Hutton Gr Sch Preston; Lon Univ; Graduate Apprentice Engl Electric 1952–54; Aerodynamicist Engl Electric Aviation 1952–58; Computer Programmer Engl Electric Aviation 1958–61; Computer Programming Instructor Engl Electric Computers 1961–68; Tr Officer Baric Computing Services 1968–70; Sen Lect Sch of Computing Staffordshire Univ 1970–95; pt Tutor Open Univ from 1972; Rtd; M Arcidiaconal Pastl Ctee from 1994; M Bp's Coun from 1994; M Dioc CSR from 1998
Tel: (01260) 272618
e-mail: atom@surfaid.org

TONBRIDGE, Bishop of [SUFFRAGAN, ROCHESTER]
Rt Revd Brian Arthur Smith, BA, MA, M LITT
Bishop's Lodge, 48 St Botolph's Rd, Sevenoaks, Kent TN13 3AG 1985–86, 1990–93 *b* 15 Aug 1943; *educ* Geo Heriot Sch Edin; Edin Univ; Fitzw Coll Cam; Jes Coll Cam; Westcott Ho Th Coll; C Cuddesdon 1972–79; Tutor and Lib Cuddesdon Coll 1972–75; Dir of Studies 1975–78; Sen Tutor Ripon Coll Cuddesdon 1978–79; P-in-c Cragg Vale Wakef 1979–85; Dir InService Tr 1979–81; Dir POT 1980–81; Dir Minl Tr Wakef 1981–87; Wrdn of Rdrs 1982–87; Hon Can Wakef Cathl 1981–87; Exam Chapl to Bp of Wakef 1983–93; Adn of Craven, dio of Bradf 1987–93; Bp of Tonbridge from 1993
Tel: (01732) 456070
Fax: (01732) 741449
e-mail: sevenoaks@clara.net

TONGUE, Mr Raymond, B SC, M SC
Church House, Great Smith St, London SW1P 3NZ [HEAD OF STATISTICS UNIT, ARCHBISHOPS' COUNCIL] *b* 25 Sep 1948; *educ* High Arcal Gr Sch; Univ Coll Lon; Birm Univ; Head of Statistics Unit, CBF 1996–98; Head of Statistics Unit, Abps' Coun from 1999
Tel: 0171–898 1542
Fax: 0171–898 1558
e-mail: raymond.tongue@stats.clara.net

TOOKE, Mr Stephen Edgar
Rectory, Church Rd, Christchurch, Cambs PE14 9PQ [ELY] 1995– *b* 21 Dec 1946; *educ* Qu Sch Wisbech; Isle of Ely Coll; Rtd Police Superintendent; Appeals Organiser The Children's Soc; Lay Chair Dioc Syn; M Dioc Stewardship Ctee
Tel: (01354) 638379
Fax: (01354) 638418

TOOP, Mrs Mary Lou (Mary Louise)
Vicarage, Clun Rd, Craven Arms, Shropshire SY7 9QW [HEREFORD] 1995– *b* 16 Feb 1955; *educ* Broxbourne Sch; W of England Min Tr Course; Accredited Lay Min Church Stretton 1993–94; Accredited Lay Min Stokesay, Sibdon Carwood and Halford from 1994; Dioc Vocations Adv from 1994; M Dioc Bd of Educ; Tutor W of England Minl Tr Course
Tel: (01588) 672797

TOVEY, Revd Phillip Noel, BC, M PHIL, MSLS, S TH
Rectory, Holton, Oxford OX33 1PR [OXFORD] 1998– *b* 4 July 1956; *educ* Lon Univ; Nottm Univ; Lon Bible Coll; St Jo Coll Nottm; C Beaconsfield 1987–90; C Banbury 1990–91, TV 1991–95; P-in-c Holton and Waterperry w Albury and Waterstock 1995–97; TV Wheatley from 1997 Tel: (01865) 872460
e-mail: phillip.tovey@virgin.net

TOWNSEND, Mrs Margot (Elizabeth Margaret Wynne)
The Cottage, Abbotts Ann, Andover, Hants SP11 7BG [WINCHESTER] 1998– *b* 6 Aug 1932; *educ* St Brandon's CDS; Qu Coll Harley St; Nor High Sch; Rdr; M DBF from 1990, Exec 1991–95; Budget 1995–97; Dioc Appts and Stg Ctees from 1995; Electoral Appeal Panel from 1996; Pastl Ctee from 1998; Chmn Andover Dny Fin Ctee from 1990 Tel: (01264) 710376

TOYNE, Professor Peter, BA, HON D ED, FRSA, CIMGT, FICPD, DL
Cloudslee, Croft Drive, Caldy, Merseyside L48 2JW [APPOINTED MEMBER, ARCHBISHOPS' COUNCIL] *b* 3 Dec 1939; *educ* Ripon Gr Sch; Bris Univ; The Sorbonne; Lect in Geography Ex Univ 1965–75, Sen Lect 1975–77; Dir Educational Credit Transfer Project DES 1977–80; Head of Bp Otter Coll Chich 1980–83; Dep Rector NE Lon Poly 1983–86; Vc Chan and Chief Exec Liv John Moores Univ from 1986; Apptd M Abps' Coun from 1999 Tel: 0151–709 3676
Fax: 0151–709 9864

TREADGOLD, Very Revd John David, LVO, BA, FRSA
The Deanery, Chichester, W Sussex PO19 1PX [DEAN OF CHICHESTER] *b* 30 Dec 1931; *educ* West Bridgford Gr Sch; Nottm Univ; Wells Th Coll; V Choral Southwell Minster 1959–64; R Wollaton Nottm 1964–74; CF (TA) 1967–72, 74–78; V Darlington 1974–81; Chmn Dur DAC 1978–81; Can Windsor, Chapl R Chapel Windsor Gt Park 1981–89; Chapl to The Queen 1982–89; Dean of Chich from 1989; Chmn Chich DAC from 1990; Chmn of Govs The Prebendal Sch Chich from 1989; Gov Wycombe Abbey Sch from 1995 Tel: (01243) 787337 (Office)
(01243) 783286 (Home)

TREMLETT, Ven Tony (Anthony Frank)
St Matthew's House, 45 Spicer Rd, Exeter, Devon EX1 1TA [ARCHDEACON OF EXETER] *b* 25 Aug 1937; *educ* Plymouth Coll; S W Minl Tr Course; Asst C Plymouth Southway 1981–82; P-in-c 1982–84; V 1984–88; RD Plymouth Moorside 1986–88; Adr of Totnes 1988–94; Adn of Exeter from 1994
Tel: (01392) 425432
Fax: (01392) 425783
e-mail: TremlettAF@aol.com

TRICKEY, Very Revd (Frederick) Marc, BA, DIP TH
St Martin's Rectory, Guernsey GY4 6RR [DEAN OF GUERNSEY] 1995– *b* 16 Aug 1935; *educ* Brs Gr Sch; St Jo Coll Dur; Cranmer Hall Th Coll; Commercial Trainee Nat Smelting Co Avonmouth 1954–59; C Lawr Alton 1964–68; R St Jo Bapt Win cum Winnall 1968–77; R St Martin Guernsey from 1977; M States of Guernsey Bd of Employment, Industry and Commerce 1982–95; Dean of Guernsey from 1995; Bp's Rep on Coun USPG; M States of Guernsey Broadcasting Ctee from 1979; Angl Religious Adv Channel TV from 1988; Hon Can Win Cathl from 1995; M Dioc Stg Ctee from 1995; Pres States of Guernsey Ecclesiastical Ctee from 1995; P-in-c Sark from 1996 Tel: (01481) 38303
Fax: (01481) 37710

TRISTAM, Brother (Tristam Keith Holland), SSF, MA
Hilfield Friary, Dorchester, Dorset DT2 7BE [RELIGIOUS COMMUNITIES, SOUTH (LAY)] 1994– *b* 20 Mar 1946; *educ* Eastwood Hall Park Sch; Trin Coll Cam; M SSF from 1967; Guardian Fiwila Friary Zambia 1973–76; Provincial Sec UK 1976–83 and 1994–96; SSF Sec for Liturgy from 1976; Gen Sec 1983–97; Guardian Alnmouth Friary 1988–91; Consultant to Liturg Commn 1992–95; M from 1995
Tel: (01300) 341345 (Friary)
(01300) 341160 (Direct Line)
Fax: (01300) 341293
e-mail: tristam@franciscan.demon.co.uk

TROTT, Revd Stephen, BA, MA, FRSA
Rectory, 41 Humfrey Lane, Boughton, Northampton NN2 8RQ [PETERBOROUGH] 1995– *b* 28 May 1957; *educ* Bp Vesey's Gr Sch Sutton Coldfield; Birm Poly; Hull Univ; Fitzw Coll Cam; Leeds Univ; Westcott Ho Th Coll; C Hessle 1984–87; C St Alb Hull 1987–88; R Pitsford w Boughton from 1988; Sec CME 1988–93; M Dioc Syn from 1990; M Exec Coun Prayer Book Soc from 1994; M Revision Ctee on Calendar, Lectionary and Collects 2000; M Legislative Ctee from 1995; M Legal Adv Commn from 1996; M CCBI and CTE from 1996; Ch Commr and

M Pastl Ctee from 1997; M CE Pensions Bd from 1998
Tel: (01604) 821387
Fax: (01604) 820637
e-mail: stephentrott@cw.com.net

TRURO, Bishop of, Rt Revd William Ind, BA
Lis Escop, Truro, Cornwall TR3 6QQ 1997– *b* 26 Mar 1942; *educ* Duke of York's Sch Dover; Leeds Univ; Coll of Resurr Mirf; C St Dunstan w St Cath Feltham 1966–70; P-in-c St Joseph the Worker Northolt 1970–73; TV Basingstoke TM 1973–87; Exam Chapl to Bp of Win 1976–82; pt Vc-Prin Aston Tr Scheme 1977–82; M Doct Commn 1980–86; DDO Win 1982–87; Hon Can Win Cathl 1985–87; Bp of Grantham 1987–97; Can and Preb of Thorngate in Linc Cathl 1987–97; Dean of Stamford 1988–97; Bp of Truro from 1997; Co-Chmn English ARC from 1993
Tel: (01872) 862657
Fax: (01872) 862037
e-mail: bishop@lisescop.demon.co.uk

TURNBULL, Ven David Charles, BA, M ED
2 The Abbey, Carlisle, Cumbria CA3 8TZ [ARCHDEACON OF CARLISLE] 1996– *b* 16 Mar 1944; *educ* K James I Gr Sch Bp Auckland; Leeds Univ; Sheff Univ; Chich Th Coll; C Jarrow 1969–74; V Carlinghow 1974–83; V Penistone 1983–86; P-in-c Thurlstone 1985–86; TR Penistone and Thurlstone 1986–93; RD Barnsley 1988–93; Hon Can Wakef Cathl 1993; Adn of Carl and Can Res Carl Cathl from 1993
Tel: (01228) 23026
Fax: (01228) 594899

TURNBULL, Revd Dr Richard Duncan, BA, PH D, CA
1 Hartswood, Chineham, Basingstoke, Hants RG24 8SJ [WINCHESTER] 1995– *b* 17 Oct 1960; *educ* Moseley Gr Sch; Normanton High Sch; Reading Univ; Dur Univ; Cranmer Hall Th Coll; Ernst and Young Chartered Accountants 1982–90; C Highfield Southn 1994–98; V Chineham Basingstoke from 1998; M CBF from 1997; M CBF Investment Management Ctee from 1997; M Dioc Pastl Ctee; M Dioc Fin Ctee; M Dioc Budget Ctee; M Steering Grp Evang Alliance Commn on Unity and Truth among Evangelicals; M CEEC
Tel: (01256) 474285
Fax: (01256) 328912
e-mail: RDTurnbull@aol.com

TYLER, Mr (John) Malcolm, FRCO, ARAM, LRAM
34 Church Way, Weston Favell, Northampton NN3 3BT [PETERBOROUGH] 1990– *b* 31 Oct 1929; *educ* K Sch Pet; R Academy of Music Lon; Asst Organist Pet Cathl 1950–53; Asst Organist Cant Cathl 1953–56; Dir of Music K Coll Taunton 1957–62; Dir of Music St Jo Coll Johannesburg 1962–64; Co Music Adv Banffshire 1964–67; Dir of Music Northants Co Coun and Dir Co Music Sch 1967–92; Rtd; M Dioc Bd of Educ from 1990; M Bp's Coun from 1995
Tel: (01604) 402589

TYRRELL, Mr Mike (Deryck Michael), BD, MA, PH D, ACIS, ACA
32 Warwick New Rd, Leamington Spa, Warws CV32 5JJ [COVENTRY] 1985– *b* 23 Jun 1948; *educ* High Storrs Gr Sch Sheff; SS Coll Cam; Aston Univ; Tr Adv Local Government Tr Bd 1975–77; Tr Services Mgr Inst of Chartered Accountants in England and Wales 1977–80; Mgr Price Waterhouse, Chartered Accountants 1980–89; Grp Development Mgr, Rugby Grp plc; Rdr; M CBF from 1986; Chr Stewardship Ctee 1986–95; M Bp's Coun from 1989; Chmn Dioc Stewardship Adv Ctee from 1990; Chmn Dioc Ho of Laity 1991–97; Chmn CEIG from 1993; M Gen Syn Stg Ctee from 1996
Tel: (01926) 429826
0836 377673 (Mobile)
Fax: (01926) 722629
e-mail: tyrrellm@rugbygroup.co.uk

VOUT, Mrs Janet Mary, BA, IDC
87 Spinneyfield, Rotherham, S Yorks S60 3LZ [SHEFFIELD] 1990– *b* 9 Feb 1944; *educ* Gainsborough High Sch; Newc Univ; Gilmore Ho Lon; Par Worker Clifton, Rotherham 1968–70; Student Nurse Middlewood Hosp Sheff 1972–73; Licensed Worker NSM Clifton, Rotherham 1985–90; Hosp Chapl Asst Rotherham Hosps from 1991
Tel: (01709) 839258 (Home)
(01709) 820000 Ext 5578(Office)

WAGSTAFF, Ven Christopher (John Harold), BA
Glebe House, Church Lane, Maisemore, Gloucester GL2 8EY [ARCHDEACON OF GLOUCESTER] 1988–98 *b* 25 Jun 1936; *educ* Bishop's Stortford Coll; St D Coll, Lampeter; C All SS Queensbury 1962–68; V St Mich Tokyngton Wembley 1968–73; RD S Forest 1975–82; V Coleford w Staunton 1973–83; Adn of Gloucester from 1982; Res Can Glouc Cathl from 1982; Chmn Glouc Dioc Trust; ABM Selector; Hon Can Njombe Cathl dio SW Tanganyika from 1993; Chmn Dioc Coun for Min
Tel: (01452) 528500
Fax: (01452) 381528

WAKEFIELD, Bishop of, Rt Revd Nigel Simeon McCulloch, MA
Bishop's Lodge, Woodthorpe Lane, Wakefield WF2 6JL 1990– *b* 17 Jan 1942; *educ* Liv Coll; Selw Coll Cam; Cuddesdon Th Coll; C Ellesmere Port 1966–70; Chapl Ch Coll Cam 1970–73; Perm to Off Dio Liv 1970–73; Dir of Th Studies Ch Coll Cam 1970–75;

Dioc Missr Nor Dioc 1973–78; R SS Thos & Edm Sarum 1978–86; Adn of Sarum 1979–86; Chmn ABM Finance Ctee 1987–92; Bp of Taunton 1986–92; Bp of Wakef from 1992; Chmn Communications Unit from 1993; Chmn BM Miss, Evang and Renewal Ctee from 1996; Lord High Almoner from 1997
Tel: (01924) 255349
Fax: (01924) 250202
e-mail: 100612.1514@compuserve.com

WALKER, Revd David
St Annes's Vicarage, 29 Park Rd West, Birkenhead, Merseyside LA43 1UR [CHESTER] **1998–** *b* 6 Aug 1948; *educ* Linc Th Coll; C Arnold 1974–77; C Crosby 1977–79; V Scrooby 1979–86; V St Mary Sutton in Ashfield 1986–94; P-in-c St Mich Sutton in Ashfield 1989–94; TR Birkenhead Priory from 1994
Tel: 0151–652 1309

WALKER, Revd Peter Stanley, B COMB STUDS, SRN, RMN
Rectory, 76 East Hill, Colchester, Essex CO1 2QW [CHELMSFORD] **1995–** *b* 20 Nov 1956; *educ* Laindon Sch; Princess Alexandra Coll of Nursing (R Lon Hosp); Nottm Univ; Linc Th Coll; C St Barn Woodford 1983–86; C St Thos Brentwood 1986–88; V St Barn Colchester 1988–94; P-in-c St Jas Colchester from 1994; P-in-c St Paul Colchester from 1995; R Colchester St Jas and St Paul w All SS, St Nic and St Runwald from 1996; M Dioc Coun for Miss and Unity 1989–92; Dioc Stewardship Support Grp 1992–94; Chapl Colchester Maternity Hosp 1993–95; Adv to DDO from 1994; M Exec CU 1992–95
Tel: (01206) 866802

WALKER, Mr William Hugh Colquhoun, MA, FCA, AIIMR
Crown Piece, Church Rd, Wormingford, Colchester, Essex CO6 3AD [CHELMSFORD] **1995–** *b* 30 Jul 1932; *educ* Wellington Coll; Selw Coll Cam; Rtd
Tel: (01787) 227337
Fax: (01787) 228413

WALLACE, Ven Martin William, BD, AKC
63 Powers Hall End, Witham, Essex CM8 1NH [ARCHDEACON OF COLCHESTER] *b* 16 Nov 1948; *educ* Varndean Gr Sch for Boys Brighton; Tauntons Sch Southn; K Coll Lon; St Aug Coll Cant; C Attercliffe Sheff 1971–74; C New Malden 1974–77; V St Mark Forest Gate 1977–83; Chapl Forest Gate Hosp 1977–80; RD Newham 1982–91; P-in-c Em Forest Gate 1985–89; P-in-c All SS Forest Gate 1991–93; Dioc Urban Officer 1991–93; Hon Can Chelmsf Cathl 1989–97; P-in-c St Lawr Bradwell and St Thos Bradwell 1993–97; Ind Chapl Maldon and Dengie 1993–97; Adn of Colchester from 1997
Tel: (01376) 513130
Fax: (01376) 500789
e-mail: a.colchester@chelmsford.anglican.org

WALTERS, Canon Michael William, B SC
Rectory, 14 Chapel St, Congleton, Cheshire CW12 4AB [CHESTER] **1980–90, 1995–** *b* 26 Nov 1939; *educ* Derby Sch; K Coll Newc; Dur Univ; Clifton Th Coll; C H Trin Aldershot 1963–66; C Ch Ch Upper Armley 1966–69; NE Area Sec CPAS 1969–75; V St Geo Hyde 1975–82; V St Jo Knutsford and Toft 1982–97; Hon Can Ches Cathl from 1994; P-in-c St Pet and St Steph Congleton and TR Designate of Congleton 1997–98; TR Congleton from 1998; M Bp's Coun; Chmn Dioc Ho of Clergy; Chmn Dioc Bd of Patronage
Tel: (01260) 273212
(01260) 290261

WALTERS, Very Revd (Rhys) Derrick Chamberlain, OBE
Liverpool Cathedral, Liverpool L1 7AZ [DEAN OF LIVERPOOL] *b* 10 Mar 1932; *educ* Gowerton Gr Sch; LSE; Ripon Hall Th Coll; C Manselton Swansea 1957–58; Anglican Chapl Univ Coll Swansea and C St Marys 1958–62; V All SS Totley 1962–67; V St Mary's Boulton by Derby 1967–74; Dioc Missnr Sarum 1974–82; V Burcombe 1974–79; Non-res Can of Sarum 1978; Can Res and Treas of Sarum Cathl 1979–82; Dean of Liv from 1982
Tel: 0151–709 6271

WALTON, Ven Geoffrey Elmer, BA
Vicarage, Witchampton, Wimborne, Dorset BH21 5AP [ARCHDEACON OF DORSET] *1990–95 b* 19 Feb 1934; *educ* W Bridgford Gr Sch; St Jo Coll Dur; Qu Th Coll, Birm; C Warsop w Sookholme 1961–65; V Norwell and Dioc Youth Chapl (Southwell) 1965–69; Recruitment and Selection Sec ACCM 1969–75; V H Trin Weymouth 1975–82; Hon Can Sarum 1981; RD Weymouth 1980–82; Adn of Dorset from 1982; P-in-c Witchampton and Hinton Parva, Long Crichel w More Crichel from 1982
Tel: (01258) 840422
Fax: (01258) 840786

WARD, Mrs Elizabeth Joyce
The Gate House, Edge, Stroud, Glos GL6 6PE [GLOUCESTER] **1995–** *b* 1 Dec 1942; *educ* Brierley Hill Gr Sch; Coll of Advanced Tech Birm; Dioc Stewardship Adv
Tel: (01452) 812188 (Home)
(01452) 410022 (Office)
Fax: (01452) 308324

WARNER, Mr David Hugh, DIP ED
41 Ox Lane, Harpenden, Herts AL5 4HF [ST ALBANS] **1995–** *b* 21 Feb 1932; *educ* St Jo Sch Leatherhead; St

Mark and St Jo Coll Chelsea; St Alb Min Tr Scheme; Dep Head St Nic CE JMI Sch 1964–71; Head Wigginton CE JMI Sch 1972–73; Head Wheathampstead CE JMI Sch 1974–93; Rtd; M Dioc Bd of Educ; Sec Wheathampstead Dny Syn; M Bp's Coun
Tel and *Fax:* (01582) 762379

WARREN, Mrs Ann, MA
Karibu, Fernhill Lane, Woking, Surrey GU22 0DR [GUILDFORD] **1980–85, 1990–95, 1997–** *b* 13 Jan 1936; *educ* Oakdene Sch Beaconsfield; St Andr Univ; BBC Radio 1958–63; Studio Manager, Scriptwriter, Producer *Children's Hour*; Editorial Bd *CE Newspaper* 1975–85; Editor company in-house magazine 1979–82; TVS *Company* 1983–85; Freelance Writer; Author; Pastl Counsellor *Tel:* (01483) 767455

WARREN, Ven Norman Leonard, MA
The Archdeaconry, Rochester, Kent ME1 1SX [ARCHDEACON OF ROCHESTER] *1974–77, 1990–95 b* 19 Jul 1934; *educ* Dulwich Coll; CCC Cam; Ridley Hall Th Coll; C Bedworth1960–63; V St Paul Leamington Spa 1963–77; R Morden 1977–89; RD Merton 1987–89; Adn of Rochester from 1989; RSCM Coun from 1989; Chmn Music in Worship Trust from 1989
Tel: (01634) 842527

WARREN, Canon Paul Kenneth, MA
Rectory, 13 Rectory Lane, Standish, Wigan, Lancs WN6 0XA [BLACKBURN] **1980–** *b* 3 May 1941; *educ* Rossall Sch; Selw Coll Cam; Cuddesdon Th Coll; C Lanc Priory 1967–70; Angl Chapl Univ of Lanc 1970–78; Prin Grizedale Coll, Univ of Lanc 1975–78; V St Leon Langho 1978–83; Chapl to Brockhall Mental Hosp 1978–83; Dom Chapl to Bp of Blackburn and Chapl Whalley Abbey 1983–88; R St Wilfrid Standish from 1988; Hon Can Blackb Cathl from 1991; RD Chorley 1992–98; Chmn Dioc Liturg Ctee 1989–98
Tel: (01257) 421396

WARREN, Canon Robert Peter Resker, MA, ALCD
16 Connaught Rd, Market Harborough, Leics LE16 7NG [NATIONAL OFFICER FOR EVANGELISM] *1975–85 b* 14 May 1939; *educ* Bradfield Coll; Jes Coll Cam; Lon-Coll of Div; C H Trin Platt 1965–68; C-in-c St Jas Fordhouses Wolverhampton 1968–71; TR St Thos Crookes Sheff 1971–93; Nat Offcr for Evang from 1993 *Tel* and *Fax:* (01858) 431947

WARRINGTON, Bishop of [SUFFRAGAN, LIVERPOOL] **Rt Revd John Richard Packer,** MA
34 Central Ave, Eccleston Park, Prescot, Merseyside L34 2QP 1985–91, 1992–96 b 10 Oct 1946; *educ* Man Gr Sch; Keble Coll Ox; Ripon Hall Th Coll; C St Pet St Helier 1970–73; Dir Pastl Studies Ripon Hall 1973–75 and Ripon Coll Cuddesdon 1975–77; Chapl St Nic Abingdon 1973–77; V Wath upon Dearne w Adwick upon Dearne 1977–86; RD Wath 1983–86; R Sheffield Manor 1986–91; RD Attercliffe 1990–91; Adn of W Cumberland 1991–96; P-in-c Bridekirk 1995–96; Bp of Warrington from 1996 *Tel:* 0151–426 1897 (Home)
0151–708 9480 (Office)

WARWICK, Bishop of [SUFFRAGAN, COVENTRY] **Rt Revd Anthony Martin Priddis,** MA, DIP TH
Warwick House, 139 Kenilworth Rd, Coventry CV4 7AP b 15 Mar 1948; *educ* Watford Gr Sch; CCC Cam; New Coll Ox; Cuddesdon Th Coll; C New Addington 1972–75; Chapl Ch Ch Ox 1975–80; TV St Jo High Wycombe 1980–86; P-in-c Amersham 1986–90, R 1990–96; RD Amersham 1992–96; Hon Can Ch Ch Ox from 1995; Bp of Warwickfrom 1996
Tel: (01203) 416200
Fax: (01203) 415254
e-mail: bishwarwick@clara.net

WATKINS, Revd Peter, BA
Vicarage, Brook St, Coventry CV8 3AD [COVENTRY] **1993–95, 1997–** *b* 24 May 1951; *educ* Monkton Combe Sch; Oak Hill Th Coll; C St Marg Whitnash Leamington Spa 1982–85; V St Marg Wolston Cov w St Pet Church Lawford Rugby from 1985; RD Rugby
Tel and *Fax:* (01203) 542722

WATSON, Very Revd Derek Richard, MA
The Deanery, 7 The Close, Salisbury, Wilts SP1 2EF [DEAN OF SARUM] *b* 18 Feb 1938; *educ* Uppingham Sch; Selw Coll Cam; Cuddesdon Th Coll; C All SS New Eltham 1964–66; Chapl Ch Coll Cam 1966–70; Dom Chapl to Bp of S'wark 1970–73; V St Andr and St Mark Surbiton 1973–78; Can Treas S'wark Cathl, DDO and POT 1978–82; R St Luke w Ch Ch Chelsea 1982–96; Dean of Sarum from 1996
Tel: (01722) 555110

WATSON, Ven Jeffrey John Seagrief, MA
1A Summerfield, Cambridge CB3 9HE [ARCHDEACON OF ELY] *1985–93, 1993–95 b* 29 Apr 1939; *educ* Univ Coll Sch Hampstead; Em Coll Cam; Clifton Th Coll; C Ch Ch Beckenham 1965–69; C St Jude Southsea 1969–71; V Ch Ch Win 1971–81; Exam Chapl to Bp of Win 1976–93; V Bitterne 1981–93; RD Southn 1983–93; Hon Can Win Cathl 1991–93; Chmn ABM Vocations Adv Sub-Ctee from 1991; M ABM Recruitment and Selection Ctee from 1991; Adn of Ely from 1993; Hon Can Ely Cathl from 1993 *Tel:* (01223) 515725
Fax: (01223) 571322
e-mail: archdeacon.ely@ely.anglican.org

WAUDE, Mr Andrew Leslie
10 Huntwick Rd, Featherstone, Pontefract WF7 5JD, and St Matthew's House, Kamloops Crescent, Leicester

LE1 2HX [WAKEFIELD] 1997– b 13 Sep 1974; educ St Wilfrid's RC High Sch Featherstone; Clerical Officer Wakef HA 1995–96; Data Preparation Asst W Yorks Central Services Agency (NHS) Leeds 1996–98; Par Asst Par of the Resurr Leic from 1998; M Dioc Syn from 1994; Sec Wakef Dioc CU Ctee 1996–98
Tel: (01977) 797059 (Featherstone)
0166– 253 9158 (Leicester)
0958 642991 (Mobile)

WEBSTER, Mr David Ernest Spencer
5 Rosehill Walk, Tunbridge Wells, Kent TN1 1HL [ROCHESTER] 1975– b 21 Sep 1930; educ Dulwich Coll; Financial Journalist; Rtd; M CBF and Exec Ctee; Chmn CBF Staff Ctee; M Budget Ctee; Ch Commr, M Bd of Govs, M Pastl Ctee; M Nat Working Party Ecum Decade of Chs in Solidarity with Women; M Invest Ctee Nat Soc; M Coun of Corp of Ch Ho and House and Accts Ctee; M CCBI; M CTE; M Coun Chr Together in Kent; Co-Chmn Tun Wells Dny Syn 1979–95; Lay Chmn Dioc Syn; M Bp's Coun; M DBF; M Coun of Min; M Coun for Miss & Unity; M Pastl Ctee; Co-ordinator of Communications and Ed Consultant Roch LINK; M Coun SAMS; Talking Newspaper Editor; Chmn Tunbridge Wells Blind Club; Rdr
Tel: (01892) 526055

WEBSTER, Mrs Diana Theresa Muriel, MBE, MA
Kilpikuja 3, 02610 Espoo, Finland [EUROPE] 1995– b 9 Jan 1930; educ Lady Eleanor Holles Sch Hampton; St Hugh's Coll Ox; Lect in Eng Lang Univ of Helsinki 1953–93; Writer; Broadcaster; Radio Dramatist
Tel: 00–358-9–520446
Fax: 00–358-9–520002
e-mail: 75337.2763@compuserve.com

WEBSTER, Canon Glyn Hamilton, SRN
22 Markham Crescent, York YO31 8NS [YORK] 1995– b 3 Jun 1951; educ Darwen Sec Tech (Gr) Sch; Cranmer Hall, St Jo Coll Dur; C All SS Huntington York 1977–81; V St Luke Ev York and Sen Chapl York District Hosp 1981–92; Sen Chapl York Health Services NHS Trust from 1992; Can York Minster from 1994; RD York from 1997
Tel: (01904) 632380 (Home)
(01904) 453120 (Office)

WEDDERSPOON, Very Revd Alexander Gillan, MA, BD
The Deanery, 1 Cathedral Close, Guildford, Surrey GU2 5TL [DEAN OF GUILDFORD] b 3 Apr 1931; educ Westmr Sch; Jes Coll Ox; Cuddesdon Th Coll; C Kingston Par Ch 1961–63; Lect in RE Lon Univ 1963–66; Educ Adv CE Schs Coun 1966–69; P-in-c St Marg Westmr 1969–70; Can Res Win Cathl 1970–87; Dean of Guildf from 1987
Tel: (01483) 560328 (Home)
(01483) 565287 (Office)
Fax: (01483) 303350

WEETMAN, Revd John Charles, MA, BA
Vicarage, Church Drive, Boosbeck, East Cleveland TS12 3AY [YORK] 1998– b 11 Apr 1966; educ Rye Hills Comp Sch Redcar; Sir William Turner Sixth Form Coll Redcar; Qu Coll Ox; Trin Coll Bris; C St Jo Newland Hull 1991–95; V Boosbeck w Moorsholm from 1995
Tel: (01287) 651728

WELLINGTON, Canon James Frederick, LL B, BA, M PHIL
Rectory, Upper Church St, Syston, Leicester LE7 1HR [LEICESTER] 1998– b 11 Feb 1951; educ Wimborne Gr Sch; Leic Univ; Fitzw Coll Cam; Ridley Hall Th Coll; Nottm Univ; C John Keble Mill Hill 1977–80; C Wood Green TM and Asst Chapl Middx Poly 1980–83; V St Luke Stocking Farm 1983–90; V Glen Magna cum Stretton Magna and Wiston cum Newton Harcourt 1990–98; Warden of Rdrs 1991–97; Hon Can Leic Cathl from 1994; RD Gartree II 1996–98; TR Syston from 1998; Chmn Ho of Clergy Dioc Syn
Tel: 0116– 260 8276
e-mail: j&hwelli@leicester.anglican.org

WELLS, Ven Roderick John, BA, MA
New Vicarage, Hackthorn, Lincoln LN2 3PF [ARCHDEACON OF STOW] 1995– b 17 Nov 1936; educ Haberdashers' Aske's Sch; Dur Univ. Hull Univ; Cuddesdon Th Coll; C St Mary at Lambeth 1965–68; P-in-c 1968–71; R Skegness 1971–78; P-in-c Winthorpe 1977–78; TR Gt and Little Coates w Bradley 1978–89; RD Grimsby and Cleethorpes 1983–89; Hon Can Linc Cathl from 1986; Adn of Stow from 1989; Adn in Lindsey from 1994; Chmn Dioc Bd of Educ
Tel: (01673) 860382

WEST, Preb Penny (Penelope) Anne Margaret, CERT ED
Vicarage, 35 Kewstoke Rd, Kewstoke, Weston-super-Mare BS22 9YE [BATH AND WELLS] 1995– b 14 Jun 1944; educ Maynard Sch Ex; City of Birm Coll of Educ; Glouc Sch for Min; Ridley Hall Th Coll; Tchr North Cerney Primary Sch 1968–85; C Portishead 1986–92; Sen C Bath Abbey 1992–95; Chapl R Nat Hosp for Rheumatic Diseases 1992–95; M Dioc Coun for Min 1991–97; V Kewstoke w Wick St Lawr from 1995; Chmn Dioc Ho of Clergy from 1994; M Bp's Coun and Joint Budget Ctee from 1994; Bp's Selector for ABM from 1993; Preb Wells Cathl from 1996; M ABM 1997–98
Tel: (01934) 416162

WESTON, Mrs Mary Louise
Carpenters House, Tur Langton, Kibworth, Leicester LE8 0PJ [LEICESTER] **1995–** *b* 4 Jul 1947; *educ* Portland Ho Sch Leic; Wroxall Abbey Sch Warwick; Nottm Univ; Co-ordinator of Organic Livestock Marketing Grp for farmers from 1996; pt Organic Farmer from 1981; Sub Postmistress 1985–98; M Gen Syn Rural Affairs Ctee from 1996; M Dioc Schs Premises and Trusts Ctee from 1997 Tel: (01858) 545564

WHEATLEY, Ven Paul Charles, BA
West Stafford Rectory, Dorchester, Dorset DT2 8AB [ARCHDEACON OF SHERBORNE] *b* 27 May 1938; *educ* Wycliffe Coll, Stonehouse, Glos; St Jo Coll Dur; Linc Th Coll; C St Mich Bishopston Bris 1963–68; Dioc Youth Chapl Bris 1968–74; TR Dorcan Tm Min Swindon 1974–79; R Ross Team Min Heref 1979–91; RD Ross and Archenfield 1979–91; Dioc Ecum Officer Heref 1987–91; Adn of Sherborne from 1991
Tel: (01305) 264637
Fax: (01305) 260640
e-mail: 101543.3471@compuserve.com

WHEATLEY, Ven Peter William, MA
27 Thurlow Rd, Hampstead, London NW3 5PP [ARCHDEACON OF HAMPSTEAD] 1975–95 *b* 7 Sep 1947; *educ* Ipswich Sch; Qu Coll Ox; Pemb Coll Cam; Asst C All SS Fulham 1973–78; V H Cross, Cromer St, St Pancras 1978–82; V St Jas W Hampstead, P-in-c St Mary w All So Kilburn 1982–95; Chmn Chr Concern for S Africa 1992–95; Dir POT Edmonton Area 1985–95; M BSR Internat Affairs Ctee 1981–96; Adn of Hampstead from 1995 Tel: 0171–435 5890
Fax: 0171–435 6049
e-mail: archdeacon.hampstead@dlondon.org.uk

WHITBY, Bishop of [SUFFRAGAN, YORK] **Rt Revd Gordon Bates**
60 West Green, Stokesley, Middlesbrough, N Yorks TS9 5BD 1988–95 *b* 16 Mar 1934; *educ* Wath-on-Dearne Gr Sch; Kelham Th Coll; C All SS New Eltham 1954–58; Asst Youth Chapl Glouc Dio 1962–64; Dioc Youth Chapl Liv 1965–69; V Huyton, Liv 1969–73; Canon Res and Prec Liv Cathl and DDO 1973–83; Bp of Whitby from 1983; Chmn Communications Officers' Panel 1990–95; M CRAC 1990–95; Trustee Sandford St Martin Trust 1990–96; M Communications Ctee 1990–95; M Rural Bps Panel from 1998
Tel: (01642) 710390
Fax: (01642) 710685

WHITE, Ven Frank (Francis), B SC
Greenriggs, Dipe Lane, East Boldon NE36 0PH [ARCHDEACON OF SUNDERLAND] **1987–** *b* 26 May 1949; *educ* St Cuth Gr Sch Newc; Consett Tech Coll; UWIST Cardiff; Univ Coll Cardiff; St Jo Coll Nottm; Dir Youth Action York 1971–73; Detached Youth Worker Man Catacombs Trust 1973–77; C St Nic Dur 1980–84; C St Mary and St Cuth Chester-le-Street 1984–87; Chapl to Dur Health Auth Hosps 1987–89; V St Jo Ev Birtley 1989–97; RD Chester-le-Street 1993–97; Hon Can Dur Cathl from 1997; Adn of Sunderland from 1997
Tel: 0191–536 2300
Fax: 0191–519 3369
e-mail: F2awhite@aol.com

WHITE, Mr Jim (James Everard), MA, B SC, FRSA
Durborough Farm, Aisholt, Spaxton, Bridgwater, Som TA5 1AP [BATH AND WELLS] **1990–** *b* 16 Oct 1927; *educ* Qu Eliz Gr Sch Gainsborough; Cam Univ; Lon Univ; Hill Farmer; Chmn Somerset NFU
Tel: (01278) 671387

WHITE, Canon Robert Charles, MA, CERT TH
St Francis House, Riders Lane, Leigh Park, Havant, Hants PO9 4QT [PORTSMOUTH] **1995–** *b* 30 Jan 1961; *educ* Portsm Gr Sch; Mansf Coll Ox; St Steph Ho Th Coll; C Forton 1985–88; C St Mark N End Portsea 1988–92; V St Clare Warren Park from 1992; P-in-c Leigh Park 1994–96; V from 1996; Hon Can Portsm Cathl from 1997; M Bp's Coun; M Dioc Bd of Educ; M Community Educ Ctee Tel: (01705) 475276
Fax: (01705) 481228

WHITEMAN, Ven Rodney David Carter
Archdeacon's House, Cardynham, Bodmin, Cornwall PL30 4BL [ARCHDEACON OF BODMIN] **1994–** *b* 6 Oct 1940; *educ* St Austell Gr Sch; Ely Th Coll; C All SS Kingsheath Birm 1964–70; V St Steph Rednal Birm 1970–79; V St Barn Erdington 1979–89; RD Aston 1981–89; Hon Can Birm Cathl 1984–89; P-in-c Cardynham 1989–94; Adn of Bodmin from 1989; Hon Can Truro Cathl from 1989 Tel: (01208) 821614
Fax: (01208) 821602

WHITWORTH, Mrs Ruth
57 North St, Oundle PE8 4AL [ELY] **1990–** *b* 1 Oct 1952; *educ* Ch High Sch Newc; Bank Clerk from 1974 Tel: (01832) 273623

WIGLEY, Canon Max (Harry Maxwell), HNC
St John's Vicarage, Barcroft Grove, Yeadon, W Yorks LS19 7SE [BRADFORD] **1990–** *b* 31 Jul 1938; *educ* K Jas Gr Sch Knaresborough; Leeds Tech Coll; Oak Hill Th Coll; C St Mary Upton, Wirral 1964–67; C Ch Ch Chadderton 1967; C St Steph Gateacre Liv 1967–69; V St Jo Ev Gt Horton Bradf 1969–88; V St Lawr and St Paul Pudsey 1988–96; V St Jo Ev Yeadon from 1996; Hon Can Bradf Cathl from 1985; Chmn Dioc Ho of Clergy; M Bp's Coun; M Dioc Evang Grp
Tel: 0113–250 2272

WILCOX, Canon Hugh Edwin, MA
St Mary's Vicarage, 31 Thunder Court, Milton Rd, Ware, Herts SG12 0PT [ST ALBANS] **1989–** *b* 11 Dec 1937; *educ* Colchester R Gr Sch; St Edm Hall Ox; St Steph Ho Th Coll; C St Jas Colchester 1964–66; Hon C St Paul Clifton and SCM Sec S England 1966–68; Exec Sec Internat Affairs Dept BCC and CBMS 1968–76; Asst Gen Sec BCC 1974–76; V St Mary Ware from 1976; M DBF from 1985; Dioc Convenor Clergy Response to Peacetime Disaster 1989–96; M Bp's Coun from 1991; Bp's Coun Agenda Grp Chmn from 1994; Gen Syn Rep CCBI 1990–96; Ch Commr from 1993, Bd of Govs from 1996: M Redundant Chs Ctee 1993–94, Assets Ctee from 1994; M Assets Ctee Ethical Investments Grp from 1995; M Liturg Publishing in 2000 Grp from 1995; M Ctee CEIG 1994–97; Convenor Affirming Catholicism Grp in Gen Syn 1991–97; Hon Can St Alban's Cathl from 1996; Prolocutor Convocation of Cant from 1996; M Gen Syn Stg Ctee from 1996; M Gen Syn Policy Ctee from 1996; M Abps' Adv Grp from 1997
Tel: (01920) 464817

WILKINSON, Mr David Blair, MA
45 Burton Rd, Repton, Derby DE65 6FN [DERBY] **1995–** *b* 16 Oct 1932; *educ* Repton Sch; Trin Coll Ox; Asst Master Repton Sch 1957–93 (Housemaster 1971–86); Chmn Bd of Visitors HM Prison Sudbury 1975–77; Rtd *Tel:* (01283) 702339

WILLESDEN, Bishop of [AREA BISHOP, LONDON] **Rt Revd (Geoffrey) Graham Dow,** MA, M SC, M PHIL, DPS
173 Willesden Lane, London NW6 7YN b 4 Jul 1942; *educ* St Geo Sch Harpenden; St Alb Sch; Qu Coll Ox; Nottm Univ; Birm Univ; Clifton Th Coll; C St Pet and St Paul Tonbridge 1967–72; Chapl St Jo Coll Ox 1972–75; Lect in Chr Doct St Jo Coll Nottm 1975–81; V H Trin Cov 1981–92; Can Th Cov Cathl 1988–92; Bp of Willesden from 1992 *Tel:* 0181–451 0189
Fax: 0181–451 4606
e-mail: bishop.willesden@dlondon.org.uk

WILLIAMS, Ms Anne
30 Blackhills Terrace, Horden, Peterlee, Co Durham SR8 4LJ [DURHAM] **1990–** *b* 16 Jan 1946; *educ* A J Dawson Gr Sch Wellfield; Purchase Ledger Controller 1989–93; Communications/PR Support for Third World charity 1993–96; Asst Bursar from 1996
Tel: 0191–586 7238 (Home)

WILLIAMS, Revd Colin Henry, BA, MA
Vicarage, 7 Vicarage Rd, Poulton-le-Fylde, Lancs FY6 7BE [BLACKBURN] **1995–** *b* 12 Aug 1952; *educ* K Geo V Gr Sch Southport; Pemb Coll Ox; St Steph Ho Th Coll; Solicitor; C St Paul Stoneycroft Liv 1981–84; TV St Aidan Walton 1984–89; Chapl Walton Hosp 1986–89; Dom Chapl to Bp of Blackb 1989–94; Chapl Whalley Abbey Retreat Ho and Conf Cen 1989–94; V St Chad Poulton-le-Fylde from 1994; M Dioc Syn; M Meissen Commn *Tel:* (01253) 883086

WILLIAMS, Canon David Gordon, MA
St Mark's Rectory, Fairmount Rd, Cheltenham, Glos GL51 7AQ [GLOUCESTER] **1990–** *b* 13 Aug 1943; *educ* Cray Valley Sch Orpington; Selw Coll Cam; Oak Hill Th Coll; C St Luke Maidstone 1968–71; C St Matt Rugby 1971–73; P-in-c Budbroke 1973–74; V 1974–81; V H Trin and The Priory Lenton 1981–87; TR St Mark Cheltenham from 1987; M CBF from 1991; Ch Commr from 1994, Bd of Govs from 1997; M Central Stewardship Ctee from 1994; M CE Pensions Bd from 1996; M Bp's Coun; M DBF
Tel: (01242) 255110

WILLIAMS, Mr David Michael, MA, DIP LIB, FSA, FRSA
Church House, Great Smith St, London SW1P 3NZ [DIRECTOR OF CENTRAL SERVICES, ARCHBISHOPS' COUNCIL] *b* 6 Apr 1950; *educ* Glyn Gr Sch Ewell; Ex Univ; Lon Univ; Employed at CCC 1972–73 and 1974–87; Dep Sec CCC 1982–87; Employed by CBF from 1987; Dep Sec CBF 1991–94; Sec CBF 1994–98; Dir Central Services, Abps' Coun and Clerk to Gen Syn from 1999; JP *Tel:* 0171–898 1559

WILLIAMS, Mr Frank John
31 Manor Park Crescent, Edgware, Middx HA8 7NE [LONDON] **1985–** *b* 2 Jul 1931; *educ* Ardingly Coll; Hendon Co Sch; Actor; Playwright; M Crown Appts Commn 1992–97; Lay Vc-Chmn Edmonton Area Coun *Tel:* 0181–952 4871

WILLIAMS, Mr Paul Lloyd, BA, DIP TH, FRMS
21 Roseway, Rosemary Lane, Burton, Rossett, Chester LL12 0LF [CHESTER] **1995–** *b* 5 Sep 1952; *educ* Ruthin Sch; Wolsey Hall Ox; Univ Coll Lon; Man Univ; Dur Univ; Proofreader/Analyst Derwent Publications Biotechnological Dept 1981–88; Clerk Intrada Shipping Co 1988; Independent Research Student Th from 1993; M Stipends Ctee from 1991; M Dioc Syn from 1991; M DBF from 1991; M Dioc BSR 1991–95; Ches Dyn Syn and Finance Link Co-ordinator from 1990 *Tel:* (01244) 570134

WILLIAMS, Mrs Shirley-Ann, LRAM, LLAM, CERT TH
Miller's Farm, Talaton, Exeter, Devon EX5 2RE [EXETER] **1985–** *b* 15 May 1933; *educ* Barr's Hill Sch Cov; Leeds Univ; Ex Univ; Freelance Tutor in

Speech and Drama, Public Speaking and Communication Skills; Broadcaster; M Gen Syn Stg Ctee and Appts Sub-Ctee; M Dioc Pastl Ctee; M Bp's Coun and Stg Ctee; Chair Dioc Bd of Patronage; M Dioc Children and Young People's Ctee; M Dioc Adult Tr Ctee; Vc-Pres and Chair Dioc Ho of Laity from 1982; M Rural Community Coun of Devon Exec Ctee; Lay Chair Ottery Dny Syn; Chair Nat Working Party Ecum Decade of Chs in Solidarity with Women; M CTE and CCBI; Editor Open Syn Grp magazine; M Dioc Liturg Ctee; M Dioc Communications Ctee; M Devon and Ex Racial Equality Coun
Tel and *Fax:* (01404) 822469

WILLIAMS, Canon Trevor Stanley Morlais, MA
Trinity College, Oxford OX1 3BH [UNIVERSITIES, OXFORD] **1990–** *b* 10 Jul 1938; *educ* Marlborough Coll; Jes Coll Ox; Univ of E Africa; Westcott Ho Th Coll; C St Paul Clifton Bris 1967–70; Asst Chapl Bris Univ 1967–70; Chapl and Fell Trin Coll Ox from 1970
Tel: (01865) 279886 (Office)
(01865) 553975 (Home)
Fax: (01865) 279911
e-mail: trevor.williams@trinity.ox.ac.uk

WILLIS, Very Revd Robert Andrew, BA
The Deanery, The Cloisters, Hereford HR1 2NG [DEAN OF HEREFORD] **1985–92, 1994–** *b* 17 May 1947; *educ* Kingswood Gr Sch; Warw Univ; Worc Coll Ox; Cuddesdon Th Coll; C St Chad Shrewsbury 1972–75; V Choral Sarum Cathl 1975–78; TR Tisbury and RD Chalke 1978–89; V Sherborne 1987–92; RD Sherborne 1991–92; Dean of Heref from 1992; M PWM Ctee from 1990; M Cathls Fabric Commn from 1993; M Liturg Commn from 1994
Tel: (01432) 359880
Fax: (01432) 355929

WILLMOTT, Ven Trevor, MA, DIP THEOL
15 The College, Durham DH1 3EQ [ARCHDEACON OF DURHAM] *b* 29 Mar 1950; *educ* Plymouth Coll; St Pet Coll Ox; Fitzw Coll Cam; Westcott Ho Th Coll; C St Geo Norton 1974–77; Asst Chapl Oslo w Trondheim 1978–79; Chapl Naples w Capri, Bari and Sorrento 1979–83; R Ecton and Warden Peterb Dioc Retreat Ho 1983–89; DDO and Dir of POT 1986–97; Can Res and Prec Peterb Cathl 1989–97; Adn of Dur and Can Res Dur Cathl from 1997
Tel: 0191–384 7534
Fax: 0191–386 6915

WILSON, Ven Mark John Crichton, MA, CERT TH
Littlecroft, Heathside Rd, Woking, Surrey GU22 7EZ [ARCHDEACON OF DORKING] **1992–** *b* 14 Jan 1946; *educ* St Jo Sch Leatherhead; Clare Coll Cam; Ridley Hall Th Coll; C St Mary Luton w E Hyde 1969–72; C Ashtead 1972–77; Chapl Epsom Coll 1977–81; RD Epsom 1987–92; V Ch Ch Epsom Common 1981–96; Adn of Dorking from 1996; M Cathls Commn Follow Up Grp from 1995
Tel: (01483) 772713
Fax: (01483) 757353
e-mail: mark.wilson@cofeguildford.org.uk

WILSON-RUDD, Miss Fay (Felicity)
c/o The Old Deanery, Wells, Som BA5 2UG [BATH AND WELLS] **1993–** *b* 15 Aug 1941; *educ* Filton High Sch; Asst Stewardship Adv St Alb dio 1981–84; Resources Adv B & W from 1984
Tel: (01749) 670777 (Office)
Tel and *Fax:* (01749) 677286 (Home)

WINCHESTER, Bishop of, Rt Revd Michael Charles Scott-Joynt, MA
Wolvesey, Winchester, Hants SO23 9ND **1993–** *b* 15 Mar 1943; *educ* Bradfield Coll; K Coll Cam; Cuddesdon Th Coll; C Cuddesdon 1967–70; Tutor Cuddesdon Th Coll 1967–72; TV Newbury 1972–75; R Bicester 1975–81; Can Res St Alb Cathl, DDO and POT 1982–87; Bp of Stafford 1987–95; Bp of Win from 1995
Tel: (01962) 854050
Tel and *Fax:* (01962) 842376
e-mail: michael.scott-joynt@dial.pipex.com

WINTERBOTTOM, Mr Michael John
15 Harper Place, Ashton-under-Lyne, Lancs OL6 6LR [MANCHESTER] **1995–** *b* 15 Jun 1959; *educ* Ashton-under-Lyne Gr Sch; Dioc Lay Chmn Forward in Faith; M Ctee Soc of Mary; M Ctee Man Branch Prayer Book Soc; Chmn Ashton-under-Lyne Conservative Assoc from 1993; Coun Tameside MBC 1991–95; JP from 1996
Tel: 0161–330 9083 (Home)
0161–253 8381 (Office)
0831 899656 (Mobile)

WOLSTENCROFT, Ven Alan
c/o The Cathedral, Manchester M3 1SX [ARCHDEACON OF MANCHESTER] *b* 16 Jul 1937; *educ* Wellington Tech Sch Altrincham; St Jo CFE Man; Cuddesdon Th Coll; C St Thos Halliwell 1969–71; C All SS Stand 1971–73; V St Martin Wythenshawe 1973–80; Chapl then Asst Chapl Wythenshawe Hosp 1973–91; AD Withington 1978–91; C St Jo the Divine Brooklands, Sale 1980–91; V St Pet Bolton w H Trin Bolton-le-Moors 1991–98; Hon Can Man Cathl 1986–98; Adn of Man and Res Can Man Cathl from 1998; M Dioc Syn; M Bp's Coun; M DBF, Trust and Fin Ctees
Tel: 0161–833 2220 (Cathedral)
Fax: 0161–839 0093 (Dioc Office)

WOLVERHAMPTON, Bishop of [AREA BISHOP, LICHFIELD] **Rt Revd Michael Gay Bourke,** MA
61 Richmond Rd, Wolverhampton WV3 9JH 1975–80, 1987–93 b 28 Nov 1941; *educ* Hamond's Gr Sch

Swaffham; Cam Univ; Tübingen Univ; Cuddesdon Th Coll; C St Jas Grimsby 1967–71; P-in-c Panshanger CD Welwyn Garden City 1971–78; V Southill 1978–86; Course Dir St Alb Minl Tr Scheme 1975–87; Adn of Bedf 1986–93; Bp of Wolverhampton from 1993
Tel: (01902) 824503
Fax: (01902) 824504

WOODHOUSE, Ven (Charles) David Stewart, MA
22 Rob Lane, Newton le Willows, Merseyside WA12 0DR [ARCHDEACON OF WARRINGTON] **1990–** *b* 23 Dec 1934; *educ* Silcoates Sch Wakef; Kelham Th Coll; C St Wilfrid's Halton 1959–63; Yth Chapl Kirkby TM 1963–66; C St Jo Pemb Bermuda 1966–69; Asst Gen Sec CEMS 1969–70; Gen Sec 1970–76; R Ideford, Luton and Ashcombe 1976–81; Dom Chapl to Bp of Ex 1976–81; V St Pet's Hindley 1981–92; Adn of Warrington from 1981; Hon Can Liv Cathl from 1983; M CBF from 1991; M Cen Ch Fund Ctee from 1992; ABM Selector from 1993; Chair Dioc Bd of Min; Gen Syn Stg Ctee Rep Chs Commn on Overseas Miss
Tel: (01925) 229247
Fax: (01925) 220423

WOOLWICH, Bishop of [AREA BISHOP, SOUTHWARK] **Rt Revd Colin Ogilvie Buchanan**, MA, DD
37 South Rd, Forest Hill, London SE23 2UJ **1970–85, 1990–** *b* 9 Aug 1934; *educ* Whitgift Sch Croydon; Linc Coll Ox; Tyndale Hall Bristol; Tutor St Jo Coll Nottm 1964–85; Prin 1979–85; Bp of Aston 1985–89; Hon Asst Bp Roch dio 1989–96; V St Mark Gillingham 1991–96; Bp of Woolwich from 1996; M CCU; M CCBI Assembly; M CMEAC
Tel: 0181–699 7771
Fax: 0181–699 7949
e-mail: bishop.colin@dswark.org.uk

WORCESTER, Bishop of, Rt Revd Peter Stephen Maurice Selby, MA, BD, PH D
Bishop's House, Hartlebury Castle, Kidderminster, Worcs DY11 7XX **1997–** *b* 7 Dec 1941; *educ* Merchant Taylors Sch; St Jo Coll Ox; Episc Div Sch Cam, Mass; Bishops' Coll Cheshunt; K Coll Lon; Asst C Queensbury 1966–69; Assoc Dir of Tr S'wark 1969–73; Asst C Limpsfield w Titsey 1969–77; Vc-Prin S'wark Ord Course 1970–72; Asst Missr S'wark 1973–77; Can Missr Newc Dio 1977–84; Bp of Kingston-upon-Thames 1984–92; William Leech Professorial Fellow in Applied Chr Th Dur Univ 1992–97; Hon Asst Bp Dur and Newc dios 1992–97; Bp of Worc from 1997; M Doct Commn from 1991; Pres Modern Churchpeople's Union 1990–96; Vis Gen CSC from 1991
Tel: (01299) 250214
Fax: (01299) 250027
e-mail: p.selby@mcmail.com

WRIGHT, Mr David John Vernon, MA
11 Davenant Rd, Oxford OX2 8BT [OXFORD] **1985–** *b* 21 Mar 1932; *educ* Cheltenham Coll; St Edm Hall Ox; Solicitor from 1958; M CE Pensions Bd from 1994; M Bp's Coun; Rdr
Tel: (01865) 556034

WRIGHT, Very Revd (Nicholas) Thomas, BA, MA, D PHIL
The Deanery, The Close, Lichfield, Staffs WS13 7LD [DEAN OF LICHFIELD] *b* 1 Dec 1948; *educ* Sedbergh Sch; Ex Coll Ox; Wycliffe Hall Th Coll; Fell Mert Coll Ox 1975–78; Asst Chapl 1976–78; Chapl and Fell Down Coll Cam 1978–81; Asst Prof NT Studies McGill Univ Montreal 1981–86; Chapl and Fell Worc Coll Ox and Univ Lect Th 1986–93; Dean of Lich from 1994
Tel: (01543) 306250
Fax: (01543) 306255
e-mail: tom.wright1@virgin.net

YATES, Canon Timothy Edward, MA, D TH
Vicarage, Great Longstone, Bakewell, Derbys DE45 1TB [DERBY] **1995–** *b* 1 May 1935; *educ* Eton; Magd Coll Cam; Ridley Hall Th Coll; C SS Pet and Paul Tonbridge 1960–63; Tutor St Jo Coll Dur and Cranmer Hall 1963–70; Warden Cranmer Hall 1970–79; R St Helen Darley 1979–90; DDO 1985–95; Hon Can Derby Cathl from 1988; Hon C Ashford w Sheldon and Longstone from 1990; M Dioc Syn
Tel: (01629) 640257

YORK, Archbishop of, Most Revd and Rt Hon David Michael Hope, KCVO, BA, D PHIL, LLD (HON)
Bishopthorpe Palace, Bishopthorpe, York YO23 2GE **1985–** *b* 14 Apr 1940; *educ* Qu Eliz Gr Sch Wakef; Nottm Univ; St Steph Ho Th Coll; C St Jo Tue Brook Liv 1965–70; Chapl Ch of the Resurr Nottm 1967–68; V St Andr Orford 1970–74; Prin St Steph Ho Ox 1974–82; V All SS Marg St Lon 1982–85; Master Guardians Shrine of Our Lady Walsingham 1982–93; Bp of Wakef 1985–91; Bp of Lon 1991–95; Dean of HM Chapels R and Prelate of OBE 1991–95; Abp of York from 1995
Tel: (01904) 707021/2
Fax: (01904) 709204
e-mail: office@bishopthorpe.u-net.com

YORKE, Very Revd Michael Leslie, MA
Provost's House, 13 Pembroke Rd, Old Portsmouth, Hants PO1 2NS [PROVOST OF PORTSMOUTH] *b* 25 Mar 1939; *educ* Brighton Coll; Magd Coll Cam; Cuddesdon Th Coll; C Croydon 1964–67; Prec Chelmsf Cathl 1968–74; R Ashdon w Hadstock 1974–78; Can Res Chelmsf Cathl 1978–88; Vc Provost 1984–88; P-in-c St Marg Kings Lynn 1988–94; Hon Can Nor Cathl 1993–94; Provost of Portsm from 1994; Bp's

Liaison Officer for Prisons; Chmn Deans and Provosts Music Working Party
Tel and Fax: (01705) 824400 (Home)
(01705) 347605 (Office)
Fax: (01705) 295480 (Office)

YOUNG, Ven Clive, BA
St Andrew's Vicarage, 5 St Andrew St, London EC4A 3AB [ARCHDEACON OF HACKNEY] *b* 31 May 1948; *educ* K Edw VI Gr Sch Chelmsf; Dur Univ; Ridley Hall Cam; C Neasden cum Kingsbury 1972–75; C St Paul Hammersmith 1975–79; P-in-c St Paul w St Steph Old Ford 1979–82; V 1982–92; AD Tower Hamlets 1988–92; Adn of Hackney from 1992; V St Andr Holborn from 1992
Tel: 0171–353 3544
Fax: 0171–583 2750
e-mail: archdeacon.hackney@dlondon.org.uk

YOUNG, Canon John David, BD, MA, DIP ED
73 Middlethorpe Grove, York YO2 2JX [YORK] **1992–** *b* 20 Feb 1937; *educ* Spring Grove Gr Sch Isleworth; Loughb Univ; Lon Univ; Sussex Univ; Clifton Th Coll; C St Jude Plymouth 1965–68; Hd of RE Northgate Gr Sch Ipswich 1968–71; Chapl and Sen Lect Bp Otter Coll Chich 1971–81; Chapl and Sen Lect Univ Coll of Ripon & York St John 1981–87; Dioc Ev from 1988
Tel: (01904) 658820 (Office)
Tel and Fax: (01904) 704195 (Home)
Fax: (01904) 671694 (Office)

YOUNG, Revd Jonathan Priestland, AKC, CERT ED
Ascension Rectory, Richmond Rd, Cambridge CB4 3PS [ELY] **1982–** *b* 12 Feb 1944; *educ* Nor Sch; K Coll Lon; St Boniface Th Coll; Whitelands Coll Lon; C Clapham 1969–73; C St Mark Mitcham 1973–74; V Godmanchester 1974–82; Chapl St Jo Coll Sch 1987–93; R Ascen Cam, TM (St Giles w St Pet, St Luke w St Aug, All Souls) from 1982; M Liturg Canons Revision Ctee, Service of the Word and Affirmations of Faith Revision Ctee; M Elections Review Grp; M Legislative Ctee; M Bp's Coun; DAC; Dioc Pastl Ctee; Dioc Bd of Educ; Dioc Bd of Patronage; Dioc Coun for Miss and Unity; Dioc Red Chs Uses Ctee; Hon Sec Dioc Liturg Ctee; M Ctee Open Syn Grp; M Bach Choir; Vc Pres Huntingdonshire Philharmonic; Chair E Anglian Praxis Ctee
Tel: (01223) 361919
Fax: (01223) 322710

LATE INFORMATION

Page

43 The following have been elected by General Synod to serve as *Church Commissioners* from January 1999: The Bishops of Bradford, Chester, London and Worcester; The Deans of Ripon and St Paul's; Canon Robert Baker; the Revd Clive Mansell and the Revd Stephen Trott; Mr Peter Bruinvels, Mr Alan Cooper, Mr Gavin Oldham and Mr David Webster.

51 From 8 May 1999, the address of Canon Michael Hodge, *Synodical Secretary of the Convocation of Canterbury*, will be Braxton Cottage, Halletts Shute, Norton, Yarmouth, Isle of Wight PO41 0RH. *Tel* and *Fax:* (01983) 761121. The e-mail address remains the same.

69 The fax number for the *Cathedral Office* has been changed to (01227) 865222.

99 The next *Bishop of Leicester* is to be the Rt Revd Timothy Stevens, currently Bishop of Dunwich. He will take up this post in the summer.

111 The next *Bishop of Hulme* is to be the Ven Stephen Lowe, currently Archdeacon of Sheffield. He will take up this post in April.

115 The Ven Anthony Foottit, *Archdeacon of Lynn*, is to be the next Bishop of Lynn with effect from January 1999.

126 The new Rural Dean of *Wensley* is the Revd Clive Mansell, Rectory, Kirklington, Bedale, N Yorks DL8 2NJ *Tel:* (018450) 567429.

131 The Rt Revd Timothy Stevens, *Bishop of Dunwich*, is to be the next Bishop of Leicester.

133 The next *Bishop of Ramsbury* is to be Canon Peter Hullah, Headmaster of Chetham's School of Music, Manchester. He will take up this post in August.

135 The *Archdeacon of Sheffield*, the Ven Stephen Lowe, is to be the next Bishop of Hulme with effect from April.

153 Canon Glynn Webster, Rural Dean of *York*, is to be a Canon Residentiary of York Minster.

148 The Ven Alan Clarkson, *Archdeacon of Winchester*, retires at the end of February 1999. His retirement address from 1 March will be: 'Cantilena', 4 Harefield Rise, Linton, Cambridge CB1 6LS. *Tel* and *Fax:* (01223) 892988.

INDEX

GENERAL INDEX

Names of dioceses are in *italic*.

Aba 298
Abakaliki 298
Aberdeen and Orkney 303
Abuja 299
Accra 322
Acorn Christian Healing Trust 215
Action for Biblical Witness to Our Nation 215
Action of Christians Against Torture 373
Action of Churches Together in Scotland 375–6
Actors' Church Union 215
Additional Curates Society 215
Addressing the clergy 157
Adelaide 280
Administry 215
Adult Theological Education Centres 373
Advertising Network 229
Advisory Board for Redundant Churches 48
Advisory Council for Local Broadcasting 177
Advisory Council on Relations of Bishops and Religious Communities 199
Affirming Catholicism 215
Africa Inland Mission International 216
African and Afro/Caribbean Churches Council 377
African Provinces
    Burundi 282, 348
    Central Africa 285, 346
    Conference of the Anglican Provinces of Africa 325
    Congo 287, 348
    Council of African and Afro/Caribbean Churches 377
    Kenya 294, 347
    Nigeria 298, 349
    Rwanda 302, 348
    Southern Africa 254, 305, 346
    Sudan 308 348
    Tanzania 309, 347
    Uganda 310, 348
    West Africa 321, 350
Afro-West Indian United Council of Churches 373
Age Concern, England 216
Agra 327
Aipo Rongo 301
Akoko 299
Akure 299
Alabama 312
Alaska 312
Albany 312
Alcuin Club 216
Algoma 284
All Africa Conference of Churches 384

All Nations Christian College 216
All Saints Educational Trust 219
All Saints Sisters of the Poor Society 207
All Souls Guild 237, 265
Almshouses Association 216
Alternative Services 175
America
    Central Region Anglican Church 287, 344
    CLAI (Latin American Council of Churches) 384
    Convocation of American Churches in Europe 314
    Episcopal Church in the USA (ECUSA) 312–18, 342–4
    South American Mission Society 254
    Southern Cone Anglican Church 307, 344
Amritsar 327
Ancient Society of College Youths 216
Andamans and Nicobar Islands 327
Anglican Association 217
Anglican Centre in Rome 276
Anglican Committee 18
Anglican Communion 271–6
    Anglican Centre in Rome 276
    churches and provinces 277–323
    Consultative Council 275–6
    extra-provincial dioceses 323–5
    Lambeth Conference 272–4
    maps of churches and provinces 337–52
    Office 274
    Primates' Meetings 274
    regional councils 325
    United Churches in Full Communion 326–31
Anglican and Eastern Churches Association 217
Anglican Evangelical Assembly 217
Anglican Fellowship in Scouting and Guiding 217
Anglican Group Educational Trust 217
Anglican Marriage Encounter 217
Anglican Pacifist Fellowship 217
Anglican Religious Communities 199
Anglican Renewal Ministries 217
Anglican Society for the Welfare of Animals 218
Anglican Stewardship Association 218
Anglican Voluntary Societies Forum 218
Anglican-Lutheran Society 218
Anglo-Catholic Ordination Candidates' Fund 246
Animal Christian Concern 218
Animal welfare organisations 211
Antananarivo 289
Antsiranana 289
Aotearoa 277
Aotearoa Bishopric 277, 341

Aotearoa, New Zealand and Polynesia Province   277, 341
Appeal Panel   52–3
Appointments Committee of the Church of England   6
Archbishop of Canterbury *see* Canterbury, Archbishop of
Archbishop of York *see* York, Archbishop of
Archbishops' (Canterbury and Westminster) Certificate in Church Music   218
Archbishop's Council   15–42
    Central Services   36–8
    Church and World   16–25
    Communications   38–9
    Finance   27–32
    Heritage   25–7
    Human Resources   39–42
    Legal Advice and Support Staff   39
    Ministry   32–6
    Structure   17
Archbishops' Examination in Theology   218
Architectural organisations   211
Archway   218
Arctic Fellowship   260
Argentina   307
Argyll and The Isles   303
Arizona   312
Arkansas   313
Armagh   290, 338, 339
Armidale   279
Army Chaplains   160
Art and Architectural organisations   211
Art and Christianity Enquiry   218
Arthur Rank Centre   219
Aruba   323
Asaba   299
Ashburnham Place   167
Assistance of Ladies in Reduced Circumstances Society   252
Associations
    of Black Clergy   219
    of Centres of Adult Theological Education   373
    of Christian Teachers   219
    of Christian Writers   219
    of Church College Trusts   219
    of Church Fellowships   221
    of the Dioceses of Singapore and West Malaysia   260
    of English Cathedrals   221
    of Hospice Chaplains   221
    of Interchurch Families   373
    of Ordinands and Candidates for Ministry   221
    for Promoting Retreats   219
Aston, Bishop of   61
Athabasca   285
Atlanta   313
Auckland   277
Australia, Anglican Church of   278–81, 340
Authorized Alternative Services   175
Authorized and Commended Services   173–6
Awka   299

Bahamas   323
Ballarat   280
Baltic Lutheran Churches   359–60
Bangladesh, Church of   326, 351
Bangor   319
Banks and Torres   297
Baptisms   188, 190
Baptist Missionary Society   374
Baptist Union of Great Britain   377
Barbados   323
Barking, Bishop of   73
Barnardo's   221
Barrackpore   327
Basingstoke, Bishop of   148
Bath and Wells   59
    Bishop of   59
    Partis College   247
Bathurst   279
Bauchi   299
BBC Local Radio   176
BBC Religious Broadcasting Dept   176
Beauchamp Community   239
Becker's (Mrs) Charity for Clergy   221
Bedford, Bishop of   129
Belize   323
    Church Association   260
Bell-Ringers, Central Council of Church   224
Bellringing organisations   211
Bendigo   280
Benedictine Communities
    Elmore Abbey   200
    Priory of Our Lady, Burford   207
    St Mary at the Cross   202
    St Mary's Abbey   202
Benin   299
Bermuda, Anglican Church of   323
Bethlehem   313
Beverley, Bishop of   152
Bhopal   327
Bible Reading Fellowship   221
Bible Society   222
Bible Study organisations   211
Birkenhead, Bishop of   76
Birmingham   61
    Bishop of   61
    Queen's College   179
Bishop Grosseteste College, Lincoln   165
Bishops
    in the House of Lords   159
    Regulations for Training   34–5
    to Prisons   164
    see also under individual dioceses
Bishops, House of   5
Bishopthorpe Palace   58
Bjørgvin   357
Black Clergy Association   219

Blackburn 63
    Bishop of 63
Blind people's organisations 211, 222
Bloemfontein 305
Bo 322
Board of Education 18–20
Board of Mission 21–2
Board for Social Responsibility 23–4
Boga 288
Bolivia 307
Bolton, Bishop of 111
Bombay 327
Bor 308
Borg 357
Borneo Mission Association 260
Botswana 286–7
Boys' Brigade 222, 375
Bradford 65
    Bishop of 65
Bradwell, Bishop of 73
Brandon 285
Brasilia 282
Bray Libraries 222
Brazil, Episcopal Anglican Church 281, 344
Brechin 304
Bridgebuilders 235
Brisbane 280
Bristol 67
    Bishop of 67
    Clerical Education Society 246
British Columbia 283, 345
British Deaf Association 222
Brixworth, Bishop of 121
Broadcasting 176
Broken Rites 222
Bromley and Sheppard's Colleges 223
Buckingham, Bishop of 118
Budget of the Archbishops' Council 28–9
Buildings organisations 211
Bujumbura 282
Bukavu 288
Bukedi 310
Bunbury 281
Bungoma 295
Bunyoro-Kitara 310
Burial fees 190, 191
Burma, Church of Burma Association 260
Burnley, Bishop of 63
Burrswood 223
Burundi, Church of the Province of 282, 348
Bush Brotherhoods 223
Business Committee of the General Synod 5
Busoga 311
Butare 302
Butere 295
Buye 282

Byumba 302

CAFOD (Catholic Fund for Overseas Development) 367, 374
Calabar 299
Calcutta 327
Caledonia 283
Calgary 285
California 313
Came's Charity for Clergymen's Widows 223
Campaigners 223
Canada, Anglican Church of 283, 284, 345
Canberra and Goulburn 279
Canterbury 57, 69–70
    Cathedral Library 262
    Christ Church College 165
    Dioceses 57
    electoral rolls 192
    Province of 57, 338, 339
    Provincial lay officers 57
    Vicar-General 57
Canterbury, Archbishop of 69
    chronology 158
    Faculty Office 170
    Personal Staff 58
Canterbury, Convocation of 51
Canterbury and York Society 223
CAPA (Conference of the Anglican Provinces of Africa) 325
Cape Coast 322
Cape Town 305
Care of Churches Council 25–6
CARE Trust 223
Careforce 223
Caribbean Conference of Churches 384
Cariboo 283
Carlisle 71
    Bishop of 71
Carlisle and Blackburn Diocesan Training Institute 179
Cashel, Waterford, Lismore, Ossory, Ferns and Leighlin 291
Catechumenate Network 223
Cathedral Camps 224
Cathedral and Church Shops Association 224
Cathedral and Clerical Libraries 262
Cathedral Statutes Commission 39
Cathedrals Administration and Finance Association 224
Cathedrals Fabric Commission for England 27
Catholic Fund for Overseas Development (CAFOD) 367, 374
Catholic Group in General Synod 224
Catholic Institute for International Relations 374
Catholic League 224
CBF Church of England Funds 31–2
CCBI (Council of Churches for Britain and Ireland) 371
CCLA Investment Management Limited 31
Central Africa, Church of the Province of 285, 346
Central Buganda 311
Central Church Fund 31–2
Central Council of Church Bell-Ringers 224

Index   **485**

Central Ecuador   313
Central Florida   313
Central Gulfcoast   313
Central Melanesia   297
Central New York   313
Central Newfoundland   284
Central Pennsylvania   313
Central Philippines   302
Central Readers' Council   35–6
Central Region of America, Anglican Church of   287, 344
Central Religious Advisory Council (broadcasting)   176
Central Solomons   297
Central Tanganyika   309
    Diocesan Association   260
Central Zambia   287
Central Zimbabwe   287
Centre for Black and White Christian Partnership   373, 374
Centre for International Briefing   225
Ceylon
    Church of Ceylon   326, 351
    Church of Ceylon Association   260
Chancery Court of York   52
Chandigarh   327
Chapel of the Royal Victorian Order   196
Chapel of the Savoy   196–7
Chapels Royal   195
Chaplains
    College of Chaplains   195–6
    Committee for Hospital Chaplaincy   25, 366
    Domestic Chaplains to The Queen   195
    Health Care Chaplains   230
    in Higher Education   161–4
    in Hospices   221
    Hospital Chaplains   24–5, 366
    to HM Services   160
    to Prison Service   164
    to The Queen   195, 196
Charitable giving statistics   186
Charterhouse (Sutton's Hospital)   225
Chelmsford   73
    Bishop of   73
Cheltenham and Gloucester College   165
Cherubim and Seraphim Council of Churches (UK)   377
Chester   76
    Bishop of   76
Chicago   313
Chichester   78
    Bishop of   78
Children's Hospice Movement   171
Children's Society   225
Childrens Work   20
Chile   307
China, Holy Catholic Church   332–4, 352
Choir Benevolent Fund   225
Choir Schools Association   225
Chota Nagpur   327

Christ Church College, Canterbury   165
Christ the King   306
Christchurch   277
Christian Adult Learning Meeting   366
Christian Aid   164, 374
Christian Approaches to Defence and Disarmament Council   231
Christian Arts   225
Christian Communities and Networks Association   373
Christian Conference of Asia   384
Christian Council on Ageing   373
Christian Education Movement   225, 373, 374
Christian Enquiry Agency   367
Christian Ethical Investment Group   225
Christian Evidence Society   226
Christian Medical Fellowship   226
Christian Research   226
Christian Socialist Movement   226
Christian Stewardship   30
Christian Teachers Association   219
Christian Unity Council   16–18
Christian Witness to Israel   226
Christian Writers Association   219
Christianity and the Future of Europe   226, 373
Christians Abroad   226, 374
Christians Aware   374
Christians for Europe   227
Christians and Jews Council   231
Christians at Work   226
Chuang Hua Sheng Kung Hui   332–4, 352
Chubu   293
Church Action on Poverty   373
Church Action with the Unemployed   227
Church Army   165
    evangelists   183
    Wilson Carlile College of Evangelism   165
Church Braillists Guild   238
Church Buildings organisations   211
Church College Trusts Association   219
Church Colleges of Higher Education   165
Church Commissioners for England   43–5
Church and Community Trust   227
Church Computer Users Group   227
Church electoral rolls   192
Church of England   377
    Children's Society   225
    Clergy Stipend Trust   228
    Evangelical Council   228
    Newspaper   172
    Record Society   228
    Schools   172
    Soldiers', Sailors' and Airmen's Clubs   228
        Housing Association Ltd (1972)   228
Church Extension Association (Sisters of the Church)   206
Church Fellowships Association   221
Church House Bookshop   37

Church House Deaneries' Group   227
Church House Publishing   37
Church Housing Trust   227
Church of Ireland *see* Ireland
Church Lads' and Church Girls' Brigade   227
Church Mission Society   227
Church Music Society   228
Church Musicians Guild   218
Church Newspapers   172
Church Pastoral Aid Society   228
    Ministers in Training Fund   246
    Patronage Trust   264
Church Schoolmasters' and Schoolmistresses' Benevolent Institution   229
Church Schools   172
Church Schools Company   229
Church of Scotland *see* Scotland
Church Services   173–6
Church societies   211
Church Society   229
Church Society Trust   265
Church Times   172
Church Trust Fund Trust   265
Church Union   229
Church Urban Fund   166
Church Welfare Association   229
Churches Advertising Network   229
Churches Advisory Council for Local Broadcasting   177
Churches for Britain and Ireland (CCBI) Council   371–3
Churches Commission on Mission   374–5
Churches Commission on Overseas Students   229, 374
Churches Commission for Racial Justice   375
Churches Committee for Hospital Chaplaincy   25, 366
Churches Community Work Alliance   367
Churches Conservation Trust   48
Churches Council for Health and Healing   230, 373
Churches East West European Relations Network   373
Churches Fellowship for Psychical and Spiritual Studies   230
Churches Group on Funeral Services at Cemeteries and Crematoria   230
Churches Joint Education Policy Committee   366
Churches Main Committee   229
Churches Millennium Group   367
Churches Rural Group   367
Churches Together in England   366–7
Churches Together for Families   367
Churches Together in Scotland   375
Churches Together in Wales   376
Church's Ministry Among Jewish People   229
CLAI (Latin American Council of Churches)   384
Cleaver Ordination Candidates Fund   246
Clergy
    addressing   157
    Appointments Adviser   166
    Associations   211
    Becker's (Mrs) Charity   221
    Black Clergy Association   219
    Came's Charity for Clergymen's Widows   223
    Clergy Stipend Fund   228
    Corporation of the Sons of the Clergy   231
    distribution statistics   182
    English Clergy Association   235
    Friends of the Clergy Corporation   236
    Holidays Society   230
    Homes for Retired Clergy   239
    Lesbian and Gay Clergy Consultation   242
    MSF Clergy and Church Workers   245
    Queen Victoria Clergy Fund   248
    Retired Clergy Association   249
    St Luke's Hospital for the Clergy   255
    Society for Relief of Poor Clergymen   253
Clergy, House of   5
Clerical Libraries   262
Clerk of the Closet   196
Clinical Theology Association   230
Clogher   290
Co-ordinating Bodies   211
Coimbatore   330
Colchester, Bishop of   73
College of Chaplains   230
College of Preachers   230
College of the Resurrection, Mirfield   179
College of St Barnabas, Lingfield   239
College of St Mark and St John   166
Colleges of Higher Education, Church   165
Collegiate Church of St Peter   193
Colombia   313
Colombo   327
Colorado   313
Commended and Authorized Services   173–6
Commission on Mission   374–5
Commission on Overseas Students   229, 374
Commission for Racial Justice   375
Committee for Hospital Chaplaincy   25, 366
Committee for Ministry Among Deaf People   33–4
Committee for Minority Ethnic Anglican Concerns   36
Committee on Roman Catholic Relations   18
Commonwealth War Graves Commission   231
Communities Consultative Council   200
Community Housing and Therapy   231
Community of
    All Hallows   202
    Companions of Jesus the Good Shepherd   204
    Epiphany   204
    Glorious Ascension (Men)   200
    Glorious Ascension (Women)   204
    Holy Cross   204
    Holy Family   204
    Holy Name   205
    Our Lady and St John   200
    Presentation   205
    Reparation to Jesus in the Blessed Sacrament   202

Resurrection, Mirfield   200
Sacred Passion   205
St Andrew   202
St Clare   202
St Denys   203
St Francis   203
St John Baptist   203
St John the Divine   203
St Laurence   203
St Mary the Virgin   203
St Peter   204
St Peter (Horbury)   204
Servants of the Cross   205
Servants of the Will of God   200
Sisters of the Love of God   205
Community and Urban Affairs Committee   23–4
Community Work Alliance   367
Company of Mission Priests   231
Compassionate Friends   231
Conference of the Anglican Provinces of Africa (CAPA)   325
Conference Centres   167
Conference of European Churches   378–9
Confirmations   189
Confraternity of the Blessed Sacrament   231
Congo Church Association   260
Congo, Church of the Province of the   287, 348
Congregational Federation   377
Connecticut   313
Connor   290
Conservation Trust   48
Consultancy   211
Convocation (Members of House of Clergy)   59–153
Cork, Cloyne and Ross   292
Corporation of the Church House   48–9
Corporation of the Sons of the Clergy   231
Corporation of SS Mary and Nicolas (Woodard Schools)   231
Costa Rica   287
Council of African and Afro/Caribbean Churches   377
Council for the Care of Churches   26
Council on Christian Approaches to Defence and Disarmament   231
Council for Christian Unity   16–18
Council of Christians and Jews   231
Council of Churches for Britain and Ireland (CCBI)   371–3
Council for Health and Healing   230, 373
Council of the Oriental Orthodox Christian Churches   377
Counselling organisations   211
Court of Arches   52
Court of Ecclesiastical Causes Reserved   52
Court of Faculties   52
Court of the Vicar-General of the Province of Canterbury   52
Court of the Vicar-General of the Province of York   52
Covenanted giving statistics   185
Coventry   81
Bishop of   81
Cranmer Hall, Durham   179

Crediton, Bishop of   91
Crosse's Charity   232
Crosslinks   232
Crown Appointments Commission   40
Crowther Hall CMS Training College   232
Croydon, Bishop of   139
Crusaders   232
CTVC   177
Cuba, Episcopal Church of   323, 344
Cueibet   308
Cuernavaca   297
Culham College Institute   232
Culham Educational Foundation   220
Cuttack   328
Cyangugu   302
Cyprus and the Gulf   294
CYTUN: Churches Together in Wales   376

Dallas   313
Damaturu   299
Dar-es-Salaam   309
Deaf people
British Deaf Association   222
Committee for Ministry Among Deaf People   33–4
National Deaf Church Conference   245
organisations for   211
Royal Association in Aid of   232
Royal National Institute for   233
Deans of Peculiars   198
Deans' and Provosts' Conference   233
Deans' and Provosts' Vergers Conference   233
Decade of Evangelism   170
Defence and Disarmament organisations   211
Delaware   313
Delhi   328
Denmark, Church of   361
Deployment, Remuneration and Conditions of Service Committee   33
Derby   83
Bishop of   83
Derry and Raphoe   291
DGAA – Homeless   233
Dhaka   326
Diaconal Association of the Church of England   233
Diakonia   233
Diocesan Associations   260
Diocesan Communications Officers Panel   39
Diocesan Conference Centres   167
Diocesan Finance Forum   28
Diocesan Institutions of Chester, Manchester, Liverpool and Blackburn   233
Diocesan Retreat Houses   167
Dioceses Commission   40–41
Dioceses in the Provinces of Canterbury and York   57
Direct giving statistics   185
Disarmament and Defence organisations   211

Distinctive Diaconate   233
Distribution of clergy   182
Doctrine Commission   41
Dogura   301
Domestic Chaplains to The Queen   195
Dominican Republic   313
Doncaster, Bishop of   135
Dorchester, Bishop of   118
Dorking, Bishop of   95
Dornakal   330
Dover, Bishop of   69
Down and Dromore   291
Drama organisations   212
Dublin and Glendalough   292, 338, 339
Dudley, Bishop of   150
Dunedin   277
Dunwich, Bishop of   131
Durgapur   328
Durham   85
    Bishop of   85
    Dean and Chapter Library   262
    North East Ordination Course   179
    St John's College and Cranmer Hall   179
Dutse   299

East Anglian Ministerial Training Course   179
East Ankole   311
East Carolina   313
East Kerala   330
East Midlands Ministry Training Course   179
East Tennessee   313
East West European Relations Network   373
Eastern Himalayas   328
Eastern Kowloon   352
Eastern Michigan   313
Eastern Newfoundland and Labrador   284
Eastern Oregon   314
Eastern Zambia   287
Eastern Zimbabwe   287
Easton   314
Eau Claire   314
Ebbsfleet, Bishop of   69
Ecclesiastical Courts   52–3
Ecclesiastical Insurance Group   234
Ecclesiastical Law Society   234
Ecclesiological Society   234
Ecumenical affairs   18
Ecumenical Canons   365
Ecumenical Councils   367–71
    for Corporate Responsibility   234, 373
Ecumenical Society of the Blessed Virgin Mary   234
Ecumenism   212
Edinburgh   304
    Theological College   179
Edmonton   285
    Bishop of   108

Education
    Adult Theological Education Centres   373
    Board of Education   18–20
    Chaplains in Higher Education   161–4
    Church Colleges of Higher Education   165
    Churches Commission on Overseas Students   229, 374
    Hockerill Educational Foundation   220
    Joint Education Policy Committee   366
    National Society for Promoting Religious Education   49–50
    organisations   212
    Regional Courses   179–80
    Theological Education and Training Committee   33
    Universities and Colleges Christian Fellowship   257
    University Representatives in Convocation   161, 165
    see also Schools; Training
Edward King Institute for Ministry Development   234
Egba   299
Egbu   299
Egypt   294
    Diocesan Association   260
Ekiti   299
El Camino Real   314
El Obeid   308
El Salvador   287
Eldoret   295
Electoral rolls   192
Elland Society Ordination Fund   246
Ely   87
    Bishop of   87
Embu   295
English Cathedrals Association*   221
English Churches Housing Group   234
English Churches Youth Service   367
English Churchman   172
English Clergy Association   235
Enquiry Centre   38
Enugu   299
Episcopal Church in the USA (ECUSA)   312–18, 342–4
Estonian Evangelical-Lutheran Church   359
Ethiopia, Order of   306
Europe   89
    Bishop in   89
    Convocation of American Churches in   314
    Suffragan Bishop in   89
European Christian Industrial Movement (Bridgebuilders)   235
Evangelical Alliance   235
Evangelical Christians for Racial Justice   235
Evangelical Church in Germany   365
Evangelical-Lutheran Churches
    of Finland   355
    of Iceland   355
    of Latvia   361
    of Lithuania   359
Evangelism, Decade of   170

Ewell Monastery   201
Exeter   91
   Bishop of   91
Expenditure statistics   186
Ezzo   308

Faculty Office and Special Marriage Licences   170
Faisalabad   329
Faith and Order Advisory Group   18
Falkland Islands   324
Family Life and Marriage Education Network   235
Family organisations   212
Family Welfare Association (FWA)   236
Federation of Catholic Priests   235
Feed the Minds   235, 373, 375
Fees   190–91
Fellowship of the Maple Leaf   260
Fellowship of Prayer for Unity   373
Fellowship for Psychical and Spiritual Studies   230
Fellowship of St Alban and St Sergius   235, 373
Fellowship of St Nicholas   236
Fidelity Trust Ltd   236
Finance Committee   30–31
Financial organisations   212
Financial statistics   185–6
Finland, Evangelical-Lutheran Church of   355
Florida   314
Fond du Lac   314
Forces Synodical Council   160
Foreign Missions Club   236
Formosa (Taiwan)   317
Fort Worth   314
Forward in Faith   236
Foundation for Christian Communication Ltd   177
Foundation of St Matthias   220
Franciscan Servants of Jesus and Mary   205
Fredericton   284
Free Churches Council   377
Freetown   322
Friends of the Church of India   260
Friends of the Clergy Corporation   236
Friends of the Diocese of Cyprus and the Gulf   260
Friends of the Diocese of Iran   260
Friends of the Diocese of Uruguay   260
Friends of the Elderly   236
Friends of Friendless Churches   236
Frontier Youth Trust   236
Fulham, Bishop of   108
Funeral fees   190, 191
FWA (Family Welfare Association)   236

Gahini   302
Gambia   322
General Synod of the Church of England   3–14
   budget   29
   committees   5–6
   composition   3
   constitution   8–10
   dates of sessions   3
   General Synod Business   10–14
   House of Bishops   5
   House of Clergy   5
   House of Laity   5
   legislation passed (1993–98)   7
   members   59–153
   non-diocesan members   4–5
   office   3
   officers   3–4
   secretariat   6–7
General Synod Fund   28
George   306
Georgia   314
Germany, Evangelical Church in   365
GFS Platform for Young Women   236
Gibraltar, Bishop of   89
Gippsland   280
Girls' Brigade   237
Gitega   282
Glasgow and Galloway   304
Gloucester   93
   Bishop of   93
GLU (Group for Local Unity)   366
Göteborg   358
Grafton   279
Grahamstown   306
Grant-Making Bodies   212
Grantham, Bishop of   104
Grassroots   375
Greater Churches Group   237
Greek Orthodox Church   377
Greenbelt Festivals   237
Gregorian Association   237
Grimsby, Bishop of   104
Group for Evangelisation   366
Group on Funeral Services at Cemeteries and Crematoria   230
Group for Local Unity (GLU)   366
Grubb Institute   237
Guatemala   287
Guides Association   237
Guild of All Souls   237
   Patronage Trust   265
Guild of Church Braillists   238
Guild of Church Musicians   218
Guild of Health   238
Guild of Pastoral Psychology   238
Guild of St Barnabas   238
Guild of St Helena   238
Guild of St Leonard   238
Guild of St Raphael   238
Guild of Servants of the Sanctuary   238
Guild of Vergers, Church of England   257
Guildford   95

Bishop of 95
Diocese Productions 238
Guinea 322
Gujarat 328
Guyana 260, 323

Haiti 314
Hamar 357
Hampton Court Palace 195
Hanuato'o 297
Harare 287
Harnhill Centre of Christian Healing 239
Härnösand 358
Harold Buxton Trust 239
Hawaii 314
Hayes Conference Centre, Swanwick 167
Health, Guild of 238
Health and Healing Council 230, 373
Health and Healing organisations 212
Helsinki 355
Hengrave Hall 167
Henry Bradshaw Society 239
Hereford 97
Bishop of 97
Hertford, Bishop of 129
High Leigh Conference Centre 167
Higher Education *see* Education
Highveld 306
Historic Churches Preservation Trust 239
Hockerill Educational Foundation 220
Hokkaido 293
Holy Cross Society 253
Holy Trinity Society 207
Home Affairs Committee 23
Homes for Retired Clergy 239
Honduras 314
Hong Kong Anglican Church Association 261
Hong Kong Sheng Kung Hui 288
Horsham, Bishop of 78
Hospice Chaplains Association 221
Hospice Movement 171
Hospital Chaplains 24–5, 366
House of Bishops 5
House of Clergy 5
House of Laity 5
House of Lords, Bishops in 159
House of St Barnabas in Soho 239
Hull, Bishop of 152
Hulme, Bishop of 111
Hulme Trustees 265
Human Resources Division 39
Huntingdon, Bishop of 87
Huron 284
Hyderabad 329
Hymn Society of Great Britain and Ireland 239
Hyndman's Trustees 265

Ibadan 299
Ibba 308
Iceland, Evangelical-Lutheran Church of 355
Idaho 314
IFCG (Inter Faith Consultative Group) 22
Ife 299
Ijebu 299
Ikale-Ilaje 299
Ilesa 299
Income statistics 185–6
Incorporated Church Building Society 239
INDEM (Group for Mission in Industry and the Economy) 367
Independent Methodist Churches 377
Independent Radio 177
Independent Television
Commission 177
Religious Programmes on 177
Indian Provinces
Bangladesh 326, 351
Ceylon 260, 326, 351
Indian Ocean 288, 346
North India 327, 351
Pakistan 328, 351
South India 329, 351
Indianapolis 314
Industry Churches Forum 239
INFORM 239
Information Technology and Office Services 36
Inner Cities Religious Council 36
Inns of Court 198
Institute for the Study of Christianity and Sexuality 240
Inter-Faith Consultative Group (IFCG) 22
Inter Faith Network 240
Interchurch Families Association 373
Intercontinental Church Society 240
Interfaith organisations 212
International and Development Affairs Committee 23
International Ecumenical Fellowship 240
International Ministerial Council of Great Britain 377
Interserve 240, 375
Iona Community 373
Iowa 314
Iran 294
Ireland
church addresses 377–8
Church of Ireland 289, 338, 339, 377
Council of Churches for Britain and Ireland (CCBI) 371–3
Hymn Society of Great Britain and Ireland 239
Irish Council of Churches 376, 376–7
Irish Missionary Union 375
Irish School of Ecumenics 373
Methodist Church 378
Roman Catholic Church 378

Index   491

Jabalpur 328
Jaffna 330
Jalingo 299
Jamaica 323
Japan, Anglican Communion in   293, 350
Jarrow, Bishop of   85
Jerusalem and the Middle East   261, 294, 350, 384
Jewish People   229
Johannesburg 306
Joint Council for Anglo-Caribbean Churches   377
Joint Education Policy Committee   366
Jos 299
Juba 308
Jubilate Hymns   240
Julian Meetings   240
Julian of Norwich, Shrine of Lady   240

Kabba 299
Kaduguli and Nuba Mountains 308
Kaduna 299
Kafanchan 299
Kagera 309
Kajiado 295
Kajo-Keji 308
Kampala 311
Kano 299
Kansas 314
Kanyakumari 330
Karachi 329
Karamoja 311
Karimnagar 330
Karlstad 358
Karnataka Central 330
Karnataka North 330
Karnataka South 330
Katakwa 295
Katsina 300
Kebbi 300
Keewatin 285
Kensington, Bishop of   108
Kentucky 314
Kenya, Anglican Church   261, 294, 347
Keston Institute   241
Keswick Convention   241
Keswick Hall Charity   220
KeyChange   241
Khartoum 308
Kibungo 302
Kigali 302
Kigeme 302
Kigezi 311
Kilmore, Elphin and Ardagh 291
Kimberley and Kuruman 306
Kindu 288
King Alfred's College, Winchester   166
King Charles the Martyr Society   253

Kingston, Bishop of   139
Kinkizi 311
Kirinyaga 295
Kisangani 288
Kita Kanto 293
Kitali 295
Kitgum 311
Kitui 295
Klerksdorp 306
Knaresborough, Bishop of   125
Kobe 293
Koforidua 322
Kolhapur 328
Kootenay 284
Korea, Anglican Church   296, 352
Korean Mission Partnership   241
Krishna-Godavari 330
Kuching 304
Kumasi 322
Kuopio 355
Kurunagala 327
Kushtia 326
Kwara 300
Kyoto 293
Kyushu 293

Lady Peel Legacy Trust   246
Lagos 300
Lahore 329
Lainya 308
Laity, House of   5
Lake Malawi 287
Lambeth Conference   272–4
    Diploma of Student in Theology (S. Th)   218
Lambeth Palace   58
    Library   262
Lancaster
    Bishop of   63
    St Martin's College   165
Langley House Trust   241
Lango 311
Lapua 355
Latimer House   241
Latin American Council of Churches   384
Latvia, Evangelical-Lutheran Church   361
Lay Workers' training   165
Lebombo 306
Lee Abbey   167
    Household Communities   241
    International Students' Club   241
Legal Advisory Commission   41
Legal Aid Commission   41
Legislative Committee of the General Synod   6
Leicester   99
    Bishop of   99
Leprosy Mission   241

Leprosy Mission International   375
Lesbian and Gay Christian Movement   242
Lesbian and Gay Clergy Consultation   242
Lesotho   261, 306
Lewes, Bishop of   78
Lexington   314
Li Tim-Oi Foundation   242
Liberia   322
Librarians' Christian Fellowship   242
Libraries   262
Licensed readers   184
Lichfield   101
    Bishop of   101
Limerick, Ardfert, Aghadoe, Killaloe, Kilfenora, Clonfert, Kilmacduagh and Emly   292
Lincoln   104
    Bishop of   104
    Theological Institute for the Study of Religion and Society   242
Linköping   358
Lithuania, Evangelical-Lutheran Church of   359
Litoral Diocese of Ecuador   314
Liturgical Commission   42
Liturgical Study Society   252
Liturgical Support and Publishing   36
Liverpool   106
    Bishop of   106
    Hope University College   165
Living Stones   373
Llandaff   320
    St Michael's College   179
Local Ministry Schemes   180
Local Non-Stipendiary Training Schemes   180
Local Unity Committee   18
Lokoja   300
London   108
    Bishop of   108
London City Mission   242
London Union of Youth Clubs   242
Long Island   314
Lord Wharton's Charity   243
Lord's Day Observance Society   243
Los Angeles   314
Louisiana   315
Lucknow   328
Ludlow, Bishop of   97
Lui   308
Luleå   358
Lund   358
Lusaka   287
Lusitanian Church (Portugal)   324
Lutheran Churches *see* Evangelical-Lutheran Churches
Lutheran Council of Great Britain   377
Luwero   311
Lynn, Bishop of   115

MACA – Partners in Mental Health   243
Machakos   295
Madhya Kerala   330
Madi and West Nile   311
Madras   330
Madurai-Ramnad   330
Mahajanga   289
Maidstone, Bishop of   69
Maiduguri   300
Main Committee   229
Maine   315
Maintenance of the Faith Society   253, 266
Makamba   282
Makurdi   300
Malaita   297
Malakal   308
Malawi   286
Malaysia   305
Managerial and Organisational Disciplines for the Enhancement of Ministry (MODEM)   244
Manchester   111
    Bishop of   111
    Northern Ordination Course   179
Mandalay   298
Maple Leaf Fellowship   260
Mara   309
Maridi   308
Marriage
    Anglican Marriage Encounter   217
    Family Life and Marriage Education Network   235
    fees   190, 191
    legal aspects   172
    organisations   212
    Relate: National Marriage Guidance   249
    special licences   170
    statistics   187
Marshall's Charity   243
Martyrs' Memorial and Church of England Trust   265
Mary and Martha, Society of   253
Mary, Society of   253
Maryland   315
Masasi   309
Maseno North   295
Maseno South   295
Maseno West   295
Massachusetts   315
Matabeleland   287
Matana   282
Mauritius   289
Mayflower Family Centre   243
Mbaise   300
Mbale   311
Mbeere   295
Meath and Kildare   292
Medak   330
Medical organisations   212

Index

493

Meditation organisations   213
Meissen Commission   18
Melanesia, Church of the Province of   296, 341
Melanesian Mission   243
Melbourne   280
Mersey Mission to Seamen   243
Meru   295
Message   243
Methodist Church   377
    in Ireland   378
Metropolitan Visiting and Relief Association   243
Mexico, Anglican Church   297, 344
Michigan   315
Mid-Africa Ministry (CMS)   243
Middle East and Jerusalem   261, 294, 350, 384
Middleton, Bishop of   111
Mikkeli   355
Millenium Group   367
Milwaukee   315
Ministry   212
Ministry Among Jewish People   229
Ministry of Women in the Church Society   253
Minna   300
Minnesota   315
Minority Ethnic Anglican Concerns   36
Mirfield
    Centre   244
    College of Resurrection   179
    Community of Resurrection   200
Mission
    Board of Mission   21–2
    Churches Commission on Mission   374–5
    Commission on Mission   374–5
    Mission, Evangelism and Renewal in England Committee   22
    Mission Theological Advisory Group   22
    overseas   212
    PWM (Partnership for World Mission)   21
    societies   212
    South American Mission Society   254
    to Seamen   243, 244
Mississippi   315
Missouri   315
Mityana   311
MODEM (Managerial and Organisational Disciplines for the Enhancement of Ministry)   244
Modern Churchpeople's Union   244
Mombasa   295
Monmouth   320
Montana   315
Montreal   284
Monument fees   190, 191
Moosonee   284
Moravian Church   378
Moray, Ross, and Caithness   304
Møre   357

Morogoro   309
Morse-Boycott Bursary Fund   244
Mothers' Union   172
Mount Kenya Central   295
Mount Kenya South   295
Mount Kenya West   295
Mount Kilimanjaro   309
Movement for Reform of Infant Baptism   244
Mozambique and Angola Anglican Association   261
Mpwapwa   309
Mrs Frances Ashton's Charity   244
MSF Clergy and Church Workers   245
Muhabura   311
Mukono   311
Multan   329
Mumias   295
Mundri   308
Murray, The   280
Musical organisations   213
Myanmar, Church of the Province of   297, 352
Myitkyina   298

Nagpur   328
Nairobi   295
Nakuru   295
Nambale   295
Namibia   306
Namirembe   311
Nandyal   330
Nasik   328
Nassau and the Bahamas   323
Natal   306
National Association of Almshouses   216
National Association of Christian Communities and Networks   373
National Christian Education Council   245, 373
National Deaf Church Conference   245
National Retreat Association   245
National Society for Promoting Religious Education   49–50
Navajoland Area Mission   315
Navy Chaplains   160
Nebbi   311
Nebraska   315
Nelson   277
Nevada   315
New Assembly of Churches   373
New England Company   245
New Guinea Islands   301
New Hampshire   315
New Jersey   315
New South Wales Province   279, 340
New Testament Assembly   378
New Westminster   284
New York   315
New Zealand Anglican Church   277, 341
Newark   315

494   Index

Newcastle 113
    Bishop of 113
Newcastle (New South Wales) 279
Newfoundland 284
Newspapers, Church 172
Newton's Trust 245
Niagara 284
Niassa 306
Nicaragua 287
Nidaros 357
Niger Delta 300
Niger Delta North 300
Niger Diocese 299
Nigeria 298, 349
Nigeria Fellowship 261
Nikaean Club 245
Nippon Sei Ko Kai 293, 350
Nnewi 300
Non-Signatory Churches 361
Non-stipendiary ministers 183
Nord Kivu 288
Nord-Hålogaland 357
Nordic Lutheran Churches 355–8
North Carolina 316
North Central Philippines 302
North Dakota 316
North East India 328
North East Oecumenical Course 179
North East Ordination Course, Durham 179
North Eastern Caribbean and Aruba 260, 323
North of England Institute for Christian Education 245
North India, Church of 327, 351
North Kerala 330
North Kigezi 311
North Mbale 311
North Queensland 280
North Queensland Auxiliary in England 261
North Thames Ministerial Training Course 179
North-West Australia 281
Northern Argentina 307
Northern California 316
Northern Indiana 316
Northern Luzon 302
Northern Malawi 287
Northern Michigan 316
Northern Ordination Course, Manchester 179
Northern Philippines 302
Northern Territory 280
Northern Uganda 311
Northern Zambia 287
Northwest Texas 316
Northwestern Pennsylvania 316
Norway, Church of 356
Norwich 115
    Bishop of 115
Nova Scotia 284

Nsukka 300
Nyahururu 296

Oak Hill Theological College 179
Ohio 316
Oke-Osun 300
Okigwe North 300
Okigwe South 300
Okinawa 293
Oklahoma 316
Old Catholic Churches of the Union of Utrecht 335
Old Testament Study Society 252
Olympia 316
OMF International (UK) 245
Ondo 300
Ontario 284, 345
Open Synod Group 246
Opportunities for Volunteering 367
Oratory of the Good Shepherd 246
Ordained Scientists Society 253
Order of Christian Unity 246
Order of Ethiopia 306
Order of the Holy Paraclete 206
Ordinands and Candidates for Ministry Association 221
Ordination Candidates Funds (General) 213, 246
Oregon 316
Oriental Orthodox Christian Churches Council 377
Orlu 300
Osaka 293
Oslo 357
Osun 300
Ottawa 284
Oturkpo 300
Oulu 355
Overseas Bishoprics' Fund 246
Overseas Missionary Fellowship (OMF International Ltd) 245
Overseas organisations 213
Overseas Settlement 23
Overseas Students Commission 229, 374
Owerri 300
Owo 300
Oxford 118
    Bishop of 118
    Pusey House 248, 263
    St Stephen's House 179
Oxford Mission 247

Pacific Conference of Churches 384
Pacifism 211
Pakistan, Church of 328, 351
Panama 287
Papua New Guinea
    Anglican Church 301, 340
    Church Partnership 247
Paraguay 308
Parish and People 247

Index   **495**

Part-time Theological Courses   180
Partis College, Bath   247
Partnership House Library   262
Partnership for World Mission (PWM)   21
Pastoral Psychology Guild   238
Patna   328
Patronage Trusts   213
Peache Trustees   265
Pelotas   282
Pennsylvania   316
Penrith, Bishop of   71
Pensions Board   46–7
Perth   281
Peru   308
Peshawar   329
Peterborough   121
      Bishop of   121
Philip Usher Memorial Fund   247
Philippines, Episcopal Church in   302, 352
Phulbani   328
Pilgrim Adventure   247
Pilgrim Trust   247
Pilgrimage organisations   214
Pilsdon Community   247
Pittsburgh   316
Plainsong and Mediaeval Music Society   248
Plymouth
      Bishop of   91
      St Mark and St John College   166
Polynesia Anglican Church   277, 341
Pontefract, Bishop of   146
Popondota   301
Port Elizabeth   306
Port Moresby   301
Port Sudan   308
Portsmouth   123
      Bishop of   123
Portuguese Episcopal Church   324
Porvoo   355
Porvoo Communion   353–4
Praxis   248
Prayer Book Society   248
Prayer and meditation organisations   213
Prayer for Unity Fellowship   373
Pre-Theological Training Course   180
Preachers at The Inns of Court   198
Precious Blood Society   207
Presbyterian Church of Wales   378
Press, Church   172
Pretoria   306
Primates' Meetings   274
Print media   172
Prison Service Chaplaincy   164
Professional groups   213
Promoting Christian Knowledge Society   252
Promoting Retreats Association   219

Protestant Reformation Society   248
Province of the Indian Ocean Support Association   261
Provincial Episcopal Visitors   69, 152
Provincial Lay Officers, Canterbury and York   57
Psychical and Spiritual Studies Fellowship   230
Public Record Office   248
Publishing organisations   37, 213
Puerto Rico   318
Pusan   296
Pusey House, Oxford   248, 263
PWM (Partnership for World Mission)   21
Pyncombe Charity   248

Quaker Peace and Service   375
Qu'Appelle   285
Quebec   284
Queen Victoria Clergy Fund   248
Queen's College, Birmingham   179
Queensland, Province of   280, 340
Quincy   316

Racial Justice Commission   375
Radio and Television   176–8
Radius (Religious Drama Society of Great Britain)   249
RAF Chaplains   160
Raiwind   329
Rajasthan   328
Ramsbury, Bishop of   133
Rayalaseema   330
Reader Missionary Studentship Association   249
Reading, Bishop of   118
Rebecca Hussey's Book Charity   249
Recife   282
Records Centre   38
Redundant Churches Advisory Board   48
Reform   249
Regional Conferences (WCC)   384
Regional Training Courses   179–80
Rejaf   308
Relate: National Marriage Guidance   249
Relief of Poor Clergymen Society   253
Religious Communities   199–207
      Advisory Council on the Relations of Bishops and   199
      Anglican   199
      Communities Consultative Council   200
      men   200–21
      mixed   207
      women   202–7
Religious Education Council of England and Wales   249
Religious Society of Friends   378
Remo   300
Renewal organisations   213
Renk   309
Repton, Bishop of   83
Research organisations   213
Residential and nursing homes   47

Resurrection, College of   179
Retired Clergy Association   249
Retirement Housing Schemes   47
Retreat Conductors Society   253
Retreat houses   167
Rhode Island   316
Rhodes House Library (USPG)   264
Richards' (Rev Dr George) Charity   249
Richborough, Bishop of   69
Richmond Fellowship for Community Mental Health   249
Ridley Hall, Cambridge   179
Rift Valley   310
Rio de Janeiro   282
Rio Grande   316
Ripon   125
    Bishop of   125
Ripon College, Cuddesdon   179
Ripon and York St John University College   166
Riverina   279
RNIB   222
Rochester   127
    Bishop of   127
Rochester USA   316
Rockhampton   280
Rockhampton Auxiliary   261
Roehampton Institute   166
Rokon   309
Roman Catholic Church
    Catholic Fund for Overseas Development   367, 374
    Catholic Group in General Synod   224
    Catholic Institute for International Relations   374
    Catholic League   224
    Committee on Roman Catholic Relations   18
    in England and Wales   378
    in Ireland   378
    Old Catholic Churches of the Union of Utrecht   335
    in Scotland   378
Royal Air Force Chaplains   160
Royal Alexandra and Albert School   250
Royal Almonry   196
Royal Association in Aid of Deaf People   232
Royal Asylum of St Ann's Society   250
Royal Chaplain   195
Royal College of Organists   250
Royal Cumberland Youths Society   253
Royal Foundation of St Katharine in Ratcliffe   197
Royal Martyr Church Union   250
Royal National Institute for the Blind   222
Royal National Institute for Deaf People   233
Royal Naval Lay Readers' Society   250
Royal Navy Chaplains   160
Royal Peculiars   193–8
Royal School of Church Music   250
RPS Rainer   250
Ruaha   310
Rumbek   309

Rupert's Land   285, 345
Rural Affairs organisations   22, 213
Rural Group   367
Rural Theology Association   250
Russian Orthodox Church   378
Ruvuma   310
Rwanda, Church of the Province of   302, 348
Rwenzori   311

Sabah   305
Sabongida Ora   300
Sacred Mission Society   201
St Aidan Trust   254
St Aidan's College Charity   254
St Alban and St Sergius Fellowship   235, 373
St Albans   129
    Bishop of   129
St Albans and Oxford Ministry Course   180
St Andrews, Dunkeld and Dunblane   304
St Asaph   320
St Barnabas Guild   238
St Christopher's College Trust   220
St Christopher's Fellowship   254
St David's   320
St Deiniol's Residential Library   263
St Edmundsbury and Ipswich   131
    Bishop of   131
St Francis Society   201
St Gabriel's Trust   220
St George's House, Windsor Castle   254
St Germans, Bishop of   144
St Helena   306
St Helena Guild   238
St Hild and St Bede Trust   220
St James's Palace   195
St John the Evangelist Society   201
St John's   306
St John's College and Cranmer Hall, Durham   179
St John's College, Nottingham   179
St John's Guild for the Blind   222
St Leonard Guild   238
St Luke's College Foundation   220
St Luke's Hospital for the Clergy   255
St Margaret Society   206
St Mark the Evangelist   307
St Mark and St John College, Plymouth   166
St Martin's College, Lancaster   165
St Mary's College Trust   220
St Mary's Convent, Chiswick   206
St Michael's College, Llandaff   179
St Michael's Fellowship   255
St Nicholas Fellowship   236
St Pancras Housing   255
St Paul's Cathedral Library   263
St Peter's Saltley Trust   220
St Raphael Guild   238

St Saviour's Priory   206
St Stephen's House, Oxford   179
St Willibrord Society   253
Salisbury   133
    Bishop of   133
Salvation Army   378
Samaritans   251
Sambalpur   328
San Diego   316
San Joaquin   316
Sandford St Martin (Church of England) Trust   178
Sandhurst, Royal Memorial Chapel   197
São Paulo   282
Sarum St Michael Educational Charity   220
Saskatchewan   285
Saskatoon   285
Scargill House   167
Scholarship and Science organisations   213
School Chaplains' Conference   251
School of Mission and World Christianity   375
Schools
    Church schools   172
    Church Schools Company   229
    see also Education
Science, Medicine and Technology Committee   24
Science organisations   213
Scotland
    Action of Churches Together in Scotland   375–6
    church addresses   377–8
    Roman Catholic Church   378
    Scottish Congregational Church   378
    Scottish Episcopal Church   303, 338, 378
    United Free Church of Scotland   378
Scout Association   251
Scripture Gift Mission (Inc.)   251
Scripture Union   251
Scripture Union in Schools   251
Seamen's Friendly Society of St Paul   251
Searches in registers   190
Secretary to the Association of Church College Trusts   221
Sekondi   322
Selby, Bishop of   152
Seoul   296
Serbian Orthodox Church   378
Servants of Christ the King   251
Servants of the Sanctuary Guild   238
Services, Authorized and Commended   173–6
Seventh Day Adventist Church   378
Seychelles   289
Shaftesbury Homes and *Arethusa*   251
Shaftesbury Society   251
Sheffield   135
    Bishop of   135
Sherborne, Bishop of   133
Sherwood, Bishop of   142
Shrewsbury, Bishop of   101

Shrine of Lady Julian of Norwich   240
Shrine of Our Lady of Walsingham   258
Shyira   302
Shyogwe   302
Sialkot   329
Sierra Leone, Inter-Diocesan Association   261
Simeon's Trustees   266
Singapore   305
Sion College Library   263
Sisters of Bethany   206
Sisters of Charity   206
Sisters of the Church   206
Sittwe   298
Skara   358
Social Concern   251
Social Concern organisations   213
Social, Economic and Industrial Affairs Committee   24
Social Responsibility, Board for   22–4
Societies
    of All Saints Sisters of the Poor   207
    for the Assistance of Ladies in Reduced Circumstances   252
    of Holy Cross   253
    of Holy Trinity   207
    of King Charles the Martyr   253
    for Liturgical Study   252
    for Maintenance of the Faith   253
    Patronage Trust   266
    of Mary   253
    of Mary and Martha   253
    for the Ministry of Women in the Church   253
    for Old Testament Study   252
    of Ordained Scientists   253
    of Precious Blood   207
    for Promoting Christian Knowledge   252
    for Relief of Poor Clergymen   253
    of Retreat Conductors   253
    of Royal Cumberland Youths   253
    of Sacred Mission   201
    of St Francis   201
    of St John the Evangelist   201
    of St Margaret   206
    of St Willibrord   253
Sodor and Man   137
    Bishop of   137
Sokoto   300
Soldiers' and Airmen's Scripture Readers Association   254
Solomon Islands   297
SOMA-Sharing of Ministries Abroad   254
Sør-Hålogaland   357
Soroti   311
South Africa, Republic of   305
South American Mission Society   254
South Australia, Province of   280, 340
South Carolina   316
South Dakota   317

South East Asia, Church of the Province of 304, 352
South East Institute for Theological Education 180
South India, Church of 329, 351
South Kerala 330
South Pacific Anglican Council 325
South Rwenzori 311
South West Ministerial Training Course 180
South Western Brazil 282
South-West Tanganyika 310
Southampton, Bishop of 148
Southeast Florida 317
Southern Africa Church Development Trust 254
Southern Africa, Church of the Province of 305, 346
Southern Brazil 282
Southern Cone of America, Anglican Church of 307, 344
Southern Malawi 287
Southern Nyanza 296
Southern Ohio 317
Southern Philippines 302
Southern Theological Education and Training Scheme 180
Southern Virginia 317
Southwark 139
    Bishop of 139
Southwell 142
    Bishop of 142
Southwest Florida 317
Southwestern Virginia 317
Spanish Reformed Episcopal Church 324
Special Marriage Licences 170
Spokane 317
Springboard 170
Springfield 317
Sri Lanka *see* Ceylon
Stafford, Bishop of 101
Standing Orders Committee of the General Synod 6
Statistics 181–92
    baptisms 188
    Church Army evangelists 183
    Church electoral rolls 192
    confirmations 189
    distribution of clergy 182
    fees 190–91
    financial 185–6
    licensed readers 184
    marriages 187
    non-stipendiary ministers 183
Statistics Unit 37–8
Stavanger 357
Stepney, Bishop of 108
Stockholm 358
Stockport, Bishop of 76
Strängnäs 358
Student Christian Movement 255
Studylink – EFAC Training Partnership 255
Sudan Church Association 261
Sudan, Church of the Province of The 308, 348

Sunyani 322
Swansea and Brecon 320
Swaziland 307
    Zululand and Swaziland Association 261
Sweden, Church of 357
Swindon, Bishop of 67
Sydney 280

Tabora 310
Taejon 296
Taita Taveta 296
Taiwan (Formosa) 317
Tamale 322
Tampere 355
Tanganyika (Central) Diocesan Association 260
Tanzania, Church of the Province of 309, 347
Tasmania 281
Taunton, Bishop of 59
Tearfund 255
Television and radio 176–8
Temotu 297
Tennessee 317
Tewkesbury, Bishop of 93
Texas 317
Theological Colleges 179
Theological Education and Training Committee 33
Theological Institute of the Scottish Episcopal Church 179
Theology and Unity Group (Ecumenical) 367
Thetford, Bishop of 115
Thika 296
Third Province Movement 255
Time Ministries International 255
Tirunelveli 331
Toamasina 289
Toc H 256
Tohoku 293
Tokyo 294
Tonbridge, Bishop of 127
Torit 309
Toronto 284
Toungoo 298
Tower of London 195
Training
    Bishop's Regulations for Training 34–5
    East Anglian Ministerial Training Course 179
    for Lay Workers 165
    Local Non-Stipendiary Training Schemes 180
    Ministers in Training Fund 246
    for Ordinands 180
    organisations 214
    Regional Courses 179–80
    see also Education; Schools
Transvaal, Zimbabwe and Botswana Association 261
Travel organisations 214
Trichy-Tanjore 331
Trinidad and Tobago 323

Index

Trinitarian Bible Society   256
Trinity College, Bristol   179
True Freedom Trust   256
Truro   144
   Bishop of   144
Tuam, Killala and Achonry   291
Tunsberg   357
Turku   355

Uganda Church Association   261
Uganda, Church of the Province of   310, 348
Ughelli   301
Ukwa   301
Umuahia   301
Umzimvubu   307
Uncovenanted giving statistics   185
Union of Utrecht, Old Catholic Churches   335
Union of Welsh Independents   378
United College of the Ascension   256
United Free Church of Scotland   378
United Nations Association of Gt Britain and Northern Ireland   256
United Reformed Church   378
United Society for Christian Literature   256
United Society for the Propagation of the Gospel   256
   Library   264
United States, Episcopal Church   312–18, 342–4
Universities and Colleges Christian Fellowship   257
University Representatives in Convocation   161, 165
Upper South Carolina   317
Uppsala   358
Urban Theology Unit   257
Uruguay   308
Utah   317
Uyo   301

Vacation Term for Biblical Study   257
Vanuatu   297
Växjö   358
Vellore   331
Venezuela   318
Vergers, Church of England Guild of   257
Vergers Guild   257
Vermont   317
Vicar-General of the Province (Canterbury and York)   57
Victoria Institute   257
Victoria Nyanza   310
Victoria, Province of   280, 340
Virgin Islands   317
Virginia   317
Visby   358
Vocation, Recruitment and Selection Committee   32–3
Volunteering, Opportunities for   367

Waiapu   278
Waikato   278

Wakefield   146
   Bishop of   146
Wales
   church addresses   377–8
   Church in   318, 338, 339
   Churches Together in Wales   376
   Roman Catholic Church   378
   Union of Welsh Independents   378
Walsingham, Shrine of Our Lady of   258
Wangaratta   281
War Graves Commission   231
Warri   301
Warrington, Bishop of   106
Warwick, Bishop of   81
Washington   318
WATCH (Women and the Church)   258
Wau   309
WCC *see* World Council of Churches (WCC)
Welfare organisations   214
Wellington   278
Wesleyan Holiness Church   378
West Africa, Church of the Province of   321, 350
West Ankole   311
West Buganda   311
West of England Ministerial Training Course, Gloucester   180
West Indies
   Church in the Province of the   323, 344
   Joint Council for Anglo-Caribbean Churches   377
West Midlands Ministerial Training Course, Birmingham   180
West Missouri   318
West Tennessee   318
West Texas   318
West Virginia   318
Westcott House, Cambridge   179
Western Australia, Province of   281, 340
Western Kansas   318
Western Kowloon   352
Western Louisiana   318
Western Massachusetts   318
Western Michigan   318
Western New York   318
Western Newfoundland   284
Western North Carolina   318
Western Tanganyika   310
Westminster Abbey   193–4
   Library   264
Whitby, Bishop of   152
Willesden, Bishop of   108
William Temple Foundation   258, 373
William Temple House   258
Willochra   280
Willochran Association   261
Winchester   148
   Bishop of   148
Windsor Castle   194, 254
Windsor Great Park   195

Windward Islands   323
       Diocesan Association   261
Wolverhampton, Bishop of   101
Women's Ministry   178
Women's World Day of Prayer   258
Woolwich, Bishop of   139
Worcester   150
       Bishop of   150
World Association for Christian Communication   178
World Conference   375
World Congress of Faiths   258
World Council of Churches (WCC)   379–80
       member churches and associate councils   381–3
       regional conferences   384
World Vision   258
Worship   173–6
Worship organisations   214
Wusasa   301
Wycliffe Hall, Oxford   179
Wyoming   318

Yambio   309
Yangon   298
Yei   309
Yewa   301
Yirol   309
YMCA   258, 259, 373, 375

Yokohama   294
Yola   301
York   57, 152–3
       Dioceses   57
       electoral rolls   192
       Minster Library   264
       Province of   57, 338, 339
       Provincial Lay Officers   57
       Registrar   57
       Vicar-General   57
York, Archbishop of   152
       chronology   158
       personal staff   58
York, Convocation of   51
York Glaziers Trust   259
Young Men's Christian Association   373, 375
Young Women's Christian Association   259, 373, 375
Youth organisations   214
Youth work   20
Ysabel   297
Yukon   283, 284, 345

Zambia   286
Zanzibar and Tanga   310
Zimbabwe   286
Zululand   307
Zululand and Swaziland Association   261

Index   **501**

Some People sail around the world for £30 or less

Pitiful wages are just the start of a seafarer's problems. Although most ships are perfectly well run, too many seafarers are trapped in a world of exploitation and abuse. Our chaplains in ports look after the physical and spiritual welfare of seafarers worldwide. Please help.

To Kathy Baldwin, The Missions to Seamen, St Michael Paternoster Royal, College Hill, London EC4R 2RL. I enclose a donation of £10 ☐ £25 ☐ £50 ☐ £ _____

Name _____

Address _____

The Missions to Seamen

CHARITY NO. 212432

THE MOTHERS' UNION
(Incorporated by Royal Charter)

The Mothers' Union (MU) is a Christian organisation which promotes the well–being of families worldwide.

❖

We achieve this by developing prayer and spiritual growth in families, studying and reflecting on family life and its place in society, and resourcing our members to take practical action to improve conditions for families, both nationally and in the communities in which they live.

❖

For further information about the MU, please contact:

Communications Organiser
The Mothers' Union
Mary Sumner House
24 Tufton Street
London SW1P 3RB
Tel 0171 222 5533
Fax 0171 222 1591
Website: www.themothersunion.org
email: mu@themothersunion.org

(Reg Charity No 240531)

NEED HELP WITH YOUR HISTORIC BUILDING?

...ORDER THE ESSENTIAL UK GUIDE TO SPECIALIST PRODUCTS, CONSULTANTS, CRAFTSMEN, COURSES and more...

Recommended by SAVE BRITAIN'S HERITAGE

The Building Conservation Directory

£16.95 including delivery from
Cathedral Communications Limited
The Tisbury Brewery, Church Street,
Tisbury, Wiltshire SP3 6NH

Telephone 01747 871717 Facsimile 01747 871718
email: bcd@cathcomm.demon.co.uk
www.buildingconservation.com

Please help Siloam to rescue 'Special' babies in the Philippines.

This is Rom-Mel, just one of the Filipino babies we have rescued.

Please send your gifts to:

SILOAM CHRISTIAN MINISTRIES

5, Clarendon Place, Leamington Spa, Warwickshire CV32 5QL
Tel: 01926 335037   Fax: 01926 431193
Registered Charity No. 327396

For the nation-wide work of the Church of England

The Central Church Fund is unique. It is the *only* fund available for the general purposes of the Church of England as a whole.

> It helps parishes and dioceses with imaginative and innovative projects of all kinds – and especially those that meet the needs of local communities.

> It provides for training for ministry in the Church (donations and bequests can be directed specifically for this purpose).

> It makes money available for those unexpected and urgent needs which cannot be budgeted for.

As a general purpose Fund, its flexibility allows it to provide, without delay, for a host of needs that no other fund is geared to cope with, and its value in this way to the Church of England is incalculable.

There are inevitably many calls upon it and funds are always urgently needed. Please help with your donation, covenanted subscription or bequest – or find out more from the Secretary.

The Central Church Fund

The Central Board of Finance of the Church of England, Church House, Great Smith Street, Westminster, London SW1P 3NZ. Tel: 0171-222 9011.

Registered. Charity No. 248711

What could be better than her own home?

Right now, nothing

Your own home is where you are independent. You have dignity, choice and memories. Which makes 'right now' the perfect time to start thinking positively about the future. Not when weakening health makes decisions urgent or stressful, but now while you can discuss with your family and friends what the next secure move should be.

Later, Trinity Care

Trinity Care Christian nursing homes are a natural and secure extension to people's lives. They are beautifully run, their values are Christian and the staff are there to serve the whole person, respecting all of her – or his – needs. **What could be better than your own home? One day, Trinity Care.**
You are welcome to visit quite informally.

Care Homes in the following locations:
Avon, Cheshire, East Sussex, Hampshire, Kent, Merseyside, Nottinghamshire, Oxfordshire, Shropshire, Somerset, South and West Yorkshire, Warwickshire, Worcestershire

TRINITY CARE
caring for the whole person

15 Musters Road, West Bridgford,
Nottingham NG2 7PP
Tel: 0800 163216 Fax: 0115 982 1919

For your FREE copy of Trinity Care's Whole Person Care guide and our FREE video, please call us now on freephone 0800 163216.

VIDEOS FOR A
Growing Church

and, especially for schools, children's and youth work
'THE MYSTERY MAN'
a new way to explore the life and meaning of Jesus.

Ring 01428 644208 for a brochure

Our videos are also on sale at
Church House Bookshop
Great Smith Street, Westminster.

And we specialise in economic tailor-made productions for a wide range of church, charitable and commercial organisations.

Ring 01428 644208

GUILDFORD DIOCESE PRODUCTIONS

Grayswood Studio, Clammer Hill
Grayswood, Surrey GU27 2DZ
Fax: 01428 656684

ADDED VALUE
FOR YOUR PARISH MAGAZINE

Why not use a parish magazine insert to improve the content of your own publication? We have two to choose from.

THE SIGN

The Sign is a really compact eight pages. Literally crammed full of good things — regular and topical features, saints' days for the month ahead, book reviews, a childrens' colouring competition and a unique classified page.

OR HOME WORDS

Home Words — 16 pages of interesting editorial. Profiles, features, stories, people and places, book reviews and loads more. 16 pages written in a lively open style.

Special sample packs are available for either, or both, publications.

Simply write or call:
The Subscription Office, 16 Blyburgate
Beccles, Suffolk NR34 9TB
Tel: 01502-711231 or 711171

For advice on advertisements — booking and copy — contact:

Stephen Dutton, c/o *Church Times*
33 Upper Street, London N1 0PN
Tel: 0171-359 4570 Fax: 0171-226 3051

The Sign and *Home Words* are published by

G. J. PALMER & SONS LTD
(A wholly owned subsidiary of Hymns Ancient & Modern Limited, a Registered Charity)

The Church of England Pensions Board
Our work is caring . . .

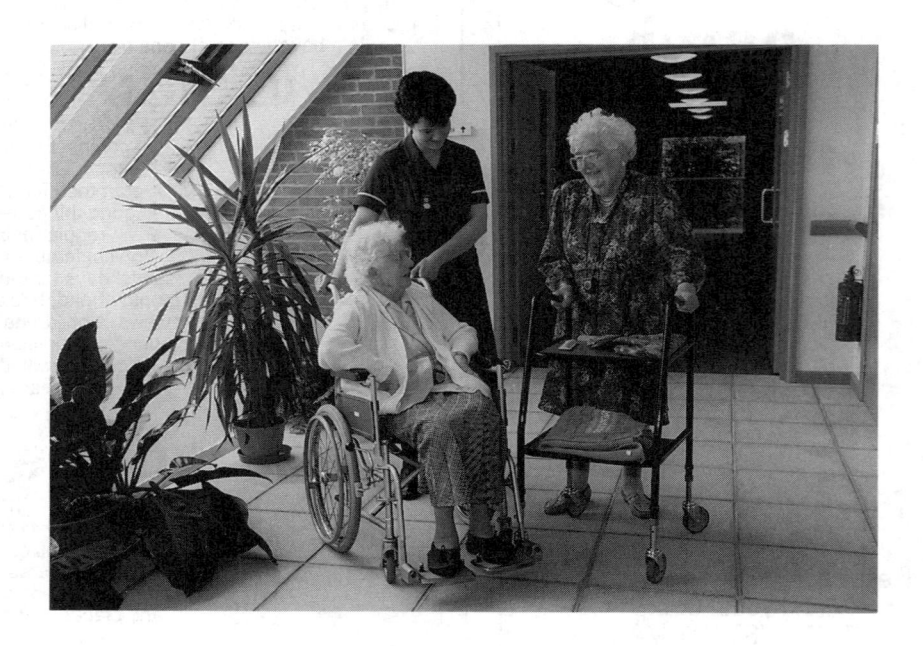

The Church of England Pensions Board offers support to those who have retired from the stipendiary ministry — clergy, deaconesses and licensed lay workers — and their spouses, or their widows and widowers.

Our greatest concern is for the welfare of our older pensioners, who because of age or infirmity need sheltered accommodation and some special care. The Pensions Board runs nine residential and nursing homes offering security and peace of mind to those who have given their lives towards helping others in the name of Christ. However, as the number of those seeking this type of care is increasing, further homes are urgently needed. The Board also gives, to a growing number of its pensioners, assistance with the fees payable for accommodation in homes run by other organisations.

The Board receives no help from central Church funds towards the cost of its residential and nursing care, and must rely on support from donations, deeds of covenant and legacies in order to continue this much needed work.

Please help us in any way you can.

For more details about our work and ways in which you can help, or a form of words for inclusion in a Will, please write to:

**The Secretary,
The Church of England Pensions Board (YB)
Freepost, 7 Little College Street, London SW1P 3SF**
reg. charity 236627

On the receiving end

The clergy are used to being on the receiving end. We take them our problems, we ask them to explain the inexplicable, we blame them for things we don't like about the church, and we expect them to behave like saints.

Small wonder that clergy sometimes wilt under the strain – a strain that can be enormously increased in times of personal crisis and financial hardship. Clergy stipends, as everyone knows, are modest, and additional calls on their resources – such as educational bills, the cost of removals and resettlement, or the expense of child-minding for the single person with young dependent children, – can be unaffordable. Without a helping hand debts may be the result of such calls on the stipend. Although we can help with debts too, we would much rather come in before the situation gets to that stage.

The Corporation was founded over 300 years ago to help Anglican clergy and their dependants in times of need. We have a wide range of grant making areas for the serving, the retired, widows and widowers, and for dependent children of any of these. If you would like to know more about this please write and ask for a copy of our Information Leaflet.

Our grants run at around £1,250,000 a year, and for clergy families at our 'receiving end' the benefits have been beyond price. But there is always more to be done, for, sadly, the stresses under which our clergy live and work ever increase. And as their need grows, so does the need grow for support from the rest of us.

Please help us to lighten their load, with a donation or covenant, or with a bequest.

Corporation of the Sons of the Clergy

Founded A.D. 1655 1 Dean Trench Street, Westminster, London SW1P 3HB. *Tel.* 0171- 799 3696. *Reg. Charity 207737*

The Church Lads' and Church Girls' Brigade
Registered Charity No. 276821

A nation-wide Anglican voluntary youth organisation offering fun and friendship and handholds to life.

Parish-based, it brings the Gospel Message to youngsters.

For further details contact:
The Church Lads' and Church Girls' Brigade
2 Barnsley Road, Wath-upon-Dearne, Rotherham S63 6PY
Telephone: Rotherham (01709) 876535   Fax: (01709) 878089
e-mail: general-secretary@churchbrigade.syol.com

BUILDING FOR PEACE IN NORTHERN IRELAND
Working to heal the hurts of years of violence

CORRYMEELA is a dispersed Christian community which feels itself called to be an instrument of God's peace. It works to break down barriers and build bridges between individuals and groups: "If Christianity has nothing to say about reconciliation then it has nothing to say" (The Revd Dr R R Davey, OBE, founder of Corrymeela).

CORRYMEELA LINK, based in Great Britain, seeks to spread the vision and support the work of the Corrymeela Community: it needs your help if this aim is to be realised.

PLEASE support us with your prayers especially on CORRYMEELA SUNDAY which is held annually on the Sunday before St Patrick's Day.

Information and donations:
Corrymeela Link (C), **PO Box 118, Reading RG1 1SL**
Tel:/Fax. 01189 261062   Charity No. XN 48052A

CORRYMEELA

WIPPELL'S

Clergy Wear & Choir Robes

Send for illustrated Catalogue
Patterns supplied on request

Church Furniture • Stained Glass
Needlework • Silverware

Exeter 88 Buller Rd. EX4 1DQ Tel.01392 254234, Fax. 1392 250868
London 11 Tufton St. SW1P 3QB Tel. 0171 222 4528 Fax. 0171 976 7536
Manchester 9-21 Princess St, M2 4DN Tel. 0161 834 7967 Fax. 0161 8351652

Inter-Church Travel

Journeys to Holy Places

Retrace Christ's footsteps in the Holy Land...follow the journeys of St Paul through Turkey and the Mediterranean...celebrate the Feast of St James in the Spanish pilgrimage city of Santiago de Compostela ... explore the Christian heritage of Italy, Poland and Croatia.

Inter-Church Travel is a long established Christian company specialising in pilgrimages and cultural tours to places of Christian interest. All our tours are expertly led by members of the clergy or senior lay people, dedicated to fostering fellowship among travellers of all ages and denominations.

We also have a wealth of experience in arranging tailor-made tours for parishes and groups and regularly organise low cost familiarisation courses for prospective group leaders.

FREE 0800 300 444

Please call FREE for our latest brochure, quoting reference A006.
Lines are open from 9am-5pm Mondays to Fridays.
Or, write to us at: Inter-Church Travel Ltd, FREEPOST, PO Box 58, Folkestone, Kent, CT20 1YB. No stamp is required.

Sunday Services at St Paul's

8.00 am	Holy Communion
10.15am	Sung Mattins
11.30 am	Sung Eucharist
3.15 pm	Sung Evensong
6.00 pm	Evening Service

Evensong is usually sung at 5pm every day (except Sunday)

St Paul's Cathedral

On Feast Days and at other times, service times may be subject to change.
For service details please contact our web site ttp://stpauls.london.anglican.org
or telephone: 0171–236 4128